"From Van Riper to oral motor therapy, Pam Marshalla has given us a 'must read' for all students and clinicians in the field of speech/articulation therapy. Pam presents not only the historical perspective of our profession but gives invaluable assessment and treatment strategies using a wide variety of methods to stimulate speech sound production. Pam was a firm believer in using what works and in this book she gives hundreds of suggestions so that the clinician can choose what works best for each client. She has given our profession a gift of her knowledge and commitment to helping children. Thank you Pam... you are missed!"

- Sara Rosenfeld-Johnson, M.S., CCC-SLP, TalkTools

"Every speech-language pathologist should have this book; it is the ultimate guide for university graduate students as well as practicing speech-language pathologists. Each section is easily navigable, containing clear, hands-on, easily-applied techniques. *The Marshalla Guide* combines research and resources from early to current speech practices, clarified by many wonderful illustrations throughout. Thank you, Pam, for leaving us with your legacy."

- Diane Bahr, M.S., CCC-SLP, CIMI, Ages & Stages

"*The Marshalla Guide* is the most comprehensive book relating to speech that we've seen in our profession. Pam's ability to see the big picture in order to remediate speech sound disorders is a rare gift. Personally, through her writings and workshops (most of which are included in *The Marshalla Guide*), she changed the course of my career and led me from having only a basic understanding of the premise and concepts of therapy to being a systematic, successful therapist who knows the reasons for what I am doing. *The Marshalla Guide* does not shy away from the oral-motor controversy; instead, it gives the history and justifications for when oral-motor techniques are appropriate and teaches how all these techniques ultimately lead to the goal of appropriate placement for speech sounds. This is a monumental work from a terrific therapist."

- Stephen Sacks, M.A., CCC-SLP, SATPAC Speech

"Anyone who knew Pam Marshalla knows how much she contributed to the remediation of speech motor skills in children. This compilation of Pam's life's work is an excellent resource especially for those who work with children who have a limited repertoire of consonants and vowels or who need refinement of these speech motor movements. I especially enjoyed the implementation of Van Riper's vision in this comprehensive guide."

- Nancy Kaufman, M.A., CCC-SLP
Kaufman Children's Center

"*The Marshalla Guide* is the 'Holy Grail' for oral motor and motor speech and may, once and for all, put an end to the oral motor controversy. As a therapist, writer, and lecturer, Pam's work has always been in my core curriculum, and this new book does wonders to solidify that core curriculum for everyone. Pam walks us through a historical journey, citing the works of all the iconic oral motor experts in one incredible book. We learn from Pam that everything old is new again and that there is, beyond any shadow of a doubt, all the evidence we need to support the use of oral motor interventions in therapy, including, but not limited to: tactile cues, reflex integration, sensory integration, motor sequencing, breath support, pre-speech training, muscle memory, phonetic and oral placement, strength training and — yes — therapy tools! Based on the information Pam presents in this book, I will from this day forward consider myself an 'elocutionist exercise expert' and I encourage other SLPs to read this book and find out why they should take on this new title as well!"

- Robyn Merkel-Walsh, M.A., CCC-SLP, COM,
TalkTools, Oral Motor Institute

"Pam wrote this Guide as her legacy to the profession she loved. In *The Marshalla Guide*, SLPs who knew Pam will recognize the precision and thoroughness of detail that was her trademark; SLPs who did not know her will have an opportunity to benefit from her extraordinary knowledge and talents. This book is well-organized with clear, compelling writing and superb illustrations — the best I have ever seen in any textbook or therapy manual. Included are detailed description of speech errors, historical precedents, theory, evolution of diagnostic and treatment methods, research, drawings, diagrams, charts, dialogue and verbal cues, and application-to-therapy sections throughout. *The Marshalla Guide* is of great value to both young SLPs and to seasoned veterans with many years experience."

- Donna Ridley, M.Ed., CCC-SLP
Presenter for Ages & Stages

"*The Marshalla Guide* is a broad-spectrum overview of the history of our profession as it relates to oral motor function as well as an extensive guide to therapeutic strategies. This is not a step-by-step "cookbook" but rather a valuable resource guide that offers a wide variety of methods for the therapeutic armamentarium of tools for today's speech-language pathologist. Within the scope of historic review, this book also includes concepts and therapeutic techniques that may or may not be utilized in today's practice, however, it is extremely valuable to know where we came from and how these concepts have influenced current thinking. This manual will prove to be a valuable reference for today's therapists."

- Leslie Faye Davis, M.S., CCC-SLP
Challenge Early Intervention Center

The Marshalla Guide

A Topical Anthology of Speech Movement Techniques for Motor Speech Disorders & Articulation Deficits

Clinically-Focused & Research-Based

By Pam Marshalla, M.A., CCC-SLP
Speech-Language Pathologist

Edited by Shanti McGinley and
Charlotte Boshart, M.A., CCC-SLP,
Speech-Language Pathologist

Illustrations by Shanti McGinley

MARSHALLA
SPEECH & LANGUAGE

The Marshalla Guide: A Topical Anthology of Speech Movement Techniques for Motor Speech Disorders and Articulation Deficits ©2019 Shanti McGinley. All rights reserved.

ISBN 978-0–9791749–5–7

Marshalla Speech & Language
2305-C Ashland St, PMB 318
Ashland, OR 97520
www.PamMarshalla.com

Printed in the United Stated of America.

Illustrations and diagrams by Shanti McGinley.

See additional copyright acknowledgements on page 495.

To Charles Van Riper
1905–1994

    Charles Van Riper wrote me a letter in 1982 after he read the therapy newsletter I had just begun to write and self-publish. He said he liked the newsletter very much and he ordered a subscription. In the letter, Van Riper said we would always need therapists to write about the discoveries they were making during the actual process of therapy and he encouraged me to keep doing so. The present manual is my latest and final attempt to carry out Van Riper's wish for my career. I have written what I know in the only way I know how. Van Riper was my muse throughout the entire process as I referred back to the many editions of his main text over and over again. I imagined him with his pipe, smiling down at me as my fingers flew over the keyboard. To him I now can say, "Thank you, my friend. You were my guiding light. I could not have done this without you."

It's very rewarding to see a troubled child
untangle his tongue.

To see him grow in self-esteem because he
can now talk like other people.

Lost children should not have to find their
way out of the swamp alone.

They need a guide who has a map.

We are that guide.

– Charles Van Riper, 1978

TABLE OF CONTENTS

PURPOSE

The purpose of *The Marshalla Guide* is to describe, categorize, and set into historic perspective many reported methods of training speech movements in light of modern research. *The Marshalla Guide* is a book by a clinician for clinicians. It is an expression of the author's 39 years of therapy experiences integrated with the evidence of research. It represents a lifelong obsession with speech movement — how it is organized, how it breaks down, how it can be assessed, and, most importantly, how speech movement errors can be remediated. This manual is a very personal account that would be written in different ways by different writers. It contains a cornucopia of ideas from a vast array of resources. The material is appropriate to clients of all ages and ability levels and to all levels of expressive output, from those who produce no phonemes at all to those who have minor single-phoneme errors.

Nearly 1000 references have been studied in the preparation of this manual including textbooks, research articles, seminar handouts, lectures, and therapy manuals that span the ages. Methods are organized by topics relevant to selected areas of articulation and motor speech training. This book is about the movements of speech sound production (phonetics); it is not about the ways in which fully formed phonemes are used within our language (phonology).

The Marshalla Guide will help professional speech-language pathologists love speech training as much as Van Riper did in his time and as much as I have in mine. It is hoped that the research community will use this manual to understand the types of information that practicing therapists still need.

Pam Marshalla, M.A., CCC-SLP
Speech-Language Pathologist
June 2015

PUBLISHER'S NOTE

I am Pam Marshalla's daughter and the designer, illustrator, editor and publisher of this book. Our beloved Pam passed away just before her 63rd birthday on June 8th, 2015, after struggling with late-stage leukemia. Pam spent her last year diligently and passionately editing this book's manuscript. With her passing, I became the sole owner of the publishing and continuing education business that she and I had managed together for over a decade and was tasked with bringing this book to print.

Over the last several years, I received numerous messages of encouragement from members of the speech community which I appreciated more than I could say at the time. Those messages were desperately cherished as I grieved Pam's passing, celebrated the birth my first child and, later, my second, all while timidly navigating the complexities of publishing a work of this volume by myself; it was a tender and bittersweet time. Developing this book was a mountain of a climb for me and it is with tremendous joy and gratitude that I finally present it as finished.

With her seminars and books, Pam taught tens of thousands of therapists to hone their craft. She was a dedicated and passionate speech pathologist and she considered *The Marshalla Guide* to be her *magnum opus*. It was her hope that this book would empower the next generation of speech-language pathologists with a deep appreciation and love for the practice of speech-language pathology. This is my wish as well.

To all speech professionals reading this today: Thank you for the work that you do — you are invaluable.

Shanti McGinley
Owner, Marshalla Speech & Language

FORWARD

I first met Pam Marshalla in California at the 1993 ASHA Convention; between sessions I was wandering the exhibit hall and noticed her company booth. Her business name, *Innovative Concepts,* intrigued me so I headed over. My first recollection of Pam is of seeing her bent over, brushing her full head of long hair upside-down. She flung it back as she stood quickly, then noticed me standing there and broke into a friendly, unpretentious smile, saying, "Oh, hello!" Little did I know that the owner of that company would later become my mentor, business partner, and lifelong friend.

Nor could I have imagined that – almost 22 years later – my bright and insightful friend would lose her hair and her life to leukemia. Two weeks before she passed away, I visited her. What did we talk about? The unsettled state within speech pathology, and about therapy; it was her life and her passion until the end.

In those intervening 22 years, Pam experienced and accomplished more than most. She raised three wonderful daughters, created and ran her own private practice, worked with countless clients, presented hundreds of seminars, and wrote prolifically. This book was her last, and her best; *The Marshalla Guide* embodies her life's work and is a true labor of love.

Pam was intimately aware of the vast variety of clients we speech-language pathologists see daily. In this book, she details therapy methods, techniques and tools: how to implement them and the rationale behind each one to better individualize therapy. Pam artfully blends knowledge from hundreds of resources with personal examples from her own first-hand experience. In my opinion, Pam's expertise was in her extraordinary ability to skillfully coax speech from a non-verbal child and in this book her masterful contributions in this area shine.

I anticipate *The Marshalla Guide* will become the quintessential handbook and go-to authority on childhood motor speech disorders and articulation deficits. Written in language that everyone can understand, this guide provides a thorough history of our profession and shares in detail the speech movement methods and methodologies that have passed from generation to generation since its inception. Pam clearly conveys how current theories and therapies have morphed and shaped into what they are today with supportive research from nearly 500 references interwoven throughout.

A massive undertaking, this practical and extensive publication is a compilation of an array of therapy options presented in three parts:

1. Traditional Approaches
2. Speech Movement
3. Vowels, Consonants, and Metaphonological Foundations

Part One: Traditional Approaches

Part One is organized for easy access and peppered with theory and therapy. It details the traditional plan and methods: phonetic placement, successive approximations, and compensation for structural differences. It also charts the stages of traditional articulation therapy. Included are methods for mumbling, auditory bombardment, auditory discrimination and training, cueing, breath support, posture, and balancing oral and nasal resonance.

Pam shows that traditional therapy approaches emerged from the foundational period of speech-discovery between 1939 and 1968:

> *"[Authors and professors, such as Charles Van Riper] worked without benefit of the kinds of formal research we have today. They wrote their textbooks from their head, from their hearts, from the experiences they had in the clinic, and from their basic understanding of anatomy"* (page 13).

Part Two: Speech is Movement

Part Two details the principles of movement and movement development, as well as critical components of jaw movement, how to facilitate tongue and lips movement, the importance of oral stability and oral perception, oral sensitivity, reflexes, swallowing and myofunctional methods, speech movement learning, and the all-important tools for speech movement training.

> *"If one accepts the premise that 'speech is movement' (Stetson, 1928) and that there are speech movement disorders called 'apraxia' and 'dysarthria' (Darley, et al, 1975), it follows that speech-language pathologists should be trained in movement"* (page 125).

Part Three: Vowels, Consonants, and Metaphonological Foundations

Part Three explores how phonemes emerge in infancy and early childhood and describes the production of phonemes. Numerous therapy methods are infused along the way. Pam teaches the foundations of pre-speech and how to teach vowels, diphthongs, stop consonants, nasal consonants, glides, and fricatives. She also covers how to work with low-cognitive and unintelligible children.

Pam tells us, "Speech training comes down to teaching phonemes" (page 317). In one sentence, she clarifies the phonetic-phonemic chain of communication:

> *"Movements create the phonemes that are used in phonological patterns to express the language for use in conversation and literacy"* (page 16).

Pam Marshalla's work is done. We are the fortunate benefactors of her gift to us – as individual speech-language pathologists and as a profession. Pam was fond of reminding us that, at any given moment in time, "we have the opportunity to make a positive difference in someone's life." She did that each and every day. Now it's time for us to carry on her legacy.

Charlotte A. Boshart, M.A., CCC-SLP
President, Speech Dynamics, Inc.

EDITORIAL NOTES

The Marshalla Guide contains numerous quotes from original resources so readers can have access to the first writers' original thoughts. Certain minor modifications were necessary to make some of these quotes readable to today's audiences but the meaning of each statement remained unaltered. No references to these minor corrections were made in the text. The following guidelines were used:

Spelling Changes

Insignificant changes in spelling were made in some of the quoted material. *The New Oxford American Dictionary* (Jewell & Abate, 2001) was used to make spelling decisions.

Print Selections

The limitations of printing presses in earlier centuries caused printers to use capitalization in order to emphasize words or to introduce new vocabulary. Here those capitals have been changed to italics.

Sentence Modifications

Elocutionists tended to write unbelievably long sentences that included many commas and semicolons. These were divided into shorter sentences set off by periods. If a quote had to be re-worded significantly for it make sense to the reader, the material was removed from quotes and the idea was paraphrased.

Person-First Labels

Early writers did not use the person-first descriptors that are in use today, and they often referred to clients by names now considered distasteful. For example, clients with cognitive deficit were called "idiots," "imbeciles," "fools," and "morons" in 19th century, and the labels "the mentally retarded," "the retarded," "the cerebral palsied," and "the handicapped" appeared in books from the middle of the 20th century. The original authors meant no offense in the use of these terms and their writing simply reflected the style of the times. The present author struggled about whether or not to change these terms when they appeared in original quotes. In the end it was decided either to omit such citations or to paraphrase them. In addition, some writers of the 20th century referred to a client as "the case" or "the speech defective." Some of these citations appear unchanged in the present manual because these were the terms Van Riper used to identify his clients.

Unsubstantiated Claims

Certain claims appear in older texts that are no longer deemed appropriate in educational or medical writing today. For example, early writers often claimed that a technique would "cure" or "heal" a client. Professionals make no such claims today, however, quotes that employ these terms are presented verbatim.

Professional Title

It is understood that *speech-language pathologist* or *SLP* is the current acceptable title of the professional who is the subject of this book. However, the reader will discover other terms such as *speech teacher, speech clinician, speech therapist, speech correctionist,* and *elocutionist.* This has been done to preserve historical accuracy and to add color to the text.

Phonetic Transcription

Writers in the field of elocution and speech correction used their own homemade methods to transcribe phonemes before the International Phonetic Alphabet was set in 1888. For example, books published before then represented phoneme /t/ in a wide variety of ways including *T, tuh, t, tee, t-t-t, tttt,* and *[T].* These original transcriptions have been retained within quoted material in order to preserve historical accuracy in most cases. However, these symbols were replaced by IPA symbols whenever the original quote might be confusing to the reader.

Conventions

There are certain conventions that practicing speech-language pathologists use everyday, which are common and very well understood between them, but which are not taught in universities as a part of standard transcription. For example, many therapists use dashes to indicate pauses between syllables or words. These and a few other nonstandard methods have been included in this text and each is explained within the text.

Gender Designations

It is understood that clinicians and clients are represented by all gender identities. However, in this text therapists generally are designated by female pronouns (she, her, hers) and clients are generally represented by male pronouns (he, him, his). This classic standard was adopted to make the text less verbally cumbersome.

Privacy

Examples of real clients from the author's clinical experiences are scattered throughout this manual. Names and all other identifying markers have been changed to protect their privacy

Precautions

This book contains methods and procedures for oral stimulation. Readers are cautioned to follow sanitary procedures at all times, to be mindful of social appropriateness regarding such methods, to heed warnings about potential allergic reactions, to avoid any and all methods that may be harmful to individual clients in any way, and to follow employment rules and regulations. These warnings must be taken into account with all clients at all times. The author, publisher, distributor, and their representatives, are not responsible for potential mishandling of the information contained herein.

Speech-language pathologists are creative and intelligent people who integrate scientific research with practical methods of speech improvement.

Introduction

*"Speech is the highest expression of all educational and emotional
attainment. The training for speech is the training for life."*

– Smiley Blanton & Margaret Blanton, 1919

The Marshalla Guide describes, categorizes, and sets into historic perspective reported methods of
speech movement training in clients with articulation and motor speech disorders in light of modern
research. It is designed as a resource for professional or student speech-language pathologists who
want more information about developing the delicate motor coordination of expressive speech. The
methods of this manual are applicable to any client regardless of the cause or severity of his speech
impairment, and no matter his chronological age, intellectual level, language background, or neuromuscular status.

Every type of speech movement is discussed in this guide, from how to stimulate voice in a client
who is non-vocal, to getting the tongue into position for a correct /r/. The manual contains a vast
amount of information from a wide variety of resources. Methods stretch way beyond those usually
covered in articulation, phonology, and motor speech texts. That is because *The Marshalla Guide* digs
deeply into the chronological record of the way speech movements have been taught by practicing
clinicians throughout the ages. The background information within each chapter can be read for a
comprehensive perspective about themes in speech movement training, or the methods sections can
be studied individually to learn precise therapy techniques.

The material of *The Marshalla Guide* has been organized into three parts. Part One describes
traditional approaches. Its chapters describe classic methods that are used with every client no matter the etiology or severity of the articulation or motor speech disorder. Part Two is called *Speech
is Movement*. It presents a broad array of methods designed to stimulate better jaw, lip, and tongue
movements for clients who cannot imitate mature phonemes on demand. Part Three concerns the
teaching of phonemes and metaphonological foundations for any type of client. These chapters
contain a catalogue of methods for teaching every consonant, vowel, and diphthong of Standard
North American English.

Speech correction is a scientific process based on natural teaching ability, creative instinct, and rapport.

PART ONE
Traditional Approaches

"To be well informed, a clinician should understand all points of view and techniques."

– Eugene T. McDonald, 1964

This first part of *The Marshalla Guide* presents traditional approaches to the remediation of speech impairment. These are the methods one employs with every client no matter if he presents with articulation impairment or motor speech disorder. Fundamental methods of teaching speech sounds according to Charles Van Riper and other important Traditional Era writers are presented. Classic techniques to improve breath support, phonation, and resonance are described. Supportive research is woven throughout the chapters when applicable.

Chapters

1

Traditional Articulation & Motor Speech Training

Methods and procedures of the Van Riper generation

> *"Any contemporary view of treatment needs to stress what is current, what is new. Thus, due to their non-contemporary roots, one might hesitate to take traditional-motor approaches seriously... Should a traditional phonetic approach still be used? The answer to this is yes."*
>
> – Jacqueline Bauman-Waengler, 2004

The profession of speech improvement is an honorable one that began in the days of ancient Greece and Rome. Seven distinct eras of speech improvement can be identified through history as summarized in Table 1 on the next page. The present chapter is about the methods of the sixth era that the present author calls *Traditional Articulation Therapy*. The Traditional Era is identified as a thirty-year period from 1939 through 1968. The focus of this era was on training one phoneme at a time no matter how severe the client's problem was. These were methods for clients with both simple articulation errors and severe motor speech disorders.

The Traditional Era opens with the publication of *Speech Correction: Principles and Methods* by Charles Van Riper (1939). This publication has been selected as the official starting point because Van Riper is considered the main architect of the traditional approach. The era closes in 1968 when phonological theory entered the field with the publication of *The Sound Pattern of English* (Chomsky & Halle, 1968) and the English translation of *Child Language Aphasia and Phonological Universals* (Jakobson, 1968). Phonology introduced ideas that took eyes off the mechanics of individual phoneme production (phonetics) and put it on patterns of phoneme use within the language (phonology).

Traditional techniques are not old-fashioned or irrelevant; they are the ones that Van Riper called "part of the standard equipment of any worker in the field" (Van Riper, 1954, p. 240). From getting a child to pay attention to a phoneme, to having him use the phoneme in spontaneous speech, all that therapists do can be traced back to Van Riper and the Traditional Era, during which speech-language pathologists were called *speech therapists*, *speech correctionists*, and *speech clinicians*.

BACKGROUND

Therapists of the Traditional Era worked without benefit of the kinds of formal research that exists today. They wrote their textbooks from their heads, from their hearts, from the experiences they had in the clinic, and from their basic understanding of anatomy. Traditional Era therapists made up their own methods and they wrote about the discoveries they were making in their schools and clinics.

A variety of research projects were undertaken in the second half of the 20th century that were designed to test the Traditional Era methods and virtually all of these projects demonstrated that they had merit. For example, Helmick (1976) studied 49 elementary children with similar types of phoneme errors. He administered basic Van-Riper-type therapy to 26 of them while 23 received no therapy. Results indicated that children receiving the therapy improved significantly over the non-therapy group.

Defective Speech Defined

Van Riper's definition of speech impairment was established at the beginning of the Traditional Era, and it became the standard for generations:

"Speech is defective when it deviates so far from the speech of other people that it calls attention to itself, interferes with communication, or causes its possessor to be maladjusted to his environment. All speech deviations are not, of course, speech defects" (Van Riper, 1939, p. 51).

Basic Elements of Therapy

The basic elements of articulation therapy according to Van Riper (1947) include the following:

1. Help the client learn that he has an error in pronunciation.

2. Eliminate the cause(s) of the disorder if possible.

3. Use ear training to teach the client to isolate, recognize, identify, and discriminate the target.

4. Teach the client to produce the target "through various methods" as described in the rest of this chapter.

5. Practice the new sound in order to "strengthen" it. This means to help the client bring the sound production under his own control, and not to

		TABLE 1 — Seven Eras of Speech Improvement		
1	Greece and Rome	500 BC to AD 01		• Pondering the nature of speech and its deficits • First remediation practices • Elocution defined
2	Pre-Renaissance	AD 01 to 1300		• Speech instruction to deaf by monks • Reports of good speech following glossectomy • First reports of oral surgery
3	European Renaissance	1300 to 1669		• Study of anatomy begins • Good speech is necessary for self growth and financial success
4	Elocution Era	1669 to 1888		• English phonetics described • Velopharyngeal (VP) surgery • Elocution and anatomy merge • Reading, writing, and speaking standards established
5	Phonetic Placement Era	1888 to 1939		• International Phonetic Alphabet (IPA) • Vowel quadrilateral (VQ) • Remediation based on the IPA, VQ, and anatomy
6	Traditional (Articulation) Era	1939 to 1968		• Van Riper defines speech impairment • Therapy progresses from isolated phoneme to conversation • Multiple methods described • Therapy described as on-going diagnosis
7	Modern Era	1968 to Present		• Phonology introduced • Motor speech therapy established • Dysphagia, feeding, and orofacial myology introduced • Research on speech movements advances

Seven eras of speech improvement can be identified. The Traditional Era of articulation therapy was dominated by the work of Charles Van Riper.

strengthen the muscles.

6. Incorporate the new sound into familiar words, and accomplish a transition of these to "normal speech." This means to establish the sound in words, phrases, sentences, paragraphs, and in conversation.

7. Habituate the new sound and eliminate the error. This means to establish carryover in all speaking situations.

The Traditional Plan

The traditional plan of articulation therapy is a simple one. Treatment revolves entirely around correct production of the individual target phoneme. It begins with production of the phoneme in isolation if it can be produced alone, or in a syllable if the sound only can be produced with an attached vowel. It ends with the phoneme produced correctly in spontaneous conversational speech outside the therapy room and with various conversational partners. Between the phoneme or syllable and conversation comes work on words, phrases, sentences, and paragraphs. Advancement through the program is based upon success at each subsequent stage.

Therapists agree that these stages are overlapping and that one can address multiple stages within individual therapy sessions. In fact, at the very end of his career, Van Riper himself said that he seldom used the plan he outlined: "Rarely did I make my clients climb that staircase step by step" (Secord et al., 2007, p. 1). Other therapists since have recommended alterations to this basic plan under certain circumstances. For example, McCabe and Bradley (1975) proposed the *multiple phonemic approach*, a plan that addresses all error phonemes simultaneously. Schissel and Doty (1979) tested this approach on one client with multiple articulation errors. The client achieved mastery over nine of his eleven error phonemes in 14 hours of direct therapy using this method.

The traditional plan is the thought process upon which is built everything therapists do in articulation therapy. It is a map, a ladder, or a staircase. The phonetic environment is controlled as clients move up the steps. See Table 2 on pages 26–27 for more details.

1. *Isolation:* The client learns to produce the target phoneme alone. (If a phoneme cannot be produced in isolation, then begin with Step 2. For example, /s/ can be produced in isolation but /b/ only can be produced with a vowel.)

2. *Syllables:* The client learns to produce the target phoneme in a CV syllable in the original plan. Therapists recognize that some clients may need to begin training with a different syllable shape.

3. *Words (both real and nonsense):* The client learns to produce the target phoneme in simple words. Real words are always used but nonsense words may be included as well. Traditional Era therapists usually began with words that contained the target phoneme in the initial position. Final position, medial position, and clusters were addressed next in that order. Therapists recognize that this order is highly variable according to client stimulability. Further, therapists understand that not all clients need training in all positions because transfer and generalization of training can occur (Ruscello, 1975).

4. *Phrases:* The client learns to produce the target phoneme in words embedded within simple phrases.

5. *Sentences:* The client learns to produce the target phoneme in words embedded within simple sentences.

6. *Paragraphs:* The client learns to produce the target phoneme in words embedded within sentences that comprise simple paragraphs. One begins with paragraphs in which the phonetic environment is tightly controlled, and progresses toward paragraphs with uncontrolled phonetic environments. The therapist and client usually write the controlled paragraphs. Uncontrolled paragraphs can be taken from any storybook, textbook, magazine article, cereal box, etc.

7. *Conversations:* The client learns to produce the target phoneme within conversations. Treatment begins with simple conversations with the therapist and within the therapy room. It progresses to more complex and uncontrolled conversations with other people outside of the therapy environment.

Charles Van Riper is considered the "father" of traditional articulation therapy.

METHODS

The rest of this chapter is devoted to practical descriptions of the methods of Traditional Era articulation therapy. Four of Van Riper's editions (1939, 1947, 1954, 1978) have been used in the preparation of this material.

The Stimulation Method / Imitation

Van Riper recommended that training begin with what he called the *stimulation method*. To stimulate a phoneme means to give an auditory and visual model of the sound for the client to imitate. Modeling is the mainstay and the most important technique of this method. Therapists model a target and instruct the client to watch, listen, and repeat after them. Van Riper said that the stimulation method is the simplest, easiest, and most natural method of phoneme instruction, and he insisted that a sound taught by this method is more stable than a sound taught by any other. Carrell (1968) called this method *stimulus-response*. Fletcher called it the process of using *speech production demonstrations*:

> *"The clinician uses speech production demonstrations as stimuli to induce images of desired articulatory actions, increase understanding of action sequences, and shape changes in the subject's articulatory skills… One of the main goals of articulatory modeling is to develop a clear mental percept or abstract visual image that represents the core elements of the postures, gestures, and movement patterns to be performed"* (Fletcher, 1992, p. 220–224).

If presenting an auditory and visual model to imitate is going to work all by itself, Van Riper said that it should work immediately. He suggested that the stimulation method be tried thoroughly before resorting to other methods. In other words, therapists should show the client how to say the phoneme by modeling it for him first, and other methods should be added to the process only if it doesn't work right away. Most writers agree: "We recommend that the clinician attempt to elicit responses through imitation as an initial instructional method for production training" (Bernthal & Bankson, 2004, p. 300). Wingo and Hoshiko (1972) tested Van Riper's concept that imitation of a direct model is the best way to begin treatment. They taught non-English phonemes to 36 college students by providing them with either imitation, tactile, or descriptive input. They found that the imitative condition proved the best.

The concept of *stimulability* reflects this basic idea. Stimulability has been defined as "a child's ability to imitate a sound absent from his/her phonetic inventory immediately following an examiner's model" (Miccio, 2002, p. 225). If a client is stimulable for a new phoneme he will learn it quickly and easily with only the auditory and visual model presented to him. Therapists model speech targets and if the client is ready he will produce it correctly right away, or he will say it correctly after just a few

presentations. Sommers et al. (1967) compared stimulability and successful therapy in young elementary school children enrolled in articulation therapy. He found that children who were not stimulable needed therapy more urgently than those who were. Arndt, Elbert, and Shelton (1971) found that children who responded well to the first few weeks of articulation training (those who were the most easily stimulated) could be predicted to do well in therapy.

> *"Imitation… requires the client to repeat a target sound after the clinician has presented one or more examples. Even when the client is not stimulable in the initial assessment, the clinician may be able to use imitation as a first step in training"* (Secord et al., 2007, p. 3).

Van Riper wrote that imitation should work successfully in all but a few cases as long as the client has no cognitive or motor impairment. This is an important point. It means that clients who *do* have cognitive or motor impairment will probably need additional techniques to achieve correct production. Remember that Van Riper was writing about elementary-age children and not preschoolers or toddlers. Nonetheless modeling still is the best place to start in order to see how well it will work with any client any time. The advice of the ages has been to try modeling first even if the client has cognitive or motor impairment, or even if he is very young, because one never knows whether or not the client will be able to imitate the sound until it is tried

The Phonetic Placement Method

Van Riper used the phrase *phonetic placement methods* to draw together the methods that had been used by the generation of speech correctionists right before his time. These methods emerged after the International Phonetic Alphabet (IPA) was accepted in 1888, and when anatomy

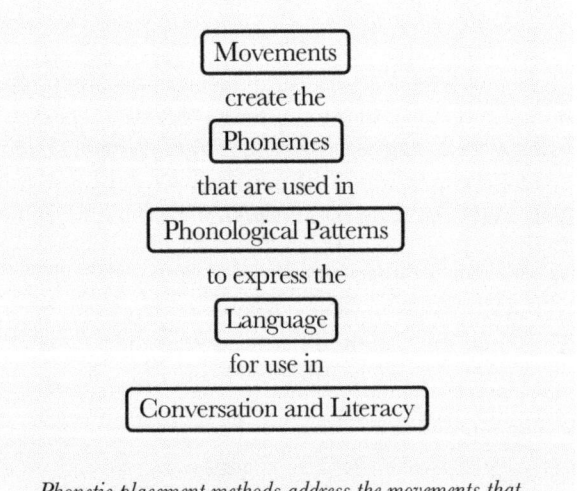

Phonetic placement methods address the movements that create phonemes.

Therapists direct speech movements much like a conductor directs an orchestra.

had become integral to the work of speech correction. The Phonetic Placement Era is located in the fifth position in Table 1 on page 14. The methods of the Phonetic Placement Era served as a bridge from the old process of elocution (the fourth era), in which anatomy was mostly ignored, to the Traditional Era of the 20th century in which anatomy had become integral to speech training.

Phonetic placement methods, therefore, have a significant focus on anatomy. They include *verbal descriptions* and *physical manipulations* to influence jaw, lip, tongue, and velar positioning.

• *Verbal descriptions:* Simple phrases are used to help the client understand the movement and position of each articulator. For example, simple directions like "Open your mouth" or "Put your tongue up here" are phonetic placement methods because they provide verbal instruction about jaw, lip, tongue, or velar movement.

• *Physical manipulations:* Tools are used in order to manipulate jaw, lip, tongue, and velar movements and positions. A simple activity like using a tongue depressor to push the tongue tip up for /l/ is considered a phonetic placement method because it uses physical manipulation to achieve the phoneme's required oral position.

There are three keys to success when using a phonetic placement method. First, the therapist must possess a clear understanding of the movements involved in a target phoneme's production. Second, the therapist must use vocabulary rich with descriptors of oral positions that match a client cognitive or intellectual capacity. Third, the SLP must understand how to use tools if necessary to manipulate the oral structures in ways that create the appropriate movements and positions of the oral structures.

Van Riper insisted that if an individual client could not imitate a therapist's phoneme model within a few minutes using the model-imitation routine or stimulation method described above, then the phonetic placement method

must be employed because the client needed more information. Van Riper preferred the phonetic placement method for clients who could not learn their phonemes from auditory information alone:

> *"Some clients are unable to perceive tiny variations in auditory experience. They are not ear-minded. They have better visual or proprioceptive imagery than auditory imagery. With these we prefer to use the phonetic placement techniques"* (Van Riper, 1978, p. 189).

Therapists use a wide variety of tools when employing phonetic placement methods. For example, many SLPs use bite blocks to set the jaw into position, they use straws to teach lip rounding, and they use Toothettes® to stimulate points of articulation on the lips, tongue, and palate. These types of phonetic placement methods have been called *oral-motor techniques* and there has been much criticism over them due to a lack of formal testing. However, these are basic Van Riper methods that have been used for decades. This topic is discussed more thoroughly in Chapter 19, *The Tools of Speech Movement Training*.

Therapists also use natural gestures to send the articulators on the right path of movement as a part of phonetic placement. This is done much like an orchestra, band, or choral conductor: "Gestural cues… provide additional information for the client" (Yorkston, Beukelman, Strand & Bell, 1999, p. 554). Gestural cues are described in more detail in Chapter 5, *Teaching Speech Movements with Cues*.

Today's phonetic placement methods also include today's technologies. Palatometry is a method that shows perhaps the most promise. Palatometry has been used to teach phonetic placement to hearing impaired students (Fletcher, Dagenais, & Critz-Crosby, 1991; Dagenais, Critz-Crosby, Fletcher, and McCutcheon, 1994) and to remediate a lateral lisp (Dagenais, Critz-Crosby, & Adams, 1994). Electronic tools such as this will add real value to phoneme training as they become more affordable to the average clinician.

A model of how the phonetic placement method fits into treatment might be described like this: Movements create the phonemes that are used in phonological patterns to express the language for use in conversation and literacy. Phonetic placement methods train the first part of this model, i.e., the movements of the phoneme.

The Sound Modification Method

Van Riper explained another method of teaching new phoneme production. That is to help the client modify the movements and positions of another sound he already can make correctly. He called this *sound modification*. Van Riper recommended that SLPs use a client's already existing sound as a point of departure, and he suggested that the beginning sound could be one of three different types. The present author has added a fourth:

• *Another phoneme:* Such as using /b/ to teach /p/.

- *A non-speech sound:* Such as using panting to teach /h/.
- *A biological noise:* Such as using coughing to teach /k/.
- *An infant pre-speech vocalization:* Such as using a voiceless lingua-labial raspberry to teach /s/.

One of these four acts is the starting point and then the sound is changed or modified until it matches the target phoneme. The process of sound modification is one of the simplest and most efficient ways SLPs have to teach a client how to produce a new phoneme. It goes straight to the heart of articulation training because it addresses the task of phoneme learning in a series of easy steps that are based on refined auditory discrimination and subtle movement changes. But the steps one takes are not spelled out like a recipe in a cookbook. The steps are highly individualistic and related directly to the client at hand. The steps will be a little different for each client. It is the job of the SLP to engage in clinical experimentation in order to determine what steps will be beneficial for the individual client.

> *"The student is asked to make a certain sound and to hold it for a short period. He is then requested to move his jaw, lips, or tongue in a definite manner while continuing to produce his first sound. This variation in articulators will produce a change in the sound, a change which often rather closely approximates the sound that is desired"* (Van Riper, 1954, p. 239–240).

The process of sound modification involves teaching clients to compare and contrast the starting sound with each subtle change that occurs. Any standard consonant chart by place of articulation can be used to select similar phonemes when one phoneme will be used to teach another. Place, manner, and voicing features are compared and contrasted. For example, SLPs can use /t/ to teach /s/ because their voice and place features are the same while their manner feature is different. Therapists help the client understand how he already is making /t/, and then teach him to modify the manner of /t/ to produce /s/. Teach him to hear himself produce /t/ and then to modify its movements and positions in order to hear himself produce a sound that gets ever closer to /s/.

The Successive Approximation Method

Van Riper also described the process of using a client's own error sound as a starting point of treatment in a process he called *successive approximations*. This method has also been called *progressive approximations* and *shaping*. The method essentially is the same as the process of sound modification described above, except now the client's error phoneme is used as the starting point.

The therapist imitates the client's error, and then changes one tiny feature at a time until the target is reached. Van Riper called successive approximation a

trail-blazing method, meaning that therapists blaze a new therapy trail that no one has ever taken before. The trail starts at the client's error and ends in production of the correct sound. Shaping is the primary tool.

Alexander Graham Bell (1906) advocated this method when working with children who were deaf. It is also especially good for tuning a hearing client's ear as he is learning to re-shape his mouth. The present author has found that it is an especially good methods for correcting distorted vowels and /r/. Success rests in one's ability to imitate the client's error exactly.

> *"Encourage [the client] to repeat the sound so that you may study it and find out how best to utilize it in his instruction… Let your pupil repeat the sound until you can imitate it yourself. Then study your own mouth"* (Bell, 1906, p. 94).

> *"The clinician joins the client and makes the same error the client makes. She then shows the client a series of transitional sounds each of which comes a bit closer to the standard sound until finally the standard sound is produced"* (Van Riper, 1978, p. 188).

The Babbling Method

Babbling can be used to introduce new phonemes to very young children, however, Van Riper recommended babbling for older clients with mild-to-moderate articulation errors. He used it to help his clients happen upon a target phoneme. Van Riper said that the babbling method is the closest to the natural process a child goes through when learning to talk.

Van Riper suggested that the clinician and student babble in unison. He stressed that one should not limit the client to the production of only the target phoneme in the babbling sequence. Instead, Van Riper recommended that SLPs use babbling to explore many oral movements and many phonemes. He said that therapists and clients "should relax, get the babbling started, and then let it continue almost automatically, ranging where it will" (Van Riper, 1954, p. 245). No attempt should be made to notice the sounds produced at first and random vocalizations should be the goal.

With time the student should be encouraged to babble by himself. The client produces this "hodgepodge of vocalizations" and then the therapist begins to encourage the client to produce the target sound with more frequency. The SLP helps the client pay attention to the target sound in the process of babbling, and then he or she helps him to stabilize it with practice.

Using Correct Phonemes in Existing Words

Van Riper recommended a process he did not name but that he described as "using words in which the usually defective sound is made correctly" (Van Riper, 1954, p. 245).

He said that words the client can speak correctly are like gold because they represent one phonetic environment in which the client has conquered his production — even if he doesn't know it.

Van Riper insisted that this method is quite valuable because there is no need to teach a phoneme that a client already can produce. The existing correct word proves that the client already can position his articulators correctly for production of the phoneme. Therapy switches, therefore, to a focus on teaching the client how to use his already correct phoneme in diverse phonetic environments or phonological neighborhoods. Van Riper's existing word approach can be used in many ways as described next.

Paired Stimuli

Weston and Irwin (1971; Irwin & Weston, 1975) formalized the process of using existing words in a process they called *paired stimuli*. The process begins by identifying one word in which the client produces the target phoneme correctly nine out of ten times. This word then is spoken in pairs with other words in which the target is incorrect. The student is given a tangible reward each time he produces the target correctly, therefore, he receives one reward for the key word and a second for the paired word if the sound is correct. This is an excellent way to help clients pay attention to what they are saying and to make comparisons between one of their correct utterances and another that is incorrect.

Abstracting a Correct Syllable

Existing words can also be used for their correct syllables. Have the client say the word he can say with his correct phoneme. Let's say, for example, that the client is working on /r/, and that he can say *church* correctly. Now, if he can say *church*, he should be able to say the simplified syllable *chur*. And if he can say *chur*, he should be able to use this syllable in other words like *teacher*, *butcher*, and *churning*. The client will pronounce these words with great pauses between the syllables: *tea—chur*, *bu—chur*, and *chur—ning*. In some cases the client will have to start with the whole word as in *tea-church* (for *teacher*) and *bu-church* (for *butcher*). Then he will have to be taught to

drop the unnecessary parts of the word. Over time the client is taught to shorten the pauses between the syllables.

Coarticulation

Another way to use a correct sound in an existing word is to pair the word with another word that needs the correct sound. Returning to /r/, if the client cannot say *car* with a correct final /r/, but he can say *ride* with a correct initial /r/, then pair the two words together in the sequence: *car-ride*. The key to success is to block the client's production of the /r/ he cannot do which in this case is the final /r/ in *car*. In other words, have the client say: *ca-ride*. Then teach him to prolong the /ɑ/ of *car* so that it runs, transitions, or sequences smoothly into to the word *ride*: *caaaaa-ride*. Then teach the client to drop *-ide* so that he says *car*. This can be done with meaningful phrases like *car ride*, or nonsense word pairings like *car robot*.

Merten (1972) expanded this method into a way to teach /s/-clusters. Her idea was to pair words together into phrases in order to help a client produce a cluster sequence he otherwise could not do. For example, if a client can produce /s/ at the end of a word, and if he can also produce /t/ at the beginning of a word, then these two words can be paired together to help him learn to produce an /st/ cluster. The key is to use two words together in a natural phrase that she called a couplet. As such, *kiss* might be paired with *Tom* to create the couplet *Kiss Tom*. This phrase then might be worked in a sentence like *You kiss Tom* and then into a longer sentence like *I saw you kiss Tom*. Natural prosody is used at each level. Merten called

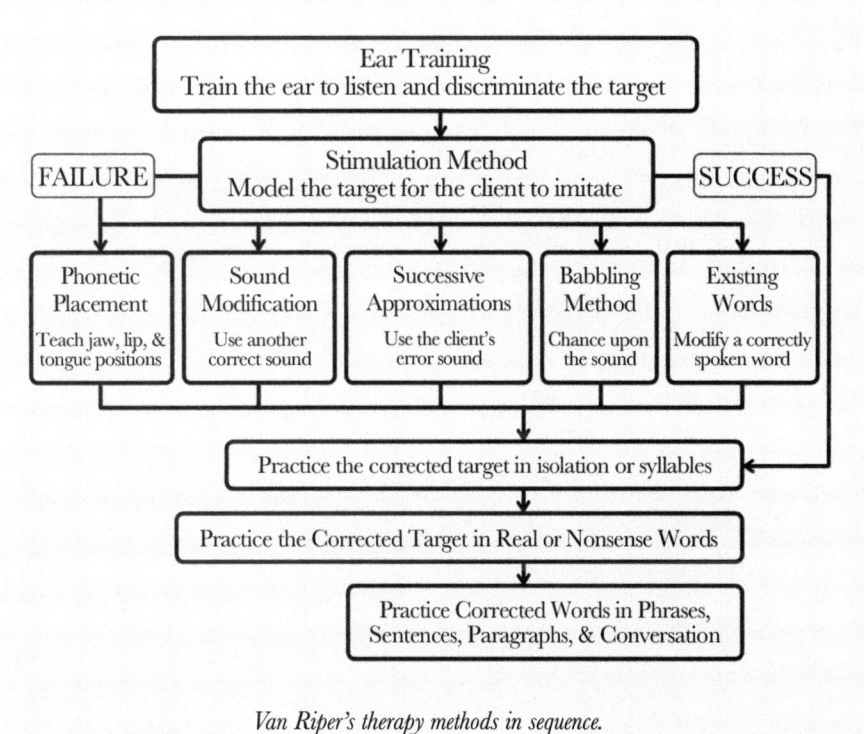

Van Riper's therapy methods in sequence.

this a "self-directing approach" and a "can do" method:

> *"The facilitating couplet provides a large enough unit to allow for the client to change and perfect the movement patterns. It also allows for a functional phrase to be used in the early sessions of treatment"* (Merten, 1972, p. 26).

Separate the Sound From an Existing Correct Word

There is another way to use existing words that can be useful for many clients. That is to separate the sound from its existing word. Begin by drawing the client's attention to the correct phoneme he is producing in his correct word. Then teach him to isolate the correct sound he is producing from that word by adding a pause.

For example, take the case of training /r/. If the client can say *car* correctly, draw his attention to his correct /r/. Then teach him to prolong the vowel as he transitions to the /r/: *caaaaaaaaar*. Then teach him to pause before /r/: *caaaaaaa—r*. Now the target phoneme is isolated from the rest of the word. Have him practice this production and make the pause longer each time. The longer the pause, the more isolated /r/ will become. Once completely isolated, the phoneme can be practiced alone, and then it can be used in other carefully selected words.

Word Selection: Simple or Complex?

Van Riper virtually always recommended beginning with simple words and progressing to more complex words over time. For example, when teaching initial /k/, words like *key* and *book* are trained before words like *Kentucky* and *asterisk*.

Words of more complexity are described as having *dense phonological neighborhoods* (Luce & Pisoni, 1998). A few studies have caused one to question the wisdom of this plan because both perception and production of vowels seems to be better in words of higher complexity. Several

theories have been proposed to explain this. One view is that more complex words are uttered more carefully, and another is that words that are spoken more often are uttered less carefully. This gets back to the general developmental principle of the drive toward economy (see Chapter 10). The more frequently a word is spoken, the more likely it is that its articulation will be slighted: "Higher frequency words are more likely to undergo reductive articulatory changes that increase the ease of articulation of a word" (Munson & Solomon, 2004, p. 1056).

The information to be taken from this is that while therapists virtually always teach target phonemes in words that were simple before they taught them in words that were complex, research suggests that perhaps the opposite should be considered. At the very least, SLPs will continue to include the density of phonological neighborhoods as a variable of speech training. In terms of the evidence-based practice model this means that each individual client will provide the evidence necessary to help the therapist determine what is the best approach for him.

Compensation for Structural Differences

Van Riper and other therapists taught that structural and medical problems related to speech impairment should be eliminated before or during the treatment process if possible: "Anything that can be done to eliminate the cause of defective articulation has first priority" (Carrell, 1968, p. 92). The reality of therapy is that many clients have structural and medical deficits that will remain unchanged. Van Riper taught that these clients must be taught compensated productions that are less that perfect but acceptable given their physical circumstances. Structural and medical problems sometimes cause the range of acceptable variations to widen.

Therapists can find themselves discouraged when working with clients who have un-repaired structural deficits but Van Riper was encouraging: "The picture is by no means hopeless… since all of the speech sounds may be made in various ways" (Van Riper, 1947, p. 163–166). Van Riper recommended the following steps when designing a compensatory plan. These notes are nearly verbatim from his 1947 publication:

1. Note how the student articulates the defective sound.

2. Make phonetic analysis to determine what the essential mechanics of the sound must be.

3. Discover what structures the student might possibly use to satisfy the mechanical requirements.

4. Give the student a thorough course in ear training.

5. Try to get the student to produce a sound similar to that made by the instructor through manipulation, phonetic diagrams, mirror work, imitation, and random activity.

6. Once achieved, do not let the student move a muscle of face or body until he prolongs, repeats, and

A mirror aids phoneme comparisons.

uses some nonsense syllables many times.

7. Build up the sound's strength. (Van Riper used the word "strength" to mean "consistency.")

8. Do not worry about exaggerated movements used by students in making the sound. This type of exaggeration usually fades in time.

9. Increase the speed with which the new performance pattern can be initiated.

10. Be careful to change the transition movements as well.

Therapy is also adjusted to meet the needs of on-going surgical repair. For example, a young client with a severe cleft palate or an adult with a severe structural deficit due to a traumatic facial injury may undergo years of reparative surgery. In these cases articulation therapy is regulated according to the changing needs. Some of these patients simply will be monitored over time to make sure they are adjusting to their new physical circumstances, and others will need to be enrolled in periods of therapy when necessary to help them adjust to the changes.

Therapy is also attuned to physical changes that are pending. For example, many children enter therapy with occlusal and dental problems that interfere with correct phoneme production. These problems usually have a significant impact on production of the sibilants because of the important role the front teeth play in the production of frication. A client with the singular problem of sibilant distortion may be served better by holding off therapy until after corrective braces or surgery takes place. On the other hand, a client with multiple misarticulations and/or significant phonological impairment can receive immediate speech therapy, even before the teeth are fixed, because other phonemes can be addressed while awaiting the dental procedures.

Some clients undergo physical alterations to their facial and oral structures that cause their phonemes to change slightly and they want to know if their speech is still good. These clients often are bothered by the subtle changes in their speech that have occurred, and they often are certain that the subtle change is making their speech stand out in undesirable ways. In short, they don't like they way they sound since the physical change was imposed upon them. For example, one adult female had an injury to her tongue tip that caused /s/ and /z/ to sound a little different but still correct. Therapy is designed to help the client understand that there are many ways to produce each phoneme and that their new production is just as good as their old one. They are helped to produce the best sound they can and they are counseled about learning to accept this unwanted change.

"Each phoneme is actually a group of sounds or allophones" (Garn-Nunn & Lynn, 2004, p. 6).

"Some… allophonic variations in a phoneme simply reflect individual differences among speakers" (Carrell & Tiffany, 1960, p. 20).

Nonsense Words

Using nonsense words was a part of therapy as recommended by Van Riper and many others, and the process has been backed by research. The use of nonsense words often has been referred to as pure speech motor practice.

Shames (1957) preferred to use nonsense words because he found that children who did not carryover from correctly produced practice words to conversational speech were often unable to maintain appropriate prosody while incorporating their new productions. Speaking words with corrected phonemes caused these clients to slow down and speak in a monotone, and they did not like this. He found that his subjects would rather produce their words incorrectly than make their prosody sound different than everyone else. Therefore, he proposed that nonsense words could serve as a link between early deliberate sound productions and automatic conversational word productions. He had 12 children produce their new sounds in nonsense words embedded within reading passages and spontaneous speech in jargon-like fashion with appropriate rate, inflection, and intonation. He called this procedure "structured jargon" and found that it aided carryover. Children were able to use their new sounds more easily with correct prosody when using nonsense words: "It seems that this technique… can build up the automaticity of correct sound productions" (Shames, 1957, p. 263).

Powell and McReynolds (1969) reported that nonsense syllable training resulted in better generalization. Krishnan et al. (2013) reviewed the literature and studied children 7–13 years of age and found that there may be a relationship between the production of nonsense words and oral movement skills. "Important aspects of language learning and consequent language deficits may be rooted in the ability to perform complex sensorimotor transformations" (p. 1800). In other words, the practice of nonsense words may be highly beneficial to clients who need to learn speech movement skills.

Exaggeration

Van Riper mentioned exaggeration of productions in the process of articulation training, and the method has had widespread representation in textbooks written in the Traditional Era. To exaggerate is to "represent (something) as being larger, greater, better, or worse than it really is" (Jewell & Abate, 2001, p. 590). Exaggeration used to be called "increasing the degree of the articulatory excursions" but a reference for this phrase could not be found when doing the background for this manual. Exaggeration often takes the form of prolongation: "When articulating a sound in isolation it is valuable to start with prolonged examples, since you can listen carefully, make the necessary adjustments, and perceive the position of your articulators" (Fairbanks, 1940, p. xxi).

Speech-language pathologists often exaggerate their own jaw, lip and tongue movements to make phonemes stand out. Therapists also exaggerate intonation, rate, rhythm, and stress patterns to make these prosodic features stand out. Exaggeration is required of the client himself in order to help him understand his own productions, to make his own speech movements consistent and precise, and to make phonemes and syllables crisp and clean. Exaggeration is also a way to work on gross speech sound production before embarking on the process of refinement.

There seems to be no research on exaggeration as a method of articulation or phonological therapy, however, it has wide spread representation in Traditional Era articulation texts and in more recent books on motor speech disorders. Some therapists worry about using exaggeration because it takes a client beyond the speech movements that would be considered optimum, but Van Riper explained this concern away when he wrote, "Do not worry about exaggerated movements... These extraneous movements drop out as the new performance patterns become habitual" (Van Riper, 1947, p. 165–166).

Exaggeration is a process of speech improvement that was carried over from the elocutionists who often used the term *just articulation* to describe expressive speech that is slightly exaggerated and well pronounced. Austin (1806) wrote one of the most poetic descriptions of well-articulated speech in which he describes the subtle art of exaggeration common to the best orators of his time. Austin's book became an immediate classic in the 19th century, and this selection from his text was repeated often in other books published throughout the elocutionary period:

> *"In just articulation, the words are not to be hurried over, nor precipitated syllable over syllable; not as it were melted together into a mass of confusion; [The words] should be neither abridged nor prolonged; not swallowed, nor forced, [nor] shot from the mouth; they should not be trailed nor drawled, nor let to slip out carelessly, so as to drop unfinished. They are to be delivered from the lips, as beautiful coins newly issued from the mint, deeply and accurately impressed, perfectly finished, neatly struck by the proper organs, distinct, sharp, in due succession, and of due weight"* (Austin, 1806, p. 38).

Creative Imagery

Therapists also used creative imagery in their training of speech sounds, especially when working with young children. The idea is to help the child understand his own speech movements by making analogies to other objects and situations with which he is familiar. Van Riper said that part of the creative process is to assign each phoneme its own "personality" (Van Riper, 1947, p. 180). These and other ways of using creative imagery are discussed more thoroughly in Chapter 5, *Teaching Speech Movements with Cues*. A few classic examples from Nemoy and Davis (1937) are presented here:

- *The image of a hill used to teach the back of the tongue to rise gently for /k/:* "The exaggerated plosion that usually accompanies excessive pressure may be overcome by suggesting that the pupil make a hill out of the back of his tongue and then to blow /k/ gently down the hill" (p. 108–109).

- *The image of a turtle used to change /s/ into /ʃ/:* "Sometimes the suggestion that the pupil make his tongue thick and bulky or that he draw it in as the turtle does when he puts his head under his shell will be effective in securing the necessary withdrawal of the tongue from that assumed in producing /s/" (p. 170).

- *The image of an apartment used to elevate the tongue tip for /l/:* "The suggestion that /l/ lives way up on the third floor and that the tongue must not forget to go up and get /l/, serves as an interesting reminder to the small child" (p. 135).

- *The image of blowing wind used to teach airflow on /w/:* "A clear mental image of the sound of /w/ may be secured through comparing the sound of /w/ with that made by the wind" (p. 64). (Note: Bilabial /w/ was rather voiceless and more aspirated in the 1930s; the 21st century's /w/ is considered a fully voiced sound.)

Trial & Error

Van Riper and virtually all writers recommended a process of *trial and error* in the remediation process. Using trial and error, a target is selected, a method is chosen, and the process begins. The response from the client gives the therapist the data she needs to make an adjustment to the method for the next trial, and so forth. Van Riper used this term frequently in his early writing.

Since the 1970s however, some SLPs have begun to view the concept of *trial and error* as out-of-date, unsophisticated, insignificant, unscientific, and non-evidence-based. Speech-language pathologists should never forget, however, that the antecedent events — the techniques themselves — are always selected through a process of trial and error; always. One makes an educated guess about the method to be used just as SLPs have always done. That guess is based upon a thorough scientific understanding of the process of speech sound production.

It is interesting to note that in the 1978 edition of his classic book, Van Riper dropped this term. Perhaps he felt pressured into doing so because he snuck the concept in anyway. Instead of using the phrase *trial and error,* he included a section called *varying and correcting* and in there he included a word about trial and error without doing so directly. He said, "Whichever approach is used — and there are times when we must try one and then another — the person must go through a process of varying his utterance" (Van Riper, 1978, p. 187). The present author believes that Van Riper was being very careful with his words. He was passing down the idea of trial and error to subsequent generations of therapists without directly saying so because the term had become dated.

Some methods should never go out of date, however, and the idea of trial and error is one of them. Speech-language pathologists of the 21st century must remember that despite a mountain of empirical evidence that may exist for a particular method, the method still has to prove itself useful for the client sitting at the table. Trial and error is the process used to discover this. Trial and error based on an educated guess has always been and always must be integral to articulation and motor speech therapy. Without the freedom to use trial and error, SLPs begin to employ rigid and robotic procedures regardless of the client's circumstance. When that happens, therapists no longer function as true problem solvers, their impact lessens, and their importance to people with speech impairment is reduced.

The process of trial and error is not random and haphazard. Logic and deductive reasoning ultimately rule the treatment of a speech disorder. Therapists use mental processes to select and modify treatment methods to fit the client's immediate needs. The ability to use logic is supreme in the process. With logic one can create methods that make sense for individual clients regardless of whether prior research exists to prove or disprove the method itself.

Practice

Van Riper and the other writers virtually always recommended practice as a regular part of speech training. To practice is to "perform an activity or exercise a skill repeatedly or regularly in order to improve or maintain one's proficiency" (Jewell & Abate, 2001, p. 1339). To practice in articulation therapy is to rehearse, repeat, exercise, or drill speech targets. Van Riper called it *strengthening* a client's responses.

Practice is not a way to create new speech movements or new phonemes. Practice is used to habituate phoneme productions or oral movements, or to improve muscular strength and endurance for performance of an oral movement. Practice is also used to improve motor memory, to increase volitional control of new movements, and to make new oral movements automatic. It is used to

improve grading, dissociation, or direction of movement for phoneme production. Practice is done in the therapy room to regularize newly-learned skills and it is used at home to habituate productions the client can produce correctly in the therapy room.

From riding a bicycle to producing a speech sound, every new motor skill requires some amount of practice in the early stages. Some clients need a lot of practice while others need hardly any at all. The speech-language pathologist's job is to determine just how much practice an individual client needs, to provide more for the client who needs it, and to provide less for the client who doesn't. The amount and type of practice is adjusted to the client at hand and the client's performance instructs the therapist as to the amount of practice needed. Flexibility is the name of the game. Practice is discussed in virtually every articulation and motor speech text ever written:

> *"Practice is the key variable thought necessary for mastery of any skilled motor behavior... Initially there is sluggishness in the execution of motor skills because the learner is acquiring the movement. With practice, the motor skill is perfected and stabilized. Ultimately, the skill becomes a part of the learner's repertoire of skilled movements and becomes automatic for the speaker"* (Bernthal & Bankson, 2004, p. 295).

Figuring Practice Percentages

Ruscello (1978) proposed the basic method most therapists use to figure a percentage correct on practice material. The method is to count the number of correct responses a client achieves in a therapy session and divide that number by the total attempts. Then multiply that number by 100 to achieve a percentage correct score. For example, a client who produces 4 correct phonemes out of 5 attempts has achieved a score of 80% correct (4/5 x 100 = 80%).

Rest During Practice

Intensive practice usually requires periods of rest. A client may perform well on one trial after another and then suddenly break down and be unable to produce correctly any more, and he needs a rest. Breakdown can be due to many factors including muscle fatigue, sensory overload, distraction, nervousness, disorganization, or sudden loss of confidence, and so forth.

SLPs allow periodic breaks in the action in order to avoid breakdown. One pauses and gives the new motor and auditory patterns a moment to settle. The client's memory for the new pattern is allowed to sink in for a moment. Van Riper commented on this: "After a successful attempt, one should insist that the student remain silent for a time before taking part in conversation. This will permit maturation to become effective" (Van Riper, 1947, p. 188).

"Do it three times." Very simple procedures can be used to encourage practice.

Negative Practice

Some writers also recommended some amount of *negative practice* during the process of phoneme correction, although no research seems to have been done to back it. Van Riper described this as "the deliberate and voluntary use of the incorrect sound or speech error" (Van Riper, 1947, p. 204). Negative practice can be useful to help clients realize what they are doing wrong and it can help them understand the difference between the old way and the new way of producing a target. Van Riper said that negative practice helps clients become more aware of their errors; it contributes to a client's determination to change and it acts as a mild penalty for not changing speech patterns. He insisted that negative practice has no harmful effect upon a client and that it merely emphasizes the distinction between correct and incorrect sounds. Van Riper recommended the following when using negative practice:

- Help the client understand why negative practice is being used.

- Never ask the client to practice the error until his correct production is under full control.

- Structure negative practice around the client's exact mispronunciation.

- Confine all negative practice to the speech room.

- Ask clients to duplicate their error immediately after they make it.

- Use negative practice to compare right and wrong productions.

- Practice correct and incorrect words back and forth in sequences.

- Work negative practice into all levels of speech, i.e., sounds, words, phrases, and sentences.

- Use negative practice to encourage carryover. Assign homework in which the client tracks his incorrect productions outside of therapy. Talk about these experiences.

Readers should be made aware that there has been one study that revealed undesirable feedback on the use of negative practice in regard to teen boys. Elliott (1960) noted that adolescent boys often associated practicing phonemes incorrectly with bad behavior, and he noted that this caused conflict and feelings of guilt within the boys. The boys and their mothers also felt that some of these purposeful errors made these adolescent males sound infantile and/or feminine. Elliott reported that the mothers relaxed when the purpose of negative practice was explained to them, and that the mothers' ease allowed the boys to feel comfortable about using the method.

Research on Types of Practice

Certain studies on various aspects of practice in speech therapy have been undertaken.

- Gordon (1960) showed that phoneme practice could be successful when done in the group setting using televised lessons.

- Carrier (1970) found that parents could administer a program of articulation practice to their own children effectively at home.

- Van Hattum et al. (1974) and Gray (1974) demonstrated that practice of words could be accomplished successfully with pre-programmed materials.

- Galloway and Blue (1975) and Costello and Schoen (1978) found that practice could be highly successful when employed by paraprofessionals.

- Gerber (1977) found that prepared practice materials are not very effective in teaching an initial target production but that they are effective after the client already has learned to produce his target using other means.

Functional Communication & Carryover

There seems to be a widespread misconception that Traditional Era therapists worked only on non-functional drill of phonemes, syllables, and words, and that they did not work on functional communication and conversational skills. For example, in an article about practice versus functional communication, one author, Kamhi, called prior decades "the days when speech-language therapy was routinely conducted in sterile, non-communicative contexts" (2000, p. 185). This is an erroneous belief that has been espoused time and again, but it simply is not true. Functional communication routines have been used in speech training since the time of the elocutionists. Van Riper himself wrote on the importance of functional communication in articulation therapy:

> *"Practice of words in word lists will produce little transfer to real speech situations unless those words are taken out of their series and made part of the actual communicative function"* (Van Riper, 1947, p. 207).

A review of the historic literature reveals that admonitions to work on conversational speech and functional communication are found all throughout historic books on articulation therapy, even in some of the oldest texts from the early 20th century, and especially in Van Riper's books. Working directly on functional communication is a procedure that therapists considered part of carryover. They taught their clients to use their new speech skills while making telephone calls and speeches, to order food in a restaurant, to ask questions during class, to speak to friends, and so forth. There is a difference in how functional communication routines were used then compared with now, however: Many therapists are taught to begin articulation training with functional communication routines whereas past therapists were taught to end with them.

Past therapists taught that new speech skills were to be carried into functional speaking arenas as soon as possible.

Dialect

European immigration was at its highest point in America during the elocutionary period and virtually all textbooks on elocution devoted considerable pages to the acquisition of an American English dialect. That perspective changed when the IPA was accepted in 1888 and the profession's focus turned to the production of individual phonemes. The speech textbooks of the Traditional Era, therefore, contained very few notes about dialect, and the few pieces of advice one finds scattered here and there are a re-hashing of the teaching methods of the elocutionists. These methods are described in Chapter 2.

Goals & Objectives

Therapists taught that long-term goals and short-term objectives were two different aspects of therapy that worked together to develop better speech. Corrected speech is the long-term goal. Short-term objectives are steps of therapy that carry the client toward the long-term goal.

For example, Van Riper taught clients to curl the tongue around a spoon in order to learn how to groove it for production of sibilants as a phonetic placement method, but he did not expect his client to walk around with a spoon in his mouth for the rest of his life. This is because placing the spoon in the mouth is not the goal; it is a short-term objective that contributes to the final goal of correct sibilant production. The spoon was faded as soon as the client was able to perform the movement without it.

Traditional Era therapists did many things that could seem unrelated to the final goal of corrected articulation, especially in their work with small children and those with cognitive deficit. They read books aloud to their clients, they taught them how to produce words that rhymed, they made funny faces together with them in front of a mirror, and they taught them to recite the alphabet. These are small steps included in treatment as short-term objectives.

Therapy was not always about repeating target phonemes and words. Traditional therapy also consisted of many diverse short-term objectives that carried the client toward his ultimate goal of improved expressive speech.

Scheduling Therapy

Traditional Era therapists generally provided articulation therapy once per week for 20–30 minutes in an individual or small group arrangement, and modifications to this basic process have been proposed ever since. Some therapists have suggested that block schedules are more effective with certain types of clients. Some have suggested that certain clients need therapy more often than once per week. One study even suggested that more frequent therapy is detrimental to clients because they do not have enough time between treatment sessions to assimilate their new skills (Weston & Harber, 1975). Today, therapists generally provide as much therapy as possible given the etiology of the disorder, the therapy environment, and the payment arrangements. This is highly variable from one setting to another. It is the present author's experience that, in the United States in most settings, the once-per-week format continues to be the norm for clients with mild problems, and twice or more per week tends to be the norm for clients with more severe problems.

SUMMARY

The methods of tradition articulation therapy are as important to speech correction today as they were in Van Riper's time and they are standard tools in the SLP's kit.

TABLE 2 — Stages of Traditional Articulation Therapy			
Level	Stage	Position	Phoneme /s/ Used in Examples
1	Isolation	Isolation	/s/ – "Sssssssss"
2	Syllables	Initial	CV – *Sah, See, Soo, So, etc.*
		Final	VC – *Ahs, Ees, Oos, Ohs, etc.*
		Medial	VCV – *Ah-sah, Ee-see, Oo-soo, etc.*
		Sequence	CVCV – *Sah-sah, See-see, So-so*
3	Words	Initial	CV – *See, Sue, So, Say, Sigh, etc.*
			CVC – *Seed, Soap, Soak, Soup, Sack, etc.*
			Complex – *Seven, Cereal, Sacramento, etc.*
		Final	VC – *Ace, Ass, Ice, Us, Ess, etc.*
			CVC – *Bus, Fuss, Kiss, Mass, Nice, Race, etc.*
			More Complex – *Curious, Playfulness, etc.*
		Medial	*Kissing, Fussing, Guessing, etc.*
4	Phrases	Initial	*See the car / Sue fell down / So what?*
		Final	*On the bus / Give a kiss / Very cold ice*
		Medial	*Hissing cat / Guessing game / A good kisser*
5	Sentences	Initial	One Phoneme – *Sue got up at eight.*
			Two Phonemes – *Sue got up at seven.*
			Three Phoneme – *Sue and Sam got up at seven.*
		Final	One Phoneme – *I got on the bus.*
			Two Phonemes – *Don't make a mess on the bus.*
			Three Phoneme – *This bus made a big mess.*
		Medial	One Phoneme – *I found a hissing cat.*
			Two Phonemes – *They were hissing and fussing.*
			Three Phonemes – *I am guessing that he could be messing up my fussy room.*

Table continues next page...

Level	Stage	Position	Phoneme /s/ Used in Examples
TABLE 2 — Stages of Traditional Articulation Therapy			
6	Paragraphs	Simple. Tightly controlled.	*Sue will come over tonight. I hope so, anyway. We are going to plan her party. Sue said I could help.*
		More difficult. More loosely controlled.	*Sue will come over at seven tonight. Yes! I hope so, anyway. We are going to plan a special party for Sam. Sam turns twelve on the seventeenth of December. Sam is so cool. He's Sue's best friend.*
		Very difficult. Completely un-controlled.	*My favorite dinosaur is the Stegosaurus. The stegosaurus walks on four legs, and has a horny collar. Sixteen stegosaurus skeletons were situated in the Soussan plain south of Soussy, France.*
7	Conversation	Structured. Within the therapy room.	Talk about the phoneme and its relevance to the child's life.
		Unstructured. Within the therapy room. Tightly controlled.	Talk about one word that has the target phoneme. For example, talk about soup. Focus on saying that word correctly throughout the conversation. Ignore all other words that contain /s/.
		Unstructured. Within the therapy room. Loosely controlled phonetic environment.	Talk about anything. Focus on saying every word with /s/ correctly throughout the conversation. This is the real bridge to conversation outside of the therapy room.
		Outside the therapy room. Somewhat structured.	Talk with others. Send the client on an errand, or assign conversations, outside of the therapy room. (Somewhat structured). The client's task is to monitor and control his /s/ as he speaks. The client will have to report back his results. (Unstructured)

2

Helping Clients Who Mumble & Slur

Lessons from the elocutionists

"Although speech departments grew out of elocutionary studies, elocution disappeared from the curriculum because of an association with excessive emphasis upon performance as performance... [But] the elocutionists encouraged and anticipated analysis now being vigorously pursued in a range extending from linguistics to nonverbal communication. Their contribution has for too long been ignored."

– G. P. Mohrmann, 1969

Speech-language pathologists serve many clients who can pass a standard test of articulation and phonology but who are very hard to understand in conversational speech. These clients mumble and slur. They trip over their words and omit everything from individual phonemes and syllables to whole words. They often talk too fast for their auditory self-monitoring and oral movement skills. Simply telling them to slow down helps for a few seconds only. These clients sometimes need help learning specific phonemes but usually they need more general instruction about how to achieve and maintain intelligibility.

Procedures for achieving broad-based intelligibility were developed by the elocutionists — the teachers of speech improvement whose work lead to the science of speech-language pathology. The elocutionists rarely are mentioned in current textbooks on articulation and phonology but their work is foundational to all aspects of expressive speech. The elocutionists were the ones who insisted that good speech was a mark of ones intelligence, educational accomplishments, and social standing (Sheridan, 1759). They were the ones who introduced the idea that anatomy and physiology must be an integral part of the speech remediation process (Thewall, 1810). They were the ones who developed the International Phonetic Alphabet (Passy, 1888), and they were the ones who documented exactly how intelligible speech is produced (e.g., Bell, 1887). This chapter describes the teachings of the elocutionists and makes applications to articulation and motor speech training.

The Elocution Era is identified as the fourth era of speech improvement as charted at the opening of Chapter 1 (page 14). For the purposes of this manual, the present author has identified the year 1669 as the beginning of the era for that was the year that the first known book on English phonetics was published (Holder, 1669). The standardization of the International Phonetic Alphabet in 1888 is considered as the end of the era, for it was then that attention was turned away from the general processes of intelligibility and pronunciation and toward the specific topic of phoneme production.

BACKGROUND

As far back as can be traced, the original concept of elocution was born in ancient Greece and Rome. The term itself is from the Latin *eloqui* meaning "to speak out." Good speech was considered a sign of one's intelligence and educational accomplishments among the educated class in those cultures and teachers of speech arose to help. Marcus Tullius Cicero was a Roman orator who was one of these teachers, and he is credited with defining the term (translated from Greek):

"Elocution is the proper and graceful management of the voice, the countenance, and gesture in speaking. These we shall be able to acquire by three ways: art, imitation, and

practice" (Sheridan, 1756, p. 49).

Cicero's definition *voice* refers to all aspects of expressive speech and language: voice, resonance, prosody, fluency, pronunciation, articulation, phonology, intelligibility, word selection, grammatical structure, and pragmatic communication. *Countenance* refers to facial expression. *Gesture* refers to the position and movements of the body and limbs. Countenance and gesture have been replaced by the term *body language* today. Cicero was saying that there are certain ways to communicate that are more effective than others, and that these skills of speech and gesture can be learned by studying the art of speaking itself, by imitating other good speakers, and by practicing.

Elocutionary practice flourished throughout the ancient world but it died off with the fall of ancient Rome and as Europe descended into the Dark Ages. It was revived again during the European Renaissance when scholarship and the arts began to flourish once more. The Renaissance re-kindled an interest in the art, architecture, and education of the ancient world, and the practice of elocution arose once again.

In the United States, it was the Revolutionary War and the US Constitution that served as the stimulus for elocutionary interests. The shedding of British aristocracy meant that social rank in the New World no longer was tied to family heritage, and people could elevate their own station in life through self-improvement. Most people wanted to develop their expressive speaking skills in order to advance their worthiness in the new intellectual and economic market places of the time and teachers of speech naturally arose again. For example, a man born a farmer could elevate himself to a teacher, preacher, or physician with a good education and good elocution. By the 19th century, elocution had risen again to a high art in both Europe and America, and it is from writers of that century that most of the material for this chapter is drawn.

Tenets

The 19th century elocutionists of Europe and America were concerned with expressive speech as a way of demonstrating one's intelligence, one's level of education, and one's importance in society. They felt that the educated person should acquire exemplary skill in speaking, reading, and writing, for these three were a reflection of a refined mind.

The elocutionists believed that well-educated young men (and women, eventually) should acquire good speech to stimulate fruitful public discourse, to develop excellent theater and vocal performances, and to give inspiring sermons. They believed that proper elocution would "make the family circle more agreeable, the social circle more desirable, the business person more successful, the teacher more instructive, and the professional man more impressive" (Hamill, 1886, p. 21).

They also believed that good speech was beneficial for gaining respect from others and that educated people should speak well so that they could be relied upon as teachers and leaders in their respective fields. They thought that correct diction impressed people more than wealth and that good speech was needed for effective government leaders. Many of the early elocutionists were Christian pastors who felt that good speech was a gift from God. They often wrote that speaking well honored God and was a way to demonstrate God's goodness toward others.

The elocutionists believed that there was a set of universal principles of speech that could be taught. They also made no bones about the destruction that poor speech could have on one's character. In fact they often stated this belief much more bluntly than one would dare today. Kofler (1887) may have made the most egregious of these statements when he described an adult who lisps:

> *"Poor creature that lisps! What frightful ungainliness he stamps upon his speech by substituting this blemished sound for S and kindred sibilants! … An intelligent person has no excuse for lacking sufficient energy and perseverance to overcome a defect that makes the speech of the wisest man appear childish and even idiotic"* (Kofler, 1887, p. 249–250).

RULES OF INTELLIGIBLE SPEECH

The elocutionists used terms like *good speech, just speech, just pronunciation, just articulation, good articulation,* and *correct articulation* to describe the aims of elocution. Their treatment protocols contained the absolute essentials of intelligible speech expressed in rules to follow. The careful reader will recognize many of their own clients' errors in the rules described below.

All the elements of expressive speech discussed by the elocutionists would make for an excellent course on speech improvement. In fact many of these topics are a continuing focus of acting and media courses offered within university departments of speech communication, and some of these ideas have resurfaced recently as new strategies for speech-language pathologists who are merging speech, conversation, and literacy in the classroom.

General Advice

The elocutionists advised their protégés to speak up, speak out, speak clearly, and resist the tendency to mumble. They told their clients to speak like they meant it, to be deliberate in their speech, and to speak with purpose and in purposeful ways. They were concerned with rate of speech and told their students to take their time, not to rush, and to take care not to speak faster than their oral control allowed.

The elocutionists taught that good speech is a sign of one's intelligence, educational accomplishments, and social standing, from elementary school through adulthood.

at the end of sentences. Rules included: do not be breathy, do not waste breath, do not produce harsh speech, do not use a glottal fry, and do not speak with too much tension. The elocutionists taught their students to engage in breathing, vocal, and whole body exercise in order to sustain the voice for the demands of speech and song. The elocutionists of yesteryear would be appalled to witness the amount of glottal fry and harshness of voice that is so popular among young speakers today.

The elocutionists warned against *elision*, which they defined as the omission of a sound, syllable, or word. They taught their clients not to mumble or slur by speaking all initial and final consonants, by including all consonants within clusters, and by including all syllables within words. Because the elocutionists dealt mostly with adults who could learn perfect speech, they also considered expressions like *I wanna* or *I gotta* to be forms of elision. They even wrote against using contractions such as *can't*, *don't*, or *won't*, although all these forms are accepted today.

Speech lessons taught by the elocutionists were energetic and deliberate, and their texts often contained information about both speaking and singing. The elocutionists taught their students how to attend to their own speech and how to study other good speakers in order to learn from them. They taught their students to watch their listeners for signs of interest or confusion and to adjust their speech accordingly.

Breath, Voice & Resonance

The elocutionists were very concerned with breath support, and they taught their students to be concerned about it first and foremost. Their lessons contained information about how to inhale an adequate amount of breath to support speech and how to use the respiratory organs without fatigue. Clients were taught to inhale and exhale in ways that supported good voice, prosody, resonance, and articulation. They also were taught to inhale between passages at appropriate syntactic markers. The elocutionists taught diaphragmatic control of the breath just as SLPs do. These methods are described in Chapter 7, *Encouraging Breath Support.*

The elocutionists advocated a strong and vigorous voice produced with correct oral and nasal resonance. They told their students to clear the nasal passageways (blow the nose) regularly for good speech, and they helped their students develop a pure vocal tone. They told them to focus the voice on the palate and not the throat. They taught students to exhale only as much air as necessary to produce clear speech and to not let the voice die out

Prosody

The elocutionists were concerned with all the supersegmentals. They instructed their students not to use a monotone but to use prosodic patterns that supported their messages. Clients were taught to be melodic and to use clear intonation patterns to their advantage when expressing attitude, emotion, interest, or passion. They also were taught to use pitch and intonation to express a wide variety of pragmatic functions such as asking, stating, requesting, refusing, denying, and so forth. The elocutionists would have spoken against the rising inflection or "up talk" that is popular now, explaining that it makes the speaker sound weak, as if he were questioning his own thoughts and opinions all the time. It was taught that loudness should be used when appropriate to deliver strong messages, and that softness, even a whisper, could be used to draw the listener into the message. Students were instructed to maintain clarity of phoneme, syllable, and word when getting louder or softer.

Elocutionists taught students to pronounce words with their proper accent and they were taught to be mindful of stress patterns in phrases and sentences and to never emphasize a word unless the utterance demanded it. They taught to place primary accent on only one syllable per word and only one word per sentence (secondary accent could be placed on a second word in a sentence). Students were taught never to place stress equally on each syllable within words, but to place it on the word that represents the main topic of thought. Words could be emphasized by speaking them a little louder or by drawing them out. The pause was of considerable interest to the elocutionists; pauses were lengthened or shortened to regulate rate and to draw attention to a word or a remark.

Phonemes & Phonology

The elocutionist's ideas about phonemes and phonological patterns are essential to clients who mumble and slur. They taught students to let their articulations be distinct and deliberate. They told their clients to pronounce all the phonemes of words, from initial to final sounds, and to produce all phonemes correctly. They taught students how to use an exact enunciation by exaggerating precise movements of the speech organs. Exaggeration was a prime method for achieving clarity of pronunciation.

Many authors of this period wrote very specific advice about consonants. Students were taught to make firm articulations in order to achieve consonants that were clean, clear, crisp, and correct. Students were also taught to make voiced and voiceless distinctions, and to produce all consonants within clusters. They were taught to keep the tongue inside the mouth except for /θ/ and /ð/. They were taught not to produce stops as trills or fricatives, and not to drop /h/ at the beginning of words — a determined rule found in most American books. Students were taught not to drag final consonants over to the next word when it began with a vowel. Interestingly, the American /r/ was taught as a trill in the 19th century.

Students were taught that the vowels should be *orotund*, meaning that they should be oral (and not nasal), made with a round oral cavity, and fully resonant. They were taught not to reduce vowels to a schwa even in unstressed syllables. Special emphasis was placed on the diphthongs, and students were taught to pronounce both the first and second vowel of diphthongs with distinction. The first vowel was to be full and the second was to be pronounced with diminishing force. They were taught not to use triphthongs because it was thought that triphthongs made a person sound too rural or pedestrian.

Oral Control

In terms of oral control, clients under an elocutionist's tutelage were taught to speak with the upper and lower teeth slightly apart, and they were told never to allow the jaw to slip left, right, forward, or too far down while speaking. They were told to speak phonemes as if they were smiling with the tongue on the inside of the mouth, and to speak with the lips slightly retracted but not quite in a grin. These are main aspects of *oral stability*, a topic that will be discussed in Chapter 14.

Students were taught that the lips do not have to move very much when speaking but that the tongue should move with vigor. They were taught not to pull the tongue back too far or to hump it up too high while speaking because it gave speech a guttural and hyponasal quality. They were taught to articulate the vowels and consonants as near the lips and as far away from the throat as possible. Authors of the late 19th century often encouraged the use of generic jaw, lip, tongue, and velar exercises or gymnastics to invigorate the articulators for phoneme production. Van Riper later taught that these calisthenics had no real value in speech correction.

RULES OF POSTURE

The elocutionists wrote about the intimate relationship between expressive speech and posture, which they called *position*, *attitude*, *bearing*, or *carriage*. They taught that posture

Melville Bell, Alexander Graham Bell's father.

should be the trainer's the first concern because it contributed to breath and voice. They taught that a speaker should not slouch forward and that the head should be erect. The head should not posture to one side or the other as if it were resting on the neck or shoulders, and it should not be held up by leaning on the hands with the elbow resting on the tabletop or podium. The elocutionists taught their lessons with students standing because their primary concerns were orating in public, acting, singing and preaching, but they also taught basic sitting positions. These rules of posture were named as important aspects of articulation therapy in Van Riper's time and they should continue to be a valuable part of articulation and motor speech training:

> *"Carry the chest easily active — avoid that extreme lifting of the chest which makes a child look pigeon breasted — and be careful that the abdomen is not thrown out in such a way that the back is curved"* (Parker, 1887, p. 3).

RULES OF GESTURE

The elocutionists taught basic rules of gesture or what is now called *body language*. They believed that body language was an integral part of intelligibility because it was a primary way in which one expressed one's feelings and passions. Many SLPs are concerned with body language when it has specific relevance for clients who lack it. The coordination of head, eye, body, arms, legs, and speech often are not expressed well in persons with certain disabilities, particularly those on the autism spectrum, and perhaps those with certain psychological disorders. Problems in these areas can cause difficulty in the communication of messages even when articulation is perfect, but therapists understand that expressive speech skills can develop adequately without good body language. In other words, a client who never looks at his communication partners can develop perfectly adequate articulation even though pragmatic communication is impaired.

Bell (1887) contains perhaps the most exhaustive descriptions of body language among the elocutionists, and his rules are listed below. He taught that mature speakers look first, then gesture, and then speak. Any good actor or public speaker follows this basic rule but there are exceptions, of course. Bell pointed out that strong emotion could be expressed by producing a word before a gesture. He also said words and gestures that do not coincide can be used in comedy.

Body Position

- The body is held easily erect to express courage, steadiness, and resolution.

- The body is held stiffly erect to denote pride, haughtiness, or the assumption of dignity.

- The body is thrown back to indicate defiance and pride.

- The body stoops forward to indicate condescension, compassion, or humility.

- The body bends forward to express respect, reverence, or salutation.

- The body is prostrated to denote moral degradation, utmost humility, or self-loathing.

Head Orientation

- The head is erect in courage, confidence, and pride.

- The head is crouched in fear.

- The head is thrown back in pride and self-conceit.

- The head hangs forward in humility, shame, or grief.

- The head is protruded in curiosity and in shortsightedness.

- The head lies to one side in bashfulness, laziness, and lethargy.

- The head rolls or tosses in anger.

- The head is averted in dislike or horror.

- The head shakes in denial or sadness.

- The head is jerked back in invitation.

- The head is forward, or nods, in assent.

- The head tosses back in dissent.

- The head sits to one side in boasting, threatening, or pigheadedness.

- The head inclines to imply bashfulness or languor.

- The head leans forward in attention.

Eyes

- The eyes beam in love.

- The eyes sparkle in mirth.

- The eyes flash and roll, and are downcast and averted in anger.

- The eyes melt in grief.

- The eyes rise in hope and in prayer.

- The eyes deject in despondency.

- The eyes measure an object from head to foot in contempt.

- The eyes stare in wonder.

- The eyes weep in sorrow.

- The eyes burn in anger.

- The eyes wink in cunning.

- The eyes are level in modesty.

- The eyes cast downward in shame.

- The eyes are restless in terror and anxiety.

- The eyes are fixed in confidence, boldness, and energy.

- The eyes look askance in suspicion and secrecy.

- The eyes are cast on vacancy in thought.

- The eyes are thrown in different directions in doubt and anxiety.

- The eyes shift left to right in dishonesty.

Mouth

- The mouth is open in fear, wonder, listening, languor, and desire.

- The mouth is shut in apathy, pride, boldness, and sullenness.

- The jaw drops in melancholy (sadness and depression).

- The teeth gnash in anger.

- The tongue is protruded with lower intelligence.

Thoughts and feelings are expressed with the face and hands.

Lips

- The lips are drawn back and raised in delight and mirth.

- The lips are depressed and projected in pain, sadness, and grief.

- The lips curl up at the corners in contempt.

- The lips curl downward at the corners in disgust.

- The lips are loose and sprawling in mental vacuity, blankness, or emptiness.

- The lips are muscular and mobile in intellectuality.

- The lips are firm in decision and energy.

- The lips are relaxed in weakness and irresolution.

- The lips are pouted in boasting and pettiness.

- The lips are bitten in vexation and discomfiture.

- The lips are compressed in agony.

Nostrils

- The nostrils are relaxed in calmness and composure.

- The nostrils are expanded and rigid in violent passion.

- The nostrils quiver in excitement.

- The nostrils twitch up in disgust and contempt.

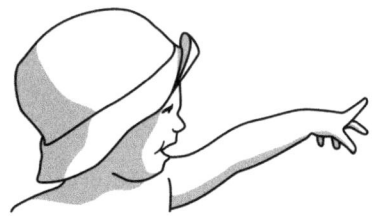

Intelligibility improves when words and gestures correspond.

Facial expressions can stimulate vocal and verbal expression.

Eyebrows

- The eyebrows are lifted in surprise, in inquiry, and in hope.

- The eyebrows are depressed in conviction, in authority, and in despair.

- The eyebrows are knitted in sorrow, in solicitude, and in anger.

- The eyebrows droop in weakness.

Arms

- The arms hang easily from the shoulders in grace.

- The arms droop listlessly in weakness and humility.

- The arms are rigid in anger.

- The arms are folded across the chest or placed in akimbo (hands on hips with elbows bent) in self-complacence.

- The arms are held forward in imploring help (entreating, requesting).

- The arms are spread or extended in welcome and in admiration.

- The arms are raised in appeal or expectancy.

- The arms fall suddenly in disappointment.

- The arms are drawn back in aversion.

- The arms shrink and bend in terror.

- The arms project forward in authority.

Hands

- The hands are open and relaxed in graceful calmness.

- The hands are locked or clasped in emotion.

- The hands are wrung in anguish.

- The hands are clenched in anger.

- The hands are raised in supplication.

- The hands descend slowly in blessing.

- The hands clasp or wring in affliction.

- The hands are held forward and are received in friendship.

- The hands fall with quiet vehemence, cursing, slander, or evil talk. The hands also fall during a threat.

- The hands are moved toward the body in invitation and in egotism.

- The hands are pushed from the body in rejection or dismissal.

- The hands start in astonishment.

- The hands wave or clap in joy. The hands also

wave in contempt.

- The hands clasp in prayer.

- The hands placed on the lips induce silence.

- The hands placed on the breast appeals to conscience or intimates desire.

- The palms are turned upwards in frankness, openness, truthfulness, and sincerity.

- The palms are cast downwards in concealment or cunning.

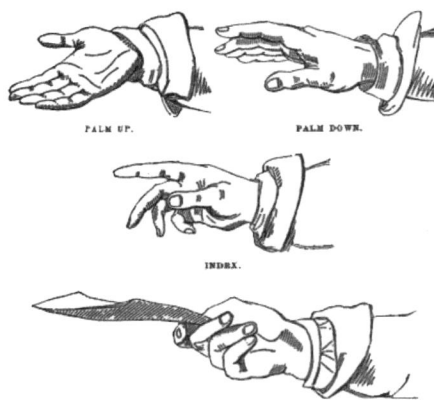

Arm, hand, leg, foot, and finger gestures from 1865 (Griffith). The man in the top middle is standing in the dancer pose known as "third position."

The right seating arrangement is important for good speech development.

- The hands are turned outwards in defense, apprehension, or aversion.

- The hands are turned inwards in boldness or confidence.

- The hand on the forehead indicates pain, confusion, or mental distress.

- The hand on the crown of the head signal giddiness or delirium.

- The hands on the side of the head indicate stupor, daze, or dream.

- The hands on the eyes signal shame or grief.

- Both hands used simultaneously intensify the expression.

- The hand supporting the cheek expresses languor or weariness.

- The hands supporting the chin indicate meditation.

- The hands laid on the breast express meekness or resignation.

- The hands pressed on the upper part of the chest, or beating it, express remorse, or acute bodily distress.

- The hands on the lower part of the chest indicate boldness or pride.

- The back of one hand laid in the palm of the other shows determination, stubbornness, and inflexibility.

- The hands applied palm-to-palm express supplication.

- The hands crossed palm-to-palm express resignation.

Fingers

- The fingers are relaxed and slightly separated in placidity.

- The fingers are rigid and separated in fear.

- The fingers are firm and bent in anger.

- The forefinger directs attention to any object by pointing.

- The pointed forefinger falls to reprove or warn.

- The pointed forefinger enumerates by successively touching the fingertips of the other hand.

- The fingers laid in the palm of the other hand specify unbending assertiveness.

- The fingers of both hands applied loosely tip-to-tip express accumulation of thought.

Legs & Feet

- In standing, the feet should be placed in *third position* just as dancers still do. The feet never should be crossed in standing. *Third position* is such: The feet should be separated by the distance of about a foot, with the forward heel pointing toward the back foot's heal and the back foot pointing slightly to the side. This indicates graceful ease.

- The feet should maintain this position gracefully as the upper body, head, and arms move in communicative gestures.

- The weight of the body supported on the retired foot indicates dignity, dislike, carelessness, disgust, horror, or defense.

- The weight of the body supported on the advanced foot indicates familiarity, attention, sympathy, listening, appeal, or attack.

- The weight of the body should generally be sustained on one foot, and it should be shifted from foot to foot over time in discourse.

- The legs held straight and rigid, in a firm position, indicate self-conceit, stubbornness, or obstinacy.

- The legs relaxed and bent show timidity, awkwardness, or fragility.

- One leg slightly bent and the other straight indicate graceful ease.

- The legs shake to express terror.

- The legs are knelt in prayer. Bent knees also indicate timidity or weakness.

- Frequent changes of foot position indicate mental agitation.

- Quick foot movements denote apprehension or violent disturbance.

- Stamping the feet indicates harsh authority, impatience, determination, or anger.

- Advancing steps denote energy, boldness, desire, and courage.

- Retiring steps denote aversion, alarm, or fear.

- Light tiptoe steps express caution or secretive intrusion.

- Heavy steps denote boasting or bravado.

- The feet turned directly forward indicate bad manners and vulgarity.

- The feet turned inward suggest deformity.

- The feet close together denote timidity or awkwardness.

- Starting movements of the legs or feet denote terror.

- In sitting, the feet should not draw back under the chair, and the soles of the feet should remain on the floor. The feet should be positioned forward from the knees.

APPLICATION TO SPEECH THERAPY

Everything that the elocutionists taught has application to speech-language therapy in one type of client or another. An elocutionary focus should dominate the work with patients who rush, slur, mumble, and lose intelligibility in conversational speech no matter the etiology. The basic message of the elocutionist is that intelligibility can be boosted significantly when due attention is paid to general enunciation, pronunciation, and prosodic factors. The elocutionists' ideas about speaking up, speaking out, making every syllable count, using stress and intonation appropriately, and speaking crisp consonants and orotund vowels are essential to clients who mumble and slur.

Rules about standing and sitting posture have perhaps more application to today's therapy than they did to the elocutionists because SLPs now treat clients with neuromuscular disorders who need assistance to achieve the best possible upper and lower body control for respiration, phonation, resonation, and articulation. SLPs also treat clients who slouch or have other bad habits of posture. The elocutionists would have taught SLPs to attend to the client's posture before working on speech so that the client has the best possible support for his speaking mechanisms. Posture for speech is an area of shared concern for speech-language pathologists, occupational therapists, and physical therapists.

The elocutionists' messages about the importance of facial expression should be a concern for clients who lack it. All manner of clients can have limited facial expression, including those with neuromuscular deficit, paralysis, depressed levels of cognition, autism, hearing impairment, blindness, depression, and other psychological disorders. Lack of facial expression and incoordination between words and facial expression can make a client's verbal expressions confusing to the listener.

Clients with motor speech disorders often demonstrate poor arm and hand movements in addition to their problems in oral control. Research indicates that hand and mouth movements develop together, and therapists often use one to teach the other. For example, it can be helpful to teach the hands to fist tightly while teaching the jaw to clench firmly. Hand gestures, natural gestures, and sign language that coordinate with expressive speech can facilitate the transmission of ideas. Gestures and facial expressions can facilitate communication when words fail. Clients who use a wide array of appropriate facial expression are more interesting to listeners. Teaching facial expression is also something SLPs do with very young children in order to stimulate more vocal and verbal output. Some clients say more when involved in movement activities.

The elocutionists' attention to the legs and feet can seem extremely out of step with speech-language therapy but the lower limbs express ideas just as arms and hands do. Many classroom teachers and therapists teach body gestures in song and story to young children as a means of simple expression, and the elocutionists' list of leg and foot positions could form the backbone of such activities. Leg and foot position are also important aspects of trunk stability. Clients with neuromuscular deficit and related motor speech disorders often lack breath support, vocal control, and sufficient oral movement because of a lack of proper lower body support. A due attention to the position of the legs and feet is appropriate in these cases, and consultation with team motor specialists should be sought about the specifics of such actions in particular clients.

Finally, the elocutionists' advice about setting head orientation, facial expression, gestures, and words in order has wide application to many different clients. For example, some children mumble a word for a desired object without appropriate gesture or head orientation and the result is failed communication. Communication of words is facilitated when clients look and gesture toward the objects to which they refer, and young children tend to talk about objects they have in their hands. The present author has found that many young children talk much more when they are allowed a toy in hand, when they are allowed to look at that toy when they are manipulating and talking about it and when they are *not* forced to look at the communication partner. Therapy might help these children develop this skill as a means of boosting the intelligibility of their messages. In other words, SLPs can work toward organizing a client's entire body to support his spoken words. This teaches habits that will remain for the rest of life as vocabulary, grammar, phonology, and communication functions are built. This training can begin in infant and preschool programs as a way to support lifelong intelligibility.

SUMMARY

The work of the elocutionists can be ignored no longer. Their rules of speech production are important elements of therapy with clients who mumble and slur, and their messages about general communication and body language are important for clients with impaired social communication skills.

3

Making Speech Units Salient

Modeling speech in effective ways for client perception and imitation

"Distinctness of articulation… is an invaluable accomplishment. It enables the speaker to express his thoughts without weariness, and the audience to hear without effort."

– S. S. Hamill, 1886

A key job of the speech-language pathologist in articulation and motor speech therapy is to use his or her own speech and voice in ways that make the movements and auditory signals of speech targets *salient* — to make them important, outstanding, prominent, leading, and/or significant. Therapists use their own utterances to highlight speech in specific ways so that clients can pay better attention to the things they are trying to learn. For example, a therapist might pronounce a phoneme louder or longer to make it stand out from the rest of a target word.

This chapter gathers together a wide range of methods designed to accomplish saliency. No one writer seems to have pulled these fundamental treatment ideas together into a comprehensive list, and perhaps that is because there might be an unlimited number of ways to go about

A wide variety of methods are employed to make speech targets salient.

this. This chapter describes methods the present author has gathered and used throughout her career. Most of these ideas are common teaching tools that therapists and teachers use every day without even thinking about it. Therapists seem to adopt favorites among these methods and use them so frequently that they become part of their own unique therapeutic or teaching style.

These methods are the bread and butter of speech training but only a select few have been studied in any kind of formal way in the speech lab. The reader should view this chapter as good advice passed on from one generation to the next.

METHODS

Methods to make phonemes and words salient are offered here in alphabetical order with no hierarchy implied. Each method is defined and described with examples. These methods can be used alone or in combinations. They can be used to highlight a correct production or an incorrect one, depending upon one's purpose. References, quoted sources, and supportive research are included where applicable.

Alliteration

Alliteration is the "repetition of the same consonant, especially an initial one, in several words within the same sentence or phrase" (Nicolosi, Harryman, & Kresheck, 1983, p. 5). Speech-language pathologists regularly use alliteration to help clients notice target phonemes and this method has been around for as long as children have been educated. For example, consider this admonition to use alliteration to practice target phonemes written in the 18th century: "These faults may be corrected by reading sentences… contrived [so as to] often… repeat the faulty sounds" (Enfield, 1780, p. vii). Articulation therapy textbooks and speech workbooks contain sentences and short paragraphs loaded with target phonemes for alliterative stimulation. Alliteration is adjusted for age and cognitive level.

Young Children

A young client might be stimulated to attend to a phoneme when the therapist, teacher, or parent alliterates the phoneme during play. For example, to highlight phoneme /b/, an adult might roll a ball back and forth with the child and, as the ball rolls away, say, "Bye-bye ball. Bye-bye ball." This alliteration of /b/ makes the phoneme stand out. Many children's songs, stories, and nursery rhymes are an excellent source of this type of alliterative material for young children. For example, consider how many times initial /r/ occurs in the children's song, *The Wheels on the Bus.*

Older Children and Adults

A tongue twister can be considered a more advanced form of alliteration that can be employed with older children and adults. For example, to highlight the differences between fricatives /s/ and /ʃ/, a therapist might utilize the classic: "She sells seashells by the seashore. Does she sell seashells by the seashore? If she sells seashells by the seashore, then how many seashells does she sell?" Tongue twisters are a practical and fun way to employ this method with clients who have the language skill and cognitive ability to appreciate them.

Amplification

To *amplify* speech is to make it louder. Amplification is one of the most direct ways to make a speech target salient, and it is mentioned often in articulation texts. Hodson and Paden recommended a low level of amplification during the auditory bombardment activities of their program of phonological training: "A low level of amplification delivered through earphones is used to increase the child's focus" (Hodson & Paden, 1983, p. 66).

The elocutionists simply spoke louder or used ear trumpets to amplify speech. Van Riper and Irwin (1958) reported that therapists of the mid-20th century were using reel-to-reel tape recorders and borrowed hearing aids. Now, therapists can use any number of digital audio or video systems. Speech should not be amplified all the as one might use for a client with a hearing impairment; speech is amplified for short periods of time or during the modeling of specific phonemes, syllables, or words.

Everything from ear trumpets to digital recording equipment has been used to amplify speech.

Aspiration

Adding a strong element of exhaled air, or *aspiration*, is an effective method of calling attention to a phoneme, especially the voiceless stops /p/, /t/ and /k/ in the word-final position. Excessive aspiration is marked as /ᶜ/. As such, SLPs might model *up* as /upᶜ/, *cat* as /kætᶜ/, and *book* as /bukᶜ/. Aspiration draws the client's auditory attention to these final voiceless sounds. The client may produce too much aspiration on a target sound as a result of this type of model, but that can always be toned down after the phoneme has been acquired; aspiration provides an easy first step.

Auditory Bombardment

Auditory bombardment, as recommended by Hodson and Paden (1983), is the process of carefully reading a list of words that contain the target in the position being stimulated. For example, if the target is /ʃ/, and the position is pre-vocalic, the client might have the following words read to him: *shoe, shop, shake, shower, shampoo, shine, shark, sharp, shove, shut, shave, sheep,* and *show.* The client's job is simply to listen to the words as he plays quietly. Auditory bombardment satisfies Van Riper's call to make the target sound "ring in the client's ear," a concept further discussed in Chapter 4.

Baby Talk

The use of *baby talk* has always caused controversy in circles of speech teachers and child development professionals. Traditional Era therapists almost always considered baby talk to be deviant. Mid-20th century writers called it *pediolalia* defined as "a syndrome composed of elisions, sound substitutions, and the omission of articles, prepositions, conjunctions, and many pronouns" (Fröeschels,

1948, p. 121). Baby talk is essentially the production of real words that are spoken with prolongation of sound (cooing), developmental consonant substitutions, and infantile pitch and intonation patterns. Baby talk can be used as a method of speech training because it calls attention to speech, and it is a way that children can have fun with speech.

The present author has used baby talk with scores of clients over 39 years and none of them was harmed by it. Most little children love to hear adults use baby talk: "Ooooo, dat puppy-doggie is soooo cuuuute! And woooook at dat titty-taaaaat. Meeeeoooo. I wuv dat titty-taaaat." Speaking this way makes speech cute and inviting to little kids. SLPs should not be afraid of using it, but should use it only with the right client at the right time. One must avoid using baby talk with older children and teens, certainly, but there is no substitute for cooing and baby talk when attempting to draw a toddler's or preschooler's attention to a speech unit. Use it where appropriate. Cooing like this is especially useful to emphasize vowels.

Ceasing Production

A simple way to help clients attend to a target phoneme is to produce it many times in sequence and then suddenly produce a different sound. The client is asked to indicate when he hears the change. This method can be used in one-on-one therapy sessions but it is also an excellent tool to use in group therapy or during classroom stimulation.

Individual Therapy

This method can be adapted to almost any activity in individual therapy. For example, consider having the client throw beanbags into a box as he listens to the therapist's productions. The client must listen to the series of target sounds. When he hears the therapist produce a different sound, he quickly tosses the beanbag into the box before he or she says the next sound. Little kids love this type of simple procedure. Take turns back and forth to make it both a listening and a production activity.

Group Games

Berry and Eisenson described the process of ceasing production of a target in a delightful game they called *Sound Chairs* that is played like *Musical Chairs:* "The children walk around the chairs as long as they hear a certain sound. When the teacher stops making the sound, the children scramble to sit down in the nearest chair. The child left without a chair is left out of the game" (Berry & Eisenson, 1956, p. 137). Continue play until there is a winner.

Chaining

Chaining targets makes the individual pieces of target words salient. Chaining is the process of "teaching an entire behavior by conditioning and reinforcing each step separately, and then bringing the steps together" (Nicolosi,

Harryman, & Kresheck, 1983, p. 48). Therapists make individual units of speech salient by saying one alone, then two in sequence, then three in sequence, and so forth. Chaining can be done forward or backward using phonemes, syllables, words, phrases, or sentences: "One behavior leads to another in a chain leading to a complex behavior" (Creaghead, Newman, & Secord, 1989, p. 188). See Table 3 on the next page for examples.

Classifying

SLPs make phonemes salient by helping clients learn to classify them by place, manner, voice, or specific distinctive feature. This exercise makes clients listen carefully and think about their productions. It stimulates cognitive functioning. Classifying is a method that has been in play for many decades, for example:

> *"[Work on] reclassification of words according to whether they begin with a vowel or a consonant [and] according to whether they begin with a voiced or voiceless consonant"* (Nemoy & Davis, 1937, p. 26).

Creative Imagery

Speech-language pathologists use creative imagery to tap the imagination and make phonemes stand out. Clients are told that a target phoneme sounds like a flat tire, a bumblebee, a hissing snake, popping popcorn, and so forth. Creative imagery helps clients attune their auditory attention to the sound quality of targets. Environmental sounds make phonemes salient because these are the types of things children understand. These ideas are discussed more thoroughly as *conceptual cues* in Chapter 5, *Teaching Speech Movements with Cues.*

Simple games can be played to make speech targets stand out.

TABLE 3 — Target Chaining Samples

Chaining phonemes in words

The phonemes of words can be chained to make them salient. For example, help a client hear the individual phonemes of the word *stop* in the following way:

- *Forward:* Model "S-," then "St-," then "Sto-," and finally, "Stop."
- *Backward:* Model "-p," then "-op," then "-top," and finally "Stop."

Chaining syllables in words

The syllables of words can be chained to make them salient. For example, help the client hear the individual syllables of the word *banana*:

- *Forward:* Model "Ba-," then "Bana-," then "Banana."
- *Backward:* Model "-na," then "-nana," then "Banana."

Chaining words in phrases

The words of phrases can be chained to make them salient. For example, help the client hear the individual words of the phrase *on the table*:

- *Forward:* Model "on-," then "on the-," and then "on the table."
- *Backward:* Model "-table," then "-the table," then "on the table."

Chaining phrases in sentences

The phrases in sentences can be chained to make them salient. For example, help the client hear the individual phrases in the sentence *That boy climbed up on the couch*:

- *Forward:* Model "That boy-," then "That boy-climbed up," and finally, "That boy-climbed up-on the couch."
- *Backward:* Model "-on the couch," then "-climbed up-on the couch," and finally, "That boy-climbed up-on the couch."

Cycles

Hodson and Paden (1983) proposed a cyclical approach in which each target phoneme and phonological process is spotlighted for one week. A new pattern is taught each week regardless of whether or not the client acquires the pattern within the particular week it is trained. There is no pre-determined level of mastery and several sounds can be targeted within one cycle. The goal is to stimulate for emergence of the target. This approach was designed for highly unintelligible children with phonological delay.

Direct Instruction

Speech-language pathologists use adjectives and adverbs to teach clients what an auditory signal should sound like. Therapists say, "That's a tiny sound" or "That's a big round sound." Therapists use vocabulary that fits the client's cognitive and developmental level, for example, SLPs tell an adult to "project your voice into the room" and tell a young child to "make a big sound." Therapists are flexible in regard to this vocabulary because one never knows what word or concept will trigger improvement.

Dramatic Flair

Dramatic flair is a very common way to make clients pay attention to speech models. Therapists produce targets with a little something extra to draw attention. They create an emotional scene to underlie the work. This is not what everyday therapy usually looks like, but dramatic flair can be used at the right moment to help treatment move forward. See examples of dramatic flair in Table 4 on the next page.

TABLE 4 — Examples of Dramatic Flair	
Sinister	Act sneaky while producing the snake sound "Sss!"
Astonishment	Act astonished while producing a final /p/, as if it was unexpected.
Sadness	Pretend to cry while producing a target sound or word incorrectly.
Happiness	Giggle while producing a funny intonation pattern.
Embarrassment	Act embarrassed while producing a pre-speech vocalization that acoustically resembles another bodily function.
Relief	Express relief while producing a phoneme correctly for the first time.
Choke	Pretend to choke while producing [+Back] sounds.
Pout	Pout while pretending to be unable to produce a certain phoneme.
General Drama	Act like producing a target phoneme causes coughing, laughing, sneezing, dropping the head, or falling asleep.

Echoing

Speech-language pathologists imitate a client's incorrect production in order to make his error stand out. Imitation of the client can facilitate development of all aspects of auditory processing and it can be quite fun for the client. The technique was called *echoing* in some literature and several types were discussed: *echo, delayed echo, echo correction, echo expansion,* and *echo expatiation.* The original author of these ideas was sought but not found during the background reading done for this manual. The following information is from an un-referenced classroom handout from the 1970s.

Echo

To *echo* is to produce the immediate and exact imitation of a client's utterance, whether correct or not. An exact echo works as a mirror to reflect back to the client that which he just said. For example, the client names *soup* as "thoup," and the therapist echoes back this incorrect production. This is an excellent way to help a client realize his error. It is intended to inform the client but not to shame him. Be careful about using this method in a group.

Delayed Echo

To provide a *delayed echo* is to present an exact imitation of a client's utterance after a momentary pause. The process creates anticipatory listening as the client awaits his mirrored sound. Van Riper and Irwin recommended the use of a tape recorder as a method of delayed echoing: "The

delay helps the [client] to be objective" (Van Riper & Irwin, 1958, p. 126). They recommended that the method be discontinued if listening to his voice causes distress in the client. SLPs can now use digital audio or video recording on a variety of devices and systems.

Echo Correction

To provide an utterance using *echo correction* means to imitate a client's utterance with correction of pronunciation. For example, when saying the word *soup*, the client says "thoup" and the therapist echoes back "soup." This method puts the child's attention on the differences between one utterance and another.

This therapist is using dramatic flair to emphasize target speech units.

Echo Expansion

To provide an utterance using *echo expansion* means to imitate a client's utterance and to add missing elements. For example, the client pronounces *elephant* as /ɛfɪn/ and the therapist echoes the word back the correct way. This is a way to help clients listen to correct models and to compare their own with the therapists. It may be the method that therapists use more often than any other.

Echo Expatiation

To provide an utterance using *echo expatiation* means to imitate a client's utterance with more detail. For example, the client says "thoup" and the therapist says, "I want soup, too. My mom makes chicken noodle soup." This method has been used to encourage more careful listening, to build vocabulary, and to develop more advanced concepts.

Emphasis

Emphasize a target by saying it a little louder and with more stress. Any speech target can become salient with emphasis. Emphasis is marked with capital letters in the chart below.

The Placement of Emphasis	
Phoneme	I live in ColoRado.
Syllable	I live in ColoRAdo.
Word	I live in COLORADO.
Phrase	I live IN COLORADO.
Sentence	Didn't you hear me? I LIVE IN COLORADO!

Exaggeration

Exaggeration is a simple way to make speech targets salient. Exaggeration makes the target more of what it already is. Any aspect of expressive speech can be exaggerated including intonation patterns, rate, rhythm, length of sound, transitional sounds, lip or tongue movements, distinctive features, and so forth. Exaggeration is especially helpful when teaching the vowels. For example, smile quite broadly for /i/, pucker very firmly for /u/, and open the mouth as wide as possible for /ɑ/.

Literacy

All the articulation literature recommends the use of jingles, poems, songs, stories, and plays to make phonemes salient, especially when working with young children and those with cognitive delay. This is called the *literacy model* and is thought of as a new idea but it isn't; many of the older articulation texts had songs, poems, and stories published in them. There is even one articulation therapy book that is an entire program of songs: *Sing Your Way to Better Speech* (Walsh, 1939).

Jingles, poems, songs, stories, and plays are broad expressions of speech and language that capture a client's attention and encourage his participation. Repetition or alliteration of the target is the key to the success when using them. Songs are an especially good way to encourage auditory processing and memory. Songs can be published ones, modifications of published ones, or new creations made up ahead of time or right on the spot. As an example of a published song, note the way syllables are repeated in the following lyrics from the song, "Do You Like Pie?" (Marshalla, 2008a):

"Do You Like Pie?"

Do-do-do-do-do-do-do-
Do you like pie?
Yea-yea-yea-yea-yea-yea-yea-
I like pie.
Wuh-wuh-wuh-wuh-wuh-wuh-wuh-
What kind of pie?
Lah-lah-lah-lah-lah-lah-lah-
Lots of different pies.

I like boo-boo-boo-boo-boo-boo-boo-
I like blueberry pie.
Puh-puh-puh-puh-puh-puh-puh-
I like pumpkin pie.
Oh! Ap-ap-ap-ap-ap-ap-ap-
I like apple pie.
I-yai-yai-yai-yai-yai-yai-
I like ice cream pie. Yea!

Homophones

A homophone is "each of two or more words having the same pronunciation but different meanings, origins, or spellings" (Jewell & Abate, 2001, p. 815). Examples include *which/witch*, *some/sum*, and *there/their/they're*. Children enjoy working with homophones once they understand them. The simple fact that the words sound the same even though they are spelled differently and mean different things causes children to listen and think hard. This is a simple way to make target sounds, syllables, or words salient with older children. Homophones have been used for many years in articulation therapy. For example, Nemoy and Davis (1937) recommended working on homophones in questions such as "Which is the witch?" (p. 26).

Intonation

To *intone* means to chant or drone an utterance. Intoning makes a target stand out. The formal intonation process known as *Melodic Intonation Therapy* (MIT) was developed as a method to stimulate expressive language in adults with acquired aphasia (Sparks & Holland, 1976). MIT is the process of using regularized intonation patterns to model speech units. The original MIT researchers were looking for ways to connect melody and language with the view that different parts of the brain control these two functions and the perspective that melodic input (right brain, so-called) could be used to help facilitate language output (left brain, so-called). Many SLPs have adopted MIT for the training of children. For example, it was recommended for children with apraxia of speech by Hall, Jordan, and Robin (1993).

Any melody can be used in this approach. The present author likes to use the high-low melodic pattern that most children adopt when they enter the phase where they tease one another:

"Nah- -nah- !"
　　nah　 nah

This high-low pattern seems to be a universal way used by children to organize language at that cognitive level. Some musicians call it the *na-na sound* and say that this is the first tonal pattern that children recognize (Reference: personal discussions with musicians and music teachers).

This high-low pattern is especially useful to highlight the individual auditory signals of syllables. For example, in the two-syllable word *peanut*, the first syllable *pea* is produced with a high note, and the second syllable *nut* is produced with a low note. This doesn't sound like singing, nor does it sound like the intonation used in speech everyday. It sounds like a regularized, somewhat robotic intonation pattern. The syllables are prolonged slightly, and the intonation is of a single note per syllable. Remember, melodic

Singing songs is a way to highlight specific aspects of speech.

intonation is used here simply to help the client hear phonemes and syllables, not intonation patterns. The client himself need not produce his utterances with the intonation pattern, although many will. The reader is reminded that this method, like so many others, will not result in a final speech product, but it is a way to help the client make a start.

Isolation

Modeling phonemes in isolation as a means of making a phoneme salient is a method that is as old as articulation therapy itself. SLPs should only model in isolation those phonemes that can be produced in isolation — the vowels, nasals, and fricatives. All other consonants are modeled in single CV or VC syllables. Train clients to hear isolated phonemes and syllables, and also train them to hear isolated words, phrases, and prosodic patterns. Select the target, train the client to hear it in isolation, then train him to hear it amid other more complex speech stimuli.

Key Words / Core Vocabulary

The key word method is used to focus the client on the correct production of a phoneme in a specific word within functional communicative contexts. For example, if a client is working on /s/, the word *please* might be chosen. Adults should encourage the client to say the key word several times throughout the day when it can be worked into natural dialogue routines:

> *"Key words are your best friend… If you can find one word the child consistently produces correctly for each sound, associate each treatment word with the key word for the sound"* (Hanson, 1983, p. 199).

A modification of this concept is the use of *core vocabulary training* for clients with phonological delay and inconsistent speech disorder. Larger sets of revolving key words are chosen to represent target phonemes and phonological patterns (Dodd et al., 2006; Crosbie, Holm, & Dodd, 2005).

> *"The Core Vocabulary Therapy procedure begins with the child, parents and teacher selecting, with the therapist's help if required, 50 words that are functionally 'powerful' for the child, and 'mean something' to him or her… Ten words are selected from the list and best production is drilled in twice-weekly sessions. At the end of the week the child produces the 10 words three times. Words produced consistently are removed from the list of 50 words. Words that are inconsistently produced remain on the list from which the next week's 10 words are randomly chosen"* (Bowen, 2011).

Modeling

Modeling a target is the most important way to make a phoneme salient. Speech-language pathologists model each and every speech unit they intend to teach. The model itself makes the sound stand out. Models are modified in various ways, according to the techniques outlined in this chapter. Therapists, teachers, parents, caregivers, paraprofessionals, siblings, or peers can provide models.

Omit Targets

A phoneme can be omitted to call attention to it. For example, to draw attention to the /r/ of the word *car*, the word is modeled without the final /r/. The client's ear is drawn to the missing phoneme, causing him to listen hard for it in other productions. This is the skill of *auditory closure* at work. (See Chapter 4 for more information on auditory skills.)

Paired Stimuli

Paired stimuli can be used to highlight phonemes (Weston, 1969). Using this method, one word the client produces with a correct phoneme is paired with another word the client produces with an incorrect phoneme. For example, if the client is working on /s/, the two words might be *sand* (a word he says with a correct /s/), and *bus* (a word the client says with an incorrect /s/). The idea is to use the correct production to teach the incorrect one. This is a basic procedure that most SLPs use regularly.

Pantomime

To *pantomime* or *mouth* a target means to produce it without breath or voice in order to draw a client's auditory and visual attention to it. Mouthing as a phoneme stimulation technique is found in articulation therapy textbooks going back to the early part of the 20th century. For example, in Blanton and Blanton (1919), each classroom activity outlined for each phoneme begins with a rhyme that highlights target words. The teacher then says the words without voice for the children to watch and guess what she is saying: "The sentinel words or phrases should then be given voicelessly" (p. 209). Going through the motions without breath or voice captures a client's visual and auditory attention. He watches and listens harder because the acoustic signal is absent.

Pause Before a Target

The simple pause is a powerful tool in articulation therapy. Pause before a target to build anticipation for it. For example, one can help a client focus on listening to /ʃ/ in the word *cash* by pausing before the /ʃ/. Longer pauses stimulate more concentrated anticipation up to a certain point, but then clients lose interest, so modify the length of the pause accordingly. Van Riper and Irwin (1958) called this *anticipatory listening*, a topic discussed further in Chapter 4.

Pause After a Target

Speech-language pathologists can pause after producing a target to extend the time during which the client's auditory system rings with the sound. For example, help a client

focus on listening to /v/ in the word *over* by pausing after the /v/. This practice divides the syllables of some words incorrectly, as would be done in this example, but that can be easily corrected once the aim has been met.

Pause Between Every Part

One of the earliest techniques for teaching sequencing skills is to add pauses between each sound or syllable. This method allows the client to hear the individual phoneme units. It is a method often recommended in early 20th century books: "It is well to break up the words into single sounds" (Ward, 1923, p. 29).

Alter Pitch

Altering pitch can make any unit of speech stand out. The pitch of any phoneme, syllable, word, phrase, sentence, paragraph, or period of conversational speech can be altered. The altering of pitch is a quick and easy way to draw a client's attention to a target. Raise pitch up to a squeak or lower it to a growl, or use any pitch in between. Pitch alterations can help a client hear the individual phonemes of a word, the individual syllables of multi-syllabic words, the individual words of multi-word phrases, or the individual phrases of multi-phrase sentences. Wild and crazy pitch alterations make clients laugh and get a little giddy as part of the listening task. Pitch alterations can make seemingly boring therapy more interesting.

Prolongation

Prolongation of a target gives clients more time to listen to it. Prolongation is a good method to use with clients who take a moment to direct their auditory attention to the therapist's models, and it gives clients more time to process what is being modeled. One can prolong any aspect of spoken language including individual phonemes. Continuant phonemes are much easier to prolong than non-continuants.

Punch Out Syllables

To "punch out" a syllable means to say it quickly, a little louder, and with a definite separation from the rest of the word or phrase. Punching out syllables is an excellent way to make them stand out. Consider the following sentence: "Jason wants to go outside today." When punching out the syllables, words are broken up into their individual syllables, and each one stands alone and has equal value with the others. The sentence would be spoken with equal punch on each syllable: "Ja-son-wants-to-go-ou-side-to-day." Punching out syllables is an excellent way to help a client slow down and over-articulate because it puts emphasis on each syllable equally. It is a fabulous method to boost intelligibility in clients with dysarthria and others who mumble and slur. Punching out syllables helps them sound better instantly. The robotic nature of these utterances may have to be toned down intentionally if the practice does not fade on its own over time.

Purposeful Phoneme Substitution

Sometime the best thing to do to make a phoneme salient is to speak another phoneme in its place. This is done in a teasing or joking fashion. For example, to highlight /d/ in the word *doggie*, perhaps say "woggie." Little children love this. When the child exclaims that the word is not "woggie," the therapist can act confused and disoriented. "Woggie? What's wrong with 'woggie?'" Purposeful substitutions help clients listen carefully to targets. They become motivated to listen in order to catch the SLP making an error.

Questions

One of the easiest ways to draw a client's attention to his target(s) is to ask him what he knows about why he comes to speech. When asked why they attend, many children will say something like "Because it's 10:30" or "Mom said I had to come." Help the client understand the real reason. Ask high-functioning clients with minor errors, "Is there something going on with your speech?" or "Is there a sound that is bothering you?" With preschool children, give them the information they need: "You are getting so big! You are learning how to say that sound!" Clients with cognitive impairment are instructed in ways that make sense to them. Therapists of the Phonetic Placement Era usually began therapy by teaching their clients that they had a problem — sometimes they even recommended scolding the child about it. Van Riper later taught that one should establish rapport first and then teach the client that he has an error in a gentle yet direct way.

Remove Distracting Elements

Parts of words can be eliminated to make targets salient. For example, one can remove one phoneme from a cluster. Consider the /pl/ cluster for a client who uses coalescence and says /fiz/ for *please*. First the /l/ might be removed and the client might be taught to say /piz/. Once this simplified version of the word is acquired, the glide is replaced. He learns to say /piz/ first and /pliz/ second. Removing distracting elements is a way to break difficult work down into smaller steps. It functions not as a final product but as a first step.

Repetition

Most therapists illuminate targets by repeating them. Some early therapists approached this idea in a fairly rigid manner. For example, Travis (1931) recommended that models be given five times in a row before a client attempted an imitation. McCabe and Bradley (1975) recommended having children repeat each of the 24 consonants five times in a row as part of the *multiple phoneme approach*. Few therapists work this formally, but SLPs certainly continue to use repetition of a model as a regular form of stimulation.

Some children's storybooks contain wonderful repetitions of words and phrases. For example, consider the

Any Speech Unit Can Be Repeated	
Phonemes in isolation	"T-T-T"
Phonemes in single words	"T-T-T-Table"
Syllables in single words	"Tay-tay-tay-table"
Whole words alone	"Table… Table… Table…."
Single words in phrases or sentences	"I see a table… table… table…and a chair."

repetitive words and phrases in the very popular book, *Goodnight Moon* (Brown, 1947). Storybooks like these can be a wonderful addition to any therapy room, and they make for great homework activities for parents.

> *"Too many clinicians produce a phoneme, syllable, or word once and then ask the client to imitate it. If you ever have studied the vocabulary in a foreign language or heard an unusual name, you may recall that you were more likely to speak the word correctly if you heard it repeated several times. Thus, when a client is learning to say a new syllable or word in a new way, several repetitions of the stimulus before production is requested probably will elicit many more accurate responses. A little experimentation will indicate the number of stimuli needed for the client to be successful"* (Bosley, 1981, p. 7).

Rhyming

Rhyming delights the imagination and is an excellent method to make words and phonemes salient. It is a method that has been used for many decades. For example, Nemoy and Davis (1937) recommended that clients be taught to recognize rhyming words in poems, complete a simple rhyme by selecting the rhyming word from a short list of words given, or make up lists of words that rhyme. Many children's storybooks contain rhyming words, and perhaps the most recognizable of these are books by the famous Dr. Seuss (Theodor Seuss Geisel). Making up lists of words that rhyme is an excellent way to work with upper-level articulation clients.

Rhythm

Rhythmic presentation of a target makes it stand out and helps to capture a client's attention. Rhythm can be

Rhymes for Vocalic /ɑr/	
Words	*Are, bar, car, far, jar, mar, par, star, tar.*
Phrases	A big *car* Go very *far* The shiny *star*
Sentences	Give me that candy *bar.* Let's go in the blue *car.*
Poems	See my toy *car.* It goes very *far.* It fits in a *jar.* It has a big *star.*
Conversations	Have a conversation that focuses around the key rhyming words.

applied to any target:

- *Isolated syllables:* "Bah-bah-bah-bah…"
- *Final consonants:* "Hat-t-t-t-t-t"
- *Every word in a sentence:* "We-went-to-the-park."
- *Morphemes:* "Walk-ing" "Eat-ing"
- *Diminutives morphemes:* "Dog-gie" "Kit-ty," "Mom-my"
- *Each syllables in multi-syllabic words:* "He-li-cop-ter"
- *Split syllables:* "Ca-r" " Ja-r" "Fa-r" "Sta-r"

Add a Schwa

A schwa can be added to a model to make a target phoneme stand out. In phonological terms, the addition of the schwa is called *epenthesis* and it is usually considered a deviant phonological pattern. However, the addition of a schwa to a model can help make target phonemes stand out, and it is a pattern that little children use to say difficult words. Epenthesis can serve as a first step toward the ultimate target.

Final Consonants

Therapists can add a schwa to draw attention to a final consonant. For example, model the word *tell* as /tɛlə/ to make the final /l/ salient. The schwa and resultant second syllable is removed from the model once the client begins to notice and say the target.

Clusters

Therapists can add a schwa to help a client hear the two individual phonemes of a cluster. For example, model *blue* as /bəlu/ so both /b/ and /l/ become salient. This added schwa makes two syllables out of the cluster at first and it is removed as the client's sequencing ability improves over time.

Shorten a Target

Shortening a target in a modeled utterance draws a client's attention. For example, some clients cannot hear vowels well, especially the short vowels. Modeling the vowel in an even more truncated manner can help them hear them better because the sounds are punctuated.

Silence

There is a certain rhythm to the back-and-forth dialogue of articulation therapy, and one of the most effective tools to help a client listen to his own productions is for the therapist to remain quiet for their turn. If a client produces a speech unit correctly, and then the SLP remains silent for a turn, it causes the client to think back on what he said, and it causes his production to resound in his ear. If one persistently speaks right after the client's turn, this echo is cut short. Take some turns in silence, and find a non-vocal or non-verbal way to let him know that he has done well, for example by nodding the head and smiling.

Slow Down

SLPs speak slowly in therapy to make everything stand out. A slower rate gives clients more time to listen, more time to engage their auditory self-monitoring skills, and more time to articulate every phoneme, syllable, and word.

Speed Up

Talking too fast so intelligibility is lost can also be an excellent tool to draw a client's attention to speech. Clients sit

Rhythmic productions highlight any speech target.

up and take notice when a therapist purposefully speaks too fast and becomes impossible to understand. This is done in a humorous manner, and on an infrequent basis, in order to make correct productions stand out.

Word Pairs

Word pairs, *nonsense word pairs*, *contrast pairs*, *minimal pairs*, *maximal pairs*, and *near-minimal pairs* have been proposed as basic tools to highlight phonemes. This method was mentioned in 1919 by Blanton and Blanton who said to teach words and phonemes by drilling in pairs such as one/once, any/many, and fought/fit.

Minimal pairs are pairs of words that "differ in just one sound and also differ in meaning" (Edwards & Shriberg, 1983, p. 57). The process of using word pairs was formalized in 1974, when *minimal pairs contrast training* was proposed by LaRiviere, Winitz, Reeds, and Herriman (1974).

Minimal pairs are used to help clients hear the difference between phonemes in similar-sounding words. The beauty of the minimal pair is that the meaning, the auditory signals, and the oral movements all change. As such, *toy* and *boy* are different in all three of these aspects. The meaning change helps the client perceive the auditory and movement changes.

The term *maximal pairs* was proposed by Elbert and Gierut (1986) and tested by Gierut (1989). Phonological instruction is designed around word pairs that demonstrated maximum phonological differences. For example, the words *can* and *man* form a maximal opposition because /k/ is back, voiceless, oral, and occluded, whereas /m/ is front, voiced, nasal, and continuant. Maximal pairs are recommended early in treatment in order to improve broad generalization of phonological processes.

The term *near-minimal pair* was proposed by Elbert and Gierut (1986). These are pairs of words that differ by more than one phoneme but the vowels stay the same, for example, *boo* and *spoon*. The terms *minimal triads* and *minimal quads* have been adopted to expand on the original idea of minimal pairs (Marshalla, 2004). For example, use the words *wack*, *lack*, *yack*, and *rack* as a four-word group to distinguish /r/ from the other glides in the prevocalic position.

Whispering

Whispering is an excellent tool for making speech units salient. Whispering almost always piques a client's general auditory attention to phonemes, syllables, whole words, phrases, and so on. Whispering is an especially good tool to highlight voiceless-ness and frication, but it can be used to draw attention to any speech target.

imitation. These methods are at the core of phoneme, syllable, and word training despite a lack of formal research to support some of them.

SUMMARY

A wide variety of methods are employed to make speech targets stand out for client attention, processing, and

4

Using the Ear to Teach Speech Movements

Classic auditory training

"It is often difficult for another person to realize how and why an individual can be blissfully unaware of defects and bad habits in his own speech when they can be so obvious and distracting to others."

– Virgil Anderson, 1953

Van Riper said that a client would not know how to change his speech movements if he was not paying auditory attention to the sound, a process called *auditory training* or *ear training*. Some of this material has morphed into the process known as *phonological awareness*, and there seems to be some misconception that clients with motor speech disorders do not need this training. However, a great number of clients with motor speech disorders and articulation impairment simply are not listening very well to themselves or others and they are not comparing their own auditory signals with enough scrutiny to benefit their own speech productions. The mouth and the ear work together in a reciprocal relationship; the ear teaches the mouth to move, and the mouth teaches the ear to hear. These clients fail to make corrections in their movements because they are not listening well. This chapter is about the traditional methods therapists have used to improve listening skill for

better articulation and motor speech skill.

BACKGROUND

Auditory training became a standard part of articulation therapy right at the beginning of the Traditional Era with an article written by Van Riper in 1939, "Ear training in the treatment of articulation disorders." Van Riper and other therapists of his era believed that it did no good to coerce the production of a new phoneme if a client was not paying auditory attention to it, and they felt that this was an element of therapy missing during the Phonetic Placement Era that had preceded theirs. They said that ear training on the targeted sound was necessary for success and that failure to complete a program of articulation therapy was almost guaranteed without it.

Therapists of the Traditional Era believed that the ear was the primary feedback mechanism and the fine tuner of speech, and that listening carefully to a target would help a client understand how he should alter his speech movements in order to achieve it. Decades later, Porter and Lubker (1980) found what they called a "very tight acoustic-motoric coupling" that speakers use to monitor their own speech, meaning that the auditory systems and the speech movement system work almost simultaneously during the monitoring process. This is what Van Riper was getting at: SLPs must get the ear to hear better so that the mouth knows what to do.

Traditional Era writers urged speech clinicians not to

Auditory training begins with helping clients listen more carefully to speech.

This therapist has seated her client for auditory advantage.

rush through ear training but to treat auditory skill management as one of the most important parts of an articulation treatment program. They understood that clients must be taught to listen to their therapists and to listen to themselves produce phonemes. The very process of articulation therapy itself is one of helping clients listen to the therapist's sounds, then to listen to their own sounds, and then to compare and contrast these productions so that refinements can be made. This is auditory training at its finest.

RESEARCH

Research on the relationship between auditory discrimination and speech production has been a long-standing part of articulation science, and much ado has been made about whether auditory training is necessary to help clients change their speech movements.

> *"A critical question that remains to be answered is whether or not speech sound discrimination training has a positive impact on the establishment or production of a target sound"* (Bernthal & Bankson, 2004, p. 297).

Do clients with specific speech deficits have difficulty with specific auditory skills and can they benefit from this training? That may vary from client to client. Therefore, the SLP must discern whether the client sitting across the table is taking advantage of the auditory capabilities he already possesses or could possess with a little training. If the individual client is not using his listening skills to capacity, then treatment includes techniques to foster them. Speech-language pathologists recognize that some clients have good listening skills and others have poor listening skills and treatment is adjusted accordingly.

Key studies on the relationship between auditory discrimination and speech production are summarized in chronological order below to illustrate the unfolding nature of this science over time. Most demonstrate

a relationship between listening and speaking, and a few show that training in listening only improves listening. Some of the studies demonstrated that children with poor speech listening have other listening and discrimination problems, too.

- Kronvall and Diehl (1954) found that elementary school children with severe functional articulation problems (speech movement problems) exhibited significantly more errors on speech sound discrimination tasks than matched peers with no speech deficit.

- Fairbanks and Guttman (1958) found that delayed auditory feedback affected articulation performance.

- Mange (1960) studied 35 children with /r/ misarticulations and found that they performed significantly lower than matched peers on a test of pitch discrimination.

- Sommers, Meyer, and Fenton (1961) found that 65 children with misarticulations on both /r/ and /s/ performed more poorly on tests of pitch discrimination that did matched peers.

- Farquhar (1961) found that kindergarten children with mild articulation deficit discriminated error phonemes better than did children who had more severe articulation deficit.

- Winitz and Bellerose (1962) found that discrimination skill is not reduced when incorrectly reinforced. In other words, children's auditory discrimination skills cannot be made poorer even when adults try to make them so.

- Cohen and Diehl (1963) found that children with functional speech defects make significantly more errors on tasks of speech sound discrimination than did matched peers with normal speech. They also found that auditory discrimination skill improves between first and third grade, and that children with speech sound errors continue to lag behind their peers even when their skills improve with age.

- Aungst and Frick (1964) found that a child's ability to discriminate another speaker's correct and incorrect productions of /r/ is not related to his ability to discriminate his own productions of /r/.

- Schlanger and Galanowsky (1966) found that children with cognitive impairment performed more poorly on a battery of auditory discrimination tests than did peers with cognition in the average range.

- Weiner (1967) reviewed the literature of the time and found that the evidence clearly pointed to a link between poor auditory discrimination ability and articulation deficit until 8 or 9 years of age.

- Sherman and Geith (1967) found that 18 children with high speech sound discrimination scores were superior in articulation ability than 18 children with low speech sound discrimination scores.

- Stitt and Huntington (1969) studied college-age students and found a relationship between auditory discrimination ability and articulation skill. They reported that their evidence supported the continued use of ear training in articulation therapy.

- Ritterman (1970) found that phoneme discrimination training improved phoneme discrimination ability.

- Williams and McReynolds (1975) found that training a client to produce a phoneme correctly develops his auditory discrimination ability, but that the opposite is not necessarily true: Auditory discrimination training did not necessarily facilitate better production.

- Doehring and Ling (1971) studied children with severe hearing impairment and found that training them to discriminate vowels did not transfer to their ability to recognize words. The authors felt that the leap between discriminating vowels and words was too large, and they recommended smaller stages of teaching to permit generalization.

- McGurk and MacDonald (1976) demonstrated that the brain collapses data when auditory signals do not match visual ones. The study showed that if a child sees a visually recorded production of "ga" and simultaneously hears a recorded auditory production of "ba," his brain interprets the syllable as "da." This is known as the *McGurk Effect*.

- Shelton et al. (1978) proposed that ear training alone will not eliminate articulation errors, meaning that one cannot simply train a client to hear a sound and then expect him to change his speech movements it all by himself.

- Polson (1980) surveyed the opinions of speech-language pathologists and found they ranked auditory self-discrimination as the most important skill needed for a child to succeed in articulation carryover.

- Phatate and Umano (1981) found that auditory perceptual skills improve with age, suggesting that auditory perception is learned.

- Broen et al. (1983) found that the ability to discriminate between /w/, /l/, and /r/ is established in children by three years of age. They also found that children with misarticulations performed much more poorly on these tasks. They concluded that the relationship between phonetic perception and articulatory development is an asymmetrical one. "Normal articulatory development is associated with the achievement of accurate phonetic perception. However, phonetic perceptual difficulties accompany some but not all articulatory problems" (p. 607).

- Elliott and Hammer (1988) studied children age 6 through 9 years of age and found that those with language-learning problems showed poorer auditory discrimination, more deviations in articulation, and lower receptive vocabulary than did their normal peers.

- Eilers, Oller, Urbano, and Moroff (1989) found that prolongation of the preceding vowel facilitated infants' perceptions of final consonants when using synthetic stimuli. They also found that altering more that one feature of presented stimuli facilitated better discrimination of final consonants.

- Rvachew and Jamieson (1989) found that children with functional (motoric) articulation deficit were significantly less capable of discriminating minimal pair words with /s/ and /θ/ contrasts, and some of these children also had difficulty with /s/ and /ʃ/ contrasts. They concluded that there might be a subgroup of children with functional articulation disorders who have difficulty with speech perception.

- Watson (1991) found that children with high intelligence and academic aptitude scored better on measures of auditory discrimination ability than did children with low intelligence and academic aptitude scores.

- Shuster, Ruscello, and Smith (1992) used real-time speech spectography successfully to enhance auditory perception of sound in the training of /r/.

- Sussmann (1993) revealed that normal young children do not necessarily discriminate better (the way adults do) when their attention is focused on the task.

- Elliott and Hammer (1993) tested children 6 through 11 years of age and found that older children performed better than younger children on selected tasks of auditory discrimination, that children with language-learning problems performed more poorly than those achieving regular school progress, and that children with moderate intellectual impairments performed more poorly than the other two groups.

- Green and Norrix (1997) found that watching a speaker's mouth as he produces a phoneme facilitates auditory discrimination of the phoneme.

- McFarland, Cacace, and Setzen (1998) found that the ability to discriminate rapid changes in auditory signals seems to be a completely separate skill than the ability to discriminate rapid changes in visual information.

- Kraus et al. (1999) found that speech sound discrimination ability is developed by age 6 years of age and does not change between 8 and 15 years of age. They also found no differences between males and females.

- Edwards, Fox, and Rogers (2002) studied word discrimination in children aged 3–8 years as well as in adults. They found that children with phonological disorders were less able to discriminate between CVC words that had different final consonants than typically developing peers. They also found that younger children performed less well than older children and adults.

- Perkell et al. (2004) found a relationship between tongue-tip placement and auditory discrimination on /s/ and /ʃ/. Subjects that were more consistent in tongue-tip placement on /s/ were also better in auditory discrimination of the two phonemes. They surmised that auditory discrimination and oral placement are integrally related in development.

- According to a review of the literature by Vihman (2004b) the few studies that have been done on the relationship between production and perception of speech reveals that some phonemic contrasts continue to be difficult to perceive by children above three years of age. These include /θ/ and /f/, /ð/ and /v/, /w/ and /r/, and so forth.

VAN RIPER AUDITORY TRAINING

Van Riper described what he called the "four main types of ear training" (Van Riper, 1939, p. 175). He called them *isolation, stimulation, identification,* and *discrimination.* Van Riper's perspective on these ideas is described first, for these four have been the very foundation of auditory training for articulation improvement.

Isolation / Sound as Signal

Van Riper used the term *isolation* to refer to the process of training a client to listen for and to recognize a target phoneme. The client is taught to actively listen for his target as the therapist presents it alone or in syllables, nonsense words, real words, phrases, sentences, paragraphs, or connected speech. The client is listening for the single or isolated target phoneme amidst many others. The client is to recognize whether the sound is present or absent from the speech production model.

The purpose of this ear training is to help the client begin to recognize the target phoneme as a unique sound and to quickly realize when he hears it. In so doing the client creates an *auditory image* of the correct production. Nemoy and Davis discussed how the auditory image fits into the *mental image* of a phoneme:

> *"There must be a correct mental image of the sound before the sound can be reproduced accurately by the voluntary muscles of speech. Ear training drills are essential in building up correct mental images of sounds"* (Nemoy & Davis, 1937, p. 26).

Van Riper and his colleagues considered this skill to be the first and most important step of ear training. It includes identification of the correct and incorrect production of the target. Activities are adjusted to the client's developmental level. For example, a very young client might be told, "Baby. Baby. Bay-bay-bay. Baby. Did you hear it? Bay-bay-bay. Baby." An older client might be asked to listen to the therapist read a paragraph loaded with words beginning with B and be required to snap his fingers every time he hears one.

Van Riper later regretted his use of the term *isolation* in this manner because it became associated with speaking the phoneme in isolation instead of listening for the individual phoneme in isolation, so he changed it. By 1958 he and Irwin had begun to use the phrase *sound as signal* (Van Riper & Irwin, 1958, p. 121). Van Riper and Irwin wrote that therapists should help clients learn to recognize a target sound as a unique auditory signal among many others. The client is taught in such a way that he has a moment of realization and thinks, "There it is!"

Stimulation / Bombardment

Van Riper used the term *stimulation* to refer to the process of bombarding the client with a "barrage of the correct sound" (Van Riper, 1947, p. 175) through his auditory channel. Earlier, Travis (1931) had written about this type of auditory stimulation, and he related it to what happens to someone when a popular song or a commercial jingle is implanted in the auditory memory:

> *"It is easily demonstrated that an individual may so learn a tune by just listening to it… It is probably the repeated [auditory] stimulation that is helpful"* (Travis, 1931, p. 228).

This is what the early writers were talking about when they discussed stimulation of a new sound. They said that the client's auditory system must be stimulated with the target sound in such a way that the sound echoes in his mind. Hodson and Paden (1983) formalized this process fifty years later and called it *auditory bombardment:*

> *"The child is introduced to the session's target phoneme or sequence by simply listening for about two minutes while the clinician slowly reads about 15 words containing that target… He only listens; he must not repeat the words"* (Hodson & Paden, 1983, p. 66).

Van Riper's main ideas about stimulating the child's ear with the target sounds continues to be supported with published research. For example, Munson, Edwards, and Beckman (2005) studied preschool children and found "the more words that the child has heard and said that contain a particular phonological pattern, the easier it will be for the child to abstract away that pattern to use for learning new words" (p. 77).

TABLE 5 — Examples of Theraplay Dialogue & Activities	
Clinician says…	Clinician does…
"Let's see if your toes make a funny noise."	Touches the child's toes and says a funny syllable using one of the child's target phonemes.
"Seep, seep! They do make a funny noise. Let's try mine."	Takes the child's hand to his/her foot, pauses, allows the child time to make the sound, or makes the sound him/herself.
"Seep, seep! You made my toes go 'Seep.'"	Together they look for sounds made by ears, fingers, tummies, and noses.
Whole words alone	"Table… Table… Table…."
Single words in phrases or sentences	"I see a table… table… table… and a chair."

Identification / Character Specification

Van Riper used the term *identification* to refer to the process of training a client to recognize the characteristics of both the correct sound and his error sound:

> "It is necessary to make the correct and incorrect sounds very vivid… This identification is largely a process of observation of the sound's characteristics, in terms of both audition and mechanics… Each correct sound and the error must come to have an individuality and an identity" (Van Riper, 1939, p. 180).

Van Riper suggested that this was a process of giving the target sound a unique status, and its own personality in terms of the way it sounds and of the way it is produced. He gave examples of this type of training for very young as well as older children. For very young children Van Riper recommended: (1) assigning a name to the phoneme such as the "snake sound" for /s/, (2) drawing a face for the sound such as a smile for /i/, (3) associating the sound with a written symbol such as the letter "P" for /p/, or (4) telling little stories that amplify the letter such

as *Little Red Riding Hood* for /r/. For older children and adults, Van Riper suggested: (1) give a name to the error, such as "the old sloppy shush" for the lateral lisp, (2) use phonetic diagrams, palatograms, and models of articulatory placement, and (3) use nonsense symbols, such as an X, to represent the error.

Theraplay

An adaptation of this idea is the *Theraplay®* model designed for preschool children (Kupperman, Bligh, & Goodban, 1980). Theraplay combines Van Riper's idea about assigning every sound a personality with playful communication routines intended to entice the attention and interest of the very young child. Table 5 above presents a sample from this article of what a clinician might say and do.

Discrimination / Comparing & Contrasting / Speech Sound Perception

The fourth type of ear training Van Riper recommended is *discrimination*. Auditory discrimination refers to the ability to compare a correctly produced sound with an incorrectly produced one and to recognize the differences between them. The topic of auditory discrimination training in speech learning goes back to the late 19th century:

> "We often find those whose ears are not trained to detect shades of vowel and consonant sounds, just as we often find those whose ears are not trained to detect shades of musical sounds or pitches. But as in the case of music, the ear, by proper methods, can be trained to detect fine shades of speech forms" (Kidder, 1896, p. 18).

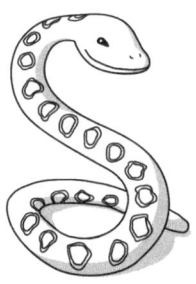

The snake image for /s/ gives the phoneme an identity.

"The case must come to match his self-heard sound against a standard pattern. He must test it, measure it, and compare it point for point with the model" (Van Riper & Irwin, 1958, p. 131).

"A primary purpose of perceptual training is to teach the individual with defective speech to attend specifically to his own speech signals, and to compare what he hears with 'memories' or percepts he has built up through training" (Carrel, 1968, p. 95).

Paired Stimuli

The technique known as *paired stimuli* is an adaptation of this idea (Weston, 1969; Irwin & Weston, 1975). Two words are spoken to the client. The first is accurate and the second is inaccurate. The client is encouraged to listen and compare the two.

An Opposite View

Bosley (1981) had a problem with the tradition of preliminary auditory training. She suggested clients be taught to discriminate phonemes *after* they have learned to produce them. This view was reinforced by research done by Williams and McReynolds (1975), and this idea is one that the present author has found useful:

"Clinic time is often used inefficiently with ear training activities. If the client can be taught quickly to produce the phoneme by a method other than auditory discrimination, the advantage of discriminating self-produced phonemes can be utilized... Such logic should encourage speech-language pathologists to begin teaching the phoneme at once and to use auditory discrimination techniques later" (Bosley, 1981, p. 6–7).

The Discrimination Process

When auditory discrimination tasks are included during the process of articulation correction (either before, during, or after production work), SLPs generally begin with sounds that are grossly different and then progress toward discrimination of very similar sounds. The ultimate step of ear training requires that the SLP have the ability to imitate the client's error production. Speech teachers should have the "ability to mimic or produce a reasonably accurate imitation of the student's error" (Van Riper & Irwin, 1958, p. 182) because this is the point at which the client's ear is most finely tuned. This progression from gross to fine auditory discrimination can occur within just a few minutes for many clients, but it can take months for others, especially those with significant cognitive deficit or auditory processing disorder. Imitating a client is also tremendously helpful in teaching therapists what their client is doing wrong. This aids the analysis, especially if the client is using a rare distortion.

"The teacher is warned that unless imitation is carefully and judiciously employed some harm may result. Care must be taken to avoid developing self-consciousness in the child or suggesting that either the child or his speech is being subjected to ridicule. It is best not to employ imitation in a group situation" (Anderson, 1953, p. 140).

"This method has certain advantages, especially for the [therapist], for in so doing she may discover how and why it is that the child speaks the way he does. When she begins to talk as the child does, she may discover, for example, the particular adjustments of the articulators that produce the observed deviations, and can thereby gain insight into the nature of the child's problem and, as a result, can assist him more effectively" (Anderson, 1953, p. 140).

There is one further advantage to imitating clients' errors, and that is that a lifetime of this practice makes one an excellent diagnostician. It allows therapists to understand speech sound errors at a level that goes far beyond any textbook description. The ability to imitate one's clients makes the treatment process much easier.

Ear Training & Motor Speech Disorders

Ear training is also recognized as an essential component of treatment for clients with motor speech disorder, even though the neuromuscular deficit is the cause of the problem and not auditory discrimination skill. Many authors have addressed this.

Van Riper (1947) explained that he liked to use auditory bombardment and modification of known sounds to teach new phonemes to children with cerebral palsy. Marie Crickmay wrote about auditory training for children with cerebral palsy in *Speech Therapy and the Bobath Approach to Cerebral Palsy* (1966). This celebrated text was one of the first American books on cerebral palsy. Crickmay said that clients with cerebral palsy often do not listen to themselves well, especially those who have been severely lacking in expressive speech. Crickmay explained that the approach taught by Van Riper and Irwin (1958) was the auditory approach with which she agreed, however, "it will be a much slower process" (p. 132):

"[Clients] are so often excited by their newly-acquired ability to vocalize that their attention is entirely focused on 'sending,' and not on 'receiving.' Even if the therapist asks such a patient to listen and to copy the sounds she is making, he simply does not receive her. He is not wishing to be uncooperative, but his mind is busy planning the sounds he is about to send" (Crickmay, 1966, p. 131).

In their ground-breaking text, *Motor Speech Disorders* (1975), Darley, Aronson, and Brown included ear training in their remediation plans. The authors explained that self-monitoring in the client with an acquired motor speech disorder is both auditory and kinesthetic:

"The speaker has a new and relentless task, that of continuously monitoring his performance, checking to see that he is attaining the standard he consciously sets for himself. He must learn to listen to himself talk… he must be self critical and recognize errors" (p. 271).

Mysak (1980) discussed the topic of auditory awareness and attention as it relates to very young children with severe neuromuscular dysfunction. He called these skills *true listening behavior.* Mysak said that some of the very earliest signs of true listening behavior included body stilling and cessation of suckling or other behavior in response to soft, soothing, or interesting sounds such as the human voice. He wrote that this type of listening behavior "should be intentionally stimulated every day by the use of novel human vocalizations, made novel by shifting pitch, loudness, quality, and time factors" (Mysak, 1980, p. 249). Mysak also wrote that these clients should be taught to listen to various types of music and interesting environmental sounds such as a ticking watch or running water.

The process of using auditory training as a prime element of therapy for clients with motor speech disorders continues. Yorkston, Beukelman, Strand, and Bell (1999) reviewed a wide variety of approaches for clients with motor speech disorders including the basics of auditory training: "Integral stimulation works well as a motor approach to treatment… The focus is on auditory and visual stimulation and repetition" (Yorkston et al., 1999, p. 553–554).

Ear Training & Phonological Deficit

Phonological skill training is also largely auditory. The study of phonology itself is the study of the sound system, and a phonological deficit is due at least in part to deficits in the client's knowledge of that sound system. Treatment of a phonological deficit is designed to awaken the client's ear to that sound system in a process now known as *phonological awareness.* According to Lowe, "… part of awareness training includes some form of ear training" (Lowe, 1994, p. 189). Auditory training of one type or another has been recommended in virtually every book written about phonological therapy. Ingram wrote about the individual nature of auditory discrimination problems in children with phonological impairment:

"Evidence that [phonologically] deviant children do not primarily have a perceptual problem challenges the widespread use of discrimination procedures. At the same time, there may be instances where individual children may have some perceptual problems with specific sounds. Given this possibility, it may be unrealistic to abandon the use of discrimination altogether. Rather, it probably should be used occasionally when evidence suggests a perceptual confusion between sounds" (Ingram, 1976, p. 152–153).

Bernthal and Bankson discussed auditory training in their wonderful text *Articulation and Phonological Disorders* (2004). They divided articulation and phonological remediation procedures into two categories: motor and linguistic:

"While the teaching of sounds may be viewed as motor oriented therapy, perceptual training (i.e., discrimination training, minimal pairs contrasts, and auditory bombardment) may be incorporated both in motor and linguistic orientated treatments. During the establishment phase of instruction, the clinician seeks to teach target behaviors and establish the awareness of phonological contrasts" (Bernthal & Bankson, 2004, p. 295).

Probably the most direct discussion of the integration of auditory training and phonological therapy is presented in Hodson and Paden's wonderful little phonology instruction book, *Targeting Intelligible Speech* (1983 & 1991). The authors begin with a discussion about auditory stimulation in their section on basic procedures:

"Since they are 'natural,' and primary, cues through which the great majority of children acquire the sound system of language, it would seem logical that the child who is phonologically disordered might also benefit from attending to the audible characteristics of sounds. Although it might be argued that the unintelligible child has probably had as much opportunity to hear language as the typical child, it may be that these children simply require more — or perhaps more concentrated or emphasized — auditory stimulation than usual" (Hodson & Paden, 1983, p. 49–50).

CLASSIC ELEMENTS OF THERAPY

Auditory training activities are grounded in those proposed by Traditional Era therapists but now there are more terms to describe the process, more materials from which to choose, and more toys and tools to employ in the work. In this chapter, the classic elements of auditory training for phoneme development are discussed.

The work of the speech-language pathologist is to identify those skills that are weak, lacking, and potentially contributing to the articulation deficit, and to encourage development of these skills while teaching the phonemes. The two skills of listening and performing usually go hand-in-hand. There are no standardized tests for most of these skills and a formal test would be unnecessary in most cases anyway. These skills are assessed informally throughout the trial-and-error process of therapy. The skills below are methods that SLPs use in therapy and are presented in alphabetical order with no hierarchy implied.

Anticipatory Listening

Van Riper and Irwin (1958) described a process they called *anticipatory listening* which is the act of getting ready to listen. The authors used several metaphors to explain this process including one about a foot race:

> *"The foot racer, crouched for the start, tenses certain muscles in anticipation of the signal to go. He also 'sharpens his ears' and anticipates with a kind of inner rehearsal the sound of the pistol. He is doing some advanced listening… This experience of pre-hearing, of auditory alertness to an expected signal, is what we mean by… anticipatory listening"* (Van Riper & Irwin, 1958, p. 130).

Speech-language pathologists use many different cues to help their clients anticipate auditory signals. Many simply say, "Listen…" just before giving a model sound or word. Other verbal cues include, "Get your ears ready…" or "Stop… Listen…" or "Okay… Sit up… Here it comes…" or "I hope you are ready…." Anticipatory listening encourages clients to settle themselves. It helps them prepare to listen to speech units modeled by the therapist. Clients who cannot prepare themselves in this way often miss important auditory cues. Methods to develop anticipatory listening are used in association with all the other methods described in this chapter.

Auditory Association

Auditory association is the ability to recognize the similarities between two sound units. It is one basis for the *association method* advocated by Van Riper. Using auditory association, the SLP teaches the client a new sound by calling attention to its similarity to another sound the client already can produce. For example, one might teach /z/ by associating it with /s/ because of their obvious phonetic similarities. Associations can be made by place, manner or voicing.

Auditory Attention

The term *auditory attention* refers to the "ability to focus on specific sound units as significant stimuli" (Nicolosi, Harryman, & Kresheck, 1983, p. 18). The ability to pay auditory attention to speech units is perhaps the most important basic skill with which to begin speech training. Speech-language pathologists train clients to pay particular attention to speech targets, be they phonemes,

Whispering captures auditory attention.

syllables, or words, or prosodic elements. Clients must be able to purposefully and actively listen to these units. This means that the SLP must make this work comprehensible and interesting to the client to grab his auditory attention. Therapists do this by structuring listening activities at the client's cognitive level.

For example, if the child's cognition is at the two-year level, then encourage him to listen in ways that normally would capture a two-year-old's auditory attention. One might produce the target louder, with a puppet, with an amusing intonation pattern, or as an environmental sound. These types of activities stretch back to the Phonetic Placement Era:

> *"The sound of the element may be likened to the sound made by some animal or by nature, or by some mechanical object such as an automobile, a train, a sawmill or an airplane"* (Nemoy & Davis, 1937, p. 36).

Auditory Awareness

Auditory awareness is a regular part of most approaches to articulation training. In essence, this skill suggests that clients must be made aware of the target phoneme and its characteristics:

> *"The articulation case should become aware of the characteristics of the standard sound in all contexts — in isolation, in nonsense syllables, in words, and in sentences. To limit the case's perceptual training to any one of these would seem most unwise"* (Van Riper & Irwin, 1958, p. 121).

Most authors agree that auditory awareness must work together with visual, tactile, and kinesthetic awareness for phoneme correction. Simple activities can be used to draw a client's auditory awareness to a target. For example, the therapists might write the letter "V" on a paper and say, "Listen while I say the sound of V…."

Auditory Blending

Therapists often note that clients can be taught to produce individual phonemes but then they have difficulty using that phoneme within a word. The clients' difficulty may be in *auditory blending*. Auditory blending refers to the "capacity to combine the phonemes of a word produced with separations between them into entire words" (Nicolosi, Harryman, & Kresheck, 1983, p. 38). For example, once a client can say /s/, he might then be taught to say the word *soap* by the use of auditory blending. His therapist might model the word by prolonging /s/ and by adding a pause between it and the rest of the word. The client might begin by speaking the word into separated units like the therapist did. But then, using his powers of auditory blending, the client will begin to blend the word back together into one single unit. Some clients can do this immediately, and others need careful guidance with slow models to learn the blending process. Clients who have difficulty may need the transition sounds produced more slowly, or they might need the word spelled out to visually see the sequence to help them hear it.

Auditory Closure

The term *auditory closure* refers to the "completion of a word or words by filling in the parts omitted when a word or words are spoken" (Nicolosi, Harryman, & Kresheck, 1983, p. 54). Therapists often leave out part of a word in order to stimulate the client to actively form the whole word in his mind and to produce it correctly with his mouth. For example, once the client can produce /t/, he might be encouraged to say the word *cat* with postvocalic /t/ when the therapist models it without the final /t/. The client's work is to speak the whole word including the final consonant. Auditory closure training forces the client to search his auditory memory for the correct auditory image and to match his production to this image.

Auditory Synthesis

The term *auditory synthesis* is similar to *auditory closure* but in this case the blending of sounds together allows the client to perceive the sequence as a single word. It refers to the "cognitive integration of phonemes that have been presented separately, resulting in recognition of a syllable or a word" (Nicolosi, Harryman, & Kresheck, 1983, p. 27). Some clients need to work on auditory blending first before they reach a moment of clarity and image of the word takes shape in their minds. In other words, a client may learn to say /k/, and then learn to say /k – æ – t/, but it will be another cognitive step for him to realize that this creates the word *cat*.

Comparing to a Community Standard

Van Riper and Irwin used the term *comparator function* to refer to the skill of comparing one's production to a community standard. The standard is "the average pronunciation of all the individuals in the group to which the speaker belongs" (Van Riper & Irwin, 1958, p. 107–108). In other words, the client must understand how most people within the speaking community pronounce a certain sound unit. The SLP tells the client what the standard is and then encourages him to meet it. For example, the community standard for *soup* is /sup/ and not /θup/.

To compare the client's habitual way of pronouncing a phoneme to the community standard, therapists throughout the years have used various terms such as the *old way* and the *new way*, or the *correct way* and the *incorrect way*. Some of the earliest writers in the field advocated that SLPs focus on the *good way* and the *bad way*.

Therapists today are more considerate of their clients' feelings, and they employ gentler approaches. In order to follow Van Riper and Irwin's directive to appeal to social norms the present author has found it best to tell clients, "Most people say it like this… and you are saying it like this…." A directive like this is especially beneficial in treatment with teens and pre-teens who are usually driven to blend in and to perform just like their peers: If they want to wear jeans and shoes like everyone else they will want to speak like everyone else. Younger children who do not yet face peer pressure can be told, "This is how mommy says it…" or "This is how big kids say it…."

Auditory Discrimination

The term *auditory discrimination* refers to the "ability to sort and sift sounds from each other [that] involves a comparison of heard sounds with other competing sounds" (Nicolosi, Harryman, & Kresheck, 1983, p. 75). *Speech sound discrimination* is "the ability to detect differences between sounds in the language, and differences between correct and incorrect productions" (Bernthal & Bankson, 2004, p. 147). This is perhaps the most important auditory skill of all. Some clients have difficulty in this area while others do not: "A relationship appears to exist between speech sound perception and articulation in some subjects" (Bernthal & Bankson, 2004, p. 154).

It is the job of the speech-language pathologist to determine whether individual clients need assistance in this area, and to build up this skill accordingly. Certain formal tests have been designed to assess skill in auditory discrimination, but usually therapists use their own informal assessment procedures during the course of therapy. Usually one tests a client's ability to discriminate a correct production of the target phoneme from others and designs a series of activities that teach the client to discriminate those phonemes or phonological patterns that are in error. For example, a client who confuses /tʃ/ and /ʃ/ will be engaged in careful listening activities that help him learn to discriminate between the two alone and in simple words. The ability to hear the differences between these two phonemes should help the client produce them discriminately.

One of the most enjoyable ways to build auditory discrimination in very young children is to model words with incorrect phonemes purposefully and teasingly. For example, a therapist might play with the word "soap" by calling it "shoap," "toap," "hoap," "choap," "moap," "loap," or "koap." Young children love this type of word play, especially if the adult is playing the role of the incredible dummy: "Yes, that is a moap! I am saying it correctly! No, it's not sssssssoap. It's mmmmmmmoap!"

Auditory Feedback / Self-Hearing / Auditory Self-Monitoring

The term *auditory feedback* is "hearing oneself talk" (Nicolosi, Harryman, & Kresheck, 1983, p. 95). Van Riper and Irwin called it *self hearing* and *simultaneous auditory feedback*. They said that clients "must learn to listen to themselves *during* the act of speaking" (1958, p. 127). This skill has also been called *auditory self-monitoring*. Deficiency in auditory self-monitoring can be a huge problem in many clients. As Fisher (1966) said, "It is especially difficult to hear yourself objectively" (p. 34). Therapists design activities to help clients listen to themselves from the onset of therapy.

"We must make his self hearing vivid and rewarding. We must teach [the client] to scrutinize his own auditory feedback…. It is not enough for [him] to be able to recognize the correct and incorrect speech sounds as they are spoken by other people. We must also help our cases to hear themselves, to listen to their own mouths" (Van Riper & Irwin, 1958, p. 116, 123).

Imitating a client's error back to him is a form of auditory feedback. In the 1950s, therapists began to use tape recorders to provide *delayed auditory feedback* after Holbrook (1954) had found that tape-recorded lessons were an effective way to reduce errors on English phonemes among Asian college students. Tape recorders provided several advantages:

"The mere act of recording his speech helps the case get set to listen, makes him pay some attention to the speech itself, and permits him to hear it again and again… The delay helps the case to be objective, to assume an experimental attitude in his scrutiny. Errors and correct sounds may be experienced again and again" (Van Riper & Irwin, 1958, p. 126).

Perhaps the most egregious example of failure to self-monitor is the client who can pass an articulation test but who becomes unintelligible in connected speech. This client can speak clearly when he carefully monitors himself as he does during the process of articulation testing. But the client fails to self-monitor during the demands of rapid conversational speech and his speech falls apart miserably; consonants are omitted, vowels and diphthongs are neutralized, and whole syllables disappear. This is not because he can't perform these skills, it is because he is oblivious to the fact that he is not performing them.

A client like this no longer needs to learn phonemes; his therapy must develop his ability to listen to himself. He must learn to monitor himself carefully as he speaks under a wide variety of speaking conditions. He also must recognize when communication partners are having difficulty understanding him, and he must take the time to

Auditory and visual feedback work together to help clients develop auditory self-monitoring.

Many different tools can be used to direct a client's sound back to his own ear for self-hearing. These include flexible tubes, toy telephones, and PVC pipes.

repair his errors during the process of conversation. Carryover depends upon auditory self-monitoring.

Auditory Figure-Ground Discrimination

The term *auditory figure-ground discrimination* refers to the "selection of the relevant from the irrelevant auditory stimuli in an environment" (Nicolosi, Harryman, & Kresheck, 1983, p. 75). It has also been called *auditory differentiation*, *selective listening*, and *competing messages integration*. An example of this skill would be the ability to discriminate between the teacher's voice giving instructions at the front of the class from the sound of other children talking nearby. Children must have good auditory figure-ground discrimination in order to actively listen to speech targets. This area continues to be of interest in the research community: "Some children, in spite of normal hearing sensitivity, report persistent listening difficulties especially in noisy environments such as classrooms" (Sharma et al., 2014, p. 1 [2308]).

Some children with articulation deficit have difficulty in this area. They treat all auditory signals as equal by listening to everything all at once or by listening to nothing at all. This is one of the reasons why all the articulation textbooks assumed that articulation therapy would take place in a quiet environment where auditory and visual distractions could be minimized.

The SLP must teach clients to listen actively to targets and to ignore all other ambient noises. A simple way to do this is to help the client seek out and discover the source of ambient noises that are distracting him, and then to tell him, "We are not listening to that. We are listening to this." For example, if the therapy room is next to a busy and noisy highway, spend a few moments at the window listening to the traffic outside. Discuss all the sounds made by vehicles. Then close the window and instruct the client to pay attention to the sounds in the room. He is being taught to actively ignore ambient noises.

Sometimes it is necessary to provide a source of *white noise* to masquerade ambient noise. The least expensive and most readily available option may be to turn on a fan in the room. Be mindful, however, that a white noise generator like a fan may also interfere with the client's ability to hear certain phonemes, and a mechanical distraction can be too powerful for some children to ignore. Other options for steady background noise include soft music playing in the background or a recording of someone reading in a monotone.

Auditory Fixing

The term *auditory fixing* refers to the process of listening while trying to produce a target, listening while oscillating around the correct position of the target, and then fixing one's auditory attention on the correct production of the target. The term comes from Van Riper and Irwin (1958).

Fixating on the target often is the very essence of articulation therapy. The client is taught to listen carefully with each trial, to think about what his production sounds like, to move slightly in one direction or another, to listen again, to move again, and so forth until he produces the target correctly. This back-and-forth between moving, producing, and listening is one of the most fundamental processes of articulation therapy. Auditory fixing on the target is especially important when clients are learning the later-developing phonemes that have to be made in precise ways.

Auditory Identification of Word Position

Mid-century SLPs developed the notion that clients should be able to discriminate whether a target phoneme occurs at the beginning, middle or end of a word:

> *"The location of the sound within the word and sentence should also be stressed. The case can learn to locate it in terms of initial, medial, or final positions within the word; he can learn to pick out the word in which the sound occurred; he can learn to know whether it occurs within a blend; he can learn to recognize that /z/, for example, as the third sound in the word 'examination'"* (Van Riper & Irwin, 1958, p. 121).

This idea appeared prominently in textbooks up into the 1970s but the idea now is challenged because no supportive research exists. However, many therapists still find that the identification of phoneme targets by word position is a simple addition to treatment with children because it helps them focus their attention on the target at hand. Identification of word position can be especially fun for children who are reading at a first or second grade level. The activity seems to help children get better orientated to their work, and it seems to foster a certain level of auditory awareness and phoneme discrimination.

Auditory Localization

The term *auditory localization* refers to the ability to locate the source of a sound by listening to it. Auditory localization is a primitive skill that develops during infancy. Children learn to turn the head in order to recognize the source of sound within their physical environment, and this allows them to associate sound with physical structures and events. Clients with poor skill in this area have great difficulty with both speech and language because the auditory signals they perceive remain unrelated to their source. In other words, the auditory world remains separate from the world perceived with the other senses. This lack of integration interferes with the development of many skills in the areas of speech, language, and cognition.

Methods to develop auditory localization are usually reserved for clients with severe receptive and expressive speech-language disorders and related sensorimotor and cognitive deficit. Training a client to localize auditory signals will not be necessary in typical articulation therapy. However, clients with motor speech disorders can have poorly developed auditory localization skills because of limitations in head control and general movement. For example, how might a very small child learn the meaning of "bell" if he cannot recognize that the ringing he hears is coming from the bell itself. SLPs can help clients to visually and aurally locate the sound they hear and integrate the two senses into one concept.

Auditory Memory

The term *auditory memory* refers to "assimilation, storage, and retrieval of previously experienced sensations and perceptions when the original stimulus is no longer present" (Nicolosi, Harryman, & Kresheck, 1983, p. 148). Clients must have an auditory memory for the sounds they are learning in speech, and this memory must extend from one minute to the next, and from one session to the next, over time. To nudge their auditory memory, therapists often ask, "Why did you come here today?" The SLP uses clients' answers to understand just how much they understand and remember about their treatment. "A primary purpose of perceptual training is to teach the [client]… to compare what he hears with 'memories' or percepts he has built up through training" (Carrell, 1968, p. 95). Auditory memory can be sub-divided into several distinct skills: auditory sequential memory, long-term auditory memory, short-term auditory memory, and rote auditory memory.

Auditory Sequential Memory

Auditory sequential memory is "storage and retrieval of information requiring a specific order of input and recall" (Nicolosi, Harryman, & Kresheck, 1983, p. 149). Clients must have good auditory sequential memory to remember the sequence of phonemes in words, of words in phrases, of phrases in sentences, and so forth. A client who say *kitten* as "nicket" may be having trouble with auditory sequential memory, and he may need help remembering information in correct sequential order. Sequential visual stimuli can help clients remember sequential auditory stimuli. Listening while following along with the printed orthographic symbols will help clients who can read. For non-readers, use blocks lined up in a row, one block per syllable, or one block per phoneme.

Long-Term Auditory Memory

Long-term auditory memory is "memory retained for an indefinite period of time" (Nicolosi, Harryman, & Kresheck, 1983, p. 149). Many clients perform well in an individual therapy session, but then return to the next session and seem to have forgotten everything that was taught earlier. This may be a client who is not putting his new speech learning skills into long-term memory. This client needs help learning speech units *and* he needs help with his long-term auditory memory. Long-term memories are created in many ways depending on the client; some clients remember better when drill is employed, some with song, and some remember better when the work involves a functional experience. Perhaps a combination of approaches is the best way to ensure long-term memory of speech units.

For example, to help a client remember to produce /b/ at the beginning of words, the therapist might have the client dab lip gloss on his lips right before he says each of ten practice words on a list. Then they might read a story about a boy named Bob, and they might sing a song about a baby bird. The gloss provides a sensory experience, the word list provides drill, and the story and song work to plant the phoneme into the child's literary world. Together, these stimuli work to build the client's long-term memory for the phoneme he is learning.

Short-Term Auditory Memory

Short-term auditory memory is "memory retained for only a relatively brief time period" (Nicolosi, Harryman, & Kresheck, 1983, p. 149). For example, when learning to produce /r/, a client might learn individual steps that are designed to get his jaw, lips, and tongue into position, and he will be taught to listen to and remember what the phoneme sounds like as he learns each individual movement. Once he moves everything adequately and produces /r/ correctly, however, the client can forget the auditory signals that resulted from each individual step. These auditory signals have served their purpose for the short term and are no longer necessary.

Clients who have severe short-term memory problems have a great deal of difficulty in articulation therapy because they usually cannot act immediately on incoming auditory signals. The most blatant example of this is the client on the autism spectrum who is verbal but who has articulation errors. Some of these clients seem unable to manipulate auditory information immediately. This makes it very difficult for them to engage in the traditional processes of articulation therapy. Yet, if long-term memory is functional, these clients can learn new phonemes because phoneme productions go into long-term memory and changes can be made. However, these changes often do not occur during therapy sessions; the client will correct his errors outside of therapy as his long-term memory allows.

Rote Auditory Memory

This is the "storage and retrieval of information without comprehension" (Nicolosi, Harryman, & Kresheck, 1983, p. 149). Clients can learn to produce speech units correctly, but carryover may be poor if meaning is not attached to them. For example, a client may learn to articulate a correct /s/ in the word *bus* when he reads the word on a list, but he may not connect this correct production to real life experiences with the word *bus*. When talking with his buddies, therefore, the client will continue to say *bus* incorrectly. He knows what a *bus* is, and he can say the word correctly, but the process of knowing and the process of producing are not connected. The client has learned in a rote way and not a functional one.

This difficulty was one of the main reasons that SLPs began to discuss the topic of *functional communication* and articulation therapy together. The best way to go about this is to do the rote work and the functional work together, perhaps going back and forth between the two. Any individual therapy session can contain both rote productions and functional conversation that contains the target. That way the client learns his new skill and simultaneously he learns to use it functionally within dialogue. This way rote auditory memory still has its utility in articulation therapy. Rote productions should be put into functional routines.

Reauditorization

The unvoiced recollection and holding of a sound production is known as *reauditorization*. It is that silent rehearsal everyone does when trying to remember something like a phone number, an address, or the spelling of a word. One rehearses the sequence to themselves in order to "hear" that which they are trying to remember. It is a method of stimulating short-term auditory memory and serves an important role in speech learning.

LISTENING TOOLS

A variety of tools can be used during the application of the methods described throughout this chapter. Some of these items are quite expensive while others cost nothing. Each has its own benefit to the client. Descriptions of these items are presented here in alphabetical order and some are pictured throughout this chapter. Young children often need time to play with these items before they are made to perform specific tasks with them. Therapists should follow sanitary procedures at all times when using these tools.

Boxes

Cardboard boxes of various sizes can be a no-cost tool for speech amplification and feedback. A small box can be held at the client's mouth, a somewhat larger box can be placed in front of or over the client's head, and a very large box can be crawled under or into. A large

The least expensive way to stimulate careful listening is to use the hands.

Cups and bowls create on-the-spot amplifiers.

Expandable tubes make listening fun.

Dampening speech with the hands and stimulate gross listening skills.

refrigerator box covered with a blanket and placed in the corner of a classroom makes a wonderful quiet workspace for speech therapy.

Cabinets

Toddlers and preschool children love to stick their heads into cabinet spaces and listen to their own sounds. The present author has always kept a lower cabinet in the therapy room empty for this purpose. Keep a few small toys in the cabinet to entice children to stick their heads in and have a mirror fastened to the back wall to get them interested in their own face and oral movements while they are making sounds in the cabinet. Little children love to crawl into a large cabinet space and close the door to play with sound inside.

Cardboard Tubes

One of the least expensive ways to amplify speech is to use the inner cardboard tubes of paper towels or wrapping paper. Hold the tube at the mouth and speak into it. These tubes will get wet with saliva as the kids place them in their mouths, so they must be used only once and then discarded. Paper towel and wrapping paper tubes are just the right size for children to hold and speak into. Van Riper used mailing tubes (Van Riper, 1947, p. 179).

Closets

Before speech-language pathologists worked in the classroom and before they had their own rooms for therapy, SLPs worked in any space that was available. In the public schools, this often meant they worked in janitorial closets. Interestingly enough, these often were excellent places to conduct articulation therapy because they are small, quiet, and contained. Nemoy and Davis called these small spaces "particular resonating chambers" (1937, p. 27).

Corners

The corner of a room makes a nice little nook for amplification. The SLP should sit the client in the corner facing outward and sit facing him (with her back to the room). The V-shaped walls of the corner act as a mini amphitheater for the SLP's voice. She can place a barrier such as a bookshelf or screen behind herself on the open side to block out extraneous noise. Place a mirror on one wall for quick visual reference.

Cups & Bowls

Cups and bowls are handy household objects that can be used to amplify speech. Hold a cup or bowl up to the mouth so that the child can make sound into the cavern. This is an excellent method to encourage feedback of gross sounds in young children. It will encourage them to make sounds into their bowls and cups every time they eat. Make sure the parents know to expect this during meals and snacks. Encourage parents to abandon sippy cups and to substitute them with regular cups for this purpose. Give the child a few sips at a time instead of a full cup to reduce the damage of spilling.

Dampeners

This playful technique can be used to heighten a client's awareness of speech targets. Use it when therapy session needs an energetic boost. The SLP closes her own ears and pretends she do not want to hear the client's productions, and allows him to do the same while listening to her. Dampening targets is an excellent method for stimulating gross listening skills in young children and those with significant cognitive delay. Use hands, fingers, earplugs, blankets, or pillows. The practice also heightens awareness of voice and resonance: "Place the student's hands over the ears and instruct him or her to hum, which heightens the sensation of vocal cord vibration" (Bleile, 2006, p. 264).

Echo Microphones

The *echo mic* is a fairly inexpensive way to amplify speech for ear training. Made of plastic, these hand-held devices are constructed somewhat like a nautilus shell with inner chambers that cause sound spoken into them to reflect back to the speaker. This echo is distorted so it cannot be used to stimulate refined phoneme amplification, but they are quite useful to orient a client to his own voice and speech in general. The echo mike is an inexpensive tool for early gross levels of auditory training.

Electronic Auditory Training Units

Electronic equipment is a much more expensive way to amplify speech. The Auditory Trainer is the professional standby in this area. An auditory trainer will give the best audio representation of speech available in the speech market. Home electronics stores also carry a variety of other products that are much less expensive and an ever-changing variety are available; some of these are even designed as toys. For years, the present author used a bright red tape recorder/radio/amplifier that had an attached yellow plastic microphone and headset that was purchased at one of these stores. Clients loved to talk and sing into this microphone to hear their own voice amplified in the room or into the headset.

An "echo mic" encourages basic listening.

Megaphones encourage playful listening.

Flexible Tubes

Any flexible tube can be used to amplify speech from mouth to ear. Tubes can be used to amplify speech from the therapist's mouth to the client's ear, from the client's mouth to the therapist's ear, or from the client's mouth to his own ear. The least expensive is flexible vinyl tubing made for plumbing projects that can be purchased at a hardware store. This inexpensive tubing comes on large rolls in a wide assortment of sizes, from ¼ inch in diameter to about one-foot in diameter. Purchase this tubing by the foot and make sure to wash and sanitize the tube before using it. Certain narrower sizes are also available at pet stores that carry aquarium supplies. One can also use more therapy-specific tools such as the Rapper Snapper (also knows as a *pop tube* or *Pull 'N Snap*), the Flex Talk Auditory Feedback Tube (SesnoryUniversity.com), and the Oral & Nasal Listener (SuperDuperInc.com).

Funnels & Megaphones

Funnels and megaphones of various shapes and sizes amplify speech outward. They are great tools to help clients listen to the SLP as she models sounds, and they are excellent to help children listen to one another in groups. Funnels can be purchases in grocery stores, drug stores and kitchen supply stores. Megaphones are harder to come by than funnels, but sometimes they are carried in toy stores. Arts and crafts stores often carry heavy-duty cardboard cones that can be used as megaphones, but for sanitary reasons they should be used only once and then discarded. A megaphone can also be made with the hands by cupping them around the mouth, or with a piece of paper by rolling it into a tube or funnel. Battery-operated megaphones are also available.

Hallways & Stairwells

Hallways and stairwells are excellent natural amplifiers of speech. They are great places to practice everything from whispering to singing to shouting and even to refined upper-level articulation work. Find a place that will not disturb others.

Hand Cupping

There is one tool that can be used to amplify speech models with no cost and that is to use the hands. Therapists can cup their hands behind a clients' ears to amplify their speech and then speak directly into one ear and then the other. Van Riper called this "cupping" and he had children do it to their own ears (Van Riper, 1947, p. 160). Cupping the hands behind the ears was a basic technique used by hearing-impaired people before hearing aids were developed. The client's own hands can also be used to feed his voice back to his ear. Have him cup one hand behind one of his own ears, and cup the other hand in front of his mouth pointing the fingers toward the cupped ear. The hand at his mouth catches his own sound and directs it right to his other hand at his ear.

Speak Directly into the Ear

The least expensive and most efficient way for a therapist to amplify her own speech is for her to place her mouth right next to the client's ear. Getting this close to a client works with developed rapport in an intimate setting.

Speak Louder

Perhaps the simplest way to amplify speech is to speak a little louder to the client. Don't talk louder all the time, just here and there to amplify this and that. Talking a little louder is something that parents and teachers can do without fuss or muss. The SLP should make sure to not abuse their vocal cords when speaking louder on a regular basis

A client can cup one hand over his mouth and the other behind his ear for on-the-spot amplification at no cost.

A toy stethoscope can be adapted to auditory training.

and should discontinue this practice if she cannot increase volume without damaging her own voice.

Toy Stethoscopes

Toy stethoscopes are usually made with hollow tubing. They can be used to amplify speech from the therapist's mouth to the client's ear, from the client's mouth to the therapist's ear, or from the client's mouth to his own ear exactly like flexible tubes described on the previous page. They are colorful and have little earpieces on one end. The other end (the part for placing near the heart) can be placed at the mouth.

Toy Telephones

Some toy telephones are constructed with a hollow tube that leads directly from the mouthpiece to the earpiece. Super Duper Publications now carries a toy telephone designed for this very purpose called the Webber Phone. Others are available as a regular children's toy.

FINAL CONCEPTS

This chapter closes with a few comments about controlling the auditory environment, auditory fatigue, and the variability of speech production.

Controlling the Auditory Environment

Early writers on the topic of articulation remediation assumed that teachers of speech would work in quiet environments, and all the early texts discussed articulation therapy as a one-on-one or small-group activity that took place in a quiet place separate from the regular classroom. This is called *pull-out* therapy. Children are pulled out of the classroom for articulation therapy to get them away from the hustle and bustle of the classroom so they can focus on their speech.

Control of the auditory environment is still one of the most important factors in articulation therapy, and it is critical that speech-language pathologist of the 21st century understand this. Articulation therapy must take place in a quiet environment so that auditory stimulation can be effective. Get the client in a place where he can hear and discriminate the phonemes and words that are being modeled. This is not an insignificant point. Top-notch articulation therapy demands quiet.

Some speech-language pathologists are required to work exclusively inside the noisy classroom using the *push-in* model. Others must share therapy rooms with other therapists and remedial teachers who provide competing auditory challenges. Many therapists wonder what to do about an administrator or supervisor who insists upon these unfavorable arrangements. The following strategies are suggested:

- Have the supervisor watch what can be accomplished with a client when given the opportunity to work privately.

- Ask the supervisor where they would prefer their own children to take violin, piano, or voice lessons. Would they want these lessons in a private room, or would they prefer their child to have their lessons in the middle of a busy classroom where they will be constantly interrupted?

- Talk about the *least restrictive environment*. Suggest that the classroom and other shared rooms are the *most restrictive environment* for learning speech sounds.

- Have an audiologist teach the staff about noise levels. Make sure the instructor talks about the optimum environment for speech sound recognition and discrimination. Have them talk about auditory distractions. Ask them to address the particular needs of children who are easily distracted by noise and those who have poor audition and limited auditory discrimination skills.

- Get parents to agree. One might drop hints or speak directly to the parents about how hard it is for the child to develop speech skills because of the classroom model. Help parents realize that their children would be much better served if they could be pulled out and instructed in an environment that is quiet. Most parents recognize this as common sense.

- If working in a classroom setting, arrange the environment to reduce interruptions. One idea is to make a heavy-duty cardboard refrigerator or stove box into a little house in which to work. One could cut a door out of one side, drape a plush quilt or blanket over the top and sides to absorb sound, and do therapy in there. Now the speech work can be done "in the classroom" but ambient sounds will be minimized.

Small enclosed spaces help control the auditory environment and amplify speech naturally.

Auditory Fatigue

The term *auditory fatigue* refers to the "normal temporary loss of sensation… following a period of stimulation" (Nicolosi, Harryman, & Kresheck, 1983, p. 94). Auditory fatigue is not a skill but a common deficient occurrence. Clients can experience auditory fatigue right in the middle of therapy as the result of a little too much auditory work. For example, a client might be listening to himself as he performs well trial after trial, and then suddenly he becomes confused. He might say, "I can't hear it" or "It doesn't sound right." Sometimes a client just shakes his head or looks confused. In these cases, the client needs a few minutes of silence or another type of activity to give time for the auditory system to recover. Allow a few silent moments to complete a turn in a game, draw a picture, or talk about something else, and then the listening or production work can continue again.

Speech-language pathologists with years of experience usually work in such a way that auditory fatigue is avoided. The SLP builds the client's work up to a point close to auditory fatigue, takes note, and then alters the activity. Therapists themselves can experience auditory fatigue during the course of therapy, especially at the end of a long and difficult week. Learn to pace the work throughout the week to avoid this auditory fatigue as a therapist.

Variability of Speech Perception

A final word about the variable nature of speech perception during conversation will conclude the discussion on auditory training. Peter Ladefoged, the great phonetician, wrote about this toward the end of his career. He said that the perception of speech is not all auditory:

> *"Although we usually perceive syllables and words as wholes, it is also true that we can listen to speech in other ways. We use whatever we can. We look at the speaker and get information from the face. We match syllables and words, using top-down and bottom-up processing. And we sometimes pick out particular sounds to get at the meaning of what we are listening to. There is no one way of perceiving speech"* (Ladefoged, 2005, p. 110).

SUMMARY

Training the ear to hear target phonemes and phonological patterns may be the most important element of speech training. It is included in therapy with clients who need it.

	Child	Therapist	Technique Used
1	This one?	Yeah. Say, *Sssssssssspoon*.	Model Prolongation
2	*Poon*	Listen again: *S–s–s ——— poon*.	Anticipatory listening Repetition Pause after target
3	*Poon—Shhhh*	Nice try. Listen again: *Sssssss* [Said louder]. Say, *Sssssss* [Said louder].	Reward Anticipatory listening Simplification of the task Modeling Isolation of target Prolongation of target Amplification of target
4	*Shhhh*	Make it tinier. *Sssssss*. Like a snake. *Sssssss*.	Direct Instruction Model Prolongation Creative imagery
5	*Sssss*	Perfect! That's it! *Sssss*.	Reward Imitation of the client
6	[Smiles]	Excellent. I love what you said that time.	Reward Rapport building
7	[Smiles more broadly]	*Sssssssssss*. Try it again. Make the snake sound.	Model Prolongation Isolation of target Creative imagery
8	*Sssssss*	Perfect! *Sssssssss*. Again.	Reward Imitation of the client Prolongation
9	*Sssssss*	Woo-hoo! You got it!	Reward
10	[Smiles again]	[Singing] Youuuu did it! Youuuuuuu made the S! S–s–s–s–s–s! Youuuuuuu made the S!	Reward Rapport building Singing Repetition of target
11	[Singing] I-I-I-I did it!	[Singing] You-woo-woo-woo did it!	Preventing auditory fatigue by switching gears into song
12	[Singing] I-yai-yai-yai did it!	[Intoning] [Singing] You-woo-woo-woo did it! Hey, check this out. [Brings out rapper snapper] [Said into tool] *Sssssssss*. [Hands tool to client]	Intoning Singing Prolongation of target Amplification of target

TABLE 6 — Sample Therapy Dialogue

Table continues next page...

TABLE 6 — Sample Therapy Dialogue

	Child	Therapist	Technique Used
13	*Sssssssss.* [Said into rapper snapper]	Again. Make that snake sound again.	Reward Amplification Creative imagery
14	*Sssssssss*	Oh no! Here comes a snake! *Sssssss!!!*	Creative imagery Dramatic flair Imitation of the client
15	*Sssssssss*	[Smile]	Silent turn
16	*Sssssssss*	[Smile] Oh, no! I don't like snakes!	Silent turn Dramatic flair
17	*Sssssssss*	Good little snake. Now try this: — *S–s–s–s–s* — *poon.*	Creative imagery Repetition of target Pause before target Pause after target Model word
18	*Poonsss*	[Whispering] Now try this: Say the snake sound and then say poon. Listen: *S–s–s–sssssssss* — *poon* [Uses a visual cue for S]	Whispering Anticipatory listening Creative imagery Direct instruction Auditory sequential memory Prolongation Pause after target Visual cue
19	*Sssss — poon*	[Whispering] There you go! *Sssss — poon.*	Reward Whispering Prolongation Pause after target
20	[Whispering] *Sssss — poon*	[Whispering] Excellent. Listen again: — *S–poon.*	Whispering Pausing before target Shortening target Pausing after target
21	*S—poon*	Now you try all by yourself: *S—*	Auditory Closure
22	*Spoon*	Nice. Again. *S—*	Auditory Closure
23	*Spoon*	*S—*	Auditory Closure
24	*Spoon*	*Spoon.*	Imitating client
25	*Spoon*	*Spoon.* You got it!	Imitating client Reward

5

Teaching Speech Movements with Cues

Giving the client more information about how and where to move

"Like two actors on stage momentarily forgetting their lines, the [therapy] scene was rescued by a whispered cue from the clinician."

– Danielle Ripich & John Panagos, 1985

This chapter discusses the use of cues in the teaching of phonemes, syllables, words, and the supersegmentals. Cues are used to teach and/or to remind clients what to say or do. Cues engage cognitive processing and can bring consistency to phoneme production. There is nothing magical about using a cue system and there are no guarantees that a client will learn a specific speech target just because a certain cue was used. Cues are a nice addition to the teaching of any phoneme because they help clients think about what they are learning. Using cues is a method that teachers have used since the beginning of recorded history.

Individual therapists develop most cue systems for their own personal use, but some systems have been formalized and described in written material. Only a few have been studied formally, yet each of these studies has demonstrated that cues have certain value in therapy. This

chapter describes the cue systems that one can learn from published manuals, research reports, and online sources. Cue systems that can be learned only by taking specific training seminars are mentioned briefly. The present author's personal set of cues for consonants and vowels is also included.

BACKGROUND

A cue is a signal, hint, prompt, or reminder. A cue is "an aid… which promotes a correct response" (Nicolosi, Harryman, & Kresheck, 1983, p. 66). A cue is "a signal for action… a piece of information or circumstance that aids the memory in retrieving details not recalled spontaneously… a hint or indication about how to behave in particular circumstances" (Jewell & Abate, 2001, p. 415).

Cues help focus a client's attention on a target or on aspects of a target, and they enhance a client's perception of the production by bringing redundancy to the learning process. Cues can be utilized to teach any aspect of speech remediation, from phonemes to syllables, words, and supersegmentals.

Cues can be verbal, visual, auditory, tactile, proprioceptive, or conceptual in nature. They may come in the form of facial expressions, signs, natural gestures, written symbols, pictures, numbers, shapes, colors, alphabet letters, toys, and more. Cues can be used to teach new skills, or they can be used to remind clients to use old ones. A cue is most effective when it matches a client's cognitive

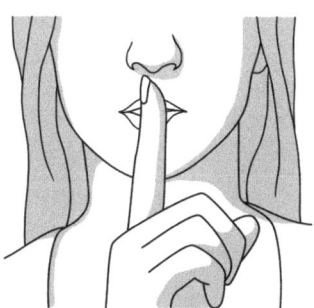

Some speech cues are universal, such as this one for /ʃ/.

Pointing to the mouth may be the simplest visual cue of all.

level and is relevant to him. Cues are usually faded over time so that clients do not continue to rely on them. Some cues are compiled into complete systems that undergo formal investigations while others are made up on the spot for single usage. Some cues are universal. Cues are used only when they are needed: "By and large, the need for [cues] should be minimal" (Hegde, 1998, p. 169).

Research on Cues

A search of the American Speech-Language-Hearing Association (ASHA) journals reveals a variety of research projects devoted to the relationship between the use of cues and speech improvement. Results of these studies are presented below in chronological order to reveal the unfolding nature of these ideas over time. Some of these studies concern language, but generalizations from these to cues for articulation and motor speech therapy can be made. Each of these studies reveals that cues may have certain benefits.

- Klick (1985) reported improved intelligibility in one five-year-old female with dyspraxia when using the *Adapted Cueing Technique* (described on page 77) during a three-month period.

- Shelton and Garves (1985) studied the effect of using the signed alphabet as cues along with traditional phoneme stimulation methods to facilitate volitional sequences of sound production in one child with apraxia. Preliminary results revealed a positive outcome.

- Weismer and Hesketh (1993) found that gestures facilitated vocabulary comprehension in kindergarten-age children with and without specific language impairment.

- Records (1994) found that visual cues improved comprehension of speech and language tasks in adults with acquired aphasia. Results showed that the more ambiguous the task, the more these clients relied upon the visual information.

- Green and Norrix (1997) reviewed the literature

and cited a number of studies showing that visual cues provided by a trainer's face facilitated auditory discrimination of a phoneme.

- Hustad and Beukelman (2001) studied the use of topic and initial-consonant alphabet cues by dysarthric patients who used them to aid in their own intelligibility. They found that both types of cues improved intelligibility in these patients, but that alphabet signs to cue the initial consonant in words was more helpful that topic cues.

- Massaro and Light (2004) demonstrated that a computer-animated talking head was a positive cue system for speech learning with clients who were hearing impaired. (Described further along in this chapter under "Computer Cues" on page 73.)

- Hustad and Garcia (2005) found that clients with cerebral palsy could be understood more easily when they accompanied their verbal speech with alphabet cues and other hand signals.

- Huber and Chandrasekaran (2006) found that cueing affects client's control of vocal loudness.

- Norrix et al. (2007) suggested that children with specific language impairment who have difficulty with speech perception also might have difficulty with broader conceptualization of speech including the processing of visual cues. They concluded that speech-learning activities that coordinate auditory and visual stimuli might be necessary for effective speech training in these children.

- Hirata and Kelly (2010) studied the process of learning vowels in a second language. They found that vowel learning improved when clients watched cues from the speakers' mouths but not from the speakers' hands, and they observed that watching the therapist's mouth helped the subjects more than listening alone.

- Picou, Ricketts, and Hornsby (2011) found that visual cues did not improve listening effort in twenty adults with normal hearing. The authors surmised that visual cues help listening behavior only when they have meaning for the client.

Learning Styles & Cue Selection

Therapists in the mid-20th century were interested in learning styles, and some devised a system for sorting clients into groups according to the types of cues that might serve them best in speech training. The following categories and notes are from Fröeschels (1948) and may help therapists with cues selection.

Audiles

Clients called *audiles* learn best through auditory input. They are *ear-minded*. Auditory cues may be quite helpful for them, as will all other methods of auditory stimulation.

Visiles

Clients called *visiles* learn best through visual stimulation. They are *eye-minded*. These clients learn best through visual models, diagrams, mouth models, hand gestures, written symbols, and so forth.

Motiles

Clients called *motiles* learn best through feeling, i.e., tactile/proprioceptive input. They are *feeling-minded*. These clients are best taught by drawing their attention to the feelings associated with movement and position of the mouth, and the tactile sensations of airflow, frication, occlusion, nasality, and so forth.

Mixed Imagery Types

Mixed imagery types are clients who learn best through a balanced auditory-visual-tactile-proprioceptive approach. Hands-on tactile cues will be a nice addition to therapy for them, and may be combined with other auditory and visual cues.

CUE OPTIONS

The rest of this chapter discusses cue options. Speech-language pathologists carry the responsibility of selecting or designing an appropriate cue system for each individual client who needs one. Cues are selected based on the client's age, areas of interest, cognitive status, learning style, and the ease with which the cues can be adapted to the learning environment. Trial and error is used throughout the process to determine if a cue or a set of cues is of benefit to the particular client at hand. The cues described in the rest of this chapter are presented in no particular order although first is one of Van Riper's most basic suggestions.

Personalities / Conceptual Cues

Van Riper taught that each individual phoneme should be given a personality to help client's pay attention to it and to mark its individual identity:

> *"All good teachers of speech correction give personalities to the sounds with which they work. They give them names, traits, and even faces. From such identification comes recognition; from recognition comes discrimination; from discrimination comes success"* (Van Riper, 1939, p. 180).

The present author uses the term *conceptual cues* for these personalities. A conceptual cue is a concrete metaphor that helps a client grasp hold of an abstract idea. In this case, the abstract idea is the phoneme. Some of the most common conceptual cues still in use include the snake for /s/, the bumblebee for /z/, the sleeping child for /ʃ/, the choo-choo train for /tʃ/, and the roaring lion for /r/. Fröeschels (1948) and Flowers (1963) were popular

sources for cues during the mid-20th century. Theirs and other conceptual cues are summarized in Table 7 on the next page.

Symbolic Cues

Any picture, object, or symbol can be used as a cue for speech learning as long as it helps the client to conceptualize the target. Here are several examples that are common.

Face Pictures

Drawings or photographs of people positioning the mouth for phonemes can be used as cues. For example, one might use a picture of an open mouth for /ɑ/ and a picture of a closed mouth for /m/.

Abstract Pictures

Abstract pictures can be used as cues. For example, one might use a picture of an open window for /ɑ/ and a picture of a closed window for /m/. Abstract pictures such as these are only used with clients who understand the analogy.

Hand-Drawn Palatograms

Palatograms can serve as very useful cues in articulation therapy. Van Riper wrote that therapists have been using hand-drawn palatograms in articulation therapy for centuries. Borden and Busse included such drawings in their text published in 1925, and Berry and Eisenson wrote about them in 1956. Marshalla used them in her classic introductory oral-motor text of 1992. Lines, shaded areas, circles, stars and other shapes can be drawn on palatograms to help clients understand place of articulation. Find a complete set of these palatograms in Chapter 13, *Facilitating Tongue Movement.*

Alphabet Cues

Alphabet letters provide simple cues for all phonemes, and some of the letters can also remind clients of mouth shape. For example, the letter "O" can cue lip rounding for /o/.

Visual Symbols on Written Letters

Therapists often draw shapes and symbols on, around, or next to written letters to signal aspects of phoneme production. For example, draw a star next to the letter "T" to remind a client to make it with a burst of air, draw a smiley face under letter "E" to remind the client to retract the lips, or draw a small circle under letter "W" to remind a client to round the lips. Berry and Eisenson described this technique as a way to teach about the escape of airflow laterally during production of a lateral /s/.

> *"A visual symbol may be used to denote the defective sound. For example, if the patient produces /s/ with a*

		TABLE 7 — Common Conceptual Cues From Fröeschels (1948), Flowers (1963), and Common Use
Category	**Phoneme**	**Common Conceptual Cues**
Stops	/p/	Balloon bursting; bubble popping; popcorn popping; motorboat sound; puffing on a pipe
	/b/	Bobbing bubble; bouncing ball; rug beating; baby babbling; sheep bleating
	/t/	Watch ticking; tsk-ing; tapping fingernails
	/d/	Broken car motor chugging; water dripping; drumming; "duh!" (no kidding); baby word *dada* or *daddy*
	/k/	Coughing; hacking; choking; clucking; crashing; "caw-caw" (crow sound)
	/g/	Gulping; water glugging out of a bottle; "guh-guh" (bullfrog sound)
Nasals	/m/	Humming; "mmmm, that's good!" (eating yummy food)
	/n/	"No-no" (negative sound); whining dog; nose sound; mosquito sound
	/ŋ/	Gong; ringing bell; auto horn; siren; "ng!" (happy newborn sound)
Glides	/w/	"Wah-wah-wah!" (crying-baby sound); "whee!" (sound of delight); "oooo!" (sound of awe); whistling
	/l/	Lullaby singing "la-la-la"; wave lapping; the "tongue sound"
	/j/	"Yes"; "yeah"; "yo"; yipping sound; "smiling sound"
	/r/	Growling dog or tiger; roaring lion; crowing rooster; "err" (self-starter sound); gearshift sound; stalled-motor sound
Voiceless Fricatives and Affricates	/θ/	Angry goose; pinwheel; radiator; "tongue-out sound"
	/f/	Angry cat; hissing cat; spitting cat; fizzing sound; falling sound
	/s/	Hissing-snake; whistling tea kettle; flat-tire sound
	/ʃ/	"Shhh!" (hush sound); sound of the wind
	/tʃ/	"Ah-choo" sneezing sound; "choo-choo" train sound; chopping sound
	/h/	Panting dog; sighing; making breath fog on a mirror or frosty window

Table continues next page...

TABLE 7 — Common Conceptual Cues
From Fröeschels (1948), Flowers (1963), and Common Use

Category	Phoneme	Common Conceptual Cues
Voiced Fricatives and Affricates	/ð/	Electric razor; motor or engine (airplane, car, jet ski, motor boat…)
	/v/	Shiver; vacuum cleaner; electric razor; motor or engine (airplane, car, jet ski, motor boat…)
	/z/	Bumble bee; electric razor; motor or engine (airplane, car, jet ski, motor boat…)
	/ʒ/	Buzzing saw; scraping; filing; electric razor; motor or engine (airplane, car, jet ski, motor boat…)
	/dʒ/	Jumping sound; jumping motor sound

left lateral emission, the symbol S may be used, with an arrow indicating the direction of the emission" (Berry & Eisenson, 1956, p. 161–162).

Colors

Therapists often write the letters of individual words with colorful markers to signal place, manner, or voice. For example, the word *cat* could be written in three colors. The "C" might be drawn in blue to remind the client to lift the back of his tongue, the "A" might be drawn in black to indicate that it is an open mouth vowel, and the "T" might be drawn in red to remind him to lift the tip of his tongue.

Toys / Objects

Toys and other objects can be used to mark sequences of sounds, syllables, or words. For example, a therapist might place three blocks in a line on the table. The three blocks could represent the three phonemes of the word *Don*, or

the three syllables of the word *banana*, or the three words in the sentence *Don likes bananas*.

Computer Cues

The burgeoning field of computer software (applications; apps) for articulation therapy is beyond the scope of this manual because development in this area is too fast to be adequately represented in printed media. Apps designed purely for fun and entertainment can be used as any game or reinforcement system of course, and apps made for educational purposes can be adapted to speech. Some apps are being designed specifically as instruction for speech production and more of these should be expected as time goes on. Any of these programs can be used as a cue system.

One such program should be mentioned by name because it has been studied in a formal way. "Baldi" is a computer-animated talking head that clients watch during speech learning activities. Baldi allows the viewer to

Some alphabet letters work nicely to cue mouth shapes.

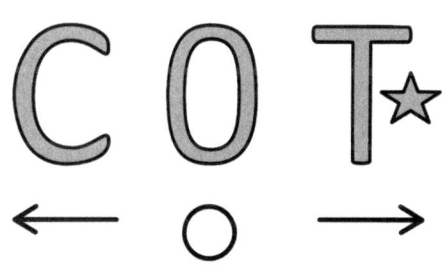

Visual symbols can help clients remember to perform certain actions. In this case: arrow (back or front of the mouth), circle (open mouth), and star (burst of air).

see jaw, lip, and tongue movement during speech in an x-ray type image called "visible speech." Massaro and Light (2004) demonstrated that Baldi was a positive addition to speech learning with clients who are hearing impaired, but it certainly could be a valuable cue system for any speech-training program.

Creative Imagery Cues

Creative imagery is a natural way of helping young children learn abstract ideas. Many SLPs have made up creative stories to help clients understand speech movements for phoneme production. For example, as long as anyone can remember, therapists have called the tongue "Mr. Tongue" and they have used him as the main character in a story designed to aid in the development of gross oral movements in young children. This concept may seem silly but many little children find this story to be delightful.

Mr. Tongue

> *Mr. Tongue lives in a house (the mouth). He washes the walls (the tongue tip sweeps against the inner cheek walls). He paints the ceiling (the tongue tip sweeps up against the palate) and arranges the curtain hanging in the back window (the velum is stroked by the tongue tip).*
>
> *The window in Mr. Tongue's house opens and closes (the front teeth come together and apart), as do the shutters (the*

Toys can be used to teach phoneme sequencing.

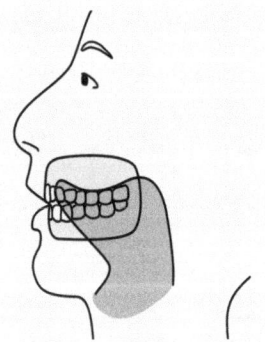

"Baldi" the computer-animated talking head provides realistic cues about jaw, lip, and tongue position. (Adapted from Massaro & Light, 2004.)

lips open and close). Mr. Tongue dances around his house (wiggles back and forth) with music on (while producing voice), but he also raps on the ceiling to keep the upstairs neighbors quiet (taps the palate with the tongue tip).

Mr. Tongue goes outside to check the weather (the tongue pokes outside the mouth), where he looks left, right, up, and down (the tongue stretches in all these directions). He stays inside if the weather is bad (the tongue retreats into the mouth), and he hides way in the back if he is scared of lightening and thunder (the tongue retracts to the back of the mouth).

Sometimes Mr. Tongue gets fat (wide), and sometimes he gets skinny (narrow). If it floods, Mr. Tongue pushes the water (saliva, water, juice) to the back of his house and down the drain (the client swallows).

Sometimes Mr. Tongue has visitors (e.g., gummy bears). He invites the visitors to sit on his chairs to the left or right (hold the bear between the molars on the left or right). Sometimes these visitors sit in the front window to look outside (hold the bear between the incisors).

Sometimes we help Mr. Tongue paint his shutters (we put lipstick or lip gloss on the lips), and we help him clean his windows (brush the teeth). Sometimes we help him clean himself (we brush the surface of the tongue with a toothbrush or Toothette®).

Mr. Tongue sleeps inside his house with the windows and shades closed (the tongue stays inside the closed mouth during oral rest).

Natural Gesture Cues

Therapists often use natural gestures to instruct many aspects of speech production. They use the arms and hands like a police officer that is controlling traffic, like a choral leader that is directing singers, or like a conductor that is leading an orchestra. Sweeping arm and hand motions signal sound prolongation for continuant sounds, quick ticks with the hands indicate the quick burst of energy for stop consonants, and shaking fingers signal frication. The arms are raised or lowered to cue high and low pitch variations. The hands are clapped to mark syllables in words. These natural gestures are usually made up on the spot, and some therapists use them unconsciously. The consistent conscious application of these cues allows therapists to develop a set that can be taught to other speech and language stimulators in the client's life.

Signed Alphabet Cues

Many speech-language pathologists use the signed alphabet as a cue system with hearing clients in articulation and

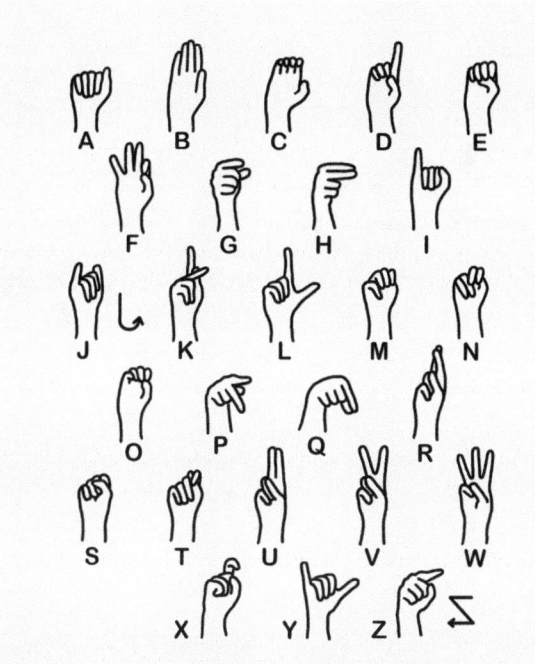

The signed alphabet makes an excellent cue system.

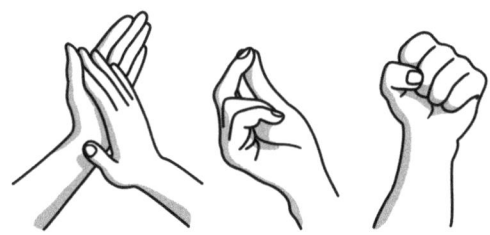

Natural gestures like hand clapping, finger snapping, and making a fist are excellent on-the-spot speech cues.

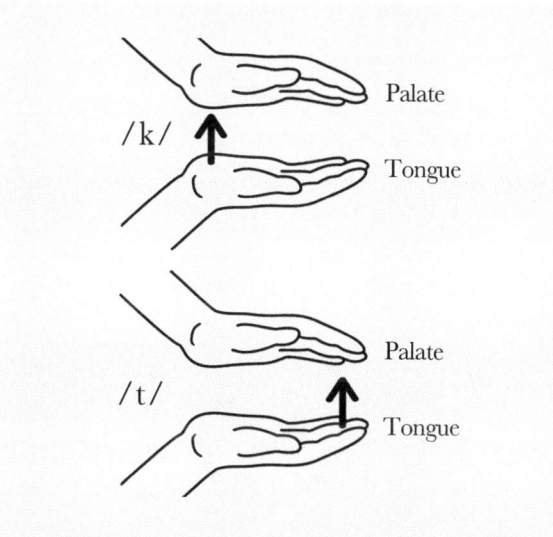

The hands can be used to cue tongue movement relative to the palate.

motor speech therapy. The signed alphabet can be used whether or not the client knows the written or signed alphabet, and whether or not he can read. Most therapists seem to sign the target phoneme but not the whole word. For example, when working on /d/ at the beginning of the word *dog*, the therapist says the whole word but signs only the /d/. The rest of the phonemes in the word go unsigned.

Organic Phonetic Cues

Most SLPs develop their own signals for the place, manner, and voicing features of consonants. The present author has asked hundreds of therapists to share their organic, self-made consonant cues and has discovered how remarkably similar they usually are: "This type of prompting tends to come naturally for most clinicians" (Pena-Brooks & Hegde, 2000, p. 410). Organic place, manner, and voicing cues are usually done on or near the therapist's face so clients can watch and imitate. The following place, manner, and voicing cues are common examples:

- *Cue bilabial contact:* Therapist places one hand next to, or in front of, her own lips. The index finger and thumb are pinched together to cue bilabial contact. The fingers are separated to cue bilabial release.

- *Cue labio-dental contact:* Therapist smiles broadly to expose the upper teeth and points to the contact made with the lower lip against the upper teeth.

- *Cue lingua-dental contact:* Therapist opens her mouth slightly and smiles to expose the teeth and tongue tip and points to her own tongue tip as it protrudes between the front teeth.

- *Cue lingua-alveolar contact:* Therapist opens her mouth fairly wide to expose the tongue and alveolar ridge and points to the alveolus to cue tongue-tip articulation there.

- *Cue lingua-palatal contact:* Therapist opens mouth wide and points to the upper side teeth to cue the sides of the tongue to stretch up to the palate.

- *Cue lingua-velar contact:* Therapist opens mouth wide to expose the back of the tongue and the velum and points to the velum to cue the back of the tongue to elevate to there.

- *Cue plosiveness:* The plosives are made with a quick burst of air, so therapists use a gestural cue that suggests a quick burst of energy. Examples include: clapping, clicking the fingers, clicking the tongue, smacking the lips, rapping on the desk or table, stomping the feet, or exploding the hands open from a fisted position.

- *Cue nasality:* The nasals are made through the nose, so most therapists develop some sort of gesture to the nose. For example, pointing to the nose or to the side of the nose to signal nasality.

- *Cue frication:* Frication is made as sound is prolonged and air turbulence is created. Many SLPs wiggle the fingers in front of the mouth to indicate the air turbulence of frication.

- *Cue gliding:* The glides are made by gliding from one vowel to another, thus many therapists develop a gesture that indicates this sliding motion. For example, the hand could move forward on the first vowel, and swoop back in transition to the second vowel.

- *Cue voice or voiceless-ness:* Therapists may point to the larynx to cue the production of voice and point away from the larynx to signal the absence of voice.

Hand Model Cues

The hands and fingers can model many elements of speech movement. Opening the hands can signal the expansion of the lungs for inhalation, and fisting of the hands can cue the compression of the lungs during exhalation. The fingers can be used to represent the vocal folds moving together or apart.

> *"One can often use the hands to demonstrate movements of the tongue relative to the palate. Let one hand represent the palate and the other the tongue... Then move the hand representing the tongue up or down as indicated"* (Bosley, 1981, p. 13).

Tactile Cues

Certain cues are tactile in nature, meaning that the client is touched on the skin to teach or to remind him of a phoneme, movement, position, or sound quality. Tactile cues have also been called *hands-on* cues. "Touch, or tactile cues, may provide a great deal of information about the way sounds are made" (Carrell & Tiffany, 1960, p. 45.) "Touch cues draw attention to an aspect of a sound's production" (Bleile, 2006, p. 8). An advantage of tactile or hands-on cues is that the therapist can control them, but a disadvantage is that the client may reject them. Another disadvantage is that the client will be exposed to them only a certain number of minutes per week when he is with the therapist. A better option for touch cues, therefore, is to have the client perform them directly on himself. This process may be the most useful to him in the long run because he can cue himself whenever he needs to.

Cues vs. Stimulation

It is important to differential between *tactile cues* and *tactile stimulation*. A tactile cue is a hint or reminder about speech movement that can be given anywhere on the skin and is the subject of this section. Tactile stimulation, on the other hand, is used to create the target speech movement. The present chapter refers to tactile cues only.

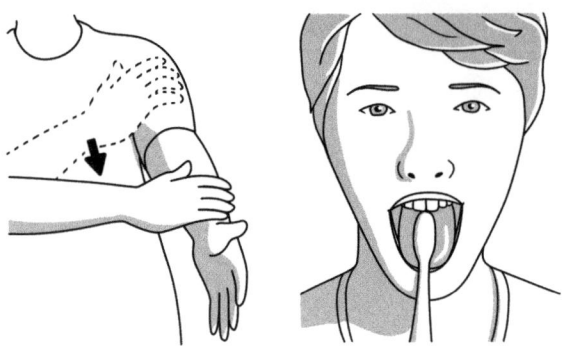

A tactile cue (left) is a hint given anywhere on the skin. Tactile stimulation (right) is designed to facilitate oral movement and position.

Gentle wipes with a dry terry washcloth can be used to mark the lips for bilabial articulation.

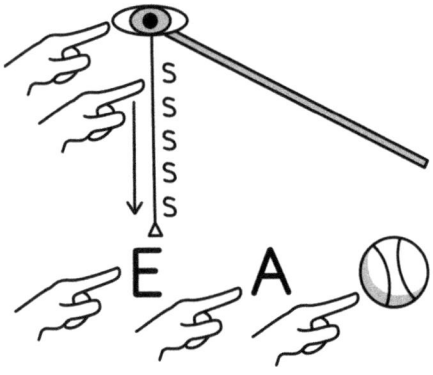

Sample of Hammer's cues for the sentence, "I see a ball."

Marshalla's place cues emphasize place of articulation from front to back.

"We use tactual cues as supplements when first presenting the new target, and fade them out as the child gains facility. Tactual cues are simply ways in which the child can, through feeling, gain additional information about the image of the target. They may take any form which seems to work with the particular child" (Hodson & Paden, 1983, p. 59).

Marking Techniques

The phrase *marking the target* means to indicate, through tactile means, the place where articulation should occur. Marking the target is a specialized form of tactile cue. Marking the target means to give tactile input directly to the target(s) of articulatory contact. Marking is a method that Van Riper and many other therapists use: "Identify contacts by stroking or pressure" (Van Riper, 1954, p. 217). The key to success in using marking cues lies in the therapist's knowledge of place of articulation.

Combining Cues

Hammer (2012) uses a combination of verbal, object, and gestural cues together for children with apraxia. He bases this speech training on the theory that children with apraxia need a multisensory approach that focuses on phoneme sequencing. His verbal cues describe the outstanding place, manner, and voicing features of target phonemes. For example, the cue for /s/ is the "smiley windy sound" and the cue for /z/ is the "buzzing windy sound." These verbal cues then are paired with simple gestures and common pictures or objects to aid in the sequencing of these sounds into words.

An example of teaching /s/ in the sentence "I see a ball" is offered in the illustration on the previous page. Clients point to the eye (for "I"), the string of the toy fishing pole (while saying /s/), the magnetic E (for /i/ in "see"), the written word "a" (for the word "a"), and then a real ball to learn how to incorporate /s/ into the sentence "I see a ball." Hammer stresses the importance of fading the cues over time and varying the context of functional work so that client will gain automatic control over their productions.

Pam's Place Cues

The present author has developed a set of cues for vowels and consonants that emphasize the place of articulation. It is based on the consonant chart and vowel quadrilateral and is arranged from front-to-back along the midline from the lips to the glottis. This is a hands-off system, so the therapist models the cues on and near her own mouth and face, and the client uses his own hands to imitate them on himself. The cues are taught in manner and voice sets that are arranged from front to back. Clients are taught only those cues they need. A few of these cues are pictured here (previous page, bottom). Pam's Place Cues are modeled in videos found online at PamMarshalla.com/cues where they are also available to download for free.

Adapted Cueing Technique

The Adapted Cueing Technique (ACT) is a visual cue system designed to teach place and manner that is done with the hands. ACT includes "manually presented visual cues created to accompany orally presented speech in the treatment of dysarthria" (Klick, 1985, p. 256). It is a modification of the signed alphabet. The therapist puts her hand in a letter shape, positions it near her own mouth, and then moves the hand to signal the trajectory of oral movement required to perform the phoneme. For example, to stimulate /l/, the therapist puts her hand in the sign for letter "L," holds the hand near her face, and then moves the hand upward in the same movement pattern required by the tongue tip to achieve lingua-alveolar contact.

Manner of articulation is stimulated by alterations in the hand's action. Quick, forward movements away from the therapist's face signal stop consonants. Slower movements that extend toward the side of the speaker mark continuants. Phoneme shapes and movements can be sequenced one-after-another to teach phoneme sequencing in words, phrases, and sentences.

Vowels are cued in the ACT system by place of articulation and jaw height. Each vowel is cued with the hand in a C-shape. The C-shape is round and full for the low vowels and squashed for the high vowels. The C-shape is held toward the lips for the front vowels, and toward the back of the cheeks for the back vowels. Sequencing two vowels one after the other in sequence cues the diphthongs.

Cued Speech

The hands-off cue system known as Cued Speech was developed as a general communication system and not necessarily to teach individual phoneme productions. It has become a worldwide phenomenon and has been adapted to 60 languages. According to the website of the National Cued Speech Association: "Cued Speech is a mode of communication based on the phonemes and properties of traditionally spoken languages. Cueing allows users who are deaf or hard of hearing or who have language/communication disorders to access the basic, fundamental properties of spoken languages through the use of vision."

Cued Speech is a gestural system.

PROMPT is a hands-on cue system.

This system employs hand gestures around the face and mouth that allow the client to see the spoken word. There are eight basic hand shapes for all consonants of English. The vowels are identified by hand placement and movement near the mouth. Cued Speech allows one to visually communicate words and sentences. It is used with both deaf and hearing individuals, and it works well when a client has a cochlear implant. The prime goal of Cued Speech is to develop literacy. General information about Cued Speech can be obtained at CuedSpeech.org.

PROMPT

The cue system known as Prompts for Restructuring Oral Muscular Phonetic Targets (PROMPT) consists of highly stylized hands-on cues designed to train phoneme position and sequence for children with apraxia (Hayden, 1984). Their website explains that PROMPT should be thought of as "a program to develop motor skill in the development of language for interaction." It is a multidimensional approach to speech production that integrates the physical aspects of speech motor performance with the cognitive, linguistic, social, and emotional aspects of speech learning. PROMPT is used to cue place of articulation, closure, manner, jaw position, tension, sequencing and timing of phonemes, and stress patterns. The cues guide the oral mechanism into phoneme positions so that imitation is avoided, and this makes it a valuable cue system for clients with apraxia. PROMPT can be used with clients of all ages and ability levels, beginning at six months of age. The cues are learned in seminars taught through the PROMPT Institute. More information can be obtained at PromptInstitute.com.

Visual Phonics

The cue system known as Visual Phonics consists of a combination of hand cues and written symbols that together represent the English phonemes. The phrase "See the sound" is used to describe it. The system can be learned in a series of training seminars offered through the International Communication Learning Institute at SeeTheSound.org. An introductory video is also offered

on the website. Visual Phonics has been discussed in a number of scientific papers, a complete list of which can be found on their website. The system is geared toward the teaching of reading.

Lindamood Phoneme Sequencing

The Lindamood Phonemic Sequencing® (LiPS®) program is an outgrowth of the original Lindamood-Bell Learning Process, and was known formally as "Auditory Discrimination in Depth" (ADD). The LiPS program is a cognitive approach to reading, spelling, and speech based on phonics, phonemic awareness, reading fluency, vocabulary, and comprehension. It includes hands-off cues designed to teach all the phonemes of the language. As of 2019, there were 50 Lindamood-Bell learning centers in the United States and over 150 seasonal learning centers ("learning camps") around the globe. The LiPS program has been involved in research endeavors involving reading skill development. A complete list of references can be found on their website, LindamoodBell.com.

Touch-Cue Method

The Touch-Cue Method (TCM) designed by Bashir, Grahamjones, and Boswick (1984) is a hands-on tactile cue system for clients with developmental apraxia. The

Visual Phonics is a symbolic visual cue system.

Lindamood Bell is a gestural system.

The Touch-Cue Method is a self-cueing system.

program is divided into three stages: (1) production of the phoneme in isolation, (2) production of the phoneme in nonsense and meaningful words, and (3) phoneme carry-over methods. These cues are done on the client's face or neck that are given simultaneously with auditory models. Cues reported in the original article were designed for eight phonemes only —/b/, /d/, /g/, /s/, /ʃ/, /f/, /n/, and /l/. After the client learns the cue for the individual targets, he then is taught to sequence two together such as /b – d/. Then he progresses to CVC words, and then to polysyllabic words and words with blends. The article that describes this process provides no research evidence to support its use; it is a descriptive article only.

SUMMARY

Therapists use a wide variety of cue systems when teaching phonemes, syllables, and words. Some are homemade, others are formal, and a few have been researched. Many SLPs select a system that they prefer, design their own system, or combine systems appropriate to their caseloads.

6

The Motokinesthetic Method

The first formalized speech movement training system

> *"The child's big task in learning or in correcting speech is to find the way to move his mouth in order to make sounds correctly."*
>
> – Edna Hill-Young & Sara Stinchfield Hawk, 1955

The classic method of articulation therapy known as *motokinesthetic speech training* (Young & Hawk, 1955) is mentioned more than any other speech movement training system in textbooks on articulation and phonology. The motokinesthetic method was the first proposed sensorimotor approach to phoneme learning. It is a method for developing speech movements through direct manipulation of the speech structures.

This chapter describes the motokinesthetic speech training method in enough detail to keep it alive into the 21st century. Most readers will discover that they are using many motokinesthetic cues already. This is because the motokinesthetic methods have become so widespread they are woven into the very fabric of articulation and motor speech therapy: "The more common movement

indicators [of motokinesthetics] have become so standard that the user may not even be aware of their source" (Bosley, 1981, p. 10). For example, if a client cannot will not press his lips together for production of a bilabial consonant, virtually every SLP eventually reaches over and uses her fingers to press the client's lips together. This is one of many very simple yet now universal techniques that Edna Hill Young and Sara Stinchfield Hawk first described in the motokinesthetic method.

BACKGROUND

The motokinesthetic system was first called the "Hill-Young" approach, named after the creator, Edna Hill-Young, who was principal at the "Hill-Young School of Speech" where she worked with cofounder and husband George Kelson Young. This private practice began in Minnesota in 1923, and it ran for some five years before they moved to Los Angeles. Dr. Sara M. Stinchfield was a psychologist from the University of Southern California who came to the new school to do research on the speech methods Young had developed for training speech movements. Stinchfield was a charter member of ASHA (Duchan, 2002).

Together, these two women worked, taught, and wrote a summary of their research in two books. The first was called *Children with Delayed or Defective Speech: Motor-Kinesthetic Factors in their Training* (Stinchfield & Young, 1938). The second, *Moto-Kinesthetic Speech Training*, explained the actual methods of therapy in the form of a manual entitled (Young & Hawk, 1955). The second book solidified the name of the procedure, described all the methods in

Edna Hill-Young (left) and Sara Stinchfield Hawk (right).

detail, and became a nationwide phenomenon. Young and Hawk's books are marvelous historical references that SLPs have returned to time and again in the decades since they were written.

THE PROCESS

The motokinesthetic system trains basic respiration, phonation, resonation, and articulation movements through simple hands-on manipulation of the organs involved. The methods are employed as the client attempts to produce the phoneme target. The system is a way of helping clients attain speech sound movements and positions that they cannot yet do on their own.

Young and Hawk described motokinesthetics as "the guidance and direction of speech muscles" (1955, p. 12). They recommended it for all types of clients with speech impairment no matter the etiology. They did not define the term *motokinesthetic* in either text, so one can only surmise. Clearly *moto* — or *motor* in the original text — refers to speech motor skill or speech movement. And the term *kinesthetic* refers to *kinesthesia* or "awareness of the position and movement of the parts of the body by means of sensory organs (proprioceptors) in the muscles and joints" (Jewell & Abate, 2001, p. 936). Thus the motokinesthetic system is a *movement* and a *sensory* system that addresses the feelings that arise in the skin, muscles, and joints during phoneme production. The term *motokinesthetic* could be translated into the more common phrase *sensorimotor*. Simply stated, the motokinesthetic system was the very first sensorimotor phoneme training system. Clients were placed in a supine position on a "speech table" while the motokinesthetic methods were applied. Methods included *guidance, direction, pressure*, and *self-monitoring*:

- *Guidance:* Therapists use their hands and fingers to physically move the articulators into positions: "One kind of stimulation actually moves the part involved, thus setting a pattern for the movement to be learned" (p. 12). In this manual, the term *assistance* has been used for this procedure. The therapist assists the movement by pushing or pulling the articulator into position. For example, they pushed the lower lip up to the upper teeth to guide it there for production of /f/ or /v/.

- *Direction:* Therapists also use their hands or fingers to touch the outside of the face in order to stimulate the tongue to move in certain directions. For example, they pressed on the skin under the nose to direct the tongue tip to press upward and forward against the alveolar ridge during production of /l/. The touch cue on the outside of the face directed the tongue's movement inside the oral cave. These direction signals make motokinesthetics a highly stylized hands-on tactile cue system.

- *Pressure:* Clinicians exerted more or less pressure as they touched in order to teach the client how hard or gentle to make the movement: "The degree of pressure used by the teacher in a stimulation tends to call forth a like degree of pressure in response" (p. 13). For example, a firm pressure was used to stimulate a stop consonant and a light touch was used to stimulate a fricative.

- *Self-monitoring:* Young and Hawk's clients also used their own fingers to feel their own oral positions. This made motokinesthetics a self-monitoring system as well.

THE METHODS

The following sections summarize all the fundamental motokinesthetic methods. Each quote is taken from their manual of 1955. The authors explained that their method caused a client to feel a movement and then to remember it. They were talking about sensory processing and motor memory. Motokinesthetics techniques create a feel and a memory for a movement that a client then attempts to achieve by himself. Young and Hawk designed their treatment methods around the four basic speech movement centers: respiration, phonation, resonation, and articulation (jaw, lip, and tongue).

> *"When the child feels the movement or movements, it is easy to reproduce the pattern, through the kinesthetic sense. The feel of what happens 'stays' in the muscles, becoming associated with the auditory patterns as the teacher speaks the words"* (Young & Hawk, 1955, p. 13).

Assisting Jaw Position

The motokinesthetic system includes a basic technique for positioning the jaw for phoneme production: "Each sound is aided by the teacher's guidance of the lower jaw, since variations for different sounds occur in the relative size of opening of the mouth" (p. 13). In essence, the authors recommended manually lowering the jaw for phonemes that required a low position, and manually elevating it for phonemes that require a high position.

Young and Hawk did not describe how to hold the jaw for these manipulations, but their photographs show them using the thumb, forefinger, and middle finger. The thumb and forefinger are placed on either side of midline on the front of the jaw, halfway between the bottom edge of the lower lip and the bottom of the chin, and the middle finger is placed under the chin. The fingers appear to be pressing downward to lower the jaw, and they appear to be pressing upward to elevate the jaw. Therefore, the present author assumes that "elevate the jaw" and "lower the jaw" simply mean to push or pull the jaw up or down in the desired direction.

Assisting Lip Position

Lip movement is stimulated in very precise yet quite simple ways using the motokinesthetic system. The therapist uses his or her own thumbs and fingers on the client's face while facing him. Two hands are used in their photos. The index fingers are placed just above and to the outsides of the upper lip. The thumbs are placed just below and to the outsides of the lower lip. All lip movements can be stimulated with the fingers thus placed. Most readers will recognize these techniques as ones they already use:

- *Closing the lips:* The thumb and forefinger are placed just below the vermilion border of the lower lip. The lower lip is pushed upward until it touches the upper lip.

- *Retracting the lips:* The thumbs and index fingers are used to spread the lips laterally for phonemes that require lip retraction.

- *Rounding the lips:* The thumbs and index fingers are used to push the lips medially into a rounded position for phonemes that require lip rounding.

- *Elevating the lower lip:* The thumbs are used to push the lower lip upward to the upper lip or teeth.

- *Lowering the lower lip:* Young and Hawk recommend lowering the lower lip by lowering the jaw. Use the jaw lowering technique described above.

- *Monitoring lip position:* Clients use their own fingers to feel their lip positions. For example, in stimulating /n/: "It helps also for the child to feel his front teeth between the parted lips with one of his fingers, to strengthen the feeling of separation of the lips for the /n/ sound" (p. 42).

Assisting Tongue Position

Young and Hawk describe a variety of methods to get the tongue to move in all its basic directions. Many readers will discover that they already use some or all of them:

- *Guiding the tongue tip to elevate:* Place the end of a tongue depressor under the tongue tip and lift it up to the alveolar ridge: "Usually the tongue depressor, inserted under the tongue and bringing it by quick upward movement to the dental ridge, brings about the necessary contact" (p. 18).

- *Directing the tongue tip to elevate to the alveolar ridge:* Touch the skin under the nose at midline to guide the tongue tip to lift and articulate with the alveolar ridge: "The child may be led into the simple suggestion of a tongue-end movement by the trainer's touching the center of the region outside and above the upper lip" (p. 18).

- *Guiding the tongue tip to lower:* Touch the skin above the upper lip at midline when the tip is elevated, and

"quickly bring the finger downward" to signal tip lowering (p. 18).

- *Guiding the back of the tongue to elevate:* Push the tongue back and up: "The tongue depressor may be placed on the tip of the tongue, holding it down, and at the same time pushing the tongue backward and upward until it comes into contact with the soft palate" (p. 18).

- *Directing the back of the tongue to elevate:* Touch the throat and push up: "Place the thumb on one side of the throat, under the back of the tongue externally, and the index finger on the opposite side. Press upward, thus suggesting that the back of the tongue move upward" (p. 18).

- *Guiding the back of the tongue to lower:* With the back of the tongue elevated as above, "move downward [with the fingers] thus suggesting a quick downward movement to the back of the tongue" (p. 18).

- *Guiding the sides of the tongue to elevate for a groove:* Use a tongue depressor to lift the sides of the tongue: "Insert a tongue depressor between the two rows of teeth at the sides, actually pressing the sides of the tongue upward against the dental ridge" (p. 20).

- *Directing the sides of the tongue to lift for a groove:* Press inward on the face at the masseters to guide the sides of the tongue to spread and elevate: "To ensure close contact of the sides to the dental ridge, the teacher may press outside on either side of the mid-line of the upper jaw. This outside pressure tends to bring the sides of the tongue upward against the dental ridge" (p. 20).

- *Guiding the tongue to create a midline depression:* Press the thin edge of a tongue depressor along the midline of the tongue: "Press at the central line lengthwise with the thin edge of the tongue depressor, drawing it along the mid-line to front between the two halves of the tongue" (p. 21).

- *Guiding the tongue to make a wider midline groove:* Use a tongue depressor to indicate a wider groove: "The tongue blade is stimulated upward along the whole front surface [of the tongue], as air comes outward, over the entire surface, not channeled along the midline as for /s/" (p. 21).

Assisting Exhalation

The authors of the motokinesthetic method based their entire program around the exhalation of air. The motokinesthetic method helps clients understand and use a constant force of exhaled air during the production of speech. The therapists used cords and pressure with the hands to help clients understand this.

- *Cords:* Young and Hawk used a cord or rope to

introduce their clients to the idea of inhaling and exhaling air for speech: "One effective stimulation for the correct use of air current during speech is to tie a thick cord or soft rope around the waist, in a loose single knot. Direct the subject to draw air through the lips, as is done in normal speech. The cord is fitted around the waistline. The subject can see it expand as he takes in the air. Immediately upon the intake, tighten the knot gradually while the subject moves the air outward through the mouth, or projects sound" (p. 8).

• *Pressure:* Once their clients began to work on phonemes, Young and Hawk used pressure applied with the hand to stimulate exhalation of air for speech: "Place one hand at the child's waistline over the diaphragm, pressing inward and upward" (p. 15). This is designed to cause awareness of exhalation, and it is to be used during phoneme stimulation.

Methods to encourage exhalation can be used discriminately with selected clients who can understand and benefit from them. To modern-day thinkers, these seem like primitive ways to encourage exhalation, and perhaps that is why these first methods will probably be the least familiar to most readers, but one can imagine a little group activity in which each child ties a small rope or ribbon around his waist and learns to feel the expansion of the belly during inhalation and the compression of the belly during exhalation.

Assisting Phonation

The Young and Hawk method also included methods to facilitate better production of voice. They explained that the prolonged voice was essential for production of vowels and voiced consonants. They gave simple ideas to help clients become aware of the production of voice that many SLPs still use:

• *Visual input:* The authors recommended that therapists draw a human figure and note the production of voice at the larynx by shading it: "A cartoon of the Disney® variety might be worked out to advantage, to clarify the uses of the air current in speech… A steady movement of the air as required for the vowel, accompanied by vibrations, might be shown in one constant color at the larynx" (p. 6).

• *Tactile feedback:* Young and Hawk directed a client's attention to the voice by having them use their hands to feel the vibrations of voice on the therapist's neck and on his own. It is safe to say that virtually every therapist uses this method at one time or another to teach voicing and voiceless-ness: "The trainer… gives the auditory pattern. [The client is helped] by feeling the vibrations" (p. 23).

Assisting Resonation

Young and Hawk were also concerned with a client's ability to control the direction of oral and nasal airflow. They designed simple methods to help clients discover and produce nasality. These are methods that most therapists still use:

• *Feeling vibration in the nasal cavities:* To help clients understand the movement of voice through the nasal cavity for production of the nasals, Young and Hawk recommended that the therapist allow the client to feel the therapist's nose: "If the teacher wishes the subject to feel her vibrations, as she makes the sounds, he may feel them more definitely by touching one of the sides of her nose" (p. 41).

• *Inducing nasality with pressure:* To facilitate nasal direction of voice, the authors recommended that gentle firm pressure be applied to the bridge of the client's nose: "Pressure on the bridge of the nose tends to send sound through the nasal chambers" (p. 13).

Assisting Sound Sequencing

Young and Hawk insisted that their method of motokinesthetic speech training was superior to all others because the emphasis was not on single phonemes, but on sequential movements from one phoneme to another. They recommended that their cues be used one-after-another in sequence as the client produces syllables, words, phrases, and sentences. To use the methods in this way means to be highly skilled in the application of the techniques in a time-oriented manner. Flexible, accurate, and fast-moving finger movements are necessary.

As simplified, condensed and illustrated on the next page, following is the order of phonemes that Young and Hawk recommended:

1. Voiceless consonants: /h/, /ʍ/, /f/, /θ/, /p/, /t/, /k/, /s/, /ʃ/, /tʃ/.

2. Voiced consonants: /v/, /ð/, /b/, /d/, /g/, /z/, /ʒ/, /dʒ/, /m/, /n/, /ŋ/, /l/, /r/, /w/, /j/.

The present author, however, suggests that phonemes be practiced in voiced and unvoiced cognate pairs by place of articulation, e.g. /p – b/, /t – d/, /k – g/, etc. (further reading on place of articulation and the functional zones of the tongue can be found on pages 189–190).

SUMMARY

The motokinesthetic system was the first sensorimotor speech training system. Most of its methods can be classified as tactile cues to assist and direct movement. The motokinesthetic cue system has maintained a constant presence in speech training since the mid-20th century.

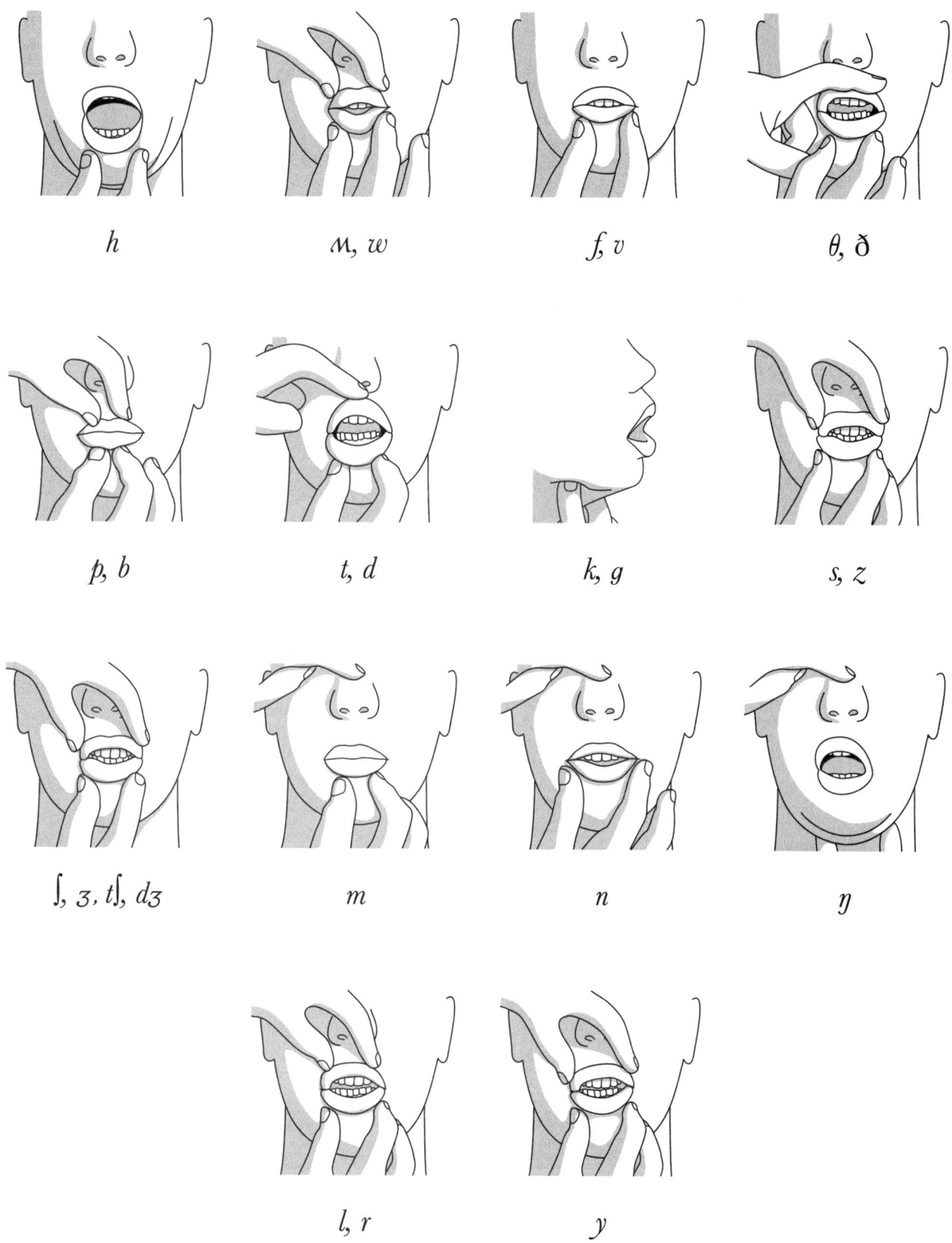

h

ʍ, w

f, v

θ, ð

p, b

t, d

k, g

s, z

ʃ, ʒ, tʃ, dʒ

m

n

ŋ

l, r

y

7

Encouraging Breath Support

Developing control of inhalation and exhalation for excellent speech production

> *"While respiration is at fault, articulation is as powerless as the fingering of a flute would be to evoke music without the stream of air."*
>
> – Melville Bell, 1916

The most fundamental speech movements are those of inhalation and exhalation. Humans inhale and exhale in various ways and for various purposes: we breathe gently and rhythmically to sustain life; we pant for faster exchange of oxygen as we recover from exertion; we hold the breath to lift heavy objects, to go under water, and to bear physical pain. We also use our breath to intensify the olfactory sense while eating and drinking, and besides all that — we breathe for speech: "The primary source of energy for speech production, of course, is air" (Zemlin, 1981, p. 36). The very foundation of all speech sound production is the sustained control of exhaled air, and this is known as *breath support*. Classic ways to facilitate breath support for improved speech is the subject of this chapter.

BACKGROUND

Speech is the modification of controlled exhalation. A vowel is breath that is voiced and shaped, a consonant is breath that is restricted or occluded, and connected speech is supported with the sustained yet interrupted outgoing breath. The written record indicates that the facilitation of breath support has been part of speech training since the elocutionists of ancient times. Articulation therapy textbooks written during the Traditional Era contained extensive sections, even entire chapters, on how to facilitate improved breath for speech. Books on singing and theater voice contain these methods as well. Current textbooks on the motor speech disorders teach that breath support is an important element of treatment.

Breath Group

Research continues to support the notion that breathing for speech is different than breathing at rest (e.g., Connaghan, Moore & Higashakawa, 2004). The elocutionists used the term *breath group* to discuss the way breathing is used to express a language. Spoken language is divided into groups that correspond with phrases and sentences. For example, consider the sentence — *She believed in every standard approach, as well as every odd technique, and even the wildest things imaginable.* A good reader might inhale at each comma thus setting the sentence into three breath groups. Henry Sweet, the principle designer of the International Phonetic Alphabet, is believed to have made the original definition of the breath group:

> *"The only division actually made in language is that into 'breath-groups.' We are unable to utter more than a certain number of sounds in succession without renewing the stock of air in the lungs. These breath-groups correspond partially with the logical division into sentences. Every sentence is necessarily a breath group, but every breath group need not be a complete sentence"* (Sweet, 1877, p. 87).

Breath Support

Exhalation must be sustained throughout the duration of each breath group. This concept is known as *breath support*. Breath support for speech is not the same as quiet breathing. During quiet breathing the breath moves in and out in a rhythmic pattern that is mostly evenly spaced, about 12–20 times per minute in adults. But breathing for speech is characterized by "rapid inhalation and a prolonged period of exhalation" (Yorkston, Beukelman, Strand, & Bell, 1999, p. 296). One of the best 20th century definitions of breath support came from Hilda Fisher, offered here and explained below:

> *"[Breath support is] the control of the force and duration of exhalation [having] to do with the time during which a single exhalation is extended, and the quantity of air being exhaled at any given moment in time"* (Fisher, 1966, p. 40).

Control

Control refers to the exercising of authority over the breath; the client who is using excellent breath support has control over his breathing for speech. He has enough control to produce all the vowels, diphthongs, syllables, consonants, distinctive features, phonological patterns, and prosodic patterns of his language as it is expressed in words, phrases, and sentences.

Force

Force refers to the physical influence the breath has upon the vocal folds, the velum, and the articulators. Clients must have enough exhalation force to make voice, to alter voice with prosody, to influence velopharyngeal movement, and to impact articulatory movement. But not too much force should be used: "It must be remembered that the least expenditure of breath necessary to produce the required energy and loudness always gives the best results" (Ross, 1886, p. 85).

Duration

Duration refers to the period of time during which the exhaled breath lasts during speech. Clients must have a duration of exhalation that is long enough to produce phonemes and syllables, to string syllables together into words and phrases, to transition from one syllable to another, to produce melodious speech, and so forth.

Breath support is the foundation of good speaking and singing.

Single Exhalation

The single exhalation refers to the *breath group*. The breath group is the word, phrase, or sentence that is held up by one exhalation. The client has to have enough control, force, and duration of breath to exhale in one breath between the markers that divide these syntactic groups, and to inhale at appropriate points between them.

Quantity

Quantity refers to the amount of air being exhaled. The client has to be able to inhale enough air to exhale for the requirements of speech. That means that inhalation skills must be sufficient to bring in enough air at each rapid inhalation.

Given Moment in Time

The *given moment in time* refers to the speech task at hand. For example, if the speech task is the production of the sentence "I want that one," then the client has to have enough control, force, duration, and quantity of breath to support the production of the breath group for that whole sentence.

Three Breathing Patterns

Articulation and speech science textbooks describe three types of breathing patterns: diaphragmatic, clavicular, and costal. Each is summarized briefly below for a quick reference. This material has been abstracted from Fisher (1966) and Zemlin (1968).

- *Diaphragmatic:* Diaphragmatic breathing is called such because the diaphragm controls the process. The diaphragm is a muscular sheath that divides the thorax from the abdominal cavity. When at rest, the diaphragm is domed upward. When in contraction, the diaphragm pulls downward. This downward pull causes the lung cavity to expand, and this causes the lungs to expand and air to rush in. Diaphragmatic breathing is used at rest, and is always recommended as the principle method for speech breathing. Diaphragmatic breathing has also been called *abdominal breathing* because the abdomen moves outward during inhalation and inward during exhalation due to the diaphragm's downward and upward movement.

- *Clavicular:* Clavicular breathing has been called *shoulder breathing* and *extreme upper chest breathing*. Clavicular breathing is used to prepare the respiratory system for strenuous activity. Clavicular breathing causes the shoulders and upper chest to rise. This causes the upper lungs to expand and an extra measure of air to be inhaled. Clavicular breathing is never recommended for conversational speech except when other breathing patterns are hindered due to injury or disease.

- *Costal:* Costal breathing involves rib (costal)

movement. It has also been called *lower thoracic breathing* because there is expansion in the lower part of the thorax. It has also been called *medial breathing* because the middle of the trunk expands, and it has been called *chest breathing, upper chest breathing,* and *thoracic breathing* because the area of greatest expansion is the upper chest. Costal breathing is used during quiet breathing. Costal breathing is also used to actively inhale a greater volume of air when necessary for speech or other purposes.

Research on Developing Breath Support

As with all motor skills, speech breathing goes through a developmental process. Changes over time are due to growth in the size and shape of the breathing apparatus, and to the natural process of developing motor skills in childhood. A researcher in the area of respiration development was asked to summarize the overall findings of developmental speech breathing research: "Basically, typical children have enough breath support to produce the appropriate number of syllables per breath group matching their linguistic complexity and speech output" (Boliek, 2008). Therefore, children at the one-word stage have enough breath support to produce single words in one breath group, children at the two-word stage have enough breath support to produce two-word combinations in one breath group, and so forth. It can be surmised from this that children without adequate breath support will demonstrate limitations in the length of utterance as measured by word or syllable when compared with age mates. A small set of selected studies on speech breathing development is summarized here:

- Hoit, Hixon, Watson, and Morgan (1990) studied lung volume, rib cage volume, and abdominal volume in children aged 7–16 years of age. In most respects, speech breathing appeared adult-like by ten years of age. No differences in sex were noted, and the size of the speech production apparatus was the most important variable. Patterns of function were generally the same for extemporaneous speaking and reading. The average number of syllables produced per breath group as a function of age were as follows (numbers rounded to the nearest whole): 7–8 syllables per breath group at age 7 years of age; 8–9 syllables per breath group at 10 years of age; 9–11 syllables per breath group at 13 years of age; 14–16 syllables per breath group at 16 years of age.

- Dromey and Ramig (1998) studied the relationship between lung volume and speech production in normal adult females and found that adjustments to lung volume had an effect on phonatory behavior but it did not have an effect on articulatory excursions and velocity of movement in the lips.

- Moore, Caulfield, and Green (2001) found markedly different patterns of movement in rest breathing and speech breathing in eighteen-month-old children. No differences were found between the breathing patterns for non-speech vocalizations, babbling, and true word productions. One can deduce from this that when a client is taught to use the breath appropriately to engage in pre-babbling vocalizations and babbling, he is learning to breath correctly for real word productions.

- Boliek, Hixon, Watson, and Jones (2009) studied the *lung volume events* of 60 children and found that the speech breathing mechanism gradually refines itself between 3 and 10 years of age: "Speech breathing, like any other motor skill, can be conceptualized as progressing through periods of emergence, refinement, and adaptation" (p. 990). Children averaged 3–4 syllables per breath group, and they produced more syllables per breath group as they aged (because speech gets faster). Inspiration durations were brief (less than 1.5 seconds), and expiration durations were longer (average of 4 seconds in length with a range of 1–9 seconds). No differences between boys and girls were noted.

- Parham, Buder, Oller, and Boliek (2011) studied breathing at rest and during speech in one-year-olds and found that tidal breathing cycles were significantly different from syllable-related cycles on all breathing measures. The researchers suggested that further research in this area might help identify infants whose coordination of voice and breathing might be delayed. These skills, therefore, could be used to identify very young clients who are at more risk for speech delay or impairment. For example, two non-verbal toddlers might be evaluated. Without samples of expressive speech to evaluate, SLPs might observe breath patterns to help determine whether either client requires early intervention. Readers are referred to the original study for data.

Blowing & Breath Support

It is important to state without hesitation early in this chapter that blowing has nothing to do with speech. Blowing is the act of exhaling with force while closing the

Let's be clear about one thing: Blowing out birthday candles has nothing to do with speech.

velopharyngeal port, opening the mouth, and rounding the lips. Blowing is used to extinguish birthday candles, to sound a horn or whistle, to blow bubbles, or to shoo away a tiny undesirable object like a fly or a dust bunny.

It is the present author's observation that blowing like this is a skill that develops by about two years of age. Evidence for this is merely anecdotal. It seems that an average child usually cannot blow out the single candle on his first birthday cake, but he can often blow out the two candles on his second birthday cake, especially if he has had a little instruction. Without more scientific evidence than that, this means that, in general, children learn to blow purposefully sometime between one and two years of age. This learning is probably both motoric and conceptual.

It seems safe to say, therefore, that the act of blowing is equivalent to the ability to produce 25–50 words, to jargon and whisper, to produce early two-word utterances, and to articulate most phonemes. It can be concluded from this that blowing is a very sophisticated skill that does not precede or act as a forerunner to speech development. In fact the opposite is true: Expressive speech could be viewed as a forerunner of blowing.

The topic of this chapter is breath support, not blowing. Therefore, SLPs are concerned with whether their clients can inhale and exhale in appropriate ways while speaking, not whether they can blow whistles, bubbles, or birthday candles. Certain objects like horns or whistles might be used as mediums to teach inhalation and exhalation patterns as detailed in sections on treatment methods below.

PROBLEMS

Speech clients can have any number of difficulties that can be attributed to difficulty with breath support. Clients with motor speech disorders usually have difficulty in several areas simultaneously and their problems are more severe. The present author's clinical observations are summarized here.

- *Voice:* Some clients with motor speech disorder move so little air with such limited force that they have difficulty setting the vocal folds into vibration and they can produce almost no voice whatsoever. No true vowels or consonants are uttered as a result. These are the clients who have the most severe forms of expressive speech incompetence. Many of them have severe neuromuscular and/or cognitive deficit and must rely on augmentative communication systems to supplement speech production.

- *Vowels and diphthongs:* Some clients with motor speech disorders can initiate voice with exhalation, but they cannot sustain exhalation well enough to support the voice needed for production of a complete vowel. Speech sounds choppy and staccato-like (rapid, brief, and clipped) because vowels are short and truncated. These clients struggle to produce diphthongs because there is not enough breath to support two vowels in sequence.

- *Projecting the voice:* Some clients with motor speech disorders produce voice but they do not have enough breath support to project the voice well. They produce speech with a quiet "muffled" quality. Some cannot shout or speak loudly. An inability to project the voice enough for intelligible speech often occurs in clients with neuromuscular deficit, but this pattern is also seen in clients who can produce all phonemes and even pass an articulation test. Sometimes it sounds as if they are swallowing their speech. Sometimes their speech is stretched and strained. Some of these clients are inhaling when they should be exhaling.

- *Intonation:* Some clients do not have enough breath support to engage a full variety of intonation patterns. Speech is produced in a monotone and intelligibility is affected accordingly. These clients may gasp between breath groups and "run out of air" mid-utterance.

- *Final Consonants:* For some clients, an inability to sustain breath throughout an entire syllable can cause final consonants to be weak or omitted. In this case, final consonant deletion and final cluster deletion become prominent phonological patterns. Some clients rapidly inhale before a final consonant, causing the final consonant to sound like an additional syllable.

- *Multi-syllabic words:* Some clients do not have enough breath support to sustain airflow throughout multi-syllabic words. Unstressed syllables may be omitted, words may be restricted to one and/or two syllables, or inhalation between syllables may occur. Speech may be slurred as the client rushes through his syllables to get them in before he runs out of usable air.

- *Multi-word phrases or sentences:* Some clients do not have enough breath support to produce multi-word phrases or sentences in one breath group. Characteristics to be expected include restriction of expression to single words, inhaling at inappropriate moments, omission of unstressed syllables, omission of unstressed words, gasping for breath between words and phrases, and limited prosodic expression.

- *Breath holding:* Some clients hold the breath and do so for various reasons. Clients with neuromuscular disorder sometimes hold the breath to stiffen the body's core muscles so they feel a greater sense of postural stability. Other clients hold the breath due to high anxiety or insecurity, or because they do not want to talk. One client who was deaf held her breath during speech simply because she did not know that she had to inhale and exhale. Significant restrictions in the use of all the distinctive features occurs when a client tries to talk and hold the breath simultaneously. Some of these clients remain non-verbal due to the holding of the breath. Glottal fry and straining may characterize the voice in the client who tries to speak and hold the breath simultaneously.

• *Slow rate:* Some clients are unable to take a rapid inhalation, so they speak slowly and take what is judged as "too long" to get to the next phrase or sentence. Slow overall rate is the main result. Vowels may become distorted during the prolongation. The client may sound dysarthric.

• *Fast rate:* Some clients rush to produce as many words as possible per utterance when breath support is lacking. Children with Down syndrome are classic examples of this. The result is that they speak too quickly for their oral movement and auditory self-monitoring capabilities. Low intelligibility, choppiness, final consonant deletion, and deletion of words and syllables are common results.

• *Lack of frication:* Some clients do not control the breath well enough to sustain airflow for frication. Fricatives and affricates may be omitted or replaced with stop consonants. The phonological patterns called *stopping* and *stridency deletion* are the result.

• *Lack of plosiveness:* Some clients do not have enough force of breath to build up air pressure for the stops. The stops are produced weakly and may be fricated. The explosion necessary for the stop consonants will be missing. The resultant phonological patterns are *frication* and *affrication.*

• *Inhaled phonemes:* Some clients inhale (instead of exhale) during the production of any one or more specific phonemes. Sometimes this sounds like a snort, a suck, or a click.

DIAGNOSIS

The diagnosis of a client's expressive speech should always include an analysis of breath support, but there are practical problems associated with this. First, speech-language pathologists do not generally have access to the laboratory equipment necessary to measure respiratory skills. Second, many SLPs find it difficult to differentiate between diaphragmatic, costal, and clavicular breathing. Without laboratory equipment or the ability to assess the client's breathing pattern, how does one know if the client has a problem with breath support for speech? The solution lies in clinical observation of expressive speech itself. One determines how well a client uses his breath as he speaks.

The following list contains a series of questions designed to guide the assessment and continual monitoring of breath support for speech. This is a checklist the present author developed by studying the articulation and

motor speech literature and by engaging in nearly forty years of assessment and treatment. Answers to these questions are obtained through careful observation of spontaneous speech during an initial evaluation session and/or during the ongoing process of treatment. One has to watch and listen with critical eyes and ears to obtain this information. Some of these questions are purposefully overlapping and redundant. Others may be difficult to answer during an initial assessment, but most can be answered throughout the course of treatment. Some of these questions will be difficult to answer by the therapist untrained in these matters, but time and experience will remedy that. For thorough discussions of assessment issues, readers are referred to the protocols of Hixon and Hoit (1999; 2000; and 2006).

Breath Support Assessment Checklist

Overall Pattern

• Is the client trying to speak while holding his breath at the same time?

• Is the client allowing too much breath to escape during speech? Is he breathy?

• Does the client inhale instead of exhale during production of any specific phonemes? If so, which ones?

• Does the client audibly gasp as he inhales during speech?

• Does the client seem to "run out of air" as he is speaking?

• Do the ends of words, phrases, or sentences fade at the end?

• Does the client resort to aphonia?

• Does the client speak in a glottal fry? When?

• Is the voice strained or strangled?

• Does the client's breath support allow him to whisper, or does he only pretend to whisper (mouth the words without air; pantomime)?

• Does it seem as if the client is "barely breathing?"

• Does breathing at rest sound strained?

• Is it nearly impossible to tell whether or not the client actually is breathing?

Breath Groups

• How many syllables are in the client's breath groups during spontaneous conversation? (Average and Range)

• How many words are in the client's breath groups during spontaneous conversation? (Average and Range)

• Do the client's breath groups correspond with the

phrases of his utterances, or does he inhale at odd times mid-phrase?

- Does the client try to speak too many syllables or words on one breath group so that he sounds like he is "running out of air" toward the end?

- Does the client talk fast in order to get as many syllables or words into one breath group as possible?

Multi-Syllabic Words

- Does the client restrict his speech to one-syllable words?

- Does the client restrict his speech to two-syllable words?

- Does the client inhale between the syllables of multi-syllabic words?

- Does the client drop unstressed syllables?

- Do syllables drop or fade out toward the end of multi-syllabic words?

- Does the client inhale on whole syllables periodically during production of multi-syllabic words?

Prosodic Factors

- Does the client have enough breath support to speak loudly?

- Does the client control airflow well enough to project his voice and reach a good conversational level, or does he mumble or sound muffled?

- Does the client's airflow allow him to produce high and low pitch, or is he stuck with limited pitch variations?

- Does the client's airflow allow him to support a variety of intonation patterns, or does he use a monotone because of poor breath support?

- Does the client speak too fast in order to not "run out of air?"

- Does the client often speak too forcefully (loud)?

- Does the client use "robotic" intonation patterns? Does he sound rigid?

- Does loudness waver because breath support is inconsistent?

- Is rate slow because his inhalations between breath groups are slow and long?

Phrases

- Does the client speak phrases in one breath group?

- Does the client inhale between the words of individual phrases?

- Do syllables drop out during production of phrases?

- Do phrases remain incomplete because breath does not support the entire phrase?

Connected Speech

- Does the client sound like he is "running out of air" during connected speech?

- Does the client pant or gasp during connected speech?

- Does the client inhale at appropriate syntactic markers during connected speech?

- Does the client inhale at inappropriate times during connected speech, such as between words of a single phrase, or between syllables of a single word?

- Do syllables drop out during connected speech?

Individual Syllables

- Does the client sustain airflow well enough to produce an individual CV syllable?

- Does the client sustain airflow well enough to produce an individual VC syllable?

- Is there enough sustained airflow to allow the client to produce a CVC?

- Are final consonant omitted because airflow is not sustained through the syllables?

- Doe the client inhale before a final consonant so that the final consonant becomes a separate syllable?

- Do individual syllables sound vigorous, or are they weak?

Vowels

- Does the client have enough breath support to produce full and resonant vowels?

- Are the vowels weak?

- Are the vowels muffled?

- Does the client have enough breath support to produce vowels that are appropriate in length, or are they cut off at the ends?

- Do vowels sound stronger or weaker depending upon word position? Specifically, are initial vowels stronger than final vowels?

Diphthongs

- Does the client sustain airflow well enough to produce both first and second vowels of diphthongs?

- Does the client have enough breath support to produce fully resonant diphthongs, or are they weak or muffled?

- Does the client have enough breath support to

maintain voice during the transition from the first to the second vowel within his diphthongs?

- Does the client's voice stop between the vowels of a diphthong?

- Does the client inhale between the vowels of his diphthongs?

Nasals

- Does the client have enough breath support to produce the nasals in isolation?

- Are the nasals weak or muffled?

- Does the client have enough breath support to produce the nasals in words, or does he substitute for them with stop consonants?

- Do the nasals fade out at the ends of words?

Glides

- Does the client have enough breath support to produce the glides in simple CV syllables?

- Does the client have enough breath support to produce the glides in words?

- Are the glides weak or muffled?

- Does the client have enough breath support to produce glides that include both parts, or is he using only one part?

- Does the client substitute stop consonants for the glides?

Fricatives and Affricates

- Does the client have enough breath support to sustain airflow for true frication?

- Is frication weak?

- Does the client rapidly "spit" out his fricatives because he cannot sustain airflow to produce them appropriately?

- Does the client substitute stop consonants for the fricatives?

Clusters

- Can the client use his breath to support two or three consonant phonemes in CC and CCC clusters, or does he use single consonants only?

- Does the client rapidly "spit" out his clusters and not allow himself enough time to produce each phoneme in the sequence?

- Does the client omit final clusters because he does not have enough airflow to sustain an entire syllable?

Phoneme Transitions

- Can the client sustain continuous airflow when transitioning from one phoneme to another within a syllable? Or does he stop airflow? For example, can the client sustain airflow between /s/ and the vowel in the word *sun*? Or does he say /stʌn/ or /sdʌn/ to stop the air?

Babbling Syllable Sequences

- Does the client have enough airflow to produce two or more syllables in a row in babbling sequences?

- How many syllables can the client produce in a babbling sequence in one breath group?

Other Practical Measures

There are a few other practical ways to assess respiratory control for speech in the clinic. Blow toys and manometers can be used, as well as consultation with motor specialists and background information about the client's medical and structural status related to breathing.

Any blow toy can give a therapist a rough idea of whether or not a client has any capacity to exhale or inhale on demand, and a manometer can be used to determine whether a client can sustain a consistent force of exhalation. The respiration sub-test of *The Marshalla Oral Sensorimotor Test* (MOST; Marshalla, 2007a) examines a child's ability to inhale and exhale through a toy harmonica and siren. This test demonstrated that children with good speech who were between the ages of 4;0 and 7;11 can inhale and exhale well enough to produce sound with selected blow toys, and they are able to sustain these sounds for three seconds with no difficulty. This benchmark can be used to judge a client's ability to produce and sustain exhalation and inhalation in children four years of age and older.

The assessment of breath support for speech can be made even more complete by consulting with team occupational and physical therapists. The team motor specialist's information, together with the SLP's speech

What looks like boredom actually may be a sign that the client has to hold up his head. This is a sign that speech breathing may be compromised.

assessment, can make for a fairly complete picture of respiratory support for speech, especially in clients with motor speech disorders. Speech-language pathologists should discuss the breathing problems they observe during speech. Discussion points for the motor specialist might include the following:

- Does the client have the hip, shoulder, and trunk support he needs for age-appropriate speech breathing?

- Does the client hold his breath during gross motor activities?

- Can the client hold his breath during heavy lifting?

- Does the client persistently hold his head up with his hands or rest his head on the table while sitting in speech or classroom lessons?

- What does his rib cage look like? Is the sternum collapsed? Are the ribs flaring?

- Are there flexion, extension, lateralization, or rotation movement activities that can be incorporated into speech-language therapy that will facilitate better support of his speech breathing?

- Are there arousal issues related to breathing that could be addressed in speech therapy?

- Could special positioning or seating arrangements benefit respiratory support for speech?

- Are there activities for adjusting muscle tone that could be included in speech-language therapy to improve trunk support for speech breathing?

- Are there activities to improve grading of respiratory control that can be assist speech breathing?

The analysis of breath support for speech also must include an inventory of medical issues related to breathing. The SLP must determine if there are any medical or structural issues that might have or might be impacting inhalation, exhalation, and/or sustained exhalation.

TREATMENT APPROACHES

The process of treating breath support for speech has many facets and varies widely depending upon the types of clients being served and the employment setting. The following methods have been drawn from textbooks and manuals on articulation therapy and the motor therapies, as well as from the present author's multidisciplinary team experiences. Virtually no research exists to support these methods and readers should view this material as advice passed down from one generation of therapists to another.

Speech-language pathologists recognize that the breathing activities presented below will not correct

speech problems as if by magic. Of course, one does not teach clients how to relax the shoulders for improved inhalation, for example, and then expect the client to speak correctly from that point forward. Therapists introduce a breathing activity to teach a breathing skill, and then they transfer that skill into specific speech tasks that become gradually more complex. For example, a tense client might be taught to relax the shoulders, inhale, and then sustain gentle exhalation. Then the client might be taught to use that skill to produce a phoneme. Then he might learn to incorporate that skill into syllables, words, and phrases, and other increasingly complex expressions, all the way to conversation and oral presentations. Speech-language pathologists understand this basic idea and none expect that a breathing activity alone will fix all their clients difficulties with expressive speech.

The methods described in the rest of this chapter are organized into six areas for the purposes of this manual. These procedures can occur simultaneously, they can overlap, or they can be sequenced over time. Areas include: *postural guidelines, pre-speech activities, classic breathing exercises, speech work, bodywork,* and *reflex stimulation.*

Even the elocutionists knew that slouching interferes with speech breathing (Griffith, 1865).

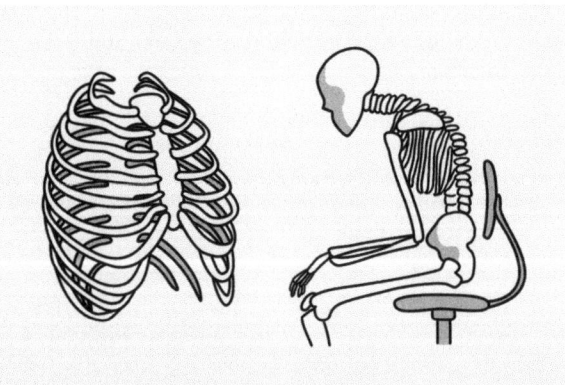

A sternum that sits high elevates and expands the rib cage while slouching collapses it.

POSTURE GUIDELINES

The term *postural guidelines* will be used here for positioning methods that ensure adequate head, neck, and trunk support for speech breathing. The classic image of a client walking around with books piled on top of the head to train an upright posture may feel out-of-date, but elocutionists and speech correctionists understood that body posture was an important element of good speech breathing and used this method to encourage such a posture. All SLP students today take classes on speech anatomy and physiology, and speech science textbooks describe the relationship between breathing for speech and the skeletal and muscular structures of the trunk. It is generally understood that these ideas for good skeletal arrangement are as important for clients today as they were in the past. Good posture for speech is necessary because inhalation and exhalation for speech is accomplished through expansion and contraction of the bony structure of the trunk. The rib cage and the lungs function best when a client has good posture. The following postural guidelines are for good breath support during articulation and motor speech therapy. These basic procedures apply to all clients regardless of age or physical condition.

Head, Neck & Upper Body Position

Articulation therapy should be done with the client's head and neck in the best alignment with the chest so that respiratory support is optimized. The head should be erect with the chin somewhat tucked, the shoulders should be back, and the upper chest should be up and forward. Have the client sit "tall and proud." Do not work with the client's head tipped backward, with the client hunched over, or with the client talking over his shoulder. Arrange the seating so these features of good posture can be attained. The trunk is in the best possible position for speech breathing when the neck is elongated in the rear with the chin slightly tucked, the shoulders down and the sternum high. This elevates the sternum, which is the high point of attachment for the rib cage. This posture, attainable through correct sitting or standing position, also aligns the larynx and velopharyngeal mechanism appropriately for good speech. Therapists often use imagery to help their clients understand this position:

> *"One good device for aligning your body frame properly is to pretend that someone is pulling you up from above like a puppet, with a string tied to the top of each of your ears (not your nose!)"* (Fisher, 1966, p. 53).

Be mindful of the client's head position as eye contact is established. Some seating positions that are face-to-face cause a small client to look up to face an adult-sized therapist. Do not sit so that the therapist's head is higher than the client's head as this will cause him to tip the head back in order to see her. With the head tipped back, the sternum collapses, the shoulders round, and respiration is

The SLP on the left is sitting too high and forcing her client to tilt her head back. She also is modeling speaking with her head tilted back. The therapist on the right has adjusted himself so that he and the client can maintain good head positions during speech training.

Boost small children to get them at eye level

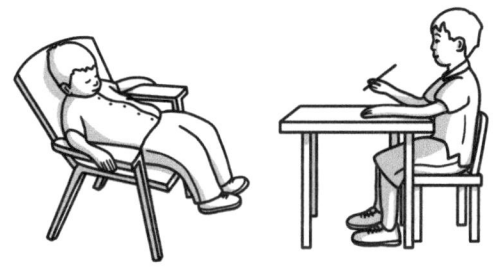

Sitting in a chair that is too big usually interferes with good speech breathing (left). A solid foot position in a chair of an appropriate size assures better upper body control for speech breathing (right).

impacted. This incorrect position often occurs when SLPs sit on the floor with children because they have to look up to see the therapist's face because she is taller. SLPs should find a work position that puts their eyes level with or slightly lower than the client's. For example, sit on the floor while the child sits in a chair. This places his head even with, or slightly above, the SLP's. If one must sit on a regular adult-sized chair, sit the client in a high chair, or in an adult-sized chair fitted with padding or a booster seat.

Chair Sitting

Hips and shoulders squared is the best possible position for respiratory support in articulation training while sitting. A client's chair should be the right size and shape for good respiratory support: the hips should fit firmly back against the back of the chair, the feet should not dangle but be planted solidly on the ground, and the trunk should be upright. Clients with balance and tone problems will be helped by a solid foot position; if the chair is too large for the client, support his feet underneath with a sturdy box or footstool. If a large stuffed chair is used with a tiny client, have the client kneel-stand or sit with crossed legs. Sometimes bolsters, pads, or cushions on a chair should be employed to adjust the client's hip or leg positions. Crossed legs may also work well if the client is seated on a sofa. A good sitting position in a chair also assures better auditory and visual attention, better distribution of tone throughout the whole body, and better oral control.

Long-leg and cross-leg sitting (left, middle) are much better for speech breathing than W-sitting (right).

Special seating arrangements provide support for better speech breathing in clients with neuromuscular deficit.

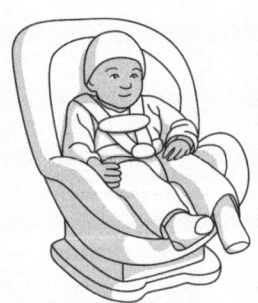

A flexed supine position is an excellent one for working on speech when a client cannot maintain an upright position by himself.

Floor Positions

Some client's have habitual floor sitting positions that have a negative impact on respiratory support for speech. Make sure to follow the occupational and/or physical therapist's recommendations for floor sitting in order to use the client's skeletal framework to his advantage. Motor specialists may recommend cross-legged sitting, side-sitting, or long-leg sitting, or they may recommend that floor sitting be avoided and that prone, supine, or side-lying positions be used instead. W-sitting (see illustration, left) is universally avoided because of its negative impact on the rib cage.

Special Seating Arrangements/Devices

Speech-language pathologists work with team occupational and physical therapists to select special seating arrangements for clients who cannot achieve a good sitting position naturally in a regular chair or on the floor. Some of these clients will need a tabletop or desktop on which to rest the arms for postural support. Others will be in wheelchairs or other individual seating arrangements. Team members will need feedback from the SLP regarding the advantage or disadvantages these devices bring to the process of building breath support for speech. Adjustments may be made as a result of the SLPs' observations.

Supine Positioning

Motor therapists often recommend that a client be seated in a flexed supine position when he cannot maintain an upright position. This is an excellent position for speech work in most cases. When using their motokinesthetic method, Young and Hawk (1955) actually had clients lie down in a supine position on a special speech table.

PRE-SPEECH ACTIVITIES

The term *pre-speech activities* will be used here to describe those activities that employ toys and other tools to prepare breath support for speech work. This is not about teaching clients to blow; this is about using certain objects to teach awareness and control over inhalation, exhalation, and prolonged exhalation for speech. A variety of toys and tools are used with clients who do not respond if given simple directions like "Take a deep breath" or "Sustain your exhalation." Therapists everywhere in the United States use these methods despite many recent outcries against them.

Working with these objects can be a lot of fun. Pre-speech activities allow SLPs to introduce concepts of breath support with clients who are very young, who speak only a few words, who have limited comprehension of language, or who have neuromuscular control problems. Think of these pre-speech activities as gross respiration

Blow toys are used to teach basic concepts about inhaling and exhaling.

work and as a part of readiness — getting the client ready for speech sound production. This type of work usually takes place simultaneously with direct phoneme stimulation.

Tools of Pre-Speech Training

A wide variety of tools can be used to develop breath support and breath control in pre-speech training activities. Readers are referred to Chapter 19, *The Tools of Speech Movement Training*, for details about how to use the following items:

- Blow toys
- Bulb syringes
- Cotton balls and feathers
- Fingers
- Kazoos
- Laryngeal mirrors
- Mirrors
- Nasal clamps
- Nasal flutes
- Rapper Snapper
- See-Scape
- Sound-activated toys
- Spirometers
- Straws
- Tissue paper
- Tubes
- Manometers

The Goals of Pre-Speech Training

Learning to blow is not the goal of this type of pre-speech training, nor is the goal to learn phonemes. The goals of this level of training are to become aware of the breath,

and to learn how to control patterns of inhalation and exhalation that will support speech. The tools listed above can be used to teach a wide variety of respiration skills. Toys that direct airflow back to the client's own ear are especially helpful in teaching him to understand his own inhalation and exhalation patterns. SLPs use the tools to teach clients how to do many things:

- Focus attention on inhalation and exhalation
- Experiment with inhalation and exhalation
- Inhale and exhale voluntarily
- Inhale rapidly, deeply, or quietly
- Sustain exhalation
- Increase pressure of exhalation
- Sustain pressure of exhalation
- Exhale instead of inhale
- Inhale or exhale through the nose
- Inhale or exhale through the mouth
- Exhale in a short, rapid burst
- Exhale in a series of short, rapid bursts
- Exhale and voice simultaneously
- Prolong (sustain) voice
- Intone voice
- Move the lips while controlling exhalation and voice
- Move the tongue while controlling exhalation and voice

Many current applications of these methods can be cited. Rosenfeld-Johnson (2001) uses horns in hierarchies that require increased duration of exhalation as clients work through her program. Increased duration allows an increase in utterance length: "Horn therapy… addresses deficits in abdominal grading, is a prerequisite for improving velopharyngeal functioning, and targets specific speech sound production" (p. 49).

Physicians at the Mayo Clinic in Florida use harmonicas with patients in respiratory therapy and found

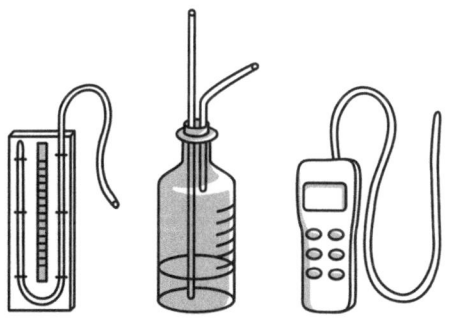

Manometers can be used to develop consistent subglottal air pressure for speech. Old-fashioned tube-type (left), home-made (middle), and electronic (right).

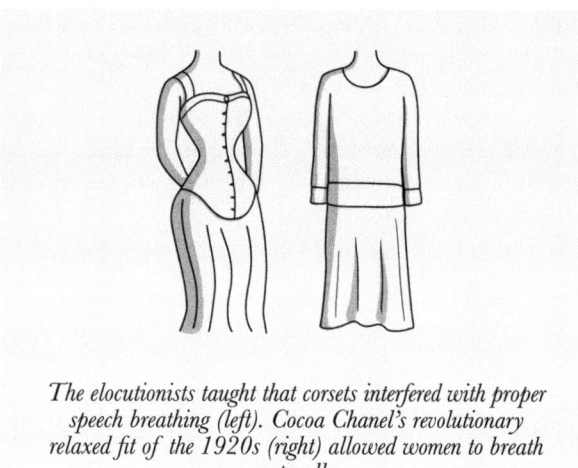

The elocutionists taught that corsets interfered with proper speech breathing (left). Cocoa Chanel's revolutionary relaxed fit of the 1920s (right) allowed women to breath naturally.

that harmonica playing can supplement a regular routine of prescribed respiratory exercises for strengthening the respiratory muscles and diaphragm (Dryer, 2017). Harmonica playing is a fun and entertaining method of pulmonary exercise.

Yorkston, Beukelman, Strand, and Bell (1999) discussed this type of pre-speech training when working with dysarthric patients:

> *"The production of a consistent level of subglottic air pressure is a primary goal of the respiratory function during speech… Rather than attempt to train them during speech, we have simplified their task by initially training them during nonspeech activities… [Then] clients can be instructed to produce consistent phonation while producing utterances"* (p. 114–115).

The authors recommended using a water manometer to train clients to sustain air pressures within the range used for speech (5–10 cm H_2O). They also recommended using a simple plastic water-filled bottle with a hole in the cap into which is inserted a tube. The same goal could be applied to any blow toy.

CLASSIC BREATHING EXERCISES

The term *breathing exercises* is assigned to activities that prepare the body and breath for articulation activities. These activities can be done with children and adults who are able to follow multi-step directions. There is no research on the effectiveness of any of these methods and they have therefore been dropped from virtually all articulation and phonology textbooks. However, these simple methods can be found all throughout the literature of speech training and they have their usefulness with the right clients at the right time. These are the types of activities

that singers, public speakers, and actors use to maintain a healthy voice during continuous performance schedules. These activities are designed to encourage the correct use of the breath for speech and to eliminate bad habits that interfere with it. Nemoy and Davis (1937) explained why in the simplest of terms: "Poor breathing habits interfere greatly with the proper functioning of the speech mechanism" (p. 23).

Many books published before the introduction of phonology could be used as sources of these exercises. The elocutionists often wrote extensive sections on respiratory support for speech and song. For example, Oskar Guttmann (1893) devoted more than 60 pages to this subject. He called these activities *respiratory gymnastics*.

Gertrude Walsh presented a succinct list of these breathing exercises in her delightful book called *Sing Your Way to Better Speech* (1939). Her organization will be used here to summarize these ideas. Her routines are divided into four basic types: *exercises to relax the body, activities to exhilarate the body, suggestions to improve posture,* and *breathing exercises*. These classic ideas will be very familiar to most readers who have been involved in any type of relaxation or therapeutic exercise program. A few ideas from other authors have been added to this list as noted. Readers will also recognize that several of these activities were demonstrated in the acclaimed movie *The King's Speech* (Hooper et al., 2010).

Clothing

To begin, a few words about clothing worn during these activities. Tight clothing constricts the body and interferes with speech breathing while loose clothing frees the body and promotes better speech breathing. This was first discussed in books on elocution when women were still wearing corsets: "We must learn to breathe properly, freely, naturally… To breathe naturally we must do away with all constriction… Off with ill-fitting corsets!" (Everts, 1908, p. 7).

Women's corsets have not been much of a concern since Coco Chanel introduced women to jersey fabric and relaxed fit during in the early 20th century. However, tight jeans and belts, restricting shirts and jackets, and ill-fitting

Stretching and shaking help loosen upper body muscles for better speech breathing.

shoes or boots might be problematic for anyone. Take a look at the clothing that clients are wearing during these breathing exercises and encourage them to wear more relaxed clothing that supports better speech breathing.

Exercises to Relax the Body

Tension is the source of many faults in speech breathing. Walsh describes the following now classic activities to relax the body for good speech. She explained that relaxation exercises should be included because "a tense muscle will not respond" (1939, p. 197). Walsh recommended that clients repeat these activities periodically throughout the day:

- Stand erect with the weight evenly distributed on the feet. Roll the head down toward the chest. Continue to roll the head down, then the shoulders and chest. Let arms and hands hang, and roll down as far forward as possible. Roll back up gently and smoothly. Take five minutes to complete this full cycle.

- Sit erect on a chair with the hands hanging limp at the side of the body. Roll the head forward. Then let it hang over the left shoulder and then the right.

- Sit quietly and release all tension in the body.

- Stand and raise the arms above the head. Inhale deeply. Then let the arms fall heavily along the body's sides.

- Shake arms and hands. Rotate them in large circles in front of the body to loosen the arms and shoulders.

Nemoy and Davis (1937) also recommended breathing exercises to relax the body in preparation for speech: "Relaxation exercises should precede breathing exercises since relaxation is the first step in correct breathing" (p. 25). They recommended the following methods:

- Lie on the floor, relax, inhale deeply and feel the action of the diaphragm and ribs as they move up and out.

- Inhale and exhale gently through the nose.

- Inhale deeply through the nose "until the chest is filled like a bag of a vacuum cleaner" (filled to capacity; taut). Exhale slowly "until the bag collapses."

- Inhale through the nose, and sustain exhalation through the mouth on a pinwheel, strip of paper, or feather. Blow long and steady.

- Repeat previous step, breathing in and out through the nose only.

- Inhale deeply, hold the breath, and rap vigorously on the chest.

- Inhale deeply, and "see how many steps you can take while holding the breath" (p. 26).

- Inhale and exhale rhythmically to music "to assist in securing rhythm in breathing" (p. 26).

- Whisper several sentences.

Activities to Exhilarate the Body

Walsh (1939) describes the following activities to exhilarate the body for good respiration:

- Lift the arms above the head and stretch until the stretch is felt throughout the entire torso. Drop the arms but sustain the torso stretch.

- Stretch the right arm up until the torso stretch is felt on that side. Repeat with the left arm.

- Stand erect and imagine a plumb line dropping through the center of the body. Get the feeling of the straightness of the plumb line. Rock back and forth from the balls of the feet to the heals, without breaking the line. Allow the arms to swing freely.

Exercises

Many elocutionists, speech-language pathologists, and vocal coaches through the ages recommended that the hands be placed on the stomach at the diaphragm in order to feel its function in breathing. The client feels the tummy

Therapists stimulate the yawn to induce deep inhalation.

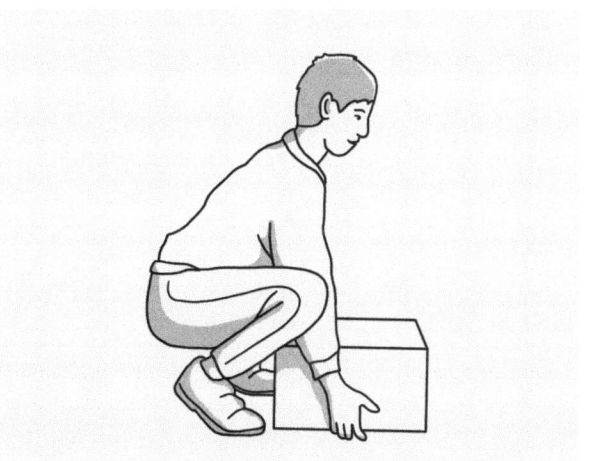

Heavy lifting is a long-standing method for increasing respiratory drive for speech.

expand and contract with each inhalation and exhalation. The present author likes to do this by laying a two-pound wristband weight on the diaphragm. The motokinesthetic approach uses cords loosely tied around the abdomen for this purpose. Walsh (1939) describes the following activities to use along with this basic idea:

- Stretch the arms over the head. Yawn. Notice the torso expansion.

- Lay flat on the floor, put the arms over the head, breath easily. Notice the expansion of the chest upon inhalation. Breathe without lifting the shoulders.

- Stand erect, chest up and forward. Raise the arms to the sides at shoulder level and inhale easily as the arms are raised. Exhale as the arms lower.

- Stand erect, chest up and forward. Place hands at the waist. Say "Ssss" and then "Shhhh" upon exhalation. Let the jaw relax.

- Repeat previous step. Don't let the chest sink in as the sounds are produced. Feel the expansion in the waist.

- Inhale and blow a fine even stream of breath, like gently blowing out a candle. Repeat and say, "Oooo." Keep everything loose.

- Inhale, then sustain an exhale for a count of three. Increase the duration of the exhale by a little every day until an exhale to a count to 20 or 30 can be sustained with one breath.

- Inhale through the nostrils. Keep the lips together and yawn. Observe the expanded intra-oral sensation. Practice words on the exhalation after the yawn.

- Whisper a favorite jingle.

- Whisper and prolong words.

- Yawn and sigh while repeat vowels.

- Keep the same open sensation of the throat as was had in the yawn while singing and speaking.

- Read aloud every day. Read as much as possible on one breath. Do not strain. Over time discover that longer and longer passages can be read without strain.

Heavy Lifting

Some breathing exercises also include pushing, pulling, lifting, or bearing-down activities to increase force of exhalation because they cause the abdomen and diaphragm to contract. This idea survives in the motor speech literature: "Pushing, pulling, and bearing down during speech or non-speech tasks may help to increase respiratory drive for speech" (Duffy, 1995, p. 390).

SPEECH WORK

Speech work is the term used here to describe the activities that are done to manipulate respiratory control during speech production. These methods are employed with clients who are ready to work at that cognitive, linguistic, auditory, motoric, phonemic, and phonological level. They are the types of activities that are found in textbooks on voice and articulation published before the phonological era. They are also still found in introductory voice and articulation books written for theater and communications majors (e.g., Crannell, 1991; Mayer, 1998).

Breath support work done at the speech level entails direct experimentation with and control of airflow during production of speech units. SLPs teach the client how to use his breath to perform specific speech skills by describing and modeling that which she wants him to learn. These ideas can be incorporated into work with many different types of clients simply by using vocabulary at the client's cognitive and receptive language level. An excellent discussion of this type of therapy is presented in Fisher (1966) and this section relies heavily on her ideas.

General Inspiratory Control

Fisher describes the essentials of correct inspiration training for speech purposes:

- *Quick inhalation:* Teach clients that inhalation during speech should be quick: "Ideally, the listener should not even be aware that the speaker is breathing, and certainly should not be aware of [inhaling] as a prominent interruption of speaking" (p. 53–54).

- *Mouth inhalation:* Fisher instructs that clients should be taught to inhale through the mouth for speech. She suggests that inhaling through the nose — as taught by the elocutionists — takes too much time and that it is more natural to inhale through the mouth while speaking.

- *Avoid inhaling too much:* Fisher wrote that untrained speakers often try to improve their speech by inhaling too deeply, and by taking in more breath than necessary for the speech task at hand. She suggested that this makes the process of inhalation too long. Fisher also warned that inhaling too deeply is usually followed by a sigh, which causes speech to be breathy: "It is better to take quick, smaller breaths more frequently (at appropriate pauses between thought-units of your speech) than to try to fill up your lungs for a nearly interminable exhalation" (p. 54).

- *Tension-free inhalation:* Do not allow a client's chest or shoulders to heave during inhalation. Fisher said that this causes too much tension and probably indicates an attempt at too much inhalation.

- *Silent inhalation:* Teach clients to inhale silently:

"Noisy inhalation is strained, since it involves tension in muscles which should be relaxed during phonation. The vocal folds should be wide open during inhalation. If they are held almost closed, inspiration will be noisy" (p. 54).

• *Inhale at syntactic markers:* Teach clients to inhale at natural syntactic markers. Fisher called them *thought units* and *sense pauses.* This means to inhale when the grammatical structure of the speech unit comes to a natural end. For example, inhale between phrases. Inhalation is marked with a forward slash in this example: "I would like to go with you / if that's okay / when you go to the store today."

• *Inhale before "running out of air":* Teach clients to inhale before gasping for breath. According to Fisher, clients should be taught to anticipate the need for oxygen and to inhale at appropriate syntactic markers before they find themselves in the middle of a phrase without breath support and before they begin gasping.

• *Inhale before register changes:* A change in vocal register usually signals that the client needs to inhale. This is especially obvious in older adult speakers. Teach clients to take the moment they need to inhale in order to avoid this occurrence.

General Expiratory Control

Fisher also describes the essentials of correct expiration during speech:

• *Exhale economically:* Teach the client to spend expiration wisely. Do not begin exhalation before the utterance begins, and do not exhale after the utterance ends.

• *Resist an "out-rush" of breath:* Pace exhalation throughout an utterance. Do not force too much exhalation too soon in an utterance. Don't waste breath early in an utterance or breath support will be lost as the utterance progresses. Count out loud to learn this and watch the abdomen in a mirror. Berry and Eisenson discussed this process at length (1956, p. 240). They suggested having the client lie down with a few books stacked on the abdomen to watch the abdomen rise during inhalation and descend during speech exhalation. Learn to exhale smoothly and steadily. Start with vowels and progress to simple syllables, words and phrases.

• *Suspend and resume expiration without wasting breath:* Do not inhale at each pause. Some pauses can be taken without inhalation. Do not waste breath by inhaling in the midst of them.

• *Regulate loudness:* Do not speak too loudly for the situation because this wastes breath.

• *Prevent fading of vocal intensity:* Fading at the end of an utterance is very annoying to listeners because it reduces intelligibility and makes them work harder to hear you. It can also lead to glottal fry and final consonant deletion. Teach the client to maintain force of exhalation steadily throughout an entire speech unit. Use simple counting or other recitation activities to practice this skill. Teach the client to learn to use his ears to self-monitor intensity.

Learning to Exhale Phonemes

One can utilize very simple activities to teach clients to exhale instead of inhale during the production of any phoneme. The basic idea is to use a small lightweight object to blow. This idea is found scattered all throughout the literature, beginning in the Phonetic Placement Era, and progressing into the Modern Era as represented in these examples from 1912 and 2003:

"Sometimes it is sufficient to explain these principles to the patient and let him feel [it] with his hand. A tissue paper flag or a light piece of cotton is also effective" (Scripture, 1912, p. 152).

"[Hold] the top corners of a paper tissue before the client so that there is a loose section of tissue hanging down before the mouth. The bottom half of the tissue should fly up on the release of the /p/" (Flowers, 2003, p. 163–164).

SLPs can use many different tools to teach exhalation and any small lightweight object will do: cotton balls, tissue paper, tiny wads of paper, hole punch paper dots, strings, string blowers, sugar, salt, and more. Use the object to teach the client about inhalation and exhalation and then use it to teach him about exhaling phonemes. Teach the client that no phonemes in English are made

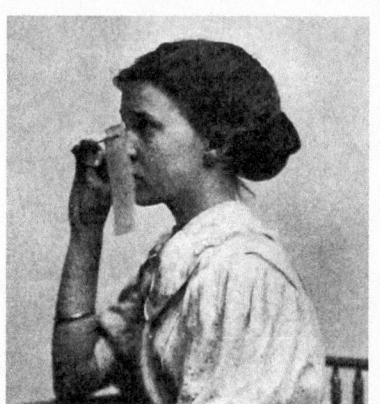

A simple "tissue flag" is a way to teach clients about exhalation during phoneme production. (Photo: Scripture, 1912)

upon inhalation. Use negative and positive practice back and forth, inhaling and then exhaling phonemes to discover their similarities and differences, then focus on exhalation of the target phoneme and progress to syllables, words, phrases, and so forth.

Visual Feedback

A mirror can help clients understand the idea of exhalation for speech. Have clients exhale to produce a cloud of fog on the mirror, then teach them that they can make the cloud larger by exhaling longer. This is a great activity for little children. Motivate them by allowing them to draw happy faces and other pictures on the fog with their fingers.

Vowels and Diphthongs

Many clients, especially those with motor speech disorders, produce weak vowels and diphthongs due to poor breath support. A speech therapy program for such clients should contain work to help them make their vowels rich and full. Make sure the client is producing vowels with a pure tone supported by adequate breath. (For additional information on vowels and diphthongs, see Chapter 21.)

Glides and Nasals

The glides and nasals may be produced weakly in clients with motor speech disorders, and they can be a problem in young clients who are just learning to talk. Make sure clients are producing these sounds with full respiratory support. Make sure the nasals are made with nasal resonance driven to full capacity and with exhalation that is strong enough that these sounds can be heard. Make sure the client's glides are made with full oral resonance on both the on-glide and off-glide segments. Functional words like *yes* and *no* are excellent selections for practicing glides and nasals.

Frication

Control of airflow for the production of the fricatives and affricates is perhaps the most sophisticated way in which the breath is used for speech. This is part of what makes these phonemes the last to emerge in normal development and the last to be remediated in clients with motor speech disorders. Clients should be taught how to inhale in preparation for isolated productions of these sounds. They also need to learn how to sustain airflow long enough that the sounds are sustained. Poor breath support may make it easier for some clients to learn the affricates /tʃ/ and /dʒ/ first because they can be "thrown out" or "spit out" quickly. But this will do only when first learning the phonemes. Sustained exhalation must be learned to help these phonemes mature. Teach clients to produce strong frication at first, and then teach them to make these sounds more softly and correctly. Recognize that production of the voiced fricatives requires that the client valve his airstream at two places simultaneously — at the glottis and in the mouth. This makes these sounds even more difficult to produce when breath support is poor, and an extra measure of attention might need to be offered to them.

Final Consonants

Teach clients to inhale an adequate amount of air so that exhalation can sustain whole syllables through to the final consonants. Do this by modeling syllables with longer duration on the vowel. Use a melodic intonation pattern to help.

Syllable Sequences

Teach clients to inhale enough air to produce multiple syllables in babbling sequences or in multi-syllabic words. Teach them "Don't stop the air" and "Keep the air going" as they practice these sequences.

Phoneme Transitions

Many clients stop airflow between phonemes in words. For example, they produce *soap* as *stoap* and use the /t/ to stop the airflow. There is a simple technique to help clients keep steady exhalation as they transition from one phoneme to another: Teach them to slow down the transition and insert /h/ in place of the stop consonant. Continuing the example, an SLP would model *soap* as "sssss-hhhhh-hh-oap" without pausing or stopping the airflow between phonemes. Producing /h/ in the transition keeps the airflow going and teaches the client to turn his voice on during the transition between the fricative and the vowel. Sustaining continuous airflow from /s/–to–/h/–to–vowel teaches the client how to sustain his exhalation during the production of the whole syllable.

Speaking

One can learn to extend the exhaled breath during speech by engaging in more complex speaking activities. The following exercises are abstracted from Mayer (1998) who wrote for college-age adults learning to improve their speaking voice:

- Read a paragraph of 40–60 words in one continuous exhalation.

- Take a deep breath and say /s/. Sustain it for as long as possible. Keep the production "even and regular, free of jerkiness and bumpiness" (p. 20). Also, try this with other voiceless fricatives.

- Count to 50, using one breath per number. Then count to 50 (or as many as possible) on one continuous breath.

- See how long of a paragraph can be read aloud in one breath if the fricatives and affricates are eliminated. These hissing sounds release much breath, so one should be able to read longer without them.

- Read aloud a list of the United States or another long, familiar list. See how many items can be read on one continuous breath. Over time, increase the number that can be read in one breath.

Singing

One can use singing to teach any breathing skill and it is a wonderful way to work on breath support with young children. Teach clients to sustain exhalation during song phrases. Clients can exaggerate the inhalation necessary between phrases to understand what is being done. In her book *Sing Your Way to Better Speech*, the author discussed how she came up with the idea of using song to teach adult clients correct breath control for speech:

> *"Although some time had been spent practicing the exercises for breath control, it was not until they sang a jingle that they realized the importance of breathing and controlling the outgoing breath, for all discovered that they did not have enough breath to sustain the phrase"* (Walsh, 1939, p. 3).

REFLEX STIMULATION

A number of reflexes can be used to stimulate inhalation and exhalation in infants and other clients with limited breath control due to low cognition or neuromuscular disability. For definitions and notes about their application, readers are referred to Chapter 17 on the speech reflexes. Reflexes related to various aspects of inhalation and exhalation include the following:

- Cough reflex
- Cry reflex
- Glottal-closing reflex
- Glottal-opening reflex
- Hand-to-mouth vocalization reflex
- Infantile-emotional reflex
- Inspiration reflex 1 and 2
- Laugh reflex
- Movement-vocalization reflex
- Yawn reflex

BODYWORK

The term *bodywork* is used here to represent the type of physical handling techniques that occupational, physical, and speech-language therapists employ to facilitate improved respiratory control in clients with neuromuscular disorder and severe motor speech problems. The development of breath support is a direct reflection of muscle tone, postural support, and the ability to achieve and maintain an upright position against gravity.

Bodywork is an area in which occupational and physical therapists have particular training while, generally, speech-language pathologists entering the field do not.

Therefore, the techniques required for this level of service necessitate teamwork. Speech-language pathologists should look to team motor specialists for methods to be used with individual clients and continuing education should also be sought to further the SLPs knowledge in this area.

The idea of including bodywork activities during speech therapy is not intended to turn speech-language pathologists into occupational/physical therapists or massage practitioners, and these activities are not to be done instead of articulation or motor speech work. In fact these activities are not recommended to replace anything in the client's speech program. Bodywork activities are to be used within or alongside the articulation or motor speech therapy program. If these positioning, handling and movement techniques distract from the required speech work, they should be abandoned for the time being, and the client's attention should be re-focused on the speech work at hand.

It should be noted that many SLPs feel awkward with these types of positioning, handling, and movement activities. This may be because college and university speech training programs generally do not include background information in this area for SLPs, and most SLPs are trained to work with clients while seated in chairs at tables. Don't let fear of these methods interfere with the speech work that must be done. It is recommended that SLPs include bodywork activities occasionally, as necessary, with occupational and physical therapy guidance and support, and that more activities be added at a comfortable pace. Over years of practice, many SLPs find that these ideas become second nature.

There are a wide variety of therapeutic activities that can be used to achieve correct skeletal support for respiration. The following sections briefly describe the types of activities that tend to be recommended. The ideas presented below should help begin team discussions about breath support remediation activities for individual clients.

Medial Trunk Elongation

Trunk elongation along the medial plane can stimulate deep inhalation. The client is stretched from the hips through the trunk, shoulders, neck, and head. This often is done while the client is lying supine or is resting on a large therapy ball.

Medial Trunk Flexion

Trunk flexion along the medial plane can stimulate deep exhalation. This can be done by having the client do sit-ups or pull-to-sits, or by rocking him gently back while he sits on a large therapy ball.

Lateral Trunk Elongation

Trunk elongation along the lateral plane can stimulate inhalation. Stabilize the hips and encourage the client to stretch up one arm on one side. This can be done while

Materials can be presented on one side and then the other so the client rotates his trunk during speech activities.

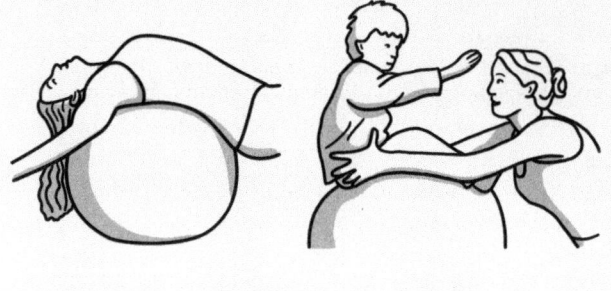

Elongating the trunk (left) stimulates inhalation while flexing the trunk (right) stimulates exhalation.

Clients of all ages can be taught to stretch the trunk for better speech breathing.

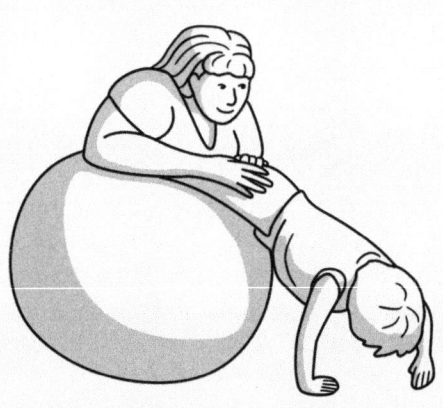

This client is being rocked toward and away from his speech materials to help develop better upper body stability for speech breathing.

the client is sitting on the floor, on the therapists lap, or on a large therapy ball.

Lateral Trunk Flexion

The trunk can be encouraged to flex along the lateral plane in order to stimulate deep asymmetrical exhalation. Stabilize the hips and encourage the client to flex-to-sit on one side. This can be done while the client is sitting on the floor, on the SLP's lap, or on a large therapy ball.

Trunk Rotation

The trunk can be rotated around the spine in order to stimulate inhalation and exhalation. Inhale as the trunk rotates from midline to one side, and exhale as the trunk rotates back from that side to midline. Repeat on the other side. Have the client smoothly rotate from left to right as he inhales and exhales in smooth sequences.

Neck Elongation

The neck can be elongated along the medial plane in order to stimulate deep inhalation. Do this in coordination with trunk elongation. Stretch the client from the hips through the trunk, shoulders, neck, and head. This can

be done while the client is lying supine on a large therapy ball. It can also be done in sitting.

Head Flexion

The head can be encouraged to flex forward along the medial plane in order to stimulate exhalation. This can be done in sitting, or during sit-ups or pull-to-sit. This work is coordinated with trunk flexion.

Shoulder Elongation

The shoulders can be stretched to encourage deeper inhalation. Have the client engage in shoulder rolls forward and backward. Head rolls can also be used to loosen up the shoulders. Make sure to consult with team motor specialists to make sure that head rolls do not cause more tone and movement problems.

Press the Shoulders Down

The shoulders can be pressed downward toward the tailbone to encourage diaphragmatic breathing instead of clavicular breathing. Face the client or work from behind. Place hands (palms down) on the top of the shoulders and press down. Encourage inhalation and exhalation.

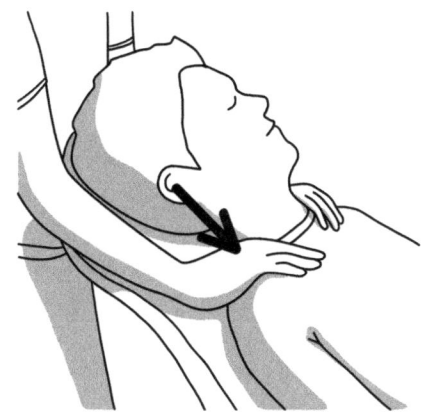

Press the shoulders down to inhibit clavicular breathing.

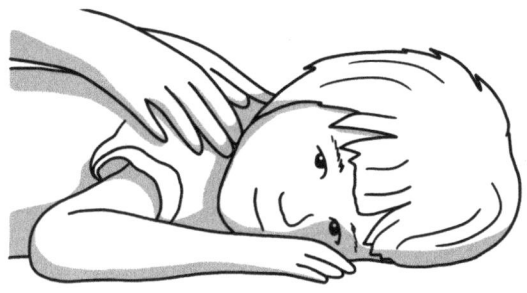

Massage can relieve tightness in the back.

Kneel-standing (left) and crawling (right) may be prescribed to facilitate better hip stability for speech breathing.

Sit-ups and airplaning are classic ways to build core strength for good respiratory support.

Sit-Ups

Performing a sit-up is a standard way to increase abdominal strength for the core. Sit-ups can be incorporated into many types of speech lessons. For example, instead of sitting at a table to manipulate speech cards, have the client lie on the floor with his knees toward the therapist. The therapist will hold the legs as the client sits up to retrieve his next card.

Airplaning

Airplaning is a classic way to increase strength of the back muscles for the core. Airplaning can be done on the floor, on a therapy ball, or in the air. Use airplaning as a reward for good speech activity or incorporate it into the therapy activity itself.

Tap the Chest

The chest can be tapped to encourage deeper inhalation. Use three fingers and tap the chest in a firm-but-comfortable hammering action with the fingertips. Tap all around the chest where the lungs sit beneath the bones.

Tap the Back

The back can be tapped to encourage deeper inhalation. Use three fingers and tap the back in a firm-but-comfortable hammering action. Tap all around the back where the lungs sit beneath the bones.

Body Massage

The body can be massaged to inhibit any stiffness or high tone that is interfering with trunk mobility and its contribution to inhalation and exhalation for speech. Use standard Swedish massage techniques on the body core.

Hip Stability

A variety of therapeutic activities can be used to develop hip stability for better speech breathing as prescribed by team motor therapists. These may include standing, kneel standing, crawling, stair climbing, and so forth.

Shoulder Stability

A variety of therapeutic activities can be used to develop shoulder strength and stability for better speech breathing. These may include but are not limited to: push-ups, pull-ups, crawling, army crawling, and prone work on a therapy ball.

Abdominal and Back Strength

A variety of therapeutic activities can be used to develop core strength of the abdominal and back muscles to support speech breathing. These may include but are not limited to: sit-ups, airplane maneuvers, trunk rotation activities, and lateral trunk activities.

SUMMARY

A wide variety of methods can be used to help clients develop the best breath support possible for speech production. These practical methods have been passed down through the generations without benefit of formal research in regard to speech therapy.

8

Balancing Oral & Nasal Resonance

Developing the distinction between "mouth sounds" and "nose sounds"

"In most cases, resonance can be improved by consciously changing unsatisfactory muscular controls."

– Hilda Fisher, 1966

This chapter discusses methods designed to help clients learn differential control of oral and nasal resonance. Errors of resonance occur in clients with both articulation deficit and motor speech disorders. Problems include clients with *hypernasality* (too much nasal resonance) and *hyponasality* (too little nasal resonance). It also includes clients who can pass an articulation/phonology test but who mumble, slur, and lose intelligibility in conversation. Clients who substitute nasal phonemes for oral phonemes are also included in this group, as are those who make nasal snorts, rustles, and other *audible nasal emissions* (ANEs). The group also contains clients with very limited speech who produce no nasal and no oral phonemes at all.

Speech teachers and speech-language pathologists throughout the ages have developed a wide variety of practical methods to facilitate correct oral and nasal resonance, but very little research has been done on the

Proper resonance is important to intelligible speech.

methods themselves. The reader, therefore, should view most of the methods of this chapter as advice passed down through the ages from one generation of therapists to another. The few studies that have been conducted along these lines are embedded within the text below where applicable.

BACKGROUND

Speech-language pathologists are taught that resonance refers to the way in which voice reverberates, vibrates, rings, echoes, resounds, or booms in the chest, throat, oropharynx, mouth, nose, and other head sinuses. According to Fisher (1966) resonance serves three main functions: (1) to increase the loudness of voice produced at the larynx, (2) to alter vocal tone, and (3) to produce separate oral and nasal phonemes. Every SLP understands that the velopharyngeal mechanism is the main organ that controls differential oral and nasal sound. Therapists also know that all vowels and consonants in English are oral except the three nasals — /m/, /n/, and /ŋ/.

Appropriate oral and nasal resonance was a primary element of speaking and singing instruction as taught by the elocutionists of the 19th century. They trained their students in the absolute basics of this skill, i.e. that oral sounds should be fully oral and nasal sounds should be fully nasal. The elocutionists helped their students accomplish good resonance by employing standard instruction methods such as ear training, modeling, and practicing during singing and speaking. These techniques are

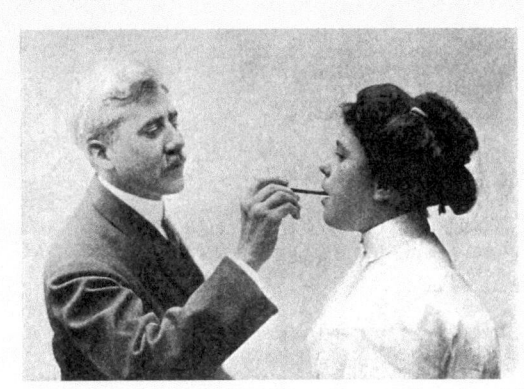

A "velar hook" was used for resonance training during the Phonetic Placement Era. (Photo: Scripture, 1912)

described in the methods cataloged below.

Anatomy became an important element of speech training by the end of the 19th century as the Phonetic Placement Era rolled in. An error of resonance began to be called *rhinolalia* and therapists of that era began to employ "soft palate exercises" and "velar gymnastics" along with their consonant and vowel training. They also used objects to manipulate the soft palate. For example, Melville Bell (1898) used a pencil and a letter opener to push the velum up, Scripture (1912) used a "velar hook" to pull it down and to resist its elevation, and Van Riper (1949) used a tongue depressor to teach his clients how to pull the velum up and away. Therapists of the Phonetic Placement Era also began to use reflex stimulation and other methods that carried into the Traditional Era. In fact, almost all of the methods that are suggested in current textbooks on articulation, voice, and resonance training can be traced back to the Phonetic Placement and Traditional Eras. These are the ideas that form the bulk of the methods described below.

Functional & Organic

The elocutionists realized that adequate treatment of a speech disorder required a differential diagnosis of its anatomical causes, and nowhere was this considered more carefully than in the area of resonance. By the early 20th century, speech correctionists of the Phonetic Placement Era began to divide problems of resonance into two types based on anatomy: *functional* and *organic*. These divisions remain.

Functional

A functional problem is a velopharyngeal movement problem that has no known cause. A functional problem of resonance now is called *velopharyngeal incompetence* or *velopharyngeal insufficiency* (VPI). The client with VPI is working with a structurally complete yet unskilled velopharyngeal mechanism. He has difficulty moving the mechanism in the right direction, with the right amount of force, with

complete closure, and/or with the correct timing necessary for expressive speech to have normal oronasal resonance. Fröeschels (1948) said that these patients "lacked the motor concept to use the soft palate" (p. 145). A problem of resonance that is functional in nature may be responsive to the types of speech therapy activities described in this chapter. Bender and Kleinfeld (1938) called this type of problem *adjustable resonance* meaning that this is the aspect of resonance that can be responsive to speech and language therapy procedures.

Therapists sometimes struggle with decision-making to determine if a client's VPI is functional or organic and what to do about it. Pannbacker (2004) pointed out that confusion may occur because some (but not all) SLPs receive extensive educational and clinical experience with these clients. She called for the development of standards in this area:

> *"There is a void in the specifications of what knowledge and skills speech-language pathologists need to make clinical decisions about VPI and improve the quality of care"* (Pannbacker, 2004, p. 199).

Organic

An organic problem of resonance is a velopharyngeal closure problem that has a known congenital or acquired physical cause. Clients with organic problems include those with cleft palate, insufficient or malformed velopharyngeal tissue, palatal fistulas, tumors, blocked or narrow nasal passageways, a deviated nasal septum, a large tongue, a small mouth, a deep pharynx, or enlarged tonsils and adenoids. Clients with paralysis, cerebral palsy, and other neuromuscular disorders that affect velopharyngeal closure are also included in this group.

Organic problems of resonance usually cannot be remediated with speech therapy activities alone. These clients need a thorough multidisciplinary team evaluation in order to determine an appropriate course of treatment. Treatment will include medical, surgical, orthodontic, and other physical interventions. Surgeries, medications, and/or specially designed oral appliances may be recommended. Occupational or physical therapy, massage, and other body therapies may also be included. Speech services help these clients learn the best oral and nasal resonance possible given their on-going structural or neuromuscular issues. The methods of this chapter can be appropriate for some of these clients when applied within the larger multidisciplinary remediation plan.

Clients

Many different types of clients have been noted as having problems in oral and nasal resonance. The following describes the resonance problems of specific populations.

Dysarthria

In their online information for the public, the American Speech-Language-Hearing Association (2012) lists "nasal speech" (hypernasality) and "sounding stuffy" (hyponasality) as two specific symptoms of dysarthria. Poor resonance in the dysarthric client is due to neuromuscular disturbance that affects the control, the completeness, and the timing of the velopharyngeal port's opening and closing movements. Yorkston et al. (1999) summarized that "velopharyngeal dysfunction is frequently, but not universally, associated with dysarthria" (p. 360). They suggested classifying dysarthric patients into five categories of velopharyngeal dysfunction: (1) consistently adequate closure, (2) consistently inadequate closure with extensive velopharyngeal dysfunction, (3) consistently inadequate closure with minimal velopharyngeal dysfunction, (4) delayed closure, and (5) inconsistent closure. The methods of this chapter are appropriate for this group.

Apraxia

Problems of resonance are *not* listed among the speech problems of apraxic adults as described in the standard set forth by Darley, Aaronson, and Brown's classic *Motor Speech Disorder* (1975). However, in regard to children, Barbara Davis reviewed the literature and found that children with apraxia may have "fluctuating nasality" but she noted that this is a controversial point (Davis, 2010). Some writers have suggested that it is the timing of transition movements between nasal and non-nasal phonemes that is the core issue in childhood apraxia. Perhaps some of these studies inadvertently have included dysarthric children in their sample. In any case the methods of this chapter are intended for apraxic clients if and when nasality is an issue.

Mumbling

There are clients who can pass a basic articulation or phonology test but who are somewhat unintelligible in conversational speech due to mumbling. Mumbling is due in part to poor control of oronasal resonance during connected speech. These clients also tend to have limited projection of the voice, restricted range of speech movements, lack of proper oral stability, and rapid rate. The velopharyngeal methods of this chapter are intended for these clients.

> *"A person with a weak voice often doesn't open the mouth widely enough in speaking. The voice does not carry because, in a sense, it doesn't have much chance to get out of the mouth in the first place"* (Mayer, 1998, p. 53).

Cul-de-Sac Resonance

> *"Cul-de-sac resonance occurs when the transmission of acoustic energy is trapped in a blind pouch with only one outlet. The speech is perceived as muffled… The sound energy is blocked and vibration occurs primarily in the pharynx"* (Kummer & Lee, 1996, p. 273).

Cul-de-sac resonance may be due to several factors including enlarged tonsils or adenoids, blocked nasal passageways, inappropriate tongue shaping (especially humping), or VPI. The methods of this chapter are intended for this category.

Nasal Twang

Some clients are quite nasal on one or more of the vowels in a pattern that has been called a *nasal twang*. The nasal twang may be due to habit, local or regional dialect, family patterns, or second-language learning. It is normal for a certain amount of nasalization to be present on vowels that occur adjacent to nasal consonants in both children and adults (Flege, 1988). But the nasal twang is nasalization of the vowels regardless of the presence or absence of neighboring nasal consonants. For example, residents of the Chicago area traditionally have been classified as having a nasal twang. Clients with a nasal twang can learn how to make their vowels fully oral if they desire. The methods of this chapter are intended for this category when the client wants to change.

Phoneme-Specific Nasal Emission

There are clients who produce only one or more specific phonemes with nasal emission in the absence of more generalized hypernasality. These clients sniff, snort, or allow some nasal sound to escape during production of their error phoneme(s). Nasal sound can occur on any one specific phoneme or on a whole category of phonemes. The escape of nasal sound on the sibilants is fairly common and has been called by various terms in the literature — *nasal lisp, nasal snort, recessive s-lisp,* and *nasal stigmatism.* More recently, Peterson-Falzone and Graham (1990) used the phrases *phoneme-specific nasal emission* and *posterior nasal frication* to describe nasalized sibilants.

What causes a phoneme-specific nasal emission? Peterson (1975) reviewed the case histories of four clients with nasal emission on sibilants. She found that some of these clients had incompetent velopharyngeal mechanisms in their past but others didn't. She postulated that phoneme-specific nasal emission might be viewed as a residual of earlier velopharyngeal incompetency that may or may not have been documented. She also found that these errors typically were accompanied by incorrect tongue placement. Peterson speculated that auditory training and the phonetic placement method might be the best approaches to treatment for these patients.

Peterson-Falzone and Graham (1990) investigated phoneme-specific nasal emission in 36 children between the ages of three and sixteen years of age in order to see how these errors related to physical findings and phonological skills. All clients had intact structural mechanisms, and no relationship between these error phonemes and phonological processes were found. Treatment recommendations included developing auditory discrimination for nasalized and non-nasalized fricatives and using bio-feedback methods as described below.

Ruscello, Shuster, and Sandwisch (1991) found that biofeedback in the form of a nasometer along with articulatory drill remediated a nasal lisp produced by one adult college student. The student was enrolled in ten weeks of biweekly 50-minute individual therapy sessions: "It appears that persons who exhibit phoneme-specific nasal emission form a subgroup of individuals who are readily amenable to articulation treatment" (p. 31). The methods of this chapter are intended for this type of client.

Upper Respiratory Problems

Clients with chronic upper respiratory problems tend to be denasal. They need medical attention so that the nature of the respiratory problem can be understood and managed through medical, surgical, environmental, and/or dietary treatments. Speech and language therapy will include methods to help these clients produce the best oral and nasal resonance possible given the condition of the upper respiratory system. The methods of this chapter are intended for this group of clients as their other conditions are managed.

Hearing Impairment / Deafness

Clients with hearing impairment or deafness virtually always have difficulty developing an appropriate balance of oral and nasal resonance. Children with cochlear implants have been found to have difficulty perceiving nasal resonance as well as producing correct resonance (Guillot, Ohde, & Hedrick, 2013). The methods of this chapter may be helpful for clients with hearing impairment.

Structural Defects

It is well-known that clients with problems of oral structure can be hypernasal or hyponasal depending upon the defect. These clients require full multidisciplinary team assessment and treatment. The methods of this chapter may be beneficial for these clients when they are used within the context of the full medical/surgical/therapeutic context.

Low Cognition

It is the present author's clinical experience that clients with cognitive skills below six months of age often produce sound without differentiated oral and nasal qualities. They continue to use the infantile quasi-resonant sounds as described on the next page. The facilitation methods described in this chapter may be helpful in developing differentiated oral and nasal sound in these clients depending upon cognitive level and neuromuscular status.

Fatigue

Kuehn and Moon (2000) studied the effects of fatigue on velopharyngeal function in adult speakers with normal mechanisms. Air was forced down onto the velopharyngeal mechanism through the nose in order to make it work harder when lifting. They found that inducing fatigue in this way negatively impacted velopharyngeal closure force within breath groups. No differences between males and females were noted.

Drugs and Alcohol

It is well known that people under the influence of certain drugs and alcohol demonstrate poor oronasal resonance at times. This area was not reviewed for inclusion in this manual, however, it is important for therapists to consider this when diagnosing the problem and when designing remedial activities. Referrals to and consultation with appropriate medical, psychological, and community help professionals should be made.

DEVELOPMENT OF RESONANCE

The ability to produce clear oral and nasal sound develops quite early. Vorperian and Kent (2007) reviewed the acoustic literature and reported that velopharyngeal function matured by about one year of age. This means that children figure out how to produce clear oral and nasal resonance during the pre-speech year so that they can produce differential oral and nasal phonemes on their first words. Correct oral and nasal resonance, therefore, is a primitive speech skill and Oller (1978) listed as metaphonological.

In terms of maturity, the velopharyngeal mechanism reaches adult shape and motion by at least five years of age although the mechanism is smaller in overall size (Tian et al., 2010). Velopharyngeal control is maintained throughout life once it is learned and velopharyngeal function does not seem to deteriorate with advancing age (Hoit et al., 1994).

Research has demonstrated that resonance characteristics unfold in developmental stages during infancy. Information about these stages was unknown in Van Riper's time, therefore, the processes of therapy that can be derived from it are not part of Traditional Era therapy. But the present author has found that the unfolding stages of oral and nasal control seen in infancy can represent levels of treatment in clients, especially those with low cognitive skill and/or severe motor speech disorder.

The stages of infant vocal development are described in Chapter 20, *Foundational Pre-Speech Platforms*. The present chapter highlights only those skills that contribute to the development of differential oral and nasal resonance. The picture that unfolds is one of producing increasingly more sophisticated sounds differentially through the mouth and nose during the first year of life. The present author has found it advantageous to the process of therapy to divide these developing skills into five stages.

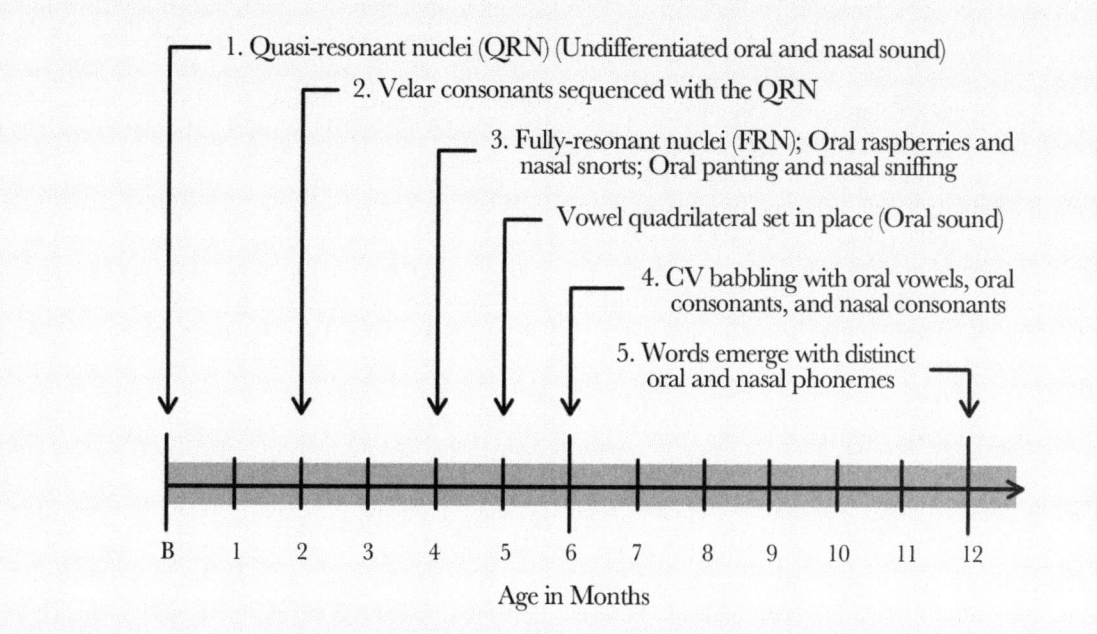

1. Quasi-resonant nuclei (QRN) (Undifferentiated oral and nasal sound)
2. Velar consonants sequenced with the QRN
3. Fully-resonant nuclei (FRN); Oral raspberries and nasal snorts; Oral panting and nasal sniffing
   Vowel quadrilateral set in place (Oral sound)
4. CV babbling with oral vowels, oral consonants, and nasal consonants
5. Words emerge with distinct oral and nasal phonemes

Age in Months

Oral-nasal differentiation develops in stages during the first year of life.

First Stage

An infant is born with the ability to produce voice but without the ability to direct it differentially through the mouth or nose. His first sounds are "quasi-resonant" meaning that they are not fully oral or fully nasal. Often these *quasi-resonant nuclei* (QRN) are simultaneously oral and nasal; a newborn exhales and produces voice while the velum and mouth remain relatively inactive. The resultant sound is simultaneously a little oral and a little nasal. Therefore, the newborn makes his first sounds without velar movement and without oral and nasal differentiation. This level of skill might represent a client before treatment begins. A client at this level must be taught to produce a good strong voice so he eventually can become differentially oral and nasal.

Second Stage

By 2–3 months of age an infant begins to produce his quasi-resonant nuclei in the same breath group with consonantal velar sounds. These occur in small sequences such as /ŋɑ/, /ɑŋ/ and /ɑŋɡɑ/. These utterances are collectively called *goo-ing*. Learning to *goo* then becomes the second level of speech training. A client at this stage might be taught to produce /ŋo/ and *no*, for example, as an initial phonological strategy.

Third Stage

By 4–6 months of age an infant has begun to produce differentiated oral and nasal sound so that true oral vowels and true nasal consonants are heard during cooing and goo-ing. These are an infant's first *fully resonant nuclei*

(FRN). According to Oller (1978), the ability to make differentiated oral and nasal nuclei is an essential metaphonological skill that serves as a foundation for all speech development in all languages from then on. The presence of FRN is strong evidence that the child can move his palate successfully to produce differentiated oral and nasal sound for speech production.

Once he can produce truly oral and truly nasal sound, an infant is free to learn all the vowels and all the nasals, and this is what a typical child does. The vowel quadrilateral is set in place by five months of age (Lieberman, 1980) and all three nasal sounds are heard in isolation.

Babies at this stage also begin to make nasal sounds while eating in a procedure the present author calls *eating-humming*. Humming while eating drives the aroma of food into the nasal cavities for enhanced olfactory perception. Food and wine tasters call it *aeration* and they engage this process silently while moving the back of the tongue and velum. Babies do it with voice and with movement of the whole mouth. As a result, primitive productions of all three nasal consonants often are heard while children are being fed.

The ability to *coo* (to prolong oral vowels and nasal consonants) might represent a third level of training for clients with resonance problems. The client at this stage needs to learn just what the elocutionists taught: to make oral sounds oral and to make nasal sounds nasal. Oral and nasal sound is acquired as the antagonistic muscles in the back of the mouth begin to operate in tandem, meaning that the velum lowers while the back of the tongue rises, and the velum elevates while the back of the tongue lowers. Eating-humming might be used as a therapeutic procedure.

Babies also begin to produce gross frication in the form of raspberries during this period, and these sounds are also produced differentially through the mouth and nose. Some of these sounds are exhaled while others are inhaled, but the important point here is that raspberries are produced exclusively through either the mouth or nose. An inhaled nasal raspberry is called a *snort*, and parents often reinforce this sound in their babies by teaching it as the "piggy sound." Panting and sniffing also arise during this time; panting is the rapid sequencing of inhalation and exhalation that occurs through the mouth and sniffing is the same thing that occurs through the nose.

In sum, the production of prolonged vowels (*cooing*), nasals, raspberries, snorts, pants, and sniffs represent a third level of control in oral/nasal differentiation.

Fourth Stage

Babies begin to babble during the 6–10 month period and they do so with both oral and nasal consonants and with oral vowels. The child is learning to sequence distinct oral and nasal sounds within and across syllables. Therefore, babbling with oral and nasal consonants and oral vowels represents a fourth level of training for a client who is learning differential oral and nasal control.

Fifth Stage

Having learned to differentially control oral and nasal resonance during the pre-babbling period, and having

A flexible tube or straw can aid the auditory assessment of nasal emission.

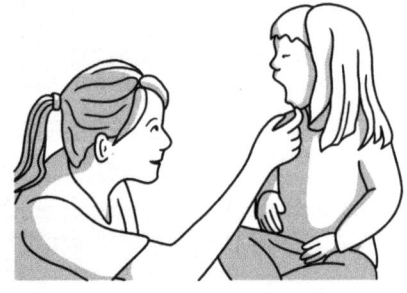

A visual inspection of the velopharyngeal mechanism is always part of the clinical assessment.

learned to sequence oral and nasal phonemes while babbling, the one-year-old is poised ready to produce his first words with vowels that are oral and consonants that are either oral or nasal. Productions include words with all oral sounds (e.g., *dada*) and words that require sequences of oral and nasal sound (e.g., *mama*). These types of words might represent a fifth level of training for a client who is learning to control resonance.

SLPs typically start resonance training at the babbling or word level and many clients can succeed at these levels. It is the present author's clinical experience, however, that certain clients cannot learn differential oral and nasal resonance at the babbling or word level right away because they have not learned the metaphonological skills of the pre-babbling stages. This group is comprised mainly of clients who have motor speech disorders and/or cognitive impairment.

ASSESSMENT OF RESONANCE

The process of assessment in the area of resonance is vastly different for researchers and clinicians. Researchers have used a wide variety of equipment to obtain precise measurements of velopharyngeal movement and sound quality. These have included magnetic resonance imagers, nasometers, manometers, x-rays, cinefluorography, pneumo-tachometers, pressure transducers, electrical analogs, endoscopes, videoendoscopy, nasopharyngoscopy, electrodes, flow meters, flow transducers, compressible bulbs, tape recordings, motion pictures, accelerometers, pneumotachograph face masks, catheters, oscilloscopes, voice synthesizers, and even capsules inserted into the nose.

Clinicians, on the other hand, often face this therapy without benefit of technological support, and they must rely upon their own auditory and visual observations. A visual inspection of the soft palate and surrounding structures is done, and therapists listen to the client during connected speech and during speech testing.

A speech test was developed to aid in the assessment of resonance that became standard in the field. The *Iowa Pressure Articulation Test* (IPAT; Morris, Spriesterbach, & Darley, 1961) is used for "assessing the adequacy of oral pressure for speech sound production and thus, inferentially, the adequacy of velopharyngeal closure" (p. 48–49). The original study demonstrated that production of the fricatives, plosives, and affricates was the best way to discriminate between speakers with adequate and inadequate velopharyngeal closure. These phonemes continue to be used as benchmarks of oral-nasal control. For a thorough discussion of the clinical assessment of resonance please see Kummer and Lee (1996) as well as Mason and Grandstaff (1971).

Therapists develop an ear for resonance that evolves during years of service. Those who are good at this can detect fine differences in resonance patterns. Just as the elocutionists could — as can singing instructors — SLPs can hear when their students are being too nasal or not nasal enough, using the ear to determine the amount of nasal resonance that occurs on vowels and consonants while clients are engaged in speech testing and conversational speech. Therapy should be done in conjunction with information from medical ear-nose-throat exams when possible.

Simple and inexpensive tools often are used during the clinical assessment of resonance. Tools reported most often in textbooks written during the Phonetic Placement and Traditional Eras include flexible hoses, tubes, and straws, as well as small handheld mirrors and cold metal spoons. Flexible tubes and straws were stretched from the client's nose to the therapist's ear in order to bring the subtle sounds of nasal emission to the therapist's auditory attention. The small mirror or metal spoon was held under the client's nose in order to observe the fog that formed on it when air escaped through the nares. Many therapists still use these simple procedures, but the See-Scape has been added to the set. The tube of the See-Scape is held at the nose while the client says sounds or words. A small plug in the tube is observed for movement since it will signal the escape of nasal air. Each of these tools and procedures is described below as well as in Chapter 19, *The Tools of Speech Movement Training.*

It has been suggested on many occasions that the perceptual (auditory) analysis alone can be problematic in the assessment of resonance. Rastatter and Hyman (1984) tested this. They assessed the speech of four groups of children — those with chronically endemic adenoids, those with allergic rhinitis, those with severely deviated septums, and those with no history of rhinologic, articulation, or resonance problems. The children were recorded during various speaking tasks and 30 graduate students analyzed the recordings. Results revealed that perceptual judgments of denasality were quite task dependent. The authors concluded, "The evaluation of nasal resonance should not be based on perceptual judgments alone" (p. 50).

It should be noted that graduate students (not professionals) made the judgments in the study; it is unlikely that these novice therapists had the discriminating ear that SLPs develop throughout years of practice. Just like the professional singer or voice teacher, SLPs get much better in this assessment over time. Further, although these students had completed their coursework in voice, and although the study demonstrated an acceptable level of examiner validity, it was tape recorders from the 1980s (of arguably low audio quality compared with today's standard) and not live performances were used to make these judgments. This study should be re-done with modern equipment and with professionals who have years of experience in this area of treatment.

TREATMENT CONSIDERATIONS

The production of speech that has appropriate oral and nasal resonance is important to all of life's endeavors. Lallh and Rochet (2000) found that the public generally has a negative view of persons with voice and resonance disturbances. They investigated whether providing these listeners with information about resonance problems helped them develop a more positive attitude about these speakers. They found that listener attitude did not change with more information. Treatment to help clients take charge of and change their resonance, therefore, is necessary so the clients can present a positive image of themselves to others.

Candidates

Certain clients are able to remediate problems in resonance from speech therapy methods alone, while others need additional medical, surgical, or orthodontic treatments. Mason and Grandstaff (1971) described the difference between these groups:

- *Clients who may benefit from speech therapy alone:* "Speakers who demonstrate reduction in hypernasality by exaggerated articulatory effort, who have a minimal nasal snort, or whose velar activity is markedly more active during gagging than voluntary phonation, may be considered especially good candidates for speech therapy" (Mason & Grandstaff, 1971, p. 60).

- *Clients who need further evaluation and a wider path of treatment:* "Those speakers who have severe amounts of nasal resonance and emission, with marked nasal grimacing, or obstructive nasal deformities, who have an anteriorly displaced velar dimple during phonation, or excessive nasopharyngeal dimensions, should be referred to a medical or dental specialist for evaluation of their candidacy for nasopharyngeal port obturation, or for other appropriate treatment" (p. 60).

Best Conditions for Treatment

Kummer and Lee (1996) proposed that therapy procedures could be effective in treating resonance under certain conditions. Treatment is more likely to be effective when the problem is mild or inconsistent, and when the client is stimulable for reduction or elimination of the problem. Treatment can help if the problem is due to faulty articulation, oral-motor dysfunction, or dysarthria. Benefit can also be expected if the resonance problem occurs primarily when the client is tired, if the velopharyngeal opening is slight or inconsistent, or if the client needs therapy to facilitate velopharyngeal movement after surgery.

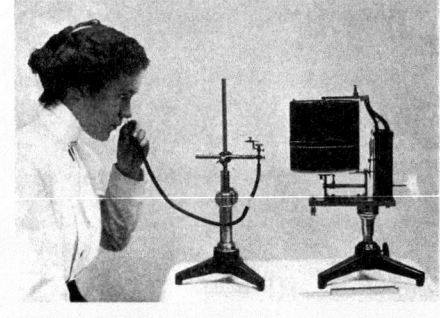

A tissue flag (above) and a breath indicator (below) were early ways to provide visual feedback of oral and nasal resonance. (Photos: Scripture, 1912)

METHODS

The rest of this chapter summarizes methods that have been used throughout the ages to develop appropriate oral and nasal resonance. The reader is reminded that this chapter presents basic speech therapy methods and not surgical, prosthetic, or medical procedures for correcting physical conditions. These are the methods of behavior management that can be found in books on articulation, the motor speech disorders, singing, and voice therapy. Virtually every modern writer in this area cautions that there is very little proof that these methods are effective, yet the same methods appear time and again in textbooks published throughout the last two centuries. The clear message one gets is that this is what SLPs have always done and continue to do despite severe gaps in supportive research.

As in most other areas, Van Riper (1939, 1947) set the foundation for this treatment process. He suggested five specific avenues of treatment: (1) get the soft palate to move, (2) teach the client to direct the air stream outward through the mouth opening, (3) increase the mobility of the jaw, lips, tongue, and cheeks, (4) teach the client to discriminate between the correct and incorrect sounds, and (5) teach the client to make target phonemes with correct resonance.

The aim of this training is to establish correct oral and

nasal resonance on all phonemes and during connected speech. This means to make oral sounds oral and nasal sounds nasal, and to make effective transitions between the two. Kummer and Lee (1996) recommended that therapy ensue as long as the client is making progress.

The treatment methods discussed below are enhanced with original quotes from textbooks and articles to demonstrate the rich presence of these ideas throughout history. They have been organized into four categories for the purpose of this manual: *Enhance biofeedback, manipulate speech, adjust supportive structures,* and *facilitate velopharyngeal movement.*

ENHANCE BIOFEEDBACK

These first treatment methods are designed to enhance auditory, visual, and tactile feedback so that clients can focus attention on patterns of oral and nasal resonance. Biofeedback came to the fore during the Phonetic Placement Era and these methods can be found in a wide variety of textbooks published then and throughout the Traditional Era. These methods have a consistent presence in research reports and in articles that outline therapy procedures. These methods of biofeedback can be employed throughout the entire process of resonance training no matter which other methods are being used.

Auditory Feedback

The concept of careful listening and auditory discrimination training starts this section because these are the most important skills taught during resonance training. Tubes and other tools have been used to provide enhanced auditory feedback during this effort for a very long time. For example, Scripture (1912) used a rubber tube in this training. One end of the tube was held at the client's nose and the other end was placed at the client's ear. The client listened to his nasal sound. Then the nasal end was brought to client's mouth so he could listen to his oral sound. The tube was used to help the client discover oral and nasal sound during correct and incorrect productions. Comparisons were made. Plastic tubes are used today, and a nasal bulb can be placed on one end to make the insertion into the nares more comfortable.

Therapists began to use microphones and earphones for this process in the 1950s (e.g., Laing, 1958), and many therapists continue to do so with the addition of computer and smartphone technologies. (For additional methods to enhance auditory feedback, see Chapter 4.)

Visual Feedback

Methods to provide visual feedback regarding oral and nasal resonance have also had a persistent presence in textbooks since the early 1900s. Objects employed in this process range from cotton balls to computers.

Lightweight Objects

The method discussed the most often during the Phonetic Placement Era was to suspend or hold a lightweight object such as a string, tissue paper, feather, or bit of cotton in front of the nose or mouth. The object moved when air exited the nose or mouth, and this helped the client understand the difference between oral and nasal airflow. Any lightweight object could do the trick. Bzoch (1989) developed a paper "air paddle" for this purpose:

> *"Place a paper paddle in front of the child's mouth during the production of pressure-sensitive phonemes. Have the child try to produce the sounds with enough pressure to force the air paddle to move"* (Kummer & Lee, 1996, p. 278).

Gestural Cues

Most therapists use gestural cues as additional visual input to teach oral and nasal resonance. The simplest way to do this is to point to the mouth for oral sounds and to the nose for nasal sounds.

Breath Indicators

Therapists have used specialized tools to help clients visually understand nasality ever since Scripture described a "breath indicator" in 1912. Therapists now use the professionally designed See-Scape. Such tools provide a visual means of understanding nasal air emission. Please see the description of the See-Scape in Chapter 19. Also, see Dworkin (1991) who presents a very detailed step-by-step description of how a See-Scape might be used with adults in motor speech therapy.

Mirrors and Metal Spoons

Cold mirrors and metal spoons are classic ways to visualize the escape of air through the nose. Place the mirror or spoon under the client's nose to observe the breath clouding that occurs with nasal exhalation. Show the smudge to the client and explain that it means air is coming out his nose. The mirror or spoon is used to teach voluntary control of velopharyngeal movement. This training often begins with vowels: "If the mirror clouds, repeat the vowel until there is no evidence of nasal emission of the breath stream" (Berry & Eisenson, 1956, p. 141).

Nasometer

"The nasometer is an excellent tool for providing visual feedback regarding oral-nasal resonance and nasal emission" (Kummer & Lee, 1996, p. 277). Seaver et al. (1991) used the nasometer to obtain normative data on 148 adults across the United States, however they also gave a caution about its use: "We feel strongly that the nasometer is not to be used as a substitute for sound clinical judgments" (p. 720). In other words, the nasometer is a helpful tool, but not as helpful as using the ear.

Accelerometers

An accelerometer is a small electronic device that can be affixed to the side of the nose to detect nasal vibration during production of speech. It is being investigated as a potential tool in research and for biofeedback during therapy. Thorp, Virnik, and Stepp (2013) noted significant variability in response of the equipment between subjects,

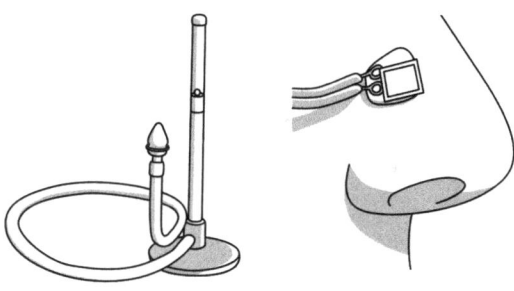

The See-Scape is a tool for assessing and monitoring nasal air emission.

An accelerometer is used to detect the vibrations of nasal resonance.

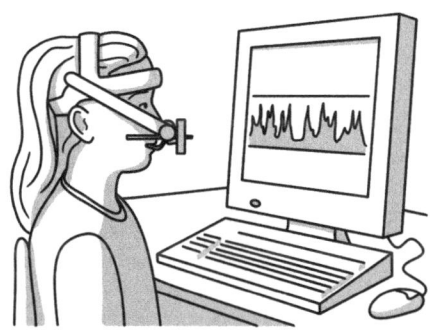

A nasometer provides visual feedback during resonance training.

The cloud that forms on a metal spoon or small mirror can teach clients about nasal air emission.

however, future improvements may make the accelerometer a useful tool for teaching appropriate oral and nasal resonance.

Computer Programs and Apps

Some computer programs have proven to be valuable tools for visual feedback regarding oral and nasal resonance. For example, Fletcher and Higgins (1980) found that their system provided useful visual feedback for clients with hearing impairment. Computer programs and apps were not reviewed for this manual because of their rapidly changing nature. Online searching and attendance at ASHA conventions will help interested therapists find the latest variety of this equipment.

Tactile Feedback

Sometimes the most effective way to provide resonance feedback is for a client to use his own fingers, and the usual way to do this is to have the client place a finger alongside his nose so he can feel nasal vibration. This is the basic motokinesthetic technique (Young & Hawk, 1955) that was used extensively throughout the 20th century:

Clients use their fingers to feel voice resonating in the nasal cavities, as well as air escaping the nose.

Simply pointing to the nose or mouth can provide sufficient visual feedback during resonance training.

A puff of air driven gently into the nose teaches a young client about nasal airflow.

"Hold the child's finger on the side of your nose as you say the sound correctly and incorrectly to contrast. Then hold his finger against his own nose and have him prolong the sound" (Hanson, 1983, p. 201).

The present author has found that this method works best when clients place their fingers right on the bottom of the nose instead of the side. Have the client place the fingers loosely enough so that sound still can escape. Voiced nasal sounds cause a stronger more obvious feeling of vibration of the nares, and oral sounds should be void of this feeling. Clients can feel vibration of their own and their clinicians' nares.

Tactile feedback can also be used to feel airflow. Have the client place his fingers under his nares so he can feel airflow as it exits. Begin with obvious airflow such as blowing through the nose. Progress onward to vowels, consonants, words, and phrases. Air that escapes through the nose is gentle and subtle, and some clients cannot feel it as a result. The back of the fingers where there are tiny hairs are usually able to detect the light touch of air much better than the non-hairy portions of the palm-side of the fingers. The sensation may also be detected better if the fingers are slightly damp.

Another way to pique tactile awareness of nasal airflow is to provide a quick and gentle puff of air shot into the nasal cavities. Use a nasal bulb or a squeeze bottle, and have the client shoot a gentle puff of air himself for safety. Place a pleasantly scented cotton ball inside the squeeze bottle to make the activity more amusing, or use several scents in different bottles for fun. Keep in mind that the olfactory mechanism habituates to odor very quickly, and that it is just the initial one or two shots that jolt a client's attention to the scent of the airflow.

MANIPULATE SPEECH

This section describes how to work with phonemes and words in order to enhance awareness and control of oral and nasal resonance. These are the model-imitate speech routines that have been employed since the days of the elocutionists. Oral and nasal sounds are modeled alone or in syllables, words, phrases, sentences, and so on, and clients are expected to imitate. Activities progress from simple to complex. Manipulating speech in these ways is a cornerstone of all resonance training. The auditory, visual, and tactile feedback methods described in the previous section are used during these activities. Creative therapists can devise many more similar activities.

Exaggerate Low Vowels & Diphthongs

Many therapists (e.g., Fisher, 1966) help clients begin to produce better oral resonance by practicing an exaggerated low jaw position during production of the low vowels: "Try to keep the jaw lowered enough for two fingers between your teeth" (p. 134). Sample practice words might

Phoneme Sequence	Sample Words
/m/ and /b/	Ember, timber, gumball, number, tumble, gamble
/b/ and /m/	Submit, submarine, Harriet Tubman
/n/ and /d/	Under, blunder, undo, candy, dandy, panda
/d/ and /n/	Good news, bad news, odd name, add none
/ŋ/ and /g/	Anger, Congo, finger, tango, mango, Bingo

is nasal and the second is oral. Bell said that these types of words could help clients discover how they can open and close the nasal port at will. Sample words are offered in the chart to the left.

Pause Between Phonemes

Teach clients to pause before or after nasal phonemes to emphasize the transition between oral and nasal sounds and to help the client gain control over velar movement. West and Ansberry (1968) had clients break a single-syllable word containing a nasal consonant into two parts by pausing before or after the nasal sound. For example, the word *beam* would be pronounced /bi/–pause–/m/, and the word *mad* would be pronounced /m/–pause–/æd/. Make sure the client is fully oral or fully nasal on each part. The vowel is prolonged and the pause between the two parts is quite long at first, but then the pause gradually is decreased over the time. Words that begin or end with nasal sounds can be used. Sample words appear in the chart below.

Use /t/

Hall and Tomblin (1975) found that /t/ was useful in remediating a nasal lisp on /s/. They had their client produce /ts-s-s-s/ to teach him how to make /s/ through the mouth instead of the nose. "Successive prolongations of the /s/ element eventually resulted in consistent oral production in isolation, and the eventual elimination of the initial /t/ element" (Hall & Tomblin, 1975, p. 30).

include: *hot, dot, not, cop, pop,* and *stop.* Once oral resonance sounded better on the low vowels, Fisher moved on to diphthongs that had a low jaw position on the first vowel. Her sample words included: *high, hide, tie, tile, die, dine, night, nice, lie, like, rye, rise, kite,* and *cow.*

Practice Sequences of Nasal Consonants

Have clients hum back and forth between the three nasal consonants — /m/, /n/, and /ŋ/. The client learns to keep the velum lowered as he transitions from one sound to another. This teaches him that he has control over his velopharyngeal mechanism even while changing oral postures.

Practice Sequences of Oral & Nasal Sound

A classic way to train oral and nasal resonance is to have the client make an oral sound like /ɑ/ and then a nasal sound like /ŋ/, and then to produce them back and forth in sequences. The client is encouraged to listen to the sounds, feel the sounds, and visualize the velopharyngeal movement during the process:

> *"Have the child try to raise and lower the velum during the production of /ɑ/ to produce nasal/oral contrasts, as in /ŋ-ɑ/, /ɑ-ŋ/. This will also increase velar sensation and control"* (Kummer & Lee, 1996, p. 278).

Use Specific Phoneme Sequences in Words

Bell (1898) used words containing specific phoneme sequences to develop control over oral and nasal resonance. Words are selected for their oral-nasal and nasal-oral sequences. For example, the word *ember* contains /m/ and /b/ in sequence. Both phonemes are bilabial but the first

Phoneme Sequence	Sample Words
Initial nasal in CV	Me, my, moo, May, knee, neigh, new, nigh, now
Final nasal in VC	Aim, am, em, in, on, an, en, own, -ing
Initial nasal in CVC	Meet, mitt, mate, met, mat, moat, mutt, mice, neat, nick, Nate, neck, knack, nuke
Final nasal in CVC	Team, Tim, tame, tam, tomb, Tom, game, gum, gun, gain, sing, ping, ring, sting, wing, walking, talking, raking, making, baking
(Pause between the nasal consonant and the oral vowel that follows or precedes)	

Intone Words

Crannell (1991) recommended intoning words that contain both oral and nasal sounds. Sing the word on one note so that each phoneme and the transitions between them are prolonged. Teach the client to maintain consistent nasality on the nasal sounds and consistent orality on the oral sounds. Also, teach him to make smooth transitions between the two so he can learn to control the resonance changes. A number of words might be used in this process: man, moon, main, mean, moan, Ming, Nome, name, numb, gnome, and Vietnam.

Focus on One Phoneme Only

Van Riper and Irwin (1958) pointed out that hypernasality is seldom evenly distributed, meaning that certain phonemes will be inappropriately more nasal than others. They suggested focusing on one phoneme only. They reported that most of their success in cases of functional hypernasality came when they focused on one or two of the most nasalized vowels. They stated that transfer of this skill to other sounds should be expected.

> *"If we can reduce the amount of hypernasality on even a single one of these especially nasal sounds, the total impression of nasality will be greatly reduced"* (Van Riper & Irwin, 1958, p. 248).

Use Quick & Light Articulatory Contacts

Reduce nasal emission by easing back on articulatory pressure:

> *"Ask the child to produce light, quick contacts during the production of pressure-sensitive phonemes. This helps to eliminate the backup of air pressure in the nasopharynx and can reduce the occurrence of nasal emission"* (Kummer & Lee, 1996, p. 278).

Use Forceful Contacts

Instruct clients to produce stop consonants more forcefully in order to decrease nasal emission on them. This method may work for some clients while lighter pressure (described above) may work for others.

Pinch the Nose Closed

Reduce nasal emission by pinching the nose while practicing words that contain no nasal sounds. Pinch the nose closed completely at first, and then fade it by pinching less firmly. For example, have the client say *cookie* while pinching the nose. If he is producing nasality on this completely non-nasal word, his fingers will feel the nasal vibration and building nasal air pressure. Encourage him to produce the words without feeling that vibration and building pressure. Advance from words to phrases, sentences, and paragraphs that contain no nasal sounds. Kummer and Lee (1996) recommend this method for cul-de-sac resonance.

> *"Have the child pinch the nostrils during the production of pressure sounds to eliminate the nasal emission. Next, try to produce the sounds in the same way with the nostrils open"* (Kummer & Lee, 1996, p. 278).

> *"Oral resonance may be achieved by occluding the child's nares while he or she makes the target production... Initially the nares may need to be occluded during the entire production. As therapy progresses, the clinician may need to occlude the client's nares only as he or she begins the production and then suddenly releases as the client is instructed to continue the production. Eventually, the clinician may need only to lightly touch the client's nares to prompt adequate oral resonance"* (Pena-Brookes & Hegde, 2000, p. 471–472).

Puff the Cheeks

Use cheek puffing to teach nasal-to-oral transitions because it only can be done if the velopharyngeal port is closed. For example, have the client produce /m-pɑ/, and have him puff out the cheeks between the two consonants. If the client can puff out the cheeks before the /p/ then he is elevating the palate. Progress to words such as *damp, camp, lamp,* and *tamp.* Fade the cheek puffing as the client gains velar control and auditory discrimination.

Study the Back Consonants

Have clients discover palatal movement by studying their production of /k/, /g/, and /ŋ/. Produce the target sound in isolation or in simple sequences like /ŋkʌ/ or /ŋ gʌ/. Auditory discrimination is the primary feedback mechanism of this activity but do the work in front of a mirror to see what can be seen. Many clients are able to make these productions slowly enough, and with the mouth open far enough, to observe palatal movement either before or after the back of the tongue elevates.

Adjust the Supersegmentals

Some clients produce better resonance patterns when the supersegmentals are altered. Van Riper and Irwin (1958) wrote that they manipulated a variety of these factors to determine if any have a positive influence on resonance. They manipulated pitch, intensity, vocal attacks, articulatory precision, oral and pharyngeal relaxation, singing, sighing, yawning, mouth opening, head posture, breathiness, and rate. Adjustments to the supersegmentals are prescribed to meet the needs of each individual client. Dwyer, Robb, O'Beirne, and Gilbert (2009) found that increasing the speaking rate of hearing impaired individuals could decrease speech nasality, but adjustment to any aspect of prosody can be helpful with just the right client at just the right time.

"Whenever we find that some one or combination of these does produce a marked reduction in nasality, we fix and stabilize it on a prolonged vowel or nonsense syllable before having the case attempt communicative speech" (Van Riper & Irwin, 1958, p. 249).

Use Negative Practice

Negative practice can be used to help clients learn to control their resonance. In other words, have the client practice his errors and listen carefully. For example, practice *oh, ah,* and *ee* with correct oral resonance, and then practice them with hypernasality. Or move the tongue into unusual positions and listen to the changes in nasality:

"Talk with the tongue retracted and bunched in the back of the mouth... Quickly move the tongue forward to the front of the mouth. Try to sense the changing focal point of tension and contrast the acoustic result" (Berry & Eisenson, 1956, p. 141).

"Have the child pretend to be 'stopped up' with a severe cold and speak accordingly. Gradually eliminate the denasality to a more oral resonance" (Kummer & Lee, 1996, p. 278).

Use Pre-Speech Vocalizations

Oral/nasal differentiation is established during the pre-speech period, and it is the proposal of this manual that a variety of pre-speech sounds can be used to teach this skill. As described in the previous section on development, oral pre-speech sounds include panting, lingual and labial raspberries, and vowels. Nasal pre-speech sounds include sniffing, snorting, and eating-humming.

Traditional Era therapists called these *non-speech* sounds because they did not understand that these were the differentiated oral and nasal sound of infancy. They claimed it helped to first teach non-speech sounds before teaching phonemes. For example, Berry and Eisenson (1956) used panting to teach oral sound, and it is now known that panting is a pre-speech sound children use when learning to be fully oral. As another example, Van Riper and Irwin (1958) used infantile raspberries, or what they called the "tongue-flutter or trill" to teach oral sound because the sound is impossible to produce if the phonation is nasal. It is now known that the raspberries are pre-speech sounds that babies use when learning to be fully oral. Teachers of acting and singing use these methods too:

"Produce a good humming sound. Do not clench the teeth. Bring the lips slightly and gently together to prepare for the hum. As you hum, get the sound in both the oral and nasal cavities. Feel the vibrating breath trying to get out between the two lips. Make sure you feel strong vibration in the nasal cavity" (Crannel, 1991, p. 57).

Eliminate Glottal Stop Replacements

Many clients with VPI substitute glottal stops for lingual and labial plosives, and this can be viewed as a problem of oral resonance. There are several methods that have been used to eliminate this habit. One can substitute /h/ for the glottal stop, or whisper the plosive. One can also delay voicing on a voiced plosive, or delay voice onset on a vowel following a voiceless plosive.

Sing

Singers learn methods of vocal production that fit nicely into the modification of resonance in articulation. These are the types of methods the elocutionists used before speaking and singing were divided into separate fields. The methods also appear periodically in books on articulation and voice therapy (e.g., Cooper, 1973; Colton & Casper, 1996).

The process is one of shifting the locus (center) of sound vibration. The client learns to modify resonance by shifting its locus from deep in the throat to high in the palate and head while holding the base of the tongue low. Opera singers speak of a "bell tone" that characterizes this optimum sound. This tone rings in the highest portions of the head while the tongue is held low.

Methods used to shift the loci of vocal tone are difficult to describe with words and the live production must be experienced. Therapists interested in these methods should observe or participate in singing classes taught by instructors who employ them. These are the methods passed down from some of the greatest singers of the early 20th century (Tetrazzini & Caruso, 1909).

ADJUST SUPPORTIVE STRUCTURES

This section presents methods designed to manipulate all the structures involved in resonance except the velopharyngeal mechanism itself. These types of methods are plentiful in articulation textbooks and some formal studies are beginning to lend support to them. For example, Rong and Kuehn (2012) called these methods "articulatory adjustments" and found that such adjustment were able to reduce the nasality of a synthetic presentation of nasalized /i/:

"Such compensatory interarticulator coordination may have an application in using articulatory adjustments to reduce hypernasality in clinical speech therapies" (Rong & Kuehn, 2012, p. 1438).

Increase Agility of Other Structures

Increasing agility and range of oral movement can have a positive affect on velar movement: "If the front of the tongue, lips, and jaw are agile, the velopharyngeal muscles also are likely to be agile" (Berry & Eisenson, 1956, p. 141). The theory is that the velum will begin to move more as the other structures move more because of the extreme amount of interdigitation that occurs in all the facial and oral musculature and because of movement overflow. This approach continues to be recommended:

> *"Increasing oral activity can increase oral resonance, because increasing anterior oral activity increases posterior oral (velar) movement and alters the path of least resistance for the air flow"* (Kummer & Lee, 1996, p. 278).

Adjust Jaw Position

The size of the oral cavity has always been considered an important factor in the development of good oral and nasal resonance, and jaw position is key. The elocutionists taught that a low jaw position facilitates oral sound and a high jaw position facilitates nasal sound. In a review of the literature Karnell, Linville, and Edwards (1988) noted that jaw movements might have a direct effect on velar position via the mechanical link between the palatoglossus and palatopharyngeus muscles. One of the first tasks of resonance training, therefore, may be to make sure the client is opening his mouth far enough to produce good oral sound and that he is closing it far enough to produce good nasal sound. This requires that the jaw be flexible and malleable:

> *"A relaxed jaw allows free action of the vocal cords and*

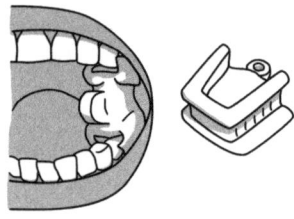

A two-way mouth prop positions the jaw low for oral sound.

Lowering the jaw is a classic way to begin teaching better oral resonance.

improves the resonance of the voice" (Greene & Wells, 1927, p. 226).

> *"Training in relaxing the jaw and throat and the production of sustained vowels with adequate breath control and improved articulation are quite sufficient to reduce or eliminate hypernasality if the case is properly motivated"* (Van Riper & Irwin, 1958, p. 249).

Teach a client to lower his jaw a little more if he sounds too nasal, and teach him to elevate the jaw a little more if he does not sound nasal enough. Van Riper called the position of the jaw the *dental opening* and said that a prop could be used to teach these positions. He used toothpicks, wooden matchsticks, pencils, and tongue depressors for this purpose. The wide side of a tongue depressor is propped between the molars for maximum jaw lowering and the toothpick is used for maximum closure. Fisher (1966) had her clients use two fingers between the molars for a wide mouth position, and a fingernail poked between the front teeth for a narrower mouth opening. Therapists can use probes of various sizes, jaw grading bite blocks and two-way mouth props for this purpose.

Clients with more severe motor speech disorders may need to exaggerate the mouth opening a lot to sound fully oral. Teach the client to open wide and produce a strong "Ahhhh!" The mental image of operatic singing helps some of these clients get the idea of full oral resonance. Also, use gestural cues to teach the concept. Having the jaw lowered as far as it can go will give an idea of how oral the client actually can become without any other adjustments. However, opening the mouth too far can lead to more hypernasality, so experiment with the client's jaw position. Adjustments to velar position will need to be made if the client continues to sound nasal when his mouth is fully open.

Lowering the jaw is important for another resonance problem, and that is the problem some clients have of pressing the whole tongue against the palate while producing /m/ or /n/. This makes these phonemes sound more like humming than the true phonemes they should be. Lowering the jaw while producing these sounds will help pull the middle sections of the tongue away from the palate and make the phonemes sound better because it will create the necessary cavity between the tongue and palate. Also, place a tongue depressor on the tongue to inhibit its elevation while the client says /m/. The tongue depressor will prevent the tongue from elevating to the palate but it will not prevent the lips from closing for /m/.

Adjust Tongue Shape

Teachers of speech and singing through the ages have noted that a tongue that arches too high along its midline interferes with good oral resonance. Guttmann (1893) and others of his generation called this a "thick" tongue: "The air poured from the lungs… should be made to pass over the flatly or, better still, concavely held tongue" (p. 93).

Bell (1887) said that the root of the tongue should be depressed as much as possible to give fullness to the vowels. Tetrazzini and Caruso (1909) said that the beautiful bell-like tones of the best singers are produced when the tongue is low, and they said that the bulging and highly arched tongue caused a *hot potato tone.* Darley, Aaronson, and Brown (1975) used similar phrases to report problems in motor speech clients, saying that those with dysarthria speak as if they had a foreign body, hot potatoes, mashed potatoes, or mush in the mouth. Oral resonance generally sounds best when the tongue is de-arching so that it sits in a bowl shape with a low root. Methods to create the tongue bowl shape are discussed in Chapter 13, *Facilitating Tongue Movement.*

Adjust the Lips

Lips that are stiff and held too close to one another restrict the mouth opening and make a client sound nasal. Help the client with stiff closed lips relax them, exaggerate their movements, and re-position them in ways that make him sound more oral. Have him lower the jaw to part the lips more. Have him watch in a mirror. In general, the lips need to be taken out of the way for better oral sound. (For more ideas see Chapters 12 and 14.)

Adjust the Cheeks

The cheeks form the outer walls of the oral cavity, and their elasticity and density can be altered to affect oral resonance. The cheeks should be held gently but firmly against the lateral teeth during good speech.

Using a neti pot to clear the nasal passageways.

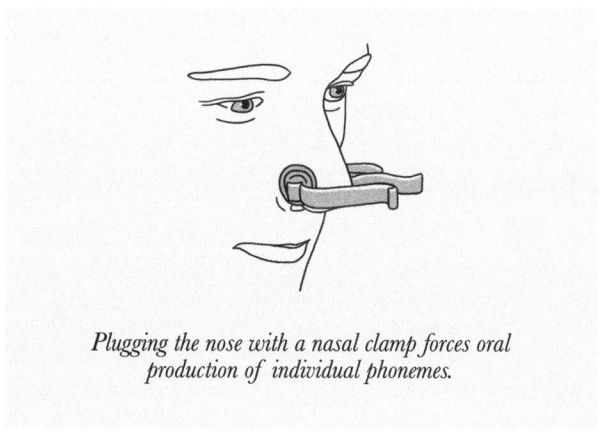

Plugging the nose with a nasal clamp forces oral production of individual phonemes.

"When they are relaxed, the cheeks are relaxed and flabby, and their inner surface has a dampening effect on sound waves… The firmer the cheeks, the more elastic and dense their inner surface becomes, and the better reflectors of sound waves they are" (Fisher, 1966, p. 99–100).

Clients with low oral tone usually present with a characteristic oral quality due to the spongy nature of their oral musculature. Activities to activate all the cheek musculature are in order so that resonance improves. Methods to stimulate better cheek function can be found in Chapter 14, *The Critical Role of Oral Stability.*

Adjust the Nasal Cavities

The nasal cavities can be adjusted in small ways to affect resonance. They can be enlarged, elongated, constricted, or narrowed slightly by contracting or relaxing the muscles that run on either side of the nose. Advanced singers learn to adjust the nares in these subtle ways but this skill may not be easy for the typical speech client: "Some individuals find it as strange as wiggling the ears" (Fisher, 1966, p. 103). Some clients have a habit of scrunching up the facial muscles during speech and they need to be taught how to relax the face and nose in these ways.

Clear the Nasal Passageways

The elocutionists taught their students to blow the nose regularly in order to keep the nasal passages in good working order for speech and song. A nasal spray or a neti pot might also be used in the process.

Plug the Nose

The simplest way to force a nasalized sound to become oral is to plug the nose. For example, if the client substitutes /m/ for /b/, simply hold his nose closed while he says /m/. The building air pressure forces the mouth to open and the sound to exit. The result will not sound like a perfect /b/ because some sound still will resonate in the nasal cavities and the phoneme will not explode properly, but it will be an important beginning. Use a nasal clamp or simply have the client hold his nose with his fingers.

Widen the Faucial Pillars

The oropharynx can be widened for good oral resonance. Therapists usually have to learn this skill themselves before they can teach it to their clients. Open the mouth wide to view the oropharynx in a mirror. Inhale quickly and deeply through the mouth or yawn to widen the pillars. Then learn to widen the pillars and expand the space voluntarily. This takes a little practice but it can be done with adequate intellectual skill and proper motivation. Once the action can be performed with the mouth wide open, try it on a vowel. Use negative practice, speaking vowels with the pillars narrow and again with them wide. Help the client learn to hear and appreciate the auditory differences. Better oral resonance should be heard when

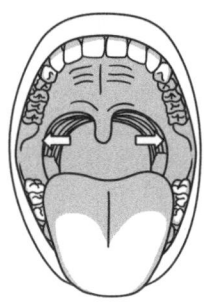

Quick deep inhalation and yawning cause the faucial pillars to widen and the oropharynx to expand.

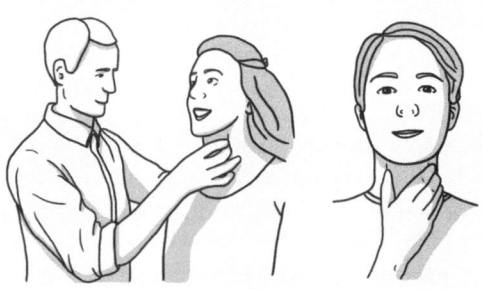

Lowering the larynx reduces the hypernasality associated with a guttural vocal quality.

the pillars take a wide stance: "The broad-resonance response of the vocal tract is best facilitated by keeping the faucial arch open" (Fisher, 1966, p. 100).

Lower the Larynx

The larynx that sits too high causes voice to sound nasal and guttural, and a low laryngeal position is best for good oral resonance. The larynx is suspended with strap muscles above and below and can be encouraged to move through massage and attention. Massage the neck around the larynx to relax the muscles for this training, and have the client palpate his hand at the larynx to help him perceive its movement up or down. Clients with adequate cognitive function and motivation can learn voluntary movement of the larynx in this way. Teach the client to listen to the changes that occur as the mechanism elevates and lowers. "The larynx, being movably seated… must always be drawn more or less downward" (Guttmann, 1893, p. 92).

Teach the Valsalva Maneuver

The Valsalva maneuver is the process of forcibly exhaling while the mouth is closed and the nose is plugged. The method is used to equalize air pressure in the middle ears and it is commonly used during airline travel and hill climbing. The method can be used in speech training to help clients perceive their oral-pharyngeal area. The

Valsalva maneuver causes a rapid change in air pressure inside the oral and pharyngeal cavities and eustachian tubes. This rapid change stimulates the tactile receptors that alert the client to movements he otherwise would not perceive. WARNING: The Valsalva maneuver should not be used with clients who have ear infections or other upper respiratory problems.

FACILITATING VELOPHARYNGEAL MOVEMENT

This final section describes direct tactile and proprioceptive methods to urge velopharyngeal movement. Van Riper called this "strengthening" the soft palate but he was not referring to muscular strength. He meant that therapists should employ methods to encourage the velum to move more often, in a greater range, with more complete velopharyngeal closure or opening, and with conscious control. Whether or not the muscles actually are strengthened is open to debate, and most researchers would argue that muscular strength has nothing to do with this problem except in cases of flaccid dysarthria.

Some therapists help their clients learn how to move the velum even though they acknowledge that this could be problematic. It is very difficult to feel these movements, but there are ways this can be done.

> *"It is difficult to isolate the control of the velopharyngeal muscles which close the nasal port because the action is not visible and not very precise"* (Berry & Eisenson, 1956, p. 141).

Locate the Soft Palate

Orientate clients to velopharyngeal movement by first helping them locate their own soft palate with a mirror and then by feeling it with the tongue:

> *"With a mirror, have the patient look at the throat and observe the uvula which is at the end of the soft palate… [Then have] the patient… locate the soft palate by pushing the tip of the tongue back until it reaches the soft surface"* (Fröeschels, 1948, p. 157).

Model Palatal Movement

Drawings can be employed to help clients visualize the actions of the velopharyngeal mechanism, but modeling with the hands can be an even better method. Use one hand to represent the palate and the other to represent the pharyngeal walls. Elevate the first hand up and down at the wrist to demonstrate velar movement, and close the fingers of the second hand around them to demonstrate medial movement of the pharynx.

Move the Velum Voluntarily

Many clients can be taught to exert voluntary control over their velar movements fairly easily. This method was advocated by Alexander Graham Bell (1906) who taught his clients to move the velum up and down voluntarily while watching in a mirror: "By watching these motions in a mirror, and attempting to control them, you will soon find yourself able to elevate or depress the palate at will" (Bell, 1906, p. 22). He said that therapists should learn how to do this themselves before they try to teach it to their students. Van Riper said that this method even could be taught to little children: "Even younger children can be made to understand something of their problem by telling them about the 'little red door to the nose-attic'" (Van Riper, 1947, p. 383).

Watch & Listen to Vowels

Once a client can begin to move the velum voluntarily, he can begin to explore its function during vowel productions. Produce the vowels alternately with the velum voluntarily pulled up and down in order to contrast and compare sound quality under both conditions.

> *"With the mouth open and looking into the mirror, say the sound /a/; notice how the uvula rises... Observe how when the uvula is raised, the soft palate spreads and forms a sort of block or curtain to the nasal passage. Now the patient must form the sound with the uvula lowered. There is a noticeable difference"* (Rich, 1979, p. 157).

Push the Velum Up

The palate can be taught to rise with assistance. Therapists can nudge the client's palate upward with any sanitary probe, or teach the client to do it to himself. Use a probe that is long enough to reach back easily to the soft palate and have the client watch himself in a mirror as he does this. The client may have to learn how to suppress his gag for this maneuver. This is a method that still makes

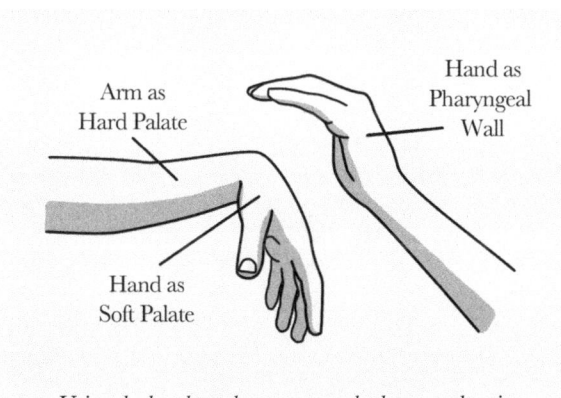

Using the hands to demonstrate velopharyngeal action.

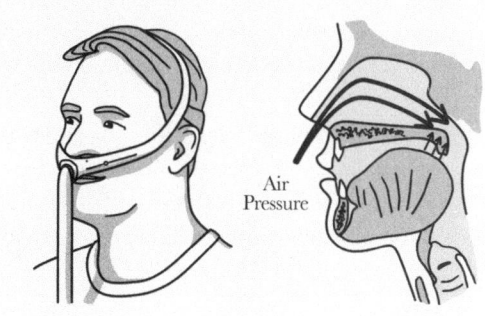

Air pressure provided by a C-PAP acts as resistance to upward velar movement.

appearances in the newest treatment regimens:

> *"Raise the velum mechanically with a tongue blade as the child is producing vowel sounds. Then have the child attempt to raise the velum without assistance to match that sound"* (Kummer & Lee, 1996, p. 278).

Lift the Velum Up & Away

Van Riper (1947) described a slightly different method for assisting velar elevation. A probe is placed against the underside of the soft palate and the client is told to lift his velum up and away from it to break contact without moving the head or jaw. Use a yawn if the client has difficulty figuring out what to do at first. The client may have to learn how to suppress his gag for this maneuver too. Allow the probe to linger up against the palate as it rises:

> *"By following the palate for part of its [upward] movement, the teacher can gradually increase the student's ability to contract the muscles"* (Van Riper, 1947, p. 382).

Resist Velar Movement

Resistance against the direction of purposeful movement is a powerful method of speech movement training and an excellent method for facilitating velar elevation and depression. As pictured in the open sections of this chapter, Scripture (1912) devised a "velar hook" to add resistance to upward velar elevation in a slightly scary way. The hook was placed in the mouth and put directly on top of the soft palate from behind. The tool then was pulled gently forward to provide resistance to the velum's upward movement. This was done while vowels were uttered. The resistance taught the client about the velum's movement and it encouraged him to lift it higher.

Scripture did not mention this, but the hook could also be used upward against the underside of the velum to encourage its downward movement. It is important to note that stimulation to the velum in these ways should elicit the gag reflex, and the presence of the gag will interfere with the purpose of the method unless the client can learn to suppress it. There are no known therapists using this method today.

Kuehn (1991) introduced a safer way to employ resistance against upward velar movement: He used a continuous positive airway pressure (C-PAP) device. This equipment was developed to force air into the nose for the treatment of sleep apnea. For speech purposes it is used to supply a steady state of positive air pressure downward against the velopharyngeal mechanism from the nasal cavities above: "The positive air pressure provides a resistance against which the muscles of velopharyngeal closure must work" (Yorkston et al., 1999, p. 380).

Kuen and Wachtel reported a positive outcome using this method with one adult speaker who had dysarthria related to a closed head injury. In a subsequent article Kuehn and Moon (2000) found that air pressure delivered in this way from above could fatigue the velopharyngeal mechanism. The C-PAP method, therefore, can be used in ways that teach closure of the velopharyngeal mechanism without causing it to fatigue.

Stretch Velar Muscles

One can also stimulate the velar muscles to activate by stretching them. Have the client extend the tongue outward to accomplish this: "Thrusting the tongue out pulls actively against the palatal elevators and tensors, thereby stretching and stimulating them" (Moore, 1971, p. 568).

Stimulate Velar Reflexes

Certain reflexes can be used to facilitate velopharyngeal movement including the yawn, gag, palatal lifting, pharyngeal, and swallow reflexes. Therapists draw attention to the movement pattern of the reflex and then teach the client to take voluntary control over its movement pattern. (For more information see Chapter 17 on the speech reflexes.) Reflexes that are mentioned the most often in the articulation and VPI literature are the yawn and the gag:

> "Have the child yawn in order to forcibly lower the back of the tongue and raise the velum. Then use this movement with the production of vowel sounds and anterior consonants, keeping that same movement in mind" (Kummer & Lee, 1996, p. 278).

> "Exercises can begin with the passive lifting of the velum with a tongue blade or the handle of a spoon. In addition, the eliciting of a gag reflex is also beneficial" (Moore, 1971, p. 535).

The Blowing Controversy

Scripture (1912) may have been the first American to write about teaching clients to blow lightweight objects as a way to encourage velar movement. He held cotton balls, feathers, and tissue paper in front of a client's mouth and nose so they could experience the movement of air in a multisensory way. The theory was that a client would be able to move objects with an oral airstream only if the velopharyngeal port was closed, so the activity was used to "exercise" velar elevation. "Blowing exercises" then became a standard way for clients to practice moving the velopharyngeal mechanism.

The Controversy

References to blowing activities can be found in textbooks from throughout the past century, however, controversy has arisen in regard to these procedures. Bell (1906) called blowing activities an "indirect method" of teaching velar control and said that they did not work to reduce hypernasality in clients with hearing impairment. Various other authors expressed the same opinion in regard to clients with cleft palate, VPI, and articulation error from then on. By the 1970s, however, blowing had been banished in most textbooks on articulation and was considered an invalid way to teach oral and nasal resonance. Since then, therapists have been cautioned away from all blowing activities in all speech remediation processes: "The difficulty with most of [these activities] was that they had no direct connection with speech" (West & Ansberry, 1968, p. 384).

Continued Use of Blowing

Why do some SLPs continue to use blowing activities in resonance training despite abundant cautions? Because blowing activities teach the simple concept of velopharyngeal function. A blowing activity does not need to be employed if a client can follow directions such as "Don't let the air come out your nose" or "Lift your velum" or "Make an oral sound." A blowing activity is employed because it is nearly impossible for many clients to do these things on demand, especially at first, and particularly if they are young or if they have a cognitive deficit. Some clients simply do not understand what the SLP wants them to do and blowing activities give them the idea. Blowing activities are not used instead of speech production activities; blowing activities are used alongside speech production activities. Blowing activities can help many clients understand the basic concept of velopharyngeal closure.

Blowing activities are used to teach clients the concept of velopharyngeal function, but not to strengthen the velopharyngeal muscles per se.

The Oral-Motor War

The re-visiting of the intense controversy over blowing activities seems to have arisen recently when these procedures began to be called *non-speech oral-motor exercises* and when some professionals began to assume that they were being advocated to "strengthen the soft palate" in lieu of speech activities. However, careful reading of texts advocating this method reveals that this never was the intent of these activities in the first place.

It's Not About Strength

Attentive reading of original texts reveals that Traditional Era therapists like Van Riper used the word "strength" in a different way than is used today. They used the word in the same way a teacher might when discussing spelling or math activities. For example, a teacher might have a group of children write selected words ten times in order to "strengthen" their spelling skills, or she might have them complete a page of multiplication problems to "strengthen" their math skills. This is the way therapists of the early 20th century used the word "strengthen" in regard to velopharyngeal activity. They used blowing activities to "strengthen" velopharyngeal closure, i.e. to hone and improve its function and the client's awareness of it, not to strengthen the muscles. They recognized that clients with resonance problems did not have enough awareness and control to close the port when necessary, so they designed activities to strengthen that awareness and control.

Van Riper's Two-Step Process

Once a client was able to understand the concept of velopharyngeal closure through a simple blowing activity and once he practiced the control a little bit without the blow toy, he was taught to transfer this skill to a speech activity. Again, the blowing activity was not employed to strengthen the muscles themselves, and it was not expected that the ability to close the port while blowing would automatically transfer to closing the velum during sound production. The blowing activity was used to strengthen the client's concept and experience with what the velopharyngeal mechanism is and what it can accomplish. Blowing activities teach the client that he has a velopharyngeal mechanism and that he can move it.

It Comes Down to Ear Training

Therapists who continue to use blowing activities engage the two-step process advocated by Van Riper. They use blowing to help clients come to an awareness of oral and nasal airflow, and then they teach them to control those movements during speech activities. Phonetic Placement Era therapists like Scripture and Traditional Era therapists like Van Riper noted that ultimately it was listening skill gained through what Scripture called "an appeal to the ear" (1912) that helps clients learn to control resonance. Blowing activities were used as one simple aspect of that training.

Adjust the Pharynx

Therapists understand that velopharyngeal movement is not just about the velum moving up and down but that this is sphincter action of the entire velopharyngeal mechanism. Problems in pharyngeal movement, therefore, can also contribute to velopharyngeal incompetency. As is now known, muscles that are either too tight or too loose tend to lack action. In the ideal case, the neck and pharyngeal muscles will have perfect muscular tone and be relaxed enough for fluid movement of the velum and the pharyngeal walls. Movement activities and massage are used to adjust tone in the face, neck, shoulders, and upper body, with the expectation that these will have a positive influence on pharyngeal tone.

Adjust Body Position

Have clients lie down in a supine position to take advantage of gravitational pull on the soft palate. Placing the client in supine position causes the velum to fall into position. The ear then is trained to hear the difference that occurs in speech, and then the client is encouraged to achieve the same sound quality while upright. Gradually shifting body position from supine to sitting may facilitate control. This method still is recommended in some texts on the motor speech disorders:

> *"Speaking in the supine position may facilitate velopharyngeal closure, although there should be no expectation that adopting this posture will eventually lead to better velopharyngeal function in the upright position"* (Duffy, 1995, p. 396).

Pushing & Lifting Exercises

Pushing and lifting heavy objects is a method used to stimulate velar movement. This method takes advantage of the fact that the velopharyngeal port typically closes when the breath is held during heavy work activities. For example, the client might clench his fists or lift a chair while producing a vowel, syllable, or word:

> *"This technique is based on the physiological law that if some muscles of the body are working vigorously they are accompanied by involuntary contraction of other muscles"* (Fröeschels, 1948, p. 146).

Electrical Stimulation

Some reports on the use of electrical stimulation directly on the soft palate for speech have been made throughout the 20th century (e.g., Scripture, 1912; Fröeschels, 1948; Yules & Chase, 1969; Peterson, 1974). More recent research has focused on the use of electrical stimulation to activate velopharyngeal muscles in sleep research. This area was not reviewed for the purposes of this manual. For introductory information on this topic please seek other professional resources and search the Internet under *electrical stimulation of the soft palate.*

Normalize Oral-Tactile Sensitivity

Dworkin (1991) pointed out that a hyperactive gag response interferes with adequate velopharyngeal movement. Activities to normalize oral-tactile sensitivity are necessary to influence velopharyngeal control in these clients. (For more information, see Chapter 16 on normalizing oral-tactile sensitivity.)

SUMMARY

A wide variety of methods have been suggested to help clients develop better resonance for speech. Most of these practical methods have been passed down through the generations without benefit of formal research.

9

Traditional Speech Movement Techniques

Classic methods to teach mouth movements for phoneme production

"Although the value of tongue, jaw, and lip exercises has been questioned and denied by many workers in the field of speech correction, [these activities] can be said to be useful in teaching the student to manipulate his articulatory apparatus in many new and unaccustomed ways."

– Van Riper, 1947

There is a widespread misconception that the stimulation of oral movements for speech is a new concept, and that Van Riper and other purveyors of Traditional Era articulation therapy did not utilize them. Nothing could be further from the truth. Many textbooks on articulation therapy, including Van Riper's, contain these activities. Some of these books mention oral movement techniques only in passing and others devote many pages to them.

Techniques to facilitate appropriate movement of the jaw, lips, tongue, and velum were a common element of articulation training beginning with the elocutionists and continuing throughout the Phonetic Placement and Traditional Eras. Unfortunately most of these methods went underground when phonology began to rule the published literature. They survived in practice however, and

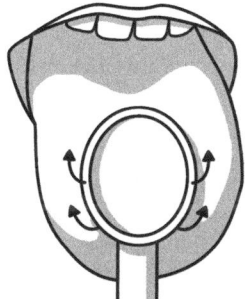

Using a spoon to teach tongue grooving was one of many methods Van Riper used to facilitate tongue movements for speech.

have been passed down from one SLP to another through continuing education programs and therapy manuals like this one, and through direct practical instruction. These types of methods are also shared online through blogs, message boards, and social media platforms.

This chapter summarizes the oral movement techniques used by Van Riper and other Traditional Era therapists and which continue to be used in therapy today. The purpose of this chapter is to demonstrate that the concept of stimulating better oral movement among certain speech-impaired individuals is not a new idea. This chapter functions to introduce the jaw, lip, and tongue movement techniques which are discussed extensively in Part Two of this manual.

BACKGROUND

In the early editions of his text, Van Riper wrote that he used methods to facilitate jaw, lip, and tongue function with a certain group of clients he called "clumsy-tongued individuals" and "the slow of tongue" (Van Riper, 1947, p. 132). "Their tongues do not move with the speed and precision demanded by good speech. They can assume only the simplest tongue positions" (Van Riper, 1947, p. 169). He said that the cause of this deficiency was unknown because these were clients with no other developmental or neurological problems.

Within a few decades these clients were being labeled

as having *functional articulation errors* (e.g., Powers, 1971a & 1971b). Today, the term *functional* has come to mean a speech problem with no known cause, but at that time the term meant that there was a speech *movement* problem that had no known cause. By the late 20th century, a new term was introduced that SLPs in the United States began to use to categorize these clients. They said they had *oral-motor* problems (e.g., Rosenwinkel Marshalla, 1985). Within the research community, these clients now are identified as having *difficulty with speech gestures* (e.g., Gibbon, 1999).

Whatever term is used to identify this group, the point is that there has always been, and probably will always be, a subgroup of clients who have difficulty with jaw, lip, tongue, and velar movements for speech in the absence of any other developmental or neurological problems. Their speech movement problems are not severe enough to classify them as having a motor speech disorder, yet speech movement is their problem. Therapists recognize this subgroup of clients just as Van Riper did. These are the clients who just cannot seem to get their oral mechanisms to do what the therapist want them to in order to produce correct phonemes. Many examples from real therapy cases could be described: the SLP wants the back of a client's tongue to elevate and the tongue tip elevates instead, the SLP want a client's tongue to groove and it humps instead, the SLP want the velar port to close and it remains inactive, the SLP want the lips to pucker and they remain stationary. This chapter summarizes the basic methods that Traditional Era therapists employed to address these speech movement problems. This is an introduction. Many more methods are discussed in Part Two in the chapters on speech movement.

METHODS

The rest of this chapter describes the specific mouth movement techniques taught by Van Riper and other therapists of his era. These are the methods therapists used to get the jaw, lips, velum, and especially the tongue to function better for phoneme production. These are presented in no particular order, although Van Riper's most basic idea appears first.

Vivify Gross Oral Movements

It is best to begin with Van Riper's idea to *vivify* movement. To vivify means to "enlighten or animate" (Jewell & Abate, 2001, p. 1889). Van Riper suggested that some clients need to move the oral mechanism in a wide variety of new ways in order to discover its movement possibilities and to break up habitual patterns that interfered with phoneme acquisition. He was especially concerned with limitations in tongue function:

> *"Many individuals have difficulty in realizing how great a repertoire of tongue movements they possess... Too many articulation cases have only one or two stereotyped*

tongue movements in their speech repertoire... They need to learn how adaptable the tongue really is" (Van Riper, 1954, p. 238–239).

The basic concept here is to get the mouth to move more before attempting to get it to do anything specific. Van Riper may have learned this concept from Stetson (1928) who seems to have proposed the idea. Stetson was one of the first great motor speech scientists and he talked about stimulating "chance success with the movement" (Hartson, 1988, p. 5). Speech therapists of the Traditional Era used their hands, fingers, food, objects, and creative imagination to vivify jaw, lip, tongue, and velar movements for speech.

Increase Range of Motion / Increase Flexibility

Therapists of Van Riper's generation and earlier also wrote about engaging activities to increase range of jaw, lip, and tongue movement so that appropriate gradation of oral movements could be achieved for speech. Range is "the area of variation between upper and lower limits on a particular scale" (Jewell & Abate, 2001, p. 1409). *Range of motion* as it relates to bodily movement refers to the extent to which the body can flex, extend, lateralize, and rotate around its axes. The phrase *flexibility of the articulators* was used by early speech therapists:

> *"Have the patient perform lip, tongue, lower jaw and soft palate exercises calculated to give these organs increased flexibility and hence greater capacity to adjust themselves in new positions"* (Borden & Busse, 1925, p. 182).

Learning to stretch the articulators to their full range is part of the early developmental process but, once the full range is learned, oral movements eventually must be restricted for speech to mature. This is a reflection of the principle that gross movements develop before refined

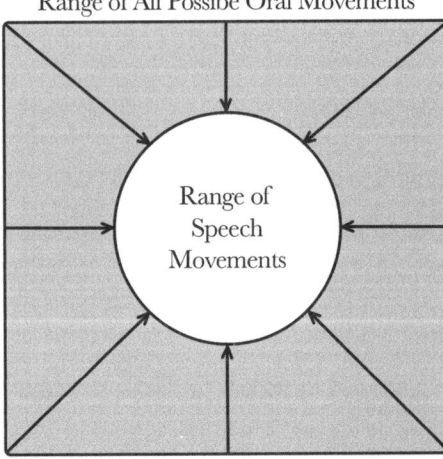

Range of All Possibe Oral Movements

Range of Speech Movements

Speech movements occur in a smaller range than do all other possible oral movements.

Therapists use active and passive physical assistance to teach new speech movements.

ones. Therapists understand that articulation for mature speech is restrained control of what the speech organs can do; a child learns to move his articulators to their full extent in pre-speech activities — during the metaphonological stage — before he learns to restrict these movements for speech production in the phonological stage.

The process of learning the full range of oral movement can be hampered by several factors including the muscle tone disturbances seen in dysarthria. In general, *hypertonicity* restricts range because of stiffness while *hypotonicity* restricts range because of looseness. Both cause weakness. Therapists understand these ideas and employ methods to remediate them:

> *"The chief enemies of clear articulation are a tight jaw, lazy tongue, and immobile lips… A large part of [this] re-education is kinesthetic: The child becomes aware, often for the first time, of what it feels like to open his mouth… to use his lips vigorously… and to perform certain important movements with his tongue"* (Anderson, 1953, p. 158).

Assist Movement

Assist clients in moving the jaw, lips, and tongue for the production of phonemes. To assist is to "help (someone), typically by doing a share of the work" (Jewell & Abate, 2001, p. 96). Generally this means to gently push or pull the articulators into position with the hands, fingers, or another tool: "The therapist assists the child in every possible way, by guiding the tongue or lips… until the required sound… is achieved" (Morley, 1972, p. 320–321). Van Riper named this as a phonetic placement method. Nemoy and Davis (1937) used term *manipulation* for this concept. They manipulated the oral mechanism by pushing or pulling the articulators into the phoneme's starting position. It is interesting to note that Nemoy and Davis recommended using this method only as a last resort when all else had failed. The motokinesthetic method (Young & Hawk, 1955) described in Chapter 6 of this manual is probably the most widely used assistance method.

Assistance can be active or passive. Active assistance requires that the client actively move his articulator at the same time the therapist moves it. Passive assistance requires that the client relax or let go of his body part so that the therapist can manipulate it all by herself. Passive movement is "any body movement, however originated, that takes place without continuing muscle contraction" (Rasch & Burke, 1978, p. 51). Active and passive assistance techniques still can be found in articulation manuals such as Secord et al. (2007) and Bleile (2006).

Resist Movement

Resistance is the process of adding weight to movement so that the client must work harder to achieve it. For example, Van Riper applied downward pressure against the tongue tip while training it to elevate for lingua-alveolar phonemes: "With spoon or tongue depressor, hold tip of tongue down. Mouth is held open. Use rhythms and increasing speed in lifting tongue against the pressure" (Van Riper, 1947, p. 170).

To resist is to "withstand the action or effect of" (Jewell & Abate, 2001, p. 1449). To resist oral movement means to apply a slight amount of pressure in the opposite direction to which the client is purposefully moving the articulator. Speech-language pathologists do resistance tasks with jaw, lip and tongue movements in order to develop new movement, to increase awareness of movement, to habituate an existing movement, to increase range of movements, and to improve strength of movement. In writing about motor speech therapy, Duffy (1995) called resistance techniques *isometric* and *isotonic* exercises: "Isometric exercise involves exertion against stationary resistance" (Duffy, 1995, p. 384). Farber (1982) suggested that isometric or isotonic activities work best when put into immediate functional use: "Resistance is applied to isotonically contracting muscles that causes the patient to exert maximum effort while his body part is moved through a functional pattern" (Farber, 1982, p. 150).

Resistance may be the simplest yet most powerful method to create new speech movements and that makes it an especially good method for clients with low oral tone

A lip trainer can be placed in the mouth and pulled outward to add resistance to lip puckering.

or weak oral strength. More weight also increases sensory feedback about movement and that makes it a good technique for clients with apraxia.

Bosley (1981) used the term *contrary direction techniques* for this method:

> "Most speakers have a poor kinesthetic awareness of the direction or degree of movement of the tongue up or down in the mouth... In the non-cerebral palsied individual, there is... a slight tendency for the articulators to respond in the same way to contrary direction techniques, and these can be used to [help] the client. Gradually the eliciting stimuli should be phased out as controlled or directed movement becomes possible" (p. 11–12).

He insisted that only a slight amount of pressure is needed:

> "Place a tongue blade lightly on the portion of the tongue that should arch or rise the highest and lightly hold the tongue blade in place without actively pressing down on the tongue. Instruct the client to raise or lower the tongue blade as he speaks. Its weight intensifies the kinesthetic sensations and gives a concrete sense of direction" (p. 31).

Mark the Target of Movement

Clients often have difficulty figuring out where to position the articulators and Van Riper said SLPs could use tactile stimulation to help. He said therapists can "identify contacts by stroking or pressure" (Van Riper, 1954, p. 217) because "tactile sensations seem to be very effective in provoking movement" (Van Riper, 1939, p. 408). This process will be called here *marking the target* of oral movement after Berry and Eisenson (1956) in their discussion of teaching /l/: "The teacher 'marks' the place on the alveolar ridge with a lollipop where the child is to place his tongue to make a correct /l/" (p. 151).

To mark the target means to indicate, through tactile means, the place where articulation should be made. Therapists often use their own fingers and foods for this purpose. Van Riper used tongue depressors, pencils, matchsticks, and toothpicks. Therapists can now use a variety of safe and sanitary probes as described in Chapter

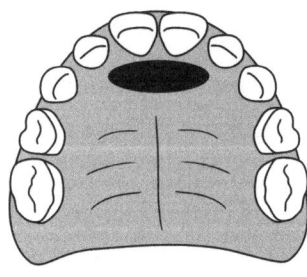

Van Riper marked what he called "the spot" with tactile stimulation when teaching tongue-tip position for lingua-alveolar phonemes.

19, *The Tools of Speech Movement Training.* Van Riper identified this method as a standard element of the phonetic placement method, and the method continues to appear in manuals on articulation therapy. Consider how marking the target is being used in this very common method for teaching place of articulation for /l/: "Touch the student's alveolar ridge with a tongue depressor, peanut butter, or lollipop to indicate the place of production for [l]" (Bleile, 2006, p. 146).

Maintain Oral Positions

Encourage clients to maintain oral positions as a way to reinforce newly learned phoneme positions. To maintain an oral posture is to hit and hold the position for increasing lengths of time. Maintaining oral positions is not used to create new speech movement but to increase awareness of a position the client already can attain, to improve voluntary control of the position, and to habituate it. Maintaining oral position is a method found scattered throughout much of the articulation therapy literature and in early books with the term *oral-motor* or similar in the title. For example, in *The Source for Oral-Facial Exercises*, Gangale (1993) used this method while teaching lingua-alveolar positioning: "Hold tip of tongue to the spot [alveolar ridge] for at least 5 seconds, or as long as possible. Increase time to 30 seconds, continuing to press tip into the spot" (p. 103).

Separate Movements

An inability to separate the movements of the organs of speech has long been considered a sign of speech movement immaturity and/or disability. Van Riper said this was a serious problem in clients with cerebral palsy and he reported that methods to aid separation were a standard element of treatment for them:

> "In general, the child with cerebral palsy has inadequate control of her tongue... In most of these cases, the essential task is to free the tongue from its tendency to move only in conjunction with the lower jaw" (Van Riper & Erickson, 1996, p. 411).

The separation of jaw and lip movements has also been recognized as an important element of speech training in children with apraxia (e.g., Winkler & Crary, 1982; Crary, 1993). Speech-language pathologists help clients separate movements of the jaw, lips, tongue, and velum so that appropriate individual movements can be made for phoneme production. The concept of separating movements is discussed further in Chapters 14 and 15.

Inhibit Unnecessary Movements

Inhibit unwanted oral movements so that those required for specific phonemes might be facilitated. To inhibit means to "slow down or prevent (a process, reaction, or function)" (Jewell & Abate, 2001, p. 873). Techniques are employed to prevent habitual, reflexive, tone-based, or undifferentiated movement patterns from overriding the

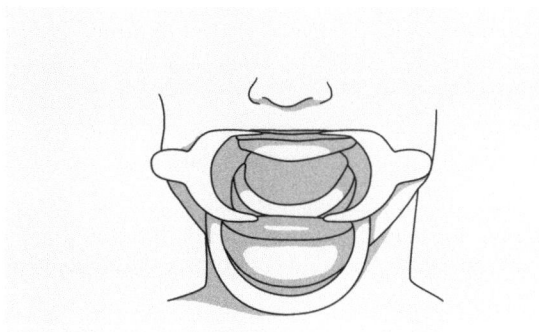

Traditional Era therapists used sticky tape to inhibit lip movements. Today's therapists can use a lip retractor.

client's attempts at new movement. For example, a therapist might ask a client to hold his lips still with his fingers as he learns to move the tongue for production of /r/.

Inhibition techniques are basic to the therapy approach known as *neurodevelopmental treatment* (NDT), a process of movement training that incorporates many goals including those to inhibit primitive reflexes, abnormal postures, and compensatory movements. For an excellent introduction to NDT, see Langley and Thomas (1991).

Although the inhibition of unwanted movement is considered a technique of modern motor therapies, speech-language pathologists began using this method decades before Van Riper's time as represented in the following example from Alexander Graham Bell's father, Melville Bell, in 1898:

> *"When a child says 'tum' for 'come,' and 'tin' for 'king,' the correct articulation will be induced almost at the first trial by the simple expedient of holding down the forepart of the tongue with the finger. [This] will then force the back of the tongue into action and in a few days at most, the child will, without any assistance, form k, g, and ng where before it could only utter t, d and n"* (Bell, 1898, p. 2–3).

Stimulate Reflexive Movements

Stimulate reflexes in order to facilitate oral movement. A reflexive action is "a response of some peripheral organ to stimulation of the sensory branch of a reflex arc, the action occurring immediately, without the aid of the will or without even entering consciousness" (Osol, 1973, p. 669). Van Riper used reflexes in a variety of ways — for example, he used the yawn reflex to facilitate velar elevation. The topic of reflex stimulation for speech production is explored more thoroughly in Chapter 17, *The Speech Reflexes.*

Speed Up or Slow Down Movements

Adjusting rate of speech production is an important element of facilitating correct speech movement:

> *"[Many clients] do not move with the speed and precision demanded by good speech… When poor muscle coordination is an important factor in producing the articulatory errors, we devote part of our therapy to improving the speed and precision of the articulatory musculature"* (Van Riper, 1954, p. 216).

Speed refers to the "rapidity of movement or action" (Jewell & Abate, 2001, p. 1639). *Rate of speech* refers to the number of syllables produced per unit of time.

Slowing rate of speech helps clients learn new phoneme movements, improve accuracy of speech movements, and improve intelligibility. Speeding up, on the other hand, makes clients sound more natural and it facilitates carryover. Traditional Era therapists often used metronomes in this process. Today's therapists are more likely to use whole body activities like bouncing to encourage better rate and rhythm.

Study Movements in a Mirror

The use of mirrors for visual feedback regarding oral movements for speech sound production was recommended beginning with the elocutionists who called a mirror a *looking glass*. Using a mirror is an especially simple method that most SLPs eventually discover for themselves although supportive research is slim. The ASHA journals report the following:

- Palmer (1952) described how to construct an inexpensive one-way mirror for observation of clients in articulation therapy that he described as "a useful item."

- Göllesz and Gáspár (1964) described their "trioptophon." This was a three-dimensional mirror with attached amplification system that they claimed provided "excellent results" in articulation training.

- Rosenbek et al. (1973) found that feedback from

Traditional Era therapists used metronomes to teach better control of speech rate. Today's therapists tend to use whole body movements like bouncing.

Therapists use mirrors to teach new speech movements.

a mirror facilitated articulation improvement in adult patients with apraxia.

- Pflaster (1979) found that mirrors neither enhanced nor detracted from articulation training in students with hearing impairment.

SUMMARY

Methods to improve jaw, lip, tongue, and velar movements have been a standard element of speech training since Van Riper's time and before. The subset of clients who need these methods have been called "the slow of tongue," "functional articulation cases," clients with "oral-motor deficit," and clients who have "difficulty with speech gestures." These methods are designed to get the jaw, lips, tongue, and velum to cooperate in speech movement learning.

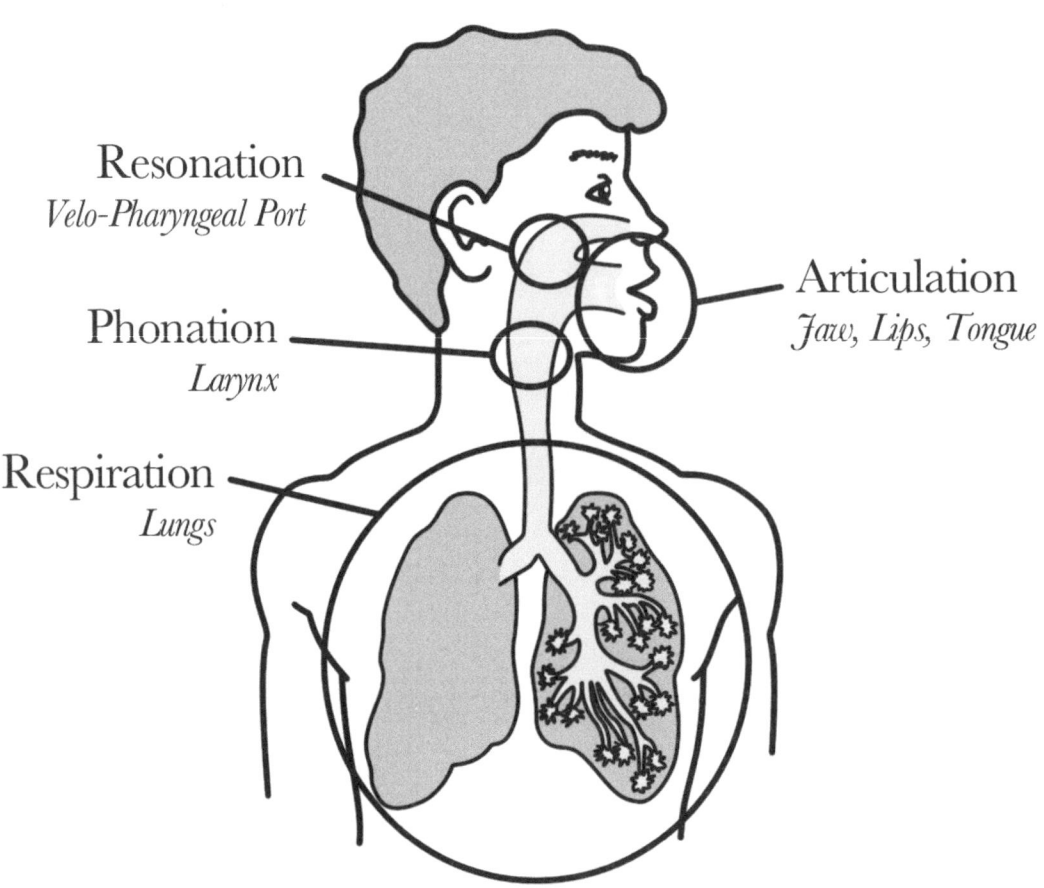

Resonation
Velo-Pharyngeal Port

Phonation
Larynx

Respiration
Lungs

Articulation
Jaw, Lips, Tongue

Speech is the coordinated effort of four speech movement centers.

PART TWO
Speech is Movement

"The SLP who is interested in correcting misarticulation should never lose sight of the fact that articulation is, among other things, a motor act."

– Rolland Van Hattum, 1980

The second part of *The Marshalla Guide* presents methods to encourage jaw, lip, and tongue movements for better speech sound production. Speech-language pathologists recognize that some clients can move their mouth easily, and with maturity, but that others cannot. Van Riper (1947) called those that had difficulty achieving the delicate mouth movements of speech "clumsy-tongued individuals" and "the slow of tongue."

It is now known that clients who have the most difficulty learning speech movements are those with the motor speech disorders known as *apraxia* and *dysarthria*. Clients with frontal lisp, lateral lisp, distorted /r/, and minor phoneme substitutions like /t/ for /k/ and /f/ for /θ/ may also need help learning the specific movements they need to correct their error(s). Part Two of *The Marshalla Guide* concerns ways to develop the intricate oral movements necessary for producing mature speech. The therapy methods presented here are integrated with the latest research on speech movements.

Chapters

10

Principles of Movement Development

Organizing factors in speech movement training

"Principles learned from studies of other motor activities may be expected to apply to those involved in speech developmental processes."

– Samuel G. Fletcher, 1992

If one accepts the premise that "speech is movement" (Stetson, 1928) and that there are speech movement disorders called *apraxia* and *dysarthria* (Darley, Aaronson, & Brown, 1975), it follows that speech-language pathologists should be trained in movement — not strength and endurance, but movement patterns themselves. SLP students are introduced to the bones, muscles, and nerves of human anatomy, but they rarely receive specific coursework on movement itself. They do not learn how movement is organized, how it develops, how it breaks down, and how it can be treated if impaired. Without this type of basic information, it would not be unusual for SLPs to struggle with remediation of movement-based speech problems that range from the severe motor speech disorder to the persistently distorted /r/. One approach to the study of movement is via the principles that underlie its development.

BACKGROUND

Movement is organized in development. This means that movements unfold along certain lines as children grow and develop. These lines can be discussed in terms of *principles*. Principles are important underlying assumptions, or main beliefs, about a particular topic which define the fundamental way in which something works. Principles are the basic propositions of a system, perhaps as yet unproven, but still valuable to the discussion. Similar to the *axiom*, a principle is a statement or idea that people accept as self-evident. For example, everyone knows that

children stand before they walk. This fact reflects the basic principle that movements develop in sequence over time. There are exceptions to this and all other basic tenets, of course; nonetheless, principles lay down a foundation of ideas from which other concepts can be judged.

Principles of movement development are not the same as *motor learning theory*. Motor learning theory (reviewed at the end of this chapter) is a discussion of how new movements skills — such as throwing a baseball or learning to produce a speech sound — are learned in children and adults through skill training and behavior management. Principles of movement development are different. They describe the way movement is organized as children naturally mature from conception onward. This chapter is not about motor learning theory; it is about motor

The development of movement skills follows certain principles that SLPs can apply to the training of speech movements.

development. It is proposed here is that there are basic governing principles of movement development that are applicable to the learning of speech movement skills.

Pathways

Most SLPs understand that movements mature over time and that immature movements present themselves in a certain way while mature movements present themselves in another, sometimes completely different way. For example, toddlers and adults both walk but they do so quite differently. A toddler's walking pattern is wide, slow, unsteady, a-rhythmical, clumsy, gross, and accomplished with hips and shoulders locked in position so that the legs rock side to side and the arms remain raised to the sides. The mature adult walking pattern is the opposite. It is narrow, fast, steady, rhythmical, smooth, refined, and accomplished with rotating hips and shoulders so that both the legs and arms move in smooth reciprocal forward-and-back swinging patterns. The adult and the toddler both ambulate, but the toddler toddles and the adult walks. These patterns represent primitive and mature patterns of the same basic movement. The line of development from the immature pattern to the mature pattern is called a *pathway of motor development*. The principles of motor development define how these pathways unfold.

Starting in the 1930s, physicians and motor specialists began to describe several lines of progression in the development of human bodily movement (e.g., Gesell & Ilg, 1937; Gesell, 1952; Illingworth, 1963). Occupational and physical therapists began to use these principles to guide their treatment of *gross motor* and *fine motor* skills. The term *oral motor* began to be used when these same principles were applied to the oral movements of feeding and speech. Because of the new term, the idea of *oral motor* problems as a basis of speech deficit has been considered a revolutionary and unproven idea in recent years, but this is not a new concept. Oral movement problems were discussed decades ago by any number of Phonetic Placement and Traditional Era therapists including ASHA president Robert West:

> "*The articulatory aspects of speech represent, from one point of view, a muscular skill… It follows that the most efficient way to correct speech defect in school children or to increase their normal speech skill is to approach the articulatory aspects of speech training as if it were a muscular skill*" (Kantner & West, 1933, p. 355–356).

Several mid-20th century studies (e.g., Dickson, 1962) demonstrated that children with speech movement problems tend to perform worse on tests of gross motor skills than do children with no speech impairment. This line of thinking — that speech movements are related to whole body movement skills in some capacity — is an area of investigation that the speech research community seems to have abandoned, but is one that practicing SLPs face in the clinic everyday. SLPs serve great numbers of clients who have concomitant speech movement and body

movement — especially hand movement — problems. Difficulty with speech movement or speech *strokes* (Tasko & Westbury, 2002) often co-occurs with gross motor and fine motor delay or disorganization, especially in children. It follows that SLPs could better understand these speech movement problems with a better understanding of general motor development as represented in the principles discussed in this chapter.

PRINCIPLES

Most of the principles presented in this chapter are well-accepted across many fields of study, but a few remain controversial to this day. When the idea that movement could be described in a set of principles was a new concept, it was understood that these principles needed to be tested: "The evidence suggests that these… principles should be examined in detail before they are accepted without question" (Cratty, 1970, p. 28). More than forty years after Cratty's plea, the evidence still has yet to come in. But like occupational and physical therapists, the speech-language pathologist of the 21st century can accept these principles as working theories because the principles have value as long as they hold up therapeutically. Therapists can use these principles as viable models of the way speech movements develop over time.

Twenty-six principles have been selected for discussion in this chapter, most of which can be supported by research as noted throughout. Each is named, defined, explained briefly, and further explained with examples. Application is made to the whole body, to speech movement development, and to articulation therapy itself. The principles are arranged to build concepts throughout this chapter, although no specific hierarchy is implied, and each section can be read and studied individually. Readers should keep in mind that as in all developmental guidelines there is overlap and there are exceptions to all these rules:

> "*The therapist must remember that no two individuals develop in exactly the same manner. Many normal children*

Toddlers and adults both ambulate but their motor patterns are very different.

bypass complete stages of development. The developmental progression is, therefore, used as a guideline to determine the direction of a patient's treatment program" (Farber, 1982, p. 122–123).

Continuity

Our first principle is a broad one: Development is a continuous process from conception to maturity. The word *continuity* in this context refers to "a connection or line of development with no sharp breaks" (Jewell & Abate, 2001, p. 372). The principle means that motor skills begin to develop in the womb, and they are refined in a continuous line until mature movements are achieved. The process includes plateaus (periods of little or no change) as well as periods of faster or slower development. The fastest time period of motor development is early childhood. After early childhood, motor development becomes a matter of refinement and integration:

> *"The overall growth rate of the child decelerates during the years one through five. In general, about twice as much growth occurs between the ages of one and three as occurs between the ages of three and five. After the age of five, however, the rate levels off to a marked degree, until the pubertal 'spurt' occurs following late childhood"* (Cratty, 1970, p. 35–36).

Body Motor Development

Infants begin to move their head, arms, fingers, legs, and toes in the womb. These rudimentary movements continue to undergo growth and development throughout childhood, and become the movements of sitting, standing, walking, running, grasping, drawing, writing, and so forth. Movements continue to develop throughout childhood, with each skill coming to a point of maturity at some point:

> *"The little fetus moves more and more every day, and the jerky body motions during the embryonic stage are now replaced, during the second trimester, by slower and apparently more goal-oriented movements"* (Nilsson & Hamberger, 2003, p. 122).

Speech Motor Development

Speech movements also begin in the womb and develop in a continuous process until maturity is reached. Jaw, lip, and tongue movements, as well as "breathing movements" of the chest begin during the second trimester (Nilsson & Hamberger, 2003). Once outside the womb, when children are exposed to air, newborns begin to develop all the respiration, phonation, resonation, and articulation movement skills of speech. At some point, all these skills reach an acceptable range of adult-level performance. Virtually every developmental study has suggested that one can expect children to make consistent adult-like productions of all the consonants by 8–9 years of age.

Application to Articulation Therapy

This principle has long been accepted in speech-language circles. The drive for speech-language therapy services to be provided during the preschool years was a direct result of broad acceptance of this principle decades ago. Most therapists try to see clients as young as possible before the motor system is set and error patterns become firmly fixed.

Sequence

The sequence of motor development is relatively the same in all children. The word *sequence* in this context refers to "a particular order in which related events, movements, or things follow each other" (Jewell & Abate, 2001, p. 1555). In normal development, movements progress through highly predictable and fairly consistent sequences that are dependent upon emerging underlying skills. This broad theory has been accepted widely for decades: "Every child goes through an orderly sequence of development" (Illingworth, 1963, p. 145).

Motor specialists have devised detailed theories that reflect this basic principle. For example, one theory described in Gallahue and Ozmun (1995) is that all movements develop in four basic sequential stages: (1) the *reflexive movement phase* of the newborn, (2) the *rudimentary movement phase* of the child until age two years of age, (3) the *fundamental movement phase* of the early childhood years, and (4) the *specialized movement phase* that emerges after seven years of age.

Body Motor Development

Experts recognize sequences in the development of hand movements, head movement, eye movements, arm movements, leg movements, and so forth. For example, children roll over, then sit, then stand, and then walk. These types of sequences are well understood in the motor therapy community and are foundational to the practices of occupational and physical therapy.

Speech and language services are provided to very young children because patterns of speech movement are established very early.

Speech Motor Development

Speech movements also develop in sequence. This is especially obvious as it concerns infant pre-speech vocal development. Oller (1978) proposed the now widely accepted *stages of development in phonetic control* that is a perfect reflection of this principle:

> *"[When infant vocalizations are studied] a remarkable set of consistent developments emerge [that can be] characterized in terms of stages of phonetic control... Children systematically introduce characteristics of speech into their vocalizations until they resemble speech in a number of crucial respects"* (p. 534–538).

Application to Articulation Therapy

A basic understanding of the sequence of speech movement development is essential for making good decisions in articulation and motor speech therapy. For example, Oller's stages of vocal development is an orderly plan for the facilitation of pre-speech vocalizations in clients with very little expressive speech. Several chapters in this manual include this type of developmental information for use as guidelines in therapy.

Rate

The rate of motor development varies from one child to another. The word *rate* in this context refers to "the speed with which something... changes" (Jewell & Abate, 2001, p. 1412). In this instance, rate refers to the time it takes for new skills to emerge and mature. Although most children acquire movement skills in a certain general sequence, the age at which they acquire these skills varies from one child to the next: "Attributes [cognitive, verbal, motor, and perceptual] emerge and mature at various rates, and at the same time overlap in time" (Cratty, 1970, p. 275).

Body Motor Development

Differences in the rate of motor acquisition become obvious when one examines any body movement. For example, some children walk as early as nine months of age while others do not walk until 14 months. Both are considered to be within normal limits.

Speech Motor Development

Differences in rate of acquisition also become obvious when speech movements are examined. A study of the acquisition of phoneme /r/ is a good example here. Some children acquire a correct /r/ in infancy during the babbling phase while others do not straighten out this phoneme until 7–8 years of age. Both are considered representative of the normal range.

Application to Articulation Therapy

A decision about when to teach an individual phoneme has been based upon developmental norms. But rigid beliefs about when phonemes should emerge must be questioned since each child is different and all movements, including speech movements, are acquired over a range of time. To say, for example, that /r/ should not be addressed in therapy until after eight years of age ignores the basic fact that most children acquire /r/ much earlier than that. Some babies babble with /r/ and some toddlers produce their first words with /r/. Based upon this principle, clients can be introduced to this phoneme at any time deemed appropriate by the SLP. An individual child's readiness to produce a particular phoneme seems to be more important than the age at which a phoneme might be expected to achieve the adult form.

Cephalo to Caudal

Movements develop from head to tail down the spine. The word *cephalo* means "relating to the head or skull" (Jewell & Abate, 2001, p. 279) and the word *caudal* means "at or near the tail or the posterior part of the body" (p. 273). The principle means that movements made at the top of the spine emerge before movements lower along the spine. This was one of the earliest lines of motor development to be identified.

Body Motor Development

The process of learning to rotate around the spine is a good example here. Babies learn to rotate the head before they learn to rotate the shoulders, and they learn to rotate the shoulders before they learn to rotate the hips. The progression of movement is from head to tail along the spine.

Speech Motor Development

The head sits at the top of the spine; therefore, oral movements are some of the earliest movements to develop. In fact, it is known that infants make oral movements in the womb, with sucking movements becoming obvious during the second trimester. Motor therapists look to oral control as an early and important factor in general motor development because oral control occurs at the top of the spine. Stimulation of oral movement is important to speech and feeding development as well as to the development of all body movement systems.

Children learn basic motor skills, such as rolling over, starting with the head.

Application to Articulation Therapy

The principle has application to the process of articulation and motor speech therapy. Pre-speech oral movements can be encouraged in the youngest clients. The carefully planned stimulation of oral movement is usually included in the treatment of premature infants in the neonatal intensive care unit.

There has been a recent troubling development within the field of speech-language therapy that violates this principle. Some therapists who work with infants, toddlers, and preschool children report that they are allowed to work on language but they are forbidden to work on speech. The rationale is that speech sound errors will continue to be made in toddlers and preschool children and, therefore, it is a waste of time to train speech sounds in these programs for the youngest clients. These therapists are allowed to work on vocabulary and concepts as well as general communication and turn taking, but they are forbidden to stimulate correct phonemes. This astounding plan runs counter to the basic principle of movement development. Oral movements are some of the earliest to be established; therefore, any educational or therapeutic program for infants and little children should include stimulation of oral movement for good speech and feeding.

Following this principle, a very young child should be taught to pronounce his emerging words the best way he can given his age and other circumstances. For example, it may not be possible to teach a one-year-old to say *shoe* with a correct /ʃ/, but certainly he can be taught to say it better if he is calling his shoe a "gaw." SLPs can teach the child to say "thoo" or "too" or "doo" or even "oo." Any of these options would put him on a correct path of speech movement development. To allow the child to continue to say "gaw" does a tremendous disservice to the child when only a little help could set his speech movements on a right course early in his treatment.

Gross to Fine

Movements begin gross and become more refined in time. The word *gross* in this context means "large-scale; not fine or detailed" (Jewell & Abate, 2001, p. 750). The word *fine* means the opposite.

This principle is perhaps the best known of all but unfortunately it has been misunderstood and the terms have been misused in recent decades. Some therapists use the term *gross motor* to refer to large body movements like walking, running, or swimming, and they use the term *fine motor* to refer to small movements of the hands, like drawing, writing, or scissoring. This division of the body into gross parts and fine parts does not represent this principle. The principle means that *all* movements begin in a gross way and *all* movements become more refined with time. All movements start out large and clumsy, and all movements become smaller and more delicate with time given growth, development, health, and adequate practice.

Body Motor Development

Many examples could be drawn from body movement development. For one, a baby can wave his hand before he can hold a crayon, and he can kick his leg before he can place his foot in a shoe. Big clumsy movements come early and small more refined movements come later. Every movement of every body part goes through this process.

Speech Motor Development

Gross speech movements also come before refined speech movements, and this pattern is reflected in many ways during speech movement development. Tongue movements are perhaps the most obvious; a baby moves his tongue in very gross ways to form early vowels during the cooing stage, and adults move the tongue in a "complex pattern of finely graded changes" (MacNeilage & Sholes, 1964, p. 29). Gross-to-fine changes require time:

> *"Time is an important factor in the development of articulation skills. Time is required for maturation and learning to occur. Motor activity becomes increasingly more specific as sensory and motor processes interact in a time dimension"* (McDonald, 1964, p. 93).

Application to Articulation Therapy

Speech-language pathologists understand that speech movements begin in gross motor patterns and develop into refined motor patterns over time. This means that certain phonemes naturally will be easier to stimulate than others. For example, many children can learn to make the relative gross labial movements of /w/ earlier than the more refined labial movements of /f/, and, therefore, therapists usually teach /w/ before /f/ in most cases.

This principle also means that all consonants can be stimulated early in life as long as therapists expect an immature and not an adult form to be produced. This is especially important to understand when treating children with motor speech disorders who take a much longer time to develop refined speech movements. Immature productions of phonemes are usually produced with a softer and sloppier quality, and they are made with broader and less

This young client is learning to say "ah" in a gross way. Over time he will learn to say it with less exaggeration and more refined oral control.

consistent points of contact than adult versions. The mature or refined form of the phoneme will develop over time and the gross form of the phoneme can be taught and accepted at first. SLPs do not need to worry about stimulating these clients to make perfect phonemes right away; clumsy ones will do for a while.

Therapists follow this principle all the time when they teach phonemes and words. For example, every SLP expects a child to say *mama* years before he is expected to say *mother*. The gross-to-fine principle also allows therapists to use exaggeration in articulation and motor speech therapy. Even Van Riper recognized that exaggerated gross speech movements developed first:

> "Do not worry about exaggerated movements made by the student in making the sound. At first, most students will use facilitating movements of other structures as a baby uses gross movements prior to specialization. We frequently encourage head and jaw movements or modifications of smiling, chewing, biting, and swallowing as accessory tools. These extraneous movements drop out as the new [more refined] performance pattern becomes habitual" (Van Riper, 1947, p. 165–166).

For example, a clumsy raspberry can serve as a substitute for a refined fricative for a while.

Proximal to Distal

Movements develop from near the trunk to further away from the trunk. The word *proximal* means "situated nearer to the center of the body" (Jewell & Abate, 2001, p. 1371) and the word *distal* means the opposite: "Situated away from the center of the body" (Jewell & Abate, 2001, p. 495). The principle means that children gain control of the core muscles first and this central stability allows for accurate and mature distal mobility to emerge. Motor therapists often call the control of the trunk *core strength*.

Body Motor Development

The development of the pencil grip and of writing exemplifies this principle. Careful study of the development of writing skill reveals four basic stages of motor control that develop from proximal to distal. At the earliest stage of writing, a child grasps the writing utensil with a gross grasp. The shoulder actually controls the movement while this one-year-old makes big left-to-right sweeping

The gross grasp (left) comes in earlier than the refined pencil grasp (right).

movements toward and away from his trunk as he marks his paper. He also takes his writing utensil and bangs it on his paper, making big dots. He is controlling both these actions at his shoulder, which is the most proximal part of the arm.

In the second stage, a child begins to control the action at his elbow, which is a point more distal than the shoulder. Now his marks on paper become a little smaller. He still sweeps toward and away from his trunk and makes dots, but his hand begins to stay on the paper, and he begins to make circles. The child is controlling movement at both the shoulder and the elbow.

In the third stage, movement control travels down to the wrist, a point more distal to the elbow. Now the child can make much smaller marks, including lines, dots, and circles. The child experiments with finger position on the utensil. Certain figures emerge, like a primitive human form. Other simple figures like suns, stars, spiders, balls, and primitive houses emerge. The bright child also begins to draw simple letters like O, M, X, and E. The child is controlling the movements of writing at the shoulder, elbow, and wrist, and perhaps at the hand as well.

In the final stage, children gain full and refined control of writing from the shoulder down to the fingers. The child experiments with many different utensil grips and his drawings get increasingly complex. His writing style may begin to vary, slanting first this way and then that, and making letters curvy one day and angular the next. The child begins to experiment with his signature. The child has gained full control of his arm from the shoulder down to the fingers.

Speech Motor Development

Speech motor control also develops from proximal to distal. To understand how this principle plays out one first must see the head as an appendage of the trunk. Biologists see the human body as having five appendages — two arms, two legs, and one head. All five bony structures extend out from the trunk, and each has proximal parts and more distal parts. The most proximal part of the speech mechanism is the diaphragm, and the most distal part is the lips. Speech movement development is from the diaphragm to the lips.

The order of infant vocal development can be viewed from proximal to distal, or from the diaphragm to the lips. The most proximal speech subsystem is the respiratory system and its control at the diaphragm and trunk. Breathing comes first, and without breathing there is no speech. The normal full-term neonate is born with the capacity to inhale and exhale, and thus his road to speech learning begins at the most proximal point.

An infant's first speech-like vocalization is the *quasi-resonant nuclei* (QRN; Oller, 1978). The QRN is made without regard to velopharyngeal or oral movement, therefore, it can be classified as a sound that is made with control only at the level of respiration and phonation, the two most proximal points on the line of proximal-to-distal

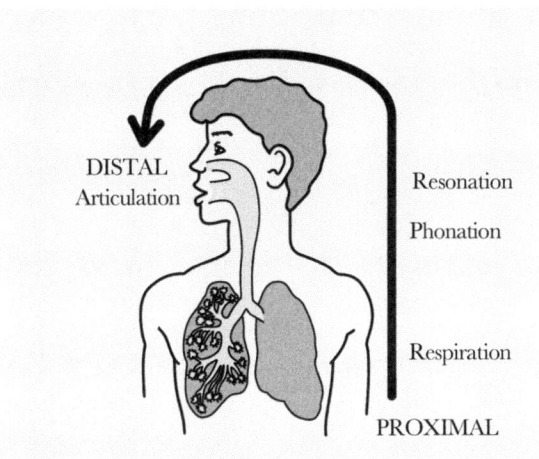

Speech movements are learned from proximal to distal, or from respiration to articulation.

development. The newborn's expression is limited to the QRN because he is using only proximal control of speech movement.

Speech movement control becomes more distal as the infant begins to experiment with velar movements. He experiments with the antagonistic movements of the velum and back of the tongue. The velum goes up while the back of the tongue lowers to make an oral sound. And the velum lowers while the back of the tongue elevates to produce a nasal sound. The infant experiments with this process of differentiating oral and nasal sound because he is learning more distal control in the oropharynx and experimenting with /ŋ/. This occurs during the first few months of life. The vowels also begin to differentiate during these first few months because the vowel quadrilateral is on the back one-third of the tongue. The phoneme /g/ is also heard at this time. All of this is sound made at the velum.

The child's speech movements become a little more distal when he begins to experiment with the temporomandibular joint, causing the jaw to move upwards and downwards. Up-and-down jaw movements cause the mouth to open and close in a wide pattern. Early babbling begins with vowels only and then consonants are added. When consonants are added, they tend to be anterior ones because the jaw is moving up and down in big sweeping patterns and banging the front structures together. These anterior sounds are primitive or gross forms of /b/, /m/, /w/, /d/, /n/, and /l/. Low vowels dominate these sequences because the jaw travels low.

The child's speech movements become even more distal when he learns to produce speech sounds by moving the tip of his tongue and his lips, the two most distal parts of the speech mechanism. With full movement capacity all the way to the tongue tip and the lips, a full range of speech sounds by place can emerge. Over time, the child will learn fully refined movement of each of these parts, from proximal to distal, and mature forms of all the

consonant phonemes will emerge and stabilize.

Application to Articulation Therapy

Severity of speech impairment can be understood along the proximal-to-distal continuum, and progress can be measured along these lines. The following represents one way that this can be done, beginning with clients who are non-verbal and non-vocal:

- *Profound:* Children with the most profound expressive speech impairments are those who breathe on their own but who produce no voice. They are using the most proximal control point only, that being respiration. Therapy is directed toward improving respiratory control and activating the voice.

- *Very severe:* Children with the next most severe speech impairments are those whose expressive speech is restricted to the QRN. These clients are using the two most proximal control points of control: respiration and phonation. Therapy focuses on improving respiration, strengthening the voice, and developing prosody. It is also directed toward stimulating tongue-back and velar movement.

- *Severe:* Children with the next most severe speech impairments are those whose speech movement control is restricted to vowels, nasals, and [+Back] consonants /k/, /g/, and /ŋ/. They are using respiration, phonation, and resonation control, as well as control of the back of the tongue. Therapy is directed toward using these phonemes and in facilitating gross movements of the more distal parts of the mouth — the jaw, lips, and front of the tongue. All the parts of the mouth need to start moving.

- *Moderate:* Children with moderate speech impairment are those who are moving the jaw up and down to create canonical babbling syllables with [+Anterior] consonants including /b/, /m/, /w/, /d/, /n/, and /l/. They are using control of respiration, phonation, and resonation, the back of the tongue, and gross up-and-down movements of the jaw that are controlled in the back. Therapy is directed toward activating more movement in the distal parts of the mouth: the lips and tongue tip.

- *Mild-to-moderate:* Children with mild-to-moderate speech impairment are those who are moving all parts of the speech mechanism, from the diaphragm to the lips, but whose movements are still somewhat unrefined and the phonemes are mixed up by place. Phonological patterns like *fronting, backing, stridency deletion,* and *final consonant deletion* are dominant, and an inability to produce refined sequences of phonemes results in patterns like *consonant cluster reduction* and *final consonant deletion.* Therapy is designed to facilitate mature movements, to produce all distinctive features and phonological patterns, to use the ear to adjust oral positions, and to produce clusters. Phonological and traditional articulation therapy approaches are recommended.

- *Mild:* Children with mild speech impairment have activated all parts of the speech mechanism from proximal to distal. Their errors are restricted to selected delayed motor patterns (e.g., frontal lisp), habituated incorrect motor patterns (e.g., lateral lisp), and minor place and manner errors (e.g., /f/ for /θ/, /θ/ for /f/, /b/ for /v/, /w/ for /l/, etc.). Many of these are simple and minor place shifts. Traditional articulation therapy approaches are recommended.

- *No speech impairment:* Children with no speech impairment are those who have activated speech movement at all points from proximal to distal. Speech movements have become refined at all places, the places of articulation are settled, and no phonemes errors are made. (No remediation is required.)

Medial to Lateral to Rotational

Movements develop from medial, to lateral, to rotational over time. The word *medial* means "situated near the median plane of the body" (Jewell & Abate, 2001, p. 1061) the word *lateral* means "situated on one side or the other of the body" (p. 962), and *rotate* means to "move in a circle around an axis" (p. 1453). This principle means that babies first gain movement in a front-to-back manner along the medial plane. With time, they learn to move side to side. With even more time they learn to rotate around the body axes through the process of midline integration.

Body Motor Development

Consider the development of purposeful trunk movements. Babies are born with excessive flexor tone that

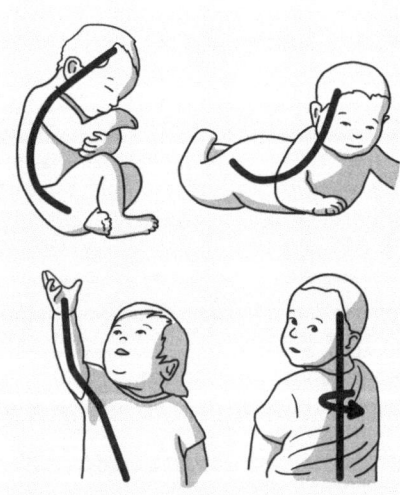

Movements emerge from medial (top left and top right), to lateral (bottom left), to rotational (bottom right).

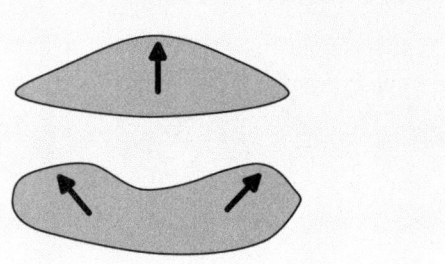

The tongue (as seen from the front) is able to elevate along its midline (top) before it can elevate along its sides (bottom).

causes them to be curled forward. Several weeks later, this high flexor tone weakens and the back extends so that by two months of age a baby begins to arch. These forward curling and backward extension movements occur with midline control, the first stage. Lateral trunk movements are the next to be seen as children learn to reach to the right and left while laterally stretching the upper body. Rotation of the trunk around the spine is the final movement plane to develop in this sequence. Rotation allows a child to turn his head and upper body in order to look around while his hips remain stationary.

Speech Motor Development

The principle also has application to the development of pre-speech movements. Twentieth century writers discussed movement of the articulators around their axes with the term "flexibility of the articulators" (e.g., Berry & Eisenson, 1956, p. 139). There is no data to demonstrate how this plays out in normal speech development but there is clear evidence of medial-to-lateral-to-rotational development in regard to oral movement skills in feeding development.

Under six months of age, infants use a suckle-swallow pattern that is medially controlled and which "involves a definite backward-and-forward movement of the tongue" (Morris & Klein, 1987, p. 28). The next to develop is sucking, and it "features a raising and lowering of the body of the tongue" (p. 28) which is also a medial movement.

By six months of age, a child starts to lateralize his tongue:

> *"Some lateralization may occur when food is placed on the side, between the biting surfaces of the gums [and at seven months the tongue] begins to show more lateralization, with a gross rolling movement or simple horizontal shift"* (Morris & Klein, 1987, p. 57).

A little later the child will learn to transfer food all the way from one side to another. These are evidence of lateral control.

Rotational feeding movements emerge last. "As

rotation develops throughout the body, we begin to see aspects of rotation emerge in the mouth" (Morris & Klein, 1987, p. 56). Rotational movements in the jaw are seen as gross rolling movements in all directions. The emergence of rotational movements reveals that the two sides of the tongue are integrating their movements together.

Application to Articulation Therapy

Clients with delayed oral movement skill often lack lateral and rotational oral movements, and this affects any phoneme that requires distinct lateral control. It also means that the two sides of the tongue may be working independently and not integrated. For example, a client who produces a bi-lateral lisp elevates the middle of his tongue instead of its lateral margins (see Chapter 13, *Facilitating Tongue Movement*) because lateral control has not developed or because the client cannot make the two sides do the same thing at the same time. Therapy to remediate this lisp may require activities to help the client develop lateral and rotational tongue movements so the groove can be created. Simple activities like wagging the tongue left and right might be used to unlock the tongue's midline control, to develop its lateral and rotational movement patterns, and to integrate the movements of the two sides in order that the groove might emerge.

Flexion & Extension

Movements develop in pairings of flexion and extension. The word *flexion* refers to "the action of bending or the condition of being bent, especially of a limb or joint" (Jewell & Abate, 2001) and the word *extension* is the opposite: "the action of moving a limb from a bent to a straight position" (p. 601).

Body Motor Development

The development of trunk movements demonstrates this principle. While acquiring the ability to sit, a baby learns to balance flexion of his trunk (bending forward) with extension of his trunk (bending back), and he learns to sit upright when this balance is achieved. The reader is probably familiar with the adorable sight of an infant of about

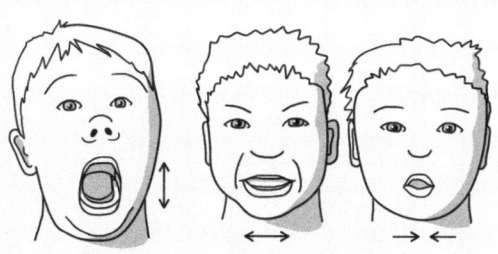

Jaw flexion and extension (left), lip extension (middle), and flexion (right) are foundational speech movement patterns.

five months of age who has not perfected this skill. After being placed in sitting, the child pulls forward in too much flexion and he topples forward onto his face, or he arches and falls backwards. Parents prop their children up with pillows and blankets during this period, and special seats are used until enough balance between flexion and extension allows the child to hold himself upright.

Speech Motor Development

The emergence and maturation of flexion and extension patterns is foundational to all speech movement development and the jaw is a good example. The jaw is in flexion when the mouth is closed, and it is in extension when the mouth is open. Babies can move the jaw up-down in a flexion-extension pattern and this is the gross jaw movement they use when babbling. Adults move the jaw in the same pattern but theirs is a much smaller movement that allows the production of mature speech.

Application to Articulation Therapy

Speech training for clients with motor speech disorders often includes activities designed to train basic flexion-extension patterns. For example, therapists often teach their clients to lift and lower the jaw, to protrude and retract the tongue, and to pucker and retract the lips in sequences. These gross flexion-extension patterns become the foundation of all more refined speech movements to be learned from that point forward.

Individual to Sequential

Individual movements are sequenced one-after-another to build linear complexity. The word *individual* means "single, separate" (Jewell & Abate, 2001, p. 865) and the word *sequential* means "forming or following in a logical order or sequence" (p. 1555). This principle means that children learn individual movements first and then they learn to sequence them one-after-another to form overlapping strings of movements.

Individual movements that are performed well contribute to sequences that are performed well, while poorly performed individual movements result in sequences that are sloppy and often contain missing elements. This is rather like the concept of part and whole; the parts have to be done well so that the whole will be successful. (It should be noted that some research has suggested that teaching the whole can be more successful for motor learning than teaching the individual parts; see Brydges et al., 2007.)

Body Motor Development

Learning to perform a cartwheel is a good illustration of this principle. Most readers are familiar with the rotating heels-over-head movement of a cartwheel. A good cartwheel is initiated with outstretched arms. A child stretches out the arms, bends over, and plants the hands down on the floor. The arms retain this flexible outstretched position as the legs push off from the ground and wheel over the head.

The ability to stretch out the arms is a critical skill in the sequence that creates the cartwheel, therefore, a good gymnastics school begins instruction for the cartwheel by teaching toddlers and preschool children how to stretch out their arms in various ways. For example, students learn to stretch out their arms to press against a wall, to perform a handstand, or to catch a ball. The ability to perform a cartwheel correctly is highly dependent upon the simple individual skill of stretching out the arms. The ability to stretch out the arms assures that the sequence of movements required for the cartwheel will be accomplished.

Speech Motor Development

The topic of *coarticulation* fits well here. Speech consists of sequences of sounds whose movements overlap and influence one another: "Articulation is a process consisting of a series of overlapping, ballistic movements" (McDonald, 1964, p. 87). The principle of individual-to-sequential skills means that a client must be able to perform the individual actions of each phoneme well so that he can put them into overlapping sequences. For example, a child will have to be able to produce /l/ correctly all by itself before he will be able to produce /l/ in clusters. There are exceptions to this rule, of course, and there are students who can produce /l/ in clusters before they can produce /l/ alone, but the principle generally holds.

Application to Articulation Therapy

Therapists have known of this principle for a long time and many methods of articulation therapy are based upon it. For example, many therapists use forward-and-backward chaining combined with sound blending to teach sequences of phonemes in words. Consider a three-letter word like *cat*. First each phoneme is practiced individually. Then the three phonemes are practiced in a sequence in which there is a pause between sounds so that each phoneme retains its original integrity. Then the sequence is practiced in a blended form where the movements of each adjacent phoneme overlap. This final step allows the production to sound more natural. This represents the perspective of traditional articulation therapy.

> "It is intuitively appealing to split a complex movement into its component parts during practice so that the learner can concentrate on a single aspect of the skill. This approach is thought to minimize the cognitive load and avoid unnecessary practice on task aspects already mastered. This part-whole approach is common in many speech remediation protocols" (Maas et al., 2008, p. 287).

Rhythmic Oscillations

Movements develop in oscillating rhythms. The word *rhythm* in this context means "a strong, regular, repeated pattern of movement" (Jewell & Abate, 2001, p. 1462). To *oscillate* means to "move or swing back and forth at a regular speed" (p. 1210). Rhythm is introduced to movement almost the moment it is learned. Rhythm is "perhaps the most basic and encompassing issue of normal development" (Morris & Klein, 2000, p. 66). Rhythm helps make movements regular, consistent, and familiar.

Infants and young children use rhythmic and oscillating movements as they play in order to enjoy virtually every movement they learn. The wonderful feelings that arise during the practice of oscillating movements help extend rehearsal of the movement, and this in itself facilitates the emergence of even more advanced movements. For example, once a child learns to hop, he hops all over the house for a while until he feels that he has reached some internal sense of rhythmic mastery over it, and then he moves on to other skills.

Body Motor Development

Infants and young children use rhythm as they practice almost every acquired movement. Babies suck on a nipple, bob the head, bounce the arms, kick the legs, and crawl along the floor in rhythmic patterns. Parents who are good at spoon-feeding their babies get through meals quickly and efficiently by timing the presentation of the spoon to fit the child's oscillating eating-and-swallowing rhythms. With development, children become good at all manner of motor skills when rhythm is added. For example, riding

Children need good arm extension (an individual movement) before their performance of a cartwheel (a sequential movement) can be well executed.

Children advance from tricycles to bicycles when pedaling becomes rhythmic and oscillating.

Rhythmic production can be added to speech work in many simple ways.

a bicycle becomes much better when the required peddling movements become rhythmic.

Speech Motor Development

"The dynamic actions of speech are intrinsically rhythmical" (Fletcher, 1992, p. 79). One of the best examples of speech developing in rhythm comes from babbling. Oller (1978) suggested that babbling begins without rhythm in a pattern he called *marginal babbling*, which he defined as babbling that has "aberrant timing properties." Once a child gets the hang of repeating syllables, he begins to do so rhythmically in the pattern Oller called *reduplicated babbling*, which consists of babbling sequences that "possess vocalic transitions which conform to the timing constraints for mature language."

Once the rhythmic pattern of the reduplicated babbling sequence is established, a baby has a platform on which to play with sounds and syllables. The rhythm of these sequences allows for more consonants and vowels to be explored in the increasingly complex babbling sequences Oller called *variegated babbling*. Rhythmic oscillation, therefore, is a key milestone in infant vocal development. Fletcher (1992) called it *pacemaker control*:

> *"A major landmark in vocal development, as in locomotion maturation, is gaining the ability to shift back and forth between alternative postures in articulatory gestures. This lays the foundation for pacemaker control of rhythmical movements"* (p. 13).

Application to Articulation Therapy

Rhythmic movement is a means of influencing higher levels of performance, and rhythm often breaks down when a client has an articulation or motor speech disorder. Therefore, SLPs often teach rhythmic speech control to many different types of clients. For example, many therapists bounce young children on their laps while teaching the syllable sequencing skills needed for babbling and early word productions.

Sensory & Motor

Movement development is both a sensory and a motor experience. The word *sensory* in this context means, "transmitted or perceived by the senses" (Jewell & Abate, 2001, p. 1553) and the word *motor* in this context means, "relating to muscular movement" (Jewell & Abate, 2001, p. 1114). This principle means that movement is simultaneously an *action* and the *feeling* of the action. During movement, muscles contract and relax, and joints bend and straighten, while pressure, movement, temperature, and texture stimulate the skin. A child moves and feels his movements simultaneously: "The learning of movement is entirely dependent upon sensory experience; sensory input which not only initiates but also guides motor output" (Fiorentino, 1972, p. 7).

Body Motor Development

Consider the act of kicking a ball. When a child kicks a ball, he actively moves his leg in a prescribed way to assure that his foot will make contact with the ball. He moves and he feels the movement at the same time. He practices kicking often in order to get the right "feel" of the leg swinging and the sensation of striking the ball. The child's sensory experiences guide him as he strives to improve his kick. His sensory experiences give him the feedback he needs to adjust his movements and kick better with each try. Experienced athletes who have a poor performance often say, "It didn't feel right," because the tactile, proprioceptive, and vestibular senses informed him that their movement was off.

Speech Motor Development

The same applies to speech movement. The production of speech is simultaneously a series of movements and the perception of those movements. During speech movement, muscles contract and relax, joints bend and straighten, and skin is stimulated. The child speaks and perceives his speech movements simultaneously. Expressive speech is both a sensory and a motor event.

Application to Articulation Therapy

Multisensory training often is the norm in articulation and motor speech therapy. The first formal approach that incorporated both sensory and motor elements was the motokinesthetic system (Young & Hawk, 1955), and newer systems like PROMPT follow this idea too (Hayden, 1984). Speech-language pathologists of the 21st century will continue to use multisensory approaches to articulation and motor speech training as they always have. Therapy should attempt to provide the sensory experiences that enhance speech movement learning.

> *"In most cases, emphasis on the auditory cues would predominate over the other senses, but it would not be unusual during the teaching of a sound to ask the child to listen, watch, feel, and touch"* (Hanson, 1983, p. 148).

Simple to Complex

Movements begin in simple patterns that become more complex with maturity. The word *simple* means "plane, basic, or uncomplicated in form, nature, or design" (Jewell & Abate, 2001, p. 1591) and the word *complex* means "consisting of many different and connected parts" (p. 351). This principle means that many developmental processes converge together over time in motor development.

Body Motor Development

All sports skills are learned in this manner, and the example of how children learn to throw a ball illustrates this principle. Cratty (1970) described the development of ball throwing skill as follows. Two-year-olds use forward-and-backward motions [and the] body remains facing the direction of the throw. There is either little or no weight shift. By three and a half years of age children usually evidence some bodily rotation that accompany their arm movements, but they do not weight shift in marked ways. By five or six years of age, children take a step before throwing and they make a pronounced weight shift as the ball is released. A child's throw improves in velocity and accuracy with age and development and the throw becomes refined over time.

Speech Motor Development

An analysis of syllable shapes illustrates the principle that speech movement progresses from simple to complex over time. Research indicates that the syllable shapes used by young children with emerging language are the V, the CV, the VC, and the CVC, with the CV used the most often. With time and maturity, syllable shapes become more complex as children acquire more complicated syllables such as CCV, CCVC, CCCV, CCCVC, VCC, CVCC, VCCC, CVCCC, CCVCC, and CCCVCCC.

An example of this can be seen in the acquisition of the word *strings*. A child might first say "ting" (CVC), and then progress to "twing" (CCVC), and then to "string" (CCCVC), and finally to "strings" (CCCVCC) over time.

Speech movements develop from simple to complex over time — just like ball throwing and most other movement skills.

Application to Articulation Therapy

Speech-language pathologists have been thinking this way for many decades, and many simple-to-complex sequences are represented throughout the course of standard articulation and motor speech practice. For example, therapists generally work from phonemes to syllables, from syllables to words, from one-syllable words to two- and more-syllable words, and from single phonemes to clusters, from two-consonant clusters to three-consonant clusters, and so forth. This sequence represents basic therapy procedures as taught by Van Riper and others of the Traditional Era.

Newer programs have also been based on this idea that speech movement skills are best taught from simple to complex. For example, Ling (1976) developed a program for the hearing impaired based upon the concept of training increasingly complex syllable shapes. SATPAC (Systematic Articulation Training Program Accessing Computers; Sacks, 2002) is a word list generation *app* (application; online software program) that allows the user to create systematic lists for specific articulation error training in increasingly difficult sequences of the therapist's selection. The app generates words, phrases, and nonsense words for phoneme targets. It allows the user to access a huge assortment of client-specific practice material for repetition and drill.

Slow to Fast

Movements are performed slowly when they are new, and they gain speed as skill improves with time and practice. The principle means that, in general, new movements are performed at a slower rate than practiced movements.

Body Motor Development

The principle has broad application to the acquisition of all body movements. For example, consider how a child learns to ride a bicycle. At first, the child's forward movement will be slow, awkward, unbalanced, and jerky because his feet are rotating slowly and a-rhythmically. With time and practice, his ability to cruise on his bike will be skilled, balanced, and smooth as his legs pedal faster and in better rhythm.

Speech Motor Development

The number of syllables produced per unit of time measures *rate of speech*. Research has demonstrated that early speech is produced with a slow rate, and that rate of speech increases as children develop over time (e.g., Smith, 1978).

Application to Articulation Therapy

Rate has two main applications in articulation therapy. First, most SLPs model new speech skills slowly so that clients can learn them, and then they increase speed over time so that the client will sound more natural. Second, problems in rate can play a significant role in unintelligibility, especially when rate is too fast for the client's own oral movement and auditory self-monitoring skills.

Therapy includes techniques to teach these clients how to recognize when they are being unintelligible and how to adjust their rate for maximum intelligibility. Rate is adjusted by slowing down the number of syllables produced per unit of time.

Mobility & Stability

Stability of movement allows for accurate and advanced mobility. The word *mobility* means "the ability to move or be moved freely and easily" (Jewell & Abate, 2001, p. 1096) and the word *stable* means "not likely to give way or overturn" (p. 1656); *stability* is "the state of being stable" (p. 1656). Mobility and stability function together in every movement. "We must have a stable base from which to develop movement and functional skills. Without that stability, our function or mobility is less controlled or even possible" (Morris & Klein, 2000, p. 62). The principle means that all movements are accomplished through interplay of mobility and stability. Stability and mobility are relative to one another; one part is more stable relative to the other part that is more mobile.

Body Motor Development

Any movement of the body can be analyzed for its mobility and stability relationships. For example, accurate arm movements are dependent upon stability at the shoulders, accurate leg movements are dependent upon stability at the hips, and accurate eye movements are dependent upon stability of the head.

Speech Motor Development

The principle also has application to all speech movements. For example, accurate breathing movements are dependent upon stability of the trunk; the movements of the respiratory system will be delayed or disordered when there is a lack of trunk stability or when it is inappropriate.

Application to Articulation Therapy

The interplay of mobility and stability in speech movement is a deep subject that has broad application in speech motor control. It is discussed in detail in Chapter 14, *The Critical Role of Oral Stability.*

Muscle Tone

Status of muscle tone contributes to movement development. The term *muscle tone* refers to the "tension present in resting muscles" (Nicolosi, Harryman & Kresheck, 1983, p. 242). Tone also refers to a muscle's readiness to respond. Normal tone allows for normal movement. Normal tone occurs in a range. The term *hypotonia* is used to describe tone that is outside that range and too low and *hypertonia* is used to describe tone that is outside that range and too high. The term *fluctuating tone* is used when a client's tone swings back and forth between the two. The term *mixed tone* is used when certain areas of the body have high tone while others have low tone. It is important to note that

muscle tone is not the same thing as muscular force or strength.

> *"Even when a muscle is 'at rest' a certain amount of contractile tension often remains. This very slight amount of contraction is called muscle tone"* (Zemlin, 1981, p. 28).

> *"Normal movement has a degree of tension to give us stability or steadiness around our joints yet it has enough relaxation to allow us to simultaneously move"* (Morris & Klein, 2000, p. 122).

Body Motor Development

Muscular tone has a direct influence on the development of all movement. Hypertonia, hypotonia, fluctuating tone, and mixed tone cause movements to be poorly graded, lacking in range, imprecise, jerky, stiff or floppy, inconsistent, weak, lacking in endurance, and slow to progress along all the developmental continuums discussed in this chapter.

Speech Motor Development

Muscular tone also seems to have a direct effect on speech movement although support research has been week (Solomon, 2004). Muscle weakness and low muscle tone seems to have an effect on the "speed, range and accuracy of speech movements" (Duffy, 1995, p. 99). The classic position has been that tone differences result in dysarthria, but a newer perspective seems to be that tone differences exist in certain types of dysarthria (Solomon, 2004). In general, hypotonicity causes speech movements to be produced in a limited range and with poor accuracy. Hypertonicity, on the other hand, tends to cause speech movements to be jerky, stiff, fixed, or absent.

> *"[With hypertonicity] speech is slow and seems to emerge [with effort], as though produced against considerable resistance... All the basic motor processes involved in speech production may be reduced in efficiency"* (Darley, Aronson & Brown, 1975, p. 134–135).

Application to Articulation Therapy

Speech-language pathologists recognize that muscle tone differences result in dysarthric speech. SLPs also recognize that these tone problems can be confined to the oral mechanism or they can envelop the whole body. All speech evaluations should include at least an informal assessment of oral and facial tone. Certainly any formal research on clients with motor speech disorders should include an assessment of muscle tone by a trained motor therapist. In therapy, referral to the team occupational or physical therapist is made in cases where severely aberrant oral/facial tone is identified. In these cases, speech therapy will include methods to adjust the muscular support for

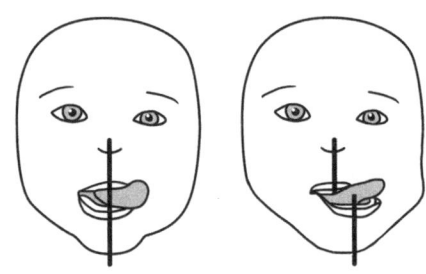

The tongue on the left is lateralizing independently whereas the tongue on the right has not separated its movements from the jaw and is moving in concert with it.

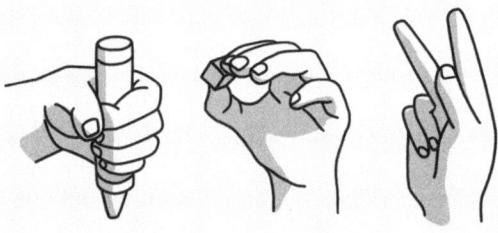

Mass to separation demonstrated in the gross grasp (left), the neat pincer (middle), and the ASL sign for K (right).

respiration, phonation, resonation, and articulation movement.

Mass to Separation

A mass action is one that incorporates many body parts. To *separate* is to "become detached or disconnected" (Jewell & Abate, 2001, p. 1553). All movements begin as mass action and separate in time to become individualized. With separation, individual body parts can make individual actions.

> "*Generalized mass activity is replaced by specific individual responses*" (Illingworth, 1963, p. 144).

> "*Precision of movement progresses from the presence of total body movement toward the refinement of specific skills*" (Morris & Klein, 2000, p. 63).

> "*The ability to dissociate one movement from another and separate the movement of different parts of the body is necessary in the developmental progression toward refinement of gross and fine motor skills*" (Morris & Klein, 2000, p. 63).

Body Motor Development

The development of hand grasping contains three levels that unfold over time and that reflect this principle. A child's earliest grasp pattern is known as a *gross grasp*. It is accomplished by flexing all the fingers simultaneously toward the palm; it is a mass movement of the whole hand. Within a few months, a child develops a more advanced grasp called the neat pincer. The *neat pincer* is a grasp of just the thumb and index finger. The neat pincer develops because the thumb and index finger begin to separate their movements from others. Hand movement skills then go beyond the gross grasp and neat pincer into more advanced separation skills. For example, the ability to sign the alphabet requires fully independent movement of each finger. Advanced sign language is possible only through a complete separation of all hand and finger movements.

Speech Motor Development

Movement patterns of the jaw, lips, tongue, and velum must also separate in order for advanced phonemes to emerge. At first, the jaw, lips, tongue, and velum function together as a single unit, a pattern that has been called the "everything moves at once" principle (Kent, 1980). The articulators then begin to separate their movements with time and maturation.

For example, consider the development of tongue-tip elevation for production of /l/. The present author has noted that the tongue-and-jaw movements for /l/ develop in three stages over time. At first an infant produces /l/ in reduplicated babbling sequences but the tongue tip actually does very little lifting. Instead the relatively flat tongue holds steady while the jaw lifts and lowers. The jaw and tongue function together as a single unit and the jaw actually is the mover at this stage. The resultant production of /l/ is a gross allophonic variation of the mature target.

Several months later, and by the time a child is producing his first words, the movements of /l/ become somewhat more refined. The jaw continues to pump up and down, but now the tongue tip elevates and depresses as well. The tongue and jaw are beginning to separate their movements. The listener's ear registers this production as /l/, but the sound is characterized by the adorable "soft" or "immature" distortion of the toddler's sound. This distortion is acceptable for a toddler but not beyond early elementary school.

When production of /l/ reaches maturity, the jaw holds itself in a partially graded stable position while the tongue alone performs all the up-and-down movement necessary for the phoneme. Movements of the tongue now are completely separated from the jaw, although their movements are interlocked through adulthood. This is the movement pattern for /l/ that classifies it as mature in an 8- to 9-year-old child. This is also the motor pattern for /l/ that is represented on the consonant chart, i.e. the ideal, fully-formed /l/.

Application to Articulation Therapy

Articulation and motor speech therapy often include methods to facilitate separation of jaw, lip, tongue, and velar movements so that phonemes can be produced with mature motor patterns. For example, many therapists use bite blocks to stabilize the jaw and force the tongue to move independently. This is a concept that has woven its way throughout the articulation and motor speech literature since the days of phonetic placement as expressed by Crary (1993) who wrote on apraxia:

> *"Using a bite block to stabilize the mandible and reduce mandibular support during speech may help to increase independent lingual movement and result in improved oral articulation for speech"* (p. 224).

Differentiation

Differentiation of movement allows for refined movements to develop. To *differentiate* is to "make or become different in the process of growth or development" (Jewell & Abate, 2001, p. 476). Immature movements are performed in a gross way by using large groups of muscles, and this principle means that with maturity comes the ability to use increasingly smaller muscle groups. The use of smaller muscle groups results in increasingly more refined movements. The process of using gradually smaller muscle groups is known as *differentiation of movement*. Differentiation should not be confused with separation as described above; *separation* involves independent movement of individual body parts while *differentiation* involves independent contraction and relaxation of muscles of the same body part.

Body Motor Development

The development of facial muscle control is a good example here. All the facial muscles function as a single unit early in development. When a baby smiles or frowns, for example, his whole face is involved. Smiling is broad and open, and frowning is narrow and closed. All the facial muscles move together in one movement pattern of either

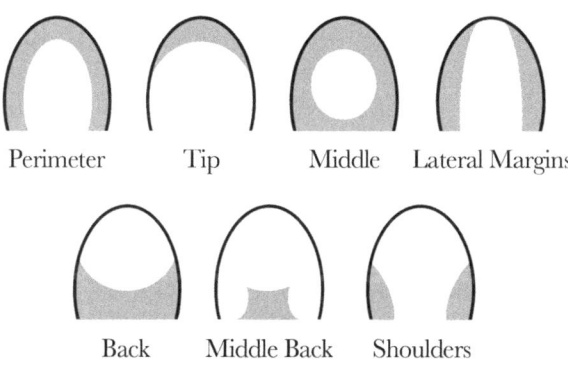

| Perimeter | Tip | Middle | Lateral Margins |

| Back | Middle Back | Shoulders |

Differential control allows parts of the tongue to elevate (gray sections) while other parts remain low (blank sections).

opening or closing. With motor maturity, an adult can smile with his mouth as he frowns with his eyes. Full differential control of all the facial muscles allows a full repertoire of facial expressions to emerge.

Speech Motor Development

The tongue and its movements are a perfect example of smaller groups of muscles functioning differentially over time. The tongue is a single body part, yet the tongue consists of several different muscle pairs, and each pair must function differentially from the rest over time. Tongue-tip control is a good example. The immature tongue cannot lift the tip to the alveolar ridge because the whole tongue moves as a single unit and it mostly moves forward and backward. Differential control of the parts of the tongue allows the tip to rise while the rest of the tongue stays low. Even more refined differential control is needed to control the tip itself so that the tip's movements for /s/ are produced differently than the tip's movements for /t/. This topic of differential tongue control is discussed more thoroughly in Chapter 13, *Facilitating Tongue Movement*.

Application to Articulation Therapy

Speech-language pathologists recognize the differential control necessary for production of all phonemes and provide activities to facilitate differential control of the speech muscles while engaging in the process of articulation therapy for clients who need it.

Combinations

Individual movements combine to create new movements. The word *combination* in this instance means "uniting different uses, functions, or ingredients" (Jewell & Abate, 2001, p. 340). The principle means that once fully separated and differentiated, new movements can be created when independent movements are newly re-combined.

Body Movement Development

The development of the hand's grasp also exemplifies this principle. Remember that the grasp begins as a mass movement and over time the fingers begin to move independently. The present principle means that once separated the individual movements of each finger can be combined back together again to create brand new movement patterns. For example, the signed alphabet requires finer movements to combine in patterns that are unique to each letter.

Speech Movement Development

The principle also applies to the development of speech movements. Once the jaw, lips, tongue, and velum function independently, they can re-combine into new movement patterns. For example, /ʃ/ can be produced when at least four individual oral movements are performed simultaneously: the jaw elevates, the velar port closes, the tongue grooves, and the lips round. Without independent action of each part, the total motor pattern will be incorrect and the sound quality of /ʃ/ will be compromised.

Synchrony of coordinated speech movements seems to improve with age. Green, Moore, Higashikawa, and Steeve (2000) demonstrated that lip and jaw synchrony steadily improves between one and six years of age. Cheng, Murdoch, Goozée, and Scott (2007a) found that tongue-jaw coordinations improved between six years of age and adulthood: "Greater movement synchrony of the articulators and a more consistent interarticulator relation appear to be emerging characteristics of speech motor maturation" (p. 352).

Application to Articulation Therapy

Following this principle, an individual phoneme can be taught by breaking down the oral position into its independent components — jaw, lips, tongue, and velum — and then these can be re-combined to develop the phoneme itself. Returning to the example above, /ʃ/ can be taught by teaching the client how to stabilize the jaw in the right position, how to close the velar port, how to anchor the tongue to form the groove, and how to round the lips while exhaling. These component movements can be taught individually, and then they can be combined together to form the whole phoneme. This process of

Extreme oral movements like this one do not occur within the phonological systems of any known language, and perhaps this is because they violate the economy principle.

Humans can flip and perform other complicated movements. But everyday activities involve movements that are simple and economical, like walking.

separating phoneme productions into individual movements and positions underlies the phonetic placement method described by Van Riper.

Economy

Economical movements are the goal of movement maturity. The word *economical* in this context means, "using no more of something than is necessary" (Jewell & Abate, 2001, p. 540). The principle means that humans tend to use only those movements that are necessary to achieve the movement goal. Economy is a driving force in the selection of movements for everyday use. The developmental drive of childhood is toward economy and efficiency: "Mechanical efficiency is an important outgrowth of motor skill learning" (Fletcher, 1992, p. 6).

Body Motor Development

For example, given good training, many young people can learn to do a summersault or "flip" in the air. But there is no reason to use this movement during the course of everyday living. There is no economy in performing a flip as one walks from the living room to the kitchen for example. One uses the flipping movement only under certain conditions, like during gymnastics, dancing, or snowboarding, or when simply showing off. A flip is not an economical movement, but walking is. People who can flip still walk as a general means of moving from one place to another because walking is simple and economical.

Speech Motor Development

Speech movements also tend toward the simple and economical as revealed in studies of tongue movements: "Much of the data reviewed has indicated that speech obeys the general rule that motor skill development is guided by movement efficiency and conservation of energy" (Fletcher, 1992, p. 92). For example, given optimum neuromuscular conditions, most people can stick the tongue out of the mouth and reach it up toward the nose; in fact some people actually can touch the nose with the tongue. But this extreme tongue movement is not used for speech in any known language because the movement is not practical, economical, or efficient. To move the tongue in such an extreme manner during the course of rapid conversational speech would be awkward, would slow speech too much, and would make sequential tongue movements more difficult. Children play with extreme oral movements like this during infancy and early childhood, but such movements drop out as speech matures. The drive toward speed and efficiency is one of the factors that move speech movement skills forward. Economy allows adult speech movements to be quick and easy. The terms *motor economy* and *underexploitation* were used by used by Lindbloom (1983) to describe this phenomena, and Ladefoged (2005) used the term *gestural economy* to describe a similar idea:

"In normal speech the production system is rarely driven

to its limits... When we examine gestures in relation to the potential capacity of the system we note a tendency toward underexploitation" (Lindblom, 1983, p. 219).

"It would be an added burden if we had to make a large number of sounds that were all completely different from one another. It puts less strain on our ability to produce speech if the sounds of our language can be organized in groups that are articulated in much the same way... This is a principle that we will call gestural economy" (Ladefoged, 2005, p. 4).

Another form of speech movement economy occurs in the way everyday words are shortened. Children and adults habitually change long complex words into simpler forms when speaking in comfortable surroundings. For example, people often say "fridge" for *refrigerator*, "kay" for *okay*, "info" for *information*, "app" for *application*, and "S'up" for *What's up?*. Different processes are at play in these instances, but economy is the driving force.

Application to Articulation Therapy

Lindblom (1983) postulated that simplification pattern errors like *assimilation* and *cluster reduction* can be seen as the incompetent speaker's way of making speech too economical. As an example, a production of /pun/ for *spoon* can be considered a more economical way to say *spoon* because it requires less movement. Phonological simplification patterns like this might be viewed as speech that is being produced with gestural economy that exceeds that which is acceptable to most speakers.

Casual to Habitual

New movements are casual but with time they become habitual. The word *casual* in this context means "not regular or permanent" (Jewell & Abate, 2001, p. 268). The term *habit* refers to "a settled or regular tendency or practice" (p. 762). This principle means that new movements eventually become habitual, but they don't start out that way. Children begin to use new movements on a casual, or irregular, basis. A new movement is used here and there until it eventually becomes a regular part of the child's movement repertoire. Once habituated, it tends to remain constant for long periods of time.

Body Motor Development

The hand's grasp on a writing utensil is illustrative here. Once a child develops past the gross grasp and he is acquiring a mature grasp, he will experiment with a wide variety of grasping patterns for a while. This experimentation can last several years. When a comfortable pattern is attained, the child tends to settle into it for many years with slight alterations as his hands grow and as he begins to use a wider assortment of writing and drawing utensils. The settled grasp eventually becomes his lifelong habit. Most adults have a habitual way of holding a writing

utensil, or they have several settled positions that are used at various times depending upon the writing task and the utensil being employed.

Speech Motor Development

This principle has widespread application to the acquisition of speech sounds.

"It is well documented that articulator movement is more variable in children than in adults... Children's articulator movements become more stable over time with a gradual progression toward adult patterns" (Grigos, 2009, p. 164).

For example, there are many ways a child might say the word *fish* before he settles on the adult form. He might call it a "tish," a "pish," or a "shishy." A child's early productions will be casual but his later correct productions will become a habit.

Application to Articulation Therapy

The application of this principle to articulation and motor speech therapy is obvious and well known. Speech therapy is a process of teaching new movements, like pressing the lips together for /b/, or lifting the tongue tip to the alveolus for /l/. Therapists expect their clients to use new speech movements irregularly at first. But over time, they expect them to make a habit of the new movement patterns. They do this by introducing gradually more intensive practice of target skills. Most SLPs realize that "a major goal of training in speech production skills is to enable articulatory execution to proceed automatically" (Fletcher, 1992, p. 159). Practice, rehearsal, and drill help ensure habituation of new phoneme movements during the speech remediation process.

Random to Controlled

The word *random* in this context means "made, done, chosen, or happening without method or conscious decision" (Jewell & Abate, 2001, p. 1409). Random movements occur haphazardly. *Control* in this context means "the power to restrain something" (p. 374). The principle means that children's movements first occur at random times but over time they become ordered to events.

Body Motor Development

The development of kicking is a simple example here. An infant kicks his legs at random intervals throughout the day but kicking is restricted to appropriate circumstances by the time a child is ready to play on a soccer team. Kicking develops from random occurrences to those that are event-specific.

Speech Motor Development

Early speech movements also occur at random times: "From birth to about one year, [speech] motor activity... is largely random" (McDonald, 1964, p. 93). With time and maturity, speech movements become controlled, regular, restricted, and organized. For example, an infant's production of /θ/ occurs randomly at haphazard times, and a preschool child might use /θ/ to substitute for other phonemes. But by 7–9 years of age the production of /θ/ is restricted to only those words that contain that phoneme. All speech movements become controlled with time given normal development.

Application to Articulation Therapy

Speech-language pathologists realize that infants, toddlers, and young preschool children often need time to produce a wide variety of pre-speech sounds and phonemes with wild abandon. They need time to make mistakes because they still are producing phonemes in a random way. Therapy is designed to help clients organize phonemes and syllables over time. Van Riper used this concept in his *babbling method*. He recommended random babbling practice to elicit new phonemes from older children:

> *"[The therapist and student] should relax, get the babbling started, and then let it continue almost automatically, ranging where it will... Random vocalizations should be the goal for the time being... The teacher's task is to get the student to select, out of the complex hodgepodge of vocalizations, the sound which he has difficulty in making, to focus his attention upon it, and to make it voluntarily"* (Van Riper, 1947, p. 193).

Reflex Foundations

Reflexes form the basis of all voluntary movement, or at least that is the theory. A *reflex* is "an action that is performed without conscious thought as a response to stimulus" (Jewell & Abate, 2001, p. 1431). Reflexes dominate the earliest motor patterns in normal development:

> *"The earliest movements that can be elicited in newborn infants consist of involuntary actions triggered by various kinds of external stimuli... Some of these reflexes... contribute in direct ways to... locomotion"* (Cratty, 1970, p. 10–27).

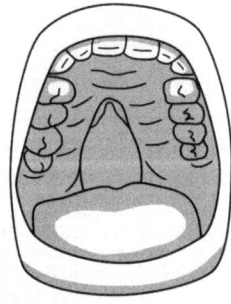

Cleft palate and other structural defects can interfere with speech movement development.

This theory means that every movement can be traced back to its triggering reflex. There are many who have argued against this principle, stating that not all movements can be traced back to a specific reflex, and, even if they could there is no proof that stimulating the reflex will stimulate the mature movement:

> *"Although it is not yet possible to determine whether there is a direct relationship between reflexive behavior and later voluntary movement, it is safe to assume that there is at least an indirect link"* (Gallahue & Ozmun, 1995, p. 163).

Despite the controversy that has surrounded this concept, occupational and physical therapists have developed many techniques of movement stimulation based upon reflex responses, and SLPs have adopted the practice.

Body Motor Development

The development of the hand's grasping pattern is useful here. The grasp begins as a reflexive movement response in the newborn. The theory is that the reflexive motor pattern of hand grasping sets up a neurological substratum that allows a child to grasp voluntarily using the same pattern.

Speech Motor Development

The tongue's grasp reflex is an excellent example to use here. The theory is that this reflexive bowl-shaped motor pattern sets up neurological tracts that are then followed as the child learns to move the tongue voluntarily in ways that support mature speech:

> *"Touching or stroking a baby's tongue elicits a spoon-shaped lingual configuration, characterized by an upraised ridge around its outer border... This basic, reflexively elicited posture, which plays an important role in sucking activities, is also found in the infant's cry posture... This lingual stance also appears to be the basis for the lingua-palatal valving in later speech production"* (Fletcher, 1992, p. 10).

Application to Articulation Therapy

Speech-language pathologists know that there are a wide variety of reflexes that may be used to stimulate movement in the four speech movement centers. Reflexes range from those that stimulate inhalation to those the cause the lips to pucker. The speech reflexes and ideas about how to use them are described in Chapter 17.

Structure & Function

Anatomy (structure) impacts movement (function), and vice versa. The principle means that adequate structure supports the natural processes of motor development and that inadequate structure interferes with it.

Body Motor Development

The length of the leg bones might be a good example: if the bones in one leg are somewhat shorter than the bones in the other leg, many movement problems will ensue. First, the hip girdle will be tilted to one side when the person is standing. This will cause a curvature of the spine as the client attempts to remain vertical and to keep his head upright. The client will tighten and loosen certain core muscles in his attempts to get as vertical as possible and to stay upright. These tone adjustments in the hips, shoulders, and trunk will cause many problems in movement of the extremities (head, arms, and legs). Development of all motor skills will be impacted.

Speech Motor Development

Speech-language professionals have differentiated between *structural* and *functional* speech problems since the elocutionists began to combine ideas of anatomy and speech. The term *organic defect* refers to speech defects that have a structural basis. Most therapists understand that adequate anatomy supports the potential for the development of adequate speech movement and that inadequate anatomy can cause problems in the development of speech movements.

Application to Articulation Therapy

In the ideal situation, structural defects are corrected before or during the course of articulation and motor speech therapy. In the less-than-ideal situation, in which the structural deficit will remain, Van Riper taught that the client should be taught "compensatory movements in speech sound production" (Van Riper, 1947, p. 162). In other words, the client is taught to produce speech that sounds and looks the best it can, given the client's permanent structural differences.

Habits

Habits can interfere with movement development under certain conditions. The word *habit* refers to "a settled or regular tendency or practice, especially one that is hard to give up" (Jewell & Abate, 2001, p. 762). Certain habits seem to cause or contribute to movement problems, and some habits actually seem to prevent new motor skill learning.

Body Motor Development

For example, chronic W-sitting on the floor can cause the core muscles necessary for mature trunk control to develop differently than if the child habitually cross-sits, side-sits, or long-sits. Elimination of the habit will facilitate appropriate trunk support for all the body's movement capabilities.

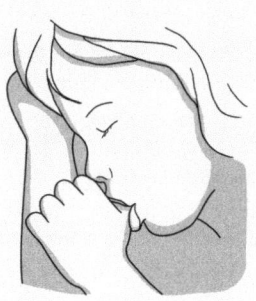

Thumb, finger, or pacifier sucking may interfere with speech movement development in individual children depending on type, frequency, duration, and intensity.

Speech Motor Development

Oral habits may interfere with speech movement development. Pacifier use, thumb sucking, and other digit sucking habits are perhaps the most common, but this area includes any chewing or sucking habit. This topic is a controversial one within the field of speech-language pathology. Clearly there are oral habits that contribute to speech developmental differences in some but not all children. For example, some toddlers suck on pacifiers with no negative impact on speech while others have the pacifier in the mouth so often that they never speak. Oral habits seem to interfere with speech movement development depending on type, frequency, duration, and intensity, although the exact nature of these relationships is uncertain at this time.

Application to Articulation Therapy

Twenty-first-century speech-language pathologists recognize that oral habits may contribute to speech movement errors in some but not all cases. When oral habits are identified and judged related to speech production errors, activities are designed to eliminate the habit either before or during the speech remediation process.

Clinicians rely on their own clinical judgments to make these decisions. The diagnostic question posed is: "Does this particular oral habit seem to be contributing to this particular speech movement problem in this particular client at this particular time?" If this question can be answered in the affirmative then speech training includes procedures designed to reduce or eliminate the habit. It is recognized that this is a weak argument, but perhaps a multidisciplinary evaluation will bring it more support. Reports on teeth, occlusion, sleep patterns, oral habits, speech, and eating/swallowing will be informative.

Health

General health contributes to the pace and certainty of movement development. The word *health* refers to "a person's mental or physical condition" (Jewell & Abate,

2001, p. 784). A healthy child can take on the world; he is prepared to engage in all the physical activities that foster growth and development of motor skills. An unhealthy child often lacks opportunity to grow and develop in these ways.

Body Motor Development

A good example here is the child with Down syndrome. A child with Down syndrome will be expected to have gross and fine motor delay, but this delay is impacted even further if the child has the types of heart defects often associated with the syndrome. The heart problem results in even more delay in motor development because the child cannot play as much or as long as other children, and he may spend certain periods of time hospitalized and/or restricted in his movements. The heart problem causes additional delays in skill acquisition.

Speech Motor Development

A client's health can contribute to speech impairment. The most common example is probably the relationship between otitis media, conductive hearing loss, auditory processing, and speech. Problems in articulation, voice, and resonance can result from chronic ear infections, allergies, and so forth.

Application to Articulation Therapy

In the ideal situation, all negative health influences are reduced or eliminated before or during the course of articulation therapy. SLPs recognize that a healthy mind and body is the ideal starting place for speech correction. In circumstances that are less than ideal, speech-language pathologists stimulate for the highest level of functioning possible given the health status of the client.

Bottom-Up & Top-Down Processing

Direct sensorimotor learning experiences (bottom) are replaced by mental functions (top) over time. When children are young, they learn through direct sensory and motor

Like solving a puzzle, speech can be processed bottom-up or top-down.

interaction with the environment. This has been called the process of *bottom-up processing*. The child's actions and his thinking are tied together when he is processing from the bottom-up in a process Jean Piaget called *sensorimotor intelligence* (Ginsburg & Opper, 1969). But at some point this need for direct action wanes, the process matures, and thinking through the consequence of motor action takes over. This is known as *top-down processing*. The child becomes able to "mentally manipulate his environment without the need for direct experience" (Cratty, 1970, p. 283). Now the child can use his mental capacities to understand future motor activities and their consequences.

> *"Bottom-up is employed to indicate the process of using available information to collect a group of details before constructing a general pattern"* (Vogel & Miller, 1991, p. 89).

> *"Top-down is used to refer to the cognitive process of using available information to construct a gestalt or whole"* (Vogel & Miller, 1991, p. 89).

> *"Top-down processing is analogous to deductive thinking"* (Wallach & Miller, 1988, p. 20).

Body Motor Development

Learning to put together a wooden form-puzzle is a good example of this principle as it applies to body skill development. A very young child places a wooden puzzle piece over a hole in a wooden puzzle form, and he tries to force it straight in. Failing that, the child begins to turn the piece this way and that until he can drop it into place. The child is using his direct physical experiences to solve his puzzle. The process is fairly slow and it can be quite frustrating for an impatient child. The child is processing from the bottom-up.

With maturation and experience, a child begins to mentally solve a puzzle before he physically manipulates it. He thinks through the size and shape of the puzzle piece in his hand, he compares it visually to the form, he twists and turns the piece first, and then he drops it straight in. The child now is using mental manipulation instead of physical manipulation to fit the piece. The child has developed the mental ability to think through the required movements and he no longer has to rely on the direct sensorimotor experience. He can direct his motor skills with top-down processing, and he can work faster and more efficiently as a result.

Speech Motor Development

The principle of bottom-up and top-down processing is reflected in the motor skill development of phoneme acquisition. Take, for example a typical four-year-old child's attempt to say the word *vacation*. Many young children substitute /b/ for /v/ and say *bacation* for a while. In order to change it, he must pay close attention to the tactile, proprioceptive and auditory sensations of changing /b/ to /v/. The child's learning comes primarily through his direct sensory and motor experimentation. He must consciously form his lips into a /v/ instead of a /b/ and he must actively listen to the result. He has to think through these movements every time he says the word for a little while. He is processing from the bottom-up.

With time and practice, the child not only says *vacation* correctly, he can also use this prior learning to think through any additional words that contain /v/, and he can produce new words correctly, immediately, and without engaging in the process of trial and error. Now the child is using his mental manipulations first. This capacity allows him to correct his potential phoneme errors before they occur. He produces new words like *vacuum* and *varnish* without error using processing that is from the top to the bottom.

Application to Articulation Therapy

Clients served by speech-language pathologists represent the full range of intellectual abilities and SLPs must design articulation and motor speech programs to reflect each client's ability to use mental manipulations. SLPs understand that direct sensorimotor experiences are not necessary when a client has the capacity to think through his articulation movement errors. Top-down processing can be used and speech movements can be adjusted in the mind before they are adjusted in the body. But direct sensorimotor learning activities are necessary with those clients who still process bottom-up because they are young, or cognitively impaired, or have some other problem that limits their capacity to understand their own speech movements. These clients still need direct motor experiences to understand and control them and bottom-up processing is used in these cases. These clients are encouraged to move first, to think about and control their movements second, and to use these movements to produce phonemes third.

Motor Learning Theory

Researchers in sports physiology and related areas study how skilled movements are learned and improved upon, and they propose *motor learning theories* to describe these processes. Motor learning theory suggests that humans of any age can acquire *specialized motor skills*. Specialized motor skills are defined as "mature fundamental movement patterns that have been refined and combined to form sport skills and other complex movement skills" (Gallahue & Ozmun, 1995, p. 386). For example, virtually any able-bodied person can learn to kick a football given instruction and practice. Motor learning theories propose various ways to accomplish and master this skill.

Motor learning theories are concerned with factors that influence skill learning within the behavior modification paradigm. Factors include: how much practice is required, how many repetitions should be included, how long practice sessions should be, how many times per week practice sessions should be held, how much rest should be

incorporated between practice sessions, and how much practice should be offered per session. It also includes: the influence of consistent practice versus variable practice schedules; random versus blocked schedules; the amount, type, and frequency of feedback offered; the use of delayed versus immediate feedback; the transfer of learning; the use of music during practice; and more.

The reader can see that elements of motor learning theory involve simple manipulations and behavior management. Motor learning theories also concern other aspects of physical and mental health including diet, nutrition, hydration, sleep, goal-setting, degree of challenge, motivation, and the mental preparation required to produce successful athletic performance.

Every trainer — from sports coaches to piano teachers — thinks through how he or she will apply these factors in the training of their protégés. Motor learning theory is behavior modification theory and it is a separate issue from the principles of movement development that have been discussed in this chapter. The principles of movement development described in this chapter concern the normal processes of motoric development in infancy and childhood. Motor learning theory concerns the acquisition of specific advanced movement skills among children and adults at any age. The principles of motor development and motor learning theories represent two different worlds of motor study. One concerns the acquisition of motor skills in normal development and the other investigates how the perfection of advanced motor skills can be changed through behavior management.

For a nice review of motor learning theories and their relevance to speech motor learning, please see Maas et al. (2008). Readers also may be interested in the topic of *neural plasticity* and are referred to Ludlow et al. (2008). Ludlow et al. define neuroplasticity as "the ability of the central nervous system (CNS) to change and adapt in response to environmental cues, experience, behavior, injury, or disease" (p. S241). It is important to note that Brunner et al. (2011) found that speakers with less articulatory skill were less able to adapt to changes imposed on their oral motor performance than were speakers with high performance skills.

Body Motor Development

Examples from general motor development are plentiful. For example, given good health, children and adults alike can learn to swim, dance, throw a ball, run, type, or eat with chopsticks. Learning any of these actions requires desire on the part of the learner, a willingness to learn, adequate instruction, time to practice, and a goal in mind. Motor learning theory proposes that any motor skills can improve given positive applications of these circumstances.

Speech Motor Development

Motor learning theory is rooted in behavior management theory, or *behaviorism*, a therapeutic approach widely attributed to Skinner (1974). Motor learning theory proposes that people can learn new speech movement skills no matter their age when given good health, instruction, and behavior management protocols. Virtually all SLPs understand this concept as demonstrated by their use of practice and rehearsal, reward charts, parent involvement, and other means to establish new speech movements. A client is taught a new speech movement alone or within a syllable or word, and then the SLP uses various motor learning theories to solidify the movement. Both children and adults can learn to produce new phonemes and they can learn to correct those acquired incorrectly given excellent behavior management of performance.

It has become popular recently to decry the use of so-called "oral-motor techniques" and to champion the use of motor learning theory, but it does no good to practice a motor skill that is wrong. For example, if a client lifts the broad surface of his tongue-blade to the palate instead of lifting the much smaller tongue tip to the palate, it will not help him to exercise this movement. The movement should be changed first and rehearsed second. The principles of motor development described in this chapter help therapists determine how to change the movement first. Motor learning theories then help therapists determine how to practice the new movement.

Application to Articulation Therapy

Speech is advanced movement skill, and, therefore, speech training should incorporate the behavior management strategies of motor learning theories. The 21st century speech-language pathologist recognizes that a certain amount of specialized practice is required for clients to learn certain speech movements. Although research in the field has not addressed the points of motor learning theory — how much actual exercise is needed or of what type and so forth — therapists know that the benefit of any technique comes down to the individual client. Therapists must discover how much exercise the particular client needs to make the expected improvements. A client's success or failure in production of the target phoneme is all the proof necessary.

Consider the simple example of teaching a client to lift the tongue tip to the alveolar ridge for production of /l/. One might argue that it is not known how many tongue-tip exercises to do in order to prepare the tongue for production of /l/, but a therapist does not need to know that information ahead of time anyway. A therapist simply integrates the movement activity with the production activity, observes the client carefully, and determines for herself whether or not the exercise is benefitting the client's phoneme productions. An SLP might ask a simple question like, "Is my client producing /l/ better after lifting his tongue tip to his alveolar ridge ten times every day for a week while watching in a mirror?" If the answer is yes, then the therapist can surmise that the exercise is being of benefit. If no, then more practice may be needed or another course of action may have to be taken.

Therapy is a mini-laboratory and the client's speech production is the measure of the success or failure of any method. There are no cookbooks to read or prescriptions to follow. Therapists observe these results while working with many clients through the years, and this develops their clinical expertise. This clinical experience becomes an element of the evidence-based practice. Therapists make increasingly sophisticated decisions about the elements of speech movement training throughout decades of service, and they develop their own motor learning theories based upon what their experiences have taught them. Some therapists keep careful records of these activities, formalize their methods, and share their programs with others (e.g., Rosenfeld-Johnson, 2014, 2005a, 2005b, 2001).

SUMMARY

Speech movements follow the same lines of development, as do all other body movements in development. These lines can be defined in terms of principles. Principles of development can be used to understand normal and abnormal development and to plan avenues of treatment in articulation and motor speech training.

11

Encouraging Jaw Oscillation for the CV

Teaching the most fundamental oral-motor pattern for the most essential syllable

"The jaw is recognized by a number of investigators as the earliest maturing articulator."

– Cheng, Murdoch, Goozée, & Scott, 2007a

The elocutionists were the first to observe that the jaw elevates for every consonant and lowers for every vowel, and this observation has been supported by all research. This means that the jaw must move in a simple up-and-down movement pattern to create the basic CV for babbling and early words like *mama* and *dada*. While clients with mild articulation deficits and/or phonological impairment generally do not have difficulty moving the jaw, clients with severe motor speech disorders usually do. This chapter describes methods to facilitate the fundamental up-down jaw movement pattern for the CV. This chapter ends with a case example of these methods at work in one child who was non-verbal and who presented with severe dysarthria.

JAW MOVEMENT BASICS

The CV has been called the *canonical syllable* meaning that it is the first officially recognized syllable and the most important of all syllable shapes in the emergence of child language. The CV is the foundational movement of babbling and any number of first words, e.g., *momma*, *dada*, and *banana*. MacNeilage and Davis (2001) called the jaw mobility that creates the basic CV in babbling a "mandibular cycle" meaning that it is up-and-down movement

of the jaw that creates this basic CV.

"In acquiring the phonetic structure of a language's sound system, the child must learn how to produce combinatorial sequences of consonants (Cs) and vowels (Vs) that constitute the syllables and words of his or her native language(s). The articulatory and acoustic origins of this motor skill have obvious roots in babbling. The rhythmic alternation of closed and open positions of the vocal tract during babbling creates the distinct impression of a series of regularly timed CV syllables... At the earliest onset of babbling at 6 to 8 months... it is generally agreed that infants do not produce independent segments, but rather undifferentiated entities... heard as syllable-like utterances consisting of consonant-like and vowel-like

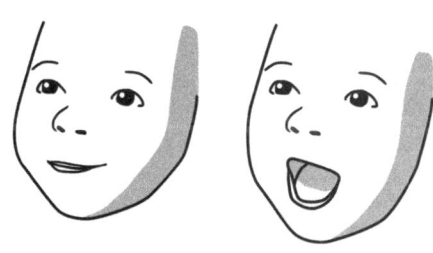

The jaw moves up and down to create the early CV sequences of babbling and early word productions.

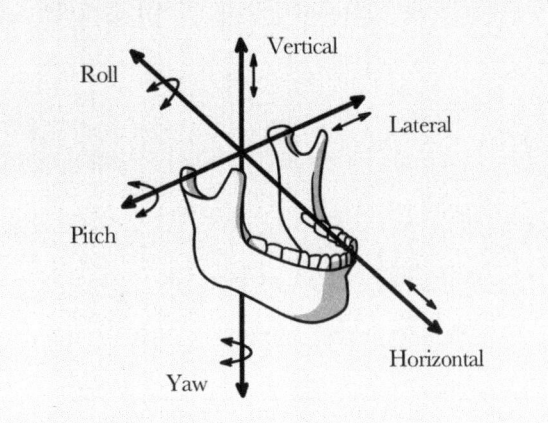

Modern equipment measures six different jaw movements.

> *sounds cyclically varying from a closed (the C) to an open (the V) position... This cyclicity has been attributed to simple oscillation of the mandible"* (Sussman, Duder, Dalston, & Cacciatore, 1999, p. 1080).

Basic Movement Patterns

The jaw comprises the bony architecture of the lower structures of the mouth. It houses the tongue, plays host to the lower lip, and has tremendous influence over both. SLPs understand that the mandible is a bone that moves in certain ways because of its attachment to the skull in the ball-and-socket arrangement that comprises the temporomandibular joint (TMJ). The TMJ allows the jaw to translate (slide or shift) and rotate in three dimensions: vertically, horizontally, and laterally (Edwards & Harris, 1990). This makes a total of six patterns of movement that are the focus of research on jaw movements in speech:

- The jaw moves upwards and downwards in the vertical plane.
- The jaw rotates around the vertical axis (called *yaw*).
- The jaw moves forward and backward (protrudes and retracts) in the horizontal plane.
- The jaw rotates around the horizontal axis (called *roll*).
- The jaw moves left to right in the lateral plane.
- The jaw rotates around the lateral axis (called *pitch*).

Research on adults has demonstrated that left-to-right translation movements are the smallest movements the jaw makes during speech while up-and-down pitching movements are the largest ones (Gibbs & Messerman, 1972). The left-to-right shifting movements are barely discernible to the naked eye while the up-and-down movements are large enough to see easily during conversational speech.

Development

The basic up-and-down jaw movement pattern of the CV has been studied in normally developing infants and children. Oller (1978) proposed that closing and opening the mouth (elevating and lowering the jaw) in sequence while phonating to create the basic CV is the third metaphonological feature to be acquired in infancy. (Phonation is the first, and opening the mouth — lowering the jaw — while phonating is the second.)

> *"All phonologies involve oppositions between high and low points in amplitude... The opening corresponds roughly with the vowels and the closure corresponds roughly with consonants"* (Oller, 1978, p. 527–528).

Other more recent studies of jaw movement in speech development reveal that the jaw is the first and largest mover in early sound production, and it does much of the work that the lower lip and tongue eventually will do (e.g., Cheng et al., 2007a). In essence, it is the large up-and-down movements of the jaw that dominate babbling and immature speech. The jaw pushes the lower structures (the lower lip and tongue) up to meet with the upper structures (the upper lip, upper teeth, and palate) for the gross and usually anterior consonants of the CV, and then it lowers them back down again for the gross and usually low vowels. Over time the jaw begins to move less (to stabilize) and this allows the tongue and lips to begin to do more of their own work. This means that the first CVs are created because the jaw begins to move up and down, and that means that early labial and lingual consonants are acquired because the jaw begins to move, not because the lips and tongue begin to move. According to Steeve (2010) these big up-and-down jaw movements are in full swing by 9 months of age.

Developmental Research

The following studies represent main ideas about the jaw-lip-tongue relationship in speech development. They are

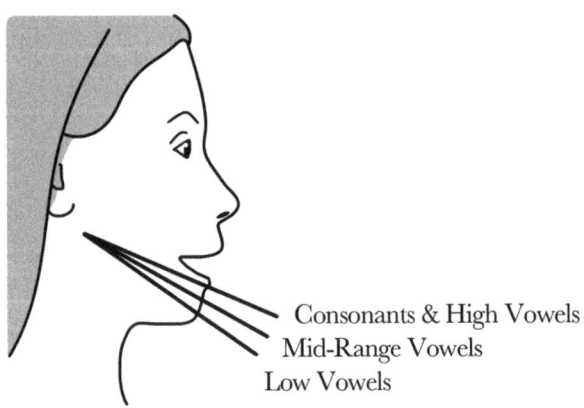

Consonants & High Vowels
Mid-Range Vowels
Low Vowels

Elocutionists established that the jaw moves up for the consonants and high vowels, and down for the mid and low vowels.

arranged chronologically to reveal the unfolding nature of these ideas over time. The interdependence of jaw, lip, and tongue movements in early speech is agreed upon, but the nature of that relationship still is under debate. Additional studies in this regard can be found in Chapters 12 and 13 on the lips and tongue, as well as in Chapter 14 on oral stability. Researchers use the term *gestures* for oral movements.

- Sharkey and Folkins (1985) measured the variability of jaw and lip movements in children and adults. They found that children used relatively consistent mouth opening movements and postures by 4 years of age. They also found that oral movements became more refined between 4 and 6 years of age, and that adults move the lips and jaw with less variability than do children during speech production tasks.

- Weber and Smith (1987) found evidence that the jaw, lips, and tongue continue to be "functionally linked" even into adulthood.

- Nittrouer (1993) found that children and adults use similar oral gestures, but that children's movements are produced more slowly and with greater "temporal variety." They also found that children acquire adult-like jaw movements before they acquire adult-like tongue movements.

- Davis and MacNeilage (1995) studied the vocalizations of six normal infants and found that "the main source of variance in reduplicated babbling is uniform amplitude of successive cycles of oscillation of the mandible" (p. 1208).

- Hinton and Arokiasamy (1997) supplied evidence of the "coordinated, compensatory relationship between the lips and jaw" even into adulthood.

- MacNeilage (1998) proposed that "cycles of mandibular oscillation" underlie the basic up-and-down jaw movement patterns of babbling and early speech in all languages. This basic up-and-down pattern is called a "frame." MacNeilage postulated that the frame evolves from chewing.

- Green, Moore, Higashikawa, and Steeve (2000) found that the bilabials were produced with jaw movements instead of lip movements in young children, but that lip function gradually took over more control with age. They also found that the synchrony of jaw and lip movements increases steadily between 2 and 6 years of age.

- Green, Moore, and Reilly (2002) studied one- and two-year-old children and found that jaw movements are established before movements of the other articulators. They suggested that jaw movements provide a necessary foundation of tongue movement.

- Smith and Zelaznik (2004) found that the jaw and lips function more as a single unit early in life, but that they function more independently with age.

- Marshalla (2007a) found that children between 4 and 7 years of age were able to imitate basic jaw positions (up, down, left, right, forward, back) with no difficulty. She also found they could imitate up-and-down jaw oscillation patterns easily with simple directions and a model.

- Takahashi, Kuribayashi, Ono, Ishiwata, and Kuroda (2005) demonstrated that masseter activity changed in association with volitional changes in tongue position. The authors speculated that chronic abnormal tongue position during childhood might affect chewing activity of the jaw.

- Cheng, Murdoch, Goozée, and Scott (2007b) studied children and adults and found that tongue-tip movement was more dependent upon jaw movement than was tongue-body movement. They also found that speech motor development undergoes a refinement period from mid-childhood to late adolescence.

- Grigos (2009) studied voice onset time in nineteen-month-old children and found that "coordinative control between the oral and laryngeal articulators [was] driven by the jaw." Results supported a relationship between the acquisition of phonemic contrasts and the variability of lip and jaw movement sequences. In other words, jaw movements are intricately associated with laryngeal control.

- Steeve (2010) found that the jaw moves less during vowel babbling than it does during babbling that includes consonants. In other words, the jaw moves less when babbling emerges with vowels only, and it moves more when CV babbling is established.

TREATMENT

The perspective of this manual is that the jaw must learn to move up and down for the CV to emerge in babbling and early words, and this section describes methods to

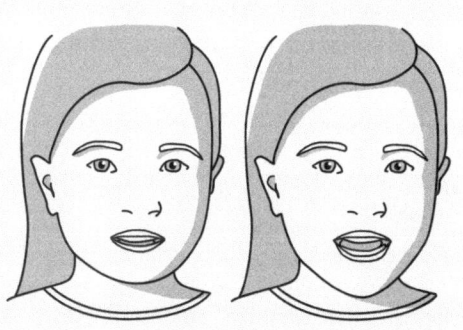

Therapists use the naked eye to observe whether the client is moving the jaw up and down to create the basic CV.

acquire it. First are described the goals of this therapy, the role of strength in this therapy, and research on stimulation methods.

Goals

The aim of these methods is to facilitate gross up-and-down jaw movements for the emergence of gross CVs. The client will be learning to elevate the jaw so consonants can emerge and to lower the jaw so that vowels can emerge. The client will also be learning to raise and lower the jaw in sequences for the emergence of babbling and multi-syllable word productions like *mamma, dada,* and *ni-ni (night-night).*

Strength

The methods of treatment described below are designed to teach the basic up-down jaw movement pattern and not to increase strength of the jaw. However, low oral strength *is* a main factor when it comes to clients with dysarthria, and in those cases several of the methods below could facilitate improved strength of up-and-down jaw movement.

Research on Treatment Methods

A small number of research projects have tested the effect of certain types of stimuli on jaw movement and the perception thereof. Each of these studies has relevance to the methods described later in this chapter.

- Kawamura and Majima (1964) studied the TMJ in a cat's jaw and found that motor control of jaw movement is perceived in the muscles and in the TMJ itself.

- Ringel, Saxman, and Brooks (1967) studied the ability of 30 normal young adult males to perceive changes in the position of their own mandibles. They concluded that the jaw movement changes are perceived in the TMJ.

- Weber and Smith (1987) found that stimulation to the jaw causes movement in the lips and tongue, but not vice versa.

- Loucks and De Nil (2001) found that tendon vibration influences jaw movements during both speech and non-speech tasks.

- Solomon and Munson (2004) found that masseter activity tended to increase when a bite block was placed between the molars during speech production.

- Rochet-Capellan, Laboissière, Galván, and Schwartz (2008) found that there is coordination in the brain between jaw movements and finger pointing. Their results suggested that the jaw might be stimulated to move if the hands are also stimulated to move.

- Pinheiro et al. (2012) reviewed 23 articles on jaw function in feeding and speech and found that: type of food influences the patterns of jaw movements in chewing; children with malocclusion can use normal mastication patterns; neck position effects jaw movement in chewing; people show preferences for chewing on one side or another (65.4% to the right and 34.6% to the left); the presence of TMJ dysfunction reduces the extent and speed of jaw movement in both feeding and speech; bruxism induces abnormal vibrations and that these vibrations may stimulate more bruxism; jaw surgery can affect jaw movement.

METHODS TO STIMULATE JAW MOBILITY

Methods to develop jaw elevation and depression are summarized here. These procedures can be found scattered throughout textbooks on articulation therapy, motor speech disorders, orofacial myology, feeding therapy, dysphagia management, neurodevelopmental treatment, and massage therapy. Quoted examples are offered throughout. Speech-language pathologists recognize that the methods described below will not automatically make speech change. As a practical matter, two processes are stimulated simultaneously: The jaw is stimulated to move upwards and downwards and the speech target itself is taught.

Modeling Jaw Movement

Modeling up-and-down jaw movement is the easiest and most common method reported in textbooks on articulation therapy and motor speech disorders. A client who can imitate the model obviously already can perform the movement, so the routine is employed simply to stimulate better conscious awareness and control over it. Gestural cues and mirror work usually accompany these activities, and short directions are given, such as "Open your mouth," "Close your mouth," or "Move your jaw up and down." These unpretentious activities function to break-up incorrect habits, to overcome inactivity, to increase flexibility, to gain control, to learn the movements, and to rehabilitate lost jaw mobility. The following quotes demonstrate this idea as represented first in the classic articulation literature and then in the motor speech literature.

> *"The teacher is safe in assuming that, in cases of oral inactivity, a reasonable amount of time spent in general articulation exercises is quite justifiable... Exercises for the jaw [include]... Drop the jaw lazily and allow the mouth to fall open... Move the relaxed jaw from side to side with the hand... Move the jaw around in a circle..."* (Anderson, 1953, p. 160–161).

This client is using a Chewy Tube to encourage the up-down jaw movement pattern.

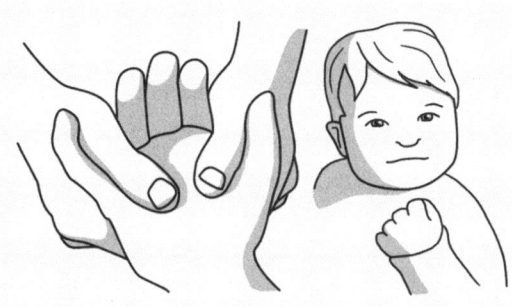

Relaxing the hand (left) is associated with jaw lowering while fisting the hand (right) is associated with jaw elevation.

"[In cases of acquired apraxia or dysarthria] one can try... to help the patient concentrate his energies first on activities preliminary to speech production, such as lowering and elevating the mandible continuously... The intent is to help the patient regain some concept of where his articulators are and of where he must put them" (Darley, Aronson, & Brown, 1975, p. 273–274).

Encouraging General Jaw Mobility

Some clients do not move the jaw much at all. In these cases there are any number of ways to encourage the jaw to begin to move more. This is Van Riper's process of vivifying movement that was discussed in Chapter 1. Prominent methods to encourage general jaw mobility include the following:

• *Munching and chewing on food:* It has been proposed that the up-down jaw movement frame evolves from chewing, so methods to develop munching and chewing often are integral to the process of CV training. Clients who are non-oral feeders are encouraged to begin oral feeding as soon as possible, and clients with limited or abnormal feeding skill receive feeding therapy to stimulate correct and more advanced munching and chewing patterns. Clients also chew on hands, feet, toys, and other safe flexible objects as another way to encourage the basic up-down jaw

movement frame.

• *Mirror play:* Children tend to move the mouth and explore its contents while looking in mirrors. Mirror play can be used to encourage increased up-down jaw mobility.

• *Tooth brushing:* Tooth brushing is a natural way to get the client to open the mouth by lowering the jaw.

• *Fisting and relaxing the hands:* Fisting the hand and closing the mouth are flexor patterns while opening the hands and opening the mouth are extensor patterns. Therapists often teach mouth and hand movements simultaneously. Even Van Riper used this method: "Chew in an exaggerated fashion with mouth openings and hand movements for thirty seconds" (Van Riper, 1947, p. 169). Therapists use flexible balls to teach clients to squeeze and relax the hands while encouraging more contraction and relaxation of the jaw muscles.

• *Normalization of oral-tactile sensitivity:* The jaw will move best when the oral-tactile system functions the way it is designed. Normalization of sensitivity in cases of hyper- or hyposensitivity should be included to reach this goal. Methods can be found in Chapter 16, *Normalizing Oral-Tactile Sensitivity.*

Assisting Jaw Movement

The jaw can be pushed or pulled gently into new positions. As described earlier in this manual, assistance like this is an essential technique of the motokinesthetic method: "Each sound is aided by the teacher's guidance of the lower jaw" (Young & Hawk, 1955, p. 13). The jaw is grasped and moved up for consonants and down for vowels. Vowel positions are set into high, mid, and low positions. The jaw is grasped by placing a thumb and index finger on the front of the chin, and the middle finger under the chin.

Assistance teaches a client where to place his jaw for target phoneme productions, and it allows him to feel the movements as the jaw is pushed or pulled into position. It is important to remember that assistance like this gives

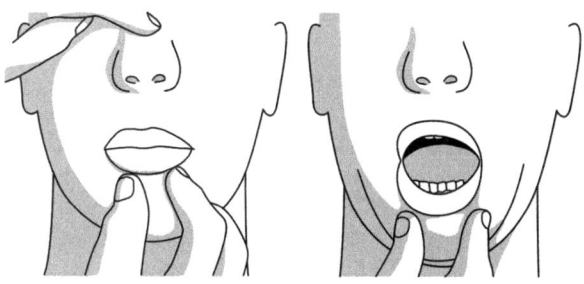

Assisting upward and downward movement of the jaw with the motokinesthetic method.

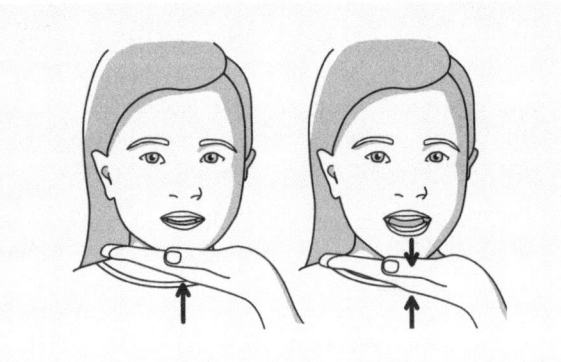

Using resistance to teach the basic up-and-down jaw movement pattern for the CV.

the client a passive movement experience. This is important for two reasons: First, the method will do nothing to build strength in cases of dysarthria and, second, a client must relax the jaw and "let go" so that the assistance can be employed. The reader is warned to take special care of the temporomandibular joint when assisting jaw movement in this way.

Resisting Jaw Movement

Resistance may be the most powerful method to help a client develop the up-and-down jaw moment pattern. Recall that to use resistance, one applies a slight amount of pressure in the opposite direction to which the client is being asked to move so that weight is added to the work. Resistance to jaw movement helps a client become more aware of his own jaw movement patterns and to move it with greater consistency and with a greater range. Resistance to up-and-down jaw movements can be accomplished with the hands, with food, or with other objects like a crossbar trainer or Jaw Exerciser. Teach the up-and-down movement pattern singly or in sequences. Use the hands in the following simple ways.

- *Jaw lowering:* Place fingers under the chin and press gently upward. Ask the client to push the jaw down against the pressure.

- *Jaw lifting:* Place one finger on the front of the chin at midline (on top of the mental protuberance) and press gently downward. Ask the client to lift the jaw up against the pressure.

- *Combining assistance and resistance:* Assistance and resistance can be used together in sequence to develop up-and-down jaw mobility. "If the speech-language pathologist wishes the mandible depressed, he can press upward firmly and then gently assist the depression of the mandible. If he wishes the mandible elevated, he presses it firmly downward, then gently assists closing" (Bosley, 1981, p. 11).

Clenching & Releasing

Voluntary clenching and releasing is another way to teach the basic up-and-down jaw movement pattern. Clenching at the molars encourages a client to bring his jaw up into a firm and high position, and it uses the molars themselves to resist that upward movement. Have the client use his fingers to feel his masseters on the outside of his face as they contract and relax with clenching and releasing. Say: "Bite hard" and then "Let it go." The SLP can also clench her own molars and allow the client to feel her masseters bulge outward as she contracts and retreats as she releases.

Clenching teaches an "up pattern" that is not appropriate for speech because it is much too high and firm, and it uses the masseters far more than they are used in speech, however, it puts internal pressure on the TMJ and, therefore, increases client perception there.

Light Touch Cues

Light touch can be used to cue the direction of jaw movement. Light touch is applied to the skin on the same side as the direction of movement. This is like touching a person gently on the right shoulder to cue him to turn to the right.

- *Lowering:* Gently touch the client under the chin at midline and say, "Lower it this way."

- *Elevating:* Gently touch the client on the top of the chin at midline and say, "Lift it up here."

Tapping

Tapping is a method that motor therapists use to stimulate joint receptors. The method is useful to encourage jaw movement because research has shown that perception of jaw movement occurs in the TMJ (see research summarized on page 162). Tapping is applied to the bones that meet in a joint, not to the joint itself. Therefore, the idea is to tap the jaw gently but firmly so that a slight jolt is sent into the TMJ. Therapists use the broad surfaces of two or three fingertips like a hammerhead to tap gently but firmly upward under the chin and backward against the mental protuberance. Tapping followed immediately by resistance is an excellent way to stimulate up-and-down jaw movements. Do not use this method if there has been damage to the TMJ or if the client complains of pain.

Vibration

A short period of vibration applied to a bone excites receptors at its joints, therefore, a vibrator can be placed anywhere on the mandible to stimulate the TMJ. Vibrators with low frequency are best, and children readily accept ones that look like toys or are embedded within stuffed animals. Press the vibrator gently but firmly against the skin so that the bone is vibrated. Allow clients to do this to themselves.

Add mandibular vibration to activities when the jaw moves very little and without much conscious control, or simply to excite general jaw activity. Be cautious in this application and do not use vibration of it causes pain, disorientation, dizziness, or seizures. Relay information about any negative reactions to other members of the team.

Reflex Stimulation

The following reflexes are thought to be foundational to up-and-down jaw movements. Readers are referred to Chapter 17, *The Speech Reflexes*, for more information about each.

- Biting reflex
- Chewing reflex
- Coughing reflex
- Crying reflex
- Face-spreading reflex
- Gag reflex
- Hand-to-mouth reflex
- Inspiration reflexes
- Jaw-lowering reflex
- Laugh reflex
- Mouth-opening reflex
- Suckling reflex
- Yawning reflex

This client is feeling his masseters bulge and retreat while clenching and relaxing the jaw.

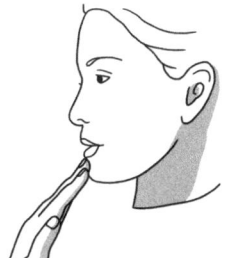

Tap the front of the mandible gently but firmly to stimulate receptors within the TMJ.

A variety of vibrating toys can be used to stimulate the TMJ.

RELAXING A STIFF JAW

Jaw mobility is impeded when its muscles are stiff. *Fixing* is the term used to describe this immobility. The jaw can be fixed in any position — high, mid, low, left, right, protruded, or retracted. Jaw fixing interferes with the mobility needed for the CV to emerge.

Methods to reduce tightness in the jaw come from many sources. Some can be traced back to the elocutionists who taught that good speech could be attained only when all the facial muscles moved fluidly and to their fullest capacity. Palmer (1949) was one of the first SLPs in the United States to discuss methods to relax a very stiff jaw in clients with cerebral palsy. The perspective that emerged out of neurodevelopmental treatment (Bobath, 1959) was that abnormal high tone must be changed before improved movement can be facilitated, therefore, any factors that caused stiffness in the jaw should be inhibited.

The following summarizes classic methods of jaw relaxation from the elocutionists and from practitioners in articulation therapy, cerebral palsy, neurodevelopmental treatment, motor speech therapy, and massage therapies.

Palpate Masseter Tension

Clients can discover their own masseter tension by feeling them with their own fingers. Have the client press his own fingertips gently but firmly onto his masseters. Use simple words like "hard" and "soft" to help him understand the relative tightness or looseness of his muscles. This method has been in play for more than a century: "Place the hands at the back of the cheeks; notice the swelling of the masseter muscles during speech" (Scripture, 1912, p. 226).

Clenching

Any muscle can be relaxed by making it contract more firmly. This is a standard muscle relaxation technique that can be applied to clients with stress-induced masseter tension and general muscle stiffness. Have the client clench and then let go. The client may need a pliable object on which to bite at the molars in order to learn how to do this, and he should use his hands on his masseters to feel the clench and release. He may also need to clench his hands simultaneously to make the clench firm. The method should be used briefly and intermittently.

WARNING: This method should not be used with clients who suffer from TMJ damage/dysfunction, neuromuscular disease, dental disease, or malocclusion that contributes to jaw tension. The method should be discontinued immediately if a client complains of soreness or pain. Appropriate medical referral should be made.

Massage

Massage is a classic method to relax stiff facial and oral muscles. An excellent practical reference on massage specific to speech is *Therapeutic Speech Massage* (Dyakova,

2013). Dyakova describes how to diagnose problems of muscle tone in the oral mechanism and supportive structures, and she thoroughly describes the process of oral-facial massage. Photographs enhance the information.

As an example of how massage might be used in motor speech therapy, Dworkin (1991) recommended massage to relieve hypertonicity of jaw function when working with hyperkinetic dysarthric patients. Therapists are advised to massage their own masseters before they use it with a client. The pressure is firm but never painful, and the rotation ranges from large to small, relative to the muscle's size. Therapists use the broad surface of two or three fingertips to apply firm but gentle pressure into the muscle belly of both masseters simultaneously. The client is told to "Let go here."

> *"The masseter muscle... is the most accessible and manipulable of all the muscles of mastication, thus lending itself to the relaxing effects of massage therapy... It may be best to use small circular strokes with moderate finger pressure for roughly 30 seconds bilaterally"* (Dworkin, 1991, p. 203).

Slow Stretch

Slow and deep stretch along the length of a muscle belly is another classic massage technique to relax stiff muscles. It works to pull the muscle fibers gently apart. This increases blood flow and releases tension. Stretch the masseters directly, and then extend the massage to the surrounding structures — the neck, shoulders, and face. Alternately, begin with the outer structures and work toward the masseters.

Neck Elongation

Neck elongation causes an overflow of relaxation to the face and jaw muscles. It is a form of slow stretch to the neck muscles. There are a number of ways to do this. One is to grasp the head at the nape and forehead, and slowly stretch the head gently away from the trunk of the body. Repeat to the left, right, forward, and back. Another is to place one hand on the client's shoulder and the other on the side of the head. Slowly and gently push these two

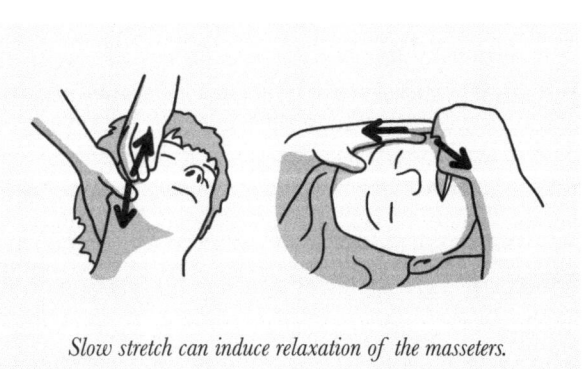

Slow stretch can induce relaxation of the masseters.

parts away from one another. Massage the neck as well.

Body Rotation

Slow rotation around the spine, from head to tail, stretches out and inhibits muscle contraction to all muscles attached to the spine, including the upper body muscles attached to the head, neck, and jaw (Farber, 1982). Clients can roll on floor mats, or they can rotate the body around the spine while sitting or standing. Body rotation should not be used if it causes more stiffness, a situation that can occur if the rotation is too fast or if the client feels insecure. Hold the client securely and be mindful that this is slow gentle work to stretch the muscles attached to the spine. This is a method that many therapists used during the Phonetic Placement and Traditional Eras, for example: "Rotate the trunk alternately to the right and to the left with arms raised" (Nemoy & Davis, 1937, p. 22).

Head & Shoulder Rolls

Rolling is another form of stretch and body rotation that is a classic method of relaxing the head, neck, and shoulder muscles. Many articulation textbooks named it as a method for relaxing a stiff jaw: "Turn the head sideways to the left and to the right looking as far backward and downward over each shoulder as possible" (Nemoy & Davis, 1937, p. 24).

Hanging Forward

Allowing the head and body to hang forward is a classic relaxation method that Traditional Era therapists used to loosen the body and the articulators including the jaw. It can be done in sitting or standing:

> *"Stand with the weight on both feet. Let your head hang on your chest. It will pull all the muscles of your shoulders. As it continues to hang, you will feel the pull in the muscles all the way down your back... Your arms will hang limp from their sockets... Let your body hang a few seconds... Come up slowly, beginning first at the base of the spine, next waist, then shoulders. Feel one vertebrae at a time going back into place"* (Walsh, 1939, p. 197).

Jaw Rotation

Rotation can also be done to the temporomandibular joint itself in order to induce relaxation of the muscles surrounding it. Certain textbooks carried simple instructions for this: "Let the lower jaw drop gradually [slowly]... Drop the jaw and protrude it... Move the jaw to the left and right" (Nemoy & Davis, 1937, p. 28).

Shaking & Swinging

Shaking and swinging a body part is a standard relaxation technique among athletes and motor therapists. The reader has probably seen world-class athletes, particularly swimmers, do this with the arms and legs just prior to the

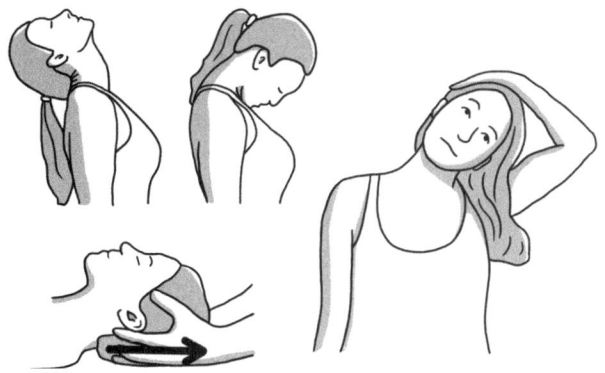

Neck elongation can relax jaw muscles.

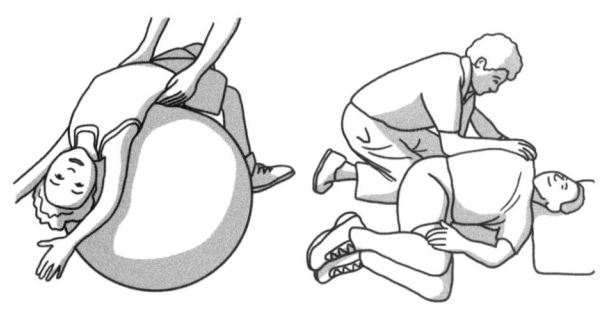

Stretching and rotating the spine induces general relaxation of all muscle groups including those that control jaw function.

Bring general relaxation to the oral musculature by hanging forward or rolling the head.

A warm towel can be used to inhibit muscle tightness in the oral area.

start of an event. The muscles of the face and jaw can be relaxed by general shaking of the arms, shoulders, upper body, and head. Also, have the client shake the head so that the jaw shakes free of the head and swings loosely back and forth. This loosens the jaw's attachment to the head. Don't use shaking if it causes more stiffening or vestibular confusion. The method can be found in many articulation texts: "Shake your arms and hands up and down. Now rotate them in a large circle crossing in front of you as you swing" (Walsh, 1939, p. 199).

Rhythmic Body Movements

Dancing and other rhythmic body movements can be used to facilitate body and oral relaxation. For example: "Rhythmic dancing especially when accompanied by movements of the arms and head is most effective in inducing relaxation of the entire body" (Nemoy & Davis, 1937, p. 24).

Move the Lips

Increasing range of lip movement can facilitate flexibility of the jaw. Get the client's lips and face to move in big facial expressions as a way to facilitate jaw relaxation. "Action of the lips… has a salutary [beneficial, productive] effect on other muscles — tongue, palate, and mandible" (Berry & Eisenson, 1956, p. 139).

Warmth

It is well known that warmth relaxes stiff muscles. Make sure to attend to the temperature of the room when attempting to relax the muscles of the jaw. Also, consider warming the hands by rubbing them briskly together before touching a client's face. Warm the neck, face, and jaw with towels or blankets heated in a microwave or clothes dryer. "Neutral warmth is an inhibitory technique" (Farber, 1982, p. 147).

Relaxing Environment

Relaxation methods are best employed in a calm environment that is free of visual and auditory distractions. The room does not have to be excruciatingly quiet, but the general atmosphere has to be conducive to the activity in terms of low levels of light, sound, and general activity. It usually is not appropriate to utilize relaxation methods in the midst of a busy classroom unless the room is calmed and the entire class is involved. It is also universally recognized that up-tempo music increases the activity of muscles and slow rhythmic music reduces it.

Vibration / Raspberries

Motor therapists teach that slow vibration can be relaxing when applied for short periods of time. Vibration can be applied to the bones of the head, to the masseters, or to the TMJ itself to affect jaw relaxation. Vibrating the lips can also help loosen the jaw. Use a slow battery operated vibrator that cycles at 60–90 Hz (Farber, 1982).

Production of the raspberries serves as a source of oral vibration that can be used to relax the oral mechanism including the jaw. Have the client produce loose and floppy bilabial and lingua-labial raspberries. This is a much safer alternative for the SLP untrained in the use of battery-operated vibrators.

Vestibular Stimulation

Occupational and physical therapists trained in these matters use swinging, spinning and other prescribed movement activities to affect the vestibular system as a means to relax muscles. These methods should be done by SLPs only when operating under the prescribed instruction of the team motor specialist who works directly with the specific client. Any further discussion of vestibular stimulation is beyond the scope of this manual. Talk to the team motor specialist to determine if these activities are appropriate for the client and use them only as prescribed.

Compensatory Lip & Tongue Movements

It is important to note that changes in sound production can be made even when the jaw cannot move at all and when there will be no opportunity to get it to move. Kelso and Tuller (1983) demonstrated that adults whose jaws were immobilized with a bite block could make compensatory lip and tongue movements to achieve acoustically correct vowels. Jaw mobility stimulates lip and tongue mobility but the jaw no longer needs to move once the lips and tongue begin to control their own actions.

TONIC BITE

A tonic bite is different than the general muscle stiffness described above. A tonic bite is an abnormal reflexive bite response that interferes with jaw mobility in clients with oral-tactile hypersensitivity. A tonic bite is a strong reflexive bite that is not immediately released. It occurs in response to tactile input to the biting surfaces of the gums or teeth, or in response to the upper and lower teeth meeting together. It does cause jaw stiffening but does so for a relatively short period of time. It can occur in clients who are hypotonic, hypertonic, or normal in tonicity. The tonic bite causes a bite to be "sudden, tense, and completed with poor release" (Morris & Klein, 2000, p. 135).

The tonic bite can interfere with the development of oral movement because it usually prevents a child from actively exploring his mouth with his own fingers, it inhibits his jaw movements while eating, it interferes with the natural movements that occur during tooth brushing and other aspects of oral care, and it can keep the jaw locked in a high position. The tonic bite, therefore, can prevent the development of the up-and-down jaw movements that should accompany early sounds and syllables and create the CV. Morris and Klein (2000) call the tonic bite a "limiting pattern" in the development of oral-motor skills. The tonic bite "disrupts the rhythm and leads to overall

disorganization" of movements in the oral mechanism (Arvedson & Brodsky, 1993, p. 276). Therapists utilize a variety of methods to treat it.

Morris and Klein (2000) recommended the following to reduce influence of the tonic bite: activities to obtain greater postural alignment, a program to normalize oral-tactile sensitivity to reduce the amount of multisensory input and distractions that the client must deal with all at the same time, controlled hand-to-mouth stimulation, firm touch to the oral mechanism, a prescribed feeding program, body massage, facial molding activities, and a graded program to handle tooth brushing.

Therapists sometimes use a bite block to inhibit or control a tonic bite reflex while engaging in lip or tongue activities. Dworkin (1991) recommended making individual bite blocks out of dental putty because they reduce the chance of tooth abrasion during a strong tonic bite, and they can be fitted exactly to the client's molars.

Release of the tonic bite can be difficult. "Release of the bite may be achieved with pressure applied at the temporomandibular joint on both sides of the face" (Arvedson & Brodsky, 1993, p. 334). The present author has found that slow deep pressure to the masseters (instead of the TMJ) is a better approach since they are the muscles that control clenching.

TMJ MALFORMATION OR DAMAGE

Jaw mobility cannot be changed by therapy methods alone when immobility is caused by TMJ damage or malformation. These clients must be referred for a full structural assessment by a medical team. The treatment methods of this chapter might be attempted before and after surgery to determine their effect as they relate to required surgical/medical procedures. Methods to facilitate jaw mobility are avoided when they cause pain or further damage.

CASE SAMPLE

The case of Kerry demonstrates the importance of facilitating jaw mobility in clients with neuromuscular disorder. Kerry was a five-year-old girl who was non-ambulatory due to cranial anomaly and severe brain damage. She was non-verbal and nearly non-vocal. Kerry made only a few sounds, mostly moans, but she was bright and could follow directions and stories. Her parents were convinced she could be taught to speak but her therapists had no success using model-and-imitate methods. Kerry came for five consultative sessions over the course of a summer.

It was immediately obvious in the first session that Kerry was beginning to "talk" but that her mouth did not move much at all and was firmly fixed in a partly open position. The only sound Kerry made was the quasi-resonant nuclei and she was fed though a gastrointestinal tube. The first session was devoted to the gathering of information and general interaction with the client and her parents. Although Kerry's skull was severely disfigured, there was no apparent structural impairment to the TMJ. A goal to facilitate more oral movement for sound production was agreed upon.

By the second session, Kerry trusted the SLP enough to sit on her lap and allow hands-on play. They worked on the floor together, and the SLP began general touch and massage to Kerry's hips, back, shoulders, neck, head, arms, and legs. This general body massage caused Kerry to loosen up, to breath more deeply, and to vocalize more. A kazoo was introduced to encourage sound production. The parents were taught to massage her at least once every day and they were to let her play with the kazoo several times per day in order to encourage sound production.

The third week revealed that Kerry was now vocalizing "all the time." The session again began with hands-on tactile play and body massage. Massage was focused on the shoulders, neck, head, face, and jaw. Buy the end of this session Kerry began to move the jaw upwards and downwards while vocalizing in a rudimentary babbling pattern of two syllables with vowels only. They used these sounds to function as words as she named pictures in a book. They rewarded her verbally and with claps and general excitement every time she "named" a picture by vocalizing in this gross two-syllable vowel sequence.

The fourth week was revolutionary. Kerry was vocalizing and moving the jaw up and down to make primitive vowel babbling on her own right from the start of the session. The therapist continued to use massage and to assist and the jaw in moving in bigger up-and-down patterns and in long rhythmic sequences. By the end of the session, Kerry was producing reduplicated babbling sequences consistently with intermittent /m/, /w/, /b/, /d/, and /n/ sounds. The parents were consulted about doing this at home once or twice every day.

During the fifth session the therapist began to use resistance to stimulate bigger up-and-down jaw movement patterns that were more consistent while Kerry produced two-syllable words: *momma, bye-bye, doggie, kitty, moo-moo,* and others. These words would have been unintelligible without context because of consonant and vowel distortion, but her intent was quite obvious. The parents were advised to continue upper body and oral massage long enough that these types of two-syllable words could solidify and increase in number. The parents were also advised to reward Kerry for moving the jaw while speaking and not to correct phonemes at this time. They were taught how to use assistance and resistance to encourage jaw movement.

The parents were thrilled at these developments and were encouraged that Kerry indeed was beginning to talk. They left knowing how to stimulate Kerry to become more vocal and verbal, and how to listen more carefully to what Kerry was saying. Now that Kerry was moving the jaw in the basic up-and-down movement frame to produce CVs, the parents were encouraged to stimulate Kerry to try to say any and all words without correction of phonemes for the time being. Exaggeration of words was encouraged as a means of moving forward, and special focus was placed on producing the right number of syllables per word. Specific functional one-, two-, and three- syllables words that were important to the client and her family were selected.

SUMMARY

Jaw mobility is an essential element of early speech development. Methods to facilitate up-down jaw movements are used to stimulate emergence the CV for babbling and early words.

12

Facilitating Lip & Cheek Movement

Getting the lips and cheeks to move successfully for speech sound production

"All of us have enormous athletic ability in the way we can move our tongue and lips. We can make rapid, precise movements that are as skilled as the finger movements of a concert pianist."

– Peter Ladefoged, 2005

Active and refined lip movement is a critical element of mature speech. The lips form all the labial consonants including /p/, /b/, /m/, /w/, /f/, and /v/, and they form the rounding necessary for the round vowels and the palatal sibilants. But the lips are even more important than that. Together the lips and cheeks form the very outer walls of the mouth and, therefore, they create the shape and texture of the oral cavity for sound amplification and modification. SLPs ask two fundamental questions in regard to lip/cheek function and speech: (1) are the lips able to form each labial phoneme and (2) are the walls of the oral cavity too soft and malleable, too tight and fixed, or just right for good sound quality?

This chapter presents an overview of lip and cheek functioning in speech including research findings, a lip and cheek movement checklist, a discussion of problems in lip and cheek movements, and methods designed to facilitate improved lip and cheek activity for speech improvement in articulation and motor speech disorders.

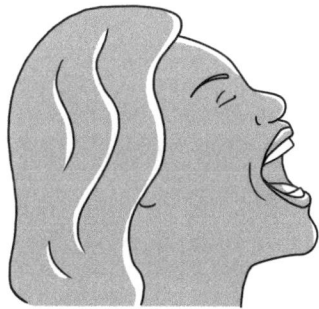

The lips and cheeks form the very outer walls of the oral cave for speech and song.

BACKGROUND

Movement of the lips and face has been a concern of speech teachers since the time of the elocutionists of the 19th century who often said that the lips should not move very much and that the best speech is produced with the lips in a slight grin:

> *"The lips should be used as little as possible in articulation; the upper lip should remain almost quiescent [calm, inactive] [except] for emotive expression... The lips should never hang loosely away from the teeth, or be pursed, pouted, or twisted, but they should maintain the form of the dental ranges as nearly as possible, lying equally and unconstrainedly against the teeth"* (Bell, 1887, p. 52).

Early in the 20th century, and after the International Phonetic Alphabet was adopted in 1888, the Phonetic Placement Era began. Stimulating for correct lip function became a principle concern as the terms *bilabial, labial-dental,* and *round* were introduced. Speech correctionists who published articulation therapy texts during this era often wrote about the deficient lip movements they noticed in clients engaged in speech and non-speech activities. For example, ASHA president Lee Edwards Travis wrote that the client with articulation deficit "frequently shows inferior ability in controlling the lips" (1931, p. 223). *Lip gymnastics* and *lip exercises* became a regular part of texts published during this period. *The Correction of Defective Consonant Sounds* by Nemoy and Davis (1937) was one such text. They described 15 specific lip exercises along

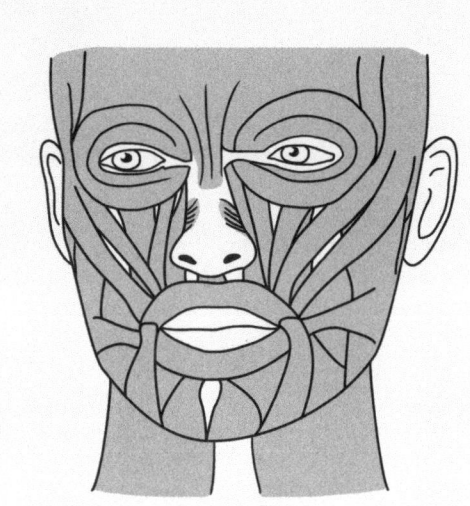

The lip and facial muscles form a complex interdigitating sunburst pattern.

with relaxation activities designed to reduce facial tension when it interfered with lip mobility.

By the mid-20th century, therapists began to realize that a problem in lip movement often was connected to problems in overall oral function. These mid-century therapists were beginning to recognize the concept of the *motor speech disorder.* For example, Mildred Berry and ASHA president Jon Eisenson (1956) wrote that lip movements needed to be improved in articulation therapy not only because lip mobility was necessary for correct production of the labial sounds, but also because labial mobility is "part of the synergy" of jaw, lip, tongue, and palatal movement. They said there were certain clients who had difficulty with all oral movements and that a problem with lip mobility may be only the first most obvious sign of it.

Occupational and physical therapists use the terms *assimilation* and *overflow* to describe some of the influences and synergies of body movements. These terms refer to the idea that movement changes in one part of the body are related to, and can cause changes to, movements of other nearby body parts. For example, given a normal mechanism, bending the pinky finger down to the palm of the hand nearly always causes the ring and middle finger to bend as well. Similarly, lip movements may be affected by other nearby structures and can provide clues about what's happening in other parts of the oral mechanism. If the lips are tight, then the tongue, jaw, and velum are probably tight as well, and if the lips are loose then the other structures are probably loose as well. This does not mean that lip movement problems cause problems of movement in the other oral structures; it simply means that these things occur together within working groups that are closely tied. Lip function can give clues about articulation and motor speech skill as well.

A specific focus on motor speech disorders was in full

swing by the second half of the 20th century and writers of that time said that patients with apraxia or dysarthria should work on lip movements as they are working on speech. *Motor Speech Disorders* (Darley, Aaronson, & Brown, 1975) was the foundational text of that era. These professors proposed that clients with apraxia should receive "multimodality stimulation together with heightened awareness of all types of sensory feedback" for relearning lip and other speech movements (p. 280). They also said that clients with dysarthria should concentrate energies "first on activities preliminary to speech production, such as... alternately pursing and retracting the lips" (p. 274). These researchers were saying that direct stimulation of lip movement was a necessary part of speech rehabilitation separate from and preliminary to phoneme production in clients with either apraxia or dysarthria.

The concept that direct stimulation of the lips was a necessary part of motor speech therapy was enmeshed in the speech community by the 1980s. Mysak (1980) discussed the methods he had developed for clients with cerebral palsy, and Dworkin (1991) described those he developed for adult patients with apraxia and dysarthria. Textbooks in other areas also discussed lip stimulation techniques, for example, Logemann (1983) in dysphagia, Hanson and Barrett (1988) in orofacial myology, and Morris and Klein (1987) in infants and children with neuromuscular dysfunction. Since then, therapists have used these methods with clients who have articulation and motor speech disorders under the umbrella term *oral motor techniques.*

LIP/CHEEK MOVEMENT BASICS

A detailed discussion of lip and cheek anatomy is beyond the scope of this manual, and it is assumed that readers have a general working knowledge of it. Speech-language pathologists understand that there is one circular muscle that comprises the lips themselves and that all other lip muscles are extrinsic and fan outward from the lips in a sunburst-like pattern that is one with the muscles of the cheeks and face.

The complex interdigitation of the lip and facial muscles makes researchers still uncertain as to which muscles function to achieve specific lip movements, but the theory of *motor equivalence* eliminates this concern in therapy. The theory of motor equivalence suggests that all muscles involved function together to achieve target movements, and that multiple patterns of movement can work together to achieve the same movement ends (Hebb, 1949). Research has substantiated this claim. For example, Stone and Vatikiosis-Bateson (1995) demonstrated that "assimilation effects on one articulator could elicit compensatory maneuvers in a related articulator to assure that key articulators reached their target" (p. 81). This means that SLPs can stimulate for the phoneme movements they are targeting without worrying which specific muscles to activate. When a specific movement is needed to accomplish a different acoustic quality, the simple concept that muscles shorten when they contract and elongate when they relax generally is enough information for the treatment of lip and cheek movement errors.

Lip & Cheek Movements

The lips move in certain patterns during phoneme production as specified in the classic phonetics literature.

- *Round:* The lips actively round (push forward toward midline) for production of selected vowels and consonants.

- *Retract:* The lips actively spread (pull away from midline toward the sides) slightly for production of selected vowels and consonants.

- *Elevate:* The lower lip actively elevates to the upper lip during production of the bilabials and to the upper teeth during production of the labial-dentals.

- *Depress:* The upper lip actively depresses to meet the lower lip during production of the bilabials.

- *Remain neutral:* The lips also must stay out of the way by actively remaining in neutral during production of a wide number of phonemes. For example, the lips must not get in the way during the production of /h/.

- *Cheek stability:* The cheeks hold a stable position while the lips move. This topic is discussed in Chapter 14.

RESEARCH ON LIP MOVEMENTS

Lip movements have been researched more than any other oral movements, and perhaps that is because of their easy access on the front of the face. Much of this research has been done to understand movements of the lips themselves, of course, but these studies have also been undertaken as representative of general oral function: "Lip gestures for speech provide a useful research topic for investigating multimodal aspects of speech production and perception" (Honda, Kurita, Kakita, & Maeda, 1995, p. 243).

The lips have been studied with force transducers, light emitting diodes, oscilloscopes, electromyography, pressure gages, magnetometers, strain-gauge systems, surface electrodes, bite blocks, tape recorders, splints, artificial palates, MRI, cinefluorography, x-rays, optical motion capture systems, miniature transducers, and through the process of cadaver dissection. Summaries of selected studies from the ASHA journals are presented below in chronological order within three categories: normal adult function,

developmental studies, and special populations. Articles are presented in chronological order within each section.

Normal Adult Lip Movement

- Daniloff and Moll (1968) studied lip rounding during the production of words and phrases. They found that the lips begin to round up to four consonants preceding the rounded vowel /u/. This study proved that phonemes are not produced as if they were beads lined up on a string, but that phoneme movements overlap in a process called *coarticulation* (McDonald, 1964).

- Sussman, MacNeilage, and Hanson (1973) found that the jaw assists the lower lip in its upward movement during production of labial phonemes. They also demonstrated that the jaw and lower lip are independently controlled articulators exhibiting their own movement characteristics.

- Folkins and Abbs (1975, 1976) demonstrated that when the jaw is stabilized with a bite block, the lips and tongue move in ways that compensate for the immobile jaw in order to achieve the same phoneme productions. They called this an "intercoordination" of the lips and the jaw.

- Barlow and Abbs (1986) found that the lower lip typically travels a distance that is roughly twice that of the upper lip for the production of /p/, /b/, and /m/.

- Barlow and Rath (1985) found that the lower lip is approximately three times stronger than the upper lip as measured by force. Males were significantly stronger than females.

- Barlow and Netsell (1986) used literature review and their own study and concluded that the lower lip had "greater strength, fine force control, and precision of movement" when compared to the upper lip. They said that the lower lip typically moves "twice as far and twice as fast" as the upper lip during bilabial contact.

- Folkins and Canty (1986) studied adult lip movements and found that the upper lip adjusted its movement downward to meet the lower lip when

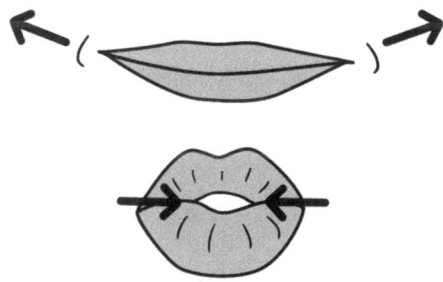

Retracting the lips pulls them back laterally (top) while rounding the lips pushes them forward medially (bottom).

the jaw was lowered with bite blocks. They also found that the lips moved less when very thin bite blocks were employed.

- Folkins, Linville, Garrett, and Brown (1988) studied movement responses in the four quadrants of the lips. They found that stimulation to the muscles of one quadrant affected a change in movement in the other quadrants, suggesting symmetry of lip movement in the four quadrants.

- Wohlert and Goffman (1994) found evidence that supported earlier studies that the superior and inferior branches of the orbicularis oris function independently in adults. They also found that the left and right sides of each branch are capable of separate activity.

- Goffman and Smith (1994) found that the four quadrants of the perioral area are organized independently of one another, and that they function independently from the jaw and other oral structures.

- Hinton and Robey (1995) reviewed the literature on labial movements and found a consistent pattern of high levels of variability in all measures. They said that research reveals "trial-to-trial [and] cross-speaker variations" in all measurements of labial muscle activity.

- Wohlert (1996a) summarized known research on the processing of spatial information by the lips and summarized that tactile and not proprioceptive stimulation is the system at play: "Muscle spindles, providing proprioceptive information, are absent in the lip musculature… but the glabrous [hairless] tissue of the lips is plentifully supplied with mechanoreceptors" (Wohlert, 1996a, p. 1191).

- Hinton and Arokiasamy (1997) studied labial movements during speech tasks and found that normal adult females typically use less than 20% of the bilabial pressure they can achieve in a nonspeech task whether or not the jaw is involved.

- Löfqvist and Gracco (1997) demonstrated that when the lips articulate during production of the bilabial stops, they move "beyond each other." In other words the lips press together beyond the point of simply touching. They press into one another in a space called "a region of negative lip aperture."

- Blair (1986) did anatomical studies on the lower lip of two cadavers and found that the lower extrinsic lip muscles interdigitated with the orbicularis oris in both cases.

- McClean (1991) observed the relationship between the perception of oral pressure and lip responses in six adults and found evidence that a common reflex pathway mediates both. They concluded that pressure sensors in the vocal tract are "significantly involved in regulating lip-muscle contraction" for speech.

- Barlow and Bradford (1996) studied the response of the lips to vibratory stimulation. They found that the sensorimotor apparatus of the lower face is very responsive to low-level mechanical inputs. Factors influencing responses included input site, amount of tissue stimulated, and subject state.

Development of Lip Movements

- Sharkey and Folkins (1985) measured the variability of jaw and lip movements in the speech of children and adults. They found that children used relatively consistent mouth opening movements and postures by four years of age. They also found that oral movements became more refined between 4 and 6 years of age, and that adults move the lips and jaw with less variability than do children.

- Sussman et al. (1996) found less anticipatory lip gestures during canonical babbling. This supports the idea that the lips move less and the jaw moves more during canonical babbling.

- Smith and Goffman (1998) studied lip movements in children and adults and found that children have larger lip movement ranges relative to the size of their mouths than do adults during speech tasks.

- Wohlert and Smith (2002) found that 7- and 12-year-old children produced labial phonemes with significantly more movement variability than adults, a result that supported earlier research. Their study supported the notion that adolescents retain more flexibility and more degrees of freedom in speech movement than adults. In other words, children use gross motor movements that occur within a larger range than the smaller more refined movements of adults.

- Walsh and Smith (2002) found that, like young children, adolescents up to 16 years of age continued to show more variability in oral movement in speech than adults. Adolescents had significantly longer movement durations, lower velocities, smaller displacements, and greater variability on these measures than young adults. There were no differences between boys and girls.

- Smith and Zelaznik (2004) found that the lips and jaw functioned with increasing independence between 4 and 21 years of age.

- Sato et al. (2007) confirmed that early words of CVCV construction contain a labial consonant in the first syllable and a coronal consonant in the second syllable more than any other pattern. They called this the *labial-coronal principle* and attributed the pattern to a developmental mechanism proposed by MacNeilage and Davis (2001).

- Marshalla (2007a) found that children between 4 and 7 years of age could produce basic lip postures easily in imitation of an adult examiner during a clinical assessment. Postures included open and close the mouth as well as pucker and retract the lips.

- Sadagopan and Smith (2008) studied lower lip movements and found further evidence that speech motor development continues well into adolescence. They also found that rate of lip movement reached adult performance levels earlier than did precision of lip movement. In other words, adolescents speak as fast as adults, but their precision of lip movement is less well developed. They concluded that their results "confirm the existence of an intricate relationship between higher level cognitive processes and speech motor output" (p. 1150).

- Green, Nip, Wilson, Mefferd, and Yunusova (2010) found that adults use significantly larger lip movements, a slower speaking rate, and an elevated pitch when speaking to infants than when speaking to adults. The greatest adult lip movements were in the vertical dimension on production of vowels. The authors speculated that exaggerated lip movements by adult models enhance speech learning in infants and very young children.

Lip Movements in Special Populations

- Hunker, Abbs, and Barlow (1982) found that the lower lips were stiffer than the upper lips in a group of dysarthric individuals with Parkinson's disease.

- McNeil, Weismer, Adams, and Mulligan (1990) investigated isometric force and static position control of the lips in normal, dysarthric, aphasic, and apraxic speakers and found that the dysarthric and apraxic speakers produced significantly greater instability in these measures than did the normal group. The pattern of instability was inconsistent.

- Wood, Hughes, Hayes, and Wolfe (1992) found that patients with Parkinson's disease had weaker force measures in the lower lip than did normal subjects.

- McHenry, Minton, Wilson, and Post (1994) found no differences in lip strength in patients with traumatic brain injury compared to normal subjects.

- Ackermann, Hertrich, and Scharf (1995) studied lower lip movements in patients with ataxic dysarthria and found weakness in the muscular forces needed to attain adequate articulatory gestures of short duration.

- Wohlert (1996b) found evidence of an increase of muscle coupling during speech in older adults, suggesting a decrease in flexibility of fine oral motor control as a function of the aging process.

- Wohlert and Smith (1998) found that strength and sensitivity in the lips decreased in aging individuals. They called this "decreased stability" of speech motor control.

LIP MOVEMENT ASSESSMENT

Speech-language pathologists usually do not have access to laboratory equipment for an assessment of lip function. A practicing therapist must rely on a simple visual analysis of lip movements by using a checklist that is part of an oral exam. It is understood that "clinical ratings are problematic due to their subjectivity and imprecision" (Solomon, Clark, Makashay, & Newman, 2008, p. 257). Nonetheless, many such checklists have been proposed and must be relied upon. Most of these checklists are based upon general observation. *The Marshalla Oral Sensorimotor Test* (**MOST**; Marshalla, 2007a) is the only standardized test that assigns a score to a client's ability to position the lips in basic ways using the simple visual analysis.

The following checklist is offered for consideration. It is a checklist of lip and cheek movement, not strength. It has been compiled for practical application from the variety of resources named in this chapter. This simple checklist is for the assessment of lip movements in speech only, but a thorough examination of lip function should also include observations of the lips at rest and during

The Lip Strength Meter is a clinical tool for measuring strength of lip pressing.

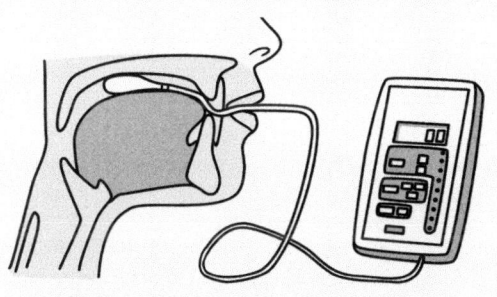

The Iowa Oral Performance Instrument (IOPI) uses a bulb to measure strength of upward tongue-tip movement. It could also be used to measure lip strength.

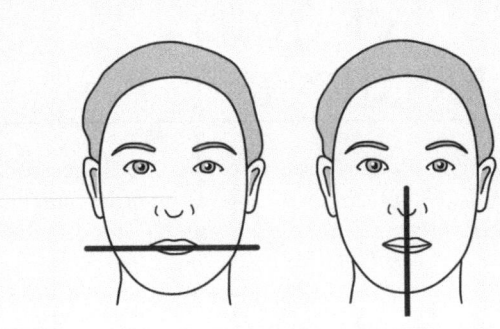

A straight probe held horizontally and vertically one inch in front of the lips aids in the visual analysis of lip function.

eating and swallowing. Patterns of lip movement during speech can be seen more easily when a probe is placed about one inch in front of the lips to mark the horizontal and vertical planes.

This assessment is not intended to measure lip strength, although there are clinical tools that can be used for that purpose. Two examples of such devices include the Lip Strength Meter and the Iowa Oral Performance Instrument (IOPI). Please see Solomon, Clark, Makashay, and Newman (2008) for information on additional tools.

Assessment Checklist

A. Correct Lip/Face Movements in Speech

- The lips maintain the form of the dental ranges as nearly as possible during speech.
- The lips round on appropriate phonemes.
- The lips retract on appropriate phonemes.
- The lower lip lifts to the upper teeth on /f/ and /v/.
- The lips stay in neutral (and out of the way) when their movements are not critical for phoneme production.
- The face expresses a variety of emotions and the lips are involved in these movements.
- Structure of the lips supports correct lip movement in speech.
- Structure of the dental ridge supports correct lip movement in speech.
- Structure of the teeth supports correct lip movement in speech.

B. Incorrect Lip/Face Movements in Speech

- The lips are relatively immobile during speech.
- The face is relatively immobile during speech.

- The lips round when they shouldn't during speech.
- The lips retract when they shouldn't during speech.
- The lips seem to move too much during speech.
- The lips hang away from the front teeth.
- The lips pull to the left during speech.
- The lips pull to the right during speech.
- The upper lip is stuck in an upward position during speech. (The upper teeth are exposed too much during speech.)
- The lower lip is stuck in a low position during speech. (The lower teeth are exposed too much during speech.)
- The lips appear to be stuck in a smile much of the time during speech. (The upper and lower teeth are exposed too much during speech.)
- The corners of the lips are pressing together during speech, pinching the mouth forward.
- The mouth is stuck in an open position. (The jaw is stuck in a low position, and the lips are stretched into an open position much of the time during speech.)
- Structure of the lips does not support correct lip movement in speech.

LIP MOVEMENT PROBLEMS

Various problems in lip movements can be observed during speech in clients with articulation and motor speech disorders. This section describes patterns that are common.

Lack of Face & Lip Movement

Lack of lip and facial movement during speech is a common problem among clients with severe expressive speech disorders. This pattern is usually called a *flaccid face*. This pattern is virtually always noted in clients with hypotonia and facial paralysis, but it is also observed in cases of

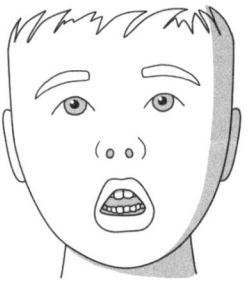

Limited lip and facial movement due to low tone is called the "flaccid face."

upper respiratory problems with obligatory mouth breathing, low cognitive skills, and in certain psychological disorders such as severe depression. Clients with functional articulation deficit can also demonstrate a lack of facial and labial movement. Clients who don't move the lips at all often move the jaw instead.

Reduced Lip Strength

Clinicians often view limited lip movement as a lack of lip strength, but lack of strength is only an issue in dysarthria.

- *Articulation:* The research cited earlier in this chapter indicates that lip strength has very little to do with lip movements during speech production in clients with articulation deficit. The lips need far less strength to move for speech than they do for pressing together during non-speech tasks. The lips only have to have enough strength to perform the basic movements required of speech — to gently articulate together, and to round, retract, elevate, and depress.

- *Apraxia:* According to the classic definition of apraxia put forth by Darley, Aaronson, and Brown (1975), clients with apraxia do not have weakness in the oral mechanism, and, therefore, they do not need assistance with lip strength.

- *Dysarthria:* According to the classic definition of apraxia put forth by Darley, Aaronson, and Brown (1975), clients with dysarthria do have a generalized lack of strength in the oral mechanism. Clients with dysarthria, therefore, do need assistance with lip strength. Weakness can be due to hypertonicity (tightness) or hypotonicity (looseness).

Poor Lip-Jaw Differentiation

Some clients hardly move the lips at all and instead allow basic up-and-down movements of the jaw to dominate speech movement. The jaw does most of the oral movement and the lips simply "go along for the ride." This pattern occurs in cases of oral motor dysfunction related to neuromuscular disorder. The pattern is also characteristic of general speech immaturity according to the research cited above.

Excessive Lip Movement

Some patients move the lips too much or in unusual patterns. Speech may look odd although it may sound adequate. The cause often is unknown although muscle tone disturbance and oral instability certainly can contribute.

Excessive Lip Rounding

Excessive lip rounding is called *labialization*. Some clients labialize when it is not required. For example, a client who rounds the lips instead of lifting the tongue tip for /l/ is labializing. The term also applies when lip rounding is used appropriately during the process of coarticulation.

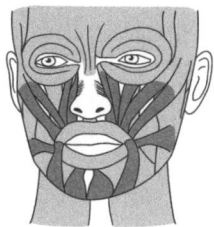

Neuromuscular disorder with high tone often causes the lips to retract in 360° causing a perpetual smile that affects labial function.

Elvis Presley was famous for his sneer. This type of unilateral upper lip retraction can be habitual and without a neuromuscular basis. It affects speech only in subtle ways.

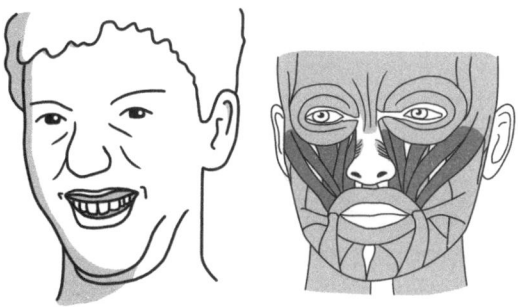

The upper lip can be fixed in a retracted position that exposes the upper teeth during speech.

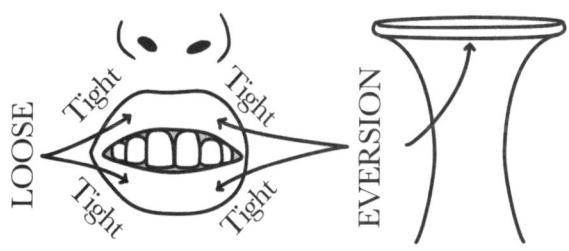

Lip eversion seems to be the result of tight extrinsic muscles and loose intrinsic muscles.

For example, one rounds the lips on /s/ in the words *soup* and *suit* because of the lip rounding required for the vowel that follows.

Lip Retraction

Some clients pull the lips back away from midline during speech in a pattern called *lip retraction*. Lip retraction is caused by excessive tightness or contraction in one or more of the extrinsic lip muscles. Lip retraction can have a neuromuscular basis or it can be the result of simple habit. Lip retraction can occur in all 360 degrees around the lips, it can be limited to either the upper or lower lip, it can be limited to either the left or right side of the lips, or it can occur in only one quadrant. Lip retraction disturbs oral resonance, it restricts lip movements for production of bilabial and labial-dental consonants, and it impacts clarity of the vowels.

Fixed Forward Positions

The lips can be fixed in a forward position that obscures most or all of the front teeth and cause the lips to pucker. Anderson (1953) pointed out that this type of excess tension in the face and lips can be the result of a client's determination to hide irregular, damaged, or diseased teeth. The lips can be clamped down in this position by tightening the orbicularis oris or by tightening the corners of the lips with the extrinsic muscles. One usually notes bulging and mottling on the face around lips as a result of the

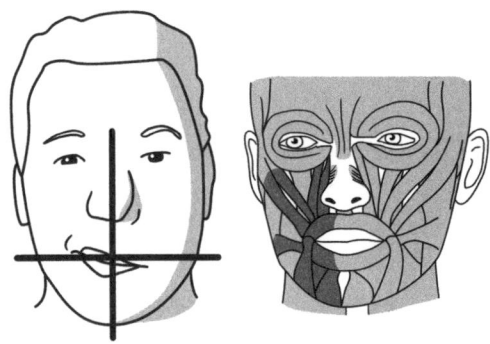

Lip asymmetry related to neuromuscular disorder. In this case the mandible is positioned at midline while the lips and facial muscles pull to the right.

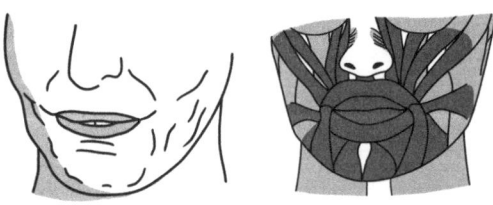

This adult has distortion of /r/, /s/, and other phonemes. She carries excessive tension in both the intrinsic and extrinsic lip muscles. Notice that tense muscles bulge outward and cause mottling on the skin.

muscular tightness under the skin.

Asymmetrical Lip Movements

Some clients move the lips in conspicuous asymmetrical patterns that some elocutionists called "twisted" (Bell, 1887, p. 52). Lip movement asymmetry can be due to neurological damage and differences on the two sides of the face. The pattern also seems to be the result of simple habit of an unknown cause. Sometimes children imitate the asymmetrical lip movements of a parent, sibling, or friend, or those of a superhero or classic "bad guy." If the inactive side of the lips is held firmly in position against the teeth the pattern makes these clients appear to be talking only out of one side of the mouth.

FACILITATING LIP MOVEMENTS

The rest of this chapter is devoted to methods of lip movement facilitation for articulation and motor speech therapy. These methods have been gleaned from a wide variety of textbooks on articulation therapy published throughout the ages, as well as from textbooks on feeding, dysphagia, orofacial myology, motor speech disorders, motor therapies, and massage. It is recognized that virtually none of these methods have undergone the rigors of research but that should not deter therapists from using these methods as needed. One of the most important researchers in the area of speech motor control expressed this idea thus:

> *"Lack of data does not mean that we should do nothing. Using the limited data that are available, along with an analysis of the motor tasks, we can assemble thoughtful paradigms for clinical application"* (Kent, 2008).

Process

The studies of lip function summarized above offer important clues about the process of stimulating lip movements in articulation therapy. The following guidelines are proposed:

- Movement patterns are the focus of these methods. These methods are used to get the lips to articulate, round, retract, elevate, depress, and remain in neutral at appropriate times before and during speech.

- Improving lip strength is not the reason these methods are used when a client has a simple articulation deficit or apraxia. In those cases the methods are used to teach the motor pattern when the client cannot imitate the movements during the demands of phoneme production.

- Most of these methods can be used to influence lip strength when it is an issue in dysarthria.

Resistance is the most influential method for building lip strength.

- Lip movements can be taught during the production of individual phonemes that require the movement and also during a co-articulating task. For example, lip rounding can be taught for the production of /u/, and also during production of the consonants in words such as *two*, *zoo*, *pools* and *scooters*.

- Stimulation in one quadrant of the lips can be used to facilitate movement of all four quadrants.

- The lips should be taught to gently articulate and then to press into and "past" one another during bilabial contact.

- More time and attention should be directed to the movements of the lower lip because it is far more active than the upper lip during speech.

- Upward jaw movement should be used to teach elevation of the lower lip, and downward jaw movement should be used to teach depression of the lower lip when a client has very limited lip mobility. Over time the jaw should be stabilized to force the lower lip to move by itself.

- Clients should be allowed to move the lips in large, slow, and irregular movement patterns (gross movements) before they are taught to move them in refined, swift, and regular patterns (fine movements).

- The lips should be expected to move with increasingly less fine motor control in aging patients.

- The lips can be encouraged to move in order to develop overall oral function: "Sharpening the action of the lips is valuable not only because the labial mobility is necessary in itself, but also because it has a salutary effect on other muscles — tongue, palate, and mandible" (Berry & Eisenson, 1956, p. 139).

Limitations

The reader is reminded that helping the lips to function better will not automatically make speech problems disappear. SLPs understand that one facilitates better lip movements at the same time other auditory, conceptual, and linguistic methods of phoneme stimulation are being employed. Therapy often is a process of presenting new oral movements in increasingly sophisticated speech tasks.

Therapy Example

Let's demonstrate how methods of lip facilitation might be incorporated into a sequence of therapy activities over several weeks. Consider how a school age client with a motor speech disorder might learn how to round his lips to produce /u/ in the target word *shoe*. The following steps might take place over a 4–6 week period:

1. The therapist models productions of *shoe*. It is discovered that the client does not round his lips on /u/.

2. The therapist then models /u/ in isolation. It is discovered that the client cannot or does not round his lips on /u/ in isolation.

3. A mirror is introduced to add visual stimulation, and more verbal descriptions of the round lip posture are given. No change is noted on /u/.

4. The therapist taps the clients lips a few times to heighten tactile sensation there. No change on lip rounding for /u/ is noted.

5. The client is shown how to round his lips around a kazoo. He is able to round his lips around the kazoo.

6. The client then is shown how to produce /u/ into the kazoo. The client and therapist together sing "Happy Birthday" by singing /u/ into kazoos. The child's kazoo is sent home for him to sing songs with his family using /u/.

7. Back in therapy the next week the client practices /u/ in front of a mirror. The child and therapist pretend to be owls saying "Ooo."

8. The client practices saying "Ooo" while drawing a picture of an owl. The picture is sent home and the client shows his parents what an owl says.

9. The next week they return to the word *shoe* and practice it with lip rounding in front of the mirror. They draw a picture of an owl wearing shoes and continue to practice "Ooo" with lip rounding.

10. Other words are introduced and drawn on picture cards — *Moo*, *new*, *Pooh*, *two*, and *zoo*. The therapist has the client tap his own lips to remind himself when he forgets to round his lips. The child practices these pictured words at home with his parents.

11. Phrases with these words are introduced and these are sent home for practice.

12. Sentences with these words are introduced and these are sent home for practice.

13. The therapist and client together write a paragraph on "my new shoes." It is loaded with these and additional words that contain /u/.

14. The client is assigned to read his paragraph aloud to his parents at home for homework.

15. The client is assigned to read his paragraph aloud to his classmates at school for show-and-tell.

16. The client is expected to produce /u/ with lip rounding in a spontaneous speaking situation.

These simple steps represent a model program for learning to produce /u/ with lip rounding. A client with a motor speech disorder might be working on /u/ as well as many other phonemes during this period. The reader can see that a small yet significant part of success on /u/ is due to the client's ability to round his lips. Lip facilitation methods are woven into the treatment sequence at

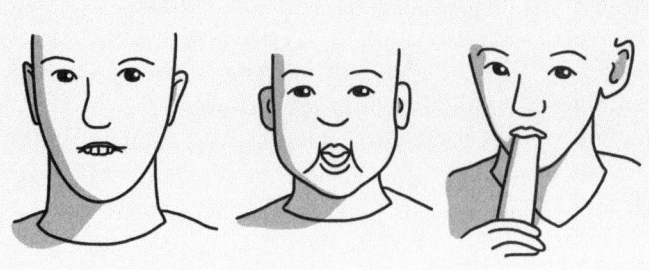

Biting the lips, puffing up the cheeks, and sucking on cold stimuli are simple ways to vivify the lips and cheeks with older children and adults.

appropriate moments to achieve the target goal of correct phoneme production. The ability to round the lips themselves is a small part of the work that represents a short-term objective in treatment. The methods described below are for that individual purpose only.

METHODS

The rest of this chapter catalogs methods to facilitate lip movement in articulation and motor speech therapy.

Vivify Lip Movement

The best place to begin is with Van Riper's directive to vivify general oral mobility. A variety of methods can be used to activate gross lip movements when clients don't move them much or when they simply need an easy warm up.

- *Mirror activities:* One of the easiest ways to vivify lip movement is to sit the client in front of a mirror and allow him time to discover his lips. Engage in activities that encourage him to watch his mouth actively — such as counting the teeth, putting on lip gloss, eating a cookie, chewing gum, sucking a popsicle, or playing with a lip retractor. Encourage the family to place a mirror on a wall that is within easy viewing for their child or have them make sure he has a stool he can use to see into a high mirror that already exists.

- *Large soft objects:* The lips of infants and other young children can be stimulated with large soft objects such as pillows, stuffed animals, or towels pressed onto the lips. Firm but safe deep pressure across the whole bottom of the face often encourages the whole oral mechanism to move forward and will provide stimulation for the lips to begin to move.

- *Mouthing toys:* Baby chew toys can be

used with infants and toddlers to encourage active lip movement.

- *Vibration:* Vibration can be used when other activities are not enough to encourage active lip mobility. "Vibration can wake up the mouth when other non-vibratory toys may be less noticed" (Morris & Klein, 2000, p. 412). Use vibrating toys and toothbrushes.

- *Raspberries:* Production of the bilabial and lingualabial raspberries is an excellent way to arouse the lips. This method has been used for decades: "Attract attention to the similarity between the sound of /p/ and the puffing sound made by a motorboat gliding over the water" (Nemoy & Davis, 1937, p. 47).

- *Puff the cheeks:* This is another method that has been used a lot. "Instruct the client to close his mouth, fill up his cheeks with air and then blow out the air in short bursts" (Secord et al., 2007, p. 16).

- *Bite the lips:* Many therapists simply have clients bite gently on their lips as a quick and easy way to enhance awareness and sensitivity.

- *Cold stimuli:* Periodic applications of cold stimuli have been used to vivify lip movements. Therapists often have clients suck on ice chips, ice cubes, ice pops, ice cream, or frozen bananas. The client puts the cold item in his own mouth, and he takes it out at his own discretion and with his own comfort in mind. Let the client handle the item himself and watch his mouth carefully for signs of over-stimulation. Too much cold stimulation will cause the lips to move less than they normally do. Remove the stimulus before that point is reached, or allow the client to have this experience and talk him through the re-warming. Consider having a warm towel or washcloth on hand to place on

Stuffed animals pressed to the face, mirrors, and mouthing toys can vivify lip movements in infants and toddlers.

the mouth alternately with the cold item. "Ice should be used around and in the mouth with extreme care" (Farber, 1982, p. 148).

• *Quick stretch:* "Lip rounding and retraction can be achieved also by appropriate stretching of the muscles to elicit the hyperactive stretch reflex" (Bosley, 1981, p. 11). "The faster the stretch is applied, the more facilitatory it will be" (Farber, 1982, p. 148). Stretch the lips from midline to the ends using two fingers simultaneously.

Old-Fashioned Lip Exercises

Writers of the Elocutionary and Phonetic Placement Eras used the term *lip exercises* and *lip gymnastics* to refer to activities designed to facilitate general awareness and gross control of the lips. The client usually performed these activities voluntarily in response to simple instructions and therapist modeling. These lip exercises are found in a wide variety of books on articulation, motor speech disorders, orofacial myology, dysphagia, and oral-motor treatment published during the 20th century. The following are from *Speech Disorders* by Berry and Eisenson (1956):

• *Vowels:* "Imitate the faces of clowns by retracting the lips, protruding the lips, and by dropping the jaw as far down as possible while producing [the basic vowels /i/, /u/, and /ɑ/]."

• *Blowing:* "Whistle with an exaggerated pucker of the lips; then retract the lips in a broad smile… Blow plastic boats across the table, directing them carefully in lanes by blowing through a glass straw… Blow Ping-Pong® balls up an inclined plane… Imitate the wind blowing first softly, then very hard."

• *Sequence:* "Imitate the sound of a squeaky see-saw: *e-oo, e-oo, e-oo*… Imitate the owl's call: *to-whit; to-whoo*."

• *Concept:* "Imitate the sound of popping popcorn by pressing the lips firmly together and then releasing them suddenly."

• *Exaggeration:* "Exaggerate the explosion of the breath stream in the consonants: *pa-pa-pa; ba-ba-ba*."

Stabilize the Jaw

The lips will fail to move if the jaw does all their work. The jaw can be stabilized utilizing the methods described in Chapter 14 on oral stability. Stabilizing the jaw to increase lip mobility is an idea that has been in play for a long time. For example, consider this sample from 1937:

> *"The use of the mirror and placing the hand upon the chin while [the phoneme] is being practiced will be of assistance in eliminating jaw action and in securing independent action of the lips"* (Nemoy & Davis, 1937, p. 48).

Encourage Lip Rounding

Lip rounding is one of the essential lip movement patterns for production of several consonants and vowels. Since Van Riper's time there have been a few common activities that therapists have used time and again to encourage and habituate this action.

• *Mirrors:* Watching in a mirror may be the simplest and most effective method for teaching lip rounding with most clients.

• *Blow toys:* Therapists often use a blow toy as a simple way to encourage lip rounding. "Blowing requires directed airflow and lip coordination. It can be a very organizing activity" (Morris & Klein, 2000, p. 434).

• *Straw drinking:* "Have the child suck different thicknesses of liquids and purees and puddings from a straw… Have the child drink from short straws, long straws, wide straws, and narrow straws. Use colored straws, straight straws, and crazy bent straws. Have the child suck from different positions on the lips: center, side, and in between" (Morris & Klein, 2000, p. 468).

• *Tubes:* "If there is muscle weakness, use tubes of varying diameters to teach successive approximation of lip rounding. Each tube, progressing from largest to smallest, is alternately inserted in the mouth and withdrawn as the sound is attempted" (Hanson,

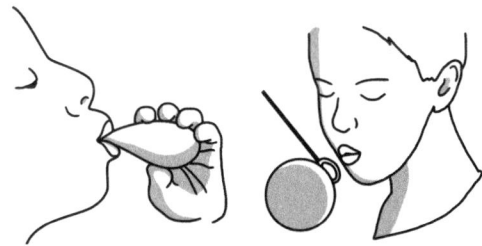

Blow toys and bubbles are classic ways to introduce lip rounding to young children.

Teach parents to encourage exaggerated lip rounding for family kisses.

1983, p. 206).

• *Kissing:* Little children love to kiss people, animals, toys, and foods like ice cream or lollipops. Teach them to round and pucker firmly each time they do, and direct the family to make a habit of this movement at home.

Mark the Target of Lip Movement

Tactile stimulation to points of articulation was a method advocated by Van Riper. It can help a client understand and control labial contact.

• *Touch both lips simultaneously:* Lightly touching and patting on both upper and lower lips can signal bilabial contact: "Use a cotton swab to lightly touch the surface of the lips where contact is made" (Secord et al., 2007, p. 16).

• *Touch the bottom lip:* Lightly touch the bottom lip to signal its articulation with the upper teeth. Use a probe to touch the lower lip or "lay an applicator horizontally across the inner surface of the lower lip and ask the client to 'touch your teeth here'" (Bosley, 1981, p. 51).

• *Place objects between the lips:* Probes can be placed between the lips to mark bilabial articulation. This is

A client can hold a probe between the lips or pat the lips to discover bilabial articulation.

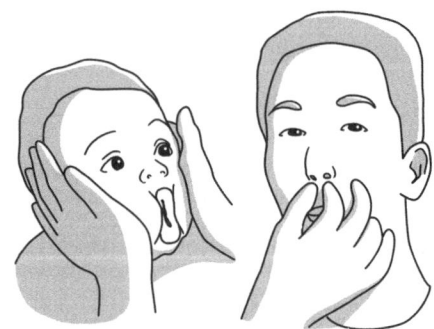

The fingers or hands can pull the face forward into a "fish face" (left). This moves the whole face forward but does not actually get the lips to round. To assist actual lip rounding, one must pull the lips forward (right).

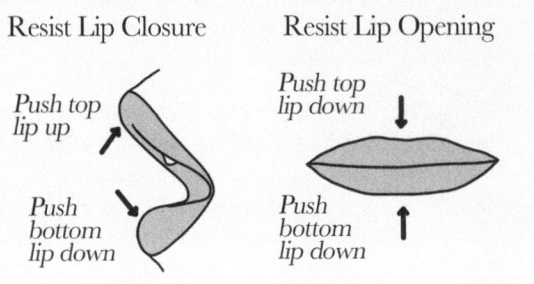

Push the lips apart to resist their closing (left) and push them together to resist their opening (right).

a standard method that still appears in guides: "Place a tongue depressor horizontally between the lips. Ask the client to close his lips on the tongue depressor" (Secord et al., 2007, p. 16).

Assist Any Lip Movement

Any lip movement can be taught with assistance. To assist lip movement means to physically push or pull the lips into the desired position. Nemoy and Davis (1937) called this "molding" the lips. The following procedures are from the motokinesthetic system and earlier resources.

• *Assist bilabial contact:* Place an index finger above the upper lip and thumb below the lower lip and press the lips together: "Place your thumb and finger under the lower lip and move the lip rapidly up and down so as to close and open the labial aperture" (Bell, 1906, p. 98).

• *Assist labial-dental contact:* Place a finger just below the vermilion border of the lower lip and press gently upward until the lower lip touches the lower margin of the maxillary (upper) central incisors.

• *Assist lip rounding:* Grasp the face with one or two hands and pull the cheeks forward into a "fish face." This will assist a gross forward position of the lips but not lip rounding per se.

• *Assist lip retraction:* Place the fingers on one side of the lips at the corners and the thumb on the other. Press the lips laterally.

Resist Any Lip Movement

Any lip movement can be taught by using resistance. Resistance is the process of adding weight or counter pressure to movement. It teaches the client what to move, in which direction, and how far. Resistance also makes muscles work harder and, therefore, it can be used to increase force of movement when weakness is present.

• *Resist bilabial contact:* Place one index finger

directly on the upper lip and the other index finger directly on the lower lip. Gently push the lips apart as he client is asked to press them together.

• *Resist labial-dental contact:* Place an index finger or other probe directly on the lower lip and press gently downward as the client is asked to push the lower lip up.

• *Resist lip rounding:* Place both index fingers on the upper lip with the fingertips on either side of midline, and place both middle fingers directly on the lower lip on either side of midline. Gently but firmly stretch the lips from midline to the lateral borders. Ask the client to pucker against this resistance. Allow the lips to round by slowly releasing the hold. Also, use a lip retractor for this purpose.

• *Resist lip retraction:* Grasp the lower lip just below the vermilion border by gently pinching the skin with the thumb and index finger. Gently but firmly pull the lower lip forward. Ask the client to smile (retract the lips) against this resistance. Allow the lips to retract by slowly releasing the hold. Repeat with the upper lip or grasp both lips simultaneously.

Reducing Lip & Cheek Tension

The motor therapy known as *neurodevelopmental treatment* proposes that abnormal movement activity should be inhibited before more normal movement is stimulated. Therefore, tight lip and cheek muscles need to be relaxed before the lips are encouraged to move more. The following methods can be employed to reduce tension in the lips and cheeks.

• *Plucking:* Some articulation therapists used *plucking* to reduce tension localized to the lips. For example, when the upper lip is tense: "Plucking the upper lip slightly with a tongue depressor and raising it slightly will tend to reduce the tension" (Nemoy & Davis, 1937, p. 48).

• *Mirror:* Help a client understand the extent of his own facial and lip tension with a mirror. Point out areas of tension, stiffness, and mottling. Provide information about the face and lip muscles so that the client can identify which muscles are holding the excess tension. Show him how specific tension interferes with his lip movements.

• *Raspberries:* Production of bilabial raspberries is a way to relax stiff lip muscles: "Trilling the lips will assist in overcoming tension of the lips" (Nemoy & Davis, 1937, p. 53). The fingers can also supply the vibration: "Trilling the lips with the finger will help to relieve the tension" (p. 61).

• *Warmth:* It is generally accepted that "neutral warm" temperatures between 95 and 98.6 °F relax muscles (Farber, 1982). Use warm hands, blankets, or towels on the face.

• *Slow stretch:* Slow stretch (elongation) of a muscle relaxes it. Identify the muscles that are holding excess tension in the lips and face and stretch them. Place the flat surfaces of the fingertips at the center of the muscle length, press into the belly of the muscle, and

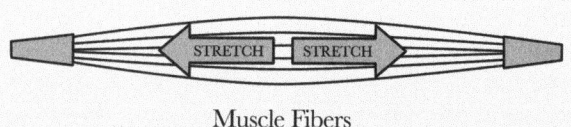

Muscle Fibers

Slow stretch relaxes muscle fibers and causes them to lengthen. Quick stretch excites muscle fibers and causes them to contract.

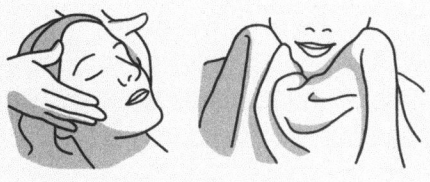

Massage and warmth reduces general tension in the face and lips.

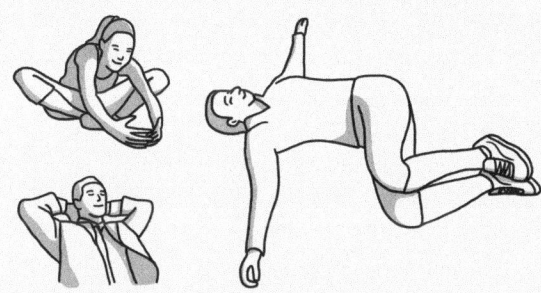

Stretch and rotation of the whole body induces general relaxation and helps reduce tension in the face and lips.

Push the lips back to resist their rounding. Use the fingers (left, middle) or a lip retractor (right).

slowly stretch from midline to the ends of the fibers.

• *Facial massage:* A general facial massage can be employed to reduce tension throughout the face and lips. Slow, deep, rotary massaging movements are used commonly. Study the anatomy of the face and make sure to reach each muscle group.

• *Body stretching and rotation:* General relaxation of the whole body that is accomplished with slow stretch and rotation can set the stage for reduction of face and lip tension.

• *Body position:* Consult with team motor specialists about the best position for lip mobility when working with clients who have neuromuscular disorder.

• *Reduction of stimuli:* Morris and Klein (2000) recommend reducing external distractions when they cause excessive face and lip tension.

• *Normalize oral-tactile sensitivity:* Employ methods to normalize oral-tactile sensitivity when it is a cause of lip retraction (see Chapter 16 for ideas).

• *Saline solution:* Hanson and Barrett (1988) used liquid inside the mouth to stretch the muscles of the lower lip. Make a saline solution by stirring several shakes of salt into a glass of warm water. Have the client take a sip of the solution and hold it between the lower lip and the lower teeth. Hold it for 10 seconds and then spit it out. Have the client continue this procedure until all the solution is used up.

Inhibiting Unnecessary Movements

Sometimes unnecessary or incorrect lip or cheek movements must be prevented or inhibited. For example many clients fail to learn production of /r/ because they keep moving the lips instead of the tongue. Inhibition of lip or cheek movements must be used in cases where a simple verbal instruction like "Don't move your lips" is insufficient. In these cases, one can utilize very specific methods to teach the client to inhibit excessive movements.

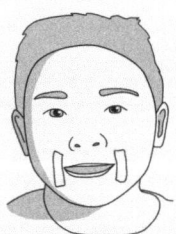

Kinesiology tape can be placed laterally to help a client recognize when he is moving the lips or cheeks unnecessarily.

• *Fingers:* The therapist's fingers can be placed on a client's lips or cheeks to hold them out of the way or in place while he produces any phoneme: "Occasionally it may be necessary to inhibit action of the lips [or the cheeks] by pressing them gently against the teeth with the fingers" (Nemoy & Davis, 1937, p. 137).

• *Tape:* A small strip of tape can be placed on either side of the lips or on the cheeks to signal a client that he is moving them unnecessarily. Traditional Era therapists used regular household sticky tape and masking tape but now there is kinesiology tape, also known as Kinesio Tape®, which is safe enough to use on a baby's skin.

Stimulating Reflexive Lip Movements

Reflexes are used to stimulate gross lip movements when they are absent. A number of reflexes are thought to be foundational to basic lip mobility. Readers are referred to Chapter 12 on these reflexes for information.

• Face-closing reflex

• Hand-to-mouth reflex

• Jaw-lowering reflex

• Lip-elevation reflex

• Lip-lowering reflex

• Lip-puckering reflex 1

• Lip-puckering reflex 2 (perioral reflex)

• Lip reflex

• Mouth-closing reflex

• Mouth-opening reflex

• Rooting reflex

• Smile reflex

• Sucking reflex

• Suckling reflex

• Swallow reflex

• Yawning reflex

SPECIAL CASES

Some cases of lip dysfunction require special consideration. The solution for all such cases is a team approach that combines speech, orthodontia, surgery, and other professional treatments. Van Riper taught that compensatory movements should be taught when orthodontic or surgical solutions cannot resolve structural issues.

Malformation & Structural Damage

Congenital malformations and acquired structural damage can have a detrimental effect on lip mobility depending upon their location, nature, and severity. These include clefts, malformations, fused bones, facial tumors, burns, lacerations, gun shot wounds, and so forth. All the facilitation methods of this chapter can be used to determine if lip movement can be taught in these cases. Results will vary depending upon the nature and severity of the disability.

Dental & Orthodontic Problems

Some problems with lip movement can be the direct result of dental or orthodontic problems. For example, some clients cannot achieve adequate lip closure because the maxillary (upper) central incisors are too large and too long. Clients with dental/orthodontic problems should be referred to appropriate professionals (dentists, orthodontists, oral surgeons) for assessment and treatment. Treatment may include tooth extraction, fitting with orthodontic appliances, surgery, and so forth. Articulation therapy should be designed with these treatments in mind. When additional services will not be utilized, Van Riper taught that clients should be taught to compensate for the structural problem, or dismissed from therapy.

Upper Respiratory Problems

Chronic upper respiratory problems can interfere with lip mobility. The most common case is the client who maintains a habitual open-lips rest posture to aid breathing. Referral for medical evaluation should be made and speech therapy plans should be designed accordingly. Clients must be taught to compensate for these problems when medical treatments to assist upper respiratory function will not be used. All the facilitation methods of this chapter can be used to encourage lip mobility in these cases.

Facial Paralysis

Facial paralysis can have a detrimental affect on labial movement in speech. Bell's Palsy, Mobius Syndrome, stroke, damage to the facial nerve, and traumatic brain injury are common causes. All the facilitation methods of this chapter can be used to rehabilitate lip mobility. Results will vary depending upon the nature and severity of the damage and the course of recovery. Severe limitations in upper lip function will have very little affect on speech since the upper lip moves very little normally. Lack of lower lip mobility is much more noticeable. However, jaw and tongue movements often can compensate for lack of lower lip movement in these cases.

Aging

Research indicates that increased muscle coupling, decreased flexibility and lower strength, and poorer sensitivity characterize lip movements among the aged. The purpose of treatment in this population is to help maintain the highest level of functioning for the longest period of time. The patient may be taught to exaggerate lip movements when necessary to improve intelligibility of short messages, but activities that cause excessive fatigue of lip and face muscles should be avoided.

Issues of Sensitivity

Tactile hypersensitivity and hyposensitivity in the face and oral mechanism can interfere with a client's ability to benefit from the techniques discussed in this chapter. These clients need help normalizing responses to tactile input before or during this period (for more information, see Chapter 16, *Normalizing Oral-Tactile Sensitivity*).

SUMMARY

The facilitation of lip and cheek movement is an integral part of articulation and motor speech therapy. A variety of methods to accomplish this have been developed through the decades.

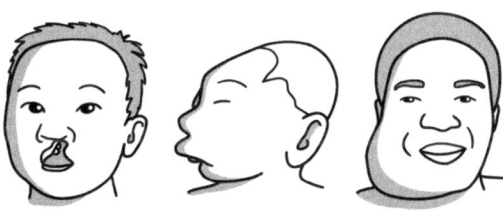

Structural problems that can interfere with lip function: Unilateral cleft lip (left), Pierre Robin Syndrome with its characteristic small mandible (middle), and facial tumor (right).

13

Facilitating Tongue Movement

Getting the tongue to move better for phoneme productions

"The tongue is without doubt the most important and the most active of the articulators."

– Willard Zemlin, 1968

An enormous part of articulation therapy is geared toward getting the tongue to move correctly. The tongue forms the floor of the oral cave and its malleable shape alters the dimension of the cavity for acoustic variability during the production of all phonemes. Sometimes the tongue stays low and other times it elevates. It elevates in the front, on the sides, and in the back depending upon the phoneme being produced. The tongue also arches and de-arches in the middle, widens and narrows from the midline, and protrudes and retracts forward and backward. A speech-language pathologist who is in charge of a range of cases with articulation and motor speech disorders must know a wide variety of ways to facilitate all basic tongue movements so that every phoneme can be produced. This is because of something that has been known for a very long time: "The tongue is the offending member in the majority of cases... of defective articulation" (Potter, 1882, p. 35).

BACKGROUND

Techniques designed to get the tongue to move better for phoneme production have been around since the 19th century, and Guttmann seems to have been the first to write about them (Guttmann, 1893). Most European and American elocutionists of his time did not believe that a teacher of speech needed to know anything about anatomy or physiology, and they greeted his book with skepticism. But Guttmann insisted that a thorough knowledge of anatomy and physiology, especially of the tongue, was important to anyone engaged in speech correction. Guttmann's book was about speech and singing, and he insisted that the process of improvement in either area called for methods to develop a malleable tongue that was

fully under the client's control. The 1859 German edition of his book was ultimately well received in Europe and then published in English in the United States in 1882. Guttmann called his methods of tongue facilitation *tongue gymnastics*:

> *"Chiefly necessary for easy speech, therefore, is a movable tongue... The correct use of the tongue is very difficult to attain, and only by means of gymnastic exercises... will the scholar be able to make it movable, so that instead of being in his way it will aid him"* (Guttmann, 1893, p. 82–83).

Guttmann's methods were carried into the 20th century by speech correctionists and singers alike. For example, Luisa Tetrazzini and Enrico Caruso were two of the very best opera stars at the turn of the last century, and they discussed some of these methods in a book they wrote on singing: "The tongue is a veritable stumbling block in the path of the singer" (Tetrazzini & Caruso, 1909, p. 9). Speech clinicians from the Phonetic Placement Era almost

The tongue is an amazing instrument that is the principle player in the production of mature speech.

Enrico Caruso (left) and Louisa Tetrazzini (right) employed tongue movement techniques in their opera training at the turn of the last century.

always recommended preparatory tongue gymnastics for those clients who needed them:

> *"Train your tongue as you would any muscle in order to gain proper control"* (Greene & Wells, 1927, p. 223).

> *"Tongue gymnastics… should be provided for better control of the muscles of the tongue"* (Nemoy & Davis, 1937, p. 137).

Charles Van Riper carried this tradition into his earliest books in which he wrote about "clumsy-tongued individuals" and the "slow of tongue." Each of the pre-phonology editions of his basic text contained tongue movement activities to employ during speech therapy. The following quotes explain Van Riper's position at that time:

> *"Although the value of tongue, lip, and jaw exercises has been questioned and denied by many workers in the field of speech correction, they can be said to be useful in teaching the student to manipulate his articulatory apparatus in many new and unaccustomed ways"* (Van Riper, 1947, p. 188).

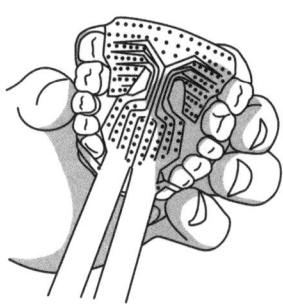

Electropalatometry is one of the best tools for studying tongue movement in speech.

> *"Many speech defectives, especially younger ones, or those with some abnormality of the tongue… need these exercises. Their tongues do not move with the speed and precision demanded by good speech. They can assume only the simplest tongue positions. Therefore, they raise the front or middle of the tongue instead of the back, and protrude it rather than lift it. It is difficult for them to curl the tip or groove the tongue. Tongue exercises are useful and necessary for these cases"* (Van Riper, 1947, p. 169).

> *"Articulation cases are occasionally seen who could truly be called the 'slow of tongue.' They can scarcely protrude the tongue even in the expression of impudence without having it loll around and droop over. Sometimes these poorly coordinated movements seem to be localized about the mouth… In modern speech correction, the emphasis on tongue exercises has almost disappeared. Yet for certain of the 'clumsy-tongued' individuals with whom we work, modern forms of these exercises are very valuable"* (Van Riper, 1947, p. 132).

> *"Many individuals have difficulty in realizing how great a repertoire of tongue movements they possess… They need to learn how adaptable the tongue really is"* (Van Riper, 1947, p. 188).

> *"[Clients with speech impairment] must not only learn some new sounds but they must also increase their repertoire of tongue movements"* (Van Riper & Irwin, 1958, p. 134).

It was only after phonological theory entered and began to dominate the field starting in 1968 that textbooks began to drop these centuries-old discussions of tongue movement. No formal research was being done on any of the methods designed to teach correct tongue function, and, therefore, no proof of their effectiveness was being established in the modern sense. These types of methods started to be treated as old-fashioned, irrelevant, and out of step with modern practice.

Methods to facilitate tongue movements have remained in practice, however, despite their elimination from articulation and phonology textbooks. Practicing SLPs continued to pass them on from one generation of therapists to the next, and by the 1980s they were being discussed along with feeding, swallowing, and orofacial myology techniques under the umbrella term *oral-motor techniques*. Speech-language pathologists in the United States were writing about them in manuals and they were teaching them in continuing education courses. The 1980s ushered in a major focus on related areas including feeding, swallowing, and tongue thrust therapy. The present author and many others began to recognize that methods to facilitate tongue function were nearly identical in five disciplines — feeding, swallowing, orofacial myology, articulation, and motor speech therapy. Speech-language pathologists continued to use practical methods to assist tongue function because clients with persistent articulation errors, motor speech disorders, developmental feeding problems, and incorrect swallow patterns still needed them.

PURPOSE

The purpose of this chapter is to bring classic methods for stimulating tongue function into the Modern Era by integrating them with research on tongue movement. Concepts and methods from four areas have been gathered and organized. This chapter integrates: (1) confirmed concepts of tongue movement now available from research, (2) methods to facilitate tongue movement that have been tested and reported in the speech science literature, (3) methods to facilitate tongue movement that were developed by therapists of the Phonetic Placement and Traditional Eras, and (4) techniques that have been developed for facilitating specific tongue movements in feeding, dysphagia, and orofacial myofunctional therapy.

TONGUE MOVEMENTS

The tongue is an amazing organ that must function in certain ways for the production of adequate speech. In the 19th century, Melville Bell said that the tongue was remarkably dexterous and he lamented the fact that he could not watch it move during articulation:

> *"Within the little compass of the mouth, [the tongue] throws itself, at the bidding of the will, into a score of different attitudes, with a dexterity, precision, and untraceable rapidity that would excite our highest admiration and astonishment, could we but witness them"* (Bell, 1916, p. 135).

Bell undoubtedly would be thrilled with the mechanisms that have been developed for studying the tongue and its three-dimensional movements. These have included electropalatometry, X-ray, cineflourography, magnetic resonance imaging, reflective-light sensing, pressure sensors, motion transducers, tissue staining, film, and other means. All these measures have confirmed what has always been known: "The tongue is a highly flexible organ that is able to deform in a complex fashion" (Iskarous, 2005, p. 363).

Normal mature tongue movements are discussed in the rest of this section. This information is based on the newest information available from research.

Functional Zones of the Tongue

The concept of *place of articulation* was based on linear divisions of the tongue that ran anterior-to-posterior. The creators of the IPA developed this simplistic concept based on the idea that place could be identified from front-to-back along the mid-sagittal line. The original definition of *place of articulation* was essentially thus: "Place or point of articulation refers to the place in the vocal tract... at which the greatest constriction is found" (Edwards & Shriberg, 1983, p. 13). This antiquated view may have been good enough for linguists to identify tongue movements in the 19th century, but knowing where the greatest constriction occurs is not good enough to describe what is now known about tongue movement for phoneme production.

It is now known know that, for the purposes of speech, the tongue elevates in certain curvilinear patterns: it bowls, grooves, attains a horseshoe-shape, elevates the tip, curls back from the tip, curls up on the sides, arches and de-arches around a pivot point in the middle, and braces at the back lateral margins. It also protrudes, retracts, widens, narrows, tenses, relaxes, and makes all its movements in stripping actions.

Marshalla (1992b) proposed abandoning the concept of place of articulation and other traditional ways of dividing the tongue into sections along linear markings. She

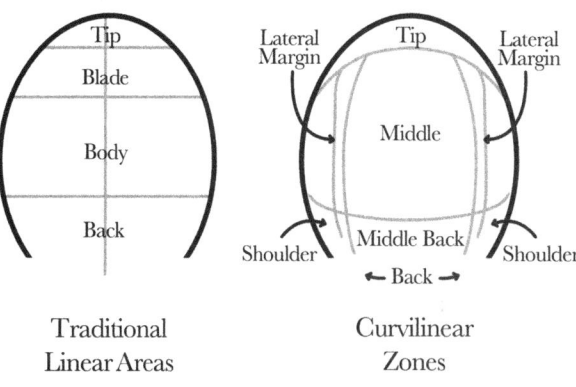

Traditional divisions of the tongue are linear (left). The proposed Functional Zones of the Tongue (right) are curvilinear and correspond to research on tongue movements in speech.

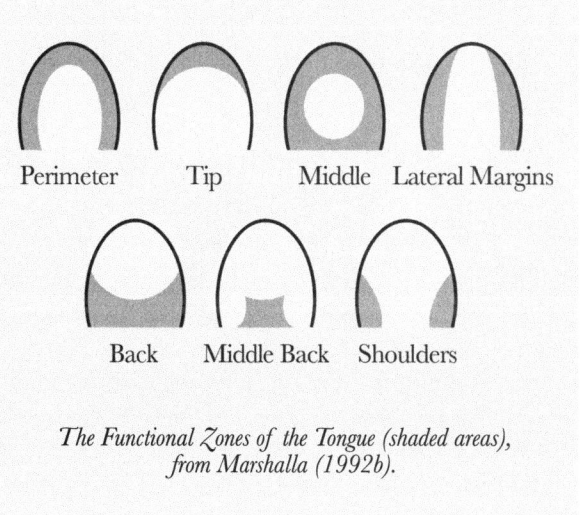

The Functional Zones of the Tongue (shaded areas), from Marshalla (1992b).

proposed organizing the tongue into curvilinear *functional zones* that correspond with elevations the tongue makes during phoneme production. The following terms for the tongue's functional zones are ones she identified: *perimeter, tip, middle, lateral margins, back, middle back,* and *shoulders.* These terms shall be used throughout this manual and are described below.

TONGUE MOVEMENT BASICS

The most fundamental concept of this chapter is that the tongue moves, and this means that tongue movements are governed by all the principles of movement described in Chapter 10. Tongue movements begin in utero, they unfold in a certain sequence in development, and they advance at a rate that is variable from one person to another. Tongue movements develop from gross to fine, from proximal to distal, and from medial to lateral to rotational. The tongue moves in mass undifferentiated simple patterns early in life, and these become separated, more complex, and refined over time. The tongue begins moving in slow simple patterns that become faster and more complex in time.

Also, the tongue must learn to move independently from the jaw and other structures. Its movements develop in flexion and extension patterns. The tongue must learn to make individual movements and to sequence these movements in overlapping patterns. The tongue must also learn to move in rhythmic oscillating patterns that occur at variable rates. The tongue contains muscles that stabilize and mobilize its actions.

The tongue's internal stabilization is responsible for its movements. According to Kier and Smith (1985) and Smith and Kier (1989) and Kent (2004b), the tongue is a *muscular hydrostat* similar to an elephant's trunk. Neither has bones or joints to help them move. "The musculature itself both creates movement and provides skeletal support for that movement" (Smith & Kier, 1989). This is a critical piece: The contraction of the intrinsic muscles of the mid-tongue — the *tongue bowl* or *groove* — enables the front-tongue to move vertically. It moves vertically through varying amounts of mid-tongue contractions for /t/, /d/, /n/, /l/, /s/, /z/, /ʃ/, /ʒ/, /tʃ/ and /dʒ/.

Variations in muscle tone affect movement of the tongue. Tongue movements are casual and random at first and they become habitual and task-specific in time. The tongue must also learn to move economically over time. Reflexes are theorized to be the basis of all tongue movements. Structure affects tongue function and vice versa. Oral habits can affect tongue movement as can the health of the individual.

Tongue Bowling

Biologists explain that the human body consists of a trunk out of which extend five appendages: two arms, two legs, and one head. Each of these appendages ends in a grasping mechanism. The arms end with the hands, the legs end with the feet, and the head biologically ends with the tongue. Each of these grasping mechanisms is designed to take hold of an object and bring it to the body. The mechanisms are called respectively the *palmer grasp*, the *plantar grasp*, and the *lingual grasp*. The lingual grasp or *tongue bowl*

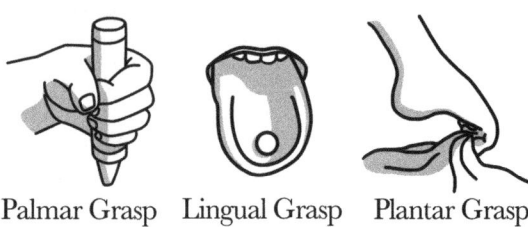

Palmar Grasp   Lingual Grasp   Plantar Grasp

The palmer grasp, the lingual grasp, and the plantar grasp all operate in the canonical bowl pattern.

The tongue bowl is evident in children and adults.

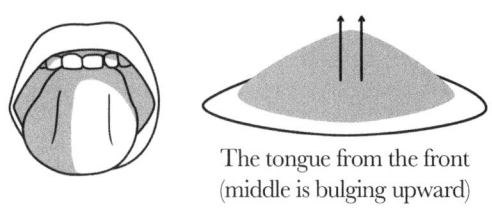

The tongue from the front (middle is bulging upward)

Absence of a dominant tongue bowl pattern causes the tongue to bulge or arch upward in its middle section. The elocutionists said this caused speech to "thicken."

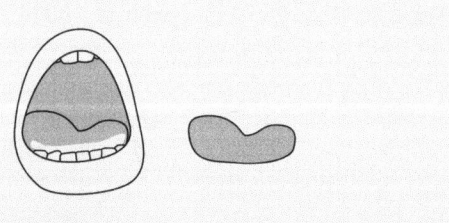

Elevation of the tongue's lateral margins with midline depression as seen from the front.

is an essential motor pattern that is necessary for the biological functions of eating and swallowing, and is integral to the higher functions of speaking and singing.

The tongue bowls by elevating its perimeter while holding its middle down. The tongue bowl contributes to the round or *orotund* quality of good speech and song noted by the elocutionists: "The root of the tongue should be depressed as much as possible to expand the back part of the mouth and give fullness to the vowel sounds" (Bell, 1887, p. 52). Elocutionists spoke of the floor of the mouth as *the bed* and described the tongue bowl as "the deepest depression in its bed" (Rush, 1855, p. 427).

Speech that is produced without tongue bowling sounds muffled, nasal, or like the client is speaking with something in his mouth. In their discussion of dysarthria,

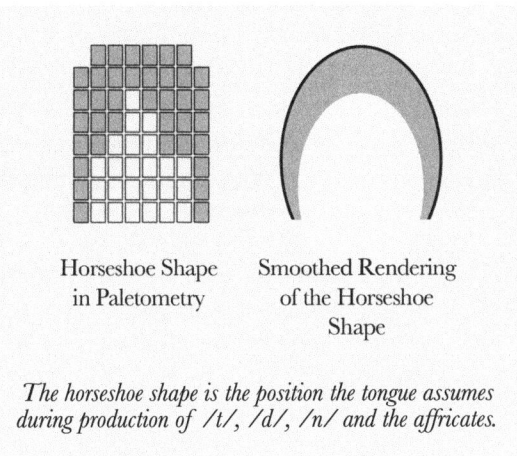

Horseshoe Shape in Paletometry   Smoothed Rendering of the Horseshoe Shape

The horseshoe shape is the position the tongue assumes during production of /t/, /d/, /n/ and the affricates.

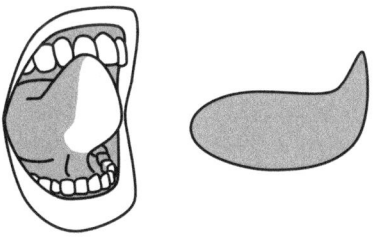

Very high tongue-tip elevation to the maxillary (upper) incisors. A smaller yet similar pattern, with the jaw in a higher position, is used inside the mouth during production of /l/.

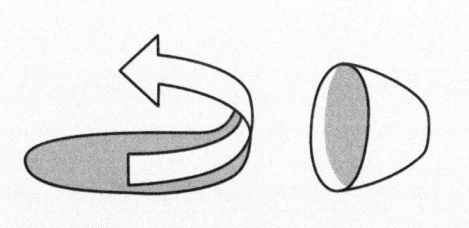

The tongue tip curls up and back in a bowl shape during production of the retroflex /ɾ/.

Darley, Aaronson, and Brown (1975) said it was like a person speaking with *mashed potatoes in his mouth*, a phrase that can be traced back to the elocutionists. The elocutionists also used the phrase *thickness of speech* to describe speech that results from raising the middle of the tongue instead of bowling it. This phrase is found articulation books through the 1960s but it seems to have been dropped when phonology entered the field: "Thickness of articulation consists of the action of the middle instead of the point of the tongue in the various lingual articulations" (Bell, 1887, p. 51).

The tongue bowl configuration is the most fundamental tongue movement pattern for all movements the tongue must do in speech and swallowing, even for /r/ (Byun, Hitchcock, & Swartz, 2014). The tongue bowl is a primitive movement pattern that is part of several infantile reflex movements including yawning, coughing, gagging, sucking, swallowing, and crying. The tongue bowl is also incorporated into the first two phases of the normal mature swallow. It is the foundational movement pattern for the production of all phonemes. Tongue-tip elevation and tongue-side elevation (grooving) are modifications of the basic tongue bowl. The tongue bowl pattern, therefore, could be considered the most fundamental of all tongue movement patterns or the *canonical tongue movement pattern*.

Horseshoe Shape

Research has demonstrated that the perimeter of the tongue lifts while the middle of the tongue holds a low position to form a basic horseshoe-shape configuration (Gibbon, 1999). The horseshoe-shape is the full expression of the tongue bowl as it is used during phoneme production. The horseshoe shape is the foundational pattern for the lingua-alveolar phonemes /t/, /d/, /n/, and the affricates /tʃ/ and /dʒ/. Since movements develop from proximal to distal and from medial-to-lateral, a tongue that can form a horseshoe-shape by extending and elevating its perimeter is functioning with full maturity.

> "School-age children with typical speech development produce anterior consonants such as /t/ and /d/ by a combination of lateral bracing and an upward movement of the tongue tip/blade to the alveolar ridge, resulting in a characteristic horseshoe-shape EPG spatial configuration" (Gibbon, 1999, p. 386).

Tip Elevation

The tongue tip lifts independently to the alveolus for production of /l/. The view that only the tongue tip contacts the palate has been held for centuries:

> "The standard sound is made with the tongue tip against the alveolar ridge, but with the tongue adjusted in such a manner that its margins do not touch the teeth and gums at the sides" (Carrell & Tiffany, 1960, p. 237).

However, electropalatometry has revealed that some

articulation may also occur at the tongue's shoulders, although this may be the result of coarticulation (McLeod & Singh, 2009).

Since movements develop from proximal to distal, a tongue that is functioning with full tip extension and elevation is functioning with full maturity. A tongue that cannot extend and elevate its very tip is showing motor immaturity.

Tongue-Tip Curling

The tongue tip lifts and curls up and back so that the tongue forms into an exaggerated bowl-shape that faces the oropharynx. This pattern is used during production of the retroflex /r/: "For the retroflex /r/ [the] spread tongue tip is curled upward toward the middle of the hard palate" (Bosley, 1981, p. 81). Retroflex /r/ is the only phoneme that requires this advanced movement pattern.

Protruding

The entire tongue shifts forward slightly so that the tip emerges between the teeth for /θ/ and /ð/. The jaw simultaneously shifts downward slightly to accommodate this forward tongue position. Shifting the whole tongue forward is a primitive movement pattern that requires only simple midline control, therefore, it is a movement often used in defective articulation. The amount of forward shifting in normal mature speech varies from one person to another:

> *"If a tongue-protruded /θ/ is made, the spread tongue tip begins to protrude between the teeth at approximately the canine or perhaps first premolar area. However, it is not necessary to protrude the tongue for a normal /θ/"* (Bosley, 1981, p. 53).

Arching, De-Arching & Pivot Point

Iskarous (2005) found that the midline of the tongue arches (bulges upward) and de-arches (withdraws downward) from a pivot point on the tongue's midline during production of phonemes. Height of the arch contributes to vowel formation. This means that the vowels are formed when the tongue braces at its lateral margins against the sides of the palate while the middle of the tongue arches and de-arches:

> *"The tongue is an elastic continuum with a very large number of degrees of freedom along its midsagittal edge… Pivoting and arching, therefore, indicate a principle of tongue movement"* (Iskarous, 2005, p. 376, 380).

The tongue de-arches to keep its middle down and away from the palate throughout speech (Fletcher, 1989). This does several things: it helps create the horseshoe-shape for /t/, /d/, and /n/, it allows the tip to elevate independently for /l/, it allows the perimeter to curl up and back in an exaggerated cup-shape for the retroflex /r/, it allows the sibilants to be produced with a central groove and creates the depressed middle which is part of the basic tongue bowl that lends itself to the orotund quality of the vowels.

A careful study of the palatography images of all consonant and vowel productions reveals that the very middle of the tongue never makes contact with the roof of the mouth in normal mature speech (McLeod & Singh, 2009). A middle that is held low is part of oral stability and tongue maturity. Since movements develop from medial-to-lateral, a tongue that is over-using or arching in its middle section is a tongue that is functioning with motor immaturity. The elocutionists' term *thickening* described speech that was produced with the tongue arching upward too much in its middle zone.

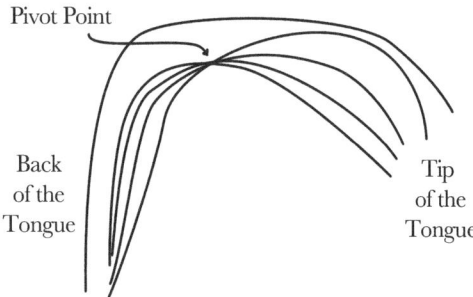

Midline arching, de-arching, and pivot point as seen from the side of the tongue (adapted from Iskarous, 2005).

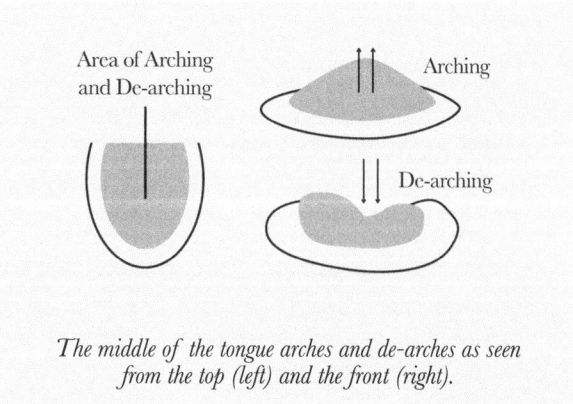

The middle of the tongue arches and de-arches as seen from the top (left) and the front (right).

Lateral Elevation

The lateral margins of the tongue must be able to elevate independently of the rest of the tongue to form the central groove and the horseshoe-shape. The lateral margins elevate in the back for /r/ and the vowels. They elevate from the back to about half-way forward for production of the palatal sounds, and they elevate all the way to the tip for the lingua-alveolar sibilants /s/ and /z/.

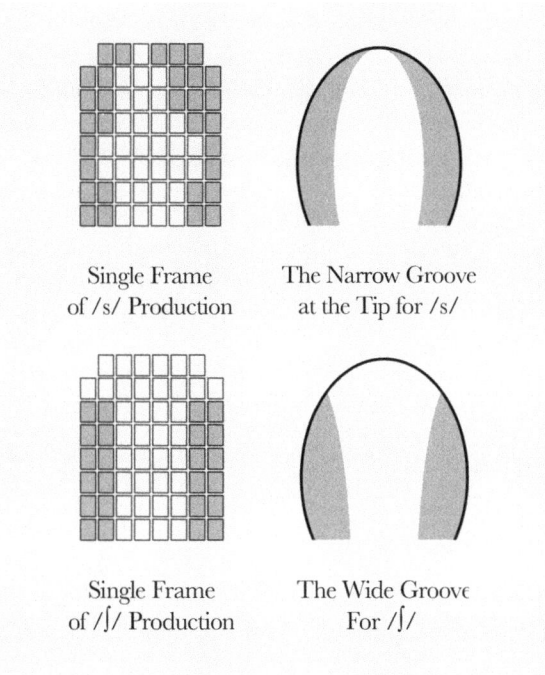

Single Frame
of /s/ Production

The Narrow Groove
at the Tip for /s/

Single Frame
of /ʃ/ Production

The Wide Groove
For /ʃ/

Palatometric and smoothed illustrations of the tongue's articulations to the palate during production of /s/ and /ʃ/.

Refined Tongue-Tip Control

The tongue tip must demonstrate extraordinary control to differentiate /s/ and /z/ from all other phonemes. Traditional phonetics dictates that the tip can be high, mid, or low during production of /s/ and /z/, i.e., the tip can be pointing toward the alveolus, toward the teeth, or toward the floor of the mouth. If the tip is pointing upward, it must stay below the alveolar ridge so that a tiny stream of air can escape. If the tip is low, then the midsagittal blade of the tongue must arch upward to create a narrow channel between it and the alveolus.

The volume of airspace between the tongue-tip constriction at the incisors is about one cubic centimeter during production of /s/ (Perkell, 1981). The sibilant groove at the tip is about 2 mm narrower for /s/ than for /ʃ/, and 1 mm narrower than each of these for /z/ and /ʒ/ (Fletcher, 1989). The size of the tip opening from widest to narrowest in sequence from gross to fine is /ʃ/, to /ʒ/, to /s/, to /z/. That makes /ʃ/ the widest and perhaps the easiest sibilant groove to learn, and it makes /z/ the most difficult.

Widening & Narrowing

The tongue must be able to widen and narrow from its midline. Since movements develop from medial-to-lateral, narrowing the tongue is considered a more primitive movement pattern and widening the tongue is considered more mature. The wide stance must be maintained most of the time during mature speech for it is integral to the tongue bowl, the horseshoe shape, lateral bracing, and the orotund quality of the vowels. The wide stance is also especially important to production of /r/: "In both retroflex and palatal [bunched] /r/ the tongue is widely spread" (Bosley, 1981, p. 81). Mature speech is always made with the tongue sitting in a wide stance except when it narrows purposefully for production of /l/.

Retracting the Entire Tongue

The whole tongue can retract toward the oropharynx, and when it does the tongue thickens, the middle bulges upward, and the tongue tip retracts into the body of the tongue so that the tongue assumes an imperfect ball-shape. In other words, the tongue can pull back into an ovoid-shape that occludes the oropharynx. Therapists often call this "bunching." This gross retracting is part of the tongue retraction reflex.

Since movements develop from proximal to distal, the tongue that habitually pulls back into a bunched position during speech is considered to be functioning immaturely. Likewise, the tongue that habitually bunches in the back for back sounds instead of elevating at the tip for front sounds is also considered to be functioning with immaturity. Clients who habitually hold the tongue in a retracted position often replace lingua-alveolar phonemes with lingua-velar ones, e.g., /k/ for /t/, /g/ for /d/, /ŋ/ for /n/,

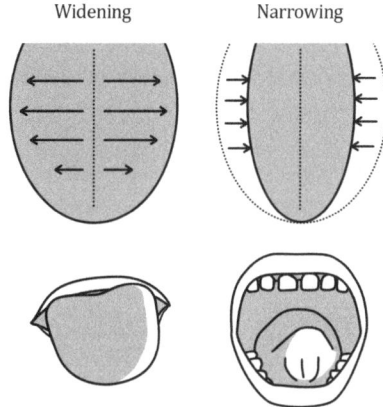

Widening   Narrowing

The tongue can widen and narrow from midline.

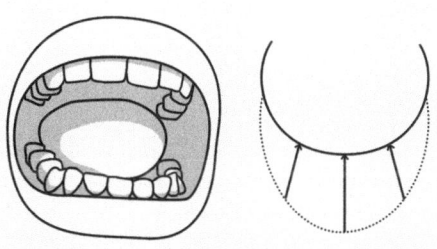

Tongue retraction (bunching) from the front (left) and top (right).

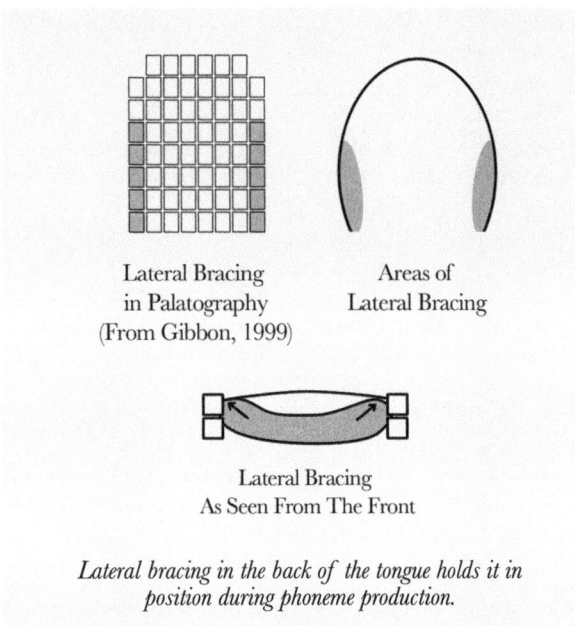

Lateral Bracing
in Palatography
(From Gibbon, 1999)

Areas of
Lateral Bracing

Lateral Bracing
As Seen From The Front

*Lateral bracing in the back of the tongue holds it in
position during phoneme production.*

and /j/ for /l/.

Back-Lateral Bracing

According to Fletcher (1989, 1992) the tongue braces itself laterally with its back lateral margins against the palate during production of all phonemes. Fletcher called this pattern *lateral bracing* and *anchoring*, and he referred to the back lateral margins of the tongue as the *fulcrums* of tongue movement:

> *"It appears that such contact may serve as an anchor for producing contrastive vowels as well as consonant tongue positioning"* (Fletcher, 1989, p. 747).

This lateral bracing was first noted by some of the elocutionists. For example Guttmann described it in 1882 when he discussed how /t/ was made:

> *"T is formed by placing the lateral edges of the tongue against the upper molars and pressing its tip against the roots of the upper incisors..."* (Guttmann, 1882, p. 116–117).

Lateral bracing was also understood by many therapists of Van Riper's time, for example, Nemoy and Davis (1937) called it "E" position. Even Chomsky and Halle, in their classic treatise on phonological theory, noted that the tongue assumes lateral bracing before the speaker produces any phoneme. They called it the *neutral position* and likened it to the position for /e/:

> *"In most X-ray motion pictures of speech, it can readily be observed that just prior to speaking the subject positions his vocal tract in a certain characteristic manner... The body of the tongue, which in quiet breathing lies in a relaxed state on the floor of the mouth, is raised in the neutral position to about the level that it occupies in the articulation of the English vowel [e] in the word bed; but the blade of the tongue remains in about the same position as in quiet breathing"* (Chomsky & Halle, 1968, p. 300).

The back lateral margins of the tongue anchor the tongue in position so that it can move with accuracy and speed while elevating to and from the palate. Just like the shoulders of the body hold the arms in correct position during their movements, the shoulders of the tongue hold the tongue in correct position during its movements. The topic of the tongue's lateral bracing is discussed in more detail in Chapter 14 on oral stability although some methods to develop this lateral bracing are presented below.

Stripping Actions

Elevation of the tongue toward the palate is made in stripping actions. For example, when the horseshoe shape is forming for production of a lingua-alveolar phoneme, the tongue begins by elevating at its shoulders for bracing, and then lifting the sides of the tongue sequentially from back-to-front. In the following quote, Fletcher describes the stripping action of the tongue as the lateral margins elevated to the palate during production of a sibilant in his study:

> *"The constriction sequence began with anchoring the tongue along the posterolateral dental-alveolar shelves. The contact then extended progressively forward to the consonant constriction position"* (Fletcher, 1989, p. 745).

In production of a lingua-palatal or lingua-alveolar phoneme, therefore, stripping is from back-to-front as the tongue approaches the palate during the on-glide movement, and it strips away from the palate from front-to-back during the off-glide movement. One can assume from this that the tongue also moves in a stripping action when it elevates to the palate from any direction. Stripping action is a rolling-type wave action that indicates that the tongue is moving in its most mature way. The reader may recall that this is called *peristalsis*. Peristalsis is a fundamental movement of the digestive tract from the mouth at the top to the anus at the bottom.

Tension & Relaxation

The tongue must be able to generate a certain amount of internal tension throughout its muscle fibers in order to achieve a correct and clear acoustic quality for all phonemes. The tongue's muscular tone creates the firmness or looseness that contributes to the way sound resonates within the oral cavity. The tongue must also relax so that it can retreat from target positions.

Tension and relaxation in the tongue occurs within a range that keeps the tongue functional and fluid during speech. A tongue that is too tense (hypertonic) is restricted in its range because of stiffness and fixing. A tongue that is too loose (hypotonic) is limited in it range because of inactivity and weakness.

Appropriate tension in the tongue allows articulatory contacts to be made more or less firmly depending upon the consonant. McGlone, Proffit, and Christiansen (1967) studied the upward pressure of the tongue against the palate during production of lingua alveolars /t/, /d/, /n/, and /s/. They found that the greatest pressure occurs with nasal /n/, that pressure is less with stops /t/ and /d/, and that pressure is the least with fricative /s/. Frication on stops and nasals occurs when upward pressure of the tongue is lacking. The dysarthric patient who has weak lingual strength is thus characterized by this sloppy quality.

Consistency

An important element of tongue movement in speech is relative consistency of placement against the upper structures. Sussman et al. (1996) studied one child beginning at 12 months of age and found that place of articulation for the stop consonants became more consistent when the child was 21 months of age. Consistency of articulatory placement is necessary for mature speech to become established. Consistency is gained when oral stability has been established, and this topic is discussed in more detail in Chapter 14.

Mid-tongue position for /s/ during a midline production

Mid-tongue position for /s/ during the bi-lateral lisp

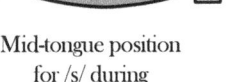

Tongue position during normal midline production of /s/ (left) and during production of a bi-lateral lisp (right) as seen from the front.

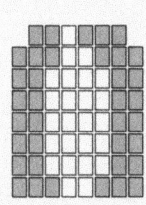
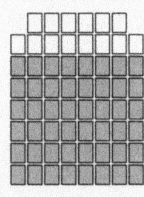

Correct production of /s/

Production of /s/ that sounds lateral

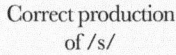

Differentiated (left) and undifferentiated (right) tongue gestures during production of normal and lateralized /s/ productions (adapted from Gibbon, 1999).

TONGUE MOVEMENT PROBLEMS

Many kinds of clients can have problems moving the tongue accurately for production of phonemes. SLPs see tongue movement problems in clients with motor speech disorders and they also see these problems among clients with so-called functional articulation errors. Even the elocutionists noted that an inactive tongue contributes to speech impairment. They said that the inactive tongue relinquishes control to the jaw and other structures:

> *"The tongue lolling on the bed of the jaw surrenders its proper functions to any part of the organs that can be got to undertake them"* (Bell, 1898, p. 56).

This section describes typical tongue movement problems noted by the present author over nearly forty years of regular client contact. Clients can have any one or all of these problems depending upon the nature and severity of their articulation or motor speech deficit. It is the present author's experience that clients with apraxia and dysarthria often have many of these problems while clients with minor phoneme errors usually have only one or two.

Problems in General Gross Tongue Mobility

Clients with the most severe motor speech disorders and cognitive dysfunction often do not move their tongues much at all during speech or feeding. The tongue may lie on the floor of the mouth and be relatively inactive, it may be fixed in a high and retracted position, it may move in gross forward-and-back movement patterns, or it may move only in tremors, tics, or primitive reflexive patterns. Sometimes the tongue is locked in position due to severe spasticity, and other times the tongue does not move at all due to very low tone. Sometimes the tongue has no purposeful movement whatsoever, and merely fasciculates (i.e., twitches slightly) in place.

Problems Developing Refined Tongue Movements

Refined tongue movements develop over time and are a sign of movement maturity. Lack of refined tongue control is a sign of immaturity, delay, or disorder in tongue movement. Cheng, Murdoch, Goozée, and Scott (2007b) found that children and adults used the same tongue-to-palate contact patterns but that children use grosser patterns with more contact surface and posterior (proximal) contact. Gibbon (1999) found evidence that children with articulation and phonological disorders of unknown origin have unrefined and gross tongue movement patterns she called *undifferentiated lingua gestures*. Gibbon's electropalatography data revealed that too much of the tongue makes contact with the palate when the tongue's movements are not well differentiated. Dagenais and Critz-Crosby (1991) found that clients with hearing impairment produced vowels that were centralized with generally undifferentiated tongue positions.

Problems Stabilizing the Tongue

Please see Chapter 14 on oral stability for in depth information on this topic.

Problems Keeping the Middle Low

Some clients occlude the oral passageway by holding the middle of the tongue high, especially in the back. The middle of the tongue arches upward when it should stay low. This position forces a muffled and nasal sound quality that the elocutionists and therapists of the Phonetic Placement Era called *thick speech* (e.g., Borden & Busse, 1925). Bell (1906) noticed this pattern in clients who are deaf. The present author has noted that this pattern is prominent in clients with dysarthria and those with oral-tactile hypersensitivity. The pattern is especially common among clients with cerebral palsy. This movement pattern can be described as midline elevation that is dominating over lateral elevation. Since midline control precedes lateral control in normal development this pattern is viewed as both a delay in tongue movement development and a deviant pattern thereof.

An inability to use the tongue in a concave position during speech or singing influences the acoustic quality of all vowels and consonants by failing to give speech its required round or orotund quality:

> *"When the tongue forms a mountain in the back part of the mouth the singer produces what you call in English slang 'a hot potato tone'—that is to say, a tone that sounds as if it were having much difficulty to get through the mouth. In very fact, it is having this difficulty, for it has to pass over the back of the tongue"* (Tetrazzini & Caruso, 1909, p. 9).

Oral resonance may become muffled when the middle back of the tongue is too high, and these clients may have difficulty making all the vowels clearly. These clients may have difficulty producing many of the anterior phonemes as well. The most severe of these clients produce distorted vowels and/or they use [+Back] consonants only. A problem depressing the middle of the tongue is a reflection of a client's inability to develop his full range of tongue movements and to integrate the tongue bowl pattern into his movements for speech.

This same movement error is seen in clients with mild articulation error as well. McGlone and Proffit (1973) used pressure transducers and found evidence that elevating the midline of the tongue upward against the palate during production of the sibilants produces the lateral lisp. Gibbon (1999) used electropalatometry and discovered the same thing. Putnam and Ringel (1976) found that the tongues of normal adult speakers began to hump excessively when deprived of sensory feedback.

Some clients also hump the middle of the tongue during feeding and swallowing:

> *"When tongue configuration is humped or bunched rather than grooved, it is difficult for... liquid to flow in an uninterrupted stream to the pharynx. It is like the difference between rain rushing down the gutter of a street into a sewer and rain that falls on top of a ridge and flows over the sides in many directions"* (Morris & Klein, 2000, p. 134).

Problems Lifting All the Way to the Palate

Some clients have an active tongue but they do not elevate it all the way to the palate during speech. For example, the client who is beginning to babble with vowels only is not articulating the lips or elevating the tongue all the way to the palate. Dagenais and Critz-Crosby (1991) used electropalatography and found that clients with hearing impairment demonstrated frequent lack of tongue-to-palate contact during production of lingua-alveolar, lingua-palatal, and lingua-alveolar consonant phonemes.

Too Much Upward Pressure

The opposite of not elevating the tongue high enough is the problem of pressing the tongue up too firmly against the palate. This pattern causes fricated sounds to become stopped. This is called *stopping* and is considered a deviant phonological pattern, but in earlier decades this was considered a problem of developing refined tongue motor control as noted in this quote from 1912:

> *"Children with this trouble substitute 't' for 's,' 'd' for 'z,' and 'd' for the two forms of 'th'... The defect arises from... the tongue pressing too tightly against the palate... In trying to make the 's,' for example, the patient [cannot] carry out the fine adjustment requisite; she presses the tongue too tightly and thus makes a 't'"* (Scripture, 1912, p. 181–182).

Problems Protruding the Tongue

Some clients do not protrude the whole tongue in the anterior direction, and, therefore, they do not produce the lingua-dental phonemes /θ/ and /ð/. A problem protruding the entire tongue also limits a client's ability to unlock the tongue from the jaw in order to develop a full range of tongue movements. Problems in protruding the whole tongue can also be related to a general problem with persistent tongue retraction: "Tongue retraction influences the freedom of movement of the tongue" (Morris & Klein, 2000, p. 367). ASHA president Lee Edwards Travis considered an inability to protrude the tongue to be a diagnostic indicator of poor tongue control: "In general, any tongue that cannot be extended beyond the teeth is not free enough for good speech" (Travis, 1931, p. 200). Problems protruding the whole tongue outside the front of the mouth may also be the result of a restricting lingua frenum or a tongue that is small, disfigured, or surgically altered.

Problems Retracting/Bunching the Tongue

Some clients do not retract or bunch the tongue back into the oral pharyngeal area. This interferes with production of the bunched (back) /r/ which requires retraction, spreading, and high elevation of the back of the tongue. A distorted /r/ may be the result, or the client may replace /r/ with the more anterior glides or another phoneme. A problem retracting the whole tongue also limits a client's ability to develop his full range of tongue movement. Some of these clients allow the tongue to hang forward outside the mouth much of the time.

Problems Elevating the Perimeter

Some clients do not simultaneously lift the entire perimeter of the tongue to create the horseshoe-shape, lifting the whole tongue instead (Gibbon, 1999). This affects speech in several ways. When the horseshoe shape cannot be achieved for production of /t/ and /d/, the result is that pressure builds too far back and the correct stop quality for these sounds cannot be achieved. Some of these clients sound like they are producing anterior and posterior sounds at the same time, and others sound like they are substituting /k/ for /t/ and /g/ for /d/. A fricated or generally distorted sound may also be the result if the perimeter elevation is not complete and the tongue does not fully seal against the palate. When a horseshoe shape cannot be created for /n/, the sound may be nasal but it its resonance will be poor, the sound may be distorted, or the error might sound like a substitution of /ŋ/ for /n/. The horseshoe shape is also the foundation of the tongue groove so lack of elevating the horseshoe shape will also result in some distortion of all the sibilants.

Problems Elevating the Tip Independently

Many clients are unable to lift the tip of the tongue for /t/, /d/, /n/, /l/, /tʃ/ and /dʒ/ while the back-lateral margins are braced. They must resort to other movement patterns in order to produce these phonemes. These clients may make these sounds by using up-and-down jaw movements instead of tongue movements, or else by lifting the middle of the tongue instead of the tip, or by shifting the whole tongue forward so that the tip protrudes instead of lifting. Some of these clients cannot lift the tip due to a restricting lingua frenum. A problem elevating the tongue tip is also an indication that the client has not developed his full range of tongue movements from proximal to distal.

Limited Tip Control

Many clients are unable to control a refined groove pattern at the tip of the tongue for production of an acoustically acceptable /s/ and /z/. They resort to other movement patterns for production of these phonemes. They might protrude the whole tongue and substitute /θ/ for /s/ and /ð/ for/z/. They might substitute lower-lip elevation for tongue-tip elevation and create a distorted sound or substitute /f/ for /s/ and /v/ for /z/. They might bang the tip of the tongue against the alveolar ridge with force enough to substitute /t/ for /s/ and /d/ for /z/. They might use the back of the tongue instead of the front and substitute /k/ for /s/ and /g/ for /z/. They might create a groove that is too wide and, therefore, substitute /ʃ/ for /s/ and /ʒ/ for /z/.

Problems Elevating the Back

Many clients do not elevate the back of the tongue for phoneme production. Sometimes these [+Back] phonemes are omitted altogether. Often the front of the tongue is used instead of the back and substitutions of /t/ for /k/, /d/ for /g/, and /n/ for /ŋ/ are noted. This pattern is called *fronting* in phonological terms. Problems elevating the back of the tongue limit the client's ability to develop his full range of tongue movements.

Problems Elevating the Sides

Many clients cannot lift the sides of the tongue upward so that a midline groove can be created for production of the sibilants. They might protrude the whole tongue forward instead and create a *frontal lisp*. They might elevate the middle of the tongue instead of the sides and produce a *bi-lateral lisp*. They might elevate one side of the tongue or the other and produce a *right* or *left unilateral lisp*. Since movements develop from medial-to-lateral, problems elevating the sides of the tongue indicate that the client's tongue has not reached full movement potential.

Problems Curling the Tip Up & Back

Many clients cannot lift and curl the tip of the tongue up and back toward the velum to produce a *retroflex* /r/. This motor pattern is unnecessary for production of any other phoneme and, since other movement patterns can be employed for /r/, most clients do not need to learn this movement. However, this movement pattern may be needed if /r/ cannot be produced any other way. Problems curling the tongue tip up and back also reflects a lack of full tongue movement development.

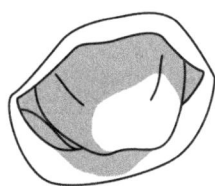

Limited widening. Notice how the sides are pulling toward midline, the tip is retracting, the middle is bulging, and the overall shape is narrow and boxy instead of wide and bowled.

Problems Widening the Tongue

Some clients cannot or do not widen the tongue during production of speech. The result is an overall distortion of the acoustic quality. Some clients squeeze medially during attempts at only one phoneme or another, for example, some clients squeeze and narrow the body of the tongue when saying /r/, and a classic distortion of this sound is the result. Problems in widening the body of the tongue is also noted when a lateral lisp is habitual.

Problems widening the tongue limit the client's ability to develop his full range of tongue movement and it may interfere with the process of forming a horseshoe-shaped seal against the palate. Alexander Graham Bell noted this problem among clients who were deaf: "The most common fault, I think, among deaf children, is an exaggerated muscular action leading to a stiffening and narrowing of the tongue" (Bell, 1906, p. 103). This is also a common problem among clients with cerebral palsy and other neuromuscular disorders. It is the main pattern of spasticity. Since movements develop from medial to lateral, an overuse of the middle of the tongue and a lack of widening is a sign of oral-motor delay.

Problems Narrowing the Tongue

Even though the tongue needs to stay wide most of the time, it must narrow for production of /l/ so the sound can escape the mouth laterally. Some clients cannot narrow the tongue body to keep it away from the palate so that the lateral sound can be produced. The result is a distorted /l/. Problems narrowing the tongue also limits a client's ability to develop his full range of tongue movement.

Lack of Tension / Strength

Some clients can perform a wide variety of tongue movements but they cannot achieve enough tension in the tongue to create the acoustic quality demanded by good speech. Low muscle tone is a major contributor to this problem. Lack of adequate tension in the tongue causes a softer, immature, slightly distorted, and somewhat muffled overall quality to speech. Lack of tension interferes with the ability to attain enough force of articulatory contact against the palate for the stops, and extra aspiration or frication may be added to these productions because of the loose contact. A lax tongue can also have a seriously detrimental effect on producing a correct /r/ and a correct midline groove for the sibilants.

Tongue strength has always been a question among speech therapists, and many SLPs report using "tongue strengthening exercises" to improve lingual control. But Clark (2008) reviewed the literature in this area and summarized that oral strength is unrelated to articulation skill. More recently, Neel and Palmer (2012) studied the relationship between tongue strength and speech rate in adults and also found strength not to be an important factor: "Focus [of treatment] must remain on factors beyond strength, such as movement precision and coordination" (p. 235). The only clients who consistently demonstrate weakness in the tongue musculature that affects both speech and swallowing are those with dysarthria (e.g., Stierwalt & Youmans, 2007).

The real difference between good and poor speakers (without dysarthria) is a matter of the tongue's movement patterns and not its strength. For example, in a client without dysarthria, an incorrect production of /l/ has nothing to do with the strength of the tongue; the only important factor is whether or not the tip actually can and does elevate to the alveolar ridge during production of the phoneme. A client with dysarthria may have weakness in the tongue that prevents his ability to lift it to the palate, but all other clients should have enough strength to accomplish this simple movement.

In other words, strength and movement patterns are two completely separate issues. Most clients have enough lingual strength to produce the movements they need for all the phonemes. After all, the articulations one makes during speech have been called "light as a butterfly." These clients just need instruction on moving the right part of the tongue in the right direction at the right time and with consistency. Only a minimum amount of strength is necessary for the tongue to move in its required patterns for speech; excessive strength is unnecessary and in fact can be quite detrimental to fluid tongue movement.

Inconsistent Points of Articulation

Many clients can perform a wide variety of tongue movements but they attain target positions inconsistently. For example, Hardcastle, Morgan Barry, and Clark (1987) studied two children with articulation deficit of unknown etiology and two with dysarthria and found that all four had difficulty maintaining consistent points of articulation of the tongue against the palate. Lack of consistent points of contact is also a pattern in younger children as noted in a single-subject study by Sussman et al. (1996).

Problems Associated with Aging

Aging and tongue mobility is a subject that has only recently become a topic of investigation. Connor, Ota, Nagai, Russell, and Leverson (2008) studied the process of aging on rat tongues and found that strength remained the same but timing became slower in the older rats.

ANKYLOGLOSSIA

The restricted lingual frenum (ankyloglossia) can impede tongue-tip movement because it holds the tongue tip to the floor of the mouth to various degrees depending upon its position, length, and thickness. But a search of the ASHA journals reveals that there has been only one study on the length of the restricting lingual frenum and its impact on speech. Fletcher and Meldrum (1968) studied the

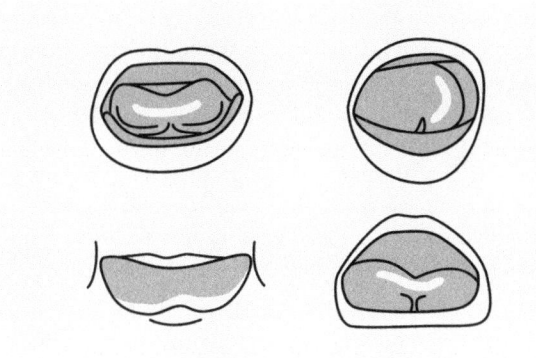

The short lingua frenum can restrict tongue-tip elevation and protrusion.

length of the lingual frenum in relation to speech skill in 40 eleven-and twelve-year-old children and found that children with more lingual restriction produced more articulation errors.

The view among SLPs in the United States of the relationship between the restricting lingua frenum and speech problems was presented in an opinion piece published in the *ASHA Leader* (Kummer, 2005). Kummer informs readers that most restricting lingua frenums have very little impact on speech except for tongue-tip placement on /l/ and /θ/. She suggested that speech problems and tongue-tie correlations are a coincidence, and she recommended teaching compensation for tongue placement:

> *"Most experienced speech-language pathologists would conclude that frenulectomy is rarely indicated for speech reasons unless it is very severe or there are concomitant oral-motor problems. It may, however, be warranted for problems with early feeding, bolus manipulation, dentition, or aesthetics. Although frenulectomy is a minor procedure with a low risk of morbidity, the true danger is the disappointment that can result when parents are led to believe that this will correct speech problems that are actually due to other causes."*

The present author would argue that this is a limited perspective because SLPs are concerned with more than just simple articulation problems. Clients now include those with motor speech disorders, issues of feeding, swallowing, and orofacial myology, oral habits, airway obstruction, dentition, and more.

References

Three books have been published that may help SLPs make treatment decisions regarding clients with ankyloglossia: *Tongue-Tie: Morphogenesis, Impact, Assessment and Treatment* by Hazelbaker (2010), *Tongue Tie: From Confusion to Clarity* by Fernando (1998), and *Demystify the Tongue Tie: Methods to Confidently Analyze & Treat a Tethered Tongue* by Boshart (2015).

Alison K. Hazelbaker is a board-certified lactation consultant who wrote a comprehensive book on the tongue-tie that was an offshoot of her doctoral dissertation. After reviewing many definitions that have been proposed through the centuries, Hazelbaker defines the tongue-tie as "impaired tongue function resulting from a tight and/or short lingual frenum, which may or may not involve fibers of the genioglossus muscles" (p. 17). This book contains information about the morphology and embryology of the disorder. It presents a summary of the suck-swallow-breath sequence and discusses how the restricting lingua frenum impacts it. It describes a screening process and various assessment procedures, and it details several different surgical solutions. The book is user-friendly and contains anecdotes of real situations faced by children and their families whose lives have been impacted by the severely restricted lingua frenum. Hazelbaker suggests that lack of information is the greatest obstacle to providing excellent treatment for tongue-tie:

> *"The sole, but huge, remaining barrier to the routine treatment of tongue-tie is ignorance. The notion that tongue-tie never causes any problems and, therefore, never needs treatment persists simply because health care professionals are not taught otherwise in their professional training programs"* (Hazelbaker, 2010, p. 187).

Another recommended book is Fernando (1998). Fernando is a speech-language pathologist who has done perhaps the most comprehensive study of ankyloglossia and speech to date and she has published her results in a manual. She reviewed the non-speech literature on ankyloglossia going back to the 17th century and she studied 256 clients referred for lingual frenectomy in her hospital clinic. She proposed a definition of the disorder.

> *"Tongue tie is the congenital condition, recognized by an unusually thickened, tightened or shortened frenum, which limits movement of the tongue in activities connected with feeding and which has an adverse impact on both dental health and speech"* (Fernando, 1998, p. 2).

Fernando developed an assessment procedure called the *Tongue-Tie Assessment Protocol* (TAP) that was administered to 200 of her patients. She found that the degree of the lingual restriction has an impact on tongue-tip movement. Some tongue tips are restricted only a little bit while others are completely pinned to the floor of the mouth:

> *"When the frenum extends right up to the tongue tip, there is, in effect, no tip; the margin of the tongue is pulled and curled under towards the buccal floor. This means that licking or lateral movements of the tongue are distorted, but may sometimes be attempted with concomitant jaw movement"* (Fernando, 1998, p. 9).

Fernando found that the restricting lingua frenum impacted her subjects' tongue movements for eating (breastfeeding, bottle feeding, eating solids, and swallowing), dental health, the management of saliva, and speech production. She also found that ankyloglossia interfered with a patient's control over dental plates, and it limited protrusion of the tongue during oral exams. She found that some children with ankyloglossia develop a lesion on the bottom of the tongue from coughing because children usually cough with the tongue protruded and the underside of the tongue is forced to rub against the mandibular (lower) incisors. Interference with patterns of facial growth has also been attributed to the problem. Of the 200 subjects in Fernando's study, 196 were referred for lingua frenectomy and she reported "all patients showed an improvement in speech after surgery" (p. 63).

ANATOMY & TONGUE MOVEMENT

It is beyond the scope of this manual to describe the anatomy of the tongue and most readers of this manual will have had coursework on such. However, two concepts from the latest research related to tongue mobility are noteworthy.

First, Takemoto (2001) proposed a new model of tongue anatomy based on five distinct strata of muscles, from deep inside the base of the tongue to the outer mucosal layer. In sum, he proposed that the inner tongue muscles ("core" and "stem" muscles) have the function of thinning, protruding, and elongating the tongue while the outer muscles ("cover" and "fringe" muscles) control the perimeter of the tongue and the tongue tip.

Second, there is new evidence about the elements that comprise tongue tissue, and a theory of how these contribute to tongue movement has been offered. Miller, Watkin, and Chen (2002) used tissue staining to study the component elements of the human tongue. They found

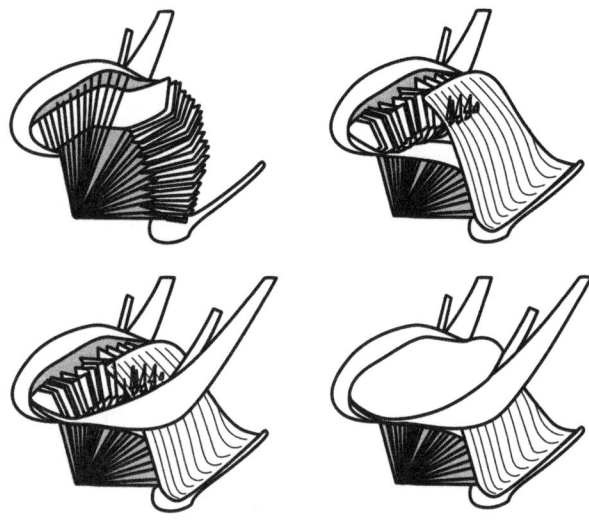

*Anatomy of the tongue
(aadapted from Takemoto, 2001).*

a higher concentration of muscle, fat, and connective tissue in the human tongue than in the tongue and striated muscles of cows. Fat contents were especially high in the tongue tip. Sex and age differences were not significant. The authors proposed that this "extracellular connective tissue matrix" might underlie the passive elastic properties of human tongue muscles by binding each muscle to its immediate neighbor and allowing the tongue musculature to function together as a single unit.

Researchers still do not understand the role each muscle plays in tongue movement, mainly because of the extreme amount of interdigitation that occurs, but the theory of *motor equivalence* allows practicing SLPs to utilize tongue movement facilitation techniques regardless. Motor equivalence (Hebb, 1949) is the theory that many different movement patterns can result in the same movement goal. This global muscle function means that it is not necessary to know which muscles cause a particular movement to occur; it is enough to know that the movement did, in fact, occur. The focus of therapy, therefore, can be on the movements themselves and not on the individual muscles per se. Therapists can rest assured that the right muscles are activating in the right ways if the tongue is moving in the right patterns.

ASSESSMENT OF TONGUE MOVEMENT

There is tremendous difference between the ways tongue movements are assessed in the research lab versus the therapy room. Numerous pieces of research equipment for studying tongue movements have been devised as mentioned throughout this chapter, however, practicing speech-language pathologists must almost always rely upon the naked eye and a simple checklist.

It is understood that "clinical ratings are problematic due to their subjectivity and imprecision" (Solomon, Clark, Makashay, & Newman, 2008, p. 257). Nonetheless, many checklists of tongue movement have been proposed and have been relied upon throughout the decades. The *Marshalla Oral Sensorimotor Test* (MOST; Marshalla, 2007a) is the only standardized test that assigns a score to a client's ability to position the tongue in basic ways using the simple visual analysis.

For the purposes of the present manual it is proposed that the basic tongue movements discussed above could make a thorough tongue movement checklist. The following features are observed as the tongue engages in speech and non-speech tasks. The most direct way to observe these movements during non-speech tasks is to have the client imitate the therapist. The checklist is designed to assess whether the tongue can move in its fundamental patterns. This checklist is not a measure of tongue strength. For information about tongue strength, please see the reference manual for the Iowa Oral Performance Instrument

(IOPI; Robin & Luschei, 1992).

Assessment Checklist

1. *Bowl shape:* The tongue utilizes a bowl- or gutter-shape as it moves around in speech and non-speech tasks. Observe the client in speech, feeding, and/or imitation tasks.

2. *Lateral bracing:* The tongue can elevate its lateral margins for lateral bracing. Have the client open his mouth wide and then say /i/ (the "E Position"). Observe the tongue as the jaw elevates and /i/ position is assumed. Check to see if the tongue spreads and elevates high on the sides as the tongue moves toward /i/ position. Alternately have the client smile with his mouth somewhat open so the back. can be seen The lateral spread should be seen during the smile.

3. *Horseshoe-shape:* The tongue can achieve a horseshoe-shape during production of /t/ or /d/. Watch and listen to the client produce these sounds. Do they look and sound correct, or is the whole tongue pressing upward without the horseshoe-shape? It may not be possible to see if the tongue is shaping into the horseshoe-shape, but if the phonemes sound correct to the ear and they look correct from the front, one can assume that the tongue is achieving the position.

4. *Lateral elevation:* The tongue is able to elevate its lateral margins to groove. Have the client open his mouth wide and then allow it to close naturally as he says /ʃ/. If the client is articulating /ʃ/ correctly, it is usually possible to see the lateral margins elevating upward toward the palate as the mouth begins to close for the sound.

5. *Tip elevation:* The tongue tip is able to elevate to the upper teeth and alveolar ridge. Have the client open his mouth wide and lift the tip to the upper teeth and then to the alveolar ridge. Does the tip do the lifting independently? The tongue will look thin if the tip lifts, but it will look thick if the blade lifts instead. The tongue will remain soft and bulbous if the jaw is doing the lifting instead of the tongue.

6. *Curl:* The tongue tip can elevate and curl up and back toward the velum. Show the client this movement and see if he can imitate you. Tell him to touch the tip of his tongue to the "punching bag" (velum) in the back. The tongue should thin and the tip should lift and curl back.

7. *Protrude:* The tongue can shift forward. Ask the client to stick out his tongue, or model it for him to imitate. It does not matter what the tip does in this case. The determination is whether the whole tongue can shift forward.

8. *Arch:* The middle of the tongue can arch upward. Observe this during production of /k/ or /g/. Ask the client to open his mouth wide and then say one of these sounds. It is usually possible to see the middle of the tongue arch upward as the mouth closes and the tongue lifts to say the sound.

9. *Groove:* The tongue tip can groove in a tiny manner to produce /s/ or /z/. The only way to test this movement is to have the client produce the phonemes. If they look and sound correct then the groove is adequate. A straw can be held in front of the maxillary (upper) central incisors for auditory assessment to determine if the groove is occurring right at the tip.

10. *Widen:* The tongue sits wide in the mouth during speech. Have the client open the mouth wide and then say /i/. The tongue should widen as the mouth closes.

11. *Narrow:* The tongue can narrow during production of /l/. Have the client open the mouth wide and then say /l/. The tongue should narrow as the tip reaches for the alveolar ridge and as the jaw elevates.

12. *Retract:* The tongue can pull back (retract) to form a ball-shape in the rear. Model this movement for the client to imitate.

13. *Tense:* The tongue can achieve enough tension for a bunched (back) /r/. The only way to test this is to ask the client to produce a bunched /r/. If the phoneme sounds correct, then the tongue is achieving enough tension.

14. *Relax:* The tongue is relaxed enough to engage in full mobility. Have the client place the tongue tip up, down, left, and right. The tongue is relaxed enough if it can achieve all these positions.

15. *Smoothness:* Observe the tongue in all the movements named above and make an assessment of the smoothness of these movements. The tongue should not demonstrate any jerkiness or hesitations.

16. *Lateral evenness:* Both sides of the tongue should move with equal range in all of the above. Some differences in movement between the two sides can be noted but they should be minimal. In other words, general symmetry is desirable but slight asymmetry is expected.

TREATMENT METHODS

The rest of this chapter is devoted to methods that have been designed to facilitate tongue movements. These techniques are scattered hither and yon throughout Phonetic Placement and Traditional Era articulation therapy textbooks, and they can also be found in more recent books on motor speech disorders, feeding therapy, dysphagia remediation, orofacial myofunctional therapy, and books with the term *oral-motor* in the title. The techniques presented below comprise a simple catalog of ideas with no hierarchy implied in their organization, although some of the earliest ideas are presented first.

When should methods to stimulate specific tongue movements be introduced in speech training? For example, how long should one model a /k/ or /g/ with no success before doing something directly to help the client lift the back of the tongue? Van Riper said that this help should be given right away. He said that a client who cannot imitate a phoneme immediately after good ear training and after being presented with a few models needs this type of instruction next. He called it the phonetic placement method as described in Chapter 1.

It is the present author's experience that together these methods can be used to teach the tongue to begin to move in all ways when it hardly moves at all, and they can be used to teach specific movements for the production of specific phonemes when a client has advanced speech skills but needs to learn a specific skill in order to produce a specific phoneme. For example, the same technique can be used to teach a client to protrude his tongue when he cannot move it at all or when he simply cannot protrude it for production of /θ/. Ideas that are not referenced are from the present author's personal clinical experiences, or they are well-known with no one citable reference. Quotes from Traditional Era textbooks are included where fitting to demonstrate that these methods have had a persistent presence throughout the history of the profession despite a lack of experimental validation.

Speech-language pathologists recognize that methods to facilitate tongue mobility will not automatically make speech change. As a practical matter, one engages in two processes simultaneously: the tongue is helped to move and the speech target is stimulated via other auditory, cognitive, and linguistic means. For example, one cannot simply teach the back of the tongue to rise and then expect a client to produce /k/. One teaches the back of the tongue to rise and one uses other input to teach the phoneme: the phoneme is modeled, a conceptual cue is offered, the ear is trained to identify the target, words are studied, and so forth. One never expects a method of tongue movement facilitation to remediate a deficiency in speech production without additional auditory, linguistic, and cognitive stimulation. To do any one of these methods alone without working directly on phonemes would make all of these

methods into *non-speech oral-motor exercises*, and that it not their purpose. These are methods to stimulate the tongue to move as needed for production of phonemes.

Visual feedback is an essential element of tongue movement therapy. The classic way to teach better tongue movement is to work in front of a mirror so clients can see all of their own tongue movements. There is also computerized equipment to help in this process. For example, the SmartPalate® is a relatively inexpensive palatometry system that can be used to monitor tongue position in real time during articulation therapy. Real-time ultrasound technology is also being used as advanced visual feedback about tongue movement for clients with articulation deficit (Byun, Hitchcock, & Swartz, 2014).

Vivify Gross Tongue Movement

Van Riper's simplest idea about stimulating tongue movement was what he called *vivifying* tongue movement (Van Riper, 1954, p. 238). To vivify means to "enliven or animate" (Jewell & Abate, 2001, p. 1889). One simply gets the tongue to move more often and with more variety before trying to get the tongue to move in specific ways for the production of specific phonemes. Van Riper explained that some clients do not recognize their tongue's full movement potential and it simply need to move more: "Variation must precede approximation" (Van Riper, 1978, p. 187). This means to pay less attention to any one specific tongue movement, to ignore the movements required for specific phonemes, and to explore and experiment with a wide variety of tongue movements instead. The idea is that any new movement is a change in the right direction. Van Riper recognized that using objects or food in the mouth to vivify its movement is a method that stretches all the way back to ancient times:

> *"The important thing about all these activities is that they introduce freedom of movement and prevent articulatory ruts. They teach the [client] to scan widely, to search far and near. New responses can only come out of variability and instability. Unless jarred out of the old pattern, the mouth can find no new ones"* (Van Riper, 1964, p. 136).

> *"Demosthenes [from ancient Greece] filled his mouth with pebbles and listened to himself as he talked. If the pebbles did anything, they probably helped to make new kinesthetic and tactile feedbacks especially vivid. And they made Demosthenes move his tongue in strange and different ways. They increased the variability of response. This stony road to success taught him to scan and search the mouth in new ways"* (Van Riper & Irwin, 1958, p. 135).

Van Riper (1954) gave advice about vivifying the tongue as follows:

- Use biological movements like chewing, swallowing, and coughing to help the client discover tongue movements.

- Encourage gross before fine tongue movements.

- Expect gradual improvement of tongue mobility over time.

- Place emphasis on tongue movements, contacts, and positions.

- Encourage movement of all parts of the tongue including the tip, blade, middle, and back.

- Work on tongue lifting, thrusting, withdrawing, curling, and grooving.

- Avoid fatigue and allow for rest periods.

- After a movement is learned, pair it with a speech sound.

- Compare, contrast, and combine various movements.

Vivify the Tongue with Creative Imagery

The classic articulation literature recommended the use of creative imagery to vivify movements of the tongue. Creative imagery is especially useful in work with young clients and older clients with limited cognitive skill. For example, many therapists use the image of *Mr. Tongue* who is always busy around his house. He "cleans the house… dusts off the roof… sweeps the floor… washes the walls… shakes out the mop… walks around the block… [and] rests behind the teeth" (Berry & Eisenson, 1956, p. 140). Mr. Tongue also opens and closes his dental door, window, or gate. He paints the interior and exterior walls of his house, and he dances, wiggles, and hops. Mr. Tongue taps on the roof to communicate with the people who live upstairs, and he searches every corner of his house for his lost socks (see full story on page 74).

Vivify the Tongue with Upward Pressure

Palmer et al. (2008) found that increasing tongue-to-palate pressure coincided with increased muscle activity in the whole tongue. They suggested that exercises in which the tongue presses against the palate could strengthen

Eating and other simple activities are used to vivify tongue movements.

This therapist is stabilizing her client's head and using food to encourage gross tongue lateralization.

floor-of-mouth muscles, tongue muscles, and jaw closing muscles. Solomon (2004) found that the tongue pressed more firmly against the palate when the jaw was not constrained by a bite block. These studies suggest that the tongue can be vivified by encouraging it to press upward against the palate without the use of a bite block. Van Riper used a sponge between the tongue tip and alveolar ridge to encourage this type of upward tongue pressure:

> *"Get a small piece of sponge rubber and sterilize it by boiling… Put it into the front of the mouth… forcing rubber to roof of mouth and compressing it with the tongue tip"* (Van Riper, 1947, p. 170).

The TonguePress® is a tool designed to teach this movement while drinking.

Vivify the Tongue with Jaw Movement

Weber and Smith (1987) found that stimulation to the jaw causes movement in the lips and tongue. Ishiwata et al. (1997) demonstrated that tongue position is reflexively controlled by jaw position. Therapeutically, these studies suggest that one of the first ways to stimulate gross early tongue movement is to stimulate gross early jaw movement: "Because the tongue rests on the jaw, tongue movement can be decomposed into movement that is due to the tongue muscles and movement that is jaw-related" (Edwards & Harris, 1990, p. 561).

Vivify the Tongue with Lip Movement

The tongue works in concert with the lips and improvements in lip function will have a positive affect on movements of the tongue. This means that one can vivify tongue movements by increasing lip mobility. (For techniques, see Chapter 12 on lip mobility.) "Labial agility has a tendency to produce lingua agility" (Berry & Eisenson, 1956, p. 139).

Vivify the Tongue with Head Movement

Therapists often get little children to move the head more as a way to encourage movement in all the oral structures including the tongue. Van Riper encouraged head movement to stimulate tongue protrusion: "Protrude tongue as far as possible… Allow head and jaw movements at first but end with head and jaw fixed" (Van Riper, 1947, p. 171).

Vivify the Tongue with Hyoid Movement

Westbury (1988) demonstrated that more hyoid bone movement occurred than did jaw movement during adult speech, suggesting that moving the hyoid bone might stimulate tongue movements while the jaw stays relatively stationary. In therapy, SLPs can use hands-on techniques to encourage the client to move the hyoid bone up and down while stabilizing the jaw on a bite block. Have the client place his fingers on his throat at the crook of the neck so he can feel the muscles move. Teach him to push the body of the tongue and hyoid up and down with the throat muscles, and to use his hands to feel the actions.

Vivify the Tongue with Hand Movements

According to a review of the literature by Rochet-Capellan, Laboissière, Galván, and Schwartz (2012) research has shown that hand and mouth movements are interrelated. Hand and mouth movements co-occur right after birth, they mutually entrain at 6–8 months during manual and oral babbling, they are produced sequentially at 9–14 months, and they are synchronized by 16–18 months of age. Therapists who work with infants, toddlers, and preschool children often take advantage of this hand-mouth relationship and vivify oral movements by stimulating hand movements. Hand movements should be of the gross motor type like squeezing clay or rummaging the hands through textured substances (sand, beans, or rice). Hand-to-mouth exploration is also encouraged with very young children through finger-feeding activities with pudding, yogurt, and other purees. With older children and adults one can rub the hands with lotions or towels, and stimulate the hands with deep pressure or vibration.

Vivify the Tongue with Cold Stimuli

Motor therapists often use cold stimuli to inhibit hypertonicity and to facilitate muscle contraction, depending upon how it is used (Farber, 1982). SLPs use cold stimuli to vivify mouth movements by having clients suck on ice, ice pops, frozen bananas, and ice cream, and by using cold metal spoons during lip and tongue movement activities.

Cold stimuli must be used cautiously. A little bit of cold stimuli seems to cause more movement, a lot of cold stimuli seems to slow and eliminate movement, and of course too much cold stimuli on the whole body can lead to hypothermia. It should be remembered that it is not the cold itself that stimulates awareness of body parts but the change in temperature (for more on this, see Chapter 16 on the tactile system). It should also be noted that there has been no research to verify that cold stimuli will improve tongue function for speech. In fact one study demonstrated that scheduled applications of cold stimuli on the tongue did not improve its swallowing movements in adults with dysphagia following stroke (Rosenbek, Robbins, Fishback, & Levine, 1991).

Increase Tongue-Jaw Independence

One of the most important elements of therapy is to help the tongue to move independently from the jaw. The principle way therapists accomplish this is to stabilize the jaw because stabilizing the jaw forces the tongue to begin to move. This is a concept that has had frequent representation all throughout the literature. Van Riper and Irwin discussed this as part of their writing on cerebral palsy:

> *"In general, the child with cerebral palsy has inadequate control of her tongue… In most of these cases, the essential task is to free the tongue from its tendency to move only in conjunction with the lower jaw"* (Van Riper & Erickson,

1996, p. 411).

Research has substantiated this idea for general tongue function. For example, Folkins and Abbs (1975) demonstrated that the lips and tongue move in ways that compensate for a jaw that is immobilized. They called this tendency "online compensatory motor reorganization" (p. 207). In other words, stabilizing the jaw forces the tongue to move more. Most therapists do this by giving the client a probe on which to bite with the molars. Other methods are described in Chapter 14 on oral stability. The following example is from Nemoy and Davis (1937):

> *"The insertion of the broad side of a tongue depressor between the side teeth and holding it steady while repeating t, t, t, in rapid succession will assist in securing independent action of the tongue"* (p. 90).

Controlling Voluntary Movement

The classic writers of articulation therapy used the term *tongue exercises* and *tongue gymnastics* to refer to the types of tongue movement activities designed to exercise weak or inactive muscles of the tongue and to learn how to control its movement. This was a process of getting the client to move his tongue in gross yet specific ways with full voluntary control. The client usually performed these activities by imitating a therapist's model. Van Riper said that these exercises were of limited usefulness yet they continue to have a small place in articulation therapy. These procedures orientate clients to their own tongue and prepare the tongue for other more intricate speech movements. The following tongue exercises are copied verbatim from ASHA president Lee Edwards Travis (1931):

- With the tongue pointed, move it outward and downward toward the chin.

- With the tongue pointed, move it outward and upward toward the nose, touching the nose if possible.

- With the tongue protruded between the lips, wag the tip up and down as rapidly as possible.

- Rotate the tongue around the outside of the mouth. This should be done in both the clockwise and counter-clockwise direction.

- Protrude the tongue and form a groove through the center by raising both sides.

- With the mouth wide open, curl the tip of the tongue back to the upper teeth.

- Press the tip of the tongue against the backs of the lower teeth until it rolls forward and out between the upper and lower front teeth.

- Move the tongue in and out of the mouth as rapidly as possible.

- Press the tip of the tongue against the backs of the upper teeth until it rolls forward and out between the upper and lower front teeth.

- With the tongue pointed, dot the roof of the mouth in three places: front, middle and back.
- Scrape the roof of the mouth with the point of the tongue going from front to back.

Increase Range of Tongue Movements

While a client is just learning to get the tongue to move, he should also be learning to increase its range of movement. This means activating the tongue muscles to contract and relax to their fullest capacity and to influence the extent to which the tongue can flex, extend, lateralize, and rotate around its axes. Increasing range of tongue movement is an application of the principle that gross movements are learned before refined movements. One works to extend tongue movements in all directions so the client can acquire its full range before he must control it in the smaller range required for speech.

Increasing range of movement is a term borrowed from the motor therapies, but the original writers in the field used this idea as well. They called it *increasing the flexibility of the articulators*. Traditional Era writers taught clients to slow down their speech in order to help them improve range of oral movement. Slowing down gives the client more time to stretch fully into the tongue positions he is trying to assume:

> *"Flexibility of the muscles involved tends to give smoothness, proper adjustment, lightness, and dexterity, all of which adds greatly to the attainment of clear distinct speech"* (Greene & Wells, 1927, p. 223).

Casual observation of countless babies in informal settings by the present author has revealed that infants often produce certain pre-speech vocalizations while learning to move the tongue to its full range. The author has named these sounds as follows: *blubbing, blalling, dlelling, lerring,* and *lateral lerring.* These are some of the gross sounds that can be stimulated when working with clients who have an extremely limited variety of tongue movements and vocal behavior. The goal for these clients is to get them to produce more sound with a wider range of gross tongue movement.

Blubbing

The child pokes the tongue forward and then brings it back into the mouth while vocalizing. The mouth is not open very much, therefore, the tongue's upper surface rubs gently forward and backward against the alveolar ridge, the upper anterior gum ridge, and the upper lip. The result is a primitive /b/-like sound as the tongue passes by the lips, and a primitive /l/-like sound as the tongue brushes against the alveolar ridge. The vowel /ʌ/ dominates throughout. The result is "bluh" as the tongue moves forward, and "lub" as the tongue moves back in. Thus "blubbing" is the name of the sound.

Blalling

The child sticks his tongue out and down as far as possible against the lower lip and chin while vocalizing. The child is seeking to discover just how far out and down his tongue will stretch. On its way out of the mouth, the tongue brushes against the lips causing a /b/-like sound, it brushes against the alveolar ridge causing an /l/-like sound, and the mouth opens to its full extent causing the vowel /ɑ/ to dominate. The result is a sound that combines primitive forms of /b/, /l/, and /ɑ/. Thus "blalling" is the name of the sound. Once fully extended, an infant often will rub the under surface of the tongue against the lower lip and chin, causing the tongue to move left and right as he "blalls."

Dlelling

Sometime between four and six months of age, the anterior teeth begin to emerge, and a baby will use the tip of his tongue to explore them. He rubs the tongue tip forward and backward against the lower surface of the emerging maxillary (upper) central incisors while vocalizing. The result is a primitive /d/-like sound, a primitive /l/-like sound, and a primitive /e/. Thus "dlelling" is the name of the sound.

Lerring

Sometime during the first year of life, while he is learning to poke his fingers into a variety of holes, an infant will begin to explore the depths of his oral cavity. He does so with his fingers, his toys, and with his tongue. He is discovering the length and breadth of his oral cavity. The tongue stretches to the back of the oral cavity by curling its tip up and back all the way to the soft palate. In the process, the infant will feel the entire length of the hard and soft palates with his tongue tip. If he does this while vocalizing, the result will be a primitive /l/-like sound when the tip is at the alveolus, a primitive /r/-like sound when the tip is at the velum, and a primitive /e/ throughout the process. Thus "lerring" is the name of the sound. Babies do this at both a fast and a slow pace.

Lateral Lerring

Infants also learn how to move their tongues left-to-right across the midline. They do this both inside and outside the mouth. Lateralizing the tongue left to right while vocalizing results in a primitive /l/-like sound that shifts in acoustic quality as the tongue tip sweeps left and right. The sound is called "lateral lerring" as a result. Babies do this both fast and slow. Many therapists have questioned the advisability of teaching clients to wag the tongue back and forth, asking, "What does this have to do with speech?" Babies figure out how to move the tongue laterally as they are learning their full range of tongue movements. This is an early step in learning to separate tongue movements from jaw movements, and it helps the tongue move in a gross manner so that it can learn to move in a small manner later.

Facilitate Tongue Bowling

The tongue's most fundamental gross movement pattern is one of bowling — elevation of the perimeter of the tongue while the middle remains depressed. Stimulating a tongue bowl has been discussed as an important component of speech, singing, and swallowing instruction by a variety of authors throughout many decades, and a wide variety of methods have been advocated to stimulate it.

Spoon

Van Riper (1947) used a spoon to teach his clients how to bowl or cup the tongue as a preliminary step toward developing a central groove. He suggested placing the bowl of the spoon on the front of the tongue after the client has relaxed it. Then he taught the client to squeeze and lift the spoon with the sides of his tongue. After success was gained, Van Riper had the client do it with an imaginary spoon, and then he did it without a spoon and with the teeth together. This spoon technique creates a very large bowl pattern that will be shaped into the central groove. Measuring spoons might be best for this activity so that the size of the spoon can be adjusted from large to small. Also, consider using infant spoons, feeding therapy spoons, or melon-ballers. Using a spoon to teach a tongue bowl is a basic feeding procedure: "Use slight downward pressure with the bowl of the spoon during feeding" (Morris & Klein, 2000, p. 435).

Light Touch

Light touch can be used to stimulate the tongue bowl reflex:

> *"Touching or stroking a baby's tongue elicits a spoon-shaped lingual configuration, characterized by an upraised ridge around its outer border... A similar posture could be elicited in adulthood by repeatedly touching, lightly stroking, or directing a stream of air across the tongue"* (Fletcher, 1992, p. 10–11).

Tap the Middle

Repetitive tapping can be used to stimulate the tongue bowl reflex:

> *"Tap the middle of the tongue with a tongue depressor... The purpose of this exercise is to stimulate the involuntary reflex, similar to the grasp reflex, that depresses the middle portion of the tongue in response to a stimulus"* (Hanson & Barrett, 1988, p. 278–279).

Feel Hyoid Movement

Lowering of the tongue's middle is caused in part by contracting the muscles that form the base of the tongue and that attach it to the hypoid bone below, and the hyoid connects to the larynx with additional muscles. Clients, therefore, can learn to lower the body of the tongue to create a bowl by discovering how to contract these lower muscles. Have the client stabilize the jaw on a bite block. Then have him place his fingers on his throat at the crook of the neck so he can feel the movements. Teach him to move the body of the tongue upwards and downwards by using the muscles attached to the hyoid bone and by lowering the larynx. His hands and fingers will feel the movement.

Bolus Control Activities

Activities to develop a tongue bowl are also found in the dysphagia literature. Jeri Logemann was a president of ASHA in 1994 and again in 2000 and she received ASHA's Honors of the Association in 2003. She was known for her expertise in articulation before she became instrumental in the establishment of dysphagia as a valid area of study for SLPs and she wrote the first major text on dysphagia assessment and treatment in the field (Logemann, 1983). To improve skill in bolus formation, Logemann recommended a series of methods she called *indirect therapy techniques*. These included activities to improve the tongue bowl.

Activities to Improve Gross Manipulation of Materials

Train clients to form the tongue into a bowl by manipulating food. Logemann suggested starting with food the therapist can control like a large flexible licorice whip. Progress to a small Life Saver® tied to a string. Then advance to a very small amount of liquid and, finally, to

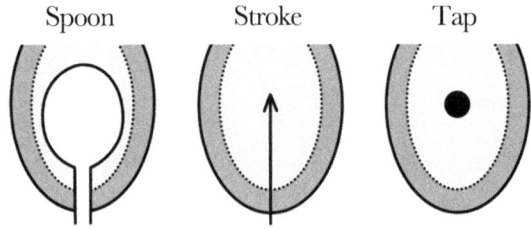

Spoon   Stroke   Tap

Van Riper (1947) used a spoon to encourage tongue bowling (left), Fletcher (1992) recommended a light stroke (middle), and Hanson and Barrett (1983) recommended tapping the middle (right).

A client can feel the action of the tongue's muscular attachments to the hyoid bone as they work to depress the middle of the tongue.

chewing gum. Encourage the client to move the tongue in all directions and to form the tongue into a bowl with each item. Include "manipulating the material from side to side in the mouth without losing control" (Logemann, 1983, p. 134).

Activities to Hold a Cohesive Bolus

Once the client can achieve the movements required in the activity described above, therapy moves on to food manipulation. Place a bolus of food on the client's tongue and encourage him to move it around in the mouth: "This requires that the patient cup the tongue around the bolus" (Logemann, 1983, p. 135). The bolus is varied in size, and the progression is from thick paste to thin liquid. Once this skill is achieved, activities to propel the bolus from the oral cavity to the oropharynx are begun.

Cough and Gag Reflexes

Van Riper (1939) suggested that coughing could be used to create a large midline bowl. Encourage the client to cough gently as he watches his tongue in a mirror. Point out the high elevation of the tongue's sides that occurs (if it does). Then encourage the client to pretend he is coughing. The sides should elevate again. Then teach him to place his tongue in that position again simply through voluntary control. Read more about the cough in Chapter 17, *The Speech Reflexes*.

Marshalla noted that the tongue also forms a deep bowl shape during the gag (Rosenwinkel Marshalla, 1985). The gag reflex is used as a last resort when the tongue functions so poorly that it does not groove or bowl; it remains thick and bunched and does not widen. The client should be reassured that it is normal to gag. Most clients prefer to gag themselves for this activity. The reader can learn more about this reflex in Chapter 17.

Verbal Instructions

Some clients can cup or bowl the tongue voluntarily when given simple verbal instructions: "Protrude the tongue and try to cup the edges. Retract the tongue inside the mouth attempting to maintain some semblance of this shaping" (Bosley, 1981, p. 67).

Coughing and gagging both cause automatic tongue bowling in clients with normal neurological function.

Schematic Illustrations and Models

Some clients can achieve a tongue bowl by imitating a physical model. The SLP can perform the movement with her own tongue for the client to imitate. Draw pictures or use an appropriate model of the tongue or mouth. Also, one can use a hand to model the similarities between the hand's ability to grasp and the tongue's ability to bowl.

Facilitate Tongue Grooving

Many writers have discussed ways to facilitate the tongue's central groove for production of the sibilants and other phonemes. As noted above, tongue grooving is not the same as tongue bowling, although they are nearly the same. *Grooving* the tongue means to lift the sides of the tongue while depressing the midline from tip to back. The *midline groove* has also been called the *central channel* or *trough*.

Some methods to develop grooving work to pull the midline of the tongue down while others work to lift the sides of the tongue up. Some of these methods are more effective than others, and some require higher levels of cognitive skill on the part of the client. No hierarchy is suggested in the following series of activities although some of the earliest and simplest methods are presented first.

Unclear Tongue Exercises

This is probably the least effective yet most widely recommended method discussed in Traditional Era articulation therapy textbooks: the generic *tongue exercise*. Many writers recommended that clients be taught to groove the tongue by engaging in tongue exercises, but they rarely told how to do this. For example, in discussing the stimulation of a groove for /s/, Nemoy and Davis wrote:

> "When the sound is not easily secured through imitation or through the additional aids suggested, it is advisable to provide exercises involving raising and lowering, widening and narrowing, and grooving the tongue" (Nemoy & Davis, 1937, p. 152).

Presumably these authors intended that the client simply imitate the therapist's model of tongue grooving. Some clients can comply with this simple direction and others cannot.

Describe the Channel

Another method that appears regularly throughout articulation books is simply to describe the groove. Again, this technique works wonderfully well as long as the client can understand what is being said and can do it without any type of assistance or stimulation. Simply telling a client to make a groove is a method that has been carried over into newer articulation guides, for example: "Tell the client to groove the tongue and then attempt /s/" (Secord et al., 2007, p. 38).

Assist Lateral Lifting

The authors of the motokinesthetic method (Young & Hawk, 1955) suggested assisting elevation of the tongue's lateral margins by placing a tongue depressor under each side of the tongue and simply lifting. The term *passive assistance* has been used to describe this method, meaning that the client must relax the tongue and let the therapist lift. Passive assistance such as this will give the client an idea of the lifting process, but it will not actually stimulate his tongue muscles to do the lifting themselves, and most clients cannot really tell what is being done with the depressors. Assistance is not nearly as effective as the method of using *resistance* as described below.

Manually lifting the lateral margins of the tongue is a common sense idea that may work for some clients but the process can be cumbersome for several reasons: (1) because there is not much room between the teeth and the sides of the tongue, (2) because it can be uncomfortable for the client when a tongue depressor is stuck between his side teeth and tongue, (3) because often the whole tongue lifts when one tries to lift the sides only, and (4) because many clients tense up the whole mouth during the process and this spoils the results.

Tactile Cue

Another motokinesthetic method for creating a central groove is to cue the sides to lift by pressing in on the outer cheeks at a point lateral to the points of articulation: "Tell the client to bite down slightly on the back teeth. Use your index finger and thumb to touch the outside of the cheeks at the location of the juncture of the upper first and second molar" (Secord et al., 2007, p. 38). Then tell him to press the sides of his tongue laterally toward the stimuli to create the central groove. The inward pressure on the cheeks works as a direction cue. It stimulates the client to understand which part of the tongue is to move and in which direction. This method works only with clients whose tongue already bowls automatically and who can understand the directions.

Draw the Central Groove on the Tongue

Most texts suggest using a tongue depressor or another probe to draw a line down the midline of the tongue in order to give the client the concept of the central groove. This method has been passed down from one therapist to another through the generations and is represented in some of the newest articulation guides, for example: "Use a tongue depressor and trace a line through the center of his tongue to give the client the idea of a trough" (Secord et al., 2007, p. 38). The method was developed for clients with upper level articulation errors and it may be useful only in the mildest of cases where the tongue bowl already is established and the client already has nearly complete control of his tongue. However, the method may also set off the tongue bowl reflex and as such may work with more severe oral-motor problems.

Visual Imagery

Speech correctionists taught the image of making the tongue into "hills and a valley" to create a central groove. The "hills" are the lateral margins of the tongue that rise up; the "valley" is the low midline. This is a creative idea that therapists have used for decades but no direct reference to it could be found in the preparation of this manual.

Illustrations and Models

Many authors have also recommended using schematic illustrations and models of the mouth and tongue to learn about the sides of the tongue and their role in creating a midline channel. Draw pictures or use an appropriate model of the tongue or mouth. Also, use a hand to model the similarities between the hands ability to groove and the tongue's ability to groove. Van Riper and others recommended drawing palatograms for this purpose: "For centuries, speech correctionists have used diagrams… to ensure appropriate tongue… placement" (Van Riper, 1954, p. 236–8).

Electropalatography

Electropalatography is being used to teach clients to lift the tongue to the palate in appropriate patterns. For example, Dagenais, Critz-Crosby, and Adams (1994) used the system to teach two clients with lateral lisps to lift the lateral margins of their tongues to their palates to create a midline groove. Their treatment results were mixed. The problem with this system is that it removes the tactile experience of the tongue touching the real palate. This equipment is also expensive although the price is reducing over time. Some outreach programs are providing this equipment for therapists to rent. Please see information about the SmartPalate in Chapter 19, *The Tools of Speech*

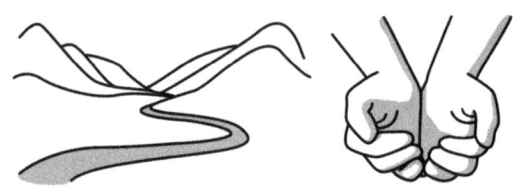

Hills and valleys as well as the hands provide appropriate imagery for developing the central groove.

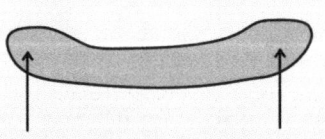

Assist elevation of the sides of the tongue by placing a probe under the sides and lifting.

Movement Training.

Sucking for a Tiny Groove at the Tip

Van Riper suggested creating a midline channel by asking the client to press the tongue tip against the upper front teeth and then to suck air in. Done correctly, air will rush in over the tip of the tongue when the tip is lowered slightly. Once the client learns to inhale in this way, teach him to exhale through that same port and a rudimentary /s/ will be produced (Van Riper, 1947, p. 172).

This type of sucking can also be done with a spoon. Place a thick puree like pudding or applesauce on the tip of a spoon bowl and place the tip at the mid-point of the lower lip. Ask the client to bring the lips and tongue tip forward to sip the puree off the spoon.

E Position (for a Wide Groove in the Back)

Using the association method, many speech correctionists and even some elocutionists used /i/ or /j/ to teach a wide groove for the palatal sibilants. It is known now that the tongue's articulation to the palate is essentially the same for /i/ as it is for the palatal sibilants. To teach a wide groove for these sibilants, have the client produce an exaggerated /i/ and then exhale in this position without voice and without moving the tongue out of its elevated lateral position. The result will be a gross non-English sound made with a wide but wonderful midline groove. The addition of lip rounding will make it sound like /ʃ/. Help the client experiment with lip rounding and retracting and with jaw elevation or depression in order to influence the width and loci of this central groove and the acoustic quality of /ʃ/. Van Riper used this procedure and described it like this: "Ask the child to round his lips, and raise the tongue, and shut the teeth, as he whispers a prolonged *ee*" (Van Riper, 1947, p 191).

T Position (for a Tiny Groove at the Tip)

Most therapists used /t/ to teach a tiny central groove at the tongue tip for /s/. This is an excellent use of the association method as long as the client is making his /t/ with correct stability in the back and correct tongue-tip placement at the alveolar ridge. One can also use /d/ to teach /z/ in the same way. This method appears time and again in articulation books old and new:

> *"Have the child begin by forming a /t/ in a word like tea. Have him pronounce it with a strong aspiration (tuh-hee), with a strong puff of breath after the explosion of the /t/, before the vowel begins. Then, instead of this sudden explosion or puff, take away the tip of the tongue from the teeth ridge slowly. This will give the sound /ts/. Hold on to this sound and you will have a prolonged /s/. The child must not think he is saying /ts/ as in the word oats or he will use his usual pronunciation"* (Van Riper, 1947, p. 190).

> *"Make /t/... with strong aspiration on the release... Prolong the strongly aspirated release... Remove the tip of the tongue slowly during the release from the alveolar ridge to make a /ts/ cluster... Prolong the /s/ part of the /ts/ cluster in a word like oats... Practice prolonging the last portion of the /ts/ production... Practice 'sneaking up quietly' on the /s/ (delete /t/)... Produce /s/"* (Bernthal & Bankson, 2004, p. 302).

Prevent Tongue-Tip Elevation

A phonetic placement technique designed to teach /s/ from /t/ is to use a thin probe to prevent the tongue tip from lifting too high as the client says /t/. A dental pick is perfect tool to use for this purpose. Poke the dental pick between the maxillary (upper) central incisors so that its tip sits between the alveolar ridge and tongue tip. Angle the handle of the pick up and down so that its tip presses down on the tongue tip as the client says /t/. It should cause the /t/ to sound more like /s/. This is one of the phonetic placement techniques that Scripture brought back from Germany and taught to Van Riper's generation:

> *"One cure consists in inserting a probe, an applicator, a toothpick, or a pencil just over the middle of the tongue and pressing it down as the person begins to speak a word beginning with 's'. [The client] cannot close the passage completely, and instead of saying 't' he is forced to say 's'"* (Scripture, 1912, p. 133).

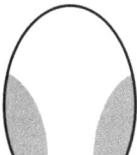

Long E   Palatal Sibilants

The tongue's points of articulation with the palate are essentially the same for long E and the palatal sibilants.

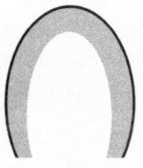
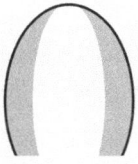

/t/ and /d/   /s/ and /z/

Tongue positions for /t/ and /d/ can be used to teach tongue position for /s/ and /z/.

Curl the Tongue Lengthwise Around an Object

Various authors have recommended teaching the central groove by having the client curl the tongue around a slender object. It is noted that some clients automatically curl the sides of the tongue up too high, creating a tongue curl that is much too exaggerated for use in speech. The procedure does train the client to pull the sides up, however, so let him do it that way at first and then teach him to pull it up more gently and with more controlled refinement.

Tongue Depressor

Place a tongue depressor flat down on the tongue at midline: "With the tongue depressor in place, the client attempts to curl the sides of the tongue up around the edges" (Hanson, 1983, p. 228).

Spoon

Van Riper used a spoon to create a central groove. Place the bowl of a spoon on the middle of the tongue with the bowl facing up and curl the lateral margins of the tongue upward and around it.

Orange Sticks

Many textbooks suggested using an orange stick to create a central groove. An orange stick is a stick of wood from an orange tree that has a tapered end and is used in nail manicuring; now they are ususaly made of plastic or metal. Place the stick lengthwise along the midline of the tongue, and ask the client to curl the tongue up along the sides to cradle it: "Groove the tongue along the median raphe with a slender orange stick, and ask the child to curl his tongue around the stick" (Berry & Eisenson, 1956, p. 148).

Probes

Swizzle sticks, lollipop sticks, toothbrush handles, and the handle of a Toothette® can be used for this same procedure.

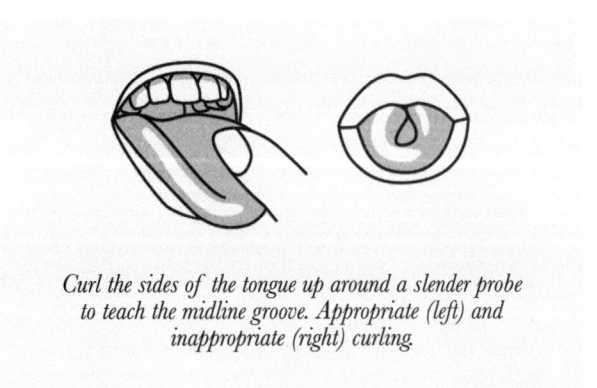

Curl the sides of the tongue up around a slender probe to teach the midline groove. Appropriate (left) and inappropriate (right) curling.

Mark the Target

Many writers have suggested using tactile stimulation on the lateral portions of the palate in order to teach the client to elevate and articulate the lateral margins of the tongue there. This process has been called *marking the target* of articulation. The idea is to provide some type of tactile stimulation to the skin on the palate just inside the molars and then to teach the client to press the lateral margins of his tongue up against those points. Use a probe to apply the stimulus or have the client use his own finger, or simply have the client use the inner surfaces of the molars themselves as his guides for the sides of his tongue.

Some authors have recommended the use of flavored cotton swabs for this procedure, however, a dry textured stimulus will be the best. Adding taste and smell to a speech movement activity increases arousal and attention to make an activity more interesting and amusing, but stimulating taste and smell actually can make perception of place of articulation more confusing for the client because the tactile stimulus occurs at one place while the taste and smell stimuli occur in many places simultaneously which can be confusing for the client. For the best results, stick to a tasteless tool with a dry, rough texture and touch exactly where the contact should be made. (See Chapter 16 more information about taste, scent, and oral movement.)

Tactile Guides

Many writers have suggesting placing a small safe object between the molars or on the inner surfaces of the molars to teach elevation of the tongue's lateral margins for the groove. The objects serve as tactile guides. People have used gum, candy, and orthodontic bands in the past. Knotted dental floss guides and interdental picks are the safest options.

- *Knotted dental floss:* Vaughn and Clark (1979, p. 56–60) described this method. They said to tie a bundle of knots at the end of a piece of dental floss 15 inches long. Place the floss between the lateral teeth on one side, and pull side so that the knot sits on the lingual surfaces of the molars. Do this on both sides: "The knot should be large enough so that it will not pull through the space, while the strand is small enough to slip easily between closely spaced teeth" (p. 56). Teach the client to reach the sides of the tongue up in order to touch the knots situated inside the upper teeth. Place the knotted dental guides between the back molars for a wide groove, and between the canine teeth and bicuspids for a narrow groove.

- *Interdental picks:* An interdental pick can be used instead of dental floss to accomplish the idea above. An interdental pick is a plastic toothpick (sometimes with soft, rubbery bristles) that is so thin that it fits between the teeth and functions like dental floss. Place an interdental pick between the upper molars

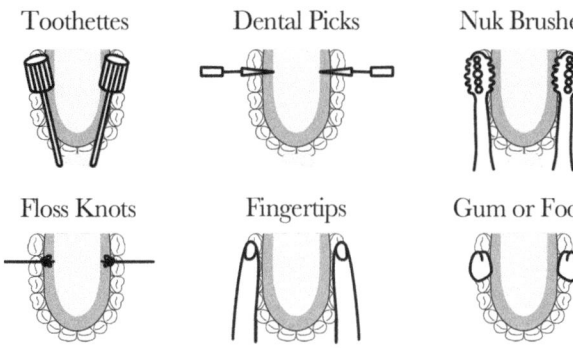

Toothettes   Dental Picks   Nuk Brushes

Floss Knots   Fingertips   Gum or Food

A variety of tools can be used to mark the target and to use as tactile guides for lateral elevation.

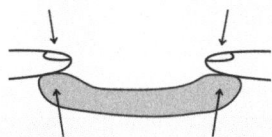

Use resistance to teach elevation of the lateral margins. The fingers push down gently while the lateral margins push up.

on both sides so that the tips poke between the teeth and touch the lateral margins of the tongue. Have the client press the sides of the tongue against the points.

• *Chewing gum:* Have the client chew a piece of gum until it is soft, then divide it into two wads. Have him place one wad between his molars on his right and the other between the molars on his left. Teach him to hold the wads in place with the sides of his tongue. This will spread the sides laterally and help the tongue form a central groove. This is a method that has been passed down from one therapist to another throughout the generations but it is one for which no written reference could be found. Make sure to use this method only with clients who have an adequate swallow.

• *Small food bits:* Use small food bits to teach lateral spreading. Use cereal O's, soft candy, raisins, or cake decorator candies. Place a food bit between the molars on both sides. Teach the client to hold the food bits in place with his teeth and the sides of his tongue. Food bits can be very motivating for some children but they are quite distracting for others and they can increase drooling, so select clients wisely for this procedure. This is another method that has been passed down from one therapist to another throughout the generations but for which no written reference could be found. Make sure to use this method only with clients who are cleared for oral swallows of small food bits.

• *Orthodontic bands:* Tiny little orthodontic elastics have been used to motivate lateral elevation of the tongue for creation of the central groove: "The elastics help the client to know when the tongue sides are in contact with the teeth or gums" (Hanson, 1983, p. 230). Swallowing these tiny bands is generally not a problem because they will simply pass through the gastrointestinal system, but make sure to use this method only with clients who have adequate swallow skill.

Bouncing and Patting

Morris and Klein discussed techniques to inhibit tongue humping or bunching in order to encourage more lateral tongue elevation and central grooving: "Treatment approaches… often include downward bouncing or patting on the tongue" (Morris & Klein, 2000, p. 607).

Resistance

As has been noted in many places throughout this manual, resistance may be the most powerful tool for helping create new oral movement. To create a central groove means to elevate the lateral margins of the tongue, therefore, use resistance against this lateral elevation, which makes the movement more distinct to the client and it helps him to lift high: "If the elevation is difficult, have him work on lifting the sides of the tongue against resistance" (Hanson, 1983, p. 228).

Use a firm probe such as a Nuk® massager brush, ARK's Oral Motor Probe, or a tongue depressor, or have the client use his own fingers. Place the tool on the lateral margins of the tongue, and ask the client to push upward with those parts of the tongue. A dental floss holder with two prongs enables pressing down on both lateral margins simultaneously. Also, use a sanitized finger: "Place your finger on the top of the tongue at the back lateral margin of one side. Push down as you ask the child to push up. Repeat on both sides" (Rosenwinkel Marshalla, 1985, p. 334). Teach clients to use their own fingers on their own tongues for the best results.

Butterfly Position

Marshalla teaches the *butterfly position* to develop lateral margin elevation (Marshalla, 1992a). The activity creates a huge central channel with high elevation of the sides and deep midline grooving. The resultant channel will be very large. Subsequent elevation of the jaw will help reduce its size.

"Teach the client to bite down with the molars on the lateral margins of the tongue on both sides simultaneously… Teach the client to use the sides of the tongue to push upwards against the upper molars in the back. When the sides of the tongue elevate, the midline should depress forming the tongue into a bowl-shaped position sometimes called the 'butterfly' position. The mouth should open wide

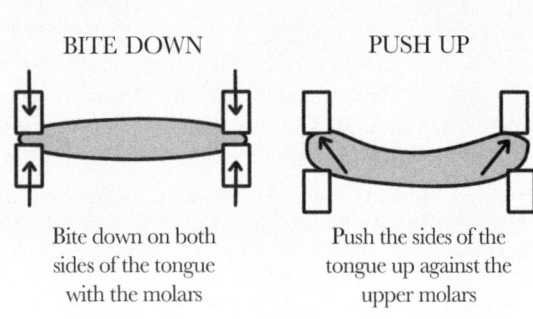

BITE DOWN   PUSH UP

Bite down on both   Push the sides of the
sides of the tongue   tongue up against the
with the molars   upper molars

The butterfly method for teaching the sides of the tongue
to elevate.

very important consideration when working with any dysarthric client, especially when muscle tone is different on the two sides.

To engage midline integration, use a rough tool like a tongue scraper with a rough shovel, place it sideways on the upper tongue surface at midline and then stroke with a little downward pressure from midline to the left. Then, in one continuous motion, sweep the scraper from left, across midline, to the right lateral margin. The tongue should flatten and flair as the scraper stimulates the midline and left, the flattening should continue as the scraper moves across midline to the right, and the right lateral margins should elevate as the scraper approaches the right lateral margin.

as the client pushes up higher and higher" (Marshalla, 1992a, p. 115).

Brushing

Sometimes the lateral placement of the tongue sides for creation of a midline groove is aided by simply enhancing the client's perception of the sides of his tongue. This is accomplished by stroking the sides of the tongue with a textured object:

> *"If the client is unable to tell whether or where lingual contact is being made, try stroking the extreme lateral, upper surface of the tongue, from back to front, alternating from one side to the other"* (Hanson, 1983, p. 229).

Many have recommended the use of flavored cotton swabs for this procedure but the dry textural stimulation works best. Cotton swabs are smooth and, therefore, less effective than a textured tool, and taste and smell do not get to the heart of the matter. The olfactory and gustatory senses do not need to be stimulated; for the best results, stick to a tool with a dry, rough texture to stimulate the tactile system. Use a toothbrush, a Nuk® massager brush, a Toothette®, wads of gum, or the client's own fingers.

Zigzag Stroke

Stimulate the lateral margins to rise by stroking the tongue up and down the midline, and then zigzagging the brush strokes toward the lateral margins. Ask the client to push the parts of the tongue being brushed up slightly toward the brush strokes. This causes the tongue to elevate from midline-to-sides in a stripping or wave pattern that ends with high elevation on the sides.

Advanced Crossing-the-Midline Stroke

The ultimate act of lateral tongue elevation is to stimulate the two sides of the tongue to elevate simultaneously. When this occurs, one can be assured that the tongue bowl response is integrated into the movements of the tongue's two hemispheres simultaneously. This can be a

Vibrate the Tongue

Vibration is more powerful than stroking and has been recommended to stimulate the tongue groove. The Z-Vibe® is an excellent tool for this procedure: "Invite the child to put a vibrating toy or massager in his mouth so that the surface of his tongue receives vibratory stimuli. This type of stimulation often activates that tongue to curl around the toy, frequently encouraging or enhancing the central groove" (Morris & Klein, 2000, p. 436).

Tubes, Straws and Circles

Writers suggested the use of tubes, straws, or circles cut in paper to direct a medial channel of air. These are phonetic placement methods that do not actually get the tongue to groove; rather, they help the client use his ear to monitor the result of producing sound through the midline groove. The method is especially good when teaching sibilants.

- *Tube:* Therapists once used rubber tubes and present-day therapists can use vinyl ones: "Have the patient practice emitting expired breath streams thru a small hole in the under surface of a hollow, hard rubber tube" (Borden & Busse, 1925, p. 184).

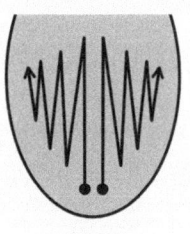 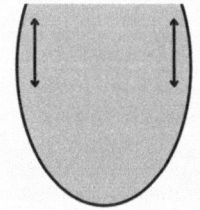

Stimulate the lateral
margins to rise by
stroking in a zigzag
pattern from midline to
one side at a time. (Start
at the dots and work
toward the sides.)

Brush along
the tongue's
lateral margins
to increase
awareness there.

- *Listening tube:* Place one end of a long narrow vinyl tube at the client's mouth, on the outside of the teeth at midline. Place the other end at his ear. Have the client make a sibilant into the tube and listen at his ear. If the client has made a midline airstream, the sound will travel through the tube. If he has not made a midline airstream, then it will not (Hanson, 1983, p. 229).

- *Circle:* "A large circle with a small hole in the center may also be placed over the mouth to suggest a central emission of the breath and to inhibit the escape of breath at the corners of the mouth" (Nemoy & Davis, 1937, p. 152).

- *Straw:* "Blow air into a straw held just in front of the space between the upper two medial incisors… The technique seems to suggest to the client centering the air and thus indirectly brings about central grooving of the tongue" (Bosley, 1981, p. 66). Use wide straws to teach the concept of the midline airstream, and use narrow straws (such as coffee stirrer straws) to teach the client to narrow the groove.

- *Fingers:* Many therapists have client's use their own fingers to discover and monitor the airflow that results from a central groove. Have the client place his fingers in front of the mouth to feel the airstream escape medially. Many clients can feel an airstream more easily when the back of the fingers or the hand is used: "The forefinger should be held vertically close to the central opening of the mouth to suggest to the pupil the presence of a narrow stream of breath emitted centrally" (Nemoy & Davis, 1937, p. 152).

Facilitate Tongue-Back Lowering

Methods to teach the back of the tongue to lower below neutral position are necessary to thin the tongue and eliminate a guttural sound. It may also be necessary for clients who elevate the back of the tongue for /l/ instead of lifting the tip in a retroflex /l/ position.

Produce /ɑ/

A client who can produce a good /ɑ/ can use it to learn how to keep the back of the tongue low. Have the client watch himself produce /ɑ/ with the mouth wide open while watching in a mirror. The base of the tongue should lower. Help him take voluntary control of the movement.

Yawn

Have the client yawn while watching in a mirror. The base of the tongue should lower. Help him take voluntary control of the movement.

Gag

Have the client gag while watching in a mirror. The base of the tongue should lower. Help him take voluntary

Straws of various diameters placed outside the teeth catch the midline airstream and teach the size of the airstream.

Extra Wide Straw   Wide Straw   Regular Soda Straw   Coffee Stirrer Straw

control of the movement.

Feel the Tongue Base

Have the client hold his neck at the crook. Teach him to lower the tongue base voluntarily. Say, "Pull this down." Have him practice the movement several times.

Facilitate Tongue Anchoring

Methods to teach the tongue to anchor at the back-lateral margins are discussed in Chapter 14 on oral stability.

Facilitate Light Tongue-to-Palate Articulation

Light tongue-to-palate articulation is an important aspect of mature speech because it allows a client to produce frication. Immature tongue movements often do not allow frication to occur because the tongue usually bangs too firmly against the palate and stops the airflow. Light touch articulation of the tongue to the palate seems to emerge as mature and refined tongue movements develop. Therefore, all the methods of this chapter that are designed to facilitate maturation of tongue movement should work to develop this type of fine motor control of the tongue. Learning to press the tongue gently toward the palate to create frication often is only a matter of ear training; therefore, use auditory discrimination methods to teach the client how to listen carefully to the frication being modeled. Slight amplification of the sound through a tube or straw is quite effective. Bosley suggested that verbal descriptions would help: "Encourage very light contact by suggestions, analogies, demonstrations, etc." (Bosley, 1981, p. 43).

Facilitate Tongue Protrusion

Protruding the tongue (moving it forward) is important for production of /θ/ and /ð/. It is also important to unlock the potential full range of tongue movements and to differentiate tongue from jaw movements. There are many simple ways to encourage tongue protrusion.

Verbal Directions

Protrusion of the tongue is a simple concept, therefore, merely telling the client to stick out his tongue may be all that is needed to get the client to do it: "Instruct the student, 'Please stick out your tongue'" (Bleile, 2006, p. 22–23).

Visual Model

Tongue protrusion can be seen and therefore the therapist's live model of tongue protrusion is always provided. For example, when teaching /θ/: "Demonstrate the difference between the place of production for /s/ and the place of production for /θ/" (Bleile, 2006, p. 22).

Assist Tongue Protrusion

To assist tongue protrusion means to give physical assistance to the tongue's forward movement. Grasp the front of the tongue and gently pull the whole tongue forward. Remember that this is passive movement on the part of the client, and he will have to relax the tongue for this to work. This type of assistance will not activate the muscles involved in protrusion, but it will give the client a sense of moving forward. Be cautious while pulling the tongue forward and see the notes on page 229 about care and best practices when grasping the tongue.

Resist Tongue Protrusion

Resistance to tongue protrusion is perhaps the easiest, most direct, and most powerful way to activate all the muscles involved in the movement. Place an object on the anterior point of the tongue tip and press back (rearward, posteriorly, toward the oropharynx). Use something that provides enough surface area for the tongue to push against, such as a fingertip or the broad side of the tongue depressor. Ask the client to push his tongue forward against the resistance.

Tease It Forward

Use treats to encourage tongue protrusion. Place a tempting treat a few inches in front of the client's mouth and

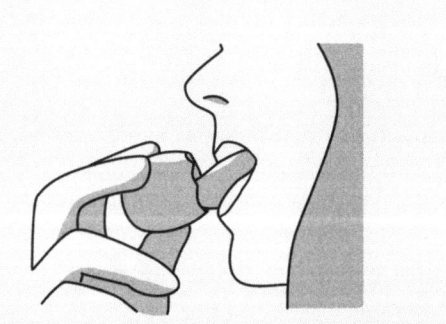

Using a cream-filled chocolate egg to encourage tongue protrusion.

encourage him to "come get it" with his tongue. Withdraw the treat a little to encourage farther protrusion. Reward him with a lick once he extends his tongue far enough to reach it. "Place a tongue depressor or piece of food in front of the student's mouth, about a half an inch before the lips... Instruct the student, 'Please touch it with your tongue'" (Bleile, 2006, p. 23).

Mark the Target

Provide an object with a hole through which the client can poke the tongue tip. This marks the target of tongue protrusion. Use a clean dry bubble wand or a baby chew toy that has a hole in it. A large straw, a piece of vinyl tubing, or a Rapper Snapper can also be used. Consider using a food the client can poke his tongue into, like a candy cream egg. Feeding therapists usually place dabs of puree on the lips to encourage tongue protrusion, and this is a method that SLPs have used in articulation therapy for decades: "Wipe candy lipstick or fudge frosting from the lips [with the tongue], carefully removing it from the corners of the mouth" (Berry & Eisenson, 1956, p. 140).

Raspberries and Creative Imagery

Using the lingua-labial raspberry along with the imagery of an "angry goose" is a classic way to teach tongue protrusion for /θ/ and /ð/ (Flowers, 2003, p. 271). Another effective image for little children is to make the "yucky" sound.

Facilitate Tongue Retraction

Retracting the tongue is necessary to establish back-lateral tongue stability, to produce the back sounds, and to activate the full range of tongue mobility. Teaching tongue retraction is a process of activating the "fringe" or extrinsic muscles that pull the tongue back. There are many ways therapists facilitate tongue retraction.

Assistance

Assistance is probably the oldest of these methods. Remember that assistance is passive and the client does not have to move anything; instead, the client has to relax the tongue for this to work. To assist tongue retraction means to push the tongue back. Use a probe to do so.

- *Push back from under the tongue:* "A flat stick or a small rod... may be put under the tongue to push it back and up" (Scripture, 1912, p. 148). The Tongue LifteR by Johnson Therapeutic is designed for this very purpose.

- *Push back from the tongue tip:* "If the child persists in placing the tongue tip against the teeth, push the tongue back with a tongue depressor" (Berry & Eisenson, 1956, p. 149). It is not uncommon when trying this method for the tongue simply to fold back upon itself. Therefore, the client will have to generate a small amount of tension in the tongue for this to work correctly.

- *Push back from on top of the tongue:* Place an object on the top surface of the tongue in the middle, and gently push the tongue back.

Resist Tongue Retraction

Once again, resistance is the most powerful method of movement facilitation and it can be used to stimulate tongue retraction. Grasp the front of the tongue gently but firmly and ease it carefully outward. Tell him, "I'm going to pull your tongue out. You pull it back away from me." With a younger client say, "I've got your tongue. I bet you can't get it back." Be cautious while pulling the tongue forward by using only a small amount of force; see the notes on page 229 about care and best practices when grasping the tongue.

Mark the Target

Clients with a long-term persistent distortion of /r/ often need help retracting the tongue to produce this elusive phoneme. The present author has found that the best way to accomplish this is to use a marking technique in conjunction with the butterfly position (Marshalla, 2004). Teach the client to butterfly (see pages 211–212 for the Butterfly Position method), then teach him to hold the butterfly while retracting the tongue. Mark the target of the retracted position, which is located on the gum tissue

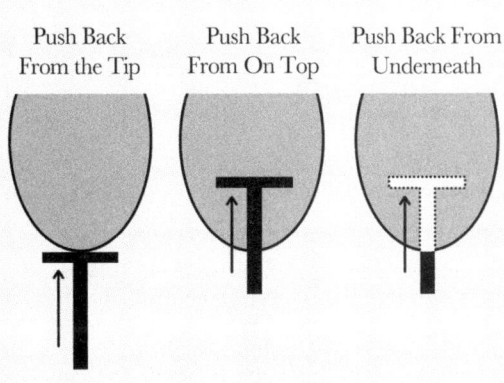

Push Back From the Tip   Push Back From On Top   Push Back From Underneath

Assist tongue retraction in three basic ways.

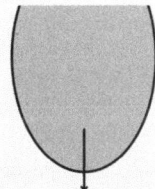

Resist tongue retraction by pulling gently outward as the client pulls it in.

up behind the upper molars in the back. Mark the gums there by having the client reach back and rub them with his index fingertip. The method is to butterfly and then retract the butterfly. The marking technique is used to teach the target position of the retracted butterfly.

Head Tapping or Pressing

A tactile cue in the form of tapping or pressing on the back of the head can inform the client about the direction of tongue movement toward the rear. This is a basic motokinesthetic method. Tap or press against the back of the head with fingers and request that the client pull the tongue back toward the stimulus. Say, "Pull your tongue back toward my fingers." This method can be used with clients learning to retract the tongue into a ball-shape or to retract the butterfly position toward the rear.

Retraction Reflex

Stimulate the tongue retraction reflex that causes the tongue to pull back into a ball-shape: "Stroke down the middle of the tongue to about half-way toward the back… The whole tongue humps up and back into a ball-shape which completely fills the posterior oral cavity and occludes the airway" (Marshalla, 1992a, p. 98). (For more information about this reflex, see Chapter 17 on the speech reflexes.)

Velar Raspberry

The lingua-velar raspberry is the pre-babbling vocalization that many clients can use as a springboard for tongue retraction. The lingua-velar raspberry is made by elevating the back of the tongue to the velum, and exhaling to cause vibration between the back of the tongue and the velum. Nemoy and Davis (1937) told clients to "cough up an imaginary fish bone" to teach the velar raspberry. The image of making "the crashing sound" of two cars colliding may be a better alternative.

Blow Toys

Certain horns and whistles can only be sounded if the tongue retracts toward the back of the mouth. They are a fun and non-invasive way of teaching retraction in both children and adults. Rosenfeld-Johnson (2001) has arranged a set of blow toys that are organized into a hierarchy to teach tongue movement skills that end in the full tongue retracted position needed for the back sounds.

Feeding Methods

Feeding therapy activities that are broad ranging sometimes are employed to teach the tongue to retract and stay inside the mouth. Sweet foods tend to encourage tongue protrusion while sour foods tend to encourage tongue retraction. Use a wedge of lemon, a squirt of lemon juice, or a sour candy to teach retraction. Simply talking about sour foods is enough to cause many people to retract the tongue and close the mouth. Bahr (2014) gives resistance to the molar area to encourage chewing movements and tongue retraction.

Facilitate Tongue-Tip Elevation

Tongue-tip elevation is one of the most important tongue movement patterns in all of articulation training. Gross tip elevation is necessary to develop the full range of tongue movement, and refined tip elevation is necessary for production of /t/, /d/, /n/, /l/, /s/, /z/, /tʃ/, /dʒ/, and the retroflex /r/. Getting the tongue tip to lift is something on which most SLPs spend considerable time, especially if the client has a motor speech disorder, interdental tongue protrusion, or a restricting lingua frenum. A wide variety of methods have been designed to facilitate tongue-tip elevation.

Use a Probe

Van Riper encouraged tongue-tip elevation with a wood match or probe:

> *"Facing a mirror, hold a sterilized probe or match horizontally about half an inch from the mouth. Reach out with the tongue and, by curling the [tip], pull it back to the teeth. The strength of this action may be increased by holding the match more firmly"* (Van Riper, 1947, p. 171).

Assist Tongue-Tip Elevation

To assist tongue-tip elevation means to place a probe under the tongue tip and push it up. This is the classic motokinesthetic method (Young & Hawk, 1955). Remember that assistance is passive movement on the part of the client. The client will have to relax the tongue for this to work and the activity will not necessarily activate the muscles involved in tip elevation, but lifting the tip for the client will give him a sense of correct movement and he may learn to do it himself as a result. It is a method that is still widely used: "Place a tongue depressor under the student's tongue tip and then raise the tongue tip behind the upper front teeth" (Bleile, 2006, p. 151).

Resist Tip Elevation

The most powerful method to facilitate tongue-tip elevation is to resist its upward movement. This is akin to lifting weights with the tip. Pressing downward on the tip teaches the client which part of the tongue to lift, how to activate that part, and how high to lift. Use a firm probe or have the client use his own finger. Simply placing an object on the tip adds weight and pressing downward slightly adds even more weight.

Resistance that is used to train tongue-tip elevation can be found in some of the earliest texts. Scripture (1912) suggested the use of a small lightweight flexible ball placed between the tongue tip and alveolar ridge (p. 131). The bulb of an eyedropper or a TonguePress® can be employed in the same way. Nemoy and Davis used a tongue depressor and Dworkin did this by making a "crossbar apparatus" out of tongue depressors (Dworkin, 1991, p. 212). The Jaw Exerciser is a plastic adaptation of the same. (For descriptions of these items, see Chapter 19 on the tools of speech movement training.)

Stimulate the Stabilizers

Muscle fibers from the palatoglossus and styloglossus muscles extend all the way to the tip of the tongue along its sides (see the illustration of the tongue's anatomy on page 200). Therefore, activation of these stabilizing muscles activates the tongue tip. In short, the better the tongue is stabilized in the back, the more assurance there is of activating the tip. Use methods to stabilize the tongue in the back against the palate and molars to activate these muscles so that the tip can become more active: "The outer musculature controls the movements of the tongue tip" (Takemoto, 2001, p. 106).

Lower the Jaw

Some clients flatten the entire tongue up against the palate instead of neatly elevating the tip to the alveolus for lingua-alveolar productions. Simply lowering the jaw a few millimeters should encourage more independent and exaggerated tip lifting. Tell the client to lower his jaw, or have him bite on a wide bite block to prop the mouth farther open: "Getting the mandible somewhat more depressed will make it difficult to flatten the whole tongue against the palate" (Bosley, 1981, p. 43).

Assisting tongue-tip elevation with a tongue depressor.

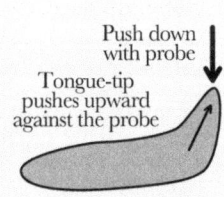

Teach tongue-tip elevation with resistance.

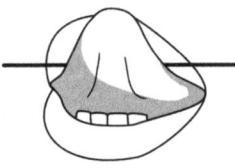

Van Riper's tongue-tip elevation exercise.

Elevate the Jaw

Problems in accurate lingua-alveolar articulation can also occur because the jaw is too low. A low jaw can cause the tongue tip to articulate with the middle of the palate instead of at the alveolar ridge. Raising the jaw can help the tip achieve better lingua-alveolar contact: "[If the tongue is making] contact too far back [because] the mandible is unduly depressed, reduce this depression" (Bosley, 1981, p. 43). In other words, raise the jaw so the tip can extend farther to the alveolus.

Mark the Target

Touch the alveolar ridge at midline to mark the target of lingua-alveolar articulation:

• *The spot:* Van Riper seems to be the one to have coined the term *the spot* to refer to the center of the anterior alveolar ridge: "With a match or tongue depressor stroke the back of the upper gum until the child touches it with the tongue. Ask him to stroke the spot with his tongue" (Van Riper, 1947, p. 191).

• *Tongue depressor:* Hanson and Barrett described how to mark the spot when teaching normal oral rest and correct swallow: "The 'spot' is against the upper gum ridge. In most patients this point is about ¼ inch posterior to the junction of alveolus and teeth… At times we press against the spot with the end of a tongue depressor, then [we] ask the patient to do the same. The parent watches closely, and may be asked to touch the child's 'spot' with a tongue depressor also" (Hanson & Barrett, 1988, p. 275).

• *Sticky food:* The spot can be marked with a sticky food to add interest: "The teacher 'marks' the place on the alveolar ridge with a lollipop where the child is to place his tongue… If the child puts his tongue in the right place he tastes the flavor of the lollipop. This also can be done with peanut butter or honey" (Berry & Eisenson, 1956, p. 151). "Syrup or some other clinging food may be placed on the alveolar ridge, and the client encouraged to lick it off" (Bosley, 1981, p. 42).

Dental Floss or Pick for /s/ and /z/ Groove

Dental floss or a dental pick can be used to teach a client how to create the minute central groove needed at the tip for production of /s/ and /z/:

• *Knotted dental floss:* Vaughn and Clark (1979) described this method. They said to tie a bundle of knots at the end of a piece of dental floss 15 inches long. Place the floss between the maxillary (upper) central incisors and pull it so that the knots sit on the lingual surfaces of the incisors right at the juncture between the teeth and alveolar ridge. Teach the client to reach the tongue tip up to the knot and tickle it with his tongue tip. Then teach him to blow a tiny bit of air against the knot as he does so and a sound nearly like /s/ will result.

• *Interdental picks:* The above technique can be done with a dental pick. Place the pick between the maxillary (upper) central incisors so that its tip pokes between them. The tip of the pick will stick out behind the incisors and sit between the tongue tip and the alveolar ridge. Teach the client to reach the tongue tip up to the pick and tickle it with his tongue tip. Then teach him to blow a tiny bit of air against the tip of the dental pick and a sound nearly like /s/ will result.

Objects with Holes

One of the easiest ways to encourage tongue-tip elevation is to provide an object with a hole through which the client can poke his tongue tip. Some swizzle sticks and bubble wands have circular shapes on the end, and many baby chew toys have holes to explore with the tongue tip.

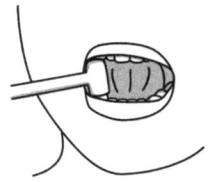

A wide bite block or bite stick placed between the molars lowers the jaw and forces the tongue tip to elevate higher. (after Dworkin, 1991).

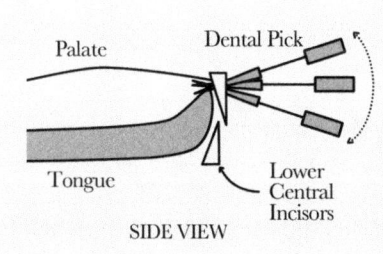

Angle a dental pick up and down between the maxillary (upper) central incisors to create a tiny central groove in the tongue for /s/ or /z/ as the client utters /t/ or /d/.

Baby chew toys and sanitized bubble wands have holes that are perfect for teaching tongue-tip protrusion and elevation.

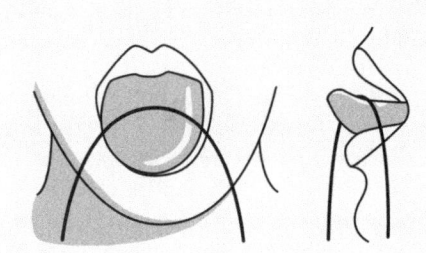

Drape a candy rope, floss ribbon, or sterilized string across the tongue to teach the tongue tip to pull upward.

Place the hole above the tongue tip and encourage the client to lift the tip straight up and into the hole.

Draped Rope Candy, Dental Ribbon or String

A long rope candy, dental ribbon, or a sterilized string can be place across the front of the tongue to teach tongue-tip lifting. Drape it across the front of the tongue. Have the client hold the item at its two ends and pull down gently as he lifts the tip up.

Tip Elevation Tool

The Tongue-Tip Elevation Tool® made by TalkTools® can be placed between the incisors to teach tongue-tip elevation. The tool is placed between the maxillary and mandibular (upper and lower) central incisors and a moveable bead is pushed up and down with the tongue tip.

Cue Tip Elevation

There are countless ways to cue tip elevation. For example: (1) point a finger upward to cue the tip to elevate, (2) point to a schematic illustration of tongue-tip elevation, (3) lift eyebrows to cue tip elevation, (4) talk about Mr. Tongue's need to stretch up and hammer a nail into the ceiling of his house (see page 74 for full story), (5) use hands to model the action. The motokinesthetic cue is to apply external pressure above the upper lip:

> *"The child may be led into the simple suggestion of a tongue-end movement by the trainer's touching the center of the region outside and above the upper lip and quickly bringing the finger downward. This external suggestion is often sufficient. The touch above the lip, outside the dental ridge, suggests that the tongue tip move upward inside, opposite the point touched, then quickly down as the finger moves down"* (Young & Hawk, 1955, p. 18).

Tapping Back

Another method for teaching tongue-tip lifting for lingua-alveolar contact was to teach the client to tap the tip of the tongue against the upper lip, the upper teeth, and then the alveolar ridge: "Ask the client to touch his upper lip with the tongue, then the upper teeth, then inside the mouth" (Bosley, 1981, p. 43).

Spitting Paper Wads

Therapists of the past have used spitballs to teach tip elevation. Place small wads of paper on the tip of the tongue and have the client expel them by spitting with the tongue tip: "Concentration of activity in the tip of the tongue may be secured through having the pupil expel small pieces of paper placed on the tip of the tongue" (Nemoy & Davis, 1937, p. 91). Don't use this activity if the client drools to excess, if he enjoys spitting as a negative social expression, or if the therapy is being done in a location that might prohibit it.

Spoon-Feeding Method

Some clients will benefit from a classic feeding therapy technique to stimulate tongue-tip elevation. This is done while feeding purees. Present the spoon at midline and hold it perpendicular to the vertical surface of the face. Place the bowl of the spoon directly on the tongue at midline so that the juncture between the bowl and its handle is positioned directly on top of the tongue tip. Press the spoon downward. Wait for the client's upper lip to lower, and then draw the spoon out, making sure to stimulate the tongue tip in the process. Both the downward pressure of the spoon on the tip, and the scraping against the tip as the spoon withdraws, should stimulate the tip to rise. A spoon with a textured convex bottom is excellent for this purpose; however, avoid using spoons that are too flexible for this application. The present author uses a Nuk® brush dipped in yogurt or applesauce for this activity.

Tongue Bowl Reflex

Stimulate the tongue bowl reflex to facilitate tongue-tip elevation. Brush the tongue from tip to about halfway back along midline. The tongue should flatten, flair and form a bowl shape with tip elevation. Read more about this in Chapter 17 on the speech reflexes.

The motokinesthetic cue for tongue-tip elevation is to press gently but firmly against the skin above the upper lip. The client presses the tongue tip toward the stimulus.

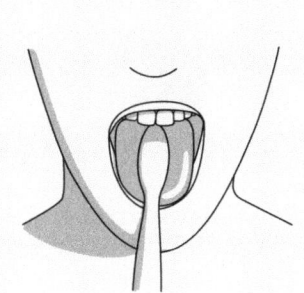

Brush down the tongue's midline to stimulate the tongue bowl reflex for tongue-tip elevation.

Associate Tip Elevation

Find one phoneme or one pre-speech vocalization in which the client already can elevate the tongue tip. Use the movements of that sound to teach the movements of the new sound. For example, if the client can lift the tip for /d/, use that phoneme to teach him to lift for /t/ or /n/.

Lingua-Alveolar Raspberry or Trill

Some early authors recommended *trilling* as a springboard for tongue-tip elevation. This sound is called a *lingua-alveolar raspberry.* Watch out for this, however, because the lingua-alveolar raspberry can be more difficult to produce than the lingua-alveolar phonemes for many clients. The Spanish /r/ is made with a lingua-alveolar trill and can also be used to encourage tip elevation by clients who can produce it.

Inhibit Lip Rounding

Many authors have noted that difficulty in lifting the tongue tip can be due to poor differentiation between the tongue tip and the lips. The client does not lift the tip because he is busy rounding the lips, or the two movements may be locked together. In this case, the lip rounding. must be inhibited This method has been around for decades and is still recommended:

> *"Because /w/ is so frequently substituted for /l/, you may need to inhibit bilabial movement by placing your gloved hands on the client's lips, by using a tongue depressor, or by having the client retract the lips"* (Secord et al., 2007, p. 90).

See Chapter 12 on the lips for more ways to inhibit labial movement.

Help the Tip Curl Up & Back

There are two reasons to teach the tongue tip to curl up and back so that the tip points back toward the velum and oropharynx. The first is to encourage maximum range of lingua movement and the second is to teach the retroflex

/r/. Van Riper called this movement *curling* (Van Riper, 1947, p. 171). There are several ways to do this as described in the articulation therapy literature. Listed here are the main concepts.

Licking

Licking is a classic Van Riper method for teaching the tongue tip to curl up and back. Licking is a fine activity for this purpose as long as the client uses the tip in performing the action. Therapists should be mindful, however, that many clients who cannot lift the tip keep it tucked down while licking and they use the blade instead. Make sure the client is using the tip to lick upward (see illustration below):

> *"Practice licking stick candy or spoon or other object held at right angles to and in contact with the upper teeth. Lick a thin scattered sprinkling of sugar from a plate"* (Van Riper, 1947, p. 171).

Slides

A classic way to stimulate tongue-tip curling up and back for the retroflex /r/ is to teach the client to slide his tongue tip from /l/ to /r/. Place the tongue tip on the alveolar ridge and produce /l/. Now slide the tip from the alveolus to the velum along the midline of the palate while

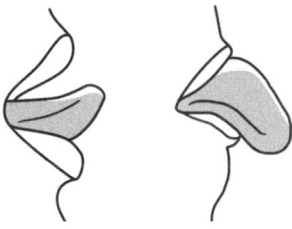

The tongue on the left is elevating its tip correctly for licking. The tongue on the right is not.

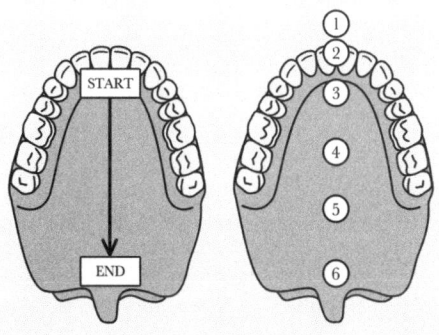

Teach the tongue tip to curl up and back by sliding it from the alveolus to the velum (left). Tap the tip of the tongue at each point 1–6 in order to teach the tongue tip to curl up and back (right).

vocalizing. One can also slide from /n/ to /r/ and from /z/ to /r/: "Have the client prolong a /z/. As he does so, he draws the tip of the tongue very slightly back, without discontinuing the /z/, but moving toward an /r/" (Hanson, 1983, p. 217). These are basic Van Riper methods.

Tapping

Bosley's method of teaching the tongue to tap from the upper lip, to the teeth, and then to the alveolar ridge, can be extended all the way back to the velum in order to teach the curl. The client taps the tip of the tongue at one point and then another down the midline of the palate. The ultimate position will be for the tip to be curled up and back and facing the velum.

Tongue Depressor

Van Riper used a tongue depressor to push the tongue tip back into a curled position to stimulate a retroflex /r/. He pushed it while it was elevated for /l/:

> "Ask child to say L. Then with the depressor gently push the tip of the tongue back until you can insert the depressor between the tip and teeth ridge or until r sound results" (Van Riper, 1947, p. 192).

Tongue Cleaner Resistance Activity

A triangle tongue cleaner is the very best tool for teaching the tongue tip to curl up and back. Place the cleaner in front of the mouth and ask the client to grasp it with his tongue tip. Then have him pull the cleaner back into the mouth by curling it back. A little outward pressure can be applied to the tool to encourage curling with resistance. This is an excellent way to teach a retroflex /r/

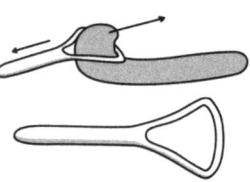

A tongue cleaner makes an excellent tool for teaching the client to curl his tongue tip up and back.

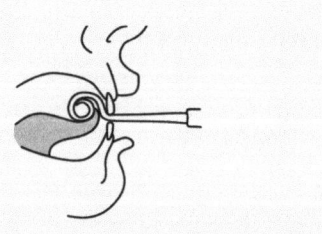

The Rabbit Buddy is designed specifically for teaching tongue-tip curling for production of retroflex /r/.

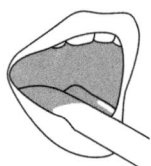

Hold the tip down to force up the back of the tongue.

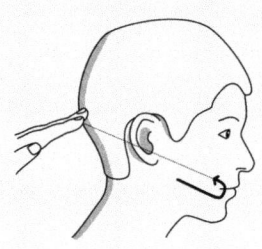

Tap the back of the head to direct the tongue tip to point rearward.

position. This method can also help generate more tone in the tongue.

Rabbit Buddy

The Rabbit Buddy from Articulate Technologies is the newest tip-curling tool. It is designed specifically for teaching tongue-tip curling for production of the retroflex /r/. The tongue tip lifts and inserts itself up into a flexible coil. The tip then curls up and back against the palate to unfurl the coil.

Lower the Jaw

Another way to encourage a client to lift and curl the tongue tip so that it faces the posterior pharyngeal wall for the retroflex /r/ is to lower the jaw while the client is making an /l/. Lowering the jaw will force the tip to curl if the client tries to keep it in contact with the palate the whole time. This will work as long as the client forms the tongue into a bowl as the jaw lowers: "While saying /l/, pull the lower jaw down slowly until [the tongue reaches] the /r/ position" (Berry & Eisenson, 1956, p. 157).

Tap or Press the Head

A motokinesthetic cue can be adapted: Tap or press against the back of the head to direct the tip to curl up and back toward the oropharynx. With a finger, press or tap against the back of the head in line with the velopharyngeal mechanism. Ask the client to stretch the tongue tip up and back toward the finger. Tap a little higher or a little lower, or to the left or right until the sound quality being sought is achieved. Sometimes the tap has to be on the very top of the head; the location will depend upon the client's response.

Facilitate Tongue-Back Elevation / Arching

Tongue-back elevation is necessary for production of /k/, /g/, /ŋ/, and /r/, and arching is needed to produce all the vowels as well as to achieve a full range of tongue movement. There are many ways to stimulate for tongue-back elevation and arching.

Inhibit Tip Elevation

Some clients cannot lift the back of the tongue because they are too busy lifting the tip of the tongue instead; help them by inhibiting tip elevation. Alexander Graham Bell's father, Melville Bell, wrote about this: "Hold down the forepart of the tongue, and the back will be compelled into action" (Bell, 1898, p. 42). The idea persisted through the ages:

> *"If there is still a problem [with tongue-back elevation], the speech-language pathologist may want to add the technique of lightly depressing the tip of the tongue with a tongue depressor until the [back] forms the habit of elevating"* (Bosley, 1981, p. 9).

Assist Back Elevation / Arching

Therapists push the back of the tongue up in one of several ways:

- *Push the tongue backward and upward from the tip:* "The tongue depressor may be placed on the tip of the tongue, holding it down, and at the same time pushing the tongue backward and upward until it comes into contact with the soft palate" (Young & Hawk, 1955, p. 18). The earliest reference to this method was found in a book published in 1874: "I request the pupil to press his tongue downwards and backwards with his index finger, while I do the same… This I have never known to fail" (Comstock & Mair, 1874, p. 21).

- *Push the back of the tongue up from under the tongue:* Place a probe under the body of the tongue and push the tongue up and back from underneath. A new tool called a Tongue LifteR is designed to serve this very purpose.

- *Push the back of the tongue up from under the chin:* A motokinesthetic method to elevate the back of the tongue was to push up from the outside: "Place the thumb on one side of the throat, under the back of the tongue externally, and the index finger on the opposite side. Press upward, thus suggesting that the back of the tongue move upward" (Young & Hawk, 1955, p. 18).

WARNING: Please notice that the authors wrote that this action should *suggest* upward movement of the back of the tongue. The method is not intended actually to push the back of the tongue upward. Such upward pressure on the back of the tongue from outside the mouth can be extremely uncomfortable, even painful, to a client. Make sure that this is used as a cue or suggestion only.

Resist Tongue-Back Elevation

Resistance is a powerful tool in the training of tongue-back elevation. Place a probe stimulus on the middle back of the tongue and press gently downward. Ask the client to push up against the stimulus.

FIRST WARNING: This stimulus should elicit a gag response. Teaching the client to do this to himself will help him suppress his gag. SECOND WARNING: Downward stimulation to the back of the tongue places the stimulus in near proximity to the epiglottis. Use this method sparingly and be careful.

Cue Tongue-Back Elevation

A wide variety of cues can teach the client to elevate the back of the tongue: (1) point a finger upward to cue the back to lift, (2) point to a schematic illustration of tongue-back elevation, (3) lift eyebrows to cue back elevation, (4) talk about Mr. Tongue's need to close the window in the back of his house by lifting the window upward (see full story on page 74), (5) tell the client to imagine that there is a string tied to the back of the tongue and it is being pulled upward, (6) use the concept of crashing.

Mark the Target of Tongue-Back Elevation

Mark the target of back elevation by touching the juncture between the hard and soft palate, or the velum itself. Procedures to inhibit the gag may need to be employed first. Berry and Eisenson recommended this marking technique for teaching /k/:

> *"Awareness of the position for the /k/ may be created by touching the back of the tongue and the soft palate with a tongue depressor and then directing the case to make contact between the touched parts"* (Berry & Eisenson, 1956, p. 164).

Motokinesthetic cue for suggesting that the back of the tongue elevate for production of /k/.

Provide a Target

Elevating the shoulders of the tongue for production of /r/ can be difficulty for many clients. The R-appliance (Clark, Schwartz, & Blakeley, 1993) is a removable acrylic palate similar to a retainer that has pieces (blocks) that extend down from the back on both sides to help with this elevation. When placed into the mouth and on the palate, the back pieces provide a target for the tongue's shoulders to hit. A mouth guard might be an inexpensive alternative. Help the client explore the guard and learn how to place it in the mouth. Examine it for identifying markers for points of elevation.

Spoon

Van Riper used a spoon facing downward to teach tongue-back elevation: "I want you to fit the back of the tongue into the bowl… and push it up until it can't go any farther" (Van Riper, 1958, p. 145).

Lower the Jaw

Sometimes opening the mouth farther will force a client who is making a front sound to make a back sound: "Asking for a greater depression of the mandible will sometimes help shift from a /t/ to /k/, since it is harder to contact the alveolar ridge with the tip of the tongue if the mandible depression is large… If the tongue contacts too far forward, depress the mandible farther. It is contacts too far back, reduce the depression of the mandible" (Bosley, 1981, p. 48).

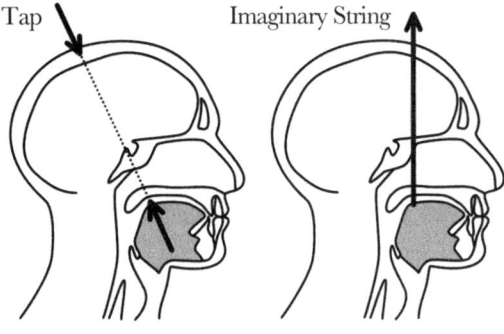

Tap the top of the head or have the client imagine a string pulling up the back of his tongue.

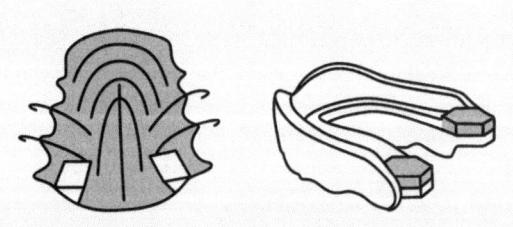

The R-appliance (left) and a mouth guard that might be used in a similar fashion.

Tap the Top of the Head

Tap or press on the top of the head, somewhat toward the back of the crown, directly above the back of the tongue. Request that the client lift and press the back of his tongue up toward the tapping point. Adjust the position of the tapping slightly forward or back, along the midline of the head, in order to find just the right place to stimulate tongue-back elevation for that client.

Imagine a String

Have the client imaging there is a string tied to the back of his tongue and extending out through the top of the head. Tell the client to imagine that the string is being pulled upward, thus pulling the back of his tongue up. This is a technique that has been passed down for generations.

Tongue Retraction Reflex

Use the *tongue retraction reflex* to stimulate elevation of the back of the tongue. Stroke down the middle of the tongue to about half way toward the back: "The whole tongue humps up and back into a ball shape which completely fills the posterior oral cavity and occludes the airway" (Marshalla, 1992a, p. 98).

Lingua-Velar Raspberry / Snoring

Traditional Era therapists recommended the idea of teaching a client to "cough up an imaginary fish bone" to stimulate for back sounds (e.g., Nemoy & Davis, 1937, p. 107). This hacking sound is called the *lingua-velar raspberry* and it is known that it is an infantile pre-babbling sound that can be thought of as a precursor to /k/ and /g/. Bosley recommended that the lingua-velar raspberry be taught by having the client inhale through the nose with the mouth wide open, which automatically brings the back of the tongue up, and then by pinching the nose closed while the client exhales (Bosley, 1981, p. 46–47). Pretending to snore sometimes can encourage the back of the tongue to lift: "The /k/ can sometimes be obtained from snoring" (Bosley, 1981, p. 47). This type of snore basically is a velar raspberry produced upon inhalation instead of exhalation. If the client can inhale and snore by vibrating the velum, the vibratory sensation produced back there during the snore can help him understand where the tongue should make contact in the back.

Facilitate Tongue Widening

Not much has been written about helping clients learn to widen the tongue but some therapists understood this concept and electropalatography has proven its necessity. The tongue must remain wide throughout all of speech production because it is part of oral stability, it is part of the round quality of all the vowels, and it allows efficient and accurate elevation of the sides of the tongue for production of all the lingua consonants. The following methods have been reported. Additional information about establishing a wide base of the tongue is available in Chapter

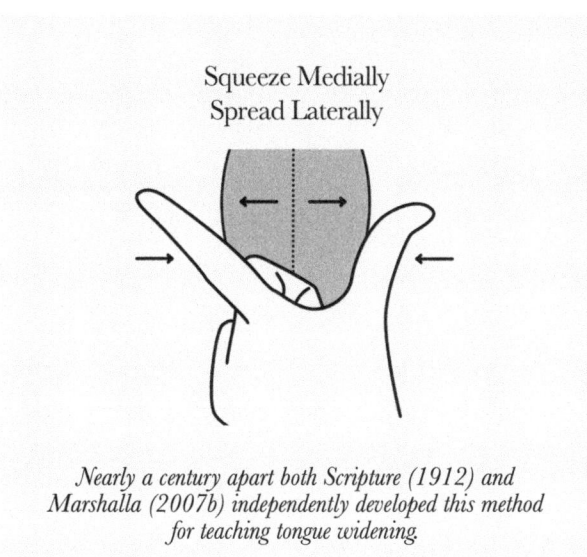

Squeeze Medially
Spread Laterally

Nearly a century apart both Scripture (1912) and Marshalla (2007b) independently developed this method for teaching tongue widening.

14 on oral stability.

E Position

Nemoy and Davis (1937) and Bosley (1981) talked about teaching clients to keep the tongue wide for production of many phonemes. They said that the way to do this was to work from /i/. The idea is to produce /i/ and then to hold the tongue in that position. Now, with the tongue in /i/ position, elevate and lower the back to produce whatever phoneme needs widening. The same E Position can be used as the beginning point of any phoneme.

Hee-Haw Activity

A method for using the fingers to teach tongue widening was described early in the 20th century:

> *"Place the thumb and finger on each side of the tongue: Broaden and narrow the tongue by use of the muscles within the tongue; this is felt by the fingers"* (Scripture, 1912, p. 225).

Marshalla added resistance to this process and called it the Hee-Haw Activity. Have the client reach into his mouth with his index finger and thumb to grasp the tongue. Have him place his index finger on one side of the tongue and his thumb on the other. Then have him squeeze and narrow the body of his tongue by squeezing the thumb and index finger toward one another. Have him say "Haw" while his fingers are squeezing. Then have him say "Hee." Saying "Hee" should cause the tongue to widen, and the client will feel this action with his fingers. Have the client alternate widening and narrowing the tongue by saying "Hee-Haw-Hee-Haw…." (See the notes on page 229 about care and best practices when grasping the tongue.)

Facilitate Tongue Narrowing

There are two basic reasons to stimulate for tongue narrowing. The first is to assure full movement capability of the tongue, and the second is to teach the tongue to narrow for production of /l/. Techniques to accomplish tongue narrowing have not been discussed much in the articulation literature but there are a few methods that can be found.

Lower the Jaw

A lower jaw position forces the tongue to narrow so that it can stretch higher to reach the alveolar ridge: "For the elimination of a flat position of the tongue, a more widely opened mouth position… should be attained" (Nemoy & Davis, 1937, p. 136).

Lighten Contact

Lack of tongue narrowing on /l/ may be due to excessive tip pressure against the alveolar ridge. In such a case, the client should be taught to lighten up his contact:

> *"Obliteration of the lateral openings [can occur] as a result of strong pressure of the tongue on the alveolar ridge. Using analogies, demonstrate strong pressure versus light touch on the hands or with a tongue blade on the alveolar ridge. Suggest 'touch very lightly'"* (Bosley, 1981, p. 78).

Tongue Curls

Van Riper's tongue curling method also works to narrow the tongue for /l/: "If there are still no lateral openings… try having the tongue curled around an applicator held horizontally across the blade of the tongue as far back as possible" (Bosley, 1981, p. 78).

Inhibit Side Elevation

Another way to narrow the tongue and create lateral spaces for air emission on /l/ is to use two sticks to hold down the sides of the tongue as the client says the sound: "Use two applicators, one on either side of the tongue, in the interest of getting the applicators placed far enough back for the lateral openings" (Bosley, 1981, p. 78).

Voluntary Narrowing

The orofacial myology literature speaks of teaching clients to narrow the tongue as part of the swallowing retraining program. The suggestion seems to be simply to model and explain the procedure for the client to perform with full voluntary control: "Demonstrate the exercise. Protrude your tongue, keeping it as narrow and pointed as possible" (Hanson & Barrett, 1988, p. 279).

Hee-Haw Activity

The Hee-Haw exercise (described previously on this page) to help widen the tongue will also work to help the client learn to narrow the tongue.

Facilitate Independent Tongue Movement

Separation of movement is a modern concept, but it was Van Riper who first said that the tongue becomes fully mature only when it moves completely independently of the other oral structures. This is accomplished by stabilizing the structures around the tongue. This subject is discussed in detail in Chapter 14 on oral stability: "It is important for good articulation that the tongue be able to move independently of the lips and jaw" (Van Riper, 1972, p. 183).

Unlock the Stiff Tongue

Some clients move the tongue very little because muscle tone is too high and there is a resultant fixing of tongue movement: "Tension is the source of so many faults in speech" (Nemoy & Davis, 1937, p. 22). "The tongue can be stiff because of hypertonicity" (Morris & Klein, 2000, p. 370).

Excessive tone in the tongue often makes it appear stiff, boxy, bunched, and positioned high at center point. When protruding the tongue, the tip may bow inward into a heart-shape or remain flat and boxy. The tongue does not flare outward toward its perimeter but instead retracts toward center point, and the sides of the tongue press toward midline giving the tongue a thick and narrow appearance. Movements are led with the whole tongue in this boxy shape and not with the tip gracefully extended.

> *"If the clinician… can inhibit central tongue thickening while facilitating spreading of the tongue surface laterally, the more mature movements of lateral tilting, rolling retrieval, and central surface grooving may be experienced"* (Jones-Owens, 1991, p. 51).

Excessive high tone in the tongue can also be unilateral in which case one side of the tongue will appear stiff as described and the other side will appear normal in appearance. The movements of both feeding and speech are usually affected when tone is high and unlocking the stiff tongue is necessary to activate the full range of movements for both. To reduce tone in the tongue, one can: reduce body tone, reduce tone in the face, relax the tongue, and/or normalize oral tactile sensitivity if it is a cause.

Reducing Overall Body Tone

Reducing tone in the tongue often means that tone must be reduced throughout the whole body. This is especially important for clients with neuromuscular deficit and motor speech disorder. Team occupational or physical therapists design these techniques on an individual client basis. Recommendations might include: (1) rocking, stretching, or slowly massaging the whole body; (2) adjusting head, shoulder, or head position; (3) massage; or (4) working in certain body positions (see Chapter 7 for more ideas for bodywork for speech therapy). SLPs can use these methods within a program of speech training to help reduce overall tone and this should have a positive effect on oral tone. Reducing overall tone sets the stage for articulation work, however, SLPs are warned not to let an emphasis on these methods overtake the necessary speech work. Sometimes co-treatment is initiated so that the motor specialist can work the body while the SLP works the mouth.

Reducing Facial Tone

Reducing tone in the tongue often means that tone must be reduced throughout the whole face and oral mechanism. This is especially important for clients with neuromuscular deficit and motor speech disorder. Reducing overall facial tone usually has an overall positive effect on reducing tone in the tongue. To reduce oral tone, work to reduce tightness in the muscles of the face and jaw with massage, shoulder rolling, head rolls, and shaking the head and face. Morris and Klein used what they called *facial molding technique* to reduce facial tone:

> *"Begin with a general massage of the child's body and face… Think of the child's face as a piece of clay that you will sculpt… The massage can be done using your palms or with your fingers… Move slowly and with the child's permission… it often helps to massage toward the closed mouth position"* (Morris & Klein, 2000, p. 415–416).

Reducing Tone Specifically in the Tongue

One can employ methods to reduce tone specifically in the tongue, i.e., get the tongue to relax. Sometimes this means grasping the tongue and slowly shaking it side to side, or stretching it forward and then side to side. Tapping the tongue can reduce its tone. Grasping the tongue, pulling it slightly forward, and then telling the client to take a deep breath and to "Let go" (relax) or "Let me have your tongue" can work. Each method needs to be evaluated for its effectiveness with the client at hand — one does not use one of these methods and then assume it will work to reduce tone; one uses the methods to *see* if it works for that client in that moment. (See the notes on page 229 about care and best practices when grasping and moving a client's tongue.)

Normalizing Oral-Tactile Sensitivity to Reduce Tone

The client with oral-tactile hypersensitivity often will present with a stiff tongue because he is working hard to avoid the gag response. Methods to normalize sensitivity should help reduce tone in the tongue and limit stiffness. (See Chapter 16 on normalizing oral-tactile sensitivity.)

Firm Up the Loose Tongue

The tongue of clients with hypotonic dysarthria has a limited range of movement because its tone is too low with weakness and general lack of movement. Reduced tone in the tongue makes it appear soft, bulbous, swollen, or too large for the oral cavity. The tongue usually sits forward

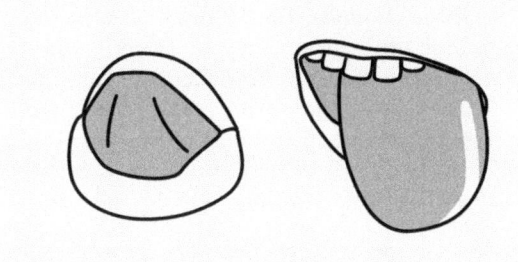

The tongue affected by high muscle tone generally is narrow, stiff, and boxy (left).

between the anterior teeth, and the lateral margins may also spill outward between the lateral teeth. The tongue tip may curl under and the tongue will appear quite bulbous as it pushes forward with its middle instead of with its tip. The lateral margins and tip of the tongue usually remain low and do not elevate well.

Movements of the tongue are slow and labored when tone and strength are low. Low tone can be unilateral, in which case one side of the tongue will appear bulbous as described, and the other side will appear normal. Firming up the loose tongue is necessary to activate the full range of tongue movements for speech. Low tone in the tongue also has an influence on feeding movements. Feeding and speech activities often go hand-in-hand for these clients. To increase tone in the tongue, increase practice trials, increase body tone, increase tone in the jaw or lips, increase tone in the tongue itself, or normalize oral tactile sensitivity:

> *"When tone is low, the tongue frequently lacks the normal, thin, cupped, or grooved configuration that assists efficient sucking. The tongue may be think and humped. Food entering the mouth falls over the edges into the buccal cavity or becomes scattered. Bolus collection is inefficient"* (Morris & Klein, 2000, p. 370).

Increase Practice Trials

Practice may not change overall tone but it may help improve tongue strength when it is low. Connor et al. (2009) and Behan et al. (2012) studied rats tongue and found that strength of the tongue increased when they were involved in a tongue-licking exercise program. In other words, a successful but soft and weak tongue movement may be improved with simple repetition.

Increasing Body Tone

Increasing overall tone in the tongue sometimes is a matter of increasing tone throughout the whole body. These methods will apply to clients with neuromuscular deficit and motor speech disorder. Team occupational or physical therapists design these techniques on an individual client basis. Recommendations might include: (1) engaging

in aerobic activities such as jumping, hopping, running, or swimming, (2) briskly massaging the body, and (3) lifting weights and engaging in weight-bearing activities. SLPs can use these methods within a program of speech training to help increase body tone and this should have a positive effect on oral tone. Often this means simply changing the speech activity. For example, instead of picking up a stimulus card from the table while in sitting position, the client can hop across the room to retrieve his card. Increasing body tone sets the stage for articulation work, however, SLPs are warned not to let an emphasis on these methods overtake the necessary speech work. Sometimes co-treatment is initiated so that the motor specialist can work the body while the SLP works the mouth.

Increasing Oral and Facial Tone

Increasing tone throughout the whole oral mechanism will have a positive effect on lingual tone. This is especially important for clients with neuromuscular deficit and motor speech disorder. To increase oral tone, work to increase firmness in the facial and jaw muscles while increasing facial expressions and lip mobility:

> *"Use the facial molding activity… Play patty-cake, peek-a-boo, and other children's games that enable patting, tapping, stroking, and other types of tactile and proprioceptive stimulation of the muscles that open and close the jaw. Tapping can be done directly around the temporomandibular joint"* (Morris & Klein, 2000, p. 444).

Increasing Tone Specifically in the Tongue

The most effective means to increase tone in the tongue is to resist tongue movements. Resistance adds weight to movement and makes the tongue work a little harder to achieve its objectives. Resistance activities are discussed below. Tone can also be built somewhat by having the client maintain tongue positions for increasing lengths of time, and by having the client repeat or practice tongue movements. Morris and Klein recommend the following for increasing tone in the tongue:

> *"Keep the child's head in a chin-tucked position… Use folk music with a clear rhythm and regular tempo while tapping or providing other sensory input directly to the tongue muscles under the chin and within the mouth… Incorporate functional oral motor activities… Increase sensory input to the tongue… Use vibration with a small massager or electric toothbrush"* (Morris & Klein, 2000, p. 445).

Increase Tongue-to-Palate Pressure

Activating jaw closing increases strength of tongue pressure against the palate. This means that jaw closure and jaw clenching can be used to teach clients to press the tongue more firmly against the palate. This is an excellent method for clients who have difficulty achieving enough upward pressure of the tongue against the palate to produce certain consonants, often the stops. Jaw clenching can also help the tongue attain enough tension for /r/ in some cases. Use a firm but flexible probe placed between the molars on one side and then the other, or between both sides simultaneously (e.g., a straw). Ask the client to clench firmly while he attempts his lingua stop consonants:

> *"In a functional system, pressing the tongue to the palate is achieved not only through the activation of tongue muscles. Floor-of-mouth muscles and jaw closing muscles also contribute to this action"* (Palmer et al., 2008, p. 834).

Normalizing Oral-Tactile Sensitivity to Increase Tone

The client with oral-tactile hyposensitivity often will present with a soft and bulbous tongue. Methods to normalize sensitivity should cause the tongue to move more; see Chapter 16 for methods to normalize oral-tactile sensitivity.

Keeping the Tongue Inside the Mouth

To keep the tongue inside the mouth means to activate oral stability. This process is discussed in Chapter 14 on oral stability.

EVOLUTION OF MOVEMENT: SIGNS OF PROGRESS

Principles of movement development can be used to monitor the development of tongue movements through time. Tongue movement can be expected to generally progress in sequences as described in this section. These types of changes can occur very quickly, even within a few minutes in many cases. Clients with motor speech disorders will take a longer course of treatment and require several weeks or even months to change their fundamental tongue movement patterns. Clients with very low cognition and severe neuromuscular disorders are the most challenged when it comes to making these changes, and some will not change depending upon their neurological status.

- *Gross to fine:* Tongue movements should begin as gross movements that become more refined with time. For example, a client may learn to elevate the entire front of the tongue upwards and downwards in a gross licking pattern. With time, he will learn to lift and lower the tongue tip in a refined pattern to produce /l/. Clients who use all the movement patterns of the tongue are showing maturity in this line of development.

- *Proximal to distal:* Tongue movements may begin in the back and progress to the tip. The tip will become a more active mover as movements mature. Infants and many clients with severe speech delay/disorder use back phonemes first. Some of the most severely impaired get stuck with back sounds only. Clients who produce both back sounds and front sounds are demonstrating maturity in this line of development.

- *Medial to lateral to rotational:* The midline of the tongue should activate first, and clients should learn to elevate the tongue along the midline early. So, for example, when a client is trying to lateralize his tongue left and right, he will first do so by elevating and rocking the middle of the tongue side to side. With maturity the lateral margins of the tongue will begin to lift and lateralize themselves toward their respective sides. With further maturity, the tongue will begin to move in rotational patterns in all directions. A client who can sweep the tongue all the way around the lips is demonstrating complete maturity in this line of development.

- *Center point:* Tongue movements are fully mature when the tongue elevates all the way around its perimeter and keeps the midline down at center point. Tongue movements are mature when the center point of the tongue stays below the center point of the palate.

- *Flexion-and-extension:* The tongue that can extend fully out and down toward the chin, and that can retract all the way back into the oral pharyngeal area is fully mature along this line of development.

- *Individual to sequential:* Sequential movements are the most advanced. Clients who can produce advanced consonant cluster sequences like /spl/ or /nts/ are demonstrating complete maturity in this line of development.

- *Arrhythmic to rhythmic:* Tongue movements will be arrhythmic early in development and rhythmic when mature. Stiff and arrhythmic movements still need work to become rhythmic.

- *Simple to complex:* Simple tongue movements are accomplished early and complex movements are accomplished late. For example, sticking out the tongue is a primitive skill while stabilizing the tongue at the back-lateral margins while elevating the tongue tip neatly for /l/ is complex. The ability to produce all consonants with adult movement patterns represents complete development along this line.

- *Slow to fast:* Tongue movements are slower when immature. Rapid tongue movement indicates maturity in this line of development. Rapid speech that is marred by mumbling, slurring, and reduced intelligibility indicates that this line of development is immature.

- *Mobility and stability:* The tongue should mobilize first and stabilize with time. A tongue that moves without back-lateral stability is moving with an immature relationship between mobility and stability. Inconsistent sound productions should be expected and stability should be taught.

- *Muscle tone:* A baby's tongue is very soft and the muscles are not well undefined. With maturity comes better definition of the tongue's muscle groups.

- *Mass to separation:* The tongue will move in tandem with the jaw and lips early in development. The tongue will move separately from the jaw and lips with maturity.

- *Differentiation:* The entire tongue will move as a single unit early in development. The individual zones of the tongue, including its tip, sides, back, lateral backs, and middle will lift differentially with maturity.

- *Combinations:* The tongue movements of adjacent phonemes overlap into co-articulated sequences with maturity. Clients with immature oral motor skills usually separate their tongue movements with the schwa. For example, *train* becomes /tʌ reɪn/. Elimination of the schwa represents maturity in this line of development.

- *Economy:* Tongue movements that are immature tend to be made in less economical ways. For example, toddlers tend to keep the jaw too low, which forces the tongue to lift very high for alveolar contact. This is not economical. With maturity, the jaw is held high more of the time so that the tongue can move much less to elevate, which brings more economy to tongue movement. Tongue movements become swift, smooth, and consistent as a result.

- *Casual to habitual:* Tongue movements occur by happenstance at first and phonemes produced with immature tongue movements are inconsistent. Tongue movements become regular and habitual when they mature and phoneme movements and positioning become consistent.

- *Random to controlled:* Immature tongue movements are marked by inconsistency. Tongue movements become more organized with time and maturity as the client learns to exercise authority over them.

- *Reflexes:* Reflexes dominate tongue movements when they are very immature. Reflexes fade and voluntary control takes over with maturity. Mature speech is produced without the influence of abnormal reflexes.

- *Top-down processing:* Clients with immature tongue movements often need direct tactile and proprioceptive input for tongue movements to occur.

With maturity the client can think through and then perform target tongue movements without this type of physical prompting. For example, a very young child may only be able to lift the sides of the tongue when he uses a tubular object around which to curl. With maturity, the client will learn to lift the sides of the tongue on command.

GLOSSECTOMY

Therapists are concerned with speech following glossectomy, including removal of part or all of the tongue. Both speech and swallowing are affected following surgical removal of parts of the tongue (Logemann et al., 1993), however, research consistently demonstrates that intelligibility can be very high even when the tongue is nearly absent in its entirety. Some speakers make up for lack of lingua tissue by engaging other oral structures and others simply use the remaining tissue to the best of their ability. There have also been attempts to create a prosthetic tongue and to use dentures to make up for tongue tissue. The following summarizes some of the basic research in this area presented in chronological order:

- Twisleton (1873) gathered dozens of anecdotal accounts of cases dating back to 1630 of people who had their tongues removed due to smallpox, cancer, and religious persecution, or who had very small tongues due to congenital malformation. Eyewitness accounts of these people from physicians, clergy, professors, and other trustworthy and learned people were gathered. High levels of intelligibility were reported in all cases.

- Goldstein (1940) studied three cases of total glossectomy following oral cancer and found that these clients were able to produce oral speech that was "understandable" and "distinct." One client even was able to use the telephone. Speech was self-taught in these cases.

- Weinberg, Christensen, Logan, Bosma, and Wornall (1969) examined one girl with limited tongue tissue (hypoplasia) since birth and found she was highly intelligible. The authors reported that the client used facial muscles, jaw movements, and lip movements to make sounds that otherwise would have been made with the tongue. She was described as making a wide variety of unusual and atypical facial movements to make up for her lack of a tongue. For example she produced /t/ by articulating the lips on one side. The authors questioned the validity of enrolling such a client in articulation treatment if intelligibility is high. The Van Riper approach would be to enroll this type of client in therapy as long as she can be taught compensatory strategies.

- Massengill, Maxwell, and Pickrell (1970) studied three cases of glossectomy and found that speech impairment depended on the amount of tissue lost. They reported that these patients retained verbal communication although speech was somewhat distorted. They also reported that patients with more radical surgery could develop speech that is better than those with lesser involvement depending upon location of excision and amount of scar tissue that forms.

- Leonard and Gillis (1982, 1983) found that a prosthetic tongue placed on a patient with total glossectomy improved intelligibility of vowel productions from 48% to 64%. Front vowels were better preserved than back or central vowels. In an addendum they noted that "at least some aspects of speech may be improved in a glossectomized talker with the use of a prosthesis" (Leonard & Gillis, 1983, p. 426).

- Imai and Michi (1992) used electropalatography to examine tongue-to-palate articulations in 17 glossectomized patients. They found that mobility of the remaining tongue is more important for better stop consonant productions than is the size of the remaining tissue.

- Logemann et al. (1993) studied patients who had undergone resection of the base of the tongue, tonsils, faucial arch, and hemimandibulectomy, and found changes in stop and fricative consonants and some minor changes in lip function for speech. They found that the nature of reconstruction might have contributed to errors on anterior consonants because reconstruction necessitates pulling the structures closer together toward the back. Scar tissue was also a factor in limiting oral movement for speech.

- One client (anecdote from a professional acquaintance) was equipped with a small set of dentures that fit inside her own set of natural teeth following removal of most of her tongue. The client learned to speak and eat well as her remaining tongue tissue learned to rely on the oral cavity formed by the set of inner false teeth.

CASE EXAMPLES

Two case studies serve as excellent examples of how to put the ideas of this chapter into practical application. Both of these clients were fifteen-year-olds, one male and one female. Sam and Abbey both had intellectual skills within the above-average range, both were sophomores in high school, and both were friendly but somewhat reserved. Sam had a persistent distortion of both consonantal and vocalic R, and Abbey had a bi-lateral lisp. Abbey had never received speech services but Sam had been in R-therapy for 8 years! Neither had been able to remediate their errors using standard model-imitation methods. Both students had excellent auditory discrimination skills

and both knew they were producing their phonemes incorrectly. Neither could get their tongues to position correctly for adequate sound production; Sam was very discouraged but Abbey seemed to take her errors in stride.

As discussed in Chapter 1 on traditional methods, Van Riper taught that listening (auditory training) should come first followed by basic model-imitation routines (stimulation method). He also taught that if these methods did not work immediately, therapists needed to switch gears and teach jaw-lip-tongue-velar positioning (phonetic placement method). These two students were ready for the phonetic placement method immediately. Methods to improve tongue function as discussed in this chapter are the types of methods required because they needed help getting their tongues to move and position correctly for the target phonemes.

Upon closer examination it was found that both students had difficulty keeping the middle of the tongue down during speech, meaning that the tongue bowl configuration was not fully integrated into their oral movement patterns for phoneme production, and they were arching instead of de-arching to make their phonemes. Sam's habit was to hump the tongue up and retract the sides when he produced both consonantal and vocalic /r/. Abbey's habit was to push the tongue's middle section up all the time so that not only did she have a bi-lateral production of all the sibilants, all other phonemes, especially the vowels, were somewhat distorted as well.

The SLP began to use methods to facilitate improved tongue function. These methods were used in conjunction with auditory stimulation, visual cues, conceptual cues, and (in Sam's case) methods to build hope. Therapy took place once per week for 30-minute sessions with minimal parent involvement. The students used mirrors as they were taught the following:

- To bowl the tongue using midline brushing.
- To widen the tongue using the Hee-Haw activity.
- To become more aware of the tongue's lateral margins using lateral brushing.
- To elevate the tongue's lateral margins independently using resistance and the Butterfly Position (see method on pages 211–212).
- To anchor the tongue at the back-lateral margins using the E Position (see method on page 209).
- Abbey was taught to make a tiny groove with the T Position and a wide groove using the E Position (see methods on page 209).
- Sam was taught to retract the whole tongue while holding the butterfly using the technique of Marking the Target, to retract the tongue tip back using the L-to-R Slide, and to pull the whole tongue back farther using the motokinesthetic method of tapping the head (see method on pages 219–220).

Both students responded positively to these methods immediately. Sam achieved a correct /r/ in 20 minutes after having been in model-imitation therapy for eight years. Sam already knew what to do with the new sound because of his extensive background in auditory discrimination, so he immediately began to figure out how to use it in both the consonantal and vocalic positions in words and phrases on his own and with no further prompting from the therapist. He took full control of the remediation process immediately and never needed another lesson.

Abbey's situation was a little more problematic since she had been humping the tongue upward on all her vowels and sibilants, and she had never been enrolled in therapy before. Abbey required 14 weeks of training to learn how to keep her tongue in correct position all the time. She learned all her sibilants and vowels and was dismissed from treatment in just over three months.

These students learned to produce correct phonemes in minimal time using appropriate methods to facilitate tongue movement and position. In Sam's case the difference was 20 minutes compared to 8 years. In Abbey's case the difference was 3 months compared to a lifetime of informal attempts. These dramatic cases have been chosen to demonstrate the critical role played by tongue movement training in articulation therapy. This concept represents the best of Van Riper-type articulation therapy. It integrates everything that has been learned about tongue function from ancient days to the present and demonstrates the effectiveness of the phonetic placement method when used skillfully.

IMPORTANT NOTES

This chapter concludes with a few words about grasping the tongue, tactile sensitivity, treating the tongue gently, and incorporating these methods into a full program of articulation therapy.

Grasping the Tongue

Several techniques described in this chapter require the tongue to be grasped. The tongue is wet, squishy, wiggly, and difficult to grasp with bare fingers. The best procedure the present author has found is to follow sanitary procedures and to use a piece of gauze. Dworkin explained this well as applied to adult patients:

> *"Request the patient to stick out the tongue so that it can be gently grasped with a gauze pad… the thumb and index fingers do the pulling as the remaining fingers of each hand are positioned gently against the undersurface of the patient's chin for leverage and head balance"* (Dworkin, 1991, p. 194–195).

This basic procedure needs to be playful when applied to young children. Close rapport, knowing the child well, creative imagery, and good timing are perhaps the keys to grasping a young child's tongue. A playful demand may encourage the child to stick it out: "Give me that tongue!"

Reverse psychology sometimes works: "Oh no, I can't find your tongue… It won't come out… I can't get it!" Playful sadness also works on occasion: "Boo-hoo... I can't get your tongue because it's hiding… Oh no, what will I do?"

Tactile Sensitivity

A great number of the methods described above require touching the tongue and certain clients will not allow this due to tactile hypersensitivity, tactile defensive behavior, or simple shyness. Direct hands-on tongue facilitation techniques may need to be withheld until the client more readily accepts tactile experiences in, on, and around the mouth. Let the client employ the methods with his own hands, employ activities to normalize tactile sensitivity, and work on developing rapport with the client first. (For details, see Chapter 16 on normalizing oral-tactile sensitivity.)

Treating the Tongue Gently

Speech-language pathologists must work cautiously when utilizing any and all of the techniques described above. The tongue is delicate and versus sensitive to movement and touch. The muscles are small, the skin tissue is thin, and the connective tissue is quite malleable. Pulling the tongue forward can cause pain and the lingua frenum can be torn if dragged too forcefully against the lower teeth. Do not cause pain or physical harm by pushing or pulling the tongue too far in any direction. Do not over-exert. A few gentle applications of any one of these techniques will suffice in most cases. Discontinue using method immediately if the client has an aversive reaction.

Engaging in a Full Program

Helping the tongue to function better by applying the methods of this chapter will not automatically make speech problems disappear. Therapy includes methods to help the tongue to function better and to help the client learn phonemes through other auditory, linguistic, and cognitive means. This is not about so-called "non-speech oral-motor exercises" or activities to "strengthen the tongue." The discussion in this chapter is about normal tongue function and methods to facilitate it for phoneme production.

An analogy to another type of movement may help the reader understand this concept. Consider the ice skater. An ice skater will work to improve movement, strength, flexibility, and control in the movement of his ankles, but these improvements will not automatically make him a better skater. The skater still has to learn how to skate forward and backward, to perform jumps, spins, and dance movements, to coordinate his skating with music, and so forth. Likewise, clients can benefit from learning better tongue movements, but better tongue movements by themselves will not automatically make the client a better speaker. Therapists still have to teach the client how to listen and think about phonemes, how to produce phonemes in syllables and words, how to repair errors in conversation, and so forth. Speech-language pathologists who work in the 21st century understand that teaching a client to move the tongue better is only one small yet valuable part of the much bigger process of articulation training.

SUMMARY

A malleable tongue is the most important aspect of mature speech production. A tremendous number of methods to facilitate tongue movement have been developed throughout the past century, many of which are supported by research on tongue function.

14

The Critical Role of Oral Stability

The next big step in articulation and motor speech therapy

> *"Speech skill building starts with learning to stabilize the jaw and anchor the tongue along the outer, lateral margins of the palate."*
>
> – Samuel Fletcher, 1992

Oral stability is an integral part of speech movement and is the next big step therapists will take in the treatment of articulation and motor speech disorders. Teaching a client to move the jaw, lips, and tongue for speech purposes as discussed in the previous three chapters is very important, but these movements will be of limited usefulness if not appropriately stabilized. Practicing SLPs have been experimenting with the concept of oral stability for many decades and this perspective has been supported by the latest research on jaw, lip, and tongue function. The present chapter describes what oral stability is, the importance of this skill to good speech, and how lack of appropriate oral stability impacts speech in negative ways. This chapter includes methods for assessing this important skill and concludes with methods for developing it.

ORAL STABILITY

Every mechanical object requires an anchor to function correctly, and examples from the industrial world are plentiful. A pendulum swings correctly only when anchored to its assembly at the top; a wheel rotates properly only when anchored by its hub in the center, a seesaw totters correctly only when anchored to its fulcrum in the middle; the arm of a crane swings accurately only when anchored at its base. A mechanical object that is suitably anchored can achieve its movement goals, but a moving object that is not appropriately anchored is much less likely to. An unanchored moving object will miss its intended target, will move too far afield, and will wobble, shake, vibrate, tremble, bob, quiver, sway, or waver as it moves.

The concept of anchoring applies to all parts of the human "machine" too, and the appropriate term for this is *stability*. All moving body parts require a certain point or points of stability, which tend to be *proximal* or near the trunk of the body. Proximal stability allows for accurate and advanced distal mobility. This means that stability of a body part that is located nearer to the trunk allows the parts that are farther away from the trunk to move with maturity, accuracy, and consistency. For one example, shoulder stability allows the arms to move accurately.

The mouth can move in a range that far exceeds that which is necessary for correct speech production, therefore it has to have mechanisms to hold each moving part in place so that articulations can be small, accurate, mature, and consistent. This is the role of oral stability. The moving parts of the mouth are the jaw, the lips, and the tongue, and the mechanisms for holding these parts in place are called *jaw stability*, *lip/cheek stability*, and *tongue stability*. Together these stabilizing mechanisms create *oral stability*.

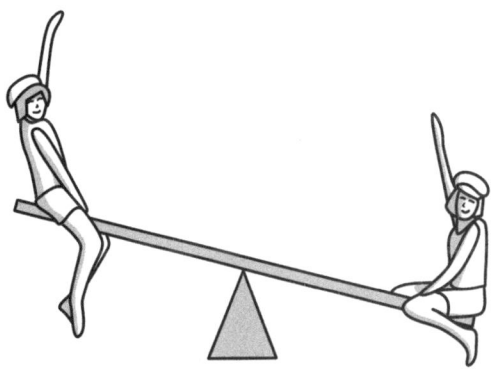

Moving objects function correctly only when appropriately stabilized.

The topic of oral stability was introduced in Chapter 10 on the principles of motor development. It is stated there that the word *mobility* refers to the capacity to move or be moved freely and easily, while the word *stable* means "not likely to give way or overturn." Body part stability denotes those factors of movement that give it anchor. Stability contributes constancy, steadiness, and firmness to movement: "All voluntary movement involves an element of stability" (Gallahue & Ozmun, 1995, p. 169).

Stability does not mean stiffness or fixedness, however. Stability is dynamic and relative to mobility; one part of the body holds relatively still so another part can be relatively more mobile:

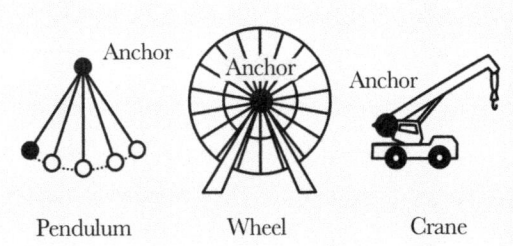

Pendulum   Wheel   Crane

Moving objects and their anchors.

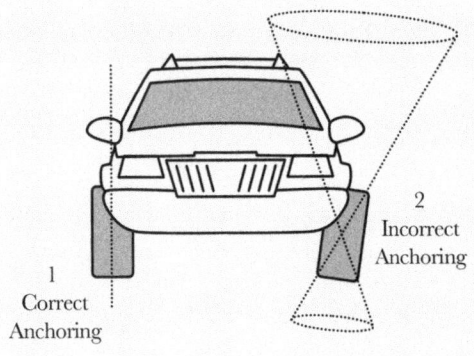

1
Correct
Anchoring

2
Incorrect
Anchoring

The wheel on the left (1) is anchored correctly and, therefore, can rotate in a straight line. The wheel on the right (2) lacks appropriate anchoring and will wobble.

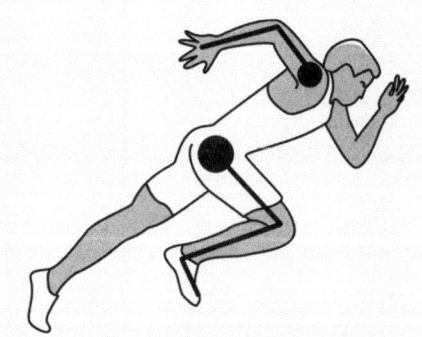

Stabilizing muscles in the shoulders and hips anchor movements of the arms and legs.

"*A fixer or stabilizer is a muscle which anchors, steadies, or supports a bone or body part in order that another active muscle may have a firm base upon which to pull... In the ideal case, a fixator or stabilizer muscle will be in static contraction. In practice, these terms are extended to include instances in which there is a slight motion in the 'stabilized' part, so as to continuously adjust the stabilization to be the requirements of the desired motion; this condition may be called 'moving fixation' or a 'guiding action'*" (Rasch & Burke, 1978, p. 47).

Mobility and stability work together in a supportive reciprocal relationship within every movement. In his treatise on speech movement, ASHA Honors winner Samuel Fletcher (1992) called it the *fixation mobilization principle.* Oral stability is an essential component of speech movement as observed by therapists and as proven by research. It is a concept that has been floating around for a long time: "Mature speech is characterized by stabilized motions" (Bosma, 1967, p. 108).

The concept of movement stability arose out of the motor therapies that emerged in the mid-20th century, but even phonologically-oriented linguists like Chomsky and Halle (1968) recognized this concept in regard to speech movement. Using the results of x-ray analysis, Chomsky and Halle stated that no matter what phoneme is being produced, the speech mechanism first shapes itself into what they called *neutral position*: "Just prior to speaking the subject positions his vocal tract in a certain characteristic manner. We shall call this configuration the 'neutral position'" (p. 300). Careful reading of their paragraph devoted to this topic reveals that Chomsky and Halle were describing some of the features that now can be identified as oral stability. However, in the entire breadth of phonological literature that has been written since Chomsky and Halle, there does not seem to be one other mention of this concept. Perhaps the mistake Chomsky and Halle made was in calling this position "neutral." They should have called it *starting position*. Every phoneme is made with a starting position, and that is the position of oral stability.

JAW STABILITY

The jaw is stabile when it moves up-down, left-right, and forward-back during speech in a very small and restricted range relative to how far it can move. Bell (1887) said that movements of the jaw in good speech are *equable*, meaning that they do not vary or fluctuate greatly. Zemlin (1968) said that jaw movements are very slight during the process of normal speech but that inadequate, inappropriate, or sluggish movements of the jaw may result in severe articulation defects. In their clinical observations of motor speech disorders, Dworkin, Meleca, and Stachler (2003) suggested that lack of appropriate jaw stability may play a leading role in the persistence of certain abnormal speech behaviors.

Jaw stability can now be defined in terms of how many millimeters the jaw moves up-down, left-right, and forward-back during the process of mature adult speech. Each of these planes of jaw stability shall be addressed individually.

Vertical Jaw Stability

The first element of jaw stability is its movement upwards and downwards in the vertical plane. Van Riper (1947) was interested in this and he called it the *proper dental opening*. He and other writers of his era said that this gap between the upper and lower teeth was generally very small but varied depending upon the phoneme being produced.

Speech movement researchers call the up-down movement of the jaw its *pitch*, and they have put numbers on these movements. Vatikiotis-Bateson and Ostry (1995) studied two English and two Japanese adult speakers uttering nonsense syllable sequences and found consistent phoneme-specific jaw movement patterning among them all. They found that the jaw pitched upwards and downwards in a maximum range of about 25 mm (0.98 inches) with the highest position occurring during production of /s/ and the lowest on /ɑ/. This range represents speech testing conditions.

From this, one can say that jaw stability in adult speech under speech production test conditions requires the jaw to restrict its up-down movements to just under 1 inch. The jaw's highest position should occur during production of /s/ and its lowest during /ɑ/. Up-down jaw movement on every other phoneme should be accomplished somewhere in between these extremes. This up-down jaw movement is fairly easy to see with the naked eye during a speech exam.

Changes to this range occur in other specific situations. The speakers in the Vatikiotis-Bateson and Ostry study moved their jaws in a wider range when speaking loudly, in a slightly smaller range when speaking normally, and in range even smaller than that when speaking fast. The present author has also noted informally that the jaw moves in a wider range when a subject is singing or engaged in public oration.

This up-down movement of the jaw during speech is much smaller than that which is used during chewing. Gibbs and Messerman (1972) studied adults and found that the range of up-down jaw movements during chewing were up to five times larger than they were during speaking. From this, one could argue that jaw movements are smaller and much more refined for speech than they are for chewing, and that jaw stability is much more restrictive for speech than for chewing.

Lateral Jaw Stability

The second element of jaw stability is its movement left and right. Lateral movement of the jaw is very slight during speech. Gibbs and Messerman (1972) measured the jaw's movement from midline to one side and found it to

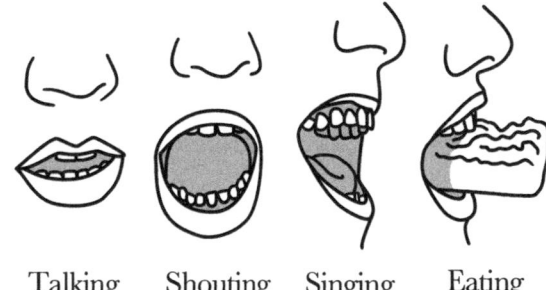

Talking   Shouting   Singing   Eating

The jaw moves up-down less than one inch during normal conversational speech but it moves much farther than that during shouting, eating, or singing.

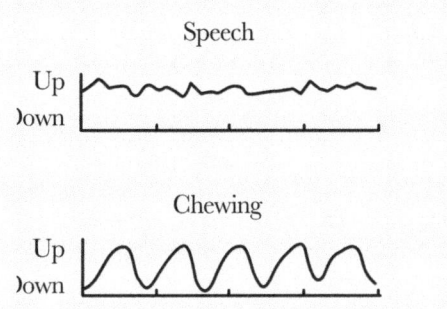

Up-down adult jaw movements are about five times larger in chewing than they are in speech (adapted from Steeve, 2010).

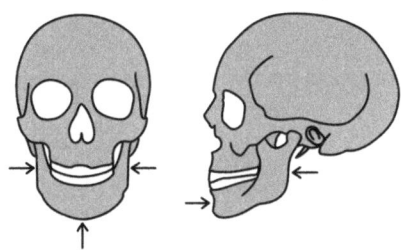

The tongue articulates with the palate correctly only when the jaw is appropriately stabilized from all directions.

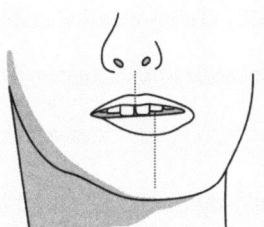

This jaw is unstable and lateralizing far outside the 2–3 mm range expected during normal adult speech.

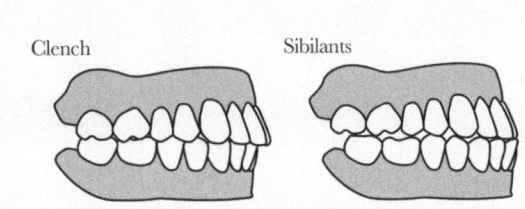

The stabile jaw shifts backward-and-forward about 0.5 mm during speech, from the clench in the rear to the vertical alignment of the incisors in the front.

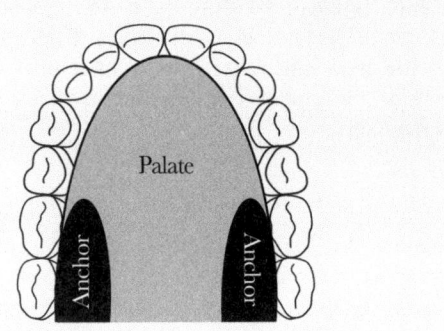

The stabilizing zones of the tongue have been called its anchors, shoulders, or fulcrums.

be one-tenth of an inch during adult speech. Vatikiotis-Bateson and Ostry (1995) measured it at 2–3 mm (about one eighth of an inch). Measured from side to side, this gives the jaw a total lateral movement of 4–6 mm (under one-quarter of an inch from left to right). This very small range of lateral jaw movement during speech generally goes unseen by the naked eye. Therefore, a therapist's eye should register the stabile jaw as functioning essentially at midline during speech testing and during conversation. A few millimeters of variation from left to right is normal and may even go unnoticed.

Anterior-Posterior Jaw Stability

The third element of jaw stability that is measured during research studies is its movements in the anterior-posterior or forward-back direction during speech. Vatikiotis-Bateson and Ostry (1995) found this range to be a maximum of about 5 mm (about 0.2 inches). The furthest back that the jaw normally moves during speech occurs when one speaks while clenching the jaw and this happens only on occasion, as, for example, when the speaker is expressing anger.

The elocutionists described the forward movement of the jaw during speech as being never so far forward as to place the lower incisors anterior to the upper incisors. The upper and lower anterior teeth align themselves in a nearly perfect vertical line when sibilants are produced. This alignment creates the anterior dental barrier against which the midline airstream strikes to create stridency.

Jaw stability in the anterior-posterior plane, therefore, can be defined as follows: During adult speech, the jaw should never position itself farther back than the clenched position, and never farther forward that vertical alignment of the upper and lower incisors.

TONGUE STABILITY

Tongue stability is the second element of oral stability. Stability of the tongue during speech keeps it in correct physical relationship to the palate at all times and thus allows tongue-palate articulations to be accurate and

1   CORONAL VIEW

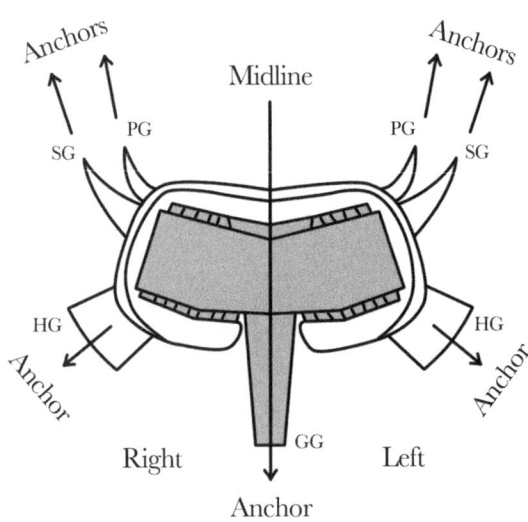

2   SIDE VIEW

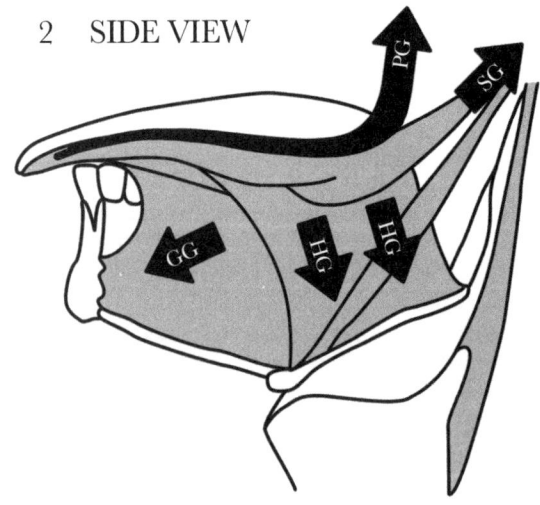

Top: Modern coronal (1) and traditional side (2) views of the extrinsic or fringe muscles that function to anchor the tongue to its surrounding hard structures. (Adapted from Takemoto, 2001.) Note: PG is Palatoglossus, SG is Styloglossus, HG is Hyoglossus, GG is Genioglossus.

consistent. Tongue stability also allows sequential lingual movements to occur smoothly, quickly, and efficiently. Tongue stability is described in four ways for the purposes of this manual: (1) the tongue is held up by the jaw, (2) the tongue anchors itself against the palate, (3) the tongue anchors itself between the side teeth, and (4) its base is held firm by attachments to lower fixed structures.

Held Up by the Jaw

The tongue sits within the frame provided by the jaw so the jaw carries the tongue wherever it goes. In the ideal situation, the jaw is stabilized as described above and this holds the tongue in place relative to the palate in all directions. With correct jaw stability the tongue can lift and make contact with the palate and upper teeth accurately, consistently, and in appropriate sequences.

Problems in the tongue-palate relationship occur when the jaw is unstable: a jaw that sits too low pulls the tongue down and away from the palate; a jaw that lateralizes too far to the right or left carries the tongue too far in these directions relative to the palate; a jaw that protrudes or retracts too far carries the tongue too far forward or back relative to the palate.

Therefore, jaw stability — as defined above — is a critical aspect of tongue stability. This concept has been stated in many ways throughout the centuries, and two examples written a century apart are presented below. Guttmann wrote about the problem of jaw lateralization and protrusion during the elocution era. McDonald and

Chance wrote one of the first texts on cerebral palsy, and they wrote about the devastation that a low jaw position has on lingual phonemes:

> *"Imperfect speech is not merely due to the defective pronunciation of the sounds, but is also, in a great measure, the consequence of keeping the lower jaw too far forward... or of moving it to one side"* (Guttmann, 1893, p. 129).

> *"Over-depression of the mandible interferes with speech production by pulling the tongue into a position which makes lingua-dental and lingua-palatal contacts difficult or impossible"* (McDonald & Chance, 1964, p. 93).

Anchored Against the Palate in the Back

The tongue stabilizes itself in three ways. First, it anchors to the palate in the back. Second, it anchors to the molars on the sides. Third, the tongue anchors itself is from below through its attachments to the jaw and hyoid bone.

Stone and Vatikiotis-Bateson (1995) demonstrated that "tongue shape is more dependent on its contact with the palate than its support from the jaw" (p. 99). This means that while jaw stability as described above is critical for accurate and advanced tongue mobility, even more important for phoneme production is the way the tongue anchors itself to the palate. The tongue anchors itself to the palate by lifting its back-lateral margins and bracing them against the hard palate's lateral margins (Fletcher, 1992). These areas of the tongue have been called the *anchors* and the *fulcrums* of tongue movement (Fletcher, 1992), and this manual has used the phrases *shoulders of the tongue* and *stabilizing zones*. The stabilizing zones are the relatively unyielding parts of the tongue that support its mobility everywhere else. Fletcher said that this *lateral lingual stability* puts restrictions on the tongue's range of motion and prevents the tongue from protruding, retracting, or lateralizing with too many degrees of freedom during speech. This back-lateral anchoring seems to be served by the palatoglossus and styloglossus fringe muscles (Takemoto, 2001).

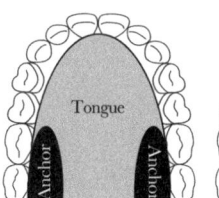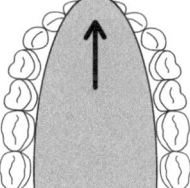

Stable Tongue   Unstable Tongue

A tongue is allowed to slip forward when not appropriately anchored in the back.

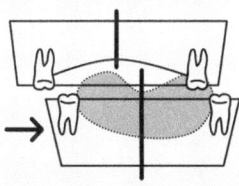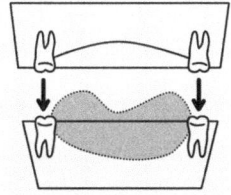

The tongue cannot anchor to the palate correctly when the jaw shifts too far to one side or the other.

The tongue cannot anchor to the palate when the jaw sits too low.

Example: /t/

Designers of the International Phonetic Alphabet used the term *place of articulation* to represent the points along midline where the primary action of a phoneme occurs. Phoneme /t/, therefore, was categorized as *lingua-alveolar* and unquestionably the place where one perceives tongue action for /t/ is at the tongue tip. However, palatometry reveals that this action at the tip is dependent upon the tongue bracing itself at the back-lateral margins. The tongue elevates and stabilizes itself on the sides in the back before, during, and after the tip elevates for production of /t/. The process is a perfect example of the stability-mobility principle: The tongue's proximal stability sets the stage for accurate distal mobility.

Palatograms from Gibbon (1999; adapted into an

illustration here) nicely demonstrate this represent one production of /t/ by an adult speaker with no speech impairment. Each picture depicts the contact points of the tongue against the palate over time during a single production of /t/. The darkened rectangles indicate points where the tongue makes contact with the palate while the empty rectangles indicate points where there is no contact. The drawings reveal that /t/ is produced in the following sequence:

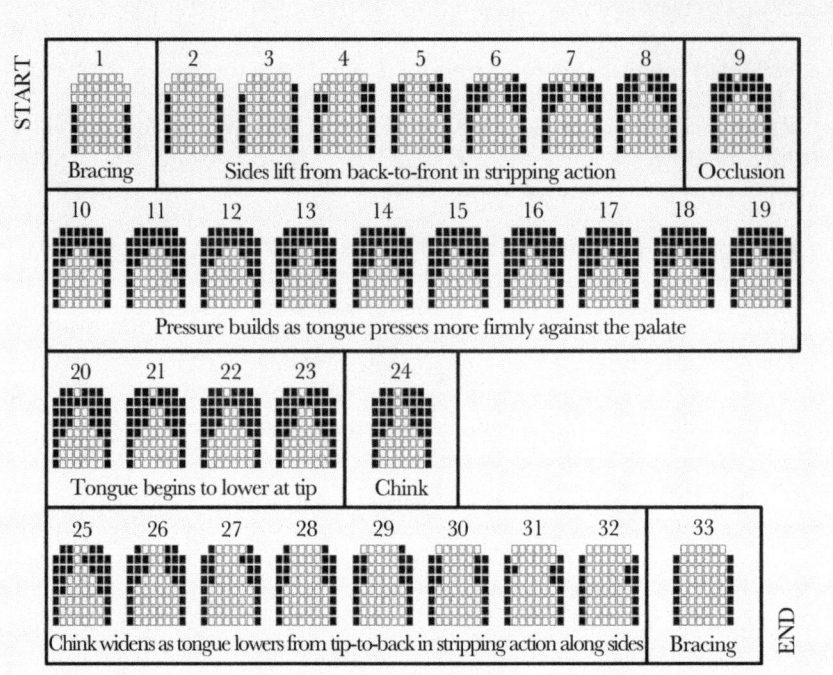

Palatograms demonstrate how the tongue's distal mobility is dependent upon its proximal stability (adapted from Gibbon, 1999).

1. Production of /t/ begins when the back-lateral margins of the tongue lift and brace against the palate to stabilize the tongue in the back (palatorgram 1).

2. With the anchors in place, the sides of the tongue lift to the palate in sequence from back-to-front (palatograms 2 through 8).

3. The target position is reached when elevation of the tongue's perimeter extends all the way from the back to the tip. This seals the tongue against the palate in a characteristic horseshoe-shape that occludes airflow (palatorgram 9).

4. The tongue continues to press upward more firmly against the palate while air pressure builds behind the horseshoe-shaped seal (palatorgrams 10 through 19).

5. The off-glide is initiated when the tongue begins to lower away from the palate at the tip (palatorgrams 20 through 23).

6. Air begins to escape the mouth when the tip descends enough to allow a tiny chink to form (palatorgram 24).

7. Then the chink widens as the tongue lowers away from the palate in reverse from the tip to the back along the sides (palatorgrams 25 through 32).

8. Production of /t/ ends when the tongue returns to a stabile position in the back (palatorgram 33). In this particular case the lateral bracing extended far to the front, but an additional slide or two that might have been reported might have shown the tongue to retreat back to its original starting position (as in palatogram 1).

Anchored Against the Molars

The second way the tongue stabilizes itself is by anchoring to the side teeth. Hasegawa-Johnson et al. (2003) used magnetic resonance imaging and demonstrated that the lateral margins of the tongue bulge outward slightly between the molars on both sides during production of all vowels. It can be deduced that this tongue position is also maintained for the consonants because the vowels shape the consonants and define oral position within each syllable. This lateral pressing is slight; the sides of the tongue do not hang out over and beyond the side teeth but simply bulge between them.

The sum of research demonstrates that the tongue anchors itself against the palate and molars in the back; a perfect example of proximal stability. Back-lateral anchoring holds the tongue in place so that it does not slide out of position relative to the palate, allowing the tongue's contact points with the upper structures to be accurate during articulation of all lingua-dental, lingua-alveolar, lingua-palatal, and lingua-velar phonemes. Therapists from 19th century forward have supported this concept as demonstrated in the following quotes. In the first, an elocutionist discusses the role of back-lateral tongue stability in preventing a frontal lisp, and, in the second, a speech researcher summarizes the role of back-lateral stability during production of all phonemes:

"I must point out the importance of this pressure of the tongue's [lateral] edges against the molars. This muscle-

action must hold the edges of the tongue in a powerful grasp, and it is the failure of this muscle action that causes a person to lisp" (Kofler, 1887, p. 250).

"This lateral lingual stability frees the tongue blade and root to produce alternative postures and reciprocal front and back articulatory gestures and action sequences required in consonant and vowel production… A reduction in the degrees of freedom in tongue movement emancipates certain portions of the tongue for precise articulatory actions" (Fletcher, 1992, p. 13).

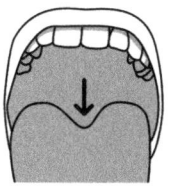 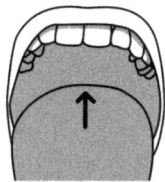

Correct   Incorrect

The base of the tongue anchors low (left) to create the orotund quality of speech. Humping in the rear (right) causes speech to sound guttural and hypernasal.

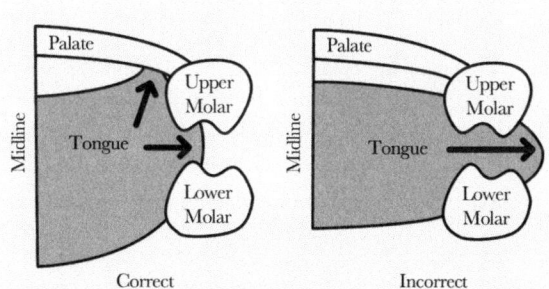

Correct   Incorrect

The tongue anchors itself by pressing its back-lateral margins upward against the palate and laterally between the back molars. The tongue does not bulge laterally past the side teeth.

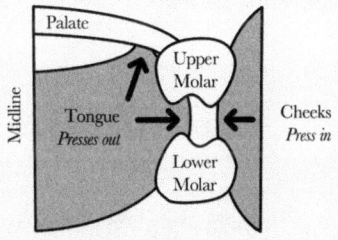

The tongue and the cheeks press toward one another to stabilize oral movements at the molars.

Held Firm From Below

The third way the tongue anchors itself is from below through its attachments to the jaw and hyoid bone via the hyoglossus and geniohyoid muscles. These lower extrinsic fringe muscles exert a staying hold on the middle back of the tongue so that it can remain low and steady while the perimeter of the tongue elevates to the palate. In other words, the tongue stabilizes its middle-back in a low position while it elevates at various points around its perimeter.

Researchers have not begun to quantify this process of middle-back anchoring but it is an essential element of the tongue bowl shape and it has been described numerous times throughout the history of speech remediation going back to the elocutionists. For example, Bell (1887) called this low middle anchoring the chief source of the orotund quality of the vowels:

"The root of the tongue should be depressed as much as possible, to expand the back part of the mouth and give fullness to the vowel sounds. This is the chief source of the mellow 'orotund' quality which distinguishes the voices of the best speakers" (Bell, 1887, p. 52).

Lack of anchoring at the base of the tongue allows the back of the tongue to press upward at incorrect moments during speech which gives speech a guttural or thick sound quality as the back of the tongue arches up too high upward, even touching the soft palate. This incorrect method of stability causes clients to produce a gross lingua-velar fricative sound while they are producing other phonemes, and it may contribute to over-use of [+Back] phonemes. Lack of low middle-back anchoring can also interfere with the refined tongue movements necessary for production of difficult phonemes like /r/. For more information on this topic, the reader is referred to the sections on tongue bowling in Chapter 13.

LIP-CHEEK STABILITY

Stability of the lips and cheeks is the third element of oral stability. The elocutionists of the 19th century used prose to describe this position. They wrote about what the lips and cheeks should and should not do during speech, and they often portrayed their correct position as forming a slight smile:

"The lips should never hang loosely away from the teeth, or be pursed, pouted, or twisted, but they should maintain the form of the dental ranges as nearly as possible, lying equally and unconstrainedly against the teeth" (Bell, 1887, p. 52).

This clinical observation has been backed by all research. Lip/cheek stability is accomplished through contraction of the cheeks, particularly the buccinator muscle that is situated laterally from the corner of the lips to the pteragomandibular raphe: "Upon contraction the buccinator compresses the lips and cheeks against the teeth and draws the corners of the mouth laterally" (Zemlin, 1968, p. 260–261).

Proper cheek stability creates a slight grin that exposes part of the front teeth. This is not a full smile that reveals all the teeth but a smaller, somewhat coy smile. A slight tightening of the cheeks against the teeth holds the mouth in position and gives the lips the stabile freedom they need to move correctly. Stability in the cheeks also helps hold the jaw in position.

The concept of lip/cheek stability emerged out of the feeding literature of the late 20th century (e.g., Morris & Klein, 1983) and some attention to this skill has arisen recently in speech research. Hasegawa-Johnson et al. (2003) found that the cheeks press inward between the upper and lower side teeth while clients produce vowels: "The

Lips that are not stabilized by the cheeks hang forward during speech.

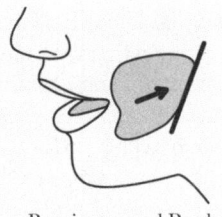

Buccinator and Raphe

The buccinator muscle presses the cheeks against the side teeth to anchor lip movements.

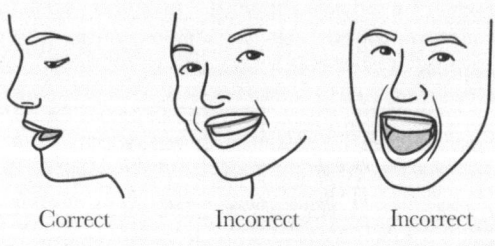

Correct   Incorrect   Incorrect

The subtle smile (left) creates appropriate stability for lip movement during mature speech.

tongue and cheeks always bulge slightly into the interdental space" (p. 741). This means that the cheeks are actively pressing inward. Here this idea is extended to all consonants since the vowels define oral position within each syllable.

THE BODY

It is beyond the scope of this manual to extend this discussion of oral stability to the rest of the body but it should be sufficient to say that oral stability is dependent upon head, neck, shoulder, trunk, and hip stability. Readers are referred to their team motor specialists for information specific to individual clients and this discussion is left to other writers who can describe these relationships thoroughly. A few activities to stabilize the hips, trunk, and upper body are described briefly in Chapter 7 on breath support.

ORAL STABILITY SUMMARY

The adult oral mechanism can be described as stabile when the jaw, lips/cheeks, and tongue are anchored in specific ways (in rounded figures):

- The jaw moves no more than 25 mm up and down, no more than 2–3 mm left and right of midline, and no more than 5 mm forward and backward.

- The back-lateral margins of the tongue anchor upward to the palate and laterally between the molars, and the middle of the tongue anchors downward via its attachments to the jaw and hyoid bone.

- The cheeks press inward against the side teeth to stabilize the lips. This also aids in stabilization of the jaw.

- Oral stability occurs relative to head, neck, shoulder, trunk, and hip stability.

ORAL STABILITY RESEARCH

Morris' classic study on feeding development (Morris, 1982) revealed that jaw, lip, and tongue stability for feeding purposes develops in stages and comes to maturity by two years of age, but there have been no specific studies on the role of oral stability in speech development. However, studies of developing phonology give hints that oral stability for speech may develop in a similar fashion. Four examples are offered here.

Davis and MacNeilage (1990) studied vowel development in one toddler and found that low vowels dominated her babbling while high vowels dominated her early words. This suggests that the jaw may be unstable and low during the babbling stage but can function with more stability and higher by the time first words emerge.

Sussman et al. (1996) studied one child beginning at 12 months of age and found that place of articulation for the stop consonants became more consistent when the child was 21 months of age. If consistency in place of articulation can be considered a benefit of oral stability, then this study would suggest that another level of oral stability is achieved some time between 12 and 21 months of age.

According to the summary of phonological development by Vihman (2004b), most children have acquired a complete phonological system by three years of age. This would suggest that another level of oral stability has been reached by then.

Finally, virtually all studies of speech development have indicated that all minor articulation errors are straightened out by around eight years of age. This may suggest that all aspects of adult oral stability have been achieved by around the third grade.

INSTABILITY & SPEECH

Oral stability can be absent, incorrect, or fluctuating, and the term *instability* is used when these occur. It is difficult to describe in words what happens to speech when instability occurs because the result is distortion. Readers, therefore, are strongly urged to read the following material carefully and to imitate these patterns themselves in order to understand the impact each has on speech. For example, hold each incorrect posture and count to 10. Study the auditory changes that occur as stability is altered in the ways described.

Lack of Stability

A complete lack of oral stability means that no amount of stability has been established. Lack of oral stability allows the jaw, lips, and tongue to move in any and all directions, often too far for correct speech, and sometimes not far enough. For example, a client with very low muscle tone often allows the jaw, lips, and tongue to hang low and forward. The client may be able to move his jaw, lips, and tongue, but the movements will be low and forward. Voice and resonance become muffled and somewhat denasal, vowels become less orotund, and consonants tend to be produced with their points of articulation sloppy and shifted forward.

Research is beginning to look at how incorrect position of one articulator affects another. For example, Solomon and Munson (2004) studied ten normal adults and found that the tongue was able to generate less upward force as the jaw lowered its position. One of the main differences

between phonemes in terms of manner of articulation is the amount of this force the tongue uses to press upward against the palate: Vowels and glides require the least upward force, fricatives require more, and stops require the most. A lack of jaw stability, therefore, may contribute to a tongue's inability to generate the right amount of upward pressure needed to differentiate these groups.

Incorrect Oral Stability

To say that an oral mechanism is stabilized incorrectly means that the client is using some measure of stability but it is being done in the wrong place, with the wrong structures, too firmly, or too loosely. These problems in oral stability cause oral movements to be incorrect. Many examples can be cited from the present author's clinical experiences.

Some clients fail to anchor the tongue upward against the palate at the back-lateral margins and they substitute it with some other tongue anchoring position. The tongue may anchor by pressing its middle against the palate (Dagenais, Critz-Crosby, & Adams, 1994). The tongue may also press its tip to the floor of the mouth, or the tip may rest its underside against the lower teeth or lip. Some clients tighten all their facial muscles to hold the mouth in place. Some draw the lips forward to create a purse-string effect. Others pull the upper lip up and fix it there to hold oral stability. Still others tilt the head back and anchor the mouth in an open position for stability. Some clients even stabilize the tongue by flipping it over onto its side during speech.

Stabilizing the tongue on the lower lip is like resting the feet on an ottoman or desk. The tongue and the legs cannot move appropriately because they are anchored in the wrong place.

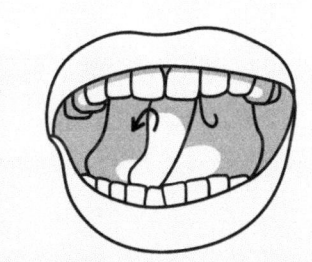

Some clients stabilize the tongue by twisting it.

Probably the most common error is the client who speaks with the jaw stabilized in a position that is too low with the result being a frontal lisp. Fröeschels and Jellinek (1941) studied 800 school children with frontal lisps to determine if the frontal lisp was the result of the anterior open bite. They discovered that the anterior open bite was a factor in only three of these cases. All the rest of the subjects (99.6%) produced sibilants with a frontal lisp because the jaw situated itself in a position that was too low.

Another common error occurs when clients use the mentalis muscle to stabilize the oral mechanism. The mentalis muscle tightens to hold the mouth in position and excessive mottling occurs on the chin as a result. The tight chin pushes upward against the underside of the lower lip, and the lower lip is driven forward so that it curls downward into a pattern called *lower lip eversion*.

A final pattern of incorrect lingual stability affects the sibilants especially. The stabilizing zones of the tongue

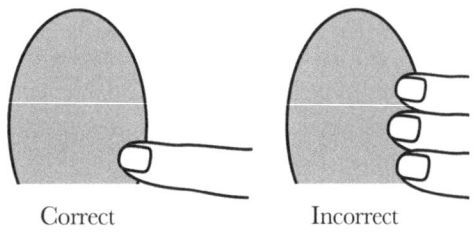

Correct   Incorrect

More than one fingertip of back-lateral tongue stability causes significant phoneme distortion, especially of the sibilants.

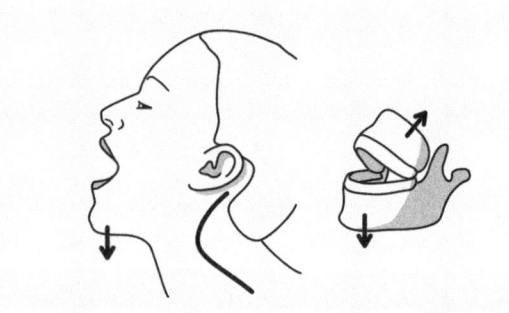

The jaw anchors too low when the head is tilted back.

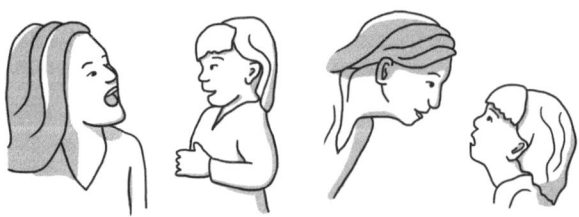

Therapists position themselves so they can get a good view of the mouth and so clients can maintain appropriate head position during the assessment of oral stability.

should be about the width of an index fingertip, and oral stability is incorrect when a client uses too much of the back-lateral margins of the tongue to accomplish this. Some clients use two, three, or even more fingertip widths in the back for stability. The longer the length of back-lateral stability from back-to-front, the more distorted the sibilants become. The tongue should hold itself stabile only in the very back. Distortion of the delicate sibilant sounds occurs when too much of the back is used. The tongue can move under these conditions but it moves from points of stability that are too large (too long). Distortion of all sounds is the result, with distortion of the sibilants being the most prominent.

Fluctuating Oral Stability

Stability can also fluctuate from one moment to the next. The jaw may be positioned too high one moment and too low the next. Or the jaw may shift left, right, forward, and back at inappropriate intervals. The tongue and the lips may also shift randomly in any and all directions. Clients with fluctuating stability speak as if they are hunting for a place to land. They sound very sloppy and dysarthric as a result.

ASSESSING ORAL STABILITY

Speech-language pathologists do not have the time or the equipment to do the types of formal evaluations of jaw, lip, and tongue function that one finds in research studies. Therapists must rely on the naked eye to assess oral stability in simple and functional ways. A clinical evaluation of oral stability is accomplished through careful observation of jaw, lip, and tongue movements during articulation testing and conversational speech. Oral stability is appraised when the client is talking calmly and not expressing wide swings in emotion, i.e., he is not laughing, crying, shouting, pouting, etc. Answers to specific questions are sought as suggested below.

Clinicians use their trained eyes to see how their clients stabilize the jaw, lips, and tongue during speech, and they compare what the client is doing with what is known about oral stability as defined above. This type of informal evaluation takes a while to master but time and practice should eventually result in excellent skill. Recording video allows one to watch a client's oral movements many times as an aid to the assessment and as a process of improving one's skills. Video is also an excellent way to educate clients and parents about oral stability and oral movements.

Recall that oral stability as defined above is the result of research on adults. There is no data on children of various ages and, therefore, there is no normative developmental data to use in assessment. What is known is that the oral stability defined above is what the child is moving toward.

Seating is an important element of the assessment of oral stability. Therapists sit in such a way that they get a good view of the client's mouth while he is talking. Do not sit above the client so he has to tilt his head back to look up at you, and do not sit to his side so that he has to turn his head and talk over his shoulder. Sit face-to-face and slightly lower than the client so that he can hold his head high and tall without straining or slouching, and so his mouth is well in view.

Simple tools can aid the assessment of oral stability. A straw, bite stick, or other straight probe can be held vertically and horizontally at various points about one inch in front of the client's face. Or dots can be placed strategically on the face. Such tools will provide reference points to help the eye see which parts of the face are pulling in which directions.

Another excellent way to assess oral stability is to imitate the client's speech pattern as exactly as possible. The SLP can observe the changes in her own oral stability as she imitates the client's speech patterns, paying close attention to hew jaw, lip, and tongue movements and stability as she imitates him, and using her own sensations to figure out what he is doing wrong. Years devoted to this type of analysis make a therapist very good at the assessment of oral movement and oral stability.

Assessing Jaw Stability

Rosenfeld-Johnson (2014) employs a bite block in the assessment of jaw stability. A bite-block is placed between the molars on one side and then the other, and it is tugged gently but firmly for 15 seconds. The client's job is to hold the block in place using isometric control. This type of

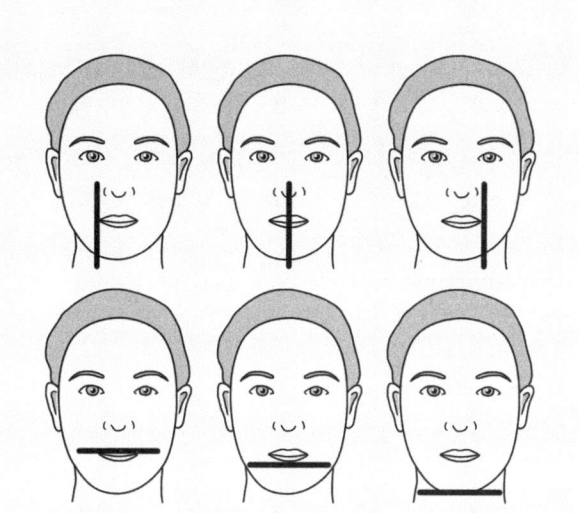

A straight probe held one inch in front of the client's face can help identify problems in oral stability.

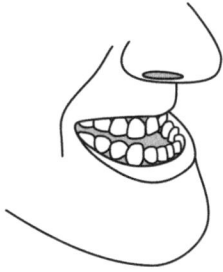

Pushing the jaw too far forward throws the tongue out of position relative to the palate. This movement error should not be confused with the Class III malocclusion.

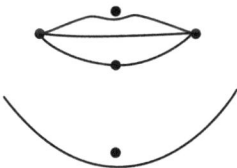

Tiny dots help the eye judge stability of the jaw and lips.

measure is a useful clinical tool to get a general idea of jaw strength for stability, but the measure is not yet standardized.

Jaw stability can also be assessed visually during speech. Watch jaw movement and the space between the maxillary and mandibular (upper and lower) incisors as the client talks. Green, Wilson, Wang, and Moore (2007) also found that the position of the chin could be used as an accurate representation of mandible movements. Use a straight probe to aid this analysis and seek answers to the following questions. Perfect symmetry is not expected.

- Is the jaw high enough for an acoustically correct /s/?

- Is the jaw low enough for an acoustically correct /ɑ/?

- Is the jaw positioning between /s/ and /ɑ/ for all other phonemes?

- Does the jaw stay within one inch of its highest position when it lowers for /ɑ/?

- Does the jaw remain essentially at midline during speech?

- Does the jaw slide to one side or the other beyond 2 mm? On which specific phonemes? On all phonemes? Which side: left, right, or both?

- Does the jaw protrude so that the mandibular (lower) incisors extend out farther than the maxillary (upper) incisors during speech? On which specific phonemes? On all phonemes?

- Does the jaw retract back beyond a clench position during speech? On which specific phonemes? On all phonemes?

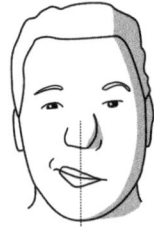

Lip asymmetry is an obvious sign of neuromuscular impairment and incorrect lip stability.

This client is stabilizing his mouth by contracting the extrinsic upper lip muscles.

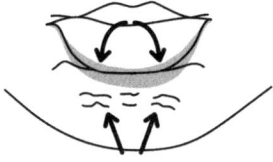

Lower lip eversion occurs when the mentalis muscle tightens as a means to hold oral stability.

Tightening all the oral and facial muscles is an inappropriate way to stabilize the mouth.

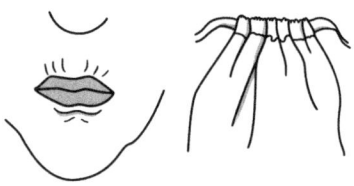

Some clients stabilize the mouth by tightening the orbicularis oris. This gives the lips a drawstring appearance.

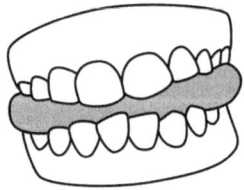

The lateral portions of this tongue are bulging incorrectly out between the side teeth. This could be the tongue's doing, or it could be due to a collapsed and narrow palate, or both.

Assessing Lip/Cheek Stability

Watch the upper and lower lips, the corners of the lips, and the cheeks during speech. Seek answers to the following questions. Perfect symmetry is not expected.

- Are the lips held in a gentle smile during speech?
- Do the lips hang forward during speech?
- Do the lips look soft and bulbous during speech?
- Do the lips pull forward medially to create a tight purse string effect during speech?
- Do the lips pull laterally beyond correct stability so that too much of the teeth are exposed during speech?
- Do the lips pull to one side or the other too much during speech? Which side? Both?
- Do the cheeks seem too inactive during speech?
- Do the cheeks seem over-active during speech?
- Does the chin tighten up and mottle the skin during speech?
- Is there lower lip eversion during speech?
- Does the upper lip pull upward to expose the upper teeth during speech?
- Does the lower lip pull downward to expose the lower teeth during speech?

Assessing Tongue Stability

Stability of the tongue can be assessed through visual analysis during speech, but special arrangements must be made. Therapists must situate themselves so that they get a good look at the outside and the inside of mouth. Sitting a little lower than the client usually works best to get a straight view inside the mouth. If recording video, make sure to have the camera set up on a tripod and level with the client's mouth. Do not ask the client to open his mouth farther in order to see the tongue as he speaks, as this will alter his stability considerably. Also, do not ask for him to imitate tongue postures and do not ask the client to speak louder or softer. His habitual tongue stability is being assessed so watch him as he speaks naturally. Watch the tip of the tongue, the sides, the blade, the middle, and the back as the tongue moves around during normal speech. Many patterns can be seen even though the tongue is buried within the oral cavity. Seek answers to the following questions. Perfect symmetry is not expected.

- Does the tongue stay inside the mouth during speech (except during production of /θ/ and /ð/)?
- Does the tongue lateralize to one side or the other during speech? If so, to which side, how far. On which phonemes does the tongue lateralize, or is this a general pattern?
- Does the tongue retract or bunch toward the rear during speech? If so, on which phonemes, or is this a general pattern?

- Does the tongue stay in a bowl-shape during speech?

- Does the middle of the tongue arch inappropriately upward during speech? On which phonemes, or is this a general pattern?

- Does the tongue anchor its back-lateral margins upward during speech?

- Is the middle-back of the tongue high or low during speech? On which phonemes, or is this a general pattern?

INTRODUCTION TO THE METHODS

Methods to stabilize the oral mechanism are employed so that jaw, lip, and tongue movements can be small, accurate, advanced, and consistent. The methods are used only when necessary, and only with clients who have certain articulation deficits or motor speech disorders. Therapists recognize that methods to facilitate oral stability by themselves will not automatically remediate speech sound errors, and one never expects that a method to stabilize the oral mechanism will remediate a deficiency in speech production without additional articulatory, phonetic, phonological, and cognitive stimulation. The methods of this chapter are employed to launch one small yet vital aspect of improved speech production.

Speech-language pathologists have been designing methods to facilitate oral stability for more than a century but virtually no controlled research has been done on any of them. The reader, therefore, should view these methods as advice passed along from SLPs who understand this concept to others who are learning it. For the purpose of this manual these methods have been separated into three categories: methods to stabilize the jaw, methods to stabilize the lips/cheeks, and methods to stabilize the tongue. It is understood that these things interact and that all these methods work together to stabilize the oral mechanism for effective speech movement. This guide leaves it to other writers to discuss how these methods are worked into a treatment program for the whole body, as one would with clients who have neuromuscular impairment.

FACILITATING JAW STABILITY

A variety of methods have been devised to help clients achieve the parameters of jaw stability described above. These are presented here in no particular order although some of the earliest and least invasive methods are presented first. Three types of methods are presented in this list: (1) methods that require the client to control his jaw

position all by himself by using internal muscular controls, (2) methods that supply the client with an external stabilizer so he can experience good oral control in a mechanical way before he can control it with his own musculature, (3) methods to stimulate the muscular actions of jaw control. Readers are warned to avoid any activities that cause pain anywhere in the oral mechanism, face, TMJ, head, neck, or rest of the body.

Verbal Instructions

Simple verbal descriptions can help clients understand jaw stability. This procedure requires full voluntary control on the part of the client and this is the type of activity one finds in most articulation texts. Verbal instructions about controlling the jaw are given with vocabulary that fits the client's cognitive level. The most important thing is to make sure the client knows what and where his jaw is, otherwise these directions will make no sense to him. An elementary school child might be told something as simple as, "You are letting your jaw go down too far... Keep it up a little higher when you talk." Therapists use plain English to describe other problems in jaw stability to their clients:

- "Your jaw is slipping to the right (or left)… Keep it in the middle."

- "Look at your jaw… I think it is pushing out too far for that sound… Keep it back so your teeth line up in the front."

- "I think you are pulling your jaw too far back… See how your lower teeth are so far back? See if you can keep your jaw a little farther forward."

- "Oops… You let your jaw slip down again… Make sure your jaw stays up so your S sounds better."

- "Most people keep the jaw right in the middle when they talk. See if you can do it that way."

Visual Feedback

Visual feedback can help clients understand their own jaw stability. The SLP can use a mirror and have clients watch their own jaw movements and compare them with hers. Draw pictures, use a mouth model or skeleton, or employ a puppet with a moveable jaw. Visual input like this is used when a client can exert his own oral stability with a little extra visual input. These are classic methods: "Mirror study [is] recommended for securing a more natural width of mouth opening" (Nemoy & Davis, 1937, p. 136).

Smile

Some therapists use a smile to pull the jaw upward into a stabile position during speech. This method is used when a client can pull his jaw up when he smiles. It is a method that has survived since the days of the elocutionists:

> *"To keep the lower jaw in the proper position… Draw back the corners of the mouth as far as possible without giving the face the appearance of a grin… By drawing*

back the corners of the mouth the speaker will be compelled to keep the lower jaw in the right position" (Guttmann, 1893, p. 131).

Physical Reminders

Some clients can achieve appropriate jaw stability but they need a reminder to carry the skill into more advanced and more relaxed speaking situations. In this case the client can use his own hands and fingers to monitor his jaw movements via the chin, and a variety of hand and finger positions can be employed as suggested in the illustration below. The beauty of this simple method is that a client can monitor his jaw position in subtle ways that can be used during any speaking situation, from practicing phonemes in therapy, to talking on the phone, or to giving an oral report. This idea seems to have arisen during the Phonetic Placement Era: "For eliminating excessive jaw action… [place] the hand upon the chin" (Nemoy & Davis, 1937, p. 48).

Study the Interdental Space

An interdental space, sometimes called the *freeway space*, should remain between the upper and lower teeth during speech. Place a very thin probe between the molars on one side and then the other to explore and talk about this space. Use a cocktail straw, coffee stirrer, toothpick, or dental pick.

Tapping the Teeth Together

The upper and lower teeth sometimes tap together when the jaw moves upward too far during speech; therefore, the tapping sensation can be used to teach jaw control. Draw the client's attention to the tactile and auditory sensations that occur when the teeth tap together. Have the client gently but firmly tap his front teeth and his back teeth, and draw his attention to the sensations that occur. "Do you feel that tap-tap-tap? Can you hear it? Do you ever experience that during speech?" Discuss how tapping the teeth together can and does occur once in a while during speech but that it should not occur on any kind of regular basis. The client is taught to bring this sensation under conscious control and to prevent himself from tapping during speech.

Imagery

The imagination can be employed when teaching the position of jaw stability. An example from Secord et al. (2007) demonstrates how this method can be represented. Found in the section on teaching /s/, included are cues about jaw, lip, and tongue stability in very practical terms, using the imagery of a closed "white gate" for the correct position of jaw stability: "Instruct the client to make a little smile and to hide his tongue behind the 'white gate' (his teeth), while resting the sides of his tongue along his upper back teeth" (p. 38).

Biting the Tongue

Another discussion that helps draw clients into the concept of proper jaw stability concerns the painful sensation of biting the tongue. Biting the tongue while talking occurs when control of jaw stability is compromised and the jaw pulls upward too far and too fast. Teach the client that this might occur periodically but that he should not bite his tongue regularly during speech. The client's desire to prevent this can be a fine motivator, so the SLP could ham it up: "I hate it when I bite my tongue. I wish I could stop doing that. How am I going to remember to stop doing that?"

Fingers & Fingernails

Speech teachers as far back as the elocutionists had clients use their fingers and fingernails to stabilize the jaw in specific positions for consonant and vowels. One or two fingers between the teeth achieved low jaw positions for vowels, and a fingernail placed between the teeth stabilized the jaw in a high position for the consonants. The fingers were usually placed between the side teeth and the fingernails were usually placed between the front teeth. The present author has observed that this method of fingers

Hands and fingers can be placed in various natural ways to monitor jaw stability.

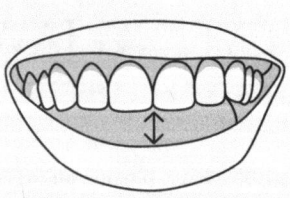

An interdental space should remain between the upper and lower teeth during speech.

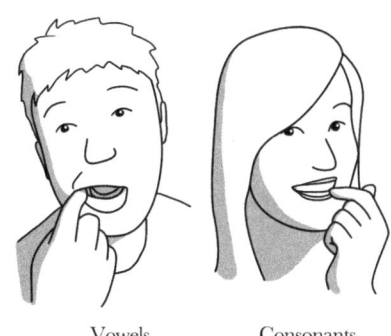

Placing fingers and fingernails between the teeth is a classic way to set the jaw in position for vowels and consonants.

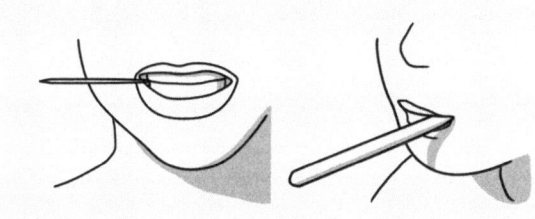

Toothpicks and bite blocks represent ways of stabilizing the jaw in a high position for consonants.

and fingernails often works better than other methods in this section because they give the client additional tactile feedback about his jaw position through his hands. This method may not be an option for clients who lack the appropriate occlusion or who have missing teeth.

Tooth Props

A wide variety of tools have been used to stabilize the jaw during speech training. Van Riper called them *tooth props*: "Tooth props of various sizes will help the student to assume a proper dental opening" (Van Riper, 1947, p. 186). Items he mentioned in his text of 1947 were made of wood and included tongue depressors, pencils, matchsticks, and toothpicks. Using wood objects to stabilize the jaw in this way is an idea that was carried over from the days of elocution. For example, Raymond (1879) described how he used matchsticks broken into various lengths to prop the jaw open at specific heights for individual vowels.

Therapists now use a variety of plastic tools to stabilize the jaw in safe and sanitary ways and these probes are described in Chapter 19 on tools. The client should bite down with the molars or side teeth on a tool of a specific size in order to stabilize the jaw at one height or another. Wide probes stabilize the jaw in low positions and narrow ones at a high position. A probe is used during the teaching of a phoneme, or it is used to stabilize the jaw throughout the practice of words and longer utterances, even conversation. The client is taught to listen carefully

to the changes in his speech that occur as a result of the stability. Then he is taught to control this position through careful auditory self-monitoring as the physical tool is faded. Rosenfeld-Johnson (2005a) presents a systematic program for teaching jaw stability by using a set of five bite blocks professionally designed to set the jaw into five basic heights.

Chin Tuck

Simple mechanics are employed to influence jaw stability in positive ways. The mouth naturally opens when the head tilts back and it naturally closes when the head tilts forward. Therefore, clients are encouraged to hold the head high with the chin slightly tucked in order to set the stage for the high jaw position necessary for mature stability. This concept harps back to the elocutionists who taught their clients to speak while balancing books on the tops of their heads. Clients with normal neuromuscular function should be able to achieve the chin tuck position easily and voluntarily. Clients with neuromuscular disorder may need additional work in occupational or physical therapy to ready the body for this position.

Classic Oral Control

Some clients, especially those with neuromuscular deficit and severe motor speech disorders, require therapists to take more control of the jaw by using hands-on methods. The classic procedure called *oral control* consists of hand positions therapists use to hold the oral mechanism in place and to influence its movement. Oral control was popularized as a feeding method during the mid-20th century and it was adapted to speech activities shortly thereafter. Oral control can be used to influence all jaw, lip, and tongue movements, but it is being discussed here just as a means for establishing jaw stability. Oral control provides external stabilization of the jaw for the client who has not as yet developed his own internal muscular controls. Morris and Klein (2000) describe two basic procedures to be used depending upon whether sitting side-by-side, behind, or face-to-face with the client.

- *Sitting side-by-side or behind the client:* Reach around

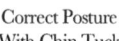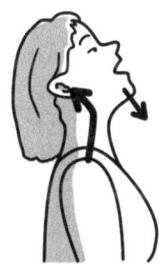

| Correct Posture With Chin Tuck | Throwing the Head Back Lowers the Jaw | Slouching and Jutting The Chin Forward |

A slight chin tuck is the best head position for accurate jaw stability during speech.

the back of the client with one arm and place the middle finger under the jaw just behind the chin and use it to assist upward movement of the jaw. Place the index finger on the chin to assist downward jaw movement. Place the thumb at the temporomandibular joint to stabilize the feeder's hand.

• *Sitting face-to-face with the client:* Place the middle finger under the jaw just behind the chin and use it to assist upward movement of the jaw. Place the index finger at the TMJ to stabilize the feeder's hand. Place the thumb below the lower lip to stabilize the lower lip.

Classic oral control positions that were developed for feeding therapy.

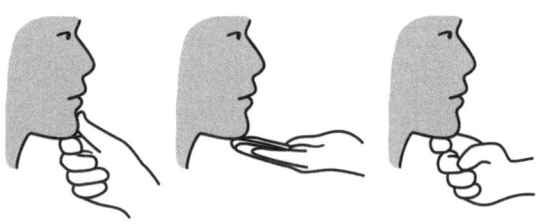

Modified oral control positions that can be less invasive for speech work.

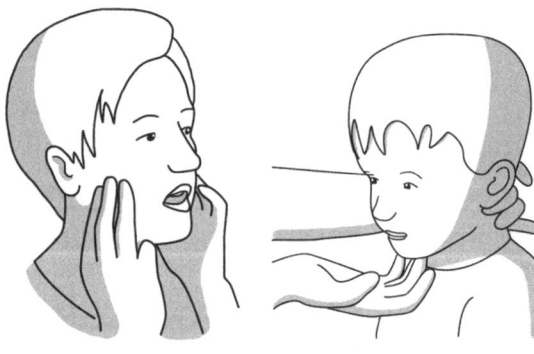

Stabilizing the head and tapping the chin to encourage active jaw stability.

Discovering the hard work of clenching vs. the light work of closing

Modified Oral Control Positions

The oral control positions described above are usually too involved and too invasive for speech work, especially when working with older children and adults who have mild-to-moderate speech movement problems. Simplified oral control positions can be used instead. These alternative hand positions will work to control the jaw if the client has full control of his head, otherwise his head may have to be held in the back, or pressed gently but firmly against the back of his chair or the wall behind it. Each of these holds is done with one hand while facing the client.

• *Thumb and finger hold:* Hold the chin by placing a thumb on the client's mentalis and curled fingers under his chin. This is rather like the hand position one employs to hold a golf club or fishing rod.

• *Open fingers hold:* Place an open hand, palm up, under the client's chin and press gently but firmly upward.

• *Bent finger hold:* Bend an index finger and place its medial side upward against the underside of the client's chin.

Press the Masseters

A bit of pressure on the masseters can help a client understand that the jaw moves as a result of muscular controls. Therapists place their fingers on the client's masseters and press into them gently but firmly as the client moves his jaw up and down. In the following example, Bosley (1981) combines this and other methods to help a client learn about his jaw so that he can stop thrusting it forward: "If [the client] still thrusts the jaw forward as the teeth are displayed, ask him to pretend he is biting or chewing his food 'back here', [and place] your index fingers against both cheeks in the molar area" (p. 65).

Clench Versus Close

Motor therapists often categorize muscle work as heavy or light. Jaw muscles do heavy work when they clench to crush hard or resilient foods, and they do light work when they lift and lower the jaw for speech. Here these will be called the *clench* and the *close*. In motor-based therapy, muscles are made to do heavy work (clench) in order to make light work (close) noticeable, easier, and more automatic. Therapy activities that are based on this concept can be approached in two different ways. One is to enroll the client in a feeding program where he can do heavy work by chewing foods of increasing hardness. Another is to teach the client the difference between clenching the jaw and closing the mouth in non-food activities.

In feeding one employs activities to develop the mature chew as opposed to the immature *munch*. (For more information, see Chapter 18 on eating, swallowing, and orofacial myofunctional methods.)

In non-food activities, the SLP asks the client to place

his fingers on her masseters so he can feel them tighten and bulge outward as she clenches. Help him place his fingers right on the center of the muscle bellies, at the point where the bulge is the greatest, and then teach him to feel this on his own masseters. Help him notice the firm bulge that occurs when he clenches his molars and then teach him to notice the lack of this bulge when he lets go and simply lifts and lowers his jaw. Teach him that the clench is hard and strong and that closing is soft and gentle. Teach him that people clench the jaw to speak when they are very angry, but that one generally closes the jaw gently when speaking in a regular tone. Garliner (1976) added isometric control to this activity in what he called the "Masseter Count to Ten" exercise. The client clenched for a count of 10 to increase awareness and strength of this action. This is an excellent way to work this activity in clients with dysarthria related to low oral tone. WARNING: Do not work on clenching if it causes pain anywhere in the mouth or TMJ.

Tap the Mental Protuberance

Jaw movement is perceived in the TMJ. Gentle but firm tapping on the jaw sends a distinct yet safe jolt into the TMJ to increase a client's perception of the jaw as a moving object. Use two or three fingertips to tap the jaw on the mental protuberance toward oral center from all sides. Tap firmly but gently, and make sure to tap the mandibular bone and not just the skin on its surface.

Reflexes

In cases of neuromuscular disorder, many therapists use reflex stimulation to facilitate the up position of jaw stability. Reflexes that function to pull the jaw up include the biting, chewing, face closing, and mouth closing reflexes. (For more information, see Chapter 17 on the reflexes.)

FACILITATING LIP-CHEEK STABILITY

Teaching lip/cheek stability can be a relatively straightforward process. The focus is on encouraging the buccinator muscles to contract in order to push the cheeks gently but firmly against the side teeth. These methods for speech therapy are adapted from feeding and myofunctional therapy and are presented in no particular order.

Vocabulary / Anatomy

A little information about the buccinator muscles (or "cheek muscles") along with an anatomical drawing will help older clients understand what they need to accomplish when stabilizing the cheeks and lips. Teach the client about the position and shape of the buccinator muscles and tell him what happens when muscles contract; tell him that buccinator contraction pushes the cheeks against

the molars to hold the jaw, lips, and tongue in position for correct speech production.

Feel the Contraction

Clients can feel the contraction of their own buccinators by using their fingers. One method is to have the client press his fingers into his cheeks from the outside. The cheeks will feel soft and pliable. Tell him to "squeeze" or "make it hard" there by smiling. They will feel their buccinators contract and pull rearward. Many clients can figure out how to tighten their buccinators with this simple direction and tactile feedback.

Another method is to have the client grasp each of his cheeks with the hand of the opposite side, i.e., use the right hand on the left cheek and left hand on the right cheek. The thumb is placed inside the mouth to press outward on the inner cheek wall and the fingers are placed outside the mouth, pressing inward on the outer cheek wall. The client then smiles broadly while he is holding the cheek gently in this manner. Smiling causes the buccinators to retract fully. The cheek will get thick and firm and it will pull back. With a few trials, the client should be able to use his fingers and thumb to feel the buccinator tighten and thicken on both sides. Encourage him to make the muscle tighter so it bulges farther.

Some clients need to learn the difference between activation of the buccinators and activation of the masseters. In this case, have the client feel buccinator activity with this method, and have him feel masseter activity with the method described in the previous sub-section, "Clench Versus Close." Do these in alternating sequences on both sides.

Patting the Cheeks

Buccinator contraction can be taught to very young children, even babies by creating playful play routines. Morris & Klein (2000) describe how to do this: "Play patty-cake, peek-a-boo, and other children's games that incorporate patting, tapping, [and] stroking [on the cheeks]" (p. 445).

Manipulate Food

Food can be manipulated in ways to encourage buccinator contraction. Morris and Klein (2000) advocated placing a piece of cookie or cheese inside the cheek pocket. The client's job is to use his cheek muscles to push the piece medially to the center of the mouth for manipulation with the tongue. Merkel-Walsh (2002) used a lollipop on a stick in the same way. Place the candy between the side teeth and cheek and encourage the client to squeeze the cheek muscles against it.

Lateral Button Pull

Dworkin (1991) used the classic *button pull* exercise to develop the buccinators in patients with low oral and facial strength; one places a button on a string between the lips and then pulls the string away and to the side. The lips and cheek on that side must tighten to hold the button in.

Straw Hierarchies

Rosenfeld-Johnson (2014) recommends straws to facilitate lateral lip stability. A series of eight straws are employed. Each subsequent straw requires slightly more sucking strength, and, therefore, more lateral lip retraction and stability. Clients are engaged in a program of ever-increasing skill with either an adult's set or a child's set of straws.

Stretch the Buccinator

The buccinator muscle lies horizontally from the pterago-mandibular raphe in the rear to the corner of the lips in the front. Stretching its muscle fibers along this horizontal line encourages its contraction and one can do so by grasping the cheeks and pulling forward. Grasp a cheek by placing the thumb inside the mouth on the inside of the cheek and by placing the fingers outside the mouth on the outside of the cheek. Grasp the cheek by squeezing the thump and fingers together and pull it forward gently but firmly while asking the client to pull it back. Use words he can understand to describe what is being done and what he is being asked to do. An older client can be told, "I'm going to grab your cheek and pull it gently forward. You pull it back away from me." A very young child can be told, "Oh-oh. I've got your cheek. I bet you can't get it back."

This activity can also be done by using the playful *fish face*. Facing the client, the SLP places the palms of

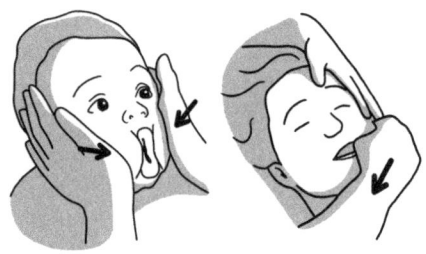

The buccinators can be stretched with the hands or fingers.

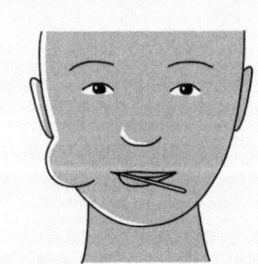

A lollipop can stretch the buccinator to encourage its active contraction.

her hands and flat fingers on his cheeks. She can pull the cheeks forward until the lips protrude forward, saying "I've got a little fishie!" and asking, "Where did that little fishie go?" as he pulls his cheeks back by contracting the buccinators.

Vibrate the Buccinators

A little vibration on the buccinators can encourage their contraction. Place the vibrator on the outside of the cheeks and press gently but firmly inward, or place it between the teeth and cheek and press outward. A small vibrator called the Z-Vibe® is good for this purpose, and there are also toy vibrators with small parts that can be useful. (For more information on vibrators, see Chapter 19.)

Normalize General Tone

Morris and Klein (2000) point out that lack of cheek compression for oral stability may be related to muscle tone that is too high or too low in the whole body. Use whole body activities prescribed by occupational and/or physical therapists in conjunction with those described in this chapter.

Cheek Puffing

Some clients puff the cheeks during production of bilabials. Cheek puffing can be a sign of generalized oral instability although it also occurs as an isolated habit during production of bilabials, especially /p/. Former United States president Barak Obama had this habit on production of /p/ as can be seen by watching several different video recordings of his early talks. Today, cheek puffing that is an isolated habit like Obama's is usually ignored in good speakers, but clinicians of the early 20th century and the elocutionists before them helped clients eliminate this problem. Therapists talked about and modeled the error, clients watched themselves in a mirror, and inhibition was used to prevent it: "Slight pressure of the thumb against one cheek and the forefinger against the other has been utilized in inhibiting puffing of the cheeks in the production of /p/" (Nemoy & Davis, 1937, p. 48). The client is then taught to use his buccinator muscles more vigorously to prevent his cheeks from doing this during the phoneme's pressure build-up phase.

FACILITATING TONGUE STABILITY

Therapists since the elocutionists have developed an assortment of methods to encourage tongue stability. The methods below are based on the concept that the tongue stabilizes itself in the back against the palate and molars, and from below with its attachments to the mandible and hyoid bones. But the reader should remember that the stabilized tongue is dependent upon the overall position of the mouth as controlled by jaw, lip, and cheek stability. Therefore, all the methods of jaw, lip, and cheek stability described above are integral to the process of developing tongue stability. This section only describes methods to stabilize the tongue itself.

Use Vowels

Probably the easiest way to work on back-lateral tongue stability is to use the vowels. Nemoy and Davis (1937) worked from production of /i/, Chomsky and Halle (1968) described tongue stability as the position for /e/, and probably any of the three highest front vowels /i/, /ɪ/, or /e/ would work for this application. The present author has found that /i/ is the best selection among these three because it is the highest and most clients already produce it correctly. Using a vowel to encourage back-lateral tongue stability only works if the client can produce the selected vowel in the first place; it will not work if the target vowel is distorted.

Have the client produce the vowel and to help him perceive how his tongue positions itself to achieve it. Teach him that the tongue is wide in the back and that the sides of the tongue in the back are high and pressing against the palate and molars. Then teach him to hold that position while attempting the other target phoneme. For example, when learning to put the tongue into correct position for /t/, a client produces an exaggerated /i/ and then holds that mouth and tongue position steady while saying /t/. The activity can be made practical by saying "Eat, eat, eat…" or "E, tea, tea…." Make sure the client is using a broad smile to exaggerate /i/, and make sure he is holding this position while saying /t/. This exaggeration may need to be softened to make the production sound more natural after some trials. The reader is encouraged to try this activity before teaching it to a client.

Toddlers and clients with low cognitive skills can learn back-lateral tongue stability with this method. The key is to over-work words that contain the high front vowel /i/. As discussed further in Chapter 21, Davis and MacNeilage (1990) found that high vowels may dominate first words, and it has been mentioned that this may be a sign that oral stability is being established. High vowels in the study occurred in the diminutive form (e.g., *kitty*) as well as in other words in which the vowel serves a regular syllabic purpose (e.g., *me, eat, teeth*). Therefore, children who have acquired correct /i/ can over-practice these types of simple words as a way to encourage and establish lingual stability. It is an effective method for them as long as the client can produce an excellent /i/. Exaggeration is key at first.

Direct Instruction

Another simple way to teach the concept of tongue stability is with direct instruction. Talk about how the tongue always stays inside the mouth during speech and model phonemes or words to demonstrate this. A simple approach is often the best approach: "Sometimes it is sufficient to show [the client] that people do not speak with

their tongue out that way" (Scripture, 1912, p. 135). This simple process can be traced back to the elocutionists and the speech correctionists of the Phonetic Placement Era: "The pupil may be directed to brace the sides of the tongue against the upper teeth" (Nemoy & Davis, 1937, p. 96).

There are many ways to do this. For example, make a list of all the consonants and talk about how all but two — /θ/ and /ð/ — are made with the tongue hidden inside the dental arches. Draw pictures of the mouth and have the client use a mirror to discover the relationship the tongue has to the mouth. Use simple phrases to label these actions like "Tongue out" and "Tongue in." Use negative practice by speaking words or by reading sentences with the tongue sticking out. Talk about the difference in tongue placement between /s/ and /θ/, and between /z/ and /ð/. Talk about how babies often speak with their tongues hanging out but big boys and big girls talk with the tongue in. Set a speech rule: The tongue always stays inside the mouth except when saying /θ/ or /ð/.

Use verbal descriptions the client can understand. Teach him the basic parts of his tongue: front, back, middle, sides, and shoulders. Teach him that the shoulders of the tongue have the responsibility of holding the tongue inside the mouth and up against the palate. Teach him to lift the sides and to touch, brace, push, or even "cram" the shoulders up there.

Engage the Imagination

The imagination can be engaged to teach the concept of back-lateral tongue stability. One therapist, Butler Hinz (2014), reported success with one boy when using the imagery of a car parking in a garage. Toys, a mouth model, and pictures were used to help the child understand that a garage is a place for a car to park and the sides of the palate are a place for the tongue to park.

Smiling

Broad smiling pulls the tongue wide in the back, and the wide tongue is more able to stabilize with its shoulders. Use broad smiling during the application of any other method in this section.

Lying Supine

Probably the earliest of all direct methods used to encourage the tongue to stay farther back inside the mouth is to have the client lie on his back during speech training. This is a classic method from the days of phonetic placement, e.g., it is an integral part of the motokinesthetic method (Young & Hawk, 1955). The theory was that lying on one's back causes the tongue to fall farther back into the oropharyngeal area.

It is true that the tongue should drop back somewhat when the body is in supine, however, it should be noted that having the tongue fall or drop farther back into the oral cavity is a passive movement experience whereas true tongue stability as described above is a very active process. It should also be noted that if this method actually worked to remediate a forward tongue position, then no client with a frontal lisp would lisp while he was lying on his back, but this generally does not happen; clients who lisp while sitting or standing usually continue to lisp while lying down. However, lying supine may help introduce the idea of keeping the tongue back and, therefore, may have some value in an initial stage of therapy. The method of lying in supine may not work if the cause of tongue instability is neuromuscular or upper respiratory, in which cases lying in supine actually may cause the client to stick the tongue out farther.

Tactile Stimulation

Tactile stimulation is used to awaken body parts and to stimulate underlying muscles. Tactile stimulation to the shoulders of the tongue can orient a client to his tongue's stability zones and can arouse the muscles there. Tactile stimulation can also be given to the palate above the shoulders: "Lateral palatal tactile feedback as the tongue is moved and positioned could substantially enhance tongue placement [in] phonetic learning" (Fletcher, 1989, p. 747). Texture is the key. Use a textured probe or the client's own fingertips to stroke or brush the tongue's shoulders or his palate above the shoulders. Clients can also use their molars to stimulate the tongue's shoulders by gently biting on them.

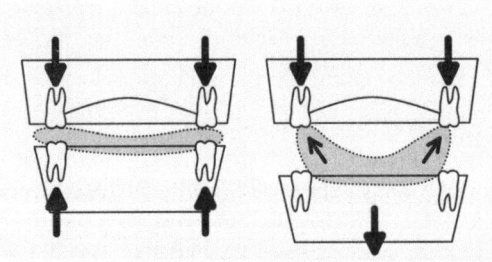

The Butterfly Procedure: Bite down on the tongue's shoulders with the molars (left) and push the shoulders up against the bottom of the upper molars (right).

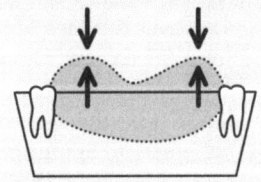

Using resistance: Ask the client to push the shoulders of his tongue up as they are being pressed down.

Clenching

Clenching also pulls the tongue wide in the back, and the wide tongue is more able to stabilize with its shoulders. Teach clenching as described on pages 246–247.

Butterfly Position

The Butterfly Position (Marshalla, 1992a) is an excellent method for teaching back-lateral tongue stability for clients who can follow the directions. There are two steps: bite and push. The client is asked to bite down on the back-lateral margins of his tongue with his very back molars, essentially squeezing the sides of the tongue between the upper and lower back molars on both sides. Then the client is asked to push the back-lateral margins of his tongue upward against the bottom of the upper molars. It is an easy methods for clients who can figure out which part of the tongue to use and which direction to push, so take some time to teach him where the shoulders of his tongue are and which teeth are his molars, and make sure he knows what direction is "up." Combine this with other methods to make it easier, for example, brush the shoulders of the tongue, have him look in a mirror, use creative imagery of a butterfly, and/or have him say /i/ while doing it.

Resistance

An effective way to encourage the back-lateral margins of the tongue to lift for lingual stability is to use counter pressure. This method is used when a client cannot figure out which part of his tongue to push and in which direction. Use a firm probe to press down on the sides of the tongue at the back-lateral margins and ask the client to push them up. This method is scattered throughout articulation therapy textbooks as represented in this quote from *Articulation* by Hanson (1983): "If the elevation is difficult, have him work on lifting the sides of the tongue against resistance. This resistance can be supplied by a pair of swab sticks pushing downward on the sides of the tongue" (p, 228). A two-pronged dental floss holder works well for this as it can be used to press down on both back-lateral margins simultaneously or have the client use his own fingers.

Popping the Tongue

Some clients need to learn how to lift the whole tongue before they can lift the sides alone for stability. Boshart (1993) used tongue popping for this purpose. To pop the tongue, one raises the jaw and presses the entire tongue up against the palate. Then the jaw is lowered while the tongue remains suctioned against the palate. Once the jaw is in its fully lowered position, the tongue is pulled down and popped away from the palate. The tongue should slap down quickly from back to front, and the tip of the tongue should be the last part to drop. The action should create a popping or clopping sound as the tongue releases its hold on the palate and as it slaps down against the floor of the mouth.

Rosenfeld-Johnson Hierarchies

Rosenfeld-Johnson (1992, 2001, 2005a) created a series of prescriptive hierarchical activities designed to develop a variety of oral movement skills including back-lateral tongue stability, a position she calls the *back-lateral side spread*. Activities include a straw drinking hierarchy, a horn blowing hierarchy, and a bubble blowing hierarchy. Each of these programs contains elements designed to teach clients how to pull the tongue up and back into a wide stabile position. Objects are presented one-at-a-time and the client progresses from one to the next when he achieves certain prescribed skills. These methods can be used with any type of client. Sequential hierarchies like these provide an effective way to track progress and collect data on developing oral stability.

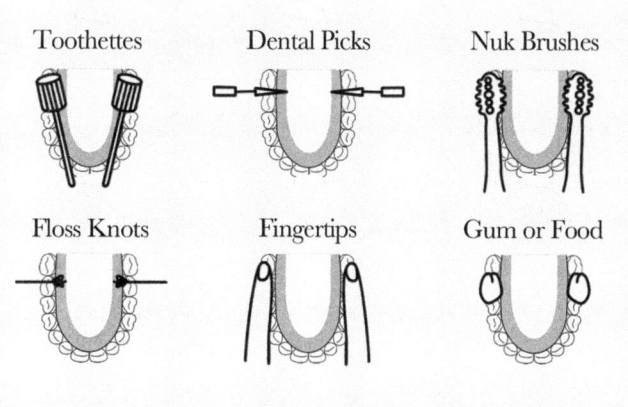

A variety of tools can be used to guide the back of the tongue to its anchor position in the back.

Tactile/Object Guides

A small object can be placed between the molars on each side to guide the shoulders of the tongue into position for stability. Therapists in the past have used gum, candy, cereal pieces, and tiny orthodontic elastics for this purpose but these can be a little dangerous if suddenly swallowed. A better idea is to use a small object that is firmly attached to a probe, like a swizzle stick with a small shape on the end, a Toothette® with its sponge, the bumpy end of a Nuk® brush, or a laryngeal mirror. Vaughn and Clark (1979) used knotted dental floss placed between the lateral teeth to guide the tongue into this position, and now a dental pick can be used. The fingers can also be used for this purpose and may be the best choice due to the additional tactile feedback they provide. A gentle vibrator like a Z-Vibe® also might be used to add more tactile stimulation. The Tongue-Tip Elevation and Lateralization Tools by Talk Tools are designed specifically for the purpose of teaching the perimeter of the tongue to elevate and push toward the sides for stability.

ORAL REST POSITION

The concept of *oral stability* should not be confused with the concept of *oral rest position*. Oral rest position is the habitual and dominant closed-lips posture assumed by the mouth when one is NOT engaged in speaking, eating, or other mouth movement activities. Oral rest position is known by other names such as *oral rest posture* and *closed lips rest posture*.

Correct oral rest can be maintained when one is upright or lying down, as well as when one is engaged in physical activities. The closed lips rest position allows one to put one's best face forward in social situations. Correct oral rest position seems to support the development of appropriate dental alignment and is critical for maintaining appropriate levels of saliva in the mouth. According to Bosma (1967), the average baby is born with an

established closed lips rest posture.

The mouth tends to open out of normal closed-lips rest posture when the head moves into extreme positions, when the body undergoes physical exertion, and when more oxygen is needed quickly. An open lips rest posture can also be a sign of low oral strength, dental malocclusion, upper respiratory problems, or other illnesses. Thumb and finger sucking during oral rest alter the oral rest position considerably. The habitually open mouth can also be a simple habit with an unknown cause. Unfortunately, an open mouth rest posture has been used to describe people with low intellectual functioning, limited social standing, low economic potential, lack of education, illiteracy, and general clueless-ness.

Correct Oral Rest Position

The mouth sits closed in a very specific way during oral rest. The following notes about this position are from Hanson and Mason (2003). Oral rest position should be assessed when the client "is in repose and unaware of our

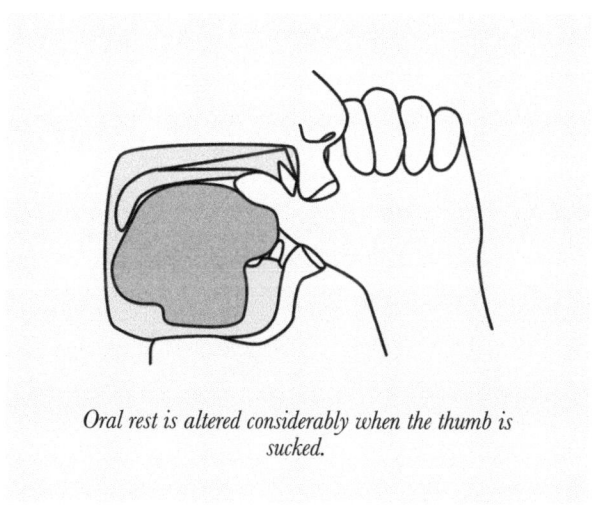

Oral rest is altered considerably when the thumb is sucked.

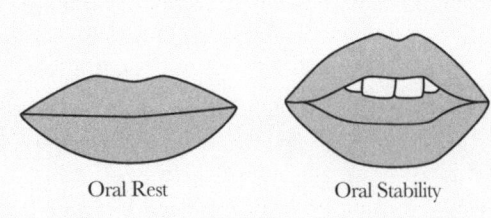

Oral Rest   Oral Stability

Lip position is quite different during oral rest (left) and oral stability (right).

scrutiny [and] distracted by interesting materials" (p. 211).

Lip Position During Oral Rest

- The facial and lip muscles should be relaxed.

- The lips should rest gently together or lightly closed so that the teeth cannot be seen.

- There should be no gap between the lips.

- If there must be a gap between the lips for breathing, it should be very slight, and the lips should be barely parted.

- The lips should attain and maintain a gentle relaxed coupling.

- The lips should not actively press together.

- There should be no stress, strain, or mottling of the lips.

Jaw Position During Oral Rest

- The jaw should sit in a neutral position during oral rest.

- The jaw should be high enough for the lips to rest gently together.

- The jaw should be low enough that the upper and lower teeth do not meet at any point around the dental arches.

- The jaw should not be clenched during oral rest.

- The jaw should not hang so low that the lips are forced apart during oral rest.

Tongue Position During Oral Rest

- The tongue should maintain a mild tonus contraction, i.e., just enough tension to elevate and remain elevated.

- The tongue should not press against the front teeth.

- The tongue should not protrude from between the front teeth.

- The tongue should not retract back toward the oropharynx.

- The lateral margins of the tongue should lightly contact the top, side teeth; it should not press or sag outward between the side teeth.

- The tongue-surface should sit comfortably nestled on top, touching the alveolar ridge and the front of the hard palate.

- The front-tongue should be aligned with the upper alveolar ridge.

- If structurally necessary, the tongue tip may gently touch the upper or lower front teeth.

Other

- The velopharyngeal mechanism should be relaxed during oral rest, and the velum should be hanging down to allow nasal breathing while the mouth is closed.

- A dimple on the chin or face is an anatomical feature that may or may not be visible during oral rest.

Teaching Correct Oral Rest

A correct oral rest posture helps to provide an optimal tongue "operating zone" so the tongue can successfully interact with the surrounding articulators. According to the American Speech-Language-Hearing Association (1993), the alteration of lingual and labial resting postures is an element of orofacial myology, and the practice of orofacial myology is within the area of practice offered by certified SLPs who have special training in that area (see American Speech-Language-Hearing Association, 2004, section 38).

Teaching correct oral rest posture begins with teaching a client what it is and why it is important. A process is engaged to eliminate oral, seating, and other habits that interfere with correct oral rest posture. Activities are used to train and habituate the physical characteristics of oral rest that are described above. Readers are referred to Hanson and Mason (2003), The International Association of Orofacial Myologists (IAOM.com), and MySwalloworks.com for the latest perspectives about and details on procedures to establish the closed lips rest posture.

SUMMARY

Oral stability (different from oral rest position) is a critical element of controlled speech movement. Oral stability allows movements of the jaw, lips, and tongue to be small, accurate, advanced, and consistent for speech. Lack of oral stability can cause significant changes to speech movement and distortion of speech. Many methods have been developed to establish appropriate jaw, lip, and tongue stability for speech. Oral stability is different from oral rest position.

15

Oral Perception
& Speech Movement Learning

Discovering the mouth during speech training

"Most authorities agree that the rich sensory information associated with speech production is particularly important in speech development and in the management of some speech disorders, as when a child must learn a new articulatory pattern."

–John Bernthal & Nicholas Bankson, 2004

The production of phonemes that have the potential for being different by place and manner requires a client to have an excellent perception of his mouth and its shaping capabilities. This is known as *kinesthesia*. Any working speech-language pathologist is aware that some clients have adequate skill in this area while others do not. For example, when asked, "Where's your mouth?" some young clients point immediately to their mouths while others point to their noses, cheeks, or ears. Failure like that can mean several things: that the client doesn't know how to answer *where?* questions, that he does not know the vocabulary word *mouth*, or that he simply is unaware he has a mouth. It is this third possibility that is the concern in this chapter. These are the clients about whom many therapists say, "He just cannot seem to get his mouth to do what I want him to." Perhaps the client simply does not know

Hand-to-mouth behavior is an early way children discover their mouths.

enough about his mouth to comply with the instructions.

The average child develops foundational perceptions of his mouth through multisensory experiences very early in life. Sensations that arise from the skin, muscles, and joints contribute to a kinesthetic percept (mental image) of the size, shape, and movement competencies of the mouth. Normal everyday experiences contribute to this percept and the average child gains this knowledge automatically during infancy. This chapter discusses basic information about the overlapping sensory and motor experiences that seem to contribute to a child's perception of his own mouth, and makes applications to articulation and motor speech training throughout.

BACKGROUND

Speech-language pathologists began to discuss the role of oral perception in articulation improvement at the turn of the last century. Therapists of the first half of the 20th century were exploring ways in which kinesthesia contributed to knowledge of one's own speech movements and certain studies were undertaken. For example, Patton (1942) administered a test of kinesthesia to 428 school children and found that the half with speech impairment had significantly more problems in kinesthetic sense than the control group, suggesting that "variation in kinesthetic sensibility may well merit consideration as a possible factor in articulatory difficulties in otherwise apparently normal children" (p. 310).

By the middle of the 20th century, some therapists were pushing and pulling the speech organs into positions so that their clients could feel oral positions before they were able to perform them:

> "When the child feels the movement or movements [provided by the therapist], it is easy for him to reproduce the pattern, through the kinesthetic sense. The 'feel' of what happens stays in the muscles, becoming associated with the auditory pattern" (Young & Hawk, 1955, p. 12–13).

Attention to oral perception increased significantly a dozen years later with the publication of *Symposium on Oral Sensation and Perception* (Bosma, 1967). A panel of physicians and other researchers who specialized in oral perception presented this conference. The conference chair, Dr. Bosma, set the tone by stating that the oral area has "an intimate interaction of sensory and motor function" (Bosma, 1967, p. 109). One presenter (Gibson, 1967) described the mouth as an active perceptual system that has many functions, both motoric and sensory, and he said that a child learns what his mouth is all about through the integration of the two.

Shortly after the Bosma symposium, Fucci and Robertson (1971) proposed that a functionally defective articulation disorder might be due to an oral sensory disturbance. By the end of the 20th century, Fletcher (1992) had used x-ray, MRI, and electropalatometry studies to discover how speech movement schemas develop, and he said that these schemas were based upon an infant's developing sense of oral perception:

> "Internally and externally perceived movement sensations and experiences are used to build and constantly update central schemata. These schemata are thought to contain the rules and other information that underpin speech production" (Fletcher, 1992, p. 21).

By the end of the 20th century, many therapists were recognizing that a perception of the mouth and its movements should be a regular part of articulation training for many different types of clients, and these activities were taking place under the umbrella term *oral motor techniques*. The topic even received some notice in certain articulation and motor speech texts, for example:

> "Tongue and lip awareness activities can often be utilized with beneficial results. They are employed not to strengthen the articulators or increase their coordination per se, but rather to heighten the child's awareness of tongue and lip movements" (Bauman-Waengler, 2004, p. 225).

EIGHT SENSORY CHANNELS

How does a person perceive his own oral mechanism? The human body acquires information about itself and the world through eight sensory systems. These are *auditory* (ears), *tactile* (skin), *muscular proprioception* (muscles), *joint proprioception* (joints), *visual* (eyes), *olfactory* (nose), *gustatory* (taste buds) and *vestibular* (inner ear). Data received via these eight sensory systems builds the oral percept. The following information about the relationship between these systems and the developing oral percept for speech is a clinical theory that has been discussed throughout the 20th century which is based upon a working knowledge of the sensory systems and simple common sense.

Auditory System

The auditory system is the hearing mechanism and it contributes to the development of the oral percept in specific ways. Infants produce voice, move the mouth, and listen to the sounds that result. This relationship between mouth movements and sound productions is reciprocal; the mouth teaches the ear to hear, and the ear teaches the mouth to move. Infant vocalizations help the child develop his oral percept, and the developing oral percept helps him produce better sound. This intimate bond between mouth movements and listening skill comprises one of the primary foundations of speech learning. It is for this reason that virtually all books written about articulation and motor speech therapy contain information about stimulating self-hearing. Self-hearing is mostly unconscious and therapy is designed to bring it to conscious awareness. The client learns to listen more carefully to his own sounds so that his oral percept and his control over his own oral movements will improve.

Tactile System

The tactile system refers to the perception, recognition, and organization of sensations that arise from the cutaneous tissue (skin). The tactile system contributes greatly to oral perception because the entire inner and outer surface of the mouth is covered in skin. The mouth is the most sensitive part of the human body because of the rich assortment and number of tactile nerves present. The skin houses these nerve endings and allows one to perceive contacts between one body part and another, such as, for example, the articulatory movements of the tongue against the palate.

Oral perception includes *oral-tactile awareness* and *oral-tactile discrimination*. The skin in, on, and around the mouth teaches a child that he has a mouth (awareness) and it contributes to perceptions of phoneme place, manner, and voice (discrimination). The tactile nerves inform as to where touch is occurring (place), the direction of movement and the amount of force being used (manner), and the moment in which articulation occurs (timing). It is for these reasons that many therapists teach that therapy should include activities designed to draw a client's attention to his mouth through the use of touch: "Touch, or tactile cues, may provide a great deal of information about the way sounds are made" (Carrell & Tiffany, 1960, p. 45).

Muscle Proprioceptive System

The muscular proprioceptive system refers to the perception, recognition, and organization of sensations that arise from muscles as they contract and relax during movement. Contraction and relaxation of the muscles of the oral musculature give information about which part of the mouth is moving, and to what direction, speed, and degree it is moving. "We do not learn a movement but the sensation of a movement" (Bobath, 1980, p. 26).

A lack of mouth movement can cause a certain lack of oral perception and it is for this reason that Van Riper said that sometimes therapists need to first get the oral mechanism to move in any way it can. He called this "vivifying" oral movement (Van Riper, 1954, p. 238). The more the mouth moves, the better the child's oral percept becomes, and the better his oral percept gets, the more opportunity he has to gain control over its movements. "We depend to a great extent upon kinesthesis to control posture and movement, including speech movements" (Carrell & Tiffany, 1960, p. 46).

Joint Proprioceptive System

The joint proprioceptive system refers to the perception, recognition, and organization of sensations that arise from joints as they bend, straighten, and rotate during movement. Movement of the jaw stimulates sensors in the temporomandibular joint and this data contributes to the developing oral percept. "It appears… that the sensory experiences of the TMJ may serve to regulate and otherwise control mandibular motor activity by means of a feedback system" (Ringel, Saxman, & Brooks, 1967, p. 641).

Visual System

A child typically cannot see his own mouth, and, therefore, he cannot use vision to discover his own mouth the way he uses his other senses. However, babies watch other adults and children who imitate the infants' facial expressions and mouth movements, and babies eventually look at themselves in mirrors. Babies who pay attention to adult faces and who enjoy playing in front of a mirror can gain visual knowledge about the functioning of their own mouth. Therefore, a working visual system can also contribute to a client's developing oral percept: "Sounds can be sensed in a number of ways, not merely through hearing. Visual cues often may help" (Carrell & Tiffany, 1960, p. 45).

Olfactory System

The sense of smell contributes to the developing oral percept in a roundabout way. The mouth and nose are right next to one another and food and other objects held near the mouth are sniffed and smelled as well as tasted and felt. Objects with pleasant odors encourage babies to put them in the mouth while objects with unpleasant odors discourage this exploration. A child who puts a wide variety of foods and other objects into the mouth has an opportunity to develop a more complex oral percept than he would if he rejects such activity. For this reason, many SLPs include mouthing play and feeding activities in phoneme-learning activities.

Gustatory System

Like the olfactory system, the sense of taste contributes to the developing oral percept in a certain way. In normal circumstances, pleasant tastes are accepted into the mouth and unpleasant tastes are rejected. Acceptance or rejection of a food or other object contributes to the amount of time a child spends exploring that item with the mouth. The theory is that the more often a child eats and mouths pleasant-tasting objects the more likely it is that he will develop a fully functioning oral percept. The more a child rejects foods and other objects in the mouth, the less complete his oral percept might be. Although this is just a working theory, many SLPs integrate speech, feeding, and mouthing work together in treatment for these reasons, especially when working with infants, toddlers, and clients with neuromuscular disorder or cognitive deficit. This aspect of treatment is especially important for clients on non-oral feeding systems who have limited experience placing various foods in the mouth.

Vestibular System

The vestibular system in the inner ear functions to perceive gravitational force. It motivates a child to achieve upright positions, helps a child understand whether he is moving or the world is moving around him, contributes to the regulation of muscle tone and arousal, and functions to organize all incoming sensations. SLPs sometimes include prescribed vestibular activities to adjust a client's state of muscular arousal, to help him organize his movements, and to adjust muscle tone. Vestibular activities are included so that the child's entire sensory system will function at maximum capability for developing the oral percept and speech movement skills. Motor specialists on the multidisciplinary team prescribe these activities for SLPs to employ in safe and useful ways.

ORAL PERCEPTION & SPEECH

According to Powers (1971a), the requirements for adequate speech articulation include accurate *precision* of movement, accurate *place* of articulation, right *direction* of movement, right amount of *contact surface* for articulation, right *shape* of lips and tongue, correct *speed* of movement, sufficient *pressure* of contacts (force), and optimal *sequencing* of movement. By extension, one could say that lack of oral perception could cause a deficiency in any or all of these speech movement skills. Powers stated that lack of skill in these areas was the basis of what began to be called the *functional articulation deficit.*

Powers explained that clients with functional articulation deficits demonstrated general oral inaccuracy as well as poor oral perception:

> "Movements are approximate rather than precise, broad rather than small surfaces are sometimes contacted, and contacts are made at the wrong place. In some cases movements are fairly accurate but are slow, weak, or under-energized, so that, although contacts are made, they are not tight or firm. The speech is spoken of as 'careless,' 'lazy,' and 'sluggish' in its milder forms; [and] 'indistinct,' 'confused,' 'mutilated,' 'distorted' and 'unintelligible' in its more severe forms" (Powers, 1971a, p. 845).

Time Frame

When does the child begin to perceive his mouth, and when does this learning process come to a conclusion? One could surmise that a child's perception of his mouth begins in utero at one of two time periods: at 7–8 weeks when the tactile system begins to awaken or at the end of the first trimester when the fetus begins to make rudimentary mouth movements. These two markers seem to be appropriate starting points for the period during which the fetus begins along the path of mouth perception development.

When does the period of developing oral perception end? Perhaps oral sensorimotor learning extends throughout life. However, the primary learning process of the typical child probably ends at about eighteen months of age, the time when, according to Jean Piaget, the sensorimotor stage of intelligence comes to its conclusion (Ginsburg & Opper, 1969). This makes a total of two years of oral sensory and motor learning, beginning during the first trimester and ending at approximately 18 months of age.

It could be speculated that it is during this two-year period that a child gains all primary concepts about his own mouth and these concepts set the stage for articulation learning. Research has shown that the bulk of phonological development takes place by three years of age in average children (summarized in Vihman, 2004b). Certainly a child's complete development of oral percept by 18 months of age contributes to his thorough phonological development by three years of age.

Every parent knows that infants and toddlers are focused on their mouths. Gesell and Ilg, two of the first writers on infant feeding development, wrote about the young child's perception of his mouth. They wrote about how children discover their tongues in the delightful dry humor of the late 1930s:

> "At about one year of age the infant becomes automatically aware of his tongue; he reaches to his mouth to grasp it with his fingers [and] he sticks it out experimentally and exploitatively... After about 15 months of age this playfulness leads to deliberate spitting with variable domestic consequences" (Gesell & Ilg, 1937, p. 79).

To summarize: A child's perception of his mouth most likely begins in utero and this learning extends through the toddler year. By the end of the second year, most children have acquired enough perception of their own mouths to produce reasonable facsimiles of almost all the consonants, vowels, and diphthongs of the language, and they can do so in single words and 2–3 word combinations. It is proposed here that the complete phoneme development that occurs by the third year of life is due in part to an intact and active oral perceptual system.

ASSESSMENT OF SENSORY SYSTEMS

Very little has been done in the way of developing a measure of oral perception. Loucks and De Nil (2001) found that *tendon vibration* influences jaw movements during both speech and non-speech tasks and they speculated that tendon vibration might be used to measure oral perception. *Oral stereognosis* used to be suggested as a way to measure oral perception but oral stereognosis is the ability to identify the size, shape, and weight of an object in the mouth, not the ability to perceive the mouth itself. SLPs each use their own mental checklist of skills that they believe might contribute to the oral percept. For example, clients who are very messy eaters often are considered to have a limited oral percept, as are clients who cannot seem to position their articulators accurately or consistently.

TREATMENT OF SENSORY SYSTEMS

Every single client the present author has seen during the past 39 years of service has needed some sort of sensorimotor activity to bring a better awareness of the mouth into focus for phoneme learning. Whether it is chewing a gummy bear, stroking the alveolar ridge, vibrating the mouth, or simply looking into a mirror to see what the lips and tongue are doing, many articulation clients seem to need a multisensory orientation to their own mouths in order to learn their movement capabilities. Articulation and motor speech therapy is not just about listening to phonemes and imitating the instructor. These processes also include activities to learn about the mouth and its movement capabilities and these lessons often are learned during oral sensorimotor activities:

> *"The learning of movements is entirely dependent upon sensory experience; sensory input… not only initiates but also guides motor output"* (Fiorentino, 1972, p. 7).

Speech-language pathologists utilize hands, food and other objects to help their clients become more aware of the different parts of the mouth and to help them learn to discriminate different parameters of the oral sensory experience during speech. These activities build a kinesthetic foundation for learning phonemes by place and manner, and not just for children. These skills have been noted to be an important element of motor speech therapy in the adult rehabilitation population, too: "The intent is to help the patient regain some concept of where his articulators are and where he must put them" (Darley, Aronson & Brown, 1975, p. 274).

In recent years, some professionals have called the sensorimotor activities of speech learning *non-speech oral-motor exercises* and they have reacted to this term as if it was an outrageous new concept. But the idea to stimulate for greater awareness of the mouth has been discussed time and again throughout the literature on articulation therapy. Traditional Era writers like Van Riper often recommended such activities to prepare the mouth for speech activity: "[These activities are used] as methods of exploration, as ways of opening up new postural feedback circuits" (Van Riper & Irwin, 1958, p. 135–136). Many other writers of the 20th century agreed:

- "[These activities are] designed to increase the child's awareness of visual-kinesthetic cues" (Berry & Eisenson, 1956, p. 138–139).

- "There is enough scientific information to say that the oral sensory channels should not be neglected or overlooked in speech habilitation or rehabilitation" (Vaughn & Clark, 1979, p. 3 and p. 13).

- "In most cases, emphasis on the auditory cues would predominate over the other senses, but it would not be unusual during the teaching of a sound to ask the child to listen, watch, feel, and touch" (Hanson, 1983, p. 148).

- "Tactile/kinesthetic and visual feedback play potentially parallel roles in articulatory movement perception and in guiding articulatory trajectories toward targeted positions" (Fletcher, 1992, p. 42).

Neuroplasticity

Scientists report that sensorimotor activity can facilitate the neurological image of a body part. In an article on neuroplasticity and the recovery of speech motor control, Ludlow et al. (2008) explained that a neural substrate that is not biologically active degrades in function over time. Conversely, he stated that cortical representation can be enhanced "by increasing environmental input," and that

functioning of a body part can be enhanced by "increased biological activity" (p. S241). SLPs, therefore, integrate biological activities into articulation and motor speech therapies in order to help their clients better understand their own mouths during phoneme instruction.

METHODS TO FACILITATE SENSORY PROCESSING

The average baby or toddler learns about his mouth through a wide variety of everyday experiences. By extension, these experiences can also be employed to enhance oral perception in articulation and motor speech therapy. Such activities are described in the rest of this chapter. The ideas have been organized into the following types: structural relationship activities, feeding experiences, mouthing experiences, visual feedback, hygiene activities, pre-speech vocalizations, and speech activities. A section on the role of saliva is also included.

The reader will discover that activities to improve oral perception are intended to prepare the oral sensorimotor mechanism for phoneme learning but not to teach specific phonemes. Speech-language pathologists recognize that stimulating oral perception is not the goal of articulation therapy; these are techniques designed to draw a clients' attention to the parts of his mouth so that knowledge can be used in phoneme learning. One uses these activities only when a client demonstrates that he needs them, and the therapeutic process of trial and error instructs therapists about this necessity. Clients who can learn phonemes without additional help developing oral perception do not need these activities; clients who fail to learn phonemes using standard auditory, visual, and conceptual therapy models may.

Speech-language pathologists working in the 21st century understand that articulation learning is a sensorimotor activity and that multiple channels of stimulation sometimes are needed to enhance the process of phoneme learning. It is important to recognize that virtually none of these ideas have undergone formal research review, and

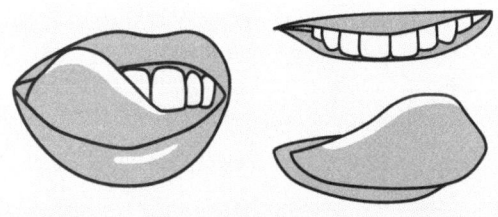

Oral structures are used to discover one another.

that there has been much outcry against them. It is understood that only certain clients need this type of input to help them learn new phonemes. The reader, therefore, should view all these ideas as practical advice to consider for certain clients. They are ideas passed down from one generation of therapists to another.

Structural Relationship Activities

A perception of the mouth is based first and foremost upon the structural relationships between the parts of the mouth. Each part is discovered as it moves around and bumps into other structures, and as other parts touch it. Just as a child comes to understand his physical body by touching it with his own hands, so too the child learns the physical parameters of his oral mechanism as one part of the oral mechanism touches another.

For example, a concept of the actual size, shape, and movement capabilities of the tongue is formed as the tongue moves around inside the oral cavity, touching the walls, palate, lips, gums, inner cheek walls, and so forth. Gaining the deciduous teeth during infancy provides additional new structures against which to press the tongue. Losing the deciduous teeth and then gaining the permanent teeth supplies even more structures to explore.

SLPs engage clients in *structural relationship activities* to take advantage of these sensory experiences. This is an idea that has been around as long as articulation therapy itself, and many examples can be drawn from the literature. Van Riper employed this concept: "The more natural landmarks of the mouth should as quickly as possible be made to serve as the check-points from which the moving postures rove and to which they return" (Van Riper & Irwin, 1958, p. 137).

There are a wide variety of ways one might go about teaching a client to use his oral structures to explore one another. The following suggestions are from Bauman-Waengler (2004, p. 255):

- *Lip-to-lip:* "Rub both lips together, first right and left, forward and backward."

- *Lip-to-teeth:* "Bite the lips" by sucking first the upper then the lower between the teeth.

- *Tongue-to-lips:* "Move tongue slowly on the outside of the mouth around the red of the lips, first clockwise, then counterclockwise."

- *Tongue-to-inner-cheek:* "Push the tongue tip against the cheeks, bulging out the cheeks to look like you have a golf ball in your mouth."

- *Tongue-to-lateral-lips:* "Tongue out, then move to the far right and far left."

- *Tongue-to-inner-lips:* "Move the tongue slowly on the inside of the lips in a clockwise, then a counterclockwise direction."

- *Tongue-to-inner-teeth:* "Let the tongue 'wash' the inside of the teeth from incisors to molars."

- *Tongue-to-palate:* "Tap the tongue against the palate."

- *Tongue-to-velum along midline:* "Move the tongue along the palate from behind the upper incisors posteriorly to the soft palate."

- *Tongue-to-palate:* "Move the tongue around the palate in circles, first clockwise then counterclockwise."

- *Tongue-to-lower teeth:* "Let the tongue tip push against the inside of the lower incisors."

Feeding Experiences

The oral percept also develops as children engage in feeding activities. These activities are of at least three different types: eating solids and semi-solids, drinking liquids, and using utensils. Food, liquid, and utensils provide children additional surfaces against which to press the articulators. The oral percept improves and gets more complex as feeding experiences expand over time. For example, a child learns a certain amount of information about his mouth when he sucks from bottle or breast, he learns more when introduced to purees on a spoon, he learns even more as he begins to finger-feed small food bits like cereal pieces, and he discovers even more when he learns to take a bite of, for example, pizza.

Young children love to stuff their mouths full of food. It is pleasurable and it teaches the child about the size and shape of the oral cavity. Feeding experiences help children develop a gross perception of the mouth, and it is the theory of this manual that it is upon this gross perception of the mouth that all subsequent speech learning will be based. This is akin to a young gymnast who first perceives his body well enough to do a somersault on the floor, but later perceives his body well enough to do a somersault in the air. Feeding activities are like somersaults on the floor because they set the foundation of oral perception. Speech activities are like somersaults in the air because they are advanced movements that require significantly more awareness and control of the moving parts.

Hunger, taste, and smell also play important roles in the feeding process, and subsequently the developing mouth percept. Hunger and the pleasure associated with the taste and smell of food causes children to accept and

Eating activities focus attention on the mouth.

explore foods of an increasingly greater variety and this in turn contributes to advances in oral percept over time. The process of oral sensorimotor learning expands as children explore the myriad options of taste, temperature, texture, and smell that mealtime activities present. Eating with the mouth is part of the normal process of mouth learning and its pay-off is a thorough perception of the physical parameters of the mouth for speech. Regardless of whether feeding problems and speech problems are inter-related, one can state with the utmost assuredness that feeding activities help an infant learn about his mouth. Children who are non-oral feeders and those who restrict their food preferences are denied aspects of these learning experiences.

Many SLPs use feeding experiences as adjuncts to articulation and motor speech therapy because they view them as a way to help clients develop mouth movement schemas. Most clients with articulation deficit do not have feeding disorder per se, and most do not need a full program of feeding therapy designed around their health, nutritional, and mealtime communication needs. Instead, the types of feeding activities that are incorporated into high-level articulation therapy are more along the lines of snacking experiences. A few simple snacking activities are added to articulation therapy to enhance a client's oral sensory perception. For more information, readers are referred to Chapter 18, *Eating, Swallowing, and Orofacial Myofunctional Methods*.

The mouthing of toys may enhance perception of the mouth.

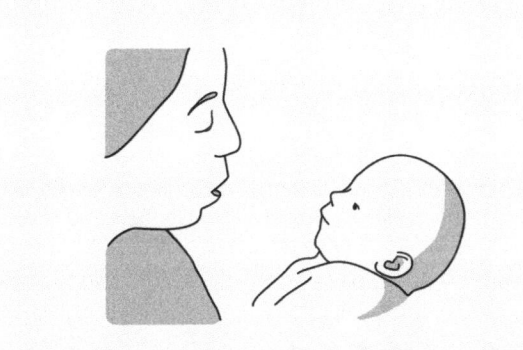

Children learn about their own mouths by watching their caregiver's mouths.

Simply pretending to eat has also been used in articulation therapy. Van Riper advocated this method — called *Fröeschels Chewing Method* — when he describe how to work with children who have severe speech delay. Fröeschels was a contemporary of Van Riper and his method was designed to relax and provide rhythmic oral movements in therapy especially in clients with fluency issues and those with motor speech disorders. Fröeschels had his patients pretend to chew, then vocalize while pretending to chew, then converse while pretending to chew.

Mouthing Experiences

A child also learns about his mouth by filling it with his own hands, feet, and other objects. Mouthing like this is a favorite pastime among infants and young children. It provides a broad platform for developing oral percept and basic oral movements. A child can put his hands and fingers into his mouth in utero, but the real mouthing period begins by about four months of age when most infants begin to grasp any object within reach and purposefully bring it to the mouth. By five months of age an infant can also bring his feet to his mouth.

Mouthing might be considered a reciprocal learning experience; the mouth is used to discover the physical properties of objects and objects are used to discover the physical properties of the mouth. Babies use objects of various size, shape, texture, temperature, elasticity, and taste parameters in order to discover all the parts of their oral cavities. Baby chew toys are specially designed with bumps, knobs, holes, scents, and tastes to entertain them during these explorations. Mouthing experiences are both tactile and proprioceptive. The size, shape, and texture of mouthed items give a child data about his mouth's shape and its movement capabilities as he sucks, bites, chews, moves, and exerts pressure against these objects. Babies stimulate the skin of the face, cheeks, jaw, lips, gums, palate, and tongue with these objects. A pleasurable experience causes children to accept and explore objects of an increasingly greater variety and this, in turn, creates more mouth movements over time.

Mouthing activities are used to facilitate primitive oral-sensorimotor learning, but they can also be used to teach very intricate oral movements. For example, a baby chew toy with a hole in it can be used to stimulate gross oral perception in a client with very little expressive speech, but it can also be used to facilitate tongue-tip extension for production of /l/ in a client with very advanced speech. Chapter 19 on the tools of articulation training contains an extensive discussion of these types of objects.

Visual Feedback

Babies generally gaze into the eyes and mouths of their loving caretakers, and children can arrive at a greater understanding of their own mouths when a caretaker provides a mirror-like image back to the child about what he, the child, is doing. Parents and other doting caretakers do this all the time. They place their faces fairly close to their baby's face and they hold their own head still. Then they use their eyes to search the baby's facial expression and oral position, and they imitate all of it. This is all a part of the parenting process and most parents do this regularly during the course of everyday activities; it is a beautiful facial dance between babies and their caretakers and infant researchers have studied it with film and video. These parent-child activities help develop the child's oral percept through visual feedback.

SLPs provide the same types of visual mouth learning activities in several ways. They engage in close visual gazing as described above, they provide mirrors for their client's own visual discoveries, they have client look at the mouths of other clients in a group, and they use photographs, drawings, and models of the mouth. Visual feedback to enhance oral percept for speech learning has been a consistent part of speech training since the elocutionists called a mirror a *looking glass*: "[Make an] appeal to the visual sense through the use of mirror, picture, diagram or directive gesture of the hand... Mirror study is essential" (Nemoy & Davis, 1937, p. 36–37).

Hygiene Activities

Babies and toddlers also learn about the mouth as they undergo the rituals of oral hygiene. Parents are charged with keeping their children clean and healthy and part of that job is to bathe the child's face, to wipe the mouth, to brush the teeth, and to clear the oral cavity of un-swallowed food. All of these activities are an important part of the early mouth learning experience because they occur several times every day under normal circumstances. Hygiene routines that are pleasurable can be an important part of developing a healthy oral percept. However, routines that are fraught with fear and anxiety affect children in negative ways, and these may be detrimental to the development of a thorough oral percept. Children who dislike these routines may begin to reject them, and this may decrease the number and variety of the child's mouth experiences.

To capitalize on the learning process that can take place during the routine events of daily oral care, therapists make sure that parents are tending to their children's oral hygiene in ways that promote pleasurable reactions for oral sensorimotor learning. This is especially important in work with babies, toddlers, and older children who

Daily hygiene routines help children discover the mouth and its parts.

have neuromuscular and cognitive disorders. Therapists make sure the parents/caretakers are washing the face, wiping the mouth, and brushing the teeth in ways that encourage healthy interactions, calm responses, and increased oral exploration. This topic is discussed more thoroughly in the next chapter.

The process of tending to oral hygiene can also be an important part of articulation training in higher functioning clients who have upper level articulation errors or mild motor speech disorders. For example, a tooth brushing routine can be done at home in which the client learns to use his brush to stimulate certain parts of the lips or tongue as well.

Pre-Speech Vocalizations

The process of producing pre-speech vocalizations also teaches a child about his mouth:

> *"The infant engages in a variety of oral exploratory movements linked with noise making activities. These activities help establish basic oral muscle control and sensory awareness of the tongue within the expanding oral space... The expansion of oral motor activities and controlled sound production during vocal play activities likely provide systematic preparatory experience for eventual emergence of specific articulation motor skills"* (Fletcher, 1992, p. 13).

There are countless examples of how pre-speech vocalizations work to develop a child's perception of his own mouth: cooing and goo-ing allow a baby to experience the deep vibration of voice in the chest, throat, face, nose, and mouth; panting and sniffing allow a baby to perceive the cool brush of voiceless-ness in the mouth and nose; humming teaches a toddler what it feels like to have sound vibration travel through the nasal cavities; an infant's production of raspberries teaches him what frication against the lips, tongue, and palate feels like; babbling allows a child to experience oscillating oral movements and the sound sequences that result. In short, the pre-speech period is the time during which an infant begins to experience the phonetic features he will later use in phoneme production. He is preparing his respiration, phonation, resonation, and articulation subsystems for the demands of speech soon to come.

SLPs often use pre-speech vocalizations to help clients on their way toward mature phoneme productions. This idea is represented all throughout the articulation literature of the 20th century. For example, Nemoy and Davis recommended using the lingua-velar raspberry to stimulate production of /k/. They called it "coughing up an imaginary fish bone" (Nemoy & Davis, 1937, p. 110).

Speech Activities

One should not forget that children learn quite a bit about their mouths simply by making phonemes. For example, babies learn about their lips by saying /b/, they learn about the tongue tip by saying /d/, and they learn about the back of the tongue by saying /g/. For this reason, many clients need no more oral-sensorimotor learning experiences than that which the process of phoneme instruction alone brings.

During the course of treatment, speech-language pathologists make judgments about the amount of mouth learning that must take place for each individual client. They observe their clients to determine if working on the phoneme alone is enough, and they determine if other activities to develop the oral percept are necessary. If a client seems to be learning all he needs about his mouth by practicing phonemes only, then nothing more than phoneme training is provided.

Saliva

Saliva plays an interesting and important role in the development of mouth perception. The mouth is bathed in an ever-changing amount of saliva. Saliva makes tongue and lip movements pleasurable as these organs slide and position themselves against one another and against other surfaces of the oral cavity. In their book entitled *A Practical Approach to Saliva Control* (1993), Johnson and Scott explain that saliva on the oral structures acts like oil on mechanical structures: "[It] lubricates the tongue and lips during speech" (p. 1). In other words, a mouth that is moist is best suited for speech movement learning. The presence of saliva in infancy encourages sound production and sound play and, in fact, certain pre-speech sounds actually are learned as a direct result of saliva play (e.g., spitting). Some clients have too little saliva in the mouth while others have too much. Both extremes can interfere with the development of the oral percept and phoneme learning.

A dry mouth makes lip and tongue movement activities downright unpleasant, and there is a natural tendency to avoid oral movement as a result. Purposeful limitations in mouth movement is natural and expected when the mouth is very dry. A dry mouth can stem from several causes; mouth breathing is a main cause. A dry mouth can also be a side effect of medications, disease, infection,

nerve damage, general dehydration, smoking, emotional states, and certain medical treatments such as radiation. Treatment for a dry mouth is designed to alter the circumstances that cause it and to increase fluid intake.

Too much saliva in the mouth causes speech to sound wet and slushy. This is most obvious during production of the sibilants, but it can also give an overall sloppy sound to speech. Too much saliva is caused by neglecting to swallow often enough or by swallowing with limited skill. Treatment is designed to teach the client to swallow more often and with greater skill. Methods to accomplish this are described in Chapter 18 on feeding and swallowing.

Speech-language pathologists recognize that management of saliva may need to be a part of articulation or motor speech therapy for some clients. This therapy might include activities to recognize the need to swallow, methods to learn how to suction, techniques to form a bolus, instruction on swallowing correctly, behavior management strategies to habituate a more frequent saliva swallow, and adjustments to medications. Very occasionally, surgery to curb excessive saliva production is recommended.

SUMMARY

An adequate perception of the mouth and its movement capabilities is necessary to develop mature speech. SLPs have developed a wide variety of multisensory methods to help clients to develop this skill.

Simple drinking activities can be used to talk about the wet and dry mouth in relation to the oral percept.

Speech activities themselves teach clients about their mouths.

16

Normalizing Oral-Tactile Sensitivity

Enhancing light-touch awareness and discrimination for phoneme learning

"Only by an integration of finely discriminated auditory, proprioceptive, and tactile stimuli can the precise ballistic, overlapping movements of mature, normal articulation be developed from the gross motor behavior of an infant."

– Eugene T. McDonald, 1964

The role of the tactile system in the training of speech movements can be ignored no longer. The skin, with its embedded nerve endings, is the organ responsible for feeling the light-as-a-butterfly touch experiences of voice, resonance, place, and manner of articulation. The concept that speech training should include methods to enhance oral-tactile sensitivity began with a few articles published in the 1940s and practicing speech-language pathologists have been developing clinical methods to assist oral-tactile perception ever since. The relationship between oral-tactile sensitivity and articulation even has received a fair amount of attention among speech researchers throughout the past sixty years, but for some reason this area continues to be a controversial one. Not everyone accepts the view that some speech clients might have difficulty with oral-tactile sensitivity despite significant evidence to the contrary.

The present chapter takes the perspective that some

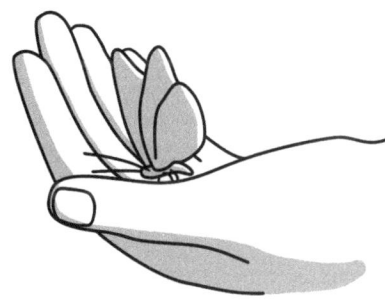

The touch experiences of articulation are as light as a butterfly and require a heightened sense of oral-tactile sensitivity.

clients, especially those with motor speech disorders, do have difficulty with oral-tactile sensitivity and that this deficit may be contributing directly to their troubles in speech movement learning. This chapter reviews aspects of normal and abnormal oral-tactile sensitivity, it explains simple procedures for clinical evaluation, and it presents practical methods to calm and/or excite oral-tactile responses. This chapter ends with two case samples that demonstrate how one might alter an articulation or motor speech program to encompass organized tactile input for improved speech movement learning.

BACKGROUND

Fairbanks (1954) was one of the first to propose that humans use three mechanisms to perceive and monitor their speech productions: the auditory system, the tactile system, and the proprioceptive system. He said that the auditory system was the most important sensor but he advised that the tactile and proprioceptive systems had their roles too. Fairbanks proposed a closed-loop theory that suggested all three sensory systems work together in the perception and self-monitoring of speech.

Fairbanks' and other similar theories have been questioned as they apply to adult speech production (e.g., Kelso & Tuller, 1983). However, many authors have suggested that the role of peripheral feedback may be very different for an adult who already produces all his phonemes correctly than for a very young child who is just learning to produce phonemes in the first place. It has been suggested that the tactile system may play a more significant role in phoneme learning than it does in phoneme maintenance:

> *"Although highly practiced speech movements can be accomplished in the absence of auditory or tactile input... the coordination of muscle activity necessary for learning and modification of speech production appears to depend on accurate perception of afferent input"* (Wohlert, 1996a, p. 1191).

Light Touch

Tactile sensitivity is important in speech development and speech therapy because articulation is all about light touch. The word *articulation* itself is rooted in the Greek word for joint (*arthron*) and refers to that place where two objects come together or touch. The articulatory touch experience required for production of /l/, for example, involves the muscles of the tongue and the bones of the palate, however, the muscles and bones never actually articulate. It is the skin on the surface of the tongue and palate that articulate, and it is the skin of these two organs that provides the data one uses to perceive the place and manner of the articulation itself. That data is tactile in nature.

It follows that some speech movement problems might be caused by a deficiency in perceiving and/or processing tactile experiences. Some clients may be unable to recognize and monitor the place, manner, resonance, and voice of their articulations as a direct result of this deficiency. This is the main idea that guides this line of thinking. Speech is a sensorimotor act and logic dictates that problems in the sensory part could lead to problems in the motor part. How could one move the oral mechanism correctly or consistently if one could not feel the result of one's movements?

> *"There are indications which seem to support the view that the quality of oral sensory function may be related to the quality of oral motor proficiency... Clinical observations and preliminary research findings encourage the speculation that there may well be a subgroup of persons with defective oral motor function such as poor articulation or poorly developed chewing, sucking, and swallowing, whose motor dysfunction is associated with defective oral sensory abilities"* (McDonald & Aungst, 1967, p. 219).

Practical Insight

The reader is encouraged to engage in the following activity before reading ahead. It is designed to help one focus on the important role oral-tactile sensitivity plays in speech production.

1. Place your mind on the sensations of your lower lip as you silently read this material and your mouth sits at rest. In this position certain tactile receptors are responding to let you know that your lower lip

is resting gently against your upper lip, assuming that you have an optimum oral rest position.

2. Now produce /f/ and note the changes in the tactile experience that occur.

3. Tactile receptors that were firing at rest cease firing when the lower lip pulls away from the upper lip in preparation for /f/.

4. Tactile receptors let you know that the lower lip changes its shape as it moves up toward the upper teeth.

5. Tactile receptors let you know that the lower lip makes contact with the upper teeth.

6. Tactile receptors allowed you to feel that air is rushing between the lips as /f/ is uttered.

7. Now add voice to this production to change /f/ to /v/. Tactile receptors in the lips allow you to feel a dramatic change in the lips that occurs when voice is added.

8. Now stop producing /v/ and go back to rest. All of these tactile experiences come to an end and the tactile system informs you that the lips have once again returned to rest position.

9. Tactile memory and tactile sequential memory allow you to remember all of this in sequence, and all future productions of /f/ and /v/ are compared against them.

What would happen to one's productions of /f/ and /v/ if these subtle tactile experiences could not be felt? What if the speaker could not tell that the lower lip was moving? What if the speaker could not tell when and if the lower lip made contact with the upper teeth? What if the speaker could not feel the sensation of air rushing over the lips, or if he could not feel the change when voice was added or taken away? What might happen to future productions if the speaker could remember none of these experiences? And what might happen if any one of these sensations caused the speaker to react in a protective way instead of a discriminatory way? In other words, for example, what would happen if these tactile experiences caused him to gag?

As elaborated below, research has indicated that adults with normal speech who are denied tactile feedback begin to produce phonemes that are somewhat distorted and they begin to have difficulty with oral placement. A child who is just developing speech is in a worse position, however. The child developing speech is denied some of the very data that would allow him to learn these phoneme in the first place. Everyone understands that a child who cannot hear has difficulty learning speech sounds. The theory iterated here is that a child who cannot feel his phoneme movements has similar problems. After all, the touch experiences of articulation are very subtle and as light as a butterfly. They would not be easy to perceive if one's tactile system was impaired even in small ways.

THE TACTILE SYSTEM

The tactile system is the largest sensory system of the human body. It includes all the skin, the tactile receptors embedded within the skin, the nerves that carry tactile messages from the skin to the midbrain where they intermingle with other sensory nerves, the nerves that carry the integrated messages from the midbrain to the cortex, and the cortex itself where the messages are organized and stored for later use.

Protection & Discrimination

The tactile system serves two principle roles: protection and discrimination. The protective function is the fight-or-flight response that serves to guard one against dangerous touch experiences. For example, the protective function alerts one to pull away from a hot surface quickly so that one will not experience too much pain or injury. The protective element of the oral mechanism includes the gag and other reflexes. These automatic mechanisms protect the airway in order to keep one breathing and alive.

The discriminatory function of the tactile system is different and more important to the discussion. The discriminatory function of the tactile system helps one perceive the way the body is touching and being touched. For example, tactile receptors in the hands allow one to find keys that have fallen to the bottom of a crowded bag as his or her fingers move around and feel the items within. Likewise tactile receptors in the mouth allow one to feel his articulators as they move around, re-shape, and make contact with one another, and as they feel the air that passes by them and the voice that passes through them.

Skin

A discussion of the tactile system's role in articulation learning begins with the skin. Phoneme production always involves manipulation and stimulation of the skin. The ear hears the sounds that result from these actions but the skin allows the speaker to feel the actions in the first place. Tactile information is one of four different mechanisms that create the internal image of the body and its movements. This is called the *body image, schema,* or *map.* Plans for each new speech movement are based on this neurological record.

Skin-Muscle Relationship

The tactile system functions protectively and discriminately as just described, but in the oral mechanism it serves an even more amazing role. According to Andreatta (2008)

TABLE 8 — Origin of Tactile Information & Perception Thereof					
Origin	Sense	#	Organ	Type	Image
Sensations that originate from outside the body	Auditory	1	Ear	Sound	Image of the world
	Visual	2	Eye	Sight	
	Olfactory	3	Nose	Smell	
	Gustatory	4	Mouth	Taste	
Sensations that originate from within the body itself	Tactile	1	Skin	Active and Passive Touch	Image of the body and its movements (body image)
	Vestibular	2	Inner Ear	Gravitational Pressure	
	Muscle Proprioception	3	Muscles	Contracting and Relaxing	
	Joint Proprioception	4	Joints	Bending, Straightening, and Rotating	

The tactile system is one of four mechanisms that contribute to the body image.

the muscles of the oral area and the skin surrounding it have a relationship that is unique among body systems. Muscle fibers in the face and oral mechanism actually insert directly into the overlying skin. This means that displacement of the skin (moving, shifting, bending, stretching, vibrating, etc.) has a direct and immediate influence on the function of the underlying muscles. This makes tactile processing integral to speech movement learning:

> *"Muscles of the lower face insert directly into the facial skin, allowing for sensory endings to encode both the static and dynamic consequences of force and movement related to orofacial behavior… The unique relationship between orofacial muscle and the overlying skin is believed to be an important factor influencing orofacial proprioception and sensorimotor control during functional behaviors… [These vast networks] of low-threshold sensory end-organs… respond vigorously to subtle mechanical events such as stretch, strain, vibration, or indentation of the skin"* (Andreatta, 2008, p. 51–52).

This means that the skin does not just help to perceive where articulations are made. It means that the skin of the oral mechanism actually serves to activate muscle contraction and relaxation during phoneme production. This makes the skin and its tactile system far more important in speech movement learning than was ever known before.

TACTILE RECEPTORS

Therapists who design methods to improve tactile processing for articulation learning need to know basic facts about the tactile receptors. Tactile nerves contain a variety of receptor end organs, or *mechanoreceptors*, that transmit different types of tactile data, and it is this data that is used in the process of speech production. One can understand why and how to design methods of tactile stimulation for speech movement learning when one understands the stimuli that cause the tactile receptor nerves to respond.

Although there is still a lot to be learned about the tactile receptors, researchers generally agree that the skin responds to specific stimuli: heat, cold, stretch, pressure, onset of pressure, sustained pressure, release of pressure, signals of various strengths, vibration of various frequencies, texture, and taste. Each type of receptor responds to several stimuli and many respond to the same stimuli. This redundancy provides humans with rich overlapping information about their own bodily experiences within the physical world, including those of expressive speech movement.

The following basic information about the tactile receptors has been gathered from a wide variety of textbooks and articles about the tactile system. This is the type of information that can be found in any basic anatomy text.

Ruffini Corpuscles

Ruffini's corpuscles are located in the stretch lines of the skin and serve several functions. They respond to temperatures of 77–113 °F, they are sensitive to skin stretching, they serve to monitor the slippage of objects along the surface of the skin, and they respond to sustained pressure. Ruffini's corpuscles have a very low threshold that allows them to respond to very weak signals. Thus they are very important to the light touch awareness and discrimination skills necessary for the perception of speech articulations. Ruffini's corpuscles are also located in ligaments and tendons where they detect mechanical deformation within joints. Ruffini's corpuscles, therefore, are important in the detection of jaw position during speech.

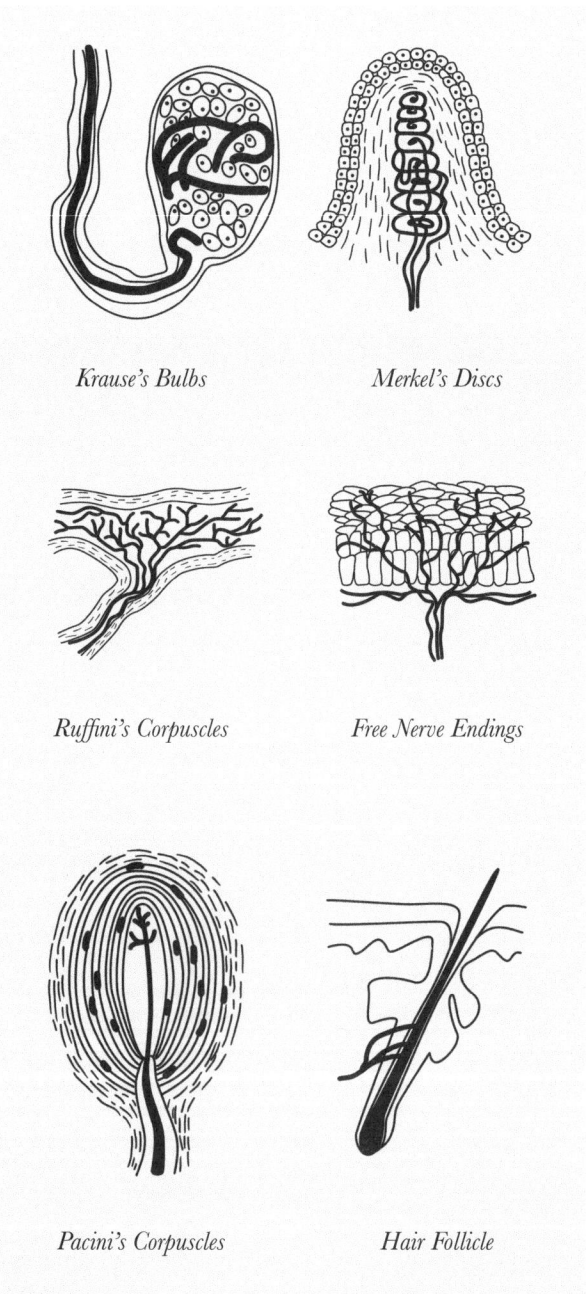

Krause's Bulbs   *Merkel's Discs*

Ruffini's Corpuscles   *Free Nerve Endings*

Pacini's Corpuscles   *Hair Follicle*

Merkel's Discs

Merkel's discs are found in the superficial layers of the skin and in the oral mucosa. They are fast to respond and are slow adapting, meaning that they respond when touch is first initiated and they continue to fire for a while with sustained stimulation. They respond to tissue displacement and vibration at low frequencies (5–15 Hz). Merkel's discs fire quickly with small points of stimulation and, therefore, are important in tactile localization and two-point discrimination. Merkel's discs on the fingertips are used to read Braille. In the tongue tip, Merkel's discs are responsible for helping a speaker detect the incredibly subtle differences in place and manner during productions of /t/, /s/, /st/, and /ts/. The ability to detect different tactile stimuli in very close proximity (two-point discrimination) means that Merkel's discs also help detect texture within the mouth.

Krause's Bulbs

Krause's bulbs are found in the mucous membranes of the lips and tongue. They are thermoreceptors that respond to temperatures less that 68 °F (cold). They also respond to touch and pressure and, therefore, play a role in the perception of all lip movements and articulations. Krause's bulbs are phasic receptors meaning that they will continue to respond with repeated stimulation (low frequency vibration). They help one perceive the size and shape of the airstream as it brushes over the lips while exiting the mouth. They also help one perceive whether the exiting airstream is voiced or voiceless.

Pacini's Corpuscles

Pacini's corpuscles often are described as having the appearance of a soft onion. They respond only to an initial touch experience and they adapt rapidly. This means that they respond only to the initial onset of pressure and to the release of that pressure, but they discontinue firing when touch is maintained. Pacini's corpuscles, therefore, allow one to perceive the initial contact or onset of speech articulations and to feel the release of that contact. Pacini's corpuscles respond to vibration and gross pressure changes and, therefore, they also play a role in the detection of voicing and voiceless-ness. They respond optimally when vibration is at 250 Hz and can detect vibration even when it is centimeters away.

Free Nerve Endings

Free nerve endings are the most common type of tactile receptors within the skin. They respond to mechanical, thermal, and noxious stimuli. These nerve endings adapt slowly, meaning that they continue to fire with sustained physical contact. They allow one to adapt to a hot bath or cold temperatures outside. Free nerve endings in the mouth play a role in the detection of saliva and in monitoring of the continuant phonemes. The role of temperature response by free nerve endings within the mouth makes cool temperatures excellent stimuli to awaken sensation in and on the mouth.

Hair Follicles

Receptors located at the base of body hairs respond to displacement or movement of the hairs. They are located on the outer surface of the face. Hair follicles fire when the hairs are bent and, therefore, they also respond when the skin is stretched or relaxed. Hair follicles play a role in the perception of oral movement because the skin on the surface of the face is in a constant state of stretching and relaxing during speech movement. Hairs on the face lean in different directions specific to the skin of each individual person.

Special Tongue Receptors

The tongue is covered in densely packed filiform (file-like) papillae. These tiny cone-shaped papillae are much smaller and more numerous that the much larger taste buds that are scattered among them on the upper surface of the tongue.

The tongue's filiform papillae are equipped with tiny hair-like projections called *secondary papillae* that extend out from the end (Manabe, Lim, Winzer, & Loomis 1999).

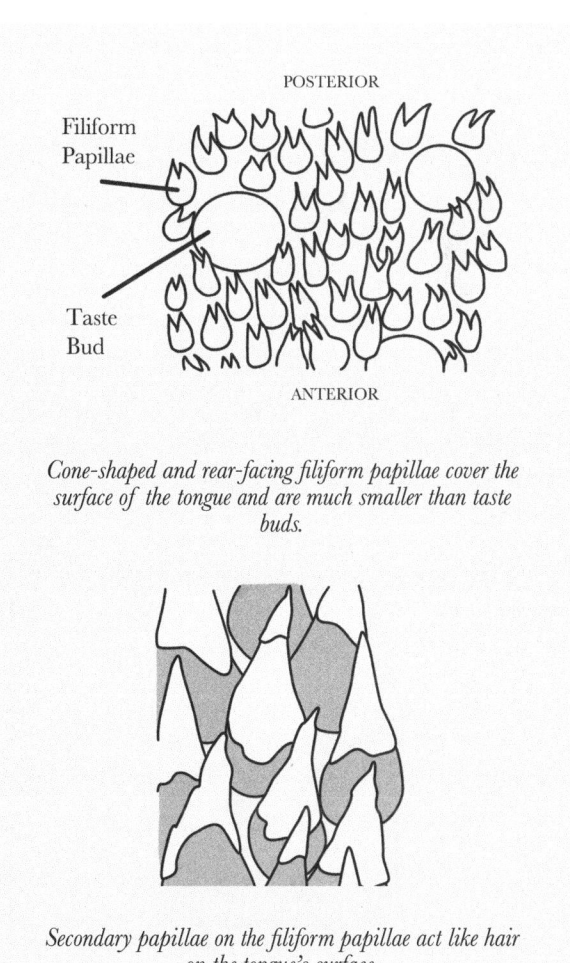

Cone-shaped and rear-facing filiform papillae cover the surface of the tongue and are much smaller than taste buds.

Secondary papillae on the filiform papillae act like hair on the tongue's surface.

These are not actual hairs but a very thin layer of epithelial (skin) tissue that moves like hair. This means that the tongue responds to touch stimulation in much the same way that hairy skin on the rest of the body does. These cone-shaped projections and their hair-like projections tilt toward the rear of the oral cavity. Therefore, stroking the upper surface of the tongue from anterior-to-posterior is inhibiting and calming, while stroking from posterior-to-anterior is exciting.

TACTILE SENSITIVITY

Researchers agree that the oral mechanism is the most sensitive part of the human body and that the tongue tip and the hard palate are the most sensitive portions that have been tested. The mouth contains very sensitive and highly discriminating cutaneous (skin) tissue. Bosma (1967) called the mouth an "oral sensorium" and explained that it has more tactile end organs than any other place on the human body. That's what makes it so sensitive: "The more end organs per unit area of skin, the more sensitive it will be" (Farber, 1982, p. 123). There is a very important tactile relationship between the tongue and palate. The tongue is richly supplied with receptors that allow one to perceive its movement and shaping capacities and the palate is richly supplied with receptors that allow one to perceive the instant it is touched.

> *"Histological and behavioral studies have shown that the lips, tongue, and fingers are more suited than other areas of the body for processing spatial information, due to dense receptive innervation and large areas of representation in the somatosensory cortex"* (Wohlert, 1996a, p. 1191).

Tactile end organs allow humans to perceive very subtle changes in tactile stimulation within the mouth. The mouth is so sensitive that a speaker can feel whether the tongue is touching the front, the back, the sides, or the middle of the palate. The mouth is so sensitive that a preschooler can feel the differences in articulations of /t/, /s/, /st/, and /ts/. The mouth is so sensitive that a slight increase in saliva sets off the swallow reflex even in a newborn. Like the fairy-tale princess who cannot sleep

when a pea is lodged under her mattress, the mouth is so sensitive that an adult will be driven to distraction until a tiny bit of popcorn kernel lodged between the teeth and gums is removed.

The tongue is so sensitive that damage to it is quite painful. The reader is probably familiar with the intense pain cause by accidentally biting the tongue. Patients who bite all the way through the tongue or who experience some other trauma to the tongue report tremendous feelings of pain that lasts many months. Some of these patients report tingling sensations that extend for years after the initial event. Inflammation, anemia, poisoning, and other life-threatening diseases can also cause tongue pain.

EARLY DEVELOPMENT

According to Gottfried (1984) the tactile system is the first sensory system to develop in utero. The system awakens at 7.5 weeks gestation and then almost the entire surface of the body becomes sensitive to touch over the next seven weeks. The earliest detectable touch responses occur at the lips, and the last ones occur at the feet and toes. This means that by the time a full-term infant is born he already has accumulated seven months of tactile experience in, on, and around the mouth. Presence of the oral reflexes at birth indicates that the oral-tactile system is functioning appropriately. The gag is elicited on the anterior half of the tongue at birth. This very sensitive nature of the oral mechanism diminishes in strength by 7–8 months of age (Crickmay, 1966) so that the gag retreats to the posterior one-third of the tongue where it will remain for the rest of life.

RESEARCH

Research has been done on the relationship between oral-tactile sensitivity and speech production in children and adults with both normal and abnormal speech. Tactile sensitivity has been measured in the research lab using a variety of tests: two-point discrimination, vibro-tactile stimulation, pain thresholds, oral stereognosis, tactile localization, consistency of tongue-to-palate articulations, simple reaction to touch, texture discrimination, nerve block injections, anesthesia, neurological test batteries, and microscopic examination of the nerves. Fucci, Harris, and Petrosino (1985) reviewed the literature in this area that had been done up until that point and found that "the majority of subjects with defective articulation had poorer oral sensory abilities than normal-speaking subjects, and that oral sensory function may be a factor in controlling speech production" (p. 331). And that is just the beginning of what is known about the relationship between oral-tactile sensitivity and speech.

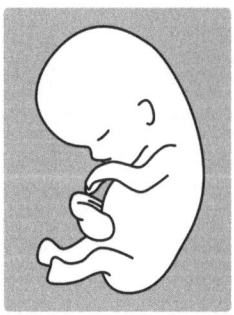

Tactile receptors in the mouth begin to respond when a child is 7.5 weeks gestation.

Case Study

MacNeilage, Rootes, and Chase (1967) did perhaps the most extensive case study of tactile sensitivity in a client with speech impairment. They studied the speech and tactile skills of a seventeen-year-old female with normal intelligence and highly unintelligible speech of unknown etiology. She had excellent auditory processing skills but produced speech that contained substituted, distorted, and omitted consonants, distorted vowels, lack of clusters, and long pauses. She also had difficulty with fine motor control of the fingers and difficulty with swallowing and chewing. Many therapists today would describe this client as having a motor speech disorder although it was not common practice to do so at the time.

Extensive testing of the client's tactile system revealed that she had impaired skill in the following areas: sensitivity to pain, tactile localization, two-point discrimination, and stereognosis. Microscopic examination revealed that the sensory receptors and nerve fibers in the client's skin and oral mucosa had a normal appearance. These results suggested that the client's skin was able to sense tactile stimuli but that this information was not transmitting to the cortex and/or processing well within the cortex itself. The authors postulated that the client's inability to move the oral mechanism correctly for sound production was directly related to a *higher order tactile deficit*. This client was having difficulty using tactile signals in meaningful ways for speech movement learning.

The authors summarized that tactile information is a necessary component of speech motor learning and that problems in this area may be directly related to impaired tactile perception in some clients.

> *"It seems likely that sensory [tactile] information accompanying early attempts at speech gestures is necessary in order for the speaker to identify more successful attempts and accordingly modify his program for future productions of the gestures"* (MacNeilage, Rootes, & Chase, 1967, p. 465–466).

Group Study

Frisch and Handler (1974) did an amazing study of tactile skills in children with speech errors. They studied 30 children with intelligence in the average range or above. The children were divided into three groups: 10 with multiple phoneme omissions, 10 with multiple phoneme substitutions, and a control group of 10 with no speech sound errors.

The children were tested with the *Reitan-Indiana Neuropsychological Test Battery*. The test measured sensory-perception and psychomotor tasks. It included sub-tests of bilateral perception, finger recognition, fingertip perception, picture matching, figure matching, copying of drawings, visual shape discrimination, analysis and integration of shape components, hand and finger tapping patterns, size recognition, color and shape perception, and visual memory.

Test results were astounding. They revealed that 16 of the 20 children with "functional speech impairment" could be classified as having cerebral damage with possible left-hemisphere lesion. Clients with a preponderance of phoneme omissions had significantly worse scores on tests of tactile performance and sensory perception than did the normal children and they demonstrated greatest difficulty with tasks that required sensory-receptive functions:

> *"These data suggest that functional articulatory disorders with multiple omissions may involve a physiological defect of a sensory-receptive and kinesthetic nature"* (p. 441).

> *"The findings of this study propose that articulatory problems of multiple omissions and substitutions involve difficulty with sensory-receptive functions, probably as a result of a dysfunction in the left hemisphere"* (p. 442).

The Frisch and Handler study suggests that up to 80% of clients with multiple phoneme omissions and substitutions may have a problem in tactile perception that underlies the speech deficit. These are children with neurological *soft signs* that are being ignored. They are students with problems in oral-tactile awareness and discrimination that simply cannot seem to make their mouths move correctly for speech. Clinicians often report that these children have difficulty with fine motor control in the hands as well.

Notes about these types of clients can be found in articulation textbooks that stretch back to the 1940s including Van Riper (1947) who called them *clumsy-tongued individuals* and *the slow of tongue*. Luria (1964, 1966) said they had *kinesthetic motor aphasia*. Powers (1971a, 1971b) said these clients had *general oral inaccuracy*. Bosley (1981) said they had lingual and alveolar *agnosia*, meaning *lack of knowledge*, and she attributed it to a lack of tactile sensation and/or difficulty localizing tactile sensations. Knickerbocker (1980), an occupational therapist, described this problem as *sensory dormancy* meaning that these clients used excessive inhibition of incoming sensory input and had a general lack of sensory arousal. For more than half a century, these cases have been treated as if they were "speech-only" clients, and the term *functional* has been equated with the concept of "no known cause." But the term *functional* meant *motoric* in Van Riper's day and difficulty with tactile processing seems to be part of it.

Some of these clients today are identified with global apraxia and/or sensorimotor integrative disorder and may receive appropriate treatment from occupational or physical therapy, but most of these clients never receive assessment or treatment for their tactile perceptual problems and are treated as "speech-only" clients. Teaching delicate and sophisticated speech movements to clients who cannot perceive them might be one reason that certain clients with severe speech impairment make very slow progress and in some cases are unable to develop certain phonemes at all. Perhaps phoneme omissions are the result of a client's inability to feel whether or not he has made articulatory contact (tactile awareness), and phoneme substitutions are the result of an inability to determine where and how contact is being made (tactile localization and tactile discrimination).

Additional Research

Selected additional research regarding oral-tactile sensitivity in normal subjects and those with speech impairment has been summarized here. It is presented in chronological order to demonstrate the unfolding nature of these ideas over time.

- Ringel and Ewanowski (1965) studied two-point discrimination in 25 normal young adults. They found the tongue tip to be the most sensitive part, followed by the finger tip, the upper lip, the soft palate, the alveolar ridge, and the base of the thumb, in that order. They also found that the midline was the most sensitive part of each area. Results revealed that the lips can perceive two points of stimuli that are only 2.5 mm apart.

- Ringel and Fletcher (1967) studied tactile sensitivity as measured by discrimination of texture in 24 young adult males. They used emery cloths of various grades and subjects judged them as more rough or more smooth relative to one another. They found that judgments were fairly accurate, that the tongue was better at this task than the lips, and that accuracy of judgment was better with rougher textures.

- Henkins and Banks (1967) used nylon filaments pressed into the skin to test oral-tactile sensitivity. They found that the tongue tip and the hard palate were the most sensitive parts of the oral mechanism, followed by the tongue blade. They also found that this process of using nylon wires was a viable method for simple clinical assessment.

- Ringel, Burk, and Scott (1968) tested adults' ability to match forms presented into subjects' mouths (oral form recognition/oral stereognosis) without being able to see them. They found that those with defective articulation were poorer at this task. This study suggested that clients with articulation

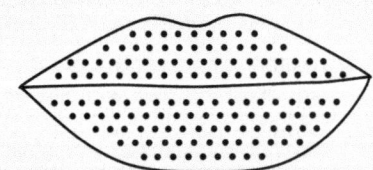

Humans can perceive touch experiences that are 2.5 mm apart on the lips.

impairment have poor oral-tactile discrimination skills.

- Locke (1969) taught average children to imitate non-English phonemes and found that those who imitated well were significantly better on a test of oral stereognosis than children who could not imitate well.

- Pleasonton (1970) used surface electrodes on the tongue and found that the tongue tip was more sensitive than the dorsum in 5 teenage girls and boys. She also found that responses in the dorsum were inconsistent from one day to the next, but that both sides of the tongue seemed equally sensitive.

- Weinberg, Liss, and Hillis (1970) found that adolescent children with /r/ misarticulation had significantly depressed levels of skill in the area of oral form recognition.

- Gammon, Smith, Daniloff, and Kim (1971) found that the administration of oral anesthesia to adults resulted in a 20% rate of consonant misarticulations. Vowels were unaffected. Misarticulation was most severe for fricatives and affricates in the labial and alveolar regions. "Articulation of consonants suffered most from tactile deprivation... Tactile feedback, information concerning articulator shape, area of contact, pressure of contact, etc., is very important to consonant production" (p. 280).

- Williams and La Pointe (1971) studied oral stereognosis, two-point discrimination, and light-touch detection on the tongue of normal adults. They found no correlations between these measures, suggesting that a test of oral stereognosis is not a good measure of oral-tactile sensitivity or two-point discrimination.

- Scott and Ringel (1971) used nerve block injections to deprive normal adult speakers of sensation from all supraglottal structures except the pharynx and posterior one-third of the tongue. They found that phonemes became distorted but that phoneme substitutions did not occur.

- Wood (1971) reported his clinical observations of patients with tongue-thrust swallow as they attempted clinical procedures involving the placement of a small elastic band on the tongue tip. He found that "some, but not all, are quite insensitive to lingual placement... Frequently, tongue-thrusting patients have difficulty with this rather simple task. The patients either will have difficulty locating the tongue tip on which to place the elastic or, if they correctly place it on the tongue tip, they will have difficulty maintaining it on the rugae long enough to get the jaws closed. Often the elastic slips off the tongue. The tongue may also slip off the spot carrying the elastic with it" (p. 83).

- Putnam and Ringel (1972) found that the lips moved less well when the trigeminal nerve was blocked with anesthesia. Rate, accuracy, and extent of lip movement were reduced.

- Lass, Kotchek, and Deem (1972) studied two-point discrimination in normal adults and found that the two sides of the face and oral mechanism have different levels of sensitivity, that the tongue tip was more sensitive than the dorsum of the tongue and lower lip, and that the middle of structures is more sensitive than the sides.

- Rosenbek, Wetrz, and Darley (1973) compared differences in oral sensation in adult patients with apraxia and aphasia with normal subjects. They studied oral form recognition, two-point discrimination, and mandibular kinesthesis. They found that the more severe the apraxia, the more difficulty apraxic clients had in all three measures, and, therefore, the more profound the oral-perceptual deficit. However, they also found that not all patients with apraxia of speech demonstrated difficulty with these tasks. They concluded that there are perhaps two groups of adults with apraxia: those with oral sensory perceptual deficit and those without.

- McNutt (1975) studied tactile discrimination in the tongues of children and adults. They found that the children had equal skills on both sides of the tongue but that the adults did not.

- Putnam and Ringel (1976) used cinefluorography to study oral movements during conditions of trigeminal nerve block anesthesia. They found that jaw movements compensated for reduced lip and tongue movements during these conditions. They also found reduced lip protrusion, loss of precision in lip closure, reduction in the precision of tongue articulations especially in the tip, and obvious alterations in jaw positions. Bunched tongue positions were noticeable. The authors suggested, "Distortion of tongue and lip activity... was due to inadequate orosensory feedback needed for the refinement of muscle activity" (p. 261).

- McNutt (1977) used tests of two-point discrimination and oral stereognosis to investigate tactile discrimination skill in children with /s/ and /r/ misarticulations. They found that those with /s/ misarticulation had tactile discrimination skills essentially the same as the control group, but that children with misarticulation of /r/ did not.

- Jordan, Hardy, and Morris (1978) found that children with relatively severe expressive speech problems performed more poorly than controls on tasks of tongue-to-palate placement. They also found that the speech-disordered subjects were able to improve this skill with training. The authors suggested that these children with speech impairment seemed to have the sensory processing skills necessary for oral placement, but that they needed more experience or training to learn the skills.

- Fucci, Small, and Petrosino (1983) found that the type of instructions given to research subjects did not affect their vibro-tactile thresholds. They found that clients could make adequate judgments as long as they were told to pay attention to the stimuli.

- Kelso and Tuller (1983) found that adults who had received topical anesthesia to the oral mucosa could produce acoustically normal vowels. Subjects also had jaw movement minimized by a bite block and auditory feedback dampened by white noise. These results suggested that adults have a motor memory that extends beyond the tactile and auditory systems. In other words adults, with normal speech could maintain good articulation despite a lack of tactile feedback.

- Hetrick and Sommers (1988) found that seven- and eight-year-old children with moderate and severe misarticulations scored more poorly on tests of oral stereognosis than did normal peers.

- Wohlert (1996a) found that oral tactile sensitivity at the lip vermillion declines with age in older adults, and that women in this group tended to have better sensitivity than men. No differences were found between upper and lower lips, or left and right sides.

- Wholert (1996b) summarized known research on the processing of spatial information by the lips and summarized that tactile and not proprioceptive stimulation is the system at play. "Muscle spindles, providing proprioceptive information, are absent in the lip musculature... but the glabrous tissue of the lips is plentifully supplied with mechanoreceptors" (p. 1191). This means that it is touch receptors and not muscle receptors that allow one to perceive movement in the lips.

- Marshalla (2007a) studied children's reactions to touch of an examiner's hands and found that children as young as four years of age with no speech impairment readily accepted and tolerated tactile stimulation to the face and mouth without overt reactions such as a gagging or pulling away.

- Andreatta and Barlow (2009) studied vibrotactile detection thresholds in young adults and found evidence to support theories of neuroplasticity in the oral sensorimotor system. The authors suggested that their results supported the clinical process of "gradual remodeling" movement responses that function to "organize the sensorimotor experiences" by controlling the "complexity, frequency, and form of the therapeutic tasks." The authors seem to be suggesting that multisensory experiences given in small steps may be the best way to stimulate new speech movement in the oral area.

HIGHER LEVEL TACTILE PROCESSING

The brain processes tactile experiences for functional application just as it organizes all other sensory experiences. The skills that result are discussed here. Collectively they are referred to as *higher-level tactile processing*.

Tactile Awareness

To be aware of touch experiences means that one is cognizant of the fact that a tactile event is occurring. One must be aware of an oral touch experience in order to consider it and to change it. The client who is unaware of incoming oral-tactile stimuli must be helped to become aware of them in order to make the changes that speech therapy requires.

Tactile Attention

Tactile experiences can be attended or ignored. One must attend an oral-tactile experience in order to adjust the movements that caused it. The client who is inattentive to oral-tactile signals is ignoring valuable information about place, manner, and voice. This client needs a program to help him pay closer attention to the incoming tactile signals of speech movements and positions.

Tactile Localization

Touch experiences can be identified by location on the body map. One must be able to locate the area of tactile experiences in and on the mouth in order to adjust place of articulation. Clients with poor localization skills need special help learning place of articulation through enhanced sensory input during the process of phoneme learning.

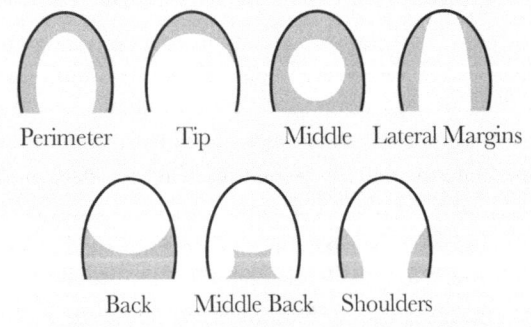

Perimeter   Tip   Middle   Lateral Margins

Back   Middle Back   Shoulders

Tactile localization allows a speaker to determine which parts of the tongue are articulating with which parts of the palate.

Tactile Discrimination

Tactile experiences can be differentiated by size, shape, depth, texture, temperature, length of time administered, location, and rate of repetition. These are important factors in learning manner of articulation. Clients with poor oral-tactile discrimination may have difficulty feeling the difference between one phoneme and another, for example, feeling the difference between /b/ and /m/. These clients need help learning to recognize these differences during the process of speech movement learning.

Two-Point Discrimination

Two-point discrimination allows humans to feel the difference between any two places of contact, for example, the touch experiences of /t/ and /k/, or between /s/ and /θ/. As another example, it is very fine two-point discrimination at the tongue tip that allows one to feel the intricate differences between /t/, /s/, /st/, and /ts/. Clients without this skill may need extra training in this area during phoneme learning activities.

Tactile Figure-Ground Discrimination

The tactile system allows one to perceive a main touch sensation while ignoring other background touch experiences. No one specific tactile sensation would stand out above others without figure-ground discrimination. For example, one could not feel speech articulations as different from the sensation of saliva bathing the entire inner surface of the mouth without figure-ground discrimination. Clients with difficulty in this area need help learning to pay attention to the main aspects of place and manner and to ignore other tactile stimuli that occur simultaneously.

Tactile Memory (Long/Short/Sequential)

Just as the ear hears and remembers, so too does the skin feel and remember. The memory of tactile experiences in the mouth makes phoneme productions and their sequences consistent. Some clients need cues and drill on phoneme sequences in order to help them remember the tactile elements involved.

Tactile Adaptation

The tactile system adapts to sensation quickly. For example, cold water may seem very cold at first but less cold after a few minutes because of adaptation. Adaptation to tactile stimuli is an aspect of normality. Tactile adaptation allows one to talk while one has food in their mouth because the mouth quickly adjusts to the differences in tactile feedback that the food brings to the speech movement experience. Clients who cannot adapt to sensations in the mouth find them irritable, and irritable sensations are usually avoided. Thus, the tactile sensations of speech articulations may be avoided if they cannot be adapted. These clients need help getting used to the feel of speech articulations so that they can respond to them discriminately and not protectively.

PROBLEMS IN SENSITIVITY

Research projects on oral-tactile sensitivity and speech impairment have generally hypothesized that under-sensitivity is the principle issue at work, but working therapists see a different picture. Clinicians report that while some of their clients are under-sensitive, others are over-sensitive, inattentive, confused, or cannot seem to remember what they feel. In addition, there are clients who avoid oral tactile experiences and, therefore, do not allow themselves enough opportunities to process what they feel.

Speech and motor therapists began to categorize clients by these sensitivity differences over four decades ago beginning at least with Morris (1977a, 1997b). Clinicians began to classify these problems as hyposensitivity, hypersensitivity, mixed sensitivity, fluctuating sensitivity, and defensiveness.

Hyposensitivity (Under-Responsiveness)

The client who is hyposensitive has a very high threshold of response to tactile input. He responds slowly or not at all. The client's gag, therefore, may be completely absent or may be tardy in its response, meaning that it takes repeated or powerful stimuli to elicit. A client who is hyposensitive has difficulty feeling place, manner, and voicing changes. He also may have trouble managing food in his mouth. This client needs a program to awaken his tactile system and to help him pay attention to oral-tactile stimuli. Clinicians and researchers have begun to use the term *under-response* for hyposensitivity. The new term takes the focus off the tactile system and places it on the client's reaction.

Hypersensitivity (Over-Responsiveness)

The client who is hypersensitive has a very low threshold of response to tactile input. He responds quickly to very little oral stimulation and, therefore, gags easily. The client even may respond negatively when he simply thinks about oral stimulation. This client usually avoids oral-tactile experiences. He may be very picky about the types of foods he eats and he may avoid certain articulatory contacts. He even may respond to tactile input with a tonic bite reflex. A hypersensitive client needs a program to calm his fight-or-flight protective responses so that the higher-order skills of tactile localization and discrimination can develop.

Mixed Sensitivity

The client with mixed sensitivity responds to touch stimuli differently depending upon where it occurs on the body map. For example a client can be over-sensitive to stimuli on the face yet under-sensitive to stimuli inside the mouth.

Some clients withdraw, hide, or protect the mouth to avoid oral-tactile stimulation.

This client needs a program to normalize his tactile responses.

Fluctuating Sensitivity

Some clients show fluctuations in their reactions to tactile input and these changes can range from complete unresponsiveness to overreactions. Such swings can be seen in any type of client, but are more common in clients on the autism spectrum and those with dementia.

Defensiveness

The client with tactile defensiveness reacts negatively and emotionally to tactile input and he avoids tactile experiences as a result. Tactile defensiveness can occur at any sensitivity level. This client needs a program to calm his defensive fight-or-flight tactile system so that he can begin to process higher-order skills like localization and discrimination. Ayres seems to have been the first to use the term *tactile defensiveness*: "Tactile defensiveness is the tendency to react negatively and emotionally to touch sensations" (Ayres, 1979, p. 107).

Tactile defensiveness is a behavioral response that ranges from mild to severe. On the mild end are subtle signs like head turning, eye blinking, gagging, or pulling away. On the severe end are children who run away, cry in pain, bite, pinch, or hit back. The present author witnessed one preschool child stand up and throw his little chair at an examiner who touched his lips. The important point is this: Children with tactile defensiveness respond protectively when they should be responding discriminatively. Tactile defensive behavior may appear in response to touch stimulation to the face and mouth more than any other place on the body: "The face has a large number of tactile receptors and is very important for survival... The tactilely defensive child is particularly defensive about his face, especially around his mouth" (Ayres, 1979, p. 110).

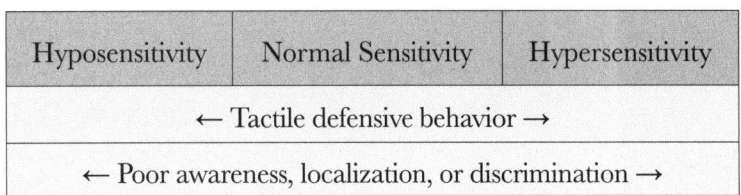

Hyposensitivity	Normal Sensitivity	Hypersensitivity
← Tactile defensive behavior →		
← Poor awareness, localization, or discrimination →		

Tactile problems can occur at any sensitivity level.

Children who prevent themselves from experiencing a wide variety of oral-tactile sensations miss out on a number of oral movement learning activities and this in turn limits their knowledge of their own mouth and its movement capabilities. The need to avoid oral-tactile sensations even may drive some clients to avoid articulations of lip and tongue.

Defensive reactions occur in clients with oral-tactile hypersensitivity but they can also occur in clients with hyposensitivity as well as those with otherwise normal sensitivity. Defensive reactions are behaviorally based, not neurologically based. Therefore, the reasons for the defensive behavior can vary widely:

- The client may be unfamiliar with the therapist and, therefore, not trusting of physical intimacy.

- The client may perceive touch experiences as socially inappropriate for the situation.

- The client may have had prior bad experiences with oral manipulation and now be afraid of them.

- The client may have had prior feeding or tooth brushing experiences that were unpleasant, and his negative reactions might simply be a carryover from these earlier events.

- The client may have had an oral injury, or he may have ongoing oral or dental pain that is causing him to withdraw.

- The client may gag easily as a general reaction to things concerning the mouth, face, neck, or hair.

- The client may be generally uncooperative in a multitude of ways and, therefore, may be unwilling to allow therapists to take the lead in any activities, including ones involving the oral-tactile system.

CLINICAL ASSESSMENT

There is an enormous difference between the types of oral-tactile sensitivity tests that can occur in the research lab and those that can be employed in the clinic. Clinicians must relay on practical tests that can be administered quickly and easily using a minimum amount of equipment and time for analysis. A clinician's test battery of oral-tactile sensitivity often includes an assessment of the gag reflex, an assessment of light touch stimulation to

oral structures, a case history specific to oral sensitivity, a feeding assessment, and consultation with motor specialists. Oral stereognosis is another simple test that has been used in the past and could still be used as discussed below.

Gag

Probably the most reliable measure of oral-tactile sensitivity is the gag reflex. As described in Chapter 17 on the speech reflexes, the gag is typically elicited when tactile stimulation is applied without warning to the posterior one-third of the oral cavity in children six months of age and older. This is stimulation to the so-called *ring of protection* in the back of the mouth, which causes a gag when unwanted stimulation occurs at the base of the tongue, on the anterior faucial pillars, or on the velum. The gag should also occur upon stimulation to any points posterior to the ring such as on the posterior pharyngeal wall. Clients who are hypersensitive tend to gag quickly when stimulation is given to points anterior to the ring. Clients who are hyposensitive tend to respond slowly or not at all to stimulation given at the ring and to points posterior to it.

Light Touch

A second practical method of assessing oral-tactile sensitivity in the clinic is to observe a client's reaction to light touch stimulation to points anterior to the ring of protection. Light touch is applied to the face, lips, gums, anterior palate, and anterior tongue. Light touch is used because it is the most irritating and because speech is a light-touch event. Test these structures by gently touching, patting, or stroking them with a textured probe.

Henkins and Banks (1967) used a graduated set of nylon filaments to test oral-tactile sensitivity. The nylon wires were poked against the area to be tested and were pushed into the skin until they just began to bend. They

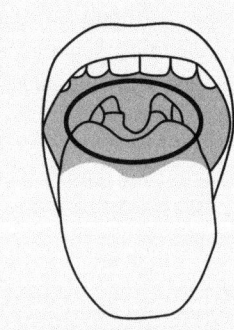

Normally the gag is elicited at the ring of protection and all points posterior to it.

tested the tongue tip and blade, and the hard palate at a site opposite the second molar. They found this to be a viable way to test oral-tactile sensitivity in the clinical setting: "We feel that these techniques can serve a useful function in the clinical evaluation of tactile perception in the oral area" (p. 186).

The Marshalla Oral Sensorimotor Test (MOST; Marshalla, 2007a) can be used to assign a score to oral-tactile sensitivity. The following describes "normal sensitivity" as defined by the present author who has observed oral-tactile responses in hundreds of children under clinical conditions. The following results should be seen in clients two years of age and older:

- *Lips:* The client with normal tactile sensitivity should tolerate and even enjoy light touch stimulation to his lips. The client may smile or laugh, or he may have very little response at all. Touching the lips seems to be no big deal to clients with normal oral-tactile sensitivity; to them it is simply an amusing event.

- *Gums:* Light touch stimulation to the gums sometimes is met with a wee bit of trepidation or thrill among clients with normal oral-tactile sensitivity, and the client's reaction may include smiling, laughing, or giggling. Some clients have no reaction at all however, and some clients look at the examiner with uncertainty because this is such an unusual occurrence; but the child with normal sensitivity will allow the stimulus. Begin by testing the upper gum. Place a textured probe at midline above the maxillary (upper) central incisors and stroke to one side all the way back to the molar region. Return to midline and stroke the upper gum to the other side. Then repeat with the lower gum, beginning at midline and stroking to one side and then the other. Clients with normal oral-tactile sensitivity often tighten the lips and hold the mouth rigidly as the stimulus reaches the posterior regions of the gums on top or bottom, but the strokes should not cause a gag.

- *Tongue:* Light touch to the tongue should be accepted and tolerated when it is applied to the anterior half. Start at the tip and stroke back down the midline. The stimulus should be accepted in the anterior half of the tongue and even should cause the tongue to bowl. The tongue retraction reflex should be elicited when the stimulus reaches about halfway back down the center of the tongue, and the gag reflex itself should be elicited on the posterior one-third of the tongue. Read more details about these reflexive responses in Chapter 17.

- *Hard palate:* Light touch stimulation to the hard palate is nearly intolerable to the client with normal sensitivity. The client should react quickly with facial grimace, shoulder elevation, or head withdrawing. The client often immediately presses and rubs his tongue up against the palate to neutralize the irritating sensations. Laughing, giggling, or calling out often accompany this stimulation.

Case History

The case history is also an excellent source of information regarding oral-tactile sensitivity. The examiner inquires about the client's responses to oral-tactile input past and present. The examiner gathers information about the client's ability to tolerate and accept divergent activities such as face-washing, tooth-brushing, tooth-flossing, dental exams, nose blowing, pulling clothing over the head and face, and kissing. Information about responses to hair washing, brushing, and cutting are also helpful. All young children have some difficulty accepting these routines. Clients with normal sensitivity and those who are hyposensitive have no significant reactions to these activities beyond those typical of average children. Clients with hyperreactive responses tend to respond in negative ways that are quick, strong, overt, excessive, dramatic, and persistent.

Feeding

A thorough examination of oral-tactile sensitivity should also include a survey of the client's feeding behaviors past and present. Information is gathered regarding a variety of subjects such as the client's ability to latch on and suck from a bottle or breast during infancy; the client's ability to adapt to a spoon; the client's food texture and taste preferences; the frequency of gagging, choking, or aspirating on foods; history of feeding assessments and therapy; and more. More detail about this assessment is beyond the scope of this manual. Morris and Klein (1987, 2000) is the best guide for this purpose.

Consultation with Motor Specialists

The examination of oral-tactile sensitivity is expanded with team consultation. The motor specialist is in a special position to assess client reaction to tactile stimulation to the rest of the body. Occupational and physical therapists with special training in sensorimotor skill are especially adept in their ability to gain this information and can provide an excellent summary of the client's overall tactile responsiveness as it may or may not relate to the mouth. Likewise, the SLPs information about tactile responses in and on the mouth helps the motor specialist make plans for treating the client's entire tactile system.

Oral Stereognosis

Oral stereognosis has been mentioned many times in the discussion above. "Stereognosis is the capacity to discern and discriminate objects by enclosing and touching them" (Hahn, 2003, p. 362). Oral stereognosis was used in the past as a means of assessing oral sensitivity. Oral stereognosis is the ability to perceive the size, shape, texture, temperature, weight, and hardness of an object placed in the mouth. A test of oral stereognosis typically involves placing an unseen object in the mouth and matching it to one of several other shapes placed within view. Imagine placing a spoon in a client's mouth while his eyes are closed. Then imagine placing an identical spoon, a Toothette®, and a Nuk® brush on the table for the client to select by matching the one he can see in front of him to the one he cannot see in his mouth.

Oral stereognosis is not a true test of tactile sensitivity but for a time it was considered so. This testing method was discontinued shortly after Williams and La Pointe (1971) found that oral stereognosis did not correlate well with two-point discrimination and light-touch detection on the tongues of normal adults.

It is important to recognize, however, that other studies named earlier in this chapter indicated that certain clients with deficient articulation performed more poorly on tests of oral stereognosis than did subjects with normal speech. The test, therefore, may still serve some purpose. The Locke study (1969) summarized on page 270 is particularly interesting in this regard. Recall that he studied English-speaking children and found that those who could imitate non-English phonemes well were significantly better on a test of oral stereognosis than children who could not. Oral stereognosis appears to be related to speech movement learning in some manner as yet to be determined. It cannot be considered a test of oral-tactile sensitivity, but perhaps it can help therapists identify clients who are less likely to outgrow their speech movement problems because of difficulty in higher level tactile processing; perhaps oral stereognosis can serve as a quick way to determine if a client is having difficulty feeling what is going on in his mouth.

INTRODUCTION TO THE METHODS

As discussed above, clinicians have been experimenting with methods to enhance oral-tactile learning in speech training since the 1940s. This section represents methods and procedures that have been in play since then. The reader is reminded that none of these ideas have been tested under formal conditions. This section, therefore, represents the state of the art despite a lack of validation from research.

Goals

The goal of this aspect of articulation and motor speech therapy is to *normalize* oral-tactile sensitivity. Therapists want the oral-tactile system of their clients to function within the parameters necessary for efficient speech movement learning. The aim of normalization is to provide the client with an oral-tactile system that is responsive enough to discriminate all aspects of phoneme place, manner, and voice. This aim plays out in different ways depending upon initial sensitivity level. Clients who are under-sensitive are helped to become more sensitive to oral-tactile

input, whereas clients who are over-sensitive are helped to become less so. Clients with mixed sensitivity are helped to bring all their tactile skills into the normal range. Clients who are inattentive to oral-tactile signals are taught to pay closer attention to them before and during speech production activities, and clients who cannot remember the oral touch experiences of phoneme production from one day to the next are engaged in activities to help them do so. Clients with oral-tactile defensiveness are helped to become less fearful and reactive to oral touch experiences so they are free to explore their mouths in ways that enhance oral movement learning.

Origin of Methods

Methods to normalize oral-tactile sensitivity have been developed by practicing clinicians who have provided hands-on training to clients of all ages and ability levels. Many therapists have contributed to this body of knowledge but not all can be mentioned here. This section will highlight some of the most important initial clinical insights that still have application to speech training.

Fay and Rood

Temple Fay (1948, 1954, 1955) and Margaret Rood (1954) were some of the first clinicians to write about the role of tactile stimulation in movement learning. Fay recognized that motor patterns could be elicited through reflex stimulation. Rood postulated that tactile stimulation could be used to develop and maintain integrated motor actions.

The Bobaths

Karl and Berta Bobath seem to be the first to report on methods to calm hypersensitivity (Bobath & Bobath, 1950; Bobath 1959, 1963, 1971, 1980). These British therapists were treating clients with cerebral palsy and had developed a method they called *neurodevelopmental treatment* (NDT). Neurodevelopmental treatment included hands-on techniques to inhibit abnormal reflex activity and to facilitate normal movement patterns. Their procedures included methods of tactile "desensitization" so

Any hands-on method to manipulate the oral structures works only if the client allows the touch experience.

that overly sensitive clients could tolerate these activities. The Bobaths began their desensitization procedures at points furthest away from the mouth and then the stimulation gradually moved toward the face and mouth. The methods of the Bobaths were introduced to the American audience in several sources especially *Speech Therapy and the Bobath Approach to Cerebral Palsy* (Crickmay, 1966). NDT persists as a standard of care for children with neuromuscular disorder.

Morris

Suzanne Evans Morris richly expanded the neurodevelopmental approach in the 1970s in continuing education coursework (e.g., Morris, 1977a) and in an early publication called *Program Guidelines for Children with Feeding Problems* (Morris, 1977b). This practical manual included ten specific suggestions for helping the hypersensitive client during feeding routines:

1. Begin at areas best tolerated by the child.

2. Use a spontaneous play and roughhouse format.

3. Gradually work toward the face.

4. Encourage the child to accept new sensations with his hands.

5. Encourage the child to play with mouth toys.

6. Begin to work the mouth after the child tolerates touch to the face.

7. Begin to work the mouth in a "sneaky" way by pretending to count the teeth with a finger while feeding him.

8. Press firmly on the tongue with a finger and walk it back.

9. Use jaw control to prevent thrusting.

10. Use food on the finger to provide additional oral stimulation inside the mouth.

Techniques for normalizing oral-tactile sensitivity disseminated rapidly among therapists practicing in North America as a result of seminars taught by Morris and others, and the ideas were greatly expanded upon in the publication of Morris' first main text called *Pre-Feeding Skills* (Morris & Klein, 1987). This groundbreaking volume described ways to treat several problems related to tactile perception: *hyperreaction, hyporeaction, sensory defensiveness,* and *sensory overload.* The manual became a standard source of information on feeding development, disorder, assessment, and treatment for children with cerebral palsy and other neuromuscular disorders as diverse professionals adopted it as a main text worldwide.

That book and its newest edition (Morris & Klein, 2000) continues to be used by speech-language pathologists, occupational and physical therapists, lactation consultants, feeding specialists, nurses, pediatricians, dental hygienists, family therapists, parents, and other professionals interested in feeding development, assessment, and therapy. Morris and Klein describe many methods for normalizing oral-tactile sensitivity as it affects feeding experiences, and many of these methods have been adapted to speech training:

- Work for better sitting posture.

- Reduce multisensory distractions.

- Use carefully graded pressure with the fingers.

- Regularize the tooth brushing routine.

- Use coated and other adapted spoons during feeding.

- Use music and rhythm to bring calm organization to the feeding experience.

- Explore ways to use touch for communication.

- Encourage hand-to-mouth and toy-to-mouth play.

- Use slow vestibular stimulation.

- Use top-down processing by warning the client of incoming stimulation.

- Press down on the front of the tongue.

- Employ jaw control procedures.

- Use guided imagery.

- Teach concentration and centering skills.

- Consult medical specialists regarding the influence of medications on sensory processing.

- Build postural tone (core strength).

- Increase the child's sensory awareness and discrimination.

Ayres

Anna Jean Ayres also contributed a great deal to the discussion of tactile sensitivity in her pioneering book *Sensory Integration and the Child* (Ayres, 1979). Ayres was an occupational therapist and developmental psychologist at the UCLA Brain Research Institute where she had developed a psychomotor test battery called the *Southern California Sensory Integration Tests* (Ayres, 1972):

> *"[Sensory integration] refers to the neural process by which input from one sensory modality is organized and integrated with input from another... The concept of sensory integration suggests that intersensory integration, particularly that which occurs at the brainstem level, lays the foundation for other neural functions such as perception... [Ayres] proposed that refined perception occurs at a cortical level, but is dependent upon filtering and integration of sensory inputs at lower brainstem levels"* (Spitzer et al., 1996, p. 124).

Ayres noted that many children with attention, movement, and learning problems have difficulty organizing sensations for functional use. She proposed that childhood apraxia was the result of problems in the nervous system's inability to integrate tactile, vestibular, and proprioceptive sensations. She said that the result was a problem of *motor planning.* Ayres postulated that children with apraxia do not perceive their movements well and, therefore, they have difficulty planning out each new movement in turn, and Ayres taught that tactile localization and discrimination were the most deficient areas in clients with apraxia. In other words, the reason the client with apraxia cannot plan movement is because he does not process tactile signals well; he has difficulty processing the tactile experience he has had, and, therefore, he has difficulty planning out each subsequent movement; he does not "feel" his movements well.

Ayres used brushing, rubbing, deep pressure, vibration, smell, and vestibular stimulation to influence tactile processing. Her central principle of therapy was "to provide and control sensory input… in such a way that the child spontaneously forms the adaptive responses that integrate those sensations" (Ayres, 1979, p. 140). Ayres noted that therapy is most effective when the child directs his own activities while the therapist unobtrusively directs the environment: "We are not trying to teach the child the activity he is doing… We want to help him become more capable of learning any motor skill" (Ayres, 1979, p. 140–141).

Sensory Overload

Ayres also wrote about the dangers of *sensory overload.* Sensory overload can occur when too much sensory stimulation causes unwanted responses such as increasing muscle tone in hypertonic children, hyper-excitement, lack of physical judgment, destructive behavior, withdrawal, seizure, flushing, blanching, unusual perspiration, nausea, yawning, profound and pervasive emotional changes, and euphoria.

A little bit of tactile stimulation supplied by an SLP in the midst of an articulation or motor speech therapy session is unlikely to cause such drastic responses. But too much oral-tactile stimulation that is applied along with other vestibular and proprioceptive stimulation can be. This might occur, for example, when speech and motor therapists work together with one child in one session, or when therapies follow one right after the other. Precaution to avoid this type of overstimulation cannot be understated.

Articulation

Methods to normalize oral-tactile sensitivity that had developed within the feeding, neurodevelopmental, and

Methods to Calm	Methods to Excite
Are used for hypersensitivity and tactile defensiveness	Are used for hyposensitivity and inattentiveness

Tactile stimulation is used to calm or excite tactile responses.

sensorimotor integration communities quickly spread to SLPs whose primary concern was speech (e.g., Marshalla, 2007e). Many therapists in the United States today use methods to normalize oral-tactile sensitivity in their work to facilitate appropriate jaw, lip, tongue, and velar movements in articulation and motor speech therapy.

Unfortunately, this is an area where formal speech research has not kept pace with the experimental findings of clinical practice, and none of these methods have undergone the scrutiny of speech research. Methods to normalize oral-tactile sensitivity have also been thrown into the basket called *non-speech oral-motor exercises* and critics of these methods do not seem to understand the difference between methods to enhance the oral-tactile system for phoneme learning and old-fashioned oral exercises like wagging the tongue or blowing bubbles.

This is not surprising, since all new ideas undergo this process. Practicing therapists first experiment clinically with new ideas for many decades and then researchers begin to develop controlled studies to test them. Although warnings to avoid all non-speech oral-motor exercises have been plentiful in recent years, many SLPs continue to use tactile stimulation in articulation and motor speech therapy because they persistently face a variety of clients who do not seem to be able to perceive their own speech movements. The research summarized above clearly demonstrates that there is a subgroup of clients who have difficulty with higher level tactile processing, and it is with those clients that these methods are employed.

Manipulating Touch Stimuli

Each therapist approaches problems in tactile perception in his or her own way but there are common procedures that have evolved based upon the history introduced above. Therapists generally add, eliminate, or enhance touch experiences in specific ways to help clients perceive place, manner, and voice features better than they would otherwise. Therapists do this by manipulating touch stimuli during the process of articulation training or by adding other methods to the therapy to substitute for the tactile experience. For example, a mirror might be used to enhance visual understanding of the oral structures when the client cannot feel them.

The manipulation of touch stimuli is accomplished in two basic ways. Methods are employed: (1) to calm hypersensitivity and defensiveness, and/or (2) to excite responsiveness in cases of hyposensitivity and inattentiveness. Better tactile awareness and discrimination is the expected result in both cases.

Certain methods tend to be used for certain effects but the specific method can vary. For example, maintained touch tends to be used for calming, and placing the hands on a client's cheeks might be calming at first, but then this stimulus may become irritating to him after a few moments. Such is the variable and ever-changing nature of the tactile system. Therapists determine how a method is affecting a client by watching his responses, and methods are modified to fit the immediate needs of the client. Therein lies the art of this therapy. "A given modality may be used for different effects depending on how, when, and where it is applied" (Farber, 1982, p. 123).

There are three other things to keep in mind when using tactile stimulation. First, the effect of a tactile stimulus can last longer than does its application: "There are times when the perception of the stimulus lasts beyond the application" (Farber, 1982, p. 123). Second, there are occasions when perception of the stimulus decreases even while the stimulus is being applied. Third, some stimuli will cause a client pain even when it does not seem that it should. A client's response to a stimulus is always its measure: "The child's response is considered the best indication of how his nervous system is interpreting the stimuli" (Ayres, 1972, p. 116).

METHODS TO NORMALIZE TOUCH RESPONSES

Specific touch variables are employed to influence tactile experiences before, during, and sometimes separate from articulation training. There are at least 12 variables of touch that can be manipulated: (1) predictability, (2) conceptualization, (3) duration, (4) surface area, (5) distance from the mouth, (6) depth, (7) recurrence, (8) vibration, (9) temperature, (10) texture, (11) movement, and (12) taste. Each variable is manipulated within a range either to calm or excite the tactile experience. See Table 9 below for a visual chart of the variables. The present author considers those that are exciting to be more powerful.

This section describes the methods specifically. The ideas have been gathered from a wide variety of textbooks

TABLE 9 — Touch Variables to Calm or Excite the Tactile System

	Touch Variable	*Calm*	← Range →		*Excite*	
1	Predictability	Predictable touch			Unpredictable touch	
2	Conceptualization	No concept of the touch experience			A rich concept of the touch experience	
3	Duration	Maintained touch			Brief touch	
4	Surface Area	Broad surfaces of touch			Small surfaces of touch	
5	Distance	Away from the mouth			Near, on, and in the mouth	
6	Depth	Deep touch			Light touch	
7	Recurrence	Tapping			Patting	
8	Vibration	Slow			Fast	
9	Temperature	Hot	Warm	Temperate	Cool	Cold
10	Texture	Smooth	Bumpy/Mixed			Rough
11	Movement	Brushing or stroking with the hair pattern		Brushing or stroking against the hair pattern		
12	Taste	Sweet	Salty	Savory	Bitter	Sour

Tactile stimulation can be altered in at least twelve different ways.

and treatment manuals on motor speech therapy, articulation therapy, neurodevelopmental treatment, sensorimotor integration therapy, neurology, kinesiology, massage, and other sources on the body and body therapies. Each method is defined and described and applications to speech training are made. Therapists are cautioned to follow sanitary procedures at all times. All these methods lack formal validation and the reader should view them as material that is being passed down from one generation of therapists to another.

Predictability

Predictability seems to be a main factor in tactile acceptance. Clients tend to be more accepting of tactile stimuli they can see and control. "The brain interprets touch sensations initiated by the person himself differently from sensations from someone else's touch" (Ayres, 1979, p. 111). For example a client may not like a Toothette® placed in his mouth by a therapist, but he may have no problem putting one into his own mouth. This is rather like the difference in comfort between brushing one's own teeth and having one's teeth brushed by someone else.

For this reason, it can be best at times to hand a stimulus to the client to perform an action on his own mouth while the therapist demonstrates with her own tool in her own mouth. If the therapist must control the stimulus, let the client hold her hand as she does so in order to let him feel as if he is controlling it. A short discussion about the tool and a few moments for the client to explore the tool itself will also help prepare him and make the activity more predictable.

Conceptualization

One of the most practical ways to enhance touch experiences is to help clients develop a concept of it, and perhaps the easiest way to do this is to develop a consistent cue system. This method seems to be particularly helpful when working with clients who have apraxia. The client is helped to organize his oral-tactile experiences through the top-down processing that cues bring to the process.

Remember, Ayres postulated that the client with apraxia has difficulty organizing tactile sensations for functional use. This means that the client can feel the sensations but he cannot organize them in his mind. One may instruct a client to "Lift your tongue up high in the back" but the client may have absolutely no idea what the SLP is talking about. He lacks the data he needs to plan out the action because of his prior lack of tactile processing.

Think about what happens to one is assigned a task that they cannot organize. Perhaps organizing information to prepare taxes seems incomprehensible to them, or perhaps their mind goes into a tailspin when they have to organize a holiday meal. *What is needed to plan this activity? What should I do first? Second? How will this activity play out? How will I get all this done? What if I fail?* The mind reels just thinking about planning the activity and sometimes one simply avoid thinking about it or doing it.

Remember: It is not that the client cannot feel with the back of his tongue — his nerves are intact and the signals are being sent to his cortex — his problem is that he is not developing a conceptual category one might call "tactile information about the back of the tongue and its movement capabilities." Activities are designed to help him conceptualize and organize the things he can feel so that he can use the sensation of the target movement again at other times. Any consistent cue system can aid in the conceptualization of speech movement. In fact, the more books on apraxia one reads, the more one finds that using cues is a consistent theme. In the example of learning to elevate the back of the tongue for production of a back phoneme, the client might be introduced to a series of activities designed to help him take hold of the concept of the movement as he is learning the phonemes. He might be helped to:

- Look at his mouth in a mirror to discover the front and back of his tongue.

- Draw a picture of a tongue and label the front and back.

- Brush his tongue in the front and back.

- Produce lingua-alveolar raspberries with the front of his tongue and lingua-velar raspberries with the back.

- Eat a cracker and follow the bolus as it travels from the front to the back of his tongue.

- Learn the verbal phrases "Back of the tongue" and "Front of the tongue."

- Learn the verbal phrases "Lift up the back" and "Lift up the front."

- Learn the phrases "Tongue-back sound" and "Tongue-tip sound."

- Learn gestural cues for the front and back of his tongue.

Duration: Maintained & Brief

To *maintain touch* means to touch and hold for a few seconds whereas *brief touch* is the process of touching and immediately releasing. Maintained touch tends to be calming while brief touch tends to be exciting, although the opposite can occur as well. Brief touch has also been called *touch-release*.

Brief touch causes attention to be drawn to the location of the stimulus; therefore, it is an excellent tool for teaching place of articulation. It stimulates the tactile receptors in the skin that respond to the initial onset of touch and thus it can be used to introduce new sensations. Brief touch is lightly applied to the skin and it does not reach into the deeper tissues of muscle and bone. It can be used on any part of the face, lips, tongue, gums, or palate.

Brief touch is one of the most common ways therapists have taught place of articulation, and it still appears in some of the newest guides. For example when teaching

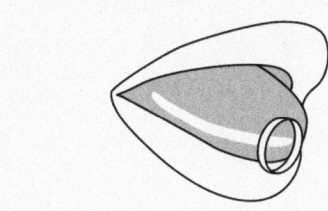

Hanson (1983) placed a small elastic band on the tongue tip (or sometimes on the tongue-blade) and had his clients hold them up against the alveolar ridge to add touch maintenance to his tongue-tip activities.

/p/: "Use a cotton swab to lightly touch the surfaces of the lips where contact is made to explode the air. Instruct the client to bring the lips together to touch that spot" (Secord et al., 2007, p. 16).

Brief touch is called *brief moving touch* when the touch is more like a quick stroke. Some SLPs used the term *plucking* for this method. Plucking was used to reduce tension and to direct the flow of voice and resonance. For example, when teaching /m/: "Trilling or plucking the lips while /m/ is being attempted will assist in directing some of the resonance to the mouth cavity and in relieving tension of the lips" (Nemoy & Davis, 1937, p. 58).

Maintained touch, on the other hand, tends to be used for calming rapid, unorganized, and hyperreactive touch responses. It is used to draw attention in a safe way to an area. Maintained touch stimulates those tactile receptors that have a long latency period and that continue to fire as touch is maintained. This calming response should override the rapid-fire initial excitatory responses that other nerves provide: "Maintained touch is an inhibitory technique useful in reducing body part disregard and in normalizing touch thresholds" (Farber, 1982, p. 126).

Articulation events are very fast and a client who cannot produce phonemes consistently by place or manner may be having difficulty because of the brief contact during speech articulations. Maintained touch can be used to enhance these experiences. Therapists sometimes do this simply by asking the client to hold an oral position longer. This method has a long-standing presence in articulation therapy. For example, when teaching /m/: "Teach the child to keep the lips closed for one or two seconds" (Hanson, 1983, p. 201). A period of bilabial contact of 1–2 seconds is longer than necessary for the natural articulation gesture of /m/ in a syllable or word, and, therefore, it is used to enhance the tactile learning experience that occurs when practicing the target phoneme.

Maintained touch for increased perception of oral placement can also be accomplished with a tool. For example, Hanson used tiny orthodontic elastics to maintain tongue-tip position during the training of /l/: "Place a tiny orthodontic elastic on the tip of the tongue. Have the client sustain an /l/, pressing the elastic moderately firmly

against the alveolar ridge" (Hanson, 1983, p. 214).

Maintained touch is used early in treatment when hands-on procedures are employed to reduce hypersensitivity and defensiveness. It is an excellent calming stimulus. Maintained touch usually helps a client settle so that he then can allow more varied touch experiences in, on, and around the mouth.

It is important to remember that touch responses change depending upon circumstances. While maintained touch is generally thought of as calming, it can be irritating to some clients. When maintained touch is irritating to a particular client, the therapist should switch to brief touch and then gradually extend the duration of the brief touch until the client can tolerate maintained touch.

Surface Area: Broad & Small

Broad surfaces of touch are generally used to introduce tactile techniques and to reduce sensitivity, whereas small surfaces of touch are used to excite awareness and to develop discrimination and localization. Broad surfaces of touch tend to be soothing while small surfaces tend to be exciting, exacting, and location specific. For example, an open hand placed on one's shoulder is soothing whereas a single finger placed on the shoulder feels like a poke. The broad surface feels safer and more comfortable while the smaller surface can feel irritating, uncertain, off-putting, and even scary.

Stimulating a small surface of skin is a perfect method for helping a client identify points of articulatory contact on the lips, tongue, and palate, and using a small surface of tactile stimulation has wide representation in the articulation therapy literature. In fact, most methods designed to help clients identify phoneme place include a small surface of stimulation. For example, the following method to teach tongue-tip placement for /t/ has been around since the turn of the last century and still appears in manuals: "Touch the alveolar ridge with the end of a tongue depressor… Ask the client to place the tip of his tongue there to begin the sound" (Secord et al., 2007, p. 23). Van Riper (1947) employed tongue depressors and wooden matches when using this method, and he may have gotten

Maintained touch provided over a broad surface is a common method for calming hypersensitivity and defensiveness.

the idea from Scripture (1912) who used a "probe" or a "stick" for the stimulus.

Small surfaces of touch can be used right away with clients who demonstrate normal sensitivity in the oral area. However, stimulating a small area can be too irritating for some clients, and then a broad surface is used instead. A client who is very sensitive, who gags easily, and who avoids all articulatory contacts usually needs to be introduced to tactile stimulation with a broad surface of touch first. This can be provided in a variety of ways, for example, a therapist might place the broad surface of her palm on a client's entire lower face several times before touching his lips specifically. The broad surface of stimuli should calm his defensive response before he is expected to process stimulation to the lips discriminatively.

Distance From the Mouth: Near & Far

As mentioned above, the Bobaths developed a method of working with severe oral-tactile hypersensitivity by starting at points distant from the mouth and working toward it. In the most severe cases, therapists should apply a broad surface of deep pressure beginning with the hands and feet and then move the stimulus up the limbs to the trunk, and then to the triangle formed by the head and shoulders. The pattern is repeated on the head, with stimulation beginning on the crown or back of the head itself, and by moving to the ears, face, and mouth, and then by moving inside the mouth. The process is repeated again inside the mouth, where therapists work from the front to the back of the gums, tongue, and palate.

"We need to introduce touch to the front half of the palate, gradually moving back along the sides where the palate borders with the upper teeth. In the extremely sensitive

mouth… the clinician will find it helpful to return to working on the cheeks and activating the tongue so that the individual will alter his or her own sensitivity level with spontaneous movement. We can gradually reach a tolerance for sustained touch on the forward half of the palate" (Nelson & De Benabib, 1991, p. 156–157).

Many therapists since the Bobaths have noted that this treatment sequence does not always have to begin with the hands and feet, and some now begin the sequence right at the head and mouth itself. Also, remember that some clients have mixed tactile sensitivity, and that some of these clients are less sensitive inside the mouth than they are outside the mouth. Stimulation can begin right inside the mouth for these clients.

Depth: Deep & Light

Deep touch (pressure) is used to stimulate the muscles underneath the skin whereas *light touch* is intended to stimulate only the skin itself. Deep pressure on a muscle belly tends to relax the muscle. It can be used to cease uncontrolled motor activity such as writhing or fasciculation. Light touch, on the other hand, is generally arousing, and it often is considered the most irritating of all touch stimuli. Light touch is used to stimulate the advanced perceptions of discrimination and localization. Light touch is used right way with clients who can handle it and deep touch is used with clients who can't.

Hypersensitivity is often associated with muscle stiffness and it can often be reduced through the relaxation of the stiff muscles. Deep pressure in the form of massage can be applied: "If the child demonstrates atypical oral motor patterns, such as a hyper-responsive gag reflex or tonic bite reaction, massage can be used to bring about an improved response" (Bahr, 2001, p. 115). Massage the face, head, neck, and shoulders. Deep pressure can also be applied inside the oral mechanism in the form of firm biting and chewing. Some children are given terry wristbands or chewy tools they can gnaw and chew on during the course of the day to provide the deep touch experiences required for their tactile normalization process.

Light touch to the skin of the face, lips, tongue, and palates is used to build oral awareness and localization once sensitivity is normalized. Therapists can give light touch stimulation with a variety of objects such as tongue depressors, Toothettes®, oral swabs, Nuk® massage brushes, toothbrushes, and washcloths. Light touch stimulation has wide

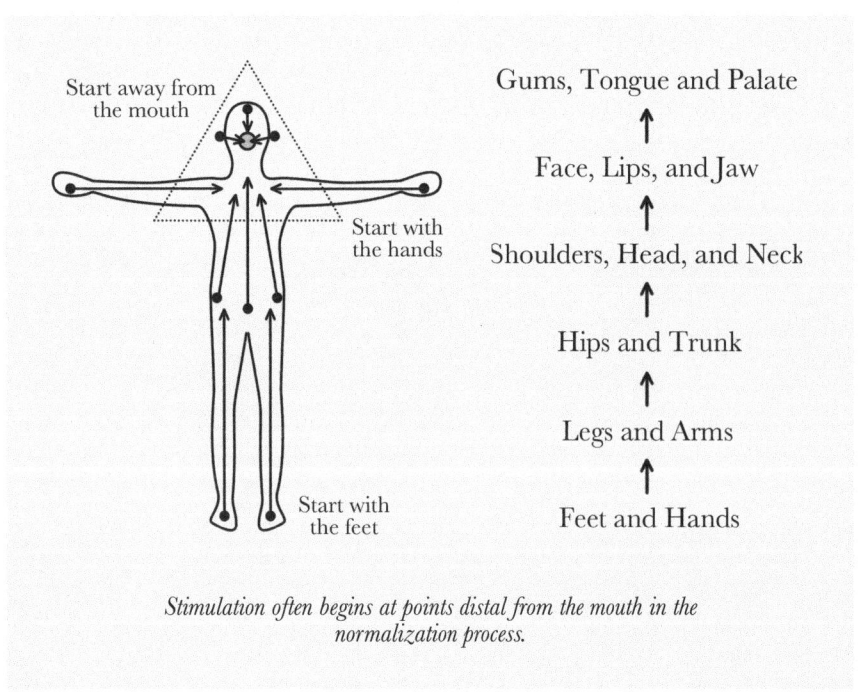

Gums, Tongue and Palate
↑
Face, Lips, and Jaw
↑
Shoulders, Head, and Neck
↑
Hips and Trunk
↑
Legs and Arms
↑
Feet and Hands

Start away from the mouth

Start with the hands

Start with the feet

Stimulation often begins at points distal from the mouth in the normalization process.

representation in the articulation literature. For example, to teach lower lip placement for /f/: "Put a piece of masking tape tightly over the lower lip to increase awareness of position of lower lip" (Berry & Eisenson, 1956, p. 156). A better alternative would be kinesiology tape for safety but in either case the tape functions as a light touch stimulus to the lower lip to teach it to move with consistency.

Recurrence: Patting & Tapping

Patting and tapping are the same basic movement done to different depths and for different purposes. Patting is a classic motor therapy technique that consists of presenting brief touch in a repeating sequence gently on the skin. Patting makes brief light touch more noticeable.

For example, if the lips are touched once but the client doesn't notice and the lips don't move, a therapist might pat 3–5 times to increase the power of the stimulus slightly. Patting has been a fairly standard tool in articulation therapy. Patting on the outside of the face and on the lips can be done with large objects such as washcloths, towels, blankets, or stuffed animals. Patting on the inside of the mouth is done with a small probe such as a finger or a Toothette®.

Tapping, the second method, is like patting but much firmer. Therapists tap firmly on the skin using three fingertips like a hammerhead in order to place deep but safe percussion on the underlying bones. Percussion on a bone sends a jolt to the joints associated with the bone and this enhances perception within the joint itself. This type of percussion on a joint adjusts tone in the muscles around it and it increases awareness of body part movement as the joint bends, straightens, or rotates.

As noted above, research has revealed that jaw position is perceived in the temporomandibular joint; therefore, tapping on the jaw can stimulate these receptors. Therapists tap on the jaw to increase the child's "internal awareness of the jaw" (Morris & Klein, 2000, p. 359). Tap firmly but gently so as not to cause any damage to the

TMJ and do not use this method if damage to or pain in the TMJ already exists or if the client complains of pain in the process. Tap the jaw a few times in all directions to affect all the receptors within the TMJ and follow the stimulus with activities to position or move the jaw.

- Tap toward the rear on the front of the chin (on the mental protuberance)

- Tap toward the front on the back of the jaw (on the back of the angles)

- Tap upward against the underside of the chin (under the mental protuberance)

- Tap downward on the front of the chin (on the top of the mental protuberance)

- Tap toward midline from one side and then the other (at the mental foramen on each side)

Vibration: Fast & Slow

Vibration is a stimulus that motor therapists use to influence both the tactile and proprioceptive mechanisms. Vibration can be relaxing or exciting "depending upon the existing state of the organism" (Ayres, 1979, p. 125). Vibration on loose muscles can tighten them yet vibration on tight muscles can loosen them. Slow vibration from a battery operated vibrator or vibrating toy can be used to normalize sensitivity of the skin and Farber (1982) recommended a frequency of 60–90 Hz for this purpose. Vibration will be loved or hated depending upon the client's tactile system:

> *"A tactile hypersensitive child may be extremely uncomfortable if she feels the vibration of cars and trucks rumbling nearby. On the other hand, a hyposensitive child might think sitting on top of the washing machine is the best feeling in the world"* (Biel & Peske, 2005, p. 30).

Speech-language pathologists often keep a battery-operated vibrator or vibrating toy in the therapy room to pull out occasionally for the purpose of arousing or calming the oral mechanism. The procedure is usually added to therapy when a client has very limited oral awareness. Morris and Klein (2000) recommend vibrating toys and toothbrushes to increase interest in the mouthing of toys and other objects: "Many times children show an interest in vibration when they have no interest in other mouthing experiences" (p. 412).

It should be noted that vibration is perhaps the most powerful of all tactile stimuli, and, therefore, some therapists have cautioned not to use it on the face or in the mouth: "It is a very potent stimulus and should be used cautiously" (Fisher, Murray, & Bundy, 1991, p. 271). Do not use vibrating objects in ways that can cause disorientation, spasticity, nausea, or seizures. Do not force a client to use vibration if he shows obvious rejection or fear. Vibration is not used every day; it is a method that is relied upon on occasion.

Speech-language pathologists of the past had a very

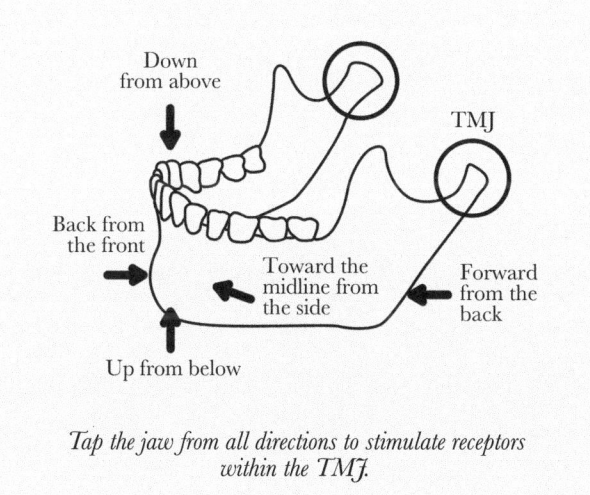

Tap the jaw from all directions to stimulate receptors within the TMJ.

safe way to introduce vibration into articulation therapy that many therapists still may opt: they had clients produce raspberries. Nemoy and Davis used bilabial raspberries ("trilling of the lips") when teaching labial phonemes, lingua-labial raspberries ("trilling of the tongue") when teaching the lingua-alveolars, and velar raspberries ("hacking up a fish bone") when teach phonemes that are [+Back]. A raspberry that a client can produce himself is a very safe alternative to a battery-operated vibrator and the stimulus is more location-specific than it is when vibrating the whole mouth with a large vibrator. The Z-Vibe® is another safe option for a small area of vibration.

Temperature: Hot, Warm, Temperate, Cool & Cold

It is understood that warm temperatures are soothing and cold temperatures are stimulating. In terms of a program to normalize oral-tactile sensitivity, warm temperatures are generally used to calm and slow down tactile responses while cold temperatures are used to alert and excite them. Warm temperatures (95–98.6 °F) are used to help normalize oral-tactile sensitivity when it is too sensitive and/or the client is defensive, and cool temperatures are used to develop the advanced skills of discrimination and localization. The reader is reminded again that opposite reactions can and do occur.

Temperature variations will influence the entire oral mechanism all at once so they are used in a gross way to stimulate overall coolness or warmth. One heats or cools the entire mouth to have an overall effect. For example, one generally does not cool only the tongue tip to stimulate tongue-tip sounds; one stimulates the entire mouth with cool or warm in order to more generally calm or alert the whole area.

The response to heating or cooling is due to the change: "Abrupt temperature changes strongly stimulate the thermoreceptors at initial contact" (Farber, 1982, p. 148). Therefore, a heating or cooling stimulus does not have to remain on the body part long and the body part itself does not have to get entirely warm or cool; the body part simply needs to be introduced to a temperature change. The change is what alerts the tactile system to notice the stimulus.

A client with severe whole-body hypersensitivity and defensiveness might be wrapped in a warm blanket during occupation or physical therapy activities to relax muscles and calm defensive responses (Farber, 1982). Likewise the head and face can be wrapped in a towel, blanket, or scarf before or during speech movement activities. A therapist will be sure to warm his or her hands when introducing tactile stimulation. A therapist might also offer the client a few sips of warm milk or tea to warm the mouth during speech activities.

A client with normal oral-tactile sensitivity who is ready to work on oral-tactile localization and discrimination activities might be introduced to cold stimuli to make oral-tactile activities more stimulating. Cold foods like ice chips, icy cold applesauce, ice pops, ice cream, or milkshakes might be employed. The present author likes to fill two-ounce paper cups halfway with water and place them in a freezer. To use, peel back the top half of the paper cup before handing it to the client for oral cooling: "Suck them, blow on them, blow raspberries on them, vocalize on them, lick them, pocket them in the mouth" (Marshalla, 1992a, p. 56).

Icy cold stimuli can be given for brief periods of time (for example, 5–10 seconds at a time) as a reward for doing speech work at hand. The mouth will get cold in one quadrant or another at first, but soon the entire mouth will be very cold. Icy cold stimuli should be discontinued before that final stage is reached or immediately afterward if it could not be avoided. The stimulus has been used too long if the pattern commonly know as "brain freeze" occurs. Do not use cold if it causes seizures, lack of movement, low affect, complaints of pain, bluing, or any other

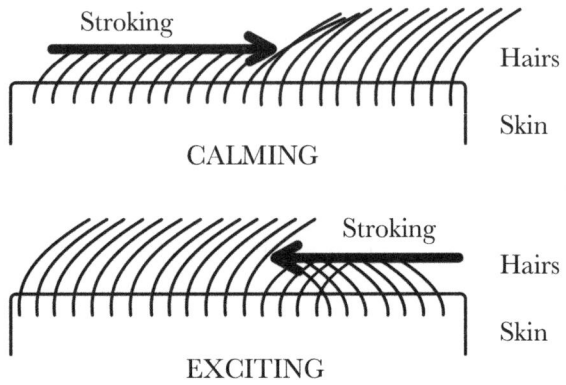

Stroking or brushing with the grain of hair is calming while against the grain is exciting.

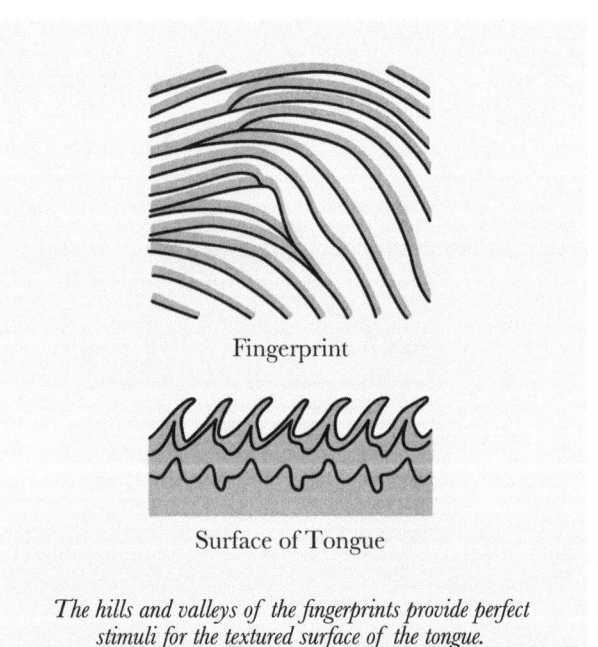

The hills and valleys of the fingerprints provide perfect stimuli for the textured surface of the tongue.

warning signs of neurological distress.

Texture: Smooth, Bumpy/Mixed & Rough

Texture variations can be used to enhance tactile input during phoneme movement training. Smooth textures are generally less readily perceptible than bumpy or rough textures, and objects with more texture provide a better stimulus for eliciting oral movement than do smooth ones. For example, stroking the tongue with a tongue depressor might not be powerful enough to elicit a tongue bowl response but stroking with a Nuk® massager might be. Therapists select tools with various textures to determine which are the best for eliciting the desired movement for the client at hand. This is part of the trial-and-error process so often recommended by preceding authors.

Considerations about texture variations plays a very important role when a client is hypersensitive because certain textures will not be tolerated in and on the mouth. Oral-tactile stimulation is arranged to help normalize the client's protective responses before he is introduced to more exciting stimuli designed to teach localization and discrimination skills. Clients with issues of severe aversion to texture variations within the mouth usually have very selective food preferences, and thus the area is addressed within the client's feeding program as well.

Movement: Brushing, Stroking & Wiping

Brushing, stroking, and wiping are calming or exciting depending upon the direction of movement. Movement in the same direction as hair growth on the hairy skin generally is calming while movement against the direction of hair growth generally is exciting. The filiform papillae on the tongue lean toward the oropharynx, therefore, stroking the tongue from anterior-to-posterior is calming whereas stroking posterior-to-anterior is exciting. The fingertips are particularly suited to stimulate the surface of the tongue. Like cogs on a wheel, the rugae of the fingerprint are a near perfect match to move the tongue's filiform papillae for tactile stimulation.

Stroking parts of the oral mechanism to teach place of articulation is a method that was used by the profession's founders including Van Riper. For example, when teaching /l/: "With a [wooden] match or a tongue depressor stroke the back of the upper gum ridge until child touches it with tongue. Ask him to stroke the spot with his tongue. Ask him to stroke it as he says *ee*" (Van Riper, 1947, p. 191).

Taste

Taste is a completely different stimulus than touch but it is included here because of its association with the tongue. Taste is an important element in feeding therapy and in the development of oral perception, but it serves only a very small role in phoneme training. Taste mainly is used to increase general interest in a speech movement activity.

Many therapists provide little snacks in articulation and

motor speech therapy in order to arouse a client's interest and to draw attention to the mouth. Mid-20th century therapists used food to teach basic tongue movements, for example, Berry and Eisenson (1956) used chocolate frosting on the lips to encourage tongue protrusion and they used vinegar on the lips to encourage tongue retraction in clients with very limited tongue movement.

The Problem with Taste

It is important to recognize that taste itself is not necessarily a good stimulus for teaching phonemes, and that adding taste to an activity even can cause more confusion about place of articulation. For example, consider the following common phonetic placement method for teaching tongue-back elevation for /k/:

> *"Rub a moist cotton swab on a flavored food, such as a Life Saver®... Then touch the soft palate near the second molars with the swab and ask the client to raise the back of the tongue to the roof of the mouth to form a seal"* (Secord et al., 2007, p. 31).

This type of activity appears time and again throughout the articulation literature but there are at least six errors of judgment related to taste and touch being made with this method:

1. The flavor is being applied to the palate, however, the palate cannot perceive flavor. Therefore, a flavor placed on the palate does not necessarily act as a stimulus for tongue movement.

2. A sweet flavor can be perceived throughout the mouth but it is primarily perceived with the front of the tongue. Therefore, once a sweet flavor is placed on the rear of the palate as prescribed, saliva causes the flavor to move to other parts of the tongue for tasting. The sweet will be perceived when it reaches the front of the tongue, and then

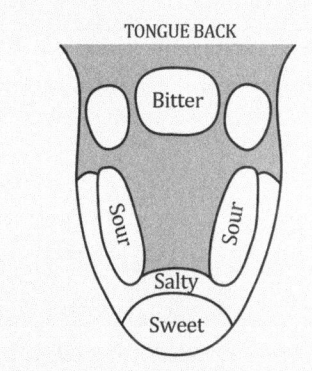

Although taste is perceived throughout, the specified areas of the tongue are the most intensive areas of recognition; the tip and sides are the most sensitive. These rarely correspond to tongue elevations for phoneme production.

the sensation will have nothing to do with tongue-back elevation to the palate.

3. Mint is perceived most prominently as odor. Placing the mint stimulus on the back of the palate causes the scent to travel immediately into the nasal cavities where the odor will become the over-riding sensation. This will cause the client to pull his attention away from his mouth or tongue and onto the inner surfaces of his nose instead.

4. If the client is hyposensitive, this flavorful stimulus may not be powerful enough to be noticed, especially because it has been put on the palate where flavor cannot be perceived in the first place.

5. If the client is hypersensitive he may not allow this stimulus at all.

6. If the client has normal oral-tactile sensitivity, this stimulation to the back of the palate should set off the gag reflex and then nothing will have been accomplished.

This simple example reveals how very important it is that SLPs understand the different roles that touch and taste play in the mouth. Lack of knowledge in this area can lead to methods that work counter to their original intent. If the method described above actually does work to elicit tongue-back elevation, the flavor will have nothing to do it. The movement will be elicited by the stroke (the tactile stimulus) and not the flavor (the taste stimulus). Flavors should be used only to stimulate general attention to the oral mechanism, to increase general arousal, and to encourage gross oral movement. A flavor can also add interest to any activity a client might find boring.

SUPPRESSING THE GAG

Many techniques discussed in this manual, and especially in this chapter, require direct stimulation of the oral mechanism and some clients cannot tolerate them because the gag is immediately triggered. Gagging is normal and the ability to *suppress* it is as well. Many clients can suppress

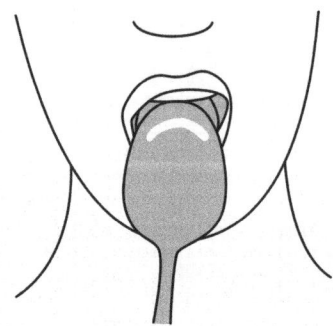

A cold spoon can be used to teach suppression of the gag.

their gag quickly and easily by simply being told, "Don't choke" or "Try not to choke when we do this."

Clients who cannot suppress the gag need a program to help them learn it so they can tolerate oral-tactile stimulation for more advanced localization and discrimination work. One should not work to *eliminate* or *desensitize* a gag because it is a protective device used to aid breathing throughout life, but a client can learn to suppress his gag during therapy activities so that tactile stimulation can be used in phoneme training. This is rather like learning to suppress one's gag during visits to the dentist.

Learning to tolerate tactile stimulation on the tongue by suppressing the gag is a regular routine in feeding therapy. The classic method is to start by placing a stimulus — usually a finger or a spoon — flat on the tongue in the front and then walking it back along the midline of the tongue in small increments. When the client begins to react, the stimulus retreats again to more anterior parts of the tongue. The movement continues a few steps forward and a few steps back until the client can tolerate the finger or spoon on the entire front half of the tongue without gagging. The spoon should be held in the normal feeding position.

The present author has developed a similar process for articulation therapy using a metal spoon chilled in ice water. Begin at the lips and then move to the tongue. On the tongue, start with the tip and move the spoon back along the midline. Work a few steps forward and a few steps back until the client can tolerate the spoon on the entire front half of the tongue without gagging. Teach the client how to suppress his gag by telling him what is being done. The present author usually makes this a little playful by saying, "You might choke… I hope you don't… You can hold it back if you try… Oh no! You choked!... Let's try it again…."

CASE SAMPLES

This chapter concludes with two case samples to demonstrate the way speech therapy might change when the tactile stimulation is included.

Case 1: Hyposensitivity

Returning to the seventeen-year-old female client from the study by MacNeilage, Rootes, and Chase (1967) from earlier in this chapter (page 269), following is discussed how her therapy might be adjusted according to the information presented in this chapter.

One always begins with assessment: The therapist first recognizes that the client's severe speech movement disorder may be related to problems in the higher-order skills of oral-tactile awareness, attention, localization, discrimination, or memory. The therapist then assesses the problem using the methods described above. She determines whether the client is hypersensitive, hyposensitive, of mixed sensitivity, and/or defensive in the oral area.

The next step is to make changes to the speech treatment protocol. The data presented in the study suggests this client was hyposensitive. Therapy might be adjusted in the following ways.

1. A mirror might become a regular part of all training activities in order to enhance her visual understanding of her own speech movements.

2. Sucking on an ice cube might be used in fifteen-second intervals as a reward or break from speech activities to alert and engage the oral-tactile system.

3. Textural stroking might be used to teach place of articulation for each phoneme taught.

4. The client might be taught to use her own fingers and other objects to touch the speech organs at places of articulation. For example, she might rub her lips with her fingers and then put lip gloss on when practicing bilabial phonemes.

5. Tapping on the jaw might be used along with a bite block to teach appropriate jaw positioning during phoneme production.

6. The client might switch to an electric toothbrush at home. She might be taught to use it to vibrate the tongue, the gums, the inner cheek walls, and the palate once per day while tooth brushing.

7. Improved chewing and swallowing might be taught within a full feeding therapy program. Food preferences would be explored and expanded with texture variations to enhance tactile learning.

8. A cue system might be designed to help her remember each phoneme or speech movement learned.

Case 2: Hypersensitivity

The second case is a client with severe tactile hypersensitivity and normal intelligence from the author's personal experience. This was a five-year-old boy who spoke only vowels in whole sentences. He had been in phonological therapy for one year with almost no change and no consonants emerging. The client barely moved his jaw, lips, and tongue to produce any phonemes and although he could eat by himself, he gagged when a utensil held by someone else approached his mouth. He had very restricted food preferences and took only minute bites of food that he could immediately liquefy with saliva. He clearly did not want to engage in hands-on speech movement training activities because they caused him to gag.

It was determined that the client was severely hypersensitive and had tactile defensive behavior. Phonological awareness activities were enhanced with methods to normalize tactile sensitivity.

1. The therapist began by sitting behind the client so his back could rest against her chest and so she could wrap her arms around him. This proved to be a safe touch position for him.

2. The therapist began hands-on stimulation with his hands, holding them firmly and squeezing them. From the hands she squeezed his forearms, then his upper arms, and then his shoulders. She squeezed firmly but gently and created a little song to explain and go along with this.

3. The client squirmed quite a bit at the shoulders, so the therapist used maintained deep pressure there until he breathed deeply and relaxed. She returned her stimulus to the hands and worked up to the shoulders several times until the client could tolerate it easily and even began to enjoy the work.

4. The firm and broad stimulus then was given to the top of the head. He tolerated touch-release much better than maintained touch so touch-release was used.

5. From the head, the therapist moved to the broad cheek area, and, from there, she place her hand broadly across his mouth. Instructions were given, "Don't choke."

6. As the client tolerated this entire procedure, from hands-to-mouth over the course of about 4 weeks, the therapist began to introduce inter-oral tactile stimulation. She used the broad surface of her finger to maintain touch on the upper gum at midline. As he tolerated this, she moved the pressure to the bottom gum at midline. From there she applied the broad firm stimulus to the gums one pressure point at a time moving gradually back toward the molar area. As he went into protection and his mouth got too tight she retreated to points more distal and started again.

7. Within 6 weeks this client could tolerate the therapist placing her hand on his jaw in a basic jaw control position, and there she began to use assistance and resistance to get the jaw to move upwards and downwards.

8. With up-and-down movement of the jaw emerged CVCV words with gross productions of /b/, /w/, and /m/. Words included /baba/ for *bye-bye*, /wawa/ for *water*, /mama/ for *mommy*, and so forth.

9. From there, chewy foods were introduced to begin the food expansion program, to further develop the jaw elevation and depression movement scheme, and to further normalize the oral-tactile response.

10. From there began a transition to more trust and more oral exploration with foods, toys, and hands-on procedures.

Procedures to normalize oral-tactile sensitivity were only one part of this client's overall phonological program that included other auditory, visual, and cognitive stimulation of phonemes and phonological processes. For example, the client worked on words like *moo*, *who* and *boo* with auditory bombardment, slight amplification, hand cues, orthographic spellings, and a storybook about a cow.

This client was seen once weekly throughout two school year schedules. In that time he gained a dozen stops, nasals, and glides, and gross fricatives. He was still very unintelligible, but consonants were emerging and he was on his way.

SUMMARY

Research and clinical experiences have indicated that higher-order tactile processing may be at the center of severe speech impairment in some clients, especially those with neurological impairment and motor speech disorders. Methods to normalize oral sensitivity have been developed and continue to be used by SLPs across North America despite lack of formal validation.

17

The Speech Reflexes

Stimulating automatic speech movements

> *"Reflexes are the first form of human movement and provide interesting insights into the process of development."*
>
> – David Gallahue & John Ozmun, 1995

Reflexes are considered the first movements in the process of human movement development. Speech is movement; therefore, reflexes can be considered the first in the line of speech movement development. It has been proposed that reflexes form the basis of all voluntary movements (e.g., Rood, 1954; Bower, 1974; Zelazo, 1976). If true, this means that all human movements may have a reflex as their beginning point. It also suggests that an absent movement pattern may be facilitated by stimulating the foundational reflex. These two ideas — that reflexes are foundational to all movement development and that reflexes can be stimulated to create new movement — have been bathed in controversy for decades. Despite the controversy, reflex stimulation has been and will continue to be used as a therapeutic tool by motor specialists and speech-language pathologists alike because it is a useful working theory in the therapy environment.

BACKGROUND

Current thinking about the relationship between reflex behavior and skilled movement development is speculative:

> *"Although it is not yet possible to determine whether there is a direct relationship between reflexive behavior and later voluntary movement, it is safe to assume that there is at least an indirect link"* (Gallahue & Ozmun, 1995, p. 163).

There isn't enough evidence to say this with certainty yet but there is some relationship between early spontaneous reflexes and mature movement patterns. It

is understood that this is a fairly inconclusive argument: "The precise role that oral reflexes play in speech production and other voluntary oral movements is unclear" (Wohlert, 1996c, p. 578).

However, the reflex foundation of speech movement does have some support in the research community. For example, Barlow and Bradford (1996) experimented with stimulation to the lips and found evidence to support the notion that reflexes may evolve into the more complex movements needed for development of more sophisticated speech motor skills. The reflex is considered part of what is called the *substrata* or underlying neurological layer of movement control. Any number of researchers in the areas of speech motor control, speech movement development, and motor speech disorders support this idea:

> *"Primitive reflexes… could provide a foundation for speech articulation motor patterns… The inborn patterns*

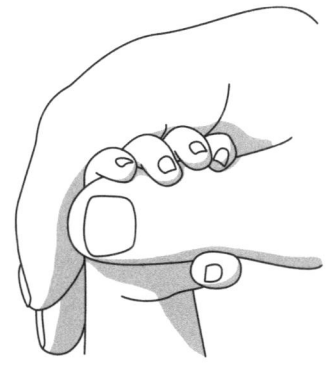

The palmer reflex is one of many that dominate newborn movement.

thus provide... substrata for developing and refining controlled movement patterns in mature body gestures... Rhythmical, temporary, and spatially patterned movement sequences are then built on this firm foundation" (Fletcher, 1992, p. 10, 14–15).

The reflex might be viewed like this: The reflex functions as the initial neurological pathway of movement. The reflex assures that the correct motor pathways for life are set up and maintained during the time when the infant can do nothing for himself. Once set, the pathways are used to direct the neurological impulses of voluntary movement as the child grows and matures. So the reflex itself does not create or evolve into the voluntary movement, but rather voluntary movements utilize the neurological roadway that is set up by the reflex initially; the reflex is part of the pre-programming for movement:

"The complexity of [speech] movement, and speed at which they are normally accomplished, make it probable that many aspects of speech movements in mature speakers are preprogrammed" (Duffy, 1995, p. 60).

Time and more research will tell the whole story eventually. Until then, speech-language pathologists of the 21st century will continue to use this as a working theory just as motor therapists do. The present author has used reflexes to stimulate new oral movements on hundreds of occasions and can attest to their clinical usefulness. Reflex responses have been used to teach all manner of speech movements as described below.

DEFINITIONS

There have been many proposed definitions of the reflex since Thomas Willis described what he called the *motus reflectus* in 1670 (Finger, 2000):

"[A reflexive action is] a response of some peripheral organ to stimulation of the sensory branch of a reflex arc, the action occurring immediately, without the aid of the will or without even entering consciousness" (Osol, 1973, p. 669).

"A reflex movement occurs when a child makes a stereotyped movement response to a stimulus without being able to control that response" (O'Brien & Hayes, 1995, p. 5).

"[Reflexes are] automatic, stereotyped movements, directed from the brain stem and executed without cortical involvement" (Goddard, 2005, p. 1).

Primitive Reflexes

The primitive reflexes are the ones that healthy, full-term, human babies display. Reflexive movement has been first

noted in fetuses of about two centimeters in length (Towen, 1976; Wolf, 1986). Most normal reflexes are present at birth and dominate movement until about four months of age when they begin to fade (Gallahue & Ozmun, 1995).

Newborns are provided with reflexes that are designed to insure immediate response to his new environment and to his changing needs (Goddard, 2005). Most of the reflexes serve an important biological and life-sustaining function. For example, the *head-turning reflex* ensures that a baby will be able to continue breathing when an obstruction is placed in front of the nose and mouth (Gallahue & Ozmun, 1995).

Certain speech reflexes reduce in strength by four months of age but maintain a presence throughout one's lifetime. Mysak (1980) said this included the *gag reflex*, the *palatal reflex*, the *yawning reflex*, and the *swallowing reflex*. The fading or inhibition of a reflex usually occurs concomitantly with the emergence of new skills (Goddard, 2005).

Abnormal Reflex Behavior

Children with neuromuscular dysfunction often continue to use the reflexes beyond four months of age. The term *retention of primitive reflexes* or *persistence of primitive reflexes* is used to describe this phenomenon. Retention of primitive reflexes can interfere with motor learning:

"If these primitive reflexes remain active beyond 6–12 months of life, they are said to be aberrant, and they are evidence of a structural weakness or immaturity within the central nervous system" (Goddard, 2005, p. 1).

Assessment of motor behavior includes an accounting of reflexes that remain because they give the SLP clues about the neurology that is actively hindering more advanced skills (Goddard, 2005). According to Gallahue and Ozmun (1995), signs of neurological dysfunction as measured by reflex stimulation include the following: perseveration of a reflex, complete absence of a reflex, unequal bilateral response to reflex stimulation, reflex responses that are too weak, or reflex responses that are too strong.

THERAPEUTIC PROCESS

The process of using a reflex to facilitate new movement is simple: One stimulates the reflex and then uses the resultant new movement pattern in a purposeful way. Functional use of the movement is emphasized in this therapeutic model: "Facilitation is always followed by purposeful activity designed to promote the desired behavior" (Farber, 1982, p. 124).

Parents instinctively use reflexes to teach their babies to do many things right from birth, for example, to suck from a bottle or breast or to grasp a rattle. Reflexes set these movement patterns into play in newborn babies, and this, at least, is established scientific fact. The extension of this idea is that reflexes can be used to teach new movements in older children. This second idea is practical theory.

For example, consider the part a reflex plays in the development of hand movements in a three-year-old client who cannot grasp an object. The palm of the hand might be stroked to facilitate the *palmer reflex.* Then the client might be encouraged to use this movement pattern for some purpose, such as holding a tambourine. Once held by the hand, the child's random arm movements will cause the tambourine to sound, or the therapists can move the arm for the child, or another reflex can be used to set the arm into motion. The sound of the tambourine that results encourages the child to shake it purposefully in a playful routine. Days or weeks later, this evolves into a simple routine of the child purposefully seeking the tambourine, picking it up, and shaking it. The theory is that the grasp reflex provided the neurological foundation (substrata) for this playful sequence to occur; it set the movement sequence into action and laid down the neurological pathway that voluntary grasping utilizes. It is recognized that this is a simplistic description of these events and is only a working theory.

Reflexes in Therapy

One discovers the origin of reflex stimulation in speech therapy by studying the history of movement therapies for clients with cerebral palsy. Fay (1948, 1954) was one of the first to describe a motor therapy approach to unlock and relax certain spastic muscle groups for children with cerebral palsy based on reflex stimulation. The program was called *neurophysical rehabilitation.* Doman et al. (1960) developed the idea further in a program called *neurological organization.*

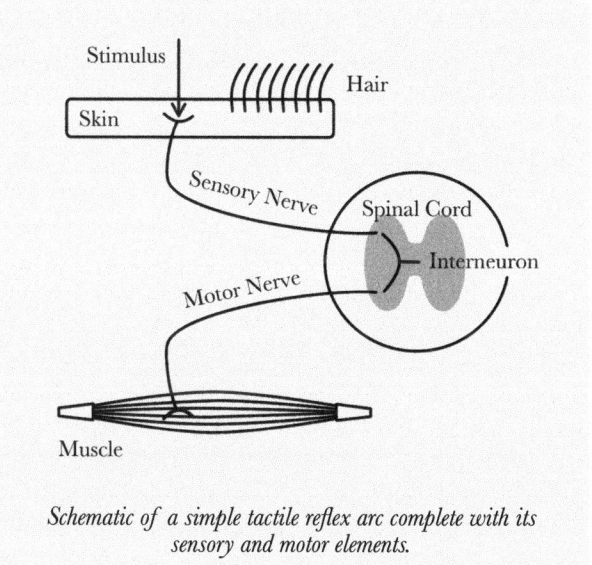

Schematic of a simple tactile reflex arc complete with its sensory and motor elements.

Karl and Berta Bobaths were perhaps the most important clinician-researchers in this line of thinking. They developed a therapeutic method called *neurodevelopmental treatment* (NDT) (Bobath & Bobath, 1950; Bobath, 1959, 1963). The NDT approach is based upon the interaction of inhibition and facilitation. Inhibition is used to suppress abnormal tonic reflex activities that are responsible for a client's patterns of hypertonicity. Facilitation of the normal, higher integrated righting and equilibrium reactions are stimulated in their proper developmental sequence.

The impact of these foundational ideas was such that, by the second half of the 20th century, occupational and physical therapists worldwide had begun to use reflex inhibition and facilitation to develop motor skills in all kinds of patients, from premature infants to geriatric patients, and from clients with brain damage to those with unknown etiologies. Several SLPs subsequently wrote books that included ideas about reflex stimulation for speech development in clients with cerebral palsy.

Reflexes in Motor Speech Therapy

Fröeschels (1952) may have been the first to name reflex stimulation for developing voluntary control in motor speech training. Fröeschels suggested, for example, that the gag reflex could be used to teach a patient how to widen the pharynx and lower the back of the tongue. Van Riper referred to Froeschel's work as important.

McDonald and Chance (1964) recommended using reflexes to stimulate new speech movements in their celebrated text *Cerebral Palsy*: "Muscles may be activated by stroking the skin area over the belly of the muscle or the area over its insertion" (p. 70).

Edward D. Mysak had affiliation with the Bobaths and extended these ideas in three classic works: *Principles of a Reflex Therapy Approach to Cerebral Palsy* (1963); *Neuroevolutional Approach to Cerebral Palsy and Speech* (1968); and *Neurospeech Therapy for the Cerebral Palsied: A Neuroevolutional Approach* (1980).

Mysak (1980) said that reflexes are the first movements of three inter-related lines of development important to oral-motor learning: (1) in feeding movements, (2) in the movements of pre-speech vocalizations, and (3) in the movements necessary to produce mature phonemes. He recommended using reflexes to stimulate movement that is completely absent: "Voluntary neuromuscular response may be facilitated through the use of reflex excitation" (Mysak, 1980, p. 150).

Suzanne Evans Morris revolutionized the understanding of feeding development and disorder in her groundbreaking research on the stages of infant feeding development (Morris, 1977a, 1982). Having studied with the Bobaths, Morris included reflex inhibition and stimulation in her therapeutic approach:

"Characteristics of cerebral palsy which may impair the development of oral-motor skills include abnormal

postural tone, abnormal oral and facial sensitivity, abnormal oral reflexes, and an inability to imitate oral movements" (Morris, 1977a, p. 163).

Reflexes in Articulation Therapy

Reflexes are not mentioned by name in textbooks on articulation therapy published in the first half of the 20th century and, therefore, reflex stimulation never is discussed as part of Traditional Era articulation therapy, but this is an oversight. There are numerous mentions of reflex stimulation that can be discovered in many textbooks, including Van Riper's. Reading carefully and thinking deeply about what the authors were saying will help in discovering them.

Scripture (1912) mentioned the tendency for the tongue to respond in certain ways when touched in specific ways. He calls the stimulation an *irritation*. For example, in his section about stimulating the tongue to form a central groove for /s/ he describes stimulating the tongue bowl reflex:

> *"The cure is often brought about by using a probe or a stick [to touch the middle of the tongue]; the irritation makes the patient narrow the channel"* (Scripture, 1912, p. 134).

Nemoy and Davis (1937) have been mentioned many times in this manual as the writers of an excellent collection of phonetic placement methods. These therapists also did not use the term *reflex* in their discussion, but they did use them and write about them. For example, they used the cough reflex to stimulate elevation of the back of the tongue for production of /k/:

> *"The pupil will find it easier to imitate the movements if he has gained control of the back of the tongue through exercises involved in raising of the back of the tongue... The suggestion that the pupil cough up an imaginary fish bone from his throat is often met with success in securing /k/"* (Nemoy & Davis, 1937, p. 107).

Van Riper noted that the oral mechanism tended to respond in certain pre-programmed ways. For example, he used the cough reflex as a means to teach a client to groove the tongue for production of a sibilant. In the following section he describes how to take this reflex response under voluntary control:

> *"Round the lips as in producing the vowel /u/, and as you do so protrude the tongue barely between teeth, then cough easily several times. Observe self in mirror and you will see that the tongue is grooved as you cough. Practice this until you can hold the groove even after the cough is completed. 'Listen' to the muscular sensations coming from the tongue when it is in this position. Shutting your eyes will help you to focus your attention. Finally, produce the groove by merely getting set to cough"* (Van Riper,

1939, p. 171).

Mid-century professor Berry and ASHA president Eisenson discussed several reflexes in their book on articulation training. For example, they used the yawn reflex to stimulate velar elevation:

> *"Begin a deep yawn with the jaw in the 'ah' position. Look into the mirror and note how the back of the tongue lowers, the velum rises, and the pillars of the fauces widen as you yawn. Repeat until you have a fairly intense feeling of the rising velum and open pharynx"* (Berry & Eisenson, 1956, p. 141).

Named Reflexes

Named reflexes began to appear in textbooks and journal articles on articulation, orofacial myology, and motor speech disorders beginning in the 1980s. Some examples:

- "Lip-rounding and retraction can be achieved also by appropriate stretching of the muscles to elicit the hyperactive stretch reflex... Yawning may achieve the desired mandible and tongue position... Coughing may help the back of the tongue to elevate for /k/ or /g/... Gargling brings the back of the tongue up and back and may assist in the production of /r/..." (Bosley, 1981, p. 11, 12).

- "In order to understand the initial development of lingual movement, therefore, one must have information about the reflexive movement patterns seen in response to touch stimulation to the tongue. The reflexes that are most relevant are the tongue bowl response (TBR), the tongue lateralization response (TLR), [the tongue retraction response (TRR)], and the tongue gag response (TGR)" (Rosenwinkel Marshalla, 1985, p. 321).

- "The purpose of this exercise is to stimulate the involuntary reflex, similar to the grasp reflex, that depresses the middle portion of the tongue in response to a stimulus... Tap the middle of the tongue with a tongue depressor... Continue tapping long enough to demonstrate the proper procedure, then have the patient do so. This is to be continued during each of the three practices each day for one minute" (Hanson & Barrett, 1988, p. 278–279).

- "Touching or stroking a baby's tongue elicits a spoon-shaped lingual configuration, characterized by an upraised ridge around its outer border... A similar posture could be elicited in adulthood by repeatedly touching, lightly stroking, or directing a stream of air across the tongue" (Fletcher, 1992, p. 10–11).

THE SPEECH REFLEXES

Mysak (1980) contains perhaps the most exhaustive discussion of the normal reflexes thought foundational to speech movement development. His complete set is the root of the material presented here and a few reflexes are added to his list as noted.

Mysak organized the speech reflexes into four types: protective reflexes, emotional reflexes, vegetative reflexes, and reflexive vocalizations. These categories have been abandoned in this chapter. The reflexes presented here are listed alphabetically in order to make the material easy to reference. Each reflex is named, defined, and explained through practical application. The present author has used almost all of these reflexes to stimulate speech movement activity in certain clients over nearly four decades and the notes about clinical applications are from her direct clinical experiences.

Biting Reflex

Placing an object between the gums causes reflexive mouth closing and holding behavior. It is thought that the reflex ensures capture of the nipple in the newborn. It is also thought to be a reflexive foundation of mouth closing, chewing, and jaw elevation for early babbling. The reflex is present at birth and reduces in strength by about four months of age. The biting reflex can be used: (1) to encourage the jaw to move upward, (2) to sustain an upward jaw position, (3) to encourage a closed-mouth rest posture, (4) to encourage an upward stable jaw position for general speech production, and (5) to encourage correct oral position for any phoneme that requires a high jaw position.

Chewing Reflex (Phasic Bite)

Stimulation to the gums or teeth causes reflexive up and down movements of the jaw. The response emerges in infants at about seven months of age. It corresponds to up-and-down jaw movement pattern of munching and babbling:

Objects placed between the teeth or gums cause biting and chewing movements.

"*Normal infants pass through a stage on the way to chewing in which stimulation of the gums elicits a rhythmical opening and closing of the jaw... This is known as the phasic bite reflex*" (Morris & Klein, 2000, p. 126).

The chewing reflex can be stimulated to encourage the mouth to open and close, and to stimulate the up-and-down oscillating jaw movements required for early babbling. It can also be used to stimulate longer strings of syllables in multi-syllabic words or multi-word phrases.

Coughing Reflex

A foreign object in the airway causes reflexive coughing. This reflex protects the airway from the inhalation of foreign objects; it is thought to be a reflexive foundation of laryngeal valving and mouth opening. Coughing causes rapid inhalation and exhalation and thus has a relationship to respiration for speech. The coughing reflex is also thought to be one cause of tongue grooving (Van Riper, 1939, p. 171). Van Riper recommended coughing as a stimulus to facilitate tongue grooving and tongue-back elevation. Others have used it to help return the voice in functional aphonia. The cough can be used to stimulate deep inhalation and many therapists use the cough to teach bursting exhalation for production of the plosives. One can also turn a client's spontaneous cough into a pre-speech turn-taking routine by imitating it. Initiate the routine by modeling it for the client to imitate.

Cry Reflex

The cry reflex consists of mouth opening, facial grimacing, sobbing, and sighing in response to fright, pain, frustration, or discomfort. It is important for cry breathing and is thought to be a reflexive foundation of breathing for speech. Mysak reports that the cry reflex signals discontentment and serves to "color" sound that will later be used in "sad talk." Reflexive crying is usually not stimulated on purpose to encourage sound production, however, when crying does occur it may be best not to discourage it in nonverbal and/or non-vocal clients because crying may be the only sound these clients produce. The cry can be imitated and played with just like any other sound. Children can take voluntary control of their cry and can learn to imitate back and forth with it just as with any other sound. Crying can be shaped into cooing using this process, and once cooing begins, the client is on his way to vocal development. Simultaneous crying often evolves into simultaneous laughing and this too can be shaped into vocal play. Crying usually opens the mouth and it causes deep inhalation and prolonged exhalation.

Face-Closing Reflex

The face-closing reflex is marked by eye closure and facial grimace in response to sudden air pressure on the face (a rush of air) or to an object suddenly approaching the face. The face-closing reflex puts the full face into flexion

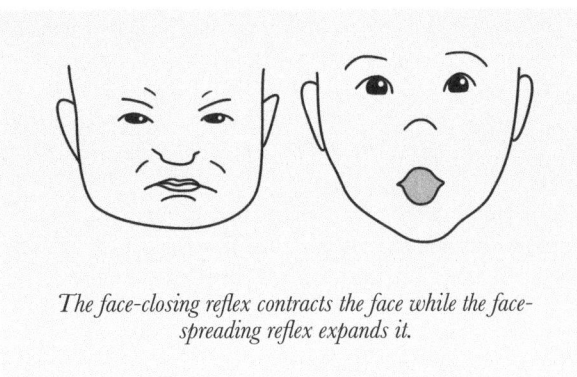

The face-closing reflex contracts the face while the face-spreading reflex expands it.

as a protective mechanism. It is thought to be a reflexive foundation of mouth closing. The face-closing reflex can be used to stimulate gross facial and oral flexor movements in clients who lack them. It can be used to stimulate the mouth to close or the lips to pucker. Stimulation of this response while the child is vocalizing can encourage production of /m/ or /u/. Blowing directly on the face is not sanitary so a bulb syringe should be used instead. Begin at the outer boarders of the face and work toward the mouth, nose, and eyes until the reflex is set off.

Face-Spreading Reflex

The face-spreading reflex involves reflexive spreading of the facial muscles to pull the face away from midline. It is an emotional reflex that is thought to be a reflexive foundation of mouth opening. Mysak discussed this reflex as a response to fear or fright, but certainly it is also seen in response to surprise. It is unfortunate that Mysak did not mention this because surprising a client is a much better therapy method than scaring him. The face-spreading reflex can be used to stimulate gross facial and oral movements in clients who lack them. Stimulation of this response while the child is vocalizing can encourage production of /ŋ/ or /ɑ/ depending upon whether the velum is raised or lowered at the same time.

Gag Reflex

Mysak did not mention the gag reflex in his text for some reason — perhaps because he did not use it — but there are many other sources for information about the gag reflex. A strong gag is present at birth, and, like all primitive reflexes, it reduces in strength by about four months of age: "In the normal infant, the reflex weakens as solid [food] intake increases" (Farber, 1982, p. 163). The gag reflex is retained all throughout life as it functions to protect the airways. Because of its complexities, the gag reflex is described here at length.

Tactile stimulation is mentioned the most often as the stimulus for the gag reflex. The gag is elicited when unannounced tactile stimulation is applied at the *ring of protection* in the back of the mouth. This ring consists of the back one-third of the tongue, the faucial pillars, and the velum. The gag can also be elicited upon tactile stimulation to the posterior pharyngeal wall. The gag can also be elicited in an emotional or conditioned way, such as when observing the choking, gagging, or vomiting of another person, or in response to the mere thought of these occurrences.

The movements of the gag reflex have been described in various bits and pieces throughout the past several centuries. Pulling all these ideas together, the gag reflex can be described in the following way (Marshalla, 1992a, p. 47):

- Downward and forward movement of the jaw

- Downward and forward movement of the anterior two-thirds of the tongue

- Rearward stretching of the posterior one-third of the tongue

- Downward pulling of the middle of the tongue

- Elevation of the hyoid bone

- Elevation of the larynx

- Medial movement of the faucial pillars

- Elevation of the velum

- The tongue takes on a predominant gutter shape with a deep midline fissure and high elevation of the lateral margins

It is the present author's observation that an infant often places his own hands and fingers into the mouth to stimulate the gag himself during the mouthing phase. Interestingly, when an adult pulls the child's hand out, the child often puts it right back in to stimulate the gag again. Marshalla calls this behavior *seeking the gag* and treats it as a part of normal development. Seeking the gag seems to be a child's way to discover the posterior limits of his oral cavity. It also seems to be a part of reducing the strength of the gag and subsequently normalizing oral-tactile sensitivity.

The gag reflex has wide applications in articulation therapy. It can be used to increase awareness of the oral mechanism, to normalize oral-tactile sensitivity, to increase oral tone, to facilitate a deep midline groove, to stimulate elevation of the tongue's lateral margins, to facilitate upward movement of the velum, to encourage downward movement of the jaw, to increase the functional size of the

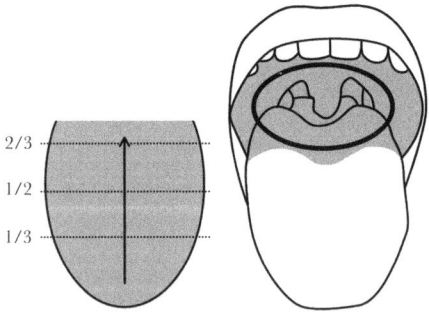

The gag reflex is elicited with stimulation down the midline of the tongue or anywhere on the "ring of protection."

oral cavity, and to stimulate tongue-tip extension. Because of its power and negative associations, stimulating the gag reflex is usually reserved as a last resort for these purposes with clients who need it.

Glottal-Closing Reflex

The glottal-closing reflex is reflexive closing of the larynx that an infant needs during aquatic fetal life. It occurs during swallowing, during sudden descent, with sudden exposure to cold water, and during heavy lifting. Mysak said that this reflex was stimulated when an infant engaged in "pushing or pulling sounds" when he is moving around. He also suggested one could stimulate glottal closing by having the child sniff vinegar fumes (Mysak, 1980, p. 209). The glottal-closing reflex is a protective reflex that is thought to be a reflexive foundation of laryngeal valving for voice.

Therapists routinely used to recommend heavy lifting as a procedure to stimulate voice in clients who had none. It is an excellent technique to use with clients who have low muscle tone, apraxia, or vocal fold paralysis, who need help adducting the larynx and producing a consistent or stronger voice. The vocalization produced during heavy lifting is basically a grunt. Clients can also be encouraged to grunt by holding their breath if they can understand that directive. The grunt can be stimulated, played with, imitated, and taken control of just like any other sound and can then can be shaped into voice for a vowel by prolonging it. WARNING: This method should be avoided in cases of vocal fold pathology.

Glottal-Opening Reflex

The glottal-opening reflex entails reflexive opening of the glottis, with rapid inhalation when there is a threat to breathing as when there is a nasal or oral obstruction. Mysak said that one could stimulate it by pinching the child's nostrils or by interfering with inhalation. It has also been called the *laryngeal reflex*. It is a protective reflex thought to be a foundation of inhalation for speech breathing.

The present author has used this reflex to stimulate inhalation in all kinds of clients by gently pressing a pillow or a stuffed animal against the face for a second or two.

WARNING: One must take special care in its

Light touch to the chest opens the glottis whereas heavy lifting closes it.

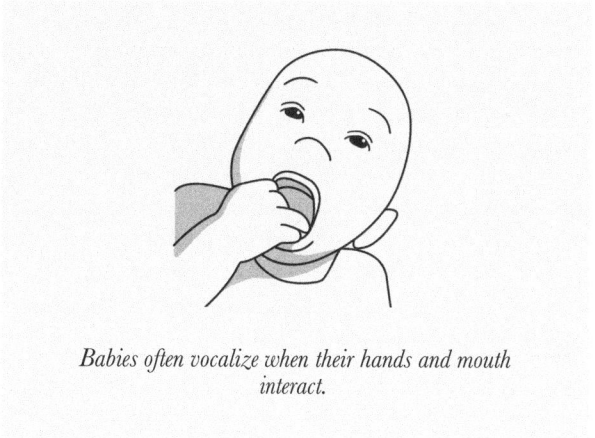

Babies often vocalize when their hands and mouth interact.

application because essentially the client's air supply is being blocked. However, clients are not endangered during this stimulation because the blocking is only for 1–2 seconds. As soon as the object is placed on the face, the client typically takes a series of tiny rapid inhalations, which are accompanied by eye widening, nasal flaring, and chin lifting. Sighing often follows, and it is this sighing that is most useful to SLPs. Sighing can be shaped into cooing, and this then can become the non-vocal client's first step toward vocal speech.

Light-touch stimulation to the face also causes this response, therefore, it often is unnecessary to close the oral and nasal ports and one can instead simply pat lightly upon the face. Light touch to the chest also causes this response. However the reflex is stimulated, the benefit of it is that the child will begin to inhale more obviously and these sounds can be imitated, played with, and taken under voluntary control.

Hand-to-Mouth Reflex

The hand-to-mouth reflex consists of mouth opening, eye closing, and head ventroflexion (flexing the spine to cause the head to lift back) in response to pressure applied to the palms of the hands. It is also called the *palmer-mandibular reflex* or *Babkin's reflex*. This reflex is present at birth and weakens during the first months of life. It disappears by the third month. The hand-to-mouth reflex is thought to be a reflexive foundation of mouth opening. It can be used to facilitate gross mouth opening in clients with very little oral movement and to provide general stimulation to the lips. This reflex can be combined with vocalization to produce /ɑ/.

Hand-to-Mouth Vocalization Reflex

The hand-to-mouth vocalization reflex causes a reflexive vocalization when an infant is engaged in hand-to-mouth play, eating, or teething. This is thought to be a reflexive foundation of voice.

The hand-to-mouth vocalization reflex has important applications in speech development for children with very little vocal output. Hand-to-mouth and object-to-mouth play can be used to stimulate voice. Touch, pressure, and movement in the mouth, especially in the gingival area, can also facilitate voice. This reflex shows that the process of feeding and the pleasure associated with it also facilitates vocal output. SLPs recognize the importance of these activities in work with infants and toddlers; therapists who work with older children with severe cognitive or neuromuscular disorder also use these techniques for the purpose of stimulating early vocalizations.

Head-Moving Reflex

Irregular head movements are caused by stimulation to the newborn's face. The head reflex is a protective reflex that ensures unobstructed breathing and that is thought to be a reflexive foundation of speech breathing. This reflex can be used to stimulate inhalation and exhalation in clients with very little control over airflow. It is used in conjunction with blow toys and tubes to play with air.

Infantile-Emotional Reflex

The infantile-emotional reflex is marked by prosodic changes to voice caused by emotional response. Mysak considered them to be important for tuning speech. He suggested that the infantile-emotional reflex influences vocal color, speech rate, and rhythm so the baby can express emotions like happiness, sadness, and fear.

This reflex demonstrates that early speech stimulation should be done in the spirit of emotional release and not rote imitation. The child who is learning to make his first sounds and words is driven by his emotions and his responses to events, not by his intellect. He wants to express joy, fear, like, dislike, amusement, and disinterest. He wants to demand, refuse, beg, cry out, and accept. Speech-language pathologists can take advantage of this by stimulating early speech with dramatic flair and by allow the child to dictate the terms of expression. In the present author's experience, this is especially important for children with apraxia who often are quite unskilled in taking turns after an adult and who perform much better if they can lead the functional communication play routines.

Inspiration Reflex 1

The inspiration reflex that Mysak described consists of reflexive inhalation that is the result of pressure on the trunk. Here this will be called *Inspiration Reflex 1*. Deep pressure applied to the chest causes deep inhalation when the pressure is released. It is first seen in the form of the primal breath, or the newborn's first breath that is the result of passing through the birth canal. This is thought to be a reflexive foundation of speech inhalation.

The present author has used this reflex response with many different types of children who, for whatever reason, were not playing with sounds and speech very much. The present author has stimulated this reflex in several ways including bear hugs, pressure to the chest with the child lying prone or supine, with children piling on top of one

another, and so forth. Any safe way to apply a broad surface of deep pressure on the chest or back, in line with the lungs, for a few seconds, can be an effective way to cause a deep inhalation when the pressure is released. Follow the release with gentle deep vibration to the chest, applied with the hands, to encourage voice. This is a great way to encourage the production and prolongation of voice.

Inspiration Reflex 2

Inhalation can also be stimulated by blowing gentle streams of air on the face. Here this will be called *Inspiration Reflex 2*. The present author learned this method from a team occupational therapist many years ago and is unsure from whom she learned it. It seems to be a traditional method many therapists have used. Parents can blow in their children's faces to stimulate inhalation. A more sanitary option for therapists is to blow air on a client's face with a bulb syringe

Jaw-Jerk Reflex

The jaw-jerk reflex is a reflexive contraction of the jaw flexors in response to steady or sudden stretch of the mandibular extensors:

> *"The jaw-jerk reflex is elicited by placing the index finger of one hand across the mental prominence of the mandible and briskly tapping the finger with the ends of the middle three fingers of the other hand"* (Mysak, 1980, p. 209).

The jaw-jerk reflex protects the jaw against damage by limiting the extension of the jaw. It is thought to be a reflexive foundation of jaw elevation.

The jaw-jerk reflex has been used to facilitate jaw mobility by occupational, physical, and speech-language therapists for many decades. Quick gentle but firm pressure (a tap) is applied downward on the chin. The jaw's response is to elevate quickly. It can be used to awaken jaw mobility.

WARNING: The temporomandibular joint is a vulnerable joint and SLPs need to be wary of causing it damage by using the jaw-jerk reflex. The jaw-jerk reflex should not be used with any client who has a history of temporomandibular joint dysfunction, structural deficit, or pain.

Jaw-Lowering Reflex

"When the center of the bottom lip is stroked [and] if the finger moves towards the chin, the mandible is lowered and the head flexes" (Illingworth, 1963, p. 133). The jaw-lowering reflex is stimulated to encourage gross mouth opening. It also causes the lips to stretch to their full capacity. Because the head also flexes forward, it is difficult to encourage specific sound at the same time, however this reflex can be used to stimulate general gross mouth opening and nonspecific sounds.

Laugh Reflex

The laugh reflex emerges in infants of about four months of age. It occurs in response to tickling and is thought to be a reflexive foundation of voice. Giggling also occurs as somewhat older infants are "tickled" by unexpected or re-curring events. For example, the game of *peek-a-boo* often elicits torrents of laughter in babies who are nearing one year of age. Mysak reports that the laugh reflex signals contentment and happiness that serves to color sound that will later be used to express happiness and excitement.

The laugh reflex is one of the most powerful to elic-it voice in non-verbal and non-vocal clients. Laughing emerges before babbling arrives and can therefore func-tion as a springboard to the development of babbling because it encourages deep inhalation and prolonged vo-cal production. A further benefit of laughter is that it is easy to elicit and family members can incorporate it into training routines at home. Speech-language sessions with children who produce little sound should be filled with laughter to encourage vocal play. Use safe and socially ac-ceptable touch and tickling as well as surprise games. The stimulation of giggling in response to funny circumstances is preferable for clients who are guarded about touch ex-periences.

Lip Reflex

The lip reflex is the source of involuntary lip movements, lip closure, and pouting, all seen in preparation for and during sucking. It is seen in children up to 12 years of age. The lip reflex is thought to be a reflexive foundation of lip closure and lower lip protrusion. This is another reflex that shows that feeding and speech work can go hand-in-hand with the youngest and lowest-functioning clients.

Lip-Elevating Reflex

Stimulation to the middle of the upper lip causes the up-per lip to elevate: "When the centre of the upper lip is stimulated, the lip elevates, baring the gums" (Illingworth, 1963, p. 133). This is a simple yet effective way to facilitate upper lip mobility, especially in clients with low tone or paralysis in the upper lip. Press a finger gently but firmly on the midpoint of the upper lip (between the nose and the lip) and flick downward.

Lip-Lowering Reflex

The lip-lowering reflex consists of reflexive lowering of the lower lip that is caused by lightly stroking outward at the angle of the mouth. It ensures that a baby will open the mouth when a nipple stimulates the lips. Stroking downward against the middle of the lower lip can also stimulate it. This is a simple yet effective way to facilitate lower lip mobility especially in clients with low tone or lip paralysis. Place a finger at the corner of the mouth and flick it downward, or press a finger gently but firmly on the midpoint of the upper lip and flick downward.

Lip-Puckering Reflex

Lip puckering is observed in response to the corners of the lips being steadily spread apart. Slow stretch of the lips toward the lateral borders causes the orbicularis oris to contract and the lips to pucker. The response has also been called the *lip counteracting response* and the *hyperactive stretch reflex*.

This reflex protects the lips against damage by putting limits on mouth opening. It is thought to be a reflexive foundation of lip puckering. SLPs can use slow stretch on the lips to activate lip puckering in clients who have little movement of the lips. Therapists can also use it to facili-tate awareness and control of this movement. The reflex can also be elicited with quick stretch. One can use a quick stretch to the corners of the mouth to stimulate the lips to pucker for the consonants and vowels that require it:

> *"The perioral reflex is elicited by a brisk mechanical tap or stretch applied to the perioral region, or by electrical stimulation of trigeminal nerve branches"* (McClean, 1978, p. 276).

Mouth-Closing Reflex

The mouth-closing reflex consists of reflexive head flexing and closing of the mouth in response to stimulation of the lower lip. Stimulate this reflex by swiping a finger from the lower lip down to the chin. The mouth-closing reflex can be stimulated when the lower lip hangs low and away from the upper lip at rest, and when lower lip movement is needed for production of the bilabials. This reflex will stimulate head flexion and jaw elevation and can also be used to stimulate early head nodding for the concept of agreement or to mean *yes*.

Mouth-Opening Reflex

The mouth-opening reflex consists of reflexive head ex-tension and opening of the mouth in response to stimula-tion of the upper lip upward. It is also seen in response to the visual stimulus of a breast, bottle, or finger, and is also seen in response to quick stimulation to the lips. This reflex is thought to be a reflexive foundation of mouth opening. There are two ways to open the mouth: by lower-ing the jaw or by elevating the head. This reflex stimulates both. It can be used to stimulate mouth opening for /ɑ/ when done with voice.

Movement-Vocalization Reflex

The movement-vocalization reflex consists of reflexive vocalizations that occur when an infant moves his head, arms, legs, or when he turns or reaches. This reflex is thought to be a reflexive foundation of voice. Clients who make very little voice or sound can be stimulated with general body movement; this client needs to get away from tabletop activities and get physically active to stimu-late more vocal expression.

Children tend to vocalize more when they are in movement.

Palatal-Lifting Reflex

The palate lifts reflexively when foreign objects stimulate the oropharynx. It is thought to be a reflexive foundation of velar valving and is maintained throughout life. This reflex occurs along with the gag reflex because stimulation to the oropharynx causes both to occur simultaneously. The palatal lifting reflex can be used to stimulate the velum to rise.

Pharyngeal Reflex

The pharyngeal reflex consists of reflexive constriction of the pharynx to protect against foreign objects entering the throat. This reflex is thought to be a reflexive foundation of velar valving and is maintained throughout life. This reflex also occurs along with the gag reflex because stimulation to the oropharynx causes both to occur simultaneously. The pharyngeal reflex can be used to stimulate gross awareness of the oropharynx.

Rooting Reflex

Tapping or stroking the head, cheek, perioral skin, or lips on one side causes reflexive turning of the head toward that side. This rooting reflex is thought to be the first in a chain of reflexive movements that result in mouth movement. The rooting reflex emerges in utero: "By mid-pregnancy, the fetus... will turn and begin to make sucking motions with its lips" (Nilsson & Hamberger, 2003, p. 141). The rooting reflex is usually described in the context of sucking but it can also be viewed as a means to stimulate primitive mouth movements for speech.

Smile Reflex

Babies begin to smile reflexively in response to a soothing maternal voice by 2–3 months of age. This *social smile* is thought to be a reflexive foundation of lip retraction and social communication. Mysak reports that the smile reflex signals contentment and happiness and serves to color sound that will later be used in happy talk. This reflex shows that making therapy pleasant and soothing in terms

of models and encouragements can stimulate gross smiling. A pleasant voice encourages primitive oral movement and sets the stage for the client to use a pleasant voice.

Sucking Reflex

Sucking and *suckling* (see below) are two very different sucking patterns. Sucking is the more mature pattern that emerges by four months of age (Morris & Klein, 2000). Three changes in oral movement mark the transition: (1) the tongue stops moving forward-back and begins to stabilize its perimeter against the palate while the midline elevates in a front-to-back stripping action, (2) the lips press into the nipple more firmly, (3) the jaw moves less as it begins to stabilize. The transition from suckling to sucking is a gradual process that occurs over several months. Sucking can be stimulated to encourage jaw stability, elevation of the tongue's perimeter, depression of the tongue's middle section, and lip rounding/closure. This reflex is discussed further in Chapter 18 on feeding.

Suckling Reflex

The suckling reflex emerges during the second trimester in utero (Morris & Klein, 2000) and consists of forward-back pumping action of the tongue coordinated with up-down movements of the jaw:

> *"The suckle appears to consist of two general phases: (a) a lowering of the jaw and forward and downward displacement of the body of the tongue, and (b) an elevation of the jaw and upward and dorsalward displacement of the tongue"* (Bosma, 1967, p. 101).

Suckling fades at about four months of age as it is overtaken by sucking, but is still seen in drowsy older children. Suckling movements are seen in newborns in response to many different stimuli including touch to the cheeks or forehead, but the response becomes limited to the oral area within a few days after birth. The suckling reflex is thought to be a reflexive foundation of general anterior-posterior tongue movement.

The infantile suckle-swallow is considered deviant or delayed when it persists into later childhood. This latent

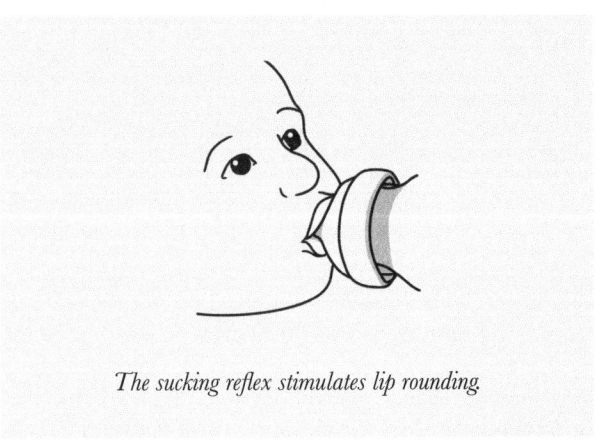

The sucking reflex stimulates lip rounding.

expression of the suckle-swallow has been called by various names over time: tongue thrust, perverted swallow, deviate swallow, deviant deglutition, horizontal swallow, reverse swallow, infantile swallow, and visceral swallow. This reflex is discussed further in Chapter 18.

The suckling reflex points to the advantage of combining feeding and speech stimulation in very young children and those with severe neuromuscular impairment and motor speech disorder. Therapists stimulate the suckle-swallow to get the jaw moving upwards and downwards, to get the tongue moving forward and backward, and to stimulate gross oral movement.

Swallow Reflex

The swallow reflex is present all through life beginning in utero. It consists of reflexive swallowing movements that occur in response to bolus formation. Coughing, sneezing, and hiccupping may also cause reflexive swallowing, as will stimulation of the palate, the fauces, the posterior pharyngeal wall, or the back of the tongue.

The swallow reflex is thought to be a reflexive foundation of tongue-tip elevation, lateral tongue elevation, and midline depression. It is also important in the differentiation of the middle of the tongue from its perimeter and also contributes to velopharyngeal closure. An *anticipatory swallowing reflex* may be seen in anticipation of food.

The swallow reflex points to the importance of facilitating both feeding and speech movements in some clients. Therapists can use the swallow reflex to stimulate gross oral movement in clients with both speech and feeding deficit. The swallow reflex is incorporated into programs designed to decrease drooling and the saliva accumulations that cause speech to sound wet. A normal mature swallow is also stimulated to facilitate differentiation of the tongue's middle from its sides and tip and to facilitate tongue-tip and lateral-margin elevation. (For more a more complete description of the swallow, see Chapter 18.)

Tongue-Bowl Reflex

Biologists say that the human body is comprised of a trunk and five limbs: two arms, two legs, and a head. Each limb ends in a grasping mechanism designed to lay hold of the environment: the hands, the feet, and the tongue. Each grasping mechanism contains within it a grasp reflex: the palmer reflex, the plantar reflex, and the lingual reflex. The lingua reflex, or what is now commonly called the *tongue-bowl reflex*, is a reflexive response to several stimuli: to pleasant oral stimuli, to tactile stimulation down the midline of the anterior half of the tongue, to coughing, and to crying. In essence, the most fundamental movement pattern of the tongue is to grasp. The tongue bowls or grasps to accept and hold objects that enter the mouth.

The tongue-bowl reflex is thought to be a reflexive foundation of tip elevation, lateral margin elevation, and midline depression of the tongue. This important reflex has been called by many names, and this may one of the

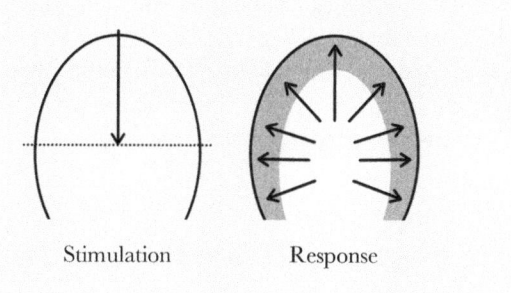

Tactile stimulation down the midline of the tongue, toward the halfway point, causes the tongue to bowl.

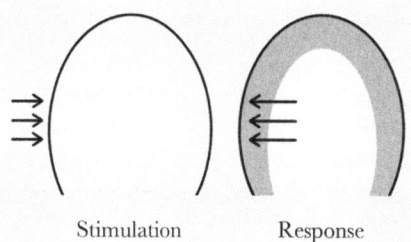

Tactile stimulation to the side of the tongue causes the tongue to move toward that side.

reasons that there has been no central body on literature about it:

- Spoon-shaped lingual configuration (Wassilieff, 1888)
- Tongue gutter (Gesell & Ilg, 1937)
- Tongue grooving (Van Riper, 1939)
- Median groove (Bosma, 1967)
- Tongue's take-in reflex (Mysak, 1980)
- Cup-shaped configuration (Morris & Klein, 1987)
- Tongue-bowl response or reflex (Rosenwinkel Marshalla, 1985)
- Horseshoe-shape configuration (Fletcher, 1992)

The tongue-bowl reflex has many applications in articulation therapy; it is used to stimulate gross tongue movement, to facilitate tongue curling, to facilitate elevation of the tongue tip and lateral margins, to increase tonus in the tongue, to create a midline depression, to widen the tongue, to create symmetrical movements of the two sides of the tongue, and to create the round oral cavity necessary for full oral resonance.

Tongue-Depression Reflex

Stimulating the middle of the lower lip causes reflexive tongue lowering. This reflex is thought to be a reflexive foundation of tongue-tip lowering; it can be thought of as the reflex that causes the tongue to move forward and down. This reflex can be used to stimulate gross move-ment of the tongue downward and forward and can also be used to increase general tone in the tongue.

Tongue-Elevation Reflex

Stimulating the middle of the upper lip causes the tongue to elevate. This reflex is thought to be a reflexive founda-tion of tongue-tip elevation. It can be used to stimulate gross movement of the tongue upward and forward. It can also be used to stimulate tongue-tip elevation for pro-duction of the lingua-alveolar consonants. It can also be used to increase general tone in the tongue.

Tongue-Lateralization Reflex

The tongue-lateralization reflex is stimulated by lightly stroking outward at the angle of the mouth (Mysak, 1980) or by stimulating the side of the tongue (Morris & Klein, 1987). The tongue-lateralization reflex is thought to be a reflexive foundation of tongue-jaw differentiation, lateral tongue movement, and lateral tongue elevation. Tongue lateralization goes through two developmental stages that can be called *immature lateralization* and *mature lateralization*:

• *Immature lateralization:* The immature form of tongue lateralization is seen as an elevation and rock-ing of the middle of the tongue toward the sides of the mouth. It can be used to unlock a jaw and tongue that are still moving in tandem, to differentiate the tongue from the jaw, to develop a full range of tongue mobility and to increase midline tone in the tongue.

• *Mature lateralization:* The mature form of tongue lateralization is seen as a lateral spreading and up-ward elevation of the sides or lateral margins of the tongue. It can be used to facilitate lateral spread and elevation of the tongue's lateral margins and to in-crease general tone in the tongue.

Tongue-Protrusion Reflex

Reflexive tongue protrusion is seen when the tongue is steadily forced into the back of the mouth. It is a protec-tive response that causes a foreign object to be rejected and pushed forward out of the mouth. The tongue-pro-trusion reflex is also called the *lingua counteracting response* and *tongue push-out reflex*. The tongue-protrusion reflex is also associated with noxious stimuli and bitter substances.

The tongue-protrusion reflex can be used to vivify tongue movement and to stimulate gross forward move-ment of the tongue in clients with little or no tongue movement. This reflex helps explain why pushing the tongue back into the oropharynx often does not work to facilitate tongue-back elevation for the back sounds.

Tongue-Retraction Reflex (TRR)

Tactile stimulation down the midline of the tongue causes the tongue to retract into the oropharynx and to hump

upward into a ball-shape. The movement occurs as the tactile stimulus reaches the posterior one-third of the tongue. The reflex causes the tongue to bunch up in the back to protect the oropharynx from foreign objects. If the tongue retraction reflex fails and the foreign object gets too far back into the oropharynx then the gag reflex is elicited. Since the tongue-retraction reflex is elicited just prior to the gag, it has also been called the *pre-gag movement* (Rosenwinkel Marshalla, 1985). The tongue-retraction re-flex can be used to facilitate gross backward movement of the tongue and tongue-back elevation. It can also be used to increase general tone in the tongue.

Tongue-Tip Protrusion & Elevation Reflex

Tongue-tip protrusion and elevation can be facilitated with stimulation to the upper lip: "When the center of the upper lip is stimulated… the tongue moves towards the place stimulated" (Illingworth, 1963, p. 133). This reflex can be used to stimulate general anterior tongue mobil-ity, to facilitate tongue-tip protrusion for the lingua-den-tal consonants, and to stimulate tongue-tip elevation for production of the lingua-alveolar consonants. This reflex causes the tongue to move out and up. It can also be used to increase general tone in the tongue.

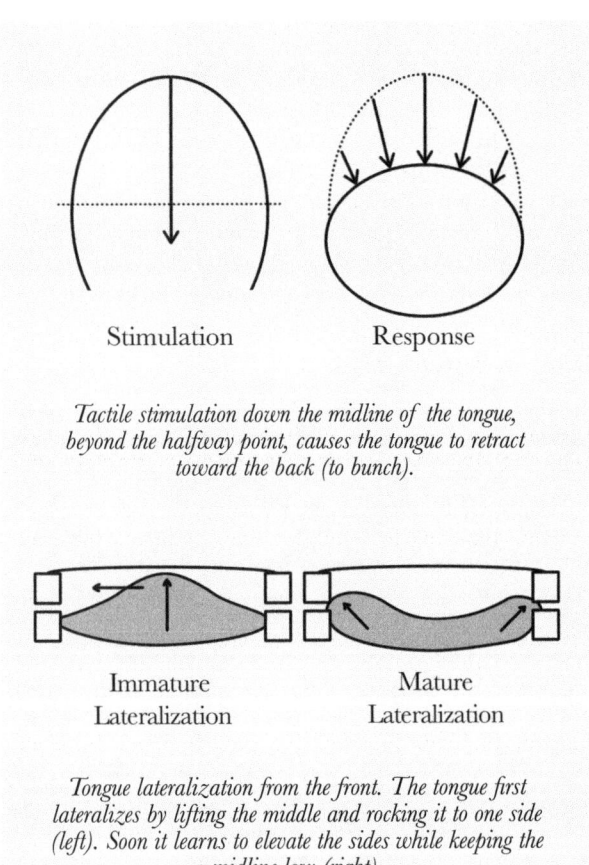

Stimulation   Response

Tactile stimulation down the midline of the tongue, beyond the halfway point, causes the tongue to retract toward the back (to bunch).

Immature   Mature
Lateralization   Lateralization

Tongue lateralization from the front. The tongue first lateralizes by lifting the middle and rocking it to one side (left). Soon it learns to elevate the sides while keeping the midline low (right).

Tongue-Tip Protrusion & Depression Reflex

Tongue protrusion and depression can be facilitated with stimulation to the lower lip: "When the center of the bottom lip is stroked… the tongue is directed to the site of stimulation" (Illingworth, 1963, p. 133). This reflex can be used to stimulate general anterior tongue mobility, and to facilitate tongue-tip protrusion for the lingua-dental consonants. This reflex causes the tongue to move outward and downward.

Tonic Bite Reflex

The tonic bite reflex is an abnormal reflex response that occurs in reaction to tactile stimulation given to the biting surfaces of the gums or teeth. This is a bite that does not release easily or has excess tension. The tonic bite is a "limiting pattern that interferes with all aspects of feeding" (Morris & Klein, 2000, p. 126). A tonic bite can cause children bite their own fingers or hands accidentally which discourages hand-to-mouth play. The tonic bite is not used as a means to develop oral movements. Rather the tonic bite is inhibited so that it does not interfere with oral motor learning. It is inhibited when the oral-tactile system is normalized as described in Chapter 16.

Yawn Reflex

The yawn reflex consists of deep involuntary inspiration while the mouth opens, the tongue lowers, the palate lifts, and the fauces narrow (Berry & Eisenson, 1956). The yawn puts the face and oral mechanism into full extension. The yawn reflex occurs when excessive carbon dioxide has accumulated and oxygen needs replenishing (Zemlin, 1968, p. 93). It is also caused by fatigue, by observing another person yawning, and even by simply thinking about yawning. The yawning reflex persists throughout adulthood. It is thought to be a reflexive foundation of jaw lowering, inhalation, velar elevation, and the exhalation of sighing. Simply talking about and modeling a yawn can elicit this reflex.

TREATMENT GUIDELINES

This final section provides guidelines for using reflexes in therapy. It discusses goals, subtlety, expectations, phoneme emergence, influence of stimuli, fading procedures, limitations, and precautions.

Goals

The goal of using a speech reflex is to facilitate speech movement or activity that is absent or weak. The next aim is to use the new movement in purposeful activity and to habituate it through repetition and practice so that the client can begin to gain voluntary control over the

The yawn stimulates mouth opening, inhalation, velar elevation, and sighing.

movement or activity. The following two examples demonstrate this idea.

- *Example 1:* Consider a client who makes no sound whatsoever. The hand-to-mouth vocalization reflex might be employed to initiate the sound-making process. An adult then imitates the child's spontaneous sound in order to create a vocal turn-taking game. The game would be initiated repeatedly and often in order to encourage practice of the vocalizations. Over time, the client should begin to gain voluntary control over the production of the vocalization so that he can initiate the game himself without the stimulus, or so that he can use the sound for some other purpose, for example, to get an adult's attention or to "talk" to a stuffed animal. The reflex stimulation activity serves as the first step in this therapeutic line of activities.

- *Example 2:* Consider the client who cannot round the lips for production of phonemes that are classified [+Round]. Lip rounding might be facilitated through stimulation of the lip-puckering reflex. The SLP then encourages the client to make a sound while the lips are rounded, for example, *ooooo*. The next step would be for the client to say this lip-rounded vowel in syllables such as *booo, gooo,* or *dooo.* The next step would be for the client to use lip rounding in words such as *two, shoe,* and *zoo.* The work would progress to phrases, sentences, paragraphs, and conversation, all with lip rounding incorporated into the work. The reflexive stimulation of lip rounding was the first step in this classic line of therapeutic activities.

Subtlety

Using a reflex to stimulate new movement is a subtle process. Other than the gag, laugh, and cry reflexes, most reflex responses are quite understated, and it can take some time to be certain of how to read the response. Just as the SLP must learn to use her ears to hear the subtle differences in phoneme productions, so does she need to learn to use the eyes to see the subtle movement changes that occur with reflex stimulation. It helps to watch another therapist use these methods before embarking on this path oneself or, at the very least, one has to have the freedom to experiment with them over time to discover their re-strained power. A reflex does not work in an obvious man-ner like a spring. Other than clients who are still operating at a reflex level, most clients will generally display only subtle changes in the actions being stimulated and it can take a while for a therapist to feel confident about what is happening.

Expectations

It is important to note that one cannot stimulate a reflex one moment and then expect a new movement pattern to emerge the next; reflexes do not work that way. One stimulates a reflex to facilitate only the subtle beginnings of new activity:

> *"The automatic reflexes that are programmed into the human system provide the building blocks from which similar responses will emerge at a voluntary level. This movement from automatic to voluntary is a slow dance gradually moving toward volitional control"* (Morris & Klein, 1987, p. 27).

For example, a client whose tongue is bunched and humped while speaking will benefit from stimulation of the tongue-bowl reflex. Stimulation of the reflex will cause the tongue to begin to function in a more concave pattern, but the presence of the bowl will not automatically ensure that all phonemes will be produced with the bowl-shape from that point forward; it will take some time for the new movement pattern to work its way into all speech pro-ductions. The length of time needed for changes to take hold will range from immediately to many months. Rate of change depends upon many factors including muscle tone, oral-tactile sensitivity, cognitive level, frequency of stimulation, influence of stimulation, and neurological status. Another factor is the client's willingness to allow the stimulation, time in treatment, treatment parameters, and so forth.

Phoneme Emergence

Stimulation of a reflex does not make phonemes appear as if by magic. The reflex only causes a more normal movement pattern to appear and this new movement pattern can be incorporated into speech activities. For ex-ample, if the client cannot close the mouth to produce /m/ because his jaw hangs low and does not elevate then the mouth-closing reflex can be employed. It is very un-likely that /m/ will emerge only because the jaw has been stimulated to elevate; the client still must be taught about /m/ through auditory, visual, and conceptual training as well. The reflex is used to facilitate one aspect of /m/ pro-duction — that of getting the jaw to elevate so the lips can articulate. This is a very important point. SLPs must make sure they understand why they are employing a reflex in speech training or the work will be futile.

Influence of Stimuli

Therapists may find that a certain type of stimuli does not set off a reflex as it should. Therefore, a stimulus with more influence, clout, or power must be selected. There are several ways to go about this: change stimuli, wait, in-crease time, and sequence stimuli.

- *Change stimuli:* One way to increase the chances of a reaction is to change stimuli. "A given modality may be used for different effects depending upon how, when, and where it is applied. The amplitude and frequency of a stimulus and the site of stimulation may determine the outcome" (Farber, 1982, p. 123). Stimuli can vary by size, weight, shape, texture, and temperature. For example, blowing air on the face may not stimulate the face-closing reflex because the stimulus is too weak. The therapist might choose a stuffed animal to brush across the face instead. If this doesn't work, she might try a slightly rough terrycloth towel rubbed briskly but gently on the face. If this doesn't work, the therapist might try a gentle vibra-tor on the cheeks. The clinician will continue to "up the power" until he or she finds one that elicits the desired response.

- *Wait:* It is not unusual for a client with a neu-romuscular disorder to have a delayed reaction to a stimulus. Therefore, it behooves the therapist to ap-ply a stimulus and then to wait to see if there is a delayed reaction. This is a very important point: One does not want to apply one stimulus after another in rapid succession without waiting to determine if the first had any effect. Applying more stimuli too quickly can be over-stimulating and can set off too much response that can be detrimental to the patient, sometimes causing disorientation, nausea, and even vomiting: "Patients should not be bombarded with input because this might cause overstimulation and confusion" (Farber, 1982, p. 120). Be patient, and work closely with the team motor specialists for guid-ance with particular children.

- *Increase time:* Another way to increase the effect of stimuli is to increase the time during which the stimulus is being applied. For example, if 5 seconds of stimuli doesn't set off a reflex, maybe 10 seconds will. Be careful with this; avoid over-stimulating by working closely with the motor specialists to find the right amount of time needed for reaction in specific clients.

- *Sequence stimuli:* One more way to increase the power of a stimulus is to sequence it with another one. If a particular stimulus does not set off a reflex, it might if it follows a different one. For example, strok-ing down the midline of the tongue might not cause the tongue bowl reflex to set off until after a gag reflex has been stimulated.

Fading the Technique

Reflexes are only used for a short while and they are faded out of the therapy routine as quickly as possible. This is because one do not want clients to become dependent upon reflex stimulation to initiate movement and because overstimulation can cause the reflex to extinguish quickly. Stimulation of a reflex facilitates new movement and the reflex is eliminated as soon as a functional routine for that movement is established. "Gradually the eliciting stimuli should be phased out as controlled or directed movement becomes possible" (Bosley, 1981, p. 11).

Limitations

It is important for SLPs to recognize that clients who function below six months of age may never get beyond the reflex level in movement patterns and habits. Some of these clients may gain splinter skills that reach beyond the reflex level but the reflex level will dominate. Some of these clients never move beyond reflexive speech movements: "Developmental stage of the patient may determine how he responds to stimulation" (Farber, 1982, p. 123).

Precautions

Application of reflex stimulation can be dangerous if used inappropriately. For example, deep pressure to the chest to stimulate Inspiration Reflex 1 would be inappropriate if the child has a heart condition, brittle bones, or another life-threatening disorder or disease. Caution should be used in the application of all reflexes and sanitary procedures should be followed at all times. Speech-language pathologists should consult with other therapeutic and medical team members when selecting reflexes for application in speech training.

Farber (1982) discusses several additional precautions: (1) do not use reflexes with a client with whom some level of rapport has not been established because fear, anxiety, and previous experiences can change the way he responds; (2) watch and learn from the client; (3) watch for delayed reactions to stimuli; (4) avoid pain; (5) be aware that the body can overcompensate for excessive stimulation and, therefore, respond in the opposite way one desires: this is called *rebound*.

CASE STUDY

The following case describes how reflexes were used to stimulate /k/ and /g/ in a high-functioning client. Brian was a child of average intelligence who started speech therapy when he was four years old due to severe phonological impairment. After three years of very successful treatment he switched to a new therapist. By that point Brian had made big strides and he had become highly intelligible, but Brian still used no [+Back] sounds — /k/, /g/, /ŋ/, /j/, and /r/ — and he had cluster reduction and cluster simplification.

After a few months of treatment with the new therapist Brian's clusters were coming along nicely but he still had gained no phonemes in the back. Brian's therapist decided to use the tongue retraction reflex to stimulate tongue-back elevation. The reflex was stimulated approximately 10 times in two weekly sessions. The tongue immediately began to elevate and make contact with the velum following the first stimulation. Brian was asked to blow over the tongue while the back was elevating in this way; a velar fricative was produced and Brian gained control over it right away.

For the next several weeks, Brian practiced the velar fricative in therapy and was encouraged to make it a few times every day at home. He then was taught to use it as a substitute for /k/ in the final position of words. He practiced *bike, book, back, make, Mike, like, look, lake* and other similar words by substituting his velar raspberry for the final /k/. Within another few weeks, final /k/ and final /g/ both were emerging in spontaneous speech. The reflex served as a powerful tool to stimulate emergence of the back sounds immediately after several years of model-and-imitate routines had failed.

SUMMARY

Reflex stimulation has been a long-standing element of articulation and motor speech therapy. Therapists use reflexes to stimulate elements of movement in all four subsystems of speech movement. Reflex stimulation is used in coordination with other cognitive, auditory, phonetic, and phonological stimuli to elicit phonemes.

18

Eating, Swallowing & Orofacial Myofunctional Methods

Stimulating the biological foundations of articulation

> *"A clinician does not have to use foods to improve speech precision; however, the use of food is a natural, functional way to facilitate the oral musculature to move in ways enhancing speech precision."*
>
> – J. Lyndelle Jones-Owens, 1991

Speech-language pathologists have speculated for decades that some kind of relationship exists between the movements of speaking and eating, especially in clients with motor speech disorders. Research suggests that speech and feeding are mediated by different control mechanisms and are, therefore, unrelated (e.g., Ruark & Moore, 1997). However, studies in neural plasticity suggest that, "training in one function may enhance related behaviors" (Ludlow et al., 2008) in a process called *transference*. This means that training oral movements in feeding may enhance movement training in speech, and vice versa. Researchers are also beginning to discuss more potential deep relationships between early feeding skill and subsequent learning processes. For example, Poore and Barlow (2009) reported that the infantile suckle pattern is being used as

a biomarker of speech, cognitive, and learning development. These researchers predicted that some day the suck might serve as an intervention point to prevent speech-language delays and disorders. At the present time, perhaps all that can be stated is that there may be a relationship between the movements of feeding, swallowing, and speech, but these are as yet unspecified.

Despite this precaution, there are tens of thousands of SLPs in the United States who already provide concurrent feeding, swallowing, and orofacial myofunctional therapy services to patients with articulation and motor speech disorders. The information of this chapter concerns ideas about eating and swallowing that have shaped the way these therapists do this. It is understood that not all therapists accept this approach nor do they function this way. This chapter represents the state of the art for therapists who *do* think and work along these lines and is intended to pass on basic information to get them started.

BACKGROUND

Who introduced the idea that eating and swallowing activities might be useful to stimulate jaw, lip, and tongue function for speech? As in so many areas, Van Riper seems to have been the one to set this stage. To stimulate tongue movements for phoneme production, for example, he wrote very specifically about using feeding methods: "Learn to recognize the [tongue] movement as part of some familiar biological movement such as

Many SLPs integrate feeding and speech routines when teaching oral movement schemes.

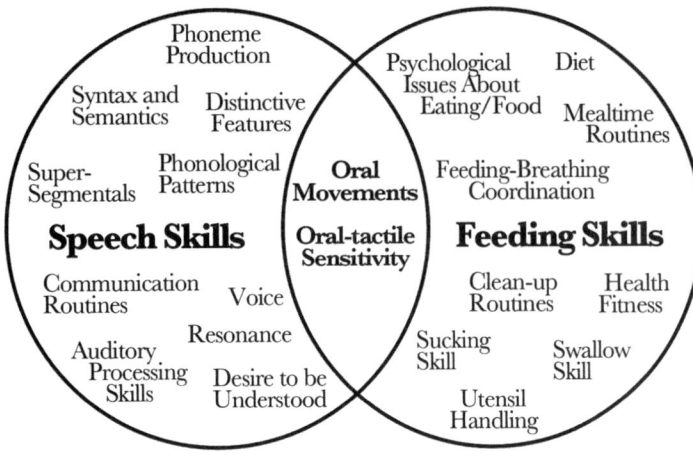

Speech and feeding share at least two common elements.

chewing, swallowing, coughing... Practice these basic activities" (Van Riper, 1947, p. 169). The early editions of Van Riper's text reveal that he used eating activities in the process of phoneme teaching when he deemed that the speech problem was the result of what he called "motor in-co-ordinations (*sic*)" (Van Riper, 1947, p. 127). Van Riper taught rhythmic chewing to clients with problems of articulation and fluency, and he advocated *Fröeschels chewing method* (Fröeschels, 1948) which was a process of pretending to chew without food in order to establish better speech rhythm. Van Riper's perspective at that time was that eating activities, whether real or pretend, could interrupt inappropriate yet habitual oral movement patterns, activate new oral movements, and help develop better speech rhythm. From his notes one might conclude that Van Riper thought feeding activities were important to speech improvement when a client had difficulty with speech movement.

Feeding activities have been included in a great number of articulation texts and manuals published since Van Riper wrote about them. Careful study of these books reveals that many of the same feeding methods appear time and again and the methods that appear most often are those that are designed to teach the basic oral movement patterns of normal eating and swallowing. For example, perhaps the most widely reported method is one of placing a sticky food such as honey or syrup on the alveolar ridge to encourage lingua-alveolar contact. This basic feeding method can be found in articulation textbooks beginning in the 1950s (e.g., Berry & Eisenson, 1956) and progressing all the way through to therapy manuals published in the current century (e.g., Secord at al, 2007). Therefore, it can be stated without hesitation that eating and swallowing methods have been a regular part of articulation therapy from the Traditional Era onward. Notions that this is a new idea can be discarded.

Not every client needs an eating experience to learn a particular oral movement. These methods are used when the therapist deems that an eating activity might be

beneficial to learning a particular movement, or if she believes that a particular client could benefit from the oral sensory input supplied by food textures, or could benefit from developing more extensive oral movement schemes, or when a client has concurrent motor speech and feeding disorder, or when it might interest an otherwise bored or distracted client. Working on speech and feeding together as representative of a single movement scheme represents the transfer process of neural plasticity at work: "Schemes develop as a result of repeated experiences that are similar but not identical" (Fletcher, 1992, p. 18). For example, lifting the tongue tip to the alveolar ridge can be considered a single movement scheme, and that scheme could be taught through a speech or an eating activity or both. Both are representative of the scheme, both contribute to the development of the scheme, and both can be used therapeutically to enhance the scheme.

Motor Speech Disorders

The concept of using feeding techniques for speech improvement was broadened in the mid-20th century when SLPs began to work with and write about children with cerebral palsy. Books began to contain recommendations to stimulate sucking, swallowing, and chewing skills as a part of *pre-speech training* when clients had this type of neuromuscular dysfunction. Clinicians began to use eating experiences to foster normality and maturity of oral movement and to prepare the oral mechanism for correct speech production.

This concept eventually extended back to speech-only clients, and therapists began to talk about using feeding methods in articulation therapy. For example, *Techniques for Articulatory Disorders* (Bosley, 1981) contains a description of Palmer's "Hard Food Orientation Program." Therapists using this program taught articulation clients how to eat foods of increasingly firmer textures in order to develop mature oral movements for speech.

Orofacial Myology

The 20th century also brought questions about the bond that may or may not exist between the lisps and the *reverse swallow* or *tongue thrust swallow*. Many SLPs in the United States now receive additional training in orofacial myology and they specialize in clients who have concurrent speech, swallowing, and dental problems. "Creating an oral environment conducive to proper facial growth and development is the goal of the orofacial myofunctional therapist" (Green, 2013). The American Speech-Language-Hearing Association (1993) has supported this view and published knowledge and skills papers in this regard. The following points are of historical interest beginning in the mid-20th century. (Readers seeking more thorough summaries of this and earlier history are referred to

Hanson and Mason [2003] and Mills [2011]).

- *1960:* Fledging articles on the speech and swallowing relationship began to appear in speech journals in the 1960s.

- *1970:* Ehrlich published an early teaching manual entitled *Training Therapists for Tongue Thrust Correction* (1970).

- *1972:* An interest group called the American Association of Oral Myo Therapists was formed in 1972 and this group eventually evolved into the International Association of Orofacial Myology (IAOM). The IAOM functions as the international professional organization that governs certification in orofacial myology and provides continuing education on the assessment and treatment of swallowing problems and oral habits, as well as information and resources for patients and their families.

- *1974:* The *Journal of Speech and Hearing Disorders* carried an article on the tongue-thrust controversy written by Mason and Proffit. This article became the standard around which everything written since has stemmed in the fields of orofacial myology, speech, and dentistry.

- *1976:* Garliner published *Myofunctional Therapy* (1976). Garliner eventually was discredited for unethical practices, but his work stands as an historic contribution.

- *1988:* Hanson and Barrett published *Fundamentals of Orofacial Myology* (1988). This textbook became the first worldwide standard.

- *1991:* ASHA published a supplement on the role of the SLP in the management of oral myofunctional disorders (American Speech-Language-Hearing Association, 1991).

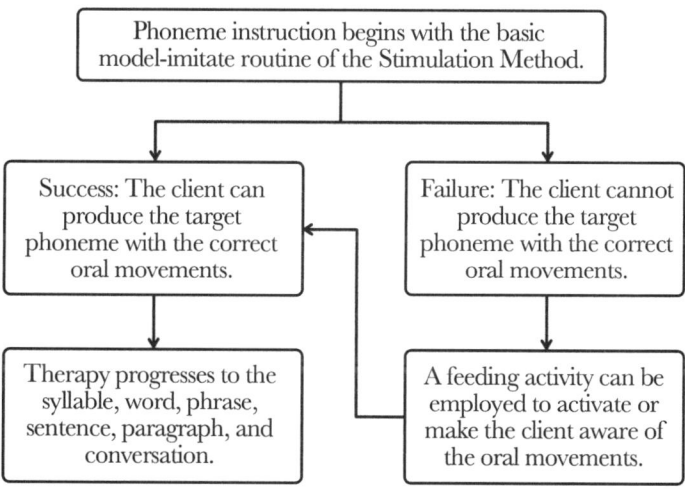

Van Riper's basic plan for incorporating feeding activities into articulation therapy.

- *1993:* ASHA published a new knowledge and skills supplement on orofacial myology (American Speech-Language-Hearing Association, 1993).

- *2003:* Hanson and Mason set a new textbook standard with *Orofacial Myology: International Perspectives* (2003). They defined orofacial myology as "the study of normal and abnormal patterns of use of the mouth and face and their relationships with dentition, speech, and vegetative functions" (p. 3).

THE MATURE SWALLOW

Therapists who want to incorporate eating and swallowing activities into articulation or motor speech therapy need to understand the mature swallow. *Swallowing* has been defined as "the entire act of deglutition from placement of food in the mouth through the oral and pharyngeal stages of the swallow until the material enters the esophagus through the cricopharyngeal juncture" (Logemann, 1983, p. 4–5). The mature swallow has been divided into three or four phases depending upon the source text. Therapists who use this information in articulation therapy are concerned only with the first two phases in which the tongue, jaw, and lips are active. The following represents idealized yet foundational ideas using a four-phase model.

Phase 1: Oral Preparatory Phase

The first stage of the mature swallow has been called the *oral preparatory phase*. This is a voluntary stage that begins when food is taken into the mouth; therefore, it includes the process of presenting and accepting food within the mouth and the act of biting. Once food enters the mouth, the tongue carries the responsibility of transferring the incoming food to the molar areas for chewing and the cheeks press in to keep food out of the sulci and over the molars. Mature chewing occurs when the jaw moves upwards and downwards, left to right, forward and backward, and diagonally in rotary patterns that are larger than those used during the process of speech. The tongue transfers food side to side during chewing so that the food becomes well masticated and mixed with saliva. Once the food has entered the mouth, the lips close, and they remain closed to prevent food from exiting the mouth throughout the entire chewing and swallowing process. The lips also remain closed to create a socially polite eating experience.

Once adequately mashed, mixed with saliva, and softened, food particles are gathered together into a *bolus* (wad; rounded mass) as a result of several coordinated and simultaneous actions. The cheeks push the particles medially, the tongue gathers the food particles together,

TONGUE MOVEMENT IN MATURE SWALLOW

Formation of the tongue bowl and the food bolus marks the end of Phase 1

The tongue's perimeter stays sealed against the palate as the middle elevates sequentially from front to back during Phase 2

Superior view of tongue position and movement during the first two phases of the normal mature swallow. The symmetry here reflects an average and idealized view.

and the lips remain closed so that suctioning can be used to draw the particles together. A bolus forms because the tongue contours itself into a bowl shape that is high around the perimeter and low in the middle. This is the *tongue bowl configuration*. Gravity and the high sides of the tongue bowl ensure that the food bolus will fall to the low center of the tongue and stay off the sides. Formation of the bolus marks the end of this first phase.

Phase 2: Oral Transit Phase

The second phase of the mature swallow has been called the *oral transit stage* or *oral propulsive stage* and it is also a voluntary stage. The phase begins after the bolus is formed. Here, the jaw elevates (the teeth close in the back) so that the tongue will be held up high near the palate. The lips remain closed. The tongue begins to push the bolus in a posterior direction from the oral cavity to the oropharynx. This push occurs in a specific way: The elevated perimeter of the tongue seals itself against the palate to keep the food bolus in the middle of the tongue and prevent food from leaking out the front or sides of the mouth; once the perimeter of the tongue seals (stabilizes) against the palate in this way, the middle of the tongue begins sequential elevation in a front-to-back pattern. This *stripping action* moves the bolus of food from the middle of the tongue to the rear, and then into the oropharynx (Chi-Fishman, Stone, & McCall, 1998). Phase 2 ends as the back of the tongue elevates and the bolus enters the oropharynx. The whole tongue is pressed upward against the palate at the end. The jaw remains elevated and the lips remain closed throughout the entire phase. The tongue bowl continues to be a critical aspect of swallowing throughout this second phase.

Phase 3: Pharyngeal Phase

The third phase of the mature swallow has been called the *pharyngeal phase*. The phase begins when the bolus passes beyond the anterior faucial pillars and over the back of the tongue. The bolus itself provides the tactile stimulus that triggers the swallow reflex. When the swallow is triggered the velum elevates to prevent food from entering the nasal port, and the respiratory sphincters close to prevent leaching of food into the trachea. Involuntary sequential peristalsis (squeezing or stripping action) pushes the bolus posteriorly through the pharynx from top to bottom. The phase ends at the cricopharyngeal sphincter when it relaxes and allows the bolus to pass from the pharynx to the esophagus.

Phase 4: Esophageal Phase

The fourth phase of the mature swallow has been called the *esophageal phase*. It is an involuntary stage. It begins as the food bolus enters the esophagus at the cricopharyngeal sphincter and ends when the bolus passes into the stomach at the gastroesophageal juncture. Peristalsis action also pushes the bolus through the esophagus in this stage. Finally, the mouth relaxes back into its rest position.

FEEDING DEVELOPMENTAL MILESTONES

Therapists who incorporate eating methods into articulation and motor speech therapy also need information about the normal process of eating development. The earliest discussion of this material seems to have begun in the 1930s with a simple description of tongue movement during infant feeding:

> *"As the tongue comes under voluntary command it is able to contract, elongate, flatten, belly, curl, lick, groove, and wag"* (Gessell & Ilg, 1937, p. 28).

Significantly more information about developing eat-

Suzanne Evans Morris' pioneering work established the normative data on feeding skill development.

ing skills came along decades later with the publication of *The Pre-Speech Assessment Scale* (Morris, 1982). Morris studied the feeding skills of children from birth through two years of age and devised a scale to qualify and quantify 28 different pre-speech skills. She found that feeding movements develop in sequential patterns like all other skills. The developmental milestones she identified gave insights into the pathways of normal oral-motor development.

The ages at which certain eating skills emerge are probably not very important to speech training but the patterns of movement development are. For example, it is not important to articulation therapy that sucking overtakes suckling at nine months of age, but it is important that the tongue first moves in a forward-back pattern (suckling) before it moves in an up-down pattern (sucking). Developmental sequences such as this reveal how oral movement skills develop over time and the general assumption is that these lines of development are the same in both eating and speech. The following summarizes developmental milestones in eating from birth through two years of age.

Newborn

Swallowing begins during the second trimester in utero when the reflexes begin to occur (Dellow, 1976). Swallowing movements occur when a fetus drinks amniotic fluid, sucks the thumb, and engages in general non-specific oral movement. A newborn, therefore, already has had several months of stereotyped suckling experiences that he carries into his first day of life. The newborn also has large sucking pads and extensive flexor tone that press the head forward and keep the lips sealed against the nipple during feeding. The suckle-swallow pattern dominates (described in Chapter 17 on the speech reflexes). The retention of the infantile suckle-swallow pattern among older children has been called by several names including the *infantile suckle-swallow pattern*, *reverse swallow*, *tongue thrust swallow*, and *tongue protrusion swallow*.

3 Months

Slight variations in oral movement appear as the suckle pattern continues with slight modifications:

- Suckling becomes less stereotyped and begins to look more like a varied volitional pattern.

- A relaxing of the infant's flexor tone makes the seal of the lips against the nipple somewhat loose, and some liquid may be lost during suckling.

- This reflex and all others begin to fade by four months of age.

6 Months

New feeding routines are introduced and new oral movements begin to emerge:

- Spoon-feeding and cup drinking are introduced.

- The early suckle pattern continues to predominate but the tongue begins to move up and down, too.

- The new up-and-down tongue movement pattern marks the beginning of a gradual shift to a more

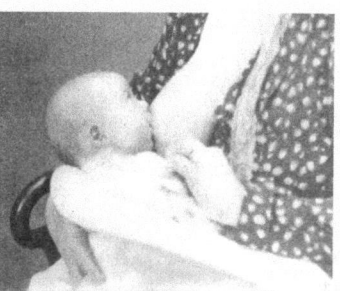

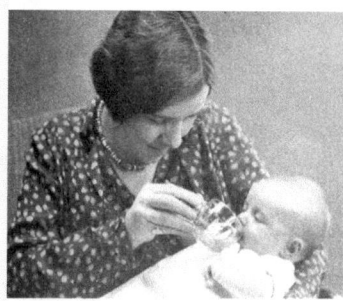

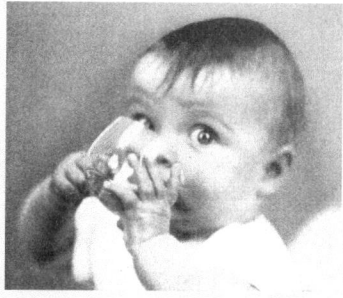

Scientists began to study feeding development early in the 20th century. (Photos: Gesell & Ilg, 1937)

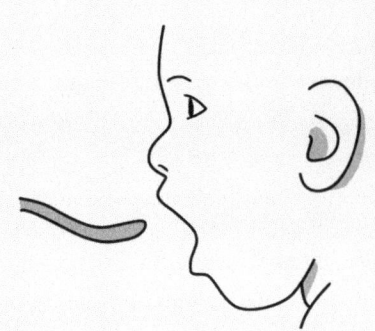

The mouth opens, the jaw stills, and the tongue quiets in anticipation of an approaching spoon beginning at about six months of age.

mature *sucking* pattern.

- In sucking, the tongue begins to stabilize its perimeter against the palate while the midline elevates in a front-to-back stripping action.

- The *tongue bowl* appears.

- Both suckling and sucking are used between 6 and 12 months of age.

- Spoon-feeding of purees is introduced, and both suckling and sucking patterns are used on the spoon. (Cups can also be used to drink sips of thick liquids.)

- Jaw movements are beginning to refine, meaning that the jaw begins to move less.

- Tongue movements begin to take over for jaw movements.

- Liquid loss is decreased because the lips are beginning to become active.

- The mouth opens, the jaw stills, and the tongue quiets in anticipation of an approaching spoon.

- The upper lip begins to move downward against the upper surface of the spoon to clear it of puree.

- The stickiness of purees causes the tongue to adhere to the palate when the jaw lowers. This soft flopping down of the tongue after the jaw has lowered is known as the *tongue lag*. This begins the separation of tongue movements from jaw movements.

- Children begin to gnaw on baby cookies by moving the jaw up and down in the first chewing pattern called *munching*.

- Cup drinking is introduced.

- Choking and coughing is common because of the rapid flow of liquid from the cup so cups with spouts are employed.

- A suckle-swallow or simple tongue protrusion is

often seen as the cup is withdrawn from the mouth.

- Presenting food on one side of the mouth causes the tongue and jaw to lateralize to that side. This has been called the *tongue lateralization response* (Rosenwinkel Marshalla, 1985). The tongue elevates its midline to lateralize before it learns to lateralize with the sides.

9 Months

New foods are introduced including chewy solids and foods for biting. Foods can vary by texture, size, shape, weight and temperature. Greater food variety provides new sensory experiences in, on, and around the mouth. This causes even more oral movements to develop:

- The protective gag reflex continues to diminish.

- Suckling fades as sucking begins to dominate.

- Lip activity increases on the spoon and cup.

- The jaw can stabilize on a cookie for breaking off pieces.

- The tongue can transfer food from midline to both sides for chewing.

- The tongue elevates its middle and shifts it to one side to make early lateral movements.

- The tongue presses outward as the cheeks press inward to keep food positioned between the gums during munching and chewing.

- *Munching* begins to change into true *chewing* because the jaw begins to move in lateral, diagonal, and rotational patterns (instead of only moving upwards and downwards).

- The tongue begins to move separately from the jaw in lateralizing and swallowing.

- The lips begin to remain closed during chewing.

- The sides, middle, and tip of the tongue begin to differentiate one from another in the process of collecting and swallowing lumpy food.

The jaw oscillates up-and-down in a munching pattern as babies begin to chew on food and everything else between six and nine months of age.

Children develop the oral stability necessary to suck from a standard straw by twelve months of age.

12 Months

Independent oral movements develop and babies begin to handle lumpy food. A wider variety of table foods that are coarsely chopped are introduced. Also:

- The tongue, cheeks, and lips learn to separate the parts of food that are ready to swallow from the lumpy parts that need to be chewed more.

- The tongue can move food to the side of the mouth and back to center again.

- The tongue tip now leads the tongue's movements.

- The lips are very active.

- A controlled bite through a soft cookie develops.

- Harder cookies can be eaten if the anterior teeth have emerged.

- The child can drink from a bottle, breast, cup, or straw.

- The suckling pattern has given way to the sucking pattern.

15 Months

Oral-motor skills for eating continue to refine as the child learns to handle foods that are more challenging in terms of texture, size, and shape:

- Chewing is refining in terms of timing.

- Coordination of food transfer improves.

- More diagonal and rotary movements are noted.

- The lips stabilize at the corners.

- The jaw stabilizes on the rim of the cup, thus allowing independent lip and tongue movements to develop for drinking.

- Tongue lateralization increasing.

- The tongue can move in all directions.

- The tip of the tongue elevates to the alveolar ridge.

18 Months

Oral-motor skills continue to refine as time passes and more foods are introduced:

- Chewing occurs with the lips closed or open.

- A closed-lips position prevents food from spilling out, however, chewing can be accomplished with the lips apart without spilling, meaning that the tongue is controlling food adequately enough itself to keep food inside the mouth.

- Jaw strength has improved enough for the child to bite through a hard cookie using a sustained bite.

- Swallowing occurs with easy lip closure.

- Tongue control increases and the tongue tip is very active.

2 Years

All the foundations for oral movement are set by two years of age:

- Chewing is comprised of vertical, diagonal rotary, and circular rotary jaw movements.

- The tongue moves independently in all directions.

- The tongue crosses the midline.

- The tongue is used to clean the lips and inner oral surfaces.

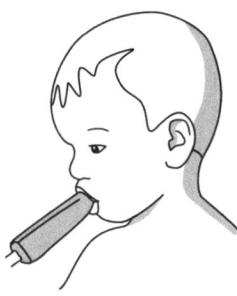

More foods are introduced and oral movements begin to refine by eighteen months of age.

Children acquire all foundational eating skills by two years of age.

- The tongue bowl configuration is integrated into all tongue movements.

- Biting is sustained and carefully graded through a variety of textures.

- Biting occurs without associated movements in the rest of the body.

- The suck is used on liquids.

- Long drinking sequences are employed.

- Drinking from an open cup without spillage is accomplished.

RESEARCH

The following selected studies explore the relationship between speech and feeding/swallowing. This body of research is expanding and becoming more sophisticated. Early studies focused mostly on the prevalence and co-occurrence of swallowing and speech problems. Newer more sophisticated equipment has allowed more recent studies to focus on fine differences between the oral movements used in speech and feeding.

- Fletcher, Casteel, and Bradley (1961) studied 1615 children and found that the prevalence of the tongue thrust swallow decreased gradually from 6 through 18 years of age. He also found that subjects with a tongue-thrust swallow were much more likely to have associated sibilant distortion than did subjects without this pattern.

- Ward, Malone, Jann, and Jann (1961) surveyed 24,657 school age children. They found 1025 with articulation deficit of which 432 were described as having atypical swallowing patterns with tongue thrust. They also studied speech, swallowing, gag, occlusion, and mouth breathing in 358 children in grades one through three. "The research indicates the emergence of a syndrome consisting of forward placement of tongue-tip sounds, tongue thrusting during the act of swallowing, and incipient malocclusion" (p. 340).

- Bell and Halle (1963) found that 82% of five- and six-year-old children used a thrusting pattern in swallowing. They also found that most (89–92%) of these children used dental or interdental tongue placement during production of the lingua-alveolar phonemes.

- Lewis and Counihan (1965) had nurses observe nearly 300 newborns and found that 97% of the babies had a tongue thrust swallow (now called the infantile suckle-swallow).

- Shriner (1966) reviewed the literature of the time and postulated that tongue thrusting is a normal pattern of development. He surmised that approximately 75% of elementary school children exhibit abnormal swallowing.

- Gibbs and Messerman (1972) studied jaw movements in adults during oral reading and eating tasks. They found that the jaw moves in a much larger range for eating than for speech in both the vertical and horizontal planes: "The maximum vertical opening was typically two to four times more for chewing than for speech" (p. 107). The jaw's lateral movements were as much as 0.7 inches during eating and less than 0.1 inch during speech.

- McGlone and Proffit (1973) found that clients with frontal lisps and reverse swallows had overall anterior tongue positioning. They also found that swallow patterns for those with lateral lisps tended to be "almost bizarre and strongly suggest overall poor coordination of tongue movements." They found that upward midline pressure of this group was stronger than the controls. They concluded that "the combination of speech and nonspeech data suggest that underlying the defective speech of children is an inability to use the muscles of the tongue properly" (p. 472).

- Mason and Proffit (1974) reviewed pertinent literature and concluded that tongue thrusting during the swallow is a normal stage: "Approximately 80% of children who have a tongue thrust and anterior open bite at age eight show improvement without therapy by age twelve" (p. 129). The authors of this landmark article recommended the following: (1) swallowing therapy is not indicated for children without speech or orthodontic problems, (2) swallowing therapy is not indicated before puberty, (3) swallowing therapy is most effective when combined with orthodontic treatment, (4) "when lisping and tongue thrusting or malocclusion coexist before puberty, we recommend initiating speech therapy in spite of concurrent problems… emphasizing phonetic placements…" (p. 129), (5) "for those older children with speech problems for whom orthodontic treatment for open bite is carried out, and in whom it is desirable to modify anterior resting posture of the tongue, the techniques of myofunctional therapy are useful. Articulation therapy techniques involving phonetic placement may also be particularly helpful in repositioning the tongue tip posteriorward" (p. 129).

- Rampp and Pannbacker (1978) reviewed aspects of the tongue thrust swallow and used the term *variation in swallowing*. This term points to the fact that not all of these deviant swallows occur because the tongue is thrusting forward. Some of these problems are lateral, and so forth.

- Dworkin and Culatta (1980) found no significant differences in tongue strength among children with normal speech, frontal lisp, tongue-thrust swallow, and open bite malocclusion. Their conclusion was that strength of the tongue has nothing to do with a frontal lisp or tongue-thrust swallow.

- Hanson and Barrett (1988) combined literature review and direct clinical experience to conclude that only one in ten children with tongue thrust problems have speech difficulty. They proposed that there is no causal relationship between speech and swallowing patterns.

- Moore, Smith, and Ringel (1988) studied jaw movements in speech and chewing and observed different muscle synergies across tasks. They believed that this indicated that there are two or more distinct coordinative systems involved in speech and chewing. They reminded SLPs that the main purpose of jaw movement in chewing is to generate upward force, and the main purpose of jaw movement in continuous speech is to move with high velocity and acceleration.

- Edwards and Harris (1990) reviewed literature and stated: "A comparison of the speech and dental literature suggests that, in many respects, jaw movement during speech appears to be more constrained than during mastication" (p. 550).

- Ostry, Vatikiotis-Bateson, and Gribble (1997) found that the jaw moves with greater range in eating than in speech. They also found that the jaw moves with less variation during mastication.

- Green, Moore, Higashikawa, and Steeve (2000) studied lip and jaw coordination during speech and noted that "features of lip and jaw coordination for sucking… are similar to those produced by the one- and two-year-olds in the present study during speech" (p. 252).

- Mizuno & Ueda (2005) found that neonates with a gestational age of 35–42 weeks who have low sucking pressure tend to have speech-language delays at 18 months of age.

- Steeve and Moore (2009) found that jaw trajectories are faster and more complex for babbling than for chewing in one child between 8 and 22 months of age. They surmised that chewing might be considered a gross and more primitive movement pattern than babbling in normal development.

- Steeve (2010) found that jaw movements in speech could not be predicted from jaw movements in feeding in one child aged 8–22 months of age. He also found that the jaw moves less during vowel babbling than it does during babbling that includes consonants.

- Poore and Barlow (2009) reviewed pertinent literature and noted that the suck is being used as a biomarker for oral feeding skills, and is also being considered as a biomarker of speech, cognitive, and learning development. They predicted that some day the suck might serve as an intervention point to prevent speech-language delays and disorders.

FEEDING ASSESSMENT CHECKLIST

Clients whose life and health are at risk as a result of eating and/or swallowing problems must be referred to a multidisciplinary team for a thorough examination of all factors that might be contributing, and a full eating/swallowing treatment program should ensue. Clients with articulation or motor speech disorders who do *not* have life-threatening eating/swallowing problems usually do not receive such a referral. Some of these clients will be referred to a certified orofacial myofunctional therapist for evaluation and treatment, but most will remain only in speech therapy. Therefore, speech-language pathologists need a simple checklist to identify minor eating/swallowing problems in their clients in order to identify potential activities for improvement within their own treatment sessions and to make appropriate outside referrals when necessary.

Bosley (1981) compiled a 15-item eating checklist for use with articulation clients and the present author has expanded it to create the more thorough checklist below. Readers familiar with feeding/swallowing therapy and orofacial myology will recognize many of the listed symptoms as indicative of a true eating/swallowing disorder. It is the present author's experience that the difference between clients with life-threatening feeding deficits and those with mild feeding problems seems to be largely a matter of degree. The problems are the same but the extent and impact are different.

Readers will also note that many of the items on the checklist below might describe any young eater. It is important to recognize that no one item on this checklist indicates that a client has an eating or swallowing problem. Diagnostic indicators must be considered together and patterns must be noted. For example, many young children are very picky eaters, but picky eating by itself is not necessarily indicative of a feeding disorder. Picky eating might be the first sign of the problem, however, and that fact would be reveled by administering and studying the rest of the checklist.

Therapists usually screen clients by observing them eat a snack or a regular meal or by observing them eat selected foods from a feeding supply cabinet. The checklist below can be used all in one session or scattered over the course of several. The checklist is for children two years of age and above who should be using all fundamental eating and swallowing patterns.

General Eating Behaviors

- The client is a picky eater and this behavior extends beyond typical childhood issues.

- The client is a very messy eater and this extends beyond an age when it would be expected to diminish.

Picky eating, using the fingers to hold food in the mouth, and very messy eating are normal behaviors that can be signs of skill deficit in older children and adults.

- The client avoids foods that require much mastication.

- The client chews stiff foods much longer than other children.

- The client stuffs the mouth with too much food and then does not manage it well.

- The client spits out his food bolus instead of swallowing it.

- The client chews only a few times and then swallows his food before it is completely masticated (the client is swallowing lumps of food instead of a thoroughly mashed product; gastrointestinal problems may result).

- The client uses his hands or fingers around the mouth to monitor or control the eating process and to keep food from falling out.

- The client makes loud smacking noises during chewing.

- The client makes loud gulping noises during swallowing.

- The client cannot suck through a straw.

- The client manages food clumsily.

- The client chokes on food periodically or regularly.

- The client makes faces while he eats. There is facial grimace or dimpling.

- The client licks the lips frequently.

Biting

- The client has difficulty using his incisors to bite off a piece of hard food (e.g., carrot sticks or pizza crust) in the absence of dental or occlusion problems.

- The client does not bite firm foods. Instead of biting through the food, he holds it between his upper and lower teeth and then he uses his hand to bend and break off a piece.

- The client bites with the molars instead of the incisors.

- The client avoids foods he cannot bite into.

- The client takes bites that are too large.

- The client takes miniscule bites of food as he "shaves" them off with his incisors.

Chewing

- The jaw does not move much as the client tries to chew; this limits food selections to purees and mushy foods.

- The client takes a bite of food and swallows it whole without chewing.

- The jaw moves only in the vertical plane (up-down) instead of in rotary movements as the client chews (the client is using the infantile *munching* pattern instead of the mature *chewing* pattern).

- Palpation of the masseters during chewing reveals little muscle action. (The fingers should feel a tightening and bulging of the masseters during each upward movement of the jaw during chewing. Absence of masseter action indicates that the client is using the infantile *munching* pattern instead of the mature *chewing* pattern.)

- The jaw protrudes too far forward while masticating.

- The jaw shifts too far to the left or right while masticating (more than 0.7 inch).

- The jaw habitually positions too low during the chewing process (the jaw never reaches a position where the lower teeth meet the upper teeth and only soft foods can be managed as a result).

- The client only masticates on one side of the mouth although examination of the teeth reveals no occlusion problems.

- The client chews in the front of the mouth, using the incisors and other front teeth instead of the molars.

- Malocclusion interferes with adequate chewing.

- Examination of an expelled bolus reveals that it is incompletely masticated.

Lip Movements

- The lips remain parted during chewing.

- The lips do not seal well and they allow food and liquid to seep out during chewing or swallowing.

- The lips and cheeks do not move adequately to push food particles medially for bolus formation.

- The lips tighten noticeably during the swallow.

- The lips protrude noticeably during the swallow.

- A protruding tongue pushes the lips forward during

or after the swallow.

- The lips are active during continuous drinking. (The lips should remain quiet and relatively unmoving during continuous drinking.)

Tongue Movements

- The tongue reaches forward outside of the mouth as food or drink approach it.

- The tongue does not transfer food to the molar area after it is bitten off or after a food bit is placed in the front of the mouth.

- The tongue does not transfer food from one side of the mouth to the other during mastication.

- The tongue presses against the front teeth during chewing and/or swallowing.

- The tongue protrudes between the anterior teeth during eating and/or swallowing.

- The sides of the tongue squeeze out between the lateral teeth during the swallow.

- The tongue tip remains low and hidden behind the mandibular (lower) incisors during eating and swallowing.

- The tongue does not bowl adequately to form a cohesive food bolus. The sides of the tongue do elevate and/or the middle does not lower.

- The tongue cannot hold the bolus up to and against the hard palate.

- If the lips are parted with the fingers during the swallow, liquid seeps out the front of the mouth because the tongue is not sealed against the palate around its perimeter. (This is a classic test of the reverse swallow.)

- The tongue positions under the cup during drinking.

- The tongue positions inside the cup during drinking.

Suctioning Movements

- The client does not suction well to aid in bolus formation.

After the Swallow

- The tongue protrudes between the anterior teeth after the swallow. (Many references refer to this as a "tongue thrust.")

- Food remains on the lips or pocketed between the teeth and cheeks after the swallow.

- Food remains on the tongue or palate after the swallow.

- The client swallows more than once on the same mouthful of food.

- The client swallows once, then spends time cleaning up around the mouth with the fingers, tongue, or lips, then swallows again. .

- The client uses his fingers to retrieve food bits left in the mouth after the swallow. He may suck these bits off his finger and then swallow again.

Seating

- The client's head is in an incorrect position during eating. He slouches forward, leans to one side, juts his head forward, or supports his head with his hands or with the tabletop while eating.

- The client cannot sit still during the eating process. He may continually fidget, get out of his chair, sit sideways in his chair, or stand while eating.

- The client is too active to sit quietly through a meal.

Other

- Excess saliva in the mouth causes a wet quality to the client's speech.

- The client drools: "Children who are unable to control their saliva have been found to have the greatest difficulty in the oral/voluntary phase of swallowing" (Arvedson & Brodsky, 1993, p. 393).

- The client demonstrates a hyper- or hypo-reactive gag reflex.

- The tongue appears heart-shaped because the tip is retracted or because the client has a short and restricting lingua frenum.

- The tongue appears boxy (the lateral margins are pulling medially).

- The mouth is habitually open (the jaw hangs low. The tongue may hang forward).

- There is a digit sucking, tooth grinding, tongue sucking, or other oral habit.

THERAPY PROCEDURES

Speech-language pathologists who integrate the treatment of feeding, swallowing, orofacial myology and speech do so in order to develop *oral movement schemes*. A scheme is a system, pattern, or organization that develops as the result of repeated activities that are similar but different. Therapists incorporate feeding and speech activities together to develop patterns of oral movement that benefit both. This working theory is open to debate, but many therapists find the process very useful therapeutically, especially for clients with motor speech disorders and/or cognitive deficit.

Snacking Activities

The following methods are designed for articulation therapy only. The clients of concern in this manual already can eat and their lives and health are not at risk because of feeding issues. These activities are not for starting from scratch as one would with a newborn or an older non-oral feeder. They also do not include the full breadth of activities that are included in a complete feeding, swallowing, or orofacial myofunctional program.

These activities are designed to boost existing skills so that jaw, lip, and tongue movements can achieve maturity during the feeding process. Activities are intended to teach mature skills and to encourage the client to utilize them each time he eats. The present author uses the term *snacking activities* to describe these undertakings. This term differentiates this work from a full feeding, swallowing, dysphagia, or orofacial myology therapy program.

The snacking activities described below are not intended to replace any other auditory, linguistic, cognitive, traditional, or phonological methods being employed to stimulate sound production, and they may be only a very small part of any one individual articulation session.

Logistics

The amount of time devoted to the eating process will vary from one client to another and from one session to the next depending upon the perceived needs of the client. Consider the following examples of how snacking activities might be included in three different 30-minute articulation therapy sessions.

- *Example 1:* The client might eat three crackers in front of a mirror and be taught how to fully extend his tongue tip to clean the entire mouth of all food particles after the swallow. This activity might take five minutes at the beginning of the speech session.

- *Example 2:* The client might suck on an ice cube, and he might be taught how to keep his lips closed while doing so. This activity might be used as a thirty-second reward or break between every five speech sound productions.

- *Example 3:* The client might eat a series of gummy bears and be taught how to bowl his tongue to cradle each one while doing so. The client might eat 10 gummy bears throughout the course of the 30-minute speech session.

Foods & Other Materials

Morris and Klein (2000) suggested that the foods to be used for clients with minimal feeding involvement should include foods with multiple textures, foods that require extended chewing, foods that can be served in many sensory variations, and foods that encourage playful exploration. The present author recommends that some or all of the following foods be on hand for snacking activities:

- *Soft foods:* Such as cheese slices or bread.
- *Crunchy foods:* Such crackers, hard cookies, or pretzels.
- *Tiny food bits:* Such as cereal pieces or raisins.
- *Spreadable foods:* Such as peanut butter, cream cheese, soft cheese, syrup, or honey.
- *Chewy foods:* Such as gummy bears, fruit roll-ups, licorice, or meat sticks.
- *Purees:* Such as yogurt, pudding, or applesauce.
- *Cold foods:* Such as ice cream, frozen bananas, ice pops, or ice cubes.
- *Vegetable sticks:* Such as carrots or celery.
- *Fruit slices:* Such as apples, pears, or bananas.
- *Thin liquids:* Such as water or thin juices (apple, grape).
- *Thick liquids:* Such as milk shakes, thick soups, or juices with thickener added.

Other Materials

Include a mirror that stands alone or is fastened to the wall, a variety of cups and spoons, straws, an eye or medicine dropper, and appropriate seating arrangements.

Allergy Alert

Do not use foods to which the client may be allergic. Include questions about allergies in the initial assessment.

SNACKING ACTIVITIES

Snacking activities are designed to achieve certain objectives and these objectives are selected from the individual elements of the mature eating process. The present author has identified 28 individual objectives that might be targeted, and these have been used to organize the activities described below. Readers trained in feeding therapy, swallowing therapy, or orofacial myofunctional therapy will recognize all the activities described below. Most of them can be done directly in therapy or they can be taught to parents and other caregivers to use at home. Consider filming the client as he eats so he can observe these things more objectively.

The emphasis of these activities is on teaching oral movement patterns and establishing mature eating habits. They are not intended to build oral strength or to teach new phonemes. They are intended to improve general eating skills for the following reason: "Good eating and drinking skills encourage the best mouth development" (Bahr, 2010, p. 20). Not every client needs to learn every step. Therapists select those skills that are absent from the client's eating repertoire or that are being done incorrectly.

Arrange appropriate seating for therapist and client.

1. Maintain Appropriate Oral Rest When Not Eating

Teach the client to attain and maintain normal oral rest position when he is not eating. (For information about the oral rest position, see Chapter 14 on oral stability.)

2. Sit Appropriately While Eating

Teach the client to sit appropriately while eating: "Proper positioning of the patient is essential to promote normal swallowing" (Groher, 1984, p. 143). Seating needs to be arranged so that the client is comfortably upright. Chair and table arrangements are preferable. The client's hips should be positioned back in the chair at a 90-degree angle and the feet should be planted firmly on the floor, stool, or other footrest. The tabletop should be level with the client's midsection so that his forearms can rest comfortably atop it. The head should be held flexibly at midline. The chin should not jut forward but be tucked downward slightly. The client should not have to look up to see the adult feeder's face, therefore, the client needs to sit high or the adult needs to sit low. The client is taught to hold his head up independently and without the support of his hands. Clients who cannot achieve good sitting with an upright head position should be referred to a motor specialist for further assessment.

3. Maintain a Quiet Mouth While Anticipating Food

Teach the client to keep his mouth still and at rest while waiting for food to approach. Use a phrase like "quiet mouth" to cue this posture. Teach the client to wait to open his mouth until just before food approaches.

4. Bring Food to the Mouth at Midline

Food pieces and spoons carrying food should be presented to the mouth at midline. The clients of this discussion all should be feeding themselves and most activities will entail them doing so. However, there are times when the adult will present food to the client's mouth during these activities to vary the activities and to challenge particular movements. Some clients habitually present spoons and finger foods to only one side of the mouth. In this case it is suggested that foods be brought to the mouth to the left, right, and midline in order to break the habit. Once the client has begun to explore food entering from all sides, then work to establish a consistent midline presentation. Some clients will need to be taught how to hold the spoon or food correctly so that it can be presented squarely to the own mouth at midline. The tip of a spoon should enter first.

5. Bite Into Firm Food with Strength at the Incisors

Teach the client to present solid foods to the incisors (not the molars) and to bite firmly into them until a snap or crunch is heard and a bite is obtained. Begin with softer foods and work toward foods of increasing firmness so that biting strength increases over time. Tell the client to "bite hard" on the food, teach him to listen for the sound of the successful bite, and praise him for doing so. Tell him, "You got it!" and "Your mouth is getting strong." Do not allow him to hold the food between his teeth and then bend and break the food instead of biting through it.

6. Bite an Appropriate Size Food Chuck

Teach the client to monitor the size of his bites. If he takes bites that are too big and unmanageable, or he stuffs his mouth, teach him to take smaller bites so that they can be handled inside the mouth with the lips closed. Use humor to discuss what a person looks like when they have too much food in the mouth. Use negative practice to watch the unpleasant results of taking too large a bite. According to Morris and Klein (2000), many clients stuff because they are in a hurry or because they have oral-tactile hypersensitivity. Help these clients slow down or help them normalize sensitivity.

7. Transfer Food From Midline to One Side

Teach the client to use his tongue tip to push the food from midline to one side or the other for chewing. Have him watch in the mirror as he learns to shift the food and as he chews with the molars on one side and then the other.

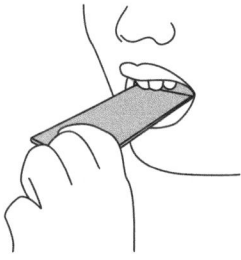

Teach the client to bite an appropriate size chunk of food with the incisors at midline.

Use resistance to teach the tongue to lateralize in this way. The client may use the middle of his tongue arched high to lateralize food at first but over time he should learn to use his tongue tip to make these transfers.

8. Transfer Food From Side to Side

Teach the client how to use his tongue to move food from the molars on one side to the molars on the other side, transferring smoothly through the midline. Teach him to do this throughout the chewing process. The client may use the middle of his tongue arched high to do this at first but over time he should learn to use his tongue tip to make these transfers.

Note: Many people prefer to chew on one side or the other and this is considered normal. This activity is not designed to force bi-lateral chewing; rather, the purpose of the activity is to help the tongue develop a full range of movement left and right, especially at the tip, and to differentiate tongue movements from jaw movements. It is also intended to help the client develop oral sensory awareness of the mouth on both sides.

9. Drink From a Cup Appropriately

Teach the client to use a cup correctly. Use a regular firm cup. Do not use a flimsy paper cup or a sippy cup with a spout or a straw for this activity; use a sippy cup with in indented opening in the lid, a *nosey cup*, or a *cut-out cup*. Teach the client to maintain a quiet mouth while waiting for the cup to approach the lips. Teach him to hold the head at midline and to tip the head forward slightly to meet the cup (slight chin tuck). Teach him to brace the rim of the cup on his lower lip, and not on his lower teeth or tongue. Teach him to keep his tongue inside his mouth, behind the rim of the cup, and to not stick the tongue into or under the cup. Consider beginning with a thick liquid or puree to teach control, then move on to thinner liquids. (For a more detailed discussion of cup variations, see Morris & Klein, 2000).

10. Teach Continuous Drinking

Teach the client to place and to maintain his tongue tip on the alveolar ridge during continuous drinking from a cup.

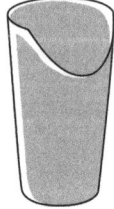

A cut-out cup can be used to teach drinking.

Teach the client to drink appropriately from a cup and a straw.

11. Drink From a Straw Appropriately

Use a cup with a separate straw, a cup with a flip-up straw, or a sippy cup with an indented opening in the lid into which a straw can be placed. Teach the client to hold the head at midline and to tip the head forward slightly to meet the straw (slight chin tuck). Teach him to place the straw to the lips at midline and to place his lips gently but firmly around the straw to grasp it. Teach him not to crush the straw and to put only about ¼ inch of the straw into the mouth between the lips. Teach him to suck the liquid in from this position. Explore both thick and thin drinks. Consider using straws of various shapes and sizes to challenge greater lip and tongue control (see Rosenfeld-Johnson, 2001).

12. Chew in a Rotary Fashion

Teach the client to unlock his habitual up-down munching pattern by encouraging him to move the jaw in more directions. Have the client make big circular (rotary) chewing motions. Show him how cows chew their cud as an example. Progress from foods that are easy to chew to that are more resilient and difficult. Expect the client's movements to get bigger at first and smaller over time.

13. Masticate Thoroughly

Teach the client to chew harder and longer if he does not chew long or hard enough to completely pulverize his food. Do this with increasingly firm foods. Also, use resistance downward on the jaw to encourage it to pull up for stronger chewing. Teach him to perceive when the crushed food has turned into a soft mushy pulp. Teach him to use his fingers to feel the tightening in his masseters during each upward movement of the jaw during chewing. Use gum as an alternative activity to teach sustained chewing over a longer period of time. A mirror is very helpful during chewing activities.

14. Maintain Lip Closure While Chewing & Swallowing

Teach the client to keep his lips closed throughout the entire eating and swallowing process, except when the mouth opens to accept food. Teach him that chewing with the lips open is impolite because it forces others to see the food being mashed up, but also teach him that it is acceptable to part the lips and open the mouth farther when necessary, as when attempting to retrieve popcorn bits stuck in difficult places. Use negative practice to discover the unpleasantness of open-lips chewing, for example challenge him to eat an entire cracker or cookie with the lips parted so he can see what it looks like in the mirror and so he can become aware of how food particles spill out the mouth. Eat purees from a spoon or use a lollipop like a spoon to practice closing the lips firmly. Light touch to the lips can help with awareness of closure: "Lightly brush the lips with your finger… to maintain lip closure during the feeding process" (Stainback & Healy, 1982, p. 42).

15. Keep the Tongue Back & Away From the Front Teeth

"Explain to the patient that there is one important principle to be remembered while eating. At no time during eating should the tongue ever touch the front teeth, for any reason" (Hanson & Mason, 2003, p. 273). This may seem a little excessive, however, it is a reoccurring theme in myofunctional therapy. Keep the tongue back as food approaches the mouth, as a bite is taken, as the food is chewed with the lips closed, and so forth.

Teach the client to keep his lips closed while chewing and swallowing.

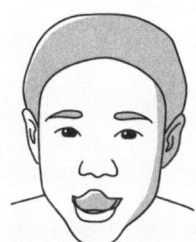

Teach the client to use the tongue to gather all remaining food particles both inside and outside the mouth.

16. Gather Food with the Tongue

Have the client learn to pay attention as he gathers food particles into a bolus. Have him eat a dry food such as a cracker or cookie. Teach the client to stretch the tongue tip in all directions inside and outside the mouth in order to gather all the bits. Teach him to swallow again to clear the mouth, and/or give him a few sips of water or juice to completely clear the mouth. Teach him to appreciate the look and feel of a completely cleared mouth. Logemann (1983) used flexible licorice whips to teach food manipulation with the tongue before using individual food pieces. Clients with a short lingua frenulum may have limitations in this area and should be referred for appropriate assessment.

17. Gather Food by Moving the Lips & Cheeks

Repeat step 16 to teach the client how to move and press his cheeks and lips against his teeth in ways that gather the remaining food bits. Teach the client to swallow several times in order to clear the mouth, and/or give him a few sips of water or juice to completely clear the mouth. Teach him to appreciate the look and feel of a completely cleared mouth. Also: "Hide pieces of cookie or cheese in the cheek pockets. Encourage the child to find them by pushing the pieces to the center of the mouth with the cheek" (Morris & Klein, 2000, p. 435). The SMILE program recommends using a lollipop or sucker in the mouth to teach more active cheek movement (Merkel-Walsh, 2002). Place the candy inside the mouth against the inner surface of the cheek. Have the client use his cheek muscles to press medially against the candy. Repeat on both sides.

18. Gather Food & Liquid by Suctioning

Repeat the activity described above and teach the client how to suction the remaining food bits. Also, teach suctioning with an eyedropper. Use the eyedropper to deliver about 2 cc of icy cold liquid between the client's closed lips. Teach the client to suction on the dropper as the drops are squeezed out. Over time, eliminate the squeeze and ask the client to suction out the drop without it. Teach the client to suction his saliva this way too, especially if he has a co-occurring problem of saliva management and drooling.

19. Form the Bolus

The SLP should describe the bolus to the client and show him how to form one with her tongue. It can be unpleasant for a child to look into an adult's mouth, so be a little playful with this so he can get through the awkwardness. This bolus formation activity will reveal whether the client has pulverized the food enough to form it. If not, continue to teach firm chewing and food transfer. More and more efficient chewing will crush the food better for the bolus. More and more efficient food transferring will mix more saliva into the mass to form a better bolus. Several things

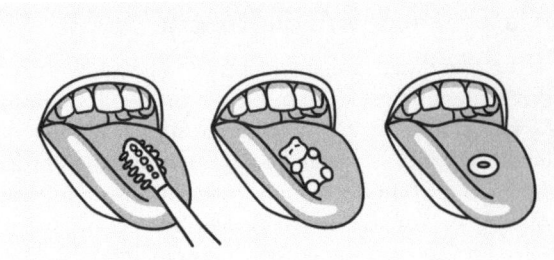

Use a Nuk® dipped in puree, a gummy bear, or a cereal piece to teach the client how to hold a bolus.

can be done if the bolus cannot be formed because the food is causing too much saliva production: Make sure not to use sweet food, have the client take smaller bites, teach him to keep his lips closed, teach him to suction better, focus on more swallowing activities, and give him a sip of liquid between trials to clear the mouth of excess food particles.

20. Cradle the Bolus

Teach the client to hold the bolus in place on his tongue as he watches in a mirror. This will allow him time to perceive the position. Logemann (1983) recommended having the client practice pushing the bolus up to the palate with the tongue. She also recommended teaching the client to manage his bolus by moving the tongue left and right while holding it. A Nuk® dipped in a puree can be used for this purpose. Also, use an individual gummy bear, mint, cereal piece, or small candy with clients who are at no risk of choking.

21. Elevate the Jaw to Initiate the Swallow

Teach the client to initiate his swallow by clenching his molars gently but firmly together. This allows the tongue to sit high enough for a correct swallow and it keeps the entire tongue within the upper dental arch. "Proper jaw control during feeding enhances the chances of correct swallowing patterns" (Stainback & Healy, 1982, p. 38). Teach the client to feel the contraction of the masseters as he clenches. "Put your hand just in front of your ear where you were shown to find the chewing muscle. Now bite your teeth together hard. You should be able to feel that muscle move. This is the muscle that should do the work when you swallow" (Ehrlich, 1970, p. 118–119). Refer to orthodontia if occlusion appears to interfere with this step.

22. Stabilize the Tongue at the Back-Lateral Margins to Initiate the Swallow

Teach the client to stabilize the tongue in the back with the back-lateral margins up against the palate to set the tongue into correct relationship with the palate when starting the swallow. (For details, see Chapter 14 on oral stability.)

23. Elevate the Tongue Tip to the Alveolar Ridge to Initiate the Swallow

Classic orofacial myology teaches clients to position the tongue tip up against the alveolar ridge to set the tongue into position for the swallow: "Patients are first taught to raise the tongue tip to 'the spot' against the alveolar ridge. This is the new resting place for the tongue tip and is its location as a swallow begins" (Hanson & Mason, 2003, p. 259). It is now known that the tongue tip elevates to the alveolar ridge while maintaining back-lateral stability. Therefore, first teach back-lateral stability (step 21) and then teach the lingua-alveolar position (step 22).

24. Lift the Bolus

Teach the client to maintain his tongue in the horseshoe shape as he lifts the bolus to the palate. This will seal the perimeter of the tongue against the palate for swallowing.

25. Engage the Stripping Action

Begin this step once the client can elevate the jaw, situate the tip of the tongue against the palate, and close the lips. Teach the client to elevate the tongue just posterior to the tip to start the stripping action and to elevate the middle of the tongue sequentially from front-to-back: "The patient learns to squeeze the dorsum of the tongue against the palate, with the tip of the tongue remaining on the spot" (Hanson & Mason, 2003, p. 259). Practice this movement with an empty mouth first. Then use purees and sips of liquid.

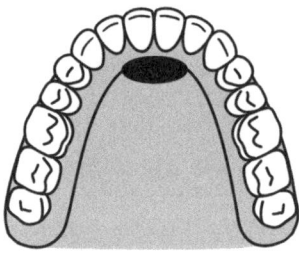

Classic orofacial myology begins by teaching the client to place the tongue tip on "the spot."

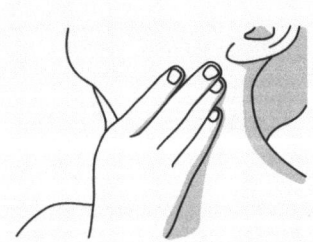

Teach the client to understand the swallow by feeling its movement with her own fingers.

Use a mirror to check for unswallowed food particles.

26. Become Aware of the Swallow Reflex

Help the client notice when his swallow reflex occurs. The SLP should use fingers to feel the reflex first by placing fingers on the crook of his neck and feeling the muscle action as he swallows. Then teach the client to feel his own neck during his swallow.

Alternately, Logemann (1983) recommended using a cold laryngeal mirror to help the client become aware of his swallow reflex. Touch the base of the anterior faucial pillars with the mirror: "Light contact is repeated 5–10 times… It is unlikely that an actual swallow will be triggered. Rather, the purpose of the exercise is to heighten the [client's] sensitivity of the reflex" (Logemann, 1983, p. 136).

It should be noted that one study demonstrated no changes in swallowing movements when cold stimuli was applied on a biweekly schedule to patients who had multiple strokes and dysphagia (Rosenbek et al., 1991). The reader is reminded that this method is being recommended in this chapter simply to increase awareness of a swallow that already exists, not to stimulate an absent swallow.

27. Notice Unswallowed Food Particles

Use a mirror to help the client discover food particles that remain on his face, lips, tongue, palate, and inner cheek walls after swallowing. Point out the messiness in a gentle way that does not break rapport or shame the client. Teach the client to take smaller bites so he can manage the food better. Teach him to pay attention while he chews and to keeps his lips closed. Teach him to gather the food particles more diligently and again teach him to appreciate the look and feel of a completely cleared mouth. Teach him that it is normal to be a little messy while eating and teach him how to use a napkin.

28. Return to Oral Rest After the Swallow

Teach the client to return to oral rest position after the mouth is cleared of all food particles.

APPLICATION TO DROOLING

All of the methods of this chapter have application to the client who drools to excess. In the final analysis, a drooling problem is a swallowing problem; the client does not swallow often enough and he doesn't swallow well enough. Frequency of swallowing is increased by normalizing his oral-tactile sensitivity so he can begin to feel when he needs to swallow, and by employing simple behavior management procedures to train him to swallow more often. Skill in swallowing is improved by using all the methods described above, especially number 18. Habituate the spontaneous swallow by using the eyedropper once every 90 seconds during any 10-minute activity. Fade the dropper over time as the client learns to initiate his own swallow without it. The client may need to learn how to make a better bolus and how to swallow it completely. All of these activities should be structured in such a way that the client becomes more conscious of the whole process.

SUMMARY

Eating and swallowing activities are integrated into articulation and motor speech therapy when the SLP predicts that the client may benefit from developing oral movement schemes. Specific skills are taught and applied to feeding, saliva management, and speech.

19

The Tools of Speech Movement Training

Using objects to teach respiration, phonation, resonation, and articulation movements

"Party horns… blow ticklers… bubbles… straws… Items like these are being used across America to treat a wide range of communication disorders… [This] has elicited spirited debate (to put it mildly) among SLPs and communication scientists."

– Thomas W. Powell, 2008a

This chapter describes how objects are being used to teach speech movements by speech-language pathologists today. It reveals how the use of tools in articulation and motor speech training has been a standard element of speech therapy since before the Traditional Era and that Van Riper himself used and advocated this process as part of the phonetic placement method. Practicing therapists began to call these methods *oral-motor techniques* in the 1980s as their knowledge of oral function expanded through new discoveries being made in feeding development, orofacial myology, and dysphagia therapy. By the 1990s, and when the evidence-based practice model hit the profession by storm, researchers began to decry the use of these methods in articulation therapy for lack of evidence. Those who spoke against them dumped them into

a new category they created called the *non-speech oral-motor exercise*. Despite ample warnings and the new atmosphere of doubt, practicing SLPs in the United States have continued to use these methods in the clinic, and they have sustained discussion about them in continuing education programs, and in articulation therapy handbooks (e.g., Bleile, 2006; Secord et al., 2007), and in online discussion groups. The new controversy over these basic Van Riper methods has caused much heartache in the field. This chapter attempts to set the record straight by explaining where the idea to use tools in therapy came from and by describing why and how SLPs use them. A catalog of sample tools comprises the bulk of this chapter.

BACKGROUND

Where did the idea to use objects to train speech movements come from? Who first advocated these practices? Is this a modern idea without historical backing? The fact is that the use of objects to teach speech movement is not a new idea. Van Riper named these as part of the "old traditional methods" (1947, p. 185) and he wrote that they had been around for hundreds of years. Van Riper discussed the use of tools in what he named the *phonetic placement method* (emphasis added by the present author):

"For centuries, speech correctionists have used diagrams,

Many SLPs use tools to teach oral movements and positions for speech sound productions just as Van Riper recommended.

applicators, and *instruments* to ensure appropriate tongue, jaw, and lip placement. [These] phonetic placement methods are indispensable tools in the speech correctionist's kit… Every available device should be used to make the student understand clearly what positions of tongue, jaw, and lips are to be assumed" (Van Riper, 1954, p. 236–8).

Van Riper explained that instruments are used in the process of phonetic placement, however, many articulation and phonology textbooks have downplayed and even eliminated the importance of using such instruments. New textbooks have focused instead on the verbal description as the essence of phonetic placement. For example, Bernthal and Bankson (2004) explained the phonetic placement method this way:

"When a client is unable to imitate a target sound, the clinician typically begins to cue or instruct the client regarding where to place his or her articulators to produce a particular sound. This type of instruction is called phonetic placement" (p. 300).

The phrase "cue or instruct" in this context sounds like a verbal cue that can be translated simply as "tell the client what to do." But that is not what phonetic placement means. These highly respected and honorable professors have overlooked Van Riper's original point in their otherwise wonderful and thorough text. They, like so many others, have ignored the important role that objects played in Van Riper's original descriptions of phonetic placement activities.

Van Riper's original writing clearly goes beyond the use of cues and verbal instruction. He said that phonetic placement is the process of using "every available device" to guide oral movement. The 1947 edition of Van Riper's book mentions the use of 22 such objects including tongue depressors, toothpicks, matchsticks, pencils, sponges, candy, sugar, tooth props, wedges, fingers, feathers, small tubes, and more. He said that objects don't need to be used if a client can produce a phoneme correctly when given an auditory and visual model alone, but that objects *must* be employed when simple model-and-imitate methods prove unsuccessful.

Van Riper devoted several pages to the use of tools in phonetic placement in the early editions of his text but apparently he felt clumsy in their use: "In our experience, they are more dramatic than useful" (1947, p. 187). Remember that Van Riper believed that ear training was the most important aspect of any regular articulation program. However, in that same paragraph, he said that objects must be employed when ear training alone fails. Van Riper wrote, "…when the stimulation method fails, they must be used" (1947, p. 186). Meaning that, in cases of persistent articulation error, and especially when the client had a "clumsy tongue" (a motor speech disorder), tools must be employed to teach specific oral movements.

Van Riper discussed the use of objects in all editions of his book from 1939 onward. By the time phonological

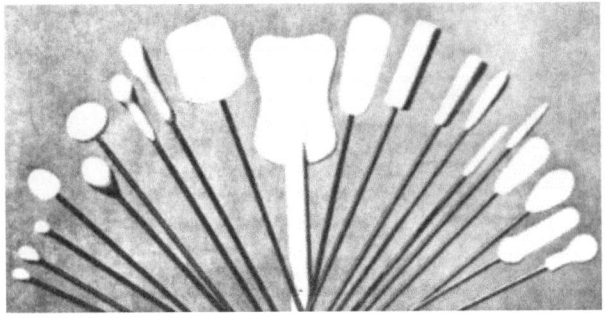

French phonetic placement tools, Borel-Maisonny, 1965.

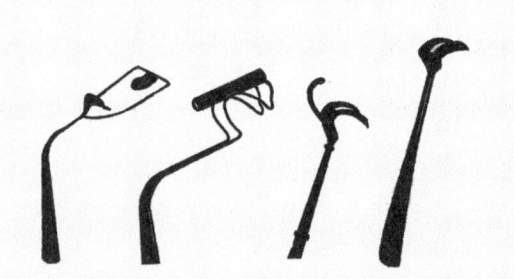

Phonetic placement tools Van Riper called "curious wire contrivances," 1925.

theory took hold in the profession, however, his textbook changed. According to Van Riper's introduction to the 1978 edition, the text changed from a collection of therapy methods to a simple introductory manual. Virtually all Van Riper's notes about his use of tools were dropped in that edition and onward. As a result, many SLP students since have graduated without an introduction to this most fundamental concept, and any discussion of tools in articulation therapy now is treated as a new idea.

To understand this history more deeply, Marshalla (2012a, 2012b) did a literature review of the phonetic placement tools that were recommended in 14 articulation textbooks published during the first half of the 20th century, including four of Van Riper's. She identified 86 different objects that were being used to stimulate correct speech movements during that period as represented in those books. These texts were published before the widespread use of plastic; therefore, named items were constructed mostly of wood, paper, metal, glass, plant materials, rubber, leather, and other animal products. They included such diverse articles as rubber tubes, rubber balls, tissue paper, toothpicks, tongue depressors, orange sticks, pencils, paper, cotton balls, Ping-Pong® (table tennis) balls, lollipops, tongue depressors, wooden matches, nasal bulbs, peanut butter, trumpets, sponges, and more. Also included were a set of wire tools developed by Borden and Busse (1925) that Van Riper called "curious wire contrivances" (Van Riper, 1947, p. 186).

European Origins

The tradition of using objects in articulation therapy came to the United States from Europe at the turn of the last century. Alexander Graham Bell's family of elocutionists moved to the United States from Scotland, and they used what they called a "manipulator" (Bell, 1906). Bell's father, Melville, said that his manipulator was a letter opener but that any similar object could be used.

Two texts from the early 20th century that Van Riper recommended were *Stuttering and Lisping* by E. W. Scripture (1912) and *Speech Correction* by R. C. Borden and A. C. Busse (1925). Scripture was an American professor who had traveled to Berlin to study the most modern speech methods being used there are the time. Borden and Busse were professors in New York City who worked with a huge European immigrant community. These books describe how they used tools with a diverse population of children and adults with acquired, habitual, second language, and medical speech problems.

In the 1960s, Suzanne Borel-Maissonny described a set of tools being used to teach speech movements in France (Borel-Maissonny, 1965). The set consisted of 24 probes made of metal and, later, of plastic. Each probe was comprised of a long thin handle with a shape on the end, those being balls and paddles of various sizes, forms, and widths. These tools were still being used in the 1980s as described by Bosley:

> *"Speech pathologists in France, called orthophonists, carry around with them a tool kit with all sorts and shapes of oral probes for pushing the tongue around and for increasing awareness of tactile sensation in the mouth"* (Bosley, 1981, p. 57).

United States

By the 1990s, the use of tools to teach oral movement for clients with articulation and motor speech disorders was being discussed along with many other methods for speech and feeding therapy under the broad heading of *oral-motor techniques* (e.g., Marshalla, 1992a, 1992b, 1992c; Rosenfeld-Johnson, 1992; Boshart, 1998). Since then, these tools have been tossed into the basket called *non-speech oral-motor exercises* (e.g., Powell, 2008a, 2008b) and this is where the trouble began. These ideas had been eliminated from textbooks in articulation and phonology for so long that newer generations of clinicians and researchers were no longer familiar with them. Speech researchers began to scorn these ideas because it was assumed they were new and were not being researched in the present day. There were also indications of misuse (Lof 2008; Lof & Watson, 2008). But textbooks from the Traditional Era are filled with these ideas.

Many "how to" articulation manuals published in the United States continued to recommend them as well. For example, Secord et al. (2007) and Bleile (2006) are therapy manuals that contain scattered examples of how to use tools in the process of phonetic placement. These books are quite popular among SLPs, and they are also used as supplemental texts in the training of university students. Two examples from each manual are offered below. These represent classic phonetic placement methods that can be traced back to some of the 20th century's earliest publications:

• *Bleile on teaching /l/:* "Touch the student's alveolar ridge with a tongue depressor, peanut butter, or lollipop to indicate place of production for [l]" (Bleile, 2006, p. 146).

• *Bleile on teaching /r/:* "Use a strip of paper, a feather, or the hand held in front of the student's mouth while you produce several glides or liquids to draw attention to the 'flowing' quality and continuous nature of the sounds. Alternately, tape a small paper flower on the end of a pencil and encourage the student to move the flower in the wind" (Bleile, 2006, p. 216).

• *Secord et al. on teaching /k/:* "Use a tongue depressor to guide the tongue toward a backward movement. [Also] rub a moist cotton swab on a flavored food, such as a Life Saver®... Then touch the soft palate near the second molars with the swab and

Wood Tools

New Tools

Original phonetic placement tools made of wood have been replaced by sanitizable ones.

ask the client to raise the back of the tongue to the roof of the mouth to form a seal" (Secord et al., 2007, p. 30–31).

- *Secord et al. on teaching /s/:* "Have the client close his teeth and direct the airstream for /s/ through a straw" (Secord et al., 2007, p. 38).

An Explosion of Ideas

The introduction of plastic, vinyl, and silicone to the manufacture of household objects has caused a virtual explosion in the number of items that might be utilized for phonetic placement. SLPs practicing in the 21st century can chose from scores of objects in order to follow Van Riper's early directive to use every available device to manipulate the articulators. For example, Van Riper used toothpicks, matchsticks, pencils, and tongue depressors to adjust jaw height, while now therapists can use safe and sanitary plastic bite sticks that are manufactured in various sizes.

Objects are being used to teach the movements and positions of any and all phoneme targets. One can use a kazoo to teach a toddler how to produce voice for a basic vowel, or an Rabbit Buddy to teach a school student to curl his tongue tip up and back for a retroflex /r/. These are the types of objects that are being used in articulation and motor speech therapy all throughout the United States and they are cataloged in the bulk of this chapter below.

Would Van Riper Approve?

It is possible that pre-phonology practitioners who taught and wrote about articulation therapy would have been thrilled to have the cornucopia of synthetic objects now available for teaching phonetic placement. It is unfortunate that these procedures have been ignored in textbooks, written against in journal articles, and re-named non-speech oral-motor exercises. The recent war over this process has caused much confusion within the profession. Tool applications were never intended to replace articulation therapy methods nor were they intended to compete with the methods of phonological therapy. SLPs who use objects in articulation and motor speech therapy are simply using new tools to carry out Van Riper's original teachings about the classic European method of phonetic placement.

Young & Severe

Nowhere has the use of tools been advocated for speech training more avidly than in the school or clinic where very young children and those with cognitive, sensorimotor, and neuromuscular deficits are the norm. Some of these clients simply cannot understand instructions about speech movements and others do not have the motor skills to perform them. Phonetic placement methods using objects often are the norm for these clients especially if feeding and swallowing skills are also impaired.

To understand why, simply consider how one might

teach a client to produce a phoneme if he could not understand the directions or if he could not move his speech mechanism in the required ways. For example, how would a client "Round your lips" if he doesn't understand what the word "round" means? And how would a client "Lift up the back of your tongue" if he did not know he had a tongue in the first place? These dilemmas greet the practicing SLP every day because their clients are younger and more severely impaired than they were in Van Riper's day. Today's caseload cries out for the tools of phonetic placement and SLPs use these tools when clients need them.

Are These Non-Speech Oral-Motor Exercises?

It is not appropriate to call the use of these tools *non-speech oral-motor exercises.* There is nothing "non-speech" about them and they are not "exercises." As summarized above, these are expanded descriptions of phonetic placement methods that have been around for hundreds of years. It is important to note that these methods are not to be used as a sole means of stimulating new phonemes. The use of these items without incorporating them into the process of good articulation therapy may have been the spark that lit the passionate flame burning against them in the first place, but no writer of these methods ever seems to have suggested that they be used alone. Instead, virtually every writer who has discussed the use of such tools has stressed that they are to be used within the context of a complete speech-training program, not instead of it. Compare how Van Riper (1958), Marshalla (1992a), and Rosenfeld-Johnson (2001) expressed this basic idea:

> "The therapist… is attempting to give the case the appropriate location and formation. As soon as this has been achieved, the therapist stimulates the case with the correct sound" (Van Riper, 1958, p. 147).

> "One does not eliminate other aspects of a client's

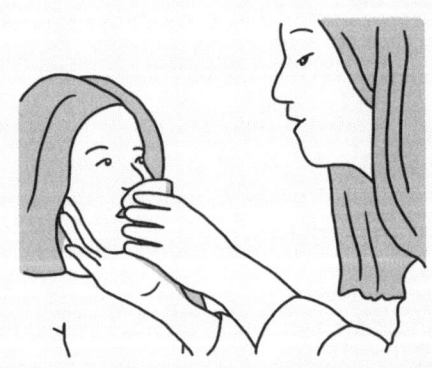

Using oral control and a cup to stimulate lip rounding for vowels.

articulation or phonological program... One utilizes [these] techniques as one engages in a program of articulation and phonological treatment" (Marshalla, 1992a, p. 16).

"It is a tactile teaching technique which supplements traditional therapy... Please remember that the exercises in this manual do not replace anything you are using now" (Rosenfeld-Johnson, 2001, p. 1).

PROCESS

The rest of this chapter is devoted to the tools of phonetic placement training presented in (mostly) alphabetical order, but first, a few important words about how to use them. The following short sections discuss sanitary procedures, safety, allergies, social appropriateness, and the goals of this work.

Sanitary Procedures

SLPs need to follow sanitary procedures at all times when touching a client in, on, or around the mouth with the hands or other objects.

Sanitizing the hands

1. Wash the hands with a sanitizing soap.
2. Dry the hands with a paper towel and dispose of it, or dry with a cloth towel and place in the laundry hamper to be washed later.
3. Slip hands into protective gloves.
4. Work with the client.
5. De-glove and dispose of gloves (one use only).
6. Wash, rinse, and dry the hands again.

Sanitizing Tools and Toys

Sanitize or discard objects that have been used in, on, or around the mouth. Use a sanitizing solution and follow its instructions or adhere to the following inexpensive guidelines:

1. Wash the object using regular dish soap and water.
2. Rinse thoroughly.
3. Soak for five minutes in a solution made of household bleach and water at a ratio of 1:10 (bleach to water).
4. Rinse thoroughly again.
5. Allow to air dry.
6. Place in a clean container and store for re-use.

Handling Tools and Toys in Sanitary Ways

Adhere to the following guidelines when handling objects that are used in, on, or around the mouth:

- *Wood, paper, cardboard, sponge, and cotton objects:* Use once and discard.
- *Plastic, rubber, vinyl, silicone and metal objects:* Use once and then sanitize before re-using.
- *Any object with interior surfaces that cannot be cleaned easily (e.g, straws, tubes, whistles, horns):* Use once and give to the client to keep or discard.
- *Uncertain composition:* Any object of uncertain composition should be used once and then discarded.

Safety

No item should be used that might cause harm to a client in any way. Use common sense in selecting objects for oral stimulation. Also, adhere to the following guidelines:

- Do not use items that are sharp.
- Do not use small items that can be swallowed, inhaled, or stuck in the throat.
- Do not use items that can burn (i.e., matches, candles)
- Do not use frozen objects for more than a few seconds at a time.
- Do not use vibrating objects, or any other objects, in ways that can cause disorientation, spasticity, nausea, or seizures.
- Do not force a client to use an object to which he shows obvious rejection or fear.
- Do not use foods or liquids with clients who are not cleared for oral swallows.
- Do not use foods, liquids, or tools constructed of materials to which the client has allergies.

Latex and Food Allergy Warning

Latex is a product to which certain people can have strong allergic reactions. Some of these reactions can be life threatening, including severe respiratory distress. Questions about allergies to latex should be part of the initial speech-language assessment. Vinyl gloves should be used instead of latex ones. Latex toys and tools should be excluded from treatment. SLPs must also carefully screen for allergies to other foods or materials that might be put into the mouth (especially peanuts, dairy products, and food dyes). Avoid all foods and materials to which the client might have an allergic reaction.

Social Appropriateness

Is it socially appropriate to introduce an object into a child's mouth and, if so, when? There seem to be no guidelines other than those introduced by

Marshalla (1992a). Those guide note and basic developmental milestones, along with common sense, can work together to help SLPs make these decisions.

Infants, toddlers, and young children usually have no problem putting objects into their mouths except food and other objects they find repulsive. Most young children love an excuse to manipulate objects in their mouths, so use them freely but make sure they are safe and sanitary. Also, make sure they are placing them appropriately in their mouths.

Older children, especially teens and pre-teens, may balk at the idea of placing an unfamiliar object into the mouth, and they may want to make their own decisions about this. They may ask what the tool is, what it is for, and why they need to use it. Be sensitive to this decision-making need. Provide information as necessary and allow the child to choose the item to be used. Let him use the tool in his own mouth as he watches the SLP demonstrate with a similar tool in hers.

It is very important to recognize that many children, especially teens and pre-teens, will not want to be embarrassed in front of their friends. For this reason, phonetic placement activities are not appropriate for presentation in casual environments. Do not use these items in the classroom in front of uninformed peers and be careful about how they are used in small groups. Individual therapy is a much better environment for introducing mouth tools to most clients. Also, do not use infantile objects like bottles or pacifiers with older children who would be embarrassed by the; select an object that is age appropriate.

Purchasing Tools

Tools can be purchased from a variety of suppliers. One of the easiest ways that the present author has found to discover new suppliers or tools is to search for an item by name on the Internet and then select the search engine's option to search for images only. One can then scan the images for the target item(s) and then click on the image link to find the supplier or discover what the object is.

Goals

The goal is always for the client to produce the speech target correctly. The goal never entails correct use of the object. For example, consider using a horn to teach lip rounding for production of /u/. An appropriate goal might contain the words "Johnny will produce /u/ with lip rounding." An inappropriate goal might contain the words "Johnny will blow a horn." This latter goal is inappropriate because blowing the horn is not the goal; producing the phoneme correctly is. The horn may be used to teach lip rounding as a step toward producing the target phoneme, but blowing the horn itself is not the goal of speech therapy. The horn is only one of many teaching methods that will be used to teach production of /u/.

THE TOYS & TOOLS

The rest of this chapter catalogs the tools of speech training that are in common use in the United States. There are hundreds of such objects now available and thus not every one could be included here. Those that have been selected represent all aspects of speech movement training that have been found to be the most useful to the present author. New toys, household objects, and speech production tools are being created all the time and any book written on the subject will be out-of-date as soon as it goes to print, therefore, this list should be used as an orientation to these items and not as a fully comprehensive set. Most of these tools are also described elsewhere in the text at points appropriate to their use.

These tools of speech training are presented alphabetically in logical working groups with no hierarchy implied. Each item is named and described, and practical applications of the tool are suggested. Brand names have generally been avoided in order to give a more generic presentation to the material although many relevant brand names have been included because of their popularity and importance to the discussion. The literature has been surveyed as thoroughly as possible to identify original sources of these ideas and references are included where available. It should be noted, however, that many of these ideas have been passed down from one therapist to another throughout generations without written origin and no original credit could be offered.

Bite Blocks / Bite Sticks / Mouth Props

A bite block, bite stick, or mouth prop is a firm object that can be placed safely between the molars to prop open the mouth. The term *bite block* originally meant *to block the bite* and they were used to prevent a client from biting his tongue during the jaw clenching that occurs during a seizure. Now, these tools and other firm probes are also used to prop the mouth open during oral surgery and dental work and they are used by SLPs to position the jaw in high, mid, and low positions for consonant and vowel productions. SLPs also use them to stabilize the jaw while teaching independent lip and tongue movements.

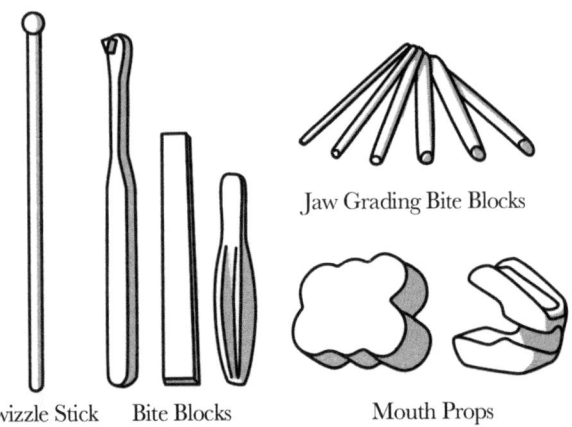

Jaw Grading Bite Blocks

Swizzle Stick   Bite Blocks   Mouth Props

These types of objects have been used throughout the profession's history. Van Riper called them *tooth props*. He placed a tongue depressor on its side between the side teeth to prop the jaw in the lowest position, and he used pencils, wooden matchsticks, and toothpicks to prop the jaw at higher elevations. Dworkin (1991) described how to make client-specific bite blocks out of dental putty pressed onto tongue depressors. Sets of *Jaw Grading Bite Blocks* were developed by Rosenfeld-Johnson (2005a). They consist of five plastic sticks of specific graded sizes bundled together and available in both firm and flexible consistencies from TalkTools® (TalkTools.com). Two-way and three-way mouth props are more classic bite blocks and available through a variety of dental suppliers and at OrofacialMyology.com.

Any firm probe can be used as a bite block including the pliable rubbery handles of toothbrushes and tongue scrapers, the rolled cardboard handles of lollipops and Toothettes®, and firm straws and coffee stirrers. Each item should be studied for its size and used accordingly.

Chewy Objects

Flexible objects are excellent tools for teaching young clients to scan and explore with the mouth and to increase general mobility of the articulators. Baby chew toys and

Chewy Tubes® are particularly good for providing resistance training of the basic up-and-down jaw movement pattern. Baby chew toys come in many sizes, shapes, colors, textures, and elastic properties; some are even flavored to encourage a child to place them in the mouth. Many therapists also use these items to feed children who are engaged in both speech and feeding therapy. Baby chew toys are available in most stores that carry baby items. More information about Chewy Tubes can be found at ChewyTubes.com.

Bubble Wands

A dry, sanitized bubble wand can be used as a tool to learn tongue-tip movements. Poke the tongue tip into the hole to learn how to extend it or to learn to curl the tip back by drawing the wand back into the mouth with the tip. Bubble wands can be purchased in bottles of bubbles in toy and department stores. Remove and sanitize the wand before using it as an oral tool.

Coffee Stirrers

The tiny sticks and straws that are used as coffee stirrers can be used in several ways.

- *Lip position in oral rest:* Ask a client to hold a coffee stirrer lengthwise between the lips to develop an appropriate lip-to-lip position during oral rest. Make sure the clients lips rest gently together against the coffee stirrer as if they were in a position of rest and not pressing together firmly.

- *Jaw stabilization:* The thin-ness of a coffee stirrer makes it just the right size for stabilizing the jaw in a high position for articulation work. Biting on the coffee stirrer with the molars brings the jaw up. This places the lower lip up near the upper lip and the tongue up near the palate. This is a perfect tool for stabilizing the jaw for the sibilants.

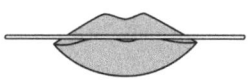

- *Tiny central groove:* Tiny coffee stirrer straws can be used to teach the concept of the very narrow central groove. Hold one end of the straw at the front teeth to catch the airstream as it exits the mouth. The narrow diameter of the coffee stirrer can help clients understand the size of the very narrow airstream he is trying to produce.

Cold Items

Cold stimuli can be used to increase oral sensory awareness, help normalize tactile sensitivity, inhibit hypertonicity, and facilitate oral movement (Farber, 1982). Use ice cubes, ice chips, ice pops, ice cream, metal spoons, metal laryngeal mirrors, or any cold commercial product. Metal spoons dipped in ice water are an excellent choice. Cold stimuli should be used with caution, and it should be reserved for children two years of age and above:

"[The mouth] is more sensitive to temperature than any other body surface area. Because of this sensitivity, ice should be used around and in the mouth with extreme care. Ice should not be used… on the face above the mouth" (Farber, 1982, p. 148).

Crossbar Trainer / Jaw Exerciser

A crossbar trainer (pictured next page, bottom illustration) is a homemade device constructed of tongue depressors (Dworkin, 1991) and a Jaw Exerciser (pictured next page, top illustration) is a plastic tool designed for the same purpose. Both are used to add resistance to jaw, lip, or tongue

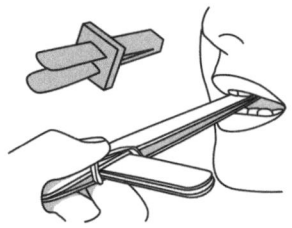

movement. Place between the upper and lower teeth to provide resistance to jaw elevation. Place between the upper and lower lips to provide resistance to lip closure. Place between the tongue tip and maxillary (upper) central incisors to provide resistance to tip elevation. To make a crossbar trainer, place one tongue depressor between two others as shown in the picture. Fasten the two together with rubber bands at the shorter end. Increase the number of tongue depressors between the outer ones to increase their distance apart.

Decorator Candies

Tiny cake decorator candies come in an assortment of colors and shapes. The flat ones are so lightweight they can stick to any wet surface of the mouth. Stick them anywhere in or on the mouth to encourage a wide variety of lip and tongue movements and positions. For example, stick one to the upper lip and en-

courage the client to retrieve it with his tongue tip. Purchase these sugary treats in grocery stores and other shops that carry baking supplies. These are a semi-hard candy so use them only with clients who are at no risk of choking. Also, remember that sugar increases saliva production so do not use these with clients who drool in excess.

Dental Floss

Dental floss is a handy tool to keep in a speech room because it can be used in many ways. For example, to facilitate tongue-tip elevation and curling, place a piece of dental floss from left-to-right across the blade of the tongue. Ask the client to elevate the tip to grab the floss and pull it into the mouth. Pull gently on both ends of the floss to add resistance to the activity. WARNING: Use ribbon floss and do not pull so hard that the tongue is in danger of being cut.

Vaughn and Clark (1979) presented a detailed description of how they used dental floss as internal cues to teach tongue position for all the consonant phonemes. The following are re-worded summaries of three of their ideas.

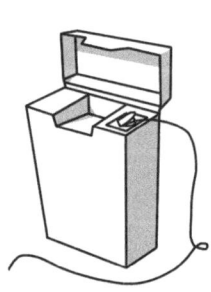

• *Tongue-tip elevation:* Take a piece of dental floss that is 7–10 inches in length. Tie 5–6 "sewer's knots" at the very end of the piece of floss, making one larger knot. Place the floss between the maxillary (upper)

central incisors so that the ball of knots is on the inner surfaces of the teeth. Pull gently outward on the dental floss so that the ball of knots sits right up next to the central incisors from behind and right in front of the tongue tip. Ask the client to extend the tongue tip upward to feel the knots (Vaughn & Clark, 1979, p. 56–59).

• *Create a central air stream:* Take a piece of dental floss that is 7–10 inches in length. Tie 5–6 "sewer's knots" at the end of the piece of floss, making one larger knot. Place the dental floss between the maxillary (upper) central incisors so that the knots are on their inner surfaces. Pull gently outward on the dental floss so that the ball of knots sits right up next to the central incisors from behind and right in front of the tongue tip. Ask the client to direct his air stream so that it hits the knots at midline (Vaughn & Clark, 1979, p. 56–59).

• *Lateral tongue spreading:* Take two pieces of dental floss that are 7–10 inches in length. Tie 5–6 "sewer's knots" at the very end of one side of each piece of floss. Place one piece of dental floss between the molars on one side so that the knots are on their inner surfaces. Pull gently outward on the dental floss so that the wad of knots sits right up next to the side teeth and near the side of the tongue. Repeat on the other side of the mouth with the other piece of dental floss. Ask the client to spread the lateral margins of the tongue so that both sides stretch outward toward the knots (Vaughn & Clark, 1979, p. 56–59).

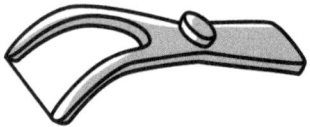

Dental Floss Handle

A dental floss handle can be used to facilitate tongue-tip and tongue-back elevation. Purchase them wherever dental floss is sold.

• *Tongue-tip elevation:* Put dental floss on the handle and place it across the blade of the tongue. Ask the client to elevate the tip to grab the floss. Pull gently on the handle of the floss holder to add resistance to the activity. Do not pull so hard that the tongue is in danger of being cut (Marshalla, 2004, p. 110).

• *Tongue-back elevation:* Use the dental floss handle without any floss to provide resistance against upward elevation. Place the ends of the two arms on top of the back lateral margins of the tongue. Push gently downward. Ask the client to push the shoulders of the tongue up against the arms.

Dental Wax

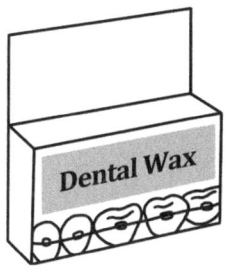

Dental wax is an inexpensive tool that can be used in articulation and motor speech therapy. Make sure to use it only with clients who will not swallow or choke on it. Dental wax comes in various flavors and colors and can be purchased wherever dental hygiene products are sold.

• *Block dental gaps during evaluation:* One of the best ways to use dental wax is to place it on the anterior teeth in such a way that it blocks gaps between the teeth. With the wax in place, the examiner can tell with certainty how the gaps affect the acoustic quality of phonemes, especially that of the sibilants. The wax will help the examiner determine if the client has achieved the best acoustic quality for these sounds given the gaps that are present because it will allow the examiner to hear what the phonemes could sound like if the gaps were closed. This activity makes an excellent demonstration to the client and his parents to explain why orthodontic or surgical procedures may help speech improvement.

• *Mark the target:* Small wads of dental wax can be used to mark the place on the palate or teeth where articulation should occur. Place a small wad behind the maxillary (upper) central incisors to help the client learn to settle the tongue tip on the alveolar ridge. Or place a wad on the inside of the upper molars on both sides to teach the client how to spread and anchor the tongue there for back-lateral stability.

• *Establish midline airflow:* Place a small wad of dental wax at midline on the lingual surface of the maxillary (upper) central incisors. Teach the client to touch the wax with the tongue tip and then to back the tip away from the wax. Teach him then to blow at the wax to create a central air stream.

• *Maintain lip closure:* Place a wad of dental wax between the lips at midline. Ask the client to press the lips together in order to hold it there. Gradually increase the time required.

Droppers & Bulbs

The bulbs of eyedroppers and medicine droppers have been used in articulation therapy at least since Scripture recommended them in 1912.

• *Tongue-tip elevation:* The dropper's small bulb is placed between the tongue tip and alveolus, and the client is taught to press the tip upward into the bulb. This procedure incorporates resistance to teach and strengthen tip elevation. The TonguePress® (upper-right illustration on this page, right-hand image) is a

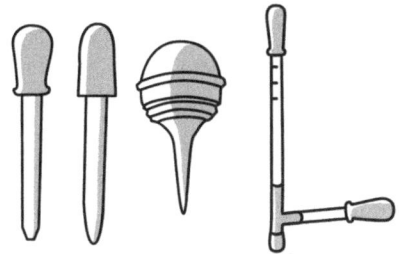

new tool with a similar bulb that is designed to train dysphagic patients to press the tongue tip up with more force when swallowing. A dropper bulb can also be placed between the upper and lower molars to encourage the jaw's chewing motions or between the lips to encourage bilabial articulation.

• *Wet speech or drooling:* Droppers can also be used with a client who drools or to teach a client to swallow more often when his speech sounds wet, slushy, and distorted because of excessive saliva. Use the dropper to squeeze 2–3 cc of icy cold water or apple juice into the mouth. Ask the client to press his lips tightly together around the very tip of the dropper. Squeeze the bulb to send the liquid into the mouth. WARNING: Use only with clients who are cleared for oral swallows.

The liquid will cause the client to swallow and clear the mouth. Use the dropper on a regular schedule throughout the session, for example, every 2 minutes. Or use it only when the client's saliva builds to a certain critical mass as measured by its effect on articulation. Train the client to hear the difference between speech that is wet and dry. Fade the dropper over time and teach the client to swallow by himself without the liquid assist.

• *Airflow:* Bulbs are also quite useful for introducing concepts about airflow. The larger bulb of an infant nasal cleaner is an especially good tool to blow a stream of air across a child's face, lips, tongue, hands, or arms, or into the nose. Squeezing a puff of air onto the face with a bulb provides a much more sanitary approach than blowing directly on a client with breath.

Electronic Equipment

A variety of specialized electronic equipment has been developed for use in speech research, assessment, and training. For example, palatometry, nasometry, and ultrasound technologies are being used during the training of lingual and velar movements in speech. This type of

equipment and the procedures being used in therapy were not reviewed for the purposes of this manual because of their ever-changing nature and because their expense is outside the range of most clinical programs. These technologies will be used more often as the 21st century unfolds. Readers interested in electronic and computerized equipment are encouraged to watch the research, to search online, and to attend the annual ASHA conventions where the latest technological models are always on display in the exhibit hall.

Finger Cot Toothbrush

The finger cot toothbrush was designed as an introductory toothbrush for infants. The tool consists of a sturdy and

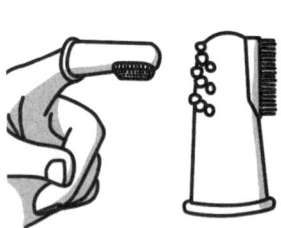

colorful finger cot with bristles and/or bumps near the tip. Place the item on the client's finger for oral self-exploration, or place it on the adult stimulator's finger. Use the infant toothbrush to provide general tactile stimulation to the oral mechanism, to stimulate the oral reflexes, or to mark the target of tongue placement on the plate. Purchase infant finger cot toothbrushes wherever baby supplies are sold. (Finger-cot toothbrushes are also manufactured in larger sizes for cleaning pet teeth, but they do not always seem to be manufactured under sanitary conditions.)

Fingers

A client's own fingers make excellent tools in articulation therapy. In fact, sometimes the client's fingers are more desirable than any other tool because he can feel his oral movements with them and because they cost nothing. Here are some of the ways that a client can use his own fingers to stimulate oral movement. Make sure the client's hands and fingers are clean before using any of these methods.

- *To monitor lip position:* Have the client place his fingers on the lips to monitor or to encourage lip position.

- *To monitor jaw position:* Have the client hold his own chin or bite gently down on his finger or fingernails to monitor or encourage jaw mobility or stability.

- *To mark the target of articulation:* Have the client use a fingertip to touch the parts to be articulated. For example, have him touch the tongue tip and then the alveolar ridge to mark the target of lingua-alveolar contact.

- *To stimulate for improved oral awareness:* Have the client rub, pat, or stretch any part of the oral

mechanism to improve tactile awareness there.

- *To resist oral movement:* Have the client use his fingers to push against the direction that the body part is moving. For example, have him push down on his lower lip as he elevates it for /f/ or /v/.

- *To assist oral movement:* Have the client use his fingers to push or pull an oral part into position. For example, have him press his lips together with his fingers to stimulate position for /m/.

- *To cue oral position:* Have the client shape his hands and fingers at his mouth to exaggerate and cue an oral movement. For example, have him shape his fingers into an "O" in front of his lips to cue /o/.

- *To cue voice:* Have the client touch his own throat to cue [+Voice].

- *To cue nasality:* Have the client touch his own nose to cue nasality: "Hold the child's finger on the side of your nose as you say [a nasal sound]… Then [have him] hold his own nose, and have him prolong the sound" (Hanson, 1983, p. 201).

Flavor

Flavor is used selectively in the detailed work of articulation therapy. It has been recommended most often to mark the target of lip or tongue position. For example, Secord et al. (2007) discuss flavoring several times in their book, as in the following description of facilitating tongue movement for /t/:

> *"To emphasize the placement of the tongue, wet the end of a cotton swab and rub it on a flavored food, such as a mint Life Saver®. Touch the client's alveolar ridge with the swab to teach correct placement"* (Secord et al., 2007, p. 23).

The present author's experience, however, is that flavor does very little to improve a client's understanding of placement, and that it is the tactile stimulation of the probe that does the trick; the flavor is just there to make the activity more interesting and perhaps acceptable to the client. But flavor can also be confusing and distracting to young clients because flavors stimulate the taste buds and the taste buds are not organized according to tongue movement. Use flavor selectively as a way to make speech movement learning activities

more interesting and amusing, but do not expect the flavor to teach movement or position; texture variations are much better for that purpose. (For more on this concept, see Chapter 15 on oral sensory awareness or pages 285–286 for a discussion on taste.)

Foods

Therapists have been using foods to vivify general oral movement since Van Riper's time. One usually categorizes foods by taste, texture, temperature, and elastic properties. A variety of foods can be used for many purposes as noted here. Be aware of food allergies when selecting foods. (For more information, see Chapter 18 on eating and swallowing methods.)

• *Chewy foods:* Chewy foods can encourage a client to make the wide up-and-down jaw movements he needs to learn babbling and the CV. Suggestions include meat jerky, dried fruit, gummy candies, caramels, and soft dried apple pieces.

• *Crunchy foods:* Biting into and chewing on crunchy foods teaches a client to pull his jaw upward into the high stabile position he needs for production of advanced phonemes. Suggestions include pretzels, hard cookies, and firm crackers.

• *Frozen treats:* Frozen treats like ice cream, frozen yogurt, ice pops, and even ice cubes made of water or juice are a fun way to orient a client to his mouth and to normalize oral tactile sensitivity. If the client is allowed to place and remove the treat from the mouth under his own control there will be no fear of over-icing the organs.

• *Gooey foods:* Gooey and gloppy foods encourage a client to move his mouth in a wide range. Selections include peanut butter, taffy, soft gum, soft caramels, and marshmallow cream. This method has been around for decades: "Wipe candy lipstick or 'fudge frosting' from the lips [with the tongue tip], carefully removing it from the corners of the mouth" (Berry & Eisenson, 1956, p. 140).

• *Hard candy:* Hard candies are useful in articulation therapy for general awareness and control as long as they are not used with any clients who may choke on them. Hard candies with holes in the center are a great way to encourage tongue-tip movement.

• *Purees:* The benefit of using purees in articulation therapy is in the tools that can be used to eat the puree for general oral stimulation. Feed purees with spoons, Nuk® massage brushes, cake decorators, swizzle sticks, tongue depressors, honey dippers, and so forth. Suggestions include applesauce, yogurt, pudding, rice cereal, mashed potatoes, and mashed yams..

• *Sticky foods:* Sticky foods can be placed on the palate to train the tongue to reach up toward specific places on the palate. They can also be spread on the lips during tongue-to-lip and lip-to-lip exercises. Suggestions include syrup, honey, peanut butter and other nut butters, jelly, cheese spreads, cream cheese, and hummus. This feeding activity is mentioned more than any others in articulation therapy textbooks across the ages.

• *Tiny food bits:* Foods that come in tiny bits (such as raisons, dried cranberries, or dry cereal pieces) are fun for children to eat because they love picking up the bits, studying them, and popping them into the mouth. Use tiny food pieces to teach refined lip and tongue control; have clients chew them, bite them, hold them between the lips, and balance them on the tip of the tongue. Also, have them deposit the food bit into the center of the tongue bowl.

Food Preparation & Service Items

There are a wide variety of food preparation and service items that can be used in articulation therapy. Some come right out of any home kitchen and others are manufactured to teach specific oral movements for eating.

• *Baby bottles:* Baby bottles are generally used as a facilitator of speech movement only when the client still is using bottles for feeding. Sometimes therapists recommend that a client continue to use a bottle longer than the parents otherwise would because the bottle helps to encourage and organize coordinated jaw, lip, tongue, and breathing movements. Preschool children may also use baby bottles, or toy baby bottles in pretend play, and these can also be used to stimulate general oral awareness and lip activity.

• *Bowls and cups:* Light plastic bowls and cups of various sizes are excellent tools to amplify speech. Have the client hold the bowl or cup at the mouth, and have him produce sound into it. His vocalization will echo directly back, making him more interested in it. The bowl or cup also helps develop jaw stability as the client bites down on the rim while drinking. A *nosey cup* or *cut-out cup* often is used to developing drinking skill with head stability.

• *Metal butter knives:* Very blunt metal butter knives with no serration can be used just like tongue depressors to stimulate lip and tongue movement. The advantage to them is that they become very cold when

dipped or soaked in ice water.

• *Honey dippers:* A honey dipper is a wooden or plastic tool for dipping honey out of a honey pot. It often is designed as a handle with a ribbed ball on one end. Use it to suck purees to encourage lip closure. The ribbing of the honey dipper also encourages tongue-tip extension into the small spaces between the ribs.

• *Spatulas:* Use a small spatula like a tongue depressor. It can be better than a tongue depressor for certain applications because it is flexible and can be chewed on.

• *Spoons:* A spoon can be used to mark the spot of articulation, to press the lips together against it, to press the tongue tip into, to stimulate tongue-back elevation, and to monitor nasal air emissions. Spoons can also be used with food for general oral stimulation. Many therapists use infant spoons that come in a wide variety of shapes, sizes, and textures. Some have nice long handles for oral work. The Duo Spoon is a flexible dipper with bumpy surfaces on both ends that are a nice addition to a therapy spoon collection (pictured above in the middle next to the baby bottle).

• *Straws:* (Please see the section on straws later in this chapter.)

• *Turkey basters:* A turkey baster is a tapered plastic tube with a large flexible bulb on one end. Turkey basters can be used to play with airflow (see the subsection "Droppers & Bulbs" on page 331) or to eat purees for activities of general oral stimulation.

Gum

Chewing and manipulating gum is a classic way to facilitate a wide variety of oral movements. Please note that young clients may need to learn how to chew gum without swallowing it before it can be used as an object of articulation learning. SLPs use gum to teach many speech movements.

• *General oral stimulation:* Have the client watch his gum-chewing in a mirror. Chew with the molars on both sides and also with the front teeth. Have him watch the tongue as it moves the gum around. Van Riper recommended to "chew in an exaggerated fashion" (Van Riper, 1954, p. 217) in order to get the mouth moving.

• *General tongue movement:* Gum chewing has been recommended to facilitate general tongue mobility. "Chew gum, rolling it to the side, 'plaster' it against the palate, slowly move the gum back over the palate, etc. Attempt to feel the tongue position with each movement" (Berry & Eisenson, 1956, p. 139).

• *Tongue-tip extension:* Learn to start a bubble by pressing the tongue against the gum to flatten it against the palate. Press the tongue tip into the flattened piece to start the bubble form.

• *Lip closure:* Learn to chew gum while maintaining lip closure. Teach the client to chew with his lips closed.

• *Lip pressing:* Learn to press the lips firmly against the teeth to hold a wad of gum against the front teeth.

• *Tongue stabilization:* Gum can be used to help stabilize the tongue at the back lateral margins. Have the client chew his gum until it's soft. Tell him to divide the wad of gum into two, and to place one on each side of his mouth, between the molars. Then tell him to stretch the back of the tongue to both sides simultaneously, pressing laterally against the two wads of gum. Teach him to hold his tongue there while producing his phonemes.

• *Rhythmic movements:* Gum chewing has been used to encourage better speech rhythm at least since Fröeschels (1933) recommended it.

• *Oral relaxation:* It has been suggested that gum chewing may relax the oral mechanism.

• *Multiple purposes:* Rosenfeld-Johnson (2001) called gum chewing a "comprehensive exercise" and has written a hierarchy of gum chewing activities for a variety of purposes: stimulating oral movements, reducing oral habits, stabilizing the body, and organizing the sensory system.

Inhalation & Exhalation Instruments, Tools & Toys

There are dozens of toys that can help clients learn to inhale and exhale with greater awareness, skill, and purpose for speech. Collectively these tools have become known as "blow toys" although improving inhalation and exhalation

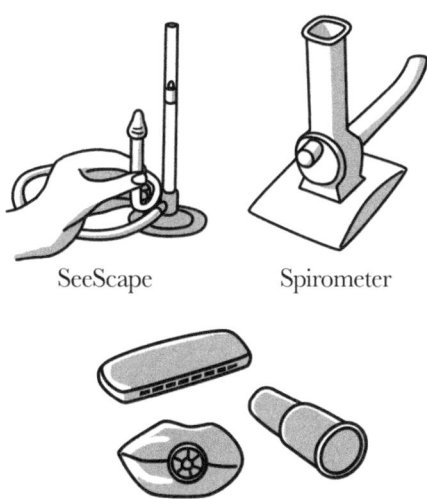

SeeScape   Spirometer

(and not blowing) are the aim. Blow toys perform some action or make some sound when air is forced through them. Some of these tools help clients discover both their inhalation and exhalation capabilities, and others work only on exhalation. Blow toys are also used to learn jaw, lip, and tongue positioning, and to experiment with velar control. Here are examples in regard to inhalation/exhalation. More can be read about these ideas in Chapter 7 on breath support, resonance, and oral movements.

• *Toys and tools that work on both inhalation and exhalation:* Harmonicas, sirens, whistle straws, spirometers, and balloons on tubes can help teach a client about the process of inhaling and exhaling. Respiration spirometers work in both inhalation and exhalation, and many of them have valves so that the amount of air needed to work them can be adjusted up or down.

• *Toys and tools that work on exhalation only:* Party horns, whistles of all sorts, singing birds, bird callers, rainbow blowers, tooting trains, bubble wands, bubble blowers, and many more items can help teach a client about exhalation. The See-Scape has been designed specifically as a way to visually monitor nasal airflow. Place the bulb of the flexible tube in the nares and observe the tiny plug move up and down in response to nasal airflow.

• *Items that facilitate sustained exhalation:* Many blow toys have a feature that encourages sustained exhalation. For example, one blower has a rainbow-colored string that moves through it as long as exhalation is sustained, and the string will not move correctly until the client has figured out how to sustain his outgoing airstream in a steady way. Any light-weight items will work for this purpose; suggestions include pinwheels, cotton balls, feathers, sheets of tissue paper, tiny bits of tissue paper, packing peanuts, Ping-Pong® (table tennis) balls, and paper boats made from folded index cards. The manometer, See-Scape, and spirometer are more professional tools that also work well in this regard.

Interdental Picks

An interdental pick is a tiny plastic tool that is smaller and thinner than a toothpick so that it can fit between the teeth like dental floss. Some are hard and sharp and somewhat dangerous to the gums, but the brand pictured (GUM® Soft Picks®, right) is firm yet flexible and it has soft bristles for safety. A dental pick can be placed between adjacent teeth so that the tip pokes inward between them to stimulate the tongue. It is an excellent way to encourage the tongue to move in specific directions.

• *Tongue tip:* Place one soft pick between the maxillary (upper) central incisors to indicate tongue-tip placement to the alveolar ridge at midline for lingua-alveolar phonemes.

• *Tongue-sides:* Place two soft picks between the maxillary (upper) molars, one on each side, to guide the sides of the tongue to the sides of the palate for phonemes that require a wide midline groove — /ʃ/, /ʒ/, /tʃ/, /dʒ/. Place the sticks more forward between the maxillary (upper) central and lateral incisors for /s/ and /z/.

Kazoos

One of the best toys to develop a client's concept of his own voice is the kazoo because a kazoo only makes sound when voice is directed through it. A company called Hohner makes the best kazoos for this purpose. A kazoo can assist in the development of many skills.

• *Vowels:* The kazoo is a fun tool for a young child who is just learning to make voice for early vowels. Say words and sing songs into the kazoo by producing /u/.

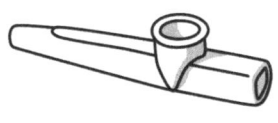

• *Prolongation of voice:* Use the kazoo to help a client learn to prolong voice so that he can produce fuller vowels and diphthongs, so he can extend his voice throughout the length of multiple-syllable words and multi-word phrases, so he can extend his vowels to reach final consonants in VC and CVC syllables, and so he can sustain voice through multiple-word phrases and sentences.

• *Intonation:* Sing songs with the kazoo to learn how to intone. Also, have "kazoo conversations" to practice more intonation patterns. Children love this.

• *Loudness:* Use the kazoo to practice getting louder and softer.

• *Pitch:* Use the kazoo to learn high, low, and

medium pitches, and to learn how to slide smoothly from one to another.

- *Lip rounding:* Use the kazoo to stimulate and strengthen lip rounding. Make sure the client is firmly rounding the lips on the mouthpiece of the kazoo and not just using his teeth to hold it in place.

- *Tongue-tip extension and retraction:* Encourage the client to extend and retract his tongue tip into and out of the mouthpiece as he plays the kazoo. Pushing the tongue tip into the kazoo will stop the airflow.

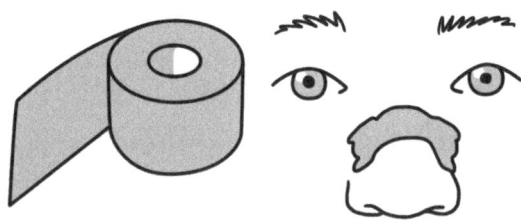

Kinesiology Tape / Nasal Strips

Regular household sticky tape and surgical tape were recommended to inhibit lip movement in many articulation therapy textbooks. Kinesiology tape, also known as Kinesio Tape®, and nasal strips are new, safer alternatives.

- *Inhibit lip rounding:* "Place a small piece of Scotch tape, vertically, at the corners of the mouth, with the lips slightly retracted. When the lips begin to move toward the /w/ position, the pulling of the tape signals the speaker that the unwanted movement is occurring" (Hanson, 1983, p. 214).

- *Remind the client of lip position:* "If all other methods fail to keep the lower lip under the upper teeth when saying /f/ or /v/, put a piece of masking tape tightly over the lower lip to increase awareness of position of lower lip" (Berry & Eisenson, 1956, p. 156).

- *Discover nasal airflow:* Use a nasal strip across the nose to increase the diameter of the nasal passageways. Discover the movement of air through the nose.

Laryngeal Mirrors

A laryngeal mirror is a long metal handle with a small mirror on the end which has long been used to inspect oral movement (e.g., Borden & Busse, 1925) but it can also be used as an oral stimulator. Laryngeal mirrors are sometimes made of plastic, however, a good quality one that is made of metal is better because it is nearly always cold and, therefore, makes a good stimulator of the tongue or soft palate. A metal laryngeal mirror can be dipped in ice water to make it even colder. Many therapists

began to use laryngeal mirrors to stimulate the back of the tongue for speech after Logemann (1983) recommended it for stimulating the back of the tongue for the swallow. Purchase laryngeal mirrors through speech or medical supply distributors.

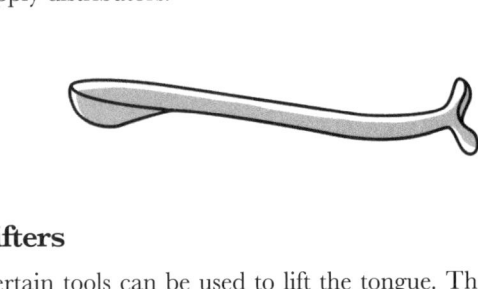

Lifters

Certain tools can be used to lift the tongue. The tongue depressor is the old standby in this regard but now there is a new tool that has been designed for this specific purpose. The Tongue LifteR is a handle with a curved crosspiece on one end. The tool can be placed under the tongue to push it up high in the back. The crosspiece is bent to accommodate the lingua frenum but the user must be careful. This lifter is available at JohnsonTherapeutic.com.

Lightweight Items

Lightweight objects such as cotton balls, feathers, thread, bits of paper, or paper boats have been used to teach aspects of airflow and frication for more than a century. Several online sites demonstrate how to make a paper boat such as that pictured below, or simply use an index card folded in half. Other objects like packing peanuts can also be used. The lighter the object, the less air required for it to move.

- *Airflow:* Blow a lightweight item off the palm or across a tabletop to discover airflow.

- *Stridency:* Produce strident sounds into a straw pointed at one of these items. Watch the item move to discover the air movement associated with stridency.

- *Voice/voiceless contrast:* Produce strident cognates /s/ and /z/, /ʃ/ and /ʒ/, /f/ and /v/, through a straw pointed at one of these items and watch it move. The item will usually move much faster and farther with the voiceless productions.

- *Purposeful exhalation:* Place tiny bits of cotton or thread in a cereal bowl. Blow into the bowl with a straw and watch the cotton bits fly up and then come

down like snow.

• *Purposeful inhalation:* Place a large ball of cotton near the end of a skinny straw. Inhale through the other end of the straw to draw the cotton ball up against the straw. Continue to inhale to hold it there. Focus on sustained inhalation. WARNING: Make sure to use a cotton ball that is too large to be drawn through the straw to avoid the possibility of choking.

Lip Gloss / Lipstick

Lip gloss or lipstick is a way to draw a client's attention to his lips; a simple home activity parents can do every day.

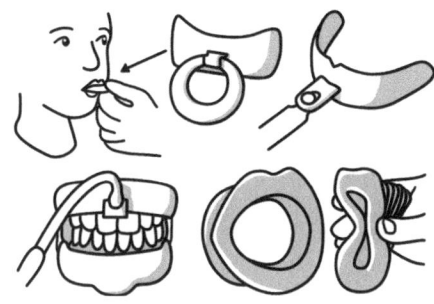

Lip Trainers & Exercisers

Specialty tools called *lip trainers* and *lip exercisers* have been around for several decades but there are new designs on the market every year. Some lip exercisers are soft and flexible while others are hard and firm, but both types use resistance as a basic training method. These tools are being marketed for improving the face and lips for rehabilitative and cosmetic purposes. The pictures above represent several different types that were available when this book went to print. Search online for these items under *lip trainer, lip exerciser, lip exercises, mouth breathing,* or *myofunctional therapy.*

Lip Retractors

Lip retractors pull the lips out of the way. They were designed for oral surgery and for orthodontists to take photographs of the teeth before and after orthodontic treatment. Several dental product companies sell different models of this tool. Kids love them because they expose all the teeth and make the child look silly and/or scary.

• *Tongue-lip differentiation:* Use the lip retractor to hold the lips out of the way when working on tongue sounds. This is especially useful to inhibit lip interference when working on /r/ (Marshalla, 2004).

• *Lip movement:* Practice lip rounding and protrusion with the lip retractor holding the

lips laterally. The retractor provides resistance to lip movement, thus making them work a little harder (Marshalla, 1992a).

• *General oral movement:* The most fun to have with a lip retractor is to place it on the client's lips and have him make faces or eat a small snack in front of a mirror. He will learn much about his mouth in the process.

Manometers

A manometer is a simple device that measures force of exhalation (pressure). The manometer has been recommended by a variety of writers for teaching dysarthric patients how to exhale steadily (e.g., Yorkston, Beukelman, Strand, & Bell, 1999).

A manometer consists of a hollow U-shaped tube partially filled with water. One end of the tube has a mouthpiece, and the other end is open to the air. The client blows into the mouthpiece and attempts to raise the water level to keep it steady at a certain level.

A simple water-based manometer can be constructed out of a plastic bottle. Drill two holes in the cap. Place a straw into one and a flexible tube through the other. Make water level marks with a permanent marker on the straw, or place stickers on the straw to mark levels. Place water into the bottle that reaches a mid-level. The client will blow into the flexible tube gently to cause the water level to rise up into the straw.

Electronic digital manometers are also available. They may be more accurate but are usually not as exciting as a water-based one to a young client who enjoys making the water rise and fall. Assembling a water manometer in therapy can be an excellent idea for drawing a bored client into the process of working on airflow.

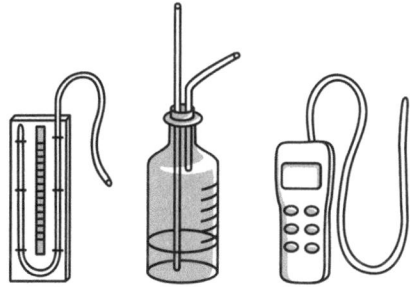

Mirrors

Mirrors are extremely valuable for helping clients understand their own speech movements. Mirrors have been used in speech training since the time of the elocutionists who called a mirror a *looking glass*. Little children often like big mirrors but a small hand-held mirror is usually better for an older client's own private inspection of his mouth.

Purchase small mirrors wherever cosmetics are sold and large mirrors at stores with furniture and/or bathroom supplies. Some speech companies provide specialized speech mirrors.

• *General oral movement:* Use a mirror to discover the oral mechanism and its parts, to learn how the oral mechanism moves, and to take control of oral movements.

• *Facial expressions:* A large mirror fastened to the wall is good for teaching big facial expressions, arm gestures, and other large body imitation work with young children who are learning how to imitate all movements, including oral movements.

• *Velar movement:* Alexander Graham Bell recommended the use of a mirror to teach velar movement with clients who were deaf: "I would recommend you to go for the soft palate itself, directly, with a hand mirror. Teach your pupil to elevate and depress it at will. Direct the action with your hand" (Bell, 1906, p. 22).

• *Group work:* A wall mirror placed lengthwise on a whiteboard or chalkboard ledge allows a small group of students to see themselves while facing the mirror together. Sit with them or behind them to model.

• *Oral and nasal airflow:* See Chapter 8 on resonance for information about how to use a small hand-held mirror to check and monitor nasality.

Nasal Clamp

The nasal clamp is a C-shaped plastic clip that fits gently over the nares and is used to pinch the nose closed. Early writers of articulation therapy recommended pinching the client's nose closed to work with inappropriate nasal air emission. For example, "Nasal emission of /l/ may be eliminated by ear training, by exercises for gaining control of the soft palate, and by the practice of /l/ with plugged nostrils" (Nemoy & Davis, 1938, p. 139). The nasal clamp allows SLPs to continue this practice in a hands-free and sanitary way. Search online for these items under nasal clamp or nasal clip. Suggested uses for a nasal clamp include:

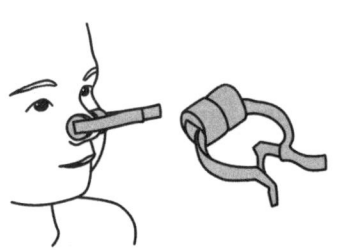

• *Discover nasal emissions:* Use the nasal clamp on the nose while practicing vowels and consonants. The client will feel air pressure against the clamp if he allows his air or sound to travel through the nasal passageways. Teach him to produce these sounds without the nasal pressure.

• *Discover how to build inter-oral air pressure:* Have the client make nasal sounds with the clamp on the nose. He will feel the build-up of air pressure in the nose.

Nuk Massage Brushes

A Nuk® massage brush (sometimes just called a Nuk) is a versatile tool in speech training. It has a flexible knobby bulb on one end of a handle. Purchase Nuks from dental hygiene suppliers, speech suppliers, or wherever baby toothbrushes are sold. A Nuk can be used in many ways:

• *Mark the target:* A Nuk is a handy probe to mark the target of articulation on the tongue, lips, or palate.

• *General oral stimulation:* Use the knobby end to eat purees as a means of general oral stimulation.

• *Lip closure:* Press the lips together on the knobby end to stimulate greater awareness of lip rounding.

• *Tip extension:* Press the tongue tip against the knobby end to facilitate extension of the tip against resistance.

• *Back elevation:* Rub the knobby end on the back of the tongue to heighten sensation of the back of the tongue. Also, use it to press down on the back of the tongue to add resistance to back elevation.

• *Suctioning:* Use the Nuk to encourage and practice suctioning for decreasing drooling. Dip the knobby end in a puree and hold it between the lips. Encourage the client to press the lips together and suction the puree off the knobby end and into the mouth.

Orthodontic Elastics

Orthodontic elastics are tiny elastic bands less than a half inch in diameter that are used in orthodontic treatments. They have been used to habituate tongue and lip positions in speech and swallowing for many decades, for example: "Place a tiny orthodontic elastic on the tip of the tongue. Have the client sustain an /l/, pressing the

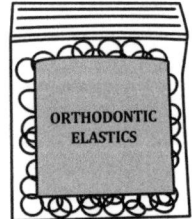

elastic firmly against the alveolar ridge" (Hanson, 1983, p. 214). Make sure to use these tiny elastics with clients who can control and not swallow them. If swallowed by mistake, however, they should do no harm and simply pass through the digestive system. Purchase orthodontic elastics at drug stores.

Pacifiers

SLPs often recommend that pacifiers be used to stimulate sucking movements when clients have severe neuromuscular and/or cognitive deficit with severe feeding disorder. In speech, one can use a pacifier to help a client eat purees for general sensory stimulation of the oral mechanism and to stimulate basic jaw, lip, and tongue mobility, especially lip puckering. It is perhaps wise to use a real pacifier only with children who are still using them at home. However, there are adult size pacifiers available in novelty gift stores, and certain candy products that come in pacifier shapes that will be acceptable to older children and can be used in fun. Do not use a pacifier when continued sucking may interfere with speech and language development.

Probes

Any firm probe can be used to stimulate the oral mechanism in any number of ways. As mentioned in the introduction, Bell used a letter opener for this purpose, but there are many better, safer options. These include ARK's Oral Motor Probe, Toothettes®, tongue depressors, oral swabs, swizzle sticks, straws, bubble wands, coffee stirrers,

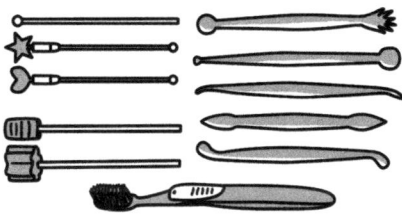

cake decorator tools, toothpicks, lollipop sticks, orange sticks, infant tongue depressors, acrylic blocks on strings or handles, corks, the handles of toothbrushes, and tongue cleaners/scrapers.

Rough Textures

Rough texture is a powerful tactile stimulator. The best rough textures for stimulation of the lips, tongue, and palate are the dry sponges of Toothettes® or oral swabs and the bristles of toothbrushes. These items should be used with care. Brush gently and do not scrub the oral mechanism. Textural input like this stimulates the light-work

muscles of the lips and tongue and stimulates the points of articulation on the palate.

• *Mark the palate:* Use the sponge or bristles to mark the lips, tongue, or palate for place of articulation. Therapists once used paintbrushes for this purpose: "Stroke back and forth, laterally, along the alveolar ridge with a tongue depressor or a water color brush, for several seconds to enhance the client's awareness of the location of lingual contact" (Hanson, 1983, p. 207).

• *General oral awareness:* Use them to stimulate the lips, count the teeth, stroke the palate, and to stimulate the inner cheek walls and velum for general oral awareness.

• *Assessment of oral-tactile sensitivity:* Toothettes® have played a key role in the assessment of oral-tactile sensitivity as described in Chapter 16.

Scents

Scent has been recommended in books on general oral stimulation but has not been seen in books on articulation therapy. Scent has a powerful effect on the arousal system and, therefore, it has been used in pre-feeding and pre-speech treatment protocols and as part of coma sequences (e.g., Farber, 1982). The present author's own experiments with scent over nearly forty years suggest that it can make lethargic and otherwise non-verbal clients more animated and expressive. However, many children get too giddy as they get caught up in the scent and then they have difficulty paying attention. Scent also permeates a room very quickly to become part of the room's ambiance and the scent receptors acclimate quickly, and then it is of little use in stimulating anything specific. Scent can be a good way to enliven and build rapport in an otherwise dull therapy routine.

It is noted that mild vanilla scent seems to be a regular addition to many baby chew toys. The manufacturers of these toys have found that vanilla is "baby-friendly" and it encourages oral exploration of these toys. The flavoring may help very young and low-functioning clients discriminate between mouth toys and non-mouth toys.

Sound-Activated Toys

Sound-activated toys move or speak in response to sound. They are a fabulous aid to therapy for children who are minimally vocal or minimally verbal because they encourage the client to produce voice. A few of these toys have been around for a while including a talking parrot, a frog band, a dinosaur band, and a butterfly. (Note that the talking parrot can be loud and obnoxious and even a little scary to some kids.) Search under "sound activated toys" to find more on the Internet. Some speech apps are also

sound-activated. Sound-activated toys and apps can help teach certain skills.

- *Voice:* Use the toy or app to teach the client how to activate his voice at will (turning the voice on).

- *Voice prolongation:* Most toys and some apps continue to respond as long as voice is produced, so they can be used to teach clients how to prolong voice.

- *Voice termination:* These toys or apps typically stop moving as soon as the client stops producing voice, so use them to teach sound termination (turning the voice off).

- *General speech stimulation:* These toys may motivate the hesitant client to begin to speak.

SmartPalate

A brand-name product that is important to this discussion is the SmartPalate. The SmartPalate is a portable electropalatometry system that can be used to teach real time tongue-to-palate articulation. The SmartPalate consists of a custom-fit mouthpiece embedded with 126 gold-plated sensors, a small hand-held display screen, and a connecting cord. This device allows clients to see exactly where they are placing their tongues against the palate.

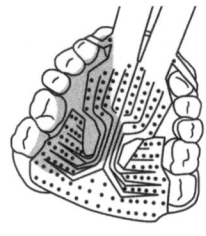

It is a commercial product modeled after the sophisticated electrometric systems used in tongue movement research.

The advantage of the SmartPalate is that it can teach the tongue where to lift. The disadvantage is that the false palate itself serves as a barrier between the tongue and the real palate, and, therefore, it interferes with the tactile sensation of the tongue touching the palate. Ultimately, the client needs to attend to the tongue placement process that is perceived through the tactile sensation on the real palate, but the Smart Palate can give the client a start. The SmartPalate is helpful for the right client at the right time. It may also reassure clients and their families that their therapist is using the most advanced techniques available.

Speech Buddies

Another 21st century brand-name product that is worth mentioning is the set of articulation tools called Speech Buddies. Speech Buddies is a set of five tools designed specifically for teaching tongue placement for individual phonemes. As of this writing, there are Speech Buddies for /s/, /ʃ/, /tʃ/, /l/, and /r/. These tools are a throwback to the original wire tools discussed on page 324 that Borden and Busse made at the early part of the 20th century. They are designed to teach individual tongue position for specific phonemes and this makes them different from all the other tools in this chapter. Research being done on SpeechBuddies makes them appealing for the clinic but the high price makes them out of reach for many clinicians and clients. The present author has used these items and found the Rabbit Buddy (for /r/) to be an excellent addition to other less expensive methods for teaching the retroflex tongue position.

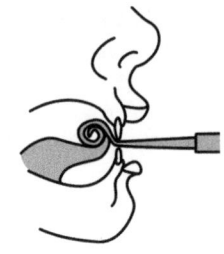

Straws

Straws have a wide variety of uses in speech training. Many different sizes are useful: cocktail straws that are quite thin, milkshake (smoothie/boba) straws that are fat, and standard soda straws that are in the middle. Firm plastic straws work best because thin straws collapse and paper straws disintegrate. Straws should be used once and then discarded. Straws can be used in many ways, such as for:

- *Airflow:* Inhale and exhale through straws to discover the movement of air in and out of the mouth and nose. Straws can be used to blow cotton balls, paper boats, feathers, pinwheels, tissues, and other light items.

- *Plosive-ness:* Straws can be used to discover, play with, and rehearse plosive-ness. For example: (1) lace one end of a wide straw at the lips and produce the plosive-ness of /p/ and /b/ into it, (2) place one end of a wide straw outside the anterior teeth and produce the plosive-ness of /t/ and /d/ into it, (3) place one end of a wide straw inside the open mouth, just in front of the back of the tongue and produce the plosive-ness of /k/ and /g/ into it.

- *Stridency and friction:* Straws can be used to discover, play with, and rehearse stridency and frication. Before straws, therapists used rubber tubes: "Have the patient practice emitting expired breath streams through a small hole in the

under surface of a hollow, hard rubber tube" (Borden & Busse, 1925, p. 184).

- *Testing and teaching the midline air channel:* The straw is a perfect tool to assess the direction of airflow when a client has a lateral lisp. Place one end of the straw against the outer surfaces of the teeth at midline. Ask the client to produce his sibilants, one at a time, the way he usually does. Move the straw from midline-to-left and midline-to-right in front of the teeth to determine where the air stream is escaping the mouth. The straw can be used to help the client discover his incorrect lateral air stream, and to teach him to produce a midline air stream. This is a classic method that the present author first read about in a book about cerebral palsy (Crickmay, 1966, p. 142).

- *Lip rounding:* Straws of various sizes can help a client learn to round the lips for vowels and consonants. Place one end of the straw between the lips and wrap the lips around it.

- *Diameter of the airstream:* Straws of various diameters can be used to help clients modify the size of the air channel needed for frication. For example, a wide straw can be used to give the idea of a wide stream of air for /ʃ/, and a narrow straw can be used to give the idea of a narrow air stream for /s/.

- *Stabilizing the jaw:* A straw is an economical tool for jaw stabilization. Place it along the length of the lateral teeth, reaching back to the back molar. Ask the client to bite down on the straw and gently crush it. Adjust the jaw forward, back, left, or right until the client bites with the best tooth alignment possible. Tug gently outward on the straw to make sure the client has grasped it with his molars.

- *Reduce tongue thrust:* Rosenfeld-Johnson (2001) uses straws of various sizes in a hierarchy of techniques designed to teach tongue retraction and to reduce tongue thrusting.

Tissues

Tissue paper draped over the nose and mouth has been used for more than a century to teach clients about inhalation and exhalation; speech correctionists called it a "tissue flag." Hold a single ply tissue by two corners and drape it across the face. Inhalation pulls the tissue toward the face and exhalation blows it away. The rapid puffs  of exhalation one uses during production of /p/ cause the tissue to pop outward playfully. Controlled exhalation causes the tissue to stand away from the face.

Tongue Cleaners & Scrapers

There are many different types of tongue cleaners and scrapers on the market; these tools come in plastic or metal and they usually have a handle and some sort of cross piece, or a curved flat shovel, or an arched end, for scraping the surface of the tongue. A tongue cleaner is an excellent tool for may uses including the facilitation of tongue-tip elevation, bowling, and lateral elevation.

- *Tongue-tip elevation:* Place the tongue cleaner from left-to-right across the blade of the tongue. Ask the client to lift his tongue tip to grasp the tool and lift it up. Provide a very slight downward tug on the tongue cleaner to add resistance to the activity while the client pulls the tip up.

- *Curling the tip back to the oropharynx:* Place the tongue cleaner from left-to-right across the blade of the tongue. Ask the client to lift his tongue tip to grasp the tool and pull the cleaner into the mouth by curling the tip back. Provide a very slight outward tug on the tongue cleaner to add some resistance to the activity while the client curls the tip all the way back so it faces the oropharynx (Marshalla, 1992a, p. 103).

- *Lateral elevation:* Place the shovel of a scraper sideways on the upper tongue surface at midline and then stroke with a little downward pressure from midline to the left. Then, in one continuous motion, sweep the scraper from left, across midline, to the right lateral margin. The tongue should flatten and flair as the scraper stimulates the midline and left, the flattening should continue as the scraper moves across midline to the right, and the right lateral margins should elevate as the scraper approaches the right lateral margin

Tongue Depressors

The tongue depressor is a time-less tool used to push or pull the articulators into any position. An SLP can do almost all the jaw, lip, and tongue activities written about in this book with only a tongue depressor. Flavored tongue depressors

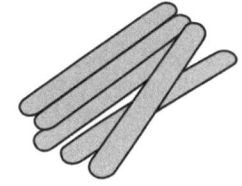

make the work somewhat fun but they don't really taste that good (they taste like flavored wood). Do not have clients bite down with the molars on the thin edge of tongue depressors as they can splinter; an unbreakable plastic probe will be preferable if the mouth needs to be propped open that wide. Discard wooden tongue depressors after a single use.

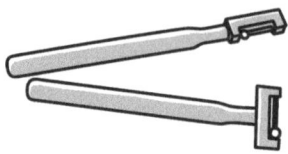

Tongue-Tip Elevation & Lateralization Tools

Another set of products worth mentioning by name are the Tongue-tip Elevation and Lateralization Tools made by TalkTools® (TalkTools.com). These tools consist of a little movable ball on the end of a probe. They are placed between the incisors and the side teeth and are used to teach the tongue to lateralization inside the mouth.

Tubing

Tubing, both flexible and firm, is one of the best tools for use in articulation therapy because it can transport sound from the mouth or nose to the ear. These are many different types. A Rapper Snapper, or *pop tube*, also called a Pull 'N Snap, is a construction toy that can be used for this purpose. The Flex Talk Auditory Feedback Tube is a plastic tube that has been designed for this purpose. A Toobaloo®, or *whisper phone*, is a new design of the popular but now-discontinued TalkBack Tool. A piece of PVC pipe with elbow joints on both ends makes a nice home-made tube.

• *Vowels:* Tubes can be used to shape basic mouth positions for the vowels. Use narrow tubes for high vowels /u/ and /ʊ/. Use wide tubes for low vowels /ɑ/ and /ɔ/. Select tubes of medium sizes for mid-range vowels.

• *Nasality:* Use flexible tubes to discover the

similarities and differences between nasal and oral airflow. Vinyl tubing works well for this. This is a standard articulation method: "Place one end at the patient's nostril and have him produce /n/ … Then place the /n/ in the arresting position in syllables, and finally in words. Emphasize self-discrimination in words" (Hanson, 1983, p. 205).

• *Central groove:* Flexible tubes of small diameter have been used for a hundred years to help clients develop a central groove for production of the sibilants. For example, in 1925 Borden and Busse described what they called an "S-Concentrator" which was nothing more than a thin, hard rubber tube that was used to achieve the tongue position and frication of /s/.

• *Simple amplification:* Inflexible tubing such as paper towel rolls, wrapping paper rolls and shipping tubes work well for general amplification of sound but they cannot reach from the client's oral mechanism to his ear. They can stretch from client-to-client or from client-to-therapist however so they have some benefit for that application.

Vibrating Objects

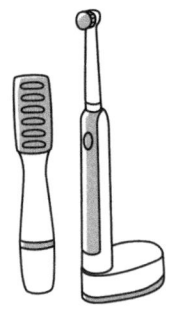

There are many vibrating objects that can be used in sanitary ways to stimulate the oral mechanism. Battery-operated vibrators, vibrating toys, the Z-Vibe®, and vibrating toothbrushes are examples. Some of these vibrators are larger and appropriate for the outside the face, and others are very small and can fit in the oral cavity and even between the teeth and lips or cheeks. Vibration is used to increase arousal, to improve oral awareness, to normalize tactile sensitivity, and to relax or excite muscles. Gentle vibration can be employed with almost any client. Do not use vibrating objects in ways that can cause disorientation, spasticity, nausea, or seizures. Do not force a client to use vibration if he shows obvious rejection or fear.

Warm Objects

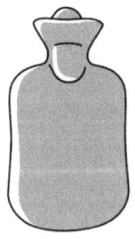

Warmth is used to relax muscles and thus increase range of oral movement. Use the hands rubbed together for greater warmth, a washcloth damp with warm water and/or warmed in the microwave, a hot-water bottle, or a heating pad on a low setting.

Washcloths

Washcloths have several uses in articulation therapy.

• *Normalization of oral-tactile sensitivity:* When

hypersensitivity is an issue, a washcloth can be used as an extra layer of material between a therapist's hands and a client's face to begin hands-on treatment procedures. When reduced sensitivity and limited awareness is the issue, a cloth can be brushed lightly against the face and lips to heighten sensitivity.

• *Jaw stabilization:* Bite on a cloth to develop jaw stability: "Have the child hold a cloth between the teeth, shake the head, and growl like a dog while you gently pull the cloth" (Morris & Klein, 2000, p. 432).

• *Lip articulation:* Press a washcloth between the lips to develop lip-to-lip articulation: "Put a corner of a piece of paper, napkin, handkerchief, or washcloth between lips. Press firmly with lips only. Hold in place 20 seconds or longer, as tolerated" (Gangale, 1993, p. 80).

SUMMARY

Many different tools have been used to teach speech movements since Van Riper recommended them. He said that every available device should be employed when a client cannot imitate a phoneme and the phonetic placement method must be used. The advancement of technology has introduced hundreds of household and medical objects made of plastic and silicone that can be employed in this type of speech training.

Speech training comes down to teaching vowels, diphthongs, and consonants in ways that clients can comprehend.

PART THREE
Vowels, Consonants
& Metaphonological Foundations

"If the acquisition of language is the highest achievement of human cognition, the acquisition of speech may be the paramount characteristic of human physiology."

– Cheng, Murdoch, Goozée, & Scott, 2007a

Speech training comes down to teaching phonemes. This final section of *The Marshalla Guide* explores the way in which the phonemes of Standard North American English are spoken with maturity as well as how they emerge in infancy and early childhood. Every phoneme is described along with many suggestions for training that can be abstracted from all the advice given in the first two parts of this manual. This part also includes chapters on the metaphonological foundations of expressive speech for clients that need them. The latest research on phoneme production is integrated throughout.

Chapters

20

Foundational Pre-Speech Platforms

The role of infant vocal development in speech remediation

"It is vitally important for the student of speech correction to know how speech develops."

– Charles Van Riper, 1947

Charles Van Riper was one of the first to recognize the importance of early pre-speech sound development in the treatment of articulation deficits: "The skills involved in speech begin to be acquired as soon as the child is born" (Van Riper, 1947, p. 69). Three decades later, Oller proposed a five-stage developmental framework for the acquisition of vocalizations during an infant's first year of life (Oller, 1978). Oller's stages are widely accepted as the basic framework of pre-speech development. The present author has found that these stages have direct application to the facilitation of expression in clients with the most severe problems in speech, especially non-verbal clients and those with severe cognitive and/or neuromuscular disorder. The stages of vocal development can be used as a road map for therapy with clients struggling to learn phonemes at the word level. Howell and Dean (1991) called this *metaphon therapy*. This chapter provides an overview of the skills learned in each of these stages. Each stage is described and ideas about how this information might apply to therapy are offered from the author's clinical experiences.

PLATFORMS OF LEARNING

Infants spend their first year of life figuring out what their body mechanisms can do and this includes the mechanisms their body has for making sound. During this first year infants explore the so-called *metaphonological skills* defined as "the most general features of phonologies [and] the background parameters upon which languages build individual concrete phonological systems" (Oller, 1978, p. 526). Oller proposed that these pre-speech and

pre-language skills develop in stages during the first year of life. The stages are described below and, for the purposes of this manual, each has been named for the primary speech movement skill being acquired during the stage: *phonating, prolonging, expanding, oscillating, variegating,* and *producing words.*

Each stage serves as a platform of learning. As in all stage frameworks, certain statements could be made about them as are detailed below. Ages of acquisition for each stage are approximate, several lessons are learned at each stage, and overlap from one stage to another is expected. Children remain at each stage as long as necessary to learn its lessons, and then they move on. The skills being practiced at each level result in the production of certain pre-speech vocalizations; these pre-speech vocal skills become increasingly more sophisticated at each subsequent stage.

The present author has found that these individual vocalizations can be used to track progress over time in the most severe clients. It has also been her experience, however, that clients with serious speech impairment do not always develop these skills in the natural order described

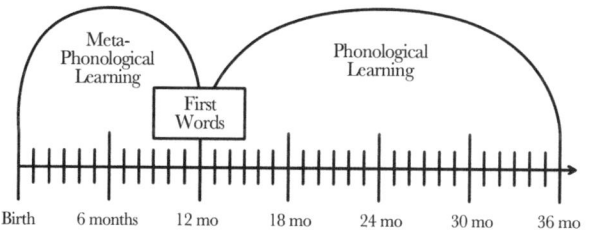

Metaphonological skills are learned before first words are produced. Phonological skills are learned during the process of word acquisition.

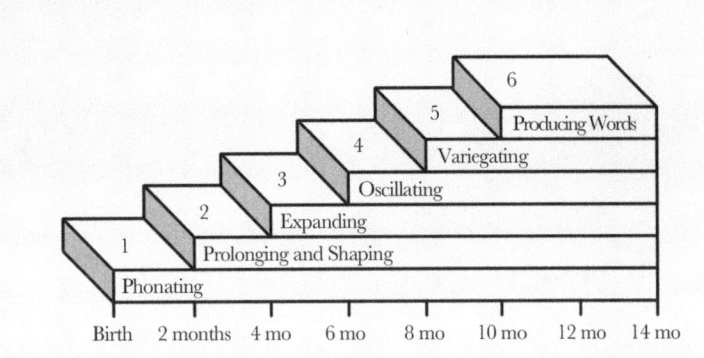

Platforms of speech movement learning govern the acquisition of pre-speech vocalizations.

below. Teaching clients to produce these preliminary sounds seems to train the auditory and speech movement systems simultaneously and in fundamental ways that enhance later articulation and phonological development. The idea that producing sound and hearing sound develops in tandem in early infancy is an idea that research is beginning to support (e.g., Kuhl et al, 2014).

Platform 1: Phonating

Expressive speech begins with exhalation and voice. Newborns produce one speech-like sound known as the *quasiresonant nuclei* (QRN) during this time. "The QRN ranges from a syllabic nasal consonant to a high, mid, un-rounded, nasalized vowel" (Oller, 1978, p. 534). The QRN dominates expression because of the newborn's governing flexor tone. High flexor tone keeps the baby curled up, and this posture restricts lung volume and oral position. Newborns also produce non-speech, vegetative, or reflexive sounds during this period including burping, sneezing, coughing, and choking. They also produce sounds of displeasure including crying, whimpering, and fussing.

Application to Therapy

Clients with the most severe forms of expressive speech impairment produce no voice at all or they produce a weak QRN. These clients need assistance with breath support and voice; they need to learn to produce the QRN.

The production of voice is stimulated in many ways depending upon etiology and therapy setting. The following main ideas are in common use and are part of the present author's clinical routine. Methods provide

Newborn: Excessive flexor tone and the QRN go hand-in-hand.

stimulation that sets the vocal mechanism into action:

• Alerting activities designed to arouse clients who are sluggish and generally unresponsive. Stimulation might come in the form of gross motor activity (jumping, bouncing, etc.) or specific vestibular stimulation (swinging, prescribed spinning, etc.). Therapists also use feeding activities for the taste and scent stimulation they contribute to arousal.

• Activities to stimulate inhalation and exhalation for speech. (For ideas, see Chapter 7 on breath support.)

• Activities to stimulate basic auditory attention to sound and speech. (For ideas, see Chapter 4 on classic auditory training.)

• Neuromuscular inhabitation and facilitation techniques when muscle tone perpetuates the excessive flexor tone that interferes with the production of voice. SLPs work with motor specialists to design these prescribed therapy activities so that the trunk supports the best possible inhalation, exhalation, and voice patterns.

• Deep pressure and/or vibration: "The most effective way that we know of facilitating voice for a [child with cerebral palsy] is through the use of vibration. As the child exhales, the therapist uses her spread hand to vibrate as rapidly as she can the patient's diaphragm, chest, spine, larynx, or the infrahyoid area, that is, underneath the lower jaw, depending upon whichever part the best and quickest results" (Crickmay, 1966, p. 120).

• Laughing, giggling, singing, and other gross pre-speech stimulation activities.

• Procedures in which communication partners respond to any and all sounds the client makes spontaneously. The idea is to reward the client for producing any and all of the sounds he can say. The goal is to get the client to produce more sound more often, and to produce sounds under a greater number of circumstances and for a greater variety of communicative purposes. Communication partners assign communicative intent to sounds these clients make spontaneously.

Platform 2: Prolonging & Shaping

A new platform of skill emerges by 2–3 months of age because of changes in postural support and oral movement. The development of trunk extension opens the chest cavity and allows a child to inhale and exhale a greater volume of air. More air allows a child to prolong sound, a process called *cooing*, and this ability to prolong voice creates a new platform for speech development. Playing with the prolonged voice creates opportunities for the child to explore his sound-making capabilities. New sound is created on these prolonged utterances as the child begins to discover the movements of his jaw, lips, tongue, and velum. The result is that the child begins to produce a few basic vowels, nasals, and grossly fricated sounds mostly in the back. These become embedded within the coos in a process known as *goo-ing*.

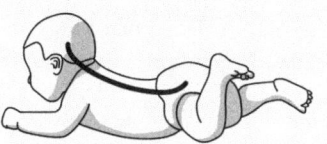

2–3 months: Extension of the trunk increases lung capacity for cooing to emerge.

Application to Therapy

A client who cannot prolong his own vocalizations is in deep trouble because he is denied access to the very playground on which he will learn the rest of his pre-speech vocal skills. Deficiency like this occurs primarily in clients who have neuromuscular disorder and/or cognitive deficit. Early vowels, diphthongs, glides, and nasals are found wanting because of this failure to prolong voice for the vowels. These clients often remain non-verbal or minimally so. Treatment of expressive speech will include methods to facilitate breath support, voice, and basic oral movements. The present author uses the following methods to stimulate prolongation of vocalization.

- *Kazoo:* The kazoo is an especially fine tool in the development of the prolonged voice. Teach the client how to make voice in the kazoo and encourage him to make the sound longer.

- *Songs:* Singing encourages a longer prolongation of voice. Use simple songs with lots of repetition. Sing by vocalizing into a kazoo.

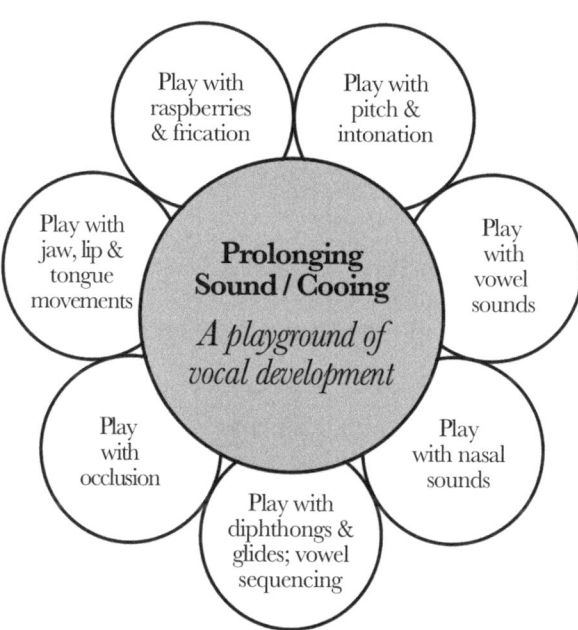

Prolongation of sound (cooing) allows children to experiment with all fundamental expressive skills.

- *Humming:* Encourage clients to hum through songs and to hum while playing and while eating.

- *Cooing:* Cooing is the essential expression of vocal prolongation, so clients at this level are taught to coo. The easiest way to do this is to use the three most basic vowels to express basic functional concepts such as "Ahhh" (meaning "I am satisfied"), "Oooo" (meaning "that is interesting"), and "Eeeee" (for excitement).

- *Sound-activated toys:* Toys that move in response to sound are an excellent way to encourage prolongation of voice. The client keeps his voice turned on so the toy keeps moving. (See pages 339–340 for more.)

- *Computer programs and apps:* There are simple computer programs and apps that have characters who activate in some way in response to voice which clients often find motivating.. (These were not investigated for this manual because of their rapidly changing nature.)

- *Recitation:* Teach the client to count and/or say the alphabet. Encourage him to turn his voice on and leave it on in the process. Instead of counting "1, 2, 3, 4, 5..." or saying "A...B...C..." he will say "Ah-ah-ah-ah-ah."

- *Babbling:* Teach the client to babble in increasingly longer strings on one breath.

- *Cues:* Develop a standard cue to indicate the short and the long voice. For example, place the palms together in praying position. Move the hands apart an inch to indicate a short sound, and move them apart a foot to indicate a long sound.

Platform 3: Expanding

Oller called the 4–6 month period the *expansion* stage because tremendous growth occurs at this time. The child's feet now are planted firmly on the vocal playground; he is prolonging sound and his oral mechanism is beginning to move quite a bit. Further development in trunk and head stability and mobility create the opportunity for vocal changes and an active velopharyngeal mechanism allows differentiated oral and nasal sound to emerge. The ability to make consistent oral sound permits a great number of pre-babbling vocalizations to occur. The following skills arise during this period. These make the child's utterances sound much more speech-like.

- *Orality:* The *fully-resonant nuclei* (FRN) is produced.

- *Nasality:* Distinct nasal sounds are produced. (They could be called *fully nasal nuclei* [FNN].)

- *Loudness:* Sound ranges from loud (yell/shout) to soft (quiet/whisper).

- *Pitch:* Sound ranges from low (growl) to high (squeal).

- *Voicing:* Sound range from voiced (mainly vowels and nasals) to voiceless (mainly panting, sniffing, snorting).

- *Vowel:* The vowel quadrilateral forms as a result of minor jaw, lip, and tongue movement. (For more information, see Chapter 21 on the vowels.)

- *Constrictions:* Sound is produced with a range of vocal tract constrictions, from no constriction (vowels) to partial constriction (raspberries) to full construction (occlusals).

- *Place:* Constrictions occur at all points along the vocal tract, from labial to glottal.

- *Emotional expression:* The sounds of pleasure begin to emerge (chortling, giggling, laughing).

- *Prosody:* This is the stage in which an infant begins to sound speech-like because he adds pitch, loudness, stress, and intonation variations to express mood and perspective.

- *Syllables:* Basic consonants and vowels are heard in CV syllables by the end of this stage. These utterances are produced in loosely-organized sequences that Oller called *marginal babbling.* These sequences lack the rhythmic oscillations and timing qualities of later babbling.

Application to Therapy

Clients who produce few consonants and who hardly babble may need help developing the pre-babbling skills of this stage and the prior two. The emphasis of treatment should be on developing a wide variety of sound. All new productions should be recognized and encouraged. Very little correction of productions should occur. The goal at this level is to produce more sound with more variety and anything that restricts this process should be avoided. Many activities are encouraged:

- Activities to develop upper body strength and control. This requires occupational/physical therapy co-treatment and consult.

- Activities to direct voice differentially through the mouth and nose (see Chapter 8 on resonance).

- Activities that encourage gross supersegmentals: shout, whisper, growl, squeal, pretend to be animals, and imitate environmental sounds.

- Activities to develop all the grossly fricated raspberries and snorts. Imitate animal and environmental sounds.

- Activities to develop basic prosodic expression in the form of high and low pitch, loudness variations, stress and emphasis, and intonation patterns. This is mostly a matter of listening and imitating these sounds within appropriate communication contexts. For example, pretend to be fairies and speak in a high pitch, pretend to be angry and speak with force, and so forth.

- Activities to activate jaw, lip, tongue, and velar movement (see corresponding chapters for methods). Van Riper recommended feeding and other activities for this purpose: "We often recommend that [therapists] combine swallowing, chewing, biting, and smiling movements with this vocal play" (Van Riper, 1947, p. 173).

Platform 4: Oscillating

By about six months of age babies develop enough hip, trunk, and shoulder support to sit upright unsupported. This level of trunk control supports the respiratory system

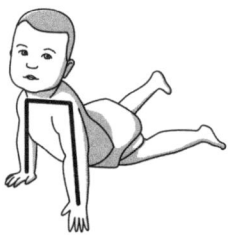

4–6 months: Expansion of the sound repertoire coincides with the development of upper body and head control.

6–10 months: The trunk control needed for sitting upright contributes to an infant's ability to speak out and babble with a rhythmically oscillating jaw.

well enough that voice can be sustained for babbling. Babbling occurs when consonants and vowels are produced in sequence upon the controlled exhalation, but very little of this has to do with lip or tongue movement. Babbling emerges because the jaw begins to oscillate upwards and downwards on the prolonged vocalization while the head and upper body remain stable. Research shows that anterior consonants and low vowels dominate these productions. (This topic is discussed in detail in Chapter 21 on vowels and Chapter 11 on jaw mobility.)

The earliest jaw oscillations are weak and small, resulting in the production of babbling sequences that are made with vowels only. This is called *vowel babbling*. Consonants in babbling emerge when the jaw begins to push upward more fully, causing the lower lip to bang against the upper lip and the tongue to bang against the palate and upper lip.

Oller called this rhythmic oscillating babbling pattern *reduplicated babbling* because the syllables repeat. It has also been called *canonical babbling* because the CV represents the most basic syllable shape. The present author also calls it *jaw babbling* for the important role that jaw mobility plays in its emergence.

The reduplicated babbling stage is characterized by identical sequences of syllables that are produced with rhythmic timing properties. Voice is produced, the mouth postures, and the jaw moves upwards and downwards to create the sequences. The length of these sequences increases with time and practice, and as breath support improves. Reduplicated babbling sometimes sounds like real words but no lexical meaning is associated with them. Reduplicated babbling is voiced and includes nasals, glides, and voiced stops. Anterior consonants dominate because of the excessive jaw mobility.

The rhythmic production of speech that begins during the babbling phase controls expressive speech for the rest of one's life. Rate and rhythm contribute to intelligibility, therefore, the oscillating and rhythmic production of individual syllables contributes to intelligibility throughout life. Lack of rhythmic oscillation causes many specific problems.

Other skills emerge during this period: children learn to speak up, speak out, and make sound with more boldness and force, and this skill carries them into and through adulthood. Bell (1898) noticed how a lack of forceful and purposeful speech leads to mumbling, or what he called "oratorical faults" and "conversational slurring."

Application to Therapy

Clients with few or no consonants need methods to stimulate them, and reduplicated babbling often is the method of choice. Prolonging sounds, speaking up and out, and getting the jaw to move up and down in sequence are keys. Jaw mobility will cause the anterior consonants and the low vowels to dominate these sequences. Therapy, therefore, should not focus on teaching specific lip and tongue movement; the focus should be on stimulating all

the anterior nasals, stops, and glides through big jaw oscillations. This topic is discussed at length in Chapter 11, *Encouraging Jaw Oscillation for the CV.*

Reduplicated babbling sequences create a new platform of phoneme learning. Once the reduplicated pattern is set, the lips and tongue can begin to move in ways that create more consonants. Trunk and head stability are important elements of this level of therapy. Rhythm is key.

> *"Talking has been computed to require many hundreds of fine coordinations to the minute; without the use of rhythm this would be obviously but a fine jumble of unintelligible sounds"* (Blanton & Blanton, 1924, p. 51).

> *"The basic unit of speech rhythm is the syllable"* (Garn-Nunn & Lynn, 2004, p. 99).

> *"The elimination of syllables is an extremely common characteristic of substandard American speech and goes along with the cluttered, rapid utterance of those who lack a sense of speech rhythm"* (Carrell & Tiffany, 1960, p. 286).

Platform 5: Variegating

To variegate means to vary. Babbling becomes variegated as the number of different consonants and vowels increases. The identical CV syllables of the earlier stage are knocked off course as children begin to move the lips and tongue in new ways while oscillating the jaw. Folklore has always postulated that babies produce all the phonemes of all the languages in the world. If so, it must be during this period because all pre-speech vocalization skills are operational by this time and many different English and non-English phonemes can be heard. Consonants vary by all place, manner, and voice features, and the complete vowel quadrilateral is set. Intonation is in place and all advanced pre-speech skills emerge. The body has completed its first year of development and has achieved an upright standing position.

Application to Therapy

The lesson to be learned from this stage is that average children are capable of producing a nearly complete collection of consonants and vowels before they ever produce words. In other words, they learn how their speech mechanism works before they learn to use these sounds to produce words that have meaning. They learn metaphonological skills in pre-language vocalizations before they use these skills phonologically within the language.

This fact runs counter to the way much therapy is done. For example, many therapists now report that they must focus on functional communication and that this has forced them to work on language and to leave remedial speech work behind. One therapist who works in a big city parent-infant program reported that she could work on "anything that has to do with words but nothing that has to do with sounds." She and the dozens of other SLPs working in this program were stimulating toddlers to produce words but they were forbidden from stimulating these children to produce sounds. This philosophy runs absolutely counter to the normal pattern of speech-language development. In normal development children acquire an expansive repertoire of pre-speech sounds and phonemes *and then* they produce words. It is this author's opinion that therapy provided in a developmental center should mimic the normal pattern.

A client who cannot produce a full repertoire of pre-speech vocalizations leading up to variegated babbling may need help with the skills of each stage. This often occurs in clients with cognitive and/or neuromuscular damage, disorder, or delay. Co-treatment with team motor specialists will reveal the neuromuscular contributions to the problems, and treatment methods will be adjusted accordingly.

Platform 6: Producing First Words

A child's first words tend to emerge within a few months before or after the first birthday. Babbling sequences continue to be produced but clear individual words are spoken. Many of these words reflect the reduplicated babbling process and contain identical CV syllables, for example, *mamma, dada, bye-bye,* and *no-no.* But these words can be in the form of V, VC, or CVC also, for example, *Oh, up,* and *dog.*

A child's very first word may contain any one or more of the 24 consonants and 11 vowels of English. This is not to say that all one-year-old children can produce every consonant and every vowel; it is to say that the one-year-old child's neuromuscular system can support the production of any consonant and vowel, but his linguistic system will limit what he chooses to say. His first word is only one word; therefore, it creates an opportunity to say only certain phonemes. The present author has observed scores of typically-developing children throughout 39 years of service and has found examples of every consonant being used at one time or another in a first word. Examples are

11–12 months: Upright body control and variegated babbling emerge together.

Walking upright and speaking first words both find expression around the first birthday.

offered in Table 10 on the next page.

Application to Therapy

The lesson to be learned here is that typically developing children learn all their expressive speech skills *before* they speak their first words. Many clients with neuromuscular impairment and/or cognitive delay do the opposite — they speak in words before they have developed a full repertoire of speech skill. Therapy approaches differ in theory as to how one might teach phonemes in words. Some therapists teach one phoneme at a time, others teach by distinctive features, some use key words, others stimulate all the consonants and vowels simultaneously. The approach should be chosen to reflect the client's learning style and the teaching environment.

FOUR BIG IDEAS

Four big ideas conclude this discussion. First, the question naturally arises about the necessity of teaching pre-speech skills to children who are older than one year of age. This is how the present author views this dilemma: Pre-speech behaviors lead to first words just as crawling leads to walking, and just as all children do not need to crawl before they walk, all children do not need to produce pre-speech vocalizations before they speak in words. Therefore, some but not all clients may need to learn pre-speech skills in order for correct word-level utterances to emerge.

No research exists to support or discredit the use of these methods, therefore, it is up to each individual therapist to determine whether the facilitation of pre-speech behavior is helpful in each case. This brings the discussion back to the creativity of therapy and the process of trial and error. If a client begins to produce more sound in a greater variety, if he begins to sound more speech-like, and if he begins to produce more consonants and vowels as a result of this work, then it can be assumed that the stimulation is helpful. If not, then the client may need more time with these methods or the methods may not be appropriate for him. In practice it can be helpful to work in three-month intervals to determine whether or not to continue along these lines.

Second, there is no reason to delay stimulating words as clients are learning their pre-speech vocalizations. In fact, the best plan may be to stimulate both at the same time.

Third, most of these clients will be using some combination of augmentative and verbal communication. The ideas of this chapter are intended to push the verbal direction. However, the development of vocal/verbal expression can progress much more slowly than an augmentative means, and the augmentative means should not be pushed aside too soon.

Most therapists agree that the use of a non-verbal, non-vocal means of communication does not have to limit expressive output unless the system is designed that way. In other words, exclusive use of pointing, touching, gesturing, or typing may cause verbal output to wane. he best solution is to work simultaneously with both systems so that verbal expression is not abandoned. Remember that an augmentative system is just that — augmentative. It is not intended to replace verbal communication but to augment, supplement, or enhance verbal communication.

Finally, it is important to recognize that stimulation of pre-speech behavior can be a bad idea in some cases. For example, pre-speech vocal productions were encouraged in one non-verbal twenty-five-year-old female who carried a diagnosis of schizophrenia and severe developmental delay. Stimulation of pre-speech vocalizations caused her to become much more vocal over a six-month period, but her utterances were loud, mostly unintelligible, and they had no communicative intent. The woman became more obnoxious as she became more vocal, and she began to appear more bizarre in public. A decision was made to allow her to remain mostly silent because this was the only way the woman could continue to function effectively in her group home, at work, and out in the community. Whether or not to encourage more sound production is a decision best made by the full team including the parents and other caretakers. Social appropriateness and the client's ability to function in society should rule this decision.

SUMMARY

Typical children learn how to control their speech mechanism before they speak words. Children with neuromuscular disorder and/or cognitive deficit often begin saying words before they learn to control their speech production mechanism. The normal platforms of pre-speech development can be used as a plan of therapy to develop these metaphonological skills.

TABLE 10 — English Consonants in First Words

Category	Consonant	Observed First Word	Category	Consonant	Observed First Word
Stop	/p/	Up	Fricative Affricate	/θ/	Tho (soap)
	/b/	Bye-bye		/ð/	Thæ (that)
	/t/	Eat		/f/	Off
	/d/	Do		/v/	Vo (no)
	/k/	Icky		/s/	Iss (kiss)
	/g/	Goggie (doggie)		/z/	Zee (zebra)
Nasal	/m/	Mama		/ʃ/	Shoe
	/n/	No		/ʒ/	ʒip (zipper)
	/ŋ/	Ŋo (no)		/tʃ/	Choo-choo
Glide	/w/	Wɔ-wɔ (water)		/dʒ/	Jo
	/l/	Lɑlɑ (name)		/h/	Hi
	/j/	Yea			
	/r/	Rɑ-rɑ (rabbit)			

Informal data collected by the present author over nearly 40 years reveals that first words can contain any of the 24 English consonants.

21

Teaching Vowels & Diphthongs

Establishing the heart of every syllable

"Consonants constitute the back-bone of spoken language — vowels the flesh and blood."
– Alexander Graham Bell, 1906

The vowels and diphthongs seem to be the most neglected topics within the field of speech correction. The vowels and diphthongs are treated as an afterthought on most tests and very little about how to fix them is included in textbooks; the attitude seems to be that vowel problems exist in very few clients and fixing the few errors that might occur is a simple task. This perspective is false. Many different types of clients have problems with vowels and diphthongs and it is not always easy to fix them because the acoustic and speech movement differences between one vowel and another are very slight. Presently, consonant problems are generally treated as very important and vowel problems are treated as very unimportant, though problems with vowels can destroy intelligibility, especially in clients with motor speech disorders.

This chapter addresses the treatment of vowels and diphthongs by focusing on their nature and development, by looking closely at the problems that occur, and by discussing remediation procedures that exist for developing

their motor patterns. Remediation of these phonemes is a subject that should alert serious concern among practicing speech-language pathologists because vowels and diphthongs form the very heart of every syllable.

CLIENTS

First, the misconception that vowel problems are a rare phenomenon must be dispelled by discussing the clients who have them. Research and clinical observations have revealed that the following types of clients have problems with vowels:

- *Apraxia:* ASHA states that apraxia is characterized by "inconsistent errors on consonants and vowels" (American Speech-Language-Hearing Association, 2007).

- *Dysarthria:* ASHA states that dysarthria is characterized by "slurred speech" and "mumbling," meaning that the vowels and diphthongs are distorted along with the consonants (American Speech-Language-Hearing Association, 2012).

- *Phonology:* Stoel-Gammon and Herrington (1990) reviewed the phonological literature and proposed that there is a group of phonologically disordered children who have vowel problems. They also found that these subjects could be divided into two groups — those with large vowel repertoires and those who use only a few lax vowels. An example of the first is described in Hargrove (1982) and an example of the latter can be found in Wolfe and Blocker (1990).

Syllable

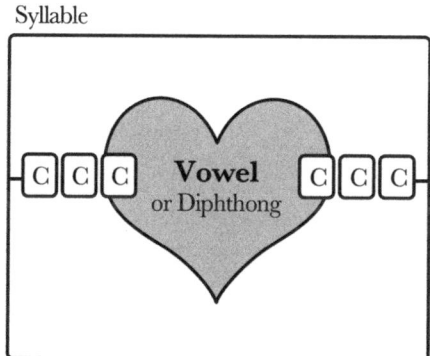

A vowel or diphthong creates the heart of every syllable.

- *Hearing impairment:* Clients with hearing impairment have difficulty producing correct vowels. This was noted as far back as Bell (1906) and all research substantiates this claim (e.g., Smith, 1975; Dagenais & Critz-Crosby, 1992).

- *Structural deficits:* Clients with oral structural anomalies can have difficulty with vowels as demonstrated in a wide variety of studies. For example, Spriestersbach and Powers (1959) found that clients with cleft palate were more nasal on vowels, and that they were more nasal on high vowels than on low vowels. Qi and Weinberg (1991) found that tracheoesophageal speakers used vowels that were more flat on spectrographic analysis. Christensen and Weinberg (1976) found that vowel duration was longer among esophageal speakers. Fernando (1998) found that clients with restricted lingua frenums often have "vowel changes due to altered lingual postures" (p. 22). Van Borsel et al. (2000) found that the large tongue of clients with Beckwith Syndrome caused vowel differences.

- *Infants and toddlers:* Otomo and Stoel-Gammon (1992) and Davis and MacNeilage (1990) demonstrated that typical toddlers can lack a complete range of vowels, therefore, toddlers enrolled in speech and language therapy undoubtedly do, especially those with severe speech-language delay/disorder.

- *Cognitive impairment:* The present author's personal clinical experiences over nearly four decades have demonstrated that clients with cognitive impairment often lack a complete vowel repertoire.

- *Fluency:* Vowel problems have been found among clients with fluency disorder. For example, Klich and May (1982) found that stutters produced vowels that were more centralized as well as spatially and temporally more restricted than hearing subjects, and Blomgren, Robb, and Chen (1998) noted a tendency for untreated stutterers to neutralize vowels. Both these studies indicate that the schwa is employed too often among clients with problems of fluency.

- *Mild articulation errors:* In their classic text on phonetics, Carrell and Tiffany (1960) reported that under-pronunciation of the diphthongs and vowels is one of the most pervasive speech faults among clients with mild-to-moderate articulation deficit. A common problem is distortion of the vowels that precede the persistent vocalic /r/ distortion.

- *Severe speech problems:* Wolfe and Blocker (1990) found that therapy progresses much more slowly when clients have difficulty with vowels and diphthongs, and this may mean that these are the clients with more severe speech problems.

- *Language impairment:* Datta et al. (2010) found that clients with atypical language development had significantly poorer identification of long vowels, and

the authors felt this might contribute to these clients' language-learning capability. (Note that this is a problem of auditory discrimination of the vowels and not necessarily of vowel production.)

- *Advanced age:* Subtle vowel changes are noticed in subjects with advancing age. For example, Kreul (1972) demonstrated limited vowel duration in aging females.

- *Second language learning:* Clients who are learning English as a second language virtually always have vowel differences as noted as far back as the 19th century American elocutionists (e.g., Bell & Bell, 1878).

- *Dialect:* Vowel differences are noted among American English dialects (Wright & Souza, 2012; Jacewicz, Fox, & Salmons, 2011). Although dialect differences are not considered a category of impairment, clients do sometimes enroll in therapy to eliminate dialect differences, and many actors enroll in speech classes to learn how to produce different dialects.

BACKGROUND

The elocutionists placed a much greater emphasis on the vowels and diphthongs than do most SLPs; the elocutionists taught that the vowels and diphthongs carry the melody, the passion, and the intelligibility of speech and song, and they devoted much attention to them in their books. In fact, some of their books are more about vowels than they are about consonants. Many of these writers called the vowels *tonics* and the consonants *atonics*. They taught that incorrect, drawn out, distorted, or sloppy vowels and diphthongs reflected negatively upon the speaker, making him difficult to understand and causing him to appear less intelligent.

The elocutionists used certain terms for vowel distortions that survive, including *drawl* and *twang*. *Drawl* refers to prolonged indistinct vowels while *twang* refers to sharp somewhat nasalized vowels.

The elocutionists also used terms that have been abandoned but that should be revived. These include *orotund* and *thickness of speech*. *Orotund* means full and round; all the vowels should be orotund meaning that they are fully oral and made with a round oral cavity. Roundness of the oral cavity occurs when the mouth opens wide and the middle of the tongue dips low and maintains a general concave appearance with a midline channel. Roundness was considered "a quality of the human voice marked by richness of overtones and sublimity of feeling and deep respect" (Bender & Kleinfeld, 1938, p. 283). The elocutionists viewed expressive speech as intimately related to human emotion.

The term *thickness of speech* refers to speech that is made with a tongue that is arching upward instead of lowering or bowling downward in the middle; it is the speech produced when the tongue is moving in a convex instead of a concave pattern. This is not referring to a tongue that is too large; it is referring instead to a tongue whose middle section is pushing or arching upward too far. Thickness of speech is a very useful term that SLPs should begin to use again because it is the sound quality that dominates in many clients. This pattern is discussed more thoroughly in Chapter 13 on the tongue and Chapter 14 on oral stability.

Rules for Vowel Production

The elocutionists gave specific advice about jaw, lip, and tongue movements for correct vowels. They said that the jaw should be low for the low vowels, high for the high vowels, and in a mid range position for the mid vowels. They said that the tongue should be low in the middle (bowled) for every vowel in order to create the orotund quality. They taught that the lips should be used as little as possible during vowel production and that only slight lip rounding or retracting is necessary to differentiate the vowels in most cases.

In regard to the diphthongs, the elocutionists taught that each diphthong should contain two distinct vowels with the first vowel prominent and the second vowel fading. They called the first vowel of a diphthong its *radical tone* and the second vowel of a diphthong its *vanishing movement.* The second vowel of a diphthong should have "that delicate expiration which may render its limit almost imperceptible" (Rush, 1855, p. 430).

The elocutionists thought that the schwa should not be overused in unaccented syllables because its overuse made a speaker sound lazy, ill informed, and poorly educated. They also warned that triphthongs should not be overused because they are mostly unnecessary and they make a speaker sound provincial and unsophisticated. The elocutionists also taught that a consonant should be attached to the vowel that follows it, and not to the vowel that precedes it. For example, one says *boa-ting* and not *boat-ing*.

Phonetic Placement Ideas

The focus of speech training shifted away from the vowels and toward the consonants with the introduction of the International Phonetic Alphabet in 1888. The IPA helped divide methods of singing from methods of speech training, and it turned the speech teacher's attention away from vowels and toward the place, manner, and voice features of consonants. Although the vowel quadrilateral was known by 1917 (Jones, 1917), speech correctionists of the Phonetic Placement Era concerned themselves mostly with consonants. This turn away from the vowels was reflected in the title of the most practical and advanced book of that period, called *The Correction of Defective Consonant Sounds* (Nemoy & Davis, 1937).

Traditional Therapy

Vowels and diphthongs had long been treated as secondary by the time Van Riper and other Traditional Era therapists began to write books. One might surmise that this occurred because of the new IPA and because therapy shifted away from private elocution lessons and singing to speech correction that took place in the public schools. The schools at that time were places where only regular education students attended; therefore, the typical caseload would have been comprised mainly of children with mild-to-moderate articulation problems who would have had very few problems with the vowels or diphthongs. Children with severe speech impairment related to neuromuscular, cognitive, or hearing problems were not enrolled in the public schools and, therefore, they did not receive the kind of speech services supplied by therapists who wrote about their public school experiences.

Modern Therapy

Phonological theory arrived on the scene in 1968 and its focus on the patterns of consonant usage in highly unintelligible clients nearly threw the vowels and diphthongs completely off the SLP's radar during the period of 1970–1990. The few books being written about cerebral palsy and other causes of motor speech disorders during that period always named vowel distortion as a prominent characteristic of dysarthria, and general advice about stimulating the vowels was offered, but virtually no books or articles about how to do this seem to have been written.

Research was affected also; toward the end of the 20th century, Davis and MacNeilage (1990) did a review of the phonological literature and found that there had been less than one study of vowels for every 20 studies of consonants. They also found that studies on children's complete phonological repertoires rarely paid any attention to the vowels — that article may have sounded the alarm, for, since then, there has been much more research on the vowels and diphthongs, especially on their emergence in infants, toddlers, and preschool children. Still, there have been few breakthroughs in terms of therapy for these phonemes (one being the course *Vowels & Intelligibility* by the present author [Marshalla, 2007c, 2018]). It is hoped that the information on therapy presented in this chapter below will help break this cycle for good.

THE VOWELS

There is important new research on vowel production that should guide treatment. It includes research on the role vowels and diphthongs play in early speech development, the way in which the vowel quadrilateral is learned, the way the tongue shapes during vowel production, and the different way that coarticulation is expressed in children and adults.

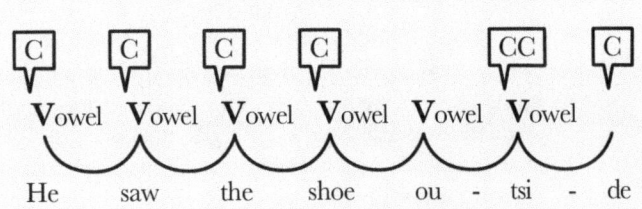

Expressive speech is comprised of a series of vowels that are interrupted by auxiliary consonant movements.

Role of Vowels in Speech Movement

Stetson (1928) was the 20th century's first great motor speech scientist and he set the stage for understanding the role vowels play in speech movement. He said that the syllable is the smallest unit of speech movement and that a vowel (or diphthong) creates each syllable. He said that consonants were extra, supplemental, secondary, or auxiliary movements added to a syllable's vowel. Stetson said that a consonant by itself could not create a syllable. He explained that words are constructed of syllables and these syllables are constructed of vowels to which the extra movements of consonants are added; consonants merely function to initiate or terminate each vowel.

This was an idea that the elocutionists of the prior century also knew: "Consonants are mere modifiers of the vowels" (Sweet, 1877, p. 87). This early idea set up the understanding of the purpose that vowels serve in expressive speech. Expressive speech is a production of vowels to which tiny consonant movements are added; consonants break up the flow of vowels into distinct syllables. Important speech researchers have reiterated this idea in various ways ever since:

> *"When we examine a sequence of sounds as they occur in contextual speech, the role of the consonants seems to be to interrupt the vowels in the utterance"* (Zemlin, 1981, p. 366).

> *"The vowel has long been recognized as the core of the syllable nucleus"* (Fletcher, 1992, p. 238).

> *"Many consonants are just ways of beginning or ending vowels"* (Ladefoged, 2005, p. 49).

The concept that expressive speech consists of the production of vowel sequences to which consonant movements are added should guide therapy. This means that vowels should rank first and foremost in therapy when lack of verbal communication and/or low intelligibility is a concern. When teaching an early word like *juice* to a client with fewer than 50 words, for example, attention should be given to the vowel first and the consonants second. This is opposite of the way most SLPs are trained

to work; most student clinicians are taught to focus on the consonants and sometimes even to ignore the vowels. This causes certain production problems.

For example, consider the process of teaching the word *boot* as an early word to a child with minimal verbal output. Most therapists model the word by saying something like, "Boot, /bʌ/ /bʌ/ boot." The focus is on the consonant and the attached vowel is changed to a schwa. This very common stimulation method works counter to the developmental pattern. In the natural order of speech acquisition, the vowel or diphthong is the main and more important member of the syllable and the consonant is secondary.

In remediation, therefore, the vowel should be straightened out first to boost intelligibility quickly and to set the production onto the normal path of development. Once the vowel is set, then the consonant movements can be added. In other words "/bʌ/ /bʌ/ boot" should not be the stimulus for the word *boot*. Instead, therapists should highlight the vowel as in "/u/ /u/ boot." The consonant should be taught after the client learns to express the word with the vowel; the vowel sets the basic oral position and then the consonant is added to it.

Embouchures

All vowels are made upon exhalation and phonation while the velar port is closed. Each individual vowel is created when the mouth forms itself into a certain shape that alters the acoustic properties of the voiced airstream: "Vowels reflect relatively slow, global changes in the vocal tract shape" (Fletcher, 1992, p. 84).

It might be useful for SLPs to adopt the term *embouchure* in discussing the vowels. The term is from the French *em-* meaning *into* and from *bouche* meaning *mouth*. An embouchure is that position the mouth assumes for directing an oral airstream into a wind instrument. Each instrument (e.g., flute, trumpet, oboe, tuba) requires a different embouchure; the mouth becomes an extension of

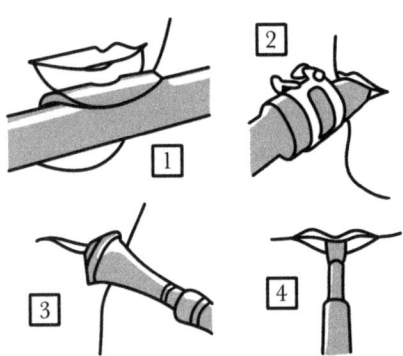

Required embouchures for the flute (1), clarinet (2), French horn (3), and oboe (4).

the instrument by shaping the airstream in a particular way. Vowels are produced in much the same way: "Different vowels are like different instruments... We can liken the air in the mouth and throat to the air in a bottle... When you blow across the top of the bottle the air inside it will be set into vibration... Producing different vowels is like altering the size and shape of the bottle" (Ladefoged, 2005, p. 32–34).

Vowel Embouchures

The classic view is that the lips and tongue are the principle actors in vowel formation. However, the view in research is that each of the articulators is involved in the production of all phonemes, therefore, each oral part is important in the shaping of vowel embouchures:

- *Jaw:* Jaw position for vowel production ranges from the high stance taken for production of /i/ to the low position required for /ɑ/. All other vowels are produced with the jaw situated at a point somewhere between these two.

- *Lips:* Lip position for vowel production ranges from the rounding necessary for /u/ to the slight retraction required for /i/. All other vowels are produced with the lips positioned between these two.

- *Cheeks:* The cheek muscles are slightly retracted during speech. This slight amount of retraction is just enough to hold the lips open during speech but not enough to cause a smile. This cheek position is a part of oral stability and is described more thoroughly in Chapter 14.

- *Tongue sides:* Every vowel is made by anchoring the tongue at the back-lateral margins, except when the jaw is very low during production of the lowest vowels (Fletcher, 1992). This topic is explained more thoroughly in Chapter 14 on oral stability.

- *Tongue middle:* The middle section of the tongue arches and de-arches to create the vowel quadrilateral (Fletcher, 1992). Arching ranges from high-to-low and from anterior-to-posterior according to the shape of the quadrilateral. Research has indicated that this arching occurs around a central pivot point (Iskarous, 2005).

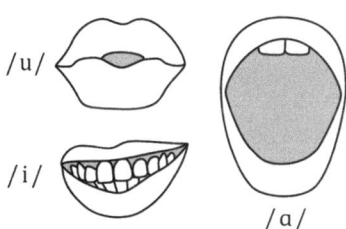

Exaggerated embouchures for the three most different vowels — /i/, /u/, and /ɑ/.

Daniel Jones is credited with developing the vowel quadrilateral.

- *Velum:* The velopharyngeal port is always closed during production of Standard North American vowels and diphthongs. Regional influences alter this feature slightly.

Three Basic Vowel Embouchures

Speech scientists, from the elocutionists to linguists, have taught that there are three basic vowel embouchures — /i/, /u/, /ɑ/.

"The three vowels of E (as in 'he'), A (as in 'ah'), and O (as in 'cool'), are the fundamental sounds on which the system of vowels rest" (Guttmann, 1882, p. 104).

"These vowels... are the extremes of the natural vowel scale: The closest lingual vowel is ee; the closest labial vowel is oo; and the most open sound is ah" (Bell, 1887, p. 26).

These three sounds represent the extreme of tongue position in all languages. They have been called the *vowel triangle* and the *vowel quadrilateral.* Daniel Jones, London-born student of Paul Passy (key developer of the IPA), is credited with developing the vowel quadrilateral (Jones, 1917). (Note of interest: He is also credited with being the first to use the word *phoneme.*)

Leading researchers in linguistics and phonetics agree with the original idea relayed in the vowel quadrilateral. Lindblom and Sundberg (1971) suggested that these three vowels were maximal distortions of the neutral vocal tract and Ladefoged (2005) wrote that the three cardinal vowels physically are "as far apart from each other as possible" and are as "auditorily distinct as possible" (p. 37). In a gross-to-fine perspective, these three vowels, therefore, represent the most gross or most extreme distinct vowel gestures. They represent the top, bottom, front, and back of midline tongue elevation; they represent the lips rounded, retracted, and neutral; and they represent the highest

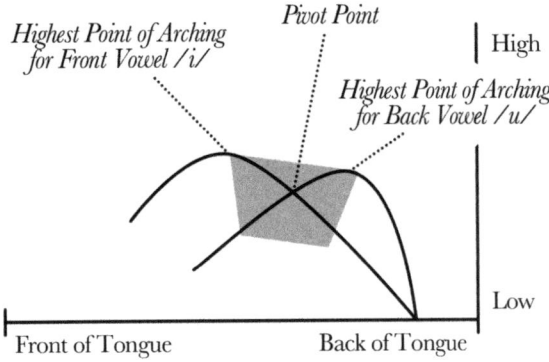

From the side: Arching of the middle of the tongue anterior and posterior to the pivot point for the front and back vowels.

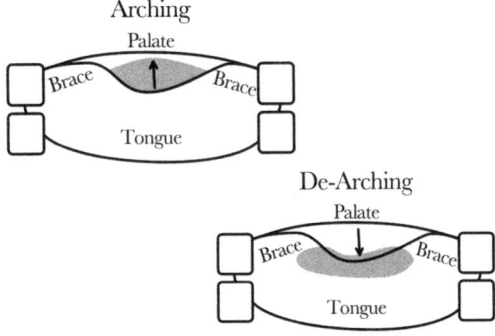

From the front: Lateral tongue bracing, arching, and de-arching together create the vowel sounds.

Arching & De-Arching

From the front: schematic illustration representing a cross section of the tongue during bracing, arching, and de-arching for production of each front and back vowel.

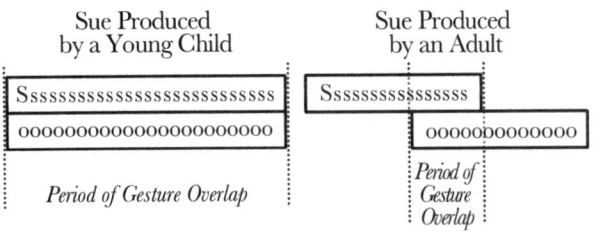

Children overlap phoneme movements more than do adults.

and lowest positions of the jaw. Each vowel that is added to a language employs vowels that are made within the movements required for these three.

Newest View of Tongue Movement

The classic vowel quadrilateral is two-dimensional and only represents a side view of midline tongue elevations during vowel productions. This model has left most therapists to think that teaching the vowels is a matter of teaching the tongue to lift and lower while teaching the lips to round or retract. This is an incorrect perspective.

Modern equipment has furthered the understanding of three-dimensional tongue movement, and it is now known that to produce vowels the tongue actually engages in two different movements patterns. First, the back-lateral margins are lifted and braced against the palate and side teeth to create a stable base. Second, from these points of stability, the middle portion of the tongue arches or de-arches to create the quadrilateral. The first movement — lateral elevation of the sides of the tongue — is very important in the tongue's bowl shape and subsequent orotund quality of vowels. Arching in the middle is that which creates each distinct vowel sound while the high sides hold the tongue in place relative to the palate. Teaching the vowels, therefore, requires instruction on two different movements: upward lateral elevation and midline arching and de-arching. The subject of how to teach the tongue to elevate and brace on the sides is discussed in Chapter 13 on tongue movement and Chapter 14 on oral stability.

Diphthongs

"Diphthongs are characterized by movement [and], like vowels, diphthongs serve as the nucleus of syllables" (Garn-Nunn & Lynn, 2004, p. 48–49). Diphthongs are produced by making two vowels in sequence. For example, "I" in the word *hi* actually consists of two basic sounds — /ɑ/ and /i/. A diphthong is different than a steady state vowel but it functions like a vowel. Traditionally five diphthongs have been identified in Standard North American English — /ɑi/, /ɑu/, /ɔi/, /ei/, and /iu/ (Garn-Nunn & Lynn, 2004). Many more diphthongs and triphthongs are used in English across the North America and the rest of the world as regional influence dictates.

Coarticulation of Cs & Vs

The movements of consonants and the embouchures of vowels overlap in syllables: "The great principle to be kept in mind is that positions do not merely succeed one another like letters on a printed page, but overlap" (Bell, 1906, p. 112). When one utters the word *Sue*, for example, the oral position for /s/ overlaps with the oral position for /u/. This process was recognized a century ago by Bell (1906), the overlap was called *coarticulation* by Miller (1951), and the concept was popularized by McDonald (1964):

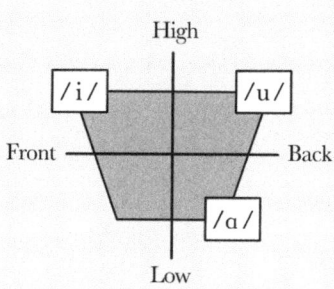

The three most different vowels define the highest, lowest, most anterior, and most posterior positions on the vowel quadrilateral.

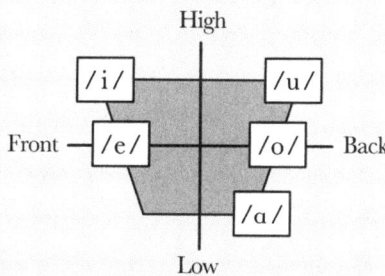

Many languages, such as Spanish, employ only these five vowels, the extreme three plus two more that cut the vertical space in half (Ladefoged, 2005).

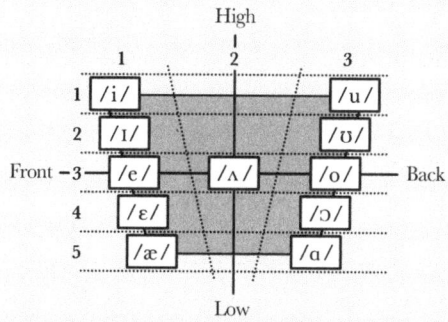

The eleven basic vowels of Standard North American English cut the quadrilateral into five vertical elevations and three horizontal areas.

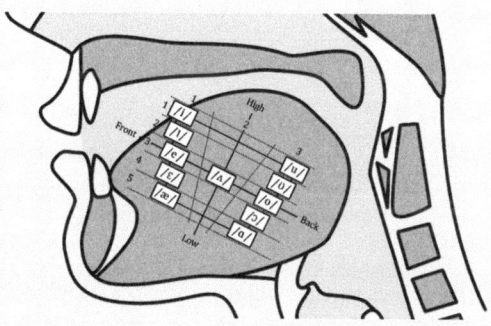

The vowel quadrilateral in situ.

"Speech is a continuous process; speech movements are modified by the movements that precede and follow them. This fact is shown clearly by the acoustic analysis... The vowel in the word 'can,' for example, appears as a steady glide from the /k/ to the /n/. Some sounds are influenced more than others by the coarticulation of the associated sounds" (Miller, 1951, p. 34).

"[Articulation is] a process consisting of a series of overlapping, ballistic movements" (McDonald, 1964, p. 87).

The reader can experience coarticulation easily with a simple experiment. Say the following sentence aloud in conversational speech style: *"Two Sues cooed."* Each of these words contains /u/ and, therefore, its oral position becomes a prominent movement feature and the main embouchure of the entire sentence. Notice that the mouth is shaped for /u/ on every consonant, even though none of these consonants require lip rounding. This is coarticulation at work; the consonant movements are added to the basic embouchure. Collapsing positions together like this allows for rapid, efficient, economical, and smooth speech productions.

There have been several studies on the development of coarticulation in children that have relevance to therapy for the vowels.

- Nittrouer et al. (1989) found that children aged 3–7 years overlap their speech gestures more than do adults.

- Nittrouer et al. (1996) found that children coarticulate consonants and vowels without the "spatial distinctiveness" and "relational timing" that characterizes adult speech.

- Sussman et al. (1996) found that this shift from more to less overlap of phoneme movements occurred in one child at 21 months of age.

- Sussman, Duder, Dalston, and Cacciatore (1999) studied one child and found that the coarticulation of labial, alveolar, and velar consonants and vowels in CVs began to trend toward adult overlap by the first birthday.

VOWEL DEVELOPMENT

Research provides insights into the sequence of natural vowel development, a sequence that offers clues about organizing therapy. Early research found that the vowels occur five times more frequently than consonants during the first two months of life (Irwin & Chen, 1946) and that children use almost all the adult vowels by 28–30 months of age (Irwin, 1948). All subsequent research has supported and expanded upon these earliest ideas as reported

Horizontal Axis
- Lip rounding and retracting
- Arching of the tongue anterior or posterior of pivot point

Vertical Axis
- Jaw pitching up and down.
- Tongue going up and down.

Tongue's Vertical Axis
Arching or de-arching toward or away from the palate

Back Vowels

Front Vowels

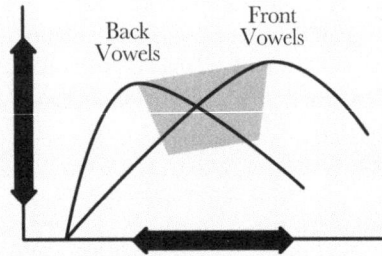

Tongue's Horizontal Axis
Arching and de-arching in front of or in back of the pivot point

Research suggests that vowels develop along the horizontal and vertical axes and that the vertical axis may develop earlier.

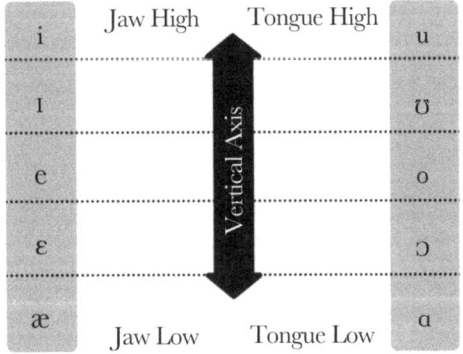

- Lip retracting
- Tongue arching toward the front

- Lip rounding
- Tongue arching toward the rear

The horizontal and vertical axes.

selectively here:

- *Emergence:* Oller (1978) noted that distinct vowels emerge by 2–3 months of age in the form of the coo and that they emerge out of the newborn's primary speech sound called the quasi-resonant nuclei.

- *Quadrilateral:* Lieberman (1980) found that a rudimentary vowel quadrilateral is set in infant vocal productions by 5 months of age.

- *First year:* Vihman (2004a) summarized known research and noted that vowels dominate infant vocalizations during the first year of life.

- *Vowel babbling:* Stoel-Gammon (1989) reported that babbling first contains vowels only.

- *Vowels in CV babbling:* Davis and MacNeilage (1990) studied one child and found that low vowels dominated her babbling. Lieberman (1980) found that vowels became gradually and consistently more adult-like from babbling onward.

- *Early words:* Davis and MacNeilage (1990) studied vowel development in one child at the early word stage. They found that certain vowel substitutions occurred. The child tended to substitute nearby vowels one for another, and she substituted the neutral vowel at a rate of 15% for all vowels except /u/. They also found that high vowels /i/ and /u/ dominated their subject's first word productions and that their subject tended to substitute the high front and the high back vowels one for another during this period. Stoel-Gammon and Herrington (1990) found that the corner vowels (the basic, extreme three: /i/, /u/, and /ɑ/) are produced more accurately than non-corner vowels in children with both normal and abnormal phonological systems.

- *Axes of learning:* Buhr (1980) proposed that vowel development could be viewed vertically and horizontally. The vertical axis consists of the jaw and tongue moving upwards and downwards. The horizontal axis consists of the tongue arching in the anterior and posterior positions on the quadrilateral, and of the lips puckering forward and retracting back. Evidence indicated that the vertical axis might develop before the horizontal.

- *High-to-low:* Lindblom and Sundberg (1969) and Buhr (1980) suggested that high front vowel /i/ is used early and that the jaw moving up and down causes the other front vowels to develop from it.

- *Second year:* Otomo and Stoel-Gammom (1992) studied six toddlers and found that high front vowel /i/ was produced the most consistently in words followed by low back vowel /ɑ/.

- *21 months:* Sussman et al. (1996) found that

vowels were more variable during babbling and they became more consistent when their subject reached 21 months of age and was producing real words. "Simply put, in babbling it does not matter what vowel sound comes out; in producing real words, it does matter" (p. 431).

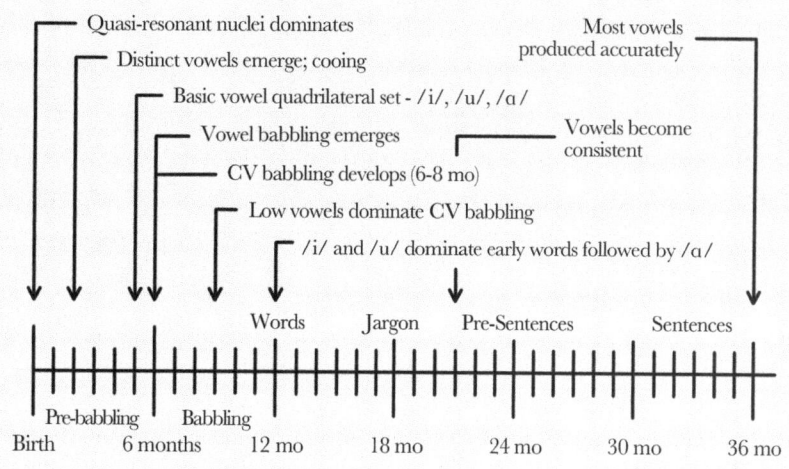

Research indicates that the vowels are acquired in a specific sequence.

• *36 months:* Various researchers from Templin (1957) to Donegan (2002) have found that children produce most vowels accurately by 36 months of age. Lieberman (1980) found that tense-lax vowel contrasts were not apparent until three years of age. McGowan, McGowan, Denny, and Nittrouer (2013) studied six children from various regional dialect groups and found that the shape of the vowel space on the quadrilateral remains qualitatively constant between 30 and 48 months of age.

Other Growth Factors

• *Growth of the vocal tract:* Ménard et al. (2009) found that "producing a given perceived vowel category likely requires different articulatory strategies throughout a speaker's lifetime" (p. 1284). In other words, an infant's vocal tract demands different positioning for the vowels than does the adult's; nonetheless, both groups can make vowels that are identifiable.

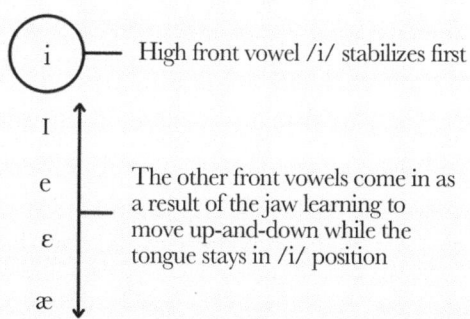

Evidence suggests that the high front vowel is established first and that other front vowels are learned off of it as the jaw lowers.

• *Shape of the palate:* Brunner et al. (2009) found that the shape of the palate influenced tongue positioning for the vowels. (Rudy and Yunusova found the same for the anterior consonants in 2013.)

• *Motherese:* Swanson, Leonard, and Gandour (1992) found that vowel prolongation is a method mothers naturally use to highlight content words when talking to their toddlers.

• *Bilingual:* Lee and Iverson (2012) found that Korean-English bilingual children developed vowel categories earlier than stop consonants.

VOWEL PROBLEMS

Vowel and diphthong problems are fairly straightforward. They are listed here and described below:

• The vowels can be substituted, omitted, or distorted.

• The full set of vowels can be under-developed so that there are vowels missing from the quadrilateral.

• Extra vowels, especially the schwa, can be added to words where they don't belong.

• The diphthongs can lack two distinct vowels.

Vowel Substitutions

The substitution of one vowel for another is quite common in the normal population. For example, many native English-speaking adults produces the word *imagine* with an initial /i/ or /ʌ/ instead of /ɪ/. The situation is more extensive in speech clients:

• The most common vowel substitution is probably

the substitution of schwa for another vowel. This has been called *centralization* (Carrell & Tiffany, 1960). The tendency to overuse the schwa is understandable from a speech economy perspective because the schwa requires less movement of the oral mechanism.

- The second most common vowel substitution pattern seems to be one of substituting a nearby vowel. For example, it is common to substitute /i/ for /ɪ/ but uncommon to substitute /u/ for /ɪ/.

- Clients speaking English as a second language tend to substitute the closest first-language vowel for the target second-language vowel.

Vowel Omissions

Vowel omission is can be observed in clients of all severity levels. On the mild end are clients who occasionally omit a vowel mid-word in an unstressed syllable, for example, telfon/telephone. This is called *syncope* (Carrell & Tiffany, 1960). On the severe end are clients who omit a word's primary vowel, for example, saying /t/ for *toy*. Omission of a word's main vowel like this means that there is no true syllable. This pattern is seen in clients with very severe speech impairment.

Vowel Distortions

Vowel distortion is a defining feature of dysarthria and is also very common in clients who mumble and slur for no known cause. A vowel can be distorted so little that it does not bother the listener or it can be distorted so much that it becomes unrecognizable. Vowels become distorted due to many different motor causes:

- The jaw is unstable.

- The lips or tongue fail to hit target positions.

- The tongue is not anchored appropriately in the back.

- The tongue habitually sits too far forward or too far back, or it lateralizes out of midline positioning.

- The tongue arches too little.

- The tongue arches too much (*thick* speech).

- The jaw, lips, or tongue move out of position in the middle of the vowel production.

- Voice is not prolonged enough during vowels so they become shortened, truncated, or lopped off. This makes the client sound choppy.

- Voice is prolonged too much during vowel production. This often makes the client slide from one vowel to another within what should be a single vowel.

- The vowel is initiated with a hard glottal stop.

- The vowel is devoiced.

- Velopharyngeal closure is inadequate or

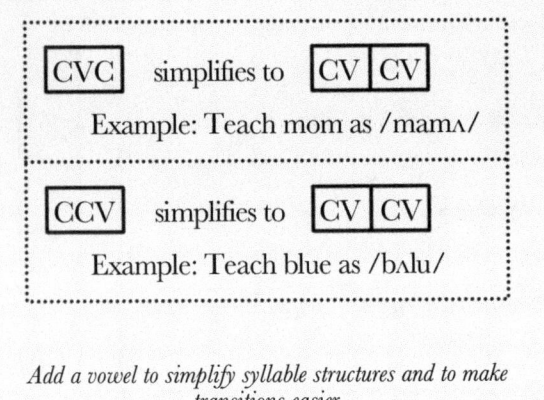

Add a vowel to simplify syllable structures and to make transitions easier.

incompetent and the vowels become nasalized.

Adding Vowels

Many clients with motor speech disorders make the error of adding a vowel to a word. For example, the client might produce /dɔgʌ/ for *dog*. The addition of the schwa like this is called *epenthesis* in phonological terms, and when /i/ is added at the end it is called the *diminutive*, e.g., *doggie*. Older phonetics texts used the term *supernumerary* to refer to the addition of any extra sounds or syllables (Carrell & Tiffany, 1960).

Epenthesis is considered a deviant phonological pattern but, from a movement perspective, both epenthesis and the diminutive can be viewed as a strategy to make speech movements simpler. It is well known that young children often add the schwa or /i/ to the ends of early words. For example, children say /mɑmʌ/ for *mom* and /dɔgi/ for *dog*. This addition of a final vowel to make the movement simpler causes the syllable shape to change. Instead of producing an advanced CVC, the child produces a sequence of two easier CV syllables.

This natural strategy for simplifying word productions can be used to teach advanced syllables. If the client cannot say *book* with a final /k/, for example, teach him to say /bʊkʌ/. It will be easier for a client with a motor speech disorder to say and will function as a step toward the correct production.

Children also add vowels in the middle of consonants clusters. This is called *consonant cluster simplification* in phonological terms and this, too, can be used as a motor teaching strategy. For example, one can teach a client to place a schwa between the movement of /b/ and the movements of /l/ in the word *blue*. This makes the CCV syllable into a simpler CVCV sequence: /blu/ changes to /bʌlu/. Again, this is not the final motor product but a step along the way.

Reducing Diphthongs

Children also reduce the complexity of speech movements by reducing diphthongs down to single vowels. For example, *hi* is produced as /hɑ/. This occurs when clients do not hear the second vowel, when they do not prolong vowels adequately to reach the second vowel, when they have very poor sequencing ability, and when they do not have enough breath support to extend exhalation through to the second vowel. This natural act of omitting a vowel to simplify syllable structures may be taught as a temporary practice for some clients who struggle to produce diphthongs. In therapy, consider adding a pause between vowels to emphasize the sounds within the syllable and make transitions easier, then combine, for example, /ha-i/ for *hi*.

TESTING VOWELS

Pollock (1991) and Eisenberg and Hitchcock (2010) reviewed tests of articulation and phonology and found that no single test took a complete inventory of the consonants, the clusters, the phonological patterns, the vowels, or the diphthongs. Both suggested that standardized tests needed to be supplemented in informal ways:

> *"Use of the data from a single standardized test of articulation or phonology would not be sufficient for completely inventorying a child's consonant and vowel production and selecting targets for therapy. It is recommended that clinicians supplement test data by probing production in additional phonetically controlled words"* (Eisenberg & Hitchcock, 2010, p. 488).

TEACHING VOWELS

This final section summarizes methods and procedures for teaching the vowels and diphthongs. These suggestions are drawn from the historic literature, they are based on the present author's nearly forty years of clinical experiences, and they are grounded in research on the vowels.

Vowel and diphthong training is subtle work that requires excellent auditory discrimination on the part of both therapist and client. Therapy includes a significant amount of ear training, many refined adjustments to jaw, lip, and tongue positions, and much trial and error regarding subtle differences. Elsewhere in this manual, the topic of *motor equivalence* (Hebb, 1949) has been discussed, a theory that suggests that every functional movement can be accomplished in many different ways. The theory applies to the learning of vowels; one adjusts the tongue, lips, jaw, velum, breath support, or phonation — or whatever combination of these is necessary, in any way necessary — to achieve the acoustic quality of the target vowel.

When to Begin

Perkins (1983) wrote on apraxia and dysarthria but his advice about when to start working on the vowels has application to most clients. Vowel training should begin early because of its importance to the development of the phonological system. Other authors have agreed:

> *"Teach vowels early when there is significant interferences with intelligibility"* (Perkins, 1983, p. 32).

> *"[The] relatively early mastery of vowels relative to many consonants gives vowels a developmental primacy in the establishment of a phonological system"* (Vorperian & Kent, 2007, p. 1511).

How to Begin

Phoneme training should always begin with advice from Van Riper, so, to start — teach the phoneme in isolation, by engaging in ear training, and by modeling the phoneme for the client to imitate (the stimulation method). Van Riper said that the importance of ear training could not be underestimated and he explained that the model-imitation routine is the most direct path of teaching. He taught that if a client cannot imitate a target from a model then mirrors, amplification, phonetic placement, and other traditional methods are employed.

A Client Who Has No Vowels

A client who uses no vowels whatsoever must learn the same basic skills that are acquired by an infant between birth and three months of age. As noted on pages 362–363, distinct vowels emerge out of the newborn's primary speech sound called the quasi-resonant nuclei. This means that before any true vowels are produced, a child first learns to produce voice while keeping the jaw, lips, tongue, and velum relatively inactive and in a neutral position. The production of voice, therefore, is the first step in learning to produce vowels.

Achieve an Orotund Quality

All vowels should be produced with a round or orotund quality. This occurs when the voice is strong, the jaw is low, and the tongue is relaxed and bowled. Teach the round oral shape and don't worry about which muscles work to achieve it.

> *"The root of the tongue should be depressed as much as possible, to expand the back part of the mouth and give fullness to the vowel sounds"* (Bell, 1887, p. 52).

> *"What matters most is the shape of the tongue rather than the particular muscles used"* (Ladefoged, 2005, p. 127).

Exaggerate Vowels

The elocutionists taught their clients to produce correct vowels by exaggerating them. "As a practice, it will be well to exaggerate the oral openings and positions of the lips for each of the vowels" (Ross, 1886, p. 76). Van Riper included exaggeration as a method of phoneme teaching and taught that it would fade on its own in most cases.

Establish the Schwa

The schwa is called the neutral vowel for a very specific reason — because the jaw, lips, and tongue remain in neutral for its production. The jaw has to lower from neutral but the lips do not have to round or retract and the tongue does not have to arch or de-arch at all. The schwa, therefore, is the simplest vowel to produce in terms of motor control. This means that most clients come to therapy with a schwa intact and the teaching of other vowels can ensue.

There are some clients who do not produce a clear schwa, however. The distorted schwa may be nasal, short in duration, lacking vigor, barely audible, or otherwise distorted due to oral instability or lack of oral movement. In these cases, the schwa needs to be improved. The SLP can teach the client to listen to his own schwa and match hers. Teach him to exhale and produce its voice with energy, to make the schwa full and round, and to make it oral and not nasal. Engage in activities to improve the tongue-bowl position and general oral control. Help the client make his schwa round and clear (just as with all other vowels). Consider selecting a few functional words for regular practice of this sound in functional routines, for example teach the client to say "uh-uh" for *no* and "uh-huh" for *yes*.

Teach /ɑ/ Early

The second easiest vowel to produce is probably /ɑ/ because the client simply has to open his mouth wide and vocalize. Clients who cannot lower the jaw far enough will need a jaw-lowering method such as any suggestion from Chapter 11 on jaw mobility. This vowel can be used to stimulate a wide assortment of early words as suggested in Table 11 on this page.

Set Up the Quadrilateral

All research supports the idea that /i/, /u/, and /ɑ/ set up the vowel quadrilateral and function as cornerstones for all subsequent vowel development. Therefore, these three should be taught early. Teach them by modeling and exaggerating these sounds in isolation or within target words.

Environmental sounds are a good way to introduce these three basic vowels in isolation. Teach /i/ as "Eeeee!" and use it while riding on a swing or going down a slide, as a response to a scary spiders, or as the mouse sound. Teach /u/ as "Ooooo!" and use it as a response to a pretty object or as the owl sound, the sound of scary ghosts, or the sound of the wind howling. Teach /ɑ/ as "Ahhhhhh!"

Target	Production
Mommy	/mɑmɑ/
Daddy	/dɑdɑ/
Bottle	/bɑbɑ/
Night-night	/nɑnɑ/
Water	/wɑwɑ/
Grandpa	/pɑpɑ/
Froggie	/gɑgɑ/
(Bowel movement)	/kɑkɑ/
(Singing)	/lɑlɑ/
Rabbit	/rɑrɑ/

TABLE 11 — /ɑ/ in Early Words

Simple early words for establishing /ɑ/.

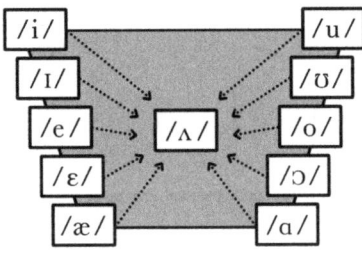

Vowels tend to collapse into the schwa because it requires less oral movement.

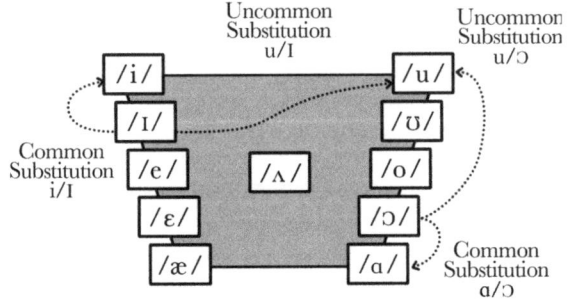

Vowels tend to be substituted for by other nearby vowels.

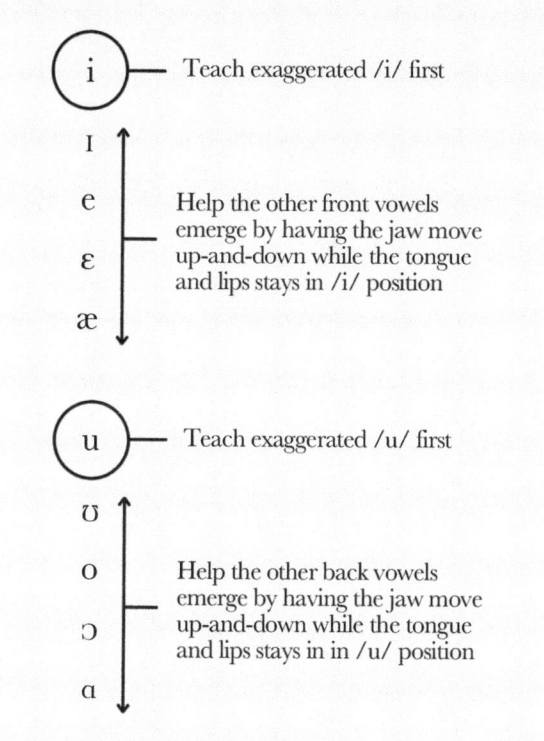

Teach exaggerated /i/ first

Help the other front vowels emerge by having the jaw move up-and-down while the tongue and lips stays in /i/ position

Teach exaggerated /u/ first

Help the other back vowels emerge by having the jaw move up-and-down while the tongue and lips stays in in /u/ position

Teach the front and back vowels as if they were on a scale. Teach clients to hear the subtle vowel differences as the jaw moves upwards and downwards.

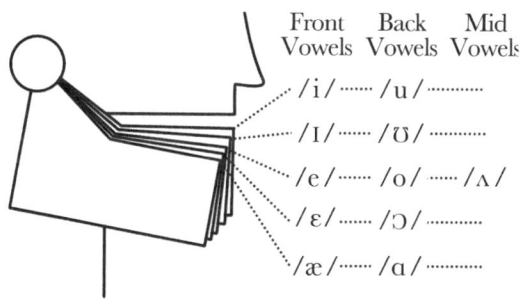

| Front | Back | Mid |
| Vowels | Vowels | Vowels |

/i/ ······ /u/ ··········
/ɪ/ ······ /ʊ/ ··········
/e/ ······ /o/ ······ /ʌ/
/ɛ/ ······ /ɔ/ ··········
/æ/ ······ /ɑ/ ··········

Exaggerated jaw positions during production of the vowels.

Vowel	i	u	ɑ
Jaw Height	High	High	Low
Lip Position	Retracted	Rounded	Neutral
Tongue Height	High Front	High Back	Low Back

Jaw, lip, and tongue positions represented in the three basic vowels.

and use it as the sound of tranquility, as the response to understanding, or to mean "no" as a sound of aversion: "Ah-ah-ahhhh!"

Consider using one-syllable words of CV or VC structure to beginning vowel training in words. For example, teach *bee* and *eat*, *boo* and *oop*, and *ma* and *on*. The diminutives (e.g., *mommy, daddy, doggie, kitty*) are also an excellent way to practice /i/ in simple early words.

Mobilize the Jaw

A classic method for teaching the vowels is the present author's favorite because it is so easy to do and because there is research to support it. The method involves manipulating jaw height. It is the present author's opinion that infants learn vowels in the first place by moving the jaw up and down. Remember, the vowel quadrilateral is acquired by five months of age and the jaw is the principle mover at that time. It seems clear from this that jaw elevation and depression is the main factor that causes early vowels to emerge and that the tongue and lips take over vowel formation much later as the jaw begins to stabilize during early word productions.

Further, Lindblom and Sundberg (1969) and Fletcher (1992) reported that different vowels may be produced solely by manipulation of jaw position. This means that up-and-down jaw mobility should be the primary concern when stimulating the vowel quadrilateral. One teaches the client to position his jaw from high-to-low while he holds lip and tongue positions steady: "Vowels are most easily taught through an understanding of their relationship to each other in terms of mandible depression and tongue arching" (Bosley, 1981, p. 36).

For the front vowels, start at the top with /i/ because research shows that this is usually the earliest prominent vowel and that all front vowels are learned off of /i/. Teach the client to make an exaggerated /i/ with a big smile. Then teach him to hold this position firmly while he lowers his jaw and lifts it again in a slow down-and-up pattern. The front vowels will be heard in sequence as the jaw lowers and elevates. The tongue does not change its position. Instead the tongue holds its position while the jaw lowers and elevates. This movement changes the distance of the tongue from the palate.

The sequence is repeated to teach the back vowels. The client assumes an exaggerated position for the highest back vowel, /u/, and he holds that embouchure while lowering and lifting the jaw. Jaw movement upwards and downwards causes all the back vowels to be produced in sequence from high-to-low.

This process is equivalent to teaching the vowels as if they operated on a musical scale, and this is the way that Alexander Graham Bell's family taught them. Just as fingering a piano up and down on a keyboard causes different sounds to be produced, so jaw elevation and depression causes different vowels to be produced. Most clients seem to need to slide the jaw down-and-up many times in sequence in order to begin to hear the subtle vowel differences that occur as they move through the scale, and therapists need to model sounds in synchrony to aid the discovery. Clients can be taught that up-and-down jaw movement is like a train running up and down a track. Each vowel is like a station along the way; the client learns to "hear" and to "stop" at each station. He learns to stop right at the point where the correct vowel is heard (see illustration on the next page).

Set Jaw Position with Bite Blocks

The vowel quadrilateral can be taught by adjusting the jaw as discussed above, or by setting the jaw into position with bite blocks or other probes of various sizes. Have the client bite down on the probe with his molars on one or both sides. Use thin objects to set the jaw high for the high vowels and use wide objects to set the jaw low for the low vowels. This is a method that was taught by some elocutionists: "Place part of a match-stick between upper and lower teeth, one to one and a half inches long for *aw*, shorter for *oh*, longer for *ah*" (Raymond, 1879, p. 25).

Van Riper used sticks, tongue depressors, pencils, wooden matches, and toothpicks for this purpose. Some

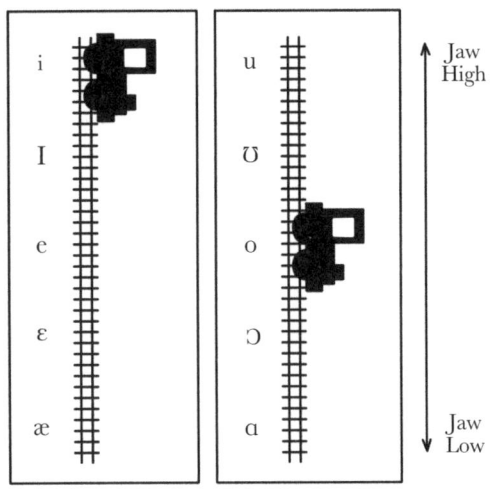

Teach the client to stop at each vowel station.

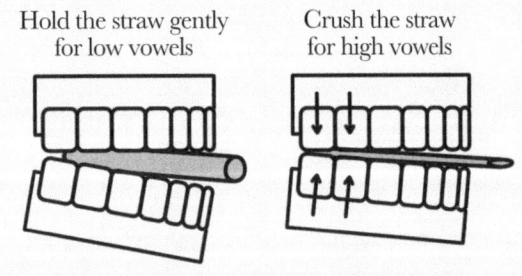

Hold the straw gently for low vowels   Crush the straw for high vowels

A flexibly firm straw provides the resistance a client may need to learn jaw height for the vowels.

therapists had their clients place a fingernail between the maxillary and mandibular (upper and lower) lateral incisors to set the jaw in a high position for the high vowels, and to place fingers between the teeth to set the jaw in a low position for the low vowels: "Can you get a finger between your upper and lower teeth in front? This is about the minimal jaw opening for the open vowels" (Fisher, 1966, p. 134).

There are better tools available now for setting the jaw into position for the vowels and TalkTools® manufactures the best; they make two sets of bite blocks that come in five sizes to set the jaw into the five elevations necessary for all the vowels.

Teach Tiny Jaw Adjustments with a Straw

A single large, flexible but firm straw is a handy and very inexpensive tool that can be used for the purpose of teaching refined jaw elevations for the vowels. Place the straw between the molars on one side. The straw will be wide when first placed and this is the position for the low vowels. Now teach the client to gently crush the straw with his molars by lifting the jaw. The higher the jaw goes, the higher the vowel that will be produced. Teach the client to produce each front and back vowel as the jaw lifts and lowers against the straw. A large firm straw is used to provide some resistance to upward jaw movement and this resistance teaches the client how to pay attention to his jaw position.

Babbling Versus Word Productions

Research suggests that low vowels dominate babbling and high vowels dominate early words. Thus babbling of basic CVCV structure should be taught with big up-and-down movements of the jaw so that /ɑ/ is encouraged. Once words emerge, the sequence of vowel maturation should reflect this research. As such, *mama* should change to *mommy*, and *dada* should chance to *daddy* over time.

Chewing Technique

Froeschel's chewing method (Fröeschels, 1948) has been used to train the vowels:

> *"As the client actually chews on gum or food, or as he pretends to chew, ask him to phonate (turn on his voice), or simply ask him to chew aloud. Listen to the vowels thus produced. You may hear one or more of the front vowels. For best results, the client is asked to chew with the lips open. If the desired vowel is heard, begin to imitate the client's chewing, producing the same vowel and gradually slowing the chewing and prolonging the vowel... Chewing with strong closing of the molars at the end of each chew will sometimes achieve an /i/ as the client forces the tongue high against the palate"* (Bosley, 1981, p. 34).

Teach the Horizontal Sets

The vowels can also be taught as they occur across the horizontal line. Begin again with an exaggerated /i/. Have the client hold that vowel while he rounds the lips tightly. If he holds the tongue firmly, then a French vowel will be heard, but a little ear training will help it change into a nice English /u/. Repeat with other sets across the horizontal axis.

Teach All the Vowels Together

The best way to teach vowels may be to present them all together as one big set and to use comparing and contrasting as a prime method. This is done with each sound produced in isolation, and by sliding back and forth between them. This process allows a client to hear and feel the vowels relative to one another.

> *"Because of the multiplicity of English vowel phonemes, the skill most important to acquire is that of making unambiguous contrasts between them… The [speaker] should practice the contrasts before attempting to achieve relative uniformity for any single vowel phoneme"* (Thomas, 1956, p. 100).

> *"Vowels are most easily taught through an understanding of their relationship to each other in terms of degree of mandible depression and tongue arching, forward movements or retraction, through auditory comparisons, and through increased kinesthetic awareness"* (Bosley, 1981, p. 36).

Two studies have backed this idea. Nishi and Kewley-Port (2008) tested adult's ability to acquire the vowels of a

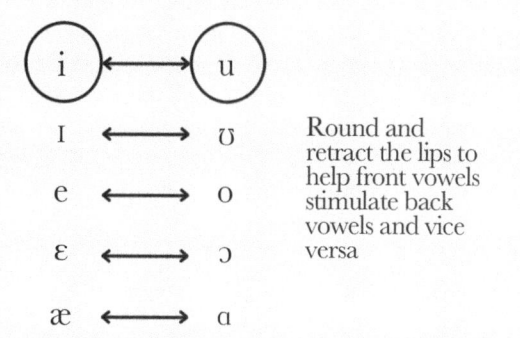

Use vowels at equivalent heights on the horizontal axis to teach one another by rounding and retracting the lips.

second language and found that better learning occurred when the all the vowels were taught together. In a second study, Nishi and Kewley-Port (2007) found that difficult vowels were acquired more skillfully when taught in comparison with other vowels:

> *"Training protocols for learning non-native vowels should present a full set of vowels and should not focus only on the more difficult vowels"* (Nishi & Kewley-Port, 2007, p. 1496).

Model Prolonged Vowels

Prolongation is one aspect of phoneme exaggeration and is a method for teaching vowels that has been used for at least a century: "Vowels and consonants are often slurred over too briefly. The training consists in reading and speaking with the vowels exaggerated in length" (Scripture, 1912, p. 159).

There is some evidence to support the use of prolongation as a good method for teaching the vowels, both in terms of learning to hear them and learning to produce them. On the input side, Swanson, Leonard, and Gandour (1992) found that vowel prolongation is a method mothers naturally use to highlight content words when talking to their toddlers in the process commonly known as *motherese* (Hoff-Ginsberg & Shatz, 1982). Therefore, prolongation of vowels is a natural method of teaching. On the output side, Ferguson and Kewley-Port (2007) found that increasing the duration of vowels to reduce rate of speech improves the production of the vowel itself and boosts intelligibility: "The slowness of clear speech is perhaps the most robust finding in studies of clear speech acoustics" (p. 1249).

Research on vowel development also suggests a sequence involving prolongation that is important to consider in therapy. Children begin to coo by 2–3 months of age and the basic vowel quadrilateral is set by 5 months of age. This succession of skills means that the prolongation of vowels while cooing may be a significant factor

TABLE 12 — Simplified Vowel Chart						
	Front Vowels		Middle Vowel		Back Vowels	
High Jaw	i	Beet			u	Boot
	ɪ	Bit			ʊ	Book
Jaw Mid	e	Bate	ʌ	But	o	Boat
Jaw Low	ɛ	Bet			ɔ	Bought
	æ	Bat			ɑ	Box

Simplified chart of Standard North American English vowels.

in a child's ability to learn differentiated vowels for the full quadrilateral. Cooing (prolonging) vowels may allow a client an opportunity hear the subtle changes in vowel formats that occur as a result of slight oral modifications. The present author has used vowel prolongation extensively throughout the past 39 years with a wide variety of clients and has found it to be perhaps the best vowel teaching method in existence.

Synchronize Vowel Productions

Jean Piaget observed that simultaneous or synchronized sound productions dominated early adult-child interactions when infants are between birth and five months of age (Ginsburg & Opper, 1969). This means that cooing develops and the vowel quadrilateral is formed during a time when adults and children produce a certain amount of sound together in synchrony. Synchronized productions, then, can be another important treatment strategy. The ear training necessary to hear the difference between one vowel and another might best be trained by cooing, chanting, or singing vowels simultaneously with the client instead of taking turns back and forth in the typical model-imitate paradigm, and it may be especially better than training vowels within words.

The present author has found this method to be very helpful in teaching vowels to clients of all ages and ability levels. Therapists and clients produce vowels together while jaw, lip, and tongue positions are altered in subtle ways. The therapist and client take turns leading and following one another's changes. This joint sound-making routine encourages the client to pay very careful attention to the sounds that he and the therapist are making. It teaches him to tune his productions in ways that match the therapist's model.

Client-Specific Oral Placement

The latest research on tongue function during production of the vowels reveals that position of the oral structures is very client-specific during production of the vowels. For example, Hasegawa-Johnson et al. (2003) looked at tongue height relative to structure of the mouth during production of vowels. They found that speech was characterized by "relatively talker-dependent vowel targets" and that "each talker adjusts his or her own tongue height to compensate for talker-dependent differences in constriction anatomy" (p. 738).

This means that there is no one oral position that is required for any particular vowel. Each client will achieve the correct acoustic quality for each vowel in his or her own unique way. Therapists must be free, therefore, to experiment with jaw, lip, and tongue position when teaching the vowels. A position that works with one client may not work with another and a new path must be sought. This is a simple idea that therapists called *trial and error;* therapists help clients learn vowels by trying one jaw, lip, or tongue position after another until the vowel sound just right.

Adjust the Lips

The lips round and retract in subtle ways to tune sound production while learning various vowels. Clients who cannot round or retract the lips may need activities to facilitate these movements. Methods are discussed in Chapter 12 on stimulating lip movement.

Mobilize the Tongue

The tongue takes over production of the differentiated vowels once the jaw begins to stabilize. Jaw elevations can be used to teach the vowels as discussed above and it is the present author's experience that, if the jaw can be used in this way, then tongue mobility does not need to be addressed. This is because the tongue naturally will take over the work as oral motor skills improve in most cases.

However, activities to activate the tongue to move for the vowels will need to be included if the tongue is very lax due to low muscle tone, too stiff due to high muscle tone, or completely immobile due to paralysis, lack of reflex response, or lack of stimulation. Methods to teach the tongue to move in all directions will be needed with special focus on vivifying, bowling, arching, and anchoring the tongue (for ideas, see Chapter 13 on facilitating tongue movements). Bosley (1981) used a tongue depressor and tactile stimulation to guide tongue arching and to mark the target of tongue position for the vowels as described in these two sections of her book:

> *"Place a tongue blade lightly on the portion of the tongue that should arch or rise the highest and lightly hold the tongue blade in place without actively pressing down on the tongue. Instruct the client to raise or lower the tongue blade as he speaks. Its weight intensifies the kinesthetic sensations and gives a concrete sense of direction"* (Bosley, 1981, p. 31).

> *"It may help to draw a line along either side of the tongue and then inside the upper [palate] where you wish the tongue to contact. Since you cannot be absolutely sure with each individual just exactly the extent of the contact that will produce the desired vowel, determine from listening if the production seems as though the tongue were too high, too low, too far forward, or too far back, and then adjust the tactile cues accordingly"* (Bosley, 1981, p. 32).

Coarticulate Early

As discussed in the research sections above, a client who is just learning his first fifty words should be taught to produce them with an emphasis on the vowel instead of the consonant and with significant coarticulation or overlap of movement. When teaching the word *shoe*, for example, teach /u/ first and then teach the client to add /ʃ/ to the vowel. Clients can be taught to say, "Oooooo-shoe." This way their mouth is in the vowel embouchure before they utter the consonant.

Presentation of the Vowels

The vowels can be taught in various ways:

- *Isolated vowels:* Teach individual vowels one-at-a-time in isolation.

- *Pairs of vowels:* Teach the vowels in pairs so that the client can discover differences in the way the two vowels sound and feel. For example, teach the difference between /u/ and /ɑ/. Call attention to distinctions in the way they sound and illustrate the dissimilarity in the high and low jaw positions required of each.

- *Sets of vowels:* Teach vowels in sets for more wide ranging comparisons. For example, consider teaching all the front vowels together as one big set using the jaw positioning method described above.

- *Real words:* Teach individual vowels within the context of real words.

- *Nonsense words:* Teach individual vowels within the context of nonsense words.

- *Minimal pair words:* Teach vowels using minimal word pairs. For example, help the client hear and comprehend the important differences between /i/ and /ɪ/ with *seat-sit, neat-knit, peach-pitch, reach-rich, leek-lick,* and *week-wick.*

Consider Word Complexity

Word complexity is a consideration in the training of vowels. The present author has found that simple CV or VC words often are the best places to begin vowel training for very young children. Tiny words like *boo* and *oop* help little children focus on the target vowel because the phonological neighborhood is so simple that the vowel can stand out.

However, Munson and Solomon (2004) found that normal adults tend to utter vowels better in words that are more complex and spoken less often. For example, the vowels in the word *Pictionary* may be uttered more carefully than those in the word *picture*. For this reason, it may be better for some clients, especially those with advanced language skills, to work on their vowels in more complex words. Words with neighborhoods of high phonological density might give these clients better results because the complexity of the words themselves causes the speaker to listen and produce their vowels more carefully.

Focus on Stressed Vowels

Alexander Graham Bell's advice about vowel training in the deaf population has value for all clients. He recommended focusing on the vowels of stressed syllables and reducing the importance of unstressed syllables. This is done to help speakers sound more natural:

"It is neither necessary... nor advisable, that every vowel in a phrase be given its full value. Unaccented syllables should be toned down like the shaded portions of a picture... Beauty of utterance depends as much upon shading as upon form... Give as definite vowels as possible in the accented syllables, but don't be too precise about the others" (Bell, 1906, p. 100).

Teach Better Substitutions

As discussed above, most clients make vowel substitutions that are nearby on the vowel quadrilateral. However, clients with severe cognitive dysfunction and/or neuromuscular disorder sometimes make wildly divergent vowel substitutions. The true target will be the first aim of treatment but there are cases in which the target simply cannot be met. In these cases, a second option is to teach the client to produce a logical substitution, and the best substitutions are those that are as close as possible to the target on the quadrilateral.

For example, if a client cannot make short vowel /ɪ/, as in the word *pig*, and he uses a schwa instead and says /pʌg/, then teach him to produce the word with the long vowel /i/ as a better substitution. He will say /pig/. This will not be a final solution, but it is a better substitute that will serve as a step in the right direction. Intelligibility should improve as a result.

Elongate Truncated Vowels

Vowel distortion occurs when clients shorten or truncate them. The vowel may fade away or be cut off with a glottal stop. Either pattern can occur when breath support is lacking; therefore, it is a pattern often noted in clients with motor speech disorders. Vowels that are produced with short duration make speech sound choppy; diphthongs are reduced to single vowels and final consonants are deleted.

Help is afforded in the form of slight prolongation of the vowel. A certain amount of work on breath support may be necessary to introduce this idea. The client should also be taught to hear his error through modeling and discussion. Negative practice can help the client hear his error, and exaggeration of the glottal stop can help the client feel and hear it. Visual cues of some sort may help the client understand what is being talked about. WARNING: Do not use exaggeration of the glottal stop if the client has vocal fold pathology.

Prolonging vowels slightly will cause a client to sound more natural and to use better prosodic expression. Vowels of slightly longer duration will also allow diphthongs and glides to emerge, and they will create a space for eventual production of final consonants.

Shortening Prolonged Vowels

Vowel distortion can also occur when clients prolong vowels unnecessarily, especially in the case of dysarthria. The

Use simple cues to signal vowel duration that is long (left) and short (right).

simplest solution to this problem is to teach the client to produce his vowels with shorter duration. Shortening the length of the vowel will eliminate the possibility that the sound will distort. Teach the client to hear how much better he sounds when his vowels are shortened just a little bit in familiar words. Open syllable words of CV or VC construction are good to use for this purpose. Use visual cues to teach the idea of long and short vowel duration, and use negative practice to compare words spoken with long and short vowels.

Teaching Exhaled Vowels

On rare occasion, a client will inhale vowels. Methods to teach proper breath support for speech are required (see Chapter 7 on breath support).

Vowels & Hearing Impairment

Auditory means are used to teach vowels even among clients with hearing impairment. Osberger (1987) demonstrated that model-imitation procedures were effective in teaching vowels to clients with hearing impairment. Tye-Murray and Kirk (1993) found that cochlear implants affected production of the vowels and diphthongs in positive ways over time.

Bell (1906) taught that one of the great problems of clients who are deaf is the tendency to stiffen and thicken the tongue during speech, what the elocutionists called *thickness of speech*: "The attempt to narrow the tongue causes it to become stiff and hard to the touch, with a rounded [bulging] surface. When it is broadened the surface becomes flat and soft" (Bell, 1906, p. 102–103). He recommended using exercises to broaden the tongue for production of the vowels in these cases. Methods for broadening, bowling, and relaxing the tongue for an orotund quality of sound can be found in Chapter 13 on facilitating tongue movement.

There have also been reports of using certain equipment to teach vowels to clients with hearing impairment with means other than auditory. Fletcher, Dagenais, and Critz-Crosby (1991) used a glossometry unit to train vowels and found that the vowels became more distinct, tongue arching improved, and the oral space expanded.

Pratt, Heintzelman, and Deming (1993) used an IBM SpeechViewer to teach vowels to subjects with hearing impairment and demonstrated some limited improvement.

Structural Defects

Van Riper wrote that clients should be taught how to compensate for their permanent structural differences by adjusting jaw, lip, and tongue positions to achieve the best acoustic quality possible. Hasegawa-Johnson et al. (2003) studied this process and found that each talker achieved acceptable vowels by adjusting the height of the tongue: "Each talker adjusts his or her own tongue height to compensate for talker-dependent differences in constriction anatomy" (p. 738).

Methods for Diphthongs

Research consistently demonstrates that the vowels, diphthongs, and glides are the earliest phonemes to be established in the creation of children's phonological systems. The diphthongs can be viewed therefore, as one of the earliest ways children learn to sequence phonemes. All the methods described above have application to the training of the individual vowels that form the diphthongs. The following additional ideas are suggested.

- *Two complete vowels:* A diphthong can only be as good as its component individual vowels. Make sure that the client can hear and produce each individual vowel of the diphthong alone before he is taught to produce them in sequence for the diphthong. Also, make sure the client maintains the integrity of each individual vowel when he sequences them together into the diphthong.

TABLE 14 — Diphthongs			
Diphthong	First Vowel	Second Vowel	Sample Word
ɑi	ɑ	i	Bye
ɑu	ɑ	u	Bout
ɔi	ɔ	i	Boy
ei	e	i	Bay
iu	i	u	Beauty

Diphthongs of Standard North American English.

- *Prominent and fading:* The elocutionists taught that the first vowel of a diphthong should be prominent and the second fading. Simply making the first somewhat louder and the second somewhat softer will achieve this pattern for many clients.

- *Exaggerate:* A simple way to teach a diphthong is to exaggerate each piece of it — the first vowel, the second vowel, and the transition sounds that occur between the two.

- *Key Words:* Select key words of high functional value to establish a habit of correct diphthong production. See Table 14 below.

- *Glides:* Glides /w/ and /j/ utilize the same movement patterns as do the diphthongs but in reverse order. For example, the words *you* and *we* both utilize /i/ and /u/ but in reverse sequence. The present author likes to teach the diphthongs and glides together in pairs of functional words that reflect the reverse sequencing. For example, teach *you* and *we* as /i/–/u/ and /u/–/i/.

Accents & Dialects

The reader is encouraged to remember that the vowels vary tremendously in different parts of North America and that adjustments to the ideas above will have to be made to account for regionalisms. This is a concept that has been in play for at least a century:

> *"The precise shade of vowel quality given in one part of the country is not heard in another... I think I am pretty safe in saying that the 'standard pronunciation,' like the 'average school boy,' nowhere exists"* (Bell, 1906, p. 111).

SUMMARY

A wide variety of methods can be used to teach the vowels. This work is based on the vowel quadrilateral and research on the sequence of vowel development.

TABLE 14 — Diphthongs in Simple Early Words	
Diphthong	Simple Words
ɑi	Hi, bye, eye
ɑu	Ow, ouch, cow
ɔi	Boy, toy, Oh boy!
ei	Hey, wait, (o)kay
iu	Pee-ooo (stinky), mee-ooo (kitty meow)

Establish each diphthong early in simple words.

22

Stimulating the Stop Consonants

Techniques for /p/, /b/, /t/, /d/, /k/, and /g/

"Think of the movements of our tongues and lips as gestures, much like the gestures we make with our hands. When we talk we use specific gestures — controlled movements — to make each sound."

– Peter Ladefoged, 2005

Many therapists have considered the stop consonants to be the easiest phonemes to teach because they are quick to recognize with the ear and simple to produce with the mouth relative to other phonemes. These phonemes may be easy to produce because the articulators can bang together in gross ways to meet the basic requirements of their production. Research has demonstrated that the voiced stops begin to emerge during the babbling phase and the voiceless stops often emerge in the final position in early words. This chapter describes methods to teach these phonemes in their emerging and mature forms.

PRODUCTION

The movements used in production of the stop consonants are described here. Details about emerging or immature production of these sounds during the babbling stage are offered first so that readers can see how these phonemes might be stimulated with clients who speak very little and

who use very few consonant phonemes. Details about mature oral movements are described next so that readers can see how these phonemes might be stimulated with clients who are quite verbal but who have articulation errors on these specific phonemes.

Respiration, Phonation, Resonation

All stops are initiated upon exhalation. The vocal folds abduct for /p/, /t/, and /k/ to make them voiceless. They adduct for /b/, /d/, and /g/ to make them voiced. All six of the stop consonants are made with velopharyngeal closure to direct the airstream through the mouth.

/p/ & /b/   *Pie, upper, top*
 Boy, rubber, cab

Emerging /p/ and /b/

Phonemes /p/ and /b/ are classified as bilabial stops. Purposeful bilabial articulation seems to begin in two ways: when raspberries emerge and when babbling emerges. The bilabial raspberry emerges at 4–6 months of age; this sound provides strong tactile stimulation to both top and bottom lips to awaken them as they articulate together. Then at 6–10 months, babbling with /b/ emerges when the jaw begins to move grossly up and down, causing the lower lip to bang into the upper lip.

Mature /p/ and /b/

A different oral-motor pattern emerges as /p/ and /b/ mature:

- *Starting position:* The jaw, lips, and tongue stabilize

Articulation therapy often is a quiet tabletop activity.

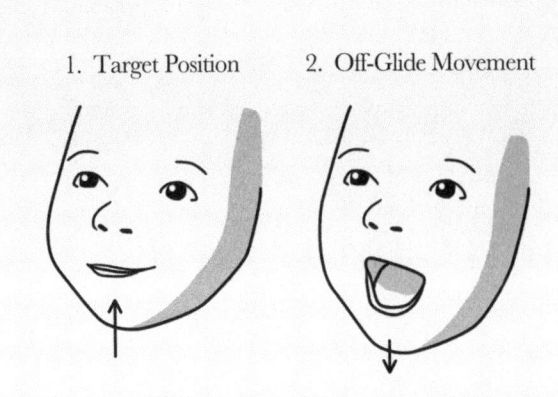

1. Target Position   2. Off-Glide Movement

The jaw is the prime mover during immature productions of /p/, /b/, and /m/.

to set the mouth in starting position (see Chapter 14 on oral stability).

• *On-glide:* The upper lip lowers and the lower lip elevates until both lips articulate together. Research has demonstrated that the lower lip moves more than the upper lip.

• *Target position:* The target position is achieved as both lips articulate together to form an anterior seal. Air pressure builds behind the seal during this phase. Research has demonstrated that the lips press into or move beyond one another during this pressure build-up phase.

• *Off-glide:* The lips quickly burst apart to release a small explosion of air. The lower lip lowers more than the upper lip elevates. The jaw, lips, and tongue adjust for coarticulating phonemes while maintaining oral stability.

/t/ & /d/   *Two, latte, hat*
                      Dog, body, mad

Emerging /t/ and /d/

Phonemes /t/ and /d/ are classified as lingua-alveolar stops. The front of the tongue begins to articulate with the upper structures between 4–6 months of age when a baby learns to press the jaw upward so that the tongue is pressed against the palate, and to exhale, thus creating a raspberry sound. This raspberry is lingua-labial by place because the front of the tongue is usually protruding slightly. Babbling with /d/ emerges between 6–10 months of age when the jaw begins moving grossly upwards and downwards which causes the tongue to bang against the upper structures in a gross, clumsy way.

Mature /t/ and /d/

A different oral-motor pattern emerges as /t/ and /d/ mature:

• *Starting position:* The jaw, lips, and tongue stabilize to set the mouth in starting position (see Chapter 14 on oral stability).

• *On-glide:* From its points of stability at the back-lateral margins, both sides of the tongue's perimeter lift simultaneously in a stripping action, from the back to the tip until the perimeter is pressed upward against the palate and a full horseshoe-shape is reached.

• *Target position:* In target position, the tongue's perimeter is pressing upward and sealed against the palate in a horseshoe-shape. This position is held briefly while air pressure builds behind the horseshoe-shaped seal.

• *Off-glide:* The off-glide begins as the tongue tip lowers to release a tiny explosion of air. The tongue lowers away from the palate in a stripping action from tip to back along the sides. The jaw and back-lateral margins of the tongue remain stable throughout, and the middle of the tongue always stays low and away from the palate.

/k/ & /g/   *Key, icky, book*
                      Go, buggy, bag

Emerging /k/ and /g/

Phonemes /k/ and /g/ are classified as lingua-velar stops. These sounds are heard during the first few months of life in the pre-cooing stage when babies are producing the *quasi-resonant nuclei* (see Chapter 20 on foundational pre-speech platforms). By 4–6 months of age, the back of the tongue rises when a child learns to produce the lingua-velar fricative or raspberry. These velar raspberries are produced alone and in sequences with vowels and that means that the back of the tongue begins to elevate and depress in sequence. By 6 months of age, the back of the tongue elevates and depresses to produce these phonemes in basic CV sequences.

Mature /k/ and /g/

A different oral-motor pattern emerges as /k/ and /g/ mature:

• *Starting position:* First the jaw, lips, and tongue stabilize to set the mouth in starting position (see Chapter 14 on oral stability).

• *On-glide:* While the tongue maintains its stable position at the back-lateral margins, the middle-back of the tongue presses upward to the velum.

• *Target position:* The entire back of the tongue

forms a seal against the velum when the tongue is in target position. This position is held briefly while air pressure builds behind it.

- *Off-glide:* The tongue's middle-back lowers quickly to release a small explosion of air in the back. The jaw and back-lateral margins of the tongue remain stabile throughout.

TREATMENT STRATEGIES

The stop consonants emerge in infancy and their relatively simple and gross nature (compared to many other phonemes) means that many therapists teach these phonemes quite early, even first, in a program for children with multiple misarticulations, severe phonological delay, or motor speech disorder. General advice for emergence of the stop consonants includes the following:

- If the entire set of stops is absent, most therapists begin with /p/ or /b/ because these two are the most visible. However, many clients find other stop consonants easier to produce. For example, clients who hold the tongue high in the back in the "high guard position" will probably will /k/ and /g/ first.

- If the entire set of stops is absent, consider addressing all six of them simultaneously and organizing them according to the client's stimulability.

- If the entire set of stops is absent, remember that these sounds emerge in babbling because the jaw begins to move up and down. Stimulate the jaw to move up and down while the child prolongs sound.

- If the entire set of stops is absent, remember that these sounds also first occur as raspberries. Consider teaching the full set of raspberries first (see Chapter 20 on pre-speech platforms).

- If the entire set of stops is absent, consider making the client's goal be one of acquiring *occlusion* instead of any one specific stop phoneme. Teach him how to stop air and voice with pillows and stuffed animals pressed safely and playfully against the face. In other words, teach the manner of stopping first, and

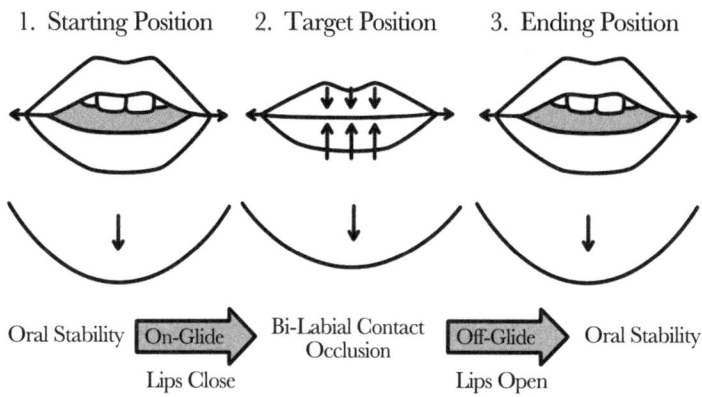

Mature productions of /p/, /b/, and /m/ are accomplished with oral stability and lip mobility.

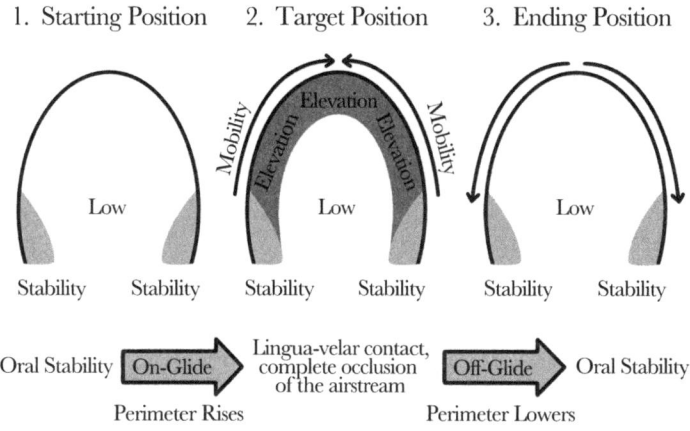

Mature productions of /t/, /d/, and /n/ are accomplished with elevation of the perimeter of the tongue

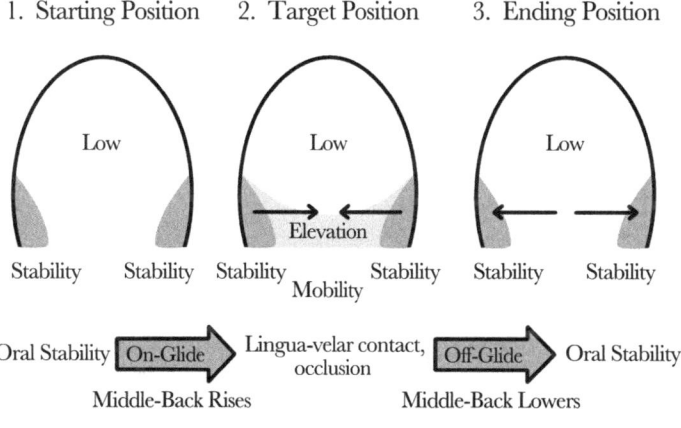

Mature productions of /k/, /g/, and /ŋ/ combine elements of mobility and stability.

worry about the place of each stop second.

- If the entire set of stops is absent, remember that babbling is produced primarily with voiced sounds, so introduce /b/, /d/, and /g/ first.

- Many therapists teach the stops in the prevocalic position first. However, it is the present author's experience that the voiceless stops — /p/, /t/, and /k/ — can be more easily learned in the postvocalic position in simple VC and CVC words. Therapy should be flexible in the ordering of targets, and engage in trial-and-error training to determine the client's readiness for either word position.

- If the entire set of stops is absent, the client may need more general information about his mouth and what it can do.

/p/

Multisensory Stimulation of /p/

- *Auditory stimulation:* Model, amplify, repeat, and bombard with this phoneme.

- *Auditory feedback:* Direct the client's production back to his ear with a tube or other tool. Imitate the client's sound.

- *Cue:* Use a cue to pique the client's interest in this phoneme.

- *Visual feedback to understand lip movements:* Watch in a mirror. Imitate the client's correct and incorrect productions and watch each other during simultaneous productions.

- *Visual feedback to understand airflow:* Hold objects in front of the lips for the client to move with his puff of air from /p/. Start with small lightweight objects like tissue paper, cotton balls, string, pieces of dental floss, tiny origami objects, etc.. If necessary, switch to heavier objects to increase strength of expiration by using items such as pinwheels or Ping-Pong® (table tennis) balls. Produce /p/ against a mirror or window and observe the fog it produces

- *Verbal:* Use vocabulary the client can understand to describe this phoneme.

- *Tactile feedback:* Have the child feel his own lip movements during production of /p/.

- *Mark the target to develop place:* Touch the upper and lower lips prior to production, or place an object between the lips against which the lips can close, such as a tongue depressor, finger, swizzle stick, coffee stirrer, or dental floss.

- *Aid lip closure:* Facilitate active lip mobility.

- *Jaw stability:* Stabilize the jaw to encourage more active lip mobility.

- *Tongue stability:* Stabilize the tongue at the back-lateral margins to keep the tongue inside the mouth during production of /p/.

Association Method for /p/

- *Place:* Help the client learn /p/ by recognizing the similarities between it and any of the other bilabial phonemes he can produce in the same place — /b/, /m/, or /w/. Also, use labio-dental /f/.

- *Manner:* Help the client learn /p/ by recognizing the similarities between it and any of the other phonemes he can produce with occlusion — /b/, /t/, /d/, /k/, or /g/.

- *Voice:* Help the client learn /p/ by recognizing the similarities between it and any of the other stops he can produce without voice — /t/ or /k/. Also, use the voiceless fricatives and affricates.

Successive Approximations for /p/

- *Build /p/ off of /b/:* Have the client produce /b/ in a whisper.

- *Build /p/ off of /m/:* Have the client prolong a whispered /m/, pinch his nose closed and lower his jaw.

- *Build /p/ off of /f/:* Have the client prolong /f/ and push his lips together.

- *Build /p/ off of /h/:* Have the client make an /h/ and then put his lips together.

- *Build /p/ off of the bilabial raspberry:* Have the client produce a voiceless bilabial raspberry and then soften it up and press his lips together.

Contrast Method for /p/

- *Place:* Contrast the lip movements of /p/ with the tongue-tip movements of /t/, with the tongue-back movements of /k/, or with the glottal movements of /h/.

- *Manner:* Contrast the occlusion of /p/ with the continuance of /f/, or contrast the plosive release of /p/ with the gliding manner of /w/.

- *Voice:* Contrast the voiceless-ness of /p/ with the voicing of /b/.

- *Resonance:* Contrast the oral quality of /p/ with

the nasal quality of /m/.

Phonological Strategies to Introduce /p/

- *Key words:* Introduce /p/ with a small set of functional key words.

- *Reduplication:* Consider teaching early /p/ in easy CVCV words, e.g., *papa, poo-poo, pee-pee*

- *Reduplication in adapted words:* Consider teaching early /p/ in easy CVCV words that are modifications of real words, e.g., *po-po* (for *open*), *pæ-po* (for *apple*).

- *Diminutive:* Consider teaching early /p/ with diminutives and similar words in CVCV, e.g., *puppy, pappy (grandpa), peepee, poopie, peppy, poppy.*

- *Baby steps:* Allow the client to use /b/ as a substitution for initial /p/, at least for a while until voiceless-ness enters his logical repertoire.

- *Aspiration:* Allow early /p/ to be produced with excessive aspiration.

- *Switch gears:* If /p/ proves to be impossible to elicit, discontinue the practice and focus on another sound for a while.

- *Introducing final /p/:* Consider introducing /p/ by using the final position in simple VC words, e.g., *up, oop.*

- *Introducing final /p/:* Consider introducing /p/ in the final position of CVC words by allowing the client to reduce words into VC syllable structure, e.g., *op* (for *open*), *up* (for *cup*), *æp* (for *cap*).

- *Closed syllables:* When moving on to CVC words with /p/, consider using those that have /p/ in both initial and final position, e.g., *pop, poop, peep, pup, pope.*

- *Introducing final position:* When stimulating final /p/, begin with simple CVC words, e.g., *cup, cap, keep, coop, cape, cop, tip, top, tape, tap, type, map, mop, nap, goop, lip, lap, rip, rap, yip, yap, zip, zap.*

- *Final position with epenthesis:* Consider allowing the client to use an extra schwa and an extra syllable to stimulate a final /p/, e.g., *ʌ-pʌ* (for *up*), *bee-pʌ* (for *beep*), *ta-pʌ* (for *top*).

- *Simplified words:* Consider teaching /p/ in the initial position by using easy words that can be spoken in CV, e.g., *poo* (for *pool*), *pay* (for *play*), *poh* (for *applesauce*).

- *Emerging /p/:* When /p/ is just emerging, consider teaching the client to use it as a substitute for other phonemes so that he can practice it in multiple ways, e.g., *pour* (for *four*), *piʃ* (for *fish*), *op* (for *off*).

- *Minimal pairs and larger sets for initial /p/:* Use contrasting word pairs and larger sets to teach initial /p/, e.g., *pee/bee*, or *pee, bee, me, tea,* and *key.*

- *Minimal pairs and larger sets for final /p/:* Use contrasting word pairs and larger sets to teach final /p/, e.g., *ape/eight*, or *ape, eight, ache,* and *aim.*

- *Reading and spelling:* Teach this phoneme as part of the client's reading and spelling program.

- *Language arts:* Teach this phoneme through stories, songs, jingles, jokes, rhymes, plays, and other material in the language arts program.

Solutions to Specific Problems on /p/

- *Weak /p/ (inadequate plosive force):* Have the client produce /p/ as he holds the back of his hand against the lips. Teach him to use greater force of exhalation.

- *Prevocalic voicing on initial /p/:* Exaggerate the voiceless-ness of /p/. Compare and contrast /p/ and /b/. Have the client hold his hands and fingers at his larynx so he can feel the voice and voiceless differences through touch; teach "motor-on" and "motor-off" (for voice on and off).

- *Too much aspiration on /p/:* Teach the client to produce final /p/ in words without releasing its occluded position. Use negative practice by amplifying the aspiration and rehearsing the sound more loudly.

- *Nasal emission on /p/:* Teach the client to control resonance.

- *Nasal substitution:* Teach the client to control resonance .

- *Inhalation on /p/:* Develop correct breath support.

- *Puffy cheeks on /p/:* Develop oral stability.

- *Asymmetrical lips on /p/:* Develop oral stability.

- *Slow release on /p/:* Build higher inter-oral air pressure by pressing the lips more firmly together. Place a probe on the midline of the lower lip and tip it downward quickly to stimulate quick release. Enhance teaching with mirrors and demonstrations.

- *Labio-dental production of /p/:* This is usually because the upper lip is pulling up out of the way, or there is a large overbite or large upper front teeth. Teach oral stability and facilitate appropriate lip mobility.

- *Malocclusion prevents bilabial contact on /p/:* Refer for orthodontia and/or teach compensation to make the best sound possible.

- *Tongue protrusion on /p/:* Develop oral stability. Establish normal swallow if deviant.

- *Glottal stop replacement:* Develop auditory discrimination, oral perception, and lip movement.

- *Client can say /p/ only with a stressed schwa (pʌ):* Allow the client to produce final /p/ words with the schwa for a while, e.g., *cap* as *ca-pʌ.* Switch to words that contain this syllable for a while, e.g., *pub, puck, puddle, puff, pug, pudgy, pumpkin, pup, puppy, puss,* and *putt.* Use amplification and negative practice and alter between the correct and the incorrect productions.

/b/

Multisensory Stimulation of /b/

- *Auditory stimulation:* Model, amplify, repeat, and bombard with the phoneme.

- *Auditory feedback:* Direct the client's production back to his ear with a tube or other tool. Imitate the client's sound.

- *Cue:* Use a cue to pique the client's interest in this phoneme.

- *Visual feedback to understand lip movements:* Watch in a mirror; imitate the client's correct and incorrect productions and watch each other during simultaneous productions.

- *Visual feedback to understand airflow on /b/:* Hold objects in front of the lips for the client to move with his puff of air from /b/. Start with small lightweight objects like tissue paper, cotton balls, string, pieces of dental floss, tiny origami objects, etc.. If necessary, switch to heavier objects to increase strength of expiration by using items such as pinwheels or Ping-Pong® (table tennis) balls. Produce /b/ against a mirror or window and observe the fog it produces

- *Verbal:* Use vocabulary the client can understand to describe this phoneme.

- *Tactile feedback to perceive lip movements:* Have the child feel his own lip movements during production of /b/.

- *Mark the target to develop place for /b/:* Touch the upper and lower lips prior to production. Place an object between the lips against which the lips can close, such as tongue depressor, finger, swizzle stick, coffee stirrer, or dental floss.

- *Proprioceptive stimulation to stimulate lip function:* Activate lip movement with resistance. Use a button

pull, crossbar apparatus, lip exerciser, and lip retractor.

- *Jaw stability:* Stabilize the jaw to encourage more active lip mobility.

- *Tongue stability:* Stabilize the tongue at the back-lateral margins to keep the tongue inside the mouth during production of /b/.

Association Method for /b/

- *Place:* Help the client learn /b/ by recognizing the similarities between it and any of the other bilabial phonemes he can produce in the same place — /p/, /m/, or /w/. Also, use labio-dental phoneme /v/.

- *Manner:* Help the client learn /b/ by recognizing the similarities between it and any of the other stops he can produce with occlusion — /p/, /t/, /d/, /k/, or /g/.

- *Voice:* Help the client learn /b/ by recognizing the similarities between it and any of the other stops he can produce with voice — /d/ or /g/. Also, use voiced /v/.

Successive Approximations for /b/

- *Build /b/ off of /p/:* Have the client produce /p/ and turn his voice on.

- *Build /b/ off of /m/:* Have the client prolong /m/, pinch his nose closed and lower his jaw.

- *Build /b/ off of /v:* Have the client prolong /v/ and push his lips together.

- *Build /b/ off of /ɑ/:* Have the client make an /ɑ/ and then put his lips together.

- *Build /b/ off of the bilabial raspberry:* Have the client produce a voiced bilabial raspberry and then soften it up and press his lips together.

Contrast Method for /b/

- *Place:* Contrast the lip movements of /b/ with the tongue-tip movements of /d/ or with the tongue-back movements of /g/.

- *Manner:* Contrast the occlusion of /b/ with the continuance of /v/. Or contrast the plosive release of /b/ with the gliding manner of /w/.

- *Voice:* Contrast the voicing on /b/ with the voiceless-ness of /p/.

- *Resonance:* Contrast the oral quality of /b/ with the nasal quality of /m/.

Phonological Strategies to Introduce /b/

- *Key words:* Introduce /b/ with a small set of functional key words.

- *Reduplication:* Consider teaching early /b/ in easy CVCV words, e.g., *bye-bye, boo-boo, ba-ba* (for *bottle*), *bʌ-bʌ* (for *brother*).

- *Diminutive:* Consider teaching early /b/ with diminutives and other similar words, e.g., *Bobby, booby, baby.*

- *Switch gears:* If /b/ proves to be impossible to elicit, discontinue it and focus on another sound for a while.

- *Early /b/ words:* Consider teaching /b/ in the initial position first by using easy CV words, e.g., *boo, bee, bow.*

- *Early /b/ adapted words:* Consider teaching /b/ in the initial position first by using easy words that can be altered to CV, e.g., *ba* (for *bye-bye*), *boh* (for *boat*), *bʌ* (for *button*).

- *Final position with epenthesis:* Consider allowing the client to use a schwa and an extra syllable to stimulate a final /b/, e.g., *ca-bʌ* (for *cab*), *cʌ-bʌ* (for *cub*), *clʌ-bʌ* (for *club*).

- *Assimilation in CVC:* When moving on to CVC words with /b/, consider using words with the target phoneme in initial and final position, e.g., *Bob, babe, bub.*

- */b/ as a substitute:* Consider helping /b/ to emerge in words by using it as a substitute, e.g., *bour* (for *four*), *by* (for *why*), *bæ-boh* (for *apple*).

- *Minimal pairs and larger sets for initial /b/:* Use contrasting word pairs and larger sets to teach initial /b/, e.g., *bee, pee, me, tea, key; boo, poo, moo, two, do; bye, pie, my, tie.*

- *Minimal pairs and larger sets for final /b/:* Use contrasting word pairs and larger sets to teach final /b/, e.g., *cab/cat, mob/mop, cub/cup.*

- *Reading and spelling:* Teach this phoneme as part of the client's reading and spelling program.

- *Language arts:* Teach this phoneme through stories, songs, jingles, jokes, rhymes, plays, and other material in the language arts program.

Solutions to Specific Problems on /b/

- *Weak /b/:* Have the client produce /b/ as his hand presses against his lips. Teach him to push harder with his lips and to use greater force of exhalation.

- *Postvocalic devoicing of final /b/:* Teach the client to keep his voice on (his "motor" on).

- *Nasal emission on /b/:* Teach client to control resonance.

- *Nasal substitution for /b/:* Teach client to control resonance.

- *Inhalation on /b/:* Develop correct breath support.

- *Puffy cheeks on /b/:* Develop oral stability.

- *Asymmetrical lips on /b/:* Develop oral stability.

- *Labio-dental production of /b/:* Teach the upper lip to relax.

- *Tongue protrusion on /b/:* Develop tongue stability.

- *Malocclusion prevents bilabial contact on /b/:* Wait until after orthodontic or surgical correction, and/or, if necessary, teach compensation to make the best sound possible. Teach the closed lips rest posture and normal oral rest position.

- *Glottal stop replacement:* Develop auditory discrimination, oral perception, and lip movement.

- *Client can say /b/ only with a stressed schwa (bʌ):* Switch to words that contain this syllable for a while, e.g., *bub, buck, buddy, buff, bug, budge, bum, bun, bus, but, butt, button,* and *buzz.* Also, allow client to produce final /b/ words with the schwa for a while, e.g., *tub* as *tu-bʌ.* Use amplification and negative practice and alter between the correct and the incorrect productions

/t/

Multisensory Stimulation of /t/

- *Auditory stimulation:* Model, amplify, repeat, and bombard with the phoneme.

- *Auditory feedback:* Direct the client's production back to his ear with a tube or other tool. Imitate the client's sound.

- *Cue:* Use a cue to pique the client's interest in this phoneme.

- *Visual feedback to understand tongue-tip elevation:* Prop the mouth open and watch in a mirror. Imitate the client's correct and incorrect productions and watch each other during simultaneous productions.

- *Visual feedback to understand airflow on /t/:* Produce

/t/ against a mirror or window and observe the fog it produces.

- *Verbal:* Use vocabulary the client can understand to describe this phoneme.

- *Tactile feedback to perceive tongue-tip movements:* Have the child use his fingers to feel his own tongue movements during production of /t/.

- *Mark the target to develop place for /t/:* Touch the tongue tip and the alveolar ridge prior to production. Place an object on the alveolar ridge against which the tongue tip can press, such as a piece of dental floss with a knot on the end or a dental pick between the maxillary (upper) central incisors.

- *Aid tongue-tip elevation:* Facilitate tongue movement and tip elevation.

- *Jaw stability to encourage more tongue activity:* Stabilize the jaw to encourage more active tongue-tip movement.

- *Tongue stability to encourage more active lip mobility:* Stabilize the tongue at the back-lateral margins to keep the tongue inside the mouth during production of /t/.

Association Method for /t/

- *Place:* Help the client learn /t/ by recognizing the similarities between it and any of the other phonemes he can produce in the same place — /d/, /n/, /l/, or /s/ and /z/.

- *Manner:* Help the client learn /t/ by recognizing the similarities between it and any of the other phonemes he can produce with the same manner — /p/, /b/, /d/, /k/, or /g/.

- *Voice:* Help the client learn /t/ by recognizing the similarities between it and any of the other stops he can produce without voice — /p/ or /k/. Also, use voiceless /s/.

Successive Approximations for /t/

- *Build /t/ off of /d/:* Have the client produce /d/ in a whisper.

- *Build /t/ off of /n/:* Have the client prolong a whispered /n/, pinch his nose closed and lower his jaw.

- *Build /t/ off of /s/:* Have the client prolong /s/ and push his tongue tip up to the alveolus.

- *Build /t/ off of /h/:* Have the client make an /h/ and then push his tongue up.

- *Build /t/ off of the lingua-labial raspberry:* Have the client produce a voiceless lingua-labial raspberry and then soften it and press his tongue tip up.

Contrasting Method for /t/

- *Place:* Contrast the tongue-tip movements of /t/ with the tongue-back movements of /k/, with the lip movement of /p/, or with the glottal movements of /h/.

- *Manner:* Contrast the occlusion of /t/ with the continuance of /s/, or contrast the plosive release of /t/ with the gliding manner of /l/.

- *Voice:* Contrast the voiceless-ness of /t/ with the voicing of /d/.

- *Resonance:* Contrast the oral quality of /t/ with the nasal quality of /n/.

Phonological Strategies to Introduce /t/

- *Key words:* Introduce /t/ with a small set of functional key words.

- *Aspiration:* Allow early /t/ to be produced with excessive aspiration.

- *Reduplication:* Consider teaching early /t/ in easy CVCV words, e.g., *ta-ta* (for *bye-bye*), *tutu*, *tee-tee* (for *kitty*), *toh-toh* (for *Toby*).

- *Diminutive:* Consider teaching early /t/ in diminutives and similar words, e.g., *kitty*, *pretty*, *bootie*, *potty*, *poopie*.

- *Baby steps:* Allow the client to use /d/ as a substitution for initial /t/, at least for a while until voiceless-ness enters his phonological repertoire.

- *Switch gears:* If /t/ proves to be impossible to elicit, discontinue the practice and focus on another sound for a while.

- *Early final /t/ words:* Consider teaching /t/ in the final position early first by using easy VC words, e.g., *eat, out, eight, ate, oat, it, at.*

- *Early final /t/ words:* Consider teaching /t/ in the final position of CVC words early by allowing the client to reduce words into VC syllable structure, e.g., *ot* (for *hot*), *æt* (for *hat*), *ight* (for *light*).

- *Final position:* When moving on to CVC words, consider using /t/ to close the syllable first, e.g., *bat, bit, bite, boat, boot, bait, cat, kit, kite, night, knit.*

- *Initial position words:* Consider teaching /t/ in the initial position early by using easy words of CV structure, e.g., *two, too, T, tea, toe, tow.*

- *Initial position in adapted words:* Consider teaching /t/ in the initial position early by using easy words that can be spoken in CV, e.g., *tee* (for *teeth*), *tay* (for *table*), *tʌ* (for *touch*), *ta* (for *helicopter*).

- *Final position with epenthesis:* Consider allowing the client to use a schwa and an extra syllable to stimulate final /t/, e.g., *hæ-tʌ* (for *hat*), *boo-tʌ* (for *boot*), *nigh-tʌ* (for *night*).

- *Assimilation in CVC:* When moving on to CVC words with /t/, consider using words with the target phoneme in initial and final position, e.g., *toot, Tate, tote, taught, tut, king Tut*.

- */t/ as a substitute:* Consider helping /t/ to emerge in words by using /t/ as a substitute, e.g., *tee* (for *key*), *teet* (for *teeth*), *mat* (for *match*), *kit* (*kiss*).

- *Minimal pairs and larger sets in initial position:* Use contrasting word pairs and larger sets to teach initial /t/, e.g., *tea, key, Dee, pee, bee, me; two, coo, poo, boo, shoe; tie, pie, bye, my.*

- *Minimal pairs and larger sets in final position:* Use contrasting word pairs and larger sets to teach final /t/, e.g., *hat/ham, light/like, coat/Coke, art/ark.*

- *Reading and spelling:* Teach this phoneme as part of the client's reading and spelling program.

- *Language arts:* Teach this phoneme through stories, songs, jingles, jokes, rhymes, plays, and other material in the language arts program.

Solutions to Specific Problems on /t/

- *Weak /t/:* Teach the client to press the tongue tip up harder.

- *Frication on /t/:* Teach the client to press the tongue tip up harder.

- *Prevocalic voicing on initial /t/:* Exaggerate the voiceless-ness of /t/ by contrasting /t/ and /d/. Have the client feel the exhaled air of /t/ versus /d/. Have the client hold his hands and fingers at his larynx so he can feel the voice and voiceless differences through touch; teach the idea of "motor-on" and "motor-off" (for voice on and off).

- *Too much aspiration on /t/:* Teach the client to produce final /t/ in words without releasing its occluded position. Use negative practice to highlight the error by amplifying the aspiration or rehearsing it louder.

- *Nasal emission on /t/:* Teach the client to control resonance.

- *Nasal substitution:* Teach the client to control resonance.

- *Inhalation on /t/:* Develop correct breath support.

- *Tongue shifts to one side on /t/:* Develop oral stability.

- *Tongue protrudes between the teeth or lips on /t/:* Develop tongue stability.

- *Glottal stop replaces /t/:* Develop auditory discrimination, oral perception, and tongue movements. Compare /t/ with the glottal stop.

- *Middle of the tongue humps up and the tip remains low on /t/:* Stimulate tongue bowling and tongue-tip elevation.

- *Client cannot elevate the tongue tip because he keeps closing the lips:* Inhibit lip closure.

- *Client can say /t/ only with a stressed schwa (tʌ):* Switch to words that contain this syllable for a while, e.g., *tub, tuck, tough, tug, tummy, ton, tusk, tut,* and *King Tut.* Also, allow the client to produce final /t/ words with the schwa for a while, e.g., *hot* as *ho-tʌ.* Use amplification and negative practice and alter between the correct and the incorrect productions.

/d/

Multisensory Stimulation of /d/

- *Auditory stimulation:* Model, amplify, repeat, and bombard with the phoneme.

- *Auditory feedback:* Direct the client's production back to his ear with a tube or other tool. Imitate the client's sound.

- *Cue:* Use a cue to pique the client's interest in this phoneme.

- *Visual feedback to understand tongue-tip elevation:* Prop the mouth open and watch in a mirror. Imitate the client's correct and incorrect productions and watch each other during simultaneous productions.

- *Visual feedback to understand airflow on /d/:* Produce /d/ against a mirror or window and observe the fog it produces.

- *Verbal:* Use vocabulary the client can understand to describe the respiration, phonation, resonation, and articulation characteristics of this phoneme.

- *Tactile stimulation to develop tongue concept:* Pat, rub, vibrate, ice, and stretch the tongue. Encourage oral play.

- *Tactile feedback to perceive tongue-tip movements:* Have the child use his fingers to feel his own tongue movements during production of /d/.

- *Mark the target to develop place for /d/:* Touch the tongue tip and the alveolar ridge prior to production. Place an object on the alveolar ridge against which the tongue tip can press, such as a piece of dental floss with a knot on the end or a dental pick between the maxillary (upper) central incisors.

- *Aid tongue-tip elevation:* Facilitate active tongue and tongue-tip movement.

- *Jaw stability to encourage more tongue activity:* Stabilize the jaw to encourage more active tongue-tip movement.

- *Tongue stability:* Stabilize the tongue at the back-lateral margins to keep the tongue inside the mouth during production of /d/.

Association Method for /d/

- *Place:* Help the client learn /d/ by recognizing the similarities between it and any of the other lingua-alveolar phonemes he can produce — /t/, /n/, /l/, or /s/ and /z/.

- *Manner:* Help the client learn /d/ by recognizing the similarities between it and any of the other stops he can produce — /p/, /b/, /t/, /k/, or /g/.

- *Voice:* Help the client learn /d/ by recognizing the similarities between it and any of the other voiced stops he can produce — /b/ or /g/. Also, use /z/.

Successive Approximations for /d/

- *Build /d/ off of /t/:* Have the client produce /t/ and turn his voice on.

- *Build /d/ off of /n/:* Have the client produce /n/, pinch his nose closed and lower his jaw.

- *Build /d/ off of /z/:* Have the client prolong /z/ and push his tongue up higher.

- *Build /d/ off of /a/:* Have the client make an /a/ and then push his tongue up.

- *Build /d/ off of the lingua-labial raspberry:* Have the client produce a voiced lingua-labial raspberry and then soften it and press his tongue tip higher.

Contrasting Method for /d/

- *Place:* Contrast the tongue-tip movements of /d/ with the tongue-back movements of /g/ or with the lip movement of /b/.

- *Manner:* Contrast the occlusion of /d/ with the continuance of /z/, or contrast the plosive release of /d/ with the gliding manner of /l/.

- *Voice:* Contrast the voicing of /d/ with the voiceless-ness of /t/. Have the client produce /t/ and then add voice to it.

- *Resonance:* Contrast the oral quality of /d/ with the nasal quality of /n/.

Phonological Strategies to Introduce /d/

- *Key words:* Introduce /d/ with a small set of functional key words.

- *Reduplication:* Consider teaching early /d/ in easy CVCV words, e.g., *daddy, dada* (for *daddy*), *dæ-dæ* (for *daddy*), *doo-doo* (for *noodle*).

- *Diminutive:* Consider teaching early /d/ with diminutives and similar words, e.g., *daddy, muddy, goodie, birdie.*

- *Baby steps:* Allow the client to use /d/ as a substitution for any other phoneme for a while to establish /d/, e.g., *doap* (for *soap*).

- *Switch gears:* If /d/ proves to be impossible to elicit, discontinue the practice and focus on another sound for a while.

- *Initial position words:* Consider teaching /d/ in the initial position early by using easy words of CV structure, e.g., *do, Dee, day, dough, dʌ, die, dye.*

- *Initial position in adapted words:* Consider teaching /d/ in the initial position early by using easy words that can be spoken in CV, e.g., *doh* (for *donut*), *day* (for *David*), *dæ* (for *that*), *doh* (for *don't*), *dow* (for *down*).

- *Final position with epenthesis:* Consider allowing the client to use a schwa and an extra syllable to stimulate a final /d/, e.g., *mæ-dʌ* (for *mad*), *bæ-dʌ* (for *bad*), *goo-dʌ* (for *good*).

- *Assimilation in CVC:* When moving on to CVC words with /d/, consider using words with the target phoneme in initial and final position, e.g., *dad, deed, did, dude, dud, Dade.*

- *Initial /d/ as a substitute:* Consider helping initial /d/ to emerge in words by using it as a substitute, e.g., *dady* (for *lady*), *do* (for *no*), *doo* (for *two*), *deeth* (for *teeth*), *doy* (for *toy*), *diss* (for *kiss*).

- *Minimal pairs and larger sets in initial position:* Use contrasting word pairs and larger sets to teach initial /d/, e.g., *Dee, bee, gee, pee, T, me; do, boo, goo, two, coo, poo, shoe; dye, bye, pie, my.*

- *Minimal pairs and larger sets in final position:* Use

contrasting word pairs and larger sets to teach final /d/, e.g., *mad, mat, ma'am; bad, bat, bam; mod, rod, god.*

• *Reading and spelling:* Teach this phoneme as part of the client's reading and spelling program.

• *Language arts:* Teach this phoneme through stories, songs, jingles, jokes, rhymes, plays, and other material in the language arts program.

Solutions to Specific Problems on /d/

• *Weak /d/:* Teach the client to press the tongue tip up harder.

• *Frication on /d/:* Teach the client to press the tongue tip up harder.

• *Prevocalic voicing on initial /d/:* Teach phonation.

• *Nasal emission on /d/:* Teach the client to control resonance.

• *Nasal substitution:* Teach the client to control resonance.

• *Inhalation on /d/:* Teach correct breath support.

• *Puffy cheeks on /d/:* Develop oral stability.

• *Tongue shifts to one side on /d/:* Develop oral stability.

• *Tongue protrudes between the teeth or lips on /d/:* Develop tongue stability.

• *Glottal stop replacement:* Develop auditory discrimination, oral perception, lip movement, and tongue movements. Compare /d/ with the glottal stop.

• *Middle of the tongue humps up and the tip remains low on /d/:* Stimulate tongue bowling and tongue-tip elevation.

• *Client cannot elevate the tongue tip because he keeps closing the lips:* Inhibit lip closure.

• *Client cannot produce /d/ because he keeps producing /g/:* Inhibit tongue-back elevation.

• *Client can say /d/ only with a stressed schwa (dʌ):* Switch to words that contain this syllable for a while, e.g., *dub, duck, dud, Duff, dug, dull, dumb, done, dust, dove,* and *does.* Also, allow the client to produce final /d/ words with the schwa for a while, e.g., *mad* as *mæ-dʌ.* Use amplification and negative practice and alter between the correct and the incorrect productions.

/k/

Multisensory Stimulation of /k/

• *Auditory stimulation:* Model, amplify, repeat, and bombard with the phoneme.

• *Auditory feedback:* Direct the client's production back to his ear with a tube or other tool. Imitate the client's sound.

• *Cue:* Use a cue to pique the client's interest in this phoneme.

• *Visual feedback to understand tongue-back elevation:* Prop the mouth open and watch in a mirror. Imitate the client's correct and incorrect productions and watch each other during simultaneous productions.

• *Visual feedback to understand airflow on /k/:* Produce /k/ against a mirror or window and observe the fog it produces.

• *Verbal:* Use vocabulary the client can understand to describe this phoneme.

• *Tactile stimulation to develop tongue concept:* Pat, rub, vibrate, ice, and stretch the tongue. Encourage oral play.

• *Tactile feedback to perceive tongue-back movements:* Have the child feel his own tongue movements during production of /k/.

• *Mark the target to develop place for /k/:* Touch the back of the tongue and the palatal notch prior to production.

• *Aid tongue-back elevation:* Facilitating tongue-back elevation and depression.

• *Jaw stability to encourage more tongue activity:* Stabilize the jaw to encourage more active tongue-back elevation.

• *Tongue stability:* Stabilize the tongue at the back-lateral margins to keep the tongue inside the mouth during production of /k/.

Association Method for /k/

• *Place:* Help the client learn /k/ by recognizing the similarities between it and any of the other lingua-velar phonemes he can produce — /g/ or /ŋ/. Have the client produce /g/ and then turn voice off. Or have the client produce /ŋ/ and then press the back of the tongue higher and harder, and then lower more quickly, then take out voice.

- *Manner:* Help the client learn /k/ by recognizing the similarities between it and any of the other stops he can produce — /p/, /b/, /t/, /d/, or /g/. Have him make a /t/ and then say, "Make a T with the back of your tongue."

- *Voice:* Help the client learn /k/ by recognizing the similarities between it and any of the other voiceless stops he can produce — /p/ or /t/.

Successive Approximations for /k/

- *Build /t/ off of /g/:* Have the client produce /g/ in a whisper.

- *Build /k/ off of /ŋ/:* Have the client prolong a whispered /ŋ/, pinch his nose closed and lower his jaw.

- *Build /k/ off of /h/:* Have the client make an /h/ and then push the back of his tongue up.

- *Build /k/ off of the lingua-velar raspberry:* Have the client produce a voiceless lingua-velar raspberry and then soften it and press the back of his tongue up.

Contrasting Method for /k/

- *Place:* Contrast the tongue-back elevation of /k/ with the tongue-tip elevation of /t/. Have him make a /t/ and then say, "Make a T with the back of your tongue."

- *Manner:* Contrast the occlusion of /k/ with the continuance of /h/, or contrast the plosive release of /k/ with the gliding manner of /r/.

- *Voice:* Contrast the voiceless-ness of /k/ with the voicing of /g/.

- *Resonance:* Contrast the oral quality of /k/ with the nasal quality of /ŋ/.

Phonological Strategies to Introduce /k/

- *Key words:* Introduce /k/ with a small set of functional key words.

- *Aspiration:* Allow early /k/ to be produced with excessive aspiration.

- *Reduplication:* Consider teaching early /k/ in easy CVCV words, e.g., *cookie, coo-coo* (meaning *loony*), *cocoa, ca-ca* (meaning *feces*).

- *Diminutive:* Consider teaching diminutives early, e.g., *icky, ucky, duckie, cookie.*

- *Adapted reduplication:* Consider teaching early /k/ in adapted CVCV words, e.g., *kee-kee* (for *kitty*), *Kay-kay*

(for *Kate*), *ka-ka* (for *helicopter*).

- *Baby steps:* Allow the client to use /t/ as a substitution for initial /k/, at least for a while until [+Back] enter his phonological repertoire.

- *Switch gears:* If /k/ proves to be impossible to elicit, discontinue the practice and focus on another sound for a while.

- *Early final /k/ words:* Consider teaching /k/ in the final position early first by using easy VC words, e.g., *eek, ick, ache, oak, uck.*

- *Early final /k/ words:* Consider teaching /k/ in the final position of CVC words early by allowing the client to reduce words into VC syllable structure, e.g., *ook* (for *look*), *ack* (for *backpack*), *ike* (for *bike*).

- *Assimilation in CVC:* When moving on to CVC words with /k/, consider using words with the target phoneme in initial and final position, e.g., *kick, cake, cook, kook, Coke.*

- *Final position:* When moving on to CVC words, consider using /k/ to close the syllable first, e.g., *back, bike, look, like, Mike, make, bake.*

- *Initial position words:* Consider teaching /k/ in the initial position early by using easy words of CV structure, e.g., *key, coo, Kay, caw, cow.*

- *Initial position in adapted words:* Consider teaching /k/ in the initial position early by using easy words that can be spoken in CV, e.g., *cæ* (for *cat*), *ca* (for *car*), *coo* (for *cookie*), *kay* (for *okay*), *ka* (for *helicopter*).

- *Final position with epenthesis:* Consider allowing the client to use a schwa and an extra syllable to stimulate a final /k/, e.g., *bæ-kʌ* (for *back*), *boo-kʌ* (for *book*), *ki-kʌ* (for *kick*).

- */k/ as a substitute:* Consider helping /k/ to emerge in words by using it as a substitute, e.g., *kop* (for *top*), *kikky* (for *kitty*), *koo* (for *two*), *kake* (for *take*), *kik* (for *kiss*).

- *Minimal pairs and larger sets in initial position:* Use contrasting word pairs and larger sets to teach initial /k/, e.g., *key, tea, me, pee, see, bee; cook, took, book, look; cat, hat, rat, bat, mat, fat, sat.*

- *Minimal pairs and larger sets in final position:* Use contrasting word pairs and larger sets to teach final /k/, e.g., *beak/beet, take/tame, ark/arm.*

- *Reading and spelling:* Teach this phoneme as part of the client's reading and spelling program.

- *Language arts:* Teach this phoneme through stories, songs, jingles, jokes, rhymes, plays, and other material in the language arts program.

Solutions to Specific Problems on /k/

- *Weak /k/:* Teach the client to press the back of his tongue up harder.

- *Frication on /k/:* Teach the client to push the back of his tongue up harder.

- *Prevocalic voicing on initial /k/:* Exaggerate the voiceless-ness of /k/ by comparing and contrasting it with /g/. Have the client feel the exhaled air of /k/ versus /g/. Have the client hold his hands and fingers at his larynx so he can feel the voice and voiceless differences through touch. Teach "motor-on" and "motor-off" for voice on and off.

- *Too much aspiration on /k/:* Teach the client to produce final /k/ in words without releasing its occluded position. Amplify the aspiration, and rehearse it louder, and negative practice so the client can hear it.

- *Nasal emission on /k/:* Teach the client to control resonance.

- *Inhalation on /k/:* Develop correct breath support.

- *Tongue protrudes between the teeth or lips on /k/:* Develop tongue stability.

- *Tongue-middle production:* Some clients produce /k/ with the middle of the tongue articulating with the middle of the palate, instead of making a clean lingua-velar articulation. Teach the tongue to bowl and to lift only the back of the tongue to the velum.

- *Client cannot produce /k/ because he keeps producing /t/:* Inhibit tip elevation while the client attempts /k/. Lower the jaw farther to make tip elevation harder and to force /k/.

- *Client can say /k/ only with a stressed schwa (kʌ):* Switch to words that contain this syllable for a while, e.g., *cub, cud, cuff, come, cup, cusp, cuss, Custer, cut, cuts,* and *cousin.* Also, allow the client to produce final /k/ words with the schwa for a while, e.g., *pick* as *pi-kʌ.* Use amplification and negative practice and alter between the correct and the incorrect productions.

/g/

Multisensory Stimulation for /g/

- *Auditory stimulation:* Model, amplify, repeat, and bombard with the phoneme.

- *Auditory feedback:* Direct the client's production back to his ear with a tube or other tool. Imitate the client's sound.

- *Cue:* Use a cue to pique the client's interest in this phoneme.

- *Visual feedback to understand tongue-back elevation:* Prop the mouth open and watch in a mirror. Imitate the client's correct and incorrect productions and watch each other during simultaneous productions.

- *Visual feedback to understand airflow on /g/:* Produce /g/ against a mirror or window and observe the fog it produces.

- *Verbal:* Use vocabulary the client can understand to describe the respiration, phonation, resonation, and articulation characteristics of this phoneme.

- *Tactile feedback to perceive tongue-back movements:* Have the child use his fingers to feel his own tongue movements during production of /g/.

- *Mark the target to develop place for /g/:* Touch the back of the tongue and the palatal notch prior to production.

- *Aid tongue-back elevation:* Facilitate tongue-back elevation and depression.

- *Jaw stability to encourage more tongue activity:* Stabilize the jaw to encourage more active tongue-back elevation.

- *Tongue stability:* Stabilize the tongue at the back-lateral margins to keep the tongue inside the mouth during production of /g/.

Association Method for /g/

- *Place:* Help the client learn /g/ by recognizing the similarities between it and any of the other lingua-velar phonemes he can produce — /k/ or /ŋ/.

- *Manner:* Help the client learn /g/ by recognizing the similarities between it and any of the other stops he can produce — /p/, /b/, /t/, /d/, or /k/.

- *Voice:* Help the client learn /g/ by recognizing the similarities between it and any of the other voiced stops he can produce — /b/ or /d/.

- *Resonance:* Have the client produce /ŋ/ and then press the back of the tongue higher and harder, and then lower more quickly.

Successive Approximations for /g/

- *Build /g/ off of /k/:* Have the client produce /k/ with voice.

- *Build /g/ off of /ŋ/:* Have the client prolong /ŋ/, pinch his nose closed and lower his jaw.

- *Build /g/ off of /ɑ/:* Have the client make an /ɑ/ and then push the back of his tongue up.

- *Build /g/ off of the lingua-velar raspberry:* Have the client produce a voiced lingua-velar raspberry and then soften it and press the back of his tongue up.

Contrasting Method for /g/

- *Place:* Contrast the tongue-back elevation of /g/ with the tongue-tip elevation of /d/. Have him make a /d/ and then say, "Make a D with the back of your tongue."

- *Manner:* Contrast the occlusion of /g/ with the continuance of /ɑ/, or contrast the plosive release of /g/ with the gliding manner of /r/.

- *Voice:* Contrast the voice of /g/ with the voiceless-ness of /k/. Have the client produce /k/ and then add voice to it.

- *Resonance:* Contrast the oral quality of /g/ with the nasal quality of /ŋ/.

Phonological Strategies to Introduce /g/

- *Key words:* Introduce /g/ with a small set of functional key words.

- *Reduplication:* Consider teaching early /g/ in easy CVCV words, e.g., gʌ-gʌ (frog sound), goo-goo (baby sound), ga-ga (baby sound).

- *Diminutive:* Consider teaching early /g/ in diminutives and other similar words, e.g., *doggie, froggie, baggie.*

- *Switch gears:* If /g/ proves to be impossible to elicit, discontinue the practice and focus on another sound for a while.

- *Initial position words:* Consider teaching /g/ in the initial position early by using easy words of CV structure, e.g., *go, goo guy.*

- *Initial position in adapted words:* Consider teaching /g/ in the initial position early by using easy words

that can be spoken in CV, e.g., *goo* (for *good*), *ga* (for *grandma*).

- *Final position with epenthesis:* Consider allowing the client to use a schwa and an extra syllable to stimulate a final /g/, e.g., ba-gʌ (for *bag*), bʌ-gʌ (for *bug*).

- *Assimilation in CVC:* When moving on to CVC words with /g/, consider using words with the target phoneme in initial and final position, e.g., *gag, gig.*

- */g/ as a substitute:* Consider helping /g/ to emerge in words by using it as a substitute, e.g., *goggie* (for *doggie*), *ga-ga* (for *grandpa*).

- *Minimal pairs and larger sets in initial position:* Use contrasting word pairs and larger sets to teach initial /g/, e.g., *goo, do, boo, two, coo, poo, shoe; guy, dye, bye, pie, my.*

- *Minimal pairs and larger sets in final position:* Use contrasting word pairs and larger sets to teach final /g/, e.g., *big, bit, Biff; bag, back, bat, bad; leg, let.*

- *Reading and spelling:* Teach this phoneme as part of the client's reading and spelling program.

- *Language arts:* Teach this phoneme through stories, songs, jingles, jokes, rhymes, plays, and other material in the language arts program.

Solutions to Specific Problems on /g/

- *Weak /g/:* Teach the client to press the back of his tongue up harder.

- *Frication on /g/:* Teach the client to press the back of his tongue up harder.

- *Prevocalic devoicing on initial /g/:* Teach the client to hold his voice on.

- *Nasal emission on /g/:* Teach the client to control resonance.

- *Inhalation on /g/:* Teach correct breath support.

- *Tongue protrudes between the teeth or lips on /g/:* Develop tongue stability.

- *Tongue-middle production:* Some clients produce /g/ with the middle of the tongue articulating with the middle of the palate, instead of making a clean lingua-velar articulation. Teach the tongue to bowl and to lift only the back of the tongue to the velum.

- *Client cannot produce /g/ because he keeps producing /d/:* Inhibit tip elevation while the client attempts /g/.

- *Client can say /g/ only with a stressed schwa (gʌ):* Switch to words that contain this syllable for a while, e.g., *gull, gum, gun, guppy, Gus, gust, gusty, gut,* and *guts.* Also, allow the client to produce final /g/ words with the schwa for a while, e.g., *bug* as *bʌ-gʌ.* Use amplification and negative practice and alter between the correct and the incorrect productions.

SUMMARY

This chapter has discussed the stop consonants /p/, /b/, /t/, /d/, /k/ and /g/. It summarized how these consonants are produced and catalogued a wide variety of methods to stimulate the infantile and adult-like productions of these sounds.

23

Stimulating the Nasal Consonants

Techniques for /m/, /n/, and /ŋ/

"Nasals… are like stops in having a complete oral closure… but are unlike stops in having an open velopharyngeal port so that sound passes through the nose rather than the mouth."

– Ray Kent, 2004a

Research has demonstrated that the nasals are some of the earliest phonemes to develop. The nasal consonants are usually considered easy to stimulate because they are auditorily distinct, they create a vibrotactile buzz, and their oral movements are as simple to make as the stop consonants. Virtually every book on phonological theory and therapy reviewed for this manual stated that the nasal consonants are rarely in error. However, these phonemes most certainly are in error or even absent in clients with motor speech disorders, those who are very young, and those with significant cognitive impairment. This chapter describes the nasal phonemes and presents methods to teach them.

PRODUCTION

The movements used in production of the nasal consonants are described here. Details about emerging/immature production of these sounds are offered first so that readers can see how these phonemes might be stimulated in clients who speak very little and/or who use very few consonant phonemes. Details about mature oral movements are described next so that readers can see how these phonemes might be stimulated with clients who have errors on these specific phonemes.

Respiration, Phonation, Resonation

All nasal consonants are initiated upon exhalation and the vocal folds adduct to make them voiced. The velopharyngeal port remains open to allow each sound to resonate through the nasal cavities.

/m/   *My, tummy, boom*

Emerging /m/

Phoneme /m/ is one of the sounds infants produce during the cooing stage and, therefore, it pre-dates babbling. A baby simply has to vocalize with his mouth closed to produce a primitive /m/; babies often do this while being fed in a process called *eating-humming*. Humming with /m/ while nursing or bottle-feeding carries scent into the nasal cavities for olfaction which is a powerful motivation for an infant to make the sound. This process continues throughout the first year of life while a child is being fed, and during the second year of life when the child begins to feed himself. Phoneme /m/ emerges in a simple CV sequence when a baby hums either before or after a vowel. Phoneme /m/ emerges in early babbling when the jaw begins to move down-and-up during humming.

The methods of resonance training are used to teach the nasals.

Mature /m/

A different oral-motor pattern emerges as /m/ matures:

- *Starting position:* First the jaw, lips, and tongue stabilize to set the mouth in starting position (see Chapter 14 on oral stability).

- *On-glide:* The upper lip lowers and the lower lip elevates until they articulate together at midline. Research has demonstrated that the lower lip generally moves more than the upper lip, and that the lips press into or beyond one another.

- *Target position:* The target position is achieved as both lips articulate together to close off and seal the oral cavity. The voiced airstream resonates simultaneously in the mouth behind the labial seal and in the nasal cavities. The airstream exits though the nasal ports while the oral port remains closed.

- *Off-glide:* The lips part after /m/ is produced. Oral stability is maintained throughout.

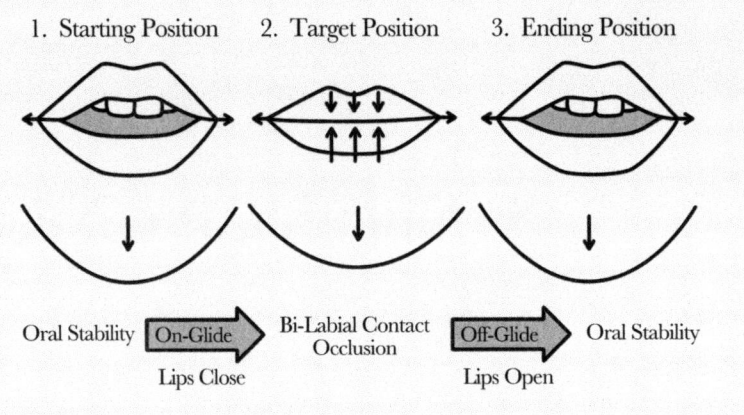

Mature productions of /m/ combine elements of oral stability and lip mobility.

/n/   *No, Anna, man*

Emerging /n/

Phoneme /n/ is one of the sounds infants produce during the cooing stage and, therefore, it also pre-dates babbling. A baby simply has to hum with his mouth closed and his tongue plastered against the palate to coo with a primitive /n/-like sound. Humming with /n/ while being fed brings scent into the nasal cavities for olfaction and this is a powerful motivation for an infant to make the sound. Phoneme /n/ emerges in a simple CV when a baby hums with /n/ and then lowers the jaw while continuing to voice. Phoneme /n/ emerges in CV babbling sequences when a child hums with /n/ and then moves the jaw down-and-up in sequences.

Mature /n/

A different oral-motor pattern emerges as phoneme /n/ matures:

- *Starting position:* First the jaw and tongue stabilize to set the mouth in starting position (see Chapter 14 on oral stability).

- *On-glide:* From its points of stability at the back-lateral margins, both sides of the tongue's perimeter lift simultaneously in a stripping action from the back to the tip in order for the tongue to create the horseshoe-shape against the palate.

- *Target position:* In target position, the tongue presses upward in a horseshoe-shaped seal against the palate. This position is held as the voiced airstream resonates in the mouth in the tongue bowl and in the nasal cavities. The sound exits through the nose.

- *Off-glide:* The off-glide begins as the tongue tip lowers away from the alveolar ridge. The sides of the tongue then simultaneously pull away from the palate in a stripping action from tip to back. The jaw and back-lateral margins of the tongue remain stable throughout.

/ŋ/   *Ringer, song*

Emerging /ŋ/

Research reveals that /ŋ/ is one of the first consonant sounds infants produce right after birth, therefore, it pre-dates both cooing and babbling. This phoneme is one of

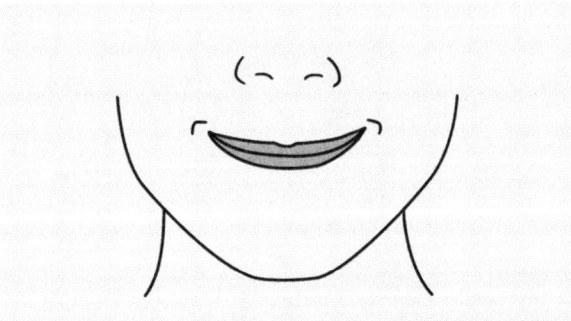

The lips do not press this hard or retract this far during production of /m/.

the newborn's first consonant sounds. It begins to occur in simple CV syllables as the baby hums with /ŋ/ and then pulls the back of the tongue down and away from the palate to create a vowel. Babbling with /ŋ/ emerges as a baby learns to move the back of the tongue down-and-up in sequences while humming with /ŋ/.

Mature /ŋ/

A different oral-motor pattern emerges as /ŋ/ matures:

- *Starting position:* First the jaw and tongue stabilize to set the mouth in starting position (see Chapter 14 on oral stability).

- *On-glide:* While the tongue maintains its stable position at the back-lateral margins, the middle-back of the tongue presses upward from sides-to-midline against the velum.

- *Target position:* The entire back of the tongue forms a seal against the velum. This position is held while the voiced airstream resonates in the nasal cavities and exits through the nose.

- *Off-glide:* The off-glide begins as the tongue's middle-back lowers away from the velum from midline-to-sides. The jaw and back-lateral margins of the

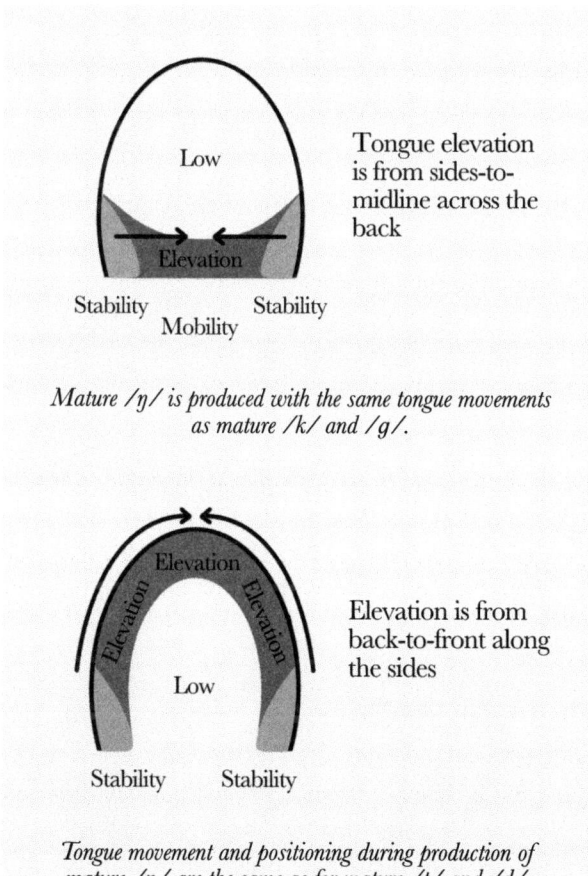

Mature /ŋ/ is produced with the same tongue movements as mature /k/ and /g/.

Tongue movement and positioning during production of mature /n/ are the same as for mature /t/ and /d/.

tongue remain stable throughout.

TREATMENT STRATEGIES

The nasals emerge early in infancy and the relative ease of their production means that they tend to be in error only in the most severe clients. Therapists tend to target /m/ and /n/ early in a program for clients with many phoneme errors but, as discussed above, /ŋ/ actually is the earliest of these sounds to emerge in pre-speech vocalizations and is very important as a means for an infant to learn how to make sound oral and nasal. The phoneme is also important as the English present progressive morpheme -*ing.* Therefore, all three nasal sounds should be addressed. The following advice for stimulating early nasals is offered:

- If the full set of nasals is completely absent, consider stimulating for general knowledge about oral and nasal airflow by using tubes and other tools.

- If a client has no nasals at all, consider addressing all three of them simultaneously and teaching the nasal feature before teaching the nasal consonants. In other words teach the client to make any "nose sound" before targeting any one specific nasal consonant.

- If no nasal sound exists, consider stimulating them while the client is eating to teach the infantile eating-humming pattern; this is sometimes is the earliest way children acquire a nasal sound.

- If the set of nasals is completely absent, consider beginning with /m/ because it is the most visible. However, many clients find others in this set easier to produce. For example, clients who keep the back of the tongue high in the "high guard position" will probably learn /ŋ/ first.

- Most therapists tend to teach these phonemes in the prevocalic position first. However, the final position in which the client can close a syllable by closing the mouth can be easier for many clients. Remember that each child takes his own path of phoneme acquisition, so be flexible in the ordering of treatment targets.

/m/

Multisensory Stimulation Techniques

- *Auditory stimulation to encourage /m/:* Model, amplify, repeat, prolong, and bombard with the phoneme.

- *Auditory feedback:* Direct the client's sound back to his ear with a tube or other tool. Imitate the client's sound.

- *Visual stimulation to teach /m/:* Use modeling, drawings, and puppets. Use a computerized sound analysis tool.

- *Visual feedback to understand /m/:* Watch in a mirror. Imitate the client's correct and incorrect productions and watch each other during simultaneous productions.

- *Visual feedback to understand airflow on /m/:* Produce /m/ with a mirror held under the nose and observe the fog it produces.

- *Verbal:* Use vocabulary the client can understand to describe this phoneme.

- *Cue:* Use a cue to pique the client's interest in this phoneme.

- *Tactile stimulation to develop lip movement for /m/:* Pat, rub, vibrate, cool, and stretch the lips, and encourage oral play.

- *Tactile feedback to perceive lip movements:* Have the child feels his own lip movements during production of /m/.

- *Mark the target to develop place for /m/:* Touch the upper and lower lips prior to production. Place an object between the lips against which the lips can close, such as a tongue depressor, dental floss, finger, swizzle stick, or coffee stirrer.

- *Aid lip closure:* Use methods to facilitate lip movement.

- *Jaw mobility:* Get the jaw to move up and down to stimulate early /m/.

- *Jaw stability:* Stabilize the jaw to encourage more active lip mobility for mature /m/.

- *Tongue stability:* Stabilize the tongue at the back-lateral margins to keep the tongue inside the mouth during production of /m/.

Association Method for /m/

- *Place:* Help the client learn /m/ by recognizing the similarities between it and any of the other bilabial phonemes he can produce — /p/, /b/, or /w/. Also, use labio-dental phoneme /v/.

- *Manner:* Help the client learn /m/ by recognizing the similarities between it and any of the other nasals he can produce — /n/ or /ŋ/.

- *Voice:* Help the client learn /m/ by recognizing the similarities between it and any of the other

voiced sounds he can produce — /n/, /ŋ/, /b/, /d/, or /g/. Also, use voiced /v/ or /z/.

Successive Approximations for /m/

- *Build /m/ off of /n/:* Have the client produce /n/ and have him close his lips.

- *Build /m/ off of /b/:* Have the client produce /b/ and keep his lips pressed together.

- *Build /m/ off of /w/:* Have the client produce /w/ and press his lips together.

Contrasting Method for /m/

- *Place:* Contrast the lip movements of /m/ with the tongue-tip movements of /n/ or with the tongue-back movements of /ŋ/.

- *Manner:* Contrast the continuance of /m/ with the stop quality of /b/.

- *Voice:* Contrast the voicing on /m/ with the voiceless-ness of /p/.

- *Resonance:* Contrast the nasal quality of /m/ with the oral quality of /ɑ/.

Phonological Strategies to Introduce /m/

- *Key words:* Introduce /m/ with a small set of functional key words, e.g., *Momma, mommy, me, my, more, move.*

- *Reduplication:* Consider teaching early /m/ in easy CVCV words, e.g., *momma, moo-moo* (for *cow*), *Mee-mee* (for *Jimmy* or *tummy*, etc.)

- *Diminutive:* Consider teaching early /m/ with diminutives and other similar words, e.g., *Mommy, tummy, gummy bear.*

- *Switch gears:* If /m/ proves to be impossible to elicit, discontinue the practice and focus on another sound for a while.

- *Early /m/ words:* Consider teaching /m/ in the initial position first by using easy CV words, e.g., *me, my, moo, May, Moe, Ma.*

- *Early /m/ adapted words:* Consider teaching /m/ in the initial position first by using easy words that can be altered to CV, e.g., *moo* (for *movie*), *moh* (for *more*), *mee* (for *tummy*).

- *Final position with epenthesis:* Consider allowing the client to use a schwa and an extra syllable to stimulate a final /m/, e.g., *gʌ-mʌ* (for *gum*), *gay-mʌ* (for *game*), *thʌ-mʌ* (for *thumb*).

• *Assimilation in CVC:* When moving into CVC words with /m/, consider using words with the target phoneme in initial and final position, e.g., *Mom, ma'am, mime, mum.*

• */m/ as a substitute:* Consider helping /m/ to emerge in words by using it as a substitute, e.g., *mo/no.*

• *Minimal pairs and larger sets for initial /m/:* Use contrasting word pairs and larger sets to teach initial /m/, e.g., *me, pee, bee, tea, key; moo, poo, boo, two, do; my, pie, bye, tie, lie.*

• *Minimal pairs and larger sets for final /m/:* Use contrasting word pairs and larger sets to teach final /m/, e.g., *gum/gut, thumb/thug, lamb/latch.*

• *Reading and spelling:* Teach this phoneme as part of the client's reading and spelling program.

• *Language arts:* Teach this phoneme through stories, songs, jingles, jokes, rhymes, plays, and other material in the language arts program.

Solutions to Specific Problems on /m/

• *Lack of labial closure:* Use methods to facilitate lip closure.

• *Weak /m/:* Use methods to facilitate stronger exhalation and voice.

• *Denasality on /m/:* Use methods to control resonance.

• *Inhalation on /m/:* Develop correct breath support.

• *Nasal snort on /m/:* A snort is inhaled, therefore, teach exhalation and voice.

• *Asymmetrical lips on /m/:* Develop oral stability.

• *Labio-dental production of /m/:* This is usually because the upper lip is pulling up out of the way. Work to develop neutral position and oral control. Refer to dental specialists if caused by malocclusion.

• *Tongue protrudes between the lips on /m/:* Develop tongue stability.

• *Bilabial raspberry for /m/:* Teach the client to press the lips together more firmly.

• *Client can say /m/ only with a stressed schwa (mʌ):* Switch to words that contain this syllable for a while, e.g., *muck, mud, muff, mug, mum, money, must, mutt,* and *muzzle.* Also, allow the client to produce final /m/ words with the schwa for a while, e.g., *gum* as *gu-mʌ.* Use negative practice and alter between the correct and the incorrect productions.

/n/

Multisensory Stimulation

• *Auditory stimulation to encourage /n/:* Model, amplify, repeat, prolong, and bombard with the phoneme.

• *Auditory feedback:* Direct the client's sound back to his ear with a tube or other tool. Imitate the client's sound.

• *Visual stimulation to teach /n/:* Use modeling, drawings, and puppets. Use a computerized sound analysis tool.

• *Visual feedback to understand /n/:* Prop the mouth open and watch in a mirror. Imitate client's correct and incorrect productions and watch each other during simultaneous productions.

• *Visual feedback to understand airflow on /n/:* Produce /n/ with a mirror under the nose and observe the fog produced by the nasal emission.

• *Verbal:* Use vocabulary the client can understand to describe this phoneme.

• *Cue:* Use a cue to pique the client's interest in this phoneme.

• *Tactile stimulation to develop tongue concept:* Encourage oral play and develop the oral percept through cold, vibration, etc.

• *Tactile feedback to perceive tongue-tip movements:* Have the child feels his own tongue movement during production of /n/.

• *Mark the target to develop place for /n/:* Touch the tongue tip and the alveolar ridge prior to production. Place an object on the alveolar ridge against which the tongue tip can press, such as a piece of dental floss with a knot on the end or a dental pick between the maxillary (upper) central incisors.

• *Aid tongue-tip elevation:* Use methods to facilitate tongue-tip elevation and the basic horseshoe-shape.

• *Jaw mobility:* Get the jaw to move up and down to stimulate early /n/.

• *Jaw stability:* Stabilize the jaw to encourage more active tongue-tip movement for mature /n/.

• *Tongue stability:* Stabilize the tongue at the back-lateral margins to keep the tongue inside the mouth during production of /n/.

Association Method for /n/

- *Place:* Help the client learn /n/ by recognizing the similarities between it and any of the other lingua-alveolar phonemes he can produce — /t/, /d/, or /l/. Also, try /s/ or /z/.

- *Manner:* Help the client learn /n/ by recognizing the similarities between it and any of the other nasals he can produce — /m/ or /ŋ/.

- *Voice:* Help the client learn /n/ by recognizing the similarities between it and any of the other voiced sounds he can produce — /m/, /ŋ/, /b/, /d/, or /g/. Also, use voiced /v/ or /z/.

Successive Approximations for /n/

- *Build /n/ off of /m/:* Have the client produce /m/ and have him bite the molars together and smile.

- *Build /n/ off of /d/:* Have the client produce /d/ and then tell him to keep the tongue tip pressed upward.

Contrasting Method for /n/

- *Place:* Contrast the tongue-tip elevation of /n/ with the lip movements of /m/ or with the tongue-back elevation of /ŋ/.

- *Manner:* Contrast the continuance of /n/ with the stop quality of /d/.

- *Voice:* Contrast the voicing on /n/ with the voiceless-ness of /t/.

- *Resonance:* Contrast the nasal quality of /n/ with the oral quality of /ɑ/.

Phonological Strategies to Introduce /n/

- *Key words:* Introduce /n/ with a small set of functional key words, e.g., *no, nose, on, one.*

- *Reduplication:* Consider teaching early /n/ in easy CVCV words, e.g., *nanna* (for *grandma*), *no-no, Nina, neigh-neigh* (for *horse*), *noo-noo* (for *noodle*).

- *Diminutive:* Consider teaching early /n/ with diminutives and other similar words, e.g., *nanny, grannie, Kenny, penny, pony.*

- *Switch gears:* If /n/ proves to be impossible to elicit, discontinue the practice and focus on another sound for a while.

- *Early /n/ words:* Consider teaching /n/ in the initial position first by using easy CV words, e.g., *no, nah* (for *no*), *knee, new, neigh, gnaw, now.*

- *Early /n/ adapted words:* Consider teaching /n/ in the initial position first by using easy words that can be altered to CV, e.g., *noo* (for *noodle*), *noh* (for *nose*), *nee* (for *needle*), *no* (for *snow*).

- *Final position with epenthesis:* Consider allowing the client to use an extra schwa and an extra syllable to stimulate a final /n/, e.g., *ca-nʌ* (for *can*), *gʌ-nʌ* (for *gun*), *bʌ-nʌ* (for *bun*).

- *Assimilation in CVC:* When moving into CVC words with /n/, consider using words with the target phoneme in initial and final position, e.g., *noon, nine, Nan, known, nun.*

- */n/ as a substitute:* Consider helping /n/ to emerge in words by using it as a substitute, e.g., *noo* (for *do*), *noon* (for *moon*).

- *Minimal pairs and larger sets for initial /n/:* Use contrasting word pairs and larger sets to teach initial /n/, e.g., *knee, me, pee, bee, tea, key; new, moo, poo, boo, two, do; nice, mice, twice, dice.*

- *Minimal pairs and larger sets for final /n/:* Use contrasting word pairs and larger sets to teach final /n/, e.g., *gun/gum, can/cat, win/whim, win/wing.*

- *Reading and spelling:* Teach this phoneme as part of the client's reading and spelling program.

- *Language arts:* Teach this phoneme through stories, songs, jingles, jokes, rhymes, plays, and other material in the language arts program.

Solutions to Specific Problems on /n/

- *Weak /n/:* Use methods to facilitate stronger exhalation and voice.

- *Lack of nasal emission on /n/:* Teach the client to control resonance.

- *Nasal snort on /n/:* Use methods to develop exhalation, voice, and nasality.

- *Inhalation on /n/:* Develop correct breath support.

- *Labio-dental production of /n/:* Develop oral stability.

- *Lingua raspberry for /n/:* Teach the client to press up more firmly with the tongue tip. Use methods to stimulate tongue-tip elevation and the horseshoe-shape.

- *Tongue protrudes between the lips on /n/:* Develop tongue stability.

- *Tongue shifts to one side on /n/:* Develop tongue stability.

• *Tongue-middle elevates instead of the tongue tip:* Lower the jaw to force the tip to lift higher. Stimulate tongue-tip elevation in other ways. Teach the horseshoe-shape position.

• *Client can say /n/ only with a stressed schwa (nʌ):* Allow client to produce final /n/ words with the schwa for a while, e.g., *gun* as *gu-nʌ*. Switch to words that contain this syllable, e.g., *nub, knuckle, 'nough, null, numb, nun, nut, nuts,* and *nuzzle*. Use negative practice and alter between the correct and the incorrect productions.

/ŋ/

Multisensory Stimulation

• *Auditory stimulation to encourage /ŋ/:* Model, amplify, repeat, prolong, and bombard with the phoneme.

• *Auditory feedback:* Direct the client's sound back to his ear with a tube or other tool. Imitate the client's sound.

• *Visual stimulation to teach /ŋ/:* Use modeling, drawings, and puppets. Use a computerized sound analysis tool.

• *Visual feedback to understand /ŋ/:* Prop the mouth open and watch in a mirror. Imitate client's correct and incorrect productions and watch each other during simultaneous productions. Use methods to develop the oral percept.

• *Visual feedback to understand airflow on /ŋ/:* Produce /ŋ/ with a mirror under the nose and observe the fog it produces.

• *Verbal:* Use vocabulary the client can understand to describe the respiration, phonation, resonation, and articulation characteristics of this phoneme.

• *Cues:* Use cues to pique the client's interest in this phoneme and to facilitate its concept.

• *Tactile stimulation to develop tongue concept:* Pat, rub, vibrate, ice, and stretch the tongue, and encourage oral play. Use methods to develop oral perception.

• *Tactile feedback to perceive tongue-back movements:* Have the child feels his own tongue-back elevation during production of /ŋ/.

• *Mark the target to develop place for /ŋ/:* Touch the back of the tongue and the palatal notch prior to production. Use methods to suppress the gag (see page 286).

• *Aid tongue-back elevation:* Use methods to facilitate tongue-back elevation.

• *Jaw stability to encourage more tongue activity:* Stabilize the jaw to encourage more active tongue-back elevation. Use methods to develop oral stability.

Association Method

• *Place:* Help the client learn /ŋ/ by recognizing the similarities between it and any of the other lingua-velar phonemes he can produce — /k/, /g/, or /r/.

• *Manner:* Help the client learn /ŋ/ by recognizing the similarities between it and any of the other nasals he can produce — /m/ or /n/.

• *Voice:* Help the client learn /ŋ/ by recognizing the similarities between it and any of the other voiced sounds he can produce — /m/, /n/, /b/, /d/, or /g/.

Successive Approximations

• *Build /ŋ/ off of /g/:* Have the client make a /g/ and hold the back of his tongue up.

Contrasting Method

• *Place:* Contrast the tongue-back elevation of /ŋ/ with the tongue-tip elevation of /n/ or with the lip movements of /m/.

• *Manner:* Contrast the continuance of /ŋ/ with the stop quality of /g/.

• *Voice:* Contrast the voicing on /ŋ/ with the voiceless-ness of /k/.

• *Resonance:* Contrast the nasal quality of /ŋ/ with the oral quality of /g/.

Phonological Strategies to Introduce /ŋ/

• *Key words:* Introduce /ŋ/ with a small set of functional key words.

• *Diminutive:* Consider teaching early /ŋ/ with real or created diminutives, e.g., *dingy, dongy, singy, songy, pingy, pongy.*

• *Switch gears:* If /ŋ/ proves to be impossible to elicit, discontinue the practice and focus on another sound for a while.

• *Early /ŋ/ words:* This phoneme occurs only in the final position. Consider teaching /ŋ/ in simple one-syllable words first, e.g., *sing, song, ring, wrong.*

- *Early /ŋ/ adapted words:* Consider teaching /ŋ/ when no other nasal sounds are emerging, e.g., *ŋoh* (for *no*), *ngee* (for *me*), *ŋat* (for *mat*).

- *Final position with epenthesis:* Consider allowing the client to use an extra schwa and an extra syllable to stimulate a final /ŋ/, e.g., *si-ŋʌ* (for *sing*), *ri-ŋʌ* (for *ring*).

- *Minimal pairs and larger sets for final /ŋ/:* Use contrasting word pairs and larger sets to teach initial /n/, e.g., *sing, sin; ring, rim; bong, bought.*

- *Reading and spelling:* Teach this phoneme as part of the client's reading and spelling program.

- *Language arts:* Teach this phoneme through stories, songs, jingles, jokes, rhymes, plays, and other material in the language arts program.

Solutions to Specific Problems on /ŋ/

- *Weak /ŋ/:* Use methods to facilitate stronger exhalation.

- *Nasal snort on /ŋ/:* Use methods to develop nasality.

- *Lack of nasal emission on /ŋ/:* Use methods to control resonance.

- *Inhalation on /ŋ/:* Use methods to develop correct breath support.

- *Velar raspberry for /ŋ/:* Teach the client to press up more firmly with the back of the tongue. Use methods to stimulate tongue-back elevation.

- *Tongue protrusion on /ŋ/:* Use methods to develop oral stability.

- *Tongue-middle elevates instead of the back of the tongue:* Lower the jaw to force the rear of the tongue to elevate. Use methods to stimulate tongue-back elevation.

- *Client can say /ŋ/ only with a stressed schwa (ngʌ):* Allow client to produce final /ŋ/ words with the schwa for a while, e.g., *song* as *so-ŋʌ*. Use negative practice and alter between the correct and the incorrect productions.

SUMMARY

This chapter has described the nasal consonants /m/, /n/, and /ŋ/. It summarized how these consonants are produced and catalogued a variety of methods to stimulate the infantile and adult-like productions of these sounds.

24

Stimulating the Glide Consonants

Techniques for /w/, /l/, /j/, and /r/

> *"Sometimes it is not so easy to feel what the tongue and lips are doing when producing a consonant. This is particularly true of the approximants [glides] in words such as what, yacht, and rot."*
>
> –Peter Ladefoged, 2005

The group of consonants known as the glides consists of four basic sounds — /w/, /l/, /j/, and /r/. These phonemes were considered vowels from the 17th to the 19th centuries, and they were called *semi-vowels* by the time the 20th century approached. Ladefoged (2005) was one of the world's greatest linguists and he called three of them *approximants*. Regardless of the name, these four consonants are very vowel-like. This group contains /w/, which may be the easiest phoneme to teach, and /r/, which can be one of the most difficult to teach. This chapter describes these phonemes and presents methods to teach them.

PRODUCTION

The movements used in production of the glide consonants are described here. Details about emerging or immature production of these sounds are offered first so that

Small groups are an excellent format for some speech production activities.

readers can see how these phonemes might be stimulated with children who speak very little and who use very few consonant phonemes. Details about mature oral movements are described next so that readers can see how these phonemes might be stimulated with clients who have minor articulation errors.

The text contains two descriptions of /r/ since it can be produced with at least two very different tongue positions. Most SLPs consider /r/ to be the very last phoneme children are able to produce correctly. However, it should be noted that Smit et al. (1990) demonstrated that the average toddler is able to produce all the glides by the time they produce their early words.

Respiration, Phonation, Resonation

All the glides are initiated upon exhalation with vocal adduction to make them voiced. The velopharyngeal port closes to direct the airstream through the mouth for each glide.

/w/   ***Water, bowing, cow***
(Considered a vowel in final position)

Emerging /w/

Phoneme /w/ first appears as vowel /u/ at 2–3 months of age when a baby learns to round the lips while cooing. The sound develops into consonant /w/ when the baby coos with /u/ and then lowers the jaw to produce a primitive CV with /ɑ/. Phoneme /w/ develops into a babbled consonant when the baby learns to move the jaw up and down while prolonging /u/.

Mature /w/

A different oral-motor pattern emerges as /w/ matures:

• *Starting position:* First the jaw and tongue stabilize to set the mouth in starting position (see Chapter 14 on oral stability).

• *On-glide:* The lips round, meaning the lips pucker without complete occlusion so that a tiny round opening is created between them.

• *Target position:* In target position the lips hold this round position. The voiced airstream exits through this small labial orifice.

• *Off-glide:* The lips relax away from target position after /w/ is produced, or they move on to the shape required of the next phoneme. The jaw and back-lateral margins of the tongue remain stable throughout.

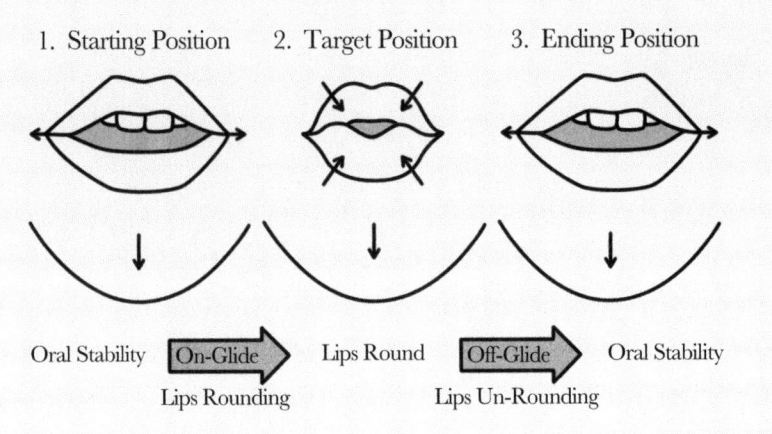

1. Starting Position   2. Target Position   3. Ending Position

Oral Stability   On-Glide   Lips Round   Off-Glide   Oral Stability
        Lips Rounding   Lips Un-Rounding

The lips are rounded during production of /w/.

/l/   *Lady, calling, bell*

Emerging /l/

Phoneme /l/ begins as a coo produced with the tongue extended out between the lips. It occurs in a simple CV when a baby learns to lower the jaw while producing this sound. It occurs during the babbling phase as babies move the jaw down-and-up in sequences while the tongue rests on the lower lip.

Mature /l/

A different motor pattern emerges as /l/ matures:

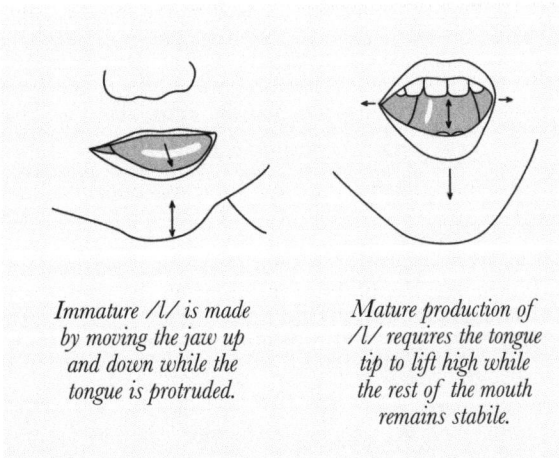

Immature /l/ is made by moving the jaw up and down while the tongue is protruded.

Mature production of /l/ requires the tongue tip to lift high while the rest of the mouth remains stabile.

• *Starting position:* First the jaw and tongue stabilize to set the mouth in starting position.

• *On-glide:* From its points of stability at the back-lateral margins, the tongue tip elevates to the alveolar ridge.

• *Target position:* In target position, the tongue tip gently presses upward against the alveolar ridge. This position is held as the voiced airstream exits laterally through the gap formed between the lateral margins of the tongue and the dental ridges on both sides of the mouth. Ideally, the sound exits laterally through both sides of the mouth simultaneously.

• *Off-glide:* The off-glide begins as the tip lowers away from the alveolar ridge and then the whole tongue retreats away from its target position. The jaw and back-lateral margins of the tongue remain stable throughout.

/j/   *Yell, mayor, day*

Emerging /j/

Phoneme /j/ first appears as vowel /i/ at 2–3 months of age when babies learn to smile (retract the lips) while cooing. The sound develops into consonant /j/ when the baby coos with /i/ and then lowers the jaw to produce a primitive CV. Phoneme /j/ develops into a babbled consonant when the baby learns to move the jaw down-and-up while prolonging /i/.

Mature /j/

A different oral-motor pattern emerges as phoneme /j/ matures:

• *Starting position:* First the jaw and tongue stabilize to set the mouth in starting position.

- *On-glide:* From its points of stability at the back-lateral margins, both sides of the tongue's perimeter elevate from the back to about half-way toward the tongue tip. Simultaneously, the middle of the tongue arches upward toward the palate but does not touch it.

- *Target position:* The opening sound of /j/ is essentially the same as the sound of /i/. Therefore, the target position at the onset of /j/ is the same as that for /i/. The lateral margins of the tongue are articulated with the palate on both sides. The middle of the tongue is arched upward but does not touch the palate.

- *Off-glide:* The off-glide consists of the second gliding sound of /j/. The lateral margins of the tongue remain stationary against the palate on the sides while the middle of the tongue lowers back to rest.

Retroflex /r/   *Run, carrot, far*

Emerging Retroflex /r/

The retroflex /r/ first appears as *lerring*. Lerring is the sound made as babies coo while rubbing the tongue tip back and forth against the palate from the alveolar ridge in the front to the velum in the back. The tongue moves in its bowl-shape during this process and the retroflex /r/ is heard when the bowl faces the oropharynx. The retroflex /r/ is also heard during babbling sequences as the jaw moves up and down while the tongue is in this rear-facing bowl position.

Mature Retroflex /r/

Mature retroflex /r/ is made as follows:

- *Starting position:* First the jaw and tongue stabilize to set the mouth in starting position.

- *On-glide:* From its points of stability at the back-lateral margins, the tongue tip curls up and back to face the oropharynx. The tongue stays wide and forms itself into a bowl-shape that faces the rear of the oral cavity.

- *Target position:* In target position, the tongue is in an exaggerated bowl-shape facing the oropharynx.

- *Off-glide:* The off-glide consists of the tongue retreating away from its target position and returning to neutral.

Bunched /r/   *Run, carrot, far*

Emerging Bunched /r/

The back or bunched /r/ first appears during the cooing stage as babies prolong a coo with the back of the tongue high. This high position of the tongue in the back is natural at this time because babies cannot yet sit up, they spend most of their time in prone or supine positions, and the tongue is quite large relative to the oral cavity. In supine, the bulk of the tongue naturally falls back to occlude most of the oropharynx. The back or bunched /r/ is also heard during babbling as the baby moves the jaw down-and-up while vocalizing in this position.

Mature Bunched /r/

Mature back or bunched /r/ is made as follows:

- *Starting position:* First the jaw and tongue stabilize to set the mouth in starting position.

- *On-glide:* From its points of stability at the back-lateral margins, the sides of the tongue reach high to press upward against the upper molars or palate to form the tongue into the butterfly (see pages 211–212). The middle of the tongue arches upward. The tongue remains in the butterfly position as it retracts farther back to produce /r/.

- *Target position:* The tongue is formed into a butterfly that is retracted toward the oropharynx.

- *Off-glide:* The off-glide consists of the tongue retreating away from its target position and returning to neutral.

TREATMENT STRATEGIES

The glides emerge in infancy. The relative ease of producing /w/ and /j/ means that these phonemes are in error only in clients with the most severe speech problems. It also means that therapists usually target these two sounds early in a program for clients with a severe lack of consonants. Many SLPs ignore /l/ and /r/ until late in a client's articulation program, however, research has shown that all the glides emerge in infancy and all of them can be stimulated early.

General advice for training infantile productions of the glide consonants includes:

- Make sure the vowels are emerging and acoustically correct because the glides are built off the vowels just like the diphthongs are.

- Consider teaching the glides and diphthongs simultaneously because the glides are essentially the opposite movement patterns of the diphthongs.

- Make sure the jaw is mobile because the glides (and the diphthongs) form when a child hits a vowel and then moves the jaw.

- Be flexible; some clients have problems that cause /w/ to be one of their most difficult challenges. If the entire set of glides is completely absent, most therapists begin with /w/ because it is so easy to produce, to see, and to cue, but this may not be the best approach for some clients.

- Remember that the developmental norms do not always apply to clients who are developing speech in abnormal ways. Most therapists treat /r/ last in the set but this is a rigid approach that can be a mistake for some clients. There are clients who find /r/ the easiest of this set to acquire. In fact, the present author worked with one client who had no consonant phonemes until seven years of age and /r/ was the very first consonant he acquired.

- If a client has no glides at all, consider addressing all four of them simultaneously and organizing them according to the client's stimulability.

- Remember that each child takes his own path of phoneme acquisition and be flexible in the target ordering. Therapists tend to teach these phonemes in the word initial position first, however, some clients acquire them more easily mid-word and even in the final position. Engage in trial-and-error training to determine the client's readiness for phoneme acquisition.

- Get the tongue moving and moving better; the advanced glides — /l/ and /r/ — emerge because the tongue begins to move with more sophistication.

/w/

Multisensory Stimulation

- *Auditory stimulation to encourage /w/:* Model, amplify, repeat, prolong, and bombard. Imitate the client's sound.

- *Auditory feedback:* Direct the client's sound back to his ear with a tube or other tool. Imitate the client's sound.

- *Visual stimulation to teach /w/:* Use modeling, drawings, puppets, etc.. Use a computerized sound analysis tool.

- *Visual feedback to understand /w/:* Watch in a mirror. Imitate client's correct and incorrect productions and watch each other during simultaneous productions.

- *Verbal:* Use vocabulary the client can understand to describe this phoneme.

- *Cue:* Use a cue to pique the client's interest in this phoneme.

- *Tactile stimulation to develop lip concept for /w/:* Pat, rub, vibrate, and stretch the lips, and encourage general oral play.

- *Tactile feedback to perceive lip movements:* Have the child feel his own lip movements during production of /w/. Develop the oral percept.

- *Mark the target to develop place for /w/:* Touch the upper and lower lips prior to production. Place an object between the lips against which the lips can close such as a tongue depressor, finger, swizzle stick, coffee stirrer, or dental floss.

- *Temperature stimulation to increase awareness of the lips:* Place the lips briefly and intermittently on an ice cube, ice pop, frozen banana, etc..

- *Aid lip movement:* Use methods to facilitate lip movement.

- *Jaw stability to encourage more lip activity:* Stabilize the jaw to encourage more active lip mobility.

- *Reflexes to activate lip movement:* Stimulate reflexes that activate upper and lower lip movement.

Association Method for /w/

- *Place:* Help the client learn /w/ by recognizing the similarities between it and any of the other voiced bilabial phonemes he can produce or compare with /u/.

- *Manner:* Help the client learn /w/ by recognizing the similarities between it and any of the other glides he can produce — /l/, /j/ or /r/.

- *Voice:* Help the client learn /w/ by recognizing the similarities between it and any of the other voiced bilabial sounds he can produce — /b/ or /m/.

Contrast Method for /w/

- *Place:* Contrast the lip movements of /w/ with the tongue-tip movements of /l/, with the tongue-to-palate movements of /j/, or with the tongue-back movements of /r/.

- *Manner:* Contrast the gliding action of /w/ with the stop quality of /b/.

- *Voice:* Contrast the voicing of /w/ with the voiceless-ness of /p/.

- *Resonance:* Contrast the oral quality of /w/ with the nasal quality of /m/.

Phonological Strategies to Introduce /w/

- *Key words:* Introduce /w/ with a small set of functional key words.

- *Reduplication:* Consider teaching early /w/ in easy CVCV words, e.g., *woo-woo* (for a train whistle), *wa-wa* (for *water*), *wee-wee* (for the little piggy's sound).

- *Diminutive:* Consider teaching diminutives and other similar words early, e.g., *owie, cowie*.

- *Baby steps:* Allow the client to use /w/ as a substitution for initial /l/ or /r/ until these phonemes come in.

- *Switch gears:* If /w/ proves to be impossible to elicit, discontinue the practice and focus on another sound for a while.

- *Early /w/ words:* Consider teaching /w/ in the initial position first by using easy CV words, e.g., *woo, weeee, we, whoa, what, where*.

- *Initial position in adapted words:* Consider teaching /w/ in the initial position early by using easy words that can be spoken in CV, e.g., *way* (for *no way*), *wʌ* (for *what*), *woo* (for *you*).

- *Final position with epenthesis:* Although /w/ does not technically occur in the final position (it is classified as a vowel in the final position), the vowel can be treated like a consonant for phoneme learning. Consider allowing the client to use an extra schwa and an extra syllable to stimulate a final /u/, e.g., *ca-wʌ* (for *cow*), *too-wʌ* (for *two*).

- *Assimilation in CVC:* When moving into CVC words with /w/, consider using words with the target phoneme in initial and final position, e.g., *wow*.

- */w/ as a substitute:* Consider helping /w/ to emerge in words by teaching it as a substitute, e.g., *wour* (for *four*), *wit* (for *fit*).

- *Minimal pairs and larger sets for initial /w/:* Use contrasting word pairs and larger sets to teach initial /w/, e.g., *we, pee, bee, me, tea, key; why, pie, bye, my, tie*.

- *Reading and spelling:* Teach this phoneme as part of the client's reading and spelling program.

- *Language arts:* Teach this phoneme through stories, songs, jingles, jokes, rhymes, plays, and other material in the language arts program.

Solutions to Specific Problems on /w/

- *Weak /w/:* Produce /w/ as the back of the hand presses against the lips to teach greater force of exhalation. Teach the client to produce a stronger voice.

- *Nasal emission on /w/:* Teach the client to control resonance.

- *Inhalation on /w/:* Develop correct breath support.

- *Puffy cheeks on /w/:* Develop oral stability.

- *Asymmetrical lips on /w/:* Develop oral stability.

- *Labio-dental production of /w/:* This is usually because the upper lip is pulling up out of the way. Develop oral stability.

- *Tongue protrusion on /w/:* Develop tongue stability.

- *Client inserts a stressed schwa after initial /w/:* Teach the client to position his mouth for the correct vowel before he says /w/. That way his vocalization will go directly from /w/ to the right vowel. Use amplification and negative practice and alter between the correct and the incorrect productions.

/l/

Multisensory Stimulation for /l/

- *Auditory stimulation to encourage /l/:* Model, amplify, repeat, prolong, and bombard. Make /l/ into a straw or small tube to amplify the sound. Direct the sound back to the ear with a tube. Imitate the client's sound.

- *Visual stimulation to teach /l/:* Use modeling, drawings, and puppets. Use a computerized sound analysis tool.

- *Visual feedback to understand /l/:* Prop the mouth open and watch in a mirror. Imitate client's correct and incorrect productions and watch each other during simultaneous productions.

- *Visual feedback to understand airflow on /l/:* Produce /l/ against a mirror or window and observe the fog it produces.

- *Verbal:* Use vocabulary the client can understand to describe the respiration, phonation, resonation, and articulation characteristics of this phoneme.

- *Cues:* Use cues to pique the client's interest in

this phoneme and to facilitate its concept.

• *Tactile stimulation to develop tongue concept:* Pat, rub, vibrate, ice, and stretch the tongue, and encourage oral play.

• *Tactile feedback to perceive tongue-tip movements:* Have the child feels his own tongue movement during production of /l/.

• *Mark the target to develop place for /l/:* Touch the tongue tip and the alveolar ridge prior to production. Place an object on the alveolar ridge against which the tongue tip can press, such as a piece of dental floss with a knot on the end or a dental pick between the maxillary (upper) central incisors.

• *Aid tongue movement:* Use methods to facilitate tongue movement.

• *Temperature stimulation to increase awareness of the tongue:* Suck or lick ice cube, ice pop, frozen banana, etc..

• *Feeding techniques for tongue movement:* Stimulate tongue movement with eating activities.

• *Jaw stability to encourage more tongue activity:* Stabilize the jaw to encourage more active tongue-tip movement.

• *Reflexes to initiate tongue-tip elevation movement:* Stimulate reflexes that activate tongue-tip elevation.

Association Method for /l/

• *Place:* Help the client learn /l/ by recognizing the similarities between it and any of the other lingua-alveolar phonemes he can produce — /t/, /d/, /n/, or /s/ and /z/.

• *Manner:* Help the client learn /l/ by recognizing the similarities between it and any of the other glides he can produce — /w/, /j/, or /r/.

• *Voice:* Help the client learn /l/ by recognizing the similarities between it and any of the vowels, or with any of the other voiced lingua-alveolar sounds he can produce — /d/ or /n/. Also, try /z/.

Contrast Method for /l/

• *Place:* Contrast the tongue-tip movements of /l/ with the tongue-back movements of /g/, /k/, or /r/, or contrast with the lip movements of /w/ or /b/.

• *Manner:* Contrast the gliding movements of /l/ with the frication of /z/ or the plosive release of /d/.

• *Voice:* Contrast the voicing of /l/ with the voiceless-ness of /t/ or /s/.

• *Resonance:* Contrast the oral quality of /l/ with the nasal quality of /n/.

Phonological Strategies to Introduce /l/

• *Key words:* Introduce /l/ with a small set of functional key words.

• *Reduplication:* Consider teaching early /l/ in easy CVCV words, e.g., *lala* (for *lollipop*), *lellow* (for *yellow*), *Lellie* (for *Nellie*), *Lay-lay* (for *lady*).

• *Diminutive:* Consider teaching diminutives and other similar words early, e.g., *dollie, lolly* (for *lollipop*), *collie, Holly, Polly, holey, rollie-pollie, Bailey, daily.*

• *Baby steps:* Allow the client to use /l/ as a substitution for initial /r/, at least until /r/ enters his phonological repertoire.

• *Switch gears:* If /l/ proves to be impossible to elicit, discontinue the practice and focus on another sound for a while.

• *Initial position words:* Consider teaching /l/ in the initial position early by using easy words of CV structure, e.g., *Lee, lay, Lou, low.*

• *Initial position in adapted words:* Consider teaching /l/ in the initial position early by using easy words that can be spoken in CV, e.g., *lo* (for *yellow*), *la* (for *lollipop*)

• *Final position with epenthesis:* Consider allowing the client to use an extra schwa and an extra syllable to stimulate a final /l/, e.g., *bɔ-lʌ* (for *ball*), *tah-lʌ* (for *tall*), *dee-lʌ* (for *deal*).

• *Initial /l/ as a substitute:* Consider helping initial /l/ to emerge in words by using it as a substitute, e.g., *labbit* (for *rabbit*), *lellow* (for *yellow*), *liss* (for *kiss*).

• *Minimal pairs and larger sets in initial position:* Use contrasting word pairs and larger sets to teach initial /l/, e.g., *Lee, knee, D, tea; Lou, do, two, new; lay, day, neigh.*

• *Minimal pairs and larger sets in final position:* Use contrasting word pairs and larger sets to teach final /l/, e.g., *tall/Tam, steal/steer, mall/Maude.*

• *Reading and spelling:* Teach this phoneme as part of the client's reading and spelling program.

• *Language arts:* Teach this phoneme through stories, songs, jingles, jokes, rhymes, plays, and other material in the language arts program.

Solutions to Specific Problems on /l/

- *Immature /l/:* Stabilize the jaw in a partially-open position.

- *Weak /l/:* Stabilize the jaw in a low position to force the tongue tip to stretch higher. Teach the client to push the tip firmly against the alveolar ridge.

- *Frication on /l/:* Teach client to press up harder with tongue, and to make a vowel-like sound and not a fricative sound. Teach auditory discrimination between gliding and fricating.

- *Prevocalic de-voicing on initial /l/:* Use methods to facilitate parameters of voicing and devoicing.

- *Nasal emission on /l/:* Use methods to control resonance.

- *Inhalation on /l/:* Develop correct breath support.

- *Tongue shifts to one side on /l/:* Develop oral stability.

- *Tongue protrusion on /l/:* Develop oral stability.

- *Client inserts a schwa after initial /l/:* Teach the client to position his mouth for the correct vowel before he says /l/, that way his vocalization will go directly from /w/ to the right vowel. Use amplification and negative practice and alter between the correct and the incorrect productions.

/j/

Multisensory Stimulation

- *Auditory stimulation to encourage /j/:* Model, amplify, repeat, prolong, and bombard. Make /j/ into a tube to amplify the sound. Direct the sound back to the ear with a tube. Imitate the client's sound.

- *Visual stimulation to teach /j/:* Use modeling, drawings, and puppets. Use a computerized sound analysis tool.

- *Visual feedback to understand /j/:* Prop the mouth open and watch in a mirror. Imitate client's correct and incorrect productions and watch each other during simultaneous productions. Develop oral percept.

- *Visual feedback to understand airflow on /j/:* Produce /j/ against a mirror or window and observe the fog it produces.

- *Verbal:* Use vocabulary the client can understand to describe the respiration, phonation, resonation, and articulation characteristics of this phoneme.

- *Cues:* Use cues to pique the client's interest in this phoneme and to facilitate its concept.

- *Tactile feedback to perceive tongue movements:* Have the child feels his own tongue movement during production of /j/.

- *Mark the target to develop place for /j/:* Touch the tongue-sides and the palate on both sides prior to production. Place an object against the lateral portions of the palate against which the sides of the tongue can press, such as a piece of dental floss with a knot on the end or a dental pick between the upper molars on each side.

- *Aid tongue movement:* Use methods to facilitate tongue movement.

- *Temperature stimulation to increase awareness of the tongue:* Suck or lick ice cube, ice pop, frozen banana, etc..

- *Feeding techniques for tongue movement:* Stimulate tongue movement with eating activities.

- *Jaw stability to encourage more tongue activity:* Stabilize the jaw to encourage more active tongue-side movement.

- *Reflexes to initiate tongue-tip elevation:* Stimulating reflexes that activate tongue-side elevation.

Association Method for /j/

- *Place:* Help the client learn /j/ by recognizing the similarities between it and /i/, or with any of the other lingua-palatal consonants he can produce — /ʃ/ or /ʒ/.

- *Manner:* Help the client learn /j/ by recognizing the similarities between it and any of the other glides he can produce — /w/, /l/, or /r/.

- *Voice:* Help the client learn /j/ by recognizing the similarities between it and any of the vowels, or with any of the other voiced lingua-palatal or lingua-velar sounds he can produce — /ʃ/, /ʒ/, /g/, /ŋ/.

Contrast Method for /j/

- *Place:* Contrast the tongue-palate movements of /j/ with the tongue-back movements of /g/, /k/, or /r/, or contrast with the tongue-tip movements of /t/, /d/ or /n/.

- *Manner:* Contrast the gliding movements of /j/ with the frication of /ʃ/ or the plosive release of /g/.

- *Voice:* Contrast the voicing of /j/ with the voiceless-ness of /ʃ/.

- *Resonance:* Contrast the oral quality of /j/ with the nasal quality of /n/ or /ŋ/.

Phonological Strategies to Introduce /j/

- *Key words:* Introduce /j/ with a small set of functional key words.

- *Reduplication:* Consider teaching early /j/ in easy CVCV words, e.g., *yo-yo, yeh-yow* (for *yellow*).

- *Baby steps:* Allow the client to use /j/ as a substitution for initial /l/ and /r/, at least until /l/ and /r/ enter his phonological repertoire.

- *Switch gears:* If /j/ proves to be impossible to elicit, discontinue it and focus on another sound for a while.

- *Initial position words:* Consider teaching /j/ in the initial position early by using easy words of CV structure, e.g., *you, yea, yeah, yo.*

- *Initial position in adapted words:* Consider teaching /j/ in the initial position early by using easy words that can be spoken in CV, e.g., *yo* (for *yellow*), *ya* (for *yes*).

- Although /j/ does not technically occur in the final position because in that case it is a vowel, the vowel can be treated like a consonant for phoneme learning. Consider allowing the client to use an extra schwa and an extra syllable to stimulate a final sound, e.g., *boh-yʌ* (for *boy*), *toh-yʌ* (for *toy*).

- *Initial /j/ as a substitute:* Consider helping /j/ to emerge in words by using it as a substitute, e.g., *yabbit* (for *rabbit*), *yeh-yow* (for *yellow*), *yiss* (for *kiss*)

- *Minimal pairs and larger sets in initial position:* Use contrasting word pairs and larger sets to teach initial /j/, e.g., *you, Lou, do, two, new; yeah, lay, day, neigh.*

- *Reading and spelling:* Teach this phoneme as part of the client's reading and spelling program.

- *Language arts:* Teach this phoneme through stories, songs, jingles, jokes, rhymes, plays, and other material in the language arts program.

Solutions to Specific Problems on /j/

- *Immature /j/:* Stabilize the jaw in a partially open position.

- *Weak /j/:* Stabilize the jaw in a low position to force the tongue tip to stretch higher. Teach the client to push the tip firmly against the alveolar ridge.

- *Frication on /j/:* Teach client to press up harder with tongue, and to make a vowel-like sound and not a fricative sound. Teach auditory discrimination between gliding and fricating. Use methods to improve tongue-tip elevation.

- *Prevocalic de-voicing on initial /j/:* Use methods to develop the voice and de-voicing.

- *Nasal emission on /j/:* Use methods to control resonance.

- *Inhalation on /j/:* Developing correct breath support.

- *Tongue shifts to one side on /j/:* Develop oral stability.

- *Tongue protrusion on /j/:* Develop oral stability.

- *Client inserts a schwa after initial /j/:* Teach the client to position his mouth for the correct vowel before he says /j/. That way his vocalization will go directly from /j/ to the right vowel. Use amplification and negative practice and alter between the correct and the incorrect productions.

RETROFLEX /r/

Multisensory Stimulation

- *Auditory stimulation to encourage the retroflex /r/:* Model, amplify, repeat, prolong, and bombard. Make /r/ into a straw or small tube to amplify the sound. Direct the sound back to the ear with a tube. Imitate the client's sound.

- *Visual stimulation to teach the retroflex /r/:* Use modeling, drawings, and puppets. Use a computerized sound analysis tool.

- *Visual feedback to understand retroflex /r/:* Prop the mouth open and watch in a mirror. Imitate client's correct and incorrect productions and watch each other during simultaneous productions.

- *Visual feedback to understand airflow on retroflex /r/:* Produce retroflex /r/ against a mirror or window and observe the fog it produces.

- *Verbal:* Use vocabulary the client can understand to describe the respiration, phonation, resonation, and articulation characteristics of this phoneme.

- *Cues:* Use cues to pique the client's interest in this phoneme and to facilitate its concept.

- *Mark the target to develop place for retroflex /r/:* There is no specific place of articulation for the tongue tip when a tip /r/ is being taught. However, there can be, if the sound is taught by training the client to touch the tip to the palate at the notch. Have the client place his tongue tip on the alveolar ridge and say /l/. Now have the client slide or tap the tongue tip back along the mid-line of the palate as he continues to voice until the tip reaches the notch. The acoustic quality of /r/ should be elicited there. Use a probe to mark the midline from the alveolar ridge to the notch beforehand.

• *Aid tongue movement:* Use methods to facilitate tongue movement.

• *Temperature stimulation to increase awareness of the tongue:* Suck or lick ice cube, ice pop, frozen banana, etc.. Stimulate oral perception.

• *Jaw stability to encourage more tongue activity:* Stabilize the jaw to encourage more active tongue-tip movement.

• *Reflexes to initiate tongue-tip elevation movement:* Stimulate reflexes that activate tongue-tip elevation.

Association Method for Retroflex /r/

• *Place:* Help the client learn retroflex /r/ by recognizing the similarities between it and any of the other voiced tongue-tip phonemes he can produce — /l/, /d/, /n/, and /z/.

• *Manner:* Help the client learn the retroflex /r/ by recognizing the similarities between it and any of the other glides he can produce — /w/, /l/, or /j/.

• *Voice:* Help the client learn the retroflex /r/ by recognizing the similarities between its voicing and that of any vowels.

Contrast Method for Retroflex /r/

• *Place:* Contrast the tongue-tip movements of retroflex /r/ with the tongue-tip movements of /l/.

• *Manner:* Contrast the gliding movements of the retroflex /r/ with the plosive release of /d/.

• *Voice:* Contrast the voicing of retroflex /r/ with the voiceless-ness of /t/.

• *Resonance:* Contrast the oral quality of retroflex /r/ with the nasal quality of /ŋ/.

Phonological Strategies to Introduce Retroflex /r/

• *Key words:* Introduce retroflex /r/ with a very small set of functional key words that all contain the same vowel.

• *Reduplication:* Consider teaching early retroflex /r/ in easy CVCV words, e.g., *ra-ra* (for *rabbit*) or *ro-ro* (for *robot*).

• *Baby steps:* Allow the client to use /l/ as a substitution for initial retroflex /r/, at least until retroflex /r/ enters his phonological repertoire.

• *Switch gears:* If retroflex /r/ proves to be impossible to elicit, discontinue the practice and focus on another sound for a while.

• *Initial position words:* Consider teaching retroflex /r/ in the initial position early by using easy words of CV structure, e.g., *row, ray, raw.*

• *Initial position in adapted words:* Consider teaching retroflex /r/ in the initial position early by using easy words that can be spoken in CV, e.g., *ro* (for *robot*), *ra* (for *rotten*)

• *Final position with epenthesis:* Consider allowing the client to use an extra schwa and an extra syllable to stimulate a final retroflex /r/, e.g., *a-rʌ* (for *car*), *ba-rʌ* (for *bar*), *dee-rʌ* (for *deer*).

• *Minimal pairs and larger sets in initial position:* Use contrasting word pairs and larger sets to teach initial retroflex /r/, e.g., *Rob, Bob, cob, knob, sob, job.*

• *Minimal pairs and larger sets in final position:* Use contrasting word pairs and larger sets to teach final retroflex /r/, e.g., *car/cat, steer/steal, mar/mall.*

• *Reading and spelling:* Teach this phoneme as part of the client's reading and spelling program.

• *Language arts:* Teach this phoneme through stories, songs, jingles, jokes, rhymes, plays, and other material in the language arts program.

Solutions to Specific Problems on Retroflex /r/

• *Immature retroflex /r/:* Make sure the jaw is stabilized in a partially open position.

• *Weak retroflex /r/:* Teach the client to push the tip more firmly and farther back toward the oropharynx. Use methods to improve tongue-tip curling.

• *Frication on the retroflex /r/:* The elocutionists sometimes called excessive frication on this sound *burring* (Bell, 1898). Teach client to lower the tongue tip away from the palate to create more room for airflow, and teach stronger tongue-tip elevation.

• *Nasal emission on retroflex /r/:* Use methods to control resonance.

• *Inhalation on retroflex /r/:* Develop correct breath

support.

• *Client inserts an unstressed schwa after initial /r/ (e.g he says "r-obot" for "robot"):* Teach the client to position his mouth for the correct vowel before he says /r/. That way his vocalization will go directly from /r/ to the right vowel. Or focus on words with initial "rʌ" for a while, e.g., *rub, rubbing, ruckus, ruddy, rough, ruff, rug, rum, run, rust, rusty,* and *rut.* Use amplification and negative practice and alter between the correct and the incorrect productions.

BUNCHED (BACK) /r/

Multisensory Stimulation

• *Auditory stimulation to encourage the bunched /r/:* Model, amplify, repeat, prolong, and bombard. Make bunched /r/ into a straw or small tube to amplify the sound. Direct the sound back to the ear with a tube. Imitate the client's sound.

• *Cues:* Use cues to pique the client's interest in this phoneme and to facilitate its concept.

• *Verbal:* Use vocabulary the client can understand to describe the respiration, phonation, resonation, and articulation characteristics of this phoneme.

• *Visual feedback to understand the bunched /r/:* Prop the mouth open and watch in a mirror. Imitate client's correct and incorrect productions and watch each other during simultaneous productions. Develop the oral percept.

• *Visual feedback to understand airflow on the bunched /r/:* Produce bunched /r/ against a mirror or window and observe the fog it produces.

• *Tactile stimulation to develop tongue concept:* Pat, rub, vibrate, ice, and stretch the tongue, and encourage oral play. Develop the oral perception.

• *Mark the target to develop place for the bunched /r/:* Touch the palate on both sides in the back at the notch.

• *Aid tongue movement:* Use methods to facilitate tongue-back elevation.

• *Temperature stimulation to increase awareness of the tongue:* Suck or lick ice cube, ice pop, frozen banana, etc.. Stimulate oral perception.

• *Feeding techniques for tongue movement:* Stimulate tongue movement with eating activities.

• *Jaw stability to encourage more tongue activity:* Stabilize the jaw to encourage more active tongue-tip movement.

• *Reflexes to initiate tongue-back elevation movement:* Stimulate reflexes that activate tongue-back elevation.

Association Method for Bunched /r/

• *Place:* Help the client learn the bunched /r/ by recognizing the similarities between it and any of the other voiced tongue-back phonemes he can produce — /k/, /g/, /ŋ/, and /j/.

• *Manner:* Help the client learn the bunched /r/ by recognizing the similarities between it and any of the other glides he can produce — /w/, /l/, or /j/.

• *Voice:* Help the client learn the bunched /r/ by recognizing the similarities between its voicing and that of any vowels.

Contrast Method for Bunched /r/

• *Place:* Contrast the tongue-back movements of bunched /r/ with the tongue-tip movements of /l/ or the retroflex /r/.

• *Manner:* Contrast the gliding movements of the retroflex /r/ with the plosive release of /g/.

• *Voice:* Contrast the voicing of the bunched /r/ with the voiceless-ness of /k/.

• *Resonance:* Contrast the oral quality of the bunched /r/ with the nasal quality of /ŋ/.

Phonological Strategies to Introduce the Bunched /r/

• *Key words:* Introduce the bunched /r/ with a very small set of functional key words that all contain the same vowel.

• *Reduplication:* Consider teaching early bunched /r/ in easy CVCV words, e.g., *ra-ra* (for *rabbit*) or *ro-ro* (for *robot*).

• *Baby steps:* Allow the client to use /j/ as a substitution for initial bunched /r/, at least until the bunched /r/ enters his phonological repertoire.

• *Switch gears:* If the bunched /r/ proves to be impossible to elicit, try the retroflex /r/.

• *Initial position words:* Consider teaching the bunched /r/ in the initial position early by using easy words of CV structure, e.g., *row, ray, raw.*

• *Initial position in adapted words:* Consider teaching the bunched /r/ in the initial position early by using easy words that can be spoken in CV, e.g., *ro* (for *robot*), *ra* (for *rotten*)

• *Final position with epenthesis:* Consider allowing the client to use an extra schwa and an extra syllable to stimulate a final bunched /r/, e.g., *ca-rʌ* (for *car*), *ba-rʌ* (for *bar*), *dee-rʌ* (for *deer*).

• *Minimal pairs and larger sets in initial position:* Use contrasting word pairs and larger sets to teach initial bunched /r/, e.g., *Rob, Bob, cob, knob, sob, job.*

• *Minimal pairs and larger sets in final position:* Use contrasting word pairs and larger sets to teach final bunched /r/, e.g., *car/cat, steer/steal, mar/mall.*

• *Reading and spelling:* Teach this phoneme as part of the client's reading and spelling program.

• *Language arts:* Teach this phoneme through stories, songs, jingles, jokes, rhymes, plays, and other material in the language arts program.

Solutions to Specific Problems on the Bunched /r/

• *Immature bunched /r/:* Make sure the jaw is stabilized in a partially open position.

• *Weak bunched /r/:* Teach the client to push the back lateral margins up more firmly. Develop the butterfly position (see pages 211–212).

• *Frication on the bunched /r/:* Teach client to lower the back of his tongue away from the palate to create more room for airflow.

• *Nasal emission on the bunched /r/:* Use methods to control resonance.

• *Inhalation on the bunched /r/:* Develop correct breath support.

• *Client inserts an unstressed schwa after initial /r/ (e.g he says "r-obot" for "robot"):* Teach the client to position his mouth for the correct vowel before he says /r/. That way his vocalization will go directly from /r/ to the right vowel. Or focus on words with initial "rʌ" for a while, e.g., *rub, rubbing, ruckus, ruddy, rough, ruff, rug, rum, run, rust, rusty, and rut.* Use amplification and negative practice and alter between the correct and the incorrect productions.

SUMMARY

This chapter has discussed the glide consonants /w/, /l/, /j/ and /r/. It summarized how these consonants are produced and catalogued a wide variety of methods to stimulate the infantile and mature productions of these sounds.

25

Stimulating the Fricated Consonants

Techniques for /θ/, /ð /, /f/, /v/, /s/, /z/, /ʃ/, /ʒ/, /tʃ/, /dʒ/, and /h/

> *"Fricatives… are made with a narrow constriction so that the air creates a noisy sound as it rushes through the narrow passage."*
>
> – Ray Kent, 2004a

This chapter is about stimulating the group of eleven consonant phonemes that are produced with a hissing element called *frication*. This is the largest group of American English consonants and it includes /θ/, /ð/, /f/, /v/, /s/, /z/, /ʃ/, /ʒ/, /tʃ/, /dʒ/, and /h/. These sounds require the articulators to approach their contacts gently and incompletely so that tiny gaps remain, which allow air to squeeze out of the oral cavity in a hiss. The hissing sounds are considered difficult to make because the oral movements required to produce them are more delicate and complex than others. These sounds require the tongue to function in a bowl shape and all of them require a gentle articulation in their mature forms.

The fricated sounds are considered later-developing, however, many toddlers produce them quite well. For example the following first words with correct phonemes are common: /θ/ for *bath*, /f/ for *off*, /s/ for *kiss*, /ʃ/ for *shoe*, /tʃ/ for *ouchie*, and /h/ for *hot*, therefore, it is not impossible for children to acquire these sounds quite early in development. In normal development, the fricated phonemes seem to emerge from the stops and the raspberries and, until the fricated phonemes emerge, most children substitute stops and raspberries for them. Sometimes, nasals and glides can also act as substitutes for these sounds.

This chapter describes the movements of these phonemes and presents methods to teach them. The descriptions of individual phonemes incorporate the newest research from studies of jaw, lip, and tongue function in adults and children.

SLPs acquire a lot of games and other activities for teaching phonemes throughout a lifetime of service.

PRODUCTION

The movements used during production of each fricated consonant are described here. Details about emerging or immature production of these sounds are offered first within each section so that readers can see how these phonemes might be stimulated with children who speak very little and who use very few consonant phonemes. Details about mature oral movements are described next so that readers can see how these phonemes might be taught to clients who are ready to produce the mature forms.

Respiration, Phonation, Resonation

All the fricated consonants are initiated upon exhalation. The vocal folds abduct for /θ/, /f/, /s/, /ʃ/, /tʃ/, and /h/ to make them voiceless. They adduct for /ð/, /v/, /z/, /ʒ/, and /dʒ/ to make them voiced. All the fricated phonemes are made with velopharyngeal closure to direct the airstream through the mouth.

/f/ & /v/   *Four, offer, off*
                                Viper, over, glove

Emerging /f/ and /v/

These two fricatives make their first appearance during infancy in the form of raspberries and spitting. Production of /f/ and /v/ might be considered refinements of these gross infantile sounds.

Mature /f/ and /v/

Specific oral-motor patterns emerge as /f/ and /v/ mature:

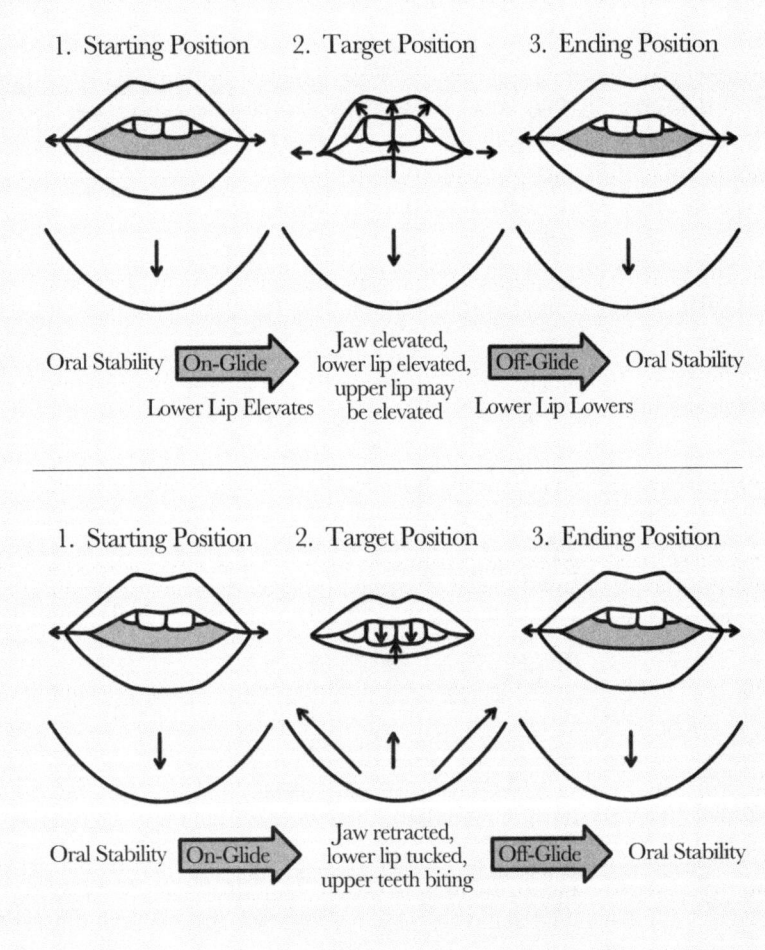

An incorrect /f/ and /v/ is often used as a gross introduction to these phonemes.

• *Starting position:* The jaw and tongue stabilize to set the mouth in starting position.

• *On-glide:* The lower lip gently elevates to the maxillary (upper) central incisors.

• *Target position:* Target position is reached when the lower lip is gently nestling against the upper teeth. This articulation forms a loose seal between the lower lip and the upper teeth through which the airstream passes. A very narrow constriction causes frication to occur.

• *Off-glide:* The lower lip returns to its neutral position.

/θ/ & /ð/   *Think, Cathy, bath*
                                That, bother, bathe

Emerging /θ/ and /ð/

These two fricatives make their first appearance during infancy in the form of raspberries and spitting. Production of mature /θ/ and /ð/ might be considered refinements of these gross infantile sounds.

Mature /θ/ and /ð/

Specific oral-motor patterns emerge as /θ/ and /ð/ mature:

• *Starting position:* The jaw and tongue stabilize to set the mouth in starting position.

• *On-glide:* The tongue shifts so that it anchors slightly forward and so the tip protrudes between the upper teeth and lower lip.

• *Target position:* Target position is reached when the tongue nestles gently between the upper teeth and lower lip from left to right. This articulation forms a loose seal at midline, and a somewhat firmer seal along the lateral borders. The loose constriction in the front causes frication to occur at the incisors.

• *Off-glide:* The tongue retreats back into the oral cavity and the mouth returns to neutral position.

/s/ & /z/

Soap, kisser, bus
Zoo, buzzer, fizz

Emerging /s/ and /z/

These two fricatives first make their appearance in infancy in the form of raspberries and spitting. Production of /s/ and /z/ might be considered refinements of these gross infantile sounds.

Mature /s/ and /z/

Specific oral-motor patterns emerge as /s/ and /z/ mature:

- *Starting position:* The jaw and tongue stabilize to set the mouth in starting position.

- *On-glide:* The tongue starts its approach to the palate by anchoring at the back-lateral margins. From these points of stability, both sides of the tongue lift simultaneously from back to front in a stripping action to form a seal along the lateral margins of the palate. This lateral lifting extends to the tip but ends before the actual tip is reached.

- *Target position:* The target position is reached when the sides of the tongue — from the back to the tip but excluding the very tip — are pressing gently upward against the palate. The midline of the tongue stays low. The combination of high sides and low midline creates a central groove, which in its final shape is wide in the back and very narrow at the tip. Frication occurs as the airstream passes through the tiny gap at the tip and strikes the anterior teeth as it escapes. The tip may be positioned high, low, or in between, and the productions that occur as a result are all considered correct allophonic variations; the only requirement for correct production is that the airstream is allowed to pass over the tongue tip to escape between the central incisors. The tongue tip may be pointing up toward the alveolus in such a way that a tiny gap is left between the tip and alveolus. Or, the tongue tip may be pointing downward and resting against the bottom of the lower teeth; in this case, the body of the tongue must arch toward the palate so that a tiny gap is created between the body of the tongue and the alveolus. Or, the tip may position itself any where between the high and low position so that the tiny gap remains between the tongue tip and front teeth.

- *Off-glide:* The tongue's retreat away from the palate is the reverse of the approach — in a stripping action from tip to back — and the tongue returns to its neutral position.

/ʃ/ & /ʒ/

Shoe, dashing, brush
Measure, beige

Emerging /ʃ/ and /ʒ/

These two fricatives first make their appearance in the form of raspberries and spitting. Production of /ʃ/ and /ʒ/ might be considered refinements of these gross infantile sounds.

Mature /ʃ/ and /ʒ/

Specific oral-motor patterns emerge as /ʃ/ and /ʒ/ mature:

- *Starting position:* The jaw and tongue stabilize to set the mouth in starting position.

- *On-glide:* From its points of stability at the back lateral margins, the perimeter of the tongue lifts sequentially from back-to-front on both sides simultaneously in a stripping action. The lifting ends about halfway toward the front of the tongue.

- *Target position:* Target position is reached when the lateral margins of the tongue, from the back to the midpoint, are nestling gently against the palate or upper side teeth. The midline stays low which causes the essential groove or channel for the midline airstream. The groove is wide all the way along the tongue, from back to tip. Air passes through this wide channel and strikes the upper and lower anterior teeth as it escapes so that frication occurs.

- *Off-glide:* The lateral margins of the tongue retreat away from the palate and the tongue returns to its neutral position.

/tʃ/ & /dʒ/

Chew, catcher, match
Jump, agile, badge

Emerging /tʃ/ and /dʒ/

These two affricates first make their appearance as spitting and raspberries. Production of /tʃ/ and /dʒ/ might be considered as refinements of these gross infantile sounds.

Mature /tʃ/ and /dʒ/

Unlike all the other phonemes in this group, these two are classified as *affricates*. This means that there exists a sequence of occlusion and frication in their production. Specific oral-motor patterns emerge as /tʃ/ and /dʒ/ mature:

- *Starting position:* The jaw and tongue stabilize to set the mouth in starting position.

- *On-glide:* From its points of stability at the back-lateral margins, both sides of the tongue's perimeter lift simultaneously in a stripping action from the back to the tip until the full horseshoe-shape is achieved.

•   *Target position:* In target position, the tongue presses upward in a horseshoe-shape that is sealed against the palate. This horseshoe-shape is thicker than that found in production of /t/ and /d/. This position is held briefly while air pressure builds behind the horseshoe-shaped seal.

•   *Off-glide:* The off-glide of these phonemes is still considered part of their production. Off-gliding begins when the tongue tip retreats down and away from the palate. The lateral margins of the tongue continue to retreat down and away from the palate in a stripping action beginning at the tip until the position for /ʃ/ or /ʒ/ are reached. The midline always remains low. This causes the groove to be very wide from back to tip. Air passes through this channel, strikes and passes through the anterior teeth and frication occurs. Following this, the lateral margins of the tongue retreat away from the palate and the tongue returns to its neutral position.

/h/   *Hot*

Emerging /h/

This fricative first makes its pre-speech appearance in the form of panting. Production of /h/ might be considered a refinement of this gross infantile sound.

Mature /h/

Specific oral-motor patterns emerge as /h/ matures:

•   *Stability:* First the jaw and tongue stabilize.

•   *On-glide:* The jaw lowers slightly, and the vocal folds approximate but do not articulate. The lips and tongue remain neutral.

•   *Target position:* Target position is reached when the jaw is positioned slightly low and the vocal folds are adducted enough to cause gentle frication to occur as the airstream passes between them.

•   *Off-glide:* The jaw and vocal folds return to neutral.

TREATMENT STRATEGIES

Many therapists hold off on teaching the fricated sounds because they generally come in later than almost all the other sounds. However, it is only the mature form of these sounds that stabilizes late.; the emergence of these sounds is actually quite early and many children's first words contain them. For example, many children produce the following types of words with fairly correct phonemes as first words: *that, bath, off, kiss, bus, shoe, ouchie,* and *jump.* The following general advice is offered:

•   If the set of fricated consonants is completely absent, consider beginning to work on exhalation.

•   If the set of fricated consonants is completely absent, consider teaching the raspberries first.

•   If the set of fricated consonants is completely absent, consider making the client's goal one of acquiring frication instead of focusing on any one specific phoneme in this group.

•   If a client has no fricated sounds at all, consider using conceptual cues to stimulate their concept, such as the snake for /s/, the bee for /z/, and so forth.

•   If a client has no fricated sounds at all, consider teaching all of them simultaneously and allowing the client time to use them as substitutes for one another for a while. In other words, teach a target word like "soap" but allow the client to say /fop/ or /ʃop/ for a while as frication enters his phonological repertoire. Encourage him to make any fricated sound and do not yet be concerned about which specific sound he is using.

•   If the set of fricated sounds is completely absent, many therapists begin with the voiceless ones because they are louder and because it seems easier for children to produce frication without voice than with voice. (A fricated sound that is voiced requires double adduction; the client has to adduct at the larynx and in the mouth at the same time. This makes the motor task more difficult.)

•   Many therapists introduce the fricated phonemes in the word initial position. However, it can be much easier for many clients to start in the final position. Developmental studies indicate that fricatives tend to emerge first in the final position, then in the intervocalic position, and finally in the initial position (Vihman, 2004b, p. 117). Use words such as *bath, off, kiss, push, ouch,* etc..

•   If the set of fricated consonants is completely absent, consider beginning with /h/ because it is so easy to perform; all the client has to do is open his mouth a little bit and exhale.

•   If the set of fricated consonants is completely absent, consider beginning with /θ/ because it is very visible and quite simple to perform; all the client has to do is to stick out his tongue and blow.

•   If the set of fricated consonants is completely absent, consider beginning with /f/ because it is the most visible and easiest to stimulate.

•   If the set of fricated consonants is completely absent, consider beginning with /s/ because it is the most frequently occurring sound in the English language. This can be a mistake for some clients, however, because /s/ requires a very refined tongue position.

- If the set of fricated consonants is completely absent, consider beginning with /ʃ/ because it is so common to tell little kids to shush, because it is a grosser sound than /s/, and because this phoneme can be produced with much distortion and still be considered adequate.

- If the set of fricated consonants is completely absent, make sure to prolong the models so clients have enough time to hear them.

/f/

Multisensory Stimulation for /f/

- *Auditory stimulation:* Model, amplify, repeat, prolong, and bombard with this phoneme. Use other methods to make it salient.

- *Auditory feedback:* Direct the client's production back to his ear with a tube or other tool. Imitate the client's sound.

- *Cues:* Use cues to pique the client's interest in this phoneme and to facilitate its concept.

- *Visual feedback to understand lower lip movements:* Watch in a mirror. Imitate the client's correct and incorrect productions and watch each other during simultaneous productions.

- *Visual feedback to understand airflow:* Hold objects in front of the lips for the client to move with his puff of air from /f/. Start with small lightweight objects like tissue paper, cotton balls, string, pieces of dental floss, tiny origami objects, etc.. If necessary, switch to heavier objects to increase strength of expiration by using items such as pinwheels or Ping-Pong® (table tennis) balls. Produce /f/ against a mirror or window and observe the fog it produces.

- *Verbal stimulation:* Use vocabulary the client can understand to describe the respiratory, phonatory, resonatory, and articulatory characteristics of this phoneme. "Bite down" is a verbal description that many therapists use to begin /f/ training, however, this description is a gross misrepresentation that is only used to introduce this phoneme — it will have to be changed over time because the upper teeth do not bite down; the lower lip pushes up.

- *Tactile feedback to perceive the lip movements:* Have the child feel his own lower lip movement during production of /f/.

- *Mark the target to develop place:* Touch the lower lip prior to production. Place an object between the lower lip and upper teeth against which the lower lip can press, such as a tongue depressor, finger, swizzle stick, coffee stirrer, or dental floss.

- *Aid lower lip elevation:* Use methods to stimulate upward movement of the lower lip.

- *Jaw stability:* Make sure the jaw is in a high position.

Association Method for /f/

- *Place:* Help the client learn /f/ by recognizing the similarities between it and any of the other labial phonemes he can produce.

- *Manner:* Help the client learn /f/ by recognizing the similarities between it and any of the other fricated sounds he can produce.

- *Voice:* Help the client learn /f/ by recognizing the similarities between it and any of the other voiceless phonemes he can produce.

Successive Approximations for /f/

- *Build /f/ off of /p/:* Teach the client to make a /p/ as a continuant instead of as a stop. Make a /p/ and hold the lips against the teeth and keep blowing, then bring the lower lip higher to push it against the upper teeth; bring the upper lip up to get it out of the way.

- *Build /f/ off of /θ/:* Have the client make /θ/, then have him push the tongue in with his lower lip while making /θ/.

- *Build /f/ off of /s/:* Have the client prolong /s/ and, as he does so, push the lower lip up to the upper teeth.

- *Build /f/ off of the bilabial raspberry:* Have the client prolong a voiceless bilabial raspberry and, as he does so, push the lower lip up to the upper teeth.

- *Build /f/ off of the lingua-labial raspberry:* Have the client prolong a lingua-labial raspberry, then, while doing so, have him push the tongue in with his lower lip.

Contrast Method for /f/

- *Place:* Contrast the lower lip movement of /f/ with the tongue-tip movements of /θ/ or /s/.

- *Manner:* Contrast the frication of /f/ with the occlusion of /p/, or contrast the frication of /f/ with the gliding manner of /w/.

- *Voice:* Contrast the voiceless-ness of /f/ with the

voicing of /v/.

- *Resonance:* Contrast the oral quality of /f/ with the nasal quality of /m/.

Phonological Strategies to Introduce /f/

- *Prolongation:* When first teaching /f/, consider modeling with excessive prolongation.

- *Key words:* Introduce /f/ with a small set of functional key words, e.g., *fun, face, fat.*

- *Final /f/:* Consider teaching early /f/ in easy VC words, e.g., *off, oaf, eff* (letter F).

- *Final /f/:* Consider introducing /f/ in the final position by allowing the client to reduce words into VC syllable structure, e.g., *aif* (for *knife*), *ʌf* (for *cuff*), *æf* (for *after*).

- *Initial /f/:* Consider teaching early /f/ in easy CV words, e.g., *fi fai foh fʌ (fum).*

- *Simplified words:* Consider teaching /f/ in the initial position by using easy words that can be spoken in CV, e.g., *fi* (for *feet*), *fu* (for *fool*), *fa* (for *far*), *foe* (for *four*), *fa* (for *five*).

- *Reduplication in adapted words:* In severe cases, consider teaching /f/ in easy CVCV that are modifications of real words, e.g., *fufu* (for *choo-choo*), *fafa* (for *fox*).

- *Diminutive:* Consider teaching early /f/ with diminutives, e.g., *fifi* (for *fishie*).

- *Baby steps:* Teach the client to use /p/ as a substitution for initial /f/ until frication enters his phonological repertoire. For example, if the client produces *bɪ* for *fish*, teach him to produce *pɪ* for *fish* instead.

- *Aspiration:* Allow early /f/ to be produced with excessive aspiration; this will be a gross production of /f/.

- *Switch gears:* If /f/ proves to be impossible to elicit, discontinue the practice and focus on another sound for a while.

- *Cluster reduction:* Allow for cluster reductions and simplifications when introducing /f/, e.g., *fawer* (for *flower*), *faon* (for *frown*).

- *Final position:* Use simple CVC words to stimulate final /f/, e.g., *knife, buff, calf, cuff, Duff, Guff, huff, 'nough* (for *enough*), *puff, tough.*

- *Final position with epenthesis:* Consider allowing the client to use a stressed schwa in an extra syllable when learning final /f/, e.g., *awfʌ* (for *off*), *naifʌ* (for

knife).

- *Minimal pairs and larger sets for initial /f/:* Use contrasting word pairs and larger sets to teach initial /f/, e.g., *fat, hat, sat, chat, mat, cat, bat.*

- *Minimal pairs and larger sets for final /f/:* Use contrasting word pairs and larger sets to teach final /f/, e.g., *eff* (letter F), *deaf, Jeff; off, cough; puff, enough, stuff.*

- *Reading and spelling:* Teach this phoneme as part of the client's reading and spelling program.

- *Language arts:* Teach this phoneme through stories, songs, jingles, jokes, rhymes, plays, and other material in the language arts program.

Solutions to Specific Problems on /f/

- *Sloppy/weak /f/:* Use resistance against lower lip elevation to make the lower lip press upwards more firmly. Teach the client to exhale more forcefully. Teach better auditory discrimination.

- *Stopping:* Teach the client to blow more air.

- *Nasal emission or substitution on /f/:* Use methods to control resonance.

- *Inhalation on /f/:* Use methods to develop breath support.

- *Puffy cheeks on /f/:* Use methods to develop oral stability.

- *Asymmetrical lips on /f/:* Use methods to develop oral stability.

- *Bilabial production of /f/:* Inhibit the upper lip from lowering.

- *Malocclusion prevents labial-dental articulation on /f/:* Teach compensation and/or refer for dental work.

- *Tongue protrusion on /f/:* Use methods to develop oral stability, specifically tongue stability.

- *Glottal stop replacement:* Use methods to develop auditory discrimination, oral perception, and lip movement.

/v/

Multisensory Stimulation for /v/

- *Auditory stimulation:* Model, amplify, repeat, prolong, and bombard with this phoneme. Use other methods to make it salient.

- *Auditory feedback:* Direct the client's production back to his ear with a tube or other tool. Imitate the client's sound.

- *Cues:* Use cues to pique the client's interest in this phoneme and to facilitate its concept.

- *Visual feedback to understand lower lip movements:* Watch in a mirror. Imitate the client's correct and incorrect productions and watch each other during simultaneous productions.

- *Visual feedback to understand airflow:* Hold objects in front of the lips for the client to move with his puff of air from /v/. Start with small lightweight objects like tissue paper, cotton balls, string, pieces of dental floss, tiny origami objects, etc.. If necessary, switch to heavier objects to increase strength of expiration by using items such as pinwheels or Ping-Pong® (table tennis) balls. Produce /v/ against a mirror or window and observe the fog it produces

- *Verbal stimulation:* Use vocabulary the client can understand to describe the respiratory, phonatory, resonatory, and articulatory characteristics of this phoneme.

- *Tactile feedback to perceive the lip movements:* Have the child feel his own lower lip movement during production of /v/. "Bite down" is a verbal description that many therapists use to begin /v/ training, however, this description is a gross misrepresentation that is only used to introduce this phoneme — it will have to be changed over time because the upper teeth do not bite down; the lower lip pushes up.

- *Mark the target to develop place:* Touch the lower lip prior to production. Place an object between the lower lip and upper teeth against which the lower lip can press, such as a tongue depressor, finger, swizzle stick, coffee stirrer, or dental floss.

- *Aid lower lip elevation:* Use methods to facilitate lower lip movement.

- *Jaw stability:* Make sure the jaw is in a high position.

Association Method for /v/

- *Place:* Help the client learn /v/ by recognizing the similarities between it and any of the other labial phonemes he can produce. Especially, teach the client to make a /b/ and hold the lips against the teeth instead of releasing into a plosive.

- *Manner:* Help the client learn /v/ by recognizing the similarities between it and any of the other fricated sounds he can produce.

- *Voice:* Help the client learn /v/ by recognizing the similarities between it and any of the other voiced fricated sounds he can produce.

Successive Approximations for /v/

- *Build /v/ off of /f/:* Have the client make /f/ and add voice.

- *Build /v/ off of /b/:* Teach the client to make a /b/ as a continuant instead of as a stop: Make a /b/ and hold the lips against the teeth and keep blowing, then bring the lower lip higher to push it against the upper teeth; bring the upper lip up to get it out of the way.

- *Build /v/ off of /ð/:* Have the client make /ð/, then have him push the tongue in with his lower lip while making /ð/.

- *Build /v/ off of /z/:* Have the client prolong /z/ and, as he does so, push the lower lip up to the upper teeth.

- *Build /v/ off of the bilabial raspberry:* Have the client prolong a voiced bilabial raspberry and, as he does so, push the lower lip up to the upper teeth.

- *Build /v/ off of the lingua-labial raspberry:* Have the client prolong a voiced lingua-labial raspberry, then, while doing so, have him push the tongue in with his lower lip.

Contrasting Method for /v/

- *Place:* Contrast the lower lip movement of /v/ with the tongue-tip movements of /z/ or with the tongue-back movements of /ʒ/

- *Manner:* Contrast the frication of /v/ with the occlusion of /b/ or the gliding manner of /w/.

- *Voice:* Contrast the voicing of /v/ with the voiceless-ness of /f/.

- *Resonance:* Contrast the oral quality of /v/ with the nasal quality of /m/.

Phonological Strategies to Introduce /v/

- *Prolongation:* When first teaching /v/ in words, consider modeling with excessive prolongation.

- *Key words:* Introduce /v/ with a small set of functional key words, e.g., *move, movie, over.*

- *Initial /v/:* Consider teaching early initial /v/ in easy CV words, e.g., *vee* (letter V), *Vi*

- *Simplified words:* Consider teaching /v/ in the

initial position by using easy words that can be spoken in CV, e.g., *vai* (for *violet*), *vei* (for *vase*).

• *Reduplication in adapted words:* In severe cases, consider teaching /v/ in easy CVCV that are modifications of real words, e.g., *væve/vacuum.*

• *Switch gears:* If /v/ proves to be impossible to elicit, discontinue the practice and focus on another sound for a while.

• *Final position:* Use simple CVC words to stimulate final /v/, e.g., *dove, give, move, have.*

• *Final position with epenthesis:* Consider allowing the client to use a stressed schwa in an extra syllable, to stimulate a final /v/, e.g., *muvʌ* (for *move*).

• *Final /v/:* Consider teaching final /v/ by allowing the client to reduce words into VC syllable structure, e.g., *ʌv* (for *glove*), *eev* (for *even*), *ʌv* (for *oven*).

• *Minimal pairs and larger sets for initial /v/:* Use contrasting word pairs and larger sets to teach initial /v/, e.g., *vee* (letter V), *me, see, she, tea, key.*

• *Minimal pairs and larger sets for final /v/:* Use contrasting word pairs and larger sets to teach final /v/, e.g., *glove/dove, cave/wave.*

• *Reading and spelling:* Teach this phoneme as part of the client's reading and spelling program.

• *Language arts:* Teach this phoneme through stories, songs, jingles, jokes, rhymes, plays, and other material in the language arts program.

Solutions to Specific Problems on /v/

• *Weak frication:* Use resistance against lower lip elevation to make the lower lip press upwards more firmly. Teach the client to produce /v/ with louder voice.

• *Stopping:* Teach the client to "keep the air going."

• *Nasal emission or substitution on /v/:* Use methods to control resonance.

• *Inhalation on /v/:* Use methods to develop breath support.

• *Puffy cheeks on /v/:* Use methods to develop oral stability.

• *Asymmetrical lips on /v/:* Use methods to develop oral stability.

• *Bilabial production of /v/:* Inhibit the upper lip from lowering.

• *Malocclusion prevents labial-dental articulation on /v/:*

Teach compensation and/or refer for dental work.

• *Tongue protrusion on /v/:* Develop oral stability.

• *Glottal stop replacement:* Develop auditory discrimination, oral perception, and lip movement.

/θ/

Multisensory Stimulation for /θ/

• *Auditory stimulation:* Model, amplify, repeat, prolong, and bombard with this phoneme. Use other methods to make it salient.

• *Auditory feedback:* Direct the client's production back to his ear with a tube or other tool. Imitate the client's sound.

• *Cues:* Use cues to pique the client's interest in this phoneme and to facilitate its concept.

• *Visual feedback to understand tongue protrusion:* Imitate the client's correct and incorrect productions and watch each other during simultaneous productions.

• *Visual feedback to understand airflow on /θ/:* Produce /θ/ against a mirror or window and observe the fog it produces.

• *Verbal:* Use vocabulary the client can understand to describe the respiratory, phonatory, resonatory, and articulatory characteristics of this phoneme.

• *Tactile feedback to perceive tongue-tip movements:* Have the child feel his own tongue movements during production of /θ/.

• *Mark the target to develop place for /θ/:* Touch the tongue tip, the lower lip, and the upper teeth prior to production.

• *Aid tongue-tip protrusion:* Use methods to facilitate tongue protrusion.

• *Jaw stability to encourage more tongue activity:* The jaw has to be able to lower slightly to produce this sound; make sure it doesn't lower too far or protrude.

Association Methods for /θ/

• *Place:* Help the client learn /θ/ by recognizing the similarities between it and any of the other tongue-tip phonemes he can produce.

• *Manner:* Help the client learn /θ/ by recognizing the similarities between it and any of the other fricated sounds he can produce.

- *Voice:* Help the client learn /θ/ by recognizing the similarities between it and any of the other voiceless fricated sounds he can produce.

Successive Approximations for /θ/

- *Build /θ/ off of /p/:* Teach the client to make a /p/ as a continuant instead of as a stop: Make a /p/ and hold the lips against the teeth and keep blowing, then push the tongue through the lips as he continues the sound, then smile slightly to pull the lips out of the way.

- *Build /θ/ off of /f/:* Have the client make /f/ and push the tongue forward between the teeth as he continues to make /f/.

- *Build /θ/ off of /s/:* Have the client prolong /s/ and push the tongue forward between the teeth while he continues to make /s/.

- *Build /θ/ off of the bilabial raspberry:* Have the client prolong a voiceless bilabial raspberry, and push the tongue forward between the teeth as he does so.

- *Build /θ/ off of the voiceless lingua-labial raspberry:* Have the client prolong a voiceless lingua-labial raspberry and then make it more quietly and gently.

Contrasting Method for /θ/

- *Place:* Contrast the tongue-tip movements of /θ/ with the labial movements of /f/.

- *Manner:* Contrast the continuance of /θ/ with the occlusion of /t/, or contrast the frication of /θ/ with the gliding manner of /l/.

- *Voice:* Contrast the voiceless-ness of /θ/ with the voicing of /ð/.

- *Resonance:* Contrast the oral quality of /θ/ with the nasal quality of /n/.

Phonological Strategies to Introduce /θ/

- *Key words:* Introduce /θ/ with a small set of functional key words, e.g., *thumb, think, thing.*

- *Protophrases:* Consider introducing /θ/ in functional protowords, e.g., ʌθæ (for *What's that?*), ʌθɪ (for *What's this?*)

- *Reduplication:* Consider teaching early /θ/ in words that can be reduced to CVCV structure, e.g., θiθi (for *fishie*).

- *Diminutive:* Consider teaching early /θ/ in a diminutive, e.g., *Bethie, bathie.*

- *Baby steps:* Allow the client to use /θ/ as a substitution for initial /s/ for a while.

- *Switch gears:* If /θ/ proves to be impossible to elicit, discontinue the practice and focus on another sound for a while.

- *Final /θ/ words:* Consider introducing /θ/ in the word final position, e.g., *bath, booth, both, math, with.*

- *Substitutions:* Consider teaching /θ/ in the initial position early by teaching θ/s substitutions, e.g., θi (for *see*), θop (for *soap*).

- *Final position with epenthesis:* Consider allowing the client to use a stressed schwa in an extra syllable to stimulate final /θ/, e.g., bæθʌ (for *bath*), buθʌ (for *booth*).

- *Minimal pairs and larger sets in initial position:* Use contrasting word pairs and larger sets to teach initial /θ/, e.g., *thumb, some, hum, gum; think, sink, wink, pink.*

- *Minimal pairs and larger sets in final position:* Use contrasting word pairs and larger sets to teach final /θ/, e.g., *bath, bass, bat.*

- *Reading and spelling:* Teach this phoneme as part of the client's reading and spelling program.

- *Language arts:* Teach this phoneme through stories, songs, jingles, jokes, rhymes, plays, and other material in the language arts program.

Solutions to Specific Problems on /θ/

- *Weak /θ/:* Teach the client to push the tongue tip up against the upper teeth a little more firmly. Teach him to blow a little harder.

- *Lack of frication on /θ/:* Teach him to blow a little harder and reduce the space between the tongue and teeth. Make sure the jaw is high enough.

- *Phoneme produced too tightly:* Teach the client to produce the lingua-labial raspberry to loosen his hold.

- *Stopping:* Teach him to blow more air.

- *Nasal emission or substitution on /θ/:* Use methods to control resonance.

- *Inhalation on /θ/:* Develop correct breath support.

- *Tongue shifts to one side on /θ/:* Develop oral stability.

- *Tongue does not come out far enough for /θ/:* Use resistance to encourage more tongue protrusion: Push the tongue tip in and ask the client to push forward against this resistance.

- *Glottal stop replaces /θ/:* Develop auditory discrimination, oral perception, and tongue movements. Compare /t/ with the glottal stop.

/ð/

Multisensory Stimulation for /ð/

- *Auditory stimulation:* Model, amplify, repeat, prolong, and bombard with this phoneme. Use other methods to make it salient.

- *Auditory feedback:* Direct the client's production back to his ear with a tube or other tool. Imitate the client's sound.

- *Cues:* Use cues to pique the client's interest in this phoneme and to facilitate its concept.

- *Visual feedback to understand tongue protrusion:* Imitate the client's correct and incorrect productions and watch each other during simultaneous productions.

- *Visual feedback to understand airflow on /ð/:* Produce /ð/ against a mirror or window and observe the fog it produces.

- *Verbal:* Use vocabulary the client can understand to describe the respiratory, phonatory, resonatory, and articulatory characteristics of this phoneme.

- *Tactile feedback to perceive tongue-tip movements:* Have the child feel his own tongue movements during production of /ð/.

- *Mark the target to develop place for /t/:* Touch the tongue tip, the lower lip, and the upper teeth prior to production.

- *Aid tongue-tip protrusion:* Facilitate tongue protrusion.

- *Jaw stability to encourage more tongue activity:* The jaw has to be able to lower slightly to produce this sound; make sure it doesn't lower too far or protrude.

Association Method for /ð/

- *Place:* Help the client learn /ð/ by recognizing the similarities between it and any of the other anterior lingua phonemes he can produce.

- *Manner:* Help the client learn /ð/ by recognizing the similarities between it and any of the other fricated sounds he can produce.

- *Voice:* Help the client learn /ð/ by recognizing the similarities between it and any of the other voiced

fricated sounds he can produce.

Successive Approximations for /ð/

- *Build /ð/ off of /b/:* Teach the client to make a /b/ as a continuant instead of as a stop. Make a /b/ and hold the lips against the teeth and keep blowing, then push the tongue forward between the lips as he continues the sound, then smile slightly to pull the lips out of the way.

- *Build /ð/ off of /v/:* Have the client make /v/ and push the tongue forward between the teeth as he continues to make /v/.

- *Build /ð/ off of /z/:* Have the client prolong /z/ and push the tongue forward between the teeth while he continues to make /z/.

- *Build /ð/ off of the bilabial raspberry:* Have the client prolong a voiceless bilabial raspberry and push the tongue forward between the teeth as he does so.

- *Build /ð/ off of the voiced lingua-labial raspberry:* Have the client prolong a voiced lingua-labial raspberry and then make it more quietly and gently.

Contrasting Method for /ð/

- *Place:* Contrast the tongue-tip movements of /ð/ with the labial movements of /v/.

- *Manner:* Contrast the continuance of /ð/ with the occlusion of /d/, or contrast the frication of /ð/ with the gliding manner of /l/.

- *Voice:* Contrast the voicing of /ð/ with the voiceless-ness of /ð/.

- *Resonance:* Contrast the oral quality of /ð/ with the nasal quality of /n/.

Phonological Strategies to Introduce /ð/

- *Key words:* Introduce /ð/ with a small set of functional key words, e.g., *the, this, that, those.*

- *Protophrases:* Consider introducing /ð/ in functional protophrases, e.g., ʌθæ (for *What's that?*) ʌθi (for *What's this?*)

- *Reduplication:* Consider teaching early /ð/ in words that can be reduced to CVCV structure, e.g., θæθæ (for *bath*).

- *Baby steps:* Allow the client to use /ð/ as a substitution for initial /z/ for a while.

- *Switch gears:* If /ð/ proves to be impossible to elicit, discontinue the practice and focus on another sound for a while.

- *Final position with epenthesis:* Consider allowing the client to use a stressed schwa in an extra syllable to stimulate final /ð/, e.g., *beðʌ* (for *bathe*), *tiðʌ* (for *teethe*).

- *Minimal pairs and larger sets in initial position:* Use contrasting word pairs and larger sets to teach initial /ð/, e.g., *that, vat, bat.*

- *Reading and spelling:* Teach this phoneme as part of the client's reading and spelling program.

- *Language arts:* Teach this phoneme through stories, songs, jingles, jokes, rhymes, plays, and other material in the language arts program.

Solutions to Specific Problems on /ð/

- *Weak /ð/:* Teach the client to push the tongue tip up against the upper teeth a little more firmly. Teach him to blow a little harder.

- *Lack of frication on /ð/:* Teach him to blow a little harder and reduce the space between the tongue and teeth. Make sure the jaw is high enough.

- *Phoneme produced to tightly:* Teach the client to produce the lingua-labial raspberry to loosen up his hold.

- *Stopping:* Teach him to blow more air.

- *Nasal emission or substitution on /ð/:* Use methods to control resonance.

- *Inhalation on /ð/:* Develop correct breath support.

- *Tongue shifts to one side on /ð/:* Develop oral stability.

- *Tongue does not come out far enough for /ð/:* Use resistance to encourage more tongue protrusion: Push the tongue tip in and ask the client to push forward against this resistance.

- *Glottal stop replaces /ð/:* Develop auditory discrimination, oral perception, and tongue movements. Compare /ð/ with the glottal stop.

/s/

Multisensory Stimulation for /s/

- *Auditory stimulation:* Model, amplify, repeat, prolong, and bombard with this phoneme. Use other methods to make it salient.

- *Auditory feedback:* Direct the client's production back to his ear with a tube or other tool. Imitate the client's sound.

- *Cues:* Use cues to pique the client's interest in this phoneme and to facilitate its concept.

- *Visual feedback to understand tongue groove:* Imitate the client's correct and incorrect productions and watch each other during simultaneous productions. Blow /s/ into a straw held outside the teeth at midline.

- *Visual feedback to understand airflow on /s/:* Produce /s/ against a mirror or window and observe the fog it produces.

- *Verbal:* Use vocabulary the client can understand to describe the respiratory, phonatory, resonatory, and articulatory characteristics of this phoneme.

- *Mark the target to develop place for /s/:* Touch the lateral margins of the tongue and the sides of the palate prior to production.

- *Aid tongue grooving:* Develop tongue grooving.

- *Jaw stability:* Make sure the jaw is in a high position.

- *Tongue stability:* Make sure the tongue is stabilizing at the back-lateral margins.

Association Method for /s/

- *Place:* Help the client learn /s/ by recognizing the similarities between it and any of the other lingua-alveolar phonemes he can produce. Phoneme /t/ is the perfect sound for this activity; have the client make a /t/ and blow more air to hear the similarity between the two.

- *Manner:* Help the client learn /s/ by recognizing the similarities between it and any of the other fricated sounds he can produce.

- *Voice:* Help the client learn /s/ by recognizing the similarities between it and any of the other voiceless sounds he can produce.

Successive Approximations for /s/

- *Build /s/ off of /z/:* Have the client produce /z/ and turn his voice off.

- *Build /s/ off of /t/:* Teach the client to make a /t/ and then blow more air as he keeps the tongue tip elevated; tell him to make a "long T."

- *Build /s/ off of /θ/:* Have the client make /θ/

and slide the tongue behind the teeth and bite the front teeth gently together.

- *Build /s/ off of /ʃ/:* Have the client make /ʃ/ and then hold this position while approaching the alveolar ridge with the tongue tip. Then have him retract the lips.

- *Build /s/ off the voiceless lingua-labial raspberry:* Have the client prolong a voiceless lingua-labial raspberry and then pull the tongue in, bite the front teeth together gently, and then make it softer.

Contrasting Method for /s/

- *Place:* Contrast the tongue-tip movements of /s/ with the lingua-dental movements of /θ/ or with the glottal movements of /h/.

- *Manner:* Contrast the continuance of /s/ with the occlusion of /t/, or contrast the frication of /s/ with the gliding manner of /l/.

- *Voice:* Contrast the voiceless-ness of /s/ with the voicing of /z/.

- *Resonance:* Contrast the oral quality of /s/ with the nasal quality of /n/.

Phonological Strategies to Introduce /s/

- *Key words:* Introduce /s/ with a small set of functional key words, e.g., *see, some, soap, kiss, bus, mouse, house.*

- *Reduplication:* Consider teaching early /s/ in words that can be reduced to CVCV structure, e.g., *sisi* (for *fishie*).

- *Diminutive:* Consider teaching early /s/ in diminutives, e.g., *sissy.*

- *CV words:* Consider teaching /s/ in the initial position early by using CV words, e.g., *see, Sue, say, sew, so, sigh.*

- *Switch gears:* If /s/ proves to be impossible to elicit, discontinue the practice and focus on another sound for a while.

- *Early final /s/ words:* Consider introducing /s/ in the final position first, e.g., *bus, mouse, house, kiss.*

- *Early final /s/ clusters:* Consider introducing /s/ in the final position first with clusters, e.g., *hats, boats, mitts, lights.*

- *Use ts/s substitution:* Consider teaching /ts/ for /s/ to get /s/ started in the initial position, e.g., teach *tsop* for *soap* and *tsa-k* for *sock.* Drop the /t/ after the pattern is consistent.

- *Final position with epenthesis:* Consider allowing the client to use a stressed schwa in an extra syllable to stimulate final /s/, e.g., *bʌsʌ* (for *bus*).

- *Minimal pairs and larger sets in initial position:* Use contrasting word pairs and larger sets to teach initial /s/, e.g., *sew, show, mow, low.*

- *Minimal pairs and larger sets in final position:* Use contrasting word pairs and larger sets to teach final /s/, e.g., *miss, mitt, Mitch, Mick.*

- *Reading and spelling:* Teach this phoneme as part of the client's reading and spelling program.

- *Language arts:* Teach this phoneme through stories, songs, jingles, jokes, rhymes, plays, and other material in the language arts program.

Solutions to Specific Problems on /s/

- *Weak /s/:* Teach the client to make the sound sharper by pushing the tongue more firmly upward toward the alveolar ridge or by pushing the tip toward the teeth and by blowing a little harder. Make sure the jaw is very high.

- *Lack of frication on /s/:* Teach him to make a /t/ and blow more air. Make sure the jaw is very high.

- *Phoneme produced to tightly:* Teach client to produce the lingua-labial raspberry to loosen up his hold.

- *Stopping:* Teach him to blow more air.

- *Nasal emission or substitution on /s/:* Use methods to control resonance.

- *Inhalation on /s/:* Developing correct breath support.

- *Tongue shifts to one side on /s/:* Develop oral stability.

- *Tongue protrudes (frontal lisp):* Establish oral stability.

- *Lateral emission of air (lateral lisp):* Build the phoneme off of /t/. Place a straw at midline outside of the incisors. Have the client make /t/ into the straw, then have him blow more air into the straw through the /t/. Finally, tell him to do this without touching the tongue tip to the alveolar ridge. Teach back-lateral tongue stability.

- *Jaw position:* Make sure the jaw is very high.

/z/

Multisensory Stimulation for /z/

• *Auditory stimulation:* Model, amplify, repeat, prolong, and bombard with this phoneme. Use other methods to make it salient.

• *Auditory feedback:* Direct the client's production back to his ear with a tube or other tool. Imitate the client's sound.

• *Cues:* Use cues to pique the client's interest in this phoneme and to facilitate its concept.

• *Visual feedback to understand tongue protrusion:* Imitate the client's correct and incorrect productions and watch each other during simultaneous productions. Blow /s/ into a straw held outside the teeth at midline. Develop the oral percept.

• *Visual feedback to understand airflow on /z/:* Produce /z/ against a mirror or window and observe the fog it produces.

• *Verbal:* Use vocabulary the client can understand to describe the respiration, phonation, resonation, and articulation characteristics of this phoneme.

• *Mark the target to develop place for /z/:* Touch the lateral margins of the tongue and the sides of the palate prior to production.

• *Aid tongue grooving:* Develop tongue grooving.

• *Jaw stability:* Make sure the jaw is in a high position.

• *Tongue stability:* Make sure the tongue is stabilized at the back-lateral margins.

Association Method for /z/

• *Place:* Help the client learn /z/ by recognizing the similarities between it and any of the other lingua-alveolar phonemes he can produce. Phoneme /d/ is the perfect sound for this activity; have the client make a /d/ and then try to continue the sound to hear the similarity between the two.

• *Manner:* Help the client learn /z/ by recognizing the similarities between it and any of the other fricated sounds he can produce. Phoneme /s/ is possibly the best for this method.

• *Voice:* Help the client learn /z/ by recognizing the similarities between it and any of the other voiced sounds he can produce.

Successive Approximations for /z/

• *Build /z/ off of /s/:* Have the client produce /s/ and turn his voice on.

• *Build /z/ off of /d/:* Teach the client to make a /d/ and then blow more air as he keeps the tongue elevated in /d/ position.

• *Build /z/ off of /ð/:* Have the client make /ð/ and slide the tongue behind the teeth and bite the front teeth together.

• *Build /z/ off of /ʒ/:* Have the client make /ʒ/ and then hold that tongue position while approaching the alveolar ridge with the tongue tip. Then have him retract the lips slightly.

• *Build /z/ off of the voiced lingua-labial raspberry:* Have the client prolong a voiced lingua-labial raspberry and then pull the tongue in, bite the front teeth, and make it more quietly and gently.

Contrasting Method for /z/

• *Place:* Contrast the tongue-tip movements of /z/ with the lingua-dental movements of /ð/ or with the glottal movements of /h/.

• *Manner:* Contrast the continuance of /z/ with the occlusion of /d/, or contrast the frication of /z/ with the glide of /l/.

• *Voice:* Contrast the voicing of /z/ with the voiceless-ness of /s/.

• *Resonance:* Contrast the oral quality of /z/ with the nasal quality of /n/.

Phonological Strategies to Introduce /z/

• *Key words:* Introduce /z/ with a small set of functional key words, e.g., *zee* (letter Z), *zero, zed, zoo, zebra, buzz.*

• *Reduplication:* Consider teaching early /z/ in words that can be reduced to CVCV structure, e.g., *zizi* (for *zebra*).

• *CV words:* Consider teaching /z/ in the initial position early by using CV words, e.g., *zee* (letter Z), *zoo.*

• *Switch gears:* If /z/ proves to be impossible to elicit, discontinue the practice and focus on another sound for a while.

• *Early final /z/ words:* Consider introducing /z/ in the final position first, e.g., *buzz, fuzz, his.*

• *Final position with epenthesis:* Consider allowing

the client to use a stressed schwa in an extra syllable to stimulate final /z/, e.g., *bʌzʌ* (for *buzz*).

- *Minimal pairs and larger sets in initial position:* Use contrasting word pairs and larger sets to teach initial /z/, e.g., *zoo, Sue, shoe, new two.*

- *Minimal pairs and larger sets in final position:* Use contrasting word pairs and larger sets to teach final /z/, e.g., *maze, made, mate, make.*

- *Reading and spelling:* Teach this phoneme as part of the client's reading and spelling program.

- *Language arts:* Teach this phoneme through stories, songs, jingles, jokes, rhymes, plays, and other material in the language arts program.

Solutions to Specific Problems on /z/

- *Weak /z/:* Teach the client to make the sound sharper by pushing harder upward toward the alveolar ridge or by pushing the tip toward the teeth and blowing a little harder. Make sure the jaw is high.

- *Lack of frication on /z/:* Teach him to make a /d/ and then to press the tongue upward and blow more air.

- *Phoneme produced to tightly:* Teach client to produce the lingua-labial raspberry to loosen his hold.

- *Stopping:* Teach him to blow more air.

- *Nasal emission or substitution on /z/:* Use methods to control resonance.

- *Inhalation on /z/:* Develop correct breath support.

- *Tongue shifts to one side on /z/:* Develop oral stability.

- *Tongue protrudes (frontal lisp):* Establish oral stability.

- *Lateral emission of air (lateral lisp):* Build the phoneme off of /d/: Place a straw at midline outside of the incisors. Have the client make /d/ into the straw, then have him blow more air into the straw through the /d/. Finally, tell him to do it without touching the tongue tip to the alveolar ridge. Teach back-lateral tongue stability.

/ʃ/

Multisensory Stimulation for /ʃ/

- *Auditory stimulation:* Model, amplify, repeat, prolong, and bombard with this phoneme. Use other methods to make it salient.

- *Auditory feedback:* Direct the client's production back to his ear with a tube or other tool. Imitate the client's sound.

- *Cues:* Use cues to pique the client's interest in this phoneme and to facilitate its concept.

- *Visual feedback to understand tongue protrusion:* Imitate the client's correct and incorrect productions and watch each other during simultaneous productions.

- *Visual feedback to understand airflow on /ʃ/:* Produce /ʃ/ against a mirror or window and observe the fog it produces.

- *Verbal:* Use vocabulary the client can understand to describe the respiration, phonation, resonation, and articulation characteristics of this phoneme.

- *Mark the target to develop place for /ʃ/:* Touch the lateral margins of the tongue and the sides of the palate prior to production.

- *Aid tongue grooving:* Develop a wide tongue groove. Begin with /i/ (see page 209 for more on the "E Position").

- *Jaw stability:* Make sure the jaw is in a high position.

- *Tongue stability:* Teach back-lateral tongue stability.

Association Method for /ʃ/

- *Place:* Help the client learn /ʃ/ by recognizing the similarities between it and any of the other lingua-palatal phonemes he can produce. Vowel /i/ is especially good for this work.

- *Manner:* Help the client learn /ʃ/ by recognizing the similarities between it and any of the other fricated sounds he can produce.

- *Voice:* Help the client learn /ʃ/ by recognizing the similarities between it and any of the other voiceless sounds he can produce.

Successive Approximations for /ʃ/

• *Build /ʃ/ off of /i/:* Have the client prolong /i/ with a big smile. Then whisper through this sound. Then round the lips while prolonging this sound.

• *Build /ʃ/ off of /ʒ/:* Have the client produce /ʒ/ and turn his voice off.

• *Build /ʃ/ off of /t/:* Have the client make a /t/ with long aspiration. Then tell him to keep the tongue tip elevated while rounding his lips.

• *Build /ʃ/ off of /s/:* Have the client produce and prolong /s/. While prolonging this new sound have him round the lips; this will often make the correct sound appear.

• *Build /ʃ/ off of /θ/:* Have the client make /θ/ and slide the tongue behind the teeth and bite the front teeth together.

• *Build /ʃ/ off of /h/:* Have the client prolong an /h/, then have him bite his molars together and make this prolonged /h/, then have him round his lips as he repeats this sound.

• *Build /ʃ/ off of /s/ and /dʒ/:* Have the client say /s/ and then /dʒ/ in sequence, then have him whisper the sequence and round his lips.

• *Build /ʃ/ off of the voiceless lingua-labial raspberry:* Have the client prolong a voiceless lingua-labial raspberry and then pull the tongue in, bite the front teeth, and make it more quietly and gently.

Contrasting Method for /ʃ/

• *Place:* Contrast the tongue position of /ʃ/ with the tongue position of /s/.

• *Manner:* Contrast the continuance of /ʃ/ with the occlusion of /t/, or contrast the frication of /ʃ/ with the gliding manner of /j/.

• *Voice:* Contrast the voiceless-ness of /ʃ/ with the voicing of /ʒ/.

• *Resonance:* Contrast the oral quality of /ʃ/ with the nasal quality of /n/ or /ŋ/.

Phonological Strategies to Introduce /ʃ/

• *Key words:* Introduce /ʃ/ with a small set of functional key words, e.g., *shoe, she, shampoo, shower, fish, bush, push.*

• *Reduplication:* Consider teaching early /ʃ/ in words that can be reduced to CVCV structure, e.g., ʃaʃa (for *shower*).

• *Diminutive:* Consider teaching early /ʃ/ in diminutives, e.g., ʃiʃi (for *fishie*).

• *CV words:* Consider teaching /ʃ/ in the initial position early by using CV words, e.g., *she, shoe, show.*

• *Switch gears:* If /ʃ/ proves to be impossible to elicit, discontinue it and focus on another sound for a while.

• *Early final /ʃ/ words:* Consider introducing /ʃ/ in the final position first, e.g., *push, bush, mush, cash, hash, fish.*

• *Final position with epenthesis:* Consider allowing the client to use a stressed schwa in an extra syllable to stimulate final /ʃ/, e.g., bʊʃʌ (for *bush*).

• *Minimal pairs and larger sets in initial position:* Use contrasting word pairs and larger sets to teach initial /ʃ/, e.g., *show, sew, mow, low.*

• *Minimal pairs and larger sets in final position:* Use contrasting word pairs and larger sets to teach final /ʃ/, e.g., *push, put, pull.*

• *Reading and spelling:* Teach this phoneme as part of the client's reading and spelling program.

• *Language arts:* Teach this phoneme through stories, songs, jingles, jokes, rhymes, plays, and other material in the language arts program.

Solutions to Specific Problems on /ʃ/

• *Weak /ʃ/:* Teach the client to make the sound sharper by pushing harder up toward the palate or by blowing a little harder. Make sure the jaw is high.

• *Lack of frication on /ʃ/:* Teach him to whisper /i/ silently with lots of air. Make sure the jaw is high.

• *Stopping:* Teach him to "keep the air going."

• *Nasal emission or substitution on /ʃ/:* Use methods to control resonance.

• *Inhalation on /ʃ/:* Develop correct breath support.

• *Tongue shifts to one side on /ʃ/:* Develop oral stability.

• *Tongue protrudes (frontal lisp):* Establish oral stability.

• *Lateral emission of air (lateral lisp):* Build the phoneme off of /i/. Have the client produce /i/ and then whisper through this position, then teach him to round the lips as he whispers through this position.

/ʒ/

Multisensory Stimulation for /ʒ/

- *Auditory stimulation:* Model, amplify, repeat, prolong, and bombard with this phoneme. Use other methods to make it salient.

- *Auditory feedback:* Direct the client's production back to his ear with a tube or other tool. Imitate the client's sound.

- *Cues:* Use cues to pique the client's interest in this phoneme and to facilitate its concept.

- *Visual feedback to understand tongue protrusion:* Imitate the client's correct and incorrect productions and watch each other during simultaneous productions.

- *Visual feedback to understand airflow on /ʒ/:* Produce /ʒ/ against a mirror or window and observe the fog it produces.

- *Verbal:* Use vocabulary the client can understand to describe the respiration, phonation, resonation, and articulation characteristics of this phoneme.

- *Mark the target to develop place for /ʒ/:* Touch the lateral margins of the tongue and the sides of the palate prior to production.

- *Aid tongue grooving:* Develop a wide tongue groove.

- *Jaw stability:* Make sure the jaw is in a high position.

Association Method for /ʒ/

- *Place:* Help the client learn /ʒ/ by recognizing the similarities between it and any of the other lingua-palatal phonemes he can produce.

- *Manner:* Help the client learn /ʒ/ by recognizing the similarities between it and any of the other fricated sounds he can produce.

- *Voice:* Help the client learn /ʒ/ by recognizing the similarities between it and any of the other voiced sounds he can produce.

Successive Approximations for /ʒ/

- *Build /ʒ/ off of /i/:* Have the client prolong /i/ with a big smile, then round the lips while prolonging this sound. Bite the teeth together to make more frication.

- *Build /ʒ/ off of /ʃ/:* Have the client produce /ʃ/ and turn his voice on.

- *Build /ʒ/ off of /d/:* Have the client make a /d/ with long aspiration, then tell him to keep the tongue tip elevated while round his lips. Tell him not to let the tip go all the way up to the alveolar ridge.

- *Build /ʒ/ off of /z/:* Have the client produce and prolong /z/. While prolonging /z/, have him curl the tongue tip upward and back slightly (only a few millimeters). Then, while prolonging this new sound, have him round the lips.

- *Build /ʒ/ off of /ð/:* Have the client make /ð/ and slide the tongue behind the teeth and bite the front teeth together.

- *Build /ʒ/ off of /ɑ/:* Have the client prolong an /ɑ/. Then have him bite his molars together and make this prolonged /ɑ/. Then have him round his lips firmly as he repeats this sound and raise his tongue toward the palate.

- *Build /ʒ/ off of /z/ and /dʒ/:* Have the client say /z/ and then /dʒ/ in sequence, then have him round his lips.

- *Build /ʒ/ off of the voiceless lingua-labial raspberry:* Have the client prolong a voiceless lingua-labial raspberry and then pull the tongue in, bite the front teeth, and make it more quietly and gently.

Contrast Method for /ʒ/

- *Place:* Contrast the tongue position of /ʒ/ with the tongue position of /i/.

- *Manner:* Contrast the continuance of /ʒ/ with the occlusion of /d/, or contrast the frication of /ʒ/ with the gliding manner of /j/.

- *Voice:* Contrast the voicing of /ʒ/ with the voiceless-ness of /ʃ/.

- *Resonance:* Contrast the oral quality of /ʒ/ with the nasal quality of /n/ or /ŋ/.

Phonological Strategies to Introduce /ʒ/

- *Key words:* Introduce /ʒ/ with a small set of functional key words, e.g., *beige*.

- *Reduplication:* Consider teaching early /ʒ/ in simple CVCV nonsense words, e.g., *ʒaʒa, ʒiʒi, ʒooʒoo*.

- *Diminutive:* Consider teaching early /ʒ/ in diminutives, e.g., *ʒiʒi* (for *fishie*).

- *Switch gears:* If /ʒ/ proves to be impossible to elicit, discontinue the practice and focus on another sound for a while.

• *Final position with epenthesis:* Consider allowing the client to use a stressed schwa in an extra syllable to stimulate final /ʒ/, e.g., be-ʒʌ (for beige).

• *Minimal pairs and larger sets in final position:* Use contrasting word pairs and larger sets to teach final /ʒ/, e.g., beige (for *bait*).

• *Reading and spelling:* Teach this phoneme as part of the client's reading and spelling program.

• *Language arts:* Teach this phoneme through stories, songs, jingles, jokes, rhymes, plays, and other material in the language arts program.

Solutions to Specific Problems on /ʒ/

• *Weak /ʒ/:* Teach the client to make the sound sharper by pushing harder up toward the palate, or by blowing a little harder.

• *Lack of frication on /ʒ/:* Teach him to make /i/ and push the tongue a little higher.

• *Stopping:* Teach him to "keep the air going."

• *Nasal emission on /ʒ/:* Use methods to control resonance.

• *Nasal substitution for /ʒ/:* Use methods to control resonance.

• *Inhalation on /ʒ/:* Develop correct breath support.

• *Tongue shifts to one side on /ʒ/:* Develop oral stability.

• *Tongue protrudes (frontal lisp):* Establish oral stability.

• *Lateral emission of air (lateral lisp):* Build the phoneme off of /i/. Have the client prolong /i/ with and big smile and exaggeration, then hold this sound and bite the molars together, then prolong that sound and round the lips.

/tʃ/

Multisensory Stimulation for /tʃ/

• *Auditory stimulation:* Model, amplify, repeat, prolong, and bombard with this phoneme. Use other methods to make it salient.

• *Auditory feedback:* Direct the client's production back to his ear with a tube or other tool. Imitate the client's sound.

• *Cues:* Use cues to pique the client's interest in this phoneme and to facilitate its concept.

• *Visual feedback to understand tongue protrusion:* Imitate the client's correct and incorrect productions and watch each other during simultaneous productions.

• *Visual feedback to understand airflow on /tʃ/:* Produce /tʃ/ against a mirror or window and observe the fog it produces.

• *Verbal:* Use vocabulary the client can understand to describe the respiration, phonation, resonation, and articulation characteristics of this phoneme.

• *Mark the target to develop place for /ʃ/:* Touch the horseshoe-shaped margins of the tongue and the sides of the palate prior to production.

• *Aid tongue grooving:* Use methods to develop a wide tongue groove.

• *Jaw stability:* Make sure the jaw is in a high position.

Association Method for /tʃ/

• *Place:* Help the client learn /tʃ/ by recognizing the similarities between it and any of the other lingua-palatal phonemes he can produce, especially /ʃ/.

• *Manner:* Help the client learn /tʃ/ by recognizing the similarities between it and any of the other fricated sounds he can produce.

• *Voice:* Help the client learn /tʃ/ by recognizing the similarities between it and any of the other voiceless sounds he can produce.

Successive Approximations for /tʃ/

• *Build /tʃ/ off of /ʃ/:* Have the client prolong /ʃ/. Then have him lift and lower the tongue tip while prolonging /ʃ/.

• *Build /tʃ/ off of /dʒ/:* Have the client produce /dʒ/ and turn his voice off.

• *Build /tʃ/ off of /t/:* Have the client make a /t/ with long aspiration. Then tell him to keep the tongue tip elevated and his jaw high while he rounds his lips.

• *Build /tʃ/ off of /t/ and /ʒ/:* Have the client make /t/ and slide into /ʒ/, then have him whisper this sequence, then have him round his lips.

Contrasting Method for /tʃ/

• *Place:* Contrast the tongue position of /tʃ/ with the tongue position of /ʃ/.

- *Manner:* Contrast the occlusion of /tʃ/ with the continuance of /ʃ/, or contrast the frication of /tʃ/ with the gliding manner of /j/.

- *Voice:* Contrast the voiceless-ness of /tʃ/ with the voicing of /dʒ/.

- *Resonance:* Contrast the oral quality of /tʃ/ with the nasal quality of /n/ or /ŋ/.

Phonological Strategies to Introduce /tʃ/

- *Key words:* Introduce /tʃ/ with a small set of functional key words, e.g., *choo-choo, chew, ouch, ouchie, itchy.*

- *Reduplication:* Consider teaching early /tʃ/ in words with reduplicated CVCV structure, e.g., *choo-choo.*

- *Diminutive:* Consider teaching early /tʃ/ in diminutives, e.g., *ouchie, itchy.*

- *CV words:* Consider teaching /tʃ/ in the initial position early by using CV words, e.g., *chew, Cho.*

- *Switch gears:* If /tʃ/ proves to be impossible to elicit, discontinue the practice and focus on another sound for a while.

- *Early final /tʃ/ words:* Consider introducing /tʃ/ in the final position first, e.g., *ouch, itch, match, couch.*

- *Final position with epenthesis:* Consider allowing the client to use a stressed schwa in an extra syllable to stimulate final /tʃ/, e.g., *kau-tʃʌ* (for *couch*).

- *Minimal pairs and larger sets in initial position:* Use contrasting word pairs and larger sets to teach initial /tʃ/, e.g., *chew, shoe, two, coo.*

- *Minimal pairs and larger sets in final position:* Use contrasting word pairs and larger sets to teach final /tʃ/, e.g., *ouch/out, pitch/pit.*

- *Reading and spelling:* Teach this phoneme as part of the client's reading and spelling program.

- *Language arts:* Teach this phoneme through stories, songs, jingles, jokes, rhymes, plays, and other material in the language arts program.

Solutions to Specific Problems on /tʃ/

- *Weak /tʃ/:* Teach the client to make the sound sharper by pushing harder up toward the palate, or by blowing a little harder. Make sure the jaw is high.

- *Lack of frication on /tʃ/:* Teach him to exhale more air. Make sure the jaw is high.

- *Nasal emission on /tʃ/:* Use methods to control resonance.

- *Nasal emission or substitution on /tʃ/:* Use methods to control resonance.

- *Inhalation on /tʃ/:* Develop correct breath support.

- *Tongue shifts to one side on /tʃ/:* Develop oral stability.

- *Tongue protrudes (frontal lisp):* Establish oral stability.

- *Lateral emission of air (lateral lisp):* Build the phoneme off of /ʃ/ which is built upon /i/. Have the client produce /i/ and then pant through this position, then teach him to round the lips as he pants through this position. Finally, teach him to lift the tip and stop the air several times as he is prolonging that sound. Make sure the jaw is high.

/dʒ/

Multisensory Stimulation /dʒ/

- *Auditory stimulation:* Model, amplify, repeat, prolong, and bombard with this phoneme. Use other methods to make it salient.

- *Auditory feedback:* Direct the client's production back to his ear with a tube or other tool. Imitate the client's sound.

- *Cues:* Use cues to pique the client's interest in this phoneme and to facilitate its concept.

- *Visual feedback to understand tongue protrusion:* Imitate the client's correct and incorrect productions and watch each other during simultaneous productions. Develop the oral percept.

- *Visual feedback to understand airflow on /dʒ/:* Produce /dʒ/ against a mirror or window and observe the fog it produces.

- *Verbal:* Use vocabulary the client can understand to describe the respiration, phonation, resonation, and articulation characteristics of this phoneme.

- *Mark the target to develop place for /dʒ/:* Touch the horseshoe-shaped margins of the tongue and the sides of the palate prior to production.

- *Tongue stability:* Develop back-lateral tongue stability.

- *Jaw stability:* Make sure the jaw is in a high position.

Association Method for /dʒ/

- *Place:* Help the client learn /dʒ/ by recognizing the similarities between it and any of the other lingua-palatal and lingua-alveolar phonemes he can produce, especially /z/, /d/, and /ʒ/.

- *Manner:* Help the client learn /dʒ/ by recognizing the similarities between it and any of the other fricated sounds he can produce.

- *Voice:* Help the client learn /dʒ/ by recognizing the similarities between it and any of the other voiced sounds he can produce.

Successive Approximations for /dʒ/

- *Build /dʒ/ off of /tʃ/:* Have the client produce /tʃ/ and turn his voice on.

- *Build /dʒ/ off of /d/:* Have the client make a /d/ with long aspiration, then tell him to keep the tongue tip elevated and his jaw high while he rounds his lips.

- *Build /dʒ/ off of /d/ and /ʒ/:* Have the client make /d/ and slide into /ʒ/, then have him make his tongue linger against the palate and round his lips while he produces this sequence.

Contrasting Method for /dʒ/

- *Place:* Contrast the tongue position of /dʒ/ with the tongue position of /ʒ/.

- *Manner:* Contrast the occlusion of /dʒ/ with the continuance of /ʒ/, or contrast the frication of /dʒ/ with the gliding manner of /j/.

- *Voice:* Contrast the voicing of /dʒ/ with the voiceless-ness of /tʃ/.

- *Resonance:* Contrast the oral quality of /dʒ/ with the nasal quality of /n/ or /ŋ/.

Phonological Strategies to Introduce /dʒ/

- *Key words:* Introduce /dʒ/ with a small set of functional key words.

- *Reduplication:* Consider teaching early /dʒ/ in words with reduplicated CVCV structure, e.g., *Jo-Jo.*

- *Diminutive:* Consider teaching early /dʒ/ in diminutives, e.g., *piʒi* (for *pigeon*).

- *CV words:* Consider teaching /dʒ/ in the initial position early by using CV words, e.g., *Joe, gee.*

- *Switch gears:* If /dʒ/ proves to be impossible to elicit, discontinue the practice and focus on another sound for a while.

- *Early final /dʒ/ words:* Consider introducing /dʒ/ in the final position first, e.g., *badge, Madge, Midge, budge.*

- *Final position with epenthesis:* Consider allowing the client to use a stressed schwa in an extra syllable to stimulate final /dʒ/, e.g., *bædʒʌ* (for *badge*).

- *Minimal pairs and larger sets in initial position:* Use contrasting word pairs and larger sets to teach initial /dʒ/, e.g., *jump, pump, dump, bump.*

- *Minimal pairs and larger sets in final position:* Use contrasting word pairs and larger sets to teach final /dʒ/, e.g., *badge/bad, budge/bud.*

- *Reading and spelling:* Teach this phoneme as part of the client's reading and spelling program.

- *Language arts:* Teach this phoneme through stories, songs, jingles, jokes, rhymes, plays, and other material in the language arts program.

Solutions to Specific Problems on /dʒ/

- *Weak /dʒ/:* Teach the client to make the sound sharper by pushing harder up toward the palate, or by blowing a little harder. Make sure the jaw is high.

- *Lack of frication on /dʒ/:* Teach him to keep the tongue up high. Make sure the jaw is high.

- *Nasal emission or substitution on /dʒ/:* Use methods to control resonance.

- *Inhalation on /dʒ/:* Develop correct breath support.

- *Tongue shifts to one side on /dʒ/:* Develop oral stability.

- *Tongue protrudes (frontal lisp):* Establish oral stability.

- *Lateral emission of air (lateral lisp):* Build the phoneme off of /ʃ/ which is built upon /i/. Have the client produce /i/, then teach him to round the lips as he prolongs the sound. Finally, teach him to lift the tip and stop the air several times as he is prolonging that sound. Make sure the jaw is high.

/h/

Multisensory Stimulation for /h/

- *Auditory stimulation:* Model, amplify, repeat, prolong, and bombard with this phoneme.

- *Auditory feedback:* Direct the client's production back to his ear with a tube or other tool. Imitate the client's sound.

- *Cues:* Use cues to pique the client's interest in this phoneme and to facilitate its concept.

- *Visual feedback to understand tongue protrusion:* Imitate the client's correct and incorrect productions and watch each other during simultaneous productions.

- *Visual feedback to understand airflow on /tʃ/:* Produce /h/ against a mirror or window and observe the fog it produces.

- *Verbal:* Use vocabulary the client can understand to describe the respiration, phonation, resonation, and articulation characteristics of this phoneme.

Association Method for /h/

- *Place:* Help the client learn /h/ by recognizing the similarities between it and /ɑ/.

- *Manner:* Help the client learn /h/ by recognizing the similarities between it and the glottal stop.

- *Voice:* Help the client learn /h/ by recognizing the similarities between it and any of the other voiceless sounds he can produce.

Successive Approximations for /h/

- *Build /h/ off of /ɑ/:* Have the client prolong /ɑ/ and turn his voice off.

- *Build /h/ off of any other voiceless fricative:* Have the client produce any voiceless fricative and open his mouth farther.

Contrasting Method for /h/

- *Place:* Contrast the open mouth position of /h/ with the closed mouth position of /p/.

- *Manner:* Contrast the continuance of /h/ with the occlusion of the glottal stop.

- *Voice:* Contrast the voiceless-ness of /h/ with the voicing of /ɑ/.

- *Resonance:* Contrast the oral quality of /h/ with the nasal quality of /m/, /n/ or /ŋ/.

Phonological Strategies to Introduce /h/

- *Key words:* Introduce /h/ with a small set of functional key words, e.g., *hi, house, ho-hum, he, hot, hʌ?* (for *huh?*).

- *Reduplication:* Consider teaching early /h/ in words with reduplicated CVs, e.g., *ho-ho-ho, he-he-he* (laughter).

- *Diminutive:* Consider teaching early /h/ in diminutives, e.g., *horsie.*

- *CV words:* Consider teaching /h/ in the initial position early by using CV words, e.g., *he, hʌ?* (for *huh?*).

- *Switch gears:* If /h/ proves to be impossible to elicit, discontinue the practice and focus on another sound for a while.

- *Minimal pairs and larger sets in initial position:* Use contrasting word pairs and larger sets to teach initial /h/, e.g., *hot, lot, pot, cot.*

- *Reading and spelling:* Teach this phoneme as part of the client's reading and spelling program.

- *Language arts:* Teach this phoneme through stories, songs, jingles, jokes, rhymes, plays, and other material in the language arts program.

Solutions to Specific Problems on /h/

- *Weak /h/:* Teach the client to exhale with more strength.

- *Nasal emission or substitution on /h/:* Use methods to control resonance.

- *Inhalation on /h/:* Develop correct breath support.

- *Glottal stop on /h/:* Tell the client to make the sound softly and gently and to keep the air going.

SUMMARY

This chapter has discussed the fricated consonants /θ/, /ð/, /f/, /v/, /s/, /z/, /ʃ/, /ʒ/, /tʃ/, /dʒ/, and /h/. It summarized how these consonants are produced and catalogued a wide variety of methods to stimulate the production of these sounds.

26

Low Cognition & Intelligibility

Guidance from studies of emerging language and phonology

"The most elementary requisite of good speech form — and there is little disagreement about this — is intelligibility."

– Carrell & Tiffany, 1960

This final chapter discusses clients with motor speech disorders who cannot attain a mature phonological system in their lifetimes because they also have significant cognitive impairment. Clients with low cognitive skills often have poor auditory processing and they may do little self-monitoring and/or self-correcting. They have limitations on their comprehension of language and therefore, they may have difficulty understanding concepts that could help their speech change, such as concepts like same/different, better/worse, or old/new. They may also have difficulty understanding simple directions such as "Put your lips together" or "Make it with two syllables" or "Remember to lift up the back of your tongue." Factors such as these can cause significant restrictions in the ability to improve phonemes and phonological processes. These clients can often get "stuck" at speech production plateaus that can last for years, and this can give the impression that the client is not changing. However, changes can be made and improvements can occur if the cognitive deficit is taken into account and problems of intelligibility are addressed in unique ways.

The present author has worked with clients with low cognitive functioning for 39 years and has found that, although change is slow, there is purpose to this work and changes can be made. This chapter presents her perspective on developing better expressive speech in this population. These ideas are rooted in research spanning three areas: cognitive development, early patterns of phonological development, and the development of imitation skills. No proof that these methods are effective can be offered other than the present author's clinical experiences, therefore, it is suggested that the reader view this chapter as practical advice passed from one therapist to another. The effectiveness of this approach comes down to the individual client. The question each therapist must ask regarding the client is: *Are these ideas helping my client become more intelligible to an increasingly wider audience?*

BACKGROUND

Children with cognitive deficit often respond differently than children whose cognition is in the average range. These clients often have difficulty learning, generalizing, and retaining new speech skills within the language context. As an example, the average child usually learns to produce /b/ quickly and easily during the babbling stage and he generalizes this sound to his first words almost immediately; he seldom "unlearns" his production of /b/ as vocabulary and grammatical skills expand. Some children with cognitive deficit perform in the opposite way: The emergence of any one phoneme can be very slow,

Clients with cognitive impairment bring unique challenges to the work of speech remediation.

phonemes may not generalize from babbling to words or from one word to another, and phonemes that have been acquired may be there one day and gone the next.

Smith and Oller (1981) demonstrated that children with Down syndrome had similar pre-speech phonological patterns as their normally-developing peers up through 15 months of age but that the babbling stage of the children with Down syndrome lasted longer and word productions emerged later. One might surmise that this is due to the cognitive dysfunction; cognitive dysfunction may allow the automatic motor skills of babbling to emerge on time but it may prevent the child from using these skills in meaningful ways. Once language does emerge, children with cognitive deficit "have difficulty relating new experiences to past learning" (Marshall & Hegrenes, 1972, p. 131) in ways that affect phonological skill acquisition.

A recent summary of pertinent literature on clients with cognitive impairment revealed a consistent high correlation between very low intelligence and severe articulation disorder:

> "Within normal limits, intelligence does not appear to be related to articulation, but when intelligence is below normal, it certainly is" (Pena-Brooks & Hegde, 2000, p. 195).

Working with clients who have limited cognitive skill can be terribly discouraging to the speech-language pathologist who aims for perfect speech. School administrators and insurance companies may not recognize that speech-language therapy is of any benefit to this population because minimal progress can be shown. There has even been some recent discussion that SLPs should not work on expressive speech in clients with cognitive impairment because no change can be expected.

Is this true? Does the stimulation of speech serve no purpose in the treatment of clients with severe cognitive impairment? What is the purpose of articulation and phonological therapy for these clients? Why should an SLP see children whose expressive speech cannot be thoroughly "fixed" because of low cognition? What skills could be targeted and how long should one persevere in training? How does an SLP even know if the client is improving?

Terminology

One of the problems therapists have always faced is what to call this population of clients. For the purposes of this manual, the phrases *cognitive impairment, cognitive disorder, cognitive disability, cognitive dysfunction, cognitive level,* and *low cognitive skills* will be used to set this group apart from others. These terms have been selected to differentiate these clients from those who have general *developmental delay.* This chapter is not about clients who simply are delayed in development. This chapter is about clients with impaired cognitive functioning who may also be delayed in development as a result; these are clients who will not reach statistically average intelligence in their lifetimes.

Cognitive level is probably the most fundamental element of goal setting in speech and language therapy. The cognitive level helps therapists understand what they are trying to accomplish. In fact, one could even say that it is impossible to identify the purpose of a client's speech training without an idea of his intellectual capabilities.

It is recognized that there is some danger in identifying a client as having a certain intellectual level because it may be a false measure and it may limit expectations for the child. However, it is equally important that the team speech-language pathologist have a general working knowledge of a client's overall intellectual capacity in order to make the work pertinent for him. Cognitive level plays an enormous role in determining the goals, objectives, methods, procedures, and expectations of treatment. It also plays a role in determining how much therapy a child actually needs. In short, the cognitive level informs the SLP about what she is doing with the client in the first place.

ALTERNATIVE SPEECH TESTING

Therapy begins with assessment, and children with severe cognitive dysfunction often do very poorly on standardized tests. Perhaps the biggest problem one faces when assessing articulation and phonology is that the word on the test may not be in the client's expressive vocabulary. One cannot test a child's production of final /s/ on the word "house," for example, if the child does not say "house" in the first place. Therapists need a better way to test speech production in these clients. They need a way to obtain a full inventory of the client's expressive speech skills without using formal tests (or in addition to them). There are various ways to do this that together give therapists a pretty good idea of the client's expressive speech capability. The following ideas are suggested.

Use Existing Words

Abandon formal articulation testing and use words from the client's existing word repertoire. Write down each word the client can say in standard orthography and in phonetic transcription. Use diacritic marks to note distortions and make notes on the client's productions.

> "Production is best examined in terms of what a client does do as well as can do... by observing a client's spontaneous communication behavior" (Owings & Guyette, 1982, p. 202).

Map the Vowels

Obtain a full inventory of all the vowels the client can say. Draw a vowel quadrilateral and circle all the vowels the client is using. Even if the client uses the wrong vowel in a word, record that he can say that vowel. For example, if the target word is *more*, and the client says /mʌ/, record that he can say /ʌ/.

Map the Diphthongs

Obtain a full inventory of all the diphthongs the client can say. Make a list of the diphthongs and circle the ones he is using. Even if the client uses the wrong diphthong in a word, record that he can say it. Listen very carefully to these and circle only the diphthongs the client is saying with two unique vowel sounds. Transcribe how the client is saying each diphthong.

Map the Consonants

Obtain a full inventory of all the consonants the client says spontaneously. List all the stops, nasals, glides, fricatives, and affricates, and circle the ones that are being used. Even if the client uses the wrong consonant in a word, record that he can say that consonant. For example, if the target is *boat*, and the client says /do/, record that he can say /d/ in the initial position.

Map the Distinctive Features

List all the distinctive features and check off the ones the child is using. Even if the client pronounces a word incorrectly, use it to record the distinctive features he has acquired. For example, if the target word is *shoe*, and the client says /su/, record that he is using the strident feature.

Map the Syllable Shapes

Make a list of all potential syllable shapes and circle the ones the client is using. Even if the client says a word incorrectly, use it to note the types of syllable shapes he is using. For example, if the target word is *stop* and he says /tɑ/, use it to record that the client can produce a CV. As another example, if the target is *crocodile* and the client says /tɑtɑ/, use it to record that he can produce words in a CVCV pattern.

Map the Phonological Error Patterns

Use the words the client says and make a list of the deviant phonological patterns that are present. For example, if the target is *boat*, and the clients says /bo/, record that he uses *final consonant deletion*.

KEYS TO TREATMENT

Our discussion of treatment begins with six proposed keys to treatment: use the existing phonological skill set, throw out the norms, combine means of expression, develop phoneme schemas, employ real words, and recognize that cognitive impairment is not apraxia.

Clients with cognitive impairment require an individual plan.

Use the Existing Phonological Skill Set

The first key to treatment proposed in this manual is to tailor therapy toward the client's existing phonological skill set. According to a summary of the literature by Vihman (2004a, 2004b), research has shown that the bulk of phonological development takes place by three years of age in average children, but some clients with very severe cognitive dysfunction do not make it past this range. Therefore, instead of trying to help these clients get past the phonological patterns of early childhood, therapy hours might be better spent by teaching these clients how to use those early patterns.

For example, returning to phoneme /b/: Once a child with normal cognition learns to make a /b/, his therapist will typically teach him to say the phoneme in a few key words. Generalization to any and all /b/-words will be expected to occur automatically within a relatively short period of time.

A child with a serious cognitive deficit may move much more slowly and generalization may never occur. Once the child learns /b/, the therapist may spend weeks, months, and even years teaching him to use /b/ in a gradually increasing set of specific vocabulary words. The client may need to learn all /b/ words individually. This may seem like a daunting and impossible task considering how many /b/-words there are in the language, but children with significant cognitive deficit will not need to say every potential /b/-word; the client's limitations in cognition will also restrict the number of different words he needs to say — he may need to say only a few /b/-words in his lifetime. Teaching the client to say the /b/-words that are important and most functional to him comprises a task that is achievable.

Throw Out the Norms

The second proposed key to treatment is to recognize that while normative studies are useful ways to obtain an overview of speech development in average children, such statistics do not reveal the way in which individual children with cognitive impairment develop their phonemes or phonological patterns. Each child with a severe cognitive impairment seems to learn to speak in his own way regardless of what the developmental trends indicate. The present author's experience is that these clients blaze their own trails through the jungle of phoneme acquisition and one often cannot predict the order in which phonemes will emerge.

The case of Michael illustrates this point. Michael was four years of age when the present author began to work with him. He carried a diagnosis of cognitive impairment and muscular dystrophy (therefore, dysarthria). At the age of four years and six months, Michael functioned more like a two-year-old. He spoke in 2–3 word utterances but was almost completely unintelligible; he spoke very quietly with distorted vowels and he produced no consonants.

Michael's expressive language grew and his vowels improved well enough that he became highly intelligible within two years, but his first consonant did not emerge until he had been in treatment for three years. The first consonant that came along was completely unexpected and untargeted: It was /r/ at the end of the word *car!* The second consonant Michael acquired that year was /ŋ/, the third was /g/, and the fourth was /k/.

Contrary to most developmental trends, Michael was learning [+Back] sounds at the ends of words first. The interesting thing about this case is that the present author also worked with this child's younger brother who presented an almost identical cognitive and neuromuscular profile. However, this second child's first consonant was /θ/ that he acquired at the beginning of the words *this, that, these,* and *those!*

The developmental norms are based on normal or typical development and these clients do not fall within that category. Further, a cognitive deficit often is compounded by other medical, structural, neuromuscular, and developmental factors. All of these things affect both the rate and the organization of phonological skill acquisition, therefore, rigid rules about the sequence of phoneme training often do not apply in these cases. Try all phonemes periodically and work on those for which the client is most stimulable.

Combine Means of Expression

The third proposed key to treatment is to recognize that many of these children will use some combination of oral and non-oral communication systems. A combination of words, sounds, gestures, signs, pictures, objects, and computerized communication devices is common. There is no reason to believe that any of these other procedures will interfere with the development of spoken speech unless the adults with whom the child works design it that way, i.e., if they only pay attention to the non-verbal system and ignore the child's vocalizations.

Many of these children will use a variety of communication modes. For example, a child might be able to say *momma*, but then he might nod his head for *yes*, say /n/ for *no*, use the standard sign for *dog*, say "meow" for *cat*, use a natural gesture for *come here*, ask to ride his bike by pointing

to a picture on a board, and use his talking software to answer questions in classroom lessons.

It is recommended that these children be made to "say it" and "show it" each time they communicate, if possible. That way the client will be saying something for each word or idea being expressed with his non-verbal system. These utterances may be unintelligible to the listener but they will lay groundwork for the concept that *one always speaks when one communicates*. The client needs to say something so that he continues to practice verbal speech even though others may understand him much better when he uses his alternative systems. His communication with the non-verbal system may be far superior to his verbal one, but his expressive speech skills may fall even further behind if he never has to talk at all.

Multisensory Stimulation

The fourth key to treatment is to recognize that instructions about phoneme productions usually must be given through multisensory stimulation. In other words, it probably will not be enough to tell the client to "Say bʌ." The client may need models, cues, tactile input, and many of the other methods that are discussed throughout this manual. Stimuli are presented in a variety of ways over many sessions until the client begins to comprehend the task and a schema for the phoneme, syllable, or word is developed. Multisensory stimulation and multiple levels of data input are faded over time as the client gains the phoneme and takes control over his own productions.

Employ Real Words

Cognitive input is more important than motor input for the client with cognitive dysfunction. Therefore, the client with cognitive deficit may perform better if real words are used to teach phonemes instead of babbling sequences. This is quite different from the client with apraxia, for example, who can usually benefit from systematic non-speech syllable training first. A decision to use words or non-words is an individual one tailored to the client at

Clients with cognitive deficit often use multiple means of communication.

hand. Therapists are cautioned not to spend too much time on babbling when work on functional words may be of more immediate benefit to the client.

Cognitive Impairment is Not Apraxia

It is important to recognize that cognitive impairment and apraxia are two very different things. A diagnosis of apraxia should not be assigned automatically to all non-verbal clients. Many problems in therapy can ensue when a cognitive impairment is ignored.

For example, one non-verbal girl came for evaluation when she was six years of age. Her former therapist had diagnosed her with apraxia but, after two years of treatment, she still had not said any words. The parents figured that they needed another opinion and/or perhaps a better therapist.

The new therapist recognized that the girl had cognitive abilities in the six- to seven-month range! As will be discussed below, a child who is functioning in this cognitive range should not be saying any words at all. The client may have had some signs of apraxia, but the biggest impediment to attaining verbal speech was that her cognitive skills were below the level at which language actually emerges.

For all clients in the population, a thorough differential diagnosis must be initiated so that the primary etiology is identified. Apraxia and cognitive deficit are two distinct disorders that require different approaches. One can debate whether five days per week of individual therapy will help the sensory processing and motor planning skills of a child with apraxia, but no amount of therapy will change the intellectual status of a client with a severe cognitive deficit. It is the present author's view that a client with low cognitive skills does not necessarily need more weekly sessions to fix his problems in expressive speech — he needs appropriate stimulation spaced over the course of his lifetime so that he can make the most of his existing skill set as it changes over time.

EXPECTATIONS BY COGNITIVE LEVEL

Appropriate treatment can be designed when a client's cognitive developmental level is known. Charles Van Riper recognized this: "Since learning and unlearning depend greatly upon intelligence, some estimate of this factor must always be made" (Van Riper, 1947, p. 47). Jean Piaget's work was very important in this regard because he identified the developmental milestones of intellectual growth (e.g., Ginsburg & Opper, 1969). His theories described the optimum capability of thought at given periods of time.

Following Piaget, therapists ask themselves what cognitive age the client expresses as he processes ideas,

information, and social situations, and as he engages in imitation routines. Does the child think like a six-month-old? A twelve-month-old? A two-year-old? If the cognitive level can be determined, this information helps therapists establish realistic expectations for expressive speech. Should the client be expected to say words? If so, how many, and how should he be expected to say them? Developmental data provides a guide for making these decisions.

The following provides general guidelines for setting goals in speech training at evolving cognitive levels. This information has been compiled from a variety of resources as named and from the present author's personal experiences. The reader will notice overlap between stages.

Cognition Under the 4-Month Level

Some clients have cognitive skills under the four-month level. This is the period in which babies begin to respond to speech: "In the baby's second and third month he begins to respond to human speech by smiling and vocalization" (Van Riper, 1947, p. 73). In terms of production, these babies make the *quasi-resonant nuclei* and they coo (Oller, 1978).

Clients whose cognition is functioning less than the four-month level should not be expected to say any words, but they should be expected to respond to speech and they should be expected to make some meaningless cooing-like

Jean Piaget defined the stages of intellectual development.

Piaget, born in 1896, was a Swiss philosopher, a natural scientist and the pioneer of the constructivist theory of knowing. He was a developmental theorist who is known for his work studying children and for his theories of cognitive development. In 1955, Piaget created the International Centre for Genetic Epistemology in Geneva, Switzerland, that he directed until 1980.

sounds.

One set of realistic goals for this client would be auditory in nature. The child might learn to stop his own activity when others speak to him ("body stilling") and he might be expected to attend to soft and soothing speech directed toward him, to orientate his gaze toward a communication partner, to show pleasure as he recognizes familiar voices, and to show signs of anticipating communication from others. These skills are a part of Piaget's *primary circular reactions* in the first stage of intellectual development called the *sensorimotor stage*. Mysak (1980) called these skills *true listening behavior.*

A second set of realistic goals would be expressive in nature. These might include that the child would show a curiosity about sound-making and that he would coo and make other sounds characteristic of the birth-to-four month period. This is not the type of speech-language therapy that needs to occur multiple times per week. The SLP might function in the role of consultant to this client, making sure that others are responding and stimulating the child in appropriate ways during the course of everyday activities.

Cognition at the 4- to 8-Month Level

Some speech-language clients function in the 4–8 month level. According to the summary by Vihman (2004a), research indicates that babies begin to respond to specific words by 4–8 months of age. At five months of age, they begin to produce sound at the same time adults produce sound in a pattern. This was called *synchronistic vocalizations* by Piaget and *socialized vocalizations* by Van Riper.

A client whose cognition functions at 4–8 months of age, therefore, should still not be expected to say any words, but he should be expected to respond appropriately to specific words and he should be expected to make general vocalizations in accord with others. Realistic goals and activities can be based on this concept: The client can be taught to participate in communication in general ways or to "go along with the crowd," so to speak.

Goals at this cognitive level may be to get the client to vocalize simultaneously with others by producing similar tones and emotional expressions. The client might be expected to coo while others coo, to "sing" while others sing, to shout as others shout, to squeal as others squeal, to laugh while others laugh, and even to cry when others cry or pretend to cry. Team members should stimulate these behaviors at various appropriate times throughout the day. Regular weekly or monthly sessions in which the SLP models and monitors these skills will be valuable.

Cognition at the 5- to 10-Month Level

Some speech-language clients function in the 5–10 month level. According to Vihman (2004a), research indicates that children show comprehension of words by 5–10 months of age but they generally do not say words. For example, a baby in this age range may orient to a cat in the room when someone says, "Kitty-kitty-kitty. Where's the kitty-cat?" But he will not attempt to say any of these words.

In terms of expression, during this period, babies begin to babble, to coo with identifiable inflection patterns, to laugh, and to make raspberries. Children at this stage also begin to take turns back and forth with others who make the child's sounds. Piaget called this *mutual imitation,* about which Van Riper wrote: "When the process of speech imitation is studied, we discover that it begins when the parents start to imitate the child" (Van Riper, 1947, p. 78).

Speech goals for clients whose cognition is at the 5–10 month level should be based upon these skills. These clients should be expected to respond in appropriate nonverbal ways to a core set of vocabulary words, to babble with some consistency, and to make sounds back and forth with others in playful routines. They should not be expected to imitate phonemes exactly and they should not be expected to practice words. Word productions can be encouraged, however, because the child is on that threshold.

Cognition at the 10- to 14-Month Level

Some speech-language clients function in the 10–14 month level, which is a time when average children generally begin to speak their first words: "The baby suddenly becomes a very human being. He learns to walk and to talk and to feed himself, three of the most fundamental of all human functions" (Van Riper, 1947, p. 76). Clients whose cognitive skills have reached the 10–14 month level should be expected to begin to say some words but not to control them. These words seem to "pop out" spontaneously when the child is in the mood and circumstances are right. In other words, the child should be expected to say words but he should not be expected to say them on demand.

A realistic goal might be to establish a few spoken words. Therapy circumstances need to be set to give the child ample opportunity to speak the words freely and without pressure. For example, it might not work to hold up a picture card of a boat and tell the child, "Say, *boat.*" A client at this cognitive level will usually be silent to this command more often than he is compliant. Therefore, therapists must find a strategy that engages the child's curiosity and interest.

For example, a toy boat might be hidden and the child might be encouraged to call for it while searching, or the boat might be placed on a high shelf and the child might be encouraged to say the word in order to get the adult to retrieve it for him. At this intellectual level the child will be internally driven to say a word because circumstances solicit the mood or desire to do so, not because someone wants him to say it.

Some time during this period, children begin to say their words on demand in a process Piaget called *spontaneous imitation within repertoire.* The adult models a word that the child already can say, and the child can repeat it back.

	TABLE 15 — Activities & Dialogues to Encourage Pop-Out Words	
Type	Activity	Sample Dialogue Turns (Target Word: *Car*)
Question-Answer-Answer	Question the name of an item, and give the answer. Expect the child to name the item.	Adult: What's this? *Car?* Child: Car.
Fill in the Blank	Make a statement and leave off the final word.	Adult: I see a... Child: Car!
Fill in the Sequence	Point to and name several items in a row, but do not name the final item. Create a pregnant pause for the child to fill with the target word.	Adult: Truck... Boat... Bike... Child: Car!
Challenge	Dare the child to say the word.	Adult: I bet you can't say *car.* Child: Car!
Reverse Psychology	Tell the child you do not want him to say the word you actually want him to say.	Adult: Please don't say *car.* Child: Car!
Amazement	Act amazed that the child actually might say the target word again.	Adult: You're not going to say *car* again, are you? Child: Car!
Awe	Act in awe that the child can say the target word, and leave a pregnant pause for him to do so.	Adult: I can't believe that you can say *car*... Child: Car!
Denial	Insist that the item is not what the child claims it to be.	Adult: This is not a car. No way! This is a boat! Child: Car!

Table continues next page...

This is a good time to introduce practice cards and the best way to do this is to make several cards for the same word.

For example, if the only word the client can say is *car*, then make five cards for this word. That way the client is being taught how to repeat his word. The repetition is the goal at this cognitive level. He is learning to imitate himself and this becomes a foundation for learning to imitate others. New vocabulary words can be stimulated too, but no assurances can be made that the child will say them on demand. Instead of assigning these refusals to personality deficiencies such as stubbornness or noncooperation, adults must realize that this is a reflection of the client's stage of cognitive development which can be played with in order to encourage vocalization.

Therapists should continue to design activities in which there are ample opportunities for new words to pop out, followed immediately by attempts to get the child to repeat the words. The present author calls them *pop-out words* (Marshalla, 2001a), and the therapy is designed to play with these words as they pop out. Table 15 on this and the next page summarizes various ways dialogues can occur in order to take advantage of a client's pop-out words. These are sample pragmatic situations that might be used to broaden the client's opportunity to say his words in a pop-out fashion. In this example, the child already knows what a car is and he already has been heard to say *car* on occasion.

Cognition at the 14- to 18-Month Level

Some speech-language clients function in the 14–18 month level. Children typically expand their spoken vocabulary from one word to a few dozen words by 18 months of age. A client whose cognition has reached the

TABLE 15 — Activities & Dialogues to Encourage Pop-Out Words

Type	Activity	Sample Dialogue Turns (Target Word: *Car*)
Act Stupid	Act like you are unsure about the item's name.	Adult: Are you sure? Are you sure this is a car? Really? Child: Car!
Say It Again	Tell the child to say the word again.	Child: Car. Adult: Say it again. Child: Car.
Alter the Prosody	Tell the child to say the word again with a change in prosody.	Child: Car. Adult: Say it big! Say CAR! Child: CAR!!
Calling	Call out the target word while searching for the item.	Adult: Car! Car!! Car!!! Child: Car! Car!!
Discovery	Find a hidden car.	Adult: Where is it? Car! Where are you, car? Car! Child (finds car): Car!
Analysis	Draw a picture of a car bit-by-bit so that the act of drawing gradually reveals what it is.	Adult: Here's a circle... I wonder what this will be. Here's another circle... Here's a roof... Maybe it's a house... Oh-oh, here's a door... Here's a steering wheel... Child: Car!

14–18 month level, therefore, can be expected to say a certain core set of vocabulary words. The child can also be expected to say new words on demand in the process Piaget called *spontaneous imitation of new repertoire*. Now the client can be expected to imitate brand-new words, however, mood and drive still play a large role in word imitation in this period. The client will say a new word because something about the circumstances causes him to take notice of the word and desire to say it — the word becomes salient for him. Clients whose cognition has reached the 14–18 month level can be expected to repeat or practice their words if the mood strikes them. Therapy is about finding and utilizing the moods that drive him to repeat words.

Cognition at the 18- to 24-Month Level

Some speech-language clients function in the 18–24 month level. Research shows that a child's expressive vocabulary surpasses 50 words in this period. These children also begin to string words together in a process called *successive single-word utterances*. In this stage, children make many production errors and they *jargon*. Van Riper spoke of the difference between jargon and vocal play: "Jargon is his vocal response to a vocal world. Vocal play is his private rehearsal" (Van Riper, 1947, p. 83). Children at this stage also begin to use 2–3 word combinations like *Uh-oh mommy* and *Doggie eat*.

Clients at this cognitive level should be expected to say words and to practice words when the approach is playful, but their words should be produced with the phonological simplification patterns described below. Piaget said that children in this stage are mostly interested in engaging in new behavior and in novel circumstances. They experiment and follow their curiosity but they don't stick with any one thing for too long. Therefore, therapy should be mostly about saying all kinds of new sounds and words, and less about repetition or drill on particular sounds or words. The novelty is what attracts the child at this stage; a few repetitions are interesting but then they move on. Expecting the child to repeat more than a few times will be met with stubborn noncooperation. The child will seem very busy: "Extremely active, he seldom plays with any one object or activity very long" (Van Riper, 1947, p. 80). This rule applies to toys as well as to the repetition of sounds and words. If he needs to practice a word 15 times, for example, spread the imitations over time within the session. Ask him to say the word three times at five different moments during the session. Do this in a playful way by playing with the sounds and words.

Clients at this level should also be expected to jargon more frequently than they say particular words. They are pretending to talk, so pretend with them in order to get them to do more of it.

Cognition at the 24- to 36-Month Level

Some speech-language clients function in the 24–36 month level. Research shows that a child's expressive vocabulary reaches 250 or more words by the end of this period and morphemes make their appearance. Children at this age range have entered Piaget's second stage of intelligence in which symbolism is key. It is in this stage that children begin to form *mental images* or *schemes* for everything, including sounds and words.

Now the client can begin to focus on sound and word productions for their own sake and he will enjoy this focus. The child wants to know what various animals say, he wants to know the names of things, and he wants to know how to say certain words. He likes to hear people talk, and asks "Why?" many times in order to get them to do so. The child may be more interested in listening than in talking as he begins to comprehend many words by listening to songs, stories, and rhymes. Children whose cognition is in the 24–36 month level can be expected to say and practice many hundreds of words but they will use restricted phonological patterns.

Cognition Above the 36-Month Level

Research has demonstrated that above three years of age "the majority of simplifying phonological processes no longer apply regularly in most cases" (Vihman, 2004b, p. 119). Typical children in this age range now use over 350 words and they are speaking in sentences that adults who are unfamiliar with them can understand easily. These children tend to be less intelligible when producing very long utterances. Cluster reduction, syllable deletion, and problems with certain later-developing phonemes are common at this stage, including /θ/, /ð/, /r/, /ʃ/, /ʒ/, /tʃ/, and /dʒ/. Clients whose cognition has reached beyond the thirty-six-month level should be expected to say words, to practice words, and to improve phonological skill in ways that gradually stretch toward maturity.

METHODS

According to what is known about emerging phonology, it is the proposal of this manual that effective treatment for clients with severe cognitive impairment lies in developing intelligibility. According to Vihman (2004a), research reveals that the first 50–100 words a child speaks represent a phonological learning period in which phonological error patterns are expected. Most clients with severe cognitive impairment speak fewer than 100 words, therefore, one might expect much similarity between the utterances of these two groups. Treatment for clients with low cognition, therefore, becomes less about helping them move past these patterns (as one would do with almost every other type of client) and more about helping them learn how to use their immature patterns in optimum ways.

For example, if a client is able to say words only by reduplicating syllables then the child could be taught to say new words if they are produced with reduplicated syllables. The child might be taught to say "bʌ-bʌ" for *peanut butter* and "mʌ-mʌ" for *Mr. Moore*. This is no different than teaching a typical one-year-old child to say "mama" for *mother* or "bɑ-boh" for *bottle*. Instead of planning for the client to leave these patterns behind, one acknowledges that the pattern may be a fairly permanent part of the client's expressive speech sound repertoire and teaches accordingly.

Consider the case of a twelve-year-old boy with Down syndrome. Bryce's cognitive skills were at the 2–3 year level and he spoke in single words that were constructed of only one and two syllables. He was just beginning to use a few two-word combinations. He produced no three-word combinations and he made no words with three syllables.

Bryce's parents were concerned about his pronunciation of *banana* which he produced as /næ-nʌ/. It was this therapist's opinion that the family should continue to help the boy say the word with three syllables, but that it should not be a high priority. They had been working on this word for many months, and he could say it with three syllables if he imitated one syllable at a time after their model of one syllable at a time. But everything else about the boy's behavior indicated that two syllables was the best he could do for now. The boy's limited cognitive abilities even might have been preventing him from understanding that "bʌ…na…nʌ" even meant the same thing as "banana."

Instead of correcting him every time he said the word, it was this therapist's opinion that the family should be celebrating the word for the skills it reflected. His production of the word meant that he knew what the object was, he knew its name, he could say its name, he was willing to say its name, and he could do so with two reduplicating syllables. These things are worthy of celebration for a client whose cognitive skills are at the two-year level.

Some might argue that to help children speak with phonological simplifications like this is a way of teaching baby talk, and this can be a concern for some. However, the children being discussed in this chapter are not those who are simply behind or developmentally delayed; these are children who will never catch up to the cognitive abilities of their peers. They are "stuck" at a certain cognitive level and this puts restrictions on what they can do phonologically. This is not like the child who is developmentally delayed who can benefit from phonological awareness and production activities that help him gain new skills within a relatively short period of time; this is also not like children with motor speech disorders who can benefit from speech motor training through repeated syllable sequence training — the children being discussed here need a phonological system that will work for them despite their lifelong cognitive restrictions. These clients need help developing a phonological system that will allow their vocabulary to grow and their speech to become as intelligible as possible given their limitations. "These people, above all others, must have the way made smooth" (Blanton & Blanton, 1919, p. 149).

Teaching children with cognitive deficit to say words with simplified phonological patterns trains the speech motor system to respond the way it does in younger children, and, therefore, allows them to be as intelligible as is any toddler. Therapy encourages the client to speak as many words as possible with the phonological skills he has so that he can learn to say many more functional words and to use them with increasing numbers of communication partners. The present author likes to imagine that each of these children is wearing a sign that says:

"This is what I can do. If you teach me at my phonological skill level I will be able to say more words and I will love communicating with you. But if you try to correct everything I say, I will shut down and come to dislike you."

New and better phonemes are also encouraged. All the phoneme stimulation techniques described in this manual will be of benefit to facilitate sound production in the client with cognitive impairment. Trial and error and careful observation of what works for the client at hand is critical. Multisensory input and the systematic use of cues are standards of treatment. As noted above, more hours of immediate therapy may not necessarily be the solution. Instead, good therapy that is well considered and consistent is recommended as an ideal approach for the long haul. The reader is reminded that this represents only the present author's clinical view. The balance of this chapter presents treatment suggestions based upon this view.

Start with Protowords

Research reveals that many early words are produced in the form of *protowords*. Protowords are attempts at real words that do not have enough adult-like phonology to be assured that the child actually was trying to say the actual word. For example, a twelve-month-old child might see a dog and say /hidɑ/. He may be attempting to say *doggie* but the phonology is too far off to say with certainty. Research reveals that protowords are produced primarily with glottal stops, /h/, and stop consonants.

Application to Therapy

The fact that first words can emerge as protowords suggests that SLPs should accept whatever production a client makes when he is learning to say his first words,

and even when he begins to say new words. For example, if the target word is *shoe*, the client should be rewarded for speaking even if he says something as far-fetched as /digɑ/. The client is attempting to say the target but his phonology does not support it and his production makes listeners question the production: "Did he say *shoe?*" If the listener does not treat the protoword as a real word, the child receives no reward for his attempt, and he may cease to say the word. Treating the protoword as a real word gives it validity in the mind of the child, and this encourages him to say it again later.

Case Example

Cindy was a non-ambulatory five-year-old female with severe brain damage. Her school therapists were teaching her to use a non-oral communication system and Cindy was beginning to make sound for the first time. The parents wondered what they could do to encourage verbal speech. The therapist noticed that Cindy was producing rudimentary vocalizations (mostly quasi-resonant nuclei), but she also noted that the parents were not responding to these sounds in any kind of consistent way.

The therapist showed the parents how they could respond to each of the child's spontaneous utterances as if they were protowords. Within the first session Cindy began to make sounds purposefully to get her mother to turn a page in a book, and she made noises and to get her mom to make animal sounds. Cindy also attempted to imitate some of these animal sounds and to say animal names with her rudimentary vocalization. The parents were instructed to spend at least five minutes three times per day responding to everything that Cindy said as if she were saying words.

Cindy was seen again one month later, and the number of vocalizations she spontaneously produced increased from 4 in 10 minutes to nearly 50 in 10 minutes! Cindy's parents were teaching her to make protowords. These would become a firm foundation upon which the rest of her expressive speech and language skills could rest.

Begin Holistically

Research reveals that typically-developing children try to say first words as whole words rather than as parts. For example, when learning to say *banana*, most children do not try to say "bʌ" or one of the other syllables. Instead they try to say the whole word *banana*. They do this even though they can't produce a /b/ or an /n/ or three syllables in a row. These whole word attempts usually come out a little soft and sloppy. This process has been called the *holistic start* (Vihman & Velleman, 1989), which is described as the "gestalt-like match of child forms to adult models" (Vihman, 2004a). A *gestalt* is a pattern or organized whole that has specific properties that cannot be derived from the summation of its component parts; here, the child is attempting to say the organized whole of the word and not the individual parts of the word. Alexander Graham Bell noted this pattern of speech acquisition as far back as 1906:

> *"Mothers do not begin with elementary sounds and then combine them into syllables and words. The mother speaks whole sentences even to the infant in arms. The child listens and listens, until a model is established in the mind. Then the child commences to imitate, not elementary sounds, but whole words. Indeed, people grow up to adult life without ever having uttered elementary sounds [i.e., phonemes]"* (Bell, 1906, p. 113).

Application to Therapy

Many therapists like to stimulate multi-syllabic words by modeling the first sound or syllable. For example, a therapist might model "mmm" for *momma* or "bʌ" for *banana*. This approach is necessary for many clients. However, therapists should keep in mind that a client with a serious cognitive impairment may not understand that an individual phoneme or syllable abstracted from a target word has anything to do with the target word. The child may not comprehend how the part (the phoneme or syllable) is related to the whole (the word). Modeling the whole word ties the child's production more obviously to the word's meaning and to the narrative. Modeling the whole word also gives the client an opportunity to make his own holistic start for the word. Therapists should stimulate both the whole word and the part to determine which way is best for the child at hand.

Case Example

At four years of age, Jerome was saying about 10 words including *elephant*. Over the course of two years, Jerome's production of *elephant* changed from /ʌ/ to /e/, to /e nʌ/, to /de-nʌ/, to /e-ʌ-ɪ/, to /de-nʌ-dɪ/, and finally to /de-nʌ-dɪnt/. Jerome was attempting to say *elephant* the best way he could throughout the entire time. If he had been trained to say only one part of the word, and if only that one part had been reinforced during those two years, he never might have developed the whole word with its three syllables the way he did. Instead, the child's expressive phonology was allowed to bloom by reinforcing his own holistic productions of the word.

Teach CV Foundations

Research reveals that the CV is the syllable shape that dominates first words in normal development. The CV is called the *canonical* syllable, which means that it is acknowledged as the first official established syllable. The CV emerges in babbling sequences before first words are produced and most first words are a reflection of this early syllable shape. The CV syllable occurs in early words in several ways:

- The CV occurs in correct one-syllable words such as *go* or *me*.

- The CV occurs in phonologically simplified words such as /dæ/ for *that* or /kʊ/ for *cookie*.

- The CV is reduplicated in early two-syllable words like *mama* and *papa*.

- The CV occurs in early diminutives such as *doggie* and *kitty*.

- The CV occurs in simplified versions of longer and more complex words such as /gæ-ge-do/ for *alligator*.

Application to Therapy

The CV is probably the most important thing a client can learn in early speech development. Many new words can be taught to a child with severe cognitive dysfunction if the syllables of those words are simplified into this individual CV, or into sequences of CVs. For example, a client might be taught to produce *truck* as /dʌ/ and *popcorn* as /pa-pa/. This gives the client an opportunity to use these words before he is able to say them correctly, and it affords him a platform on which to practice a variety of words. CVs can continue to be used as word length increases. For example, the client might be taught to say *spaghetti* as /bʌ-ge-di/. CVs even can continue to be used as children develop phrases and early sentences; he could say the pre-sentence *that dog barking* as /dæ dɔ ba-di/. Broadening the client's applications of basic CV syllables allows him to develop words and word ordering while phonological skill remains seriously impaired.

Case Example

Sandra Rose was a five-year-old with cognitive deficit that caused her to function more like a three-year-old. She talked quite a bit but produced all words with CVs only. *Dog* was /dɔ/, *pigeon* was /pɪ/, and *crocodile* was /ka/. The CV syllable was used to expand her vocabulary and concepts. For example, she was taught her colors and shapes: /ba/ for *brown*, /pi/ for *pink*, /tʊ/ for *circle*, and /ta/ for *triangle*. This practice allowed Sandra Rose to participate

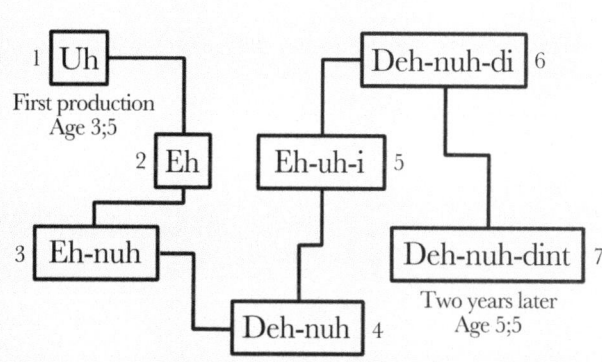

One client's productions of "elephant" over a two-year period reveal systematic patterns of syllable change.

in classroom activities before she could pronounce any of these words correctly.

Prioritize Vowels

Research shows that vowels are organized before consonants emerge (as discussed in Chapter 21 on the vowels) and that vowels are easier to perceive than consonants (Goodglass, 1973).

Application to Therapy

This means that teaching vowels may be more important to improving intelligibility than teaching consonants. For example, consider the client who pronounces *shoe* as /di/. It will be better to change the vowel and help him say /du/ than it would be to change the consonant and help him say /ʃi/.

Case Example

Mark was four years old. He had muscular dystrophy and cognitive skills in the two-year range. Mark spoke about 15 words one of which was *Dee*, which was the name of the building secretary. Mark called her /ʌ/. He first changed her name to /dʌ/, but the secretary still did not understand that he was saying her name. Then he was taught to call her /i/ and she got it. "He said my name!" exclaimed the secretary when she first heard it. This was despite the fact that he already had been saying it for several months. In other words, intelligibility did not change when the consonant was added, but it did improve when the vowel was straightened out, even though the consonant was dropped again.

Let Anterior Sounds Dominate

Research demonstrates that labial consonants dominate the CV syllables of early words. Oller (1981) studied the pre-speech vocalizations of typical infants and those with Down syndrome and found that, between 6 and 12 months of age, those with Down syndrome produced a substantially greater percentage of lingua-labial and bilabial trills than did the typical children. Many theories have been proposed to account for these occurrences. The present author's view is that this occurs because the jaw is still unstable and it moves in wide up-and-down patterns in both speech and feeding during the babbling and first word stages (see Chapter 11 on jaw mobility and Chapter 14 on oral stability). When the jaw's principle movement pattern is up-and-down, the lower lip bangs against the upper lip and upper teeth, and the front of the tongue bangs against the palate and teeth in the front. As long as an infant or one-year-old child is trying to speak with jaw instability — which he should be doing at this age — anterior sounds should dominate.

Application to Therapy

Therapists interested in helping a client's first consonants emerge in words often focus on the anterior consonants and they often do this by teaching the lip and tongue movements necessary to produce these phonemes. Instead, the focus of treatment should be placed on big up-and-down movements of the jaw. In other words, /b/, /p/, /m/, /w/, /t/, /d/, /n/, and /l/ emerge in CVs because the jaw begins to move up and down, not because the lips and tongue begin to move. More early consonants may be stimulated in the CV by getting the jaw to move instead of by getting the lips or tongue to move when a client has fewer than 50 words.

Case Example

Danny was a seven-year-old boy who produced no consonants other than /n/ and he made this sound in isolation with no vowel. Danny's cognitive skills were at the three-year level. He was trying to say many words, but everything came out as "Nnn." His therapists used moto-kinesthetics procedures to lower the jaw as Danny made his sound to help him say /n/+vowel which they counted as *no*. Next the therapist repeated the activity, this time moving the jaw down twice as Danny said *no-no*. Then they played a game: The therapist playfully asked Danny ridiculous questions to which he responded *no-no* each time. The questions got increasingly outrageous with time and Danny's productions of *no-no* got faster and faster. The therapist faded her assistance and Danny took over control of his up-and-down jaw movement. Danny's word was distorted because the vowel wasn't quite right, but moving the jaw was the first step to help him move forward from an isolated consonant to a basic reduplicated CV sequence that could be used as an intelligible word. The next step of therapy was to teach others how they could encourage Danny to say *no-no* many times every day.

Encourage Reduplication

Reduplication of phonemes or syllables is one of the most common patterns noted in the early words productions of typical children. For example, some one-year-olds say /dɔ-dɔ/ for *doggie* and /ti-ti/ for *kitty*. Reduplication of syllables allows children to practice the correct number of syllables in words and to sound like they are saying certain words before they can pronounce all the various phonemes or syllables of them.

Application to Therapy

Reduplication of sounds or syllables can be a strategy of therapy. New words can be taught in reduplicated patterns in order to establish them, and they can be improved upon later. For example, *butter* can be taught as /bʌ-bʌ/ to start.

Case Example

Bart was a six-year-old boy with cognitive skills at the 18- to 24-month level. He produced only three words at the beginning of the school year (*Bart, no,* and *bus*), and he was producing each word with three reduplicated CV syllables. He produced *Bart* as /bababa/, *no* as /nanana/, and *bus* as /bababa/.

After many frustrating months of no change, his therapist decided to teach him to say more words by allowing him to use his triple reduplicated CV pattern. By the end of two years, Bart could say two and three word phrases with this pattern. For example, when asked, "Who's ready for speech?" he responded by saying, "Me go speech" as /mimimi dododo bibibi/.

Intelligibility still was very low and only familiar listeners could understand him, but at least his expressive speech was changing and moving forward. Bart had to use basic signs and gestures along with each word to aid intelligibility. His teachers had been convinced that Bart wasn't really talking, but they finally understood that he was once they were trained to hear this very unusual reduplicated pattern. Having knowledge of his idiosyncratic pattern they then could use it to teach him many new words in the classroom.

Expect Syllable Deletion

Research reveals that the omission of syllables in longer words is very common in early word productions, for example, /efi/ for *elephant*. Producing words with missing syllables is one way that very young children allow themselves to make a holistic start of new words. According to Vihman (2004a), syllable deletion is common even in three-year-olds. Roberts et al. (2005) found that children with Down syndrome omit syllables in words. Syllables that tend to be deleted most often are the unstressed ones and those that occur before stressed syllables.

Application to Therapy

One can encourage the production of more advanced words by teaching words with purposefully deleted syllables. For example, one might teach the client to say /tɪ-ri/ for *cafeteria*, or to say /wɔ-dɪ/ for *Washington*. Teach all the adults who are involved with the child to listen for, to expect, and to reward these productions.

Case Example

The ability to say the names of one's siblings and friends is very important to children. Arielle was six years old. She had Down syndrome and a cognitive age of about 3 years. She pronounced her own name /ewi/. Arielle was very social and there were many names she wanted to say, but she couldn't pronounce them because of their length; this was the early 1990s and a tremendous number of girl names had three and more syllables. The most important names to Arielle were those of her best friends: Jennifer, Stephanie, Annabelle Lee, and Christina.

Arielle's parents helped her therapist make a list of all the names important in Arielle's life, and together they decided which syllables to omit. It was understood that Arielle would need to shorten these names for many years, so some of the other parents were included in this project so they could agree about what to call their child. The following decisions were made: Jennifer was called "Jen," Stephanie was called "Steph," Anabelle Lee was called "Ann," and Christina was called "Chris."

Next, each child and her parents were taught how Arielle would say their name: Jen was pronounced /dɛ/, Steph was pronounced /tɛ/, Ann was pronounced /æ/, and Chris was pronounced /ki/. This plan allowed Arielle to say all these names in effective communication routines. The activity also helped all these communication partners begin to listen more carefully to the things Arielle said. The whole team began to realize that Arielle needed to be given credit for saying much more than they thought she was saying.

Expect Manner Before Place

Research demonstrates that children acquire manner before place of articulation. This means toddlers who have fewer than 50 words bring in the manner features with a variety of phonemes before they settle on the right phoneme to be used within specific words. For example, in learning to say *no*, a very young child might say /mo/ or /ŋo/ just as readily as he says /no/. The child recognizes and honors the nasality but he cannot produce the right phoneme because place of articulation is uncertain. A young child who is learning his first 50 words freely marks one phoneme with any of the other phonemes that have the same manner. The presence of the correct manner makes the word intelligible even though the phoneme was wrong by place.

Application to Therapy

A client who is still learning his first 50–100 words should be allowed and encouraged to make this same type of error. Therapy should include activities to stimulate for manner first and place second. This is done by modeling all phonemes that have the same manner, by encouraging the client to try them all, and by allowing him to mix them up for a while. Following this plan, the client is rewarded when he produces any nasal sound to mark the presence of any other nasal sound, he is rewarded when he produces any voiceless sound to mark the presence of any other voiceless sound, he is rewarded when he produces any strident sound to mark the presence of any other strident sound, and so forth.

Case Example

This process often is the most striking when children are gaining stridency and Latoya was such a case. Latoya was five years old. She had a cerebellar disorder with cognitive skills just below average and she was learning to say her first 50 words. Four of Latoya's spontaneous words required strident phonemes: *spoon, soap, bus,* and *kiss*. She produced these words as /fun/, /ʃop/, /bʌts/, and /kɪtʃ/. These substitutions were encouraged and not corrected as long as Latoya's expressive language skills were limited to so few words. This allowed Latoya the opportunity to use these words freely without worrying about saying them correctly — a freedom that encouraged more word attempts.

Accept Consonant Deletion

Consonant deletion is also very common in early word acquisition in young children. This occurs primarily as final consonant deletion (e.g., /dæ/ for *dad*) and as consonant cluster reduction (e.g., /pun/ for *spoon*). Clients with motor speech disorders also seem to have a high rate of initial consonant deletion (e.g, /ʌp/ for *cup*).

Application to Therapy

Teaching clients to practice words with deleted consonants is another strategy one can employ to help these clients produce words at their cognitive skill level but beyond their phonological capacity. For example, one might teach a child to say /tɑ/ for *star* when he has no initial s-cluster and no final /r/.

Case Example

Josh had a cognitive developmental level of about four years when he was six years old. He spoke hundreds of words and phrases. Josh's biggest problem was cluster deletion, and his brother was making fun of him for saying "ease" instead of "please." Knowing that it might be a while before Josh could produce the /pl/ cluster, his therapist taught him to say /piz/. In other words, she taught him to say the word with a /p/ but not the /l/, i.e., the simplified cluster pattern. This allowed Josh to use the word intelligibly. Six months later, the word *please* was emerging correctly with the cluster. The therapist was able to make progress with Josh by accepting the fact that syllable deletion was the best he could do at the time and she laid the foundation for the cluster by teaching the reduction pattern first.

Treating Vowel Distortions

Clients with low cognitive functioning often produce distorted vowels, especially when they have concomitant neuromuscular disorder and subsequent dysarthria. Incorrect vowels can be the most destructive elements of intelligibility and they need to be remediated whenever possible. Readers are referred to Chapter 21 on the vowels for more information on this important topic.

TRACKING PROGRESS

Children with significant cognitive impairment often do not say enough words to take a standard articulation test and this makes it difficult to determine if progress is being made. The following methods for tracking progress are recommended. These are simple ways to demonstrate that the client is making progress even when his skills appear no better on a standardized test.

Track Difficult Words & Phrases

Make phonetic transcriptions of the client's production of difficult words and phrases and monitor these over time. Select popular words and phrases that contain phonetic and phonological elements that are beyond his phonological skill level. Samples might include: *helicopter, crocodile, alligator, peanut butter, dictionary, hamburger, cheeseburger, applesauce, orange juice, pancake syrup, Superman, The Incredible Hulk, Buzz Lightyear, I'm ready, I want that one, Time to go outside,* and *To infinity and beyond.* Alternately, or in addition, track his recitation of the alphabet, his ability to count to 10, his way of saying his teacher's name, or the way he spells his own name aloud. Test the client's production of these utterances every few months. Transcribe them fully so that the phonetic and phonological changes can be tracked over time. These often will demonstrate progress when a standardized articulation test won't.

Practice Cards

Make picture cards of words the client says. Place or draw a picture of the word on one side of the card, and write the word below the picture. Then write down how the child says the target word on the back of the card. Use orthographic symbols on both sides so anyone can read them. For example, if the target word is *computer*, and the client says /pu/, write this on the back as "Poo." Write the date of the production next to the word. As time passes and the client's pronunciations get better, cross out (without making illegible) this record and write the new pronunciation below with the new date. The progression of pronunciations for the target word proves that the client is responding positively to therapy. The cards will demonstrate progress and give others appropriate expectations on practice material. Nancy Kaufman's practice cards use the same idea in ready-made cards with common vocabulary words (Kaufman, 2006).

Phoneme Charts

Draw simplified versions of the consonants, vowels, and diphthongs using standard orthographic symbols and real words so parents and other team members can understand them. Consider making one chart for initial consonants and another for final consonants. Circle each phoneme as it emerges in the child's repertoire. Use this during the diagnostic session to pinpoint the client's initial skills and update it as time passes in therapy. Consider writing the date next to each sound as it emerges so that the development of the client's phonetic system can be tracked over time.

Communication Chart

Create a chart that summarizes all the sounds and words expressed by the client categorized by type. Use the chart to monitor progress and to teach team members the client's capabilities and practice routines.

SUMMARY

Clients with significant cognitive dysfunction require special procedures. Speech testing needs to be supplemented and individualized. Speech is stimulated in ways that foster improved intelligibility using simplified phonological patterns and concepts from normal development are understood and incorporated.

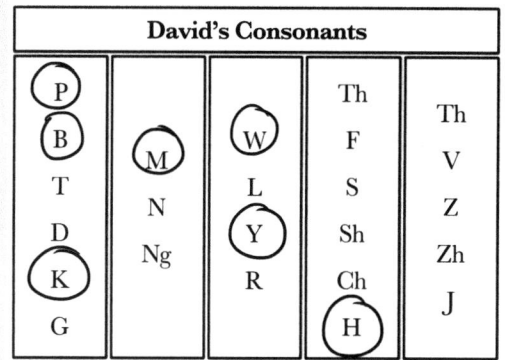

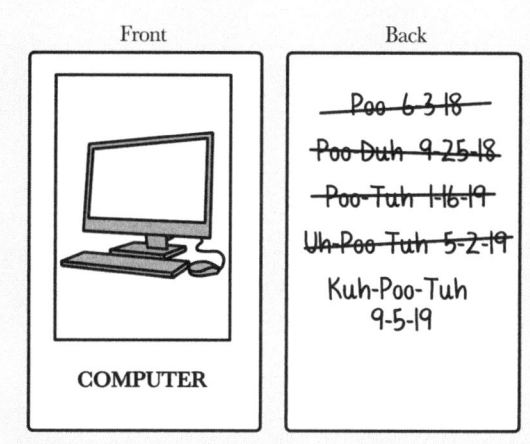

Make practice cards that reflect the client's progress.

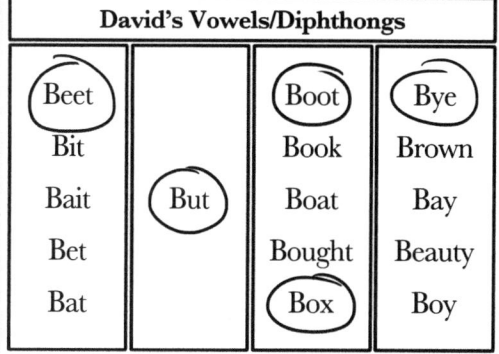

Draw simple charts to track the client's progress.

Standard orthographic symbols and real words make this information accessible to other team members.

Consider making two consonant charts, one for initial consonants and one for final consonants.

David's Communication Skills					
Spoken Words	Signed Words	Meaningless Sounds	Meaningful Sounds	AAC Words	Facial Expressions
Apple- a	All Gone	Cry	E-e- Mouse	Milk 4/19	Open (pleased)
Bird- bo	Telephone	Whine	Growl- Lion	OJ 5/19	Closed (not pleased)
Cat- tae	Shoe	Fuss	Oo-oo- Owl	AJ 5/19	Smile (happy)
No- mo	Bath	Bah-bah	Thh- Snake	Cookie 7/19	Frown (sad)
Mom- mah	Night-night	Nah-nah	H-h-h- Dog	Cracker 8/19	Nod (yes)
Dad- dah	Cookie	Go-go-go	Sh- Quiet	Cheerios	Shake (no)
All Done- duh	More	Bi-lab Rasp	Spit- Reject	Grandma	
Up- p		Nasal Snort		Grandpa	
Eat- t		Laugh		Bus	
				Outside	

A simple communication chart can help all team members understand what a client can do.

POSTSCRIPT

"We recognize, of course, that in many cases the whole process of establishing adequate controls for correct articulation moves very swiftly. Our analysis of the basic principles underlying this process may seem unnecessarily detailed or cumbersome. But blind therapy often fails with those who most need help. The therapist must know what is needed, and what he must do. Far too many teachers and therapists rely on massed repetition and repeated experiences as their basic training procedure. Success may come after such crude [teaching methods], but not because of it. The good therapist tries to arrange his stimulus conditions so that the [client] can get the vivid experience he needs."

– Charles Van Riper & John Irwin, 1958

REFERENCES

Ackermann, H., Hertrich, I., & Scharf, G. (1995). Kinematic analysis of lower lip movements in ataxic dysarthria. *Journal of Speech and Hearing Research, 38*(6), 1252–1259.

American Speech-Language-Hearing Association. (1991). The role of the speech-language pathologist in assessment and management of oral myofunctional disorders. *ASHA, 31*(11 Suppl 5), 91.

American Speech-Language-Hearing Association. (1993). Orofacial myofunctional disorders: knowledge and skills. *ASHA, 35*(3 Suppl 10), 21–23.

American Speech-Language-Hearing Association. (2004). Preferred practice patterns for the profession of speech-language pathology [Preferred Practice Patterns]. Retrieved from https://www.asha.org/policy/PP2004-00191.htm

American Speech-Language-Hearing Association. (2007). Childhood apraxia of speech [Position Statement]. Retrieved from http://www.asha.org/policy/PS2007-00277

American Speech-Language-Hearing Association. (2012). Dysarthria [Information for the Public, Disorders and Diseases]. Retrieved from http://www.asha.org/public/speech/disorders/dysarthria

Anderson, V. A. (1953). *Improving the child's speech.* New York, NY: Oxford University Press.

Andreatta, R. D. (2008). Sensorimotor elements of the orofacial system: Reviewing the basics. *Perspectives on Speech Science and Orofacial Disorders, 18*(2), 51–61.

Andreatta, R. D., & Barlow, S. M. (2009). Somatosensory gating is dependent on the rate of force recruitment in the human orofacial system. *Journal of Speech, Language, and Hearing Research, 52*(6), 1566–1578.

Arndt, W. B., Elbert, M., & Shelton, R. L. (1971). Prediction of articulation improvement with therapy from early lesson sound production task scores. *Journal of Speech and Hearing Research, 14*(1), 149–153.

Arvedson, J. C., & Brodsky, L. (1993). *Pediatric swallowing and feeding: Assessment and management.* San Diego, CA: Singular Publishing Group.

Aungst, L. S., & Frick, J. V. (1964). Auditory discrimination ability and consistency of articulation of /r/. *Journal of Speech and Hearing Disorders 29*(1), 76–85.

Austin, G. (1806). *Chironomia: A treatise on rhetorical delivery.* London, England: W. Bulmer & Company.

Ayres, A. J. (1972). *Sensory integration and learning disorders.* Los Angeles, CA: Western Psychological Services.

Ayres, A. J. (1979). *Sensory integration and the child.* Los Angeles, CA: Western Psychological Services.

Bahr, D. C. (2001). *Oral motor assessment and treatment: Ages and stages.* Boston, MA: Allyn & Bacon.

Bahr, D. (2010). *Nobody ever told me (or my mother) that! Everything from bottles and breathing to healthy speech development.* Arlington, TX: Sensory World/Future Horizons.

Bahr, D. (2014, May). Prevention of Feeding, Speech, and Mouth Development Problems (Birth to Age 2). International

Association of Orofacial Myology (IAOM), Calgary, Alberta, Canada.

Barlow, S. M., & Abbs, J. H. (1986). Fine force and position control of select orofacial structures in the upper motor neuron-syndrome. *Experimental Neurology, 94*(3), 699–713.

Barlow, S. M., & Bradford, P. T. (1996). Comparison of perioral reflex modulation in the upper and lower lip. *Journal of Speech and Hearing Research, 39*(1), 55–75.

Barlow, S. M., & Netsell, R. (1986). Differential fine force control of the upper and lower lips. *Journal of Speech and Hearing Research, 29*(2), 163–169.

Barlow, S. M., & Rath, E. M. (1985). Maximum voluntary closing forces in the upper and lower lips of humans. *Journal of Speech and Hearing Research, 28*(3), 373–376.

Bashir, A. S., Grahamjones, F., & Boswick, R. Y. (1984). A touch-cue method of therapy for developmental verbal apraxia. *Seminars in Speech and Language, 5*(2), 127–137.

Bauman-Waengler, J. (2004) *Articulatory and phonological impairments: A clinical focus* (2nd ed.). Boston, MA: Pearson.

Behan, M., Moeser, A. E., Thomas, C. F., Russell, J. A., Wang, H., Leverson, G. E., & Connor, N. P. (2012). The effect of tongue exercise on serotonergic input to the hypoglossal nucleus in young and old rats. *Journal of Speech, Language, and Hearing Research, 55*(3), 919–929.

Bell, A. G. (1906). *Lectures upon the mechanism of speech.* New York, NY: Funk & Wagnalls.

Bell, A. M. (1887). *Elocutionary manual: The principles of elocution, with exercises and notations, for pronunciation, intonation, emphasis, gesture and emotional expression.* Salem, MA: James P. Burbank. (Original text published in 1849).

Bell, A. M. (1898). T*he faults of speech: A self-corrector and teacher's manual.* Washington, DC: The Volta Bureau. (Original text published in 1880).

Bell, A. M. (1916). *Principles of speech and dictionary of sounds: Including directions and exercises for the cure of stammering and correction of all faults of articulation.* Washington, DC: The Volta Bureau. (Original work published in 1849).

Bell, D., & Halle, A. (1963). Observations of tongue-thrust swallow in preschool children. *Journal of Speech and Hearing Disorders, 28,* 195–197.

Bell, D. C., & Bell, A. M. (1878) *Bell's Standard elocutionist. Principles and exercises.* London, England: William Mullan & Son.

Bender, J. F., & Kleinfeld, V. M. (1938). *Principles and practices of speech correction.* New York, NY: Pitman Publishing Company.

Bernthal, J. E., & Bankson, N. W. (2004). *Articulation and phonological disorders* (5th ed.). Boston, MA: Pearson.

Berry, M. F., & Eisenson, J. (1956). *Speech disorders: Principles and practices of therapy.* New York, NY: Appleton-Century-Crofts. (Original text published in 1942).

Biel, L., & Peske, N. (2005). *Raising a sensory smart child.* New York, NY: Penguin.

Blair, C. (1986). Interdigitating muscle fibers throughout orbicularis oris inferior: Preliminary observations. *Journal of*

Speech and Hearing Research, 29(2), 266–269.

Blanton, M. G., & Blanton, S. (1919). *Speech training for children: the hygiene of speech.* New York, NY: The Century Company.

Bleile, K. (2006). *The late eight.* San Diego, CA: Plural Publishing.

Blomgren, M., Robb, M., & Chen, Y. (1998). A note on vowel centralization in stuttering and nonstuttering individuals. *Journal of Speech, Language, and Hearing Research, 41*(5), 1042–1051.

Bobath, K. (1959). The effect of treatment by reflex-inhibition and facilitation in cerebral palsy. *Folia Psychiatrica, Neurologica et Neurochirugica Neerlandica, 62,* 448–457.

Bobath, K. (1963). A neuro-developmental treatment of cerebral palsy. *Physiotherapy, 49,* 242–244.

Bobath, K. (1971). The normal postural reflex mechanism and its deviation in cerebral palsy. *Physiotherapy, 57*(11), 515–525.

Bobath, K. (1980). *A neurophysiological basis for the treatment of cerebral palsy* (2nd ed.). London, England: Spastics International Medical Publications.

Bobath, K., & Bobath, B. (1950). Spastic paralysis treatment of by the use of reflex inhibition. *British Journal of Physical Medicine, 13*(6), 121–127.

Boliek, C. (2008) Personal correspondence.

Boliek, C. A., Hixon, T. J., Watson, P. J., & Jones, P. B. (2009). Refinement of speech breathing in healthy 4- to 6-year-old children. *Journal of Speech, Language, and Hearing Research, 52*(4), 990–1007.

Borden, R. C., & Busse, A. C. (1925). *Speech correction.* New York, NY: F.S. Crofts & Company.

Borel-Maisonny, S. (1965). Pourquoi des guide-langue et pourquoi ces formes? Correction des erreurs motrices de la parole. *Rééducation orthophonique, 10,* 2–14.

Boshart, C. (1993). *Oral-motor techniques: Remediate your single-sound artic cases in half the time!* [Seminar handbook]. Seattle, WA: Innovative Concepts.

Boshart, C., (1998). *Oral-motor analysis & remediation techniques* (2nd Ed.). Ellijay, GA: Speech Dynamics, Inc.

Boshart, C. (2015). *Demystify the tongue tie: Methods to confidently analyze & treat a tethered tongue.* Ellijay, GA: Speech Dynamics, Inc.

Bosley, E. C. (1981). *Techniques for articulatory disorders.* Springfield, IL: Charles C. Thomas.

Bosma, J. (Ed.). (1967). *Symposium on oral sensation and perception.* Springfield, IL: Charles C. Thomas.

Bowen, C. (2011, November 23). *Core vocabulary therapy.* Retrieved from https://www.speech-language-therapy.com/index.php?option=com_content&view=article&id=74

Bower, T. G. R. (1974). *Development in infancy.* San Francisco, CA: W. H. Freeman & Company.

Broen, P. A., Strange, W., Doyle, S. S., & Heller, J. H. (1983). Perception and production of approximant consonants by normal and articulation-delayed preschool children. *Journal of Speech and Hearing Research, 26*(4), 601–608.

Brown, M. W. (1947). *Goodnight moon.* New York, NY: Harper & Row.

Brunner, J., Fuchs, S., & Perrier, P. (2009). On the relationship between palate shape and articulatory behavior. *The Journal of the Acoustical Society of America, 125*(6), 3936–3949.

Brunner, J., Ghosh, S., Hoole, P., Matthies, M., Tiede, M., & Perkell, J. (2011). The influence of auditory acuity on acoustic variability and the use of motor equivalence during adaptation to a perturbation. *Journal of Speech, Language, and Hearing Research, 54*(3), 727–739.

Brydges, R., Carnahan, H., Backstein, D., & Dubrowski, A. (2007). Application of motor learning principles to complex surgical tasks: Searching for the optimal practice schedule. *Journal of Motor Behavior, 39*(1), 40–48.

Buhr, R. D. (1980). The emergence of vowels in an infant. *Journal of Speech, Language, and Hearing Research, 23*(1), 73–94.

Butler Hinz, S. (2014). Personal email correspondence.

Byun, T. M., Hitchcock, E. R., & Swartz, M. T. (2014). Retroflex vs. bunched in treatment for rhotic misarticulation: Evidence from ultrasound biofeedback intervention. *Journal of Speech, Language, and Hearing Research, 57*(6), 2116–2130.

Bzoch, K. R. (1989). *Communicative disorders related to cleft lip and palate* (3rd ed.). Austin, TX: Pro-Ed.

Carrell, J., & Tiffany, W. R. (1960). *Phonetics: Theory and application to speech improvement.* New York, NY: McGraw-Hill.

Carrell, J. A. (1968). *Disorders of articulation.* Englewood Cliffs, NJ: Prentice-Hall.

Carrier, J. K. (1970). A program of articulation therapy administered by mothers. *Journal of Speech and Hearing Disorders, 35*(4), 344–353.

Cheng, H. Y., Murdoch, B. E., Goozée, J. V., & Scott, D. (2007a). Physiologic development of tongue-jaw coordination from childhood to adulthood. *Journal of Speech, Language, and Hearing Research, 50*(2), 352–360.

Cheng, H. Y., Murdoch, B. E., Goozée, J. V., & Scott, D. (2007b). Electropalatographic assessment of tongue-to-palate contact patterns and variability in children, adolescents, and adults. *Journal of Speech, Language, and Hearing Research, 50*(2), 375–392.

Chi-Fishman, G., Stone, M., & McCall, G. N. (1998). Lingual action in normal sequential swallowing. *Journal of Speech, Language, and Hearing Research, 41*(4), 771–785.

Chomsky, N., & Halle, M. (1968). *The sound pattern of English.* New York, NY: Harper & Row.

Christensen, J. M., & Weinberg, B. (1976). Vowel duration characteristics of esophageal speech. *Journal of Speech and Hearing Research, 19*(4), 678–689.

Clark, C. E., Schwarz, I. E., & Blakeley, R. W. (1993). The removable r-appliance as a practice device to facilitate correct production of /r/. *American Journal of Speech-Language Pathology, 2*(1), 84–92.

Clark, H. M. (2008). The role of strength training in speech sound disorders. *Seminars in Speech and Language 29*(4), 276–283.

Cohen, J. H., & Diehl, C. F. (1963). Relation of speech-sound discrimination ability to articulation-type speech deficits. *Journal of Speech and Hearing Disorders, 28,* 187–190.

Colton, R., & Casper, J. K. (1996). *Understanding voice problems: A physiological perspective for diagnosis and treatment.* Baltimore, MD: Williams & Wilkins.

Comstock, A., & Mair, J. A. (1874). *The model elocutionist: A manual of instruction in vocal gymnastics and gesture.* London: William Collins, Sons & Company.

Connaghan, K. P., Moore, C. A., & Higashakawa, M. (2004). Respiratory kinematics during vocalization and nonspeech respiration in children from 9 to 48 months. *Journal of Speech, Language, and Hearing Research, 47*(1), 70–84.

Connor, N. P., Ota, F., Nagai, H., Russell, J. A., & Leverson, G. (2008). Differences in age-related alterations in muscle contraction properties in rat tongue and hindlimb. *Journal of Speech, Language, and Hearing Research, 51*(4), 818–827.

Connor, N. P., Russell, J. A., Wang, H., Jackson, M. A., Mann, L., & Kluender, K. (2009). Effect of tongue exercise on protrusive force and muscle fiber area in aging rats. *Journal of Speech, Language, and Hearing Research, 52*(3), 732–744.

Cooper, M. (1973). *Modern techniques of vocal rehabilitation.* Springfield, IL: Charles C. Thomas.

Costello, J., & Schoen, J. (1978). The effectiveness of paraprofessionals and a speech clinician as agents of articulation intervention using programmed instruction. *Language, Speech, and Hearing Services in Schools, 9*(2), 118–128.

Crannell, K. C. (1991). *Voice and articulation* (2nd ed.). Belmont, CA: Wadsworth Publishing Company.

Crary, M. A. (1993). *Developmental motor speech disorders.* San Diego, CA: Singular Publishing Group.

Cratty, B. J. (1970). *Perceptual and motor development in infants and children.* Los Angeles, CA: MacMillan.

Creaghead, N. A., Newman, P. W., & Secord, W. A. (1989). *Assessment and remediation of articulatory and phonological disorders* (2nd ed.). Columbus, OH: Merrill.

Crickmay, M. C. (1966). *Speech therapy and the Bobath approach to cerebral palsy.* Springfield, IL: Charles C. Thomas.

Crosbie, S., Holm, A., & Dodd, B. (2005). Intervention for children with severe speech disorder: A comparison of two approaches. *International Journal of Language and Communication Disorders, 40*(4), 467–491.

Dagenais, P. A., & Critz-Crosby, P. (1991). Consonant lingual-palatal contacts produced by normal-hearing and hearing-impaired children. *Journal of Speech and Hearing Research, 34*(6), 1423–1435.

Dagenais, P. A., & Critz-Crosby, P. (1992). Comparing tongue positioning by normal-hearing and hearing-impaired children during vowel production. *Journal of Speech and Hearing Research, 35*(1), 35–44.

Dagenais, P. A., Critz-Crosby, P., & Adams, J. B. (1994). Defining and remediating persistent lateral lisps in children using electropalatography: Preliminary findings. *American Journal of Speech-Language Pathology, 3*(3), 67–76.

Dagenais, P. A., Critz-Crosby, P., Fletcher, S. G., & McCutcheon, M. J. (1994). Comparing abilities of children with profound hearing impairments to learn consonants using electropalatography or traditional aural-oral techniques. *Journal of Speech and Hearing Research, 37*(3), 687–699.

Daniloff, R., & Moll, K. (1968). Coarticulation of lip rounding. *Journal of Speech and Hearing Research, 11*(4), 707–721.

Darley, F. L., Aronson, A. E., & Brown, J. R. (1975). *Motor speech disorders.* Philadelphia, PA: Saunders.

Datta, H., Shafer, V. L., Morr, M. L., Kurtzberg, D., & Schwartz, R. G. (2010). Electrophysiological indices of discrimination of long-duration, phonetically similar vowels in children with typical and atypical language development. *Journal of Speech, Language, and Hearing Research, 53*(3), 757–777.

Davis, B. L. (2010, March 8–9). *Assessment and intervention issues in CAS* [Seminar handbook]. Retrieved in person, summary available online at https://pammarshalla.com/evaluation-diagnosis-the-best-list-of-cas-characteristics/

Davis, B. L., & MacNeilage, P. F. (1990). Acquisition of correct vowel production: A quantitative case study. *Journal of Speech and Hearing Research, 33*(1), 16–27.

Davis, B. L., & MacNeilage, P. F. (1995). The articulatory basis of babbling. *Journal of Speech and Hearing Research, 38*(6), 1199–1211.

Dellow, P. (1976). The general physiological background of chewing and swallowing. In B. Sessle & A. Hannan (Eds.), *Mastication and swallowing: Biological and clinical correlates.* Toronto, ON: University of Toronto Press.

Dickson, S. (1962). Differences between children who spontaneously outgrow and children who retain functional articulation errors. *Journal of Speech and Hearing Research, 5,* 263–271.

Dodd, B., Holm, A., Crosbie, S., & McIntosh, B. (2006). A core vocabulary approach for management of inconsistent speech disorder. *Advances in Speech–Language Pathology, 8*(3), 220–230.

Doehring, D. G., & Ling, D. (1971). Programmed instruction of hearing-impaired children in the auditory discrimination of vowels. *Journal of Speech and Hearing Research, 14*(4), 746–754.

Doman, R. J., Spitz, E. B., Zucman, E., Delacato, C. H., & Doman, G. (1960). Children with severe brain injuries; Neurological organization in terms of mobility. *JAMA. 174*(3), 257–262.

Donegan, P. (2002). Normal vowel development. In M. J. Ball & F. Gibbon (Eds.), *Vowel disorders* (pp. 1–35). Boston, MA: Butterworth-Heinemann.

Dromey, C., & Ramig, L. O. (1998). The effect of lung volume on selected phonatory and articulatory variables. *Journal of Speech, Language, and Hearing Research, 41*(3), 491–502.

Dryer, J. (2017, Oct. 17). Harmonicas help transplant patients learn to breathe again. *First Coast News,* Retrieved from https://www.firstcoastnews.com/article/news/health/harmonicas-help-transplant-patients-learn-to-breathe-again/484088662

Duchan, J. F. (2002). What do you know about your profession's history? And why is it important? *The ASHA Leader, 7*(23), 4–29.

Duffy, J. R. (1995). *Motor speech disorders: Substrates, differential diagnosis, and management.* St. Louis, MO: Mosby Publishing Company.

Dworkin, J. P. (1991). *Motor speech disorders: A treatment guide.* St. Louis, MO: Mosby Publishing Company.

Dworkin, J. P., & Culatta, R. A. (1980). Tongue strength: Its relationship to tongue thrusting, open-bite, and articulatory proficiency. *Journal of Speech and Hearing Disorders, 45*(2), 277–282.

Dworkin, J. P., Meleca, R. J., & Stachler, R. J. (2003). More on the role of the mandible in speech production: Clinical correlates of Green, Moore, and Reilly's (2002) findings. *Journal of Speech, Language, and Hearing Research, 46*(4), 1016–1019.

Dwyer, C. H., Robb, M. P., O'Beirne, G. A., & Gilbert, H. R. (2009). The influence of speaking rate on nasality in the speech of hearing-impaired individuals. *Journal of Speech, Language, and Hearing Research, 52*(5), 1321–1333.

Dyakova, E. (2013). *Therapeutic speech massage.* Bloomington, IN: Xlibris.

Edwards, J., Fox, R. A., & Rogers, C. L. (2002). Final consonant discrimination in children: Effects of phonological disorder, vocabulary size, and articulatory accuracy. *Journal of Speech, Language, and Hearing Research, 45*(2), 231–242.

Edwards, J., & Harris, K. S. (1990). Rotation and translation of the jaw during speech. *Journal of Speech and Hearing Research, 33*(3), 550–562.

Edwards, M. L., & Shriberg, L. D. (1983). *Phonology: Applications in communicative disorders.* San Diego, CA: College-Hill Press.

Ehrlich, A. B. (1970). *Training therapists for tongue thrust correction.* Springfield, IL: Charles C. Thomas.

Eilers, R., Oller, D. K., Urbano, R., & Moroff, D. (1989). Conflicting and cooperating cues: Perception of cues to final consonant voicing by infants and adults. *Journal of Speech and Hearing Research, 32*(2), 307–316.

Eisenberg, S. L., & Hitchcock, E. R. (2010). Using standardized tests to inventory consonant and vowel production: A comparison of 11 tests of articulation and phonology. *Language, Speech, and Hearing Services In Schools, 41*(4), 488–503.

Elbert, M., & Gierut, J. (1986). *Handbook of clinical phonology: Approaches to assessment and treatment.* San Diego, CA: College-Hill Press.

Elliott, F. (1960) Clinical observations regarding negative practice.

Journal of Speech and Hearing Disorders, 25(2), 196–197.

Elliott, L. L., & Hammer, M. A. (1988). Longitudinal changes in auditory discrimination in normal children and children with language-learning problems. *Journal of Speech and Hearing Disorders, 53*(4), 467–474.

Elliott, L. L., & Hammer, M. A. (1993). Fine-grained auditory discrimination: Factor structures. *Journal of Speech and Hearing Research, 36*(2), 396–409.

Enfield, W. (1780). *The speaker*. London, England: J. Johnson.

Everts, K. J. (1908). *The speaking voice: Principles of training*. New York, NY: Harper.

Fairbanks, G. (1940). *Voice and articulation drillbook*. New York, NY: Harper & Brothers.

Fairbanks, G. (1954). Systematic research in experimental phonetics: I. A theory of the speech mechanism as a servosystem. *Journal of Speech and Hearing Disorders, 19*(2), 133–139.

Fairbanks, G., & Guttman, N. (1958). Effects of delayed auditory feedback upon articulation. *Journal of Speech and Hearing Research, 1*(1), 12–22.

Farber, S. D. (1982). *Neurorehabilitation: A multisensory approach*. Philadelphia, PA: W. B. Saunders Company.

Farquhar, M. S. (1961). Prognostic value of imitative and auditory discrimination tests. *Journal of Speech and Hearing Disorders, 26*, 342–347.

Fay, T. (1948). The neurophysical aspects of therapy in cerebral palsy. *Archives of Physical Medicine and Rehabilitation, 29*(6), 327–334.

Fay, T. (1954). The use of pathological and unlocking reflexes in the rehabilitation of spastics. *American Journal of Physical Medicine, 33*(6), 347–352.

Fay, T. (1955). The origin of human movement. *American Journal of Psychiatry, 111*(9), 644–652.

Ferguson, S. H., & Kewley-Port, D. (2007). Talker differences in clear and conversational speech: Acoustic characteristics of vowels. *Journal of Speech, Language, and Hearing Research, 50*(5), 1241–1255.

Fernando, C. (1998). *Tongue tie: From confusion to clarity*. Sydney, Australia: Tandem Publishing Group.

Finger, S. (2000). *Minds behind the brain: A history of the pioneers and their discoveries*. New York, NY: Oxford University Press.

Fiorentino, M. R. (1972). *Normal and abnormal development: The influence of primitive reflexes on motor development*. Springfield, IL: Charles C. Thomas.

Fisher, H. B. (1966). *Improving voice and articulation*. New York, NY: Houghton Milton.

Fisher, A. G., Murray, E. A., & Bundy, A. C. (1991). *Sensory integration: Theory and practice*. Philadelphia, PA: F. A. Davis.

Flege, J. E. (1988). Anticipatory and carry-over nasal coarticulation in the speech of children and adults. *Journal of Speech and Hearing Research, 31*(4), 525–536.

Fletcher, S. G. (1989). Palatometric specification of stop, affricate, and sibilant sounds. *Journal of Speech and Hearing Research, 32*(4), 736–748.

Fletcher, S. G. (1992). *Articulation: A physiological approach*. San Diego, CA: Singular Publishing Group.

Fletcher, S. G., Casteel, R. L., & Bradley, D. P. (1961). Tongue-thrust swallow, speech articulation, and age. *Journal of Speech and Hearing Disorders, 26*(3), 201–208.

Fletcher, S. G., Dagenais, P. A., & Critz-Crosby, P. (1991). Teaching consonants to profoundly hearing-impaired speakers using glossometry. *Journal of Speech, Language, and Hearing Research, 34*(4), 943–956.

Fletcher, S. G., & Higgins, J. M. (1980). Performance of children with severe to profound auditory impairment in instrumentally guided reduction of nasal resonance. *Journal of Speech and Hearing Disorders, 45*(2), 181–194.

Fletcher, S. G., & Meldrum, J. R. (1968). Lingual function and relative length of the lingual frenulum. *Journal of Speech and Hearing Research, 11*(2), 382–390.

Flowers, A. M. (1963). *The big book of sounds*. Danville, IL: Interstate Printers & Publishers.

Flowers, A. M. (2003). *The big book of sounds*. Austin, TX: Pro-Ed.

Folkins, J. W., & Abbs, J. H. (1975). Lip and jaw motor control during speech: Responses to resistive loading of the jaw. *Journal of Speech and Hearing Research, 18*(1), 207–220.

Folkins, J. W., & Abbs, J. H. (1976). Additional observations on responses to resistive loading of the jaw. *Journal of Speech and Hearing Research, 19*(4), 820–821.

Folkins, J. W., & Canty, J. L. (1986). Movements of the upper and lower lips during speech: interactions between lips with the jaw fixed at different positions. *Journal of Speech and Hearing Research, 29*(3), 348–356.

Folkins, J. W., Linville, R., N., Garrett, J. D., & Brown, C. K. (1988). Interactions in the labial musculature during speech. *Journal of Speech and Hearing Research, 31*(2), 253–264.

Frisch, G. R., & Handler, L. (1974). A neuropsychological investigation of "functional disorders of speech articulation." *Journal of Speech and Hearing Research, 17*(3), 432–445.

Fröeschels, E. (1933). *Speech therapy*. Boston, MA: Expression Company.

Fröeschels, E. (Ed.). (1948). *Twentieth century speech and voice correction*. New York, NY: Philosophical Library.

Fröeschels, E. (1952). *Dysarthric speech: Speech in cerebral palsy*. Magnolia, MA: Expression Company.

Fröeschels, E., & Jellinek, A. (1941). *Practice of voice and speech therapy: new contributions to voice and speech pathology*. Boston, MA: Expression Company.

Fucci, D., Harris, D., & Petrosino, L. (1985). Threshold and suprathreshold correlations for the oral tactile sensory mechanism. *Journal of Speech and Hearing Research, 28*(3), 331–335.

Fucci, D., & Robertson, J. H. (1971). Functional defective articulation: An oral sensory disturbance. *Perceptual Motor Skills, 33*(3), 711–714.

Fucci, D., Small, L. H., & Petrosino, L. (1983). Effects of practice and instructional set on the measurement of lingual vibrotactile thresholds. *Journal of Speech and Hearing Research, 26*(2), 289–293.

Gallahue, D. L., & Ozmun, J. C. (1995). *Understanding motor development* (3rd Ed.). Madison, WI: William C. Brown Publishing.

Galloway, H. F., & Blue, C. M. (1975). Paraprofessional personnel in articulation therapy. *Language, Speech, and Hearing Services in Schools, 6*(3), 125–130.

Gammon, S. A., Smith, P. J., Daniloff, R. G., & Kim, C. W. (1971) Articulation and stress-juncture production under oral anesthetization and masking. *Journal of Speech and Hearing Research, 14*(2), 271–282.

Gangale, D. (1993). *The source for oral-facial exercises*. East Moline, IL: Linguisystems.

Garliner, D. (1976). *Myofunctional therapy*. Philadelphia, PA: Saunders.

Garn-Nunn, P. G., & Lynn, J. M. (2004). *Calvert's descriptive phonetics*. New York, NY: Thieme.

Gerber, A. (1977). Programming for articulation modification.

Journal of Speech and Hearing Disorders, 42(1), 29–43.

Gesell, A. (1952). *Infant development: The embryology of early human behavior.* New York, NY: Harper.

Gesell, A. & Ilg, F. L. (1937). *Feeding behavior of infants.* Philadelphia, PA: Lippincott.

Gibbon, F. E. (1999). Undifferentiated lingual gestures in children with articulation/phonological disorders. *Journal of Speech, Language, and Hearing Research, 42*(2), 382–397.

Gibbs, C. H., & Messerman, T. (1972). Jaw motion during speech. In American Speech and Hearing Association (Ed.), *ASHA Reports 7: Proceedings of the conference: Orofacial function: Clinical research in dentistry and speech pathology (pp. 104–112).* Retrieved from https://www.asha.org/uploadedFiles/ASHAReports7 .pdf

Gibson, J. J. (1967). The mouth as an organ for laying hold on the environment. In J. Bosma (Ed.), *Oral sensation and perception* (pp. 111–136). Springfield, IL: Charles C. Thomas.

Gierut, J. A. (1989). Maximum opposition approach to phonological treatment. *Journal of Speech and Hearing Disorders, 54*(1), 9–19.

Ginsburg, H., & Opper, S. (1969). *Piaget's theory of intellectual development: An introduction.* Englewood Cliffs, NJ: Prentice-Hall.

Goffman, L., & Smith, A. (1994). Motor unit territories in the human perioral musculature. *Journal of Speech, Language, and Hearing Research, 37*(5), 975–984.

Goddard, S. (2005). *Reflexes, learning and behavior: Non-invasive approach to solving learning & behavior problems.* Eugene, OR: Fern Ridge.

Goldstein, M. A. (1940). Speech without a tongue. *Journal of Speech and Hearing Disorders, 5*(1), 65–69.

Göllesz, V., & Gáspár, Á. (1964). "Trioptophon"—Three-dimensional "phonetic mirror" combined with amplifier. *Journal of Speech and Hearing Disorders, 29*(3), 338–340.

Goodglass, H. (1973). Developmental comparison of vowels and consonants in dichotic listening. *Journal of Speech and Hearing Research, 16*(4), 744–752.

Gottfried, A. W. (1984). Touch as an organizer for learning and development. In C. C. Brown (Ed.), *Pediatric round table 10: The many facets of touch.* New York, NY: Johnson & Johnson Baby.

Gordon, M. J. (1960). Third grade television-classroom articulation program. *Journal of Speech and Hearing Disorders, 25*(4), 398–404.

Gray, B. B. (1974). A field study on programmed articulation therapy. *Language, Speech, and Hearing Services in Schools, 5*(3), 119–131.

Green, K. P., & Norrix, L. W. (1997). Acoustic cues to place of articulation and the McGurk effect: The role of release bursts aspiration, and format transitions. *Journal of Speech and Hearing Research, 40*(3), 646–665.

Green, J. R., Moore, C. A., Higashikawa, M., & Steeve, R. W. (2000). The physiologic development of speech motor control: Lip and jaw coordination. *Journal of Speech, Language, and Hearing Research, 43*(1), 239–255.

Green, J. R., Moore, C. A., & Reilly, K. J. (2002). The sequential development of jaw and lip control for speech. *Journal of Speech, Language, and Hearing Research, 45*(1), 66–79.

Green, J. R., Nip, I. S., Wilson, E. M., Mefferd, A. S., & Yunusova, Y. (2010). Lip movement exaggerations during infant-directed speech. *Journal of Speech, Language, and Hearing Research, 53*(6), 1529–1542.

Green, J. R., Wilson, E. M., Wang, Y. T., & Moore, C. A. (2007). Estimating mandibular motion based on chin surface targets during speech. *Journal of Speech, Language, and Hearing Research, 50*(4), 928–939.

Green, S. (2013). Case history: Improved maxillary growth and development following digit sucking elimination and orofacial myofunctional therapy. *International Journal of Orofacial Myology, 39*, 45–54.

Greene, J. S., & Wells, E., J. (1927). *The cause and cure of speech disorders: A text book for students and teachers on stuttering, stammering, and voice conditions.* New York, NY: The Macmillan Company.

Griffith, A. A. (1865). *Lessons in elocution.* Chicago, IL: Adams, Blackmer, & Lyon.

Grigos, M. I. (2009). Changes in articulator movement variability during phonemic development: A longitudinal study. *Journal of Speech, Language, and Hearing Research, 52*(1), 164–177.

Groher, M. E. (Ed.). (1984). *Dysphagia: Diagnosis and management.* Boston, MA: Butterworth-Heinemann.

Guttmann, O. (1893). *Gymnastics of the voice for song and speech: Also a method for the cure of stuttering and stammering.* New York, NY: Werner.

Guillot, K. M., Ohde, R. N., & Hedrick, M. (2013). Perceptual development of nasal consonants in children with normal hearing and in children who use cochlear implants. *Journal of Speech, Language, and Hearing Research, 56*(4), 1133–1143.

Hahn, V. (2003) Oral stereognosis. In M. Hanson & R. Mason (Eds.), *Orofacial myology: International perspectives* (pp. 362–368). Springfield, IL: Charles C. Thomas.

Hall, P. K., Jordan, L. S., & Robin, D. A. (1993). *Developmental apraxia of speech: Theory and clinical practice.* Austin, TX: Pro-Ed.

Hall, P. K., & Tomblin, J. B. (1975). Case study: Therapy procedures for remediation of a nasal lisp. *Language, Speech, and Hearing Services in Schools, 6*(1), 29–32.

Hamill, S. S. (1886). *New science of elocution.* New York, NY: Hunt & Eaton.

Hammer, D. (2012). Childhood apraxia of speech: A multisensory approach to achieving speech outcomes [Seminar handbook]. Retrieved in person. Lectures ongoing: https://www.mrhassociates.com/education.html

Hanson, M. L. (1983). *Articulation.* Philadelphia, PA: W. B. Saunders Company.

Hanson, M. L. (1988). Orofacial myofunctional disorders: Guidelines for assessment and treatment. *International Journal of Orofacial Myology, 14*(1), 27–32.

Hanson, M. L., & Barrett, R. H. (1988). *Fundamentals of orofacial myology.* Springfield, IL: Charles C. Thomas.

Hanson, M. L., & Mason, R. M. (2003). *Orofacial myology: International perspectives.* Springfield, IL: Charles C. Thomas.

Hardcastle, W. J., Morgan Barry, R. A., & Clark, C. J. (1987). An instrumental phonetic study of lingual activity in articulation-disordered children. *Journal of Speech and Hearing Research, 30*(2), 171–184.

Hargrove, P. M. (1982). Misarticulated vowels: A case study. *Language, Speech, and Hearing Services in Schools, 13*(2), 86–95.

Hartson, L. D. (1988). Stetson: A biographical sketch. In J. A. S. Kelso & K. G. Munhall (Eds.), *R. H. Stetson's Motor Phonetics.* Boston, MA: College-Hill Press.

Hasegawa-Johnson, M., Pizza, S., Alwan, A., Cha, J. S., & Haker, K. (2003). Vowel category dependence of the relationship between palate height, tongue height, and oral area. *Journal of Speech, Language, and Hearing Research, 46*(3), 738–753.

Hayden, D. (1984). The PROMPT system of therapy: Theoretical framework and applications for developmental apraxia of speech. *Seminars in Speech and Language, 5*(2), 139–156.

Hazelbaker, A. K. (2010). *Tongue-tie: Morphogenesis, impact, assessment and treatment.* Columbus, OH: Aidan & Eva Press.

Hebb, D. O. (1949). *Organization of behavior: A neuropsychological theory.*

New York, NY: Psychology Press.

Hegde, M. N. (1998). *Treatment procedures in communication disorders.* Austin TX: Pro-Ed.

Helmick, J. W. (1976). Effects of therapy on articulation skills in elementary-school children. *Language, Speech, and Hearing Services in Schools, 7*(3), 169–172.

Henkins, R. I., & Banks, V. (1967). Tactile perception on the tongue, palate and the hand of normal man. In J. Bosma (Ed.), *Oral sensation and perception* (pp. 182–187). Springfield, IL: Charles C. Thomas.

Hetrick, R. D., & Sommers, R. K. (1988). Unisensory and bisensory processing skills of children having misarticulations and normally speaking peers. *Journal of Speech, Language, and Hearing Research, 31*(4), 575–581.

Hinton, V. A., & Arokiasamy, W. M. (1997). Maximum interlabial pressures in normal speakers. *Journal of Speech, Language, and Hearing Research, 40*(2), 400–404.

Hinton, V. A., & Robey, R. R. (1995). Parameter estimation of labial movements in speech production: Implications for speech motor control. *Journal of Speech and Hearing Research, 38*(4), 812–820.

Hirata, Y., & Kelly, S. D. (2010). Effects of lips and hands on auditory learning of second-language speech sounds. *Journal of Speech, Language, and Hearing Research, 53*(2), 298–310.

Hixon, T. J., & Hoit, J. D. (1999). Physical examination of the abdominal wall by the speech-language pathologist. *American Journal of Speech-Language Pathology, 8*(4), 335–346.

Hixon, T. J., & Hoit, J. D. (2000). Physical examination of the rib cage wall by the speech-language pathologist. *American Journal of Speech-Language Pathology, 9*(3), 179–196.

Hixon, T. J., & Hoit, J. D. (2006). A clinical method for the detection of quick respiratory hyperkinesia. *American Journal of Speech-Language Pathology, 15*(1), 15–19.

Hodson, B. W., & Paden, E. P. (1983). *Targeting intelligible speech.* San Diego, CA: College-Hill Press.

Hodson, B. W., & Paden, E. P. (1991). *Targeting intelligible speech.* Austin, TX: Pro-Ed.

Hoff-Ginsberg, E., & Shatz, M. (1982). Linguistic input and the child's acquisition of language. *Psychological Bulletin, 92*(1), 3–26.

Hoit, J. D., Hixon, T. J., Watson, P. J., & Morgan, W. J. (1990). Speech breathing in children and adolescents. *Journal of Speech, Language, and Hearing Research, 33*(1), 51–69.

Hoit, J. D., Watson, P. J., Hixon, K. E., McMahon, P., & Johnson, C. L. (1994). Age and velopharyngeal function during speech production. *Journal of Speech, Language, and Hearing Research, 37*(2), 295–302.

Holbrook, A. (1954). A study of the effectiveness of recorded articulation exercises. *Journal of Speech and Hearing Disorders, 19*(1),14–16.

Holder, W. (1669). *Elements of speech.* London, England: Royal Society.

Honda, K., Kurita, T., Kakita, Y., & Maeda, S. (1995). Psychology of the lips and modeling of lip gestures. *Journal of Phonetics, 23*(1–2), 243–254.

Hooper, T. (Director), Canning, I. (Producer), Sherman, E. (Producer), Unwin, G. (Producer), Seidler, D. (Writer). (2010). *The King's Speech* [DVD]. Molinare, London: Momentum Pictures.

Howell, J., & Dean, E. (1991). *Treating phonological disorders in children: Metaphon, theory to practice.* San Diego, CA: Singular Publishing Group.

Huber, J. E., & Chandrasekaran, B. (2006). Effects of increasing sound pressure level on lip and jaw movement parameters and consistency in young adults. *Journal of Speech, Language, and Hearing Research, 49*(6), 1368–1379.

Hunker, C. J., Abbs, J. H., & Barlow, S. M. (1982). The relationship between Parkinsonian rigidity and hypokinesia in the orofacial system: A quantitative analysis. *Neurology, 32*(7), 749- 754.

Hustad, K. C., & Beukelman, D. R. (2001). Effects of linguistic cues and stimulus cohesion on intelligibility of severely dysarthric speech. *Journal of Speech, Language, and Hearing Research, 44*(3), 497–510.

Hustad, K. C., & Garcia, J. M. (2005). Aided and unaided speech supplementation strategies: Effect of alphabet cues and iconic hand gestures on dysarthric speech. *Journal of Speech, Language, and Hearing Research, 48*(5), 996–1012.

Illingworth, R. S. (1963). *The development of the infant and young child: Normal and abnormal* (2nd Ed.). Baltimore, MD: Livingstone.

Imai, S., & Michi, K. (1992). Articulatory function after resection of the tongue and floor of the mouth: Palatometric and perceptual evaluation. *Journal of Speech and Hearing Research, 35*(1), 68–78.

Ingram, D. (1976). *Phonological disability in children.* New York, NY: Elsevier.

Irwin, O. C. (1948) Infant speech: Development of vowel sounds. *Journal of Speech and Hearing Disorders, 13*(1), 31–34.

Irwin, O. C., & Chen, H. P. (1946) Infant speech: Vowel and consonant frequency. *Journal of Speech Disorders, 11*(2), 123–125.

Irwin, J. V., & Weston, A. J. (1975). The paired stimuli monograph. *Acta Symbolica, 6*(4), 1–76.

Ishiwata, Y., Hiyama, S., Igarashi, K, Ono, T, & Kuroda, T. (1997). Human jaw- tongue reflex as revealed by intraoral surface recording. *Journal of Oral Rehabilitation, 24*(11), 857–862.

Iskarous, K. (2005). Patterns of tongue movement. *Journal of Phonetics, 33*(4), 363–381.

Jacewicz, E., Fox, R. A., & Salmons, J. (2011). Regional dialect variation in the vowel systems of typically developing children. *Journal of Speech, Language, and Hearing Research, 54*(2), 448–470.

Jakobson, R. (1968). *Child language aphasia and phonological universals.* The Hague, Netherlands: Mouton Publishers.

Jewell, E. J., & Abate, F. (Ed.). (2001). *The new oxford American dictionary.* New York, NY: Oxford University Press.

Johnson, H., & Scott, A. (1993). *A practical approach to saliva control.* San Antonio, TX: Communication Skill Builders.

Jones, D. (1917). *Everyman's English pronouncing dictionary.* London, England: J.M Dent & Sons Ltd.

Jones-Owens, J. L. (1991). Prespeech assessment and treatment strategies. In M. B. Langley & L. J. Lombardino (Eds.), *Neurodevelopmental strategies for managing communication disorders in children with severe motor* dysfunction (pp. 49–80). Austin, TX: Pro-Ed.

Jordan, L. S., Hardy, J. C., & Morris, H. L. (1978). Performance of children with good and poor articulation on tasks of tongue placement. *Journal of Speech and Hearing Research, 21*(3), 429–439.

Kamhi, A. G. (2000). Practice makes perfect: The incompatibility of practicing speech and meaningful communication. *Language, Speech, and Hearing Services in the Schools, 31*(2), 182–186.

Kantner, C. E., & West, R., (1933). *Phonetics.* New York, NY: Harper & Brothers.

Karnell, M. P., Linville, R. N., & Edwards, B. A. (1988). Variations in velar position over time: A nasal videoendoscopic study. *Journal of Speech and Hearing Research, 31*(3), 417–424.

Kaufman, N. (2006). *The Kaufman speech praxis workout book: Treatment materials and a home program for childhood apraxia of speech.* Gaylord,

MI: Northern Rehabilitation Services.

Kawamura, Y., & Majima, T. (1964). Temporomandibular-joint sensory mechanisms controlling activities of the jaw muscles. *Journal of Dental Research, 43*, 150.

Kelso, J. A. S., & Tuller, B. (1983). "Compensatory articulation" under conditions of reduced afferent information: A dynamic formulation. *Journal of Speech and Hearing Research, 26*(2), 217–224.

Kent, R. D. (1980). Articulatory and acoustic perspectives on speech development. In A. P. Reilly (Ed.), *Pediatric round table 4: The communication game* (pp. 38–42). New York, NY: Johnson & Johnson Baby.

Kent, R. D. (2004a). Normal aspects of articulation. In J. E. Bernthal & N. W. Bankson, *Articulation and phonological disorders* (pp. 1–62). Boston, MA: Pearson.

Kent, R. D. (2004b). The uniqueness of speech among motor systems. *Clinical Linguistics & Phonetics, 18*(6–8), 495–505.

Kent, R. D. (2008). Personal correspondence.

Kidder, C. W. (1896). *An outline of vocal physiology and Bell's visible speech.* Boston, MA: Charles W. Kidder.

Kier, W. M., & Smith, K. K. (1985). Tongues, tentacles and trunks: the biomechanics of movement in muscular-hydrostats. *Zoological Journal of the Linnean Society, 83*(4), 307–324.

Klich, R. J., & May, G. M. (1982). Spectrographic study of vowels in stutterers' fluent speech. *Journal of Speech and Hearing Research, 25*(3), 364–370.

Klick, S. L. (1985). Adapted cuing technique for use in treatment of dyspraxia. *Language, Speech, and Hearing Services in Schools, 16*(4), 256–259.

Knickerbocker, B. M. (1980). *A holistic approach to learning disabilities.* Thorofare, NJ: C. B. Slack.

Kofler, L. (1887). *Art of breathing: As the basis of tone-production.* New York, NY: Edgar S. Werner & Compay.

Kraus, N., Koch, D. B., McGee, T. J., Nicol, T. G., & Cunningham, J. (1999). Speech-sound discrimination in school-age children: Psychophysical and neurophysiologic measures. *Journal of Speech, Language, and Hearing Research, 42*(5), 1042–1060.

Kreul, E. J. (1972). Neuromuscular control examination (NMC) for Parkinsonism: Vowel prolongations and diadochokinetic and reading rates. *Journal of Speech and Hearing Research, 15*(1), 72–83.

Krishnan, S., Alcock, K. J., Mercure, E., Leech, R., Barker, E., Karmiloff-Smith, A., & Dick, F. (2013). Articulating novel words: Children's oromotor skills predict nonword repetition abilities. *Journal of Speech, Language, and Hearing Research, 56*(6), 1800–1812.

Kronvall, E. L., & Diehl, C. F. (1954). The relationship of auditory discrimination to articulatory defects of children with no known organic impairment. *Journal of Speech and Hearing Disorders, 19*(3), 335–338.

Kuehn, D. P. (1991). New therapy for treating hypernasal speech using continuous positive airway pressure (CPAP). *Plastic and Reconstructive Surgery, 88*(6), 967–969.

Kuehn, D. P., & Moon, J. B. (2000). Induced fatigue effects on velopharyngeal closure force. *Journal of Speech, Language, and Hearing Research, 43*(2), 486–500.

Kuhl, P. K, Ramírez, R. R., Bosseler, A., Lotus Lin, J., & Imada, T. (2014). Infants' brain responses to speech suggest analysis by synthesis. *Proceedings of the National Academy of Science, 111*(31), 11238–11245.

Kummer, A. W. (2005). Ankyloglossia. To clip or not to clip? That's the question. *The ASHA Leader, 10*(17), 6–30.

Kummer, A. W., & Lee, L. (1996). Evaluation and treatment of resonance disorders. *Language, Speech, and Hearing Services In Schools, 27*(3), 271–281.

Kupperman, P., Bligh, S., & Goodban, M. (1980). Activating articulation skills through Theraplay. *Journal of Speech and Hearing Disorders, 45*(4), 540–548.

Ladefoged, P. (2005). *Vowels and consonants: An introduction to the sounds of languages.* Malden, MA: Blackwell Publishing.

Laing, J. M. (1958). Therapy techniques for better nasal resonance. *Journal of Speech and Hearing Disorders, 23*(3), 254–256.

Lallh, A. K., & Rochet, A. P. (2000). The effect of information on listeners' attitudes toward speakers with voice or resonance disorders. *Journal of Speech, Language, and Hearing Research, 43*(3), 782–795.

Langley, M. B., & Thomas, C. (1991). Introduction to the neurodevelopmental approach. In M. B. Langley & L. J. Lombardino (Eds.), *Neurodevelopmental strategies for managing communication disorders in children with severe motor dysfunction.* Austin, TX: Pro-Ed.

LaRiviere, C., Winitz, H., Reeds, J. & Herriman, E. (1974). The conceptual reality of selected distinctive features. *Journal of Speech and Hearing Research, 17*(1), 122–133.

Lass, N. J., Kotchek, C. L., & Deem, J. F. (1972). Oral two-point discrimination: Further evidence of asymmetry on right and left sides of selected oral structures. *Perceptual and Motor Skills, 35*(1), 59–67.

Lee, S. A. S., & Iverson, G. K. (2012). Vowel category formation in Korean–English bilingual children. *Journal of Speech, Language, and Hearing Research, 55*(5), 1449–1462.

Leonard, R., & Gillis, R. (1982). Effects of a prosthetic tongue on vowel intelligibility and food management in a patient with total glossectomy. *Journal of Speech and Hearing Disorders, 47*(1), 25–30.

Leonard, R., & Gillis, R. (1983). Effects of a prosthetic tongue on vowel formants and isovowel lines in a patient with total glossectomy (an addendum to Leonard and Gillis, 1982). *Journal of Speech and Hearing Disorders, 48*(4), 423–426.

Lewis, J. A., & Counihan, R. F. (1965). Tongue-thrust in infancy. *Journal of Speech and Hearing Disorders, 30*, 280–282.

Lieberman, P. (1980). On the development of vowel production in young children. In G. Yeni-Komshian, J. Kavanaugh, & C. A. Ferguson (Eds.), *Child phonology, volume one: production.* New York, NY: Academic Press.

Lindblom, B. (1983). Economy of speech gestures. In P. F. MacNeilage (Ed.), *The production of speech* (pp. 217–245). New York, NY: Springer-Verlag.

Lindblom, B., & Sundberg, J. (1969). A quantitative method of vowel production and the distinctive features of Swedish vowels. *Speech, Music, and Hearing Quarterly Progress and Status Report, 10*(1), 14–32. Retrieved from http://www.speech.kth.se/prod/publications/files/qpsr/1969/1969_10_1_014-032.pdf

Lindblom, B., & Sundberg, J. (1971). Acoustical consequences of lip, tongue, jaw, and larynx movement. *Journal of the Acoustical Society of America, 50*(4), 1166–1179.

Ling, D. (1976). *Speech and the hearing-impaired child: Theory and practice.* Washington, D.C.: The Alexander Graham Bell Association for the Deaf.

Locke, J. L. (1969). Short-term auditory memory, oral perception, and experimental sound learning. *Journal of Speech and Hearing Research, 12*(1), 185–192.

Lof, G. L. (2008). Controversies surrounding nonspeech oral motor exercises for childhood speech disorders. *Seminars in Speech and Language 29*(4), 253–255.

Lof, G. L., & Watson, M. M. (2008). A nationwide survey of nonspeech oral motor exercise use: Implications for evidence-based practice. *Language, Speech, and Hearing Services in Schools, 39*(3), 392–407.

Löfqvist, A., & Gracco, V. L. (1997). Lip and jaw kinematics in bilabial stop consonant production. *Journal of Speech and Hearing Research, 40*(4), 877–893.

Logemann, J. A. (1983). *Evaluation and treatment of swallowing disorders.* San Diego, CA: College-Hill Press.

Logemann, J. A., Pauloski, B. R., Rademaker, A. W., McConnel, F. M., Heiser, M. A., Cardinale, S., … Baker, T. (1993). Speech and swallow function after tonsil/base of tongue resection with primary closure. *Journal of Speech Hearing Research 36*(5), 918–926.

Loucks, T. M., & De Nil, L. F. (2001). The effects of masseter tendon vibration on nonspeech oral movements and vowel gestures. *Journal of Speech, Language, and Hearing Research, 44*(2), 306–316.

Lowe, R. J. (1994). *Phonology, assessment and intervention applications in speech pathology.* Baltimore, MD: Williams & Wilkins.

Luce, P. A., & Pisoni, D. B. (1998). Recognizing spoken words: The neighborhood activation model. *Ear and Hearing, 19*(1), 1–36.

Ludlow, C. L., Hoit, J., Kent, R., Ramig, L. O., Shrivastav, R., Strand, E., … Sapienza, C. M. (2008). Translating principles of neural plasticity into research on speech motor control recovery and rehabilitation. *Journal of Speech, Language, and Hearing Research, 51*(1), supplement 240–258.

Luria, A. (1964). Factors and forms of aphasia. In A. V. S. DeReuck & M. O'Conner (Eds.), *Disorders of language.* Boston, MA: Little, Brown, & Company.

Luria, A. R. (1966). *Higher cortical functioning in man.* New York, NY: Basic Books.

Maas, E., Robin, D. A., Austermann Hula, S. N., Freedman, S. E., Wulf, G., Ballard, K. J., & Schmidt, R. A. (2008). Principles of motor learning in treatment of motor speech disorders. *American Journal of Speech-Language Pathology, 17*(3), 277–298.

MacNeilage, P. F. (1998). The frame/content theory of evolution of speech production. *Behavioral and Brain Sciences, 21*(4), 499–511.

MacNeilage, P. F., & Davis, B. L. (2001). Motor mechanisms in speech ontogeny: Phylogenetic, neurobiological, and linguistic implications. *Current Opinion in Neurobiology, 11*(6), 696–700.

MacNeilage, P. F., Rootes, T. P., & Chase, R. A. (1967). Speech production and perception in a patient with severe impairment of somesthetic perception and motor control. *Journal of Speech and Hearing Research, 10*(3), 449–467.

MacNeilage, P. F., & Sholes, G. N. (1964). An electromyographic study of the tongue during vowel production. *Journal of Speech and Hearing Research, 7*, 209–232.

Manabe, M., Lim, H. W., Winzer, M., & Loomis, C. A. (1999). Architectural organization of filiform papillae in normal and black hairy tongue epithelium: Dissection of differentiation pathways in a complex human epithelium according to their patterns of keratin expression. *Archives of Dermatology, 135*(2), 177–181.

Mange, C. V. (1960). Relationships between selected auditory perceptual factors and articulation ability. *Journal of Speech and Hearing Research, 3*, 67–74.

Marshall, N. R., & Hegrenes, J. R. (1972). A communication therapy model for cognitively disorganized children. In B. M. McLean (Ed.), *Language intervention with the retarded* (pp. 130–150). Baltimore, MD: University Park Press.

Marshalla, P. (1992a). *Oral-motor techniques in articulation and phonological therapy.* Mill Creek, WA: Marshalla Speech & Language.

Marshalla, P. (1992b). *Oral-motor techniques in articulation and phonological therapy* [2-day Educational Workshop on VHS]. United States: Innovative Concepts.

Marshalla, P. (1992c). Oral-motor techniques in articulation and phonological therapy [Seminar handbook]. Seattle, WA: Innovative Concepts.

Marshalla, P. (2001a). *Becoming verbal with childhood apraxia.* Mill Creek, WA: Marshalla Speech & Language.

Marshalla, P. (2004). *Successful r therapy.* Mill Creek, WA: Marshalla Speech & Language.

Marshalla, P. (2007a). *Marshalla oral sensorimotor test.* Greenville, SC: Super Duper Publications.

Marshalla, P. (2007b). *Frontal lisp, lateral lisp.* Mill Creek, WA: Marshalla Speech & Language.

Marshalla, P. (2007c) *Vowel Tracks for Improving Intelligibility* [CD]. Mill Creek, WA: Marshalla Speech & Language.

Marshalla, P. (2008a). *Do you like pie?* Mill Creek, WA: Marshalla Speech & Language.

Marshalla, P. (2012a). Horns, whistles, bite blocks, and straws: A review of the objects/tools used in articulation therapy by Van Riper and other traditional therapists. *International Journal of Orofacial Myology, 37*, 69–96.

Marshalla, P. (2012b). Horns, whistles, bite blocks, and straws: A review of the objects/tools used in articulation therapy by Van Riper and other traditional therapists. *Oral Motor Institute, 4*(2). Retrieved from http://www.oralmotorinstitute.org/mons/v4n2_marshalla.html

Marshalla, P. (2018) Vowels & Intelligibility [CD]. Ashland, OR: Marshalla Speech & Language.

Mason, R. M., & Grandstaff, H. L. (1971). Evaluating the velopharyngeal mechanism in hypernasal speakers. *Language, Speech, and Hearing Services in Schools, 2*(4), 53–61.

Mason, R. M., & Proffit, W. R. (1974). The tongue thrust controversy: Background and recommendations. *Journal of Speech and Hearing Disorders, 39*(2), 115–132.

Massaro, D. W., & Light, J. (2004). Using visible speech to train perception and production of speech for individuals with hearing loss. *Journal of Speech, Language, and Hearing Research, 47*(2), 304–320.

Massengill, R., Maxwell, S., & Pickrell, K. (1970). An analysis of articulation following partial and total glossectomy. *Journal of Speech and Hearing Disorders, 35*(2), 170–173.

Mayer, L. V. (1998). *Fundamentals of voice and articulation.* Boston, MA: McGraw-Hill.

McCabe, R. B., & Bradley, D. (1975). Systematic multiple phoneme approach to articulation therapy. *Acta Symbolica, 6*, 1–18.

McClean, M. (1978). Variation in perioral reflex amplitude prior to lip muscle contraction for speech. *Journal of Speech and Hearing Research, 21*(2), 276–284.

McClean, M. D. (1991). Lip muscle EMG responses to oral pressure stimulation. *Journal of Speech and Hearing Research, 34*(2), 248–251.

McDonald, E. T. (1964). *Articulation testing and treatment: A sensory-motor approach.* Pittsburgh, PA: Stanwix House.

McDonald, E. T., & Aungst, L. S. (1967). Studies in oral sensorimotor function. In J. Bosma (Ed.), *Oral sensation and perception* (pp. 202–220). Springfield, IL: Charles C. Thomas.

McDonald, E. T., & Chance, B. (1964). *Cerebral palsy.* Englewood Cliffs, NJ: Prentice-Hall.

McFarland, D. J., Cacace, A. T., & Setzen, G. (1998). Temporal-order discrimination for selected auditory and visual stimulus dimensions. *Journal of Speech and Hearing Research, 41*(2), 300–314.

McGlone, R. E., & Proffit, W. R. (1973). Patterns of tongue contact in normal and lisping speakers. *Journal of Speech and Hearing Research 16*(3), 456–473.

McGlone, R. E., Proffit, W. R., & Christiansen, R. L. (1967). Lingual pressures associated with alveolar consonants. *Journal of Speech and Hearing Research, 10*(3), 606–615.

McGowan, R. W., McGowan, R. S., Denny, M., & Nittrouer, S. (2014). A longitudinal study of very young children's vowel production. *Journal of Speech, Language, and Hearing Research, 57*(1) 1–15.

McGurk, H., & MacDonald, J. (1976). Hearing lips and seeing voices. *Nature, 264*(5588), 746–748.

McHenry, M. A., Minton, J. T., Wilson, R. L., & Post, Y. V. (1994). Intelligibility and nonspeech orofacial strength and force control following traumatic brain injury. *Journal of Speech and Hearing Research, 37*(6), 1271–1283.

McLeod, S., & Singh, S. (2009). *Speech sounds: A pictorial guide to typical and atypical speech.* San Diego, CA: Plural Publishing.

McNeil, M. R., Weismer, G., Adams, S., & Mulligan, M. (1990). Oral structure nonspeech motor control in normal, dysarthric, aphasic and apraxic speakers: Isometric force and static position control. *Journal of Speech and Hearing Research, 33*(2), 255–268.

McNutt, J. C. (1975). Asymmetry in two-point discrimination on the tongues of adults and children. *Journal of Communication Disorders, 8*(3), 213–220.

McNutt, J. C. (1977). Oral sensory and motor behaviors of children with /s/ or /r/ misarticulations. *Journal of Speech and Hearing Research, 20*(4), 694–703.

Ménard, L., Davis, B. L., & Boë, L. J., & Roy, J. P. (2009). Producing American English vowels during vocal tract growth: A perceptual categorization study of synthesized vowels. *Journal of Speech, Language, and Hearing Research, 52*(5), 1268–1285.

Merkel-Walsh, R. (2002). *SMILE: Systematic intervention for lingual elevation, a fun therapy program for tongue-thrust remediation.* Tucson, AZ: TalkTools.

Merten, K. (1972). A self-directing approach to articulation therapy: Theoretical and practical considerations. *Language, Speech, and Hearing Services in the Schools, 3*(3), 24–31.

Miccio, A. W. (2002). Clinical problem solving: Assessment of phonological disorders. *American Journal of Speech-Language Pathology, 11*(3), 221–229.

Miller, G. A. (1951). *Language and communication.* New York, NY: McGraw-Hill.

Miller, J. L., Watkin, K. L., & Chen, M. F. (2002). Muscle, adipose, and connective tissue variations in intrinsic musculature of the adult human tongue. *Journal of Speech, Language and Hearing Research, 45*(1), 51–65.

Mills, C. S. (2011). International Association of Orofacial Myology History: Origin, background, contributors. *International Journal of Orofacial Myology, 37,* 5–25.

Mizuno, K., & Ueda, A. (2005). Neonatal feeding performance as a predictor of neurodevelopmental outcome at 18 months. *Developmental Medicine and Child Neurology, 47*(5), 299–304.

Mohrmann, G. P. (1969). Introduction. In T. Sheridan, *Elocution and the English language* (pp. vii). Los Angeles, CA: The Augustan Reprint Society.

Moore, C. A., Caulfield, T. J., & Green, J. R. (2001). Relative kinematics of the rib cage and abdomen during speech and nonspeech behaviors of 15-month-old children. *Journal of Speech, Language, and Hearing Research, 44*(1), 80–94.

Moore, C. A., Smith, A., & Ringel, R. L. (1988). Task-specific organization of activity in human jaw muscles. *Journal of Speech and Hearing Research, 31*(4), 670–680.

Moore, G. P. (1971). Voice disorders organically based. In L. E. Travis, *Handbook of speech pathology and audiology* (pp. 535–570). Englewood Cliffs, NJ: Prentice-Hall.

Morley, M. (1972). *The development and disorders of speech in childhood.* Baltimore, MD: Williams & Wilkins.

Morris, H. L., Spriestersbach, D. C., & Darley, F. L. (1961). An articulation test for assessing competency of velopharyngeal closure. *Journal of Speech and Hearing Research, 4*(1), 48–55.

Morris, S. E. (1977a). Assessment of children with oral-motor dysfunction (Section II), & Treatment of children with oral-motor dysfunction (Section III). In J. M. Wilson (Ed.), *Oral-motor function and dysfunction in children* (pp. 106–208). Chapel Hill, NC: University of North Carolina.

Morris, S. E. (1977b). *Program guidelines for children with feeding problems.* Edison, NJ: Childcraft.

Morris, S. E., (1982). *Pre-speech assessment scale: A rating scale for the measurement of pre-speech behavior from birth through two years, revised edition.* New York, NY: J. A. Preston Corp.

Morris, S. E., & Klein, M. D. (1987). *Pre-feeding skills: A comprehensive resource for feeding development.* Austin, TX: Pro-Ed.

Morris, S. E., & Klein, M. D. (2000). *Pre-feeding skills: A comprehensive resource for mealtime development.* Austin, TX: Pro-Ed.

Munson, B., Edwards, J., & Beckman, M. E. (2005). Relationships between nonword repetition accuracy and other measures of linguistic development in children with phonological disorders. *Journal of Speech, Language, and Hearing Research, 48*(1), 61–78.

Munson, B., & Solomon, N. P. (2004). The effect of phonological neighborhood density on vowel articulation. *Journal of Speech, Language, and Hearing Research, 47*(5), 1048–1058.

Mysak, E. D. (1963) *Principles of a reflex therapy approach to cerebral palsy.* New York, NY: Teachers College.

Mysak, E. D. (1968). *Neuroevolutional approach to cerebral palsy and speech.* New York, NY: Teachers College.

Mysak, E. D. (1980). *Neurospeech therapy for the cerebral palsied: A neuroevolutional approach.* New York, NY: Teachers College.

Neel, A. T., & Palmer, P. M. (2012). Is tongue strength an important influence on rate of articulation in diadochokinetic and reading tasks? *Journal of Speech, Language, and Hearing Research, 55* (1), 235–246.

Nelson, C. A., & De Benabib, R. M. (1991). Sensory preparation of the oral-motor area. In M. B. Langley & L. J. Lombardino (Eds.), *Neurodevelopmental strategies for managing communication disorders in children with severe motor dysfunction* (pp. 131–158). Austin, TX: Pro-Ed.

Nemoy, E. M., & Davis, S. F. (1937). *The correction of defective consonant sounds.* Magnolia, CA: Expression Company.

Nicolosi, L, Harryman, E., & Kreshek, J. (1983). *Terminology of communication disorders: Speech-language-hearing.* Baltimore, MD: Williams & Wilkins.

Nilsson, L., & Hamberger, L. (2003). *A child is born.* New York, NY: Random House.

Nishi, K., & Kewley-Port, D. (2007). Training Japanese listeners to perceive American English vowels: Influence of training sets. *Journal of Speech, Language, and Hearing Research, 50*(6), 1496–1509.

Nishi, K., & Kewley-Port, D. (2008). Nonnative speech

perception training using vowel subsets: Effects of vowels in sets and order of training. *Journal of Speech, Language, and Hearing Research, 51*(6), 1480–1493.

Nittrouer, S. (1993). The emergence of mature gestural patterns is not uniform: Evidence from an acoustic study. *Journal of Speech and Hearing Research, 36*(5), 959–972.

Nittrouer, S., Studdert-Kennedy, M., & McGowan, R. S. (1989). The emergence of phonetic segments: Evidence from the spectral structure of fricative-vowel syllables spoken by children and adults. *Journal of Speech and Hearing Research, 32*(1), 120–132.

Nittrouer, S., Studdert-Kennedy, M., & Neely, S. T. (1996). How children learn to organize their speech gestures: Further evidence from fricative vowel syllables. *Journal of Speech and Hearing Research, 39*(2), 379–389.

Norrix, L. W., Plante, E., Vance, R., & Boliek, C. A. (2007). Auditory-visual integration for speech by children with and without specific language impairment. *Journal of Speech, Language, and Hearing Research, 50*(6); 1639–1651.

O'Brien, C., & Hayes, A. (1995). *Normal and impaired motor development: Theory into practice.* New York, NY: Chapman & Hall.

Oller, D. K. (1978). Infant vocalizations and the development of speech. *Allied Health and Behavioral Sciences Journal, 1*(4), 523–549.

Osberger, M. J. (1987). Training effects on vowel production by two profoundly hearing-impaired speakers. *Journal of Speech and Hearing Research, 30*(2), 241–251.

Osol, A. (1973). *Blakiston's pocket medical dictionary.* New York, NY: McGraw-Hill.

Ostry, D. J., Vatikiotis-Bateson, E., & Gribble, P. L. (1997). An examination of the degrees of freedom of human jaw motion in speech and mastication. *Journal of Speech, Language, and Hearing Research, 40*(6), 1341–1351.

Otomo, K., & Stoel-Gammon, C. (1992). The acquisition of unrounded vowels in English. *Journal of Speech and Hearing Research, 35*(3), 604–616.

Owings, N. O., & Guyette, T. W. (1982). Communication behavior assessment and treatment with the adult retarded: An approach. In N. J. Lass (Ed.), *Speech and language: Advances in basic research and practice* (pp. 185–216). New York, NY: Academic Press.

Palmer, M. F. (1949). Studies in clinical techniques IV: Rapid repetitive manipulation of the mandible in dysphonia. *Journal of Speech and Hearing Disorders, 14*(3), 260–261.

Palmer, M. F. (1952). Construction of one-way vision mirrors. *Journal of Speech and Hearing Disorders, 17*(2), 138.

Palmer, P. M., Jaffe, D. M., McCulloch, T. M., Finnegan, E. M., Van Daele, D. J., & Luschei, E. S. (2008). Quantitative contributions of the muscles of the tongue, floor-of-mouth, jaw, and velum to tongue-to-palate pressure generation. *Journal of Speech, Language, and Hearing Research, 51*(4), 828–835.

Pannbacker, M. (2004). Velopharyngeal incompetence: The need for speech standards. *American Journal of Speech-Language Pathology, 13*(3), 195–201.

Parker, F. S. (1887). *Order of exercises in elocution: Given at the Cook County Normal School.* Chicago, IL: Donohue & Henneberry.

Parham, D. F., Buder, E. H., Oller, D. K., & Boliek, C. A. (2011). Syllable-related breathing in infants in the second year of life. *Journal of Speech, Language, and Hearing Research, 54*(4), 1039–1050.

Passy, P. (1888). Our revised alphabet. *The Phonetic Teacher*, 57–60.

Patton, F. E. (1942). A comparison of the kinesthetic sensibility of speech-defective and normal-speaking children. *Journal of Speech and Hearing Disorders, 7*(4), 305–310.

Pena-Brooks, A., & Hegde, M. N. (2000). *Assessment and treatment of articulation and phonological disorders in children.* Austin, TX: Pro-Ed.

Perkell, J. S. (1981). On the use of feedback in speech production. In T. Myers, J. Laver, & J. Anderson (Eds.), *The cognitive representation of speech* (pp. 45–57). Amsterdam, Netherlands: Elsevier.

Perkell, J. S., Matthies, M. L., Tiede, M., Lane, H., Zandipour, M., & Marrone, N., … Guenther, F. H. (2004). The distinctness of speakers' /s/– /ʃ/ contrast is related to their auditory discrimination and use of an articulatory saturation effect. *Journal of Speech, Language, and Hearing Research, 47*(6), 1259–1269.

Perkins, W. H. (1983). *Dysarthria and apraxia.* New York, NY: Thieme-Stratton.

Peterson, S. J. (1974). Electrical stimulation of the soft palate. *The Cleft Palate Journal, 11*(1), 72–86.

Peterson, S. J. (1975). Nasal emission as a component of the misarticulation of sibilants and affricates. *Journal of Speech and Hearing Disorders, 40*(1), 106–114.

Peterson-Falzone, S. J., & Graham, M. S. (1990). Phoneme-specific nasal emission in children with and without physical anomalies of the velopharyngeal mechanism. *Journal of Speech and Hearing Disorders, 55*(1), 132–139.

Pflaster, G. (1979). Mirror, mirror on the wall…? *Journal of Speech and Hearing Disorders, 44*(3), 379–387.

Phatate, D. D., & Umano, H. (1981). Auditory discrimination of voiceless fricatives in children. *Journal of Speech, Language, and Hearing Research 24*(2), 162–168.

Picou, E. M., Ricketts, T. A., & Hornsby, B. W. Y. (2011). Visual cues and listening effort: Individual variability. *Journal of Speech, Language, and Hearing Research, 54*(5), 1416–1430.

Pinheiro. P. F., da Cunha, D. A., Filho, M. G. D., Caldas, A. S. C., Melo, T. M. A., & da Silva, H. J. (2012). The use of electrognathography in jaw movement research: A literature review. *The Journal of Craniomandibular Practice, 30*(4), 293–303.

Pleasonton, A. K. (1970). Sensitivity of the tongue to electrical stimulation. *Journal of Speech and Hearing Research, 13*(3), 635–644.

Pollock, K. E. (1991). The identification of vowel errors using traditional articulation or phonological process test stimuli. *Language, Speech, and Hearing Services in Schools, 22*(2), 39–50.

Polson, J. M. C. (1980). A survey of carryover practices of public school clinicians in Oregon (Unpublished master's thesis). Portland State University, Portland, OR. Retrieved from https://pdxscholar.library.pdx.edu/open _access_etds/2972/

Poore, M. A., & Barlow, S. M. (2009). Suck predicts neuromotor integrity and developmental outcomes. *Perspectives on Speech Science and Orofacial Disorders, 19*(1), 44–51.

Porter, R. J., & Lubker, J. F. (1980). Rapid reproduction of vowel-vowel sequences: Evidence for a fast and direct acoustic-motoric linkage in speech. *Journal of Speech and Hearing Research, 23*(3), 593–602.

Potter, S. (1882). *Speech and its defects: considered physiologically, pathologically, historically, and remedially.* Philadelphia, PA: P. Blakiston, Son & Company.

Powell, J., & McReynolds, L. (1969). A procedure for testing position generalization from articulation training. *Journal of Speech and Hearing Research, 12*(3), 629–645.

Powell, T. W. (2008a). The use of nonspeech oral motor treatments for developmental speech sound production disorders: Interventions and interactions. *Language, Speech and Hearing Services in the Schools, 39*(3), 374–379.

Powell, T. W. (2008b). An integrated evaluation of nonspeech oral motor treatments. *Language, Speech and Hearing Services in the Schools, 39*(3), 422–427.

Powers, M. H. (1971a). Functional disorders of articulation—Symptomatology and etiology. In L. E. Travis (Ed.), *Handbook of speech pathology and audiology* (pp. 837–875). Englewood Cliffs, NJ: Prentice-Hall.

Powers, M. H. (1971b). Clinical and educational procedures in functional disorders of articulation. In L. E. Travis (Ed.), *Handbook of speech pathology and audiology* (pp. 875–910). Englewood Cliffs, NJ: Prentice-Hall.

Pratt, S. R., Heintzelman, A. T., & Deming, S. E. (1993). The efficacy of using the IBM Speech Viewer Vowel Accuracy Module to treat young children with hearing impairment. *Journal of Speech and Hearing Research, 36*(5), 1063–1074.

Putnam, A. H. B., & Ringel, R. L. (1972). Some observations of articulation during labial sensory deprivation. *Journal of Speech and Hearing Research, 15*(3), 529–542.

Putnam, A. H. B., & Ringel, R. L. (1976). A cineradiographic study of articulation in two talkers with temporarily induced orosensory deprivation. *Journal of Speech and Hearing Research, 19*(2), 247–266.

Qi, Y., & Weinberg, B. (1991). Spectral slope of vowels produced by tracheoesophageal speakers. *Journal of Speech and Hearing Research, 34*(2), 243–247.

Rampp, D. L., & Pannbacker, M. (1978). Indications and contraindications for tongue thrust therapy. *Language, Speech, and Hearing Services in Schools, 9*(4), 259–264.

Rasch, P. J., & Burke, R. K. (1978). *Kinesiology and applied anatomy.* Philadelphia, PA: Lea & Febiger.

Rastatter, M. P., & Hyman, M. (1984). Effects of selected rhinologic disorders on the perception of nasal resonance in children. *Language, Speech and Hearing Services in Schools, 15*(1), 44–50.

Raymond, G. L. (1879). *The orator's manual.* Chicago, IL: S. C. Griggs.

Records, N. L. (1994). A measure of the contribution of a gesture to the perception of speech in listeners with aphasia. *Journal of Speech and Hearing Research, 37*(5), 1086–1099.

Rich, K. (1979). *The art of speech: A handbook of elocution.* Surry, England: Gresham Books.

Ringel, R. L., Burk, K. W., & Scott, C. M. (1968). Tactile perception: Form discrimination in the mouth. *British Journal of Disorders of Communication, 3*(2), 150–155.

Ringel, R. L., & Ewanowski, S. J. (1965). Oral perception: I. Two-point discrimination. *Journal of Speech and Hearing Research, 8*(4), 389–398.

Ringel, R. L., & Fletcher, H. M. (1967). Oral perception: III. Texture discrimination. *Journal of Speech and Hearing Research, 10*(3), 642–649.

Ringel, R. L., Saxman, J. H., & Brooks, A. R. (1967). Oral perception: II. Mandibular kinesthesia. *Journal of Speech and Hearing Research, 10*(3), 637–641.

Ripich, D. N., & Panagos, J. M. (1985). Accessing children's knowledge of sociolinguistic rules for speech therapy lessons. *Journal of Speech and Hearing Disorders, 50*(4), 335–346.

Ritterman, S. I. (1970). The role of practice and the observation of practice in speech-sound discrimination learning. *Journal of Speech and Hearing Research, 13*(1), 178–183.

Robin, D. A., & Luschei, E. S. (1992). *IOPI: Iowa oral oerformance instrument, model 1.5 reference manual.* Oakdale, IA: Breakthrough.

Roberts, J., Long, S. H., Malkin, C., Barnes, E., Skinner, M., Hennon, E. A., & Anderson, K. (2005). A comparison of phonological skills of boys with Fragile X Syndrome and Down Syndrome. *Journal of Speech, Language, and Hearing Research, 48*(5), 980–995.

Rochet-Capellan, A., Laboissière, R., Galván, A., & Schwartz, J. L. (2008). The speech focus position effect on jaw finger coordination in a pointing task. *Journal of Speech, Language, and Hearing Research, 51*(6), 1507–1521.

Rong, P., & Kuehn, D. (2012). The effect of articulatory adjustment on reducing hypernasality. *Journal of Speech, Language, and Hearing Research, 55*(5), 1438–1448.

Rood, M. S. (1954). Neurophysiological reactions as a basis for physical therapy. *Physical Therapy Review, 34*(9), 444–449.

Rosenbek, J. C., Lemme, M. L., Ahern, M. B., Harris, E. H., & Wertz, R. T. (1973). A treatment for apraxia of speech in adults. *Journal of Speech and Hearing Disorders, 38*(4), 462–472.

Rosenbek, J. C., Robbins, J., Fishback, B., & Levine, R. L. (1991). Effects of thermal application on dysphagia after stroke. *Journal of Speech and Hearing Research, 34*(6), 1257–1268.

Rosenbek, J. C., Wertz, R. T., & Darley, F. L. (1973). Oral sensation and perception in apraxia of speech and aphasia. *Journal of Speech and Hearing Research, 16*(1), 22–36.

Rosenfeld-Johnson, S. (1992). *A three-part treatment plan for oral-motor therapy* [Seminar handbook]. Seattle, WA: Innovative Concepts.

Rosenfeld-Johnson, S. (2001). *Oral-motor exercises for speech clarity.* Tucson, AZ: TalkTools.

Rosenfeld-Johnson, S. (2005a). *Assessment and treatment of the jaw: Putting it all together: Sensory, feeding and speech.* Tucson, AZ: TalkTools.

Rosenfeld-Johnson, S. (2005b). *Drooling remediation program for children and adults.* Tucson, AZ: TalkTools.

Rosenfeld-Johnson, S. (2014). *A therapist's guide to rehabilitative feeding and speech techniques for teens and adults.* Tucson, AZ: TalkTools.

Rosenwinkel Marshalla, P. (1985). The role of reflexes in oral-motor learning: Techniques for improved articulation. *Seminars in Speech and Language 6*(4), 317–336.

Ross, W. T. (1886). *Voice culture and elocution.* New York, NY: Baker and Taylor.

Ruark, J. L., & Moore, C. A. (1997). Coordination of lip muscle activity by 2-year-old children during speech and nonspeech tasks. *Journal of Speech, Language, and Hearing Research, 40*(6), 1373–1385.

Rudy, K., & Yunusova, Y. (2013). The effect of anatomic factors on tongue position variability during consonants. *Journal of Speech, Language, and Hearing Research, 56*(1), 137–149.

Ruscello, D. M. (1975). The importance of word position in articulation therapy. *Language, Speech, and Hearing Services in Schools, 6*(4), 190–196.

Ruscello, D. M (1978). Recording articulation training sessions. *Language, Speech, and Hearing Services in Schools, 9*(2), 133–136.

Ruscello, D. M., Shuster, L. I., & Sandwisch, A. (1991). Modification of context-specific nasal emission. *Journal of Speech and Hearing Research, 34*(1), 27–32.

Rush, J. (1855). *The philosophy of the human voice.* Philadelphia, PA: Lippincott.

Rvachew, S., & Jamieson, D. G. (1989). Perception of voiceless fricatives by children with a functional articulation disorder.

Journal of Speech and Hearing Disorders, 54(2), 193–208.

Sacks, S. (2002). Computerized program for articulation therapy. *ADVANCE Magazine for Speech Language Pathologists and Audiologists, 12*(6), 10.

Sadagopan, N., & Smith, A. (2008). Developmental changes in the effects of utterance length and complexity on speech movement variability. *Journal of Speech, Language, and Hearing Research, 51*(5), 1138–1151.

Sato, M., Vallée, N., Schwartz, J. L., & Rousset, I (2007). A perceptual correlate of the labial-coronal effect. *Journal of Speech, Language, and Hearing Research, 50*(6), 1466–1480.

Schissel, R. J., & Doty, M. H. (1979). Application of the systematic multiple phonemic approach to articulation therapy: A case study. *Language, Speech, and Hearing Services in Schools, 10*(3), 178–184.

Schlanger, B. B., & Galanowsky, G. I. (1966). Auditory discrimination tasks performed by mentally retarded and normal children. *Journal of Speech and Hearing Research, 9*(3), 434–440.

Scott, C. M., & Ringel, R. L. (1971). Articulation without oral sensory control. *Journal of Speech and Hearing Research, 14*(4), 804–818.

Scripture, E. W. (1912). *Stuttering and lisping.* New York, NY: Macmillan.

Seaver, E. J., Dalston, R. M., Leeper, H. A., & Adams, L. E. (1991). A study of nasometric values for normal nasal resonance. *Journal of Speech and Hearing Research, 34*(4), 715–721.

Secord, W. A., Boyce, S. E., Donohue, J. S., Fox, R. A., & Shine, R. E. (2007). *Eliciting sounds: Techniques and strategies for clinicians.* New York, NY: Thomson Delmar Learning.

Shames, G. H. (1957). Use of the nonsense-syllable in articulation therapy. *Journal of Speech and Hearing Disorders, 22*(2), 261–263.

Sharkey, S. G., & Folkins, J. W. (1985). Variability of lip and jaw movements in children and adults: Implications for the development of speech motor control. *Journal of Speech and Hearing Research, 28*(1), 8–15.

Sharma, M., Dhamani, I., Leung, J., & Carlile, S. (2014). Attention, memory and auditory processing in 10- to 15-year-old children with listening difficulties. *Journal of Speech, Language, and Hearing Research, 57*(6), 2308–2321.

Shelton, I. S., & Garves, M. M. (1985). Use of visual techniques in therapy for developmental apraxia of speech. *Language, Speech, and Hearing Services in Schools, 16*(2), 129–131.

Shelton, R. L., Johnson, A. F., Ruscello, D. M., & Arndt, W. B. (1978). Assessment of parent-administered listening training for preschool children with articulation deficits. *Journal of Speech and Hearing Disorders, 43*(2), 242–254.

Sheridan, T. (1759). *A discourse being introductory to his course of lectures on elocution and the English language.* London, England: Miller.

Sherman, D., & Geith, A. (1967). Speech sound discrimination and articulation skill. *Journal of Speech and Hearing Research, 10*(2), 277–280.

Shriner, T. H. (1966). Tongue thrusting and articulatory deficits. *Journal of Speech and Hearing Disorders, 31*(2), 206–207.

Shuster, L. I., Ruscello, D. M., & Smith, K. D. (1992). Evoking [r] using visual feedback. *American Journal of Speech-Language Pathology, 1*(3), 29–34.

Skinner, B. F. (1974). *About behaviorism.* New York, NY: Knopf.

Smit, A. B., Hand, L., Freilinger, J. J., Bernthal, J. E., & Bird, A. (1990). The Iowa articulation norms project and its Nebraska replication. *Journal of Speech and Hearing Disorders,*

55(4), 779–798.

Smith, A., & Goffman, L. (1998). Stability and patterning of speech movement sequences in children and adults. *Journal of Speech, Language, and Hearing Research, 41*(1), 18–30.

Smith, A., & Zelaznik, H. N. (2004). Development of functional synergies for speech motor coordination in childhood and adolescence. *Developmental Psychobiology, 45*(1), 22–33.

Smith, B. L. (1978). Temporal aspects of English speech production: A developmental perspective. *Journal of Phonetics, 6*(1), 37–67.

Smith, B. L., & Oller, D. K. (1981). A comparative study of pre-meaningful vocalizations produced by normally developing and Down's syndrome infants. *Journal of Speech and Hearing Disorders, 46*(1), 46–51.

Smith, C. R. (1975). Residual hearing and speech production in deaf children. *Journal of Speech and Hearing Research, 18*(4), 795–811.

Smith, K. K., & Kier, W. M. (1989). Trunks, tongues, and tentacles: Moving with skeletons of muscle. *American Scientist, 77,* 29–35.

Solomon, N. P. (2004). Assessment of tongue weakness and fatigue. *International Journal of Orofacial Myology, 30,* 8–19.

Solomon, N. P., Clark, H. M., Makashay, M. J., & Newman, L. A. (2008). Assessment of orofacial strength in patients with dysarthria. *Journal of Medical Speech-Language Pathology, 16*(4), 251–258.

Solomon, N. P., & Munson, B. (2004). The effect of jaw position on measures of tongue strength and endurance. *Journal of Speech, Language, and Hearing Research, 47*(3), 584–594.

Sommers, R. K., Leiss, R. H., Delp, M. A., Gerber, A. J., Fundrella, D., Smith, R. M., … & Haley, V. A. (1967). Factors related to the effectiveness of articulation therapy for kindergarten, first, and second grade children. *Journal of Speech and Hearing Research, 10*(3), 428–437.

Sommers, R. K., Meyer, W. J., & Fenton, A. K. (1961). Pitch discrimination and articulation. *Journal of Speech and Hearing Research, 4*(1), 56–60.

Sparks, R. W., & Holland, A. L. (1976). Method: Melodic Intonation Therapy for aphasia. *Journal of Speech and Hearing Disorders, 41*(3), 287–297.

Spitzer, S., Roley, S. S., Clark, F., & Parham, D. (1996). Sensory integration: Current trends in the United States. *Scandinavian Journal of Occupational Therapy, 3*(3), 123–138.

Spriestersbach, D. C., & Powers, G. R. (1959). Nasality in isolated vowels and connected speech of cleft palate speakers. *Journal of Speech and Hearing Research, 2*(1), 42–45.

Stainback, S. B., & Healy, H. A. (1982) *Teaching eating skills: A handbook for teachers.* Springfield, IL: Thomas.

Steeve, R. W. (2010). Babbling and chewing: Jaw kinematics from 8 to 22 months. *Journal of Phonetics, 38(3),* 445–458.

Steeve, R. W., & Moore, C. A. (2009). Mandibular motor control during the early development of speech and nonspeech behaviors. *Journal of Speech, Language, and Hearing Research, 52*(6), 1530–1554.

Stetson, R. (1928). *Motor phonetics: A study of speech movements in action.* Amsterdam, Netherlands: Martinus Nijhoff.

Stierwalt, J. A., & Youmans, S. R. (2007). Tongue measures in individuals with normal and impaired swallowing. *American Journal of Speech-Language Pathology, 16*(2), 148–156.

Stinchfield, S. M., & Young, E. H. (1938). *Children with delayed or defective speech: Motor-kinesthetic factors in their training.* Stanford, CA: Stanford University Press.

Stitt, C. L., & Huntington, D. A. (1969). Some relationships among articulation, auditory abilities, and certain other variables. *Journal of Speech and Hearing Research, 12*(3), 576–593.

Stoel-Gammon, C. (1989). Prespeech and early speech development of two late talkers. *First Language, 9*(26), 207–223.

Stoel-Gammon, C., & Herrington, P. B. (1990). Vowel systems of normally-developing and phonologically-disordered children. *Clinical Linguistics and Phonetics, 4*(2), 145–160.

Stone, M., & Vatikiotis-Bateson, E. (1995). Trade-offs in tongue, jaw, and palate contributions to speech production. *Journal of Phonetics, 23*(1–2), 81–100.

Sussman, H. M., Duder, C., Dalston, E., & Cacciatore, A. (1999). An acoustic analysis of the development of CV coarticulation: A case study. *Journal of Speech, Language, and Hearing Research, 42*(5), 1080–1096.

Sussman, H. M., MacNeilage, P. F., & Hanson, R. J. (1973). Labial and mandibular dynamics during the production of bilabial consonants: Preliminary observations. *Journal of Speech and Hearing Research, 16*(3), 397–420.

Sussman, H. M., Minifie, F. D., Buder, E. H., & Stoel-Gammon, C., & Smith, J. (1996). Consonant-vowel interdependencies in babbling and early words: Preliminary examination of a locus equation approach. *Journal of Speech and Hearing Research, 39*(2), 424–433.

Sussman, J. E. (1993). Auditory processing in children's speech perception: Results of selective adaptation and discrimination tasks. *Journal of Speech and Hearing Research, 36*(2), 380–395.

Swanson, L. A., Leonard, L. B., & Gandour, J. (1992). Vowel duration in mothers' speech to young children. *Journal of Speech and Hearing Research, 35*(3), 617–625.

Sweet, H. (1877). *A handbook of phonetics.* Oxford, England: Clarendon Press.

Takahashi, S., Kuribayashi, G., Ono, T., Ishiwata, Y., & Kuroda, T. (2005). Modulation of masticatory muscle activity by tongue position. *Angle Orthodontist, 75*(1), 35–39.

Takemoto, H. (2001). Morphological analyses of the human tongue musculature for three-dimensional modeling. *Journal of Speech, Language, and Hearing Research, 44*(1), 95–107.

Tasko, S. M., & Westbury, J. R. (2002). Defining and measuring speech movement events. *Journal of Speech, Language and Hearing Research, 45*(1), 127–142.

Templin, M. C. (1957). *Certain language skills in children: their development and interrelationships.* Minneapolis, MN: University of Minnesota Press.

Tetrazzini, L., & Caruso, E. (1909). *The art of singing.* New York, NY: Metropolitan Company.

Thewall, H. (1810). *A letter to Henry Cline, Esq.* London, England: Richard Taylor & Company.

Thomas, C. K. (1956). *Handbook of speech improvement.* New York, NY: Ronald Press Company.

Thorp, E. B., Virnik, B. T., & Stepp, C. E. (2013). Comparison of nasal acceleration and nasalance across vowels. *Journal of Speech, Language, and Hearing Research, 56*(5), 1476–1484.

Tian, W., Yin, H., Redett, R. J., Shi, B., Shi, J., Zhang, R., & Zheng, Q. (2010). Magnetic resonance imaging assessment of the velopharyngeal mechanism at rest and during speech in Chinese adults and children. *Journal of Speech, Language, and Hearing Research, 53*(6), 1595–1615.

Towen, B. (1976). *Neurological development in infancy.* London, England: Heinemann.

Travis, L. E. (1931). *Speech pathology: A dynamic neurological treatment of normal speech and speech deviations.* New York, NY: Appleton-Century.

Twisleton, E. (1873). *The tongue not essential to speech.* London, England: Murray.

Tye-Murray, N., & Kirk, K. I. (1993). Vowel and diphthong production by young users of cochlear implants and the relationship between the phonetic level evaluation and spontaneous speech. *Journal of Speech and Hearing Research, 36*(3), 488–502.

Van Borsel, J., Morlion, B., Van Snick, K., & Leroy, J. S. (2000). Articulation in Beckwith-Wiedemann Syndrome: Two case studies. *American Journal of Speech-Language Pathology, 9*(3), 202–213.

Van Hattum, R. J. (1980). *Communication disorders: An introduction.* New York, NY: Macmillan.

Van Hattum, R. J., Page, J., Baskervill, R. D., Duguay, M., Schreiber Conway, L., & Runzo Davis, T. (1974). The Speech Improvement System (SIS) taped program for remediation of articulation problems in the schools. *Language, Speech, and Hearing Services in Schools, 5*(2), 91–97.

Van Riper, C. (1939). Ear training in the treatment of articulation disorders. *Journal of Speech Disorders, 4*(2), 141–142.

Van Riper, C. (1978, 1954, 1947, 1939). *Speech correction: Principles and methods.* New York, NY & Englewood Cliffs, NJ: Prentice-Hall.

Van Riper, C. & Erickson, R. L. (1996, 1990, 1984). *Speech correction: An introduction to speech pathology and audiology.* Boston, MA: Allyn & Bacon.

Van Riper, C. & Irwin, J. V. (1958). *Voice and articulation.* Englewood Cliffs, NJ: Prentice-Hall.

Vatikiotis-Bateson, E., & Ostry, D. J. (1995). An analysis of the dimensionality of jaw motion in speech. *Journal of Phonetics, 23*(1–2), 101–117.

Vaughn, G. R., & Clark, R. M. (1979). *Speech facilitation: Extraoral and intraoral stimulation technique for improvement of articulation skills.* Springfield, IL: Thomas.

Vihman, M. M. (2004a). Early phonological development. In J. E. Bernthal & N. W. Bankson, *Articulation and phonological disorders* (pp. 63–104). Boston, MA: Pearson.

Vihman, M. M. (2004b). Later phonological development. In J. E. Bernthal & N. W. Bankson, *Articulation and phonological disorders* (pp. 105–138). Boston, MA: Pearson.

Vihman, M. M., & Velleman, S. L. (1989). Phonological reorganization: A case study. *Language and Speech, 32*(2), 149–170.

Vogel, D., & Miller, L. (1991). A top-down approach to treatment of dysarthric speech. In D. Vogel & M. P. Cannito (Eds.), *Treating Disordered Speech Motor Control: For Clinicians by Clinicians.* Austin, TX: Pro-Ed.

Vorperian, H. K., & Kent, R. D. (2007). Vowel acoustic space development in children: A synthesis of acoustic and anatomic data. *Journal of Speech, Language, and Hearing Research, 50*(6), 1510–1545.

Wallach, G. P., & Miller, L. (1988). *Language intervention and academic success.* Austin, TX: Pro-Ed.

Walsh, B., & Smith, A. (2002). Articulatory movements in adolescents: Evidence for protracted development of speech motor control processes. *Journal of Speech, Language, and Hearing Research, 45*(6), 1119–1133

Walsh, G. (1939). *Sing your way to better speech: A jingle sequence for the improvement of articulation and rhythm in speaking.* New York, NY: Dutton.

Ward, I. C. (1923). *Defects of speech: Their nature and their cure.* London, England: Dent.

Ward, M. M., Malone, H. D., Jann, G. R., & Jann, H. W. (1961). Articulation variations associated with visceral swallowing and malocclusion. *Journal of Speech and Hearing Disorders, 26*(4), 334–341.

Watson, B. U. (1991). Some relationships between intelligence and auditory discrimination. *Journal of Speech Hearing Research, 34*(3), 621–627.

Wassilieff, N. W. (1888). Wo wird der schluckereflex ausgelöst? In Mittheilungen der Naturforsch Gessellsch [Conference Proceedings]. Bern, Switzerland: P. Haller.

Weber, C. M., & Smith, A. (1987). Reflex responses in human jaw, lip, and tongue muscles elicited by mechanical stimulation. *Journal of Speech and Hearing Research, 30*(1), 70–79.

Weinberg, B., Christensen, R., Logan, W., Bosma, J., & Wornall, A. (1969). Severe hypoplasia of the tongue. *Journal of Speech Hearing Disorders, 34*(2), 157–168.

Weinberg, B., Liss, G. M., & Hillis, J. (1970). A comparative study of visual, manual, and oral form identification in speech impaired and normal speaking children. In J. Bosma (Ed.), *Second symposium on oral sensation and perception* (pp. 350–356). Springfield, IL: Thomas.

Weiner, P. S. (1967). Auditory discrimination and articulation. *Journal of Speech and Hearing Disorders, 32*(1), 19–28.

Weismer, S. E., & Hesketh, L. J. (1993). The influence of prosodic and gestural cues on novel word acquisition by children with specific language impairment. *Journal of Speech, Language, and Hearing Research, 36*(5), 1013–1025.

West, R. W., & Ansberry, M. (1968). *The rehabilitation of speech* (4th Ed.). New York, NY: Harper & Row.

Westbury, J. R. (1988). Mandible and hyoid bone movements during speech. *Journal of Speech, Language, and Hearing Research, 31*(3), 405–416.

Weston, A. J. (1969). The use of paired stimuli in the modification of articulation. (Unpublished doctoral thesis). University of Kansas, Lawrence, KS.

Weston, A. J., & Harber, S. K. (1975). The effects of scheduling on progress in paired-stimuli articulation therapy. *Language, Speech, and Hearing Services in Schools, 6*(2), 96–101.

Weston, A. J., & Irwin, J. V. (1971). Use of paired stimuli in modification of articulation. *Perceptual Motor Skills, 32*(3), 947–957.

Williams, G. C., & McReynolds, L. V. (1975). The relationship between discrimination and articulation training in children with misarticulations. *Journal of Speech and Hearing Research, 18*(3), 401–412.

Williams, W. N., & La Pointe, L. L. (1971). Correlations between oral form recognition and lingual touch sensitivity. *Perceptual and Motor Skills, 32*(3), 840–842.

Wingo, J. W., & Hoshiko, M. (1972). Differential effectiveness of six information-input procedures utilized to teach unfamiliar sounds in isolation. *Journal of Speech and Hearing Research, 15*(2), 256–263.

Winkler, A., & Crary, M. A. (1982). *Developmental verbal dyspraxia: A therapy study* [Seminar handbook]. Retrieved in person at the American Speech-Language-Hearing Association Convention, Toronto, Canada.

Winitz, H., & Bellerose, B. (1962). Sound discrimination as a function of pretraining conditions. *Journal of Speech and Hearing Research, 5*(4), 340–348.

Wohlert, A. B. (1996a). Tactile perception of spatial stimuli on the lip surface by young and older adults. *Journal of Speech and Hearing Research, 39*(6), 1191–1198.

Wohlert, A. B. (1996b). Perioral muscle activity in young and older adults during speech and nonspeech tasks. *Journal of Speech, Language, and Hearing Research, 39*(4), 761–770.

Wohlert, A. B. (1996c). Reflex responses of lip muscles in young and older women. *Journal of Speech, Language, and Hearing Research, 39*(3), 578–589.

Wohlert, A. B., & Goffman, L. (1994). Human perioral muscle activation patterns. *Journal of Speech, Language, and Hearing Research, 37*(5), 1032–1040.

Wohlert, A. B., & Smith, A. (1998). Spatiotemporal stability of lip movements in older adult speakers. *Journal of Speech, Language, and Hearing Research, 41*(1), 41–50.

Wohlert, A. B., & Smith, A. (2002). Developmental change in variability of lip muscle activity during speech. *Journal of Speech, Language, and Hearing Research, 45*(6), 1077–1087.

Wolf, P. H. (1986). The maturation and development of fetal motor patterns. In M.G. Wade & H. T. A. Whiting (Eds.), *Motor development in children: Aspects of coordination and* control (pp. 77–96). Dordrecht, Netherlands: Martinus Nijhoff.

Wolfe, V. I., & Blocker, S. D. (1990). Consonant-vowel interaction in an unusual phonological system. *Journal of Speech and Hearing Disorders, 55*(3), 561–566.

Wood, J. M. (1971). Tongue thrusting: Some clinical observations. *Journal of Speech and Hearing Disorders, 36*(1), 82–89.

Wood, L. M., Hughes, J., Hayes, K. C., & Wolfe, D. L. (1992). Reliability of labial closure force measurements in normal subjects and patients with CNS disorders. *Journal of Speech and Hearing Research, 35*(2), 252–258.

Wright, R., & Souza, P. (2012). Comparing identification of standardized and regionally valid vowels. *Journal of Speech, Language, and Hearing Research, 55*(1), 182–193.

Yorkston, K. M., Beukelman, D. R., Strand, E. A., & Bell, K. R. (1999). *Management of motor speech disorders in children and adults*. Austin, TX: Pro-Ed.

Young, E. H., & Hawk, S. S. (1955) *Moto-Kinesthetic Speech Training*. Stanford, CA: Stanford University Press.

Yules, R. B., & Chase, R. A. (1969). A training method for reduction of hypernasality in speech. *Plastic and Reconstructive Surgery, 43*(2), 180–185.

Zelazo, P. (1976). From reflexes to instrumental behavior. In L. P. Lipsett (Ed.), *Developmental psychobiology: The significance of infancy.* Hillsdale, NJ: Erlbaum.

Zemlin, W. R. (1968). *Speech and hearing science: Anatomy and physiology*. Englewood Cliffs, NJ: Prentice-Hall.

Zemlin, W. R. (1981). *Speech and hearing science: Anatomy and physiology*. Englewood Cliffs, NJ: Prentice-Hall.

SUPPLEMENTAL BIBLIOGRAPHY

Abbs, J. H., & Hughes, O. M. (1980). Labial-mandibular motor equivalence in speech: A response to Sussman's evaluation. *Journal of Speech and Hearing Research, 23*(3), 702–704.

Akin, J. (1958). *And so we speak: Voice and articulation.* Englewood Cliffs, NJ: Prentice-Hall.

Albert, M., Sparks, R., & Helm, N. (1973). Melodic intonation therapy for aphasia. *Archives of Neurology 29*(2), 130–131.

Alexander, A. W., Anderson, H. G., Heilman, P. C., Voeller, K. S., & Torgesen, J. K. (1991). Phonological awareness training and the remediation of analytic decoding deficits in a group of severe dyslexics. *Annals of Dyslexia, 41*(1), 193–206.

Alexander, R. (1987). Oral motor treatment for infants and young children with cerebral palsy. *Seminars in Speech and Language, 8*(1), 87–100.

Alexander, R. (1990). Oral-motor and respiratory-phonatory assessment. In E.D. Gibb & D. M. Teti (Eds.), *Interdisciplinary assessment of infants.* Baltimore, MD: Paul H. Brookes Publishing.

American Speech-Language-Hearing Association. (2002). Knowledge and skills needed by speech-language pathologists providing services to individuals with swallowing and/or feeding disorders. Retrieved from http://www.asha.org /policy/KS2002-00079.htm

American Speech-Language-Hearing Association. (2005). (Central) auditory processing disorders – the role of the audiologist. Retrieved from http://www.asha.org/policy /PS2005-00114.htm

American Speech-Language-Hearing Association. (2010). Evidence-Based Practice. Retrieved 24 July, 2014 from http:// www.asha.org/members/ebp/

Amos, H. D. (1996). *These were the Greeks.* Chester Springs, PA: Defour Editions Inc. (Original work published in 1979).

Ansel, B. M., Windsor, J., & Stark, R. E. (1992). Oral volitional movements in children: An approach to assessment. *Seminars in Speech and Language, 13*(1), 1–13.

Arey, L. B. (1966). *Developmental anatomy: A textbook and laboratory manual of embryology.* Philadelphia, PA: W. B. Saunders Company. (Original work published in 1934).

Arlt, P. B., & Goodban, M. T. (1976). A comparative study of articulation acquisition as based on a study of 240 normals, aged three to six. *Language, Speech, and Hearing Services in the Schools, 7*(3), 173–180.

Asher, I. E. (1984). Management of neurologic disorders: The first feeding session. In M.E. Groher (Ed.), *Dysphagia: diagnosis and management* (pp. 133–155). Boston, MA: Butterworths.

Asher, R. E., & Henderson, E. J. A. (1981). *Towards a history of phonetics.* Edinburgh, Scotland: Edinburgh University Press.

Ayres, A. (1897). *The essentials of elocution.* New York, NY: Funk & Wagnalls Company.

Ayres, A. J. (1972). *Southern California sensory integration tests.* Los Angeles, CA: Western Psychological Services.

Bae, Y., Kuehn, D. P., Sutton, B. P., Conway, C. A., & Perry, J. L. (2011). Three-dimensional magnetic resonance imaging of velopharyngeal structures. *Journal of Speech, Language, and Hearing Research, 54*(6), 1538–1545.

Bahr, D., & Rosenfeld-Johnson, S. (2010, May). Treatment of children with speech oral placement disorders (OPDs): A paradigm emerges. *Communication Disorders Quarterly, 31*(3), 131–138.

Bahr, D. (2003, Mar.). Typical versus atypical oral motor function in the pediatric population: Beyond the checklist. *Perspectives on Swallowing and Swallowing Disorders (Dysphagia), 12*(1), 4–12.

Bahr, D. (2006, Sept.). Coordinated oral-motor treatment. *ADVANCE for Speech-Language Pathologists and Audiologists, 16*(36), 10–11.

Bahr, D. (2007, Sept). Could an ad-hoc committee define oral-motor? *ADVANCE for Speech-Language Pathologists and Audiologists, 17*(36), 4.

Bahr, D. (2008). A topical bibliography on oral motor assessment and treatment: To help address the current controversy regarding oral motor research. *Oral Motor Institute, 1*(2). Retrieved from http://www.oralmotorinstitute.org/mons /v2n1_bahr.html

Bahr, D. (2008, Nov.). "The Oral Motor Debate: Where Do We Go From Here?" Poster session with extensive handout presented at the annual meeting of the American Speech-Language-Hearing Association, Chicago, IL.

Bahr, D. (2011). The oral motor debate part I: Understanding the problem. *Oral Motor Institute 3(1).* Retrieved from http:// www.oralmotorinstitute.org/mons/v3n1_bahr.html

Bahr, D. (2011). The oral motor debate part III: Exploring terminology and practice patterns. *Oral Motor Institute 3(2).* Retrieved from http://www.oralmotorinstitute.org/mons /v3n2_bahr.html

Bahr, D., & Banford, R. J. (2012). The oral motor debate part III: Exploring research and training needs/ideas. *Oral Motor Institute, 4*(1). Retrieved from http://www.oralmotorinstitute .org/mons/v4n1_bahr.html

Ballard, K. J., Granier, J. P., & Robin, D. A. (2008) Understanding the nature of apraxia: Theory, analysis, and treatment. *Aphasiology, 14*(10), 969–995.

Balmuth, M. (1982). *The roots of phonetics: A historical introduction.* London, England: McGraw-Hill.

Barnes, S. (1995). *Taming the tongue thrust: Video and handbook for tongue thrust correction and oral motor therapy.* Arcadia, CA: Suzanne M. Barnes.

Bell, A. M. (1867) *Visible speech: The science of universal alphabets.* London, England: Simpkin, Marshall & Company.

Bird, J., & Bishop, D. V. M., & Freeman, N. H. (1995). Phonological awareness and literacy development in children with expressive phonological impairments. *Journal of Speech and Hearing Research, 38*(2), 446–462.

Blache, S. E. (1982). Minimal word-pairs and distinctive features. In M. A. Crary (Ed.), *Phonological intervention: Concepts and procedures* (pp. 61–96). San Diego, CA: College-Hill Press.

Blakely, R. (1983). Treatment of developmental apraxia of speech. In W. H. Perkins (Ed.), *Dysarthria and apraxia: Current therapy speech disorders in children.* New York, NY: Thieme.

Cermak, S. A. (1991). Somatodyspraxia. In A. G. Fisher, E. A. Murray, & A. C. Bundy, *Sensory integration: Theory and practice.* Philadelphia, PA: F. A. Davis Company.

Chance, P. (Ed.). (1979). *Pediatric round table 3: Learning through play.* New York, NY: Johnson & Johnson Baby.

Cody, S. (1905). *The art of writing and speaking the English language.* New York, NY: Funk & Wagnalls Company.

Cole, R. A. (1973). Perceiving syllables and remembering phonemes. *Journal of Speech and Hearing Research, 16*(1), 37–47.

Comstock, A. (1853). *Comstock's phonetic reader no. 1.* Philadelphia, PA: Andrew Comstock.

Comstock, A., Pitman, B., & M'Lean, J. (1855). *A treatise on phonology: Comprising a perfect alphabet for the English language* (2nd ed.). Philadelphia, PA: E. H. Butler & Company.

Cooper, R. (1968). The method of meaningful minimal contrasts in functional articulation problems. *Journal of the Speech and Hearing Association of Virginia, 10,* 17–22.

Cornett, R. (1972). *Cued speech parent training and follow-up program.* Washington, DC: Bureau for Education of Handicapped.

Costello, J. M. (Ed.). (1984). *Speech disorders in children: Recent advances.* San Diego, CA: College-Hill Press.

Costello, J. & Onstine, J. M. (1976). The modification of multiple articulation errors based on distinctive feature theory. *Journal of Speech and Hearing Disorders, 41*(2), 199–215.

Crary, M. (Ed.). (1982) *Phonological intervention: Concepts and procedures.* San Diego, CA: College Hill Press.

Crowner, T. A. (1977). Mealtime skills program at a public school. In R. Perkse, A. Clifton, B. McLean, & J. Stein (Eds.), *Mealtimes for severely and profoundly handicapped persons.* Baltimore, MD: University Park Press.

Czesak-Duffy, B. (1993). *Triathlon articulation training.* Kearney, NJ: Creative Communication Concepts.

Dalston, R. M., Warren, D. W., & Dalston, E. T. (1991). A preliminary investigation concerning the use of nasometry in identifying patients with hyponasality and/or nasal airway impairment. *Journal of Speech and Hearing Research, 34*(1), 11–18.

Dangennes, B. (1915). *Speech: How to use it efficiently, by Xanthes.* New York, NY: Funk & Wagnalls Company.

Daniloff, R. G. (1984). *Articulation assessment and treatment issues.* San Diego, CA: College-Hill Press.

Davis, B., & Velleman, S. (2008). Establishing a basic speech repertoire without using NSOME: Means, motive, and opportunity. *Seminars in Speech and Language 29*(4), 312–319.

DeThorne, L. S., Johnson, C. J., Walder, L., & Mahurin-Smith, J. (2009). When "simon says" doesn't work: Alternatives to imitation for facilitating early speech development. *American Journal of Speech Language Pathology, 18*(2), 133–145.

Diedrich, W. M. (1971). Procedures for counting and charting a target phoneme. *Language, Speech, and Hearing Services in Schools, 2*(5), 18–32.

Dinnsen, D. A., Chin, S. B., Elbert, M., & Powell, T. W. (1990). Some constraints on functionally disordered phonologies: Phonetic inventories and phonotactics. *Journal of Speech and Hearing Research, 33*(1), 28–37.

Dionne, W. (2001). *Little thumb.* Gretna, LA: Pelican Publishing Company.

Dollaghan, C. (2004). Evidence-based practice: Myths and realities. *The ASHA Leader, 9*(7), 4–12.

Dollaghan, C. A. (2007). *The handbook for evidence-based practice in communication disorders.* Baltimore, MD: Paul H. Brooks Publishing Company.

of communication disorders. New York, NY: Thieme Medical Publishers.

Bleile, K. (1995). *Manual of articulation and phonological disorders: infancy through adulthood.* San Diego, CA: Singular Publishing Group.

Blockcolsky, V. D., Frazer, J. M., & Frazer, D. H. (1979). *30,000 selected words: Organized by letter, sound, and syllable.* Tucson, AZ: Communication Skill Builders.

Boehme, R. (1990). Integration of neurodevelopmental treatment and myofascial release in adult orthopedics. In J. F. Barnes (Ed.), *Myofascial release, the search for excellence: A comprehensive evaluatory and treatment approach,* (pp. 209–217). Peoli, OH: John F. Barnes.

Boehme, R. (1990). *The hypotonic child.* Tucson, AZ: Therapy Skill Builders.

Borden, G. (1984). Consideration of motor sensory targets and a problem in perception. In H. Winitz (Ed.), *Treating articulation disorders: For clinicians by clinicians* (pp. 51–66). Baltimore, MD: University Park Press.

Boshart, C. (1999). *Treatise on the tongue.* Temecula, CA: Speech Dynamics.

Bosma, J. (1978). Structure and function of the infant oral and pharyngeal mechanism. In J. M. Wilson (Ed.), *Oral-motor function and dysfunction in children* [conference proceedings] (pp. 33–65). Chapel Hill, NC: University of North Carolina.

Bowen, C. (2005, Oct.). What is the evidence for oral motor therapy. *Acquiring Knowledge in Speech, Language and Hearing, 7*(3), 144–147.

Bower, T. G. R. (1977). *A primer of infant development.* San Francisco, CA: W. H. Freeman & Company.

Bower, T. G. R. (1989). *The rational infant: Learning in infancy.* New York, NY: W. H. Freeman & Company.

Boyce, E. M. (1889). *Enunciation and articulation: A practical manual for teachers and schools.* Boston, MA: Ginn & Company.

Bricker, W. A., & Bricker, D. D. (1972). Assessment and modification of verbal imitation with low-functioning retarded children. *Journal of Speech and Hearing Research, 15*(4), 690–698.

Brooks, A. R., Shelton, R. L., & Youngstrom, K. A. (1966). Tongue-palate contact in persons with palate defects. *Journal of Speech and Hearing Disorders, 31*(1), 14–25.

Brookshire, R. H. (1992). *An introduction to neurogenic communication disorders.* St. Louis, MO: Mosby.

Brown, C. (1955). *My left foot.* New York, NY: Simon and Schuster.

Brown, C. C. (Ed.). (1984). *Pediatric round table 10: The many facets of touch.* New York, NY: Johnson & Johnson Baby.

Brown, R. (1973). *A first language.* Cambridge, MA: Harvard University Press.

Bunton, K. (2008). Speech versus nonspeech: Different tasks, different neural organization. *Seminars in Speech and Language 29*(4), 267–275.

Bunton, K., & Weismer, G. (1994). Evaluation of a reiterant force-impulse task in the tongue. *Journal of Speech and Hearing Research, 37*(5), 1020–1031.

Campbell, S. K. (1977). Oral sensorimotor physiology. In J. M. Wilson (Ed.), *Oral-motor function and dysfunction in children* [conference proceedings], (pp. 1–11). Chapel Hill, NC: University of North Carolina.

Cantu, R. I., & Grodin, A. J. (1992). *Myofascial manipulation: Theory and clinical application.* Gaithersburg, MD: Aspen Publishers.

Carson, M. K. (2007). *Alexander Graham Bell: Giving voice to the world.* New York, NY: Sterling Publishing Company.

Caruso, A. J., & Strand, E. A. (1999). *Clinical management of motor*

Dougherty, D. P. (2005). *Teach me how to say it right: Helping your child with articulation problems.* Oakland, CA: New Harbinger Publications.

Duchan, J. F. (2005). The phonetically-based speech therapy methods of Alexander Graham Bell. *Canadian Journal of Speech Language Pathology and Audiology, 29,* 70–72.

Duchan, J. F. (2006). The phonetic notation system of Melville Bell and its role in the history of phonetics. *Journal of Speech Language Pathology and Audiology, 30*(1), 14–17.

Duchan, J. F. (2009). The conceptual underpinnings of John Thelwall's elocutionary practices. In S. Poole (Ed.), *John Thewall: Radical romantic and acquitted felon* (pp. 139–145). London, England: Pickering & Chatto.

Duchan, J. F. (2011, May 12). A history of speech-language pathology. Retrieved from https://www.acsu.buffalo .edu/~duchan/new_history/ overview.html

Dunn, C., & Till, J. A. (1982). Morphophonemic rule learning in normal and articulation-disordered children. *Journal of Speech and Hearing Research, 25*(3), 322–333.

Dworkin, J. P. (1996). Bite block therapy for oromandibular dystonia. *Journal of Medical Speech-Language Pathology, 4*(1), 47–56.

Dworkin, J. P., Aronson, A. E., & Mulder, D. W. (1980). Tongue force in normals and in dysarthric patients with amyotrophic lateral sclerosis. *Journal of Speech and Hearing Research, 23*(4), 828–837.

Dworkin, J. P., & Culatta, R. A. (1985). Oral structural and neuromuscular characteristics in children with normal and disordered articulation. *Journal of Speech and Hearing Disorders, 50*(2), 150–156.

Dworkin, J. P., & Culatta, R. A. (1996). *The Dworkin-Culatta oral mechanism examination and treatment system.* Farmington Hills, MI: Edgewood Press.

Dwyer, J. H. (1853). *An essay on elocution.* Albany: Weare C. Little.

Sexton, S. M. (2006). *Five-minute kids: Drill based program for students with speech sound disorders.* Lapeer, MI: 5-Minute Kids.

Eisenson, J. (1965). *The improvement of voice and diction.* New York, NY: Macmillan.

Eisenson, J. & Ogilvie, M. (1957). *Speech correction in the schools.* New York, NY: Macmillan.

Eldridge, M. (1968). *A history of the treatment of speech disorders.* Edinburgh, Scotland: Livingstone.

Faber, A. & Mazlish, E. (1980). *How to talk so kids will listen and listen so kids will talk.* New York, NY: Avon.

Fenno, F. H. (1876). *The science and art of elocution: How to read and speak.* Philadelphia, PA: Potter.

Ferguson, C. A., & Farwell, C. B. (1975). Words and sounds in early language acquisition. *Language, 51*(2), 419–439.

Finnie, N. R. (1975). *Handling the young cerebral palsied child at home.* New York, NY: Dutton.

Fiorotti, R. C. (2004). Early lingua frenectomy assisted by Co2 Laser. *International Journal of Orofacial Myology, 30,* 64–71.

Fisher, H. B., & Logemann, J. (1971). *The Fisher-Logemann test of articulation.* Austin, TX: Pro-Ed.

Fletcher, S. G. (1972). Time-by-count measurement of diadochokinetic syllable rate. *Journal of Speech and Hearing Research 15*(4), 763–770.

Fletcher, S. G., McCutcheon, M. J., & Wolf, M. B. (1975). Dynamic palatometry. *Journal of Speech and Hearing Research, 18*(4), 812–819.

Folk, J. (1992) *Straight speech.* Vero Beach, FL: Speech Bin.

Folkins, J. W., & Linville, R. N. (1983). The effects of varying lower-lip displacement on upper-lip movements: Implications for the coordination of speech movements. *Journal of Speech and Hearing Research, 26*(2), 209–217.

Forrest, K., & Iuzzini, J. (2008). A comparison of oral motor and production training for children with speech sound disorders. *Seminars in Speech and Language 29*(4), 304–311.

Frick, S., Frick, R., Oetter, P., & Richter, E. (1996). *Out of the mouths of babes.* Hugo, OK: PDP Press.

Friedland, D. J. (Ed.). (1998). *Evidence-based medicine: A framework for clinical practice.* New York, NY: McGraw-Hill.

Friedman Narr, R. A. (2006). Teaching phonological awareness with deaf and hard-of-hearing students. Teaching Exceptional Children, 38(4), 53–58.

Friedman Narr, R. A. (2008). Phonological awareness and decoding in deaf/hard of hearing students who use visual phonics. *Journal of Deaf Studies and Deaf Education, 13*(3), 405–416.

Fry, E. B., Polk, J. K., & Fountoukidis, D. (1984). *The reading teacher's book of lists.* Englewood Cliffs, NJ: Prentice-Hall.

Fudala, J. B., & Reynolds, W. M. (1986). *Arizona articulation proficiency scale.* Los Angeles, CA: Western Psychological Services.

Fujimura, O. (1961). Bilabial stop and nasal consonants: A motion picture study and its acoustical implications. *Journal of Speech and Hearing Research, 4*(3), 233–247.

Gagnon, E. (2001). *Power cards: Using special interests to motivate children and youth with asperger syndrome and autism.* Shawnee Mission, KS: Autism Asperger Publishing Company.

Gage, C. (1984). *The last northwoods reader.* Au Train, MI: Avery Color Studios.

Garber, S. W., Garber, M. D., & Spizman, R. F. (1990). *Good behavior.* New York, NY: Villard Books.

Gierut, J. A., Elbert, M., & Dinnsen, D. A. (1987). A functional analysis of phonological knowledge and generalization learning in misarticulating children. *Journal of Speech and Hearing Research, 30*(4), 462–479.

Gierut, J. A., Morrisette, M. L., Hughes, M. T., & Rowland, S. (1996). Phonological treatment efficacy and developmental norms. *Language, Speech, and Hearing Services in the Schools, 27*(3), 215–230.

Gierut, J. A., Morrisette, M. L., & Ziemer, S. M. (2010). Nonwords and generalization in children with phonological disorders. *American Journal of Speech-Language Pathology, 19*(2), 167–177.

Gilbert, D. W., & Swiney, K. A. (2007). *Sound strategies for sound production.* Austin, TX: Pro-Ed.

Gilpin, R. W. (1993). *Living and loving with autism: A collection of real life warm and humorous stories.* Arlington, TX: Future Horizons.

Grandin, T. (1996). *Thinking in pictures: And other reports from my life with autism.* New York, NY: Vintage Press.

Gray, H. (1901). *Anatomy: Descriptive and surgical.* Philadelphia, PA: Running Press.

Grosvenor, E. & Wesson, M. (1997). *Alexander Graham Bell: The life and times of the man who invented the telephone.* New York, NY: Harry Abrams.

Guiard-Marigny, T., & Ostry, D. J. (1997). A system for three-dimensional visualization of human jaw motion in speech. *Journal of Speech, Language, and Hearing Research, 40*(5), 1118–1121.

Guisti Braislin, M. A., & Cascella, P. W. (2005). A preliminary investigation of the efficacy of oral motor exercises for children with mild articulation disorder. *International Journal of Rehabilitation Research, 28*(3), 263–266.

Gunzenhauser, N. (Ed.). (1990). *Pediatric round table 14: Advances in touch: New implications in human development.* New York, NY: Johnson & Johnson Baby.

Guyton, A. C. (1981). *Basic human neurophysiology.* Philadelphia, PA: W. B. Saunders Company.

Hagbarth, K. E. (1952). Excitatory and inhibitory skin areas for flexor and extensor motor neurons. *Acta Physiologica Scandinavica Supplementum 26(94),* 1–58.

Hardy, J. C. (1983). *Cerebral palsy (remediation of communication disorders series.* Englewood Cliffs, NJ: Prentice-Hall.

Harper, C. A. (1939). *A century of public teacher education: The story of the state teachers colleges as they evolved from the normal schools.* Normal, IL: Hugh Birch-Horace Mann Fund for the American Association of Teachers Colleges, a Department of the National Education Association of the United States.

Harrington, R, & Breinholt, V. (1963). The relation of oral mechanism malfunction to dental and speech development. *American Journal of Orthodontics, 49(2),* 84–93.

Helfrich-Miller, K. R. (1994). A clinical perspective: Melodic intonation therapy for developmental apraxia. *Clinics in Communication Disorders, 4(3),* 175–182.

Hillard, S. W., & Goepfert, L. P. (1979). Articulation training: A new perspective. *Language, Speech, and Hearing Services in Schools, 10(3),* 145–151.

Hockett, C. D. (1960). The origin of speech. *Scientific American, 203(3),* 88–96.

Hodge, M. (1993). Assessment and treatment of a child with developmental speech disorder: A biological-behavioral perspective. *Seminars in Speech and Language, 14(2),* 128–141.

Hodson, B. W. (1975). *Aspects of phonological performance in four-year-olds* [Unpublished doctoral dissertation]. Urbana-Champaign, IL: University of Illinois.

Hodson, B. W. (1984). Facilitating phonological development in children with severe speech disorders. In H. Winitz (Ed.), *Treating articulation disorders: For clinicians by clinicians.* Baltimore, MD: University Park Press.

Hodson, B. W., & Edwards, M. L. (1997). *Perspectives in applied phonology.* Gaithersburg, MD: Aspen Publishers.

Hodson, B. W. (Writer), & Whitmire, K. A. (Writer). (2005). *Enhancing phonological & metaphonological skills of children with highly unintelligible speech* [DVD & Book]. Rockville, MD: American Speech-Language-Hearing Association.

Hoffman, P. R., Schuckers, G. H., & Daniloff, R. G. (1989). *Children's phonetic disorders.* Boston, MA: College-Hill Press.

Hoffmann, H. (1995). *Struwwelpeter: In English translation.* New York, NY: Dover Publications. (Original text published in German in 1845).

Hoit, J. D., & Hixon, T. J. (1986). Body type and speech breathing. *Journal of Speech, Language, and Hearing Research, 29(3),* 313–324.

Holbrook, A. (1859). *The normal: Or methods of teaching the common branches, orthoepy, orthography, grammar, geography, arithmetic and elocution.* New York, NY: A. S. Barnes & Burr.

Hopper, R., & Naremore, R. C. (1978). *Children's speech: A practical introduction to communication development* (2nd Ed.). New York, NY: Harper & Row.

Huer, M. B. (1989). Auditory tracking of articulation errors: [r]. *Journal of Speech and Hearing Disorders, 54(4),* 530–534.

Hulme, C., Thomson, N., Muir, C., & Lawrence, A. (1984). Speech rate and the development of short-term memory span. *Journal of Experimental Child Psychology, 38(2),* 241–253.

Illingworth, R. S. (1962). *An introduction to developmental assessment in the first year.* London, England: Heinemann Medical.

Illingworth, R. S. (1983). *The normal child: Some problems of the early years and their treatment.* Edinburgh, Scotland: Churchill Livingstone.

Ingram, D. (1982). The assessment of phonological disorders in children: State of the art. In M. Crary (Ed.), *Phonological intervention: Concepts and procedures* (pp. 1–12). San Diego, CA: College Hill Press.

Institute of Educational Sciences. (2010). *What works clearinghouse intervention report: Lindamood phonemic sequencing (LiPS).* Retrieved from https://ies.ed.gov/ncee/wwc/Docs/InterventionReports/wwc_lindamood_031610.pdf

International Communication Learning Institute. (1981). *Visual phonics.* Edina, MN: Communication Arts, Inc.

Irwin, J. V. (1972). *Disorders of articulation.* Indianapolis, IN: Bobbs-Merrill.

Irwin, J. V., Weston, A. J., Griffith, F. A., & Rocconi, C. (1976). Phoneme acquisition using the paired-stimuli technique in the public school setting. *Language, Speech, and Hearing Services in the Schools, 7(4),* 220–229.

Irwin, J. V., & Wong, S. P. (1983). *Phonological development in children 18 to 72 months.* Carbondale, IL: Southern Illinois University Press.

Jaffe, M. B. (1984). Neurological impairment of speech production: Assessment and treatment. In J. Costello (Ed.), *Speech disorders in children.* San Diego, CA: College-Hill Press.

Jakobson, R. (1949). On the identity of phonemic entities. *Traveaux du Cercle Linguistique de Prague, 5,* 205–213.

Jakobson, R. (1971). *Studies on child language and aphasia.* The Hague, Netherlands: Mouton Publishers.

Jakobson, R., & Waugh, L. R. (1987). *The sound shape of language* (2nd Ed.). New York, NY: Mouton de Gruyter.

Jenkins, E., & Lohr, F. E. (1964). Severe articulation disorders and motor ability. *Journal of Speech and Hearing Research, 29(3),* 286–292.

Jenkins, R. L. (1940). The rate of diadochokinetic movement of the jaw at the ages of seven to maturity. *Journal of Speech Disorders, 6,* 13–22.

Jesperson, O. (1889). *The articulations of speech sounds: Represented by means of analphabetic symbols.* Marburg, Germany: N. G. Elwert.

Johnson, J. P. (1980). *Nature and treatment of articulation disorders.* Springfield, IL: Charles C. Thomas.

Justice, L. (2008). Evidence-based terminology. *American Journal of Speech-Language Pathology, 17(4),* 324–325.

Kabat, H. (1952). Central facilitation: The basis of treatment for paralysis. *Permanente Foundation M. Bull. 19,* 190–204.

Kamhi, A. G. (2006). Treatment decisions for children with speech-sound disorders. *Language, Speech, and Hearing Services in the Schools, 37(4),* 271–279.

Kamhi, A. G. (2008). A meme's-eye view of nonspeech oral-motor exercises. *Seminars in Speech and Language 29(4),* 331–338.

Kaplan, A. S., & Williams, G. (1988). *The TMJ book.* New York, NY: Pharos Books.

Kaplan, H. M. (1960). *Anatomy and physiology of speech.* New York, NY: McGraw-Hill.

Karlan, G. R., Lloyd, L. L., & Fristoe, M. (1983). The effects of presentation modality upon learning in a comprehension task using oral, manual, and dual modes stimulus cues. *Journal of Speech and Hearing Research, 26(3),* 436–443.

Kaufman, N. (1995). *The Kaufman speech praxis test for children.* Detroit, MI: Wayne State University Press.

Kawamura, Y. (1965). Oral physiology and clinical dentistry. *Journal of Dental Education, 29,* 179–185.

Keller, E. (1987). Factors underlying tongue articulation in speech. *Journal of Speech and Hearing Research, 30*(2), 223–229.

Kelso, J. A. S., & Munhall, K. G. (Eds.). (1988). *R. H. Stetson's motor phonetics: A retrospective edition.* Boston, MA: College-Hill Press.

Kelsey, C. A., Minifie, F. D., & Hixon, T. J. (1969). Application of ultrasound in speech research. *Journal of Speech and Hearing Research, 12*(3), 564–575.

Kennedy III, J. G., & Kent, R. D. (1985). Anatomy and physiology of deglutition and related functions. *Seminars in Speech and Language, 6*(4), 257–274.

Kent, R. D. (1999). Motor control: Neurophysiology and functional development. In A. J. Caruso & E. D. Strand (Eds.), *Clinical management of motor speech disorders in children.* New York, NY: Thieme.

Kent, R. D., & Moll, K. L. (1972). Cinefluorographic analyses of selected lingual consonants. *Journal of Speech and Hearing Research, 15*(3), 453–473.

Kent, R. D., & Vorperian, H. K. (2013). Speech impairment in Down syndrome: A review. *Journal of Speech, Language, and Hearing Research, 56*(1), 178–210.

Kirshner, H. S. (1992). Apraxia of speech: A linguistic enigma (A neurologist's perspective). *Seminars in Speech and Language, 13*(1), 14–24.

Kline, P. (1972). *The theater student: The actor's voice.* New York, NY: Richards Rosen Press.

Krafnick, A. J., Flowers, D. L., Napoliello, E. M., & Eden, G. F. (2011). Gray matter volume changes following reading intervention in dyslexic children. *Neuroimage, 57*(3), 733–741.

Kranowitz, C. S. (2005). *The out-of-sync child.* New York, NY: Penguin.

Krupke, D. (2008). What exactly is visual phonics? *Communication Disorders Quarterly, 29*(3), 177–182.

Kuehn, D. P. & Moon, J. B. (1998). Velopharyngeal closure force and levator veli palatini activation levels in varying phonetic contexts. *Journal of Speech, Language, and Hearing Research, 41*(1), 51–62.

Kuehn, D. P., & Wachtel, J. M. (1994). CPAP therapy for treating hypernasality following closed head injury. In J. A. Till, K. M. Yorkston, & D. R. Beukelman (Eds.), *Motor speech disorders: Advances in assessment and treatment* (pp. 207–212). Baltimore, MD: P. H. Brookes Publishing Company.

Kumin, L., & Bahr, D. C. (1999). Patterns of feeding, eating, and drinking in young children with Down syndrome with oral motor concerns, *Down Syndrome Quarterly, 4*(2), 1–8.

Kumin, L., & Chapman, D. (1996, May/June). Oral motor assessment and treatment in children with Down syndrome. *Communicating Together* [a parent magazine].

Kumin, L., Von Hagel, K. C., & Bahr, D. C. (2001). An effective oral motor protocol for infants and toddlers with low muscle tone. *Infant-Toddler Intervention, 11*(3), 181–200.

Ladefoged, P. (1957). Use of palatography. *Journal of Speech and Hearing Disorders, 22*(5), 764–774.

Langley, J. (1987). *Working with swallowing disorders.* London, England: Winslow Press.

Langley, M. B., & Lombardino, L. J. (Eds.). (1991). *Neurodevelopmental strategies for managing communication disorders in children with severe motor dysfunction.* Austin, TX: Pro-Ed.

Larson, C. (1985). Neurophysiology of speech and swallowing. *Seminars in Speech and Language, 6*(4), 275–292.

Lass, N. J., & Pannbacker, M. (2008). The application of evidence-based practice to nonspeech oral motor treatments. *Language, Speech and Hearing Services in the Schools, 29*(3), 408–421.

LeComer, L. (2006). *A parent's guide to developmental delays.* New York, NY: Berkeley Publishing Group.

Lee, L. (1974). *Developmental sentence analysis: A grammatical assessment procedure for speech and language clinicians.* Evanston, IL: Northwestern University.

Leonard, L. (1973). Referential effects on articulatory learning. *Language and Speech, 16*(1), 44–56.

Leonard, L. B., & Webb, C. E. (1971). An automated therapy program for articulatory correction. *Journal of Speech and Hearing Research, 14*(2), 338–344.

Lindsay, L. (2012). *Speaking of apraxia: A parent's guide to childhood apraxia of speech.* Bethesda, MD: Woodbine House.

Logemann, J. A. (1984). Evaluation and treatment of swallowing disorders. *NSSLHA Journal,* 38–50.

Logemann, J. A. (1985a). The relationship of speech and swallowing in head and neck surgical patients. *Seminars in Speech and Language, 6*(4), 351–359.

Logemann, J. A. (1985b). Preface. *Seminars in Speech and Language, 6(4),* 253–255.

Love, R. J. (1992). *Childhood motor speech disability.* New York, NY: Macmillan.

Love, R. J., & Webb, W. G. (1992). *Neurology for the speech-language pathologist.* Boston, MA: Butterworth-Heinemann.

Lowe, R. J., & Weitz, J. M. (1994). Intervention. In R. J. Lowe, *Phonology, assessment and intervention applications in speech pathology* (pp. 175–206). Baltimore, MD: Williams & Wilkins.

Lubker, J. F., & Morris, H. L. (1968). Predicting cinefluorographic measures of velopharyngeal opening from lateral still x-ray films. *Journal of Speech and Hearing Research, 11*(4), 747–753.

Lynch, J. I. (1990). Tongue reduction surgery: Efficacy and relevance to the profession. *ASHA, 32*(1), 59–61.

Macie, D., & Arvedson, J. (1993). Tone and positioning. In J. C. Arvedson & L. Brodsky (Eds.), *Pediatric swallowing and feeding* (pp. 209–247). San Diego, CA: Singular Publishing Group.

MacKay, J. A. (1997). *Sounds out of silence: A life of Alexander Graham Bell.* Edinburgh, Scotland: Mainstream.

MacNeilage, P. F. (Ed.). (1983). *The production of speech.* New York, NY: Springer-Verlag.

MacNeilage, P. F., & Davis, B. L. (1990). Acquisition of speech production: The achievement of segmental independence. In W. J. Hardcastle & A. Marchal (Eds.), *Speech production and modeling* (pp. 55–68). Dordrecht, Netherlands: Kluwer Academic.

MacNeilage, P. F., & Davis, B. L. (2000). Deriving speech from non-speech: A view from ontogeny. *Phonetica, 57*(2–4), 284–96.

MacNeilage, P. F., Davis, B. L., Kinney, A., & Matyear, C. L. (1999). Origin of serial-output complexity in speech. *Phonological Science, 10*(5), 459–460.

Malone, R. (1999). *The first 75 years, American Speech-Language-Hearing Association, an oral history.* Washington, DC: American Speech-Language-Hearing Association.

Marchesan, I. Q. (2004). Lingua frenulum: Classification and speech interference. *International Journal of Orofacial Myology, 30,* 31–38.

Marshalla, P. (2001b). *How to stop drooling.* Mill Creek, WA: Marshalla Speech & Language.

Marshalla, P. (2001c). *How to stop thumbsucking.* Mill Creek, WA: Marshalla Speech & Language.

Marshalla, P. (2007d). Oral motor techniques are not new. *Oral-Motor Institute, 1*(1). Retrieved from http://www.oralmotorinstitute.org/mons/v1n1_marshalla.html

Marshalla, P. (2007e). *Apraxia uncovered: The seven stages of phoneme development.* Mill Creek, WA: Marshalla Speech & Language.

Marshalla, P. (2007f). *The complete newsletter archives: 1983–1989: The innovative concepts speech and language therapy newsletter.* Mill Creek, WA: Marshalla Speech & Language.

Marshalla, P. (2008b). Oral motor techniques vs. non-speech oral-motor exercises. *Oral-Motor Institute, 2*(1). Retrieved from: http://www.oralmotorinstitute.org/mons/v2n2_marshalla.html

Marshalla, P. (2009). *Improving intelligibility in apraxia and dysarthria.* Mill Creek, WA: Marshalla Speech & Language.

Martin, K. L. (1997). *Does my child have a speech problem?* Chicago, IL: Chicago Review Press.

Mason, R. M. (2011) Myths that persist about orofacial myology. *International Journal of Orofacial Myology, 37*, 26–38.

Mason, R. M, & Simon, C. (1977). An orofacial examination checklist. *Language, Speech and Hearing Services in the Schools, 8*(3), 155–163.

Massaro, D. W., & Chen, T. H. (2008). The motor theory of speech perception revisited. *Psychonomic Bulletin & Review, 15*(2), 453–457.

Massler, M., & Schour, I. (1982). *Atlas of the mouth.* Chicago, IL: American Dental Association.

Matthews, J., & Byrne, M. C. (1953). An experimental study of tongue flexibility in children with cleft palates. *Journal of Speech and Hearing Disorders, 18*(1), 43–47.

Mayer, C. A., Brown, B. E., & Brown, A. C. (1997). *My thumb and I: A proven approach to stop a thumb or finger sucking habit for ages 6–10.* Chicago, IL: Chicago Spectrum Press.

McCauley, R. J., & Strand, E. A. (2008). Treatment of childhood apraxia of speech: Clinical decision making in the use of nonspeech oral motor exercises. *Seminars in Speech and Language 29*(4), 284–293.

McCauley, R. J., Strand, E. A., Lof, G. L., Schooling, T., & Frymark, T. (2009). Evidence-based systematic review: Effects of non-speech oral motor exercises on speech. *American Journal of Speech-Language Pathology, 18*(4), 343–360.

McClean, M. D. (1984). Recruitment thresholds of lower-lip motor units with changes in movement direction. *Journal of Speech and Hearing Research, 27*(1), 6–12.

McClowry, D. P., Guilford, A. M., & Richardson, S. O. (1982). *Infant communication: Development, assessment and intervention.* New York, NY: Grune & Stratton.

McLean, J. E. (1970). Extending stimulus control of phoneme articulation by operant techniques. *ASHA Monographs, 14,* 24–47.

McNeil, M. R. (1997). *Clinical management of sensorimotor speech disorders.* New York, NY: Thieme.

McNeil, M. R., Rosenbek, J. C., & Aronson, A. E. (1984). *The dysarthrias: Physiology, acoustics, perception, management.* San Diego, CA: College-Hill Press.

Miccio, A. W., & Ingrisano, D. R. (2000). The acquisition of fricatives and affricates: Evidence from a disordered phonological system. *American Journal of Speech-Language Pathology, 9*(3), 214–229.

Mitchell, H. L., Hoit, J. D., & Watson, P. J. (1996). Cognitive-linguistic demands and speech breathing. *Journal of Speech and Hearing Research, 39*(1), 93–104.

Modisett, N. F., & Luter, J. G. (1988). *Speaking clearly: The basics of voice and articulation.* Edina, MN: Burgess.

Monahan, D. (1986). Remediation of common phonological processes: Four case studies. *Language, Speech, and Hearing Services in the Schools, 17*(3), 199–206.

Monsen, R. B. (1976). Normal and reduced phonological space: The production of English vowels by deaf adolescents. *The Journal of the Acoustical Society of America, 59(S1),* S86-S86.

Moore, C. A., Yorkston, K. M., & Beukelman, D. R. (1991). *Dysarthria and apraxia: Perspectives on management.* Baltimore, MD: Paul H. Brookes Publishing Company.

Morris, S. E. (1981). *The normal acquisition of oral feeding skills: implications for assessment and treatment* [Seminar handbook]. New York, NY: Therapeutic Media.

Morris, S. E. (1985). Developmental implications for the management of feeding problems in neurologically impaired infants. *Seminars in Speech and Language, 6*(4), 293–315.

Morris, S. E. (1991). Facilitation of learning. In M. B. Langley & L. J. Lombardino (Eds.), *Neurodevelopmental strategies for managing communication disorders in children with severe motor dysfunction* (pp. 251–296). Austin, TX: Pro-Ed.

Morris, S. E. (2009, February). Personal email correspondence.

Morrison, D., Pothier, P., & Horr, K. (1978). *Sensory-motor dysfunction and therapy in infancy and early childhood.* Springfield, IL: Charles C. Thomas.

Mowrer, D. (1984). Correcting multiple misarticulations. In H. Winitz (Ed.), *Treating articulation disorders: For clinicians by clinicians* (pp. 91–103). Baltimore, MD: University Park Press.

Mowrer, D. E., Baker, R., & Shultz, R. (1968). *S-programmed articulation control kit.* Tempe, AZ: Educational Psychological Research Associates.

Murdoch, J. E., Rush, J., & Webb, G. J. (1923). *Orthophony.* United States.

Murry, T., & Murry, J. (1980). *Infant communication: Cry and early speech.* Houston, TX: College-Hill Press.

Nathani, S., & Stark, R. E. (1996). Can conditioning procedures yield representative infant vocalizations in the laboratory? *First Language, 16*(48) 365–387.

Newman, P. W., & Creaghead, N. A., & Second, W. (1985). *Assessment and remediation of articulatory and phonological disorders.* Columbus, OH: Charles E. Merrill.

Northrup, P. S. (2006). *The literacy link: A multisensory approach to sound-symbol connections.* Greenville, SC: Super Duper Publications.

Oetter, P., Richter, E. W., & Frick, S. M. (1988). *M.O.R.E: Integrating the mouth with sensory and postural function.* Hugo, MN: PDP.

O'Neill, J. J. (1987). The development of speech-language pathology and audiology in the United States. In H. J. Oyer (Ed.), *Administration of programs in speech-language pathology and audiology.* Boston, MA: Allyn & Bacon.

Orlikoff, R. F. (1992). The use of instrumental measures in the assessment and treatment of motor speech disorders. *Seminars in Speech and Language, 13*(1), 25–38.

Orton, S. T. (1937). *Reading, writing, and speech problems in children.* New York, NY: Norton.

Paden, E. P. (1970). *A History of the American Speech and Hearing Association 1925 to 1958.* Washington, DC: American Speech and Hearing Association.

Paget, R. (1963). *Human speech.* London, England: Routledge & Kegan Paul.

Palmer, M. F. (1948). Studies in clinical techniques III: Mandibular facet slip in cerebral palsy. *Journal of Speech and Hearing Disorders, 13*(1), 44–48.

Panagos, J. M., Bobkoff, K., & C.M. Scott (1986). Discourse analysis of language intervention. *Child Language Teaching and Therapy, 2*(2), 211–229.

Passy, J. (1986). *Cued articulation.* Melbourne, Australia: ACER

Press.

Passy, J. (1990). *Cued vowels.* Melbourne, Australia: ACER Press.

Peppard, H. M. (1925). *The correction of speech defects.* New York, NY: Macmillan.

Perlman, A. L., Luschei, E. S., & Du Mond, C. E. (1989). Electrical activity from the superior pharyngeal constrictor during reflexive and nonreflexive tasks (1989). Journal of Speech and Hearing Research, 32(4), 749–754.

Piaget, J. (1962). *Play, dreams and imitation in childhood.* New York, NY: Norton.

Piaget, J. (1975). *The child's conception of the world.* Totowa, NJ: Littlefield, Adams & Company.

Poole, I. (1934). Genetic development of articulation of consonant sounds in speech. *Elementary English Review, 11*(6), 159–161.

Porter, E. (1839). *The rhetorical reader.* Andover, MA: Gould & Newman

Powell, T. W. (1992). Planning for phonological generalization: An approach to treatment target selection. *American Journal of Speech-Language Pathology, 1*(1), 21–27.

Prather, E. M., Hedrick, D. L., & Kern, C. A. (1975). Articulation development in children aged two to four years. *Journal of Speech and Hearing Disorders, 40*(2), 179–191.

Proffit, W. R., & Mason, R. M. (1975). Myofunctional therapy for tongue-thrusting: Background and recommendations. *Journal of the American Dental Association, 90*(2), 403–411.

Quiros, J. B., & Schrager, O. L. (1979). *Neuropsychological fundamentals in learning disabilities.* Novato, CA: Academic Therapy Publications.

Redstone, F. (1991). Respiratory components of communication. In M. B. Langley & L. J. Lombardino (Eds.), *Neurodevelopmental strategies for managing communication disorders in children with severe motor dysfunction.* Austin, TX: Pro-Ed.

Reilly, A. P. (Ed.). (1980). *Pediatric Round Table 4: The communication game: Perspectives on the development of speech, language, and nonverbal communication skills.* New York, NY: Johnson & Johnson Baby.

Reitan, R. (1966). Diagnostic inferences of brain lesions based on psychological test results. *Canadian Psychologist, 7*, 368–383.

Rice, M. L., & Haight, P. L. (1986). "Motherese" of Mr. Rogers: A description of the dialogue of educational television programs. *Journal of Speech and Hearing Disorders, 51*(3), 282–287.

Robin, D. A., Goel, A., Somodi, L. B., & Luschei, E. S. (1992). Tongue strength and endurance: Relation to highly skilled movements. *Journal of Speech and Hearing Research, 35*(6), 1239–1245.

Robbins, J. (1985). Swallowing and speech production in the neurologically impaired adult. *Seminars in Speech and Language, 6*(4), 337–350.

Robbins, J. (1992). The impact of oral motor dysfunction on swallowing: From beginning to end. *Seminars in Speech and Language, 13*(1), 55–69.

Rood, M. S. (1956). Neurophysiological mechanisms utilized in the treatment of neuromuscular dysfunction. *American Journal of Occupational Therapy, 10*(4), 220–225.

Rosenbek, J. C., Kent, R., & LaPointe, L. (1984). Apraxia of speech: An overview and some perspectives. In J. C. Rosenbeck, M. R. McNeil, & A. E. Aronson (Eds.), *Apraxia of speech: Physiology, acoustics, linguistics, management* (pp. 1–71). San Diego, CA: College Hill Press.

Rosenbek, J. C., McNeil, M. R., & Aronson, A. E. (1984). *Apraxia of speech.* San Diego, CA: College-Hill Press.

Rosenfeld-Johnson, S. (1997, August 4). The oral-motor myths of Down Syndrome. *ADVANCE Magazine for Speech Language Pathologists and Audiologists.*

Rosenwinkel, P. (1976). Phonologically-based therapy for children with multiple misarticulations (Unpublished master's thesis). University of Illinois, Urbana, IL.

Rosenwinkel, P. (1982). *Tactile-proprioceptive stimulation techniques in articulation therapy* [Seminar handbook]. Champaign, IL: Innovative Concepts.

Rosenwinkel, P., Kleinert, J. E. O., & Robbins, R. L. (1978). Tactile-proprioceptive stimulation techniques and the frontal lisp [Paper]. Chicago, IL: Illinois Speech and Hearing Association Convention.

Rosenwinkel, P., Kleinert, J. E. O., & Robbins, R. L. (1979). Remediation of severe speech and language disorders: A pre-speech sensorimotor developmental model. In M. S. Burns & J. R. Andrews (Eds.), *Selected papers: Current trends in the treatment of language disorders presented at the 1979 Annual Convention of ASHA, Atlanta, GA.* Evanston, IL: Institute For Continuing Professional Education.

Rosenwinkel), P., Kleinert, J. E. O., & Robbins, R. L. (1980). Remediation of severe speech and language disorders: A pre-speech sensorimotor developmental model. *The Illinois speech and hearing journal, 13*(2), 45–66.

Ruscello, D. M. (1984). Motor learning as a model for articulation instruction. In J. Costello (Ed.), *Speech disorders in children: Recent advances* (pp. 129–156). San Diego, CA: College-Hill Press.

Ruscello, D. M. (1993). A motor skill learning treatment program for sound system disorders. *Seminars in Speech and Language, 14*(2). 106–118.

Ruscello, D. M. (2008). An examination of nonspeech oral motor exercises for children with velopharyngeal inadequacy. *Seminars in Speech and Language 29*(4), 294–303.

Russell, W. (1833). *Lessons in enunciation: comprising a course of elementary exercises and statements of common errors in articulation.* Boston, MA: Carter/Hendee.

Rutherford, B. R. (1940). The use of negative practice in speech therapy with children handicapped by cerebral palsy, athetoid type. *Journal of Speech and Hearing Disorders, 5*(3), 259–264.

Ryan, B. P. (1971). A study of the effectiveness of the S-Pack program in the elimination of frontal lisping behavior in third-grade children. *Journal of Speech and Hearing Disorders, 36*(3), 390–396.

Sackett, D.L., Rosenberg, W.M.C., Gray, J.A.M., & Richardson, W.S. (1996). Evidence-based medicine: What it is and what it isn't. *British Medical Journal, 312*(7023), 71–72.

Sackett, D. L., Richardson, W.S., Rosenberg, W., & Haynes, R.B. (1997). *Evidence-based medicine: How to practice and teach EBM.* Edinburgh, Scotland: Churchill Livingstone.

Salek, B., Braun, M. A., & Palmer, M. M. (1982). *Early detection and treatment of the infant and young child with neuromuscular disorders: Based upon transcriptions of June 1982 Boston conference.* New York, NY: Therapeutic Media.

Sakada, S. (1971). Response of Golgi-Mazzoni corpuscles in the cat periostea to mechanical stimuli. In R. Dubner & Y. Kawamura (Eds.), *Oral-facial sensory and motor mechanisms.* New York, NY: Appleton-Century-Crofts.

Sander, E. (1972). When are speech sounds learned? *Journal of Speech and Hearing Disorders, 37*(1), 55–63.

Scripture, E. W. (1895). *Thinking, feeling, doing.* New York, NY: Flood & Vincent.

Secord, W. (2007). Dedication. In W. A. Secord, S. E. Boyce, J. S.

Donohue, R. A. Fox, & R. E. Shine, *Eliciting sounds: Techniques and strategies for clinicians* (pp. vii). New York, NY: Thomson Delmar Learning.

Secord, W., & Donohue, J. S. (2002). *Clinical assessment of articulation and phonology: Examiner's manual.* Greenville, SC: Super Duper Publications.

Shelton, R. L. (1993). Grand rounds for sound system disorder. Conclusion: What was learned. *Seminars in Speech and Language, 14*(2), 166–178.

Sheridan, T. (1803). *A course of lectures on elocution.* Troy, NY: Obidiah Penniman.

Siegel, I. M. (2000). *All about muscle: A user's guide.* New York, NY: Demos.

Smart, B. H. (1826). *The practice of elocution, or a course of exercises for acquiring the several requisites of a good delivery.* London, England: Royal Exchange.

Smith, A., & Luschei, E. S. (1983). Assessment of oral-motor reflexes in stutterers and normal speakers: Preliminary observations. *Journal of Speech and Hearing Research, 26*(3), 322–328.

Smith, N. V. (1973). *The acquisition of phonology: A case study.* London, England: Cambridge.

Solomon, N. P. (2000). Changes in normal speech after fatiguing the tongue. *Journal of Speech and Hearing Research, 43*(6), 1416–1428.

Solomon, N. P., Drager, K. D. R., & Luschei, E. S. (2002). Sustaining a constant effort by the tongue and hand: Effects of acute fatigue. *Journal of Speech, Language, and Hearing Research, 45*(4), 613–624.

Solomon, N. P., Robin, D. A., Mitchinson, S. I., VanDaele, D. J., & Luschei, E. S. (1996). Sense of effort and the effects of fatigue in the tongue and hand. *Journal of Speech and Hearing Research, 39*(1), 114–125.

Sommers, R. K. (1983). *Articulation disorders.* Englewood Cliffs, NJ: Prentice-Hall.

Sommers, R. K., Leiss, R. H., Fundrella, D., Manning, W., Johnson, R., Oerther, P., … & Siegel, M. (1970). Factors in the effectiveness of articulation therapy with educable retarded children. *Journal of Speech and Hearing Research, 13*(2), 304–316.

Sommers, R. K., Shilling, S. P., Paul, C. D., Copetas, F. G., Bowser, D. C., & McClintock, C. J. (1959). Training parents of children with functional misarticulations. *Journal of Speech and Hearing Research, 2*(3), 258–265.

Sparks, R. W., Helm, N., & Albert, M. (1974). Aphasia rehabilitation result from melodic intonation therapy. *Cortex, 10*(4), 303 316.

Steefel, J. S. (1981). *Dysphagia rehabilitation for neurologically impaired adults.* Springfield, IL: Thomas.

Stinchfield, S. M. (1933). *Speech disorders: A psychological study of the various defects of speech.* New York, NY: Harcourt, Brace and Company.

Stoddard, C. B. (1940). *Sounds for little folks: speech improvement, speech correction.* Boston, MA: Expression Company.

Stone, M., Faber, A., Raphael, L. J., & Shawker, T. H. (1992). Cross-sectional tongue shape and linguopalatal contact patterns in [s], [(esh)], and /1/. *Journal of Phonetics, 20*(2), 253–270.

Straub, W. J. (1951). Etiology of the perverted swallow habit. *American Journal of Orthodontia, 37*, 603–610.

Subtelny, J. D. (1965). Examination of current philosophies associated with swallowing behaviors. *American Journal of Orthodontia, 51*, 161–182.

Sweet, H. (1888). *A history of English sounds: From the earliest period.* Oxford, England: Clarendon Press.

Sweet, H. (1890). *A primer of spoken English.* Oxford, English: Clarendon Press.

Travis, L. E. (Ed.). (1957). *Handbook of speech pathology.* New York, NY: Appleton-Century-Crofts.

Travis, L. E. (Ed.). (1971). *Handbook of speech pathology and audiology.* Englewood Cliffs, NJ: Prentice-Hall.

Tuchman, D. N., & Walter, R. S. (1994). *Disorders of feeding and swallowing in infants and children.* San Diego, CA: Singular Publishing Group.

Van Norman, R. (1999). *Help for the thumb-sucking child.* New York, NY: Avery Publishing Group.

Van Riper, C. (1953). *Speech therapy: A book of readings.* Englewood Cliffs, NJ: Prentice-Hall.

Van Riper, C. (1993). Personal correspondence to Wayne Secord. In W. A. Secord, S. E. Boyce, A. S. Donohue, R. A. Fox, & R. E. Shine, *Eliciting sounds: Techniques and strategies for clinicians* (2nd Ed.)(pp. viii). Clifton Park, NY: Thomas Delmar Learning.

Vealey, J., & Bailey, C., & Belknap, L. (1966). Rheadeik: To detect the escape of nasal air during speech. *Journal of Speech and Hearing Disorders, 30*(1), 82–84.

Walk, R. D., & Pick, H. L. (1981). *Intersensory perception and sensory integration.* New York, NY: Plenum

Warner, J. L. (Producer), & Cukor, G. (Director). (1964). *My Fair Lady* [Motion Picture]. United States: Warner Bros Pictures.

Watson, M. M., & Lof, G. L. (2008). Epilogue: What we know about nonspeech oral motor exercises. *Seminars in Speech and Language 29*(4), 339–344.

Weiner, F. (1981). Treatment of phonological disability using the method of meaningful minimal contrasts: Two case studies. *Journal of Speech and Hearing Disorders, 46*(1), 97–103.

Weiss, C. E., Gordon, M. E., & Lillywhite, H. S. (1987). *Clinical management of articulatory and phonological disorders* (2nd Ed.). Baltimore, MD: Williams & Wilkins.

Weiss, C. E., Lillywhite, H. S., & Gordon, M. E. (1980). *Clinical management of articulation disorders.* St. Louis, MO: Mosby.

Werner, D. (1987). *Disabled village children: A guide for community health workers.* Berkeley, CA: The Hesperian Foundation.

West, R., Kennedy, L., Carr, A., & Backus, O. (1937). *The rehabilitation of speech.* New York, NY: Harper.

Weston, A. J., & Leonard, L. B. (1976). *Articulation Disorders: Methods of Evaluation and Therapy.* Lincoln, NE: Cliffs Notes.

Whately, R. (1861). *Elements of rhetoric.* Nashville, TN: Southern Methodist Publishing House.

White, R. (1994). *Sensory Integration and Neurodevelopmental Therapy* [Seminar handbook]. Seattle, WA: Innovative Concepts.

Wilbarger, P., & Wilbarger, J. L. (1991). *Sensory defensiveness in children aged 2–12: An intervention guide for parents and other caregivers.* Santa Barbara, CA: Avanti.

Wilson, E. M., Green, J. R., Yunusova, Y. Y., & Moore, C. A. (2008). Task specificity in early oral motor development. *Seminars in Speech and Language 29*(4), 257–266.

Wilson, J. M. (1977). *Oral-motor function and dysfunction in children.* conference proceedings. Chapel Hill, NC: University of North Carolina.

Winitz, H. (1969). *Articulatory acquisition and behavior.* New York, NY: Appleton-Century-Drofts.

Winitz, H. (1975). *From syllable to conversation.* Baltimore, MD: University Park Press.

Winitz, H. (Ed.) (1984). *Treating articulation disorders: For clinicians by clinicians.* Baltimore, MD: University Park Press.

Worth, B. (1996). *Bye-bye, thumb-sucking*. New York, NY: Western Publishing Company.

Wright, V., Shelton, R. L., & Arndt, W. B. (1969). A task for evaluation of articulation change. III. Imitative task scores compared with scores for more spontaneous tasks. *Journal of Speech and Hearing Research, 12*(4), 875–884.

Wyllie, J. (1894). *The disorders of speech*. Edinburgh, Scotland: Oliver & Boyd.

Yavas, M. (1998). *Phonology development and disorders*. San Diego, CA: Singular Publishing Group.

Young, E. C. (1987). The effects of treatment on consonant cluster and weak syllable reduction processes in misarticulating children. *Language, Speech, and Hearing Services in the Schools, 18*(1), 23–33.

Žagar, L. L., & Locke, J. L. (1986). The psychological reality of phonetic features in children. *Language, Speech, and Hearing Services in the Schools, 17*(1), 56–62.

Zehel, Z., Shelton, R. L., Arndt, W. B., Wright, V., & Elbert, M. (1972). Item context and /s/ phone articulation test results. *Journal of Speech and Hearing Research, 15*(4), 852–860.

Zimmerman, J. (1993). *The tongue, the teeth and resistant speech problems* [Seminar handbook]. Seattle, WA: Innovative Concepts.

AUTHOR INDEX

INDEX

TABLES, CHARTS & DIAGRAMS